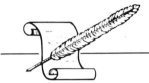

HISTORIC
DOCUMENTS
OF
1975

Cumulative Index 1972-75

Congressional Quarterly, Inc.

Historic Documents of 1975

Major Contributor: Elizabeth Wehr

Other Contributors: Buel W. Patch, Diantha Johnson Allenby
Cumulative Index: Diane Huffman
Cover Design: Howard Chapman
Production Manager: I. D. Fuller
Assistant Production Manager: Kathleen E. Walsh

Library of Congress Cataloging in Publication Data

Historic documents. 1972—
    Washington. Congressional Quarterly Inc.

    1. United States—Politics and government—1945—   —Yearbooks.
2. World politics—1945—   —Yearbooks.   I. Congressional Quarterly Inc.

E839.5.H57   917.3′03′9205   72-97888
ISBN 0-87187-090-8

FOREWORD

Publication of *Historic Documents of 1975* carries through a fourth year the project launched by Congressional Quarterly Service and Editorial Research Reports with *Historic Documents 1972.* The purpose of this continuing series of volumes is to give students, scholars, librarians, journalists and citizens convenient access to documents of basic importance in the broad range of public affairs.

To place the documents in perspective, each entry is preceded by a brief introduction containing background materials, in some cases a short summary of the document itself and, where necessary, relevant subsequent developments. We believe this editorial input will prove increasingly useful in future years when the events and questions now covered are less fresh in one's memory and the documents may be hard to find or unobtainable.

The year 1975 marked the conclusions of both the Watergate scandal and the long and bitter struggle in Vietnam. With the conviction and sentencing of the Watergate cover-up conspirators early in the year and the issuance of the Special Prosecutor's report in October, the final curtain came down on the Watergate drama. The Saigon government fell April 29. President Ford and Secretary of State Kissinger spent much of the remainder of the year trying to reassure allies about American commitments abroad.

The year's most sensational headlines reported the findings of unprecedented government inquiries into alleged improper and unlawful activities of the Central Intelligence Agency, the National Security Agency, the Federal Bureau of Investigation and the Internal Revenue Service. Throughout the year, the economy continued to suffer from the double burden of inflation and recession.

These developments added substantially to the usual outpouring of presidential statements, court decisions, commission reports, special studies and speeches of national or international importance. We have selected for inclusion in this book as many as possible of the documents that in our judgment will be of more than transitory interest. Where space limitations prevented reproduction of the full texts, the excerpts used were chosen to set forth the essentials and, at the same time, preserve the flavor of the materials.

Robert E. Cuthriell
Editor

Washington, D.C.
January 1976

How to Use This Book

The documents are arranged in chronological order. If you know the approximate date of the report, speech, statement, court decision or other document you are looking for, glance through the titles for that month in the Table of Contents below.

If the Table of Contents does not lead you directly to the document you want, make a double check by turning to the subject Index at the end of the book. There you may find references not only to the particular document you seek but also to other entries on the same or a related subject. The Index in this volume is the fourth of a projected **five-year cumulative index** of Historic Documents.

The introduction to each document is printed in italic type. The document itself, printed in roman type, follows the spelling, capitalization and punctuation of the original or official copy. Where the full text is not given, omissions of material are indicated by the customary series of dots.

TABLE OF CONTENTS

January

April

May

June

July

August

September

October

November

December

HISTORIC
DOCUMENTS
OF
1975

 HISTORIC DOCUMENTS OF 1975

January

KISSINGER AND THE OIL CARTEL

January 2, 1975

By January 1975 exorbitant oil prices, in effect since October 1973 when they were imposed by the Arab-dominated Organization of Petroleum Exporting Countries (OPEC), threatened major global economic and political dislocations. In a statement made public Jan. 2, Secretary of State Henry A. Kissinger said it was possible the United States would resort to military action if that was necessary to avert "strangulation of the industrialized world by Arab oil producers." But he added that "the use of force would be considered only in the gravest emergency." Kissinger's remarks—the first official admission of the possibility of U.S. armed intervention to resolve the oil crisis—came during an interview on international economic policy with editors of Business Week.*

Reaction from OPEC members was swift and angry. The influential Iranian newspaper Kahyam *characterized Kissinger's statement as a thinly veiled threat. Egyptian President Anwar Sadat observed that in the event of an invasion, "We will not need armies, because it is much easier to blow up oil wells...."*

OPEC Embargo

OPEC had precipitated an acute crisis in October 1973 when, during the Arab-Israeli war, it banned oil shipments to the United States and the Netherlands, supporters of Israel. Coupled with the embargo, later extended to a few other countries, were substantial production cutbacks and

---

* Reprinted in Department of State *Bulletin.*

sharp price rises which drained the financial reserves of developed nations and pushed impoverished governments toward bankruptcy. The price of oil had shot up from $1.99 to $11 a barrel by the end of 1974. Estimates placed that year's oil bill of underdeveloped countries of Asia, Africa and Latin America at $10-billion, a sum which almost equaled their combined foreign aid income of $11.4-billion.

When the embargo against the United States was lifted in March 1974 (see Historic Documents of 1974, p. 221), *the oil producers had learned to appreciate the force of their oil weapon. Prices remained high. Nor was the lesson lost on third-world suppliers of other raw materials, such as Algeria, which proposed "producer associations" to reinforce their negotiating power with industrialized nations and multinational corporations.* (See Historic Documents of 1974, p. 255.)

OPEC nations experienced an unprecedented inflow of wealth, much of which they were unable to absorb in spite of lavish spending on domestic projects and foreign investments. The Economist *of London estimated that OPEC, with its then-current income and at current stock-exchange quotations, could gain a controlling interest in all the major companies of the world in about 15 years. OPEC's accumulation of unused capital was the major if not sole cause of a steadily worsening global recession.*

Previous Warnings

After eleven months of elevated oil prices, President Gerald R. Ford in September 1974 warned that continued high oil prices could provoke a "confrontation" and a "breakdown of world order and safety." In subsequent months speculative articles on the "military option" were published widely but, less than two weeks before his Business Week *interview, Kissinger had brushed aside the suggestions of a* Newsweek *interviewer that the financial bankruptcy of the West would be a* casus belli. *"We will find other solutions," Kissinger said.*

The secretary cautioned in his later interview that military action would be "a very dangerous course" and said: "We should have learned from Vietnam that it is easier to get into a war than to get out of it."

In the course of the Business Week *interview Kissinger emphasized the urgent need of halting the escalation of oil prices but acknowledged that a reduction of oil prices could not be expected for several years. The secretary sharply criticized Western European nations for initially ignoring his advocacy of a coordination of economic policies. Their refusal to support this country's Middle East policy, he said, reflected their "enormous feeling of insecurity" vis-à-vis the United States.*

Kissinger also scored congressional intervention in foreign affairs. "The attempt to prescribe every detail of policy by congressional action can...so stultify flexibility that you have no negotiating room," he said. (Two weeks later, on January 14, Kissinger announced that the Soviet Union had rejected certain conditions laid down by the 1974 Trade Act and, consequently, would prevent putting into effect an important Soviet-American trade agreement negotiated in 1972.

For several months after Kissinger's statement, the theme of U.S. military intervention recurred in administration statements. At a Jan. 21 news conference, President Ford stressed the hypothetical nature of Kissinger's statement on the use of force, but affirmed that "a country has a right to protect itself." Defense Secretary James R. Schlesinger said on Mar. 31 that this country would not "tolerate" another Arab oil embargo, adding that "the reaction of the United States might be far more severe this time than last time."

OPEC Action

Meanwhile, OPEC ministers meeting in Algeria agreed on Jan. 26 to maintain then-current oil prices through 1975 and gradually increase them in 1976 and 1977. However, only nine months later OPEC ministers meeting in Vienna adopted a further 10 per cent price hike effective Oct. 1. The compromise measure was expected to raise the annual world oil bill by approximately $10-billion.

> *Excerpts from Secretary of State Kissinger's interview with* Business Week *editors on international economic policy, made public January 2, 1975. Reprinted from the* Department of State Bulletin *of Jan. 27, 1975:*

Q. *Until recently it was the U.S. position that the energy crisis could be solved only by an immediate and substantial reduction in the price of imported oil. Why has that policy changed?*

Secretary Kissinger: I would disagree with the word "immediate." It has been the U.S. position that the energy crisis cannot be fundamentally changed without a substantial reduction in the price of oil. This remains our view. It is also our view that the prospects for an immediate reduction in oil prices are poor. I have always had the most serious doubts that an immediate reduction in oil prices could be achieved, because I did not see the incentives for the oil producers to do this in the absence of consumer solidarity. A reduction in energy prices is important. It must be achieved, and we must organize ourselves to bring it about as rapidly as possible.

Q. *Why was it impossible to reduce the price of oil immediately?*

Secretary Kissinger: Because in the absence of consumer solidarity, pressures required to bring oil prices down would create a political crisis of the first magnitude. And this would tempt other consuming countries to simply step into the vacuum created by the United States and would therefore not be effective.

Q. *Can you describe the kind of political problems that would develop without consumer solidarity?*

Secretary Kissinger: The only chance to bring oil prices down immediately would be massive political warfare against countries like Saudi Arabia and Iran to make them risk their political stability and maybe their security if they did not cooperate. That is too high a price to pay even for an immediate reduction in oil prices.

If you bring about an overthrow of the existing system in Saudi Arabia and a Qadhafi takes over, or if you break Iran's image of being capable of resisting outside pressures, you're going to open up political trends which could defeat your economic objectives. Economic pressures or incentives, on the other hand, take time to organize and cannot be effective without consumer solidarity. Moreover, if we had created the political crisis that I described, we would almost certainly have had to do it against the opposition of Europe, Japan, and the Soviet Union.

Q. *In your University of Chicago speech [Nov. 14, 1974], you said, "The price of oil will come down only when objective conditions for a reduction are created, and not before." What are these objective conditions, and when do you think they will be achieved?*

Secretary Kissinger: The objective conditions depend upon a number of factors: One, a degree of consumer solidarity that makes the consumers less vulnerable to the threat of embargo and to the dangers of financial collapse. Secondly, a systematic effort at energy conservation of sufficient magnitude to impose difficult choices on the producing countries. Thirdly, institutions of financial solidarity so that individual countries are not so obsessed by their sense of impotence that they are prepared to negotiate on the producers' terms. Fourth, and most important, to bring in alternative sources of energy as rapidly as possible so that that combination of new discoveries of oil, new oil-producing countries, and new sources of energy creates a supply situation in which it will be increasingly difficult for the cartel to operate. We think the beginning of this will occur within two to three years....

The Use of Political Pressures

Q. *Are there any political pressures the United States can bring to bear on the oil cartel?*

Secretary Kissinger: A country of the magnitude of the United States is never without political recourse. Certainly countries will have to think twice about raising their prices, because it would certainly involve some political cost. But I don't want to go into this very deeply.

Q. *Businessmen ask why we haven't been able to exploit King Faisal's fear of communism to help lower prices.*

Secretary Kissinger: We have a delicate problem there. It is to maintain the relationship of friendship that they have felt for us, yet make clear the consequences of these prices on the structure of the West and of the non-Communist world.

I think we will find that Saudi Arabia will not be the leader in the reduction of prices but that it will not be an impediment to a reduction if enough momentum can be created in the Arab world—indeed, it will be discreetly encouraging.

The Saudi Government has performed the enormously skillful act of surviving in a leadership position in an increasingly radical Arab world. It is doing that by carefully balancing itself among the various factions and acting as a resultant of a relation of forces and never getting too far out ahead. Therefore I never for a moment believed, nor do I believe today, that the lead in cutting prices will be taken by Saudi Arabia. On the other hand, the Saudis will happily support a cut in prices proposed by others. The Saudis have no interest in keeping up prices. They don't know what to do with their income today....

Recycling Oil Money

Q. *Many bankers claim that all the schemes for recycling oil money—including the one you suggested in the University of Chicago speech—are only band-aids because each scheme piles bad debt on top of good. Most of the countries have no way to ever repay the loans. Do you see how the $25 billion fund you proposed could be repaid?*

Secretary Kissinger: We have two problems. We have an economic problem, and we have a political problem. The political problem is that the whole Western world, with the exception perhaps of the United States, is suffering from political malaise, from inner uncertainty and a lack of direction. This also affects economic conditions because it means that you have no settled expectations for the future and therefore a lowered willingness to take risks.

One of the principal objectives of our energy policy is to restore among the industrialized countries some sense that they can master their own fate. And even if this would involve some questionable debts, these are debts that have to be met somehow. It would be enormously important for the general cohesion of the industrialized world, and for its capacity to deal with the future, that they are dealt with systematically and not as the outgrowth of some crisis. Moreover, one way of disciplining some of the industrial countries is by the conditions that are attached to the funds that might be available.

Q. *Where would this $25 billion come from?*
Secretary Kissinger: The United States, the Federal Republic of Germany, small sums from other countries....

Q. *Will this require congressional approval?*
Secretary Kissinger: I'm told that we could actually do it by borrowing and not require congressional approval. However, we have decided that in undertaking even potential obligations of this magnitude we'd better seek some congressional concurrence....

7

Q. *Have you had any discussion with the Soviets about what their position would be if there were a confrontation between the oil cartel and the Western consumer governments?*

Secretary Kissinger: No, and I think it would be a very foolish question to ask them.

Q. *Do you know if the Arabs are using their petrodollars to force a favorable resolution of the Arab-Israeli conflict?*

Secretary Kissinger: I don't think they've done it up to now. If we don't have consumer solidarity that may happen eventually....

Q. *Is it possible that we may have to engage in an emergency financial bailout of Italy or Britain before the financial facility is in place?*

Secretary Kissinger: Very possibly, in this sense, the proposed facility merely institutionalizes what will have to happen anyway, because if present trends continue, there will have to be a bailout sooner or later. But it makes a lot of difference whether you bail somebody out in an emergency and therefore enhance the sense of vulnerability and create conditions for a new emergency. Or whether, having perceived the emergency, you can convey to the public that there is a structure that makes it possible to master your fate and to deal with difficulties institutionally.

Q. *How do you rate the chances for another Arab-Israeli war in the spring?*

Secretary Kissinger: In the absence of a political settlement there is always the danger of another Arab-Israeli war. On the other hand, war is talked about much too loosely. Both sides lost grievously in the last war. Neither side really won. I think the readiness of either side to go to war is often exaggerated. I also believe that there is some possibility of political progress before the spring.

Q. *Then you don't anticipate the possibility of another oil embargo soon?*
Secretary Kissinger: Not unless there is a war.

Q. *Well, what about after the spring?*

Secretary Kissinger: I don't anticipate an oil embargo in the absence of war. I am not even sure of an oil embargo in the event of war. It would now be a much more serious decision than it was the last time....

Military Action

Q. *One of the things we also hear from businessmen is that in the long run the only answer to the oil cartel is some sort of military action. Have you considered military action on oil?*

Secretary Kissinger: Military action on oil prices?
Q. *Yes.*

Secretary Kissinger: A very dangerous course. We should have learned from Vietnam that it is easier to get into a war than to get out of it. I am not saying that there's no circumstance where we would not use force. But it is one thing to use it in the case of a dispute over price; it's another where there is some actual strangulation of the industrialized world.

Q. *Do you worry about what the Soviets would do in the Middle East if there were any military action against the cartel?*
Secretary Kissinger: I don't think this is a good thing to speculate about. Any President who would resort to military action in the Middle East without worrying what the Soviets would do would have to be reckless. The question is to what extent he would let himself be deterred by it. But you cannot say you would not consider what the Soviets would do. I want to make clear, however, that the use of force would be considered only in the gravest emergency.

Q. *What do you expect is going to be achieved in the first meeting between the consumers and the producers?*
Secretary Kissinger: The industrialized nations suffer in general from the illusion that talk is a substitute for substance. And what *might* happen is used as an excuse for not doing what *can* happen. What can happen at a consumer-producer meeting depends entirely upon whether the consumers manage to bring about concrete cooperation and whether they can concert common positions *before* the conference. In the absence of these two conditions, the consumer-producer conference will not take place with our participation. If it did take place, it would only repeat in a multilateral forum the bilateral dialogues that are already going on.

There is too much talk to the effect that there is no consumer-producer dialogue now. There's plenty of dialogue. We talk to *all* of the producers. We have excellent relations with Iran and Saudi Arabia. The Europeans are talking to the producers; the Japanese are talking to the producers.

We do not suffer from the absence of dialogue, but from the absence of a systematic approach, the lack of a clear direction in which to go. If you don't have a systematic coordinated approach, then a consumer-producer conference can only repeat in a multilateral forum under worse circumstances what is already going on bilaterally. So you ought to ask me the question again in about two months, when we're further down the road.

But I want to make absolutely clear that the United States is willing to have this conference. It is in fact eager to have a consumer-producer dialogue. In our original proposals to the Washington Energy Conference in February, we argued that consumer cooperation must lead as soon as possible to a consumer-producer dialogue. At that time we envisaged it for the fall of 1974. But we also want the dialogue to be serious and concrete.

It must deal with the problem of recycling. It must deal with the problem of the less developed countries. It must deal with the problem of price over a period of time. In terms of the producers, we can consider some assurance of long-term development for them. But all this requires some very careful preparation....

Q. *Many people have felt that the U.N. meeting on population in Bucharest last summer and the meeting on food in Rome were unsuccessful* *because there were too many countries represented at them. Will this problem plague the oil meetings, too?*

Secretary Kissinger: ...In general I would say the larger the membership the more unwieldy the procedures are likely to be and the more difficult it will be to achieve a consensus.

We worked hard to make the World Food Conference a success. I think that the proposals we made in Rome will probably be the basis of food policy for some time to come. Our basic point was that there already exists a large global food deficit which is certain to grow. The gap cannot be closed by the United States alone or even primarily. Whether our food aid is 4 million tons or 3 million tons is important for moral and humanitarian reasons; it is not decisive in dealing with the world food deficit, which is already approaching 25 million tons and which can grow to 80 million tons in 10 years.

What we need is a systematic effort to increase world food production, especially in the less developed countries, to have the exporting countries organize themselves so that they know where to put their efforts, and to improve world food distribution and financing. That was the major thrust of our ideas....

Raw Materials

Q. *What policy do you think the world has to adopt for making sure countries have access to raw materials?*

Secretary Kissinger: Last year at the special session of the General Assembly, I pointed out that we are facing a substantial change in world economic patterns. In the past, even the very recent past, almost all producing countries were afraid of surpluses. We're now in a period in which the idea of surpluses will seem a relic of a golden era. The pressures of population, industrialization, and increasing interdependence of the world economy impose on us some form of rational planning and interaction.

I proposed a systematic study of world resources, of raw materials, to obtain a systematic estimate of what we will be up against, even with good will, over a period of the next decade or so. I believe that we need the sort of coherent approach which is now being attempted in the field of energy; it will either be imposed on us or we will have to take the lead in developing it in other fields, including food. One of our efforts at the Rome food conference was to show how a constructive approach might work in contrast to a restrictive cartel approach of the energy producers.

Policy and Congress

Q. *Do you think there will be any legislation in the United States because the food situation, in which we have the position of the OPEC countries, is an explosive political question domestically?*

Secretary Kissinger: We're going to face a problem. We have to come to an understanding with the Congress about the proper relationship between the executive and the legislative functions—what Congress should legislate and what should be left to executive discretion. The attempt to prescribe every detail of policy by congressional action can, over a period of time, so stultify flexibility that you have no negotiating room left at all. We recognize that the Congress must exercise ultimate policy control. But what is meant by that, how much detail, is what we intend to discuss very seriously with the congressional leadership when it reassembles. I would hope that the Congress would keep in mind that we need some flexibility.

Now back to your question of how we can allocate food for use abroad and yet not drive food prices too high in this country. That's a tough problem. We have to make decisions on that periodically in the light of crop reports, in the light of sustainable prices....

Impact on Europe

Q. *How long do you think the economies of Italy, the United Kingdom, and France can go without serious trouble because of the strains imposed by the oil deficits?*

Secretary Kissinger: All West European economies, with the exception of the Federal Republic of Germany, are going to be in more or less serious trouble within the next 18 months. Which is another reason for striving for a much closer coordination of economic policies.

Q. *Can this economic trouble lead to political trouble?*

Secretary Kissinger: Without any question. Every government is judged not only by its performance but whether it is believed to be trying to master the real problems before it. F. D. Roosevelt could go along for several years without a great improvement in the economic conditions because the public *believed* he was dealing with the problems. The danger of purely national policies is that they are patently inadequate for dealing with economic problems—especially in Europe—and as the sense of impotence magnifies, the whole political base will erode.

As it is, the Communist vote in Italy, and to some extent in France, has remained constant regardless of economic conditions. A substantial proportion of the population has felt sufficiently disaffected with the system, even when the system was performing well, that they voted Communist in order to keep pressure on. As the Communist vote grows, the flexibility of the political system diminishes. Economic decline in Europe would therefore have serious political consequences.

Q. *There appears to be a rise in enthusiasm for the far right, too, a feeling that what is needed is an authoritative man that can cope with these labor problems, these inflation problems, et cetera.*

Secretary Kissinger: If you have a major economic crisis, the emergence of authoritarian governments of the left or the right is a distinct possibility.

Q. *In Europe, the charge is made that you have sold out Western civiliza-tion for 18 months of peace in the Middle East. Why do Europeans feel this hostility toward the United States and toward you?*

Secretary Kissinger: Well, of course I'd like to know who these Europeans are—for my own education. What would they have had us do?

Q. *They're talking about military action.*

Secretary Kissinger: The fact of the matter is that the governments they represent systematically opposed every move we made in the Middle East; every strong action that was taken in the Middle East was taken by the United States. Had we taken military action in the Middle East, we would have faced violent opposition from their own governments.

Our difficulty in the Middle East is caused in part by our inability to organize cooperation even for nonmilitary action. The efforts the ad-ministration made diplomatically to lift the oil embargo reduced, at least for a time, the dangers in the Middle East. It gave everyone a breathing space. We gave up nothing. Except the possibility of military action, which was a chimerical idea....

Why are the Europeans so hostile to the United States? I think they suffer from an enormous feeling of insecurity. The recognize that their safety depends on the United States, their economic well-being depends on the United States, and they know that we're essentially right in what we're doing. So the sense of impotence, the inability to do domestically what they know to be right, produces a certain peevishness which always stops just short of policy actions. No foreign minister ever says this.

Trade

Q. *Even though the trade bill [of 1974] has been passed, do you think the economic difficulties here in the United States and abroad will make it possible to reduce tariffs and nontariff barriers?*

Secretary Kissinger: I think it is essential that we go into these trade negotiations with the attitude of creating a new international trading system. It is the only hope we have of avoiding the political consequences we talked about earlier. If we begin to draw into ourselves, we will cause a loss of confidence. We must act as if these problems can be overcome. Maybe they can't be, but they will never be licked if we do not build a new inter-national economic environment with some conviction.

Q. *Will Congress' restrictions on Export-Import Bank credits* have any impact on trade with the Soviet Union or detente?*

Secretary Kissinger: The congressional restrictions have deprived the United States of important and maybe fundamental leverage. The Soviet Union was much more interested in credits than it was in trade, because for the next four or five years it will have very little to give in reciprocal trade.

---

* The Trade Act of 1974 provided that any country denying its citizens the right to emigrate would be prohibited from receiving U.S. government credits and credit or investment guarantees from the Export-Import Bank and the Commodity Credit Corporation. The measure was directed toward Soviet restrictions on the emigration of its Jewish citizens.

And this is one of those examples I had in mind before. If the Congress cannot trust the executive enough to use its credit authority with discretion, then Congress will not be able to deal with the problem by the sort of restrictions it put on aimed at depriving the credit authority granted by Congress of any effective meaning.

Three hundred million dollars over a period of four years is simply not enough to use as a bargaining chip with a major country. It has no significant impact on its economy, and therefore it is the surest guarantee it will be wasted.

For two years, against the opposition of most newspapers, we refused to extend credit to the Soviet Union until there was an amelioration of its foreign policy conduct. You remember various congressional amendments were introduced urging us to liberalize trade. The corollary of this was if there was more moderate Soviet conduct, trade and credits could open up. I believe that the recent Soviet statements on Jewish emigration have been caused, in part, by Soviet disappointment with the credit restrictions.

But beyond that, a President who has only $300 million of credit flexibility over four years is forced in a crisis more and more to rely on diplomatic or military pressures. He has no other cards. The economic card has been effectively removed from his hand....

Q. *Do you think that Soviet disappointment over credits will cause a hardening of their position on emigration of Jews?*

Secretary Kissinger: If these trends continue in the United States, you can expect a general hardening of the Soviet position across the board over a period of time. They will not go back to the cold war in one day. But there are many things the Soviet Union could do that would make our position much more complicated. What could happen in Europe, in the Middle East, in Southeast Asia, if the Soviet Union pursued a policy of maximizing our difficulties? Most of the criticism leveled at the Soviet Union these days is that they are not solving our difficulties, not that they are exacerbating them. I think the restrictions on Exim credits will have an unfortunate effect on U.S.-Soviet relations.

Q. *Do you see any way that the countries of the world can better coordinate their economic and financial policies?*

Secretary Kissinger: One interesting feature of our recent discussions with both the Europeans and Japanese has been this emphasis on the need for economic coordination. In April 1973, in my "Year of Europe" speech, I proposed the coordination of economic policies and of energy policies. At that time, the proposal was generally resisted on the grounds that we were trying to produce a linkage where the obligations had never run to economic matters. In all the recent meetings of the President with heads of government, and all the meetings I have had with Foreign Ministers, our allies and friends have absolutely insisted that we coordinate economic policies. So you have had a 180-degree turn in one year.

How you in fact coordinate policies is yet an unsolved problem, but it must be solved. Otherwise we will have a succession of beggar-thy-neighbor policies and countries trying to take a free ride on the actions of their partners.

Q. *Do you believe we have to go beyond what is done at the Organization for Economic Cooperation and Development?*

Secretary Kissinger: I don't know if we need new structures, but I think we need new approaches to existing structures. I haven't thought through whether we need new structures.

In the next 10 years you will have coordinated fiscal policy, including ours. I am not saying they have to be identical, but they have to be coordinated.

We have greater latitude than the others because we can do much on our own. The others can't. But it is an important aspect of leadership to exercise our freedom of action with restraint and to let others participate in decisions affecting their future.

Q. *Is there any chance of coordinating better U.S. international economic policy, particularly since the Council on International Economic Policy seems to be losing its power?*

Secretary Kissinger: You can't look at policies of a government in terms of organizational mechanisms. The Council on International Economic Policy was created at a time when the National Security Council was essentially divorced from economic policies. Then it became clear that every economic policy had profound foreign policy implications and really required political inspiration and leadership to make it effective. You could never implement the energy policy as a purely economic matter; it has been a foreign policy matter from the beginning....

Arab Investments

Q. *Should there be additional legislation to protect U.S. industry from ownership by Arab oil money? If so, what shape should the legislation take?*

Secretary Kissinger: We are now studying the ways that oil producers' money could be invested in the United States and what we should protect against. We haven't come to any conclusions because if you get a manageable minority interest, that would be in our interest. If you get actual control over strategic industries, then you have to determine how that control would be exercised before you know how to avoid it. There are some industrial segments we would not want to be dominated by potentially hostile investors. Since we haven't completed the study, I can't give you a conclusive answer....

STATE OF THE UNION, ECONOMY MESSAGES—AND REBUTTAL

January 13 and 15, 1975

In mid-January 1975, neither President Ford nor congressional Democrats could point to a rosy state of the union. The United States remained mired in economic recession and plagued by difficulties involved in assuring sufficient energy supplies for the future. The real gross national product (GNP) had declined 9.1 per cent in the last quarter of 1974, inflation continued high at an annual rate of 13.7 per cent and unemployment had risen in December to 7.1 per cent.

When President Ford delivered his first State of the Union address to Congress Jan. 15, he declared, "I've got bad news and I don't expect much if any applause." He presented tough measures aimed at stabilizing the economy and achieving national self-sufficiency in energy. His message focused almost exclusively on economic and energy matters. Other proposals for domestic legislation would be sent to Congress later, in separate messages, he said.

Congressional Democrats had already sought to upstage Ford with proposals of their own to improve the economic and energy outlooks. At a news conference Jan. 13 House Speaker Carl Albert (D Okla.) unveiled alternatives that had been designed by a 10-member task force of the House Democratic Steering and Policy Committee. Not to be outdone, Ford attempted to blunt the impact of the Democratic proposals by previewing his state-of-the-union remarks in a televised address to the nation only hours after the Democratic plan had been announced.

Ford and the Democrats were in agreement on quick action to cut taxes and save energy. There was no quarrel with the President's request, in his

State of the Union address, for action by Congress within 90 days on recession-fighting tax cuts and energy-conserving measures. There was also common determination to reduce unemployment, foster energy self-sufficiency and push the economy out of its precipitous 1974-75 decline.

However, there were differences of opinion over how far the government could go in trying to stimulate recovery without setting off a fresh burst of inflation. Emboldened by their swollen House and Senate majorities, Democratic leaders were vowing to press their own program for bringing the economy out of its deep downturn. Ford and the Democratic 94th Congress still appeared headed for a renewed struggle over the long-term course of economic and energy policies.

Ford's Economic Proposals

After declaring that "the state of the Union is not good," the President abandoned his earlier position that curbing inflation was the most immediate priority. "The emphasis of our economic efforts," he said, "must now shift from inflation to jobs." Because increased consumer demand and business flexibility would tend to create more jobs, he proposed a one-shot $16-billion tax reduction effective only for 1975. Twelve per cent of 1974 income taxes paid by individuals would be refunded up to a $1,000 limit, thereby reducing total personal taxes by $12-billion. In addition, business would be stimulated by raising the business investment tax credit to 12 per cent during 1975, thus cutting 1975 federal taxes paid by businesses and farmers by about $4-billion.

The proposed tax reductions were to be accompanied by a $30-billion package of increased oil and gasoline taxes designed to discourage consumption by raising energy prices. Because those levies would be inflationary, Ford proposed to offset the $30-billion drain on purchasing power through permanent income tax reductions, direct payments to the poor and a 6 per cent reduction in the corporation income tax rate. To deal with the continuing threat of inflation, the President challenged Congress to come to grips with "a fundamental issue we . . . must jointly solve." That issue, he said, was the self-sustaining growth of federal budget spending and the inflationary strains of federal borrowing on financial markets.

Ford's Energy Proposals

Ford blamed the nation's economic troubles in part on the fact that the price of oil had quadrupled in the past year. With domestic oil production declining and demand growing, the country was increasingly dependent for its fuel on a cartel of foreign producers. To remedy that situation, the President outlined a comprehensive energy program that he said would ease the immediate supply-demand squeeze, "make us invulnerable to cut-offs of foreign oil" by 1985 and turn the United States into a major supplier of "free world" energy needs by the end of the century. His program contained three phases: short-term, mid-term and long-range policies.

For the short term, Ford said he would take immediate administrative steps to reduce the nation's dependence on foreign oil, stimulate domestic production and reduce consumption. He announced an increase of $3 a barrel in the import fee on foreign crude oil and petroleum products, to be imposed on a graduated basis between February and April, and he outlined a second series of proposals geared to making the United States independent of foreign fuel supplies by 1985. To increase domestic supplies, the administration would step up exploration and leasing of oil and gas resources on the Outer Continental Shelf, take steps to speed coal leasing and production and review the financial and regulatory status of electric utilities.

Along with his proposals for increasing supplies, the President listed several administrative and legislative proposals aimed at conserving energy. A White House fact sheet on the subject noted that the major automobile companies had agreed to increase auto fuel economy by 40 per cent by the model year 1980 if Congress relaxed clean air standards. The administration was also working on "energy efficiency goals" for electric appliances.

For the long term, Ford outlined a program to promote production of synthetic fuels. He called for increased funding of energy research and development, to be coordinated by the new Energy Research and Development Administration (ERDA). The synthetic fuels program would include government incentives such as capital subsidies and price guarantees to encourage production, with a goal of one-million barrels of synthetic fuel a day by 1985.

Reaction to Ford's Message

Republicans generally praised the President for not trying to gloss over the nation's problems. "It was a tough speech and he has put the ball right in our court," said Sen. Edward W. Brooke (R Mass.). "Now it is up to Congress to act." The tax-cutting proposal won quick support from members of both parties, but reaction to the plan for increasing oil prices was skeptical. Rep. Al Ullman (D Ore.), chairman of the House Ways and Means Committee, said he hoped the House would be able to vote on the tax cut by March. But he was not impressed by other presidential proposals: "It is far from the broad definitive program the nation needs," he said. "To do the job, we will have to have a more dynamic program."

Democratic Alternatives

"We mean business," Speaker Albert declared in making public the Democratic "emergency" plan for bringing the economy out of recession, checking inflation and conserving energy. "We intend to act," he said. "The state of the economy is probably worse than it's ever been since before World War II." Major aspects of the Democratic plan included a $10- to $20-billion tax cut for lower- and middle-income persons, closing of corpora-

tion tax loopholes, reduced interest rates, additional public service jobs and aid to the ailing housing industry.

To curb a continuing wage-price spiral, House Democrats called for a "tough but selective program." They vigorously opposed a return to the policies of the Nixon administration which, they said, had resulted in "a cruel diminution of the wage-earner's purchasing power." At the same time they opposed the "toothless tiger" approach of the Ford administration.

Another target for specific action was "those industries where near monopoly and 'administered' prices render the forces of true competition inoperable." Because "voluntary [energy] restrictions simply have not worked," proposals also were offered for mandatory allocation of petroleum and other fuels, increased gasoline taxes, rationing of gasoline and home heating oil, higher taxes on power boats and high-powered cars and redesign of utility rates to discourage excess use.

Action on Energy and Economic Proposals

By July 1975, the Democratic leadership's economic and energy program was in disarray because Democrats themselves could not agree to an increase in taxes on gasoline as the central pillar of their plan to reduce energy demand. They also had had only limited success with their proposals to lessen the impact of the recession. Their more far-reaching measures to create jobs and assist home buyers were vetoed by President Ford. And Ford's vetoes stuck, despite earlier Democratic warnings about a "veto-proof" Congress.

The Democrats did manage to gain enactment of an income-tax cut for individuals and businesses totaling $22.8-billion. The bill signed into law by President Ford on March 29 also withdrew oil and gas depletion allowances enjoyed by major petroleum companies and curbed tax preferences of multinational corporations.

Following are the texts of President Ford's first State of the Union address as delivered to Congress Jan. 15, 1975, Ford's televised address on economic and energy proposals Jan. 13, 1975, and alternative economic and energy proposals put forth Jan. 13, 1975, by the Democratic leadership of the House of Representatives:

STATE OF THE UNION MESSAGE

Mr. Speaker, Mr. Vice President, members of the 94th Congress and distinguished guests:

Twenty-six years ago, a freshman Congressman, a young fellow with lots of idealism who was out to change the world, stood before Sam Rayburn in the well of the House and solemnly swore to the same oath that all of you took yesterday—an unforgettable experience, and I congratulate you all.

Two days later, that same freshman sat at the back of this great chamber—over there someplace—as President Truman, all charged up by his single-handed election victory, reported as the Constitution requires on the State of the Union.

When the bipartisan applause stopped, President Truman said:

"I am happy to report to the Eighty-first Congress that the State of the Union is good. Our Nation is better able than ever before to meet the needs of the American people and to give them their fair chance in the pursuit of happiness. It is foremost among the nations of the world in the search for peace."

Today, that freshman member from Michigan stands where Mr. Truman stood and I must say to you that the state of the union is not good.

Millions of Americans are out of work. Recession and inflation are eroding the money of millions more. Prices are too high and sales are too slow.

This year's federal deficit will be about $30-billion; next year's probably $45-billion. The national debt will rise to over $500-billion.

Our plant capacity and productivity are not increasing fast enough. We depend on others for essential energy.

Some people question their government's ability to make hard decisions and stick with them. They expect Washington politics as usual.

Yet, what President Truman said on January 5, 1949, is even more true in 1975.

We are better able to meet our peoples' needs.

All Americans do have a fairer chance to pursue happiness. Not only are we still the foremost nation in the pursuit of peace, but today's prospects of attaining it are infinitely brighter.

Bad News

There were 59,000,000 Americans employed at the start of 1949. Now there are more than 85,000,000 Americans who have jobs. In comparable dollars, the average income of the American family has doubled during the past 26 years.

Now, I want to speak very bluntly. I've got bad news, and I don't expect much if any applause. The American people want action and it will take both the Congress and the President to give them what they want. Progress and solutions can be achieved. And they will be achieved.

My message today is not intended to address all of the complex needs of America. I will send separate messages making specific recommendations for domestic legislation, such as the extension of General Revenue Sharing and the Voting Rights Act.

The moment has come to move in a new direction. We can do this by fashioning a new partnership between the Congress on the one hand, the White House on the other and the people we both represent.

Let us mobilize the most powerful and creative industrial nation that ever existed on this earth to put all our people to work. The emphasis on our economic efforts must now shift from inflation to jobs.

Tax Cut

To bolster business and industry and to create new jobs, I propose a one-year tax reduction of $16-billion. Three-quarters would go to individuals and one-quarter to promote business investment.

This cash rebate to individuals amounts to 12 per cent of the 1974 tax payments—a total cut of $12-billion, with a maximum of $1,000 per return.

I call on the Congress to act by April 1. If you do, and I hope you will, the Treasury can send the first check for half the rebate in May and the second by September.

The other one-fourth of the cut, about $4-billion, will go to business, including farms, to promote expansion and to create more jobs. The one-year reduction for businesses would be in the form of a liberalized investment tax credit increasing the rate to 12 per cent for all business.

This tax cut does not include the more fundamental reforms needed in our tax system. But it points us in the right direction—allowing taxpayers rather than the government to spend their pay.

Cutting taxes, now, is essential if we are to turn the economy around. A tax cut offers the best hope of creating more jobs. Unfortunately, it will increase the size of the budget deficit. Therefore, it is more important than ever that we take steps to control the growth of federal expenditures.

Spending Growth

Part of our trouble is that we have been self-indulgent. For decades, we have been voting ever-increasing levels of government benefits—and now the bill has come due. We have been adding so many new programs that the size and the growth of the federal budget has taken on a life of its own.

One characteristic of these programs is that their cost increases automatically every year because the number of people eligible for most of the benefits increases every year. When these programs were enacted, there was no dollar amount set. No one knows what they will cost. All we know is that whatever they cost last year, they will cost more next year.

It is a question of simple arithmetic. Unless we check the excessive growth of federal expenditures or impose on ourselves matching increases in taxes, we will continue to run huge inflationary deficits in the federal budget.

If we project the current built-in momentum of federal spending through the next 15 years, state, federal and local government expenditures could easily comprise half of our gross national product. This compares with less than a third in 1975.

I have just concluded the process of preparing the budget submissions for fiscal year 1976. In that budget, I will propose legislation to restrain the growth of a number of existing programs. I have also concluded that no new spending programs can be initiated this year, except for energy. Further, I will not hesitate to veto any new spending programs adopted by the Congress.

As an additional step toward putting the federal government's house in order, I recommend a five per cent limit on federal pay increases in 1975. In all government programs tied to the consumer price index—including social security, civil service and military retirement pay, and food stamps—I also propose a one-year maximum increase of 5 per cent.

None of these recommended ceiling limitations, over which Congress has final authority, are easy to propose, because in most cases they involve anticipated payments to many, many deserving people. Nonetheless, it must be done. I must emphasize that I am not asking to eliminate, to reduce, to freeze these payments. I am merely recommending that we slow down the rate at which these payments increase and these programs grow.

Only a reduction in the growth of spending can keep federal borrowing down and reduce the damage to the private sector from high interest rates. Only a reduction in spending can make it possible for the Federal Reserve System to avoid an inflationary growth in the money supply and thus restore balance to our economy. A major reduction in the growth of federal spending can help dispel the uncertainty that so many feel about our economy, and put us on the way to curing our economic ills.

If we do not act to slow down the rate of increase in federal spending, the United States Treasury will be legally obligated to spend more than $360-billion in fiscal year 1976—even if no new programs are enacted. These are not matters of conjecture or prediction, but again a matter of simple arithmetic. The size of these numbers and their implications for our everyday life and the health of our economic system are shocking.

I submitted to the last Congress a list of budget deferrals and rescissions. There will be more cuts recommended in the budget I will submit. Even so, the level of outlays for fiscal year 1976 is still much, much too high. Not only is it too high for this year but the decisions we make now will inevitably have a major and growing impact on expenditure levels in future years. I think this is a very fundamental issue we, the Congress and I, must jointly solve.

Energy

The economic disruption we and others are experiencing stems in part from the fact that the world price of petroleum has quadrupled in the last year. But in all honesty, we cannot put all of the blame on the oil exporting nations. We, the United States, are not blameless. Our growing dependence upon foreign sources has been adding to our vulnerability for years and years and we did nothing to prepare ourselves for an event such as the embargo of 1973.

During the 1960s, this country had a surplus capacity of crude oil, which we were able to make available to our trading partners whenever there was a disruption of supply. This surplus capacity enabled us to influence both supplies and prices of crude oil throughout the world. Our excess capacity neutralized any effort at establishing an effective cartel, and thus the rest of the world was assured of adequate supplies of oil at reasonable prices.

21

By 1970 our surplus capacity had vanished and, as a consequence, the latent power of the oil cartel could emerge in full force. Europe and Japan, both heavily dependent on imported oil, now struggle to keep their economies in balance. Even the United States, our country, which is far more self-sufficient than most other industrial countries, has been put under serious pressure.

I am proposing a program which will begin to restore our country's surplus capacity in total energy. In this way, we will be able to assure ourselves reliable and adequate energy and help foster a new world energy stability for other major consuming nations.

But this nation and, in fact, the world must face the prospect of energy difficulties between now and 1985. This program will impose burdens on all of us with the aim of reducing our consumption of energy and increasing our production. Great attention has been paid to considerations of fairness and I can assure you that the burdens will not fall more harshly on those less able to bear them.

I am recommending a plan to make us invulnerable to cut-offs of foreign oil. It will require sacrifices. But it—and this is most important—will work.

Proposals

I have set the following national energy goals to assure that our future is as secure and as productive as our past:

• First, we must reduce oil imports by 1 million barrels per day by the end of this year and by 2 million barrels per day by the end of 1977.

• Second, we must end vulnerability to economic disruption by foreign suppliers by 1985.

• Third, we must develop our energy technology and resources so that the United States has the ability to supply a significant share of the energy needs of the free world by the end of this century.

To attain these objectives, we need immediate action to cut imports. Unfortunately, in the short term there are only a limited number of actions which can increase domestic supply. I will press for all of them.

I urge quick action on the necessary legislation to allow commercial production at the Elk Hills, California, Naval Petroleum Reserve. In order that we make greater use of domestic coal resources, I am submitting amendments to the Energy Supply and Environmental Coordination Act which will greatly increase the number of power plants that can be promptly converted to coal.

Obviously voluntary conservation continues to be essential, but tougher programs are also needed—and needed now. Therefore, I am using presidential powers to raise the fee on all imported crude oil and petroleum products. Crude oil fee levels will be increased $1 per barrel on February 1, by $2 per barrel on March 1 and by $3 per barrel on April 1. I will take action to reduce undue hardships on any geographic region. The foregoing are interim administrative actions. They will be rescinded when the broader but necessary legislation is enacted.

New Taxes

To that end, I am requesting the Congress to act within 90 days on a more comprehensive energy tax program. It includes:
- Excise taxes and import fees totalling $2 per barrel on product imports and on all crude oil.
- Deregulation of new natural gas and enactment of a natural gas excise tax.

I plan to take presidential initiative to decontrol the price of domestic crude oil on April 1. I urge the Congress to enact a windfall profits tax by that date to insure that oil producers do not profit unduly.

The sooner Congress acts, the more effective the oil conservation program will be and the quicker the federal revenues can be returned to our people.

I am prepared to use presidential authority to limit imports, as necessary, to guarantee success.

I want you to know that before deciding on my energy conservation program, I considered rationing and higher gasoline taxes as alternatives. In my judgment, neither would achieve the desired results and both would produce unacceptable inequities.

Increasing Supply

A massive program must be initiated to increase energy supply, to cut demand and provide new standby emergency programs to achieve the independence we want by 1985. The largest part of increased oil production must come from new frontier areas on the Outer Continental Shelf and from the Naval Petroleum Reserve No. 4 in Alaska. It is the intent of this administration to move ahead with exploration, leasing and production on those frontier areas of the Outer Continental Shelf where the environmental risks are acceptable.

Use of our most abundant domestic resource—coal—is severely limited. We must strike a reasonable compromise on environmental concerns with coal. I am submitting Clean Air amendments which will allow greater coal use without sacrificing clean air goals.

I vetoed the strip mining legislation passed by the last Congress. With appropriate changes, I will sign a revised version when it comes to the White House.

I am proposing a number of actions to energize our nuclear power program. I will submit legislation to expedite nuclear licensing and the rapid selection of sites.

In recent months, utilities have cancelled or postponed over 60 per cent of planned nuclear expansion and 30 per cent of planned additions to non-nuclear capacity. Financing problems for the industry are worsening. I am therefore recommending that the one year investment tax credit of 12 per cent be extended an additional two years to specifically speed the construction of power plants that do not use natural gas or oil. I am also submitting proposals for selective reform of state utility commission regulations.

To provide the critical stability for our domestic energy production in the face of world price uncertainty, I will request legislation to authorize and require tariffs, import quotas or price floors to protect our energy prices at levels which will achieve energy independence.

Conservation

Increasing energy supplies is not enough. We must take additional steps to cut long-term consumption. I therefore propose to the Congress:

- Legislation to make thermal efficiency standards mandatory for all new buildings in the United States.
- A new tax credit of up to $150 for those home owners who install insulation equipment.
- The establishment of an energy conservation program to help low income families purchase insulation supplies.
- Legislation to modify and defer automotive pollution standards for 5 years which will enable us to improve new automobile gas mileage by 40 per cent by 1980.

These proposals and actions, cumulatively, can reduce our dependence on foreign energy supplies to 3-5 million barrels per day by 1985. To make the United States invulnerable to foreign disruption, I propose standby emergency legislation and a strategic storage program of 1 billion barrels of oil for domestic needs and 300 million barrels for national defense purposes.

I will ask for the funds needed for energy research and development activity. I have established a goal of 1 million barrels of synthetic fuels and shale oil production per day by 1985 together with an incentive program to achieve it.

I have a very deep belief in America's capabilities. Within the next ten years, my program envisions:

- 200 major nuclear power plants,
- 250 major new coal mines,
- 150 major coal-fired power plants,
- 30 major new refineries,
- 20 major new synthetic fuel plants,
- the drilling of many thousands of new oil wells,
- the insulation of 18 million homes,
- and the manufacturing and sale of millions of new automobiles, trucks and buses that use much less fuel.

I happen to believe that we can do it. In another crisis—the one in 1942—President Franklin D. Roosevelt said this country would build 60,000 [50,000] military aircraft. By 1943, production in that program had reached 125,000 airplanes annually.

They did it then; we can do it now.

If the Congress and the American people will work with me to attain these targets, they will be achieved and will be surpassed.

From adversity, let us seize opportunity. Revenues of some $30-billion from higher energy taxes designed to encourage conservation must be refunded to the American people in a manner which corrects distortions in our tax system wrought by inflation.

People have been pushed into higher tax brackets by inflation with consequent reduction in their actual spending power. Business taxes are similarly distorted because inflation exaggerates reported profits resulting in excessive taxes.

Tax Relief

Accordingly, I propose that future individual income taxes be reduced by $16.5-billion. This will be done by raising the low income allowance and reducing tax rates. This continuing tax cut will primarily benefit lower and middle income taxpayers.

For example, a typical family of four with a gross income of $5,600 now pays $185 in federal income taxes. Under this tax cut plan, they would pay nothing. A family of four with a gross income of $12,500 now pays $1,260 in federal taxes. My plan reduces that total by $300. Families grossing $20,000 would receive a reduction of $210.

Those with the very lowest incomes, who can least afford higher costs, must also be compensated. I propose a payment of $80 to every person 18 years of age and older in that very limited category.

State and local governments will receive $2-billion in additional revenue sharing to offset their increased energy costs.

To offset inflationary distortions and to generate more economic activity, the corporate tax rate will be reduced from 48 per cent to 42 per cent.

International Problems

Now, let me turn, if I might, to the international dimension of the present crisis. At no time in our peacetime history has the state of the nation depended more heavily on the state of the world. And seldom if ever has the state of the world depended more heavily on the state of our nation.

The economic distress is global. We will not solve it at home unless we help to remedy the profound economic dislocation abroad. World trade and monetary structure provides markets, energy, food and vital raw materials—for all nations. This international system is now in jeopardy.

This nation can be proud of significant achievements in recent years in solving problems and crises. The Berlin Agreement, the SALT agreements, our new relationship with China, the unprecedented efforts in the Middle East—are immensely encouraging. But the world is not free from crisis. In a world of 150 nations, where nuclear technology is proliferating and regional conflicts continue, international security cannot be taken for granted.

So let there be no mistake about it: international cooperation is a vital factor of our lives today. This is not a moment for the American people to turn inward. More than ever before, our own well-being depends on America's determination and America's leadership in the whole wide world.

We are a great nation—spiritually, politically, militarily, diplomatically and economically. America's commitment to international security has sustained the safety of allies and friends in many areas—in the Middle East, in Europe, in Asia. Our turning away would unleash new instabilities, new dangers around the globe, which would, in turn, threaten our own security.

At the end of World War II, we turned a similar challenge into an historic opportunity and, I might add, an historic achievement. An old order was in disarray; political and economic institutions were shattered. In that period, this nation and its partners built new institutions, new mechanisms of mutual support and cooperation. Today, as then, we face an historic opportunity. If we act imaginatively and boldly as we acted then, this period will in retrospect be seen as one of the great creative moments of our nation's history.

The whole world is watching to see how we respond.

A resurgent American economy would do more to restore the confidence of the world in its own future than anything else we can do. The program that this Congress passes can demonstrate to the world that we have started to put our own house in order. If we can show that this nation is able and willing to help other nations meet the common challenge, it can demonstrate that the United States will fulfill its responsibilities as a leader among nations.

Quite frankly, at stake is the future of the industrialized democracies, which have perceived their destiny in common and sustained it in common for 30 years.

The developing nations are also at a turning point. The poorest nations see their hopes of feeding their hungry and developing their societies shattered by the economic crisis. The long-term economic future for the producers of raw materials also depends on cooperative solutions.

Our relations with the Communist countries are a basic factor of the world environment. We must seek to build a long-term basis for coexistence. We will stand by our principles. We will stand by our interests; we will act firmly when challenged. The kind of world we want depends on a broad policy of creating mutual incentives for restraint and for cooperation.

Strength and Diplomacy

As we move forward to meet our global challenges and opportunities, we must have the tools to do the job.

Our military forces are strong and ready. This military strength deters aggression against our allies, stabilizes our relations with former adversaries and protects our homeland. Fully adequate conventional and strategic forces cost many, many billions, but these dollars are sound insurance for our safety and a more peaceful world.

Military strength alone is not sufficient. Effective diplomacy is also essential in preventing conflict and building world understanding. The Vladivostok negotiations with the Soviet Union represent a major step in moderating strategic arms competition. My recent discussions with leaders of the Atlantic Community, Japan and South Korea have contributed to meeting the common challenge.

But we have serious problems before us that require cooperation between the President and the Congress. By the Constitution and tradition, the execution of foreign policy is the responsibility of the President.

In recent years, under the stress of the Vietnam war, legislative restrictions on the President's ability to execute foreign policy and military decisions have proliferated. As a member of the Congress, I opposed some and approved others. As President, I welcome the advice and cooperation of the House and Senate.

But, if our foreign policy is to be successful, we cannot rigidly restrict in legislation the ability of the President to act. The conduct of negotiation is ill-suited to such limitation. Legislative restrictions, intended for the best motives and purposes, can have the opposite result, as we have seen most recently in our trade relations with the Soviet Union. For my part, I pledge this administration will act in the closest consultation with the Congress as we face delicate situations and troubled times throughout the globe.

Renewed Pledge

When I became President only five months ago, I promised the last Congress a policy of communication, conciliation, compromise and cooperation. I renew that pledge to the new members of this Congress.

Let me sum it up:

America needs a new direction which I have sought to chart here today—a change of course which will:
- put the unemployed back to work;
- increase real income and production;
- restrain the growth of federal government spending;
- achieve energy independence; and
- advance the cause of world understanding.

We have the ability. We have the know-how. In partnership with the American people, we will achieve these objectives.

As our 200th anniversary approaches, we owe it to ourselves, and to posterity, to rebuild our political and economic strength. Let us make America, once again, and for centuries more to come, what it has so long been—a stronghold and beacon-light of liberty for the whole world. Thank you.

GERALD R. FORD

Beginning on the next page is the White House text of President Ford's Jan. 13 address, broadcast on nationwide television and radio, on new economic and energy proposals:

Good evening.

Without wasting words, I want to talk with you tonight about putting our domestic house in order. We must turn America in a new direction. We must reverse the current recession, reduce unemployment and create more jobs.

We must restore the confidence of consumers and investors alike. We must continue an effective plan to curb inflation. We must, without any delay, take firm control of our progress as a free people.

Together we can and will do this job. Our national character is strong on self-discipline and the will to win. Americans are at their very best when the going is rough. Right now, the going is rough, and it may get rougher. But if we do what must be done, we will be on our way to better days. We have an historic opportunity.

On Wednesday I will report to the new Congress on the State of the Union and ask for its help to quickly improve it. But neither Congress nor the President can pass laws or issue orders to assure economic improvement and instant prosperity. The Government can help by equalizing unfair burdens, by setting an example of sound economic actions and by exerting leadership through clear and coordinated national recovery programs.

Tonight I want to talk to you about what must be done. After all, you are the people most affected.

Since becoming your President five months ago, economic problems have been my foremost concern. Two elements of our problem are long-range—inflation and energy. Both are affected not only by our actions, but also by international forces beyond our direct control.

The new and disturbing element in the economic picture is our worsening recession and the unemployment that goes with it. We have made some progress in slowing the upward spiral of inflation and getting interest rates started down, but we have suffered sudden and serious setbacks in sales and unemployment.

Shift of Emphasis

Therefore, we must shift our emphasis from inflation to recession, but in doing so, we must not lose sight of the very real and deadly dangers of rising prices and declining domestic energy supplies.

Americans are no longer in full control of their own national destiny, when that destiny depends on uncertain foreign fuel at high prices fixed by others. Higher energy costs compound both inflation and recession, and dependence on others for future energy supplies is intolerable to our national security.

Therefore, we must wage a simultaneous three-front campaign against recession, inflation and energy dependence. We have no choice. We need within 90 days the strongest and most far-reaching energy conservation program we have ever had.

Yes, gasoline and oil will cost even more than they do now, but this program will achieve two important objectives—it will discourage the unnecessary use of petroleum products, and it will encourage the development and substitution of other fuels and newer sources of energy.

To get started immediately on an urgent national energy plan, I will use the Presidential emergency powers to reduce our dependence on foreign oil by raising import fees on each barrel of foreign crude oil by $1 to $3 over the next three months.

Energy Taxes

A more comprehensive program of energy conservation taxes on oil and natural gas to reduce consumption substantially must be enacted by the Congress. The revenues derived from such taxes will be returned to the economy. In addition, my energy conservation program contains oil allocation authority to avoid undue hardships in any one geographic area, such as New England, or in any specific industry or areas of human need where oil is essential.

The plan prevents windfall profits by producers. There must also be volunteer efforts to cut gasoline and other energy use.

My national energy conservation plan will urge Congress to grant a five-year delay on higher automobile pollution standards in order to achieve a 40 percent improvement in miles per gallon.

Stronger measures to speed the development of other domestic energy resources, such as coal, geothermal, solar and nuclear power are also essential.

This plan requires personal sacrifice. But if we all pitch in, we will meet our goal of reducing foreign oil imports by one million barrels a day by the end of this year and by two million barrels before the end of 1977. The energy conservation measures I have outlined tonight will be supplemented by use of Presidential power to limit oil imports as necessary to fully achieve these goals.

By 1985—10 years from now—the United States will be invulnerable to foreign energy disruptions or oil embargoes such as we experienced last year. Of course, our domestic needs come first. But our gains in energy independence will be fully coordinated with our friends abroad. Our efforts should prompt similar action by our allies.

If Congress speedily enacts this national energy program, there will be no need for compulsory rationing or long waiting lines at the service station. Gasoline prices will go up, though not as much as with a 20 cent a gallon gas tax. Furthermore, the burden of the conservation taxes on oil will be shared by all petroleum users, not just motorists.

Tax Cut

Now, let me talk about the problem of unemployment. This country needs an immediate Federal income tax cut of $16 billion. Twelve billion dollars, or three-fourths of the total of this cut, should go to individual tax-payers in the form of a cash rebate amounting to 12 percent of their 1974 tax payments—up to a $1,000 rebate. If Congress acts by April first, you will get your first check for half the rebate in May and the rest by September.

The other one-fourth of the cut, about $4 billion, will go to business tax-payers, including farmers, to promote plant expansion and create more jobs. This will be in the form of an increase in the investment tax credit to 12 percent for one year. There will be special provisions to assist essential public utilities to step up their energy capacity. This will encourage capital spending and productivity, the key to recovery and growth.

As soon as the new revenues from energy conservation taxes are received, we will be able to return $30 billion to the economy in the form of additional payments and credits to individuals, business and State and local governments. Cash payments from this total also will be available to those who pay no income taxes because of low earnings. They are the hardest hit by inflation and higher energy costs. This combined program adds up to $46 billion—$30 billion in returned energy tax revenues to compensate for higher fuel costs and $16 billion in tax cuts to help provide more jobs. And the energy conservation tax revenues will continue to be put back into the economy as long as the emergency lasts.

Bigger Deficits

This economic program is different in emphasis from the proposals I put forward last October. The reason is that the situation has changed. You know it, and I know it. What we need most urgently today is more spending money in your pockets rather than in the Treasury in Washington. Let's face it, a tax cut to bolster the economy will mean a bigger Federal deficit temporarily, and I have fought against deficits all my public life. But unless our economy revives rapidly, Federal tax revenues will shrink so much that future deficits will be even larger. But I have not abandoned my lifelong belief in fiscal restraint. In the long run, there is no other real remedy for our economic troubles.

While wrestling with the budgets for this year and next, I found that at least three-quarters of all Federal expenditures are required by laws already on the books. The President cannot, by law, cut spending in an ever-growing list of programs which provide mandatory formulas for payments to State and local governments and to families and to individuals. Unless these laws are changed, I can tell you there are only two ways to go—still higher Federal taxes or the more ruinous hidden tax of inflation. Unchecked, Federal programs mandated by law will be prime contributors to Federal deficits of $30 to $50 billion this year and next. Deficits of this magnitude are wrong—except on a temporary basis in the most extenuating circumstances.

Reform of these costly mandated Federal spending programs will take time. Meanwhile, in order to keep the budget deficit as low as possible, I will do what I can.

Spending Moratorium

In my State of the Union and subsequent messages, I will not propose any new Federal spending programs except for energy, and the Congress—your representatives in Washington—share an equal responsibility to see that no new spending programs are enacted.

I will not hesitate to veto any new spending programs the Congress sends to me. Many proposed Federal spending programs are desirable and have had my support in the past. They cost money—your tax dollars. Mainly it is time to declare a one-year moratorium on new Federal spending programs.

I need your support in this. It is vital that your representatives in Congress know that you share this concern about inflation.

I believe the Federal Government ought to show all Americans it practices what it preaches about sacrifices and self-restraint. Therefore, I will insist on a 5 percent limit on any Federal pay increases in 1975, and I will ask Congress to put the same temporary 5 percent ceiling on automatic cost of living increases in Government and military retirement pay and Social Security.

Government alone cannot bring the cost of living down, but until it does start down, Government can refrain from pushing it up. For only when the cost of living comes down can everybody get full value from a pension or a paycheck. I want to hasten that day.

New Programs

Tonight I have summarized the highlights of my energy and my economic programs. They must go hand in hand, as I see it.

On Wednesday I will spell out these proposals to the Congress. There will be other recommendations, both short-term and long-range, to make our program as fair to all as possible.

I will press for prompt action and responsible legislation. The danger of doing nothing is great. The danger of doing too much is just as great.

We cannot afford to throw monkey wrenches into our complex economic machine just because it isn't running at full speed. We are in trouble, but we are not on the brink of another Great Depression.

Our political and economic system today is many times stronger than it was in the 1930s. We have income safeguards and unemployment cushions built into our economy. I have taken and will continue to take whatever steps are needed to prevent massive dislocations and personal hardships and, in particular, the tragedy of rising unemployment.

But sound solutions to our economic difficulties depend primarily on the strong support of each one of you. Self-restraint must be exercised by big and small business, by organized and unorganized labor, by State and local governments, as well as by the Federal Government

No one will be allowed to prosper from the temporary hardships most of us willingly bear, nor can we permit any special interests to gain from our common distress.

To improve the economic outlook we must rekindle faith in ourselves. Nobody is going to pull us out of our troubles but ourselves, and by our own bootstraps.

In 200 years as a Nation we have triumphed over external enemies and internal conflicts and each time we have emerged stronger than before. This has called for determined leaders and dedicated people, and this call has never gone unheeded.

In every crisis, the American people have closed ranks, rolled up their sleeves and rallied to do whatever had to be done.

I ask you and those who represent you in the Congress to work to turn our economy around, declare our energy independence and resolve to make our free society again the wonder of the world.

The beginning of our Bicentennial is a good time to reaffirm our pride and purpose as Americans who help themselves and help their neighbors no matter how tough the task. For my part, I will do what I believe is right for all our people—to do my best for America as long as I occupy this historic house.

We know what must be done. The time to act is now. We have our Nation to preserve and our future to protect. Let us act together.

May God bless our endeavors. Thank you, and good night.

> *Text of Democratic alternative plans presented by House Speaker Carl Albert (D Okla.) at a news conference Jan. 13, 1975:*

The 94th Congress, convening at a moment of historic challenge to the American economy, must assume a responsibility for decisive and resourceful leadership. The critical problems of this immediate time will not yield to half-way measures, timid initiatives or public relations appeals to voluntarism. The nation at this juncture could ill afford a passive Congress which did no more than await and then react in leisurely, piecemeal fashion to executive recommendations. The public expects and is fully entitled to a coordinated program of legislative action beginning immediately and clearly designed to rebuild a healthy and stable economy in the United States. We are determined that the American people shall not be disappointed in this rightful expectation.

For too long has the economy been allowed to drift, devoid of purposeful direction. For four consecutive quarters the gross national product has shrunk. Unemployment has mounted steadily while the debilitating increase in the basic cost of living continues, its rate abated only slightly. During the past year, the purchasing power of real wages has declined by 5.6 percent. Bankruptcies and foreclosures have grown alarmingly. Residential housing starts have been cut approximately in half. Waning business investments in new plants and equipment and sagging consumer purchases reflect a lack of confidence in the future.

Mirroring the general economic malaise, the federal budget has become a principal victim of the inflation-recession. Declining economic output and rising joblessness have diminished government revenues while the extortionate and unprecedented level of interest rates has added many billions of dollars to the cost of public debt service and the swelling ranks of unemployed have added extra billions to the cost of providing unemployment compensation and public assistance. It is clear that the government cannot realistically expect to balance its budget until it comes to grips with the recessionary forces which have contributed so massively to the budgetary imbalance.

The Democratic majority in the 94th Congress totally rejects the theory that the tides of economic decline are inexorable. We do not believe that the nation has grown old and tired and incapable of a vigorous economic revival. We shall not recline in supine acquiescence to forecasts which point toward an 8 percent unemployment rate by the end of 1975. We believe that there are things which can be done to reverse the trends of deterioration. We are determined that these things shall be done. To the maximum extent consistent with the responsibility of careful legislative draftsmanship, we shall insist that several of them be done very quickly.

As one of the three equal and coordinate branches of government, we invite and wholeheartedly welcome the cooperation of the Executive branch in supporting the following legislative recommendations, in suggesting refinements and improvements, and finally in faithfully and diligently executing such programs as we shall enact. Meanwhile, the Democratic congressional leadership calls upon various committees of the Congress to begin immediately in the implementation of the following agenda.

I. IMMEDIATE ACTION GOALS

Due to the critical state of the nation's economy, we urgently request the committees of respective jurisdiction to prepare for presentation to the House the following items as soon as possible and in no case later than 90 days after our convening:

A. Tax Relief and Reform

The quickest way to generate the added purchasing power needed to counter the current recession and to ease the burden of those most damaged by inflation is through *tax relief* for low and middle income families. This can be achieved by increasing the personal income tax exemption, the standard deduction and minimum income allowance, by reducing the weight of payroll tax liabilities upon the working poor, and/or by a system of individual tax credits. The committee may wish to consider alternate or additional proposals. In any event, the amount of purchasing power released to the hands of Americans of modest income should be substantial and made quickly available.

The revenue loss thus suffered should be recouped to the extent reasonably possible by closing the loopholes that now enable large corporations and wealthy individuals to pay little or no taxes at all.

Action: Committee on Ways and Means.

33

B. Lower Interest Rates

A primary cause of the nation's simultaneous suffering from both inflation and recession is the misbegotten and prolonged policy of attempting to halt inflation solely by monetary restrictions and high interest rates. Manifestly, this policy has been counterproductive. It has not abated inflation. It has fed its fires, adding an extra layer of cost at every level of the market place. It has contributed cruelly to the massive tide of small business bankruptcies, brought homebuilding to a virtual halt, dipped a heavy hand into the pockets of most American families, added a multi-billion dollar burden to the national budget through increased debt service costs, and actually set in motion a retrogressive redistribution of national income, widening the gap between rich and poor and largely undoing the beneficial results of a decade of costly public programs.

Two immediate steps are needed to reduce interest rates and stimulate the flow of credit to vital economic sectors:

1) **Increase the Supply of Credit.** Between July 1 and October 1 of 1974, the Federal Reserve Board constricted the growth of the money supply to less than 2 percent per year at an annual rate, far below the 4-6 percent growth rate needed to finance the long-run needs of the economy. Furthermore, the stop and go policies of the Federal Reserve Board and the uncertainty generated by these policies have contributed in a major way to excessive inflation, combined with excessive unemployment. Steady and stable economic growth requires a steady and stable policy and a gradual but determined reduction of interest rates to a liveable level.

2) **Credit Allocation.** With any given supply of new money overall, a credit allocation program is needed to channel credit *away from* speculative and inflationary uses—ranging from conglomerate take-overs to gambling in foreign exchange or gold—and *toward* vital credit-starved areas, such as housing, small business, food production, power generation, state and local governments, and productive capital investment. The expanded supply of credit for these purposes could be expected to lower interest rates for these necessary activities, thus lowering costs and reducing inflationary pressures, stimulate production of vital commodities and generate jobs in the private sector.

Action: Committee on Banking, Currency and Housing.

If the combination of these actions has not begun an appreciable reversal in interest rates by July 1 of this year, we recommend the serious consideration of more dramatic remedies, including the possibility of a progressive tax on interest income which would be prohibitive on income derived from excessive rates of interest (9 percent and above) and evolving downward to nominal on income derived from low rates of interest (below 6 percent).

Action: Committee on Ways and Means.

C. The Problem of Rising Unemployment

The Democratic majority in the Congress is unequivocally dedicated to the task of increasing productive jobs and reducing unemployment. The rate of unemployment hovers today at approximately 7.1 percent. Even by the optimistic forecasts of Administration economists, this figure is expected to exceed 7.5 percent by mid-1975. This is intolerable. The recent report of the Joint Economic Committee portrays an even grimmer picture, estimating that the modest goal of a 5 percent unemployment rate cannot be expected before 1980 in the absence of a sustained overall economic growth rate of 5 to 6 percent. As a direct immediate attack on this problem we propose two approaches:

1) **Additional Public Service Jobs.** The Joint Economic Committee last month estimated the overall national need for public service jobs at 750,000. Since then the number of unemployed has increased dramatically and the need for public service jobs is correspondingly greater, outstripping even the emergency programs enacted by the 93rd Congress. The stagnating state of the economy is distressingly revealed in the ratio of funds provided in the most recent appropriation, which earmarked roughly three times as much for unemployment compensation as for public service employment. While clearly the duty of a humane nation which cannot provide useful and remunerative work, unemployment compensation is by comparison economically non-productive and personally unsatisfying. Public service jobs, admittedly second best to gainful and lasting employment in private industry, should be provided in an adequate dimension to fill the slack productively while other policies are generating a revival of the private sector.

Action: Committee on Education and Labor.

2) **Acceleration of Approved Public Works.** It is ironic that the nation suffers increasing unemployment in the building trades and a growing inventory of idle construction equipment, with ever mounting public costs for unemployment payments, at the very time that literally billions of dollars worth of badly needed and Congressionally approved civil works projects (water pollution abatement, flood control, highway, public mass transit and other constructive works) suffer unconscionable delays in administrative processing of grant applications. Legislation should be enacted to mandate early administrative funding of such projects already authorized by Congress. Such legislation should dramatically reduce the time lag created by redundant reports and proliferating paperwork and mandate a swift acceleration of construction starts.

Action: Committee on Public Works and Transportation.

D. An Emergency Housing Program

Probably the most seriously depressed sector of our economy is the housing and construction industry. Performance has fallen fully 60 percent below our national commitment to meet the need for 2.3 million new housing starts each year. As in the automotive industry, depression in housing starts has widespread "ripple" effects throughout countless other sectors of the economy. It is imperative, therefore, that significant stimulus be applied rapidly. We ask the appropriate committees to consider and recom-

35

mend emergency housing measures, including such alternatives as (1) increasing the ability of savings and loan and thrift institutions to attract adequate capital in this era of escalating interest rates which have starved the mortgage markets, (2) interest rate subsidies for low and medium priced housing for the near term until concerted effort succeeds in reducing interest rates to an acceptable level, (3) incentives for the preservation and rehabilitation of older existing housing, including multi-family dwellings, and (4) short term assistance to homeowners having difficulty making mortgage payments because of unemployment or a significant drop in income. Recognizing the complexities of the housing market and the mortgage market which fuels it, we expect the appropriate committees to exercise broad judgment and discretion in weighing these and other alternatives and to report specific recommendations to the Congress for action early in this session.

Action: Committees on Banking, Currency and Housing, Ways and Means.

E. Emergency Energy Conservation Measures

It now is apparent to all with the will to see that the alarmingly increasing gap between domestic production and domestic consumption of energy (especially petroleum) in the United States threatens not only our basic national economy but our national security as well. Just as the long term solution must lie in discovering ways to increase our production of energy, our interim salvation can be found only in vastly more effective conservation measures. We must control runaway energy consumption if the nation is to retain economic independence, let alone achieve stable and enduring economic growth. Voluntary restrictions simply have not worked. More stringent short-term measures are imperative.

To reduce our immediate energy usage and our resulting dependence on foreign oil sources, we commend to the appropriate committees for their consideration and recommendation one or more of the following courses: (1) mandatory allocation of petroleum and other forms of energy, 2) enactment of higher gasoline taxes, 3) gasoline and home fuel oil rationing, 4) higher manufacturer's excise taxes on pleasure craft and private automobiles of high horsepower, 5) restricting the sale of gasoline on certain days such as week-ends, 6) long term, low interest loans for home insulation improvements, and 7) a national examination of utility rate structures of a type that encourage energy wastefulness by rewarding large usage with low rates.

We recognize that the above include hard and in some cases unpalatable choices and that the range of options should not be limited to those here enumerated. In specific connection with 2) above, we urge very cautious and careful consideration of the effect of any proposed fuel tax increase upon the millions of working Americans who have no available or practical alternative to the use of their automobiles in getting to and from their daily work and in the conduct of their necessary business activities. A punitive retail sales tax in the range of an additional 20¢ per gallon on gasoline, as advocated by some, predictably would penalize most harshly those whose consumption of fuel is directly related to their essential employment, while providing a relatively negligible disincentive to the use of scarce fuel by the wealthy for purposes of pleasure. We suggest, therefore, that some consideration might be given to dedicating revenues from any increase in the retail gasoline tax to a trust fund for a sharply accelerated program to develop alternative fuel sources (See II B below). In the alternative, we would strongly recommend rebates adequate to compensate workers for their loss of income.

Action: Committees on Commerce and Health, and Ways and Means.

F. Wage and Price Stability

We need a tough but selective program to halt the current wage-price spiral. Phases I and II of the Nixon Administration program controlled wages with a vengeance while permitting prices to rise, resulting in a cruel diminution of the wage earner's purchasing power. There must be no return to such a policy. The present Council on Wage and Price Stability is a toothless tiger. The need is for an independent agency with subpoena power, the resources to hold extensive hearings, the authority to delay price increases up to 90 days, and in extreme cases the authority to impose controls more permanently on a selective basis. The selectivity should be aimed at those industries where near-monopoly and "administered" prices render the forces of true competition inoperable.

Action: Committees on Banking, Currency and Housing, and Government Operations.

G. Programs for the Needy

While utilizing every effective means to bring about a national economic revival, we cannot lose sight of the anguish of those whose vulnerability to the twin menaces of recession and inflation has made them the principal victims of the nation's present economic plight. We urge in particular the early enactment of legislation to forestall the apparent intention of the administration to increase the price of food stamps to low income Americans, and a more realistic measure of help to the needy aged, blind, and disabled.

Action: Committees on Agriculture, and Ways and Means.

II. OTHER IMPERATIVE GOALS OF THE 94TH CONGRESS

While the six goals listed above claim a priority of very early attention due to the impelling need for swift and decisive action to begin the economic revival, there are other goals no less imperative and no less important to the nation's economic growth and health. These goals, too, should be effectively addressed by the 94th Congress during its 1975 session.

A. Health and Medical Care

Circumstances dictate the timely enactment of a comprehensive national program to assure adequate health and medical care for all. The ravages inflicted upon family income by the steadily rising costs of medical care are well known to most Americans. Less well recognized is the significant impact such a plan could have on the nation's economy. The job-creating effects of public works programs, housing and other construction activities are easily apparent, but none of these exceeds health and medical care programs in the potential for generating useful employment. Health care is one of the most labor-intensive industries in the entire economy.

Action: Committees on Ways and Means, and Commerce and Health.

B. New Sources of Energy

In addition to the strictly conservation methods outlined above (Part I, Item E) it is obvious that the nation urgently needs to take major steps toward energy self-sufficiency. We ask the appropriate committees to consider and report their recommendations on ways to encourage exploration for new domestic oil and gas supplies, to encourage the development of secondary and tertiary recovery techniques for existing wells, to develop a national strategic energy reserve, and to mandate a concentrated program of research and development aimed at other sources and methods of energy production.

In the intermediate time frame, it is obvious that the nation shall depend to a profoundly greater degree upon coal and nuclear power. We, therefore, recommend to the appropriate Committees the early perfection of responsible surface mining legislation and the improvement of regulatory procedures relative to the construction of energy production facilities.

The long term solution must of necessity feature the earliest possible development of energy alternatives to petroleum. This concentrated effort should include the rapid perfection of economically viable methods of coal conversion and levels of funding adequate to accelerate pure and applied research in solar energy, nuclear fusion, geothermal power, the environmentally acceptable recovery of oil from shale, and any other alternatives that committees may choose to consider.

Twice before in our history we have made monumental achievements through concentrated "crash" programs: the Manhattan Project which resulted in unlocking the secrets of the atom and the Space Program spurred by President Kennedy's audacious promise to put man on the moon in less than a decade. Our present crisis involving the need for energy self-sufficiency is surely no less urgent and is vastly more complicated and predictably more costly. To guarantee the steady and consistent maintenace of effort, free from starts and stops, we have suggested the possibility of a trust fund dedicated expressly to this singularly vital endeavor.

Action: Committees on Science and Technology, Interior, Ways and Means, Appropriations, and the Joint Committee on Atomic Energy.

C. Anti-Trust Legislation

Mindful of the recent action of Congress in increasing penalties under existing anti-trust laws, we feel the time has come for a broad new look aimed at tightening and strengthening these basic laws. Increasing sectors of our economy have become alarmingly vulnerable to monopoly and effective oligopoly conducive to administered pricing practices based solely on the seller's determination regardless of the efficiency of production. We have witnessed the systematic development of planned obsolescence in a variety of products and a growing tendency to reduce output rather than prices and thus make the growing unit of profit compensate for a declining volume of sales.

These practices manifestly contribute to inflation and mitigate against national economic recovery and against the best interest of consumers everywhere. The fundamental laws of competitive marketplace economics are effectively repealed where such concentrated economic might is permitted to operate. Without attempting an all-inclusive list, we feel that this condition has come to apply particularly in the sectors of steel, automobile production, communications, food processing, banking, oil and electrical production and marketing, as well as in certain multi-national corporations. We ask the appropriate committee to initiate careful oversight hearings on the effectiveness of present anti-trust laws and where justified to report new legislation to tighten and strengthen those laws so as to make these economically destructive practices impossible.

Action: Committee on the Judiciary.

D. Consumer Protection

It is manifestly in the interests of the consumer that safeguards be established against inferior goods as well as deceptive advertising and merchandising techniques. Equally important to the long-run health and vibrancy of our economy is insistence that the nation's manpower and material resources be expended to produce durable, high-quality goods and services at prices affordable by the mass market. In pursuit of this goal, the Congress should promptly enact legislation establishing an effective and workable Consumer Protection Agency.

Action: Committee on Government Operations.

E. Food Production

In the past decade sweeping changes have dictated dramatic reversal in our basic agricultural policies—away from efforts aimed at curtailing excess production to avoid surpluses and toward the new goal of maximizing the nation's agricultural production to avoid shortages. The old programs contained certain built-in incentives not to produce. The new programs must feature incentives to achieve greater production from the nation's agricultural acreage. We request the appropriate committees, therefore, to conduct a careful review of such basic agricultural programs as acreage allotments, soil bank and acreage reserves in light of the nation's present and future requirements.

We also recommend that consideration be given to: 1) establishing a food export monitoring and management system to anticipate and prevent the development of domestic food shortages, 2) reestablishing a national grain reserve system to stabilize supplies, and 3) appropriate ways to guarantee a significant increase in competition and efficiency in the processing and distribution sectors of the food industry and an equitable rate of return to the growers themselves.

Action: Committee on Agriculture.

F. Aid to Specific Industries

Some industries that are presently depressed due to the slack economy and/or the energy shortage may in fact be faced with even more profound long term problems. Automobile production, where massive lay-offs recently have occurred, is a prime example. This particular industry looks to Congress for future guidance and direction. We request the appropriate committees to consider carefully what incentivies may be provided to assist this industry in meeting the public need for less expensive and more energy efficient vehicles.

We also ask the appropriate committees to consider and recommend means of assistance to such other industries as are vital to the nation's economic health, including both existing programs and the possible need for new programs.

Action: Committees on Banking, Currency and Housing, Commerce and Health, Ways and Means.

G. Help for Senior Citizens

Of all of our population, the elderly are among the hardest hit by inflation. Most of them are living on fixed incomes, and the cost of living adjustments provided in Social Security benefits in the past have not been sufficient nor made quickly enough to prevent extreme hardship in many cases. Improvements in the Social Security system are thus urgently needed.

Action: Committee on Ways and Means.

The above action agenda is not intended as an exhaustive recitation of the problems confronting the nation or of the important legislation to be considered by the 94th Congress. Its purpose is to bring direct and immediate focus upon the truly urgent problems of the nation's economy which demand creative initiative and swift, decisive action on the part of the people's elected representatives in Congress. Some of the problems have been years in developing. They cannot be solved in a day. But they are not insoluble. Every day of unnecessary delay in coming directly to grips with them will only aggravate their dimensions. So let us begin.

NEW CONSTITUTION FOR PEOPLE'S REPUBLIC OF CHINA

January 19, 1975

The People's Republic of China (PRC) on Jan. 19 made public a new constitution, approved two days earlier at a secret Peking meeting of the National People's Congress Jan. 13-19. The meeting was the first of that legislative body since 1965. The intervening years had been marked with the disruptions of the Cultural Revolution and the alleged coup attempt of Marshal Lin Piao. (See Historic Documents of 1974, p. 271.)

Convening of the congress suggested, as did the constitution's provisions and a new, moderate slate of government ministers, that the severe tensions within the Communist Party leadership had abated. Press comments generally rated the congress and the constitution as a victory for moderates, but Taiwan's ambassador in Washington, James C. H. Shen, dissented sharply from this interpretation. He said: "The [PRC] regime is still beset with a power struggle of undiminished intensity [which] the fourth National People's Congress...has done little or nothing to change.

Though the new constitution echoed Maoist principles, such as ongoing revolution, the aging Communist Party chairman did not put in an appearance at the congress sessions. No official explanation was made for his absence and reasons of health seemed ruled out by Mao's well-publicized meetings with several visiting heads of foreign governments in the preceding week. Mao's absence was judged significant by China-watchers, but informed guesses as to its meaning ranged from an assertion by the Far Eastern Economic Review *of Hong Kong that "Mao Tse-tung can at last sit back in the sun and watch his once-quarreling sons working together...." to speculation by* The New York Times *that Mao's absence was somehow related to the abortive "Criticize Confucius" campaign he launched in 1974. That national drive for ideological purification faded out when factional struggles began to disrupt industrial production.*

Provisions of Constitution

The new constitution, first circulated in draft form in 1970, replaced a previous constitution of 1954. It confirmed major structural changes in the government, including abolition of the long-vacant post of head of state. The functions of this position were assigned to the People's Congress, which was described as "the highest organ of state power" subject only to the "leadership of the Communist Party." The former head of state, Liu Shao-chi, had been stripped of power during the Cultural Revolution.

The constitution stressed the primacy of the party. Revolutionary committees—a legacy of the Cultural Revolution—were recognized as part of the government machinery. Clauses guaranteed collective ownership of agricultural resources by villagers and authorized relative economic autonomy. Both provisions apparently reflected an agrarian conservatism less influenced by the Cultural Revolution than was urban life.

Other major provisions of the constitution included qualified permission for farm workers to keep private garden plots and engage in "sideline production." Industrial workers also won a limited right to work for themselves, and a right to strike. The latter measure seemed to legalize reported labor stoppages and slowdowns. The constitution repudiated any Chinese pretension to the role of "superpower." Further, the nation would "strive for peaceful coexistence with countries having different social systems" but would resist "the hegemony of the superpowers."

In other business the congress heard a basic report on the government from Premier Chou En-lai, re-elected Chou and endorsed a group of deputy premiers and ministers drawn almost entirely from elderly officials. Radical leaders who had been close to Mao were conspicuously absent from the slate.

> *The Constitution of the People's Republic of China, adopted Jan. 17, 1975, by the Fourth National People's Congress, published Jan. 19, 1975, by Hsinhua, the official Chinese press agency:*

Preamble

The founding of the People's Republic of China marked the great victory of the new-democratic revolution and the beginning of the new historical period of socialist revolution and the dictatorship of the proletariat, a victory gained only after the Chinese people had waged a heroic struggle for over a century and, finally, under the leadership of the Communist Party of China, overthrown the reactionary rule of imperialism, feudalism and bureaucrat-capitalism by a people's revolutionary war.

For the last twenty years and more, the people of all nationalities in our country, continuing their triumphant advance under the leadership of the Communist Party of China, have achieved great victories both in socialist revolution and socialist construction and in the Great Proletarian Cultural Revolution, and have consolidated and strengthened the dictatorship of the proletariat.

Socialist society covers a considerably long historical period. Throughout this historical period, there are classes, class contradictions and class struggle, there is the struggle between the socialist road and the capitalist road, there is the danger of capitalist restoration and there is the threat of subversion and aggression by imperialism and social-imperialism. These contradictions can be resolved only by depending on the theory of continued revolution under the dictatorship of the proletariat and on practice under its guidance.

We must adhere to the basic line and policies of the Communist Party of China for the entire historical period of socialism and persist in continued revolution under the dictatorship of the proletariat, so that our great motherland will always advance along the road indicated by Marxism-Leninism-Mao Tsetung Thought.

We should consolidate the great unity of the people of all nationalities led by the working class and based on the alliance of workers and peasants, and develop the revolutionary united front. We should correctly distinguish contradictions among the people from those between ourselves and the enemy and correctly handle them. We should carry on the three great revolutionary movements of class struggle, the struggle for production and scientific experiment; we should build socialism independently and with the initiative in our own hands, through self-reliance, hard struggle, diligence and thrift and by going all out, aiming high and achieving greater, faster, better and more economical results; and we should be prepared against war and natural disasters and do everything for the people.

In international affairs, we should uphold proletarian internationalism. China will never be a superpower. We should strengthen our unity with the socialist countries and all oppressed people and oppressed nations, with each supporting the other; strive for peaceful coexistence with countries having different social systems on the basis of the Five Principles of mutual respect for sovereignty and territorial integrity, mutual non-aggression, non-interference in each other's internal affairs, equality and mutual benefit, and peaceful coexistence, and oppose the imperialist and social-imperialist policies of aggression and war and oppose the hegemonism of the superpowers.

The Chinese people are fully confident that, led by the Communist Party of China, they will vanquish enemies at home and abroad and surmount all difficulties to build China into a powerful socialist state of the dictatorship of the proletariat so as to make a greater contribution to humanity.

People of all nationalities in our country, unite to win still greater victories!

CHAPTER ONE

General Principles

Article 1

The People's Republic of China is a socialist state of the dictatorship of the proletariat led by the working class and based on the alliance of workers and peasants.

Article 2

The Communist Party of China is the core of leadership of the whole Chinese people. The working class exercises leadership over the state through its vanguard, the Communist Party of China.

Marxism-Leninism-Mao Tsetung Thought is the theoretical basis guiding the thinking of our nation.

Article 3

All power in the People's Republic of China belongs to the people. The organs through which the people exercise power are the people's congresses at all levels, with deputies of workers, peasants and soldiers as their main body.

The people's congresses at all levels and all other organs of state practise democratic centralism.

Deputies to the people's congresses at all levels are elected through democratic consultation. The electoral units and electors have the power to supervise the deputies they elect and to replace them at any time according to provisions of law.

Article 4

The People's Republic of China is a unitary multi-national state. The areas where regional national autonomy is exercised are all inalienable parts of the People's Republic of China.

All the nationalities are equal. Big-nationality chauvinism and local-nationality chauvinism must be opposed.

All the nationalities have the freedom to use their own spoken and written languages.

Article 5

In the People's Republic of China, there are mainly two kinds of ownership of the means of production at the present stage: socialist ownership by the whole people and socialist collective ownership by working people.

The state may allow non-agricultural individual labourers to engage in individual labour involving no exploitation of others, within the limits permitted by law and under unified arrangement by neighbourhood organizations in cities and towns or by production teams in rural people's communes. At the same time, these individual labourers should be guided onto the road of socialist collectivization step by step.

Article 6

The state sector of the economy is the leading force in the national economy.

All mineral resources and waters as well as the forests, undeveloped land and other resources owned by the state are the property of the whole people.

The state may requisition by purchase, take over for use, or nationalize urban and rural land as well as other means of production under conditions prescribed by law.

Article 7

The rural people's commune is an organization which integrates government administration and economic management.

The economic system of collective ownership in the rural people's communes at the present stage generally takes the form of three-level ownership with the production team at the basic level, that is, ownership by the commune, the production brigade and the production team, with the last as the basic accounting unit.

Provided that the development and absolute predominance of the collective economy of the people's commune are ensured, people's commune members may farm small plots for their personal needs, engage in limited household sideline production, and in pastoral areas to keep a small number of livestock for their personal needs.

Article 8

Socialist public property shall be inviolable. The state shall ensure the consolidation and development of the socialist economy and prohibit any person from undermining the socialist economy and the public interest in any way whatsoever.

Article 9

The state applies the socialist principle: "He who does not work, neither shall he eat" and "from each according to his ability, to each according to his work."

The state protects the citizens' right of ownership to their income from work, their savings, their houses, and other means of livelihood.

Article 10

The state applies the principle of grasping revolution, promoting production and other work and preparedness against war; promotes the planned and proportionate development of the socialist economy, taking agriculture as the foundation and industry as the leading factor and bringing the initiative of both the central and the local authorities into full play; and improves the people's material and cultural life step by step on the basis of the constant growth of social production and consolidates the independence and security of the country.

Article 11

State organizations and state personnel must earnestly study Marxism-Leninism-Mao Tse-tung Thought, firmly put proletarian politics in command, combat bureaucracy, maintain close ties with the masses and wholeheartedly serve the people. Cadres at all levels must participate in collective productive labour.

Every organ of state must apply the principle of efficient and simple administration. Its leading body must be a three-in-one combination of the old, the middle-aged and the young.

Article 12

The proletariat must exercise all-round dictatorship over the bourgeoisie in the superstructure, including all spheres of culture. Culture and education, literature and art, physical education, health work and scientific research work must all serve proletarian politics, serve the workers, peasants and soldiers, and be combined with productive labour.

Article 13

Speaking out freely, airing views fully, holding great debates and writing big-character posters are new forms of carrying on socialist revolution created by the masses of the people. The state shall ensure to the masses the right to use these forms to create a political situation in which there are both centralism and democracy, both discipline and freedom, both unity of will and personal ease of mind and liveliness, and so help consolidate the leadership of the Communist Party of China over the state and consolidate the dictatorship of the proletariat.

Article 14

The state safeguards the socialist system, suppresses all treasonable and counter-revolutionary activities and punishes all traitors and counter-revolutionaries.

The state deprives the landlords, rich peasants, reactionary capitalists and other bad elements of political rights for specified periods of time according to law, and at the same time provides them with the opportunity to earn a living so that they may be reformed through labour and become law-abiding citizens supporting themselves by their own labour.

Article 15

The Chinese People's Liberation Army and the people's militia are the workers' and peasants' own armed forces led by the Communist Party of China; they are the armed forces of the people of all nationalities.

The Chairman of the Central Committee of the Communist Party of China commands the country's armed forces.

The Chinese People's Liberation Army is at all times a fighting force, and simultaneously a working force and a production force.

The task of the armed forces of the People's Republic of China is to safeguard the achievements of the socialist revolution and socialist construction, to defend the sovereignty, territorial integrity and security of the state, and to guard against subversion and aggression by imperialism, social-imperialism and their lackeys.

CHAPTER TWO

The Structure of the State

SECTION I

The National People's Congress

Article 16

The National People's Congress is the highest organ of state power under the leadership of the Communist Party of China.

The National People's Congress is composed of deputies elected by the provinces, autonomous regions, muncipalities directly under the Central Government, and the People's Liberation Army. When necessary, a certain number of patriotic personages may be specially invited to take part as deputies.

The National People's Congress is elected for a term of five years. Its term of office may be extended under special circumstances.

The National People's Congress holds one session each year. When necessary, the session may be advanced or postponed.

Article 17

The functions and powers of the National People's Congress are: to amend the Constitution, make laws, appoint and remove the Premier of the State Council and the members of the State Council on the proposal of the Central Commitee of the Communist Party of China, approve the national economic plan, the state budget and the final state accounts, and exercise such other functions and powers as the National People's Congress deems necessary.

Article 18

The Standing Committee of the National People's Congress is the permanent organ of the National People's Congress. Its functions and powers are: to convene the sessions of the National People's Congress, interpret laws, enact decrees, dispatch and recall plenipotentiary representatives abroad, receive foreign diplomatic envoys, ratify and denounce treaties concluded with foreign states, and exercise such other functions and powers as are vested in it by the National People's Congress.

The Standing Committee of the National People's Congress is composed of the Chairman, the Vice-Chairmen and other members, all of whom are elected and subject to recall by the National People's Congress.

SECTION II

The State Council

Article 19

The State Council is the Central People's Government. The State Council is responsible and accountable to the National People's Congress and its Standing Committee.

The State Council is composed of the Premier, the Vice-Premiers, the ministers, and the ministers heading commissions.

Article 20

The functions and powers of the State Council are: to formulate administrative measures and issue decisions and orders in accordance with the Constitution, laws and decrees; exercise unified leadership over the work of ministries and commissions and local organs of state at various levels throughout the country; draft and implement the national economic plan and the state budget: direct state administrative affairs; and exercise such other functions and powers as are vested in it by the National People's Congress or its Standing Committee.

SECTION III

The Local People's Congresses and the Local Revolutionary Committees at Various Levels

Article 21

The local people's congresses at various levels are the local organs of state power.

The people's congresses of provinces and municipalities directly under the Central Government are elected for a term of five years. The people's congresses of prefectures, cities and counties are elected for a term of three years. The people's congresses of rural people's communes and towns are elected for a term of two years.

Article 22

The local revolutionary committees at various levels are the permanent organs of the local people's congresses and at the same time the local people's governments at various levels.

Local revolutionary committees are composed of a chairman, vice-chairmen and other members, who are elected and subject to recall by the people's congress at the corresponding level. Their election or recall shall be submitted for examination and approval to the organ of state at the next higher level.

Local revolutionary committees are responsible and accountable to the people's congress at the corresponding level and to the organ of state at the next higher level.

Article 23

The local people's congresses at various levels and the local revolutionary committees elected by them ensure the execution of laws and decrees in their respective areas; lead the socialist revolution and socialist construction in their respective areas; examine and approve local economic plans, budgets and final accounts; maintain revolutionary order; and safeguard the rights of citizens.

SECTION IV

The Organs of Self-Government of National Autonomous Areas

Article 24

The autonomous regions, autonomous prefectures and autonomous counties are all national autonomous areas; their organs of self-government are people's congresses and revolutionary committees.

The organs of self-government of national autonomous areas, apart from exercising the functions and powers of local organs of state as specified in Chapter Two, Section III of the Constitution, may exercise autonomy within the limits of their authority as prescribed by law.

The higher organs of state shall fully safeguard the exercise of autonomy by the organs of self-government of national autonomous areas and actively support the minority nationalities in carrying out the socialist revolution and socialist construction.

SECTION V

The Judicial Organs and the Procuratorial Organs

Article 25

The Supreme People's Court, local people's courts at various levels and special people's courts exercise judicial authority. The people's courts are responsible and accountable to the people's congresses and their permanent organs at the corresponding levels. The presidents of the people's courts are appointed and subject to removal by the permanent organs of the people's congresses at the corresponding levels.

The functions and powers of procuratorial organs are exercised by the organs of public security at various levels.

The mass line must be applied in procuratorial work and in trying cases. In major counter-revolutionary criminal cases the masses should be mobilized for discussion and criticism.

CHAPTER THREE

The Fundamental Rights and Duties of Citizens

Article 26

The fundamental rights and duties of citizens are to support the leadership of the Communist Party of China, support the socialist system and abide by the Constitution and the laws of the People's Republic of China.

It is the lofty duty of every citizen to defend the motherland and resist aggression. It is the honourable obligation of citizens to perform military service according to law.

Article 27

All citizens who have reached the age of eighteen have the right to vote and stand for election, with the exception of persons deprived of these rights by law.

Citizens have the right to work and the right to education. Working people have the right to rest and the right to material assistance in old age and in case of illness or disability.

Citizens have the right to lodge to organs of state at any level written or oral complaints of transgression of law or neglect of duty on the part of any person working in an organ of state. No one shall attempt to hinder or obstruct the making of such complaints or retaliate.

Women enjoy equal rights with men in all respects.

The state protects marriage, the family, and the mother and child.

The state protects the just rights and interests of overseas Chinese.

Article 28

Citizens enjoy freedom of speech, correspondence, the press, assembly, association, procession, demonstration and the freedom to strike, and enjoy freedom to believe in religion and freedom not to believe in religion and to propagate atheism.

The citizens' freedom of person and their homes shall be inviolable. No citizen may be arrested except by decision of a people's court or with the sanction of a public security organ.

Article 29

The People's Republic of China grants the right of residence to any foreign national persecuted for supporting a just cause, for taking part in revolutionary movements or for engaging in scientific activities.

CHAPTER FOUR

The National Flag, the National Emblem and the Capital

Article 30

The national flag has five stars on a field of red.

The national emblem: Tien An Men in the centre, illuminated by five stars and encircled by ears of grain and a cogwheel.

The capital is Peking.

JURY SERVICE FOR WOMEN
January 21, 1975

More than 13 years after it upheld a Florida law which tended to keep women from serving on juries, the Supreme Court found a similar Louisiana law unconstitutional. The Court ruled 8-1 that exclusion of women from juries deprived defendants tried by those juries of their right to a fair trial. But more important to the women's rights movement than the law itself was the Court's acknowledgment that the concept of "the woman's role" upon which the earlier decision was based had become extinct. "If it ever was the case that women were unqualified to sit on juries, or were so situated that none of them should be required to perform jury service, that time has long passed," Justice Byron R. White said in delivering the opinion of the Court.

The lone dissenter, Justice William H. Rehnquist, was not persuaded that "things have changed in constitutionally significant ways." Further, since the appellant alleged no prejudice or bias on the part of his all-male jury, Rehnquist asserted, the decision "smacks more of mysticism than of law."

Impact

The immediate impact of the ruling was slight since at the time no states—including Louisiana—specifically excluded women from jury service, although some states allowed women to claim exemptions not extended to men. The appellant in the Louisiana case, Billy J. Taylor, had been convicted of "aggravated kidnaping" by an all-male jury in 1972. At that time Louisiana law excluded women from jury duty unless they filed a written declaration of a desire to serve. Women comprised 53 per cent of the population of the parishes from which the Taylor jury panel was drawn, but no women were included in the 175-person panel.

Justice White pointed out that while the state's jury selection system did not disqualify women, its practical effect was that the number of women called for jury service was "grossly disproportionate to the number of eligible women in the community." Excluding an "identifiable class of citizens" from jury service violated constitutional requirements that a jury represent a "fair cross-section," said White, because "the purpose of a jury is...to make available the commonsense judgment of the community." The Court's opinion made it clear that states still had "much leeway" in granting exemptions and setting standards for jurors. But, at a time when 54.2 per cent of all women between the ages of 18 and 64 worked outside the home, it was "untenable to suggest...that it would be a special hardship for each and every woman to perform jury service or that society cannot spare any women from their present duties."

The Court ordered the case remanded to the Louisiana supreme court. The ruling raised the possibility that thousands of prison inmates in Louisiana and other states convicted by similar juries might demand new trials. But a week later, on Jan. 27, the Court warned that the Taylor ruling could not be used to reverse earlier convictions.

Sex Discrimination Rulings

The Taylor case was one of three decisions of the 1974-75 term in which the Supreme Court ruled out different treatment of the sexes. However, it did not rule on the general question of whether sex-based classifications were inherently suspect, and in one case (Schlesinger v. Ballard), *the Court upheld separate Navy discharge procedures for men and women.*

At a time when the momentum behind ratification of a constitutional amendment to guarantee equal rights for women was faltering, the Court's decisions suggested that the amendment's goals might finally be obtained through judicial action. Only a few weeks later, the Court in a unanimous decision invalidated a 36-year-old Social Security regulation which awarded survivor's benefits to widows but not to widowers. That regulation, the Court held, violated women's rights to equal protection under the law by denying them the opportunity to provide for their survivors, even though they paid the same taxes as men. (See p. 177) In Stanton v. Stanton, *moreover, the Court on April 14 rejected a Utah statute setting different majority ages for men and women. The law was based on the assumption that men, as primary providers for families, needed a longer period of dependency in which to prepare for that responsibility. However, the Court ruled: "No longer is the female destined solely for the home and the rearing of the family, and only the male for the marketplace in the world of ideas."*

Excerpts from Supreme Court decision on Louisiana law tending to bar women from jury duty, handed down Jan. 21, 1975:

No. 73-5744

Billy J. Taylor, Appellant,	On Appeal from the Su-
v.	preme Court of Louisi-
State of Louisiana.	ana.

[January 21, 1975]

MR. JUSTICE WHITE delivered the opinion of the Court.

When this case was tried, Art. VII, § 41, of the Louisiana Constitution, and Art. 402 of the Louisiana Code of Criminal Procedure provided that a woman should not be selected for jury service unless she had previously filed a written declaration of her desire to be subject to jury service. The constitutionality of these provisions is the issue in this case.

I

Appellant, Billy J. Taylor, was indicted by the grand jury of St. Tammany Parish, in the Twenty-second Judicial District of Louisiana, for aggravated kidnapping. On April 12, 1972, appellant moved the trial court to quash the petit jury venire drawn for the special criminal term beginning with his trial the following day. Appellant alleged that women were systematically excluded from the venire and that he would therefore be deprived of what he claimed to be his federal constitutional right to "a fair trial by jury of a representative segment of the community...."

The Twenty-second Judicial District is comprised of the parishes of St. Tammany and Washington. The appellee has stipulated that 53% of the persons eligible for jury service in these parishes were female, and that no more than 10% of the persons on the jury wheel in St. Tammany Parish were women. During the period from December 8, 1971, to November 3, 1972, 12 females were among the 1,800 persons drawn to fill petit jury venires in St. Tammany Parish. It was also stipulated that the discrepancy between females eligible for jury service and those actually included in the venires was the result of the operation of La. Const., Art. VII, § 41, and La. Code Crim. Proc., Art. 402. In the present case, a venire totalling 175 persons was drawn for jury service beginning April 13, 1972. There were no females on the venire.

Appellant's motion to quash the venire was denied that same day. After being tried, convicted, and sentenced to death, appellant sought review in the Supreme Court of Louisiana, where he renewed his claim that the petit jury venire should have been quashed. The Supreme Court of Louisiana, recognizing that this claim drew into question the constitutionality of the provisions of the Louisiana Constitution and Code of Criminal Procedure dealing with the service of women on juries, squarely held, one justice dissenting, that these provisions were valid and not unconstitutional under federal law. *State* v. *Taylor...(1973).*

Appellant appealed from that decision to this Court. We noted probable jurisdiction...(1974), to consider whether the Louisiana jury selection system deprived appellant of his Sixth and Fourteenth Amendment right to an impartial jury trial. We hold that it did and that these amendments were violated in this case by the operation of La. Const., Art. VII, § 41, and La. Code Crim. Proc., Art. 402. In consequence, appellant's conviction must be reversed.

II

The Louisiana jury selection system does not disqualify women from jury service, but in operation its conceded systematic impact is that only a very few women, grossly disproportionate to the number of eligible women in the community, are called for jury service. In this case, no women were on the venire from which the petit jury was drawn. The issue we have, therefore, is whether a jury selection system which operates to exclude from jury service an identifiable class of citizens constituting 53% of eligible jurors in the community comports with the Sixth and Fourteenth Amendments.

The State first insists that Taylor, a male, has no standing to object to the exclusion of women from his jury. But Taylor's claim is that he was constitutionally entitled to a jury drawn from a venire constituting a fair cross section of the community and that the jury that tried him was not such a jury by reason of the exclusion of women. Taylor was not a member of the excluded class; but there is no rule that claims such as Taylor presents may be made only by those defendants who are members of the group excluded from jury service. In *Peters* v. *Kiff*...(1972), the defendant, a white man, challenged his conviction on the ground that Negroes had been systematically excluded from jury service. Six Members of the Court agreed that petitioner was entitled to present the issue and concluded that he had been deprived of his federal rights. Taylor, in the case before us, was similarly entitled to tender and have adjudicated the claim that the exclusion of women from jury service deprived him of the kind of fact finder to which he was constitutionally entitled.

III

The background against which this case must be decided includes our holding in *Duncan* v. *Louisiana*...(1968), that the Sixth Amendment's provision for jury trial is made binding on the States by virtue of the Fourteenth Amendment. Our inquiry is whether the presence of a fair cross section of the community on venires, panels or lists from which petit juries are drawn is essential to the fulfillment of the Sixth Amendment's guarantee of an impartial jury trial in criminal prosecutions.

The Court's prior cases are instructive. Both in the course of exercising its supervisory powers over trials in federal courts and in the constitutional context, the Court has unambiguously declared that the American concept of the jury trial contemplates a jury drawn from a fair cross section of the community. A unanimous Court stated in *Smith* v. *Texas*...(1940), that "[i]t is part of the established tradition in the use of juries as instruments of public justice that the jury be a body truly representative of the community." To exclude racial groups from jury service was said to be "at war with our basic concepts of a democratic society and a representative government." A state jury system that resulted in systematic exclusion of Negroes as jurors was therefore held to violate the Equal Protection Clause of the Fourteenth Amendment. *Glasser* v. *United States*...(1942), in the context of a federal criminal case and the Sixth Amendment's jury trial requirement, stated that "our notions of what a proper jury is have developed in harmony with our basic concepts of a democratic system and representative government," and repeated the Court's understanding that the jury "be a body truly representative of the community...and not the organ of any special group or class."

A federal conviction by a jury from which women had been excluded, although eligible for service under state law, was reviewed in *Ballard* v. *United States*...(1946). Noting the federal statutory "design to make a jury a cross section of the community" and the fact that women had been excluded, the Court exercised its supervisory powers over the federal courts and reversed the conviction. In *Brown* v. *Allen*...(1953), the Court declared that "[o]ur duty to protect the federal constitutional rights of all does not mean we must or should impose on states our conception of the proper source of jury lists, so long as the source reasonably reflects a cross-section of the population suitable in character and intelligence for that civic duty."

Some years later in *Carter* v. *Jury Comm'n*...(1970), the Court observed that the exclusion of Negroes from jury service because of their race "contravenes the very idea of a jury—'a body truly representative of the community....' " (Quoting from *Smith* v. *Texas, supra.*) At about the same time it was contended that the use of six-man juries in noncapital criminal cases violated the Sixth Amendment for failure to provide juries drawn from a cross section of the community, *Williams* v. *Florida*...(1970). In the course of rejecting that challenge, we said that the number of persons on the jury should "be large enough to promote group deliberation, free from outside attempts at intimidation, and to provide a fair possibility for obtaining a representative cross section of the community." ...In like vein, in *Apodaca* v. *Oregon*...(1970) (plurality opinion), it was said that "a jury will come to such a [commonsense] judgment as long as it consists of a group of laymen representative of a cross section of the community who have the duty and the opportunity to deliberate...on the question of a defendant's guilt." Similarly, three Justices in *Peters* v. *Kiff*...observed that the Sixth Amendment comprehended a fair possibility for obtaining a jury constituting a representative cross section of the community.

The unmistakable import of this Court's opinions, at least since 1941, *Smith* v. *Texas, supra,* and not repudiated by intervening decisions, is that the selection of a petit jury from a representative cross section of the community is an essential component of the Sixth Amendment right to a jury trial. Recent federal legislation governing jury selection within the federal court system has a similar thrust. Shortly prior to this Court's decision in *Duncan* v. *Louisiana, supra,* the Federal Jury Selection Act of 1968 was enacted. In that Act, Congress stated "the policy of the United States that all litigants in Federal courts entitled to trial by jury shall have the right to grand and petit juries selected at random from a fair cross section of the community in the district or division in which the court convenes." ...In that Act, Congress also established the machinery by which the stated policy was to be implemented. ...In passing this legislation, the Committee Reports of both the House and the Senate recognized that the jury plays a political function in the administration of the law and that the requirement of a jury's being chosen from a fair cross section of the community is fundamental to the American system of justice. Debate on the floors of the House and Senate on the Act invoked the Sixth Amendment, the Constitution generally, and prior decisions of this Court in support of the Act.

We accept the fair cross-section requirement as fundamental to the jury trial guaranteed by the Sixth Amendment and are convinced that the requirement has solid foundation. The purpose of a jury is to guard against the exercise of arbitrary power—to make available the commonsense judgment of the community as a hedge against the overzealous or mistaken prosecutor and in preference to the professional or perhaps overconditioned or biased response of a judge. *Duncan* v. *Louisiana....* This prophylactic vehicle is not provided if the jury pool is made up of only special segments of the populace or if large, distinctive groups are excluded from the pool. Community participation in the administration of the criminal law, moreover, is not only consistent with our democratic heritage but is also critical to public confidence in the fairness of the criminal justice system. Restricting jury service to only special groups or excluding identifiable segments playing major roles in the community cannot be squared with the constitutional concept of jury trial. "Trial by jury presupposes a jury drawn from a pool broadly representative of the community as well as impartial in a specific case.... The broad representative character of the jury should be maintained, partly as assurance of a diffused impartiality and partly because sharing in the administration of justice is a phase of civic responsibility." *Thiel* v. *Southern Pacific Co....*(1946) (Frankfurter, J., dissenting).

IV

We are also persuaded that the fair cross-section requirement is violated by the systematic exclusion of women, who in the judicial district involved here amounted to 53% of the citizens eligible for jury service. This conclusion necessarily entails the judgment that women are sufficiently numerous and distinct from men that if they are systematically eliminated from jury panels, the Sixth Amendment's fair cross-section requirement cannot be satisfied. This very matter was debated in *Ballard* v. *United States, supra.* Positing the fair cross-section rule—there said to be a statutory one—the

Court concluded that the systematic exclusion of women was unacceptable. The dissenting view that an all-male panel drawn from various groups in the community would be as truly representative as if women were included, was firmly rejected:

"The thought is that the factors which tend to influence the action of women are the same as those which influence the action of men—personality, background, economic status—and not sex. Yet it is not enough to say that women when sitting as jurors neither act nor tend to act as a class. Men likewise do not act as a class. But, if the shoe were on the other foot, who would claim that a jury was truly representative of the community if all men were intentionally and systematically excluded from the panel? The truth is that the two sexes are not fungible; a community made up exclusively of one is different from a community composed of both; the subtle interplay of influence one on the other is among the imponderables. To insulate the courtroom from either may not in a given case make an iota of difference. Yet a flavor, a distinct quality is lost if either sex is excluded. The exclusion of one may indeed make the jury less representative of the community than would be true if an economic or racial group were excluded."

In this respect, we agree with the Court in *Ballard:* If the fair cross-section rule is to govern the selection of juries, as we have concluded it must, women cannot be systematically excluded from jury panels from which petit juries are drawn. This conclusion is consistent with the current judgment of the country, now evidenced by legislative or constitutional provisions in every State and at the federal level qualifying women for jury service.

V

There remains the argument that women as a class serve a distinctive role in society and that jury service would so substantially interfere with that function that the State has ample justification for excluding women from service unless they volunteer, even though the result is that almost all jurors are men. It is true that *Hoyt* v. *Florida*...(1961), held that such a system did not deny due process of law or equal protection of the laws because there was a sufficiently rational basis for such an exemption. But *Hoyt* did not involve a defendant's Sixth Amendment right to a jury drawn from a fair cross section of the community and the prospect of depriving him of that right if women as a class are systematically excluded. The right to a proper jury cannot be overcome on merely rational grounds. There must be weightier reasons if a distinctive class representing 53% of the eligible jurors is for all practical purposes to be excluded from jury service. No such basis has been tendered here.

The States are free to grant exemptions from jury service to individuals in case of special hardship or incapacity and to those engaged in particular occupations the uninterrupted performance of which is critical to the community's welfare. *Rawlins* v. *Georgia*...(1906). It would not appear that such exemptions would pose substantial threats that the remaining pool of jurors would not be representative of the community. A system excluding all women, however, is a wholly different matter. It is untenable to suggest these days that it would be a special hardship for each and every woman to perform jury service or that society cannot spare *any* women from their present duties. [Footnote: ...Statistics compiled by the Department of Labor indicate that in October 1974, 54.2% of all women between 18 and 64 years of age were in the labor force....] This may be the case with many, and it may be burdensome to sort out those who should not be exempted from those who should serve. But that task is performed in the case of men, and the administrative convenience in dealing with women as a class is insufficient justification for diluting the quality of community judgment represented by the jury in criminal trials.

VI

Although this judgment may appear a foregone conclusion from the pattern of some of the Court's cases over the past 30 years, as well as from legislative developments at both federal and state levels, it is nevertheless true that until today no case had squarely held that the exclusion of women from jury venires deprives a criminal defendant of his Sixth Amendment right to trial by an impartial jury drawn from a fair cross section of the community. It is apparent that the first Congress did not perceive the Sixth Amendment as requiring women on criminal jury panels; for the direction of the First Judiciary Act of 1789 was that federal jurors were to have the qualifications required by the States in which the federal court was sitting and at the time women were disqualified under state law in every State. Necessarily, then, federal juries in criminal cases were all-male, and it was not until the Civil Rights Act of 1957...that Congress itself provided that all citizens, with limited exceptions, were competent to sit on federal juries. Until that time, federal courts were required by statute to exclude women from jury duty in those States where women were disqualified. Utah was the first State to qualify women for juries; it did so in 1898.... Moreover, *Hoyt* v. *Florida* was decided and has stood for the proposition that, even if women as a group could not be constitutionally disqualified from jury service, there was ample reason to treat all women differently from men for the purpose of jury service and to exclude them unless they volunteered.

Accepting as we do, however, the view that the Sixth Amendment affords the defendant in a criminal trial the opportunity to have the jury drawn from venires representative of the community, we think it is no longer tenable to hold that women as a class may be excluded or given automatic exemptions based solely on sex if the consequence is that criminal jury venires are almost totally male. To this extent we cannot follow the contrary implications of the prior cases, including *Hoyt* v. *Florida*. If it was ever the case that women were unqualified to sit on juries or were so situated that none of them should be required to perform jury service, that time has long since passed. If at one time it could be held that Sixth Amendment juries must be drawn from a fair cross section of the community but that this requirement permitted the almost total exclusion of women, this is not the case today. Communities differ at different times and places. What is a fair cross section at one time or place is not necessarily a fair cross section at another time or a different place. Nothing persuasive has been presented to us in this case suggesting that all-male venires in the parishes involved here are fairly representative of the total population otherwise eligible for jury service.

VII

Our holding does not augur or authorize the fashioning of detailed jury selection codes by federal courts. The fair cross-section principle must have much leeway in application. The States remain free to prescribe relevant qualifications for their jurors and to provide reasonable exemptions so long as it may be fairly said that the jury lists or panels are representative of the community. *Carter* v. *Jury Comm'n, supra,* as did *Brown* v. *Allen, supra; Rawlins* v. *Georgia, supra,* and other cases, recognized broad discretion in the States in this respect. We do not depart from the principles enunciated in *Carter.* But, as we have said, Louisiana's special exemption for women operates to exclude them from petit juries, which in our view is contrary to the command of the Sixth and Fourteenth Amendments.

It should also be emphasized that in holding that petit juries must be drawn from a source fairly representative of the community we impose no requirement that petit juries actually chosen must mirror the community and reflect the various distinctive groups in the population. Defendants are not entitled to a jury of any particular composition, *Fay* v. *New York*...(1947); *Apodaca* v. *Oregon*...(plurality opinion); but the jury wheels, pools of names, panels or venires from which juries are drawn must not systematically exclude distinctive groups in the community and thereby fail to be reasonably representative thereof.

The judgment of the Louisiana Supreme Court is reversed and the case remanded to that court for further proceedings not inconsistent with this opinion.

So ordered.

MR. JUSTICE REHNQUIST, dissenting.

The Court's opinion reverses a conviction without a suggestion, much less a showing, that the appellant has been unfairly treated or prejudiced in any way by the manner in which his jury was selected. In so doing, the Court invalidates a jury selection system which it approved by a substantial majority only 13 years ago. I disagree with the Court and would affirm the judgment of the Supreme Court of Louisiana.

The majority opinion canvasses various of our jury trial cases, beginning with *Smith* v. *Texas*...(1940). Relying on carefully chosen quotations, it concludes that the "unmistakable import" of our cases is that the fair cross-section requirement "is an essential component of the Sixth Amendment right to a jury trial." I disagree. Fairly read, the only "unmistakable import" of those cases is that due process and equal protection prohibit jury selection systems which are likely to result in biased or partial juries. *Smith* v. *Texas, supra,* concerned the equal protection claim of a Negro who was indicted by a grand jury from which Negroes had been systematically excluded. *Glasser* v. *United States...*(1942), dealt with allegations that the only women selected for jury service were members of a private organization which had conducted pro-prosecution classes for prospective jurors. *Brown* v. *Allen...*(1953), rejected the equal protection and due process contentions of several black defendants that members of their race had been discriminatorily excluded from their juries. *Carter* v. *Jury Comm'n...*(1970), similarly dealt with equal protection challenges to a jury selection system, but the persons claiming such rights were blacks who had sought to serve as jurors.

In *Hoyt* v. *Florida...*(1961), this Court gave plenary consideration to contentions that a system such as Louisiana's deprived a defendant of equal protection and due process. These contentions were rejected, despite circumstances which were made more suggestive of possible bias and prejudice than are those here—the defendant in *Hoyt* was a woman whose defense to charges of murdering her husband was that she had been driven temporarily insane by his suspected infidelity and by his rejection of her efforts at reconciliation.... The complete swing of the judicial pendulum 13 years later must depend for its validity on the proposition that during those years things have changed in constitutionally significant ways. I am not persuaded of the sufficiency of either of the majority's proffered explanations as to intervening events.

The first determinative event, in the Court's view, is *Duncan* v. *Louisiana...*(1968). Because the Sixth Amendment was there held applicable to the States, the Court feels free to dismiss *Hoyt* as a case which dealt with entirely different issues—even though in fact it presented the identical problem. But *Duncan's* rationale is a good deal less expansive than is suggested by the Court's present interpretations of that case. *Duncan* rests on the following reasoning:

> "The test for determining whether a right extended by the Fifth and Sixth Amendments with respect to federal criminal proceedings is also protected against state action by the Fourteenth Amendment has been phrased in a variety of ways in the opinions of this Court. The question has been asked whether a right is among those 'fundamental principles of liberty and justice which lie at the base of all our civil and political institutions,' *Powell* v. *Alabama...*(1932); whether it is 'basic in our system of jurisprudence,' *In re Oliver...*(1948); and whether it is 'a fundamental right, essential to a fair trial,' *Gideon* v. *Wainwright...*(1963); *Malloy* v. *Hogan...*(1964); *Pointer* v. *Texas...*(1965).... Because we believe that trial by jury in criminal cases is fundamental to the American scheme of justice, we hold that the Fourteenth Amendment guarantees a right of jury trial in all criminal cases...." ...(Emphasis added.)

That this a sturdy test, one not readily satisfied by every discrepancy between federal and state practice, was made clear not only in *Williams* v. *Florida*...(1970), and *Apodaca* v. *Oregon*...(1972), but also in *Duncan* itself. In explaining the conclusion that a jury trial is fundamental to our scheme of justice, and therefore should be required of the States, the Court pointed out that jury trial was designed to be a defense "against arbitrary law enforcement,"...and "to prevent oppression by the Government." The Court stated its belief that jury trial for serious offenses is "essential for preventing miscarriages of justice and for assuring that fair trials are provided for all defendants."

I cannot conceive that today's decision is necessary to guard against oppressive or arbitrary law enforcement, or to prevent miscarriages of justice and to assure fair trials. Especially is this so when the criminal defendant involved makes no claims of prejudice or bias. The Court does accord some slight attention to justifying its ruling in terms of the basis on which the right to jury trial was read into the Fourteenth Amendment. It concludes that the jury is not effective, as a prophylaxis against arbitrary prosecutorial and judicial power, if the "jury pool is made up of only special segments of the populace or if large, distinctive groups are excluded from the pool." ...It fails, however, to provide any satisfactory explanation of the mechanism by which the Louisiana system undermines the prophylactic role of the jury, either in general or in this case. The best it can do is to posit "a flavor, a distinct quality," which allegedly is lost if either sex is excluded.... However, this "flavor" is not of such importance that the Constitution is offended if any given petit jury is not so enriched.... This smacks more of mysticism than of law. The Court does not even purport to practice its mysticism in a consistent fashion—presumably doctors, lawyers, and other groups, whose frequent exemption from jury service is endorsed by the majority, also offer qualities as distinct and important as those...here.

In *Hoyt*, this Court considered a stronger due process claim than is before it today, but found that fundamental fairness had not been offended. I do not understand how our intervening decision in *Duncan* can support a different result. After all, *Duncan* imported the Sixth Amendment into the Due Process Clause only because, and only to the extent that, this was perceived to be required by fundamental fairness.

The second change since *Hoyt* that appears to undergird the Court's turnabout is societal in nature, encompassing both our higher degree of sensitivity to distinctions based on sex, and the "evolving nature of the structure of the family unit in American society." ...There are matters of degree, and it is perhaps of some significance that in 1961 Mr. Justice Harlan saw fit to refer to the "enlightened emancipation of women from the restrictions and protections of bygone years, and their entry into many parts of community life formerly considered to be reserved to men." *Hoyt, supra*.... Nonetheless, it may be fair to conclude that the Louisiana system is in fact an anachronism, inappropriate at this "time or place." ...But surely constitutional adjudication is a more canalized function than enforcing as against the States this Court's perception of modern life.

Absent any suggestion that appellant's trial was unfairly conducted, or that its result was unreliable, I would not require Louisiana to retry him (assuming the State can once again produce its evidence and witnesses) in order to impose on him the sanctions which its laws provide.

SUPREME COURT ON
RIGHTS OF SUSPENDED STUDENTS
January 22, 1975

The Supreme Court ruled Jan. 22 that public school pupils who are suspended from school for disciplinary reasons are entitled to the protections of due process of law. Splitting 5-4, the Court held that suspended students have the right to notice of the charges against them, an explanation of any adverse evidence and an opportunity to tell their side of the story.

The decision was the first by the high court to equate constitutional protections for adults deprived of their rights with safeguards for students against unfair interference with their education. It was only the second time the Court had acted to enforce the constitutional rights of high school students. In 1969, the Court held that suspension of students wearing black armbands in peaceful Vietnam protests abridged First Amendment rights to freedom of speech.

The ruling on student rights coincided with public debate over student suspensions. A study by the Children's Defense Fund, published in December 1974, had shown that eight per cent of secondary school students had been suspended at least once during the 1972-1973 school year. The study also showed that six per cent of white students, in contrast to 12 per cent of black students, had been suspended. Civil rights groups accused school authorities of using suspensions to discriminate against black students.

The decision handed down Jan. 22 involved nine students suspended from school in Columbus, Ohio, in 1971 during a period of racial unrest. The plaintiffs challenged an Ohio law allowing suspensions of up to 10 days without a hearing. They contended that they had been deprived of their right to property—a statutory right to education—and their right to liberty—through damage to their school records without proof of wrong-doing. Both rights, they said, had been abridged without due process of law, in violation of the Fourteenth Amendment.

The Supreme Court held in favor of the students, affirming a lower court decision that found the Ohio law unconstitutional. "Young people do not shed their rights at the schoolhouse door," wrote Justice Byron R. White for the majority. Once a state guarantees its residents free primary and secondary education, the state "may not withdraw that right on grounds of misconduct, absent fundamentally fair procedures to determine whether the misconduct has occurred."

The Court specified three "fair procedures" to ensure due process of law: oral or written notice of the charges against a student, an explanation of the evidence against him and an opportunity to present his side of the story. The Court said students were entitled to these "rudimentary precautions against unfair findings of misconduct and arbitrary exclusions from school." Charges of misconduct on students' records "could seriously damage the students' standing with their fellow pupils and their teachers as well as interfere with later opportunities for higher education and employment," White said.

However, the Court stopped short of requiring a right to counsel, formal hearings, or an opportunity for students to cross-examine witnesses who appeared for the school authorities. "Further formalizing the suspension process and escalating its formality and adversary nature may not only make it too costly as a regular disciplinary tool, but also destroy its effectiveness as part of the teaching process," it pointed out. But additional procedures might be in order for more extensive suspension, the Court held. "Nor do we put aside the possibility that in unusual situations, although involving only a short suspension, something more than the rudimentary procedures will be required."

Dissent: Dangers of "New Thicket"

The four Nixon appointees to the Court—Chief Justice Warren E. Burger and Associate Justices Harry A. Blackmun, William H. Rehnquist and Lewis F. Powell Jr.—dissented from the majority opinion. Speaking for the minority, Justice Powell warned that "No one can foresee the ultimate frontiers of the new 'thicket' the Court now enters."

"The decision unnecessarily opens avenues for judicial intervention in the operation of our public schools that may affect adversely the quality of education," Powell said. "The Court holds for the first time that the federal courts, rather than educational officials and state legislatures have the authority to determine the rules applicable to routine classroom discipline." Judicial intervention in the suspension process, Powell asserted,

could open the way for further involvement in such questions as grading, grade promotion or failure and assignment to vocational or college-preparatory curricula.

Powell also contended that education must include a comprehension of the necessity of discipline. "In an age when the home and church play a diminishing role in shaping the character and value judgments of the young, a heavier responsibility falls upon the schools," he said. "When an immature student merits censure for his conduct, he is rendered a disservice if appropriate sanctions are not applied or if procedures for their application are so formalized as to invite a challenge to the teacher's authority—an invitation which rebellious or even merely spirited teenagers are likely to accept." Because teachers serve as advisers, friends and even parent substitutes, Powell faulted the Court's ruling as casting student-teacher roles in an adversary relationship.

Excerpts from the Supreme Court's Jan. 22, 1975, opinion concerning rights of suspended students and from the dissenting opinion written by Justice Lewis F. Powell Jr.:

No. 73-898

| Norval Goss et al., Appellants,
v.
Eileen Lopez et al. | On Appeal from the United States District Court for the Southern District of Ohio. |

[January 22, 1975]

...MR. JUSTICE WHITE delivered the opinion of the Court.

This appeal by various administrators of the Columbus, Ohio, Public School System ("CPSS") challenges the judgment of a three-judge federal court, declaring that appellees—various high school students in the CPSS—were denied due process of law contrary to the command of the Fourteenth Amendment in that they were temporarily suspended from their high schools without a hearing either prior to suspension or within a reasonable time thereafter, and enjoining the administrators to remove all references to such suspensions from the students' records.

I

Ohio law...empowers the principal of an Ohio public school to suspend a pupil for misconduct for up to 10 days or to expel him. In either case, he must notify the student's parents within 24 hours and state the reasons for his action. A pupil who is expelled, or his parents, may appeal the decision to the Board of Education and in connection therewith shall be permitted to be heard at the board meeting. The board may reinstate the pupil following the hearing. No similar procedure is provided in...state law for a suspended student. Aside from a regulation tracking the statute, at the time of the imposition of the suspensions in this case the CPSS had not itself issued any written procedure applicable to suspensions. Nor, so far as the record reflects, had any of the individual high schools involved in this case. Each, however, had formally or informally described the conduct for which suspension could be imposed.

The nine named appellees, each of whom alleged that he or she had been suspended from public high school in Columbus for up to 10 days without a hearing...filed an action against the Columbus Board of Education and various administrators of the CPSS.... The complaint sought a declaration that [the state law] was unconstitutional in that it permitted public school administrators to deprive plaintiffs of their rights to an education without a hearing of any kind, in violation of the procedural due process component of the Fourteenth Amendment. It also sought to enjoin the public school officials from issuing future suspension...and to require them to remove references to the past suspensions from the records of the students in question.

The proof below established that the suspensions in question arose out of a period of widespread student unrest in the CPSS during February and March of 1971. Six of the named plaintiffs...were each suspended for 10 days on account of disruptive or disobedient conduct committed in the presence of the school administrator who ordered the suspension.... None was given a hearing to determine the operative facts underlying the suspension, but each, together with his or her parents, was offered the opportunity to attend a conference, subsequent to the effective date of the suspension, to discuss the student's future.

...Dwight Lopez...was suspended in connection with a disturbance in the lunchroom which involved some physical damage to school property. Lopez testified that at least 75 other students were suspended from his school on the same day. He also testified below that he was not a party to the destructive conduct but was instead an innocent bystander. Because no one from the school testified with regard to this incident, there is no evidence in the record indicating the official basis for concluding otherwise. Lopez never had a hearing....

On the basis of this evidence, the three-judge court declared that plaintiffs were denied due process of law because they were "suspended without hearing prior to suspension or within a reasonable time thereafter," and that §3316.66 Ohio Rev. Code and regulations issued pursuant thereto were unconstitutional in permitting such suspensions. It was ordered that all references to plaintiffs' suspensions be removed from school files.

Although not imposing upon the Ohio school administrators any particular disciplinary procedures and leaving them "free to adopt regulations providing for fair procedures which are consonant with the educational goals of their schools and reflective of the characteristics of their school and locality," the District Court declared that there were "minimum requirements of notice and hearing prior to suspension, except in emergency situations." In explication, the court stated that relevant case authority would: (1) permit "immediate removal of a student whose conduct disrupts the academic atmosphere of the school, endangers fellow students, teachers or school officials, or damages property"; (2) require notice of suspension proceedings to be sent to the students' parents within 24 hours of the decision to conduct them; and (3) require a hearing to be held, with the student present, within 72 hours of his removal. Finally, the court stated that, with respect to the nature of the hearing, the relevant cases required that statements in support of the charge be produced, that the student and others be permitted to make statements in defense or mitigation, and that the school need not permit attendance by counsel.

The defendant school administrators have appealed the three-judge court's decision.... We affirm.

II

At the outset, appellants contend that because there is no constitutional right to an education at public expense, the Due Process Clause does not protect against expulsions from the public school system. This position misconceives the nature of the issue and is refuted by prior decisions. The Fourteenth Amendment forbids the State to deprive any person of life, liberty or property without due process of law. Protected interests in property are normally "not created by the Constitution. Rather, they are created and their dimensions are defined" by an independent source such as state statutes or rules entitling the citizen to certain benefits....

Accordingly, a state employee who under state law, or rules promulgated by state officials, has a legitimate claim of entitlement to continued employment absent sufficient cause for discharge may demand the procedural protections of due process.... In like vein was *Wolff* v. *McDonald*, ...where the procedural protections of the Due Process Clause were triggered by official cancellation of a prisoner's good-time credits accumulated under state law, although those benefits were not mandated by the Constitution.

Here, on the basis of state law, appellees plainly had legitimate claims of entitlement to a public education.... It is true that §3313.66 of the code permits school principals to suspend students for up to two weeks; but suspensions may not be imposed without any grounds whatsoever. All of the schools had their own rules specifying the grounds for expulsion or suspension. Having chosen to extend the right to an education to people of appellees' class generally, Ohio may not withdraw that right on grounds of misconduct absent fundamentally fair procedures to determine whether the misconduct has occurred....

Although Ohio may not be constitutionally obligated to establish and maintain a public school system, it has nevertheless done so and has required its children to attend. Those young people do not "shed their constitutional rights" at the schoolhouse door.... The authority possessed by

71

the State to prescribe and enforce standards of conduct in its schools, although concededly very broad, must be exercised consistently with constitutional safeguards. Among other things, the State is constrained to recognize a student's legitimate entitlement to a public education as a property interest which is protected by the Due Process Clause and which may not be taken away for misconduct without adherence to the minimum procedures required by that clause.

The Due Process Clause also forbids arbitrary deprivations of liberty.... School authorities here suspended appellees from school for periods of up to 10 days based on charges of misconduct. If sustained and recorded, those charges could seriously damage the students' standing with their fellow pupils and their teachers as well as interfere with later opportunities for higher education and employment. It is apparent that the claimed right of the State to determine unilaterally and without process whether that misconduct has occurred immediately collides with the requirements of the Constitution.

Appellants proceed to argue that even if there is a right to a public education protected by the Due Process Clause generally, the clause comes into play only when the State subjects a student to a "severe detriment or grievous loss." The loss of 10 days, it is said, is neither severe nor grievous and the Due Process Clause is therefore of no relevance. Appellee's argument is again refuted by our prior decisions.... The Court's view has been that as long as a property deprivation is not *de minimis,* its gravity is irrelevant to the question whether account must be taken of the Due Process Clause.... A 10-day suspension from school is not *de minimis* in our view and may not be imposed in complete disregard of the Due Process Clause.

A short suspension is of course a far milder deprivation than expulsion. But, "education is perhaps the most important function of state and local governments." *Brown* v. *Board of Education,*...and the total exclusion from the educational process for more than a trivial period, and certainly if the suspension is for 10 days, is a serious event in the life of the suspended child. Neither the property interest in educational benefits temporarily denied nor the liberty interest in reputation, which is also implicated, is so insubstantial that suspensions may constitutionally be imposed by any procedure the school chooses, no matter how arbitrary.

III

"Once it is determined that due process applies, the question remains what process is due." ...We turn to that question, fully realizing as our cases regularly do that the interpretation and application of the Due Process Clause are intensely practical matters and that "the very nature of due process negates any concept of inflexible procedures universally applicable to every imaginable situation."...

...*Mullane v. Central Hanover Trust Co.*.....said that "many controversies have raged about the cryptic and abstract words of the Due Process Clause but there can be no doubt that at a minimum they require that deprivation of life, liberty or property by adjudication be preceded by notice and opportunity for hearing appropriate to the nature of the case." ...At the very minimum, therefore, students facing suspension and the consequent interference with a protected property interest must be given *some* kind of notice and afforded *some* kind of hearing. "Parties whose rights are to be affected are entitled to be heard; and in order that they may enjoy that right they must first be notified."...

It also appears from our cases that the timing and content of the notice and the nature of the hearing will depend on appropriate accommodation of the competing interests involved.... The student's interest is to avoid unfair or mistaken exclusion from the educational process, with all of its unfortunate consequences. The Due Process Clause will not shield him from suspensions properly imposed, but it disserves both his interest and the interest of the State if his suspension is in fact unwarranted. The concern would be mostly academic if the disciplinary process were a totally accurate, unerring process, never mistaken and never unfair. Unfortunately, that is not the case, and no one suggests that it is. Disciplinarians, although proceeding in utmost good faith, frequently act on the reports and advice of others; and the controlling facts and the nature of the conduct under challenge are often disputed. The risk of error is not at all trivial, and it should be guarded against if that may be done without prohibitive cost or interference with the educational process.

The difficulty is that our schools are vast and complex. Some modicum of discipline and order is essential if the educational function is to be performed. Events calling for discipline are frequent occurrences and sometimes require immediate, effective action. Suspension is considered not only to be a necessary tool to maintain order but a valuable educational device. The prospect of imposing elaborate hearing requirements in every suspension case is viewed with great concern, and many school authorities may well prefer the untrammeled power to act unilaterally, unhampered by rules about notice and hearing. But it would be a strange disciplinary system in an educational institution if no communication was sought by the disciplinarian with the student in an effort to inform him of his defalcation and to let him tell his side of the story in order to make sure that an injustice is not done. "[F]airness can rarely be obtained by secret, one-sided determination of the facts decisive of rights.... Secrecy is not congenial to truth-seeking and self-righteousness gives too slender an assurance of rightness. No better instrument has been devised for arriving at truth than to give a person in jeopardy of serious loss notice of the case against him and opportunity to meet it." *Anti-Fascist Committee* v. *McGrath*....

We do not believe that school authorities must be totally free from notice and hearing requirements if their schools are to operate with acceptable efficiency. Students facing temporary suspension have interests qualifying for protection of the Due Process Clause, and due process requires, in connection with a suspension of 10 days or less, that the student be given oral or written notice of the charges against him and, if he denies them, an explanation of the evidence the authorities have and an opportunity to present his side of the story. The clause requires at least these rudimentary precautions against unfair or mistaken findings of misconduct and arbitrary exclusion from school.

There need be no delay between the time "notice" is given and the time of the hearing. In the great majority of cases the disciplinarian may informally discuss the alleged misconduct with the student minutes after it has occurred. We hold only that, in being given an opportunity to explain his version of the facts at this discussion, the student first be told what he is accused of doing and what the basis of the accusation is.... Since the hearing may occur almost immediately following the misconduct, it follows that as a general rule notice and hearing should precede removal of the student from school. We agree with the District Court, however, that there are recurring situations in which prior notice and hearing cannot be insisted upon. Students whose presence poses a continuing danger to persons or property or an ongoing threat of disrupting the academic process may be immediately removed from school. In such cases, the necessary notice and rudimentary hearing should follow as soon as practicable, as the District Court indicated.

In holding as we do, we do not believe that we have imposed procedures on school disciplinarians which are inappropriate in a classroom setting. Instead we have imposed requirements which are, if anything, less than a fair-minded school principal would impose upon himself in order to avoid unfair suspensions....

We stop short of construing the Due Process Clause to require, countrywide, that hearings in connection with short suspensions must afford the student the opportunity to secure counsel, to confront and cross-examine witnesses supporting the charge or to call his own witnesses to verify his version of the incident. Brief disciplinary suspensions are almost countless. To impose in each such case even truncated trial type procedures might well overwhelm administrative facilities in many places and, by diverting resources, cost more than it would save in educational effectiveness. Moreover, further formalizing the suspension process and escalating its formality and adversary nature may not only make it too costly as a regular disciplinary tool but also destroy its effectiveness as part of the teaching process.

On the other hand, requiring effective notice and informal hearing permitting the student to give his version of the events will provide a meaningful hedge against erroneous action. At least the disciplinarian will be alerted to the existence of disputes about facts and arguments about cause and effect. He may then determine himself to summon the accuser, permit cross-examination and allow the student to present his own witnesses. In more difficult cases, he may permit counsel. In any event, his discretion will be more informed and we think the risk of error substantially reduced.

Requiring that there be at least an informal give-and-take between student and disciplinarian, preferably prior to the suspension, will add little to the factfinding function where the disciplinarian has himself witnessed the conduct forming the basis for the charge. But things are not always as they seem to be, and the student will at least have the opportunity to characterize his conduct and put it in what he deems the proper context.

We should also make it clear that we have addressed ourselves solely to the short suspension, not exceeding 10 days. Longer suspensions or expulsions for the remainder of the school term, or permanently, may require more formal procedures. Nor do we put aside the possibility that in unusual situations, although involving only a short suspension, something more than the rudimentary procedures will be required.

IV

The District Court found each of the suspensions involved here to have occurred without a hearing, either before or after the suspension, and that each suspension was therefore invalid and the statute unconstitutional insofar as it permits such suspensions without notice or hearing. Accordingly, the judgment is

Affirmed.

MR. JUSTICE POWELL, with whom THE CHIEF JUSTICE, MR. JUSTICE BLACKMUN, and MR. JUSTICE REHNQUIST join, dissenting.

The Court today invalidates an Ohio statute that permits student suspensions from school without a hearing "for not more than ten days." The decision unnecessarily opens avenues for judicial intervention in the operation of our public schools that may affect adversely the quality of education. The Court holds for the first time that the federal courts, rather than educational officials and state legislatures, have the authority to determine the rules applicable to routine classroom discipline of children and teenagers in the public schools. It justifies this unprecedented intrusion into the process of elementary and secondary education by identifying a new constitutional right: the right of a student not to be suspended for as much as a single day without notice and a due process hearing either before or promptly following the suspension.

The Court's decision rests on the premise that, under Ohio law, education is a property interest protected by the Fourteenth Amendment's Due Process Clause and therefore that any suspension requires notice and a hearing. In my view, a student's interest in education is not infringed by a suspension within the limited period prescribed by Ohio law. Moreover, to the extent that there may be some arguable infringement, it is too speculative, transitory and insubstantial to justify imposition of a *constitutional* rule.

I

...State law...extends the right of free public school education to Ohio students in accordance with the education laws of that State. The right or entitlement to education so created is protected in a proper case by the Due Process Clause.... In my view, this is not such a case.

In identifying property interests subject to due process protections, the Court's past opinions make clear that these interests "are created and their *dimensions are defined* by existing rules and understandings that stem from an independent source such as the law." ...The Ohio statute that creates the right to a "free" education also explicitly authorizes a principal to suspend a student for up to 10 days. ...Thus the very legislation which "defines the "dimension" of the student's entitlement, while providing a right to education generally, does not establish this right free of discipline imposed in accord with Ohio law. Rather, the right is encompassed in the entire package of statutory provisions governing education in Ohio—of which the power to suspend is one.

The Court thus disregards the basic structure of Ohio law in posturing this case as if Ohio had conferred an unqualified right to education, thereby compelling the school authorities to conform to due process procedures in imposing the most routine discipline.

But however one may define the entitlement to education provided by Ohio law, I would conclude that a deprivation of not more than 10 days' suspension from school, imposed as a routine disciplinary measure, does not assume constitutional dimensions. Contrary to the Court's assertion, our cases support rather than "refute" appellant's argument that "the Due Process Clause...comes into play only when the State subjects a student to a 'severe detriment or a grievous loss.' "...

The Ohio suspension statute allows no serious or significant infringement of education. It authorizes only a maximum suspension of eight school days, less than 5% of the normal 180-day school year. Absences of such limited duration will rarely affect a pupil's opportunity to learn or his scholastic performance. Indeed, the record in this case reflects no educational injury to appellees....

The Court also relies on a perceived deprivation of "liberty" resulting from any suspension, arguing again without factual support in the record pertaining to those appellees—that a suspension harms a student's reputation. In view of the Court's decision in *Board of Regents* v. *Roth,* ...I would have thought that this argument was plainly untenable. Underscoring the need for "serious damage" to reputation, the *Roth* Court held that a nontenured teacher who is not rehired by a public university could not claim to suffer sufficient reputational injury to require constitutional protections. Surely a brief suspension is of less serious consequence to the reputation of a teenage student.

II

In prior decisions, this Court has explicitly recognized that school authorities must have broad discretionary authority in the daily operation of public schools. This includes wide latitude with respect to maintaining discipline and good order.... Such an approach properly recognizes the unique nature of public education and the correspondingly limited role of the judiciary in its supervision. In *Epperson* v. *Arkansas*, ...the Court stated:

> "By and large, public education in our Nation is committed to the control of state and local authorities. Courts do not and cannot intervene in the resolution of conflicts which arise in the daily operation of school systems and which do not directly and sharply implicate basic constitutional values."

The Court today turns its back on these precedents. It can hardly seriously be claimed that a school principal's decision to suspend a pupil for a single day would "directly and sharply implicate basic constitutional values.".....

Moreover, the Court ignores the experience of mankind, as well as the long history of our law, recognizing that there *are* differences which must be accommodated in determining the rights and duties of children as compared with those of adults. Examples of this distinction abound in our law: in contracts, in torts, in criminal law and procedure, in criminal sanctions and rehabilitation, and in the right to vote and to hold office. Until today, and except in the special context of the First Amendment issue in *Tinker*, the educational rights of children and teenagers in the elementary and secondary schools have not been analogized to the rights of adults or to those accorded college students. Even with respect to the First Amendment, the rights of children have not been regarded as "coextensive with those of adults.".....

A

...The State's interest, broadly put, is in the proper functioning of its public school system for the benefit of *all* pupils and the public generally. Few rulings would interfere more extensively in the daily functioning of schools than subjecting routine discipline to the formalities and judicial oversight of due process. Suspensions are one of the traditional means—ranging from keeping a student after class to permanent expulsion—used to maintain discipline in the schools. It is common knowledge that maintaining order and reasonable decorum in school buildings and classrooms is a major educational problem, and one which has increased significantly in magnitude in recent years. Often the teacher, in protecting the rights of other children to an education (if not his or their safety), is compelled to rely on the power to suspend.... [I]f hearings were required for a substantial percentage of short-term suspensions, school authorities would have time to do little else.

B

The State's generalized interest in maintaining an orderly school system is not incompatible with the individual interest of the student. Education in any meaningful sense includes the inculcation of an understanding in each pupil of the necessity of rules and obedience thereto. This understanding is no less important than learning to read and write. One who does not comprehend the meaning and necessity of discipline is handicapped not merely in his education but throughout his subsequent life. In an age when the home and church play a diminishing role in shaping the character and value judgments of the young, a heavier responsibility falls upon the schools. When an immature student merits censure for his conduct, he is rendered a disservice if appropriate sanctions are not applied or if procedures for their application are so formalized as to invite a challenge to the teacher's authority—an invitation which rebellious or even merely spirited teenagers are likely to accept.

The lesson of discipline is not merely a matter of the student's self-interest in the shaping of his own character and personality; it provides an early understanding of the relevance to the social compact of respect for the rights of others. The classroom is the laboratory in which this lesson of life is best learned....

In assessing in constitutional terms the need to protect pupils from unfair minor discipline by school authorities, the Court ignores the commonality of interest of the State and pupils in the public school system. Rather, it thinks in traditional judicial terms of an adversary situation. To be sure, there will be the occasional pupil innocent of any rule infringement who is mistakenly suspended or whose infraction is too minor to justify suspension. But, while there is no evidence indicating the frequency of unjust suspensions, common sense suggests that they will not be numerous in relation to the total number, and that mistakes or injustices will usually be righted by informal means.

C

One of the more disturbing aspects of today's decision is its indiscriminate reliance upon the judiciary, and the adversary process, as the means of resolving many of the most routine problems arising in the classroom. In mandating due process procedures the Court misapprehends the reality of the normal teacher-pupil relationship. There is an ongoing relationship, one in which the teacher must occupy many roles—educator, adviser, friend and, at times, parent-substitute. It is rarely adversary in nature except with respect to the chronically disruptive or insubordinate pupil whom the teacher must be free to discipline without frustrating formalities....

D

In my view, the constitutionalizing of routine classroom decisions not only represents a significant and unwise extension of the Due Process Clause; it also was quite unnecessary in view of the safeguards prescribed by the Ohio statute....

The Ohio statute, limiting suspensions to not more than eight school days, requires *written* notice including the "reasons therefor" to the student's parents and to the Board of Education within 24-hours of any suspension. The Court only requires oral *or* written notice to the pupil, with no notice being required to the parents or the Board of Education. The mere fact of the statutory requirement is a deterrent against arbitrary action by the principal. The Board, usually elected by the people and sensitive to constituent relations, may be expected to identify a principal whose record of suspensions merits inquiry. In any event, parents placed on written notice may exercise their rights as constituents by going directly to the Board or a member thereof if dissatisfied with the principal's decision.

Nor does the Court's due process "hearing" appear to provide significantly more protection than that already available. The Court holds only that the principal must listen to the student's "version of the events," either before suspension or thereafter—depending upon the circumstances.... Such a truncated "hearing" is likely to be considerably less meaningful than the opportunities for correcting mistakes already available to students and parents....

In its rush to mandate a constitutional rule, the Court appears to give no weight to the practical manner in which suspension problems normally would be worked out under Ohio law. One must doubt, then, whether the constitutionalization of the student-teacher relationship, with all of its attendant doctrinal and practical difficulties, will assure in any meaningful sense greater protection than that already afforded under Ohio law.

III

No one can foresee the ultimate frontiers of the new "thicket" the Court now enters. Today's ruling appears to sweep within the protected interest in education a multitude of discretionary decisions in the educational process. Teachers and other school authorities are required to make many decisions that may have serious consequences for the pupil. They must decide, for example, how to grade the student's work, whether a student passes or fails a course, whether he is to be promoted,....

In these and many similar situations claims of impairment of one's educational entitlement identical in principle to those before the Court today can be asserted with equal or greater justification. Likewise, in many of these situations, the pupil can advance the same types of speculative and subjective injury given critical weight in this case....

It hardly need be said that if a student, as a result of a day's suspension, suffers "a blow" to his "self esteem," "feels powerless," views "teachers with resentment," or feels "stigmatized by his teachers," identical psychological harms will flow from many other routine and necessary school decisions. The student who is given a failing grade, who is not promoted, ...is unlikely to suffer any less psychological injury than if he were suspended for a day for a relatively minor infraction.

If, as seems apparent, the Court will now require due process procedures whenever such routine school decisions are challenged, the impact upon public education will be serious indeed.... If the Court perceives a rational and analytically sound distinction between the discretionary decision by school authorities to suspend a pupil for a brief period, and the types of discretionary school decisions described above, it would be prudent to articulate it in today's opinion. Otherwise, the federal courts should prepare themselves for a vast new role in society.

IV

...In recent years the Court, wisely in my view, has rejected the "wooden distinction between 'rights' and 'privileges,' "...and looked instead to the significance of the state created or enforced right and to the substantiality of the alleged deprivation. Today's opinion appears to abandon this reasonable approach by holding in effect that government infringement of any interest to which a person is entitled, no matter what the interest or how inconsequential the infringement, requires *constitutional* protection. As it is difficult to think of any less consequential infringement than suspension of a junior high school student for a single day, it is equally difficult to perceive any principled limit to the new reach of procedural due process.

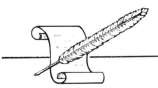

February

FORD'S 1976 BUDGET

February 3, 1975

President Ford sent his 1976 budget requests to Congress Feb. 3, asking a record $349.4-billion in expenditures for the fiscal year starting July 1, 1975. In blunt but forthright fashion, Ford's requests laid out bleak economic prospects for Congress and the nation to ponder. While projecting a near-record $51.9-billion federal deficit resulting from a serious recession, the President passed along his economic advisers' estimate that unemployment still would average 8 per cent in 1975 and 1976. (Economic Report, see p. 99.) And while urging federal spending restraint to keep that deficit from approaching $70-billion, he nonetheless acknowledged that the double-digit inflation rates that plagued the nation in 1974 actually would accelerate in 1975 under the impact of his own energy conservation strategy. Unpleasant as those prospects were, the budget spelled them out to show the prolonged and painful recovery the administration envisioned from the nation's twin troubles of recession and inflation.

More than most budgets, the fiscal 1976 recommendations took a long-term view of economic policy requirements. Mindful of the risks posed by inflationary pressures and energy deficiencies, the administration's program shaped its response to immediate economic needs to fit the more distant dangers and objectives as well. "My budget recommendations are designed to meet longer-term national needs as well as immediate, short-run objectives," Ford told Congress in his budget message. The nation's serious problems can be solved, he insisted, "if we exercise reasonable patience and restraint."

In charting that course, the President was reluctantly accepting back-to-back fiscal 1975 and 1976 federal deficits of $34.7-billion and $51.9-billion.

Those estimates were provisional figures, premised both on the administration's economic assumptions and on congressional approval of Ford's Jan. 15 recommendations for temporary tax cuts, for energy conservation levies offset by permanent tax reductions, and for budget reductions to curb spending by $6.1-billion in fiscal 1975 and by $17.5-billion in fiscal 1976. (Ford's energy and economic proposals, see p. 102.) *Making those assumptions, the budget forecast fiscal 1976 outlays of $349.4-billion and revenues of $297.5-billion. Those estimates covered the 12-month period ending June 30, 1976, although Congress had shifted the start of subsequent fiscal years to Oct. 1. The President's budget estimated receipts of $84.4-billion and outlays of $94.3-billion in the transition quarter to run from July 1 to Sept. 30, 1976. For fiscal 1975, ending June 30, 1975, the budget projected $313.4-billion in outlays and $278.8-billion in revenues.*

In light of Ford's self-declared moratorium on new federal spending programs except for energy development, the fiscal 1976 budget offered few innovative proposals, conspicuously omitting previously discussed plans for national health insurance and welfare reform. While taking a hold-the-line stance on most domestic programs, the budget proposed an $8-billion increase in defense outlays—to a total of $92.8-billion in fiscal 1976. Ford defended the increase as necessary to "maintain defense preparedness and preserve manpower levels in the face of rising costs." For energy, the budget proposed an $805.5-million increase to $3.9-billion in outlays for conservation research and the development of new fossil fuels, nuclear energy and solar and geothermal energy.

Fiscal Restraints

To hold the over-all increase in spending to $36-billion, the budget included a package of spending restraints calculated to pare a total of $17.5-billion off potential outlays: $2.1-billion through administrative action; $2.6-billion through rescissions and deferrals of budget authority; and $12.4-billion through enactment of new legislation. Almost one-half of the latter sum, $6.1-billion, would be saved by Ford's controversial proposal to put a 5 per cent ceiling, through June 1976, on federal pay raises and on cost-of-living increases in federal benefit programs, including Social Security. Roy L. Ash, then director of the Office of Management and Budget, explained at a briefing Feb. 1 that curbing of federal outlays for Medicare, child nutrition, educational impact aid and public assistance programs also would contribute to the required savings.

To provide the funding for part of the fiscal 1976 outlays—and for spending in future years as well—the President proposed budget authority of $385.8-billion, with $253.3-billion requiring action by Congress. Of that $385.8-billion in budget authority, $237.8-billion would be used for fiscal 1976 outlays, in combination with $111.6-billion in funds appropriated in prior years. The remaining $148.1-billion in fiscal 1976 appropriations would be available for spending in future fiscal years.

Democratic Response

United as they were in opposition to President Ford's economic program, congressional Democrats still could not agree on what to put in its place. Most Democrats, however, were convinced of the need for a federal budget large enough to force unemployment down quickly, even at the expense of more inflation. It was this issue that dominated the Democrats' response to the Ford budget.

"The trouble with the Ford budget," said Sen. Walter F. Mondale (D Minn.), "is that he listened to those Republicans who still pray to the god of balanced budgets." Mondale contended that the economy could tolerate a deficit much bigger than Ford's projected $52-billion for the 1976 fiscal year. Sen. William Proxmire (D Wis.), chairman of the Senate Banking, Housing and Urban Affairs Committee, saw disaster in the President's projection of 7 per cent unemployment or more through 1977. "The President's budget is a tragic confession of failure," said Proxmire. "It admits that the richest and most powerful country in the world cannot provide useful work for millions of those who seek work."

A second major theme for Democrats grew out of their dislike for Ford's use of cutbacks in social welfare programs as a means of keeping the deficit down. Rep. Morris K. Udall (D Ariz.), for example, called the budget "a bloated, saddening document replete with monumentally misplaced priorities reflecting a sorry insensitivity to the needy, the elderly and the disadvantaged."

Text of President Ford's budget message to Congress, Feb. 3, 1975 (some tables omitted):

THE BUDGET MESSAGE

The President's Message to the Congress Transmitting the Budget for Fiscal Year 1976. February 3, 1975

To the Congress of the United States:

The year 1976 will mark the bicentennial of this country. With this budget we shall begin our third century as a Nation.

In our first two centuries we have developed from 13 struggling colonies to a powerful leader among nations. Our population has increased from three million to more than 213 million. From a simple agricultural society we have grown into a complex industrialized one.

Our Government—and its budget—have grown with the Nation, as the increasing complexity of modern society has placed greater responsibilities upon it. Yet our society has remained free and democratic, true to the principles of our Founding Fathers.

As we approach our third century as a Nation, we face serious economic difficulties of recession and inflation. I have a deep faith, however, in the fundamental strength of our Nation, our people, our economy, and our institutions of government. I am confident that we can overcome today's challenges as we have overcome others in the past—and go on to greater achievements.

My budget recommendations are designed to meet longer-term national needs as well as immediate short-run objectives. It is vital that they do so. Because of the size and momentum of the budget, today's decisions will have far-reaching and long-lasting effects.

The recommendations set forth in this budget are an integral part of the broader series of proposals outlined in my State of the Union address. These proposals provide for:

—fiscal policy actions to increase purchasing power and stimulate economic revival, including tax reductions and greatly increased aid to the unemployed;

The Budget at a Glance

[In billions of dollars]

Item	1974 actual	1975 estimate	1976 estimate	Transition quarter
Receipts	264.9	278.8	297.5	84.4
Outlays	268.4	313.4	349.4	94.3
Deficit (−)	−3.5	−34.7	−51.9	−9.8

—a major new energy program that will hold down energy use, accelerate development of domestic energy resources, and promote energy research and development;

—an increase in outlays for defense in order to maintain preparedness and preserve force levels in the face of rising costs;

—a one-year moratorium on new Federal spending programs other than energy programs; and

—a temporary 5% ceiling on increases in pay for Federal employees, and on those benefit payments to individuals that are tied to changes on consumer prices.

These policies call for decisive action to restore economic growth and energy self-reliance. My proposals include a one-time $16 billion tax cut—$12 billion for individual taxpayers and $4 billion for businesses—to stimulate economic recovery.

Total Federal outlays are estimated to increase 11% between 1975 and 1976. It is essential that we keep a tight rein on spending, to prevent it from rising still further and making tax reduction imprudent. I believe that tax relief, not more Government spending, is the key to turning the economy around to renewed growth.

I regret that my budget and tax proposals will mean bigger deficits temporarily, for I have always opposed deficits. We must recognize, however, that if economic recovery does not begin soon, the Treasury will lose anticipated receipts and incur even larger deficits in the future.

My energy program calls for an increased fee on imported oil, and an excise tax on domestically produced petroleum and natural gas. The proposals also call for decontrol of oil prices—coupled with a windfall profits tax—and deregulation of prices on new natural gas. These measures will discourage excessive energy use and reduce our dependence on imported oil. The $30 billion in receipts these measures will produce will be refunded to the American people—refunded in a way that helps correct the distortions in our tax system created by inflation. Special provisions will ensure that low-income Americans and State and local governments are compensated equitably. All of these compensatory measures will be in addition to the $16 billion in tax relief I have proposed.

My budget recommendations provide for total outlays of $349.4 billion in 1976, an increase of $35.9 billion over 1975, and anticipate receipts of $297.5 billion, an increase of $18.8 billion over 1975.

The Congressional Budget and Impoundment Control Act of 1974 provides for major reforms in the budget process. As part of these reforms, it changes the fiscal year for the Federal budget from the present July-through-June basis to an October-through-September basis, beginning with the 1977 fiscal year. This requires that there be a separate transition quarter, extending from July through September of 1976, after fiscal year 1976 ends and before fiscal year 1977 begins. Estimates for the transition quarter are included in this budget. In general, they anticipate continuing the 1976 program levels unchanged for the additional three months. Because outlays and receipts vary seasonally—that is, they do not occur at uniform rates during the year—the estimates for this quarter (and particularly the deficit) are not representative of a full year's experience.

The Budget and the Economy

If the Congress acts decisively on the new policies I have announced in my State of the Union address, and if we exercise reasonable patience and restraint, we can go far toward solving the broad range of economic problems our Nation now faces.

It must be clearly understood that these problems are serious and that strong remedies are fully justified. The economy is now in a recession. Unemployment is far too high and productivity has declined. At the same time, inflation, a serious and growing problem for nearly a decade, continues to distort our economy in major ways. Underlying these problems is the fact that we are far from self-sufficient in energy production, and even with the measures I have proposed, regaining the capacity for self-sufficiency will take years to achieve. Imported fuel supplies have been interrupted once and remain vulnerable, and oil prices have been increased fourfold.

The increased unemployment and continued price increases from which we now suffer are problems we share with much of the rest of the world. The roots of these problems are complex. The steep rise in the price of imported oil, for example, while directly increasing prices, has also acted like a tax increase by reducing the real income of American consumers and transferring that income to oil exporting countries. Lower real incomes, combined with consumer resistance to rising prices, has reduced the demand for goods in the American marketplace. Such factors, superimposed on the inevitable slowdown in economic growth following the boom of 1972-73, underlie the recession we are now in.

The weakening of consumer demand and investment, in turn, is beginning to exert a dampening effect on price and wage increases. Thus, inflationary pressures are already beginning to recede and are likely to continue to do so. The one-time increase in fuel costs needed to constrain excessive energy usage will not reverse this basic trend.

Aiding economic recovery.—In view of this situation, I have proposed a $16 billion rebate of personal and corporation income taxes that will help reduce unemployment without rekindling inflation. This tax cut will contribute to deficits, adding $6 billion in 1975 and $10 billion in 1976.

Aside from the effects of the proposed tax reduction, the deficits anticipated for 1975 and 1976 are in large part the result of those aspects of the budget and the tax system that respond automatically to changes in the economy. When an economic slowdown occurs, Federal tax collections slow down more than incomes and profits do, and unemployment benefit payments rise sharply. These factors tend to cushion the economic downturn and help sustain individual and corporate incomes.

These stabilizing influences are substantial. If the economy were to be as fully employed in 1976 as it was in 1974, we would have $40 billion in additional tax receipts, assuming no change in tax rates. Aid to the unemployed, including the special measures I proposed and the Congress enacted last December, will be $12.7 billion larger in 1976 than in 1974, providing income support for 14.7 million beneficiaries and their families. In 1975, receipts would be $30 billion higher and aid to the unemployed is up $9 billion over 1974. These factors alone more than account for the deficits expected in both 1975 and 1976.

The Government must act decisively to help restore economic health, and act compassionately to aid those most seriously affected by unemployment. It does not make economic sense to insist on cutting a dollar out of the budget for each dollar of tax receipts lost just because of decreases in incomes and profits resulting from the economic downturn. Nor does it make sense arbitrarily to offset each dollar of increased aid to the unemployed by a reduction elsewhere in the budget.

Last October, I proposed a National Employment Assistance Act, which provided for liberalized unemployment benefits and coverage and for more public employment. Congress has since enacted, and I have signed into law, two employment assistance acts derived from my proposals. One of these measures, the Emergency Jobs and Unemployment Assistance Act, provides unemployment benefits to workers not covered by the regular unemployment insurance system and provides increased job opportunities in the public sector. The other measure, the Emergency Unemployment

Compensation Act, extends the length of time that workers covered by the regular unemployment insurance system are eligible for benefits. My budget recommendations include outlays of $17.5 billion in 1976 for income support for the unemployed, both under these two acts and under the regular unemployment compensation programs. Another $1.3 billion will be spent for increased public sector jobs.

Budget reductions.—While recommending temporary measures to help the economy and to provide greater assistance to the unemployed, I have sought, on an item-by-item basis, to eliminate nonessential spending and avoid commitment to excessive growth of Federal spending in the long run. I am proposing no new spending initiatives in this budget other than those for energy. I am also proposing that the allowable increase in Federal pay and in benefit payments to individuals that currently are linked by law to increases in consumer price levels be limited to 5% through June 30 of next year. To be equitable, this ceiling should apply to all these programs. This limit will save $6 billion in 1976 and permit us to concentrate maximum resources on direct efforts to speed economic recovery, including tax reduction.

In addition, I have previously asked the Congress to agree to a series of measures that would reduce outlays. In some cases the Congress has done so; in others it has overturned my proposals. Those economy measures to which Congress has not objected are reflected in my budget recommendations. These measures will provide $8 billion in savings in 1976. Further program reductions recommended in this budget will save another $3 billion. Unless the Congress concurs with the proposals now before it, including those advanced in this budget, outlays—and thus the deficit—will be about $17 billion greater in 1976 than the figure estimated in this budget. It is therefore essential that the tax cuts I am proposing be considered in conjunction with these savings proposals.

My proposal to place a temporary limit on civil service and military pay increases recognizes that the Federal Government must set an example for the rest of the economy, and that Federal employees generally enjoy considerably greater job security than the average worker under current economic conditions. I believe that most Federal employees will understand that some restraint on their pay increases is appropriate now to help provide benefits and increased job opportunities for those who are unemployed.

I urge the Congress to accept this recommendation. I especially urge the private sector—labor and management alike—to follow this example and minimize price and wage increases.

I have proposed a similar temporary limit on the automatic increases in benefit programs linked to changes in consumer prices. These programs include Social Security, Railroad Retirement, Federal employee retirement and disability systems, military retired pay, Supplemental Security Income, and the food stamp and child nutrition programs. My proposal is made in the context of the very large increases that have occurred in these programs in recent years—increases well in excess of the rate of inflation.

89

For example, between 1970 and 1975, average payments per Social Security beneficiary have increased 22% in constant prices—that is, *after* adjusting for the 38% rise in consumer prices. Both benefit increases and growth in the number of beneficiaries have contributed to an increase in outlays for these programs from $39 billion in 1970 to an estimated $91 billion in 1975.

With thousands of workers being laid off while considerable inflationary momentum persists, I believe that modest restraint on Federal pay raises and on the growth of Federal benefit programs is an equitable way to keep the budget from perpetuating inflation.

Budget Trends and Priorities

The Federal budget both reflects our national priorities and helps to move the Nation toward their realization. Recent years have seen a significant shift in the composition of the Federal Budget. The proportion of the budget devoted to defense has declined substantially since 1964, with a corresponding increase in the nondefense proportion of the budget. This shift has been particularly rapid since 1969, due in part to the end of American combat involvement in Vietnam.

Defense outlays remained virtually level in current dollar terms from 1969 to 1974, absorbing substantial cost increases—including the pay raises necessary to establish equitable wage levels for our servicemen and women and to make possible the transition to an all-volunteer armed force. Defense programs have undergone large reductions in real terms—reductions of about 40% since 1969 in manpower and materiel. In consequence, defense outlays have been a decreasing share of our gross national product, falling from 8.9% in 1969 to 5.9% in 1976.

At the same time, Federal nondefense spending has increased substantially in both current and constant dollar terms, growing from 11.6% of the gross national product in 1969 to an estimated 16.0% in this budget. In the process, the form that Federal spending takes has shifted dramatically away from support for direct Federal operations and toward direct benefits to individuals and grants to State and local governments. About a third of the latter also help to finance payments to individuals. Both legislated increases and built-in program growth have contributed to the doubling of outlays for domestic assistance in the past five years. The sharp drop in defense manpower and procurement has helped make this possible without tax increases or larger deficits.

It is no longer realistically possible to offset increasing costs of defense programs by further reducing military programs and strength. Therefore, this budget proposes an increase in defense outlays in current dollars that will maintain defense preparedness and preserve manpower levels in the face of rising costs. These proposals are the minimum prudent levels of defense spending consistent with providing armed forces which, in conjunction with those of our allies, will be adequate to maintain the military balance. Keeping that balance is essential to our national security and to the maintenance of peace.

In 1969, defense outlays were nearly one-fifth more than combined outlays for aid to individuals under human resource programs and for aid to State and local governments. Despite the increase in current-dollar defense outlays, this budget—only seven years later—proposes spending twice as much money for aid to individuals and State and local governments as for defense.

Outlays for assistance to individuals and to State and local governments will rise from $140 billion in 1974 to $173 billion in 1975, and $190 billion in 1976. These increases include the costs of the emergency unemployment assistance measures enacted last December, together with increased outlays under the regular unemployment insurance system. Outlays for other benefit programs, including Social Security, Supplemental Security Income, Medicare, and Medicaid, will also increase substantially.

The budget carries forward a philosophy that stresses an appropriate separation of public and private sector responsibilities. Within the sphere of public sector responsibilities, it calls for Federal emphasis on meeting national problems and encourages State and local responsibility and initiative in meeting local and statewide needs. Broader Federal aid to States and localities and a reduction in the Federal restrictions imposed as requirements for this aid are key elements of this philosophy. In 1974, Federal aid supplied 21% of total State and local government receipts, more than twice the percentage of two decades earlier. My budget recommends Federal grants-in-aid of $56 billion in 1976.

Energy

The fourfold increase in oil prices dictated by oil-exporting countries has been a major factor in the sharp inflationary surge of the past year and a half. It endangers the health of world trade and is creating significant financial and economic disruption throughout the world. Among other things, the resulting high fertilizer prices are hampering efforts to increase world agricultural production, thereby aggravating the world food problem.

Fuel conservation.—I continue to believe that fuel conservation and a reduction of world oil prices are in the long-term interest of both consumer and producer countries. Accordingly, I have proposed a series of stringent fuel conservation measures, including taxes on petroleum and natural gas offset by income tax reductions, payments to low-income individuals, and increased aid to State and local governments. On balance, this program will preserve consumer and business purchasing power while strongly discouraging petroleum consumption. Amendments to the Clean Air Act and other measures I have proposed will contribute to substantial improvement in automobile gasoline mileage and allow greater use of domestic coal for electric power generation, thus further reducing our need for imported oil.

At the same time, my Administration is pursuing diplomatic efforts to alleviate financial and supply problems in the industrialized world.

Development of domestic energy sources.—Fuel conservation measures and stronger diplomatic efforts are only part of the solution to the energy problem. Vigorous efforts to speed development of our vast domestic energy resources—particularly oil, gas, coal, and nuclear—are also essential. As part of these efforts, my Administration has worked out a comprehensive plan for leasing the offshore oil and gas resources of our Outer Continental Shelf. Studies are underway to insure that development and production will be accomplished safely and in an environmentally acceptable manner. We also seek responsible use of our extensive Naval Petroleum Reserves in California and Alaska and are taking steps to increase our use of our vast domestic coal reserves. These measures, including workable and precise legislation regulating strip mining, seek a proper balance between energy needs and environmental considerations. I will propose legislation to assist certain utilities facing serious financial difficulties and to encourage utilities to use fuels other than oil and natural gas. Increased domestic supplies, including establishment of a strategic petroleum storage system, coupled with fuel conservation, will help reduce our dependence upon petroleum imports and our vulnerability to interruption of foreign supplies.

In addition, the Federal Government has further expanded its research and development program to provide the new and improved technologies necessary for increasing the use of our domestic energy resources. Outlays for energy research and development will be $1.7 billion in 1976, an increase of 36% over 1975 and 102% over 1974. My budget recommendations continue our vigorous nuclear research and development program and further accelerate nonnuclear energy research and development—particularly in coal and solar energy. To provide a better organizational framework for this effort, last October I signed into law an act creating the Energy Research and Development Administration, which brings together within a single agency the Government's various research and development programs relating to fossil fuels, nuclear energy, and other energy technologies such as geothermal and solar. An independent Nuclear Regulatory Commission has also been established to improve the regulatory process associated with nuclear plant licensing, safety, and nuclear materials safeguards, and to separate this function from nuclear power development activities.

Agriculture.—Besides fuel costs, the cost of food has been the other special problem in the inflationary surge of the past two years. A worldwide decline in agricultural production due in part to adverse weather conditions has created shortages that have been critical in some areas and have sent world food prices soaring.

In response to these shortages, we have stimulated U.S. production by eliminating Government-imposed crop restrictions originally designed to prevent surpluses. Our increased production will help to curb inflation and will aid in relieving severe food shortages abroad. To the extent that we can produce beyond our domestic needs, we will be able to increase our agricultural exports and share our increased supplies with hungry peoples overseas.

National Security and Foreign Relations

The ultimate goal of American foreign policy is to ensure the freedom, security, and well-being of the United States as part of a peaceful and prosperous international community. Our diplomacy, backed by a strong national defense, strives to strengthen this international community through the peaceful resolution of international disputes, through arms control, and by fostering cooperation and mutual restraint. We seek a healthy world economy through expanded trade, cooperative solutions to energy problems, and increased world agricultural production to meet mankind's need for food. In today's interdependent world, each of these objectives serves our own national interest even as it helps others.

National security.—The Vladivostok understanding, which I reached with General Secretary Brezhnev of the Soviet Union, represents a major step on the long and arduous road to the control and eventual reduction of nuclear arms. For the first time, we have reached an understanding on specific and equal limitations on strategic nuclear weapons. Once we have concluded an agreement based on these understandings, we will be prepared to take the next step—to seek further reductions, as we have already done in the case of antiballistic missile launchers.

The progress we have already made along the road to eventual strategic arms reductions has been possible only because we have remained strong. If we are to make further progress, we must act to preserve our strategic strength. My defense proposals provide for necessary force improvements and for the development of strategic alternatives necessary to maintain, within the limits of the Vladivostok agreement, a credible strategic deterrent.

More attention must now be given to maintaining an adequate balance in general purpose forces. In this area we share the burden of defense with our allies. The United States has entered into negotiations between members of NATO and of the Warsaw Pact on mutual and balanced force reductions. If those negotiations are successful, some U.S. forces stationed in Europe could safely be withdrawn. For the time being, however, the United States and its allies must maintain present manpower levels and continue to strengthen conventional combat capabilities.

In an effort to increase efficiency and achieve greater combat capability with existing manpower levels, the Army has undertaken to provide 16 active combat divisions by June of 1976 with approximately the same total number of Army personnel as was authorized for 13 divisions in June of 1974. This 16-division combat force will require additional equipment, which is provided for in my budget recommendations.

Because the welfare and survival of the United States and its allies depend upon the flow of ocean-going trade and supplies, strong naval forces are required. In recent years, the number of Navy ships has decreased, primarily as a result of the retirement of many aging ships built during

World War II. The savings from this action have been used to strengthen the combat capabilities of the remaining force. This budget provides for a vigorous program of new ship construction and modernization necessary to maintain the naval balance in the future.

Foreign relations.—In addition to maintaining a strong defense capability, the United States strives, through its diplomacy, to develop and maintain peaceful relationships among nations. Foreign assistance is both an expression of our humanitarian concern and a flexible instrument of diplomacy. Our assistance in Indochina is making an essential contribution to the security and reconstruction of the countries in that region. Additional military assistance is now necessary to enable the South Vietnamese and Cambodian Governments to defend themselves against increasing military pressure. Our assistance in the Middle East is an integral part of our diplomatic effort to continue progress toward a peaceful solution to the area's problems. An increasing portion of our economic aid program is devoted to helping developing countries improve their agricultural productivity.

Higher oil prices, widespread food shortages, inflation, and spreading recession have severely strained the fabric of international cooperation. The United States has undertaken several major diplomatic initiatives designed to help restore international economic stability. Our diplomatic efforts were instrumental in the establishment of the International Energy Agency and its program, which provides for emergency oil sharing, conservation efforts, and development of alternative energy sources. More recently, the United States proposed a $25 billion special financing facility to assist industrialized countries in dealing with balance of payments difficulties. This new facility will supplement expanded operations of the International Monetary Fund. At the World Food Conference, in Rome, the United States proposed a number of measures to deal with the world food problem, including creation of an international system of grain reserves.

In addition, the Trade Act passed by the Congress last December will make possible a strengthening of international trade relations by enabling the United States to work with other nations toward reducing tariff and nontariff barriers to trade and improving access to supplies.

The strengthening of international trade and financial cooperation is essential if we and other nations are to cope successfully with current economic stresses. It is a prerequisite for renewed economic progress at home and abroad.

Domestic Assistance

The enormous growth in recent decades of Federal programs for assistance to individuals and families, and to State and local governments, has placed heavy demands on the budget. This growth expressed the desire of a compassionate society to provide well for its retired workers, veterans, and less fortunate members without sacrificing our proud and productive tradition of individual initiative and self-reliance. In the process, we have built a stronger partnership among the various levels of government: Federal, State, and local.

Human resources programs.—The rapid growth of human resources programs in recent years has brought about many improvements in the well-being of the American people. Benefits under Social Security, Medicare, Medicaid, Supplemental Security Income, food stamps and veterans programs have increased substantially. In just seven years, cash benefits under social security programs will have risen from $26 billion in 1969 to $70 billion in 1976. They now reach 28 million beneficiaries. By 1976, six social security benefit increases will have occurred since 1969. Automatic cost-of-living adjustments to benefits are now provided by law. Allowing for the temporary 5% ceiling I have proposed on benefit increases between now and July 1976, the increases from 1970 through 1976 in the average recipient's social security benefits, taken together, will total 77%. This far exceeds the increases in the cost of living (51%) estimated for this period.

The Supplemental Security Income program began operation a year ago, replacing the various State public assistance programs for the aged, the blind, and the disabled with a more uniform and equitable national system. This broad reform has provided higher benefits for these disadvantaged groups. In addition, Federal assumption of responsibility for these programs has provided significant fiscal relief to State and local governments. This budget provides for substantial increases in administrative personnel necessary to improve services to beneficiaries both of this program, and of social security.

Outlays for the food stamp program have increased from $248 million in 1969 to an estimated $3.6 billion in 1976. I have undertaken reforms to simplify the administration of this program and reduce costs, while providing for more equitable treatment of beneficiaries.

Over the years, the income security of our labor force has been enhanced by liberalization of benefits and coverage under our unemployment insurance system, while increased employment opportunities have been created in areas of high unemployment. Programs derived from the special unemployment assistance measures I proposed last October have been enacted into law as the Emergency Jobs and Unemployment Assistance Act and the Emergency Unemployment Compensation Act. With these new acts, total unemployment assistance, including employment programs, will expand 207%, from $6.1 billion in 1974 to $18.8 billion in 1976.

Our present welfare system is inefficient and inequitable. It is wasteful not only of tax dollars but, more importantly, of human potential. Left unchanged, over the long run the situation will almost surely continue to deteriorate. I urge the Congress to work with my Administration to develop reforms that make the system simple, fair, and compassionate. This

95

approach need not cost more, but rather can use our welfare dollars more effectively.

America needs to improve the way it pays for medical care. We should begin plans for a comprehensive national health insurance system. However, in view of the economic developments and the measures I have proposed to combat recession and inflation, I cannot now propose costly new programs. Once our current economic problems are behind us, the development of an adequate national medical insurance system should have high national priority. I urge the Congress to work with my Administration in order to devise a system that we will be able to afford.

The major existing Federal programs for financing medical care, Medicare and Medicaid, are now 10 years old. Medicare outlays of $15 billion in 1976 will help to meet the medical costs of an estimated 13.3 million aged and disabled Americans, 29% more people than were aided in 1971. Medicaid outlays of $7.2 billion will help to pay medical care for 26 million low-income Americans in 1976—a 40% increase in beneficiaries since 1971. Federal health programs also provide health care and insurance for Federal employees, veterans, and other groups. In total, existing Federal health programs now pay about 27% of the Nation's total health bill.

General Revenue Sharing.—General Revenue Sharing has become an integral and important part of the Federal grants-in-aid system. This program has been highly successful, providing fiscal assistance that can be applied flexibly to meet the needs of States and localities according to their priorities. It has distributed assistance more equitably than before, reaching many local governments that had not received Federal aid in the past.

Current authority for general revenue sharing will expire at the end of calendar year 1976. Because I believe in the soundness of this program, I shall propose legislation extending general revenue sharing through fiscal year 1982. Prompt action by the Congress on the proposed extension will permit State and local governments to plan their future budgets more effectively and avoid the waste and inefficiencies that prolonged budgetary uncertainties would create. In addition, the energy tax equalization payments to State and local governments will be distributed according to the formula used for general revenue sharing.

Transportation.—My budget recommendations anticipate legislation that I shall propose to extend the Highway Trust Fund through 1980 for the Interstate Highway System only, and increase its funding. My proposal will focus trust fund assistance on completion of key segments of the Interstate Highway System needed to link the national system together. They will also combine a number of narrow categorical grant programs to eliminate red tape and allow localities greater flexibility in meeting their transportation problems. In 1978, States will be permitted, under this proposal, to assume over $1 billion of Federal motor fuel tax receipts for local needs.

In order to improve the safety and efficiency of the Nation's aviation system, and to increase its responsiveness to current needs, I will propose legislation to restructure Federal airport and airway development programs. My proposal will broaden the range of aviation activities that may be financed from the Airport and Airway Trust Fund, eliminate unnecessary Federal involvement in airport investment decisions, and allocate user fees more equitably among aviation system users.

Budget Reform

As demands on the budget have grown, the need for better congressional procedures for considering the budget has become increasingly clear. In the past the Congress has acted upon the budget in a piecemeal fashion, with far too little attention to the total. The Congressional Budget and Impoundment Control Act, passed last summer, mandates changes in the Federal budget and major reforms in congressional procedures for dealing with it. Under the new procedures, the Congress will have a larger and better-defined role in developing sound budget and fiscal policies. Congressional organization and procedures will focus greater attention on the budget totals early in the legislative process.

Major provisions of the act require greater attention to the future-year costs of legislative proposals and ongoing programs, and establish a budget committee in each Chamber and a Congressional Budget Office to aid Congress in its consideration of budget recommendations. The shift of the fiscal year to an October-to-September basis will give the Congress more time to complete action on the budget before the fiscal year begins.

The act also provides for a closer working relationship between the Congress and the executive branch in controlling outlays. I look forward to a new era of fruitful cooperation between the legislative and executive branches on budgetary matters, a cooperation that will enhance fiscal responsibility, make the budget a more useful instrument of national policy, and promote a more careful allocation of limited resources.

During the past six years, the budget has become increasingly forward-looking, focusing attention on the future effects of budget proposals. The new act builds upon this initiative with the requirement that the budget present more extensive five-year projections of outlays and receipts. These projections indicate the large natural increase in receipts resulting from rising incomes and profits as the economy recovers. These increased receipts, coupled with *prudent fiscal restraint,* will make it possible to avoid deficits that would be inflationary when the economy returns to high employment.

The Government strongly affects the economy in many ways not fully reflected in the budget. These influences include tax expenditures such as those that encourage homeownership and business investment; and the operations of Federal or Government-sponsored enterprises, particularly in the credit field, that are excluded from the budget. The new act recognizes the importance of these factors by requiring that they be given greater consideration in connection with the budget.

Conclusion

As we approach our national bicentennial, difficult challenges lie before us. The recommendations in this budget address the Nation's problems in a direct, constructive, and responsible fashion. They are designed to move the Nation toward economic health and stability. They meet human needs. They provide for the strong defense essential to our national security and to our continuing efforts to maintain world peace.

Looking beyond the bicentennial, toward the year 2000, the practical limits to the growth of the Federal Government's role in our society become increasingly clear. The tremendous growth of our domestic assistance programs in recent years has, on the whole, been commendable. Much of the burden of aiding the elderly and the needy has been shifted from private individuals and institutions to society as a whole, as the Federal Government's income transfer programs have expanded their coverage.

These programs cannot, however, continue to expand at the rates they have experienced over the past two decades. Spending by all levels of government now makes up a third of our national output. Were the growth of domestic assistance programs to continue for the next two decades at the same rates as in the past 20 years, total government spending would grow to more than half of our national output. We cannot permit this to occur. Taxation of individuals and businesses to pay for such expansion would simply become insupportably heavy. This is not a matter of conservative or liberal ideology. It is hard fact, easily demonstrated by simple extrapolation. We must begin to limit the rate of growth of our budgetary commitments in the domestic assistance area to sustainable levels.

The growth of these domestic assistance programs has taken place in a largely unplanned, piecemeal fashion. This has resulted in too many overlapping programs, lack of coordination, and inequities. Some of the less needy now receive a disproportionate share of Federal benefits, while some who are more needy receive less. We must redouble the efforts of the past five years to rationalize and streamline these programs. This means working toward a stable and integrated system of programs that reflects the conscience of a compassionate society but avoids a growing preponderance of the public sector over the private. It also means decentralizing Government operations and developing a closer partnership among the Federal Government, State and local governments, and the individual private citizen.

The Congress will approach this budget in a new way, with new legislative machinery and procedures. I pledge to work in a spirit of cooperation with the Congress to make this effort a success. The tasks before us provide difficult tests: to meet immediate economic problems; to relate our limited Federal resources more clearly to current national priorities; and to develop long-term strategies for meeting Federal responsibilities as we begin our third century. I am confident of success.

February 3, 1975   GERALD R. FORD

THE ANNUAL ECONOMIC REPORT
February 4, 1975

The President's Council of Economic Advisers issued its annual report Feb. 4, urging caution in the federal government's efforts to speed economic recovery. "The policies that we use to support the economy in 1975 must be consistent with a further reduction in inflation in 1976 and thereafter," the advisers warned. The economy would continue to decline for "several more months," they predicted, but it should "move onto the road of recovery in the second half" of the year.

The council termed a reversal of the downward trends of production and employment "the most pressing concern of policy." But it added that "the momentum of the decline is so great that a quick turnaround and a strong recovery in economic activity aren't yet assured." The council predicted a second annual decline in gross national product (GNP), which had dropped 2.2 per cent in 1974. Inflation would be slowed, but only to about 7 per cent by the end of 1975.

"Consumers hold the key to the strength of the economic recovery," the advisers noted. "If they respond as expected to the stimulus of the tax cuts proposed by the administration for the spring and summer, real GNP should record a good-sized advance in the second half, but if not, the 1975 recovery could be a sluggish one."

In his message to Congress accompanying the council's report, President Ford described the grim nature of the nation's economy: "The economy is in a severe recession," he said. "Unemployment is too high and will rise higher. The rate of inflation is also too high although some progress has been made in lowering it." A third area of concern, he said, was "the newer problem of reducing America's vulnerability to oil embargoes."

To meet these problems, Ford asked Congress to approve his economic and energy proposals and "to help me follow through with further measures that changing circumstances may make desirable." While his economic package, if enacted, "will not produce swift and immediate results," the President conceded, efforts to remedy recession "must be both effective and consistent with the long-term objectives that are important for the future well-being of our economy." Cautioning against action to stimulate the economy too quickly, he concluded: "For the sake of one step forward, we must not adopt policies which will eventually carry us two steps backward."

Council's Forecast for 1975

In its report, the Council of Economic Advisers predicted a continued economic plunge in the first half of 1975, although acknowledging that the decline in the last part of 1974 "gathered so much momentum that developments beyond the current quarter are difficult to gauge." It appeared "quite likely," the council said, "that the contraction of business activity and rising unemployment will continue for several months." While the downturn was expected to be reversed in the second half of 1975, "the first half decline is likely to be severe...and the subsequent recovery will still leave the level of output in the fourth quarter about the same as a year earlier," the report said.

For the year, the actual GNP would be about 3 per cent below its 1974 average, the council predicted, with unemployment moving above 8 per cent by July before starting a slow decline. The inflation rate in the meantime would be "very high in the first half of the year," but it was likely to subside to a 7 per cent rate by the year's final quarter. For all of 1975, prices as measured by the inflation component of the GNP were expected to rise 11 per cent.

While keeping a vigilant eye on inflation, the report continued, the nation must accept some immediate and painful price increases in the even longer-term interest of energy sufficiency. The council predicted that President Ford's energy program, if put into effect, would add 1.3 per cent to the consumer price index by midyear. That program, it pointed out, was based on "creating market conditions that will have a lasting influence, rather than relying on allocations and rationing which at best are only short-term solutions."

Surveying the economy for 1975, the economic advisers forecast a 9 per cent reduction in real business investment, a substantial reduction in business inventories, reversal of the housing industry's decline, little change in actual government outlays and an upturn in consumer spending. But they emphasized the uncertainties of the predictions. Questions of consumer and business confidence, the severity of the economic decline and the money-mangement policies of the Federal Reserve Board made the forecast "subject to an unusually wide margin of error."

By May, unemployment had risen to 9.2 per cent nationwide and the rate of inflation had slowed slightly to a seasonally adjusted rate of 11.3 per cent. As the council had predicted, GNP continued to decline in the first quarter of 1975, falling at an annual rate of 3.9 per cent. That figure reflected an inflation rate of 8.4 per cent and a decline of 11.4 per cent in real GNP.

There were strong indications by mid-1975 that the recession had bottomed out, as the council had forecast. Housing starts increased by 14 per cent in May. And on May 29, the Ford administration published a list of leading economic indicators—comprised of a composite of 12 indices that tend to foreshadow economic trends—showing a composite 4.2 per cent increase in April, the second increase in a row after 11 months of decline.

Excerpts from Chapter One of the 1975 Report of the Council of Economic Advisers, issued Feb. 4, 1975:

CHAPTER 1

Economic Policy and Outlook

The story of the past year was one of inflation and recession. Several of the forces that added to the rate of inflation also exerted downward pressure on economic activity. The sharp rise in oil prices resulted in a large transfer of purchasing power to the oil-producing countries. Inflation, strong demands for credit, and the unwillingness of the monetary authorities to underwrite a continued acceleration of inflation drove interest rates upward, causing a slump in housing. Another debilitating effect of the higher and variable rate of inflation was the sharp rise in uncertainty regarding future rates of price increase. The general rise in prices was instrumental in reducing real incomes in another way. Inflation pushed individuals into higher tax brackets thereby causing a significant transfer of real income from individuals to the government sector. Inflation also caused a similar updrift in the tax liabilities of business. The result was to shift the budget in the direction of restraint, by considerably more than had been anticipated at this time last year.

As 1975 begins, the unemployment rate stands at its highest level since 1958 and production and employment are declining sharply. The decline in activity during the closing months of the year gathered so much momentum that developments beyond the current quarter are difficult to gauge. It is quite likely, however, that the contraction of business activity and rising unemployment will continue for several more months. Although the rate of inflation is still high, it has begun to moderate. One can observe actual declines in prices of crude industrial materials and a slowdown in the rate of price advance among important categories of goods sold in wholesale and retail markets.

The most pressing concern of policy is to halt the decline in production and employment so that growth of output can resume and unemployment can be reduced. The momentum of the decline is so great that a quick turnaround and a strong recovery in economic activity are not yet assured. But prompt action on the Administration's proposals to stimulate the economy should hasten the end of the recession and contribute to the pace of recovery during the second half of the year. The policies that we use to support the economy in 1975 must be consistent with a further reduction in inflation in 1976 and thereafter. This will obviously require discipline both in the Federal budget and in the monetary policies of the Federal Reserve.

The formulation of economic policy is complicated by the need for much stronger actions to tackle the Nation's energy problems. New energy policies have been proposed which will provide an enduring framework for the adjustment that began after the oil embargo. The adjustment to lower levels of consumption and importation will impose further costs upon the economy in the short run in order to avoid mounting political and economic costs in the long run. The energy program will raise prices at a time when inflation is serious. On balance, however, the program will provide important benefits. Moreover, as formulated, it is consistent with the values and the objectives of an efficient market-oriented economy.

PROGRAMS TO STIMULATE THE ECONOMY AND CONSERVE ENERGY

To provide support for the economy, the President on January 13 proposed tax relief for individuals and business. For individuals the program calls for a tax rebate equivalent to 12 percent of total 1974 personal tax liabilities up to a limit of $1,000 per return....

For business the President proposed a 1-year increase in the investment tax credit to 12 percent. Except for utilities, which now have a 4 percent credit, the present credit is equal to 7 percent of investment in equipment. For electric utility investment in generating capacity that does not use oil or gas, the higher tax credit would remain in force through 1977. The increase in the tax credit is expected to reduce tax liabilities of businesses by approximately $4 billion during 1975. The credit will apply to machinery and equipment put into service during 1975, as well as to orders placed during 1975 and put into service by the end of 1976.

The tax cut will not prevent a decline in real output from 1974 to 1975 but it will reduce the extent of the year-over-year decline—perhaps by one-half of 1 percent to 1 percent in terms of real GNP—and will contribute to the recovery in the second half of 1975. An assessment of the economic effects of the stimulus program is complicated by a number of factors. We cannot be certain how much of the tax cut will be saved rather than spent, but past experience suggests that most of the tax cut will be spent, and a large fraction of it this year. Saving will be high initially, but as the year progresses spending will increase.

The investment tax credit may have some immediate effect in stimulating purchases of certain types of equipment, but it is most likely to begin to affect spending appreciably in the second half of 1975. Because of the time limitations applicable to the tax credit, businessmen have an incentive to undertake some investment now that they would otherwise have undertaken only later. In view of the fact that new orders for durable goods generally and for machinery and equipment specifically have fallen rapidly in recent months, any addition to orders at the present time is quite important in itself, even if it does not raise fixed investment immediately.

The Administration's energy program aims at discouraging energy consumption and encouraging domestic production by raising the relative price of energy. Prices are increased through removal of controls in combination with a series of taxes, but the tax proceeds are refunded so as to keep consumer purchasing power roughly unchanged once the program has become fully effective. The major components of the Administration's energy program are:

> —Price decontrol for crude oil and deregulation for new natural gas.
> —A windfall profits tax on crude oil.
> —An import fee which will rise to $2 per barrel on imported oil, accompanied by an excise tax of $2 per barrel on domestic oil and an equivalent tax of 37 cents per thousand cubic feet on natural gas.
> —Creation of a strategic oil reserve of up to 1.3 billion barrels with early action to require the stepped-up holding of private oil inventories.
> —Protection of domestic energy producers against excessive risks from abrupt declines in prices of imported petroleum.
> —Expanded production from the Naval Petroleum Reserves and other Federal oil deposits.
> —Expanded production and use of coal and nuclear energy.
> —Development of a synthetic fuels industry.
> —Various measures designed to increase the efficiency of energy consumption.

An important source of uncertainty regarding the stimulus program concerns the timing of the energy package. The reasoning behind the decision to embark on an energy conservation program is outlined further on. Here we note some of the price and fiscal aspects of the energy program.

It is estimated that the imposition of import fees, excise taxes on crude oil and natural gas, and the decontrol of domestic crude oil by April 1, 1975, will directly add about $30 billion (annual rate) to the Nation's oil and gas bill. Ultimately prices should rise by an equivalent amount. The windfall profits tax (WPT) is designed to capture the increase in profits of domestic oil producers attributable to decontrol. The increase in receipts from import fees, excise taxes, and the windfall profits tax will be returned to individuals, businesses, and governments mainly through a set of tax reductions, with a portion taking the form of increased Federal Government expenditures....

The initial effect of the import fee will be to raise prices of imported oil and of domestic oil that is now uncontrolled. Together these constitute some 60 percent of total U.S. oil consumption. This effect will be reinforced on April 1 by the decontrol of the remaining part of domestic petroleum production. In the second quarter of the year, the average price of crude oil is expected to rise by approximately $4.20 per barrel over current levels as a result of decontrol and the $2 per barrel excise tax. It is expected that the increase will be reflected with a lag in higher prices for gasoline, fuel oil, and other petroleum products and eventually in higher electricity prices. By the end of the second quarter of 1975, when all of the program will be effective, the consumer price index is estimated to be 1.3 percent higher than it would be without the proposed program. Not all of the higher price of crude oil and natural gas will affect prices in final markets this quickly. At first some of the higher petroleum prices will reduce profits rather than increase the prices charged by users of refined petroleum inputs, especially where prices are regulated. The profits squeeze is not expected to last long, however, and by the latter part of 1976 all of the increased cost should show up in the form of higher prices of those goods and services that consume crude oil and natural gas directly and indirectly. The $30-billion impact is estimated to be about 2 percent of GNP. About 90 percent of it will be reflected in higher prices by the fourth quarter of this year. For all of 1975 we estimate that the GNP deflator will be about 1 percent higher than it would have been without the program.

Rising prices not compensated for by offsetting tax cuts will reduce real incomes to a slight extent in the first half of 1975. Consequently, the effect of the stimulus proposals will be partially offset by the energy proposals during the first half of the year. On the other hand, to the extent that oil imports and hence the transfer of purchasing power to foreign oil producers are reduced the demand for domestic goods would be increased. By the third quarter the stimulus from both programs will be substantially greater.

The Energy Tax Offsets

The energy taxes are to be turned back to the economy in a variety of ways. (Estimates below are annual rates based on calendar year 1975.)

—For individual taxpayers, rates are being reduced and the low-income allowance is being raised in such a way that total taxes will be cut by an estimated 12 percent from what they would otherwise be in 1975....

—Low-income households that pay no taxes and certain low-income taxpayers will receive a special distribution of up to $80 per adult after application to the Internal Revenue Service....

—The program calls for a tax credit of 15 percent of expenditures—up to a maximum expenditure of $1,000 per homeowner—for outlays that improve residential thermal efficiency....

—The Federal Government would use $3 billion to cover its share of the costlier energy bill, while State and local governments would receive an additional $2 billion in revenue sharing grants.

—Business would receive $6 billion through a reduction in the corporate tax rate from 48 percent to 42 percent....

The Fiscal 1976 Budget

Because of concern that a too expansionary budget carries the risk of worsening the inflation, the Administration has proposed a slower rate of increase in spending from fiscal 1975 to fiscal 1976 than from fiscal 1974 to fiscal 1975. The new budget calls for outlays of $349.4 billion, a rise of 11.5 percent compared to a rise of 16.8 percent from fiscal 1974 to fiscal 1975. The President has proposed a moratorium on new spending programs except for energy as well as numerous actions to reduce spending in existing programs. The reductions total $17.5 billion and embrace $7.8 billion in proposals made last year and $9.7 billion in new reductions. Taking into account the $16 billion in tax cuts to stimulate the economy, receipts are expected to total $297.5 billion, a rise of 6.7 percent over fiscal 1975.

The deficit is expected to rise from an estimated $34.7 billion to $51.9 billion. These are large deficits but they reflect the shortfall in receipts and increased unemployment benefits stemming from the weak economy. For the calendar year the full-employment surplus on a national income accounts basis is expected to decline by $9 billion from 1974 to 1975.

Financing the Deficit

The financing of the large deficits will pose problems which are not easy to evaluate. The economic circumstances of 1975 are quite different from those encountered in past recessions, like the recession of 1958. If prices are stable, any large decline in output lowers the demand for private credit, and this slack is taken up only in part by the normal increase in the budget deficit resulting from lower tax collections and higher unemployment benefits. Even a discretionary stimulus that would partly counteract rather than merely cushion a large decline of aggregate demand would probably not create serious financing problems under such conditions. The reason is that if unemployment is widespread and factors of production are in highly elastic supply, cost pressures are minimal and private investment and credit demands are likely to be low.

The present situation is far different from past recessions, but the deficit as presently estimated can probably be financed without serious problems in 1975. The private demand for credit will decline at least somewhat, and probably substantially, as the direct result of the low level of housing, reduced consumer purchases of durable goods, and the sharp swing from inventory accumulation to inventory liquidation. The drop in real output, however, has brought less relief in the credit markets than it would have under less inflationary conditions. Furthermore, imbalances have developed in the financial structure of businesses in recent years because of the disproportionate reliance on debt financing in general and short-term debt in particular. As the desired private refinancing is made more difficult by the deficit financing, businesses may abandon investment projects more readily than in the past, rather than risk further unbalancing their capital structure and increasing their credit market exposure.

One way of preventing significant displacement of private investment in a substantially underemployed economy would be to increase the rate of money supply growth to reduce Federal financing pressures. Under such conditions, an increase in monetary growth need not be inflationary in the short run, especially if there is a large unsatisfied demand for liquidity. On the other hand, should large deficits continue well after the recovery has taken hold, maintaining such a course of monetary accommodation could spark an increase in the rate of inflation. For this reason it is essential that any monetary accommodation to large fiscal deficits be permitted only so long as the effective underemployment of resources remains large and there is ample room for above-average growth. Otherwise, future price level trends will be affected adversely and the deficit will become increasingly "unproductive" in real terms.

Monetary policy faces great difficulties in the year ahead and will require careful and continuous evaluation by the Federal Reserve. The uncertainties that underlie the outlook for 1975 add to the importance of a flexible monetary policy. Monetary policy must be conducted so as to encourage a near-term recovery in the economy and a resumption of sustainable economic growth. Toward this end, reasonable growth in money and credit will be required—growth which, one hopes, will encourage a freer flow of credit and lower interest rates in private credit markets. Whether more accommodating credit conditions will in fact develop depends importantly on the ease with which the enlarged Federal deficit is financed, and also on the progress that is achieved in moderating the Nation's rate of inflation as 1975 progresses.

A special problem for monetary policy is posed by the energy conservation program, the initial effects of which will be to raise the price level. To a degree, this one-time increase in prices will require additional financing, so as to avoid a contractive effect on the real economy. However, rapid monetary growth would run the risk that inflationary pressures would once again be increased, later on if not in 1975, undermining the Nation's fundamental need to regain the basis for reasonable price stability. That must not be permitted to happen.

Aid to the Unemployed

In response to the sharp rise in unemployment in the latter part of 1974, and in anticipation of further increases in 1975, the Administration initiated legislation to increase the duration and coverage of unemployment insurance benefits and to create employment by funding additional public service jobs. In December 1974, the President signed the Emergency Unemployment Compensation Act, which extends the duration of benefits by 13 weeks beyond the prevailing limits. Unemployed workers can now receive up to 52 weeks of benefits. The Emergency Jobs and Unemployment Assistance Act, also signed in December, grants unemployment benefits, for up to 26 weeks, for the first time to workers in occupations and industries that were not covered by the regular State or Federal programs. This act provides coverage for an estimated 12 million workers, primarily agricultural, domestic, and State and local government employees. While these programs are administered by the States, the funds are entirely from Federal sources.

The Emergency Jobs and Unemployment Assistance Act also amends the Comprehensive Employment and Manpower Training Act (1973) to expand Federal funding for State and local public service jobs. The budget provides funds that will permit an increase in the number of public service jobs from 85,000 in fiscal 1974 to 280,000 in 1975 and 1976.

THE OUTLOOK WITH NEW POLICIES

Given the above assumptions regarding energy, fiscal, and monetary policies, the economy is likely to continue its downward course in the first half of 1975 and to move onto the road of recovery in the second half. The first-half decline is likely to be severe, however, and the subsequent recovery will still leave the level of output in the fourth quarter about the same as a year earlier. For 1975 as a whole real GNP will probably be about 3 percent below the average of 1974. The rate of inflation will be very high in the first half of the year—higher than it would be in the absence of the energy policy—but it should subside in the second half. For all of 1975, prices as measured by the GNP deflator should be 11 percent higher than prices in 1974. By the final quarter an inflation rate of about 7 percent is projected, not counting the pay increase scheduled for Federal civilian and military personnel. The projections of real GNP and the deflator yield a nominal GNP of about $1,500 billion, which is some 7¼ percent greater than the 1974 figure. Given the large decline in real output, the unemployment rate should average about 8 percent for the year, moving above that level before midyear but coming down from the peak in the second half.

The uncertainties are so great at the present time that the projections cited above, although presented as specific numbers, are subject to an unusually wide margin of error. The past several months have witnessed a progressive scaling down of output projections and a scaling up of unemployment projections.

Nonresidential Fixed Investment

Early in January the Department of Commerce published a survey of plant and equipment plans that projected a rise of 4½ percent in nominal outlays from 1974 to 1975. In view of the prospective rise in capital goods prices the survey results imply a sizable decline in real outlays. Large nominal increases ranging from 14 to 28 percent were scheduled by producers of basic materials, such as steel, paper, chemicals and petroleum, and by mining firms, railroads, and gas utilities. Very small rises or decreases were projected by electric utilities, air transport, and commercial firms. The deterioration of sales, output, and profits since this survey was taken will probably lead to a scaling down of even this small overall planned increase, although the large expansion plans of a number of basic industries will provide an element of stability. The plans reported in this survey came in too early to be affected by the proposed investment tax credit.

There seems little likelihood of preventing a decline in real nonresidential investment in the first half of 1975. The pronounced slump in real outlays for producers' durable equipment in the final quarter of 1974 was heavily concentrated in outlays for automobiles and trucks. But the closing months of the year also witnessed decreases in the production of a broad range of machinery and equipment as businessmen canceled orders or delayed deliveries on contracts made earlier. These cutbacks will take the form of reduced deliveries in the first half. The liberalization of the investment tax credit, coupled with the turnaround in economic activity and a rebound in profits, should bring rising real outlays in the second half. The main impact of a liberalized investment tax credit will be felt late in the year. For 1975 the projection foresees nominal investment about 4 percent above the 1974 total but real investment down approximately 9 percent.

Inventories

The behavior of inventory investment is likely to be the dominant influence on the course of production over the coming year. At the start of 1975 the ratio of nonfarm inventories to GNP in real terms was the highest since the end of World War II. It seems fairly likely that the physical volume of inventories will fall during most and perhaps all of the coming year, with especially large reductions in the first half. Even with a decline in stocks and above average growth in demand in the second half of the year, the ratio of stocks to output at year-end would still be high by post-World War II standards. Although stocks may well decline throughout the year, the impact of inventory behavior on the change in output should be greatest early this year, when inventory investment turns negative following a high rate of involuntary accumulation in the fourth quarter of 1974. What is already happening to automobile stocks will be reinforced by similar but less pronounced adjustments in other industries. By mid-year, shifts in inventory investment should be contributing to rising overall production. All told, current dollar inventory liquidation could approach $5 billion in 1975.

Housing

Underlying conditions seem ripe for a reversal of the housing decline, even though the prospect of a sharp upturn appears small at this time. The stock of housing increased very little during the past year because of the low rate of starts. Despite very weak demand the low rate of housing completions kept vacancy rates from rising; the vacancy rate in rental housing, for example, stabilized from the first to the fourth quarter of 1974. The rate of housing starts in the fourth quarter of 1974 was about one-half the estimated underlying demand indicated by prospective household formation and replacement demand.

The projection for 1975 calls for private starts to begin rising this spring up to an annual rate of 1.6 to 1.7 million units in the final quarter, with single-family homes likely to be in the forefront of the recovery. Because of financing problems and reduced profitability, apartment house construction is not likely to recover until the second half of 1975, although it may show a very weak recovery in the first half. Real outlays for residential construction in 1975 are projected to be about 15 percent below those of 1974, and current dollar outlays, about 5 percent.

Government Purchases

Federal outlays for goods and services are expected to rise by about 8½ percent from 1974 to 1975, while State and local purchases are expected to rise by about 12 percent. Each includes an allowance for the higher cost of energy under the new energy program. In real terms, combined government purchases are expected to show little change from 1974 to 1975, with offsetting decreases and increases in the Federal, and State and local totals.

Consumption

Consumers hold the key to the strength of the economic recovery. If they respond as expected to the stimulus of the tax cuts proposed by the Administration for the spring and summer, real GNP should record a good-sized advance in the second half, but if not, the 1975 recovery could be a sluggish one. The effect of the tax cut on consumer incomes should be reinforced by a turnaround in gross private domestic investment, which has undergone a steep decline since the final quarter of 1973. In the meantime the loss of earned income is being cushioned by increases in unemployment benefits. Last year such benefits totaled more than $7 billion, but with this year's high unemployment they are projected to total more than $18 billion. The latter figure includes, in addition to regular State programs, about $2½ billion of extended State benefits and $3¼ billion in special unemployment benefits for those not previously eligible for unemployment compensation.

Consumer income will be bolstered on July 1, 1975, by a scheduled increase of $3.0 billion (annual rate) in social security benefits (excluding medicare benefits). One offset is the increase in social security taxes due to the rise in the taxable earnings base from $13,200 to $14,100 effective January 1, 1975. This tax increases Federal receipts by about $1½ billion, about half of which represents a reduction in personal income.

Consumers should be aided by a slower rate of inflation in the second half of 1975 compared with the first. The rate of inflation will be highest at midyear because it will reflect the main impact of the higher energy prices. The rate of increase should taper off considerably, even though the energy program will be adding to the level of prices throughout the year. The rise in disposable income and the slower rise in prices yield a substantial increase in real income in the second half.

Despite the possible negative aspects of the energy program this spring, we foresee some improvement in consumer spending in the second quarter occasioned by the refunds of 1974 tax liabilities. To some extent the refunds will induce additional purchases of automobiles, furniture, and appliances, even though initially the greater part of the refunds is likely to be saved. In the third quarter, however, the further stimulus scheduled for September, coupled with the rebates of the windfall profits tax and the stronger recovery, should bring a step-up in consumption that carries into the fourth quarter. For all of 1975 the personal saving rate is likely to be higher than in 1974.

Real consumer spending in 1975 may fall slightly below the corresponding total for 1974. If so, this would mark the second year of decline in real consumer spending. In nominal terms the increase over 1974 should be close to 10 percent.

ECONOMIC ASPECTS OF THE ENERGY PROGRAM

The economy surmounted the energy crisis with which 1974 began, but the energy problems of 1975 and beyond may prove more intransigent.

Now, a year after the embargo, there is widespread agreement that the oil-exporting nations will maintain restrictions on oil supplies and thus be able to hold prices far above the pre-embargo level for at least the period immediately ahead. It is also agreed that the demand for goods and services by the oil exporters will rise, but not enough to offset the large money flows received in exchange for oil exports. Finally, it is realized that supplies of oil from foreign sources are unreliable and will remain so into the indefinite future. For these reasons, the Administration's energy policy is designed to lower imports and thereby reduce our vulnerability to interruptions in the supply of petroleum. In achieving this goal, the Administration is placing maximum reliance on creating market conditions that will have a lasting influence, rather than relying on allocations and rationing which at best are only short-term solutions.

An acceptable level of security can be achieved in the longer run with a combination of measures, including standby domestic capacity and strategic oil reserves for an emergency, as well as reduced consumption and increased production from conventional and new energy sources. Except for reduced consumption, none of these measures will increase security quickly. Consequently, it is essential that we begin to reduce import vulnerability by reducing demand, and that we promptly initiate programs to establish standby capacity and to increase energy production and stocks.

Short-Run Policies

To curtail petroleum imports in the short run, the energy program would reduce total energy consumption by raising its price to the equivalent of the world market price plus $2 per barrel. This policy is better than restricting petroleum imports directly. If petroleum imports are rigidly controlled, unexpected variations in energy supply or demand would cause large disruptive effects because oil imports could not serve their usual role of offsetting these fluctuations. Restraining general energy consumption by raising its price is more equitable and more efficient than restraining specific energy uses. The diverse uses to which energy is put and the complex patterns of its consumption create extraordinary difficulties, administrative costs, and inefficiencies when administrative allocation is attempted. The burden falls more broadly and is handled more efficiently by the economy when it is imposed through the operation of market forces. Purchasers of energy can decide for themselves where they can best reduce consumption.

The elimination of price controls on crude oil (effective April 1) will increase the price of energy and reduce its consumption. The Administration has renewed its recommendation that the price of new natural gas be freed from controls, and that prices of regulated gas be decontrolled when existing contracts expire under their own terms. This will lead to a gradual but eventually large increase in natural gas prices. These actions will have some effect on the price of substitute fuels, such as coal, but price increases will come with some delay and will gradually induce additional supplies of energy.

The windfall profits tax in the President's energy program is designed to prevent increases in profits on existing oil production that would have little, if any, short-term impact on production. The tax is levied on the difference between a base price and the price actually received. The marginal tax rate rises with the size of the gap, reaching 90 percent on that portion of the price received which is more than $3 per barrel greater than the base price. The tax will be phased out over a period of several years, as the base is gradually adjusted upward.

In the near term, oil producers will not receive additional revenues on existing production from the combination of decontrol and the WPT. But they will have a powerful incentive to make new investments, because they will receive higher prices when new ventures come into production.

Decontrol of old oil will be insufficient in the short run to bring about the reduction in imports that energy security requires. The $2 per barrel tax on crude oil and the 37 cents per thousand cubic feet tax on natural gas will raise the price paid by consumers above that received by producers in order to reduce consumption and imports further. The revenue from this tax, like other proposed energy tax revenues, would be returned to consumers of energy so that they would have roughly as much purchasing power as they had before the tax.

Longer-Run Measures

The costs of energy security are lower in the long run than in a short period because security can be achieved by measures that do not rely so heavily on demand restraint. The keystone to long-run policy is a storage program of up to 1.3 billion barrels, a strategic reserve which is large enough to replace imports for an extended period. This will permit the Nation to continue to import some oil from unreliable sources indefinitely without the potential costs of interruption.

Domestic production encouraged by eliminating both price controls and relaxing restrictions on exploration in promising areas, would respond still more if investors were assured that the price they would receive for oil would not be temporarily driven below the long-run supply price by events in the world market. For this reason protection against large downside price risks for conventional oil production are proposed. Producers would thus be assured that large drops in the world price of oil would not disrupt the domestic market. Businesses that invested in energy-saving equipment would also be protected against competitors who avoided such expenditures.

A reduction in standards of living and potential output compared to what we would otherwise enjoy is inevitable with a program to achieve a greater degree of energy security, though the program announced by the Administration is designed to hold such effects to a minimum. The alternative approach—allocations and rationing—would give rise to structural changes in the economy that could have serious, long-run consequences.

A productive economy is one which readily responds to change and is open to growth, development, and new initiatives. Those characteristics are weakened when market allocation of resources is supplanted by administrative control. The restrictions on individual choice that are caused by further centralization of decision making are obvious. Not so obvious, but potentially far larger, are the economic losses if the economy becomes bound to rigid patterns by these measures. An allocation system tends to favor large and established entities. It is likely to discriminate against small firms and the potential entrants from whom innovation could otherwise be expected. With quasi-permanent controls, the benefits of competitive markets would be lost, superior performance might not be rewarded; inefficiency would not be punished by losses or bankruptcy. The Administration's program emphasizes the creation of incentives for individuals and firms to act in a way consistent with energy security, rather than mandating particular behavior.

There are risks in the Administration's energy program. If the world price of energy were to fall dramatically, the United States would be left with high energy costs relative to those of other countries. If the demand and supply response to higher energy prices is far lower than predicted, then additional actions may be necessary. If the response is higher, of course, the oil tax can be reduced or eliminated. If the world price of oil fell to acceptable levels, and if imports were never interrupted, the program would have caused unnecessary costs. The program balances the extra costs from lack of preparation for import disruptions against the costs of preparing for them. The balance struck does not protect against all contingencies, but it will lead to less vulnerability to import cutoffs.

The energy program will speed the transition to a new energy reality that was started by the embargo. The energy situation in 1975 and beyond is markedly different from that of 1973 and before, because energy prices are much higher. These higher prices will call forth substantial increases in investment for both greater energy production and for producing less energy-intensive goods and services.

INTERNATIONAL ECONOMIC RELATIONS

Rising unemployment, rapid inflation, and the energy crisis have placed heavy strains on the fabric of international economic relationships. The pressures on the world capital markets resulting from the financing of large deficits of the oil-importing countries are growing and may threaten to undermine the past liberalization of capital flows among the industrial countries. The acquisition of large amounts of liquid assets by the Organization of Petroleum Exporting Countries (OPEC) has posed a risk of financial and exchange rate instability that must be contained through increased cooperation among the oil-importing countries as well as with the OPEC countries. Some encouraging steps have been taken in this direction....

Economic problems experienced by many countries have created pressures for governments to adopt restrictive trade measures. The resolve of government leaders to avoid such self-defeating measures was considerably strengthened by a decision 3 years ago among U.S., Canadian, Japanese and European leaders to convene a new round of multilateral trade negotiations to continue the process of trade liberalization begun after World War II. U.S. participation, however, was contingent upon passage of legislation by the Congress granting the President authority to undertake such negotiations. The Congress passed the Trade Reform Act of 1974 at the end of last year, opening the way for full-scale multinational negotiations to begin later this year.

The recent decline in economic growth around the world and the parallel increase in unemployment might make it more difficult for most governments to commit themselves in the coming year to major reductions in trade barriers. It is generally recognized, however, that any reductions resulting from such commitments will be sufficiently gradual to allow firms and workers to adjust to the change in competitive conditions over a period of years. Finally, the major focus of a new round of multilateral negotiations is likely to be on nontariff barriers, which are frequently motivated by objectives other than the protection of domestic industries. While the reduction of such barriers can make an important contribution to a more efficient allocation of world resources, it will frequently not require major changes in the structure of domestic industry.

SOCIAL SECURITY DILEMMA
February 12, 1975

The future of the Social Security program that provides monthly benefits for retired and disabled workers came under serious scrutiny early in 1975. A panel appointed by the Senate Finance Committee reported Feb. 12 that over the next 75 years—through 2050—the program would no longer pay for itself. On the contrary, the payments to beneficiaries would rapidly outpace the program's income from payroll taxes. As a result, depletion of trust fund reserves and mounting deficits were in the offing. Two other reports—by the Advisory Council on Social Security on March 7 and by the Social Security Board of Trustees on May 5—confirmed the panel's findings and likewise predicted large deficits. It appeared that the federal government was faced with the long and complex task of revamping the program to assure future retirement security.

Experts divided the Social Security dilemma into two parts—the short-range picture covering the years 1975-1980 and the long-range picture covering the program through 2050. The short-term problem of rapidly disappearing trust fund reserves was considered the easier one to solve, with a wide range of alternatives available. The long-range problem was viewed as more complex, dependent on economic and demographic trends—such as future wage and price increases and birth-rate figures—which were difficult to project.

Roots of the problem could be found in the economic and demographic trends of the 1970s. Increasing inflation, growth in the number of Social Security beneficiaries and declining birth rates were the major factors underlying the dilemma. Rapid inflation had diminished the purchasing power of retirees on fixed incomes, prompting Congress in 1972 to approve a cost-of-living clause to keep benefits in line with inflation. Although the payroll tax base also was adjusted to help meet the cost-of-living increases, the added revenue from payroll taxes was not expected to match the larger outlays.

The problem was compounded by declining birth rates, which foreshadowed a decrease in the number of people who would be paying into the system. And it was feared that the situation would become acute when the "war babies," the exceptionally large number of persons born during the 1940s and 1950s, began to retire from the work force. In 1975, the number of recipients of Social Security payments already was rising at a greater rate than the number of contributors. In 1955, for example, there were seven workers paying into the system for every recipient, according to the Department of Health, Education and Welfare (HEW). But HEW forecast that by the first decade of the 21st century—when the war babies begin to retire —only two workers would be paying Social Security taxes for every person drawing benefits.

Report of Senate Finance Committee's Panel

"While the long-range financing problem is far more serious than the short-range one, we believe the benefit structure of the Social Security system should be overhauled in the near future along with additional financing," said the Senate Finance Committee's experts. They added: "Unless this is done, the present trust fund will be seriously eroded in the years immediately ahead, and will be exhausted by the late 1980s." In their report, issued Feb. 12, the experts said that over the next 75 years the income from Social Security taxes would fall far short of benefits. They estimated that the income would have to be increased by about 20 per cent in the first half of the period and by 100 per cent in the second half. The panel also predicted that the cost-of-living escalator clause would respond irrationally to changes in the inflation rate, giving large numbers of lower-paid workers a higher standard of living immediately after retirement than they enjoyed immediately before retirement.

Report of Social Security Advisory Council

Agreeing with earlier findings that the Social Security system would incur deficits over the period from 1975-2050, the Social Security Advisory Council issued a report March 7 making recommendations to correct the underfunding. The council's key recommendation was to rework the formula for computing benefits so that it would be less sensitive to fluctuations in the economy. The 12-member council headed by W. Allen Wallis faulted the existing formula for permitting some retirees to receive more money from Social Security than they earned prior to retirement.

A second significant and extremely controversial recommendation was to finance the costs of hospitalization insurance from general federal tax revenues rather than from that part of the proceeds of the Social Security payroll tax earmarked for Medicare. Such action would solve the immediate deficit problem without raising payroll taxes, the council said. At the same time, the council rejected a proposal to raise the taxable wage base from $14,100 to $24,000 because, it said, such action would interfere with private savings for retirement. But it favored increasing the rate of taxation on the $14,100 base from the existing rate of 9.9 per cent (not counting the present 1.8 per cent for hospital insurance under Medicare) to 10.9 per cent in 1976 and to 16.1 per cent by 2025. Existing law would raise the tax to 11.9 per cent in 2025.

Report of Social Security Board of Trustees

A third report on the health of the nation's retirement insurance program, the gloomiest forecast of the three, was made public May 5 by the Board of Trustees of the Social Security system. The board predicted that without legislation to provide additional financing, the assets of the trust funds would be exhausted soon after 1979. The trustees—Treasury Secretary William E. Simon, HEW Secretary Caspar W. Weinberger and Labor Secretary John T. Dunlop—also asserted that without financing and benefit modifications, the costs of the program would surpass its income in every year between 1975 and 2050.

For calendar year 1975, the trustees estimated that benefits paid out would exceed taxes collected by almost $3-billion. By 1979, benefits would exceed income by almost $7-billion, leaving the trust fund almost empty. Between 1975 and 2050, the trustees estimated that the average annual deficit would amount to 5.32 per cent of taxable payroll—a substantial monetary amount considering that the existing taxable payroll was more than $600-billion and was expected to top $1-trillion in 1979.

Citing the Advisory Council's report of March 7, the trustees agreed that the deficit problem could be solved in part by altering the existing benefit payment structure "to avoid the probability of future unintended and excessively costly benefit payments." For the long range, the trustees urged Congress to establish a stable relationship between the amount of benefits received by a retired worker and his past earnings. The trustees rejected proposals made by the Advisory Council and others to fund deficits through an infusion of general revenues.

> Following are excerpts from the three reports on the Social Security system: the Feb. 12 report by the Senate Finance Committee's panel; the March 7 report by the Advisory Council on Social Security; and the May 5 report by the Board of Trustees of the Social Security system:
>
> Excerpts from the Report of the Panel on Social Security Financing to the Senate Finance Committee, Feb. 12, 1975:

Report of the Panel on Social Security Financing

Preamble

The panel was appointed as a result of a Senate Resolution of June 26, 1974 sponsored by the Senate Committee on Finance, for the purpose of giving to that Committee "an expert, independent analysis of the actuarial status of the social security system."

The request for this evaluation arose from the Finance Committee's examination of the 1974 Annual Report of the Board of Trustees of the Federal Old-Age and Survivors Insurance and Disability Insurance Trust Funds. Specifically, the following statement in that Report (at page 38) precipitated the request:

> The long-range actuarial cost estimates...show an actuarial balance of − (minus) 2.98 percent of taxable payroll over the valuation period of 75 years, which substantially exceeds the acceptable limit of variation....

This panel's study has been limited to the OASI segment of the OASDI system. The estimate in the Trustees' Report attributed more than 85 percent of the projected average deficit to the OASI segment, and only the remaining 15 percent to the Disability Insurance segment.

This Report supports the conclusion that a long-range deficit of material size is likely. It recommends that attention be given to means of financing this deficit; but, equally of importance, it recommends that changes in benefit structures be sought to reduce the present undue sensitivity of the benefit structure to fluctuations in economic conditions.

This Report contains no specific proposals for the means of removing or narrowing the expected financial gap; such proposals are outside this Panel's charge.

In view of limitation of time, the Panel concentrated its study on the structure of the retirement benefits and its impact on the financing of the program. Other benefit formulas such as survivor benefits may deserve an equally thorough study.

I. Summary of Findings and Recommendations

FIRST FINDING: THE ACTUARIAL STATUS OF THE OASDI SYSTEM IS UNSATISFACTORY

Our studies suggest that the income to the OASDI program over the next 75 years, arising from the payroll tax rates scheduled under present law, will fall considerably short of the amounts needed to pay the benefits provided by that same law. Our best estimate is that this income will need to be increased by an average of about 20 percent during the first half of this period, and to be about doubled during the second half.

Thus, we not only confirm the seriousness of the long range financing problem indicated in the 1974 Trustees' Report, but we believe that the size of the deficit may be even greater than predicted in that Report. Following is a brief comparison, for selected years, of payroll tax rates scheduled under present law, and projected expenditures expressed as percentages of taxable payrolls from the 1974 Trustees' Report and from this Panel's analysis:

[In percent]

Calendar year	Combined pay-roll tax rate	Expenditures as a percent of taxable payroll	
		1974 Trustees' Report	This panel
1975	9.9	10.2	10.2
1990	9.9	11.0	11.5
2010	9.9	12.7	14.6
2030	11.9	17.6	23.3
2050	11.9	17.2	23.9
Average	10.9	13.9	16.9
Average deficit		3.0	6.0

Our estimates of expenditures as percentages of taxable payrolls exceed those in the Trustees' Report for two principal reasons. First, we assumed that fertility rates would continue their downward trend until 1980 before beginning an upswing. The 1974 Trustees' Report assumed that the trough in fertility rates had already been reached. Second, we assumed a long term average inflation rate of 4 percent per year compared to the Trustees' 3 percent assumption. These assumptions are discussed fully in Section VII of this report.

We conclude, as others have, that the serious long range financing difficulties of the OASDI program are attributable jointly to the expectation of an increasing ratio of OASDI beneficiaries to the working population, and the nature of the benefit formula. Our figures suggest that each of these two factors accounts for about half of the problem.

While the long range financing problem is far more serious than the short range one, we believe the benefit structure of the social security system should be overhauled in the near future along with additional financing. Unless this is done the present Trust Fund will be seriously eroded in the years immediately ahead, and will be exhausted by the late 1980's.

SECOND FINDING: THE PRESENT FORMULA FOR DETERMINING BENEFIT AWARDS AT RETIREMENT RESPONDS IRRATIONALLY TO CHANGES IN THE RATE OF INFLATION

The present Social Security benefit formula, legislated in 1972, automatically adjusts benefits to reflect changes in the Consumer Price Index. Also the maximum taxable earnings base rises according to increases in average wages under covered employment. These "indexing" provisions were introduced to provide a more orderly and timely means of adjusting benefit levels in response to inflation, rather than the ad hoc increases voted from time to time by the U.S. Congress. An automatic mechanism for this purpose is commendable, but only if it operates in a rational manner.

One measure of the rationality of a retirement benefit formula is the so-called "replacement ratio." This is simply the ratio of the benefit award at retirement to the worker's earnings just before retirement. The general level of these ratios, how they vary for workers whose earnings histories differ or who retire at different times, and how they vary under differing economic conditions, are important indicators of the ability of the system to achieve its intended purpose.

We find that the present benefit formula responds irrationally to changes in the rate of inflation, and can produce patterns of replacement ratios inconsistent with the generally understood purpose of the social security system. As we see it, there are two problems.

First, the benefit formula is hypersensitive to changes in the rate of inflation. The present automatic provisions operate to increase replacement ratios when the rate of inflation increases, and they do so even when real wage growth (i.e., wage growth after adjustment for increases in the price level) remains constant. For example, if the real wage growth of an individual were a constant 2 percent, a low earnings worker without a spouse who retired in the year 2050 would have a replacement ratio of 65, 86, or 109 percent, depending on whether the rate of inflation during his working years was 2, 3, or 4 percent. Thus, large changes in replacement ratios can arise from small changes in the inflation rate. Of course, large changes in replacement ratios imply large changes in the financial cost of the Social Security system.

Second, the operation of the formula easily leads to numerous instances where replacement ratios—for many workers who had experienced no fall-off in earnings just before retirement—approach and even exceed 100 percent. This results in the anomaly of large numbers of workers having standards of living just after retirement higher than just before retirement. The problem would be further aggravated of course, in the case of workers with spouses eligible for the additional 50 percent benefit.

We have no objection to a benefit formula which automatically increases the dollar amount of benefit awards at retirement or after retirement to properly reflect inflation. Our objection is to a benefit formula which automatically changes replacement ratios when there are changes in the rate of inflation. We believe that any general changes in the level or pattern of replacement ratios are of such fundamental importance to a social insurance program, that they should be made only as a direct result of conscious policy decisions by the U.S. Congress.

Unless material changes are made in the present benefit formula, Congress will not have the appropriate control over the reasonableness and consistency of benefits and it will be difficult, if not impossible, to finance the system on a satisfactory actuarial basis.

THIRD FINDING: PRESENT METHODOLOGY FOR FORECASTING AND ANALYSIS PURPOSES IS INADEQUATE FOR THE SYSTEM'S MAGNITUDE AND COMPLEXITY

Although recognizing that present mathematical and statistical procedures may indeed have been appropriate in the past, we believe that these procedures are no longer adequate to the tasks rightly demanded of them for validity of estimation, and for understanding of the workings of the system under different demographic and economic conditions and with alternative benefit and tax structures.

Recommendations—This Panel's recommendations are:

1. That strong measures be taken to restore the financial health of the OASDI Program.
2. That the benefit structure be changed to eliminate its irrational response to changes in the rate of inflation. This is essential to achieve financial soundness. The first step should be a prompt thorough study of several possible changes in benefit structure.
3. That improved procedures be adopted to reveal the costs, implications and controllability of this program.

These recommendations flow directly and logically from our three findings. We believe that exploration and research will result in orderly transition to a new benefit structure and new forecasting procedures which will enable this country's Social Security system to serve the best interests of our people.

The rest of this Report describes the present financing method and retirement benefit structure of the OASI segment of the system, and amplifies the three findings and the recommendations already discussed....

Excerpts from the March 7, 1975 report of the Quadrennial Advisory Council on Social Security:

...The short-range actuarial cost estimates indicate that the assets of both the old-age and survivors insurance trust fund and the disability insurance trust fund will decline during the 5-year period 1975-79. Without legislation to provide additional financing, the assets of both trust funds will be exhausted soon after 1979.

The Board recommends that prompt action be taken to strengthen the financing of the old-age, survivors, and disability insurance system over the near term. The required additional income to the trust funds should be obtained through increases in the tax rate, in the taxable earnings base, or in both rate and base. The Board opposes the use of additional general revenue financing for the old-age, survivors, and disability insurance program. The Board noted that the amount of additional income required for the program would be reduced if the Congress adopted the President's proposal to limit to 5 percent the automatic benefit increase scheduled for June, 1975.

The long-range actuarial cost estimates indicate that for every year in the future the estimated expenditures will exceed the estimated income from taxes. This excess increases with time and is estimated to average about 1.3 percent of taxable payroll over the next 25-year period (1975-1999). All reasonable alternative actuarial assumptions indicate that over the remainder of this century the financing of the old-age, survivors, and disability insurance program will need additional revenues equivalent to about 1.3 percent of taxable payroll.

The long-range cost of the OASDI program projected to occur after the turn of the century will substantially exceed the taxes scheduled in present law. Although those projected costs are highly sensitive to variations in the actuarial assumptions, all reasonable assumptions indicate that there will be significant excesses of expenditures over income. This report is not intended to provide an indication of the fullest possible range of variation in the long-range cost estimates. (Appendix A provides some information on the sensitivity of the long-range cost estimates to alternative assumptions.)

To some extent the high cost of the old-age, survivors, and disability insurance program projected to occur after the turn of the century is due to unintended results in the automatic benefit adjustment provisions enacted in 1972, which cause future projected benefits to increase out of proportion to levels of wage replacement established by benefits currently paid under the program. The Board fully concurs with the intent of the recommendation by the 1975 Advisory Council on Social Security that the benefit structure be revised to maintain the levels of benefits in relation to preretirement earnings levels that now prevail.

The Board recommends that development of specific plans for strengthening of the long-range financing of the old-age, survivors, and disability insurance program be pursued immediately with special priorities given to ways of modifying the automatic benefit adjustment provisions in present law.

In this regard, the Board is pleased to note that the Administration has already begun studies of the possible means of accomplishing this objective. The Board also welcomes the cooperative efforts now under way between the Social Security Administration and the actuarial and economic consultants appointed by the Congressional Research Service of the Library of Congress at the request of the House Committee on Ways and Means and the Senate Committee on Finance to study this matter.

The Board also concurs with the 1975 Advisory Council on Social Security in the recommendation that the OASDI tax rate applicable to self-employment income be set at a level equivalent to 150 percent of the tax rate applicable to wages.

Excerpts from the annual report of the Board of Trustees of the Social Security System, issued May 5, 1975:

CHAPTER 7—FINANCING

Section 1. Basic Characteristics of Old-Age, Survivors, and Disability Insurance Program

1.1 CURRENT COST FINANCING

The financing of the OASDI system is based on the "current cost" method. Under this approach, no fund is created during the life of a worker from which his benefits are ultimately paid. Instead the social security taxes he pays are immediately paid out by the government to persons who are already beneficiaries. His own benefits will be paid from taxes that are collected in the future from persons who are then working. The tax rate is set so as to provide tax receipts that approximate current expenditures. In essence, the plan transfers money from one generation to another with the amount taken from the one generation being measured by the other generation's benefit requirements.

The current cost method would be unacceptable for a private pension plan, but it is a sound alternative for OASDI, because the government has the continuing power to tax future workers in order to pay benefits in the future to those who are now working....

1.2 MEASURING LONG-RANGE COSTS

In discussing the "cost" of the OASDI system, the use of numbers in absolute dollars is of little help, because there are constant changes in the number of workers, beneficiaries, wage and benefit levels and other factors. Throughout this report, therefore, we will be expressing "cost" as a percentage of total covered earnings, meaning earnings subject to the OASDI tax.

1.3 OASDI TAX RATES

The current tax rate for OASDI is 9.9 percent, payable on all earnings up to $14,100. The total tax is split equally between the employer and employee, with each paying 4.95 percent. (To this is added .9 percent for hospital insurance making a total social security tax of 5.85 percent borne by each.)...

1.4 WEIGHTED BENEFIT STRUCTURE

While the tax rate for all employees is the same, the benefits are not equal. They are weighted in favor of lower-paid workers and those with dependents. The low-paid worker receives a benefit that is a higher percentage of his (or her) average earnings than does the higher-paid employee, even though the latter receives a larger absolute amount. This weighting of the benefit schedule represents society's recognition of "adequacy" as a criterion of the plan, and is a departure from the strict principle of individual equity. Another such social concept is found in the fact that a married worker receives certain protection for his dependents without paying any more premium than a single worker who receives no such protection.

The entire social security program is necessarily a blend of social goals and individual equity. Maintaining the proper blend is very important if we are to sustain the workers' support of the plan. To date, most workers feel responsible for the system because, while aware of the social weighting within the program, they still view their protection as being reasonably related to the taxes they pay. This attitude is important to the success of social security. It becomes an important factor when considering the introduction of additional welfare-type benefits or methods of financing from general revenues.

Section 2. Automatic Adjustment to Inflation

2.1 BENEFITS

In 1972, Congress made a basic change in the system. It modified the *ad hoc* approach and provided that thereafter benefits would increase automatically in accordance with changes in the cost of living, without any action by Congress. The cost of living is to be measured by the Consumer Price Index (CPI). The first such automatic increase is now scheduled to take place for the month of June 1975, with the increase in benefits to be payable in early July.

2.2 TAXES

Congress is relying on the fact that, as prices increase, wages will also increase, thereby raising the total wage base and providing the needed additional revenue to cover the automatic increase in benefits. The social security law provides that whenever benefits are automatically increased, the base for the following year is raised by the amount of the increase in wages in covered employment.

2.3 EFFECT OF WAGE AND PRICE INCREASES ON COST ESTIMATES

Adoption of this automatic method has made the future cost of the system dependent upon future changes in prices and in wages. The cost can no longer be determined on the basis of today's benefit schedule, because it will move up automatically with changes in the CPI. In determining the long-range financial soundness of the system, therefore, estimates of the movements of prices and wages are made for a 75-year valution period. This long period of time is used because the inter-generational transfers and the impact of the controlling factors are best reflected when measured over a very long time frame.

Section 3. 1974 Trustees' Report on the Financial Condition of OASDI

3.1 ASSUMPTIONS

In the first part of 1974, the trustees of the OASDI system made their regular actuarial review of the plan and projected its cost over the period beginning with 1974 and ending with the year 2048. Their projections were based on four major assumptions:

   1. Wages will increase over the 75-year period at an average rate of 5 percent;

   2. The CPI will increase at an average rate of 3 percent;

   3. Real wages will increase at an average rate of 2 percent;

   4. The total fertility rate will rise from 1.9 in 1974 to 2.1 by 1985 and remain there.

3.2 ESTIMATED DEFICIT

Based upon these assumptions, the trustees have computed the cost of the system....

The difference between the costs and the tax rates...represent a financing deficit of 2.98 percent.

3.3 PATTERN OF THE DEFICIT

It is not enough, however, to say that the long-term deficit is 2.98 percent. The "shape" of that deficit is very important. It is clear...that the deficit does not occur evenly over the period. This is a vital factor in determining future tax rates....

The deficit is the spread between the tax and cost curves. The graph shows that a relatively small amount of the deficit occurs in the next 30 years, but thereafter the deficit increases rapidly.

The most important reason for this shape of the deficit is demographic. Relatively few people were born during the great depression of the 30's. After the war, the total fertility rate rose sharply to a peak of 3.77 in 1957. Thereafter it began to decline and it has recently reached the very low rate of 1.9 which is below the population replacement rate. The trustees have estimated that this rate will gradually rise to 2.1, which is the rate at which the population will eventually stabilize itself, and will remain there indefinitely.

It is this historic birth rate pattern that largely shapes the deficit. The working population has been growing rapidly as the "war babies" have entered the work force, and this will continue for some years. This means that there is a relatively large number of people who will be paying the benefits of a relatively small number of people, and for this reason the cost will not rise materially, even with automatic increases in benefits. After all of the war babies have entered the work force, costs will still rise slowly for a short period during which the relatively small number of depression babies start to draw benefits.

Starting about 2005, however, the process reverses itself. Then the war babies begin to draw social security benefits in ever larger numbers, while the work force is not increasing at a commensurate rate because of the low fertility rate now existing and forecasted for the future.

These demographic changes are reflected in two important statistics:

1. Today there are 30 beneficiaries for every 100 workers.

2. In the year 2030 it is estimated that there will be 45 beneficiaries for each 100 workers....

It is possible, of course, that greater immigration or greater than anticipated participation by women in the work force may solve the problem. If not, [the data suggest] that around the year 2005, pressures may well develop to increase the retirement age beyond 65. This would modify the ratio between workers and beneficiaries and reduce the high benefit costs that will otherwise have to be met. Today, of course, the general demand is to *reduce* the retirement age, not increase it, because the work force is expanding.

Obviously the demographic projection has an almost overwhelming effect on the costs of the system....

3.5 REVISIONS OF THE ESTIMATE OF THE DEFICIT

As this is being written the social security staff is well along in its work on the 1975 trustees' report. It is already quite clear that the assumptions as to wage and price increases in that study will be higher than the 5 percent and 3 percent used in the 1974 study. It seems possible that new demographic projections may reflect lower fertility rates than those used in the 1974 trustees' report. Thus, the 1975 trustees' report will almost certainly show a significantly higher long-term deficit than is currently projected.

Our primary problem is covering the estimated deficit, but the 2.98 percent, forecasted by the trustees, is not the full amount. There are other factors which add to and subtract from that deficit, and which must be included in any proposed solution. One of these factors is the effect of the unexpectedly high benefit increase for June of 1975.

Under the present law, benefits are scheduled to rise automatically with the CPI. The first such automatic increase will occur for the month of June 1975, and will be measured by the rise in the CPI between the second quarter of 1974 and the first quarter of 1975. The trustees originally estimated in early 1974 that such increase would be 4.4 percent. It is now estimated that the increase will be 8.5 percent and this, in turn, will cause an increase of .51 percent of covered wages in the estimated long-term deficit.

It is important to note that this increase in the deficit has an *immediate* impact on the cost of the plan. It is not deferred like so much of the 2.98-percent deficit computed by the trustees. Provision for this addition to the deficit cannot be long delayed.

Section 4. Council Recommendations Affecting Financing

4.1 STABILIZATION OF REPLACEMENT RATIOS

A "replacement ratio" is the relationship between a worker's initial monthly benefit and the monthly wage he earned just before he retired, died, or was disabled. For example, if a worker earned $600 per month just before he retired and received a benefit of $300 per month, his replacement ratio would be 50 percent. Replacement ratios are an important criterion of the effectiveness of an earnings replacement system, and they should be stable, even though benefit levels will continue to rise with wages and prices.

The system at present contains a flaw which can cause replacement ratios to fluctuate widely, both up and down, depending on movements of wages and prices....

If the inflation rate is 4 percent, the replacement rate for the low earner will grow from .615 to 1.647, and he will receive a benefit in 2050 that is more than 60 percent above his final earnings level. On the other hand, if the inflation rate is 2 percent, his replacement rate in 2050 will be only 27 percent of what it would have been under a 4-percent inflation rate.

...Replacement ratios can move capriciously, either *up or down*, and they can move in a broad range depending upon the movements of prices and wages, two factors over which the system has no control. This is a very undesirable characteristic in the system and was probably not intended.

The cause of this instability is found in the automatic benefit increase mechanism. Whenever the CPI rises under today's system, benefits will automatically rise. The increase in benefits is accomplished, in effect, by raising the entire benefit schedule. This increases the benefits for all persons who are already retired, *but it also increases the future benefits for those who are still working*, because they will eventually obtain the advantages of the higher benefit schedule when they retire. At the same time, however, those who are still working will also receive an increase in wages, and this will increase their average monthly earnings and thereby further increase their future benefits. In other words, the benefit increases for those still working are coupled with the benefit increases for retired persons, and this produces the instability in replacement ratios....

To correct this flaw requires a new method of computing benefits and the Council has already proposed such a method....

Briefly summarized, the starting point in computing the benefit of an individual today is the determination of his average monthly earnings (AME) by using the actual taxable earnings for years after 1950 down through the year before retirement occurs. That AME is then applied to a benefit schedule which is set out below:

119.89 percent of first $110.00 of AME;

43.61 percent of next $290.00 of AME;

40.75 percent of next $150.00 of AME;

47.90 percent of next $100.00 of AME;

26.64 percent of next $100.00 of AME;

22.20 percent of next $250.00 of AME; and

20.00 percent of next $175.00 of AME.

As explained earlier, this benefit table is intentionally weighted in favor of the low-paid employee.

The proposed system (sometimes referred to as the "decoupled" system) uses the same earnings for the years after 1950, but it indexes those earnings to the year before the year in which retirement occurs. Let us assume, for example, that a man retires in 1975 at age 65. If he earned $3,500 in 1960 and the average 1973 covered wage is 80 percent higher than the average 1960 covered wage, then the employee's earnings of $3,500 will be multiplied by 1.8 and the resulting $6,300 will be used as his earnings for 1960 in computing his average earnings. These are now referred to as his average monthly *indexed* earnings, referred to as AMIE.

This AMIE will always be higher than the AME, formerly used, and will usually be substantially higher. Therefore, it would be improper to use the schedule of benefit percentages used under today's method. Instead, a new formula has been developed which can be expressed as follows:

A percent of the first $X of AMIE

plus

B percent of all AMIE over $X

The numbers represented above by A and B are fixed, but the X would increase as average covered wages increased.

The fixing of the exact amounts of A and X and B, in the above formula, will depend on the precise objectives to be met, as ultimately determined by Congress. They will also depend on the actual date on which the new system is installed. If the system became effective in 1976 and was designed to meet the objectives thus far proposed by the Council, here is an approximation of the formula in numerical terms:

100 percent of the first $123 of AMIE

plus

31 percent of all AMIE above $123

(The $123 is adjusted upward each year as average covered wages rise.)

Again it is emphasized that this specific formula is presented here solely to facilitate discussion and not to indicate that it is the only one that can be used, or even that it is the best. For example, there is some opinion to the effect that we need a three factor formula, such as the following:

100 percent of the first $X of AMIE

plus

31 percent of the next $Y of AMIE

plus

20 percent of all AMIE above $Y

The new system will not freeze benefits in any sense of the word; it will merely stabilize at the various levels the relationship of the benefits to the earnings of the recipient just prior to retirement. Furthermore, the proposed system can be implemented in such a way as not to reduce anyone's benefits as computed under the formula presently applicable to persons now retiring.

Whether the proposed system would produce lower or higher benefits and costs than the present system depends upon the relationship between future movements in wages and prices, factors which no one can predict with certainty. Under the assumptions of the trustees, as to wage and price increases, the long-term benefits and costs of the proposed system will not be as high as under the present plan, but if the movements of wages and prices follow a different pattern, the benefits and costs could be higher under a decoupled system than under the present system....

In summary, the new formula will cause benefits to rise solely in keeping with wages during an individual's working years, and after retirement his benefits will increase solely on the basis of increases in the CPI. The Council strongly recommends that such a decoupled system be adopted. In fact, the Council is convinced that decoupling is by far the most important step to be taken to improve the system.

4.2 OTHER BENEFIT RECOMMENDATIONS

Compulsory Coverage of Government Employees—Some 90 percent of the working population is today covered by social security. By far the largest segment that remains uncovered is composed of government employees, Federal, State, and local. The Council has recommended that social security coverage of these employees be made compulsory in order to prevent the windfall benefits which they frequently receive at the expense of the social security system....

Liberalization of the Retirement Test—Under the retirement test today, a retiree loses one dollar of benefits for each two dollars he earns above the exempt amount, which is $2,520 in 1975. Such exempt amount rises each year with average covered wages. The Council has recommended that for earnings above the exempt amount, but not in excess of twice the exempt amount, the loss of benefits be limited to one dollar for each three dollars of earnings. For earnings above twice the exempt amount the one-for-two reduction in benefits would again apply.

Equalizing Dependency Requirements—The Council has voted to recommend that the support test for husbands and widowers benefits be eliminated and that benefits be provided for fathers and certain divorced men, so as to provide equal treatment of the sexes.

Liberalization of the Disability Test—The Council has recommended a somewhat less stringent test of disability for workers who are 55 years of age and older....

4.4 SHIFT OF HOSPITAL INSURANCE CONTRIBUTION RATE TO OASDI

The OASDI program is financed from taxes on covered earnings, because the benefits of the program are always related to the earnings of a worker-taxpayer. This is true even when the beneficiary is a spouse or dependent survivor. The same principle does *not* apply to benefits under part A of the Medicare program. There the amount of the benefits is determined by the hospital and related health care costs of a particular person, and bears no relationship whatsoever to his wages or those of anyone else.

Under such circumstances there does not seem to be any real reason for funding such costs by a tax on wages. Hospital insurance expenditures would seem to be more properly funded from general revenues, and the Council recommends such a proposal to the Congress. If adopted it could make an important contribution to the solution of the financial problems of the OASDI program without an immediate increase in total social security tax rate....

It is obvious that the shifting of the hospital insurance tax to general revenues would create a need for higher income taxes or other levies. Depending on how this need is met, it is quite possible that for many persons the proposal would mean just a shift in the type of tax that is paid. In fact, some persons or employers would incur a higher aggregate tax burden than they would if the OASDI tax were simply increased.

However, to the extent that general revenues are derived from progressive taxes, those in the lower economic groups would almost certainly benefit from the shift of the hospital insurance tax to general revenues. These groups include the persons that would have the greatest difficulty in handling a .5 percent increase in the social security tax. For many of them that tax is already a greater burden than the income tax....

Section 5. Meeting the Estimated Deficit

5.1 SHORT-TERM DEFICIT

The short-term deficit (again, based on the 1974 trustees' report...) does require a prompt increase of 1.0 percent in the OASDI tax rate. This means an increase of .5 percent for both the employer and the employee. This increase should not be delayed, because the deficit is already here, not in the future. It arises largely from existing factors, such as the 8.5 percent increase in benefits scheduled for mid-1975. These factors are not delayed in their effect on the system; they cause a prompt increase in the cost and must be offset by higher tax rates. Based on present projections, the rate will also have to rise by an additional .2 percent in 1980 and by a .7 percent more in 1985.

If the 1.0 percent increase in the OASDI tax rate is not enacted by 1976, the OASDI fund will start to go down in absolute terms by several billion dollars per year. It will go down even more in relation to the expenditures for a year, because those expenditures will be rising by several billion dollars per year. This produces a double-barrelled effect on the important ratio of the fund to expenditures. Today the trust fund stands at about $50 billion, or about 2/3 of one year's expenditures. If the tax rate is not increased, the fund will fall below 1/3 of one year's expenditures by early 1978. Even at this level, the system could probably still meet its payment obligations without interruption, but it will certainly cause concern among both workers and beneficiaries. Furthermore, there is no sound reason for letting the fund deteriorate in that way. The deficit exists and should be met now with a reasonable tax increase.

5.2 LONG-TERM DEFICIT

The long-term deficit has its roots in the demographic projection.... Whether that deficit actually occurs will depend on the validity of the estimated future fertility rates and their effect on the composition of the population. It is very difficult to forecast fertility rates with any confidence and the Council recognizes that such forecasts are always subject to error. For that reason the Council's recommended tax rate schedule, below, does not contain any immediate increase in order to handle the long-term portion of the deficit. Such increases are scheduled for later years when the cost increase has been more clearly established.

If all of the various assumptions are borne out, this delaying approach will result in a higher eventual tax rate than we might obtain by an immediate increase now of 2.50 percent. However, the latter procedure would be quite inconsistent with the "current cost" method of financing the OASDI program, because the taxes collected would immediately exceed expenditures by a substantial amount, and a large surplus would be created in the near term.

5.3 PROPOSED TAX RATES

Having in mind both the long- and short-term estimated deficits, the Council now proposes a new tax schedule that would handle the problem to the extent that its dimensions are known to us:

Proposed tax rate expressed
as a percent of covered
wages

[percent]

1976-1984	10.9
1985-1994	11.1
1995-2004	11.8
2005-2014	12.3
2015-2024	14.2
2025-2050	16.1

These proposed rates approximate the estimated cost curve. By this approach no increase in the tax is provided before it is actually needed, and if future trends differ from the various assumptions herein, the rate can be modified before the fund has risen too high or fallen too low....

It is recognized that an increase of 1.0 percent in the OASDI tax is a significant increase, but the direct impact in terms of social security tax rates can be eliminated through the implementation of the Council's proposal to fund at least part of the hospital insurance program from general revenues.

Section 6. Other Financing Proposals Considered

6.1 GENERAL REVENUE FINANCING OF OASDI

One method of dealing with the long-range actuarial deficit in the social security cash benefits program that has been advocated by some, including several members of this Council, is the use of substantial amounts of general revenues. After consideration of this method of financing, a majority of the Council decided against the use of additional general revenue financing in the social security cash benefits program. The Council believes that the deficit can and should be dealt with through the conventional system of ear-marked payroll contributions.

General revenues are used in the present social security cash benefits program only to a very limited extent and only to finance benefits in special cases. General revenues are used in the cash benefits program to finance (a) special payments made on a transitional basis to certain uninsured people age 72 and over, (b) benefits attributable to military service before 1957, and (c) noncontributory wage credits provided for members of the military service after 1956, and (d) noncontributory wage credits for persons of Japanese ancestry interned during World War II. The Council believes that it is entirely appropriate to finance these kinds of benefits from general revenues.

The Council believes that there are compelling reasons against the use of substantial amounts of general revenues in the cash benefits program. Such indirect financing would tend to obscure the true cost of additional benefit liberalizations and could easily lead to pressures for unwarranted increases in benefits. Financing the program entirely from payroll contributions serves to prevent unreasonable demands for increases in benefits. The tie between benefit payments and contributions under the present method of financing fosters a sense of responsibility since the worker knows that higher benefits mean higher contributions. At present when the program must deal with a substantial long-range deficit it is particularly important that any liberalizations be financed in a manner that will not obscure the relationship between benefits and contributions.

Substantial general revenues would also have a detrimental effect on the insurance nature of the program. While there is recognition of the social role of social security through such elements as the weighted benefit formula and provision for dependents, the program is essentially one in which the worker earns the right to benefits through his work in covered employment. The fact that the program is supported almost exclusively from the contributions of covered workers and their employers accords with the insurance aspects of the program. It is this earned-right, contributory principle which is one of the primary reasons for the widespread public acceptance of and confidence in the program.

The introduction of a substantial general revenue contribution in the cash benefits program might lead to strong pressures for the introduction of a needs test for many social security benefits. It would be difficult to justify the use of general revenues derived largely from the progressive income tax to pay benefits to middle- and upper-income workers who are not in financial need.

In addition, the use of large amounts of general revenues would place the social security system in competition with all other govenment programs for such funds. For budgetary reasons, the Government's contributions might not be paid in the amount or at the time required. There would not necessarily be any guarantee that this money would be available to the social security program when it is needed. In the absence of assurance that these funds would be forthcoming as needed, confidence in the financial integrity of the system would seriously be undermined.

6.2 RAISING THE MAXIMUM COVERED WAGE

Today, only earnings up to $14,100 per year are covered by social security. Under the automatic changes in the law, this amount will rise each year in the same proportion as average wages rise. This will gradually increase the amount of maximum taxable earnings over the years to come.

There is nothing sacred in the figure, $14,100; it is largely arbitrary. To help cover the deficit, the Council, at one point, considered raising the maximum covered wage to $24,000 per year in 1976. It was eventually abandoned because there were formidable arguments against this proposal.

Social security was designed from the beginning as only one of three elements in the income-maintenance system, the other two being: (1) private savings, pension, etc., and (2) public assistance programs. It was logically argued that raising the limit to $24,000 would cause social security to interfere with the private savings element. It certainly would extend coverage to a level of income where "enforced" savings seems inappropriate, and where it could further reduce needed capital formation.

The only real argument in its favor was that it would hold down the increase in the tax rate which is necessary to cover the long-term deficit. If it were adopted, it would cut the short-term deficit by .89 percent and the long-term deficit by .49 percent.

6.3 INCREASING THE RETIREMENT AGE

After the year 2005, the system will incur substantially higher costs and this will require substantially higher taxes at that time. The high costs and taxes are due to the sharp changes after 2005 in the ratio of workers to beneficiaries, as described earlier herein. If it is desired to minimize those later high costs, the Council recommends that serious consideration be given to gradually extending the retirement age, starting in the year 2005.

The Council is well aware that today most social and economic pressures are directed toward *reducing* the retirement age. Those pressures arise, however, because the work force is now growing, and there are only 30 beneficiaries for every 100 workers. After 2005, however, the number of people drawing benefits will be growing proportionately faster than the number of people paying taxes, and by the year 2030 there will be 45 beneficiaries for every 100 workers, and the tax burden on the workers will have risen substantially. In such a situation, and given the expected advances in health care and longevity, it seems sensible to at least consider some modest increase in the retirement age so as to maintain a reasonable ratio of workers to beneficiaries and thereby hold down the tax rates....

COURT ON IMPOUNDMENT
OF FUNDS
February 18, 1975

Ruling for the first time on the power of the President to refuse to spend certain funds provided by Congress for a particular purpose, the Supreme Court Feb. 18 held unanimously that President Nixon exceeded his authority when he refused in 1972 to allocate to the states $9-billion in water pollution funds.

The Court's ruling appeared to rely upon the wording of the particular law authorizing such spending, the Water Pollution Control Act Amendments of 1972 (PL 92-500). In that law, said the Court, Congress gave the President no leeway to withhold any funds. Left unresolved was the question of presidential authority to withhold funds provided by Congress through the ordinary appropriations process.

Delivering the opinion of the Court, Justice Byron R. White wrote that the 1972 legislation "was intended to provide a firm commitment of substantial funds within a relatively limited period of time in an effort to achieve an early solution of what was deemed an urgent problem." He added: "We cannot believe that Congress at the last minute scuttled the entire effort by providing the Executive with the seemingly limitless power to withhold funds from allotment and obligation."

Uses of Impoundment

Impoundment as a financial management technique had been used occasionally by Presidents since 1803, when Thomas Jefferson left unspent $50,000 appropriated for gunboats which he deemed "unnecessary." But Richard M. Nixon's frequent impoundment of appropriated funds provoked charges that he was resorting to the practice as a means of substituting his *own priorities for those of Congress. Citing inflation to justify his actions, Nixon claimed a presidential right to control the timing and distribution of federal expenditures. He held back funds from a variety of programs, including food stamps, highway construction and military projects. Estimates of funds impounded by Nixon reached a high of $12-billion (for 1972). Of $18-billion (for fiscal 1973, 1974 and 1975) allotted for sewage treatment by the 1972 water pollution control amendments, Nixon ordered the impoundment of $9-billion after Congress had overridden his veto of the act. In May 1973, a U.S. district court judge in the District of Columbia ordered the funds in question to be released, but the administration appealed the ruling.*

The Nixon administration had often cited a clause in the Anti-Deficiency Act of 1950 allowing the executive branch to withhold funds to take account of changing circumstances or to save money. However, in 1974 Congress, in a major budget reform bill, repealed the 1950 provision and restricted presidential impoundments. Under the 1974 law (PL 93-344), a President can defer certain expenditures unless either house forces release of the funds by adopting a simple resolution. In order to cut total spending or terminate a program, a President must request Congress to rescind its appropriation.

President Gerald R. Ford, citing the poor state of the economy, had written substantial rescissions and deferrals into his fiscal 1976 budget, including $5-billion of the controversial sewage treatment funds. However, Ford had also said he would free an additional $4-billion.

Limits of the Ruling

The Court took care to limit the reach of its decision to the 1972 law and the funds authorized by that act. After a lengthy discussion of the arguments concerning what Congress had intended to provide in the law, White refused to read more into the legislative language than he saw: "Legislative intention, without more, is not legislation." The Court directed release of the funds.

In a related case announced the same day, Train v. Campaign Clean Water, *the Court similarly held that the "Administrator has no authority...to allot less than the full amounts sought to be appropriated...."*

Excerpts from Supreme Court opinion on impoundment in the case of Train v. City of New York et al., *Feb. 18, 1975:*

No. 73-1377

Russell E. Train, Administrator, United States Environmental Protection Agency, Petitioner, v. City of New York et al.	On Writ of Certiorari to the United States Court of Appeals for the District of Columbia Circuit.

[February 18, 1975]

MR. JUSTICE WHITE delivered the opinion of the Court.

This case poses certain questions concerning the proper construction of the Federal Water Pollution Control Act Amendments of 1972, ...which provide a comprehensive program for controlling and abating water pollution. Title II of the 1972 Act, §§201-222, makes available federal financial assistance in the amount of 75% of the cost of municipal sewers and sewage treatment works. Under §207, there is "authorized to be appropriated" for these purposes "not to exceed" $5 billion for fiscal year 1973, "not to exceed" $6 billion for fiscal year 1974, and "not to exceed" $7 billion for fiscal year 1975. Section 205 (a) directs that "[s]ums authorized to be appropriated pursuant to §207" for fiscal year 1973 be alloted "not later than 30 days after October 18, 1972." The "[s]ums authorized" for the later fiscal years, 1973 and 1974, "shall be allotted by the Administrator not later than the January 1st immediately preceding the beginning of the fiscal year for which authorized...." From these allotted sums §201 (g) authorized the Administrator "to make grants to any...municipality...for the construction of publicly owned treatment works...," pursuant to plans and specifications as required by §203 and meeting the other requirements of the Act, including those of §204. Section 203 (a) specifies that the Administrator's approval of plans for a project "shall be deemed a contractual obligation of the United States for the payment of its proportional contribution to such project."

The water pollution bill that became the 1972 Act was passed by Congress on October 4, 1972, but was vetoed by the President on October 17. Congress promptly overrode the veto. Thereupon, the President, by letter dated November 22, 1972, directed the Administrator "not [to] allot among the States the maximum amounts provided by Section 207" and, instead, to allot "[n]o more than $2 billion of the amount authorized for the fiscal year 1973, and no more than $3 billion of the amount authorized for fiscal year 1974...." On December 8, the Administrator announced by regulation that in accordance with the President's letter he was allotting for fiscal years 1973 and 1974 sums not to exceed $2 billion and $3 billion respectively.

This litigation, brought by the city of New York and similarly situated municipalities in the State of New York followed immediately. The complaint sought judgment against the Administrator of the Environmental Protection Agency declaring that he was obligated to allot to the States the full amounts authorized by §207 for fiscal years 1973 and 1974, as well as an order directing him to make those allotments. In May 1973, the District Court denied the Administrator's motion to dismiss and granted the city's motion for summary judgment. The Court of Appeals affirmed, holding that "the Act requires the Administrator to allot the full sums authorized to be appropriated in §207."

Because of the differing views with respect to the proper construction of the Act between the federal courts in the District of Columbia in this case and those of the Fourth Circuit in No. 73-1378, *Train* v. *Campaign Clean Water*, *post*,—,we granted certiorari in both cases..., and heard them together. The sole issue before us is whether the 1972 Act permits the Administrator to allot to the States under §205 less than the entire amounts authorized to be appropriated by §207. We hold that the Act does not permit such action and affirm the Court of Appeals.

I

Section 205 provides that the "sums authorized to be appropriated pursuant to §207...shall be allotted by the Administrator." Section 207 authorizes the appropriation of "not to exceed" specified amounts for each of three fiscal years. The dispute in this case turns principally on the meaning of the foregoing language from the indicated sections of the Act.

The Administrator contends that §205 directs the allotment of only "sums"—not "all sums"—authorized by §207 to be appropriated and that the sums that must be allotted are merely sums that do not exceed the amounts specified in §207 for each of the three fiscal years. In other words, it is argued that there is a maximum, but no minimum, on the amounts that must be allotted under §205. This is necessarily the case, he insists, because the legislation, after initially passing the House and Senate in somewhat different form, was amended in Conference and the changes, which were adopted by both Houses, were intended to provide wide discretion in the Executive to control the rate of spending under the Act.

The changes relied on by the Administrator, the so-called Harsha amendments, were two. First, §205 of the House and Senate bills as they passed those Houses and went to Conference, directed that there be allotted "all sums" authorized to be appropriated by §207. The word "all" was struck in Conference. Second, §207 of the House bill authorized the appropriation of specific amounts for the three fiscal years. The Conference Committee inserted the qualifying word "not to exceed" before each of the sums so specified.

The Administrator's arguments based on the statutory language and its legislative history are unpersuasive. Section 207 authorized appropriation of "not to exceed" a specified sum for each of the three fiscal years. If the States failed to submit projects sufficient to require obligation, and hence the appropriation, of the entire amounts authorized, or if the Administrator, exercising whatever authority the Act might have given him to deny grants, refused to obligate these total amounts, §207 would obviously permit appropriation of the lesser amounts. But if, for example, the full amount provided for 1973 was obligated by the Administrator in the course of approving plans and making grants for municipal contracts, §207 plainly "authorized" the appropriation of the entire $5 billion. If a sum of money is "authorized" to be appropriated in the future by §207, then §205 directs that an amount equal to that sum be allotted. Section 207 speaks of sums authorized to be appropriated, not of sums that are required to be appropriated; and as far as §205's requirement to allot is concerned, we see no difference between the $2 billion the President directed to be allotted for fiscal year 1973 and the $3 billion he ordered withheld. The latter sum is as much authorized to be appropriated by §207 as is the former. Both must be allotted.

It is insisted that this reading of the Act fails to give any effect to the Conference Committee's changes in the bill. But, as already indicated, the "not to exceed" qualifying language to §207 has meaning of its own, quite apart from §205, and reflects the realistic possibility that approved applications for grants from funds already allotted would not total the maximum amount authorized to be appropriated. Surely there is nothing inconsistent between authorizing "not to exceed" $5 billion for 1973 and requiring the full allotment of the $5 billion among the States. Indeed, if the entire amount authorized is *ever* to be appropriated, there must be approved municipal projects in that amount, and grants for those projects may *only* be made from allotted funds.

As for striking the word "all" from §205, if Congress intended to confer any discretion on the Executive to withhold funds from this program at the allotment stage, it chose quite inadequate means to do so. It appears to us that the word "sums" has no different meaning and can be ascribed no different function in the context of §205 than would the words "all sums." It is said that the changes were made to give the Executive the discretionary control over the outlay of funds for Title II programs at either stage of the process. But legislative intention, without more, is not legislation. Without something in addition to what is now before us, we cannot accept the addition of the few words to §207 and the deletion of the one word from §205 as altering the entire complexion and thrust of the Act. As conceived and passed in both Houses, the legislation was intended to provide a firm commitment of substantial sums within a relatively limited period of time in an effort to achieve an early solution of what was deemed an urgent problem. We cannot believe that Congress at the last minute scuttled the entire effort by providing the Executive with the seemingly limitless power to withhold funds from allotment and obligation. Yet such was the Government's position in the lower courts—combined with the argument that the discretion conferred is unreviewable.

The Administrator has now had second thoughts. He does not now claim that the Harsha amendments should be given such far-reaching effect. In this Court, he views §205 and 207 as merely conferring discretion on the Administrator as to the timing of expenditures, not as to the ultimate amounts to be allotted and obligated. He asserts that although he may limit initial allotments in the three specified years, "the power to allot continues" and must be exercised, "until the full $18 billion has been exhausted." ...It is true that this represents a major modification of the Administrator's legal posture, but our conclusion that §205 requires the allotment of sums equal to the total amounts authorized to be appropriated under §207 is not affected. In the first place, under §205 the Administrator's power to allot extends only to "sums" that are authorized to be appropriated under §207. If he later has power to allot, and must allot, the balance of the $18 billion not initially allotted in the specified years, it is only because these additional amounts are "sums" authorized by §207 to be appropriated. But if they are "sums" within the meaning of §205, then that section requires that they be allotted by November 17, 1972, in the case of 1973 funds and for 1974 and 1975 "not later than the January 1st immediately preceding the beginning of the fiscal year for which authorized." The November 22 letter of the President and the Administrator's consequent withholding of authorized funds cannot be squared with the statute.

Second, even assuming an intention on the part of Congress, in the hope of forestalling a veto, to imply a power of some sort in the Executive to control outlays under the Act, there is nothing in the legislative history of the Act indicating that such discretion arguably granted was to be exercised at the allotment stage rather than or in addition to the obligation phase of the process. On the contrary, as we view the legislative history, the indications are that the power to control, such as it was, was to be exercised at the point where funds were obligated and not in connection with the threshold function of allotting funds to the States. The Court of Appeals carefully examined the legislative history in this respect and arrived at the same conclusion, as have most of the other courts that have dealt with the issue. We thus reject the suggestion that the conclusion we have arrived at is inconsistent with the legislative history of §§205 and 207.

Accordingly, the judgment of the Court of Appeals is affirmed.

So ordered

MR. JUSTICE DOUGLAS concurs in the result.

WATERGATE CONSPIRACY SENTENCING

February 21, 1975

Three of former President Richard M. Nixon's closest aides were sentenced Feb. 21 for their part in the Watergate cover-up conspiracy, bringing to an apparent end the national scandal that forced Nixon to resign from the presidency. Sentenced were former Attorney General and 1972 Nixon campaign manager John N. Mitchell, former White House chief of staff H.R. Haldeman and former White House chief domestic adviser John D. Ehrlichman. Also sentenced was Robert C. Mardian, a former assistant attorney general. All four had been convicted Jan. 1, 1975, on charges of conspiracy in the Watergate affair. Mitchell, Haldeman and Ehrlichman were also convicted on all charges of conspiring to obstruct justice and lying to various congressional committees and officials. A fifth defendant, Kenneth W. Parkinson, a lawyer retained by the 1972 Nixon re-election committee, was acquitted. (Watergate cover-up verdict, Historic Documents of 1974, p. 991-1002; Watergate cover-up indictments, Historic Documents of 1974, p. 157-184.)

"It is the intention of the Court that the defendant will serve not less than 30 months and not more than eight years," said District Judge John J. Sirica as each of the three key defendants was summoned before him. Mitchell, Haldeman and Ehrlichman were each sentenced to a term of 20 months to five years for conspiracy and obstruction of justice in seeking to impede the investigation of the June 1972 Watergate break-in and to cover up White House involvement in that break-in. In addition, the three defendants received sentences of 10 months to three years for perjury counts against them. Mardian was given a prison term of 10 months to three years for conviction on the single count of conspiracy.

Sirica also ordered that Ehrlichman's sentence be served concurrently with an earlier sentence stemming from the White House-orchestrated burglary of the office of Daniel Ellsberg's psychiatrist. Ehrlichman had been convicted and sentenced in 1974 for his role in that 1971 break-in. (Indictments and trial for 1971 break-in, Historic Documents of 1974, p. 205-214, 411-417 and 661-669.) *The defendants were all released on their personal recognizance pending appeals, a process that was predicted to take at least a year.*

Prior to sentencing, lawyers for the defendants were given an opportunity to present statements on their clients' behalf. Haldeman's counsel, John J. Wilson, asked the court to consider that "whatever Bob Haldeman did, so did Richard Nixon; that Nixon has been freed of judicial punishment, yet Bob Haldeman has had to endure agony and punishment by the trial and conviction." At another point, Wilson said that Haldeman "was caught up in a political maelstrom that engulfed a lot of other good people." Ehrlichman's lawyer, Ira N. Lowe, capped his presentation with a surprise suggestion that Ehrlichman be "sentenced" not to prison, but to serve the Pueblo Indians in New Mexico. That plan wouldn't cost "the taxpayers a peso" and would enable Ehrlichman to impart his knowledge of land use to the Indians, Lowe said.

Sentencing Decision

Without commenting on the nature of the Watergate scandal, the judge said he had "given careful and serious thought" to the length of the defendants' sentences. He listed four factors pertinent to sentencing, but did not comment on the relationship of the factors to the case at hand. Those factors were: incarceration for the protection of society; punishment; the possibility of rehabilitation versus the effect of the sentence on the defendant and his family; and the deterrent effect on others who may be tempted to commit the same type of crime.

For Mitchell, Haldeman and Ehrlichman, Sirica imposed sentences that were equivalent to the most severe sentence handed down in the Watergate trials. One of the original Watergate burglars, E. Howard Hunt Jr., had been sentenced to an identical 30-month to eight-year prison term for his part in the break-in at Democratic National Committee headquarters.

Only Mitchell spoke with reporters following the sentencing. Of his sentence, he quipped: "It could have been much worse...a hell of a lot worse. They could have told me to spend the rest of my life with Martha Mitchell." Martha Mitchell was John Mitchell's wife, although the couple had separated. Martha Mitchell had become a prominent figure in Washington for her outspoken and sometimes indiscreet comments on activities within the Nixon administration. At one time, she had contended that her husband was shielding Nixon himself in the Watergate affair.

Although the defendants were expected to appeal, the sentencing of Mitchell, Ehrlichman and Haldeman was the final climax of the Watergate ordeal. Former President Nixon, who resigned from office Aug. 9, 1974, and was pardoned by President Gerald R. Ford on Sept. 8, 1974, remained secluded at his San Clemente, California, estate. (Nixon resignation and pardon, Historic Documents of 1974, p. 683-693, 811-817.) *Three former members of Nixon's cabinet, in addition to Mitchell, had been tried for Watergate-related crimes. Former Commerce Secretary Maurice H. Stans had been acquitted April 28, 1974, of charges of conspiracy, obstruction of justice and perjury. Those charges had stemmed from allegations that Stans, together with Mitchell, had attempted to block a government investigation into the activities of financier Robert L. Vesco in return for a campaign contribution. Former Treasury Secretary John B. Connally was acquitted April 17, 1975, of charges that he accepted a $10,000 bribe from the dairy industry in return for recommending in 1971 that the Nixon administration raise federal milk price supports. And former Attorney General Richard G. Kleindienst had pleaded guilty May 16, 1974, to refusing to testify fully to a congressional committee on the Justice Department antitrust case involving International Telephone and Telegraph (ITT). Kleindienst was sentenced to one month unsupervised probation.* (Kleindienst guilty plea, Historic Documents of 1974, p. 407-410.)

On Jan. 8, 1975, Judge Sirica had ordered John W. Dean III, Jeb Stuart Magruder and Herbert W. Kalmbach released from prison after serving only a part of their sentences. Dean, who had been presidential counsel to Nixon, was Nixon's prime accuser in the Watergate affair. Dean himself pleaded guilty to charges of conspiracy to obstruct justice and to defraud the United States and was sentenced to one to four years in prison. (Dean's Watergate testimony, Historic Documents 1973, p. 659-679.) *Magruder, a former White House aide and former deputy director of the Committee for the Re-election of the President, had pleaded guilty to charges of conspiracy to obstruct justice and to defraud the United States. He was sentenced to 10 months to four years in prison. Kalmbach, Nixon's personal attorney, pleaded guilty to charges of violating the Federal Corrupt Practices Act and to a charge of promising federal employment in return for political activity and for support of a candidate. He was sentenced to a prison term of six to 18 months, which he had begun serving on July 1, 1974.*

Charles W. Colson, the former special counsel to President Nixon, who had pleaded guilty to obstruction of justice for disseminating damaging information about Daniel Ellsberg, was sentenced to one to three years in prison and fined $5,000. But he served only seven months because his sentence was ordered reduced. (Colson indictments and guilty plea, Historic Documents of 1974, p. 157-167, 205, 443-447.)

Following are excerpts from the official court transcript of the sentencing of John N. Mitchell, H. R. Haldeman, John D. Ehrlichman and Robert C. Mardian by U.S. District Court Judge John J. Sirica on Feb. 21, 1975:

UNITED STATES DISTRICT COURT
FOR THE DISTRICT OF COLUMBIA

UNITED STATES OF AMERICA

vs.   Criminal No. 74-110

JOHN N. MITCHELL, et al.,

    Defendants.

Friday, February 21, 1975

The defendants in the above-entitled cause appeared before the HONORABLE JOHN J. SIRICA for sentencing at 9:30 o'clock a.m.

On Behalf of the United States:

JILL WINE VOLNER, Assistant Special Prosecutor
GEORGE FRAMPTON, Assistant Special Prosecutor
GERALD GOLDMAN, Assistant Special Prosecutor
JUDY DENNY, Assistant Special Prosecutor...

PROCEEDINGS

JUDGE SIRICA: Good morning.... The defendants and their counsel will first be given the opportunity to make any statements they wish for the record and the Court will then proceed with the sentencing.

Mr. Clerk, will you call the defendants and their attorneys to the lectern.

THE DEPUTY CLERK: Defendant John N. Mitchell, represented by William Hundley and Plato Cacheris.

Harry R. Haldeman, represented by John J. Wilson, Frank Strickler and Ross O'Donoghue.

Defendant John Ehrlichman, represented by Ira M. Lowe.

Robert C. Mardian, represented by Thomas C. Green and David Ginsburg.

THE COURT: I will ask Mr. Mitchell's counsel if he wishes to make a statement at this time.

MR. HUNDLEY: Mr. Mitchell has no statement.

THE COURT: I take it the Government has nothing to say then?

MRS. VOLNER: Correct, Your Honor.

MR. HUNDLEY: Your Honor, as his counsel, I would like to say briefly that Mr. Mitchell and I have tried to cooperate completely with Mr. Vogt of the Probation Office in the preparation of the Court's presentence report and I believe that we have brought to Mr. Vogt's attention for Your Honor's ultimate consideration all of the factors that are relevant to today's proceedings and I know Your Honor has studied and weighed the personal factors that we submitted in that regard and since sentencing is a difficult time not only for us but for the Court and since I don't think there is anything to add to it that hasn't already been said, I would just as soon not prolong the difficulties and move on.

THE COURT: Very well.

All right, I am going to ask counsel for Mr. Haldeman if he wishes to make a statement on behalf of Mr. Haldeman?

MR. WILSON: I do, sir.

THE COURT: I will hear you, sir.

MR. WILSON: May it please the Court, as we come to the end of a long road, a road that began with the grand jury proceedings in May of 1973 and is ending with the sentencing ceremony today, we are now at the point where a convicted defendant is given an opportunity to say what he wishes before sentence is pronounced.... I have always felt the opportunity of this moment was a meaningless one.... As for myself making an appeal for mercy and compassion comes too late. Not meaning any criticism whatever, Your Honor, like all other sentencing Judges, very likely decided upon the sentence before you left your chambers and entered the courtroom, and rarely, if ever, is a change brought by elocution of counsel either by persuasion or supplication or by offensiveness. I intend neither, since I am disciplined to respect the justice process from its beginning to its end.... And so I address Your Honor on the plane of what I hope—I repeat—what I hope that Your Honor considered when you reached your judgment—an awesome judgment in the exercise of the power of life and death—either literally in the sentence or in the effect upon the individual. Reverently and respectfully, I hope Your Honor took into consideration that never before has Bob Haldeman been in trouble, that he has lived an honorable and fruitful life; he is married to a wonderful woman and they together have raised a wonderful family of four children, one of whom you saw daily in the courtroom during the trial using the partial knowledge of the law to assist her father's counsel in his defense.

I hope that Your Honor considers whatever Bob Haldeman did, he did not for himself but for the President of the United States, that the virtue of loyalty is not to be forgotten when evaluating all the attending circumstances; that he was caught up in a political maelstrom that engulfed a lot of other good people. I hope that Your Honor without the need to be egotistical felt as you pondered Bob Haldeman's fate that to a degree you were holding a power not dissimilar from that of pardon, that whatever Bob Haldeman did so did Richard Nixon. Nixon has been freed of judicial punishment. Yet Bob Haldeman has had to endure agony and punishment by the trial and conviction.

This is not to say Nixon has not suffered agony and punishment of a kind, but while Bob Haldeman was not toppled from the highest office in the land, he was toppled from the highest office that he had achieved and, as a human being he has suffered at least the equivalent of what Richard Nixon has suffered, and he stands before Your Honor today facing the possibility of suffering far more than Richard Nixon will ever suffer. I hope that Your

145

Honor considered that Bob Haldeman was not to be punished for standing trial and testifying in his own defense, at all times maintaining a maximum respect for the dignity of Your Honor's courtroom and for the processes of justice. I hope that Bob Haldeman's unwillingness to plead guilty when, as he wrote Your Honor, he did not consider himself guilty, is not to be taken as a black mark upon his conduct at this moment. And I hope that the treatment which Your Honor has determined to accord Bob Haldeman comes out of the same compassion which Your Honor showed toward Dean, Magruder and Kalmbach.

While Your Honor is of course not bound by the compassion which another Judge exhibited towards another defendant, certain contrasts come to mind. That other defendant did not cooperate with the Ervin Committee and the grand jury while Bob Haldeman did. That other defendant pled the Fifth Amendment, or warned that he would do so, thus avoiding exposure to perjury charges, albeit weak ones supported by perjured testimony.

I mentally thrash myself for not giving Bob Haldeman the same advice, which, by the way, he would not have taken since the same loyalty for Nixon which got him into trouble was the same loyalty which caused him to stand up and be counted by every process which was being invoked at the time. He may not have pled guilty or testified for the prosecution, thus morally assuring himself of lenient treatment by the Court, but he did not defy the normal process by refusing to tell his story as he honestly saw it.

I hope that all of these matters have been considered by Your Honor and that as a result Bob Haldeman's fate may have been weighed on the scales of justice and found to be tipped in his favor.... I express the final hope that I shall not have hoped in vain. Thank you, Your Honor.

THE COURT: Now I will ask Mr. Haldeman if he wishes to make a statement in his own behalf or offer any information in mitigation of punishment. Do you wish to make a statement?

DEFENDANT HALDEMAN: As Your Honor knows, I submitted a written statement to the Court.

THE COURT: I have considered that.

DEFENDANT HALDEMAN: As counsel indicated, I know you have given that consideration. I appreciate it.

THE COURT: All right. Counsel for the Government, do you wish to reply?

MRS. VOLNER: As Your Honor knows, it has been the consistent policy of the Office of the Special Prosecutor not to make any recommendations upon sentencing. We have not done so in the past and will not make any recommendations today. Thank you.

THE COURT: Thank you.

Mr. Ehrlichman, would you step forward. I will ask counsel for Mr. Ehrlichman if he wishes to make a statement in behalf of the defendant.

MR. LOWE: Your Honor, I would make a statement. In arguing before Your Honor this morning on behalf of John Ehrlichman, I am not making an appeal for needs, nor am I asking he be placed on probation. I discussed this matter of sentence with Mr. Ehrlichman at length before undertaking his representation and he requests no less than a strict sentence for a period of time to be determined by Your Honor on the basis of his actions, carefully supervised. I would like to detail to you the request for an alternative sentence in a few moments.

This case has been and is one of the most important and far-reaching cases in the annals of United States history and I submit the hope that it will also be remembered for something else—as a catalyst for the beginning of the demise of the prison system as we know it. I will discuss that further.

One of your colleagues on this Court has stated: The increase in our crime rate indicates that the possibility of imprisonment is not necessarily a deterrent to criminal conduct and that such punishments may be devised as will restore them to virtue.... The question then is: Is imprisonment the only, or the best deterrent? I believe the answer to that is that it is within the power of the Court to make sentences long and strict as well as useful without incarceration. Now, Your Honor, of course this requires ingenuity, it requires cooperation of the defendant, it requires imagination, requires initiative, and requires a sense of humanity, all of which, Your Honor, is present in abundance in this case.

Mr. Ehrlichman has spent his time profitably, I believe, in the recent weeks considering what he might or what he could do to comport with the old Hassidic command of a good deed for a bad. In this search he met Chief Agoyo, one of the chiefs of the eight Northern Pueblos in the area of Espinola, New Mexico. These Puebloes are Taos, Picuris, San Juan, Santa Clara, San Ildefonso, Tesuque, Pojoaque, and Nambe, all in an area of several hundred miles in New Mexico. He determined by discussing with them that there is a crucial need that they have, and it happens that the need coincides almost precisely with the qualifications of Mr. Ehrlichman.

Now, in order to put these two together, I must give a little background, and I will make it as brief as I can. Mr. Ehrlichman attended several post-law school courses on the law of land use and controls, environmental law and real property, and was an instructor at the University of Washington, and in continuing legal education courses on land use and controls, and I believe it is a correct statement to say that he is one of the few specialists in this country in this field of land use law. His practice in law was limited to problems of real property and of land use from 1960 to 1969, regarding water rights title, natural resource development, industrial siting and environmental law.

The problems of the Pueblos are the need for basic research, legal research, and of course this would not be practicing law because Mr. Ehrlichman would not be able to practice law, but basic legal research into the establishment of the eight Northern Pueblos location of external and internal boundaries. Apparently they have never been fixed by the normal way. It has been by statute or Act of Congress. So there is a great need to determine that.... Putting those needs and qualifications together, it seems to match.

Your Honor, the Pueblo area is very remote. They cannot obtain the services that they need. They can hire a law firm living a distance away, number one, but that is very expensive; number two, it is not the same as being on the reservation. The suggestion therefore, is—and I believe Your Honor has a letter from Chief Agoyo, requesting Mr. Ehrlichman's services....

Your Honor, there are some precedents to this request. Prior to February 3 when Mr. Ehrlichman sent a letter to Your Honor, there was one case of a Doctor Jack Lorry, in Phoenix, Arizona, I believe, where he is serving a sentence for federal and state narcotics violations. He is not serving it in prison, he is not costing the taxpayers a peso, he is not rehabilitating himself by staring at the walls or writing letters to his lawyer trying to get out and his family is not adrift to suffer. He is serving as the only doctor in the town of Tombstone, Arizona, a population of 4,000 people, which means a population of 4,000 patients, he being the only doctor and which also means 4,000 supervisors or probation officers.... I think I could say correctly that everything is a question of timing, and is this a time to consider the question of prisons and what our society requires in terms of punishment?... I am directing his argument to the vast majority of persons who may provide a compensatory service, or if you want to call it alternative sentence. I am not concerned with the wording, but an alternative to confinement, to despair, to apathy and to frustration.... Your Honor, we are suggesting that this may be a perfect situation for just such an alternative sanction. I think all the requirements for such a sentence, and I do call it a sentence, we are not asking for anything other than a strict sentence.... I think he wants to show that this project, this kind of sentence can work.

Now I would like to, for the record, I think it is very important, read just a short part of the letter of February 3, 1975, that Mr. Ehrlichman sent to Your Honor. I think it is very important for this record:

> "With regard to my personal reform I have given the whole Watergate episode deep thought during the past year and a half. I profoundly regret my part in it. It is clear to me from the jury verdicts in the two cases I was a defendant my public life was deceived in such a way that my peers find me unworthy of their trust and belief. For me that realization is more punishing than any sentence Your Honor could impose. My 17 years of practice were based on my personal integrity. When I left my hometown to come to Washington, I did not leave behind my fidelity to truth, yet I have been found to be a perjurer and no reversal on appeal alone can expunge the stigma of those verdicts. I also stand convicted of denying a man of civil rights, of obstructing the cause of justice. As you know even better than I do, finding the balance between the needs of the nation and the rights of the individual is a never finished quest. The basic liberties which comprise the genius of our national society can only be preserved by resolving all doubt in favor of the individual citizen. I see that clearly.
>
> The opportunity to do public service for the Pueblos is a way to specifically and tangibly express my respect for this truth. Their

rights are in question every day. It seems to me appropriate to show my understanding of the principles involved through actions of this kind....

While prison might knock out of me a lot of my pride and self will, I truly would like to be able to do that rehabilitation myself. I believe I have begun that, that I can do it, and that if I do it myself I will be infinitely better for it.

At the same time I believe this self-rehabilitation and usefulness is possible for many thousands of others now serving prison time were they given the chance. I would take your sentence to this work as responsibilities to all those people.

If I prove to be a successful experiment perhaps other Judges would notice and would grant similar opportunities to those who seem to be good prospects."

So in closing, Your Honor, I would like to say that we are requesting, respectfully requesting Your Honor, that Mr. Ehrlichman be sentenced to work for these eight Northern Pueblo Indian group[s] in New Mexico for a length of time to be determined by Your Honor, to deal with the matters that there is a need to be dealt with, that he can do, that he can substantially assist in, under supervision by the way of 6,000—that is all there are left—6,000 of these eight Pueblo tribe members.... Now if Your Honor feels that what we are asking is a little beyond what Your Honor feels able to do, although I respectfully request that it is something that should be done, or at least to consider it, I would even request Your Honor to take it under advisement for a short period of time. But in any case, the alternative it seems to me would be a deferred sentence. So we respectfully request, if Your Honor feels unable to grant the first request that you grant a deferred sentence, or you give Mr. Ehrlichman a deferred sentence and give him the opportunity to go out to these Pueblos, to spend a few months there, to report back to Your Honor, to have the local probation officer check to see whether or not this is a worthy cause, whether he could convince Your Honor, let the burden of proof be on him, let him convince Your Honor that he has performed a worthy service.

The only reason that I can see of not doing this is for some reason you think that the American people would not understand, would not appreciate, would not accept this kind of a sentence, and I submit to Your Honor that I think maybe they would, maybe they would understand it.... Of course as an aside, if this was done, it would probably moot an appeal and again result in a great amount of saving. In the event that Your Honor again still is unable to grant this request, and I respectfully request that Your Honor consider it and even possibly take it under advisement then we request that Mr. Ehrlichman be able to remain on his personal recognizance pending appeal and be allowed to live in with the Pueblos and work there so that he may on his own perform his penance, again under the supervision of 6,000 Pueblos and the American people.... Thank you.

THE COURT: Mr. Ehrlichman, do you wish to make a statement in your own behalf or offer any information in mitigation of punishment other than what has been said?

DEFENDANT EHRLICHMAN: I have nothing to add.

THE COURT: Thank you.

Mr. Mardian, would you step up to the lectern? I will ask counsel for Mr. Mardian at this time if he wishes to make a statement on behalf of Mr. Mardian?

MR. GINSBURG: In direct answer to your question, Your Honor, the answer is no....

THE COURT: The Court has for many days now given careful and serious thought to what the proper sentences to impose in this case should be. It has carefully read and considered all of the presentence reports and has conferred with the probation officers. In addition, the Court has read the vast number of letters written on behalf of the defendants, by people who know them and who wished to state their opinions as to the good character, reputation and background of each of these men.

In an attempt to arrive at a just and fair sentence, a Court of criminal justice usually takes into consideration the purpose or purposes to be served by imposing a particular sentence on a particular individual. There may be said to be, among others, four primary reasons that are normally considered in this respect. These are: First incarceration for the protection of society; second, the matter of punishment; third, the possibility of rehabilitation and the effect of the sentence on the defendants and their families; and fourth, the deterrent effect that the sentence may have on others who may be tempted to commit the same types of crimes for which these defendants now stand convicted. Therefore, having in mind these reasons for imposing sentences in the administration of criminal justice, and having carefully reviewed all of the other facts before it in this proceeding, the Court will now proceed with the sentencing.

Mr. Mitchell, would you mind stepping in front of the lectern? In Criminal Case Number 74-110, the Court sentences the defendant John N. Mitchell on each of Counts One and Two to be incarcerated for a period of not less than 20 months and not more than five years. Said sentences to run concurrently with each other and are to be served in an institution to be designated by the Attorney General or his authorized representative. On each of Counts Four, Five, and Six, the Court sentences the defendant to be incarcerated for a period of not less than ten months and not more than three years, and the sentences on Counts Four, Five and Six are to run concurrently with each other and consecutively with the sentences imposed on Counts One and Two. It is the intention of the Court that the defendant will serve not less than thirty months and not more than eight years.... In view of the fact the Court has been informed at the bench at the beginning of the proceedings that each defendant intends to appeal, Mr. Mitchell will be permitted to remain on his own personal recognizance.

MR. HUNDLEY: Thank you, Your Honor.

THE COURT: ....Just one further thing: The Court recommends to the Director of the Bureau of Prisons that he study this case from the standpoint of a suitable place of confinement in a federal institution.

Mr. Haldeman, in Criminal Case Number 74-110, the Court sentences the defendant Harry R. Haldeman on each of Counts One and Two to be incarcerated for a period of not less than twenty months and not more than five years. Said sentences to run concurrently with each other and are to be served in an institution to be designated by the Attorney General or his authorized representative. On each of Counts Seven, Eight and Nine the Court sentences the defendant to be incarcerated for a period of not less than ten months, not more than three years, and the sentences on Counts Seven, Eight and Nine are to run concurrently with each other and consecutively with the sentences imposed on Counts One and Two. It is the intention of the Court that the defendant will serve not less than thirty months nor more than eight years.... If the defendant desires to appeal, he may remain on his own personal recognizance....

Mr. Ehrlichman.

In Criminal Case Number 74-110, the Court sentences the defendant John D. Ehrlichman on each of Counts One and Two to be incarcerated for a period of not less than twenty months and not less than five years, said sentences to run concurrently with each other and are to be served in an institution to be designated by the Attorney General or his authorized representative. On each of Counts Eleven and Twelve, the Court sentences the defendant to be incarcerated for a period of not less than ten months and not more than three years and the sentences on Counts Eleven and Twelve are to run concurrently with each other and consecutively with the sentences imposed on Counts One and Two. The sentences imposed in this case are to run concurrently with the sentence imposed in Criminal Case Number 74-116. It is the intention of the Court that the defendant will serve not less than thirty months and not more than eight years.... The defendant also may remain on personal recognizance....

Mr. Mardian.

In Criminal Case 74-110, the Court sentences the defendant Robert C. Mardian to be incarcerated for a period of not less than ten months and not more than three years in an institution to be designated by the Attorney General or his authorized representatives.... The defendant may of course remain on his personal recognizance pending appeal....

Announce adjournment, Mr. Marshal.

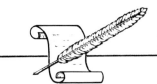 **HISTORIC DOCUMENTS OF 1975**

March

WALLACE ON FOREIGN POLICY
March 3, 1975

In a rare discussion of American foreign policy, Alabama Governor George C. Wallace told a group of foreign journalists March 3 that he "wished" the United States had fought "on the same side" with Japan and Germany—instead of with the Soviet Union—during World War II. Wallace's remarks on wartime alliances began and ended a rambling discussion of foreign and domestic issues with 25 visiting journalists on a United States Information Agency tour of the South. In the interview Wallace deplored post-World War I developments which, in his opinion, had needlessly alienated the Japanese and German people and had fostered the rise of their "nationalistic feeling."

The interview went unreported in the American press until May 8 when the Washington Post *published a controversial article which emphasized Wallace's statements about World War II alliances. A* Post *"ombudsman" later accused the newspaper of having sensationalized Wallace's remarks. The day after the article appeared, Wallace told a Washington audience that his views had been misunderstood. His criticism, he said, had been directed toward American foreign policy in general, which "for the last 50 years...[has] utterly failed."* Post *political reporter David Broder subsequently wrote that on "at least three occasions" in recent years Wallace had "volunteered the observation that the United States misidentified its real enemy in World War II."*

The March interview was notable for reasons that went beyond the question of press ethics. At the time of the interview Wallace was, according to the Gallup Poll, a front-runner for the Democratic presidential nomination

155

in 1976, and he had never before expressed himself at length on American foreign policy.

Wallace the Candidate

Wallace first came to national attention in 1963 when, as governor of Alabama, he attempted to bar black students from enrolling at the University of Alabama. He campaigned as a spoiler in the presidential elections of 1964 and 1968. In 1968 Wallace led a sizable third-party movement, the American Independent Party; however, by 1972 he was running for President once again as a Democrat. In early party primaries that year, he scored impressive victories but his campaign was cut short by an assassination attempt which left him paralyzed from the waist down. In 1974 Wallace won the governorship of Alabama for a third time and by a landslide vote, but his health remained an issue as he launched his drive for the 1976 presidential nomination.

Detente, Vietnam and Foreign Aid

During the interview Wallace repeatedly expressed his distrust of communism and said if he were President he would base his foreign policy on American military superiority. "You never have been able to trust [the Communists]," Wallace asserted, adding that he believed in détente. "But while I'm détenting...I wouldn't turn my back on them." On the other hand, thanks to postwar aid to Japan "today we have a good buffer against Soviet and Chinese expansion." As for Germany, Wallace considered the Versailles treaty unjust and responsible for Hitler's rise to power. On Vietnam (the interview took place prior to the fall of the South Vietnamese government and the end of the war, see p. 279), Wallace said the United States should either have won the war with conventional weapons or "gotten out." He scored India for spending money on a "nuclear weapon" rather than on food, and he rebuked other nations that had criticized the United States while accepting assistance.

In October Wallace made his first trip to Europe, a two-week tour during which he met with government leaders in Britain, Belgium and Italy. His itinerary also included West Germany and France.

> *Excerpts from the transcript made by the Foreign Press Center of the United States Information Agency (USIA) of an interview granted by Alabama Governor George C. Wallace to visiting foreign journalists, March 3, 1975:*

WALLACE: We do a lot of business with the Japanese. We ship a lot of coal. We have a lot of Japanese. The President of Nippon Steel was here the other day. We send a lot of coal to them. We have to keep it and use it ourselves, you know, but we sell you a lot of coal. We're glad to do business with you. In fact, I wish we'd been on the same side in World War II. Instead of being on the side [of] China and Russia....

Race Not an Issue

...In 1963, when I was first Governor, my fight was not against black people. It was against Big Government. And as a consequence, having lost the so-called legal battle, we have smoother conditions. They say—Why is that? Well, in the first place, the media didn't listen...when we first told them. We have nothing against black people. We're against Big Government.... Now,...where are you folks from, England? You raise more sand about race in England—than any place in the country. Don't even want citizens of your Commonwealth to come in your country. I think that's abhorrible [sic]. I think people ought to be able to come into that country. They're citizens.

We have no objections to Puerto Ricans coming to the United States from Puerto Rico. Never has been a question raised in this state or in the Congress, as I know of, because they're citizens, and they're entitled to come here....

CORRESPONDENT: Would you tell us about your viewpoint on international affairs? At the present time.

WALLACE: Well, my viewpoint on international affairs is that I think the best foreign policy we can have at the present time, with the situation of the Soviet and the Red Chinese, is to be the strongest nation on the face of the earth—because the people we're dealing with don't understand anything but strength. And any of you folks that believe otherwise will wind up like people in Finland. Anybody from Finland here? They know. Every move they have to make they almost have to clear it with the Soviet—because of that strength. I think this nation ought not to be on a parity.... I think it ought to be superior. So, I think the first foreign policy matter should be number one in strength militarily. Until the time truly comes that there is bilateral disarmament. We don't have any bilateral disarmament. We have a unilateral disarmament in a way on the part of the United States, but we don't have it in the Soviet Union, and we don't have it in Red China. And, of course, our foreign policy to be strong—necessarily insures the umbrella that the Japanese themselves who are now conquering Southeast Asia in a business fashion, that couldn't conquer it in war, but almost did—and I'll tell you what—You did a great job to be a little country. I'll tell you. You can certainly hand it to you.

But our nuclear umbrella is your shield, and that's part of our foreign policy. I believe in support of NATO, and I believe that people in West Germany and East and Western Europe ought to, ought to help us with the cost involved—because, after all, it's for their protection, and our interest too. I'm not [for] withdrawing troops from NATO.... I was against this country getting involved in Vietnam, militarily bogged down in a land war in Asia, but once they got bogged down, I was for them winning it, and if they couldn't win it, they should have gotten out. And I think they stayed too long, in dissipating our resources, and what I would have liked to have seen done was the United States win the war, with whatever necessary with conventional weapons, and if they got to the point where you can't win a war with conventional weapons in Vietnam, then we should have withdrawn then. I don't believe in the Paris Peace Accords...I knew that the Communists never would keep a single agreement....

Doubts Communists

So, my foreign policy if I were the President would be based on the fact that you can't trust a Communist. You never have been able to trust them. I don't believe in confrontation. I believe in negotiation. I believe in détente. But while I'm "détent'ing," as they say, I wouldn't turn my back on them. And I don't trust the Communists. I don't want any war with them. I'd like to see them truly spend many of their resources on consumer and on people and on human resources....

Don't get the attitude the United States thinks it's better than you [West Germans] are. We think you're great. But we are magnanimous. We've been to India—given them $10-billion—and they make fun of us. And they've spit in our face, and they built a nuclear weapon with it.

So, if I were the President, I would do foreign policy on the basis of what was in the interest of this country—because the survival of this country is in the interest to the free world, and I'd stop worrying about whether the Netherlands liked what we did or not. I'd stop worrying about whether Czechoslovakia liked it or not. And the Russians didn't give a damn about what they thought.... Nobody raised any sand about it. So, I'd like to have respect. I'd like to have love on the part of other peoples in the world. I'd like to have them respect me. And nobody can make fun of this country for being materialistic because, India—some of her Communists make fun of us, but they take all the materials we give them....

Nuclear Weapons in India

And let me say this—I have a great respect for the Indian people, don't forget that. In fact, I just think all people in the world are great—because they're the handiwork of a Supreme Being, but I do criticize the Indian government, as you criticize it—have a right to—you can criticize me and the Alabama Governor, but the money you spent on the nuclear weapon. I don't know that you need one. I saw on the television people in India starving to death, actually starving to death while they're building a nuclear weapon, and I just don't know....

And I say this because we've got a lot of things you can criticize us about—but if we're going to keep on giving India money to feed starving people who then propagate to the point where another 20 million are starving next year, you're going to have some population control programs.

CORRESPONDENT: We have.

WALLACE: Well, you have them, but they're not very effective because your population goes up. You've got them in the cities where people's educational level is uncertain, but for the mass of Indians, evidently, it's not working—because you wouldn't be increasing 15 or 20 million people a year, however many it is. Over and above Western countries, and over that of the United States. So, what I'm trying to say is—that we can't give everything because we've run out. You know. We just have certain limitations...and I'll tell you another thing: While we were in the Vietnam, people in your government, including your government, criticized us and even, in effect, gave aid and comfort to the North Vietnamese. And many other countries here did the same thing. Sweden did. They [were not] getting anything from us. We just saved them from the Germans back in World War II, but that was a long time ago.... You people in Scandinavia were mighty glad when we came over and saved you from the Germans, but when we go to Vietnam, to save the Vietnamese, you give us hell. So, what's the difference? Why didn't we just let you go to the Germans as we let them go to the Communists? I don't see any difference. I don't think we ought to have the kind of criticism we get from your country for doing to other people what we did for you—because it was humanitarian then. And, now, we're supporting a corrupt government—and I don't know what is the difference.

Now, that's my attitude....

CORRESPONDENT: I'm from Yugoslavia.

WALLACE: Yes, you're a country that they sold out, too. Over here I'm talking about. (laughter) I say that you're a country that the Western World—although Tito and the Yugoslav Communists are supposed to be different. What I'm saying is—let me say not Yugoslavia but Eastern Europe—we made so many mistakes back there at Yalta and Potsdam and all those places, when Eastern European people ought to be free today like West Germans. And if I had been the President then, I'd never have let the Russians come in and take Berlin first—because we were the strongest, and I certainly would have preserved the security of Eastern Europe....

Other Forms of Government

And let me say this about...communism. I don't care what kind of government any country has—that's their own business. I don't think they ought to try to export through subversion and other means that sort of government to other parts of the world. I think one mistake our government makes is that they think maybe—some of the liberals think maybe that they ought to have a certain type of government in—well, South Vietnam, for instance. In Cambodia. Like ours. Well, everybody don't want a government like ours. The people are conditioned over centuries for other type governments. If they want to have that type of government, that's one thing. So, I think we try to push our form on too many people through persuasion and through otherwise.

And I want to say this about the Soviet Union—because you've got a member of the Soviet press here. I'm not anti-Soviet Union...I watched the Soviet athletes on television and I marvel at them. I think they're great, and the people are great. But I do think that the government of Soviet Russia has not been, shall I say on the table? They just haven't kept their agreements. Now, I can understand why we shouldn't keep an agreement if it was going to be at our disadvantage. But I do think that if the time comes when the Soviet Union makes agreements with our country, that we can trust and they can be kept, we'll come closer to having what we call "true détente"—and I think it's necessary for the whole peace of the world....

Mistaken Foreign Policy

About foreign policy—I want to tell you something—I do not believe in Nazi-ism—just like maybe you don't believe in Wallace-ism. But that was not the German people. The German people were mistreated after World War I. The Versailles Treaty, that was imposed on them by France and Britain and the United States—and, mainly, France and Britain, was a treaty that brought Hitler to power. And if it hadn't been Hitler, his name would have been Jones—it would have been Schmidt—it would have been somebody else because it was only sure that nationalistic feeling of the German people would be aroused from the mistreatment they got.

And so our foreign policy over the years made a mistake in allowing that to happen. We ought to have [been]—after World War I [as we were] after World War II—magnanimous.... And the Japanese people, in my judgment, were provoked to a certain extent by people, by interests in this country that helped to bring about Pearl Harbor. And what I'm saying is that our true foreign policy in those years ought to have been [cultivating] the friendship of the Japanese and of the Germans instead of being antagonistic....

I think we were fighting the wrong people, maybe, in World War II, and I say that with all due regard to the Soviet person here. What I'm saying is—We fought on your side, but I wish the Soviet Union, or government rather, had been contained somewhat. And I do think we helped build up enemies in Western Europe, and in Germany, and in Japan, that we ought to have been friendly to 50 years ago. And then there wouldn't have been any Hitler, and there wouldn't [have been] any Jewish tirade.

ROSTROPOVICH ON FREEDOM
March 9, 1975

When Soviet cellist Mstislav Rostropovich started on what he described as a "prolonged concert tour" in the West in May 1974, it was the first time in three years that he and his wife, opera singer Galina Vishnevskaya, had been allowed by the Soviet government to perform abroad. Both had brilliant artistic reputations; Rostropovich was, to many critics, the best cellist alive. But for the preceding five years the two musicians had incurred official harassment for supporting Soviet dissidents, including Nobel laureate Alexander I. Solzhenitsyn. (See Historic Documents 1972, p. 727; 1973, p. 791; 1974, p. 129.) *In addition to the ban on foreign travel, their concert schedules were disrupted and their appearances unpublicized and unreviewed. "We were," Vishnevskaya told* The New York Times, *"surrounded by a wall of silence."*

By March 1975 Rostropovich had taken several steps which raised doubts about his return to the Soviet Union. He accepted the post of music director and conductor of a major American orchestra, the National Symphony, beginning with the 1977-78 season. And, early in the month, he made public a letter deploring the Soviet tactics which had curtailed his and his wife's artistic growth. The letter was a response to an article critical of Soviet emigrants like Rostropovich which had been published in the Paris news-paper Le Monde *by Igor Shafarevich. The Moscow University mathe-matician, also a leader in the Soviet human rights movement, had asserted that Soviet artists and intellectuals who chose voluntary exile lacked "spiritual values" and therefore could not contribute to world culture.*

"I Never Was Political"

"What should you do then," Rostropovich wrote in reply, "if you are perhaps not bereft of these 'spiritual values,' but are restrained from sharing them with your people?" He stressed that the reasons for his departure from the Soviet Union were not political—"as a musician, I never was political"—but artistic. "How much," he wrote, "I could have done for my country had I been given just 'musical freedom' without being regulated or tripped up, without someone trying to destroy me as a person and a musician just to prove that even a talented man can be destroyed if he is not obedient, that such a man can be replaced with a mediocrity...."

Rostropovich's letter, published first by the Paris newspaper Le Monde, *also appeared in the Russian-language New York newspaper* Novoye Russkoye Slovo. *The* Washington Post *published the* Le Monde *letter March 9.*

Rostropovich joined a growing number of exiled Soviet artists distinguished by their brilliant international reputations, including dancers Valery and Galina Panov and Mikhail Baryshnikov and the novelist Solzhenitsyn. The same day that the Post *carried an account of Rostropovich's letter it reported that the eminent Soviet sculptor Ernst Niezvestny was seeking an exit visa. The limits set on his artistic development by the Soviet establishment were, he reportedly said, too severe.*

> *Text of letter by Mstislav Rostropovich to the Paris newspaper* Le Monde, *reprinted by the* Washington Post *March 9, 1975:*

Dear Mr. Editor:

I have read in your newspaper Yuly Daniel's brilliant answer to the article written by Igor Shafarevich on the issue of the emigration by Soviet cultural figures. I am much concerned with this issue. That is why I think it my duty to take part in this discussion. Having read a statement by Shafarevich, whom I deeply respect, I realized that even those who feel as kindly to me as he neither know nor understand the real causes that made me take such a crucial step as my extended separation from my Motherland.

I. Shafarevich writes: "The best representatives of our literature, criticism, music...left of their own free will. And if now some say that they were exiled, others that they were almost exiled, and a third group is filled with indignation about their being deprived of citizenship, that means that the first, second and third groups themselves feel that they did something they should not have done."

Did I really take a wrong step? Could my friends have found me a better way out? What else could I do?

For the last five years my family was in a special position, unlike that of other Soviet artists and musicians. The reason was that being a musician, I have never been a politician. My life was dictated by my heart and my conscience. I had never signed any officially prefabricated letters, whether they were against "the Israeli aggressors," or [Boris] Pasternak, or [Andrei D.] Sakharov.

I had never participated in the officially organized campaigns of persecution against composers, writers, artists, scientists, and as is well known, I gave shelter to my friend, Alexander Solzhenitsyn in my country house, where he spent four winters. All these are my "crimes," that were followed by a whole tail of events. The result was that with my family, I embarked on an extended departure from Russia.

I do think that it is necessary for me to answer all the guesses and rumors surrounding my departure.

I. Shafarevich writes: "(They) left...of their own free will." What does that mean "of free will?"

I now want to talk not about the form of the departure but what forced the two Russian artists to ask the government's permission for the whole family to leave Russia on a "long-term basis."

"Deprived of Self-Expression"

I would like to get an answer from I. R. Shafarevich: How do you imagine my creative life was in my Motherland if, as an artist, I was deprived of the possibility of self-expression? What can one do if the art of the performer-musician gets older and dies together with him? Only on records (although it is not good enough) one could leave a "print" which could even "survive" the artist himself. But what if the recording simply is stopped by somebody's order literally on half-a-word, and you practically get kicked out of the studio, as it once happened when my wife was recording Puccini's "Tosca," with me as conductor, at the Bolshoi Theater?

Once Herbert von Karajan asked whether Galina Vishnevskaya [Rostropovich's wife] could come to Vienna to record "Boris Godunov" by Mussorgsky. The Ministry of Culture of the USSR, of course without asking Vishnevskaya, replied to Karajan that she is a "soprano" and cannot sing the part of Marina Mnishek, as that part is not for her voice. It's too bad that H. Karajan happened not to be a well enough educated musician for our ministry of culture, which surely knows best. After a further scandal the recording session took place. It surely is brilliant proof of which of those arguing knows more about music.

I wonder what Leontyne Price would do if the State Department, without telling her anything, simply prohibited some record company from recording the opera "Carmen" because, in their judgment, her voice was of too low range?

And how long could I be treated, in the planning of my concerts abroad, as a marionette in the hands of the state organization "Gosconcert?" Only they could say, depending on their (or someone else's) wish, where I could go and where I could not, which parts I could play and which ones not.

When they did not wish me to go to Paris (in January 1974) to perform the Beethoven trios with Yehudi Menuhin and Wilhelm Kempff for the

UNESCO jubilee, they sent an official telegram to Menuhin saying that I could not come as I was sick, but in reality I was absolutely healthy.

How long is it possible to ruin my creative plans and "punish" me by the different terms of quarantine for my tours abroad and by repeated disruptions of my concert engagements in my Motherland?

But maybe I was always eager to go abroad without giving enough of my time and energy to my own countrymen? In 25 years with the Moscow Conservatory, I prepared more than 20 international prize laureates. I tried to stimulate composers to produce new works for the cello. I was one of the initiators of the first music festival in Gorkiy. I never refused to perform in the most remote parts of Siberia, Chukotka and the Far East.

In the places where they didn't have a piano, I played the accordion.

But for me as a musician and an artist, for my professional growth, it is necessary to do the more important projects, with the great orchestras and the top conductors and soloists, in my country as well as abroad.

"How Much I Could Do"

I am only 47 and in my prime. How much I could do for my country, had I been given just "musical freedom" without being regulated or tripped up, without someone trying to destroy me as a person and a musician just to prove that even a talented man can be destroyed if he is not obedient, that such a man can be replaced with a mediocrity, obeying the bosses, like a slave and blindly walking the narrow and often stupid official line.

So much mistrust, so much control, and over-cautiousness, towards their own countrymen!

I was carrying out hundreds of plans. I dreamed to conduct the opera "Ekaterina Ismailova" by Shostakovich, all of his symphonies, "Queen of Spades" by Tchaikovsky, "Boris Godunov" by Mussorgsky. When I was fired from the Bolshoi Theater, I didn't lose hope. I contacted the opera theaters of Tashkent ("Queen of Spades") and a production group came to see me in Moscow to discuss the staging in advance; in Baku—again "Queen of Spades"; in Vilnus—a new staging of "Prince Igor."

But I was once again forbidden to do all of that. I was even kicked out of Moscow's Operetta Theater a week before the premiere of "Fledermaus" by Strauss on whose staging I had been working for months.

I could endlessly go on but it would be disgusting. It is not my fault that these dreams of my life will have to come true not in my Motherland, but on the stages of New York, San Francisco, London, Paris, Milan, Vienna and Munich. Not long before my departure, the assistant minister of culture of the USSR told me: "Who cares that you want to play in the theaters or conduct the best orchestras of our country. They do not want you." To which Galina Vishnevskaya replied: "That is why we must leave. Rostropovich is wanted in Paris, London and New York."

G. Vishnevskaya, in the prime of her creative life, had found herself in the position of an actress whose work was deliberately surrounded by silence. In fact she was exiled from radio and television.

And so in the opinion of my friend Igor Shafarevich I should sit at home until I grow old or die and wait to become "wanted" again. And before I die with none of my dreams come true, I would think: "Oh, how well I could play such and such work."

I. Shafarevich writes: "Those creative figures who have voluntarily departed simply couldn't stand the pressure that for decades had been borne by millions of believers."

"Almost Anything Can Be Borne"

Is there anything in my case that suggests I cannot bear pressure? Almost anything can be borne physically. My wife lived through the blockade of Leningrad.

Together with our people we lived through starvation and all the bitterness of the war. But it must be possible for one's hope and belief to come true. A musician cannot close himself up in four walls and create for himself: he must pass his art on to the people. Otherwise, his art, not finding an outlet, destroys the artist.

My wife and I left for a few years, but not from our people, but from the officials, who are given the right to mock at the people of art. We left not because of the lack of recognition, comfort or money. Not at all. Just the opposite. Our life abroad became a lot harder for us: our children are now staying in the boarding school in Switzerland, we continuously change the cities, living in the hotels for several days in each, and surely without such a comfort as we had in our excellent apartment and our huge villa.

We left only in order to make our musical plans come true. To live a life like a plant, whose only goal is to hold onto life as it is, cannot become the fate of those able to lead a creative life.

I. Shafarevich writes that "those creative figures who have voluntarily departed...did not have enough spiritual values so that they could endure the threat of tests—very severe tests but ones not beyond human power to endure—as has been proven by numerous people. And if so, what valuable contributions to world culture are there to talk about? Those without these values cannot accomplish anything in the culture, regardless of what side of the border they are on."

But what can you do if you do not lack these spiritual values, but simply cannot transmit them physically to your people?

There is no way you can jump over the wall created by the ruling system, no matter how you suffer and try.

I do not know whether I have made the slightest contribution to music, but everything I shall do on the other side of our Motherland's border will always be Russian. For my wife and me, being abroad is not an escape from Russia, but the only way to realize our musical dreams, by which we express our love for Russia and our great people.

165

SUPREME COURT ON OFFSHORE OIL
March 17, 1975

Oil and gas resources beneath the continental shelf and beyond the three-mile limit are within the sole jurisdiction of the federal government, not the coastline states, the Supreme Court ruled March 17. In a unanimous opinion, the Court rejected claims to those resources put forward by 13 Atlantic states. Justice Byron R. White delivered the Court's opinion, which was based on decisions handed down in 1947 and 1950.

Protection and control of marginal sea areas (within the three-mile limit) "has been and is a function of national external sovereignty," the Court had ruled in 1947 in a case involving California's claims to the Pacific seabed off its shores. "In our constitutional system," it said, "paramount rights over the ocean waters and their seabed were vested in the federal government." In 1950, the Court similarly rejected claims by Louisiana and Texas to sovereignty over 27 miles of seabed areas in the Gulf of Mexico. In reaffirming those decisions, Justice White said, "These cases, unless they are to be overruled, completely dispose of the states' claims of ownership here." He added: "Under our constitutional arrangement, paramount rights to the lands underlying the marginal sea are incident to national sovereignty and...their control and disposition in the first instance are the business of the federal government." Any prior ownership of such areas during the colonial period "did not survive becoming a member of the Union."

This ruling had the effect of clearly placing in federal hands the control over exploration and development of offshore resources beyond the three-mile limit. It thus removed one obstacle from the path to production of oil and gas from the continental shelf. Deposits were thought to exist off the

167

Atlantic Coast as well as Southern California and Alaska. The Department of the Interior had announced plans to exploit seabed oil and gas deposits in an effort toward making the country independent of foreign energy sources. More immediately, the Court's March 17 decision opened the way for leasing of tracts off the mid-Atlantic coast for exploration and production. Leasing was expected to begin in 1976. In the event that oil was discovered immediately, significant production could begin as early as 1978 or 1979. However, difficulty in locating large oil reserves, potential state and environmentalist law suits and technical difficulties could delay significant production until the early or mid-1980s.

Although the Court's decision disappointed officials in the Atlantic states, the ruling apparently did not put an end to federal-state wrangling over the offshore drilling question. State officials indicated that they would continue their efforts to establish environmental safeguards affecting such drilling. Gov. Hugh L. Carey of New York called for strict regulation of oil exploration. "I'd like to see the creation of a federal corporation responsible for the proper supervision of oil resources along the lines of the federal Atomic Energy Commission," he said. A second line of contention between state and federal officials was the economic impact of offshore drilling. State officials had demanded a share of federal revenues from leasing rights in order to ease the cost of services that would be needed once drilling began.

The oil industry, by contrast, welcomed the Court's decision. Frank Ikard, president of the American Petroleum Institute, said the decision had eliminated "a major stumbling block in the path of achieving a greater degree of energy self-sufficiency."

Events Leading to Offshore Oil Ruling

Despite the Court's rulings in 1947 and 1950 denying state claims to offshore resources, Maine moved in 1969 to lease lands on the outer continental shelf off its coast for private development. In response, the United States government brought a complaint in the Supreme Court against the 13 states with Atlantic coastlines. The government asked for a declaration of its ownership of the seabed and subsoil under the Atlantic Ocean from a point beyond the statutory three-mile limit to the outer edge of the continental shelf. Twelve of the 13 states—Florida excepted—responded with a claim that the same area had been included in grants to the original colonies from the kings of England and Holland. As successors to the colonies, the states claimed they retained ownership of the seabeds. Florida filed a separate claim based on an 1868 federal law approving the boundaries of that state.

As is the practice with many cases involving competing state and federal boundary claims, the Supreme Court referred the matter to a retired federal judge, a special master. The special master, Albert B. Maris, upheld the *federal claim to the Atlantic territory. The states took exception to Maris' report, and the Court listened to arguments on Feb. 24 and 25. The Court's decision on the case came with unusual speed, apparently due in part to a Justice Department request for quick action so that the Ford administration could proceed with its accelerated offshore leasing program.*

Additional Arguments

In addition to arguing that rights to territory under the adjacent seas were derived from the mother countries of colonial times, the states contended that legislation passed by Congress in 1953 had given them title to offshore resources beyond the three-mile limit. But the Court insisted the assumption of federal ownership of contested offshore areas was "embraced rather than repudiated by the Congress in the Submerged Lands Act of 1953." That statute granted the states a right only to the offshore seabed within three miles from shore or, in the cases of Texas and Florida, three leagues (about nine miles) from shore.

The Court asserted that the right of the United States to the resources of the seabed beyond the three-mile limit was confirmed not only by the Submerged Lands Act, but also by the Outer Continental Shelf Lands Act of 1953. Through that act, White said, "Congress emphatically implemented its view that the U.S. has paramount rights to the seabed beyond the three-mile limit." He went on to say "we are convinced" that the position announced by the Court in the California case in 1947 "has peculiar force and relevance in the present context. It is apparent that in the almost 30 years since California, a great deal of public and private business has been transacted in accordance with those decisions.... Both the Submerged Lands Act and the Outer Continental Shelf Lands Act which soon followed proceeded from the premises established by the prior court decisions and provided for the orderly development of offshore resources."

Since 1953, the Court noted, 33 lease sales had been held, embracing over eight million acres and 1,940 leases. For that reason, the Court concluded, "we are quite sure that it would be inappropriate to disturb our prior cases, major legislation, and many years of commercial activity, by calling into question, at this date, the constitutional premise of prior decisions."

> *Following are excerpts from the Supreme Court's decision March 17 on the federal government's ownership of offshore oil and gas resources:*

No. 35, Orig.

United States, Plaintiff,
v.
State of Maine et al.

On Exceptions to Report of
Special Master

[March 17, 1975]

MR. JUSTICE WHITE delivered the opinion of the Court. [JUS-
TICE DOUGLAS took no part in consideration or decision of the case.]

Seeking to invoke the jurisdiction of this Court...the United States in
April 1969 asked leave to file a complaint against the 13 States bordering on
the Atlantic Ocean—Maine, New Hampshire, Massachusetts, Rhode
Island, New York, New Jersey, Delaware, Maryland, Virginia, North
Carolina, South Carolina, Georgia, and Florida. We granted leave to file...
on June 16, 1969. The complaint asserted a separate cause of action
against each of the States, and each alleged that:

> "The United States is now entitled, to the exclusion of the
> defendant States, to exercise sovereignty rights over the
> seabed and subsoil underlying the Atlantic Ocean, lying
> more than three geographical miles seaward from the or-
> dinary low watermark and from the outer limits of inland
> waters on the coast, extending seaward to the outer edge of
> the Continental Shelf, for the purpose of exploring the area
> and exploiting the natural resources."

It was further alleged that each of the states claimed some right or title to
the relevant area and was interfering with the rights of the United States. It
was therefore prayed that a decree be entered declaring the rights of the
United States and that such further relief be awarded as may prove proper.

The defendants answered, each generally denying proprietary rights of
the United States in the seabed in the area beyond the three-mile marginal
sea. Each of them, except Florida, claimed for itself, as successor in title to
certain grantees of the Crown of England (and in the case of New York, to
the Crown of Holland), the exclusive right of dominion and control over the
seabed underlying the Atlantic Ocean seaward from its coastline to the
limits of the jurisdiction of the United States, asserting as well that any
attempt by the United States to interfere with these rights would in itself
violate the Constitution of the United States.

Without acting on the motion for judgment filed by the United States
that asserted that there was no material issue of fact to be resolved, we
entered an order appointing the Honorable Albert B. Maris as Special
Master and referred the case to him with authority to request further
pleadings, to summon witnesses and to take such evidence and submit such
reports as he might deem appropriate.... Before the Special Master, the
United States contended that based on *United States* v. *California*,...
(1947), *United States* v. *Louisiana*,... (1950), and *United States* v.
Texas,...(1950), it was entitled to judgment in accordance with its motion.
The defendant States asserted that their cases were distinguishable from
the prior cases and that in any event, *California, Louisiana,* and *Texas*
were erroneously decided and should be overruled. They offered, and the

Special Master received, voluminous documentary evidence to support their claims that, contrary to the Court's prior decisions, they acquired dominion over the offshore seabed prior to the adoption of the Constitution and at no time relinquished it to the United States. At the conclusion of the proceeding before him, the Special Master submitted a Report which the United States supports in all respects but to which the States have submitted extensive and detailed exceptions. The controversy is now before us on the Report, the exceptions to it and the briefs and oral arguments of the parties.

In his Report, the Special Master concluded that the *California, Louisiana* and *Texas* cases, which he deemed binding on him, governed this case and required that judgment be entered for the United States. Assuming, however, that those cases were open to re-examination, the Special Master went on independently to examine the legal and factual contentions of the States and concluded that they were without merit and that the Court's prior cases should be reaffirmed.

We fully agree with the Special Master that *California, Louisiana,* and *Texas* rule the issues before us. We also decline to overrule those cases as the defendant States request us to do.

United States v. California,...involved an original action brought in this Court by the United States seeking a decree declaring its paramount rights, to the exclusion of California, to the seabed underlying the Pacific Ocean and extending three miles from the coastline and from the seaward limits of the State's inland waters. California answered, claiming ownership of the disputed seabed. The basis of its claim, as the Court described it, was that the three-mile belt lay within the historic boundaries of the State; "that the original thirteen states acquired from the Crown of England title to all lands within their boundaries under navigable waters, including a three-mile belt in adjacent seas; and that since California was admitted as a state on an 'equal footing' with the original states, California at that time became vested with title to all such lands." ...The Court rejected California's claim. The original Colonies had not "separately acquired ownership of the three-mile belt or the soil under it, even if they did acquire elements of the sovereignty of the English Crown by their revolution against it.".... As the Court viewed our history, dominion over the marginal sea was first accomplished by the National Government rather than by the Colonies or by the States. Moreover, the Court went on to hold that the "protection and control of [the marginal sea] has been and is a function of national extended sovereignty,"... and that in our constitutional system paramount rights over the ocean waters and their seabed were vested in the Federal Government.

The United States later brought actions to confirm its title to the seabed adjacent to the coastline of other States. *United States v. Louisiana,*...was one of them. There Louisiana claimed title to the seabed under waters extending 27 miles into the Gulf of Mexico, the basis of the claim being that before and since the time of her admission to the Union, Louisiana had exercised dominion over the ocean area in question and that her legislature had formally included the 27-mile belt within the boundaries of the State. The

Court gave judgment for the United States, holding that *United States* v. *California* was controlling and emphasizing that paramount rights in the marginal sea and seabed were incidents of national sovereignty.... Louisiana had "no stronger claim to ownership of the marginal sea than the original 13 Colonies or California had,"...;and its claim, like theirs, gave way to the overriding rule that "the three-mile belt is in the domain of the Nation rather than of the separate States,"... [T]he waters and seabed beyond that limit were governed by the same rule.

In a companion case, *United States* v. *Texas,*...the Court again reaffirmed the holding and rationale of *United States* v. *California* and again rejected the claims of the State based on her historic boundaries at the time of the State's admission to the Union:

> "If the property, whatever it may be, lies seaward of low-water mark, its use, disposition, management, and control involve national interests and national responsibilities. That is the source of national rights in it. Such is the rationale of the *California* decision which we have applied to Louisiana's case. The same result must be reached here if 'equal footing' with the various States is to be achieved....

The Special Master was correct in concluding that these cases, unless they are to be overruled, completely dispose of the States' claims of ownership here. These decisions considered and expressly rejected the assertion that the original States were entitled to the seabed under the three-mile marginal sea. They also held that under our constitutional arrangement paramount rights to the lands underlying the marginal sea are an incident to national sovereignty and that their control and disposition in the first instance are the business of the Federal Government rather than the States.... Whatever interest the States might have had immediately prior to statehood, the Special Master was correct in reading the Court's cases to hold that as a matter of "purely legal principle...the Constitution...allotted to the federal Government jurisdiction over foreign commerce, foreign affairs and national defense" and that "it necessarily follows, as a matter constitutional law, that as attributes of these external sovereign powers of the federal government has paramount rights in the marginal sea."....

United States v. *Texas* unmistakably declares this constitutional proposition. There, Texas claimed that prior to joining the Union, she was an independent sovereign with boundaries extending a substantial distance in the Gulf of Mexico—boundaries which Congress had allegedly recognized when Texas was admitted to the Union. In deciding against the State, the Court did not reject the prestatehood rights of Texas as it had the rights of the 13 original States in the *California* case. On the contrary, the Court was quite willing to "assume that as a republic she had not only full sovereignty over the marginal sea but ownership of it, of the land underlying it and of all the riches which it held.... Such prior ownership nevertheless did not survive becoming a member of the Union:

"When Texas came into the Union, she ceased to be an independent nation. She then became a sister State on an 'equal footing' with all the other States. That act concededly entailed a relinquishment of some of her sovereignty. The United States then took her place as respects foreign commerce, the waging of war, the making of treaties, defense of the shores, and the like. In external affairs the United States became the sole and exclusive spokesman of the Nation. We hold that as an incident to the transfer of that sovereignty any claim that Texas may have had to the marginal sea was relinquished to the United States"....

Assuming the possibility, however, that the Court might re-examine the constitutional premise of *California* and similar cases, the Special Master proceeded, with admirable diligence and lucidity, to address the historical evidence presented by the States aimed primarily at establishing that the Colonies had legitimate claims to the marginal sea prior to independence and statehood and that the new States never surrendered these rights to the Federal Government. The Special Master's ultimate conclusion was that the Court's view of our history expressed in the *California* case was essentially correct and that if prior cases were open to re-examination, they should be reaffirmed in all respects.

We need not retrace the Special Master's analysis of historical evidence, for we are firmly convinced that we should not undertake to re-examine the constitutional underpinnings of the *California* case and of those cases which followed and explicated the rule that paramount rights to the offshore seabed inhere in the Federal Government as an incident of national sovereignty. That premise, as we have indicated, has been repeated time and again in the cases. It is also our view, contrary to the contentions of the States, that the premise was embraced rather than repudiated by Congress in the Submerged Lands Act of 1953. In that legislation, it is true, Congress transferred to the States the rights to the seabed underlying the marginal sea; but this transfer was in no wise inconsistent with paramount national power but was merely an exercise of that authority. As the Special Master said, the Court in its prior cases "did not indicate that the federal government by Act of Congress might not, as it did by the subsequently enacted Submerged Lands Act, grant to the riparian states rights to the resources of the federal area, subject to the reservation by the federal government of its rights and powers of regulation and control for purposes of commerce, navigation, national defense, and international affairs."... The question before the Court in the *California* case was "whether the state or the Federal Government has the paramount right and power to determine in the first instance when, how, and by what agencies, foreign or domestic, the oil and other resources of the soil of the marginal sea, known or hereafter discovered, may be exploited."... The decision there was that the National Government had the power at issue, the Court declining to speculate that "Congress, which has constitutional control over Government property, will execute its power in such a way as to bring about injustices to states, their subdivisions, or persons acting pursuant to their permission."...

The Submerged Lands Act did indeed grant to the States dominion over the offshore seabed within the limits defined in the Act and released the States from any liability to account for any prior income received from state leases that had been granted with respect to the marginal sea. But in further exercise of paramount national authority, the Act expressly declared that nothing in the Act.

> "shall be deemed to affect in any wise the rights of the United States to the natural resources of that portion of the subsoil and seabed of the Continental Shelf lying seaward and outside of [the marginal sea] all of which natural resources appertain to the United States, and the jurisdiction and control of which by the United States is confirmed."...

This declaration by Congress is squarely at odds with the assertions of the States in the present case. So too is the provision of the Act by which the grant to the States is expressly limited to the seabed within three miles (or three marine leagues in some cases) of the coastline, whether or not the States' historic boundaries might extend farther　into the ocean.... Moreover, in the course of litigation dealing with the reach and impact of the Act, the Court has said as plainly as may be that "the Act concededly did not impair the validity of the *California, Louisiana* and *Texas* cases, which are admittedly applicable to all coastal States...."... We agree with the Special Master when he said that "[i]t is quite obvious that Congress could reserve to the federal government all the rights to the seabed of the continental shelf beyond the three-mile territorial belt of sea (or three leagues in the case of certain Gulf States) only upon the basis that it already had the paramount right to that seabed under the rule laid down in the *California* case."...

Congress emphatically implemented its view that the United States has paramount rights to the seabed beyond the three-mile limit when a few months later it enacted the Outer Continental Shelf Lands Act of 1953.... Section 3 of the Act

> "declared [it] to be the policy of the United States that the subsoil and seabed of the Outer Continental Shelf appertain to the United States and are subject to its jurisdiction, control, and power of disposition as provided in this subchapter."

The Act then proceeds to set out detailed provisions for the exercise of exclusive jurisdiction in the area and for the leasing and development of the resources of the seabed.

Of course, the defendant States were not parties to *United States* v. *California* or to the relevant decisions and they are not precluded by *res adjudicata* from litigating the issues decided by those cases. But the doctrine of *stare decisis* is still a powerful force in our jurisprudence; and although on occasion the Court has declared—and acted accordingly—that constitutional decisions are open to re-examination, we are convinced that the doctrine has peculiar force and relevance in the present context. It is apparent that in the almost 30 years since *California,* a great deal of public and private business has been transacted in accordance with those decisions and in accordance with major legislation enacted by Congress, a principal purpose of which was to resolve the "interminable litigation" arising over the controversy of the ownership of the lands underlying the marginal sea.... Both the submerged Lands Act and the Outer Continental Shelf Lands Act which soon followed proceeded from the premises established by prior Court decisions and provided for the orderly development of offshore resources. Since 1953, when this legislation was enacted, 33 lease sales have been held, in which 1940 leases, embracing over eight million acres, have been issued. The Outer Continental Shelf, since 1953, has yielded over three billion barrels of oil, 19 trillion m.c.f. of natural gas, 13 million long tons of sulfur, and over four million long tons of salt. In 1973 alone, 1,081,000 barrels of oil and 8.9 billion cubic feet of natural gas were extracted daily from the Outer Continental Shelf. Exploitation of our resources offshore implicates a broad range of federal legislation, ranging from the Longshoremen's and Harbor Workers' Compensation Act, incorporated into the Outer Continental Shelf Lands Act, to the more recent Coastal Zone Management Act. We are quite sure that it would be inappropriate to disturb our prior cases, major legislation, and many years of commercial activity by calling into question, at this date, the constitutional premise of prior decisions. We add only that the Atlantic States, by virtue of the *California, Louisiana,* and *Texas* cases, as well as by reason of the Submerged Lands Act, have been on notice of the substantial body of authoritative law, both constitutional and statutory, which is squarely at odds with their claims to the seabed beyond the three-mile marginal sea. Neither the States nor their putative lessees have been in the slightest misled. Judgment shall be entered for the United States.

So ordered.

SOCIAL SECURITY FOR WIDOWERS
March 19, 1975

In its strongest ruling against sex discrimination to date, the Supreme Court March 19 held unconstitutional a 1939 Social Security regulation providing survivors' benefits to widows with children but denying those benefits to widowers. The Court ruled unanimously that by taxing women workers at the same rate as men—but paying their surviving husbands, left with small children, less than widows in similar circumstances receive—the Social Security system was guilty of sex discrimination.

Although the most direct beneficiaries were men, the decision was a major victory for the women's rights movement. It was one of several sex-discrimination decisions handed down in the 1974-75 term in which the Court held that "gender-based distinction" was permissible only if non-discriminatory in its consequences (see p. 55). "If that distinction prevails in pending cases, very few such [sex-based] distinctions are likely to survive," commented The New York Times.

As late as 1971 the Advisory Council on Social Security had rejected support for surviving widowers with dependent children. In the Council's judgment it was "unnecessary to offer the same choice [whether to work or stay home with dependent children] to a man...[because] the customary and predominant role of the father is not that of a homemaker but rather that of the family breadwinner."

The plaintiff, Stephen C. Wiesenfeld, left with an infant son on the death of his wife, challenged this assumption when he found available household help unsatisfactory. Paula Wiesenfeld, a teacher, had been the couple's primary source of support before her death.

Speaking for the court, Justice William J. Brennan Jr. said that "the notion that men are more likely than women to be the primary supporters" of their families is "a gender-based generalization [which] cannot suffice to justify the denigration of the efforts of women who do work." Like armed forces regulations struck down by the Court earlier in the case of Frontiero *v.* Richardson (1973), *these provisions, Brennan wrote, deprived women "of protection for their families which men receive as a result of their employment" and violated the constitutional guarantee of due process.*

The purpose of the payment was to enable women to choose not to work but to stay home and care for young children, Brennan asserted. "Since this purpose in no way is premised upon any special disadvantages of women, it cannot serve to justify a gender-based distinction which diminishes the protection afforded to women who do work," he stated. Any gender-based distinction in providing for children to have the care of the surviving parent is irrational, he continued: "It is no less important for a child to be cared for by its sole surviving parent when that parent is male rather than female."

The ruling, which could cost an estimated $20-million in expanded Social Security benefits, applied to all widowers with dependent children. But since the individual benefit was small—under $3,000 per year—and there were stringent limitations on supplemental income, not many men were expected to claim the benefit. The Court did not rule on whether Wiesenfeld or other widowers in similar circumstances should receive retroactive benefits.

In a concurring opinion Justice Lewis F. Powell Jr. and Chief Justice Warren E. Burger took a narrower view of the "impermissible discrimination" in question, stating that the statute was designed "for the protection of the family." Therefore benefits could not be denied to a surviving parent—regardless of whether that parent chose to stay at home or work. Justice William H. Rehnquist also concurred but observed in a separate opinion that it was unnecessary to rule on the constitutionality of the statute in question.

> *Excerpts from the Supreme Court's March 19, 1975, decision on Social Security benefits for widowers with dependent children:*

No. 73-1892

Caspar W. Weinberger,
  Secretary of Health,
  Education, and Welfare   On Appeal from the United
      Appellant,   States District Court for
        v.   the District of New
Stephen Charles Wiesenfeld,   Jersey.
        Etc.

[March 19, 1975]

MR. JUSTICE BRENNAN delivered the opinion of the Court. [JUSTICE DOUGLAS took no part in the consideration of the case.]

Social Security Act benefits based on the earnings of a deceased husband and father covered by the Act are payable, with some limitations, both to the widow and to the couple's minor children in her care. 42 U.S.C. §402 (g). Such benefits are payable on the basis of the earnings of a deceased wife and mother covered by the Act, however, only to the minor children and not to the widower. The question in this case is whether this gender-based distinction violates the Due Process Clause of the Fifth Amendment.

A three-judge District Court for the District of New Jersey held that the different treatment of men and women mandated by §402 (g) unjustifiably discriminated against women wage-earners by affording them less protection for their survivors than is provided to male employees.... We noted probable jurisdiction.... We affirm.

I

Stephen C. Wiesenfeld and Paula Polatschek were married on November 5, 1970. Paula, who worked as a teacher for five years before her marriage, continued teaching after her marriage. Each year she worked maximum social security contributions were deducted from her salary. Paula's earnings were the couple's principal source of support during the marriage, being substantially larger than those of appellee.

On June 5, 1972, Paula died in childbirth. Appellee was left with the sole responsibility for the care of their infant son, Jason Paul. Shortly after his wife's death, Stephen Wiesenfeld applied at the Social Security office in New Brunswick, New Jersey, for social security survivors' benefits for himself and his son. He did obtain benefits for his son...and received for Jason $206.90 per month until September 1972, and $248.30 per month thereafter. However, appellee was told that he was not eligible for benefits for himself, because §402 (g) benefits were available only to women. If he had been a woman, he would have received the same amount as his son as long as he was not working, ...and, if working, that amount reduced by $1.00 for every $2.00 earned annually above $2,400....

Appellee filed this suit in February, 1973...on behalf of himself and of all widowers similarly situated. He sought a declaration that §402 (g) is unconstitutional to the extent that men and women are treated differently, an injunction restraining appellant from denying benefits under 42 U.S.C. §402 (g) solely on the basis of sex, and payment of past benefits commencing with June, 1972, the month of the original application. Cross motions for summary judgment were filed. After the three-judge court determined that it had jurisdiction, it granted summary judgment in favor of appellee, and issued an order giving appellee the relief he sought.

II

The gender-based distinction made by §402 (g) is indistinguishable from that invalidated in *Frontiero* v. *Richardson*...(1973). *Frontiero* involved statutes which provided the wife of a male serviceman with dependents' benefits but not the husband of a servicewoman unless she proved that she supplied more than one-half of her husband's support. The Court held that the statutory scheme violated the right to equal protection secured by the Fifth Amendment. *Schlesinger* v. *Ballard*...(1975), explained: "In...*Frontiero* the challenged [classification] based on sex [was] premised on overbroad generalizations that could not be tolerated under the Constitution.... [T]he assumption...was that female spouses of servicemen would normally be dependent upon their husbands, while male spouses of servicewomen would not." ...A virtually identical "archaic and overbroad" generalization, *id.*, at—, "not...tolerated under the Constitution" underlies the distinction drawn by §402 (g), namely, that male workers' earnings are vital to the support of their families, while the earnings of female wage-earners do not significantly contribute to their families' support.

Section 402 (g) was added to the Social Security Act in 1939 as one of a large number of amendments designed to "afford more adequate protection to the family as a unit." ...Monthly benefits were provided to wives, children, widows, orphans, and surviving dependent parents of covered workers.... However, children of covered women workers were eligible for survivors' benefits only in limited circumstances...and no benefits whatever were made available to husbands or widowers on the basis of their wives' covered employment.

Underlying the 1939 scheme was the principle that "under a social-insurance plan, the primary purpose is to pay benefits in accordance with the *probable needs* of beneficiaries rather than to make payments to the estate of a deceased person regardless of whether or not he leaves dependents." ...(Emphasis supplied.) It was felt that "[t]he payment of these survivorship benefits and supplements for the wife of an annuitant are...in keeping with the principle of social insurance...." ...Thus, the framers of the Act legislated on the "then generally accepted presumption that a man is responsible for the support of his wife and child."....

Obviously, the notion that men are more likely than women to be the primary supporters of their spouses and children is not entirely without empirical support.... But such a gender-based generalization cannot suffice to justify the denigration of the efforts of women who do work and whose earnings contribute significantly to their families' support.

Section 402 (g) clearly operates, as did the statutes invalidated by our judgment in *Frontiero*, to deprive women of protection for their families which men receive as a result of their employment. Indeed, the classification here is in some ways more pernicious. First, it was open to the servicewoman under the statutes invalidated in *Frontiero* to prove that her husband was in fact dependent upon her. Here, Stephen Wiesenfeld was not given the opportunity to show, as may well have been the case, that he was dependent upon his wife for his support, or that, had his wife lived, she would have remained at work while he took over care of the child. Second, in this case social security taxes were deducted from Paula's salary during the years in which she worked. Thus, she not only failed to receive for her family the same protection which a similarly situated male worker would have received, but she also was deprived of a portion of her own earnings in order to contribute to the fund out of which benefits would be paid to others. Since the Constitution forbids the gender-based differentiation premised upon assumptions as to dependency made in the statutes before us in *Frontiero*, the Constitution also forbids the gender-based differentiation that results in the efforts of women workers required to pay social security taxes producing less protection for their families than is produced by the efforts of men.

III

The Government seeks to avoid this conclusion with two related arguments. First, it claims that because social security benefits are not compensation for work done, Congress is not obliged to provide a covered female employee with the same benefits as it provides to a male. Second, it contends that §402 (g) was "reasonably designed to offset the adverse economic situation of women by providing a widow with financial assistance to supplement or substitute for her own efforts in the marketplace," ...and therefore does not contravene the equal protection guarantee.

A

Appellant relies for the first proposition primarily on *Flemming* v. *Nestor*...(1960). We held in *Flemming* that the interest of a covered employee in future social security benefits is "noncontractual," because "each worker's benefits, though flowing from the contributions he made to the national economy while actively employed, are not dependent upon the degree to which he was called upon to support the system by taxation." ...The Government apparently contends that since benefits derived from the social security program do not correlate necessarily with contributions made to the program, a covered employee has no right whatever to be treated equally with other employees as regards the benefits which flow from his or her employment.

We do not see how the fact that social security benefits are "noncontractual" can sanction differential protection for covered employees which is solely gender-based. From the outset, social security old age, disability, and survivors' (OASDI) benefits have been "afforded as a matter of right, related to past participation in the productive processes of the country." ...It is true that social security benefits are not necessarily related directly to tax contributions, since the OASDI system is structured to provide benefits in part according to presumed need. For this reason, *Flemming* held that the position of a covered employee "cannot be soundly analogized to that of the holder of an annuity, whose right to benefits is bottomed on contractual payments." ...But the fact remains that the statutory right to benefits *is* directly related to years worked and amount earned by a covered employee, and not to the need of the beneficiaries directly. Since OASDI benefits do depend significantly upon the participation in the work force of a covered employee, and since only covered employees and not others are required to pay taxes toward the system, benefits must be distributed according to classifications which do not without sufficient justification differentiate among covered employees solely on the basis of sex.

B

The Government seeks to characterize the classification here as one reasonably designed to compensate women beneficiaries as a group for the economic difficulties which still confront women who seek to support themselves and their families. The Court held in *Kahn* v. *Shevin, supra,* ...that a statute "reasonably designed to further a state policy of cushioning the financial impact of spousal loss upon that sex for which that loss imposes a disproportionately heavy burden" can survive an equal protection attack. See also *Schlesinger* v. *Ballard, supra.* But the mere recitation of a benign, compensatory purpose is not an automatic shield which protects against any inquiry into the actual purposes underlying a statutory scheme. Here, it is apparent both from the statutory scheme itself and from the legislative history of §402 (g) that Congress' purpose in providing benefits to young widows with children was not to provide an income to women who were, because of economic discrimination, unable to provide for themselves. Rather, §402 (g), linked as it is directly to responsibility for minor children, was intended to permit women to elect not to work and to devote themselves to the care of children. Since this purpose in no way is premised upon any special disadvantages of women, it cannot serve to justify a gender-based distinction which diminishes the protection afforded to women who do work.

That the purpose behind §402 (g) is to provide children deprived of one parent with the opportunity for the personal attention of the other could not be more clear in the legislative history. The Advisory Council on Social Security, which developed the 1939 amendments, said explicitly that "[s]uch benefits [§402 (g)] are intended as supplements to the orphans' benefits *with the purpose of enabling the widow to remain at home and care for the children."* ...(Emphasis supplied.) In 1971, a new Advisory Council, considering amendments to eliminate the various gender-based distinctions in the OASDI structure, reiterated this understanding: "Present law provides benefits for the mother of young...children...if she chooses to stay home and care for the children instead of working. In the Council's judgment, it is desirable to allow a woman who is left with the children the *choice* of whether to stay at home to care for the children or to work." ...(Emphasis supplied.)

Indeed, consideration was given in 1939 to extending benefits to all widows regardless of whether or not there were children. The proposal was rejected, apparently because it was felt that young widows without children can be expected to work, while middle-aged widows "are likely to have more savings than young widows, and many of them have children who are grown and able to help them." ...Thus, Congress decided *not* to provide benefits to all widows even though it was recognized that some of them would have serious problems in the job market. Instead, it provided benefits only to those women who had responsibility for minor children, because it believed that they should not be required to work.

The whole structure of survivors' benefits conforms to this articulated purpose. Widows without children obtain no benefits on the basis of their husband's earnings until they reach age 60 or in certain instances of disability, age 50.... Further, benefits under §402 (g) cease when all children of a beneficiary are no longer eligible for children's benefits. If Congress were concerned with providing women with benefits because of economic discrimination, it would be entirely irrational to except those women who had spent many years at home rearing children, since those women are most likely to be without the skills required to succeed in the job market.... Similarly, the Act now provides benefits to a surviving divorced wife who is the parent of a covered employee's child, regardless of how long she was married to the deceased or of whether she or the child was dependent upon the employee for support.... Yet, a divorced wife who is not the mother of a child entitled to children's benefits is eligible for benefits only if she meets other eligibility requirements *and* was married to the covered employee for 20 years.... Once again, this distinction among women is explicable only because Congress was not concerned in §402 (g) with the employment problems of women generally but with the principle that children of covered employees are entitled to the personal attention of the surviving parent if that parent chooses not to work.

Given the purpose of enabling the surviving parent to remain at home to care for a child, the gender-based distinction of §402 (g) is entirely irrational. The classification discriminates among surviving children solely on the basis of the sex of the surviving parent. Even in the typical family hypothesized by the Act, in which the husband is supporting the family and the mother is caring for the children, this result makes no sense. The fact that a man is working while there is a wife at home does not mean that he would, or should be required to, continue to work if his wife dies. It is no less important for a child to be cared for by its sole surviving parent when that parent is male rather than female. And a father, no less than a mother, has a constitutionally protected right to the "companionship, care, custody, and management" of "the children he has sired and raised, [which] undeniably warrants deference and, absent a powerful countervailing interest, protection." *Stanley* v. *Illinois,...* (1972). Further, to the extent that women who work when they have sole responsibility for children encounter special problems, it would seem that men with sole responsibility for children will encounter the same child-care related problems. Stephen Wiesenfeld, for example, found that providing adequate care for his infant son impeded his ability to work....

Finally, to the extent that Congress legislated on the presumption that women as a group would choose to forego work to care for children while men would not, the statutory structure, independent of the gender-based classification, would deny or reduce benefits to those men who conform to the presumed norm and are not hampered by their child-care responsibilities. Benefits under §402 (g) decrease with increased earnings.... According to the Government, "the bulk of male workers would receive no benefits in any event," Brief for Appellant, at 17, because they earn too much. Thus, the gender-based distinction is gratuitous; without it, the statutory scheme would only provide benefits to those men who are in fact similarly situated to the women the statute aids.

Since the gender-based classification of §402 (g) cannot be explained as an attempt to provide for the special problems of women, it is indistinguishable from the classification held invalid in *Frontiero*. Like the statutes there, "[b]y providing dissimilar treatment for men and women who are...similarly situated, the challenged section violates the [Due Process] Clause." *Reed* v. *Reed*...(1971).

Affirmed.

MR. JUSTICE POWELL, with whom THE CHIEF JUSTICE joins, concurring.

I concur in the judgment and generally in the opinion of the Court. But I would identify the impermissible discrimination effected by §402 (g) somewhat more narrowly than the Court does. Social Security is designed, certainly in this context, for the protection of the *family*. Although it lacks the contractual attributes of insurance or an annuity, *Flemming* v. *Nestor*...(1960), it is a contributory system and millions of wage earners depend on it to provide basic protection for their families in the event of death or disability.

Many women are the principal wage earners for their families, and they participate in the Social Security system on exactly the same basis as men. When the mother is a principal wage earner, the family may suffer as great an economic deprivation upon her death as would occur upon the death of a father wage earner. It is immaterial whether the surviving parent elects to assume primary child care responsibility rather than work, or whether other arrangements are made for child care. The statutory scheme provides benefits both to a surviving mother who remains at home and to one who works at low wages. A surviving father may have the same need for benefits as a surviving mother. [Footnote: I attach less significance to the view emphasized by the Court that a purpose of the statute is to enable the surviving parent to remain at home to care for a child. In light of the long experience to the contrary, one may doubt that fathers generally will forgo work and remain at home to care for children to the same extent that mothers may make this choice. Under the current statutory program, however, the payment of benefits is not conditioned on the surviving parent's decision to remain at home.] The statutory scheme therefore impermissibly discriminates against a female wage earner because it provides her family less protection than it provides that of a male wage earner, even though the family needs may be identical. I find no legitimate governmental interest that supports this gender classification.

MR. JUSTICE REHNQUIST, concurring in the result.

Part III B of the Court's opinion contains a thorough examination of the legislative history and statutory context which define the role and purpose of §402 (g). I believe the Court's examination convincingly demonstrates that the only purpose of §402 (g) is to make it possible for children of deceased contributing workers to have the personal care and attention of a surviving parent, should that parent desire to remain in the home with the child. Moreover, the Court's opinion establishes that the Government's preferred legislative purpose is so totally at odds with the context and history of §402 (g) that it cannot serve as a basis for judging whether the statutory distinction between men and women rationally serves a valid legislative objective.

This being the case, I see no necessity for reaching the issue of whether the statute's purported discrimination against female workers violates the Fifth Amendment as applied in *Frontiero* v. *Richardson...*(1973). I would simply conclude, as does the Court in its Part III B, that the restriction of §402 (g) benefits to surviving mothers does not rationally serve any valid legislative purpose, including that for which §402 (g) was obviously designed. This is so because it is irrational to distinguish between mothers and fathers when the sole question is whether a child of a deceased contributing worker should have the opportunity to receive the full-time attention of the only parent remaining to it. To my mind, that should be the end of the matter. I therefore concur in the result.

FOREIGN ECONOMIC POLICY REPORT
March 20, 1975

President Ford sent to Congress March 20 the third annual report of the
Council on International Economic Policy. In a message accompanying the
council's report, Ford stressed the need for the nations of the world to work
together to achieve an open world economy. "Improved living standards
and a more peaceful world are the rewards of an open world economy based
on international cooperation," he said. "Such rewards are too great to allow
short-sighted distractions to alter our course." He cautioned against
economic nationalism as a response to the problems of inflation, recession
and the energy and food shortages. Such a trend, he said, would frustrate
the goal of an open economy.

The council's report outlined economic trends in 1974 and discussed the
major economic problems that emerged during the year. The report cited
energy costs as the major disruptive force in the world economy. "On the
global scale," the report said, "OPEC's [Organization of Petroleum Exporting Countries] fourfold oil price increase in late 1973 and subsequent
rises in prices are having a more pervasive and far-reaching impact on the
international economic system than any single event since World War II."
But the council forecast development of alternative energy sources: "For
the next few years, oil importing countries undoubtedly will suffer both
economically and financially in the face of sustained high oil prices. In the
long run, however, structural changes wrought by current crude [oil] prices
will work to the disadvantage of the OPEC."

The report also explored the reasons behind various economic trends.
Included were analyses of inflation, the on-going recession, the world-wide
food shortage and the long-range availability of raw materials. Also in-

cluded was a discussion of the possibility that producer groups other than OPEC would seek to raise prices of commodities artificially. Listing the necessary prerequisites for such action, the council reiterated its doubt that producers of other raw materials could intervene in the market to drive up the cost of their materials. (For council's earlier reports, see Historic Documents 1973, p. 379, and Historic Documents of 1974, p. 113.)

> *Following are the text of President Ford's International Economic Report, sent to Congress March 20, and excerpts from the third annual report of the Council on International Economic Policy that accompanied the President's message:*

THE INTERNATIONAL ECONOMIC REPORT OF THE PRESIDENT

To the Congress of the United States:

America must adjust to turbulent global economic events. The world has moved from a period of slow economic growth in 1971 through a two-year expansionary boom to a sudden and pervasive recession. Recent events have caused the United States, as well as other countries, to reappraise international economic policies.

This, the third annual International Economic Report, describes the very difficult situation confronting us. It also reflects the progress made toward achieving our goal of an open world economy to serve the interdependent needs of all countries.

In 1974, most of the world's economies were beset by problems flowing from the unprecedented combination of recession and inflation. Additional pressures, including precipitous increases in energy costs and disappointing food harvests further strained the world economy, particularly in the areas of trade and monetary flows and adjustments. Moreover, these factors contributed to the trend towards increasing economic nationalism which could frustrate our desire for an open world economy.

In recent years, many governments have elected more direct involvement in economic activities, notably through restrictive supply and pricing practices and, sometimes, by the expropriation of foreign investment. When governments manipulate international markets to maximize short-term benefits, they often do so at the expense of others and, ultimately, of themselves. Improved living standards and a more peaceful world are the rewards of an open world economy based on international cooperation. Such rewards are too great to allow shortsighted distractions to alter our course.

Building effective economic institutions and policies in today's economic environment is more difficult, but also more necessary, than ever. Unless we act constructively, energy and food problems, growing economic nationalism, the possibility of increased protection for trade, and the prospects of world recession and unemployment will jeopardize the world cooperation developed after World War II.

The United States does not and cannot govern the world economy. But it should fulfill its responsibility as an economic leader among nations. The Administration recognizes this responsibility. We have taken steps to turn the difficult food, energy, trade and investment issues into positive opportunities for achieving cooperation with trading partners and coordination between the Nation's domestic and international economic policies. Specifically, the Trade Act of 1974—which exemplified constructive cooperation between the Executive and Legislative Branches—reflects the U.S. commitment to an open and equitable world trading system.

The World Food Conference, proposed by the United States, set in motion international activities to improve world food reserves, agricultural assistance, crop information systems and increased food production. At the time I signed the Foreign Investment Study Act of 1974 which authorized the collection and analysis of data on foreign investment in the United States, I reaffirmed American support for the operation of free market forces to direct worldwide investment flows in the most productive way. Therefore, we will oppose any new restriction on foreign investment in the United States except where absolutely necessary on national security grounds or to protect an essential national interest.

The goal of normalization of economic relations with the Communist countries has been reaffirmed. America also has continued its commitment to help the less developed countries. Moreover, we have proposed that an International Monetary Fund trust be established to provide special assistance to the least developed countries. We will shortly implement a generalized system of preferences in trading with less developed countries. We are also continuing our cooperative efforts to achieve equitable treatment for U.S. investment abroad.

Recently, I sent to the Congress a comprehensive energy and economic program. It is designed to reduce our dependence on imported oil. The plan provides incentives to increase domestic energy production and conserve energy use. The United States is meanwhile developing joint policies with other major oil-consuming countries aiming at increased resource development and more efficient use of energy. The major consuming countries must act jointly to build a constructive relationship with the oil producing nations. Such actions are essential to restore the international confidence in adequate and reliable energy sources.

These interrelated economic activities are aimed at achieving an improved international economic system. They are part of a balanced policy. They also accentuate the positive initiatives being taken to cope with the specialized problems of food, assistance to less developed countries and East-West economic relations.

The United States firmly believes that our own problems, and those of the rest of the world, can be dealt with most effectively through international cooperation. We lead in the pursuit of peace. Therefore, our motivating principles, our standards of conduct and the guidelines we set for the conduct of international economic development are ever more crucial to our national well being, and that of the world.

The White House,
March 1975   (Signed) GERALD R. FORD

Following are excerpts from the report of the Council on International Economic Policy, March 20, 1975:

I. PROGRESS TOWARD ACHIEVING THE NATION'S INTERNATIONAL ECONOMIC GOALS

INTRODUCTION

Nineteen seventy-four may prove to have been one of the most crucial years in the development of the U.S. economy. Fast-moving and far-reaching changes tested the Nation's capability to maintain progress consistent with its long-term economic goals and to deal effectively with relatively short-term situations impacting the global and domestic economies.

Most industrialized nations faced serious problems of skyrocketing energy costs and steadily rising food prices. These problems, coupled with general inflation and recession, posed threats to employment, income, and economic stability for many countries, more severe than any encountered in the postwar period of general world prosperity. While these problems could have jeopardized international economic relations, they in fact acted as a catalyst for the formation of many new international cooperative structures, such as the World Food Conference and the International Energy Agency.... In response to the enormous increase in the price of imported oil, the United States has asked all oil-importing nations to reevaluate their domestic and international energy policies. In the United States, the complex situation of an unacceptably high inflation rate coupled with a recession has been met by an energy and tax program designed to deal with many aspects of a currently imbalanced economy....

INTERNATIONAL ECONOMIC SITUATION—1974

Overview: From Boom to Recession

In the past three years, the world's economies have moved between extreme economic conditions and have been subjected to fundamental shocks. In this short period they have gone through a complete economic cycle—from a period of slow economic growth, through an expansionary boom, to a sudden and major recession....

Recession

At the start of 1974, weakening demand in certain sectors, shortages in some key commodities, continued market dislocations, an energy shortage, and sharply higher prices for energy and agricultural products, did not portend well for the year. In fact, by midyear the major industrial countries were sliding into what has since become the most widespread recession since World War II. Contrary to general expectations, the slowdown was accompanied by a persistent inflation.

By August 1974, the combined developed countries' monthly output fell slightly below the year-earlier level, and by December it was declining at an estimated annual rate of 7 percent. The United States, West Germany, and Japan—the three largest trading economies—registered declines in that month of 6.5, 7, and 13 percent respectively below previous year's levels. For the entire year, real economic activity stagnated in the developed countries. The United States, the United Kingdom, and Japan experienced actual declines and West Germany remained at its 1973 level. Although France and Italy showed real growth rates of 4 percent for the entire year, both were experiencing negative growth rates by year's end.

The decline in 1974 was due to a number of distinct but related factors. The intensity of the previous boom was a major contributor as higher prices, shortages, high interest rates, and market dislocations set the stage for a precipitous decline. Added to these were restrictive monetary and fiscal policies aimed at controlling inflation and the impact of the oil crisis. By mid-1974, as soft spots were perceived, business and consumer confidence began to erode, leading to a decline in consumption outlays. As inventories mounted, output was reduced. The strength of the capital goods market, which had been masking soft spots in some industrial countries, finally succumbed in the third quarter to these adverse pressures and investment plans were curtailed.

The industrial capacity utilization rates declined rapidly thereafter and by year-end excess capacity in most industrial countries was near or above the highest levels reached in the previous 20 years....

The result was a cutback in industrial expansion programs and a fall off in new orders for machinery and equipment. This decline accelerated and spread in the fourth quarter....

Unemployment rates in most developed countries did not increase appreciably until the last half of 1974....

The decline in real earnings aggravated the adverse impact of increased unemployment on spending. Rising consumer prices and shorter work hours, for the most part, completely offset record wage settlements. Real incomes fell in the United States and the United Kingdom and rose only slightly in Canada, France, Italy, and Japan.

Foreign trade, bolstered by efforts to secure scarce commodities together with large deliveries of investment goods ordered earlier, sustained economic activity in both developed and less developed countries through the first half of 1974.... World trade volume increased more than 9.5 percent on an annual basis during the first half of 1974, compared to a 7.9 percent average annual rise from 1961-72. Growth then slowed markedly in the second half as demand in non-OPEC countries slipped. Although Organization of Petroleum Exporting Countries (OPEC) imports continued to climb rapidly, the dollar volume of this trade is not large enough to have a major impact on world trade trends. By the end of 1974, trade in volume terms had increased by only 6 percent from the previous year's level....

Inflation

Prices, which had begun accelerating in mid-1972, gained momentum in 1973, and continued to rise rapidly through 1974.... By the end of 1974, consumer prices in industrial countries on average were 25 percent above mid-1972 levels, marking the steepest and most sustained price spiral in postwar history....

The impetus to inflation over this two and one-half year period came from a number of extraordinary and largely unrelated events in different parts of the world at different times. These included national decisions to stimulate demand, lagging investment for new capacity, adverse weather conditions which reduced agricultural output, and the decision by the OPEC nations to raise prices on crude oil.

Governments of most industrial countries simultaneously adopted expansionist policies in 1972. The resulting surge in demand strained production capacity, especially in basic industries, causing shortages and delivery delays.

Available capacity was unable to meet these demands for a number of reasons. Growing excess capacity in the late 1960's led to a sluggish growth in investments in the early 1970's, so that spending for plant and equipment rose only 3.8 percent annually in 1970-72, a rate roughly half the long-term rate. Although investment generally recovered in 1973, growth in plant capacity continued below normal. This is explained partly by the long lead times needed to complete investment projects, the growing share of investment going into equipment to control pollution, the high costs of investments, and the limited supply and high cost of investment funds.

Since capacity shortages were worldwide, especially in the basic and raw materials industries, imports provided little relief and, in fact, aggressive bidding characterized many international markets. This resulted in inventory drawdowns and left commodity markets tight even before the oil crisis hit in late 1973. Commodity prices surged an average of 50 percent through the first half of 1974, primarily because of heavy speculative buying to hedge against future shortages and price increases. This dramatic price rise occurred even though final demand was beginning to level off or decline. By mid-1974, when speculation eased, raw material prices generally turned down.

Although apparent demand for foodstuffs increased in 1974, the major reason for higher prices throughout much of the year was that harvests were not up to expectations. Given estimates of significantly more planted acreage for most agricultural products, it was believed that the food shortages prevalent during 1973 would be overcome in 1974. These expectations of record crops were not realized as poor weather sharply cut into expected yields throughout the world. Thus, with grain inventories already low, prices for most agricultural products continued to rise and not until late in 1974 did the composite price index for agricultural commodities fall.

By far the most significant single factor affecting inflation in 1974 was the OPEC price increases on crude oil.... Since October 1973, the fourfold increase in the price of crude oil approximately tripled the delivered cost of imported crude oil. Japan and Italy were particularly hard hit because oil imports supply the overwhelming share of their energy requirements. In all countries the surging demand for alternative energy sources caused a sympathetic rise in the price of other fuels.

Most of the oil-induced inflation occurred during the first half of 1974. For example, it has been estimated that nearly half the wholesale price rise in West Germany in the first half of 1974 was due to higher oil prices. In the United States they accounted for 20 percent, in Japan 40 percent, and in the United Kingdom 25 percent.

Balance of Payments

The large OPEC price jump meant that oil importing countries in 1974 had to pay $75 billion more for the oil they bought. Less than 10 percent of these higher costs were financed by higher exports to OPEC. The remainder was financed through borrowing on international markets, from international institutions, or from the oil exporting countries. The impact on each importing country varied widely. Although the developed countries imported about 85 percent of the higher priced oil, the poorest of the less developed ones were more seriously affected because of their more limited ability to sell goods to OPEC and their difficulties in obtaining needed financing....

EXTRAORDINARY INTERNATIONAL
ECONOMIC PROBLEMS—1974
ENERGY

Until 1973, most industrial nations assumed that inexpensive and apparently limitless foreign oil would continue to satisfy ever-growing world demand for energy. Environmental policies, especially in the United States, also spurred the demand for oil as industry moved from the use of coal to oil for electrical production and heating. Adding to oil consumption were more stringent emission controls that reduced automobile and truck efficiencies. During this time, the United States was becoming increasingly dependent on foreign oil as domestic production fell and the search for new oil reserves declined.

At the time of the Arab oil embargo in 1973, imported oil accounted for over one-third of U.S. petroleum consumption, as well as 17 percent of total U.S. energy consumption. ...This dependence was projected at that time to increase still further during the next several decades. This oil policy, combined with the increased relative concentration of oil production in a handful of Middle Eastern states, set the stage for the events of 1973-74.

On the global scale, OPEC's fourfold oil price increase in late 1973 and subsequent rises in prices are having a more pervasive and far-reaching impact on the international economic system than any single event since World War II. ...The price and balance of payments changes wrought by OPEC's actions have been widespread and without recent precedent. Existing inflation in developed countries has been greatly accelerated. Similarly, the cyclical downturn in the world economy, which developed in 1974, has been severely aggravated by the cartel's actions. The enormous impact of these price increases on the value of world trade can be seen in figure 8 [omitted], which shows how crude oil costs dwarf the value of other major-traded basic commodities.

U.S. Policy

The general principles of U.S. energy policy are now in focus. The United States is actively seeking to bring about lower international oil prices and to reduce its dependence on foreign sources of supply. Priority development of domestic energy sources is imperative to meet both these goals. The United States also must move to conserve energy both through "belt-tightening" and through more efficient use of energy. A comprehensive plan to achieve these goals has been set forth by the President. He has called for the United States to develop its energy technology and resources so that it will have the ability to supply a significant share of the energy needs of the free world by the end of this century.

The United States is developing joint energy policies with other consuming countries to counter the effects of any future embargoes, to establish financial solidarity, to effect savings in energy consumption through conservation, and to develop alternate sources of energy. A cooperative consumer program based on these elements provides the necessary underpinning for a mutually beneficial consumer-producer conference.

Changing Conditions

...For the next few years oil importing countries undoubtedly will suffer both economically and financially in the face of sustained high oil prices. In the longer run, however, structural changes wrought by current crude prices will work to the disadvantage of the OPEC. As the United States and other consuming countries move to promote conservation, develop methods of production that use less energy, and develop non-OPEC energy sources, OPEC's market share will decline. In 1974, preliminary efforts by consuming countries have already caused OPEC producers to shut in an estimated 8 million barrels per day of potential production. ...[O]il consumption fell from between 3.2 percent for the United States to 7.5 percent for Japan. Stiffer conservation measures and the current economic downturn could significantly increase OPEC's excess capacity. A continuation of this trend would cause OPEC earnings to fall sharply by the early 1980's, adversely affecting the development prospects of some of these countries.

Large, untapped oil resources off the U.S. shores and in the Arctic, coupled with improved recovery methods from other sources, may place the United States in a favorable position to meet more of its energy requirements. Elsewhere, oil discoveries in the past year alone may have added some 30 billion barrels of oil to proven reserves—an amount approaching current U.S. reserves. These recent finds have a 1980 production potential of six million barrels per day—approximately the current level of U.S. imports or about half of current Western European oil imports....

To assure development of non-OPEC energy sources, fossil-based and others, the International Energy Agency (IEA) member countries are holding preliminary discussions on the desirability of common incentive programs. In his 1975 State of the Union message, the President asked Congress for legislation that would enable the United States to institute such programs.

AGRICULTURE

At the start of 1974 all indications pointed to record production. No major problems were anticipated in the agricultural sector. Widespread adverse weather conditions, however, significantly reduced harvests and contributed to higher food prices....

But 1974 was not simply a year of shortages. Grains and sugar were in tight supply, while beef and cotton were in surplus. Consequently, international cooperation was sought by all nations to deal with agricultural shortages and surpluses. Recognition of this need, especially by nations heavily dependent upon food imports, led to the convening of the World Food Conference (WFC). For many, the Conference was the first tangible step toward increased international cooperation in dealing with the problems of feeding the world's people in years to come.

The U.S. role in these efforts is crucial, since it is the world's largest producer and exporter of agricultural goods. ...Its importance in the international grain and oilseed trade is as great as the Persian Gulf countries in crude oil trade....

Supply Conditions
Adverse weather conditions cut grain production below forecasted levels in South Asia, North America, and the U.S.S.R. World grain production in 1974 was 4.5 per cent under 1973 totals, and 3.5 percent below its long-term average trend. ...Much of this decline resulted from a 13 percent drop in U.S. grain production, the largest one-year setback in 40 years. An extremely wet spring in major growing areas led to late planting. This was followed by the worst summer drought since 1936. Moreover, there were early frosts and freezing in the Midwest....

In marked contrast to these situations, the meat industry experienced record production and sagging demand. The EC [European Communities], Japan and Canada took actions to limit imports of beef and cattle in 1974, leaving the United States as the only major unrestricted import market. This gave rise to concern among U.S. producers that imports would be up sharply. However, low U.S. market prices were a disincentive to imports and U.S. total red meat imports in 1974 were 17 percent below 1973 imports despite the absence of quantitative restrictions.

The current food problems began in 1972 when world agricultural output declined after 20 years of uninterrupted increases. Although production rose again in 1973, it was only enough to compensate for 1972's shortfall and not enough to allow stocks to be rebuilt. Preliminary data for 1974 indicate that total production of all agricultural products failed to increase. Both total and per capita agricultural production for the developed countries declined in 1974. The less developed countries (LDC) saw a rise in total agricultural production but a decline in per capita production.

Significant agricultural shortages on the world market in two of the last three years have raised fundamental questions regarding the stability of the food supply. Long-term climate changes have been cited by some as the reason why this matter should be considered as more than a temporary phenomenon. While the weather during the 1951-71 period appears to have been unusually good by historical standards, there is insufficient evidence available to conclude that fundamental climate changes have occurred or are occurring.

The food supply problems of the past three years have underscored the interdependence of the international economy. Food shortages coincided with and significantly contributed to unacceptably high rates of inflation in most countries. The high commodity prices benefited the world's exporters. But LDC's that did not have high-priced commodities to export were faced with staggering new problems. These will be compounded in the future by the weekly addition of 1.4 million people to the world's population.

The quadrupling of oil prices in the three-month period following the start of the embargo not only was a major contributor to inflationary pressures worldwide, but it had a direct impact on agricultural inputs. Some of these were fuel for tractors and irrigation pumps, raw materials for fertilizer production, and transportation costs....

The U.S. Response

Faced with the serious world supply problems of the past few years, the U.S. response has been to set policies with the intention of increasing production and removing impediments to trade. Increasing emphasis has been placed on incentives to produce for the market. This concept is an integral part of the Agriculture and Consumer Protection Act of 1973 with its system of loans and target prices for major crops.

As part of this response, all production restraints on grains were removed in 1974. As recently as 1972 U.S. farmers were holding out of production, under Government programs, about one out of every five acres that normally would have been cropped. Stimulated by the potential for profitable sales, U.S. farmers in the past two years brought into production 33 million acres of cropland formerly held in reserve. Additional land is expected to be planted for production in 1975.

Other steps taken by the U.S. Government to increase food output and availability included:

- Allocating fuel to agriculture at 100 percent of requirements during the oil embargo.
- Making additional natural gas available to fertilizer plants, whenever shortages were a problem in assuring maximum fertilizer production.
- Making additional rail cars available to transport fertilizer to U.S. farmers.
- Increasing, temporarily, import quotas for dairy products.
- Suspending meat import quotas for 1974.
- Releasing all agricultural commodities in short supply that are held by the U.S. Government.
- Terminating all export payments programs that artificially stimulated farm exports.
- Suspending indefinitely quotas on wheat imports....

The Search for International Cooperative Solutions

The recent food supply problems have intensified the search for greater international cooperation to lessen the impact of periodic supply shortfalls and surpluses and to improve the diets of the millions of poorly fed people in the LDC's. The burden of meeting these goals should be shared equitably among all nations. The United States has sought the needed cooperation in numerous bilateral and multilateral forums. Most notable in 1974 were the cooperation achieved at the U.S.-proposed WFC held in Rome in November 1974, and the discussions with our main foreign grain customers to avoid U.S. short-supply export controls. Also of importance was the passage of the Trade Act of 1974 which will allow negotiations directed at greater trade liberalization....

INDUSTRIAL RAW MATERIALS

Although OPEC's actions on oil prices received the lion's share of attention and caused the most disturbance to world trade in 1974, similarly significant developments were occurring in other raw materials.

From 1972 through the middle of 1974 prices of all basic raw materials rose rapidly. ...This rise was triggered by simultaneous demand increases in all industrialized countries with suppliers unable to expand production quickly because of capacity constraints, plant closures due to environmental requirements, and the decision by some raw material producing countries to take advantage of the excess demand situation and speculative buying by outsiders. Market intervention actions were threatened, heightening concern about the use of raw materials as a political weapon. Consequently, trade policy discussions and actions in 1974 focused on these questions.

Over the last half of the year, as demand slackened, some improvement in supply occurred, and liquidations of speculative holdings took place. The prices of many raw materials topped out or declined from their midyear peaks. During the year, however, careful reassessments were undertaken regarding the long-term supply security of raw materials....

Long-Term Supply

Amidst the sharp price upswings and prevailing scarcity psychology of early 1974, concern was expressed about the longer term adequacy of the world's raw material base.

Estimates of long-term availability and demand for natural resources are hazardous to make. Furthermore they tend to ignore a basic function of the price mechanism in the face of limited supply, which is to restrain demand and encourage the development of additional or alternate sources of supply. Estimates of proved reserves can also be misleading, since they include only those resources that can be profitably exploited at current prices with present technology.... At this time world reserves of most commodities at current prices appear to be sufficient to meet world needs at least through the end of the century....

Market Intervention

The Arab embargo served as a strong temptation to other raw material producers to form similar organizations of their own to raise prices, profits, or revenues. The success of such actions, however, depends on the following conditions:

● The producer, or producer organization, must control a significant portion of the export market, production, and in the case of minerals, reserves.
● The producers, or their organization, must be able to forego export earnings, and be immune to retaliation on imports or on other economic fronts.
● Consumer demand must be relatively unresponsive to price changes. That is, the demand for the product changes much less than proportionately with the change in price.
● Substitute, or alternate products, must not be too readily available to the consumer. That is, the consumer will continue to pay higher prices for some time before seeking a substitute.
● Members of the producer organization must have similar, strongly held economic or political objectives....

From an economic standpoint, therefore, the prospects of producing countries impeding raw materials markets over the long run are not favorable. Eventually, cartels must face the economic reality that artificially high prices will discourage demand and encourage the development of new sources of supply and of substitute products and technologies that will compete with and limit the market for the controlled commodity.

Political, nationalistic, or personal factors, however, could bring about attempts at market intervention, however ill advised, at least over the short run. Consequently, the United States and other industrialized countries face the possibility of supply interruptions in a few instances where dependence is on individual countries that could have political motives for curtailing raw material supply or whose domestic political situation is so unstable as to disrupt normal production processes.

An overall assessment of the raw materials situation indicates that the United States should focus its policy actions on countering the effects of short-term supply disruptions and discouraging unilateral producer actions. If these efforts are successful, then the longer term objectives of establishing and securing freer world trade will be closer to realization....

LAST FLIGHT FROM DA NANG
March 29, 1975

One of the grimmest documents to come out of the Vietnamese war was an eyewitness account of the last refugee flight out of Da Nang, March 29. In a sequence of events which mirrored the collapsing nation's panic, marauding South Vietnamese troops forced their way onto an American mercy flight intended for civilians, primarily women and children. "Only the fastest, the strongest and the meanest got out," reported United Press International (UPI) correspondent Paul Vogle, who was on board the chaotic flight. "People fought one another and died trying to get aboard. Others fell thousands of feet to their deaths in the sea because they could no longer cling to the [airplane's] undercarriage," Vogle wrote. Of the plane's 270 passengers, two were women, one an infant. The rest were soldiers from the Black Panthers, the "toughest" unit of the prestigious South Vietnamese First Division.

Three weeks earlier the Communists had launched a last, major offensive which, by April 30, was to bring down South Vietnam's government and end the interminable war (see p. 279). On March 5 North Vietnamese troops attacked heavily in the Central Highlands. Between March 13 and March 28 Viet Cong and North Vietnamese units swept over 12 provincial capitals and gained control of the Central Highlands and northern coastal regions, roughly 40 per cent of South Vietnamese territory. After a largely uncoordinated withdrawal of its troops from the Central Highlands in mid-March, the Saigon government was never again able to reestablish effective control over the army.

Da Nang Overrun

Refugees from the fighting swarmed into Da Nang, South Vietnam's second largest city and once the largest U.S. Marine base in Vietnam. The city was glutted with displaced civilians—perhaps as many as one and one-half million—and demoralized South Vietnamese troops. Conditions were chaotic. For a week prior to the fall of Da Nang, mutinous soldiers looted the city, raped and fired indiscriminately on their compatriots. Ordered back to barracks the night before the Communist attack, most troops simply deserted, according to an Agence France-Presse report. The report also indicated that the advancing Communist troops met little resistance, contrary to U.S. and South Vietnamese claims that the city fell only after heavy fighting.

The Communist assault on Da Nang began with a rocket attack on March 26. The same day an American-operated airlift began. While intended only to relieve the massive overcrowding by transferring refugees south, the evacuation was apparently interpreted as a signal that the city would be abandoned, touching off mass panic.

American consular officials left Da Nang March 28. Tens of thousands of South Vietnamese jammed the airport until enemy shelling prevented further flights. The frantic refugees then mobbed the city docks where the struggle to escape by sea produced more violence. Whereas earlier evacuations of provincial capitals had been kept in order by disciplined troops, at Da Nang it was the troops themselves who fought the civilians to escape. In one of many incidents, UPI reported that South Vietnamese marines on board an American evacuation ship so terrorized the passengers that the crew "barricaded" itself in a cabin.

American sources estimated April 1 that 30,000 to 50,000 refugees had escaped from Da Nang by sea and an additional 2,000 to 4,000 by air. As the military situation deteriorated in April, the United States launched a massive evacuation from Vietnam to temporary resettlement centers in the United States and Guam.

The total number of refugees from South Vietnam was placed at 130,000, according to a June 8 estimate of the U.S. Interagency Task Force for Indochina Refugees.

In the first few months after the fall of South Vietnam there were few reports of Communist reprisals against the population, and no incidents could be confirmed. A spokesman for the Provisional Revolutionary Government (Viet Cong) had given assurances in Paris on April 1 that the Viet Cong would protect the rights of all South Vietnamese (see p. 301).

Report on refugee flight from Da Nang, March 29, 1975, by Paul Vogle, correspondent for United Press International:

DA NANG, South Vietnam, March 29—Only the fastest, the strongest and the meanest got out on what may be the last refugee plane from Da Nang today.

I saw a South Vietnamese soldier kick an old woman in the face to get aboard.

In the movies somebody would have shot the soldier and helped the old woman aboard. But this was no movie—he flew and the old woman tumbled down the tarmac, her fingers clawing toward the plane as it rolled away.

People fought one another and died trying to get aboard. Others fell thousands of feet to their deaths in the sea because they could no longer cling to the undercarriage.

It was a flight out of hell and only the expertness of the American pilot got us back to Saigon's Tan Son Nhut air base alive—with the Boeing 727's flaps jammed and the wheels fully extended.

I was aboard because I had asked the World Airways vice president, Charles Patterson, whether he had anything going to Da Nang. He said, "Get on that truck and you've got yourself a ride."

It was a ride I'll never forget.

The airline's president, Ed Daley, was aboard. He was angry and tired after a night of arguing with American and Vietnamese officials for permission to make the refugee flight. Finally, he decided to forget about paperwork, clearances and caution, and we were on our way.

It seemed peaceful enough as we touched down at the Da Nang airport, 370 miles northeast of Saigon.

More than a thousand people had been waiting around a quonset hut several hundred yards away. Suddenly it was a mob in motion, roaring across the tarmac on motorbikes, jeeps, scooters—and on foot.

"There Wasn't Room"

Mr. Daley and I stood near the bottom of the 727's tailramp. He held out his arms while I shouted in Vietnamese, "One at a time. There's room for everybody."

There wasn't room for everybody and everybody knew it.

We were knocked aside and backward. In an instant the plane was jammed with troops of the First Division's toughest unit, the Black Panthers.

A British television cameraman who flew up with us made the mistake of getting off the plane when we landed to take pictures of the loading. In the pandemonium he could not get back aboard, so he threw his camera into the closing door and watched us take off.

We heard later than an Air America helicopter picked him up and carried him to safety.

As we started rolling, insanity gripped those who had missed their chance. Government troops opened fire at us. Somebody lobbed a hand grenade toward the wing. The explosion jammed the open flaps. The undercarriage was in full extension.

Communist rockets began exploding at a distance.

Our pilot, Ken Healy, 52 years old, of Oakland, Calif., opened the throttles wide and lurched into the air.

Ammunition Collected

Another 727 had flown behind us but had been ordered not to land when the panic broke out. The pilot radioed that he could see people hanging from the undercarriage of our plane.

Lien Huong, a photographer who was in the cockpit of the backup plane, saw at least one person lose his grip and plummet into the South China Sea.

About 270 people were jammed into the cabin of our little 727, only two women and one baby among them. The rest were soldiers. They didn't talk to each other or us.

I saw that one of them had a clip of ammunition and asked him to give it to me. He handed it over. As I walked up the aisle, other soldiers started loading my arms with clips of ammunition, pistols, grenades. There was no more fight left in the Black Panthers this day.

We flew down the coast, the backup plane behind us. Our pilot circled the Phan Rang air base 165 miles northeast of Saigon, hoping to put down for an emergency landing.

The photographer served as interpreter on the backup plane, radioing the Phan Rang control tower that our 727 had to land there. The reply was that there was no fire-fighting equipment. Our pilot headed the plane for Tan Son Nhut.

I heard our pilot on the radio telling Tan Son Nhut, "I've got control problems." The backup plane was shepherding us in. The photographer told me after we had touched down safely that the pilot and crew on his plane pulled off their headphones, some of them crossed themselves, and all thanked God for a small miracle.

When we landed, the troops who had stormed on the plane were unloaded and put under arrest.

The mangled body of one soldier, his rifle still strapped to his shoulder, was retrieved from the undercarriage.

About 20 soldiers came out of the baggage compartment, cold but alive. Somebody told me that four others crawled out of the wheel wells alive. One died.

The last flight from Da Nang was quite a ride.

April

SENATE REPORT ON SCHOOL VIOLENCE

April 9, 1975

Violence and vandalism in American public schools have reached epidemic proportions in recent years. Statistics demonstrating the extent of this widely recognized development were cited in a preliminary report issued April 9 by the U.S. Senate Judiciary Subcommittee to Investigate Juvenile Delinquency. The figures on violence and vandalism showed shocking increases between 1970 and 1973 in assaults on students and on teachers, smaller but substantial increases in rapes, robberies and homicides, and a rise in the costs of school vandalism to $500-million a year. Responses from more than 500 of 757 school districts questioned by the subcommittee, the records of earlier committee hearings, and evidence from independent studies spelled out in detail the mounting upward trend in school violence in urban, suburban and rural districts across the country.

Outlays for repairing damage to school property in 1972 equaled the total national expenditure for school books in that year, Sen. Birch Bayh (D Ind.), chairman of the subcommittee, noted in releasing his staff's findings. Bayh characterized the problem of school violence as one of "crisis proportions."

Between 1970 and 1973—the base period of the study—homicides in public schools increased by 18.5 per cent, rapes and attempted rapes by 40.1 per cent and robberies by 36.7 per cent in the 516 school districts which responded to the subcommittee's questionnaire. Data from the study also showed that the number of physical attacks on teachers jumped dramatically, by 77.4 per cent. But students themselves were more often the victims in the schools, for recorded attacks on them during the three-year

*period rose by 85.3 per cent. Apart from the human toll, the violence im-
posed financial hardship on many educational systems. Scarce operating
funds had to be diverted from teaching and equipment to pay for repairs,
skyrocketing insurance premiums and tighter security measures. The report
cited the ominous conclusion of one study that "the most serious aspect of
vandalism is the set of messages it conveys: that students look upon the
school as alien territory...."*

Causes

*At a public hearing on school violence held by the subcommittee on April
16, 1975, Albert Shanker, president of the American Federation of
Teachers, attributed the rise in school violence to judicial leniency and a
popular culture which idealized students as "a kind of...colonial minority."
(Several months earlier, the students' rights movement had won a major victory when the Supreme Court held that students suspended for disciplinary
reasons had a right to due process, see p. 67). James A. Harris, president of
the National Education Association, laid the blame on failure of the schools
themselves to serve the students. But Dr. Irving Anker of the New York City
Board of Education—a system which reported 474 assaults on teachers in
the first five months of 1975—asserted that the troubled inner-city school
was "an arena in which many of the crushing social problems of the city
itself intrude...."*

*The subcommittee's April report focused on the extent and nature of
crime in the schools. The question of what caused the sharp rise in violence and the issues of student rights and security measures were scheduled for consideration in a final subcommittee report to be issued in
1976.*

> *Excerpts from* Our Nation's Schools—A Report Card: "A"
> in School Violence and Vandalism, *Preliminary Report of
> the U.S. Senate Judiciary Subcommittee to Investigate
> Juvenile Delinquency, released April 9, 1975:*

INTRODUCTION

The purpose of this preliminary report by the Senate Subcommittee to
Investigate Juvenile Delinquency is to direct the attention of the Congress
and the American people to a most disturbing and costly problem—violence
and vandalism in the schools of our nation. Since 1971 the Subcommittee
has been involved with a variety of issues which have a very fundamental
and critical bearing upon the causes, prevention and treatment of delinquent behavior exhibited by young citizens in every region of our country.

During the past four years the Subcommittee has held 55 days of hearings and received testimony from 419 witnesses on numerous topics; some of which involved the extent and causes of drug abuse, runaway youth, school dropouts, and the confinement of juveniles in detention and correctional facilities.

The legislation developed to deal with these problems and which promises to greatly assist our efforts to combat and prevent juvenile delinquency is the Juvenile Justice and Delinquency Prevention Act of 1974 (P.L. 93-415). This Act is designed to prevent young people from entering our failing juvenile justice system, and to assist communities in creating more sensible and economic approaches for youngsters already in the juvenile justice system. Thus, the Juvenile Justice and Delinquency Prevention Act of 1974 provides incentives to develop delinquency prevention programs and community based alternatives to incarceration of youthful offenders.

During the course of our hearings, the Subcommittee developed a serious concern over the rising level of student violence and vandalism in our nation's public school systems. Since many aspects of juvenile problems are intimately connected with the nature and quality of the school experience, it became apparent that, to the extent our schools were being subjected to an increasing trend of student violence and vandalism, they would necessarily be contributing to the underlying causes of juvenile delinquency. The President's Commission on Law Enforcement and the Administration of Justice, 1967, found that:

> Recent research has related instances of delinquent conduct to the school-child relationship and to problems either created or complicated by schools themselves. First, in its own methods and practices, the school may simply be too passive to fulfill its obligations as one of the last social institutions with an opportunity to rescue the child from other forces, in himself and in his environment, which are pushing him toward delinquency. Second, there is considerable evidence that some schools may have an indirect effect on delinquency by the use of methods that create the conditions of failure for certain students.

In order to more fully understand the nature and extent of this problem, the Subcommittee sent a questionnaire in August 1973, to the superintendents of 757 public school districts throughout the country with an enrollment of 10,000 pupils or more ranging from grades K-12. The questionnaire was designed to obtain categorized information to determine the extent and scope of violence, vandalism, and dropouts in the systems surveyed for the school years 1970-71, 1971-72, and 1972-73. A Subcommittee follow-up letter was mailed to the non-respondent school districts in December 1973. To date, 516 school districts or 68.1 percent of the school districts surveyed have responded to the questionnaire. Several districts found it necessary to refer the study instruments to the municipal police department because the school did not maintain records of certain school-related offenses. Of the 516 respondents, 220 school districts returned incomplete questionnaires. Useful information was, however, gleaned from these incomplete responses. The incomplete questionnaires were primarily from school districts which were unable to provide the Subcommittee with the information requested due to the lack of adequate recordkeeping procedures for the entire three years or from districts which had not implemented recordkeeping systems pertaining to school crimes until 1972 or 1973.

Also in August 1973, the Subcommittee corresponded with 50 school security directors requesting their assistance in furnishing the Subcommittee with any available information they desired to contribute to the discussion of crimes committed by youngsters in the public school systems. (The directors were informed that a Subcommittee questionnaire had been circulated to over 700 school superintendents.) The Subcommittee was particularly interested in receiving the school security directors recommendations for developing federal legislation to provide the research, coordination, and resources necessary for the prevention and deterrence of crimes and violence in our nation's schools. Twenty school security directors responded to the Subcommittee's request for assistance.

This preliminary Subcommittee report discusses the information obtained from these sources, together with various additional studies of school violence and vandalism gathered by the Subcommittee. The report is divided into several sections, the first of which is a general overview of some of the trends and causes of school violence and vandalism throughout the country. The second section is a regional breakdown of the Subcommittee's findings on how school violence and vandalism is affecting the Northeast, Northcentral, South and West areas of the country. The third and fourth sections deal with federal and state legislation in this area under study. Our final section details the subcommittee's future goals.

NATIONAL TRENDS

There has always been a certain level of violence and vandalism in our nation's public school system. Professor Alar. F. Westin of Columbia University in a study of urban school violence in the years between 1870 and 1950 has found a rather steady stream of disruptions occurring throughout that entire period. If, however, the system has never been totally immune from incidents of student misbehavior such problems have historically been viewed as a relatively minor concern seldom involving more than a few sporadic and isolated incidents. As recently as 1964 a survey of the nation's teachers found that only 3 percent of their students could be considered discipline problems. Overall, teachers were able to rate 70-80 percent of their classes as exhibiting good to excellent behavior.

Today, however, the situation has changed and the level of violence and vandalism in our schools is rapidly increasing in both intensity and frequency. Dr. Frank Brown, Chairman of the National Commission for Reform of

Secondary Education, contends, "The major concern confronting secondary schools today is the climate of fear where the majority of students are afraid for their safety." A Grand Jury in San Francisco issued a report last January which declared, "The most serious problem facing the city is the deterioration of its public school system." In a survey of teacher needs conducted in 1972 fully 54 percent of the teachers found student disruption of their classrooms to be a problem of moderate to critical proportions. Syracuse University Research Corporation conducted a survey of urban secondary schools which found that 85 percent of these institutions had experienced some type of student disruption in the period between 1967 and 1970. The Syracuse report concluded, "The disruption of education in our high schools is no longer novel or rare. It is current, it is widespread and it is serious."

Growth and Types of Violence

It is alarmingly apparent that student misbehavior and conflict within our school system is no longer limited to a fist fight between individual students or an occasional general disruption resulting from a specific incident. Instead our schools are experiencing serious crimes of a felonious nature including brutal assaults on teachers and students, as well as rapes, extortions, burglaries, thefts and an unprecedented wave of wanton destruction and vandalism. Moreover our preliminary study of the situation has produced compelling evidence that this level of violence and vandalism is reaching crisis proportions which seriously threaten the ability of our educational system to carry out its primary function.

Quite naturally the rising tide of violence in our schools has engendered an increasing awareness and concern among the American people. In a 1974 Gallup poll most adults and high school students surveyed cited the lack of discipline as the chief problem confronting schools today. In fact three of the top four problems cited by most of those polled were directly related to various problems of student behavior.

Our recently completed nationwide survey of over 750 school districts demonstrates that this concern is well founded. The statistics gathered by the Subcommittee indicate that violence in our schools affects every section of the nation and, in fact, continues to escalate to even more serious levels. The preliminary Subcommittee survey found that in the three years between 1970 and 1973:

> (A) Homicides increased by 18.5 percent;
> (B) Rapes and attempted rapes increased by 40.1 percent;
> (C) Robberies increased by 36.7 percent;
> (D) Assaults on students increased by 85.3 percent;
> (E) Assaults on teachers increased by 77.4 percent;
> (F) Burglaries of school buildings increased by 11.8 percent;
> (G) Drug and alcohol offenses on school property increased by 37.5 percent; and
> (H) Dropouts increased by 11.7 percent.

An even more ominous statistic for the future course of school safety is the fact that by the end of the 1973 school year the number of weapons confiscated by school authorities had risen by 54.4 percent in three years. These weapons include knives, clubs, pistols and even sawed-off shotguns designed to be easily concealed within a student's locker.

The conclusions to be drawn from the Subcommittee survey are supported by other studies of these problems. Simply put, the trend in school violence over the last decade in America has been, and continues to be, alarmingly and dramatically upward.

In a 1964 survey by the National Education Association (NEA), 14.7 percent of the teachers surveyed reported that a teacher had been physically assaulted in their schools. By 1973 a similar survey showed that 37 percent of the nation's public school teachers reported an incident of teacher-oriented assault in their schools, and almost 50 percent of the teachers in the larger school systems (over 25,000 students) were aware of specific assaults on other teachers in their schools. Data from an earlier survey of large urban school districts conducted by the Subcommittee showed that assaults on teachers in those systems increased 612 percent between 1964 and 1968. In Chicago alone the number of such assaults went from 135 to 1,065 in that same period.

The returns from the Subcommittee's current nationwide survey show that this problem continues to exist and in fact to worsen. Between 1970 and 1973 assaults on teachers in school systems throughout the country increased again over previous levels by 77.4 percent. The NEA estimates that in the 1972-73 school year alone 69,000 teachers were physically attacked by students and 155,000 teachers had their personal property maliciously damaged. Another study found that 75,000 teachers are injured badly enough each year to require medical attention.

In response to this increase in assaults on teachers, the United Federation of Teachers recently issued to its members a booklet on how to handle violence in a variety of school situations including hallways, lunchrooms and classrooms. The booklet also contains advice to teachers on how best to combat sexual assaults:

> This is especially true for female teachers. Most rapes and other sex crimes occur in classrooms, faculty rooms and workrooms—when the teacher is alone. *The surest means of preventing sexual attacks is never to be alone.*
> The teacher who is confronted by a sexual assailant should take account of Police Department recommendations. If a rapist is armed, the police urge that his victim offer no resistance, lest she be maimed or fatally injured. If he is *not* armed, a woman should remember that her knee or almost any instrument can become a weapon: a Bic pen will open a beer can—or a kidney or an eye.

There are indications that student violence and vandalism occurs more often in larger urban secondary schools. A survey of newspaper articles between October 1969 and February 1970 revealed that 63 percent of the major school disruptions occurred in urban areas. A Vandalism and Violence study published by the School Public Relations Association estimated that 55 percent of the major incidents of disruption occurred in cities larger than one million people and 26 percent occurred in cities of less than 100,000 population. It should be emphasized, however, that this is not a problem found exclusively in large cities or solely involving older students. A guidance counselor for a school system on the West coast commented:

> We get thousands of reports on assaults. It's astonishing to see what happens in the elementary grades, teachers being hit and called filthy names, assaulted by little kids who really can't hurt them much. But the thing is, what are you going to do about these kids so they change their way of thinking about things, their attitude and behavior?

Although the level of violence, directed against teachers revealed by these statistics, is indeed alarming, the principal victims of the rising tide of crime in our schools are not the teachers, but the students. The Subcommittee's survey found that violent assaults on students increased by 85.3 percent over a three year period, while reported robberies of students increased by 36.7 percent.

The Subcommittee survey found that incidents involving the use of drugs and alcohol on public school property went up 37.5 percent. A study released this year by the NEA estimates that drug-related crimes in schools had increased by 81 percent since 1970, and that 30 percent of the 18 million students in secondary schools use illegal drugs.

The National Highway Safety Administration estimates that 50 percent of the nation's high school students go to drinking parties every month and that 61 percent of that group gets drunk once a month. The Highway Safety Administration also found that these students represent a remarkable cross-section of our schools:

> They are not far out, drop out alienated or under achieving types. On the contrary, they represent all levels of scholastic achievement and aspiration. They report the same range of sport and extracurricular activities as the students who are not involved with drinking.

It is important to stress that the Subcommittee survey findings, as well as those of other surveys on violence within the school system, are only estimates of the nature and extent of the problem. A report on the New York City school system found that the rate of unreported incidents ranged between 30 percent and 60 percent. Albert Shanker, President of the American Federation of Teachers, explained teachers' reluctance to fully report such incidents as follows:

> Teachers find that if they report to the principal an assault, the principal who feels that his own reputation or her reputation or the school's reputation is at stake here, will very frequently turn around and start harassing the teacher by saying, "Well, if you had three assaults, how come you are the one always complaining. You must have more observation or better planning, or this or that." So the teacher soon finds out that bringing these reports to the attention of the principal is something that is not wanted and tends to suppress that information.

In conducting our survey, the Subcommittee found that many of the schools contacted did not keep records of violent incidents involving their students or personnel, which obviously makes the task of gauging the levels and directions of violence a difficult one. A uniform, national reporting system for our schools would be particularly helpful in this regard.

Costs of Vandalism

In addition to the violence directed against both teachers and students within the school system, there is also a continuing and rapidly increasing level of destruction and theft of school property. A survey conducted by the Baltimore, Maryland, public schools of 39 cities across the country found that in 1968-69 these cities had reported vandalism losses of over $12,000,000. In a 1971 report prepared by Education U.S.A. and the National School Public Relations Association, it was estimated that vandalism was costing $200 million annually. Barely two years later Dr. Norman Scharer, President of the Association of School Security Directors, stated:

> A conservative estimate of the cost of vandalism, thefts and arson to schools in this country this year will reportedly be over a half a billion dollars. I say conservative because out of the almost 15,000 school systems the top five account for $15-20 million dollars of this cost.

This $500 million vandalism cost represents over $10 per year for every school student, and in fact equals the total amount expended on textbooks throughout the country in 1972.

A 1970 survey conducted by the School Product News found that damages from vandalism cost an average of $55,000 for every school district in the country. By the end of the 1973 school year the average cost per district had risen to $63,031. Although these figures indicate that the incidents of vandalism are certainly widespread, it is in the larger urban districts with upwards of 25,000 students where the most costly destruction occurs. Almost 60 percent of all vandalism takes place in these larger districts with an average cost per district in 1973 at $135,297.

The source of this destruction ranges from broken windows, found in over 90 percent of our districts, to fires reported by 35 percent of the districts. Significant incidents of theft and malicious destruction of educational equipment occur in 80 percent of the school districts in the country.

Staggering as these figures are they undoubtedly represent a very conservative estimate of economic loss attributable to school vandalism. A study of school vandalism by Bernard Greenberg of the Stanford Research Institute found:

> It should be noted that the cost figure is grossly understated because it does not include in all instances losses attributable to burglary, theft and property damage repaired by resident maintenance staffs. Nor does it take into account costs to equip and maintain special security forces, which are considerable for

the larger school districts, and law enforcement costs to patrol and respond to calls reporting school incidents. Many school districts carry theft insurance, but the costs are exceedingly high. Where data on selected school districts theft losses are available, the dollar amounts are significantly high.

Spiraling insurance rates are a significant, but often overlooked, factor in the overall cost of vandalism. The Greenberg study found a West Coast state which underwent a 40 percent rise in fire insurance costs within one year. Another survey stated:

> Many school administrators point out that only a few years ago schools were wooed by the insurance industry as good risks. Now this has changed. And school districts all over the country are reporting difficulty in obtaining insurance. Half the districts answering the Education U.S.A. survey said rates have increased. Many are either paying higher premiums, higher deductibles, or in all too many instances, having policies cancelled or flatly rejected.

In addition to insurance rates, school districts are facing increasing costs for security guards, fencing, intrusion and fire detectors, special lighting, emergency communications equipment and vandalism resistant windows. In 1965, for instance, the Los Angeles school system had a total of 15 security guards, but in six years that force was compelled to increase to over 100 members at a cost of over $1 million per year. During the 1972-73 school year Los Angeles spent over $2 million for security agents. A report of the Panel on School Safety for New York City found that in 1971 the taxpayers had paid $1,300,000 for security guards, over $3,500,000 for police stationed in schools, and in spite of such effort incurred at least $3,700,000 worth of vandalism damage. It was estimated that New York City schools had over 248,000 window panes broken at a replacement cost of $1.25 million. Over 65 percent of the urban districts polled in the 1973 School Product News survey reported they were using special vandalism resistant windows, and 62 percent had at least one security guard assigned to their schools.

The overall impact of violence and vandalism on our educational system cannot, of course, be adequately conveyed by a recitation of the numbers of assaults and the dollars expended. Every dollar spent on replacing a broken window or installing an alarm system cannot be spent on the education of students. J. Arlen Marsh, editor of a study on school security costs estimates that:

> The cost of replacing broken windows in the average big city would build a new school every year.

The School Public Relations Association study found that a $60,000 loss, approximately the average loss for a school district, could pay for eight reading specialists or finance a school breakfast program for 133 children for a year. It is quite clear that in some areas of the country the high cost of vandalism is resulting in the reduction or elimination of needed educational programs.

215

The natural reaction to these enormous amounts of wasted money is to wonder over the apparently senseless nature of this destruction. A study entitled Urban School Crisis, however, questions whether vandalism is as irrational as it may appear:

> Perhaps the most serious aspect of vandalism is the set of messages it conveys: that students look upon the school as alien territory, hostile to their ambitions and hopes; that the education which the system is attempting to provide lacks meaningfulness; that students feel no pride in the edifices in which they spend most of their days.

In addition to requiring the diversion of funds from academic and scholastic projects to security and repair programs, the atmosphere of violence and vandalism has a devastating impact on the ability of our educational system to continue with the instruction of its students. The extent to which this atmosphere permeates our children's educational experience can perhaps be best illustrated by a letter sent to the Subcommittee from a West Coast police official:

> It isn't only in the school or the schoolyard that the students are likely to be exposed to violence. School buses, in addition to being mechanically unsound and totally devoid of the slightest semblance of safety devices, are frequently a terrifying experience for the children who are captive passengers. They are the scene of rip-offs for lunch money, physical violence, and pressure to indulge in the illegal use of drugs or narcotics. We appear to have accepted without effective challenge this mass intimidation simply because, naively, some of us hope it will "go away." Students who are normally nonviolent have started carrying guns and knives and lengths of bicycle-chains for protection on campus. Though I am obviously concerned about the millions of dollars of property loss which occurs in our schools, I am far more concerned about our apparent willingness to accept violence as a condition of our daily existence.

Few students can be expected to learn in an atmosphere of fear, assaults and disorder. There can be little doubt that the significant level of violent activity, threats and coercion revealed by the Subcommittee's preliminary survey would have a detrimental effect on the psychological and educational development of children and young adults. Moreover a continuous pattern of destruction of school equipment and buildings naturally makes nearly impossible the already challenging process of education. The extent and continued growth of this chaotic and threatening climate in our schools is a serious threat to our educational system.

CAUSES

Not surprisingly, the underlying causes for this wave of violence and vandalism in our schools is a subject of intense debate and disagreement. In a certain sense the school system may be viewed as merely a convenient battleground for the pervasive societal problem of juvenile crime. As this Subcommittee pointed out in its recent Annual Report, violent juvenile crime has increased by 246.5 percent in the last thirteen years. Over the same period crimes directed against property by youths increased by 104.6 percent. Today persons under 25 years old are committing 50 percent of all violent crimes and 80 percent of all property crimes. Since our school systems are charged with the care and custody of a large percentage of our young people it is reasonable to assume that the incidents of violence and vandalism within our educational institutions would follow patterns similar to those developing in the society at large. A study conducted in 1973 by Paul Ritterbrand and Richard Silberstein concluded that the roots of school problems could be traced to problems existing in the general American society rather than to conditions or failures within the school system itself.

Other studies, however, while acknowledging the substantial effect general societal conditions would have on the conduct of school behavior, have indicated the existence of several "in school" conditions which may contribute to the level of youthful disorder. One possible contributing factor is the various methods of excluding students from school. A 1974 report entitled, "Children Out of School in America," prepared by the Children's Defense Fund, estimates that hundreds of thousands of students are removed from schools each year by short-term, long-term or indefinite expulsions and suspensions. While most educators concur in the necessity for the exclusion of seriously disruptive troublemakers from the school environment, the Children's Defense Fund study found the numbers of students being suspended were far in excess of those who must be removed as a means of maintaining order. The study recounted the history of one youngster's long-term suspension:

Dale McCutcheon, 13, is in the eighth grade of his local public school. He is an eneuretic, a bedwetter.

Dale's school had a policy requiring every eighth grade boy to spend a long weekend in the country to learn to live outdoors. Most boys adore this trip. Dale dreaded it as early as fifth grade after he heard it was compulsory. When the time came, he begged his mother to keep him home, but she refused.

The first night of the excursion, Dale woke several times and cautiously felt around his waist, but everything was dry. The next day his spirits were high and he enjoyed learning how to make food from wild plants and to classify mushrooms. The secret problem he had carried for so long seemingly had vanished.

It was different the second night. He did not awake until morning when the sounds of boys talking and laughing startled him. The two boys sharing his tent had discovered the wetness. They hounded Dale mercilessly and he wept. The boys told the counselors, who lectured him. Later, someone cracked a joke about Dale's accident and all the boys exploded with laughter. Humiliated, he wanted to run away and dreaded the thought of returning to school. The third night he remained dry but the damage had been done.

Dale never told his parents about the incident. He refused to go to school for two days and pretended he was sick. But by the end of the week, his sister had become the butt of other children's insults about Dale, and she reported the incident to her parents who were painfully embarrassed and angry with Dale.

Two weeks after the excursion, the principal of Dale's school asked his parents to come in for a meeting. The principal wasted no time outlining the seriousness of Dale's situation for the boy as well as for the school. The problem was not, he explained, the other children. "They'll probably forget the whole thing in another week or so. It's Dale's teachers—how do we know he won't just, you know, pop off at any time in one of his classes?" Mrs. McCutcheon explained that it was only a nighttime problem but the principal replied, "We can't take any chances. I can't stop him from going to school. But I can stop him from going to this school and that's exactly what I'm doing. The boy's out for a month, or until a time you can prove to us that he is able to control himself, night and day."

And so Dale was out of school.

There are in fact so many students being subjected to expulsive disciplinary practices that the phenomenon has been referred to as the "Pushout" problem.

Another facet of the pushout problem which may operate as a contributing factor to school disorders was revealed in a report recently released by the Department of Health, Education, and Welfare. In statistics gathered at the end of the 1973 school year it was demonstrated that while Blacks represent only 27 percent of the total student enrollment in the 3,000 school districts surveyed, they accounted for 37 percent of the expulsions and 42 percent of the suspensions from those districts. The disparity among these figures raises serious questions concerning possible widescale bias in the administration of suspension and expulsion. Such policies can only result in anger and hostility on the part of students.

In addition to these forms of compulsive absence from schools there are the related problems of "force outs" and truancy which contribute to the large numbers of children and young adults who attend school in only a very irregular fashion. The "force out" concept is the educational system's version of a plea bargain, so common in our criminal justice system. A student involved in academic or behavioral difficulty may be informally presented with the options of failing courses, facing expulsion or voluntary removal from school. In many instances the student will opt for "dropping out" and therefore be removed temporarily or permanently. Truancy, of course, is an accepted and traditional fact of life in schools, but the modern rates of truancy especially in the large urban systems, reveal numerous students attend school only in the most erratic fashion.

At first glance it might appear that the expulsion, suspension, pushout, force out and truancy phenomenon, although certainly tragic for those involved, might at least create a somewhat more orderly atmosphere for those remaining in school as a result of the absence of youngsters evidently experiencing problems adjusting to the school environment. The opposite, however, appears to be the case. The Syracuse study, for instance, found that in schools where the average daily attendance was lower, the disruptions, violence and vandalism rates were higher. This may be explained by the fact that the vast majority of students who are voluntarily or compulsively excluded from schools do, in time, return to those schools. In many instances their frustrations and inadequacies which caused their absence in the first place have only been heightened by their exclusion and the school community will likely find itself a convenient and meaningful object of revenge.

As the subcommittee's statistics reveal, the use of drugs and alcohol by students in secondary schools continues to increase. These trends cannot be ignored as a contributing factor to the problems confronting the schools. A report on violence in the Boston Public Schools, for example, states:

> Regarding behavior, most administrators and teachers felt a person occasionally "high on drugs" could be very difficult to handle. There was no question that drugs were a very important cause for the increase in stealing and fighting in the schools.

Another cause of disruption and violence found mainly in large urban centers on the East and West Coasts is the presence of youthful, but highly organized, gangs within the school system. A school which finds itself being used as the center of a gang's illegal activities can quickly develop a very hostile environment. A security director for a metropolitan school system in a letter to the Subcommittee states:

> Although the number of gang members, in proportion to the overall student population in most schools is minimal, the trouble they cause is at times, cataclysmic. Students are robbed, intimidated, raped, bludgeoned and sometimes fatally wounded. Teachers and other adults in the schools are threatened and on occasions, physically assaulted. The peace of any school is breached and the learning climate seriously polluted by gang activity, however slight.
> In some schools, gang activity is so intense that it is necessary for school security officers and the local police to escort one gang through the territory of a rival gang at dismissal time. At certain schools, Safety Corridors have been established which provide safe passage for neutral students under the protection of school security personnel and police, through the hostile territory. Needless to say, these measures provide at best, temporary relief. They do not begin to attack the root causes of the problem.

Schools, of course, cannot escape the impact of racial and ethnic dislike and distrust of contemporary American society. Moreover, the intense concentration of individuals within the school confines coupled with the naturally vigorous personalities of students exacerbate these antagonisms. Following a fight at one of its schools, involving more than seventy students in October 1974, a suburban school district in Virginia conducted a thorough investigation into the incident. Their report, released earlier this year, concluded that racial tensions and antagonisms were a significant cause of the disruptions at the school. The report found that students were being bullied and intimidated in the halls of the school and a widely held belief existed among students of both races that disciplinary measures were not being fairly administered. It must be emphasized that this situation is in no way unique to this particular district, but, in fact, represents a widespread problem confronting schools across the country.

Rules and Disciplinary Problems

One common thread of particular interest to the Subcommittee running through many of the underlying causes of school violence and vandalism is

219

what may be called the crisis of Due Process. Quite naturally schools, like other institutions, are compelled to issue rules and regulations concerning the conduct of persons within their jurisdiction. It is clear that without fair and meaningful control and discipline the schools would quickly lose their ability to educate students. Increasingly, though, educators and administrators are finding that the extent of student conduct which is sought to be regulated, as well as the methods of regulation, are causing more problems than they are controlling. A 1975 NEA study interviewed a large number of students from different schools and found that, "Many students spoke of the need for consistent, fair discipline."

For example, the Subcommittee found that in numerous institutions across the country, students, administrators and teachers are embroiled in constant ongoing disputes over restrictions on dress, hair style, smoking, hall passes, student newspapers and a myriad of other aspects of school life. The Syracuse study observes that intense efforts to control clothes or hair styles may, in fact, be counterproductive to a well ordered environment:

> This remains a constant bone of contention between students and staff, and when it takes on racial or ethnic features, the contention becomes far more serious. We suspect that everyone would agree that nakedness at school is prohibited because, by itself, it disrupts education. On the other hand, restrictions against bell bottom pants, long hair, 'Afros', and beads are probably useless and offensive.

In another area, administrative attempts to control student publications have at times appeared to be overly restrictive and conducted in a capricious manner. A 1974 report by the Commission of Inquiry Into High School Journalism found that:

> Censorship and the systematic lack of freedom to engage in open, responsible journalism characterize high school journalism. Unconstitutional and arbitrary restraints are so deeply embedded in high school journalism as to overshadow its achievements, as well as its other problems.

As discussed earlier, the manner in which suspensions and expulsions are administered have in some instances been arbitrary and discriminatory. Students in some schools are suspended without being given an opportunity to answer or explain charges against them, while other students are suspended for improper conduct which results only in a reprimand for other students engaging in identical activity. A study of the student pushout phenomena undertaken by the Southern Regional Council and the Robert F. Kennedy memorial found that:

> Most observers acknowledge the need for rules and the power to enforce them. The pragmatic observer will concede that there are those individual students just as some older citizens, who finally will not or cannot conform to any societal standards. The misuse of discipline, however, often occurs because racial, cultural and generation differences cloud the judgment and actions of teachers and administrators alike.

On a more positive level certain efforts have been made to rationalize and reform the rule making and disciplinary functions in our schools. The Supreme Court held recently in *Gross* v. *Lopez* 95 S. Ct. 729 (1975) that student expulsion or suspension procedures must be governed by at least the minimal standards of Due Process. The Court stated:

> In holding as we do, we do not believe that we have imposed procedures on school disciplinarians which are inappropriate in a classroom setting. Instead we have imposed requirements which are, if anything, less than a fair minded school principal would impose upon himself in order to avoid unfair suspensions.

The NEA has developed a Student Rights and Responsibility statement which recommends that the standards of conduct to be followed at a particular school be drawn up with participation by student representatives, and that they be distributed to all members of the school community in written form. This practice would insure that students as well as teachers have a clear and understandable statement of the rules and regulations governing their conduct while in school. Many schools have in fact amended or instituted written student codes which contain a statement of student rights and responsibilities and which set forth the grounds for suspension and expulsion along with whatever procedural protections are to be used prior to such action. The mere practice of committing school regulations to writing helps insure an even-handed administration of student discipline within the institution.

In addition to students, many teachers are anxious for clear and closely followed disciplinary codes within schools. Following the shooting death of a teacher in Philadelphia by a junior high school student who had continuously caused trouble at the school, both principals and teachers within that system demanded a new and stricter code for dealing with repeatedly disruptive students. Many teachers feel that only when seriously disruptive students are properly controlled can the remainder of the school community continue the task of education.

The proper response to the problem of the seriously disruptive student is a difficult and complex issue. On the one hand, a small group of disruptive and violent students can create conditions which make the task of education impossible and dangerous for both teachers and other students. On the other hand, however, several studies indicate that mass expulsions of these students from schools often creates groups of resentful youngsters who return to the school community to seek vengeance.

Unfortunately, not all the sources of school violence and vandalism discussed in this report are as amenable to solution as the promulgation and fair administration of rules and regulations affecting both teachers and students. Some of these causes are obviously beyond the direct control of administrators or teachers, while others no doubt remain largely unidentified. Many school districts are attempting to identify and confront those problems, but their nature and cure are not readily treatable solely by teachers or administrators. What is shockingly apparent from the Subcommittee survey, however, is that our school system is facing a crisis of serious dimensions, the solutions to which must be found if the system is to survive in a meaningful form. It is essential that the American public school become a safe and secure environment where education, rather than disruption, violence, and vandalism, is the primary concern....

CONCLUSION

The preliminary findings of the Subcommittee present clear and dramatic evidence that violence and vandalism in the schools of our country has reached a level of crisis that demands immediate comprehensive review and legislative action. To accomplish this the Subcommittee will proceed immediately with hearings to obtain the views of all affected parties, and to develop a comprehensive record that will serve as a basic reference source on the many interrelated components of these very complex problems. As evidenced in this preliminary report, the etiology of school violence is as complex as the structure of our society. We intend to examine thoroughly the categories of school problem areas which we believe must be singularly and collectively understood before any legislative proposal can be finalized. These areas include pushouts, dropouts, forceouts, truancy, gang violence and terrorism, student rights, teacher rights, parent rights, alcohol and drug abuse, community involvement, and alternative approaches to correct the devastating patterns of violence in our nation's schools.

FORD'S ADDRESS TO CONGRESS ON U.S. FOREIGN POLICY
April 10, 1975

President Ford delivered a foreign policy address to Congress April 10, emphasizing the need for cooperation between the executive and legislative branches in the area of foreign affairs. "I am here to work with Congress," he told a joint session of the House and Senate, but he cautioned that "in the conduct of foreign affairs, presidential initiative and ability to act swiftly are essential to our national interest." Ford's speech continued the practice initiated by President Nixon in 1970 of presenting Congress each spring with an overview of U.S. foreign policy.

During conversations with congressional leaders before the speech, Ford described it as the "most serious" he would make. The address dealt largely with longstanding areas of conflict between Congress and the executive branch—Indochina, Turkey, trade restrictions, Soviet relations and congressional oversight of intelligence-gathering agencies.

At one point, the President theorized on the impact of American setbacks in Vietnam. "Above all, let's keep events in Southeast Asia in their proper perspective," he said. "The security and the progress of hundreds of millions of people everywhere depend importantly on us. Let no potential adversary believe that our difficulties or our debates mean a slackening of our national will."

Ford asked Congress to make available to South Vietnam $722-million in emergency military aid and an "initial" $250-million in economic and humanitarian aid. Saying that "assistance to South Vietnam at this stage must be swift and adequate," he called on Congress to complete work on his proposals within nine days—by April 19—a deadline Congress did not meet.

The President at the same time urged Congress to clarify restrictions it had placed on the use of U.S. military assistance in Southeast Asia, so as not to impede the evacuation of Americans and South Vietnamese "whose lives may be endangered, should the worst come to pass." Ford voiced regret that a request he had made in January for "food and ammunition for the brave Cambodians" had not been fulfilled, for it "may soon be too late." On the day the President spoke, rebel forces had already surrounded the Cambodian capital of Phnom Penh. South Vietnam succumbed to the Communists on April 29. (See p. 251 and p. 279.)

Additional Requests

In his address to Congress, the President also called for the resumption of military aid to Turkey, which had been cut off by Congress on Feb. 5 because of Turkey's use of American arms in the invasion of Cyprus in 1974. Ford asked, in addition, for authority to waive restrictions in the Trade Act of 1974 which he said were incompatible with this country's national interests. He referred specifically to the denial of trade preferences to Ecuador and Venezuela by the act's ban on extension of such preferences to members of the Organization of Petroleum Exporting Countries (OPEC). Ecuador and Venezuela, although OPEC members, had not participated in the embargo on oil shipments to the United States. Ford said this situation had "seriously complicated our new dialogue with our friends in this hemisphere."

The President likewise asked for "remedial legislation" in the case of the trade bill's provision that linked trade preferences for the Soviet Union to its policy on emigration of Jewish citizens and limited the amount of U.S. credits and investment guarantees that might be extended to Russia. Because of those restrictions, Moscow had opted to accept credits offered by Western European countries and Japan. The United States thus lost "economic opportunities, jobs, and business which could have gone to Americans," Ford said.

Intelligence Activities

In the only major departure from his prepared text, the President told Congress it would be "catastrophic" if the Central Intelligence Agency (CIA) were "in effect" to be dismantled, in the course of congressional inquiries, by the use of procedures that make "the protection of vital information very, very difficult." He said that "any investigation [of intelligence activities] must be conducted with maximum discretion and dispatch to avoid crippling a vital national institution." He pledged to work with Congress to devise procedures that would permit congressional oversight of intelligence activities while providing for "an effective intelligence service." (CIA investigations, see pp. 401, 709 and 873.)

Congressional Action on Ford's Requests

Congress outrightly rejected Ford's request for additional military aid for South Vietnam, but it attempted to clear legislation approving $327-million for humanitarian and evacuation assistance. However, in the latter case, events in Indochina outpaced congressional action. The House dropped the proposal for humanitarian aid on May 1 following the completion of evacuation efforts and the unconditional surrender of the South Vietnamese government to the Communists. However, on May 21, Congress cleared a bill authorizing funds to cover evacuation costs and the costs of resettling Vietnamese refugees brought to this country.

Congress adjourned in 1975 without taking action to ease trade restrictions relating to the Soviet Union as requested by President Ford. Another presidential request—to lift the prohibition on arms to Turkey—was eventually agreed to on Oct. 2, 1975, but only after extensive wrangling between the White House and the House of Representatives, which had previously rejected the proposal.

Following is the text of President Ford's foreign policy address to Congress April 10, 1975:

UNITED STATES FOREIGN POLICY

The President's Address Delivered Before a Joint Session of the Congress. April 10, 1975.

Mr. Speaker, Mr. President, distinguished guests, my very good friends in the Congress, and fellow Americans:

I stand before you tonight after many agonizing hours in very solemn prayers for guidance by the Almighty. In my report on the State of the Union in January, I concentrated on two subjects which were uppermost in the minds of the American people—urgent actions for the recovery of our economy and a comprehensive program to make the United States independent of foreign sources of energy.

I thank the Congress for the action that it has taken thus far in response to my economic recommendations. I look forward to early approval of a national energy program to meet our country's long-range and emergency needs in the field of energy.

Tonight it is my purpose to review our relations with the rest of the world in the spirit of candor and consultation which I have sought to maintain with my former colleagues and with our countrymen from the time that I took office. It is the first priority of my Presidency to sustain and strengthen the mutual trust and respect which must exist among Americans and their Government if we are to deal successfully with the challenges confronting us both at home and abroad.

The leadership of the United States of America since the end of World War II has sustained and advanced the security, well-being, and freedom of millions of human beings besides ourselves. Despite some setbacks, despite some mistakes, the United States has made peace a real prospect for us and for all nations. I know firsthand that the Congress has been a partner in the development and in the support of American foreign policy, which five Presidents before me have carried forward with changes of course but not of destination.

The course which our country chooses in the world today has never been of greater significance for ourselves as a nation and for all mankind. We build from a solid foundation.

Our alliances with great industrial democracies in Europe, North America, and Japan remain strong with a greater degree of consultation and equity than ever before.

With the Soviet Union we have moved across a broad front toward a more stable, if still competitive, relationship. We have begun to control the spiral of strategic nuclear armaments.

After two decades of mutual estrangement, we have achieved an historic opening with the People's Republic of China.

In the best American tradition, we have committed, often with striking success, our influence and good offices to help contain conflicts and settle disputes in many, many regions of the world. We have, for example, helped the parties of the Middle East take the first steps toward living with one another in peace.

We have opened a new dialog with Latin America, looking toward a healthier hemispheric partnership. We are developing closer relations with the nations of Africa. We have exercised international leadership on the great new issues of our interdependent world, such as energy, food, environment, and the law of the sea.

The American people can be proud of what their Nation has achieved and helped others to accomplish, but we have from time to time suffered setbacks and disappointments in foreign policy. Some were events over which we had no control; some were difficulties we imposed upon ourselves.

Building on Past Successes

We live in a time of testing and in a time of change. Our world—a world of economic uncertainty, political unrest, and threats to the peace—does not allow us the luxury of abdication or domestic discord.

I recall quite vividly the words of President Truman to the Congress when the United States faced a far greater challenge at the end of the Second World War. If I might quote: "If we falter in our leadership, we may endanger the peace of the world, and we shall surely endanger the welfare of this Nation."

President Truman's resolution must guide us today. Our purpose is not to point the finger of blame, but to build upon our many successes, to repair damage where we find it, to recover our balance, to move ahead as a united people. Tonight is a time for straight talk among friends, about where we stand and where we are going.

Tragedy of Vietnam and Cambodia

A vast human tragedy has befallen our friends in Vietnam and Cambodia. Tonight I shall not talk only of obligations arising from legal documents. Who can forget the enormous sacrifices of blood, dedication, and treasure that we made in Vietnam?

Under five Presidents and 12 Congresses, the United States was engaged in Indochina. Millions of Americans served, thousands died, and many more were wounded, imprisoned, or lost. Over $150 billion have been appropriated for that war by the Congress of the United States. And after years of effort, we negotiated, under the most difficult circumstances, a settlement which made it possible for us to remove our military forces and bring home with pride our American prisoners. This settlement, if its terms had been adhered to, would have permitted our South Vietnamese ally with our material and moral support, to maintain its security and rebuild after two decades of war.

The chances for an enduring peace after the last American fighting man left Vietnam in 1973, rested on two publicly stated premises: first, that if necessary, the United States would help sustain the terms of the Paris accords it signed 2 years ago, and second, that the United States would provide adequate economic and military assistance to South Vietnam.

Let us refresh our memories for just a moment. The universal consensus in the United States at that time, late 1972, was that if we could end our own involvement and obtain the release of our prisoners, we would provide adequate material support to South Vietnam. The North Vietnamese, from the moment they signed the Paris accords, systematically violated the cease-fire and other provisions of that agreement. Flagrantly disregarding the ban on the infiltration of troops, the North Vietnamese illegally introduced over 350,000 men into the South. In direct violation of the agreement they sent in the most modern equipment in massive amounts. Meanwhile, they continued to receive large quantities of supplies and arms from their friends.

In the face of this situation, the United States—torn as it was by the emotions of a decade of war—was unable to respond. We deprived ourselves by law of the ability to enforce the agreement, thus giving North Vietnam assurance that it could violate that agreement with impunity. Next, we reduced our economic and arms aid to South Vietnam. Finally, we signaled our increasing reluctance to give any support to that nation struggling for its survival.

Encouraged by these developments, the North Vietnamese, in recent months, began sending even their reserve divisions into South Vietnam. Some 20 divisions, virtually their entire army, are now in South Vietnam.

The Government of South Vietnam, uncertain of further American assistance, hastily ordered a strategic withdrawal to more defensible positions. This extremely difficult maneuver, decided upon without consultations, was poorly executed, hampered by floods of refugees, and thus led to panic. The results are painfully obvious and profoundly moving.

In my first public comment on this tragic development, I called for a new sense of national unity and purpose. I said I would not engage in recriminations or attempts to assess the blame. I reiterate that tonight.

In the same spirit, I welcome the statement of the distinguished majority leader of the United States Senate earlier this week, and I quote: "It is time for the Congress and the President to work together in the area of foreign as well as domestic policy."

So, let us start afresh.

I am here to work with the Congress. In the conduct of foreign affairs, Presidential initiative and ability to act swiftly in emergencies are essential to our national interest.

Appeal to Honor Vietnam Peace Accord

With respect to North Vietnam, I call upon Hanoi—and ask the Congress to join with me in this call—to cease military operations immediately and to honor the terms of the Paris agreement.

The United States is urgently requesting the signatories of the Paris conference to meet their obligations to use their influence to halt the fighting and to enforce the 1973 accords. Diplomatic notes to this effect have been sent to all members of the Paris conference, including the Soviet Union and the People's Republic of China.

The situation in South Vietnam and Cambodia has reached a critical phase requiring immediate and positive decisions by this Government.

The options before us are few and the time is very short.

—On the one hand, the United States could do nothing more; let the Government of South Vietnam save itself and what is left of its territory, if it can; let those South Vietnamese civilians who have worked with us for a decade or more save their lives and their families, if they can; in short, shut our eyes and wash our hands of the whole affair—if we can.

—Or, on the other hand, I could ask the Congress for authority to enforce the Paris accords with our troops and our tanks and our aircraft and our artillery and carry the war to the enemy.

There are two narrower options:

—First, stick with my January request that Congress appropriate $300 million for military assistance for South Vietnam and seek additional funds for economic and humanitarian purposes;

—Or increase my requests for both emergency military and humanitarian assistance to levels which, by best estimates, might enable the South Vietnamese to stem the onrushing aggression, to stabilize the military situation, permit the chance of a negotiated political settlement between the North and South Vietnamese, and, if the very worst were to happen, at least allow the orderly evacuation of Americans and endangered South Vietnamese to places of safety.

Let me now state my considerations and conclusions.

Ford's Plan for Vietnam

I have received a full report from General [Frederick C.] Weyand, whom I sent to Vietnam to assess the situation. He advises that the current military situation is very critical, but that South Vietnam is continuing to defend itself with the resources available. However, he feels that if there is to be any chance of success for their defense plan, South Vietnam needs urgently an additional $722 million in very specific military supplies from the United States. In my judgment, a stabilization of the military situation offers the best opportunity for a political solution.

I must, of course, as I think each of you would, consider the safety of nearly 6,000 Americans who remain in South Vietnam and tens of thousands of South Vietnamese employees of the United States Government, of news agencies, of contractors and businesses for many years whose lives, with their dependents, are in very grave peril. There are tens of thousands of other South Vietnamese intellectuals, professors, teachers, editors and opinion leaders, who have supported the South Vietnamese cause and the alliance with the United States to whom we have a profound moral obligation.

I am also mindful of our posture toward the rest of the world, and particularly of our future relations with the free nations of Asia. These nations must not think for a minute that the United States is pulling out on them or intends to abandon them to aggression.

I have, therefore, concluded that the national interests of the United States and the cause of world stability require that we continue to give both military and humanitarian assistance to the South Vietnamese.

Assistance to South Vietnam at this stage must be swift and adequate. Drift and indecision invite far deeper disaster. The sums I had requested before the major North Vietnamese offensive and the sudden South Vietnamese retreat are obviously inadequate. Half-hearted action would be worse than none. We must act together and act decisively.

I am, therefore, asking the Congress to appropriate without delay $722 million for emergency military assistance and an initial sum of $250 million for economic and humanitarian aid for South Vietnam.

The situation in South Vietnam is changing very rapidly, and the need for emergency food, medicine, and refugee relief is growing by the hour. I will work with the Congress in the days ahead to develop humanitarian assistance to meet these very pressing needs.

Fundamental decency requires that we do everything in our power to ease the misery and the pain of the monumental human crisis which has befallen the people of Vietnam. Millions have fled in the face of the Communist onslaught and are now homeless and are now destitute. I hereby pledge in the name of the American people that the United States will make a maximum humanitarian effort to help care for and feed these hopeless victims.

And now I ask the Congress to clarify immediately its restrictions on the use of U.S. military forces in Southeast Asia for the limited purposes of protecting American lives by ensuring their evacuation, if this should be necessary. And I also ask prompt revision of the law to cover those Vietnamese to whom we have a very special obligation and whose lives may be endangered should the worst come to pass.

I hope that this authority will never have to be used, but if it is needed, there will be no time for Congressional debate. Because of the gravity of the situation, I ask the Congress to complete action on all of these measures not later than April 19.

"Tragic" Situation in Cambodia

In Cambodia, the situation is tragic. The United States and the Cambodian Government have each made major efforts, over a long period and through many channels, to end that conflict. But because of their military successes, steady external support, and their awareness of American legal restrictions, the Communist side has shown no interest in negotiation, compromise, or a political solution. And yet, for the past 3 months, the beleaguered people of Phnom Penh have fought on, hoping against hope that the United States would not desert them, but instead provide the arms and ammunition they so badly needed.

I have received a moving letter from the new acting President of Cambodia, Saukham Khoy, and let me quote it for you:

"Dear Mr. President," he wrote, "As the American Congress reconvenes to reconsider your urgent request for supplemental assistance for the Khmer Republic, I appeal to you to convey to the American legislators our plea not to deny these vital resources to us, if a nonmilitary solution is to emerge from this tragic 5-year-old conflict.

"To find a peaceful end to the conflict we need time. I do not know how much time, but we all fully realize that the agony of the Khmer people cannot and must not go on much longer. However, for the immediate future, we need the rice to feed the hungry and the ammunition and the weapons to defend ourselves against those who want to impose their will by force [of arms]. A denial by the American people of the means for us to carry on will leave us no alternative but inevitably abandoning our search for a solution which will give our citizens some freedom of choice as to their future. For a number of years now the Cambodian people have placed their trust in America. I cannot believe that this confidence was misplaced and that suddenly America will deny us the means which might give us a chance to find an acceptable solution to our conflict."

This letter speaks for itself. In January, I requested food and ammunition for the brave Cambodians, and I regret to say that as of this evening, it may be soon too late.

Impact of Indochina Events on U.S. Resolve

Members of the Congress, my fellow Americans, this moment of tragedy for Indochina is a time of trial for us. It is a time for national resolve.

It has been said that the United States is over-extended, that we have too many commitments too far from home, that we must re-examine what our truly vital interests are and shape our strategy to conform to them. I find no fault with this as a theory, but in the real world such a course must be pursued carefully and in close coordination with solid progress toward overall reduction in worldwide tensions.

We cannot, in the meantime, abandon our friends while our adversaries support and encourage theirs. We cannot dismantle our defenses, our diplomacy, or our intelligence capability while others increase and strengthen theirs.

Let us put an end to self-inflicted wounds. Let us remember that our national unity is a most priceless asset. Let us deny our adversaries the satisfaction of using Vietnam to pit Americans against Americans. At this moment, the United States must present to the world a united front.

Above all, let's keep events in Southeast Asia in their proper perspective. The security and the progress of hundreds of millions of people everywhere depend importantly on us.

Let no potential adversary believe that our difficulties or our debates mean a slackening of our national will. We will stand by our friends, we will honor our commitments, and we will uphold our country's principles.

The American people know that our strength, our authority, and our leadership have helped prevent a third world war for more than a generation. We will not shrink from this duty in the decades ahead.

Strengths and Difficulties of U.S. Foreign Policy

Let me now review with you the basic elements of our foreign policy, speaking candidly about our strengths and some of our difficulties.

We must, first of all, face the fact that what has happened in Indochina has disquieted many of our friends, especially in Asia. We must deal with this situation promptly and firmly. To this end, I have already scheduled meetings with the leaders of Australia, New Zealand, Singapore, and Indonesia, and I expect to meet with the leaders of other Asian countries as well.

A key country in this respect is Japan. The warm welcome I received in Japan last November vividly symbolized for both our peoples the friendship and the solidarity of this extraordinary partnership. I look forward, as I am sure all of you do, with very special pleasure to welcoming the Emperor when he visits the United States later this year.

We consider our security treaty with Japan the cornerstone of stability in the vast reaches of Asia and the Pacific. Our relations are crucial to our mutual well-being. Together, we are working energetically on the international multilateral agenda—in trade, energy, and food. We will continue the process of strengthening our friendship, mutual security, and prosperity.

Also, of course, of fundamental importance is our mutual security relationship with the Republic of Korea, which I reaffirmed on my recent visit.

U.S. Relations With Europe

Our relations with Europe have never been stronger. There are no peoples with whom America's destiny has been more closely linked. There are no peoples whose friendship and cooperation are more needed for the future. For none of the members of the Atlantic community can be secure, none can prosper, none can advance unless we all do so together. More than ever, these times demand our close collaboration in order:

—to maintain the secure anchor of our common security in this time of international riptides;

—to work together on the promising negotiations with our potential adversaries;

—to pool our energies on the great new economic challenge that faces us.

In addition to this traditional agenda, there are new problems involving energy, raw materials, and the environment. The Atlantic nations face many and complex negotiations and decisions. It is time to take stock, to consult on our future, to affirm once again our cohesion and our common destiny. I therefore expect to join with the other leaders of the Atlantic Alliance at a Western summit in the very near future.

U.S. Policy in the Greek-Turkish Dispute Over Cyprus

Before this NATO meeting, I earnestly ask the Congress to weigh the broader considerations and consequences of its past actions on the complex Greek-Turkish dispute over Cyprus. Our foreign policy cannot be simply a collection of special economic or ethnic or ideological interests. There must be a deep concern for the overall design of our international actions. To achieve this design for peace and to assure that our individual acts have some coherence, the Executive must have some flexibility in the conduct of foreign policy.

United States military assistance to an old and faithful ally, Turkey, has been cut off by action of the Congress. This has imposed an embargo on military purchases by Turkey, extending even to items already paid for—an unprecedented act against a friend.

These moves, I know, were sincerely intended to influence Turkey in the Cyprus negotiations. I deeply share the concern of many citizens for the immense human suffering on Cyprus. I sympathize with the new democratic government in Greece. We are continuing our earnest efforts to find

equitable solutions to the problems which exist between Greece and Turkey. But the result of the Congressional action has been:
  —to block progress towards reconciliation, thereby prolonging the suffering on Cyprus;
  —to complicate our ability to promote successful negotiations;
  —to increase the danger of a broader conflict.

Our longstanding relationship with Turkey is not simply a favor to Turkey; it is a clear and essential mutual interest. Turkey lies on the rim of the Soviet Union and at the gates of the Middle East. It is vital to the security of the eastern Mediterranean, the southern flank of Western Europe, and the collective security of the Western Alliance. Our U.S. military bases in Turkey are as critical to our own security as they are to the defense of NATO.

I therefore call upon the Congress to lift the American arms embargo against our Turkish ally by passing the bipartisan Mansfield-Scott bill now before the Senate. Only this will enable us to work with Greece and Turkey to resolve the differences between our allies. I accept and indeed welcome the bill's requirement for monthly reports to the Congress on progress toward a Cyprus settlement, but unless this is done with dispatch, forces may be set in motion within and between the two nations which could not be reversed.

At the same time, in order to strengthen the democratic government of Greece and to reaffirm our traditional ties with the people of Greece, we are actively discussing a program of economic and military assistance with them. We will shortly be submitting specific requests to the Congress in this regard.

A vital element of our foreign policy is our relationship with the developing countries in Africa, Asia, and Latin America. These countries must know that America is a true, that America is a concerned friend, reliable both in word and deed.

As evidence of this friendship, I urge the Congress to reconsider one provision of the 1974 Trade Act which has had an unfortunate and unintended impact on our relations with Latin America where we have such a long tie of friendship and cooperation. Under this legislation, all members of OPEC [Organization of Petroleum Exporting Countries] were excluded from our generalized system of trade preferences. This, unfortunately, punished two South American friends, Ecuador and Venezuela, as well as other OPEC nations, such as Nigeria and Indonesia, none of which participated in last year's oil embargo. This exclusion has seriously complicated our new dialog with our friends in this hemisphere. I therefore endorse the amendments which have been introduced in the Congress to provide Executive authority to waive those restrictions on the Trade Act that are incompatible with our national interest.

Concern Over the Middle East

The interests of America as well as our allies are vitally affected by what happens in the Middle East. So long as the state of tension continues, it threatens military crisis, the weakening of our alliances, the stability of the world economy, and confrontation with the nuclear super powers. These are intolerable risks.

Because we are in the unique position of being able to deal with all the parties, we have, at their request, been engaged for the past year and a half in the peacemaking effort unparalleled in the history of the region. Our policy has brought remarkable successes on the road to peace. Last year, two major disengagement agreements were negotiated and implemented with our help. For the first time in 30 years, a process of negotiation on the basic political issues was begun and is continuing.

Unfortunately, the latest efforts to reach a further interim agreement between Israel and Egypt have been suspended. The issues dividing the parties are vital to them and not amenable to easy and to quick solutions. However, the United States will not be discouraged.

The momentum toward peace that has been achieved over the last 18 months must, and will, be maintained. The active role of the United States must, and will, be continued. The drift toward war must, and will, be prevented.

I pledge the United States to a major effort for peace in the Middle East, an effort which I know has the solid support of the American people and their Congress. We are now examining how best to proceed. We have agreed in principle to reconvene the Geneva Conference. We are prepared as well to explore other forums. The United States will move ahead on whatever course looks most promising, either towards an overall settlement or interim agreements should the parties themselves desire them. We will not accept stagnation or stalemate with all its attendant risks to peace and prosperity and to our relations in and outside of the region.

U.S.-Soviet Relations

The national interest and national security require as well that we reduce the dangers of war. We shall strive to do so by continuing to improve our relations with potential adversaries.

The United States and the Soviet Union share an interest in lessening tensions and building a more stable relationship. During this process, we have never had any illusions. We know that we are dealing with a nation that reflects different principles and is our competitor in many parts of the globe. Through a combination of firmness and flexibility, the United States, in recent years, laid the basis of a more reliable relationship, founded on mutual interest and mutual restraint. But we cannot expect the Soviet Union to show restraint in the face of the United States' weakness or irresolution.

As long as I am President, America will maintain its strength, its alliances, and its principles as a prerequisite to a more peaceful planet. As long as I am President, we will not permit détente to become a license to fish in troubled waters. Détente must be—and I trust will be—a two-way relationship.

Central to U.S.-Soviet relations today is the critical negotiation to control strategic nuclear weapons. We hope to turn the Vladivostok agreements into a final agreement this year at the time of General Secretary Brezhnev's visit to the United States. Such an agreement would, for the first time, put a ceiling on the strategic arms race. It would mark a turning point in postwar history and would be a crucial step in lifting from mankind the threat of nuclear war.

Our use of trade and economic sanctions as weapons to alter the internal conduct of other nations must also be seriously reexamined. However well-intentioned the goals, the fact is that some of our recent actions in the economic field have been self-defeating, they are not achieving the objectives intended by the Congress, and they have damaged our foreign policy.

The Trade Act of 1974 prohibits most-favored-nation treatment, credit and investment guarantees and commercial agreements with the Soviet Union, so long as their emigration policies fail to meet our criteria. The Soviet Union has, therefore, refused to put into effect the important 1972 trade agreement between our two countries.

As a result, Western Europe and Japan have stepped into the breach. Those countries have extended credits to the Soviet Union exceeding $8 billion in the last 6 months. These are economic opportunities, jobs, and business which could have gone to Americans.

There should be no illusions about the nature of the Soviet system, but there should be no illusions about how to deal with it. Our belief in the right of peoples of the world freely to emigrate has been well demonstrated. This legislation, however, not only harmed our relations with the Soviet Union but seriously complicated the prospects of those seeking to emigrate. The favorable trend, aided by quiet diplomacy, by which emigration increased from 400 in 1968 to over 33,000 in 1973 has been seriously set back. Remedial legislation is urgently needed in our national interest.

Shanghai Communique: Blueprint for U.S.-China Ties

With the People's Republic of China, we are firmly fixed on the course set forth in the Shanghai communique. Stability in Asia and the world require our constructive relations with one-fourth of the human race. After two decades of mutual isolation and hostility, we have, in recent years, built a promising foundation. Deep differences in our philosophy and social systems will endure, but so should our mutual long-term interests and the goals to which our countries have jointly subscribed in Shanghai. I will visit China later this year to reaffirm these interests and to accelerate the improvement in our relations, and I was glad to welcome the distinguished Speaker and the distinguished minority leader of the House back today from their constructive visit to the People's Republic of China.

New Challenges Ahead

Let me talk about new challenges. The issues I have discussed are the most pressing of the traditional agenda on foreign policy, but ahead of us also is a vast new agenda of issues in an interdependent world. The United States, with its economic power, its technology, its zest for new horizons, is the acknowledged world leader in dealing with many of these challenges.

If this is a moment of uncertainty in the world, it is even more a moment of rare opportunity:

—We are summoned to meet one of man's most basic challenges—hunger. At the World Food Conference last November in Rome, the United States outlined a comprehensive program to close the ominous gap between population growth and food production over the long term. Our technological skill and our enormous productive capacity are crucial to accomplishing this task.

—The old order—in trade, finance, and raw materials—is changing and American leadership is needed in the creation of new institutions and practices for worldwide prosperity and progress.

—The world's oceans, with their immense resources and strategic importance, must become areas of cooperation rather than conflict. American policy is directed to that end.

—Technology must be harnessed to the service of mankind while protecting the environment. This, too, is an arena for American leadership.

—The interests and the aspirations of the developed and developing nations must be reconciled in a manner that is both realistic and humane. This is our goal in this new era.

One of the finest success stories in our foreign policy is our cooperative effort with other major energy consuming nations. In little more than a year, together with our partners,

—we have created the International Energy Agency;

—we have negotiated an emergency sharing arrangement which helps to reduce the dangers of an embargo;

—we have launched major international conservation efforts;

—we have developed a massive program for the development of alternative sources of energy.

But the fate of all of these programs depends crucially on what we do at home. Every month that passes brings us closer to the day when we will be dependent on imported energy for 50 percent of our requirements. A new embargo under these conditions could have a devastating impact on jobs, industrial expansion, and inflation at home. Our economy cannot be left to the mercy of decisions over which we have no control. And I call upon the Congress to act affirmatively.

Intelligence Operations: "Information Is Power"

In a world where information is power, a vital element of our national security lies in our intelligence services. They are essential to our Nation's security in peace as in war. Americans can be grateful for the important, but largely unsung, contributions and achievements of the intelligence services of this Nation.

It is entirely proper that this system be subject to Congressional review. But a sensationalized public debate over legitimate intelligence activities is a disservice to this Nation and a threat to our intelligence system. It ties our hands while our potential enemies operate with secrecy, with skill, and with vast resources. Any investigation must be conducted with maximum discretion and dispatch to avoid crippling a vital national institution.

Let me speak quite frankly to some in this Chamber and perhaps to some not in this Chamber. The Central Intelligence Agency has been of maximum importance to Presidents before me. The Central Intelligence Agency has been of maximum importance to me. The Central Intelligence Agency and its associated intelligence organizations could be of maximum importance to some of you in this audience who might be President at some later date. I think it would be catastrophic for the Congress or anyone else to destroy the usefulness by dismantling, in effect, our intelligence systems upon which we rest so heavily.

Now, as Congress oversees intelligence activities, it must, of course, organize itself to do so in a responsible way. It has been traditional for the Executive to consult with the Congress through specially protected procedures that safeguard essential secrets. But recently, some of those procedures have been altered in a way that makes the protection of vital information very, very difficult. I will say to the leaders of the Congress, the House and the Senate, that I will work with them to devise procedures which will meet the needs of the Congress for review of intelligence agency activities and the needs of the Nation for an effective intelligence service.

Need For Strong Defense Posture

Underlying any successful foreign policy is the strength and the credibility of our defense posture. We are strong and we are ready and we intend to remain so. Improvement of relations with adversaries does not mean any relaxation of our national vigilance. On the contrary, it is the firm maintenance of both strength and vigilance that makes possible steady progress toward a safer and a more peaceful world.

The national security budget that I have submitted is the minimum the United States needs in this critical hour. The Congress should review it carefully, and I know it will. But it is my considered judgment that any significant reduction, revision would endanger our national security and thus jeopardize the peace.

Let no ally doubt our determination to maintain a defense second to none, and let no adversary be tempted to test our readiness or our resolve.

History is testing us today. We cannot afford indecision, disunity, or disarray in the conduct of our foreign affairs. You and I can resolve here and now that this Nation shall move ahead with wisdom, with assurance, and with national unity.

The world looks to us for the vigor and for the vision that we have demonstrated so often in the past in great moments of our national history. And as I look down the road,

—I see a confident America, secure in its strengths, secure in its values—and determined to maintain both.

—I see a conciliatory America, extending its hand to allies and adversaries alike, forming bonds of cooperation to deal with the vast problems facing us all.

—I see a compassionate America, its heart reaching out to orphans, to refugees, and to our fellow human beings afflicted by war, by tyranny, and by hunger.

As President, entrusted by the Constitution with primary responsibility for the conduct of our foreign affairs, I renew the pledge I made last August: to work cooperatively with the Congress. I ask that the Congress help to keep America's word good throughout the world. We are one Nation, one government, and we must have one foreign policy.

In an hour far darker than this, Abraham Lincoln told his fellow citizens, and I quote: "we cannot escape history. We of this Congress and this Administration will be remembered in spite of ourselves. No personal significance or insignificance can spare one or another of us."

We who are entrusted by the people with the great decisions that fashion their future can escape neither responsibilities nor our consciences. By what we do now, the world will know our courage, our constancy, and our compassion.

The spirit of America is good and the heart of America is strong. Let us be proud of what we have done and confident of what we can do.

And may God ever guide us to do what is right.

Thank you.

DUBCEK PROTEST LETTER
April 13, 1975

Late in the night of Aug. 20, 1968, Czechoslovakia was invaded without warning by Warsaw Pact troops led by the Soviet Union. Within days Czechoslovakia's eight-month experiment with economic and political reforms—the "Prague Spring"—was over. Alexander Dubcek, the Communist Party First Secretary who had launched the Czech liberalization, at first sought through compromises to salvage some of the reforms. But less than a year after the invasion he was replaced by Gustav Husak. Little was heard of Dubcek thereafter, except that he was working as a mechanic for the Bratislava forest service.

In October 1974, six years after the Soviet invasion, Dubcek broke his long silence with a bitter letter of protest addressed to the federal assembly in Prague. He assailed the political clampdown in effect since 1968 as an abuse of power and a violation of socialist principles.

Dubcek's letter was subsequently smuggled out of Czechoslovakia, and portions of it were published by The New York Times *April 13, 14 and 15, 1975. The Czechoslovak Socialist Opposition, reportedly a dissident group within Czechoslovakia, was believed responsible for circulating the letter in the West. The text also appeared in the London* Observer, *the German weekly* Der Spiegel, *and other major European publications.*

Official Czech reaction came from Communist Party leader Husak himself. He declared April 16 that Dubcek was free to "pack his bags tomorrow and go to any bourgeois state." But if he chose to stay, he would have "to fully respect Czechoslovak laws." On May 20 the Prague underground journal Narodni Noviny (National News) *reported that Dubcek had been reassigned to a tree-planting section in the forestry service. Further, it was reported that approximately 100 suspected Czechoslovak supporters of Dubcek had been targets of police raids and interrogation.*

Prague Spring

The "Prague Spring" of 1968 began with Dubcek's election as First Secretary of the Czechoslovak Communist Party in January of that year. He had come to power as head of a moderate party faction which sought economic reforms, equalization of Slovak status in the Czech-dominated state, and liberalization of Communist Party procedures. During Dubcek's eight months in office, Czech censorship ended. Prominent liberals were placed throughout the conservative bureaucracy and independent political groups, many openly anti-Soviet, flourished.

Soviet displeasure with these developments led to Czech-Soviet talks in the Czech border town of Ciena at the beginning of August 1968. There the Soviet delegation led by Leonid Brezhnev reportedly forced Dubcek to promise to purge key reform leaders from the government, curb the political groups and muzzle the free-wheeling Czech press. (The contents of these secret pledges, rumored at the time, were confirmed in February 1975 when an Italian Communist newspaper published an account of the events surrounding the 1968 invasion written by one of Dubcek's former associates, the late Josef Smrkovsky). When Dubcek failed to carry out the secret agreements, the Soviet Union launched the invasion and Husak dismantled the Dubcek government.

After 1968, official criticism of Dubcek was rare. Husak censured the reformist movement and its leader at a 1971 party congress in Prague, and in 1974 the party newspaper Rude Pravo *characterized Dubcek and his associates as "liquidators" of the Communist Party. Meanwhile, Czechoslovakia developed one of the highest standards of living in Eastern Europe and began normalizing relations with Western governments, none of which commented on Dubcek's letter.*

Suspicion, Fear, Hypocrisy

In his lengthy communication Dubcek asserted his own loyalty to communism and to the socialist bloc. But he pointed out that whereas his government had "stressed...the Leninist principle of inner-party democracy," the Husak regime suppressed any discussion of party policy. Citing "misuse" of state security forces for surveillance and intimidation, Dubcek deplored the resulting "atmosphere of suspicion, fear, hypocrisy and police-informing." Social values were "destroyed," he said; moreover, without the assent of the majority the party would fail to achieve "progressive development."

On July 5, Dubcek sent an appeal to the Communist Party leaders of Italy and East Germany. He asked that the situation of Czechoslovakia, still occupied by Soviet troops, be reviewed at a Communist summit conference scheduled for the end of the summer. The expected meeting did not take place.

> Excerpts from letter by Alexander Dubcek as published by The New York Times April 13, 14 and 15, 1975. The letter had been addressed to the Czechoslovak Federal Assembly and the Slovak National Council under date of Oct. 28, 1974:

At May 1 and anniversary celebrations, and on other occasions our party leaders justly demand freedom for the Chilean patriots. But how is one to judge such appeals considering the things happening in a Socialist state under Communist leadership, aimed at other Communists, internationalists and patriots of their own country and party? They are part of the method of governing in a system of personal power and are being carried out against hundreds of thousands of Communists with the aim of strengthening and confirming old practices, already condemned by the party and the Communist movement, which have caused the Communist movement so much harm in the past.

During the post-August, 1968, period, under the pretext of struggle against counter-revolution from a sectarian position, advantage was taken of the situation that had arisen to liquidate the official policy of the Central Committee of the Communist party of Czechoslovakia (C.C. of the C.P.), the Government and the National Front. This led to the victimization of not only ex-functionaries of the party, Government, National Assembly, revolutionary trade-union movement, the youth movement, women's movement, antifascist federations, cultural and artistic and other bodies comprising the National Front, but also of hundreds of thousands of rank-and-file members of the party and the said organizations.

Furthermore, the official line of the present party leadership still threatens their social existence and civil rights. Officially this is called systematic implementation of the party's leading role and *restoration* of its standing and influence in society.

Abuses of Husak Regime

Certain sections of the state security organs are misused for the conduct of illegal activities, and forces within those organs are attempting to seize sole control of political and public life. That is why these components of armed power feel called upon again to direct their activities against the "enemy" inside the party. That is why surveillance webs have been spun and informants have been planted not only where I work but throughout our society.

This hinders the activity and the education and political work of the party, stultifying its main function, which is replaced by rule based on coercion. This is much simpler and at the same time extremely harmful to Socialism, not only in Czechoslovakia. Corruption inevitably spreads in a party deprived of the possibility of open discussion and of regular and effective control of even its highest offices.

Fear for their means of existence leads a great number of members to endorse decisions they do not agree with. Duplicity becomes general. An atmosphere of suspicion, fear, hypocrisy and police-informing is created. In that kind of situation it is impossible to obtain a *democratic majority* in the party, and therefore it must lack drive toward progressive development.

We have gained enough experience to grasp that Marxism-Leninism is not a blind dogma, a textbook and a primer, in which the *same* prescription and procedure is given for every Communist party irrespective of where it is, what stage of development it has reached, and in what historical and economic situation it finds itself. We know that Marxism-Leninism is in itself a *guide* for the activity of each particular Communist party, even if it has generally valid maxims and principles.

I mention this because it is hard for me to bear being lumped together with party traitors because I, like so many others, differed with the present party leadership in our view of the implementation of party policy at a given stage of development and the method of solving difficulties and surmounting obstacles.

Under conditions of Socialist power and Socialist development—especially in view of today's level of development and of the history of our working-class and Socialist movement—agreement with party politics and determination of its correctness in the party and society cannot and may not be obtained by force, especially armed force.

It is totally inadmissible to achieve this by calling in "aid" from the outside, as happened in August 1968.

The post-January policy of the C.C. and the Government [the period following Dubcek's election in 1968] constituted a solution to the crisis in the party and society. This policy was a logical consequence of the crisis that began in the 1950s and culminated in the 1960s [apparently a reference to the de-Stalinization process begun by Soviet leader Nikita S. Khruschev in 1956]. A deeper and qualitatively new crisis was brought about by the August intervention. But a solution to this new crisis is not to be found in the policy formulated in ["Lessons From the Crisis Period of 1968-69", an official repudiation of Dubcek's policies and justification of the 1968 invasion, adopted December 1970]; the way out of the post-August crisis situation was outlined in the November, 1968, resolution of the C.C. [A moderate document adopted under Dubcek after the 1968 invasion.] I said then and reiterate today that I could not, and would not, go beyond that resolution. I said openly at the autumn, 1969, session of the C.C. (during the debate that followed the Presidium's proposal to annul the resolution) that to go further than the resolution would create real havoc in the party and society.

That is why trumped-up charges of "betrayal of the party, the working class, the people and our nation" were laid against me and others; in the eyes of the new leadership I was a threat to the existence of Socialism, and I was undermining our alliance [with the Soviet Union], Socialism, and the efforts to achieve normalization. I am convinced that the November, 1968, resolution, which *was a consequence of the August intervention, came the nearest to achieving the political unification of the vast majority of the party and society. It could have led the party out of this new crisis,* which was in part precipitated by a certain faction who aimed to annul the principles of the post-January policies of the C.C. through the entry of the troops.

The November resolution did not nullify the post-January policy and the Action Program [program of the Dubcek-led reform movement] as the present party leadership did in ["Lessons From the Crisis Period"]. This resolution pointed a finger not only at right-wing opportunism, but also at sectarianism *in relationship to the official policy of the C.C.* As far as I know, the resolution was supported even by those members of the C.C. who later rejected it as well as the whole Action Program. Under the new conditions growing sectarianism became the main threat to the post-January policies, especially after the April, 1969, C.C. session.

Husak's Policies Divisive

The new party leadership adopted sectarian opportunism as its main ally when forming new policies, and very soon merged with it. On the basis of sectarianism and dogmatism, under the pretext of a struggle against "right-wing opportunism" and "counter-revolution," the new party leadership *repudiated* the November resolution as a political base and as a *platform for consolidation* (under the new post-August conditions), and adopted instead a *divisive policy* based on sectarian and dogmatic principles *with a view to annulling the post-January official policy of the C.C.* This led logically to a conception in which, in *their* view, "the opportunists" were not those forces who had opposed the post-January policy of the C.C. but the leaders of the Government themselves. The "opportunist" label was then extended to their policy, which had been founded on a realistic assessment of the internal situation and the possible solution to the [economic] crisis of the 1960's, based on equal cooperation within the Council of Mutual Economic Aid, [Comecon, the Eastern European trade organization] and respecting our treaties of alliance with the other members of the Warsaw Pact.

Let us not forget that in those tragic days of August, 1968, our state security organs did not apprehend a *single* counter-revolutionary. On the other hand, a group of state security members in Bohemia and Slovakia knew exactly where to find and arrest a large part of the leadership of the Communist party, the Government, the National Assembly and the Czech National Council.

If the invasion by Warsaw Pact armies did take place at the invitation of *a self-appointed group* of Czechoslovak representatives, as was announced by the official Soviet news agency, then I can only call such a procedure factional activity—to put it mildly—and the consequences of this step an affront and humiliation, the moral and ideological humiliation of the entire party of Czechoslovakia and the Czech and Slovak people.

Aftermath Of Invasion

It was a heavy blow to the Communist and Socialist movement. A severe blow was likewise dealt to Czechoslovak-Soviet relations, relations with a long tradition behind them, strengthened by gratitude for our liberation. One can only regret that so many founding members and representatives of the party and Czechoslovak-Soviet friendship, as well as the younger generation of Communists from the antifascist and national-liberation struggle, and people who worked so hard in the years of building of Socialism, have had their honor besmirched.

All these people have proved in practice their relation to our party and the Soviet Union but have now—thousands of them—been branded as anti-Soviet elements; they have been morally, socially and materially punished in a Socialist state to which they have devoted a large part of their lives. This is *revenge* for January and its principles, carried out by supporters of the dogmatic approach to the problems of further Socialist development, upholders of the system of personal power and of suppression of the democratic aspects of Marxism-Leninism.

No, we cannot draw lessons from the "Lessons," which document has been adopted as the political platform of the present party leadership, either for an assessment of the crisis in our party and society, or for our future development. Insofar as this platform does determine present policy, it can only lead to moral, ideological and cultural stagnation of our society and to the degradation of human personality.

Dubcek's Reforms

The post-January policy grew out of an ideological struggle based on true political forms and methods; this struggle extended from the plenary sessions of October, 1967, and January, 1968, and the April plenary session on the Action Program and also the May plenum of the C.C. Of course there was no time to work out all the details in such a short period. It was all enacted in front of the whole party and the people, with their active participation. The party and state leadership defended this line because they regarded the whole thing as their offspring. There were undeniable successes. These cannot be diminished even if the party looks back and sees deficiencies and distortions, as a consequence of which the results accomplished in the national economy and in political education and artistic and cultural endeavor were not so great as Socialism and government by the people make possible.

The impetus for the post-January policy was, and remains, the serious contradiction between the development of the means of production on the one hand, and the system of planning, the organization and system of political power on the other. The crux of the matter is to utilize more fully the possibilities that Socialism gives our society to rid Socialism, with regard to the contradiction, of outdated aspects, distortions and one-sided theoretical and practical implementation of the tenets of Marxism-Leninism, which are being used subjectively to justify the present course in that some aspects are emphasized and others are suppressed.

Democracy and Socialism

The post-January [Dubcek] policy of the party and the Government was not a revision of Marxist fundamentals, which is the way it is presented to-day to the party at home and to the international Communist and working-class movement; but it did give weight to aspects of Marxism-Leninism that had been suppressed, and began to democratize the political system. The post-January leadership stressed in theory and practice the Leninist principle of inner-party democracy, without the implementation of which there can be no talk of a new type of party. This basic principle of party life and creative approach to the fulfillment of its mission, suppressed in the past, is being suppressed again today. This is why the crisis in the party has sharpened. In stipulating the line of Socialist development, the leadership has come into conflict with the party rank and file and the broad masses of the working people, youth and students, the trade unions and the women's movement. One cannot look upon the rank and file as a blind mass to whom the leaders pass down chewed-over morsels for them to swallow. The party and its leadership can be strong only when the latter does not have a monopoly of vision, but the whole membership has eyes.

Disagreement with a new line while it is being formulated cannot be regarded as an "anti-party attitude" and members should not be punished for it. It is absurd to threaten their social existence as the present party leadership did when creating and implementing a different internal political course. That is not a political method. That is *coercion* used against the party and against our Socialist society.

Perhaps the most audacious accusations in the "Lessons" and voiced by the present party leadership is that plans were afoot to tear Czechoslovakia away from the community of Socialist countries.

I hesitate to call this by its right name and to point out the consequences that this demagogy produces and the harm it does to internationalism in this sphere. I could give the names of many important revolutionaries, founders of the party, artists, academicians, partisans, people who took part in the antifascist resistance at home and abroad, writers, dramatists and composers. But where could I find the time and space to draw up a complete list of silenced political activists and creative workers? This label ["anti-Soviet elements"] has been given to hundreds of thousands who fought for the liberation of our country side by side with Soviet troops and partisans, fighters for Socialism, Communists and non-Communists. More than a half million are expelled Communists accused of "anti-Sovietism." If people of this caliber are branded thus in the eyes of their milieu, what other result can this have than to evoke anti-Sovietism in other members of the party and the public?

Foreign Policy

Today, just as at the time when the Action Program was drawn up, I realize—and I am convinced that the other representatives of the former official policy of the party and Government share my opinion—that the Czechoslovak Socialist Republic cannot base its policy on withdrawal from the community of Socialist countries; on the contrary, it vitally needs this cooperation, particularly with the Soviet Union; this was and will continue to be the foundation stone of Czechoslovakia's foreign policy. I therefore reject most emphatically every fabrication about Czechoslovakia's endeavors to withdraw from the community of Socialist countries as well as the false accusation of anti-Sovietism leveled against me and the comrades with whom I created and tried to implement the short-term post-January program of the party, the Government and the National Front [union of all legal Czechoslovak political parties].

We did not try to revise Czechoslovak foreign policy; we were striving for fuller activity and equality in relations among the Socialist countries, while preserving the right of every party to solve its internal problems in harmony with the needs of society and the will of the people.

Impact of Current Party Line

I find [the present leadership] morally guilty of imposing their conception by the use of force and undemocratic means, the incorrectness of their conception having been demonstrated over a span of six years. On what criteria does the present leadership judge fitness for continued membership in the party and the member's Marxist-Leninist standpoints? 1. Agreement with the procedure of the group who invited the troops of the five Warsaw Pact countries. 2. Agreement with the expulsion from the party of the revisionist and opportunistic leadership headed by A. Dubcek. 3. Admission that the official post-January policy and the Action Program were of an opportunistic and revisionist character. 4. Support for the present line, based on the "Lessons," which is—unlike the post-January line—as much Marxist-Leninist as those who created it. Whoever agrees with this is a Marxist-Leninist and whoever does not harms the interests of the party and is a political opportunist.

The enforced dismissal from the industrial and cultural spheres of large numbers of qualified people who have expressed and continue to express a different *opinion* from the leadership will continue to cause immense damage. The creative intelligentsia are the hardest hit; the hands of those who can create and write are tied. The greatest threat to means of existence concerns those capable of creating socially committed works. I think that the working class and its leading role has been morally affected. I should like to be mistaken when I say that the working class, as the most important component and nominal bearer of power in a Socialist state, feels that it is being thoroughly manipulated. It has been deprived of what it regarded as progressive and has had a different conception forced upon it. Worker participation in public affairs and state administration has been reduced to a minimum insofar as it exists at all.

In my view the most serious consequence of the present policy is *the fact that the people have been deprived of the possibility of discussing party policy without fear, i.e., freely,* and thus of making decisions about matters affecting society.

I am forced to conclude that the present party line has been successfully implemented, social values have been successfully destroyed, but none of the conflicts that led to the crisis in the party and society in the sixties (before 1968) *has been solved.*

[The party's development has been set back] not only to the stage prior to 1968, but to a situation the like of which has not been seen during the whole of its history. Since April, 1969, the party, having failed to solve the existing crisis, has fallen into an even deeper crisis the seriousness of whose consequences it has not yet fully appreciated.

Internal Differences Valid

To disregard the differences between countries endangers the party and the development of Socialism and the fate of the whole Socialist revolution. Underestimating or ignoring internal differences in the activity of the Communist party as the leading force in society after the victory of the working class leads inevitably to a gradual weakening of the party's influence on the masses, to a decline in initiative and initial enthusiasm, and mainly to a gradual loss of the voluntary spirit with which the masses launched the revolution and the building of Socialism.

The party leadership becomes divorced from the rank and file, and the party line from the working class and the people as a decisive basis of power. *The masses cease to understand the party.* The party and state leadership, seeing no other way out, resort to the exercise of administrative power through which it imposes respect for its line, and the obedience and "uniform discipline" of Communists. This provides the basis for violating Leninist norms in the party (though they may be formally upheld); some aspects of Marxism are stressed and others suppressed. This is how power begins to be exercised over those in whose hands power ought to be invested....

Would it be right for us to instruct the comrades in Poland how to collectivize their agriculture, a problem that we solved a long time ago and that has not yet been solved in Poland? And if we were to construe a theory that they were thereby conserving capitalism and private enterprise? No, this would not be right, for they know best why, when and how they will solve this problem. It was not right of the leadership of the Polish United Workers' party to attempt to drive us to ill-considered actions in 1968 while we were trying to solve our own problems, when at that time all the universities in Warsaw were closed, the lecturers had been dismissed from their posts, and there was general dissatisfaction with policy that eventually led to such tragic events as shooting at workers. Perhaps the party leadership in Poland at that time thought that by attacking our policy and our leadership they would solve their own domestic conflicts.

We had only to *consider* a not very large loan from an advanced country for this to be described as a danger of becoming dependent on capitalism, although it was obvious to every reasonable economist that these means could help to renew our technological base. Today it is a matter of course not only to accept loans but even to open foreign banks in the Socialist countries. Since the principle of peaceful coexistence of states with different systems has been accepted, economic and technological cooperation and trade among these states is not only necessary but unavoidable.

Non-Intervention Essential

If there are to be good relations between Communist parties, the principle should be observed that the solution of internal problems in a party and a country is the exclusive concern of the respective party. Perhaps this principle should be chronicled in a resolution at a world or European forum of Communist parties.

Regarding principles governing the mutual relations between Communist parties, a factional policy inside another C.P. should not be supported: I mean by this the actions of a group who six years ago formulated a conception of the solutions of our internal problems differing from that of the C.C., the Government and the National Assembly, and going as far as military intervention by some Warsaw Pact countries. [The Soviet Union in 1968 claimed that the Warsaw Pact intervention had been requested by "Czechoslovak party and government leaders."] This group took upon itself too great a responsibility without the knowledge of the authorities competent to take this step. Although today they brandish Leninism, they have jettisoned the principle of a democratic majority. Today they cry out that they are loyal to the Warsaw Pact. This is common demagogy. Did such a question ever arise in our party and state leadership? Did our leadership violate this pact? There has been no violation on our part. This fully attests to our internationalism.

I understand now more than ever that the *system of personal power* is an amalgamation of political, ideological, organizational, cadre and other instruments and measures wielded primarily from a position of power. It is not enough to agree with this analysis: It is necessary to consciously overcome this system, to thwart it through legal norms, prevent its perpetuation and existence; we tried to do this partly. This method is incompatible with Marxism-Leninism. What is important is not so much the individuals and personalities who put this system into operation under the pretext of protecting orthodox Leninism, threatened by various "improvers," although this factor is by no means negligible. It is crucial that the very concept behind this method of governing, based, among other things, on manipulating the masses into obedience and discipline "in order that Socialism may not be threatened," be destroyed theoretically, organizationally and politically.

I have written about my political reflections and views also to show that I am not a case for the state security forces. What I have written here is not and cannot be a subject for political agitation at chance meetings with workers in the state forests commission or in the streets, or with the friends I run into sometimes when swimming at Senec, or when I go to see my relatives or the grave of my parents and brother at Uhrovec, as the surveillance officers who have spun so many webs around me clearly imagine.

If they want to know my views, they are here at their disposal; it is partly due to them that I have expressed myself. The main content of this letter is intended to show more clearly that *my "guilt" (and not mine alone) consists of a different evaluation of our development than the one expressed in the* ["Lessons From the Crisis Period of 1968-69"] *and a different view of the necessity to overcome the lasting and deepening crisis in the party and in society than that held by the present leadership of the party.*

I reject the injustice shown toward me and comrades who think the same way, including even the use of the security organs. (In their defense it would perhaps be more correct to say that they are misused.) It is worth mentioning that the President of the Republic had the habit of placing transistor radios at the windows before opening any discussions. This requires no comment and speaks for itself....

FORD AND KISSINGER:
POST-VIETNAM OUTLOOK
April 17, 23 and 29, 1975

In the final days before the collapse of anti-Communist governments in Cambodia and South Vietnam, President Gerald R. Ford and Secretary of State Henry A. Kissinger warned Americans against what Kissinger called a "precipitate and dangerous withdrawal" from world affairs. Both men declared that the United States would honor its foreign alliances and urged Americans to look to the future and avoid recriminations.

From 1950, when American arms were first shipped to the colonial French battling insurgents in Indochina, until 1973, Congress had gone along with virtually every presidential request relating to Indochina policies and funding. However, legislation enacted after the Paris peace accord was signed in January 1973 (see Historic Documents 1973, p. 115) explicitly barred further use of funds for U.S. combat activities in Indochina. And in November 1973 Congress limited the President's authority to commit U.S. troops anywhere outside the United States and provided for congressional termination of such a commitment (PL 93-148, see Historic Documents 1973, p. 923).

Against a background of mounting truce violations by both sides, Congress in 1974 cut military aid to Vietnam and in 1975 rejected Ford's request for additional emergency military aid to South Vietnam and Cambodia (see p. 223). When the Cambodian government collapsed in mid-April under renewed Khmer Rouge assaults, its last official message to the United States called American inaction a "heartbreaking betrayal." And South Vietnamese President Nguyen Van Thieu, resigning nine days before the surrender of his country, bitterly charged the United States with abandoning a pledge to redress Communist violations of the Paris accord (see p. 279)

Response to Surrender

International reaction at the time of the South Vietnamese surrender, April 29, ranged from praise for the Communist victory to concern over the future course of American foreign policy. South Korean President Park Chung Hee told his people April 29 that "Although South Vietnam is far removed, we cannot regard the situation there as a fire across the river," The New York Times *reported. Cairo radio termed the Vietnam outcome a victory and predicted that the event would undercut Kissinger's credibility in Egypt. Britain's* Daily Telegraph *asserted that "America has received a fearful jab in the face, from which it will take years to recover."*

Kissinger on U.S. Credibility

Kissinger dealt with the issue of U.S. credibility in a major address to the American Society of Newspaper Editors (ASNE) in Washington April 17. Any new American commitments, Kissinger said, "must be carefully weighed.... But after our recent experiences we have a special obligation to make certain that commitments we have made will be rigorously kept and that this is understood by all concerned. Let no ally doubt our steadfastness." Kissinger faulted the other signatories of the Paris accord for failing to protest North Vietnamese violations of the agreement. In an apparent reference to the Soviet Union and China, Kissinger declared: "We shall not forget who supplied the arms which North Vietnam used to make a mockery of its signature on the Paris accords." American priorities for the future included reform of the international economic system, support of existing alliances, and solutions for energy and food crises, Kissinger said.

Ford on Reconciliation

On April 23 President Ford told a Tulane University audience that the Vietnam war was over "as far as America is concerned." Americans should "begin a great national reconciliation," Ford said, by turning to "problems of today and the future." Ford's statements did not mean he was abandoning his emergency request for aid to Southeast Asia (still pending before Congress), a White House spokesman said the following day. The speech was simply a call for "people to shift their attention."

Evacuation

When the South Vietnam surrender finally came on April 29, administration statements dealt primarily with the last-minute American evacuation operation in Saigon. U.S. policy in the final weeks of the war had been to achieve "as humane a political evolution as we could," Kissinger told a Washington news conference that day. The American evacuation had included some 56,000 South Vietnamese who, because of their wartime associations with Americans, were considered to be "in the most severe jeopardy," Kissinger said.

Panic had erupted in the last stages of the evacuation as thousands of Vietnamese sought places on the U.S. helicopters that were completing the operation. President Ford had ordered an emergency airlift from the American embassy in Saigon to U.S. warships off the Vietnamese coast after Tan Son Nhut airport was closed by enemy shelling. U.S. Marines and civilians fought off desperate Vietnamese with pistols and rifle butts to prevent their overrunning the U.S. compound as the last helicopters lifted off. When questioned about this aspect of the evacuation, Kissinger said "it was always foreseen that a helicopter lift for some contingents would be necessary" and pointed out that earlier stages of the evacuation had been accomplished "without any substantial opposition." Kissinger also defended the 1973 Paris accord as appropriate at the time it was signed. Assumptions valid then were later "falsified by events...unforeseeable by anybody who negotiated these agreements," said Kissinger.

Also at the Kissinger news conference, White House press secretary Ronald Nessen read a brief statement from President Ford announcing his evacuation order and calling on Americans "to close ranks, to avoid recrimination about the past, to look ahead...."

> *Address by Secretary of State Henry A. Kissinger to the American Society of Newspaper Editors in Washington on April 17, 1975:*

I am here to sound a note of hope about the future of our foreign policy despite the fact that we are now going through a period of adversity.

A nation facing setbacks can submerge itself in acrimony, looking for scapegoats rather than lessons. It can ignore or gloss over its difficulties and fatuously proceed as if nothing serious had happened.

Or it can examine its situation dispassionately, draw appropriate conclusions, and chart its future with realism and hope.

President Ford has chosen this latter course. A week ago he called upon Congress and the American people to turn this time of difficulty into a demonstration of spirit—to prove once again our devotion and our courage and to put these into the service of building a better world.

For the entire postwar period our strength and our leadership have been essential in preserving peace and promoting progress. If either falters, major shifts in political alignments will occur all around the world. The result will be new dangers for America's security and economic well-being. The Middle East war and oil embargo of 1973 demonstrated how distant events can threaten world peace and global prosperity simultaneously. A reduction of American influence in key areas can have disastrous consequences.

How other nations perceive us is thus a matter of major consequence. Every day I see reports from our embassies relaying anguished questions raised by our friends. What do events in Indochina, the southern flank of NATO, and the Middle East signify for America's competence—constancy—credibility—coherence? How will Americans react? What are the implications for future American policy? We can be certain that potential adversaries are asking themselves the same questions—not with sympathy, but to estimate their opportunities.

It is fashionable to maintain that pointing to dangers produces a self-fulfilling prophecy, that the prediction of consequences brings them about. Unfortunately, life is not that simple. We cannot achieve credibility by rhetoric; we cannot manufacture coherence by proclamation; and we cannot change facts by not talking about them.

We can do little about the world's judgment of our past actions. But we have it within our power to take charge of our future: if the United States responds to adversity with dignity, if we make clear to the world that we continue to hold a coherent perception of a constructive international role and mean to implement it, we can usher in a new era of creativity and accomplishment. We intend to do just that.

I know that it is not easy for a people that faces major domestic difficulties to gear itself up for new international efforts. But our economic future is bound up with the rest of the world—and with international developments in energy, trade, and economic policy. Our economic health depends on the preservation of American leadership abroad.

This country has no choice. We must, for our own sake, play a major role in world affairs. We have strong assets: a sound foreign policy design, major international achievements in recent years, and the enormous capacities of an industrious and gifted people. We have the resources, and the will, to turn adversity into opportunity.

Indochina

Let me start with our most tragic and immediate problem.

I can add nothing to the President's request for military and humanitarian assistance for the anguished people of South Viet-Nam. I support this appeal and have testified at length to that effect before congressional committees over the past several days.

The time will come when it will be clear that no President could do less than to ask aid for those whom we encouraged to defend their independence and at whose side we fought for over a decade. Then Americans will be glad that they had a President who refused to abandon those who desperately sought help in an hour of travail.

In Indochina our nation undertook a major enterprise for almost 15 years. We invested enormous prestige; tens of thousands died, and many more were wounded, imprisoned, and lost; we spent over $150 billion; and our domestic fabric was severely strained. Whether or not this enterprise was well conceived does not now change the nature of our problem. When such an effort founders, it is an event of profound significance—for ourselves and for others.

I, for one, do not believe that it was ignoble to have sought to preserve the independence of a small and brave people. Only a very idealistic nation could have persevered in the face of so much discouragement.

But where so many think that the war was a dreadful mistake, where thousands grieve for those they loved and others sorrow over their country's setback, there has been sufficient heartache for all to share.

The Viet-Nam debate has now run its course. The time has come for restraint and compassion. The Administration has made its case. Let all now abide by the verdict of the Congress—without recrimination or vindictiveness.

The Design

Let us therefore look to the future. We start with a sound foreign policy structure.

We are convinced that a continuing strong American role is indispensable to global stability and progress. Therefore the central thrust of our foreign policy has been to adjust our role in the world and the conceptions, methods, and commitments which define it to the conditions of a new era—including an America fatigued by Indochina.

The postwar order of international relations ended with the last decade. No sudden upheaval marked the passage of that era, but the cumulative change by the end of the 1960's was profound. Gone was the rigid bipolar confrontation of the cold war. In its place was a more fluid and complex world—with many centers of power, more subtle dangers, and new hopeful opportunities. Western Europe and Japan were stronger and more self-confident; our alliances needed to be adjusted toward a more equal partnership. The Communist world had fragmented over doctrine and national interests; there were promising prospects for more stable relations based on restraint and negotiation. And many of our friends in other parts of the globe were now better prepared to shoulder responsibility for their security and well-being, but they needed our assistance during the period of transition.

At home, the American people and Congress were weary from two decades of global exertion and years of domestic turmoil. They were not prepared for confrontation unless all avenues toward peace had been explored.

The challenge for our foreign policy has been to define an effective but more balanced U.S. role in the world, reducing excessive commitments without swinging toward precipitate and dangerous withdrawal.

We have come a long way.

Our major allies in the Atlantic world and Japan have grown in strength politically and economically; our alliances are firm anchors of world security and prosperity. They are the basis for close cooperation on a range of unprecedented new problems, from détente to energy.

We have launched a hopeful new dialogue with Latin America.

We are looking to a new era of relations with Africa.

We have taken historic steps to stabilize and improve our relations with our major adversaries. We have reduced tensions, deepened dialogue, and reached a number of major agreements.

We have begun the process of controlling the rival strategic arms programs which, unconstrained, threaten global security. When the Vladivostok agreement is completed, a ceiling will have been placed for the first time on the level of strategic arsenals of the superpowers.

We have helped to ease longstanding political conflicts in such sensitive areas as Berlin and the Middle East.

And we have taken the major initiatives to mobilize the international response to new global challenges such as energy, food, the environment, and the law of the sea.

In all these areas the American role has frequently been decisive. The design still stands; our responsibilities remain. There is every prospect for major progress. There is every reason for confidence.

The Domestic Dimension

If this be true, what then is the cause of our problem? Why the setbacks? Why the signs of impasse between the executive and the Congress? What must we do to pull ourselves together?

Setbacks are bound to occur in a world which no nation alone can dominate or control. The peculiar aspect of many of our problems is that they are of our own making. Domestic division has either compounded or caused difficulties from the southern flank of NATO to the Pacific, from the eastern Mediterranean to relations between the superpowers.

Paradoxically, herein resides a cause for optimism. For to the extent that the causes of our difficulties are within ourselves, so are the remedies.

The American people expect an effective foreign policy which preserves the peace and furthers our national interests. They want their leaders to shape the future, not just manage the present. This requires boldness, direction, nuance, and—above all—confidence between the public and the government and between the executive and the legislative branches of the government. But precisely this mutual confidence has been eroding over the past decade.

There are many causes for this state of affairs. Some afflict democracies everywhere; some are unique to America's tradition and recent history. Modern democracies are besieged by social, economic, and political challenges that cut across national boundaries and lie at the margin of governments' ability to control. The energies of leaders are too often consumed by the management of bureaucracy, which turns questions of public purpose into issues for institutional bargaining. Instant communications force the pace of events and of expectations. Persuasion, the essential method of democracy, becomes extraordinarily difficult in an era where issues are complex and outcomes uncertain. A premium is placed on simplification—an invitation to demagogues. Too often, the result is a disaffection that simultaneously debunks government and drains it of the very confidence that a democracy needs to act with conviction.

All of this has compounded the complex problem of executive-legislative relations. In every country, the authority of the modern state seems frustratingly impersonal or remote from those whose lives it increasingly affects; in nearly every democracy, executive authority is challenged by legislators who themselves find it difficult to effect policy except piecemeal or negatively. Issues become so technical that legislative oversight becomes increasingly difficult just as the issues become increasingly vital. The very essence of problem-solving on domestic issues—accommodation of special interests—robs foreign policy of consistency and focus when applied to our dealings with other nations.

Statesmen must act, even when premises cannot be proved; they must decide, even when intangibles will determine the outcome. Yet predictions are impossible to prove; consequences avoided are never evident. Skepticism and suspicion thus become a way of life and infect the atmosphere of executive-legislative debate; reasoned arguments are overwhelmed by a series of confrontations on peripheral issues.

America faces as well the problem of its new generation. The gulf between their historical experience and ours is enormous. They have been traumatized by Viet-Nam as we were by Munich. Their nightmare is foreign commitment as ours was abdication from international responsibility. It is possible that both generations learned their lessons too well. The young take for granted the great postwar achievements in restoring Europe, building peacetime alliances, and maintaining global prosperity. An impersonal, technological, bureaucratized world provides them too few incentives for dedication and idealism.

Let us remember that America's commitment to international involvement has always been ambivalent—even while our doubts were being temporarily submerged by the exertions of World War II and the postwar era. The roots of isolationism, nourished by geography and history, go deep in the American tradition. The reluctance to be involved in foreign conflicts, the belief that we somehow defile ourselves if we engage in "power politics" and balances of power, the sense that foreign policy is a form of Old World imperialism, the notion that weapons are the causes of conflict, the belief that humanitarian assistance and participation in the economic order are an adequate substitute for political engagement—all these were familiar characteristics of the American isolationism of the twenties and thirties. We took our power for granted, attributed our successes to virtue, and blamed our failures on the evil of others. We disparaged means. In our foreign involvement we have oscillated between exuberance and exhaustion, between crusading and retreats into self-doubt.

Following the Second World War a broad spectrum of civic leaders, professional groups, educators, businessmen, clergy, the media, congressional and national leaders of both parties led American public opinion to a new internationalist consensus. Taught by them and experience of the war, the nation understood that we best secured our domestic tranquility and prosperity by enlightened participation and leadership in world affairs. Assistance to friends and allies was not a price to be paid, but a service to be rendered to international stability and therefore to our self-interest.

But in the last decade, as a consequence of Indochina and other frustrations of global engagement, some of our earlier impulses have reasserted themselves. Leadership opinion has, to an alarming degree, turned sharply against many of the internationalist premises of the postwar period. We now hear, and have for several years, that suffering is prolonged by American involvement, that injustice is perpetuated by American inaction, that defense spending is wasteful at best and produces conflict at worst, that American intelligence activities are immoral, that the necessary confidentiality of diplomacy is a plot to deceive the public, that flexibility is cynical and amoral—and that tranquility is somehow to be brought about by an abstract purity of motive for which history offers no example.

This has a profound—and inevitable—impact on the national mood and on the national consensus regarding foreign policy. In the nation with the highest standard of living and one of the richest cultures in the world, in the nation that is certainly the most secure in the world, in the nation which has come closest of all to the ideals of civil liberty and pluralist democracy, we find a deep and chronic self-doubt, especially in the large urban centers and among presumptive leaders.

Will the American people support a responsible and active American foreign policy in these conditions? I deeply believe that they will—if their leaders, in and out of government, give them a sense that they have something to be proud of and something important to accomplish.

When one ventures away from Washington into the heart of America, one is struck by the confidence, the buoyancy, and the lack of any corrosive cynicism. We who sit at what my friend Stewart Alsop, a great journalist, once called "the center" tend to dwell too much on our problems; we dissect in overly exquisite detail our difficulties and our disputes.

I find it remarkable that two-thirds of the Americans interviewed in a nationwide poll in December, at a time of severe recession, still thought an active role in the world served their country's interests better than withdrawal. Even as other nations are closely watching the way we act in Washington, I suspect they marvel at the resiliency of our people and our institutions.

There is a great reservoir of confidence within America. We have the values, the means, and we bear the responsibility to strive for a safer and better world. And there is a great reservoir of confidence around the globe in this country's values and strength.

Where Do We Go From Here?

So, let us learn the right lessons from today's trials.

We shall have to pay the price for our setbacks in Indochina by increasing our exertions. We no longer have the margin of safety. In the era of American predominance, America's preferences held great sway. We could overwhelm our problems with our resources. We had little need to resort to the style of nations conducting foreign policy with limited means: patience, subtlety, flexibility. Today, disarray, abdication of responsibility, or short-sightedness exact a price that may prove beyond our means.

We are still the largest single factor in international affairs, but we are one nation among many. The weight of our influence now depends crucially on our purposefulness, our perseverance, our creativity, our power, and our perceived reliability. We shall have to work harder to establish the coherence and constancy of our policy—and we shall.

We must give up the illusion that foreign policy can choose between morality and pragmatism. America cannot be true to itself unless it upholds humane values and the dignity of the individual. But equally it cannot realize its values unless it is secure. No nation has a monopoly of justice or virtue, and none has the capacity to enforce its own conceptions globally. In the nuclear age especially, diplomacy—like democracy—often involves the compromise of clashing principles. I need not remind you that there are some 140 nations in the world, of which only a bare handful subscribe to our values.

Abstract moralism can easily turn into retreat from painful choices or endless interference in the domestic affairs of others; strict pragmatism, on the other hand, robs policy of vision and heart. Principles without security spell impotence; security without principles means irrelevance. The American people must never forget that our strength gives force to our principles and our principles give purpose to our strength.

Let us understand, too, the nature of our commitments. We have an obligation of steadfastness simply by virtue of our position as a great power upon which many others depend. Thus our actions and policies over time embody their own commitment whether or not they are enshrined in legal documents. Indeed, our actions and the perception of them by other countries may represent our most important commitments.

At the same time, diplomacy must be permitted a degree of confidentiality, or most serious exchange with other governments is destroyed. To focus the national debate on so-called secret agreements which no party has ever sought to implement and whose alleged subject matter has been prohibited by law for two years is to indulge what Mencken called the "national appetite for bogus revelation." It goes without saying that a commitment involving national action must be known to the Congress or it is meaningless.

One lesson we must surely learn from Viet-Nam is that new commitments of our nation's honor and prestige must be carefully weighed. As Walter Lippmann observed, "In foreign relations, as in all other relations, a policy has been formed only when commitments and power have been brought into balance." But after our recent experiences we have a special obligation to make certain that commitments we have made will be rigorously kept and that this is understood by all concerned. Let no ally doubt our steadfastness. Let no nation ever believe again that it can tear up with impunity a solemn agreement signed with the United States.

We must continue our policy of seeking to ease tensions. But we shall insist that the easing of tensions cannot occur selectively. We shall not forget who supplied the arms which North Viet-Nam used to make a mockery of its signature on the Paris accords.

Nor can we overlook the melancholy fact that not one of the other signatories of the Paris accords has responded to our repeated requests that they at least point out North Viet-Nam's flagrant violations of these agreements. Such silence can only undermine any meaningful standards of international responsibility.

At home, a great responsibility rests upon all of us in Washington.

Comity between the executive and legislative branches is the only possible basis for national action. The decade-long struggle in this country over executive dominance in foreign affairs is over. The recognition that the Congress is a coequal branch of government is the dominant fact of national politics today.

The executive accepts that the Congress must have both the sense and the reality of participation; foreign policy must be a shared enterprise. The question is whether the Congress will go beyond the setting of guidelines to the conduct of tactics; whether it will deprive the executive of discretion and authority in the conduct of diplomacy while at the same time remaining institutionally incapable of formulating or carrying out a clear national policy of its own.

The effective performance of our constitutional system has always rested on the restrained exercise of the powers and rights conferred by it. At this moment in our history there is a grave national imperative for a spirit of cooperation and humility between the two branches of our government.

Cooperation must be a two-way street. Just as the executive has an obligation to reexamine and then to explain its policies, so the Congress should reconsider the actions which have paralyzed our policies in the eastern Mediterranean, weakened our hand in relations with the U.S.S.R., and inhibited our dialogue in this hemisphere. Foreign policy must have continuity. If it becomes partisan, paralysis results. Problems are passed on to the future under progressively worse conditions.

When other countries look to the United States, they see one nation. When they look to Washington, they see one government. They judge us as a unit—not as a series of unrelated or uncoordinated institutions. If we cannot agree among ourselves, there is little hope that we can negotiate effectively with those abroad.

So one of the most important lessons to be drawn from recent events is the need to restore the civility of our domestic discourse. Over the years of the Viet-Nam debate rational dialogue has yielded to emotion, sweeping far beyond the issues involved. Not only judgments but motives have been called into question. Not only policy but character has been attacked. What began as consensus progressively deteriorated into poisonous contention.

Leaders in government must do their share. The Administration, following the President's example, will strive for moderation and mutual respect in the national dialogue. We know that if we ask for public confidence we must keep faith with the people.

Debate is the essence of democracy. But it can elevate the nation only if conducted with restraint.

The American people yearn for an end to the bitterness and divisiveness of the past decade. Our domestic stability requires it. Our international responsibilities impose it.

You, in this audience, are today in a unique position to contribute to the healing of the nation.

The Coming Agenda

Ralph Waldo Emerson once said "No great man ever complains of want of opportunity." Neither does a great nation.

Our resources are vast; our leadership is essential; our opportunities are unprecedented and insistent.

The challenges of the coming decades will dwarf today's disputes. A new world order is taking shape around us. It will engulf us or isolate us if we do not act boldly. We cannot consume ourselves in self-destruction. We have great responsibilities:

—We must maintain the vigor of the great democratic alliances. They can provide the anchor of shared values and purposes as we grapple with a radically new agenda.

—We must overcome the current economic and energy crisis. A domestic energy program is thus an urgent national priority. Looking ahead, we envisage a fundamentally reformed international economic system, a Bretton Woods for the 1980's and beyond.

—We must stand up for what we believe in international forums, including the United Nations, and resist the politics of resentment, of confrontation, and stale ideology. International collaboration has a more vital role now than ever, but so has mutual respect among nations.

—We must meet our continuing responsibility for peace in many regions of the world, especially where we uniquely have the confidence of both sides and where failure could spell disaster beyond the confines of the region, as in the Middle East. We will not be pushed by threats of war or economic pressure into giving up vital interests. But equally, we will not, in the President's words, "accept stagnation or stalemate with all its attendant risks to peace and prosperity."

—We must stop the spiral, and the spread, of nuclear weapons. We can then move on to a more ambitious agenda: mutual reductions in strategic arms, control of other weaponry, military restraint in other environments.

—We must overcome two scourges of mankind: famine and the vagaries of nature. We reaffirm the food program announced at the World Food Conference last November. Our fundamental challenge is to help others feed themselves so that no child goes to bed hungry in the year 2000.

—We must continue to reduce conflict and tensions with our adversaries. Over time, we hope that vigilance and conciliation will lead to more positive relationships and ultimately a true global community.

—We must insure that the oceans and space become areas of cooperation rather than conflict. We can then leave to future generations vast economic and technological resources to enrich life on this earth.

261

Our nation is uniquely endowed to play a creative and decisive role in the new order which is taking form around us. In an era of turbulence, uncertainty, and conflict, the world still looks to us for a protecting hand, a mediating influence, a path to follow. It sees in us, most of all, a tradition and vision of hope. Just as America has symbolized for generations man's conquest of nature, so too has America—with its banner of progress and freedom—symbolized man's mastery over his own future.

For the better part of two centuries our forefathers, citizens of a small and relatively weak country, met adversity with courage and imagination. In the course of their struggle they built the freest, richest, and most powerful nation the world has ever known. As we, their heirs, take America into its third century, as we take up the unprecedented agenda of the modern world, we are determined to rediscover the belief in ourselves that characterized the most creative periods in our country.

We have come of age, and we shall do our duty.

Excerpts from address by President Gerald R. Ford at a convocation at Tulane University, April 23, 1975 (introductory remarks omitted):

On January 8, 1815, a monumental American victory was achieved here—the Battle of New Orleans. Louisiana had been a State for less than three years, but outnumbered Americans innovated, outnumbered Americans used the tactics of the frontier, to defeat a veteran British force trained in the strategy of the Napoleonic wars.

We, as a Nation, had suffered humiliation and a measure of defeat in the War of 1812. Our national capital in Washington had been captured and burned. So the illustrious victory in the Battle of New Orleans was a powerful restorative to our national pride.

Yet, the victory at New Orleans actually took place two weeks after the signing of the Armistice in Europe. Thousands died although a peace had been negotiated. The combatants had not gotten the word, yet the epic struggle nevertheless restored America's pride.

War "Finished"

Today, America can regain the sense of pride that existed before Viet-Nam, but it cannot be achieved by refighting a war that is finished as far as America is concerned.

As I see it, the time has come to look forward to an agenda for the future, to unify, to bind up the Nation's wounds and to restore its health and its optimistic self-confidence.

In New Orleans, a great battle was fought after a war was over. In New Orleans tonight, we can begin a great national reconciliation. The first engagement must be with the problems of today, but just as importantly, the problems of the future.

That is why I think it is so appropriate that I find myself tonight at a university which addresses itself to preparing young people for the challenge of tomorrow.

I ask that we stop refighting the battles and the recriminations of the past. I ask that we look now at what is right with America—at our possibilities and our potentialities for change and growth, achievement and sharing. I ask that we accept the responsibility of leadership as a good neighbor to all peoples and an enemy of none.

I ask that we strive to become, in the finest American tradition, something more tomorrow than we are today.

New Agenda

Instead of my addressing the image of America, I prefer to consider the reality of America. It is true that we have launched our Bicentennial celebration without having achieved human perfection, but we have attained a very remarkable self-governed society that possesses the flexibility and the dynamism to grow and undertake an entirely new agenda, an agenda for America's third century.

So, I ask you to join me in helping to write that agenda. I am as determined as a President can be to seek national rediscovery of the belief in ourselves that characterizes the most creative periods in our Nation's history. The greatest challenge of creativity, as I see it, lies ahead.

We, of course, are saddened indeed by the events in Indochina, but these events, tragic as they are, portend neither the end of the world, nor of America's leadership in the world.

Let me put it this way, if I might. Some tend to feel that if we do not succeed in everything everywhere, then we have succeeded in nothing anywhere.

I reject categorically such polarized thinking. We can, and we should help others to help themselves, but the fate of responsible men and women everywhere in the final decision rests in their own hands, not in ours.

America's future depends upon Americans, especially your generation, which is now equipping itself to achieve the challenges of the future, to help write the agenda of America.

Earlier today, in this great community, I spoke about the need to maintain our defenses. Tonight, I would like to talk about another kind of strength, the true source of American power that transcends all of the deterrent powers for peace of our Armed Forces. I am speaking here of our belief in ourselves and our belief in our Nation.

Abraham Lincoln asked, in his own words, "What constitutes the bulwark of our own liberty and independence?" He answered, "It is not our frowning battlements or bristling seacoasts, our Army or our Navy. Our defense is in the spirit which prized liberty as the heritage of all men, in all lands everywhere."

It is in this spirit that we must now move past the discords of the decade. It is in this spirit that I ask you to join me in writing an agenda for the future.

I welcome your invitation, particularly, tonight because I know it is at Tulane and other centers of thought throughout our great country that much consideration is being given to the kind of future that Americans want and, just as importantly, will work for.

Each of you are preparing yourselves for the future, and I am deeply interested in your preparations and your opinions and your goals. However, tonight, with your indulgence, let me share with you my own views.

Goals

I envision a creative program that goes as far as our courage and our capacities can take us, both at home and abroad. My goal is for a cooperative world at peace, using its resources to build, not to destroy.

As President, I am determined to offer leadership to overcome our current economic problems. My goal is for jobs for all who want to work, and economic opportunity for all who want to achieve.

I am determined to seek self-sufficiency in energy as an urgent national priority. My goal is to make America independent of foreign energy sources by 1985. Of course, I will pursue interdependence with other nations and a reformed international economic system.

My goal is for a world in which consuming and producing nations achieve a working balance. I will address the humanitarian issues of hunger and famine, of health and of healing. My goal is to achieve or to assure basic needs and an effective system to achieve this result.

I recognize the need for technology that enriches life while preserving our natural environment. My goal is to stimulate productivity, but use technology to redeem, not to destroy our environment.

I will strive for new cooperation rather than conflict in the peaceful exploration of our oceans and our space. My goal is to use resources for peaceful progress, rather than war and destruction.

Let America symbolize humanity's struggle to conquer nature and master technology. The time has now come for our Government to facilitate the individual's control over his or her future and of the future of America.

"New Knowledge"

But the future requires more than Americans congratulating themselves on how much we know and how many products that we can produce. It requires new knowledge to meet new problems. We must not only be motivated to build a better America, we must know how to do it.

If we really want a humane America that will, for instance, contribute to the alleviation of the world's hunger, we must realize that good intentions do not feed people. Some problems, as anyone who served in the Congress knows, are complex. There are no easy answers. Willpower alone does not grow food.

We thought, in a well-intentioned past, that we could export our technology lock, stock and barrel to developing nations. We did it with the best of intentions, but we are now learning that a strain of rice that grows in one place will not grow in another; that factories that produce at 100 percent in one nation produce less than half as much in a society where temperaments and work habits are somewhat different.

Yet, the world economy has become interdependent—not only food technology, but money management, natural resources and energy, research and development—all kinds of this group require an organized world society that makes the maximum effective use of the world's resources.

I want to tell the world: let's grow food together, but let's also learn more about nutrition, about weather forecasting, about irrigation, about the many other specialties involved in helping people to help themselves.

We must learn more about people, about the development of communities, architecture, engineering, education, motivation, productivity, public health and medicine, arts and sciences, political, legal and social organization. All of these specialties and many, many more are required if young people like you are to help this Nation develop an agenda for our future, your future, our country's future.

Challenges

I challenge, for example, the medical students in this audience to put on their agenda the achievement of a cure for cancer. I challenge the engineers in this audience to devise new techniques for developing cheap, clean and plentiful energy and as a by-product, to control floods.

I challenge the law students in this audience to find ways to speed the administration of equal justice and make good citizens out of convicted criminals.

I challenge education, those of you as education majors, to do real teaching for real life.

I challenge the art majors in this audience to compose the great American symphony, to write the great American novel and to enrich and inspire our daily lives.

America's leadership is essential. America's resources are vast. America's opportunities are unprecedented.

As we strive together to perfect a new agenda, I put high on the list of important points the maintenance of alliances and partnerships with other people and other nations. These do provide a basis of shared values, even as we stand up with determination for what we believe.

This, of course, requires a continuing commitment to peace and a determination to use our good offices wherever possible to promote better relations between nations of this world.

Arms Control

The new agenda, that which is developed by you and by us, must place a high priority on the need to stop the spread of nuclear weapons and to work for the mutual reduction in strategic arms and control of other weapons.

I must say parenthetically, the successful negotiations at Vladivostok, in my opinion, are just a beginning.

Your generation of Americans is uniquely endowed by history to give new meaning to the pride and spirit of America. The magnetism of an American society, confident of its own strength, will attract the good will and the esteem of all people wherever they might be in this globe in which we live.

It will enhance our own perception of ourselves and our pride in being an American. We can—we can, and I say it with emphasis—write a new agenda for our future.

I am glad that Tulane University and other great American educational institutions are reaching out to others in programs to work with developing nations, and I look forward, with confidence, to your participation in every aspect of America's future, and I urge Americans of all ages to unite in this Bicentennial year to take responsibilities for themselves, as our ancestors did.

Let us resolve tonight to rediscover the old virtues of confidence and self-reliance and capability that characterized our forefathers two centuries ago.

I pledge, as I know you do, each one of us, to do our part. Let the beacon lights of the past shine forth from historic New Orleans, and from Tulane University, and from every other corner of this land to illuminate a boundless future for all Americans and a peace for all mankind.

Thank you very much.

> *Transcript of Secretary of State Henry A. Kissinger's April 29, 1975, press conference in Washington, including a statement by President Gerald R. Ford which was read by Mr. Ford's press secretary, Ronald H. Nessen:*

MR. NESSEN: The briefing was delayed until the evacuation was completed, and the last helicopters are now in the air.

I would like to read a statement by the President:

"During the past week, I had ordered the reduction of American personnel in the U.S. Mission in Saigon to levels that could be quickly evacuated during an emergency, while enabling that mission to continue to fulfill its duties.

"During the day on Monday, Washington time, the airport at Saigon came under persistent rocket, as well as artillery, fire and was effectively closed. The military situation in the area deteriorated rapidly.

"I therefore ordered the evacuation of all American personnel remaining in South Viet-Nam.

"The evacuation has been completed. I commend the personnel of the Armed Forces who accomplished it, as well as Ambassador Graham Martin and the staff of his mission, who served so well under difficult conditions.

"This action closes a chapter in the American experience. I ask all Americans to close ranks, to avoid recrimination about the past, to look ahead to the many goals we share, and to work together on the great tasks that remain to be accomplished."

Copies of this statement will be available as you leave the briefing.

Now, to give you details of the events of the past few days and to answer your questions, Secretary of State Kissinger.

American Objectives

SECRETARY KISSINGER: Ladies and Gentlemen, when the President spoke before the Congress [April 10], he stated as our objective the stabilization of the situation in Viet-Nam.

We made clear at that time, as well as before many congressional hearings, that our purpose was to bring about the most controlled and the most humane solution that was possible and that these objectives required the course which the President had set.

Our priorities were as follows: We sought to save the American lives still in Viet-Nam. We tried to rescue as many South Vietnamese that had worked with the United States for 15 years in reliance on our commitments as we possibly could. And we sought to bring about as humane an outcome as was achievable under the conditions that existed.

Over the past two weeks, the American personnel in Viet-Nam have been progressively reduced. Our objective was to reduce at a rate that was significant enough so that we would finally be able to evacuate rapidly but which would not produce a panic which might prevent anybody from getting out.

Our objective was also to fulfill the human obligation which we felt to the tens of thousands of South Vietnamese who had worked with us for over a decade.

Finally, we sought, through various intermediaries, to bring about as humane a political evolution as we could.

By Sunday evening [April 27], the personnel in our mission had been reduced to 950 and there were 8,000 South Vietnamese to be considered in a particularly high-risk category—between 5,000 and 8,000. We do not know the exact number.

On Monday evening, Washington time, around 5 o'clock, which was Tuesday morning in Saigon, the airport in Tan Son Nhut was rocketed and received artillery fire.

The President called an NSC [National Security Council] meeting. He decided that if the shelling stopped by dawn Saigon time, we would attempt to operate with fixed-wing aircraft from Tan Son Nhut Airport for one more day to remove the high-risk South Vietnamese, together with all the Defense Attache's Office [DAO], which was located near the Tan Son Nhut Airport. He also ordered a substantial reduction of the remaining American personnel in South Viet-Nam.

I may point out that the American personnel in Saigon was divided into two groups; one with the Defense Attache's Office, which was located near the Tan Son Nhut Airport; the second one, which was related to the Embassy and was with the U.S. Mission in downtown Saigon.

The shelling did stop early in the morning on Tuesday, Saigon time, or about 9 p.m. last night, Washington time. We then attempted to land C-130's but found that the population at the airport had got out of control and had flooded the runways. It proved impossible to land any more fixed-wing aircraft.

The President thereupon ordered that the DAO personnel, together with those civilians that had been made ready to be evacuated, be moved to the DAO compound, which is near Tan Son Nhut Airport; and at about 11:00 last night, he ordered the evacuation of all Americans from Tan Son Nhut and from the Embassy as well.

This operation has been going on all day, which of course is night in Saigon, and under difficult circumstances, and the total number of those evacuated numbers about 6,500—we will have the exact figures for you tomorrow—of which about 1,000 are Americans.

Our Ambassador has left, and the evacuation can be said to be completed.

In the period since the President spoke to the Congress, we have therefore succeeded in evacuating all of the Americans who were in South Viet-Nam, losing the two marines last night to rocket fire and two pilots today on a helicopter.

We succeeded in evacuating something on the order of 55,000 South Vietnamese. And we hope we have contributed to a political evolution that may spare the South Vietnamese some of the more drastic consequences of a political change, but this remains to be seen. This last point remains to be seen.

As far as the Administration is concerned, I can only underline the point made by the President. We do not believe that this is a time for recrimination. It is a time to heal wounds, to look at our international obligations, and to remember that peace and progress in the world has depended importantly on American commitment and American conviction and that the peace and progress of our own people is closely tied to that of the rest of the world.

I will be glad to answer questions.

Q. Mr. Secretary, you made some reference a few weeks back to those who believe in the domino theory, and while I don't remember exactly your words, the point was it is easy to laugh at it but there is some justification for subscribing to that theory. Now that this chapter is over, can you give us your estimate of the security of Thailand and other countries in the area, or the near area?

SECRETARY KISSINGER: I think it is too early to make a final assessment.

There is no question that the outcome in Indochina will have consequences not only in Asia but in many other parts of the world. To deny these consequences is to miss the possibility of dealing with them.

So, I believe there will be consequences. But I am confident that we can deal with them, and we are determined to manage and to progress along the road toward a permanent peace that we have sought; but there is no question that there will be consequences.

Final U.S. Efforts

Q. Now that it is over, could you tell us, or elaborate in more detail, what we did through various intermediaries to bring about, I think you said, as humane a political solution as possible, and why those efforts seem to have failed?

SECRETARY KISSINGER: I would not agree with the proposition that these efforts have failed because at least some of the efforts, especially those related to evacuation, were carried out through intermediaries. I think it is premature for me to go into all of the details, but we did deal with Hanoi and with the PRG [Provisional Revolutionary Government] through different intermediaries, and we were in a position to put our views and receive responses.

Q. May I follow on that by saying, why, then, was it necessary to stage a rescue operation in the final stages?

SECRETARY KISSINGER: In the final stages, it was always foreseen that a helicopter lift for some contingents would be necessary. I believe that the dynamics of the situation in South Viet-Nam and the impatience of the North Vietnamese to seize power brought about an acceleration of events in the last day and a half.

But you will remember there was a period of about five days when both civilian and U.S. personnel were evacuated without any substantial opposition—in fact, more than five days, about a week.

Q. Mr. Secretary, on that point, do you now anticipate that the North Vietnamese intend to move in and forcefully seize Saigon? Do you anticipate there will be a bloody battle of Saigon, or is there still a chance for an orderly transition?

SECRETARY KISSINGER: This is very difficult to judge at this moment. I think it is important to point out that the Communist demands have been escalating as the military situation has changed in their favor.

So, a week ago they were asking only for the removal of President [Nguyen Van] Thieu. When he resigned, they immediately asked for the removal of his successor, specifying that General [Duong Van] Minh would be acceptable. When President [Tran Van] Huong resigned in favor of General Minh, he was now described as a member of a clique which includes all the members of his administration.

A week ago, the Communist demand was for the removal of American military personnel. This quickly escalated into a removal of all American personnel.

Then a new demand was put forward for the dismantling of the South Vietnamese military apparatus. When that was agreed to, they added to it the demand for the dismantling of the South Vietnamese administrative apparatus. So, it is clear that what is being aimed at is a substantial political takeover.

Now, whether it is possible to avoid a battle for Saigon, it is too early to judge. I would hope—and we certainly have attempted to work in that direction—that such a battle can be avoided. And it is basically unnecessary because it seems to us that the South Vietnamese Government is prepared to draw the conclusions from the existing situation and, in fact, look forward to correspond to the demands of the Communist side.

Q. Mr. Secretary, do you consider the United States now owes any allegiance at all to the Paris pact? Are we now bound in any way by the Paris agreements?

SECRETARY KISSINGER: Well, as far as the United States is concerned, there are not many provisions of the Paris agreement that are still relevant. As far as the North Vietnamese are concerned, they have stated that they wish to carry out the Paris accords, though by what definition is not fully clear to me. We would certainly support this if it has any meaning.

Q. May I ask one follow-up? Do you now favor American aid in rebuilding North Viet-Nam?

SECRETARY KISSINGER: North Viet-Nam?

Q. North Viet-Nam.

SECRETARY KISSINGER: No, I do not favor American aid for rebuilding North Viet-Nam.

Q. South Viet-Nam?

SECRETARY KISSINGER: With respect to South Viet-Nam, we will have to see what kind of government emerges and indeed whether there is going to be a South Viet-Nam. We would certainly look at particular specific humanitarian requests that can be carried out by humanitarian agencies, but we do believe that the primary responsibility should fall on those who supply the weapons for this political change.

Evacuation

Q. Mr. Secretary, I would like to ask a question about the length of time that it took to complete this evacuation. First, the question of whether days went by after the end became obvious before ordering the evacuation; second, if after ordering it there was a one-hour delay in helicopter landings, apparently caused by military confusion; third, whether the evacuation was prolonged by picking up thousands of Vietnamese instead of concentrating on Americans; and fourth, whether this was delayed even further by Ambassador Martin's desire to be the last man to leave the sinking ship.

In other words, I tried to put the specifics in order to ask you, did it take too long to get out of there, to write this last chapter?

SECRETARY KISSINGER: We got out, with all of the personnel that were there, without panic and without the substantial casualties that could have occurred if civil order had totally broken down. We also managed to save 56,000 people whose lives were in the most severe jeopardy.

We had to make a judgment every day how many people we thought we could safely remove without triggering a panic and at the same time still be able to carry out our principal function and the remaining functions.

I think these objectives were achieved and they were carried out successfully. Therefore I do not believe that there was an undue delay, because an evacuation has been going on for two weeks.

The difference between the last stage and the previous period was that the last stage was done by helicopter and the previous stage had been done by fixed-wing.

I think the ability to conduct a final evacuation by helicopter without casualties during the operation, at least casualties caused by hostile action, is closely related to the policies that were pursued in the preceding two weeks.

As for Ambassador Martin, he was in a very difficult position. He felt a moral obligation to the people with whom he had been associated, and he attempted to save as many of those as possible. That is not the worst fault a man can have.

Q. Mr. Secretary, there have been numerous reports of American appeals to the Soviets, to the Chinese. Can you say today in the evacuation effort were either the Soviets or the Chinese helpful or unhelpful in this diplomatic effort?

SECRETARY KISSINGER: I think that we received some help from the Soviet Union in the evacuation effort. The degree of it we will have to assess when we study the exchanges.

Paris Accords

Q. Mr. Secretary, what caused the breakdown of the intent which was spoken of earlier on the Hill to try to achieve a measure of self-determination for the people of South Viet-Nam, and what is your total assessment now of the effectiveness or the noneffectiveness of the whole Paris accord operation, which you said at the outset was intended to achieve peace with honor for the United States?

SECRETARY KISSINGER: Until Sunday night we thought there was some considerable hope that the North Vietnamese would not seek a solution by purely military means, and when the transfer of power to General Minh took place—a person who had been designated by the other side as a counterpart worth talking to, they would be prepared to talk with—we thought a negotiated solution in the next few days was highly probable.

Sometime Sunday night the North Vietnamese obviously changed signals. Why that is, we do not yet know, nor do I exclude that now that the American presence is totally removed and very little military structure is left in South Viet-Nam, that there may not be a sort of a negotiation, but what produced this sudden shift to a military option or what would seem to us to be a sudden shift to a military option, I have not had sufficient opportunity to analyze.

As to the effectiveness of the Paris accords, I think it is important to remember the mood in this country at the time that the Paris accords were being negotiated. I think it is worth remembering that the principal criticism that was then made was that the terms we insisted on were too tough, not that the terms were too generous.

We wanted what was considered peace with honor, was that the United States would not end a war by overthrowing a government with which it had been associated. That still seems an objective that was correct.

There were several other assumptions that were made at that time that were later falsified by events that were beyond the control of—that indeed were unforeseeable by—anybody who negotiated these agreements, including the disintegration of or the weakening of executive authority in the United States for reasons unconnected with foreign policy considerations.

So, the premises of the Paris accords, in terms of aid, of the possibility of aid, and in terms of other factors, tended to disintegrate. I see no purpose now in reviewing that particular history. Within the context of the time, it seemed the right thing to do.

Q. Mr. Secretary, a follow-up question on that. What is the current relationship of the United States to the South Vietnamese political grouping, whatever you would call it?

SECRETARY KISSINGER: We will have to see what grouping emerges out of whatever negotiations should now take place between the two South Vietnamese sides. After we have seen what grouping emerges and what degree of independence it has, then we can make a decision about what our political relationship to it is. We have not made a decision on that.

Q. Would you say diplomatic relations are in abeyance with the government in South Viet-Nam?

SECRETARY KISSINGER: I think that is a fair statement.

Q. Mr. Secretary, looking back on the war now, would you say that the war was in vain, and what do you feel it accomplished?

SECRETARY KISSINGER: I think it will be a long time before Americans will be able to talk or write about the war with some dispassion. It is clear that the war did not achieve the objectives of those who started the original involvement nor the objectives of those who sought to end that involvement, which they found on terms which seemed to them compatible with the sacrifices that had been made.

What lessons we should draw from it, I think we should reserve for another occasion. But I don't think that we can solve the problem of having entered the conflict too lightly by leaving it too lightly, either.

Future U.S. Commitments

Q. Mr. Secretary, looking toward the future, has America been so stunned by the experience of Viet-Nam that it will never again come to the military or economic aid of an ally? I am talking specifically in the case of Israel.

SECRETARY KISSINGER: As I pointed out in a speech a few weeks ago [April 17], one lesson we must learn from this experience is that we must be very careful in the commitments we make but that we should scrupulously honor those commitments that we make.

I believe that the experience in the war can make us more mature in the commitments we undertake and more determined to maintain those we have. I would therefore think that with relation to other countries, including Israel, that no lessons should be drawn by the enemies of our friends from the experiences in Viet-Nam.

Q. Mr. Secretary, in view of the developments in the last week or so, would you agree that there was never any hope of stabilizing the South Vietnamese military situation after the withdrawal from the northern region?

SECRETARY KISSINGER: When the President met with General Weyand [Gen. Frederick C. Weyand, Chief of Staff, U.S. Army] in Palm Springs, the judgment was that there was a slim hope, but some hope. Somewhat less than 50-50, but still some hope.

The situation deteriorated with every passing day. Those of you whom I briefed at that time will remember that I said that whatever—and I said it in public testimony on innumerable occasions—that whatever objective we may set ourselves and whatever assessment we make about the outcome, the Administration had no choice except to pursue the course that we did, which was designed to save the Americans still in Viet-Nam and the maximum number of Vietnamese lives, should the worst come to pass.

Q. Mr. Secretary, could you tell us, are you now reassessing the amount of humanitarian aid which Congress should give to the South Vietnamese, and also, can you tell us the President's reaction and mood during the past 24 hours?

SECRETARY KISSINGER: With respect to humanitarian aid for South Viet-Nam, we spoke to the congressional leadership this morning, and we urged them to pass the humanitarian part of the aid request that we have submitted to the Congress.

The President pointed out that he would make a later decision as to what part of that humanitarian aid could be used in South Viet-Nam after the political evolution in South Viet-Nam becomes clearer.

The President's mood was somber and determined, and we all went through a somewhat anxious 24 hours, because until the last helicopter had left, we could not really know whether an attack on any of these compounds might start and whether missiles might be used against our evacuation.

Q. Mr. Secretary, could I ask you to clarify something that seems rather important at this point? You said here and in the past that a weakening of the American executive authority was a factor in this whole outcome. Now, there have been reports that former President Nixon, with your advice, had decided in April of 1973 to resume the bombing of North Viet-Nam but that Watergate intruded and he could not carry through on that. Is that a historic fact or not?

SECRETARY KISSINGER: To the best of my knowledge, President Nixon had never actually decided on any particular action. The Washington Special Action Group at that period was considering a number of reactions that could be taken to the beginning flagrant violations of the agreements. This was done on an interdepartmental basis—including the Department of State, my office, the Department of Defense—and had reached certain options.

Then President Nixon, as it turned out, never made a final decision between these options. To what extent it was influenced by Watergate is a psychological assessment that one can only speculate about.

Q. Mr. Secretary, there is a new Asia developing after the Indochina situation. What will the priorities of the United States be in recognizing its existing commitments and in making new ones?

SECRETARY KISSINGER: We will have to assess the impact of Indochina on our allies and on other countries in that area and on their perceptions of the United States, and we will have to assess also what role the United States can responsibly play over an indefinite period of time, because surely another lesson we should draw from the Indochina experience is that foreign policy must be sustained over decades if it is to be effective, and if it cannot be, then it has to be tailored to what is sustainable.

The President has already reaffirmed our alliance with Japan, our defense treaty with Korea, and we, of course, also have treaty obligations and important bases in the Philippines. We will soon be in consultation with many other countries in that area, including Indonesia and Singapore and Australia and New Zealand, and we hope to crystallize an Asian policy that is suited to present circumstances with close consultation with our friends.

Q. Mr. Secretary, are you confident that all the Americans that wanted to come out are out of Saigon, and do you have any idea of the number of Americans who remained behind?

SECRETARY KISSINGER: I have no idea of the number of Americans that remained behind. I am confident that every American who wanted to come out is out, but how many chose to stay behind we won't know until tomorrow sometime. The last contingent that left was the Ambassador and some of his immediate staff, and we won't know really until we get the report from them.

Q. Mr. Secretary, is President Thieu welcome to seek asylum in this country, and is there any possibility that the United States would recognize an exile government of South Viet-Nam?

SECRETARY KISSINGER: If President Thieu should seek asylum in the United States, he would be, of course, received.

The United States will not recognize an exile government of South Viet-Nam.

"What Went Wrong?"

Q. Mr. Secretary, could you tell us what went wrong, what were the flaws in American foreign policy toward Indochina all these years? Why was it that so many Administrations repeatedly underestimated the power of the North Vietnamese and overestimated the capability on the part of the South Vietnamese?

SECRETARY KISSINGER: As I said earlier, I think this is not the occasion, when the last American has barely left Saigon, to make an assessment of a decade and a half of American foreign policy, because it could equally well be argued that if five Administrations that were staffed, after all, by serious people dedicated to the welfare of their country came to certain conclusions, that maybe there was something in their assessment, even if for a variety of reasons the effort did not succeed.

As I have already pointed out, special factors have operated in recent years. But I would think that what we need now in this country, for some weeks at least, and hopefully for some months, is to heal the wounds and to put Viet-Nam behind us and to concentrate on the problems of the future. That certainly will be the Administration's attitude. There will be time enough for historic assessments.

Q. Mr. Secretary, you have repeatedly spoken of the potential consequences of what has happened in Southeast Asia. I would like to ask if you feel that your personal prestige and therefore your personal ability to negotiate between other countries has been damaged by what has happened?

SECRETARY KISSINGER: If I should ever come to the conclusion that I could not fulfill what the President has asked of me, then I would draw the consequences from this. Obviously, this has been a very painful experience, and it would be idle to deny this has been a painful experience for many who have been concerned with this problem for a decade and a half.

I think the problems in Viet-Nam went deeper than any one negotiation and that an analysis of the accords at the time will require an assessment of the public pressures, of what was sustainable, but I don't think, again, that we should go into this at this particular moment, nor am I probably the best judge of my prestige at any particular point.

Q. Mr. Secretary, what was it in particular that led you to believe until Sunday night that Hanoi might be willing to go for a nonmilitary solution? Did you have some specific information from them to indicate that, because certainly the battlefield situation suggested otherwise?

SECRETARY KISSINGER: Maybe to you, but the battlefield situation suggested that there was a standdown of significant military activity, and the public pronouncements were substantially in the direction that a negotiation would start with General Minh. There were also other reasons which led us to believe that the possibility of a negotiation remained open.

Implications For Detente

Q. Mr. Secretary, you have blamed the Soviets and the Red Chinese for breaking faith with the letter and the spirit of the Paris peace accords. The Soviet Union has apparently, through its broadcasts, encouraged a Communist takeover in Portugal. The Chinese have signed a joint communique with North Korea encouraging North Korea to unify South Korea by force.

My question is, why, in view of these violations in both the letter and in the spirit of détente, does the United States continue to believe in détente; secondly, are we ever going to take some obvious action showing American displeasure at the behavior of the two Communist superpowers?

SECRETARY KISSINGER: First, I think it is important to keep in mind that our relationship with both the Soviet Union and the People's Republic of China is based on ideological hostility but practical reasons for cooperation in certain limited spheres.

With respect to the Soviet Union, they and we possess the capability to destroy mankind. The question of how to prevent a general nuclear war is a problem that some Administration must solve before consequences that would be irremedial. Therefore there is always a common interest, and indeed a common obligation, to attempt to deal with this particular problem.

With respect to the various points you made, it is important for us to recognize that we cannot, in this situation, ask of the Soviet Union that it does our job for us. On the one hand, as I pointed out previously, of course the Soviet Union and the People's Republic must be responsible for the consequences of those actions that lead to an upset of the situation in Indochina, or maybe in the Middle East; that is, the introduction of massive armaments that will in all probability be used offensively is an event that we cannot ignore.

On the other hand, I think it would be a grave mistake to blame the Soviet Union for what happened in Portugal. It may have taken advantage of the situation in Portugal, but the fact that the Communist Party in Portugal has emerged despite the fact that it, in recent elections, had only 12 per cent of the votes cannot be ascribed to Soviet machinations primarily, but due to causes that are much more complicated and also due to evolutions in Europe that have roots quite different from Soviet pressures.

So, we must not make the mistake of ascribing every reverse we have to our Communist opponents, because that makes them appear 10 feet tall. On the other hand, we must not make the mistake of lulling ourself, with a period of détente, into believing that all competition has disappeared.

Between these two extremes, we must navigate, seek to reduce tensions on the basis of reciprocity, and seek to promote a stabler world. When either of the Communist countries have attempted actively to bring foreign policy pressures, the United States has resisted strenuously, and again we have called their attention to the fact that the fostering of international conflict will certainly lead to a breakdown of détente. But the individual examples which you gave cannot be ascribed to Communist actions primarily.

Q. In ordering the evacuation, to what extent were you responding exclusively to the military situation and to what extent were you responding either to a request by "Big" Minh for all Americans to get out or to your own feeling that a total evacuation might facilitate a political settlement?

SECRETARY KISSINGER: When the President ordered total evacuation, it was done on the basis that Tan Son Nhut Airport had already been closed and that therefore the American personnel in Saigon—and there were 45 in the province—might soon become hostage to the approaching Communist forces.

The order to evacuate was made before any request had been received from General Minh, and the principal, indeed the only, reason was to guarantee the safety of the remaining Americans.

Q. Mr. Secretary, there was a report last night that the Communists were backing away from the airport, the rockets seemed to be moving back. Was that a direct result of negotiations and were they prepared to let us move refugees out or Americans out on fixed-wing aircraft?

SECRETARY KISSINGER: I don't know that particular report, but the shelling stopped about 9 p.m., last night. We could not operate fixed-wing aircraft, because the control at the airport broke down. And it was at this point that the President decided that with Communist forces approaching on all sides and with the airport being closed that we had to go to helicopter evacuation.

Q. Mr. Secretary, there is a report in New York that last week you sent a further request for the good offices of the Council of Ministers of the Nine, the European Communities.

SECRETARY KISSINGER: We did not approach the Nine last week.

Q. Mr. Secretary, do you see any possibility of a negotiated settlement, and also, with respect to that, what can and should the South Vietnamese Government do now?

SECRETARY KISSINGER: I have already pointed out that the Communist demands have been escalating literally with every passing day, that as soon as one demand is met, an additional demand is put forward. So, we should have no illusions about what the Communist side is aiming for.

The South Vietnamese, as far as I can tell, have met every demand that has so far been put forward on the radio. There have not been any direct negotiations with which I am familiar.

What is attainable in the transfer of power that would preserve a vestige of other forces than the Communist forces. that remains to be seen.

THIEU'S RESIGNATION SPEECH AND NIXON'S LETTERS

April 21, 1975

With Communist troops less than 40 miles from Saigon, South Vietnamese President Nguyen Van Thieu resigned from office April 21. Thieu's resignation had been demanded by his political opponents, who blamed him for the disastrous military situation, and by the Provisional Revolutionary Government (PRG, Viet Cong), which refused to negotiate with him. A week later Thieu's successor, former Vice President Tran Van Huong, was also rejected by the PRG and ceded the presidency to opposition leader Gen. Duong Van Minh. Minh announced Saigon's surrender April 29 (April 30, Saigon time).

The day of his resignation Thieu delivered a bitter two-hour speech in which he accused the United States of breaking its promises to support an anti-Communist South Vietnamese government. According to Thieu, former President Richard M. Nixon had promised that the United States would always stand ready to help South Vietnam in the event that the Communists violated the 1973 Paris cease-fire pact. "The Americans," said Thieu, had pledged to "react violently and immediately to check North Vietnamese aggression." U.S. failure to do so constituted "an injustice, lack of responsibility and inhumanity toward an ally...the shirking of a responsibility."

Basis of Thieu's Allegations

The basis of Thieu's allegations became known April 30, a day after South Vietnam's surrender, when a former South Vietnamese government official released in Washington two previously unpublished letters from Nixon to

Thieu. Written during the period of the final negotiations leading to the 1973 cease-fire (see Historic Documents 1973, p. 115), the letters pressured the reluctant Thieu to accept the terms which the United States had worked out in secret talks with the North Vietnamese.

Thieu had objected strenuously to the truce provisions for a coalition government in South Vietnam. He had also protested the continued presence of North Vietnamese troops in the South, which was sanctioned by the accord, and to the makeup of the truce observation group (the International Commission of Control and Supervision, ICCS). Nixon acknowledged Thieu's objections but insisted that the terms were the best that could be achieved and said that Thieu risked losing American support if he rejected them. Should North Vietnam violate the truce, Nixon added, "you have my assurance...that we will respond with full force...." The White House said, April 30, 1975, that the Nixon letters were authentic and asserted that their contents did not differ from publicly stated administration policy.

Reluctance of Congress to Give Further Aid

All U.S. combat troops had been withdrawn from Vietnam two months after signature of the cease-fire agreement on Jan. 27, 1973. The flood of American aid, estimated at $160 billion for the period 1961 to April 30, 1975, had slowed to a trickle following the cease-fire. By May 1974 United States military aid was limited to ammunition and fuel. Even the flow of replacement parts for equipment was stopped, as Thieu bitterly noted in his April 21 speech. In one year his armed forces had lost "some 60 per cent of their combat potential," Thieu said.

When North Vietnamese and Viet Cong troops launched a major offensive in the northern and central provinces March 5, 1975, they met only token resistance. By the following week, after the fall of Ban Me Thuot in the Central Highlands, Thieu had ordered South Vietnamese forces to abandon Pleiku and Kontum provinces in the North. The retreat disintegrated into a rout of marauding soldiers and refugees streaming south to Saigon.

"Secret Agreements"

This was the situation when, on April 8, Sen. Henry M. Jackson (D Wash.) directed attention to what he called "secret agreements" involving renewed U.S. military assistance to South Vietnam. The senator cited administration "intimations" that Congress had reneged on "commitments" to the Saigon government—commitments that Congress "never heard of," according to Jackson. The following day the White House acknowledged that former President Nixon had privately assured Saigon in 1973 that the United States would "react vigorously" to North Vietnamese violations of the cease-fire. As it was to say later of the Nixon letters, the White House maintained that the private assurances did not go beyond publicly stated policies. A presidential spokesman noted that Congress had barred U.S. combat activities anywhere in Indochina after Aug. 15, 1973.

South Vietnamese officials nevertheless demanded that the United States make good the Nixon "assurances." On April 4, 1975, Thieu declared that "the American people as well as the American Congress must now see that they have got to do something...to keep from earning the label of traitors."

On May 1, the House rejected a compromise aid bill which would have provided $327-million for evacuation of Americans and endangered Vietnamese and for humanitarian relief. Many members argued that much of the bill had become moot once the evacuation had been completed and the Republic of South Vietnam had unconditionally surrendered to the Communists. Earlier, Congress had rejected Ford's April 10 appeal for $722-million in military aid to allow South Vietnam to "save itself" (see p. 223). In his resignation speech, Thieu had referred angrily to the congressional debate over the amount of aid. He had challenged Congress to provide massive military assistance and prove that American attacks on his regime were not merely "a pretext to abandon Vietnam."

Thieu left Saigon April 26 for Taipei, Taiwan.

> *Excerpts from South Vietnamese President Nguyen Van Thieu's resignation speech of April 21, 1975, delivered at the Presidential Palace, Saigon. The translation was provided by the U.S. Department of State:*

Mr. Vice President, Mr. President of the Senate, Mr. Acting Speaker of the lower House, Mr. President of the Supreme Court, Mr. Prime Minister, Mr. President of the Inspectorate, Dear Senators and Deputies, Dear Supreme Judges and Inspectors, Dear Members of the government and advisers to the government, Dear brother armymen and policemen, dear compatriots, dear brother and sister combatants and cadres:

First of all, I apologize for addressing you directly today without preparing a message for you, the compatriots nationwide and the brother and sister combatants and cadres. Because the urgent issue required an urgent decision and maximum secrecy, for reasons of national security, I permitted myself to invite members of both chambers of the National Assembly, members of the Supreme Court, members of the constitutional institutions and all of you on very short notice to come to a setting that should have been different from that of Independence Palace. This is also true with the compatriots and the brother and sister combatants. This is a very important talk, but it had not been announced beforehand. For reasons of national security and because of the importance of the talk to national security, I ask the compatriots and the brother and sister combatants, cadres and members of the national police to appreciate that.

Had time permitted, I would have convened a plenary session of both chambers of the National Assembly with the presence of the Supreme Court and various mass and religious organizations, so I could deal with the situation that I am going to elaborate on today. May I ask you to generously excuse me for dealing with this urgent issue in such a way that, it is reasonable to say, is not fully consistent with etiquette.

Gentlemen, compatriots, brothers and sisters:

Today, may I summarily review the developments in our country since the day of my assumption of leadership. I have gone through two presidential terms and my second term will expire in 6 months.

In 1965, in this South Vietnam, we controlled only half of the entire population and about half of our territory. The situation was very serious. The Communist aggressors had the upper hand and were able to win over us militarily within a very short period of time.

At that time, thanks to the vigorous intervention and firm determination of our U.S. ally and other allies, thanks to the presence of half a million allied troops from six allied countries, and thanks to the effective use of U.S. air and naval forces to punish the North Vietnamese aggressors both in the North and the South, we advanced toward a very fine situation up to 1968.

At that time, Communist North Vietnam was in a weakened position. Unable to endure the bombing raids, North Vietnam agreed to go to Paris for negotiations. The Communists agreed to do so because they had a sole aim: To have the United States end unconditionally and permanently its airstrikes against North Vietnam. Only when the U.S. airstrikes had ended could North Vietnam have the opportunity to stand up again and rebuild its aggressive potential in preparation for unleashing a new, even more vigorous aggression against the RVN. Thus, the Communists had an aim. What was their aim? They wanted—the U.S. ally only wanted peace talks, although it foresaw that they would help achieve nothing.

For this reason, it is no wonder that from 1968 to 1972, the peace talks made no progress. The Communists became more and more stubborn, fighting while talking and talking while fighting. They skillfully applied this tactic. They succeeded in deceiving the world and the United States.

In 1972, when the Communists became strong, that is, after they had 4 years to build regular units at the corps and division levels and received thousands of tanks and artillery pieces from the Soviet Union and Red China, they launched a general offensive in the summer.

The Communists wanted to reverse the trend by a military victory. Nevertheless, we subsequently drove the Communists out of Binh Long, Kontum, Binh Dinh, and Quang Tri. As a result, they agreed to negotiate because they were subject to renewed, even more heavier airstrikes, and their potentials did not permit them to continue their aggression. If they had not agreed to negotiate seriously, they would have been permanently annihilated.

The Communist strategy is as follows: when they are strong militarily, they fight vigorously while holding talks perfunctorily. And when they are weak militarily, they fight that way but come on strong in the talks. They agreed to resume the peace talks. But after the talks between the South Vietnam-U.S. side and the Communist side resumed at the Paris conference table, we realized they were stalling.

"South Vietnam Sold to Communists"

At the time, there was collusion between the Communists and the United States with a view to reaching the agreement of 26 October 1972. This agreement, which I spent much time explaining to our compatriots—I am sure that my compatriots still remember it—was an agreement by which the United States sold South Vietnam to the Communists.

I had enough courage to tell [U.S.] Secretary of State [Henry A.] Kissinger at that time the following: If you accept this agreement, this means you accept to sell South Vietnam to the North Vietnamese Communists. As for me, if I accept this agreement, I will be a traitor and seller of the South Vietnamese people and territory to the Communists. If you accept it, this is for U.S. interests or for some private reason which I do not know about. It is a sharing of interests among you powers that I do not know about. You make concessions or exchanges among you. You want to sell the interests and lives of the South Vietnamese. As for me, a Vietnamese, I cannot do so.

I refused to accept this agreement. I opposed this agreement for 3 months. During these 3 months, I struggled vigorously for three main points....

First was the three-segment government at the top which would direct the two governments of the RVN [Republic of Vietnam (South)] and the NFLSV [National Liberation Front]. And this three-segment coalition government would exercise its power downward to the provincial, district, village and hamlet levels. In my opinion, this was a coalition government I could not accept, regardless of its form or its level.

I did not accept such a government 5 or 7 years ago. I did not accept such a government at the central level—this is not to mention the village or hamlet level. I also refused to accept a three-segment, or four-segment, or two-segment government. I stressed that I could not accept it.

Second, they said that there were only three countries in Indochina: Cambodia, Laos and Vietnam. Thus, I asked Secretary of State Kissinger: Which Vietnam? Is it the Vietnam of the Saigon government or of the Hanoi government? If you accept this agreement, this means that you accept the Vietnam of Hanoi. According to the Communists, this Vietnam includes both the North and the South. I cannot accept it. I want to return to the Geneva agreement [of 1954] according to which there are two Vietnams and two administrations—the Hanoi and Saigon administrations. I call the Communist country the DRV [Democratic Republic of Vietnam (North)] and they must call this country the RVN. Neither country must invade the other. The 17th parallel and the Geneva agreement must serve as a basis, pending the day of national reunification through peaceful and democratic means. The date of reunification is unknown. The North and the South—that is, two separate countries—will apply for U.N. membership. The 17th parallel and the demilitarized zone will be maintained until the day of national reunification.

North Vietnamese Troops

The third point was that with regard to the North Vietnamese troops, Secretary of State Kissinger acknowledged that they had the right to remain in the South legally and as a matter of course. As I said, this was the most important point. Nothing was more weird than the fact that the aggressors, after the war had been ended and peace restored, had the right to leave their troops forever on the territory of someone else.

I said then that a most important prerequisite was the withdrawal of North Vietnamese troops to the North. Mr. Kissinger replied to me that the United States had negotiated this issue for 3 years with the Soviet Union and Red China, but no avail. That was why the United States had given up.

I said: Ah! This is why the U.S. President at the outset raised the following condition for North Vietnam: The North Vietnamese troops, as the aggressor troops, must withdraw first, before the United States would withdraw its troops. This sounded sensible and logical. It sounded very resolute. But later, the United States gradually deescalated its demand, saying that the U.S. and North Vietnamese troops would be bilaterally and simultaneously withdrawn. This also sounded reasonable, logical and peaceful. However, why was it that President [Richard M.] Nixon said in a speech that the United States would unilaterally withdraw its troops? He did not demand that North Vietnam withdraw its troops.

I asked Mr. Kissinger if the United States no longer demanded that North Vietnam withdraw its troops. He said yes. That was why I disagreed. I said: You gentlemen agree, but I don't. North Vietnam must withdraw its troops. This is an inevitable and normal condition to be met when the war ends, especially when the war in this South is a war of aggression waged by the North Vietnamese Communists.

Finally, we had to reach a compromise solution. I said that I would only agree to a solution whereby the problem of North Vietnamese troops was settled. This solution was: The problem concerning the armed forces of the two South Vietnamese parties and concerning the armed forces of South and North Vietnam shall be settled by the Vietnamese governments, the Vietnamese elements themselves, on the basis of gradual reductions in the troop strength and demobilization.

I believe that this was not our desired solution to the problem concerning the North Vietnamese troops and was not an ideal solution. But we could do nothing better. We could not drive all of them out of the South at a time when the United States had stopped fighting and stopped aiding us. That was why I considered this solution acceptable if North Vietnam had good will....

With regard to the proposed three-segment coalition government, I categorically rejected it. That was why it was subsequently changed into a three-segment National Council of National Reconciliation and Concord, charged solely with holding elections. It would have no ruling power in this South. Therefore, as I recall, I said: Our government, our constitution, our regime, our armed forces, our police, our administrative system and our people remain. Nothing will change.

I also said that when general elections are held, we will struggle against the Communists politically....

"Worthless Papers"

Three months elapsed before my demand was met. There was untold menace and pressure. With regard to pressure, let me say frankly, and let you gentlemen here be witnesses, that Mr. Nixon told me as follows: All accords are, in the final analysis, mere sheets of papers. They will be worthless, if they are not implemented and if North Vietnam violates them. Therefore, the important thing is what you will do after signing the agreement, and what facilities we will make available to you if North Vietnam reneges on and violates the agreement and renews its attacks against the South. So, you should not be concerned about the signing of this agreement which, in my view, is the best. There can be no better agreement. We want it to be better, but we cannot make any more moves vis-a-vis the Soviet Union and Red China; and we have given up. Furthermore, President Thieu, you should know that no matter how good the agreement you draft may be, the problem will not be for you to refer to the signed agreement if the Communists fail to respect it and send troops to attack you again. They would not be afraid of the agreement. The real problem is: What will the Americans make available to you, President Thieu, and the Vietnamese people so they can resist the Communist attacks? This is the really important matter. And I invite you to Washington to lay the new groundwork for the relations between Vietnam and the United States in the postwar period, and for the commitments to provide mutual assistance in protecting the freedom and independence of South Vietnam, should the Communists violate the agreement.

I thought that I was practical and I know that our southern compatriots are practical, too.

Actually, if the Communists violated the agreement using the abundant aid they received from the Soviet Union and Red China and if we showed them the beautifully worded agreement, they would not be afraid of it. But if we received adequate U.S. military aid, if the Vietnamization Plan and the plan to modernize the RVN armed forces were carried out, and if the Americans resumed their assistance to us with their air force facilities to punish the aggressors, this would be more practical for us, I thought.

Our survival depended on bombs and ammunition needed on the battlefield, on economic facilities, and on U.S. backing. This was more practical than having a beautifully worded agreement but nothing with which to cope with the enemy. That sounded very enticing and logical. And the most important pressure on me at that time was that if the RVN government refused to sign the agreement, the U.S. Congress would certainly and immediately cut all U.S. military and economic aid to the RVN government—"and even if later on you agree to sign the agreement, you will be unable to get U.S. aid. That is an irreversible decision by the U.S. Congress. And when the Communists again launch attacks against you, you will have no military and economic aid for defense, and we will not intervene. Do you think that the future or the present is important?"

Doubt About U.S. Commitments

Those were the conditions and solemn commitments made not between, I think, the persons of Mr. Nixon and Mr. Nguyen Van Thieu or between two individuals or two administrations, but between a U.S. President and a Vietnamese President; between a representative of our great U.S. ally, leader of the free world, and one of its allies which was fighting—the RVN. The commitments were made with the honor of two countries, particularly the honor of a superpower, leader of the free world. What were these commitments about?

First, when Communist North Vietnam renewed its aggression and violated the agreement, the Americans would react violently and immediately to check the aggression.

Second, the Americans would recognize only the RVN government as the sole government in South Vietnam.

Third, the Americans would promptly provide abundant military and economic aid to the South Vietnamese people to help them fight the Communist aggressors in case of renewed Communist aggression. The Americans would provide the South Vietnamese people with sufficient economic aid to help them develop their country.

He [Nixon] also said Vice President [Spiro T.] Agnew would come to Vietnam in a few days and would publicly announce these three commitments in Saigon. But when Mr. Agnew arrived, he only talked about two commitments and he failed to mention the third one: he ignored the one dealing with U.S. interference, reaction, and vigorous retaliation. I became doubtful about the U.S. commitments at that point.

Gentlemen, compatriots, brothers and sisters:

Dealing with the agreement of 26 October 1972, I did not think that a Secretary of State like Mr. Kissinger could not realize that it was an agreement leading the nation and country of Vietnam to its death. I believe he realized this. I do not want to stress that he accepted this, but since everyone realized this, he must have realized it....

Request for Aid

I told President Nixon and the U.S. government and Congress that I did not request from them endless aid for 20 or 30 years, because the economic potential and natural resources of South Vietnam are very abundant. If they wanted South Vietnam to develop vigorously without needing their aid for 20 or 30 years like the ROK [Republic of Korea] and Nationalist China or any country after World War II, they should give us a lot of aid for 3 or 5 years so that we could develop our economy, and then gradually reduce it to zero by 1980....

However, I regret that later on Watergate occurred in the United States. The U.S. political situation has prevented abundant economic aid and the continuation of the Vietnamization program and the program to modernize the RVN armed forces. In addition, international economic changes concerning energy and food have created difficulties and contradictions among the U.S. people.

The Communists are not so stupid as to fail to recognize all this. They are very cunning and have fully exploited these events.

U.S. military and economic aid has decreased, the Vietnamization program has not been properly carried out, and the program to modernize the RVN armed forces has not been implemented. While 300,000 North Vietnamese troops are still here, the allied troops have gone. Prior to the cease-fire, the Communists had stored in the South five times more munitions than we had. Since then, they have repaired their airfields, built highways, laid oil pipelines, and continued to receive tanks and artillery pieces from the Soviet Union and Red China while the Americans have pretended not to notice any of these activities and have remained inactive. They have succeeded in building their army in the South to the 570,000 mark, forming more divisions and army corps, bringing in more tanks, artillery pieces, rockets, and antiaircraft guns, and building more highways and airfields. They have added various types of modern weapons and equipment to their arsenal in the South. Meanwhile, all types of U.S. aid to the South have decreased and so has the U.S. determination to cope with the Communists.

We are now in a very difficult position. We desire to show that we respect the Paris agreement so as to please the world and U.S. public opinion, and we want to prove that we love peace and respect the Paris agreement. Therefore, we have kept inviting the Communist side to negotiate, advancing one proposal after another and we have adopted a defensive rather than offensive attitude. Even if we wanted to launch attacks, we lack enough facilities to launch vigorous and deep thrusts against the enemy's rear area. We cannot bomb North Vietnam because we lack facilities to do so. If we had done that, the Americans would have cut aid more rapidly. Therefore, the Communists have gained the upper hand....

There can be no magic in combat. In combat, there must be an equilibrium in the balance of forces. Combat requires bombs, ammunition and other facilities.

In addition to the will to fight and gallantry, we must be realistic. We cannot just bite others to demonstrate our gallantry. We are fighting the Communists who possess facilities made available to them by the Soviet Union and Red China. We are not fighting an enemy possessing just primitive weapons and machetes, as he did in the past. The Communists now possess more abundant, more modern and more powerful facilities and have more troops.

Therefore, the time has come when the Communists have compelled us to use our regular units to defend our territory. We have been fully aware that the Communists were laying a trap. However, because we have the territory, the people, the communications, the bridges, the economy, the rice paddies and the rivers, we have had to defend this by spreading out our armed forces. And we have effectively defended our territory for 2 years until recently.

Outnumbered by Communists

Meanwhile, the Communists have steadily introduced into the South more troops, more tanks, more heavy artillery pieces, more antiaircraft guns and more rockets. In certain areas, the Communist forces were one and a half, two and even three times larger than ours. In certain province capitals, district capitals or military bases, if we had one division, the Communists deployed two divisions to confront us; if we had one regiment, they deployed one division; if we had one battalion, they deployed one regiment; if we had 15 tanks, they deployed 20 tanks; if we had 10 heavy guns, they deployed two divisions to confront us; if we had one regiment, they As a result, the balance of forces has tilted toward the Communists. Consequently, a number of our bases and province capitals have inevitably been overrun.

The time had come when we had to make up our minds. Realizing that with aid and will it intervene after all? Shall we sit by and wait for the United States to provide us with aid so we can fight and launch counterattacks? If the United States did not intervene, we would at some future time lose everything. If the province capitals, the district capitals and the RVN units were lost, the head of South Vietnam—the capital and this prosperous region—would be lost.

The time had come when we had to make up our minds. Realizing that the Americans had adopted a defeatist attitude toward the Communists' acts of aggression, we had to decide our own affairs. Therefore, after Ban Me Thuot—the most important, prosperous and densely populated area of the Central Highlands—came under Communist attack, we wondered if our forces could defend Kontum and Pleiku. Our forces could not defend Kontum and Pleiku which, we believed at that time, would fall sooner or later. After Ban Me Thuot had fallen [March 13, 1975], we wondered where we could get troops to recapture it. We came to a political decision not to insure the life or death defense of Kontum and Pleiku....

Defeatist Commanders

In Hue and Danang, the problem also concerned the balance of forces between us and the enemy [Hue fell to the Communists March 25, 1975; Danang was taken March 30.] I readily acknowledge that a few other factors were involved in the loss of Hue and Danang: Specifically, some commanders had adopted a defeatist attitude; some disturbances were caused by the compatriots' evacuation. I am speaking frankly. I am not trying to lay the blame on the troops or the compatriots. I want to say that some developments on the battlefield were foreseeable and some others were not. Faced with the enemy pressure and his artillery attacks on Danang, we could not insure a protracted life or death defense of our positions.

It is true that we at the central level had given the life or death defense orders; however, when the field commanders, who were closely associated with the troops and the people, could not fulfill their missions despite their determination, we had no way of having them fulfill their missions unless we could send them additional troops, which we did not have; unless we could provide them with additional aircraft and bombs, which we did not have; and unless we provided them with additional tanks and heavy guns, which we did not have either.

It is recalled that the U.S. troops were regularly provided with more B-52 support than were our RVN troops. That was why the U.S. troops could win victories easily and succeeded in forcing the enemy to bow his head.

After 1973, our troops had fought many battles that won the admiration of the U.S. generals who returned to South Vietnam, especially since I ordered our forces to fight the enemy in economical Vietnamese ways. These U.S. generals said that even U.S. Marines supported by B-52's could hardly fight so victoriously....

Lost Combat Potential

Nevertheless, during that period, when we asked for $1.4 billion in U.S. aid, the United States reduced this requested amount to $700 million, and the $300 million has been hanging in air for about 1 year now. During that period, the RVN armed forces have lost some 60 per cent of their combat potential: It is like a boxer who has lost some 60 per cent of his strength.

Militarily, when an army is strong, it will remain strong, and if it is weak, it will get weaker. It is like a patient: If a patient remains strong enough, he will recover, and if he is weak, he will get weaker. When the United States reduced its aid to us and we consequently lost some 60 per cent of our combat potential, you can imagine what had to happen. Our casualties have increased manifold, because we have not had enough air support. Furthermore, our artillery has been inferior to that of the enemy. The casualties inflicted on us by the enemy artillery have soared. The fatality rate among the wounded has increased because we have not had enough helicopters to evacuate the wounded. Worse still, at the hospitals, bandages have been used and reused two or three times. This is inhuman to a wounded combatant: it is inhuman to use a bandage, then wash it and use it again.

Because of the shortage of ammunition, we have had to count every single cartridge. We have lost a certain number of our tanks and artillery pieces. The United States undertook in the Paris agreement to carry out replacements on a piece-to-piece basis, but it has not made these replacements: It has stopped providing us with these means.

As a matter of course, our war materiel has gradually decreased: That is why we have lost. On the contrary, the Communists at the outset had an amount of war materiel which has steadily increased. Therefore, they have gained a dual advantage—that is, they have obtained more war materiel, whereas our volume of war materiel has decreased.

Thus, no matter how brave our combatants may be and no matter how skillful our commanders may be, we must suffer losses and lose land and people. We have realized this fact and we cannot endure it. Many times, we have seen that we must resort to an illogical tactic to defend our land and to protect our people. We have had to fight an illogical war because this is our responsibility. The Communists have no responsibility....

I have therefore, told [the Americans]: You have asked us to do something that you failed to do with half a million powerful troops and skilled commanders and with nearly $300 billion in expenditures over 6 long years. If I do not say that you were defeated by the Communists in Vietnam, I must modestly say that you did not win either. But you found an honorable way out. And at present, when our army lacks weapons, ammunition, helicopters, aircraft and B-52's, you ask us to do an impossible thing like filling up the ocean with stones.... This is an impossible, absurd thing.

Also, you have let our combatants die under a hail of shells. This is an inhumane act by an inhuman ally. Refusing to aid an ally and abandoning it is an inhumane act. This is the reason why, on the day a U.S. congressional delegation came here, I told the congressmen that it was not the problem of $300 million in aid, but it was the question of complying with the U.S. pledge to assist the Vietnamese people in the struggle to protect their independence and freedom and the ideal of freedom for which the Americans fought together with our people here and for which some 50,000 U.S. citizens were sacrificed.

The United States is proud of being an invincible defender of the just cause and the ideal of freedom in this world and will celebrate its 200th anniversary next year. I asked them: Are U.S. statements trustworthy? Are U.S. commitments still valid? Some $300 million is not a big sum to you. Compared with the amount of money you spent here in 10 years, this sum is sufficient for only 10 days of fighting. And with this sum, you ask me to score a victory or to check the Communist aggression—a task which you failed to fulfill in 6 years with all U.S. forces and with such an amount of money. This is absurd!...

All this has led to the current situation in our country. I accept the criticism of the people of the world and our ally as well as the correct criticism of our Vietnamese people. I admit that some, but not all, of our military leaders were cowardly and imbued with a defeatist spirit and lacked the bravery of combatants in recent battles. In some areas our combatants fought valiantly and I don't think that our allied troops could have fought as valiantly as they did.

We must be just. Therefore, I have said that wrongdoers must be properly awarded. We do not try to conceal the shortcomings of those wrongdoers. We are proud to say that we scored achievements in some of the recent battles that our U.S. allied troops probably could not have scored if they had been here.

Let us now again talk about the general situation in our country. The Communists have introduced into South Vietnam 20 divisions and numerous rockets, antiaircraft guns, artillery pieces and tanks. We regret that the situation has changed so rapidly in central Vietnam. However, as a President and a man with some military knowledge, I have the courage to say that the current situation would be the same regardless of the rate of development of the situation in the recent past....

Therefore, under the current conditions, we must try to redeploy our troops to defend MR [Military Regions] III and IV. We are now in a position in which we must rely on the valor and determination of our combatants, the support of our compatriots, and the utmost sacrifice of our combatants. We cannot say that we can defend these areas by reliance on our troops' strength and weapons....

Resignation

Gentlemen: Today, before both chambers of the National Assembly, before the Supreme Court, before the government, before the compatriots and before the brother and sister combatants and cadres nationwide, I declare my resignation as President, and, in accordance with the Constitution, Vice President Tran Van Huong will assume the position of President....

As you know, I am not a man who lacks courage. I can proudly affirm that I have ample physical courage, because I have been a combatant for 20 years now. If I were doomed to death, I would have died while I was a second lieutenant. At that time, with the blessing of providence, I survived. I have lived to this day, undergoing untold trials in combat. In my military career, I have spent little time in the office. I have spent most of the time in combat....

With regard to my political and moral courage, let me recall—not merely to cite the meritorious service I have rendered to the compatriots and the brothers and sisters—that on 2 November 1968, the United States strongly pressured me into heading a delegation to Paris to attend the four-party conference on the same footing as the NFLSV. I balked at going, and you may recall the speech I delivered before both chambers of the National Assembly on 2 November 1968. It is reasonable to say that my life was at stake, because those who wanted to kill me had ample means to do so, and those who wanted to overthrow my regime also had ample means and the experience to do so. But I was not afraid.

In 1971, when the presidential election was described as a solo race, I was being pressured into giving up the solo campaign after the other two slates had withdrawn. Despite this pressure, I believed that if I withdrew, a political vacuum would inevitably have arisen. I still recall that I told the compatriots at that time that I was not greedy for power and status. I also told the compatriots, however, that this political vacuum would lead the country to an incalculable political adventure, and that this political vacuum was a setting that people were attempting to create in order to impose a disadvantageous political solution, called a peace solution, on the RVN in 1971-1972. Therefore, I resolutely ran alone so as to maintain the constitutional and legal position of the President of the South and to successfully defend our position, should negotiations be held.

With my resolve and courage, I disregarded untold pressure and threats. At that time, although I had my own solution, they had already laid the groundwork for attaining a solution. Owing to my resolve and courage, a tentative political solution was reached in October 1972. At that time, they were seeking a solution. Therefore, had the opportunities presented themselves—namely, internal political disturbances in the South—they would have imposed their own solution. If the South remained politically stable, they would take their time in finding a solution. They were ready to seize every opportunity that would allow them to impose an undesirable political solution on the South.

In 1972, once again, I proved to the compatriots that I did not lack courage and clearsightedness in the political sphere and that I did not fear any threat to my life. I only feared the threat that they would immediately cut off all economic and military aid and that, later on, if the Communists restarted the fight, the U.S. Congress would not correct its decision on an aid cut and there would not be a single cent in economic aid.

Please excuse me for telling this: I only feared that after signing the Paris agreement in 1973, the South would be lost and the Americans would wash their hands of the situation if the Communists resumed the war and if we did not receive any economic and military aid. I dared not say this was an empty threat. I thought that this was an opportunity for the Americans to wash their hands, because they said that I was stubborn and refused to achieve peace and to sign the agreement when there was a good opportunity. They described the Paris agreement as very fine before U.S. and world public opinion. Thus, when I dealt with a point, a comma or a word in the agreement, they blamed me for being stubborn and bellicose. If I refused to sign and waited for something else, this was a pretext for them to cut their economic and military aid and to abandon us definitively....

Some U.S. people and some U.S. congressmen hold that so long as Mr. Thieu remains in power, there can be no negotiations; Mr. Thieu is not the man to agree to negotiate; Mr. Thieu is bellicose and refuses to implement the Paris agreement. So long as Mr. Thieu remains in power, U.S. aid cannot be given in full because so long as he receives U.S. aid, he will continue to fight and will not agree to negotiate.

This is the U.S. scheme to stop providing us with aid and to wash their hands of us. This is a scheme of people who have completely lost their conscience and humanity, or this may be the opinion of people who misunderstand me. Therefore, I resign today.

We will see whether or not negotiations will be satisfactorily conducted with the agreement of the Communists and South Vietnam when Mr. Thieu is no longer in power. If the answer is in the affirmative, it is something that our people and the world people would gladly welcome. If, with Mr. Thieu's departure, abundant U.S. aid will be provided immediately to help the RVN armed forces conduct the fight, this is something very lucky for us, and my departure is just like a grain of sand in the desert.

It is an insignificant act on my part, but a very well-worthwhile sacrifice. Exchanging a presidential position for adequate, and even abundant, aid to help the southern armed forces and people continue the fight to defend their country and then to negotiate a solution guaranteeing a free and democratic South Vietnam which will not be ruled by the Communists—that's beyond my expectations and I would be really grateful to the Americans.

But, if they say that so long as Mr. Thieu remains in power, negotiations cannot be conducted and U.S. aid cannot be provided and if they use me as an excuse for their disengagement and to wash their hands of us in disregard of their conscience, their sense of responsibility, justice and humanity, this is another matter which will be judged by history and the people of the world.

Decreased Aid

Now that more than half of our country has been lost to the Communists, the U.S. government has said that the situation must be stabilized in order to conduct negotiations and that stabilization of the situation and our military position must precede the negotiations. We cannot stabilize our military position with saliva, but with guns, munitions and plenty of weapons which must be rapidly provided us in sufficient quantities. We cannot stabilize our military position with the debates, which have lasted for 1 year, over the U.S. aid which has decreased from $700 million to $300 million. The Americans have refused to accord us that amount and they are now bargaining for $340 million, $350 million, $355, or $360 million.

The honor of an allied country and the fate of one of its allies are being bargained in the same manner as the purchase of fish at the market. I am very sorry that I cannot accept that, I cannot, on account of my presidential position, do harm to the Vietnamese people and sacrifice the lives of our combatants who lack munitions while fighting. I cannot let people bargain the destiny of our people with offers of $10 million, $2 million and $1 million and conduct debates for months when the results have not been determined and no guarantee is in sight. This is one of the reasons for my resignation. I will see if I was merely a pretext or the real cause....

Some [South Vietnamese] religious groups, some politicians, some mass organizations and some well-known persons have said: Mr. Thieu should step down and let us negotiate with the Communists. South Vietnam will certainly have freedom and democracy and the Communists will have to agree to that. There will be no coalition. The Communists are afraid of us and respect us. Although we do not share their views, the Communists will respect us and accept our proposals. We will score achievements without a fight.

These people and groups are now vigorously voicing their opinions. I don't know whether they have said this because they are too self-confident, because they suffer illusions, or because they were compelled to say so by some motivating force....

Even some of our brother army men, either because they are rather credulous or victimized by propaganda—a vigorous propaganda drive is being launched to put all the blame on Mr. Thieu just as Mr. Diem was the one blamed for everything in 1963. [Ngo Dinh Diem, President of South Vietnam was assassinated in 1963.] Gentlemen and compatriots, you probably know the origin of this propaganda—some have said that so long as President Thieu remains in power, the Americans will be killed and so will our wives and children. If no fighting can be conducted, the military situation will not be stabilized and no negotiations will be held. Therefore, President Thieu should step down so that we will have sufficient aid to conduct the fighting to stabilize the situation, conduct negotiations, and protect the free South.

The Communists have succeeded in using these arguments in their propaganda to poison world and U.S. public opinion. In Vietnam, I find that there has been a strong tendency for everything. Peace cannot be achieved because of me. People want to fight and win, but they are prevented from doing so. That is also because of me. Therefore, I have performed a righteous act in sacrificing my person and my position.

Why have I resigned today? The aid problem is being carefully discussed in the United States today and such figures as $350 million, $355 million and $360 million have been advanced just like people bargaining when they buy something. But none of the figures surpass the $722 million mark requested by the U.S. President from the Congress.

The figure of $722 million which U.S. President Gerald Ford asked from the Congress will not suffice for South Vietnam and its armed forces to check the North Vietnamese Communists and to stabilize the military situation in order to start serious negotiations. The Communists know this, and they have only to take advantage of their victories to push for a military victory without negotiations.

To achieve the goal expected by the United States—that is, to stabilize the military situation in order to get negotiations underway on the basis of the Paris agreement and thus achieve a political solution—there must be more than $722 million. Moreover, there must be B-52's to punish the Communists in the South and, if possible, also the Communists in the North. It is also necessary to have tanks, heavy artillery, equipment, small and big guns, signal equipment and ammunition. These things must be sent in continuously, continuously, continuously and immediately, immediately, immediately. It is not a matter of months or weeks, but rather a matter of days. This materiel must be abundant enough to reequip the divisions that are being equipped and to activate more regular divisions to fight the 20 North Vietnamese divisions....

Reaction Promised

The Americans fought a war here without success and went home. The Vietnamization Plan was worked out and we accepted it, but its implementation has been suspended. After suspension of Vietnamization, there was a promise that if the Communists intruded and invaded again, there would be a reaction. But there has been no reaction. Thus, the minimum thing to do is to give us equipment to fight with, but they have not given it. What does this amount to? This amounts to a breach of promise, injustice, lack of responsibility and inhumanity toward an ally who has suffered continuously—the shirking of responsibility on the part of a great power....

The reason I resign today is the fact that today the U.S. Congress is going to scrutinize the problem of aid. I think that after my resignation today, maybe tomorrow the $300 million will be raised to $722 million or to more than a billion and then a continuous airlift will bring in tanks and heavy artillery. Since Mr. Thieu is gone, here comes the aid, aid and more aid. I hope so. Let us wait and see whether the U.S. Congress will do so....

I call on all people, organizations, religions and politicians who have so far referred to me as an impediment to peace and considered me impotent in bringing about peace and protecting the South and unable to defeat the Communists and restore peace, and thus only causing mourning and misery, for the sake of patriotism and love for the people, to assist President Tran Van Huong in bringing about peace, honor, freedom, prosperity and democracy, in insuring strict implementation of the Paris agreement with the Communists forced to respect it, and in achieving the realization of the southern people's national right to self-determination as specified in the Paris agreement. In short, I do not want anybody to use me—President Nguyen Van Thieu—personally as an excuse to maltreat this nation. Those persons, from this moment onward, can no longer use that excuse and must now show their sincerity and honesty.

Ladies and Gentlemen, compatriots, brothers and sisters: I have served the compatriots, brothers and sisters for the past 10 years. As I have said, I do not lack courage. It is not that any demonstration or slander can discourage and demoralize me and prompt me to step down in a nonsensical and irresponsible manner, it is not due to the pressure of our ally or the difficult and hard struggle against the Communists that I have to avoid responsibility and leave my office.

The presidents of some big countries are proud of the fact that they have undergone 6, 7 or 10 crises. They have written books in which they proudly offer themselves as heroes and outstanding politicians. As for me, over the past 10 years, all years, months, days and all hours in my life have been bad, as my horoscope forecast. As regards my fate, I can enjoy no happiness; I have enjoyed no happiness, yet I have not sought ways to enjoy life. A ruler of a country can enjoy either honor or disgrace. He must accept this so he can lead the people. If I have some good points the compatriots will praise me even if I do not want it, but if I have some bad points and errors, I am ready to accept judgments and accusations from the compatriots....

I am resigning but not deserting. From this moment, I place myself at the service of the President, the people and the army. As I step down, Mr. Tran Van Huong will become President and our nation will not lose anything. Perhaps, our country will gain another combatant on the battlefront. I will stand shoulder to shoulder with the compatriots and combatants to defend the country....

Texts of two letters from then United States President Richard M. Nixon to then Republic of Vietnam (South Vietnam) President Nguyen Van Thieu, released April 30, 1975, in Washington by Nguyen Tien Hung, former Minister of Planning of the Republic of Vietnam:

November 14, 1972

Dear Mr. President:

I was pleased to learn from General Haig [Alexander M. Haig Jr., then deputy assistant to the President for national security affairs], that you held useful and constructive discussions with him in Saigon in preparation for Dr. Kissinger's [Henry A. Kissinger, then the President's national security adviser] forthcoming meeting with North Vietnam's negotiators in Paris.

After studying your letter of November 11 with great care I have concluded that we have made substantial progress towards reaching a common understanding on many of the important issues before us. You **can be sure** that we will pursue the proposed changes in the draft agreement that General Haig discussed with you with the utmost firmness and that, as these discussions proceed, we shall keep you fully informed through your Ambassador to the Paris conference on Vietnam who will be briefed daily by Dr. Kissinger.

I understand from your letter and from General Haig's personal report that your principal remaining concern with respect to the draft agreement is the status of North Vietnamese forces now in South Vietnam. As General Haig explained to you, it is our intention to deal with this problem first by seeking to insert a reference to respect for the demilitarized zone in the proposed agreement and, second, by proposing a clause which provides for the reduction and demobilization of forces on both sides in South Vietnam on a one-to-one basis and to have demobilized personnel return to their homes.

Additional Clauses

Upon reviewing this proposed language, it is my conviction that such a provision can go a long way toward dealing with your concern with respect to North Vietnamese forces. General Haig tells me, however, that you are also seriously concerned about the timing and verification of such reductions. In light of this, I have asked Dr. Kissinger to convey to you, through Ambassador Bunker, some additional clauses we would propose adding to the agreement dealing with each of these points. In addition, I have asked that Dr. Kissinger send you the other technical and less important substantive changes which General Haig did not have the opportunity to discuss with you because they had not yet been fully developed in Washington. With these proposed modifications, I think you will agree that we have done everything we can to improve the existing draft while remaining within its general framework.

You also raise in your letter the question of participation by other Asian countries in the international conference. As you know, the presently contemplated composition are the permanent members of the United Nations Security Council, the members of the I.C.C.S. [International Commission of Control and Supervision, the truce observation group], the parties to the Paris conference on Vietnam, and the Secretary General of the United Nations. We seriously considered Cambodian and Laotian participation but decided that these would be unnecessary complications with respect to representation. We do not, however, exclude the possibility of delegations from these countries participating in an observer status at the invitation of the conference.

As for Japan, this question was raised earlier in our negotiations with Hanoi and set aside because of their strenuous objections to any Japanese role in guaranteeing the settlement and also because it inevitably raises the possibility of Indian participation. I have, however, asked that Dr. Kissinger raise this matter again in Paris and he will inform your representative what progress we make on this. What we must recognize as a practical matter is that participation of Japan is very likely to lead to the participation of India. We would appreciate hearing your preference on whether it is better to include both countries or neither of them.

Truce Observation Group

Finally, in respect to the composition of the I.C.C.S. I must say in all candor that I do not share your view that its contemplated membership is unbalanced. I am hopeful that it will prove to be a useful mechanism in detecting and reporting violations of the agreement. In any event, what we both must recognize is that the supervisory mechanism in itself is in no measure as important as our own firm determination to see to it that the agreement works and our vigilance with respect to the prospect of its violation.

I will not repeat here all that I said to you in my letter of Nov. 8, but I do wish to reaffirm its essential content and stress again my determination to work toward an early agreement along the lines of the schedule which General Haig explained to you. I must explain in all frankness that while we will do our very best to secure the changes in the agreement which General Haig discussed with you and those additional ones which Ambassador Bunker will bring you, we cannot expect to secure them all. For example, it is unrealistic to assume that we will be able to secure the absolute assurances which you would hope to have on the troop issue.

But far more important than what we say in the agreement on this issue is what we do in the event the enemy renews its aggression. You have my absolute assurance that if Hanoi fails to abide by the terms of this agreement it is my intention to take swift and severe retaliatory action.

I believe the existing agreement to be an essentially sound one which should become even more so if we succeed in obtaining some of the changes we have discussed. Our best assurance of success is to move into this new situation with confidence and cooperation.

With this attitude and the inherent strength of your government and army on the ground in South Vietnam, I am confident this agreement will be a successful one.

If, on the other hand, we are unable to agree on the course that I have outlined, it is difficult for me to see how we will be able to continue our common effort towards securing a just and honorable peace. As General Haig told you, I would with great reluctance be forced to consider other alternatives. For this reason, it is essential that we have your agreement as we proceed into our next meeting with Hanoi's negotiators. And I strongly urge you and your advisers to work promptly with Ambassador Bunker and our mission in Saigon on the many practical problems which will face us in implementing the agreement. I cannot overemphasize the urgency of the task at hand nor my unalterable determination to proceed along the course which we have outlined.

"The United States Will React Very Strongly"

Above all we must bear in mind what will really maintain the agreement. It is not any particular clause in the agreement but our joint willingness to maintain its clauses. I repeat my personal assurances to you that the United States will react very strongly and rapidly to any violation of the agreement. But in order to do this effectively it is essential that I have public support and that your government does not emerge as the obstacle to a peace which American public opinion now universally desires. It is for this reason that I am pressing for the acceptance of an agreement which I am convinced is honorable and fair and which can be made essentially secure by our joint determination.

Mrs. Nixon joins me in extending our warmest personal regards to Madame Thieu and to you. We look forward to seeing you again at our home in California once the just peace we have both fought for so long is finally achieved.

Sincerely,
RICHARD NIXON

His Excellency
Nguyen Van Thieu
President of the Republic of Vietnam
Saigon.

Nothing Substantial to Add

January 5, 1973

Dear Mr. President:

This will acknowledge your letter of December 20, 1972.

There is nothing substantial that I can add to my many previous messages, including my December 17 letter, which clearly stated my opinions and intentions. With respect to the question of North Vietnamese troops, we will again present your views to the Communists as we have done vigorously at every other opportunity in the negotiations. The result is certain to be once more the rejection of our position. We have explained to you repeatedly why we believe the problem of North Vietnamese troops is manageable under the agreement, and I see no reason to repeat all the arguments.

We will proceed next week in Paris along the lines that General Haig explained to you. Accordingly, if the North Vietnamese meet our concerns on the two outstanding substantive issues in the agreement, concerning the DMZ [demilitarized zone] and the method of signing and if we can arrange acceptable supervisory machinery, we will proceed to conclude the settlement. The gravest consequence would then ensue if your government chose to reject the agreement and split off from the United States. As I said in my December 17 letter, "I am convinced that your refusal to join us would be an invitation to disaster—to the loss of all that we together have fought for over the past decade. It would be inexcusable above all because we will have lost a just and honorable alternative."

As we enter this new round of talks, I hope that our countries will now show a united front. It is imperative for our common objectives that your Government take no further actions that complicate our task and would make more difficult the acceptance of the settlement by all parties. We will keep you informed of the negotiations in Paris through daily briefings of Ambassador Lam.

I can only repeat what I have so often said: The best guarantee for the survival of South Vietnam is the unity of our two countries which would be gravely jeopardized if you persist in your present course. The actions of our Congress since its return have clearly borne out the many warnings we have made.

Should you decide, as I trust you will, to go with us, you have my assurance of continued assistance in the post-settlement period and that we will respond with full force should the settlement be violated by North Vietnam. So once more I conclude with an appeal to you to close ranks with us.

Sincerely,
RICHARD NIXON

FUTURE OF SOUTH VIETNAM UNDER THE PRG

April 30 and May 1, 1975

Hours after jubilant Communist troops swept into Saigon, a Provisional Revolutionary Government (PRG) spokesman in Paris pledged the new government to a policy of nonalignment and national unity. The assurance came in a victory statement issued April 30 by Dinh Ba Thi, head of the Paris PRG delegation. Foreigners and their property in South Vietnam would be safe, Thi said, provided they "observe the policies of the revolutionary power." Also, the new nation would accept economic and technical aid from "any country with no political conditions attached."

On the same day, the PRG radio in Vietnam rebroadcast a "ten-point program" of domestic policy. The ten-point program had been broadcast earlier on April 3. At that time the Communists had already taken Da Nang and were in control of two-thirds of South Vietnam. The broadcast instructed "newly liberated areas" to dismantle the previous government's agencies, and declared its laws abolished and its property confiscated. Rural areas were urged to increase production—South Vietnam was suffering severe food shortages at the time—and a qualified amnesty was offered to soldiers who had "quit the enemy ranks."

Subsequent PRG broadcasts May 1 announced nationalization of property and warned of heavy penalties for crimes such as arson, looting and "spreading rumors." Prostitution and "all decadent slave cultural activities of the American variety" were banned. Publication of newspapers and other printed materials by private citizens was suspended.

After the Takeover

In the weeks following the takeover, the PRG apparently pursued a moderate course in accordance with its stated policies. Unlike neighboring Cambodia, where victorious Communists dealt harshly with the civilian population, South Vietnam seemed to have escaped the retributive "bloodbaths" which had been widely predicted.

Hanoi reportedly controlled the area through local military committees, but the timetable for final reunification with North Vietnam was not known. The remaining foreigners, largely French and Chinese businessmen, were subjected to restrictions on travel and transport, and the military government censored news dispatches. The Paris newspaper Le Monde *reported Aug. 20 that commercial properties of "capitalist patriots" had remained in private hands but their operations were severely limited because the military government had closed all banks and frozen capital assets. Low-ranking soldiers and civil servants in the previous government underwent short-term "reeducation"—often lasting no more than a day. However, high-ranking military and civilian officials were removed for reeducation to camps scattered throughout the countryside. Although PRG officials indicated that these persons would be held for approximately a month, the vast majority had still not returned by the end of the year, nor had they communicated with their families.*

Official reaction of foreign governments to the fall of South Vietnam was muted, with many governments declining to comment. But in the weeks following the capture of Saigon a number of governments which had not previously recognized the PRG agreed to establish diplomatic relations. By September some 70 nations, including Great Britain, Canada, Japan and India, had recognized the new government.

> *Text of statement released in Paris, April 30, 1975, on behalf of the Provisional Revolutionary Government of the Republic of South Vietnam by its representative Dinh Ba Thi:*

The long war of resistance of the Vietnamese people against the American aggression for its independence and its freedom has just ended victoriously. The population of the People's Liberation Armed Forces of South Vietnam, supported and staunchly helped by their brothers in the North, have brought the uprising and attacks against the repressive war machine set up by the U.S. in South Vietnam to a successful end.

The capital of South Vietnam, Saigon, was liberated. The U.S. aggressors were compelled to pull out. The puppet administration in Saigon as a whole, which is a tool of the U.S. neocolonialist policy, has fully collapsed. This is a complete bankruptcy of the strategy of neocolonialist aggression carried out by the U.S. for more than a decade.

Henceforth, South Vietnam is free and independent. The sacred testament of our beloved President Ho Chi Minh is realized. This is a victory of historic significance for the South Vietnamese population and for the Vietnamese nation as a whole. It is at the same time a just victory of the cause of peace, national independence and justice of the peoples over the world.

"Union and National Concord"

In this eventful day, I want to reaffirm that the policy of the P.R.G. has always been and will be a policy of great union and national concord. Yesterday, the P.R.G. rallied with this policy all strata of the population with a view to achieving the struggle of the population for its legitimate aspirations for peace, independence, democracy and national concord.

Today and tomorrow, it will mobilize with this policy all forces in order to build, in recovered peace, a peaceful, independent, democratic, neutral and prosperous South Vietnam and to progress toward peaceful reunification of Vietnam.

This policy of great union and national concord of the P.R.G. specially aims at erasing hatred and divisions and offering a place and a role to all inhabitants irrespective of their past in the tremendous task of reconstruction and building.

Policy on Foreigners

With regard to foreigners present in South Vietnam, according to the 10-point policy of the P.R.G., their lives and property are protected but they are asked to respect the independence and sovereignty of Vietnam and to observe the policies of the revolutionary power.

In international affairs, South Vietnam will carry out a foreign policy of peace and nonalignment. It will be prepared to establish relations with all countries irrespective of their political and social systems on the basis of mutual respect for independence and sovereignty and accept economic and technical aid from any country with no political conditions attached.

Allow me, in the name of the P.R.G. and the people of South Vietnam, to express our warm thanks to all socialist countries of national independence and all peace and justice-loving peoples, including the American people who have supported our just struggle.

The victory gained today is also theirs. We are convinced that they will continue to support and help our people in the building and reconstruction of our country.

Text of a broadcast of the 10-Point Policy Toward the Newly Liberated Areas of the Provisional Revolutionary Government of the Republic of South Vietnam, as monitored April 3, 1975, by the Foreign Broadcast Information Service and rebroadcast April 30, 1975:

Over the past more than 2 years, the U.S. imperialists and the puppet Nguyen Van Thieu clique have continued the war, constantly sabotaged the Paris agreement on Vietnam and perpetrated untold crimes against our people.

Our armed forces and people have valiantly launched offensives and staged uprisings to punish the clique; have won many more great victories; and have liberated many more provinces, cities and towns and many large rural areas in the mountainous, forest and delta regions. Our people now live in independence and freedom in the newly liberated areas under PRGRSV [Provisional Revolutionary Government of the Republic of South Vietnam] control.

In order to protect and develop the revolutionary gains, stabilize the people's livelihood, positively protect and implement the Paris agreement on Vietnam and advance the South Vietnamese revolution toward even greater victories, the PRGRSV hereby makes public its following 10-point policy toward the newly liberated areas:

1. Completely eradicate the regime and its ruling apparatus, the armed forces, organizations, and rules and regulations and forms of repression and control of the puppet administration, and quickly establish the people's revolutionary administration at all levels in the newly liberated areas. All puppet agencies must come under revolutionary administration management. Public officials who worked for the puppet machinery are allowed to continue to work under the revolutionary administration and must correctly implement its policies and lines. Abolish all reactionary political parties and factions and all other political organizations which were lackeys of the U.S. imperialists and the puppet administration.

2. Implement the people's democratic liberties and achieve equality between men and women. Insure freedom of faith and unity and equality among the various religions. Respect the people's freedom of worship and protect pagodas, churches and temples.

3. Implement a policy to achieve all-people unity and national reconciliation and concord and oppose aggressive imperialism. Strictly forbid all activities creating divisiveness, hatred, and suspicion among the people and among the various nationalities. Everyone, regardless of financial situation, nationality or political tendency, must unite, love and assist one another in developing the liberated areas and a peaceful, joyful and healthy life. Implement equality among the people of various nationalities, large and small. Positively assist the ethnic minority compatriots to develop their economic and cultural activities and improve their livelihood.

4. Everyone in the liberated areas will be allowed to continue their activities to earn a living and must maintain public order and security and support the revolution. The people's revolutionary administration will resolutely and promptly smash all enemy schemes and acts of sabotage and counterattacks; and it will severely punish those who oppose the revolutionary administration, sabotage public order and security, encroach on the people's livelihood, property and dignity and encroach or sabotage property managed by the revolutionary administration.

5. The property of the puppet administration will be managed by the PRGRSV.

6. Enterprises, industries and handicrafts, trading, and communications and transportation enterprises and other public utility projects must continue their activities to support the people's economy and normal activities. Restoration of production will be actively carried out and the urban people's livelihood will be stabilized. Unemployed workers and other working people will be given jobs. Industrialists' and traders' property will be guaranteed. They will be allowed to continue their business transactions if these are beneficial to national plans and the people's livelihood. Orphans, invalids, and the old and weak will be cared for.

7. Encourage and assist peasants in restoring and developing agricultural production, fishery, salt production and forestry; encourage the owners of plantations to grow industrial crops and fruit trees and continue their business.

8. All cultural, scientific and technical installations, schools and hospitals must continue their operations to serve the people. All reactionary, depraved and brain-poisoning organizations and activities of the U.S. imperialists and the puppet administration are banned. Encourage and develop healthy national cultural activities. Appreciate and employ persons of talent in the scientific and technical domains who are useful to national development.

9. Strictly implement the PRGRSV's policy promulgated on 25 March 1975 toward officers and soldiers of the puppet administration. All servicemen, officers, policemen, disabled troops, veterans and personnel of the puppet administration who have quit the enemy ranks to join the liberated areas, who have volunteered to stay in the liberated areas, who have reported to the organs of the revolutionary administration in accordance with regulations, or who have seriously complied with the laws of the revolutionary administration will be provided assistance in their business or allowed to return to their homes and participate in various activities according to their desires and ability. Those who have scored merits or who have atoned for their faults by achieving merits will be commended and rewarded. Those who resist the revolution will be seriously punished. Those guilty persons who have sincerely repented will be granted leniency.

10. Insure the lives and property of foreigners. All foreigners must respect the independence and sovereignty of Vietnam and must seriously implement all lines and policies of the revolutionary administration. Those foreigners who have contributed to the struggle for independence and freedom and in the national building of the South Vietnamese people will be welcomed.

The liberated zone in South Vietnam is the brilliant achievement of all the Vietnamese people and a stable prop for the revolutionary undertaking to completely liberate South Vietnam.

The PRGRSV appeals to all compatriots to strictly respect and fully implement these policies, to achieve solidarity and singlemindedness, to resolutely struggle to protect and consolidate the liberated zone. All of the cadres, combatants and personnel of the revolutionary administration must set an example in implementing these policies and must make positive efforts to explain and guide the people in implementing these policies.

The PRGRSV will duly commend and reward those who have scored merits for the revolution or outstanding achievements in protecting and building the liberated zone.

> *Texts of broadcasts of May 1, 1975, by various agencies of the Provisional Revolutionary Government of the Republic of South Vietnam as monitored by the Foreign Broadcast Information Service:*

Property

The Ministry for Foreign Affairs of South Vietnam declares: All the property in South Vietnam as well as abroad including real estate and movable property, money, and transport means previously belonging to the Saigon administration from now on belongs to the South Vietnamese people and [is to] be managed by the Provisional Revolutionary Government. This is an inalienable right of property inheritance of the Provisional Revolutionary Government recognized by international law.

In their flight, many elements of the Saigon puppet administration brought tens of warships, cargo ships and hundreds of cargo planes and jet fighters to Thailand and other countries and stole and brought along dozens of tons of gold and other property to foreign countries. These properties must be returned to the Provisional Revolutionary Government of the Republic of South Vietnam.

The Provisional Revolutionary Government of the Republic of South Vietnam solemnly declares to reserve for it the right to recover all these properties now in many foreign countries as well as the property recently stolen and brought along by members of the puppet army and puppet administration when they fled to foreign countries.

Publications

[Military Management Committee decision] During this period of military management, in order to stabilize the situation and to maintain order and security, the Military Management Committee has decided the following:

1. To temporarily suspend publication of all kinds of books, newspapers, magazines and other printed material privately owned during this period.

2. The distribution of all printed material already published without authorization from the Military Management Committee and at variance with this decision must be stopped and these materials must be withdrawn at once.

Security

[Communique of the Saigon-Gia Dinh Military Management Committee] In order to protect and develop the accomplishments of the revolution, to protect the lives and property of the people, to protect the property of the revolutionary administration, and in order to rapidly stabilize order and security and assure the people's normal activities, the Saigon-Gia Dinh City Military Management Committee stipulates that:

1. Everyone has the obligation and responsibility to defend the revolutionary administration, to preserve order and security; and to stabilize the newly liberated city.

2. The lives and property of the people are to be protected.

3. Until a new decree is issued, the people are allowed to temporarily retain their identification cards and family registration documents and other individual and family documents, including photographs, used for family registration for each person, family and dwelling.

4. From now on, anyone who plots or acts to sabotage the city's security, by such acts as collecting intelligence, creating armed disturbances, harming revolutionary cadres or soldiers, carrying out psychological warfare, spreading false rumors, coercing the people to flee with the enemy, dividing the popular solidarity bloc, or sabotaging the implementation of the policies and stipulations of the revolutionary administration, will be severely punished.

5. From now on, anyone who disturbs order, sets fires, causes explosions, poisons or kills people, extorts money, steals, rapes women, takes advantage of the situation to loot, or commits other acts which violate the lives and property of the people or the property of the revolutionary administration, will be severely punished.

6. Anyone who commits illegal acts in the name of the revolutionary administration will be severely punished.

7. All activities of houses of prostitution, dance halls, smoking dens, and all decadent slave cultural activities of the American variety are strictly forbidden.

8. People who have achieved merit in opposing all activities of the enemy, maintaining order and security, protecting the lives and property of the people, or protecting the property of the revolutionary administration, will be appropriately rewarded.

May

THE MAYAGUEZ AFFAIR

May 15, 1975

Seven years after North Korea captured the American intelligence ship Pueblo, *Cambodian forces on May 12 seized a U.S. merchant ship, the* Mayagüez, *in the Gulf of Siam. In this case, unlike that of the* Pueblo, *the United States responded with force and on May 14 secured release of the ship and its crew some 50 hours after their capture. (The* Pueblo *crew was detained almost a year.)*

The incident called into play the procedures of the 1973 War Powers Resolution (PL 93-148), which requires a President to consult with Congress "in every possible instance" before committing U.S. troops overseas (see Historic Documents 1973, p. 923). On the evening of May 14, more than 15 hours after the military operation was launched, President Ford followed a series of telephone calls to Capitol Hill with a brief White House meeting attended by selected congressional leaders. Some leaders later objected to the notification procedure. "I was not consulted. I was notified after the fact about what the administration had already decided to do," Senate Majority Leader Mike Mansfield (D Mont.) told The New York Times.

During the operation 15 U.S. servicemen were killed and later three more were reported missing. A helicopter crash related to the rescue effort claimed an additional 23 lives in Thailand. Total costs for the operation and losses reached $9.5-million. When these figures became known, a House subcommittee undertook an investigation, beginning June 19. However, prevailing opinion in the international press and among members of Congress was that the success of the mission justified the way President Ford handled it.

Sequence of Events

In compliance with a war powers act provision requiring the President to report within 48 hours to the House speaker and Senate president pro tempore any U.S. troop commitment abroad, Ford submitted a brief letter, dated May 15, which outlined the rescue operation and events leading to it. After .being notified May 12 of Cambodia's "illegal and dangerous act," Ford reported, the U.S. demanded "both publicly and privately, without success" that the ship and crew be freed. According to a New York Times dispatch, the United States tried to approach Cambodia through third countries, primarily China.

On May 13, in an attempt to prevent the transfer of the ship or its crew to a mainland port, U.S. forces fired across the bow of the Mayagüez and shortly after midnight, on May 14, bombed the surrounding area. Three Cambodian gunboats were sunk and four others damaged. However, the Mayagüez crew had already been removed from the ship, and late in the afternoon of the 14th Ford ordered a U.S. Marine attack on a nearby island, Koh Tang, where the men were thought to be held. U.S. aircraft also bombed mainland targets to prevent Cambodian interference in the rescue operation. By midnight Marines from a U.S. destroyer had boarded and secured the empty Mayagüez, and a small Cambodian boat had returned the crew to a second U.S. vessel.

Cambodian Response

The Cambodians broke their silence shortly after the U.S. raids on the mainland began. In a radio broadcast from Phnom Penh the government, "wishing to provoke no one or to make trouble," promised to release the ship. One explanation for Cambodia's previous silence emerged some months later when a high Cambodian official, in New York to attend a United Nations meeting, said that a local army unit had decided to take the Mayagüez without the knowledge of the Phnom Penh government. Ieng Sary, deputy premier and foreign minister, said on Sept. 6 that Cambodian authorities first learned of the capture "through American broadcasts, because the American technology is able to convey information much faster than our armed forces can." (The seizure occurred less than a month after insurgent Khmer Rouge forces had toppled the Cambodian coalition government.) Ieng Sary also said that, before the new government could act, the local commander who had taken the American ship had to travel to the capital to explain his action. He was then instructed to return and release the ship.

In a May 15 communique, however, Cambodian Information Minister Hu Nim had accused the United States of spying systematically on Cambodia "with a view to committing subversion, sabotage and provocation." Although he asserted that the Mayagüez itself was a spy ship sent into Cambodian waters to "create a pretext for attacking the Cambodian *nation," Hu Nim said the ship and crew would be freed. Cambodia never intended "to detain it permanently.... We only wanted to know the reason for its coming and to warn it."*

Text of the letter on the Mayagüez rescue operation sent by President Gerald R. Ford to House Speaker Carl Albert (D Okla.) and Senator James O. Eastland (D Miss.), president pro tempore of the Senate, at 2:30 a.m. May 15, 1975:

May 15, 1975.

DEAR MR. SPEAKER: (DEAR MR. PRESIDENT PRO TEM:) On 12 May 1975, I was advised that the S.S. Mayaguez, a merchant vessel of United States registry en route from Hong Kong to Thailand with a U.S. citizen crew, was fired upon, stopped, boarded, and seized by Cambodian naval patrol boats of the Armed Forces of Cambodia in international waters in the vicinity of Poulo Wai Island. The seized vessel was then forced to proceed to Koh Tang Island where it was required to anchor. This hostile act was in clear violation of international law.

In view of this illegal and dangerous act, I ordered, as you have been previously advised, United States military forces to conduct the necessary reconnaissance and to be ready to respond if diplomatic efforts to secure the return of the vessel and its personnel were not successful. Two United States reconnaissance aircraft in the course of locating the Mayaguez sustained minimal damage from small firearms. Appropriate demands for the return of the Mayaguez and its crew were made, both publicly and privately, without success.

In accordance with my desire that the Congress be informed on this matter and taking note of Section 4(a) (1) of the War Powers Resolution, I wish to report to you that at about 6:20 a.m., 13 May, pursuant to my instructions to prevent the movement of the Mayaguez into a mainland port, U.S. aircraft fired warning shots across the bow of the ship and gave visual signals to small craft approaching the ship. Subsequently, in order to stabilize the situation and in an attempt to preclude removal of the American crew of the Mayaguez to the mainland, where their rescue would be more difficult, I directed the United States Armed Forces to isolate the island and interdict any movement between the ship or the island and the mainland, and to prevent movement of the ship itself, while still taking all possible care to prevent loss of life or injury to the U.S. captives. During the evening of 13 May, a Cambodian patrol boat attempting to leave the island disregarded aircraft warnings and was sunk. Thereafter, two other Cambodian patrol craft were destroyed and four others were damaged and immobilized. One boat, suspected of having some U.S. captives aboard, succeeded in reaching Kompong Som after efforts to turn it around without injury to the passengers failed.

American Objectives

Our continued objective in this operation was the rescue of the captured American crew along with the retaking of the ship Mayaguez. For that purpose, I ordered late this afternoon [May 14] an assault by United States Marines on the island of Koh Tang to search out and rescue such Americans as might still be held there, and I ordered retaking of the Mayaguez by other marines boarding from the destroyer escort HOLT. In addition to continued fighter and gunship coverage of the Koh Tang area, these marine activities were supported by tactical aircraft from the CORAL SEA, striking the military airfield at Ream and other military targets in the area of Kompong Som in order to prevent reinforcement or support from the mainland of the Cambodian forces detaining the American vessel and crew.

At approximately 9:00 P.M. EDT on 14 May, the Mayaguez was retaken by United States forces. At approximately 11:30 P.M., the entire crew of the Mayaguez was taken aboard the WILSON. U.S. forces have begun the process of disengagement and withdrawal.

This operation was ordered and conducted pursuant to the President's constitutional Executive power and his authority as Commander-in-Chief of the United States Armed Forces.

Sincerely,

GERALD R. FORD

Text of communique promising release of the Mayagüez *and its crew, broadcast by Cambodian Information Minister Hu Nim at 7:07 p.m. May 14, 1975 (6:07 a.m. May 15, Cambodian time):*

Since we liberated Phnom Penh and the entire country, U.S. imperialism has conducted repeated, successive intelligence and espionage activities with a view to committing subversion, sabotage and provocation against the newly liberated New Cambodia in an apparent desire to deny the Cambodian nation and people, who have suffered all manner of hardships and grief for more than five years because of the U.S. imperialist war of aggression, the right to survive, to resolve the problems of their livelihood, to restore their economy and build their country on the basis of independence and initiative as an independent, peaceful, neutral and non-aligned nation. Specifically, the U.S. imperialists have tried to block our sea routes and ports as part of the above-mentioned strategic goal.

In the air, U.S. imperialist planes have been conducting daily espionage flights over Cambodia, especially over Phnom Penh, Sihanoukville, Sihanoukville port and Cambodia's territorial waters. They even resorted to an insolent show of force, trying to intimidate the Cambodian people. On the ground, U.S. imperialism has planted its strategic forces to conduct subversive, sabotage and destructive activities in various cities by setting fire to our economic, strategic and military positions and so forth.

On the sea, it has engaged in many espionage activities. U.S. imperialist spy ships have entered Cambodia's territorial waters and engaged in espionage activities there almost daily, especially in the areas of Sihanoukville port, from Pring, Tang and Wai Islands to Pres Island, south of Sihanoukville.

These ships have been operating as fishing vessels. There have been two or three of them entering our territorial waters daily. They have secretly landed Thai and Cambodian nationals to contact their espionage agents on the mainland. Those who were captured have confessed all of this to us.

Some ships carry dozens of kilograms of plastic bombs and several radio-communication sets with which they try to arm their agents to sabotage and destroy our factories, ports and economic, strategic and military positions. These persons have successively confessed to us that they are C.I.A. [Central Intelligence Agency] agents based in Thailand and that they entered Cambodia's territorial waters through Thai waters.

Previous Incursions

On 11 May 1975 our naval patrol captured one ship near Prince Island facing Sihanoukville port. This ship, disguised as a fishing boat, was manned by a crew of seven heavily armed Thais carrying, among other things, two 12.7-mm machine guns and a quantity of plastic bombs, grenades and mines. At the same time, we found a powerful U.S.-built radio-teletype set capable of maintaining communications from one country to another.

These people have admitted that they are C.I.A. agents sent out to conduct sabotage activities and to make contact with the forces set up and planted by U.S. imperialism before it withdrew from Cambodia. Later on, at dawn on 12 May, another ship manned by seven Thai nationals and disguised as a fishing vessel reached Pres Island near Sihanoukville port with the same intention as the previous ships.

All this forms part of U.S. imperialism's ceaseless, premeditated and well-organized attempts to violate Cambodia's territorial waters bent on destruction. These activities are not common mistakes. These ships were operating in the territorial waters of Cambodia. At certain points they moved within only four or five kilometers from the coast; at other times they even accosted Cambodian islands and landed at these islands. Such was the case at Pring, Pres, Tang and other islands.

This is a definite encroachment on Cambodia's sovereignty—an encroachment they dare to make because they are strong and because Cambodia is a small and poor country with a small population that has just emerged from the U.S. imperialist war of aggression lacking all and needing everything. The Cambodian nation and people, though just emerging from U.S. imperialist war of aggression and needy as they are, are determined to defend their territorial waters, national sovereignty and national honor in accordance with the resolutions of the N.U.F.C. [National United Front of Cambodia] and of the successive national congresses. Accordingly, Cambodia's coast guard has never ceased its relentless patrols inside Cambodia's territorial waters.

As part of the U.S. imperialists' espionage activities in our territorial waters, on 7 May 1975 a large vessel in the form of a merchant ship flying the Panamanian flags entered deeply into Cambodian territorial waters between Wai and Tang Islands and intruded about 50 kilometers past Wai Island coastward. Seeing that this ship had intruded too deeply into Cambodian territorial waters, our patrol then detained it in order to examine and question the crew and then report to higher authorities, who would in turn refer the matter to the R.G.N.U.C. [Royal Government of National Union of Cambodia] for a decision. We did not even bother to inquire about the ship's cargo.

The crew was composed of Thais, Taiwanese, Filipinos and Americans. It was evident that this ship, having intentionally violated Cambodian territorial waters, had only two possible goals: either to conduct espionage or to provoke incidents. It certainly did not lose its way. If it did it would not have entered our waters so deeply. However, the R.G.N.U.C. has decided to allow this ship to continue its route out of Cambodia's territorial waters. This is clear proof of our goodwill. Though this ship had come to provoke us inside our territorial waters, we still showed our goodwill.

Capture of Mayaguez

Then on 12 May 1975 at 1400 our patrol sighted another large vessel steaming toward our waters. We took no action at first. The ship continued to intrude deeper into our waters, passing the Wai Islands eastward to a point four or five kilometers beyond the islands. Seeing that this ship intentionally violated our waters, our patrol then stopped it in order to examine and question it and report back to our higher authorities so that the latter could report to the Royal Government. This vessel sails in the form of a merchant ship code-named *Mayagüez*, flying American flags and manned by an American crew.

While we were questioning the ship, two American F-105 aircrafts kept circling over the ship and over the Wai and Tang Islands until evening. From dawn on 13 May between four and six American F-15's and F-111's took turns for 24 hours savagely strafing and bombing around the ship, the Wai and Tang Islands and Sihanoukville port area. At 0530 on 14 May six U.S. F-105 and F-111 aircraft resumed taking turns strafing and bombing. According to a preliminary report, two of our patrol vessels were sunk. We still have had no precise idea of the extent of the damage done or the number killed among our patrolmen and the American crewmen.

This is one of the most savage, barbarous acts of U.S. imperialism. Because they have all types of modern weapons the U.S. imperialists think they can threaten, intimidate and kill other people at will inside other people's territories and waters, without allowing other people the right to self-defense or to investigate their espionage, intelligence and encroachment activities. U.S. imperialism and the Ford Administration must bear full responsibility for this act before the Cambodian nation and people, before the world people as well as before the American people and politicians.

What was the intention, the reason, for this ship entering our territorial waters? We are convinced that this American ship did not lose its way, because the Americans have radar, electronic and other most sophisticated scientific instruments. It is therefore evident that this ship came to violate our waters, conduct espionage and provoke incidents to create pretexts or mislead the opinion of the world people, the American people and the American politicians, pretending that the Cambodian nation and people are the provocateurs while feigning innocence on their part.

A Provocation

The world peoples, the American people and the American politicians have already seen the U.S. imperialists successfully bullying the peoples of small countries who refused to bow to their will. The U.S. imperialists used to bully Russia in the past. Cuba, China, North Korea, North Vietnam and other countries loving independence and honor were also bullied by them. Now they have invented the incident in Cambodian territorial waters to create a pretext for attacking the Cambodian nation and people. However, we are confident that the world peoples as well as the American people, youth and politicians who love peace and justice will clearly see that the Cambodian people—a small, poor and needy people just emerging from the U.S. imperialist war of aggression—have no intention and no wherewithal, no possibility of capturing an American ship cruising the open seas at large. We were able to capture it only because it had violated our territorial waters too flagrantly, and had come too close to our nose.

Therefore, the charge leveled by the U.S. imperialists—that we are sea pirates—is too much. On the contrary, it is the U.S. imperialists who are the sea pirates who came to provoke the Cambodian nation and people in Cambodian territorial waters, just as they had only fomented subversion in our country, staged a coup d'état destroying independent, peaceful and neutral Cambodia, and committed aggression against Cambodia causing us much destruction and suffering. Now they are looking for pretexts to deceive world opinion and that of the American people and politicians so as to destroy a country which refuses to bow to their will. We are confident in the good sense of the world peoples and the American people, youth and politicians who love peace and justice.

Regarding the *Mayagüez* ship, we have no intention of detaining it permanently and we have no desire to stage provocations. We only wanted to know the reason for its coming and to warn it against violating our waters again. This is why our coast guard seized this ship. Their goal was to examine it, question it and make a report to higher authorities who would then report to the Royal Government so that the Royal Government could itself decide to order it to withdraw from Cambodia's territorial waters and warn it against conducting further espionage and provocative activities.

This applies to this *Mayagüez* ship and to any other vessels, like the ship flying Panama flags that we released on 9 May 1975.

Wishing to provoke no one or to make trouble, adhering to the stand of peace and neutrality, we will release this ship, but we will not allow the U.S. imperialists to violate our territorial waters, conduct espionage in our territorial waters, provoke incidents in our territorial waters or force us to release their ships whenever they want, by applying threats.

No country cherishing its honor and sovereignty can abide by the orders of the U.S. imperialists. The Cambodian nation and people demand that the world peoples and the American people, youth and politicians who love peace and justice bear witness to our good faith, and we demand that they refuse to believe the U.S. imperialists and sternly condemn them in any future such incidents they may provoke. The Cambodian nation and people have no intention of provoking anybody, nor do we have the wherewithal to provoke anybody. We only exercise the right to defend our sovereignty and territorial integrity, which we hardly manage to defend, having just emerged from the war of destruction of U.S. imperialism.

Phnom Penh, 15 May 1975.

HU NIM

R.G.N.U.C. Information and Propaganda Minister

CONTROLS ON GENETIC ENGINEERING

May 20, 1975

Because of health risks inherent in new techniques of genetic manipulation of living cells and viruses, a group of prominent scientists—meeting at the Asilomar Conference Center near Pacific Grove, California, at the end of February—called for stringent controls on certain types of experiments. This largely unprecedented action—medical researchers recommending that their own investigations be rigorously controlled, or in certain cases abandoned, because of possible hazards to the health of laboratory personnel or the public—followed an eight-month moratorium on such high-risk research observed at the request of a National Academy of Sciences committee.

The move brought sharp objections from such scientists as Nobel laureates Joshua Lederberg and James Watson, who argued that the risks were too remote to justify limiting the absolute freedom of scientific inquiry. In an interview with Science *magazine, Watson said "the dangers" were "probably no greater than working in a hospital."*

The controversial research involved constructing new combinations of genes ("recombinant DNA molecules") by snipping the genetic material DNA and rejoining the resulting molecular segments in altered sequence. The new technique enabled researchers for the first time to unite genetic material from two different species. The resulting recombinant DNAs were inserted into fast-growing viruses or bacteria which would produce the new genetic entity in quantity.

Such research could lead to a less expensive process of manufacturing insulin or to improved agricultural productivity. But it could also result in

*new, untreatable infections if it created genes which confer resistance to an-
tibiotic drugs or form new types of poisonous substances. In addition to
these dangers suggested by current research, the procedures were so new
that scientists could not predict all of the potential hazards. "It is this ignorance that has compelled us to conclude that it would be wise to exercise
considerable caution in performing this research," the Asilomar scientists
said.*

Voluntary Moratorium

*In July 1974 a committee of the National Academy of Sciences (the Com-
mittee on Recombinant DNA Molecules), chaired by Paul Berg of the Stanford University Medical Center, had recommended that the biohazards of
such research be evaluated by an international scientific conference. To
prevent the construction of "dangerous molecules" in the interim before the
conference, the Berg committee asked for a voluntary suspension of certain
types of experiments involving the recombinant DNA molecules. Its appeal
was published in an open letter to the American journal* Science *and its
British counterpart,* Nature. *The recommended research moratorium was
believed to have been observed worldwide.*

*The 140 conferees at Asilomar, including 53 foreign scientists, debated
reports evaluating the hazards of the three types of experiments covered by
the Berg letter. Opponents of specifying controls for experiments raised the
problem of who should regulate scientific research. Lederberg and other opponents expressed fear that the mere act of spelling out procedures for certain types of research would open scientific investigation to interference by
non-scientists. In fact, several months later, on April 22, the Asilomar conference was criticized by Sen. Edward M. Kennedy (D Mass.) for having
reached its conclusions without broader consultation. Other critics dis-
counted the hazards to health or asserted that standard precautions were
adequate.*

Safeguards

*A major new discovery reported at the February meeting was the
feasibility of constructing biological safety barriers; that is, developing
strains of host organisms which could not survive outside of laboratory conditions. This would promise a greater degree of control or "containment" of
the hybrid molecules when combined with such standard precautions as
specially equipped laboratories isolated from other areas, protective
laboratory clothing, and stringent decontamination procedures for
laboratory personnel.*

*The combination of biological and physical safeguards appeared to the
conferees "adequate," in most cases, "to contain the newly created organisms." A summary statement voted by the conference concluded that*

"most of the work on construction of recombinant DNA molecules should proceed." The statement ranked experiments by potential risk and specified containment procedures for each level. But it continued to ban those experiments which, while "feasible...present such serious dangers that their performance should not be undertaken at this time."

In its final form the document was approved May 20 by the Executive Committee of the Assembly of Life Sciences of the National Academy of Sciences. The National Institutes of Health subsequently appointed an advisory committee to develop guidelines, using the Asilomar statement, for funding recombinant DNA research.

Excerpts from Summary Statement *of the Asilomar Conference on Recombinant DNA Molecules, approved May 20, 1975, by the Executive Committee of the Assembly of Life Sciences of the National Academy of Sciences:*

I. Introduction and General Conclusions

This meeting was organized to review scientific progress in research on recombinant DNA molecules and to discuss appropriate ways to deal with the potential biohazards of this work. Impressive scientific achievements have already been made in this field and these techniques have a remarkable potential for furthering our understanding of fundamental biochemical processes in pro- and eukaryotic cells. The use of recombinant DNA methodology promises to revolutionize the practice of molecular biology. While there has as yet been no practical application of the new techniques, there is every reason to believe that they will have significant practical utility in the future.

Of particular concern to the participants at the meeting was the issue of whether the pause in certain aspects of research in this area, called for by the Committee on Recombinant DNA Molecules of the National Academy of Sciences, U.S.A. in the letter published in July, 1974, should end; and, if so, how the scientific work could be undertaken with minimal risks to workers in laboratories, to the public at large and to the animal and plant species sharing our ecosystems.

The new techniques, which permit combination of genetic information from very different organisms, place us in an area of biology with many unknowns. Even in the present, more limited conduct of research in this field, the evaluation of potential biohazards has proved to be extremely difficult. It is this ignorance that has compelled us to conclude that it would be wise to exercise considerable caution in performing this research. Nevertheless, the participants at the Conference agreed that most of the work on construction of recombinant DNA molecules should proceed provided that appropriate safeguards, principally biological and physical barriers adequate to contain the newly created organisms, are employed. Moreover, the standards of protection should be greater at the beginning and modified as improvements in the methodology occur and assessments of the risks change. Furthermore, it was agreed that there are certain experiments in which the potential risks are of such a serious nature that they ought not to be done with presently available containment facilities. In the longer term serious problems may arise in the large scale application of this methodology in industry, medicine and agriculture. But it was also recognized that future research and experience may show that many of the potential biohazards are less serious and/or less probable than we now suspect.

II. Principles Guiding the Recommendations and Conclusions

Though our assessments of the risks involved with each of the various lines of research on recombinant DNA molecules may differ, few, if any, believe that this methodology is free from any risk. Reasonable principles for dealing with these potential risks are: 1) that containment be made an essential consideration in the experimental design and, 2) that the effectiveness of the containment should match, as closely as possible, the estimated risk....

Containment of potentially biohazardous agents can be achieved in several ways. The most significant contribution to limiting the spread of the recombinant DNAs is the use of biological barriers. These barriers are of two types: 1) fastidious bacterial hosts unable to survive in natural environments, and 2) non-transmissible and equally fastidious vectors (plasmids, bacteriophages or other viruses) able to grow only in specified hosts. Physical containment, exemplified by the use of suitable hoods, or where applicable, limited access or negative pressure laboratories, provides an additional factor of safety. Particularly important is strict adherence to good microbiological practices which, to a large measure can limit the escape of organisms from the experimental situation, and thereby increase the safety of the operation. Consequently, education and training of all personnel involved in the experiments is essential to the effectiveness of all containment measures....

III. Specific Recommendations for Matching Types of Containment with Types of Experiments

No classification of experiments as to risk and no set of containment procedures can anticipate all situations. Given our present uncertainties about the hazards, the parameters proposed here are broadly conceived and meant to provide provisional guidelines for investigators and agencies concerned with research on recombinant DNAs. However, each investigator bears a responsibility for determining whether, in his particular case, special circumstances warrant a higher level of containment than is suggested here....

Experiments to be Deferred: There are feasible experiments which present such serious dangers that their performance should not be undertaken at this time with the currently available vector-host systems and the presently available containment capability. These include the cloning of recombinant DNAs derived from highly pathogenic organisms....,DNA containing toxin genes and large scale experiments (more than 10 liters of culture) using recombinant DNAs that are able to make products potentially harmful to man, animals or plants.

IV. Implementation

In many countries steps are already being taken by national bodies to formulate codes of practice for the conduct of experiments with known or potential biohazard. Until these are established, we urge individual scientists to use the proposals in this document as a guide. In addition, there are some recommendations which could be immediately and directly implemented by the scientific community.

A. Development of Safer Vectors and Hosts

An important and encouraging accomplishment of the meeting was the realization that special bacteria and vectors can be constructed genetically, which have a restricted capacity to multiply outside the laboratory, and that the use of these organisms could enhance the safety of recombinant DNA experiments by many orders of magnitude. Experiments along these lines are presently in progress and in the near future, variants of λ bacteriophage, non-transmissible plasmids and special strains of *E. coli* will become available....

B. Laboratory Procedures

It is the clear responsibility of the principal investigator to inform the staff of the laboratory of the potential hazards of such experiments, before they are initiated. Free and open discussion is necessary so that each individual participating in the experiment fully understands the nature of the experiment and any risk that might be involved. All workers must be properly trained in the containment procedures that are designed to control the hazard, including emergency actions in the event of a hazard. It is also recommended that appropriate health surveillance of all personnel, including serological monitoring, be conducted periodically....

V. New Knowledge

This document represents our first assessment of the potential biohazards in the light of current knowledge. However, little is known about the survival of laboratory strains of bacteria and bacteriophages in different ecological niches in the outside world. Even less is known about whether recombinant DNA molecules will enhance or depress the survival of their vectors and hosts in nature. These questions are fundamental to the testing of any new organism that may be constructed. Research in this area needs to be undertaken and should be given high priority. In general, however, molecular biologists who may construct DNA recombinant molecules do not undertake these experiments and it will be necessary to facilitate collaborative research between them and groups skilled in the study of bacterial infection or ecological microbiology. Work should also be undertaken which would enable us to monitor the escape or dissemination of cloning vehicles and their hosts....

RESTRUCTURING OF UNITED NATIONS

May 20, 1975

The first major attempt to effect basic changes in the structure of the 30-year-old United Nations was set in motion in the spring of 1975. An international panel of consultants in May recommended reforms aimed at bypassing the conflict-ridden parliamentary processes of the General Assembly in favor of negotiated settlements of disputes. This proposal and others for overhauling the existing system of international economic relations constituted the most substantial U.N. response to date to Third World demands for a radical redistribution of the world's wealth. U.N. Secretary-General Kurt Waldheim termed submission of the panel's report, entitled A New United Nations Structure for Global Economic Cooperation, *"a historic moment" in the life of the international institution. But the proposed changes faced an uncertain fate because they seemed unlikely to be entirely satisfactory either to the industrialized nations or to the developing nations which dominate the General Assembly.*

Three decades after its formation the U.N. had tripled its membership and the long-dominant bloc of Western powers was challenged by a new majority of underdeveloped Latin, Asian and African states. Over strenuous U.S. objections these states, often allied with the Arab oil-producing nations and Communist members, had carried a number of controversial actions in the 1974 session, including:

●Adoption of a Charter of Economic Rights and Duties, *Dec. 12, 1974, following up a special session the previous April dealing with raw materials* (see Historic Documents of 1974, p. 255). *According to a State Department evaluation, the United States found the charter objectionable because it "encouraged formation of raw material cartels similar to the oil cartel;"*

● *Exclusion of South Africa for the latter part of the session because of that nation's discriminatory racial policies. The United States opposed the move because of its belief that U.N. interference in members' domestic affairs would sap the organization's effectiveness;*

● *Extension of participant or observer status to the Palestine Liberation Organization (PLO) in several U.N. forums, and adoption by the General Assembly of a resolution affirming an "inalienable right of Palestinians to return to their homes and property..."—both measures considered by the United States to be contrary to U.N. rules and prejudicial to ongoing negotiations in the Middle East;*

● *Exclusion of Israel from regional meetings and programs of the United Nations Educational, Scientific and Cultural Organization (UNESCO).*

"A Tyranny of the Majority"

In a major address Dec. 6, 1974, John Scali, then U.S. ambassador to the United Nations, denounced the foregoing actions as "a tyranny of the majority." He described them as "one-sided, unrealistic solutions that cannot be implemented and that disregarded the U.N. Charter." The Algerian representative called Scali's remarks "unjust, exaggerated...."

What lay behind these confrontations was the crushing poverty of the Third World and—paradoxically—the recent successes of the oil cartel in forcing fourfold price increases on the global market (see Historic Documents of 1974, p. 221). While the price rise had plunged the underdeveloped nations into desperate financial straits, it also had given a dramatic example of joint action against the industrialized states.

The year 1975 witnessed a proliferation of programs for a "new economic order," proclaimed at conferences of developing nations in Africa, South America and Asia. At these meetings, discussions of allocation of food and resources resulted in adoption of at least five separate declarations demanding concessions from industrialized nations. Major reforms called for in these documents included:

● *Stabilization of prices of raw materials. One method often proposed was to link commodity prices to the world inflation index;*

● *Control of multinational corporations to prevent their manipulation of the commodities markets, and to halt the flow of profits out of underdeveloped countries by forcing their reinvestment in those countries;*

● *Reform of the world monetary system;*

● *Cushions—"buffer stocks"—to absorb sharp drops in world prices or demand;*

● *"Transfer of technology" to provide non-industrialized nations with the capacity to process their own commodities, thereby freeing them from the necessity to buy back their own materials, processed, at high prices.*

Just a month before the U.N. reorganization plan was released, efforts of oil-producing and oil-consuming nations in Paris to draw up an agenda for energy negotiations had foundered on the insistence of Third-World representatives that raw materials and industrial development be included on the agenda.

Panel Recommendations

The U.N. panel had been instructed by a December 1974 resolution to recommend "structural changes within the United Nations system so as to make it fully capable of dealing with problems of international cooperation." The key to the proposed reforms was consensus. As the report noted, "no amount of restructuring can replace the will of Member States to discharge their obligations...." Under the proposed reorganization, which would not require amendments to the U.N. Charter, differences would be reconciled by small groups consisting of representatives of interested parties. Once a group had reached unanimous agreement, its solution would be submitted to a vote by the General Assembly.

A second major proposal was to create a new post of Director-General for Development and International Economic Cooperation who would report directly to the Secretary-General. This position would be filled by a representative from one of the developing nations in years when the Secretary-General came from an industrialized state. The group recommended "the consolidation of funds for technical cooperation and pre-investment activities" under a new United Nations Development Authority which would work in coordination with the World Bank and the International Monetary Fund, both U.N. affiliates. These lending institutions would restructure their voting procedures, which were weighted in favor of developed nations.

A seventh special General Assembly session on raw materials, in September 1975, established a U.N. committee to initiate the process of restructuring the U.N. so as to render it "more responsive" to a "new economic order" (see p. 587). Observers noted that the session was marked by a conciliatory atmosphere in distinct contrast to the bitter proceedings at the sixth special session on raw materials, in April 1974, which had ended without any substantial agreement.

Excerpt from A New United Nations Structure for Global Economic Cooperation, *the report of a U.N. panel released May 20, 1975:*

Chapter I

Why Restructuring?

Introductory Remarks

In its thirtieth anniversary year the United Nations has reached a turning point. In one direction lies the prospect of new capacity to cope with the central issues facing mankind in the decisive last quarter of the twentieth

327

century. In the other direction lies the danger of a decline in the effectiveness of the United Nations. Which direction the Organization takes will be significantly influenced by the decisions on policy and structural questions which its Member States take in the months and years ahead. The proposals in this report are designed to assist in rectifying certain weaknesses in the United Nations structure which we sought to identify and which we believe are preventing it from becoming a more effective instrument for the promotion of international economic and social co-operation and development.

A world without a strong United Nations, in the opinion of our Group, is inconceivable. It is in the interest of every Member of the United Nations to make the Organization a more effective instrument for the strengthening of international peace and security and for international economic and social co-operation.

The founders of the United Nations, in the very first paragraph of Article 1 of the Charter, defined the first purpose of the United Nations as the maintenance of international peace and security. At the same time they recognized that peaceful and friendly relations among nations also require co-operation in the economic and social area. Thirty years after the Charter was signed at San Francisco, the intimate relationship between peace and security issues and economic and social issues is clearer than ever.

At least four fifths of the approximately $1.5 billion now spent each year by the system, exclusive of its international financial institutions, is devoted to economic and social activity. In addition, the World Bank [International Bank for Reconstruction and Development, IBRD] and the International Monetary Fund [IMF] are currently making available over $5 billion in medium- and long-term loans to Member countries. Yet the members of the Group recognize all too well that even this level of activity is not adequate to meet fully the challenges of our times.

Even more importantly, the United Nations system now has an impact on the world economic scene which cannot be measured merely in terms of financial expenditures. For years the work of the specialized agencies in health, agriculture, education, labour, communications and other fields has provided indispensable services to Member States and their citizens. Global conferences under United Nations auspices on the environment, population, food, trade and industrialization have influenced national policies by gathering scientific evidence, mobilizing public opinion, recommending lines of action and focusing the attention of political leaders on hitherto neglected national and international problems.

Recently the United Nations has become the centre of far-reaching debate, negotiations and decisions leading towards the establishment of a more rational and just international economic order. The sixth special session of the General Assembly and the forthcoming seventh special session, devoted to economic issues, represent the focal points in this process. The Declaration and Programme of Action on the Establishment of a New International Economic Order, the Charter of Economic Rights and Duties of States, and the International Development Strategy for the Second

United Nations Development Decade constitute major attempts to fashion a new framework of international economic relations. Developing countries have made it clear that structural changes should be made in the international system so that it will become a supportive factor in their efforts to construct their own development models requiring control of their national resources and general policies of national self-reliance, including the mobilization of internal resources.

Need for Action

It is now widely accepted that the major challenges faced by the human race can only be met through multilateral action, and that a logical place for this action is the United Nations system. Yet it is a paradox that at the very moment when this recognition is becoming widespread there are growing doubts about the capacity of the United Nations system as an instrument to meet these challenges.

The concern to strengthen the capacity of the United Nations system to meet present and future challenges was reflected in the General Assembly's request in resolution 3343 (XXIX) for a "study containing proposals on structural changes within the United Nations system so as to make it fully capable of dealing with problems of international economic co-operation in a comprehensive manner".

Our Group has sought to comply with this request by offering a number of specific proposals for structural change. But we wish to emphasize at the outset that no amount of restructuring can replace the political will of Member States to discharge their obligations under Article 56 of the Charter to "take joint and separate action in co-operation with the Organization for the achievement of...higher standards of living, full employment, and conditions of economic and social progress and development." In this connexion, the fact that United Nations decisions are not uniformly implemented is, in the view of many members of the Group, a factor leading to a lack of confidence in the effectiveness of the system.

We would also emphasize that most of the structural deficiencies of the United Nations system are the result of actions by its Member States, and the correction of these deficiencies will require action by the same States. Every serious reform proposal (as opposed to marginal proposals that amount to mere "tinkering") is bound to cut across someone's vested interest in the *status quo*. A meaningful reform of the system, to take account of new requirements and developments, may involve the forgoing of some short-term interests and entrenched habits in favour of long-term interests in a workable international economic order.

Our Group began its task with a shared recognition that institutions are not ends in themselves but only means to the fulfilment of human needs, and that there is no ideal institutional design for the United Nations. Our principal aim has not been organizational neatness or even the achievement of financial economies—although we believe the latter to be an important subsidiary purpose. Our principal criterion in evaluating proposals has been to enhance the effectiveness of the system in promoting the goals of "social progress and better standards of life in larger freedom" mentioned in the Preamble to the United Nations Charter. Since the United Nations is not, and was not intended to be, a world government, the Organization can only seek those ends by promoting international economic co-operation. In evaluating structural proposals, therefore, we have placed particular emphasis on enhancing the effectiveness of the United Nations system in influencing its Members to undertake appropriate policies in development and international economic co-operation to enable the Organization, in the words of the Charter, "to be a centre for harmonizing the actions of nations in the attainment of these common ends."

The ability of mankind to master the awesome challenges confronting it depends largely on the political will of Member States. International institutions can be an important factor in mobilizing that political will. If the United Nations system is to play a central part in meeting the challenges of our time, it must reflect a number of realities in the present world situation—the trend towards relaxation of tensions and universality of participation in the international community, the growing interdependence between Member States, the increasing interrelationship between sectoral issues, the active discontent of a substantial segment of mankind with the present status of international economic relations and the fact that not only is the world now divided between developed and developing countries but that the composition of each of these groups reflects an increasingly variegated pattern of countries with different levels of wealth, development and technological capability and diverse social systems. It will also have to reflect the differences which exist among countries as to the degree of interest they have in different subjects.

We mentioned at the outset that four fifths of the $1.5 billion a year spent by the United Nations system is devoted to economic and social activities. But it is useful to record that the expenditures of the United Nations system during the past three decades have amounted to only 0.4 per cent of the total gross national product of Member States in the single year of 1974 and that current United Nations expenditures barely equal the sum spent on armaments by Members in only 36 hours. The priorities of Members clearly need to be redirected towards development. Disarmament could provide additional resources for this purpose. Restructuring is of significance because a more efficient and effective United Nations system could be an important factor in redirecting priorities in favour of development and could attract additional financial support needed to build the economic foundations of world peace envisaged in the United Nations Charter.

Goals of Proposals

Our proposals for structural change are designed to enable the United Nations system to:

(a) Deal with international economic and social problems in a more effective and comprehensive manner, with better co-ordination throughout the United Nations system as a whole;

(b) Harmonize, as far as possible, the views and approaches of Member countries towards these problems;

(c) Contribute to a significant improvement in the transfer of real resources and technology to developing countries;

(d) Promote economic co-operation between States, including those with different social systems;

(e) Increase the capacity of the United Nations system to provide essential services for all its Members;

(f) Improve the management of United Nations resources available for assistance to the developing countries so as to maximize the benefit to these countries;

(g) Respond effectively to new opportunities, problems and challenges arising from changing requirements of world economic co-operation;

(h) Foster better utilization of the capabilities of developing countries for economic and technical co-operation among themselves;

(i) Make the United Nations a more effective instrument for the establishment of a new, more rational and just international economic order.

While the members of our Group may place somewhat different emphasis on the factors mentioned below, we are in agreement that the following represent major problem areas where structural improvements will be necessary if the United Nations system is to realize its potentialities as an instrument for development and international economic co-operation.

1. Fragmentation of Effort

During the past decade, hardly a year has gone by without the establishment of one or two new United Nations bodies. Today the United Nations system embraces 12 organizations and operational programmes, five regional commissions, 14 specialized agencies and the International Atomic Energy Agency, a multiplicity of special funds, and various semi-autonomous bodies within the central secretariat, not to mention several hundred intergovernmental committees, co-ordinating bodies and *ad hoc* groups. It must be recognized that the system is more a product of historical circumstances than of a rational design. The development of this very complex institutional system can be regarded as a sign of vitality and is the result of well-intended *ad hoc* actions to deal with growing problems of development and international economic co-operation. At the same time, the proliferation of intergovernmental bodies and secretariats represents an increasing burden on Governments in terms of both cost and physical capacity to participate. Moreover, the diffusion of responsibility among so many institutions, many of which are dealing with the same or related subjects, inevitably reduces the impact of all of them. We believe some regrouping and some consolidation of institutions should be possible which would both enhance the effectiveness and coherence of the system and preserve a degree of healthy institutional pluralism on the basis of recognized competence in specialized areas. Development is, after all, a comprehensive process encompassing economic, cultural, social, environmental, political and institutional elements which cannot successfully be tackled except through integrated treatment.

As will be elaborated later in this report, one of the main weaknesses of the system as it has developed over the years is the absence of an effective set of central institutions to shape the various elements affecting development into coherent global policies. As the Secretary-General himself recognized in his statement to the fifty-fifth session of the Economic and Social Council:

"Any dispassionate appraisal of the United Nations system must admit that we are today better equipped to deal with the parts than we are with the whole, and any comfort we derive from the knowledge that we dispose of unrivalled specialized expertise must be weighed against an acute awareness that we are in danger of losing our way through excessive fragmentation."

2. Decision Making

The system of decision making of the United Nations on economic and social questions places insufficient emphasis on the search for consensus. As a result, it does not always produce the desired results. The Group of Experts was concerned about the need to provide within the United Nations for a system of meaningful negotiations to facilitate agreement on issues on which there is wide divergence of opinion and interest among Member States. The expansion of membership has made this problem more acute and urgent. The Group believes that the remedy may lie in new consultative procedures, consistent with the Charter of the United Nations, that permit small negotiating groups to work under a full-time chairman for specified periods during which interested parties would seek to reconcile their differences. The solutions agreed to by these groups could then be voted on by the Economic and Social Council and the General Assembly. Such a procedure would enhance the prospects of speedy implementation of United Nations decisions. At the same time, the Group believes that the distribution of voting rights under the weighted voting system in the World Bank and the International Monetary Fund (IMF) needs to be revised to reflect the new balance of economic power and the legitimate interests of developing countries in a greater voice in the operation of these institutions.

3. Methods of Work

The Group recognizes that public debate in United Nations intergovernmental bodies is of great value in creating public awareness of important economic issues. It further recognizes the value of arrangements that permit all countries to participate in a universal process of decision making. At the same time, the negotiation of solutions on specific problems may require greater use of small negotiating groups which are reasonably representative of the membership as a whole and include an adequate representation of countries with a particular interest in the subject under consideration. It also requires that such groups be permitted to operate in closed session to facilitate negotiations, it being understood that the results of such negotiations should be submitted to the entire membership for decision.

4. Levels and Types of Representation

The experience of recent years suggests that international organizations work best, particularly in economic and technical fields, when they attract appropriate officials from capitals having the required expertise, flexible instructions and the capacity to follow up directly the implementation of the decisions that may be agreed upon. Governments should be encouraged to secure, to a greater extent than in the past, the participation of such representatives, including ministers where appropriate, in the deliberations of the United Nations.

5. Artificial Separation of Planning and Operations

In the United Nations today there is little or no relationship between those institutions that are concerned with planning and those that are concerned with operations. To take the most obvious example, the Department of Economic and Social Affairs (ESA), which is supposed to function as the central "brain" for economic research and analysis and to provide support facilities for policy planning at the intergovernmental level, has very little practical impact on the administration of the principal operational programme run from the centre, the United Nations Development Programme (UNDP). In turn, the UNDP experience in operations rarely feeds back into the work of ESA. Some restructuring is clearly required to integrate planning and operations not only at the centre and in the regions but also between the centre and the various specialized organs.

6. Quality of the International Staff

Throughout its history the United Nations has been served, and continues to be served, by individuals of extraordinary ability and dedication. Nevertheless, the work of certain portions of the Secretariat has on occasion been regarded by groups of Members as not reflecting adequately their concerns and priorities. The Charter requires that due regard be paid to the importance of recruiting the staff on as wide a geographical basis as possible. At the same time, the Charter demands the "highest standards of efficiency, competence and integrity" as the "paramount consideration" in the staffing of the international civil service. What is now required is a new commitment to excellence in the staffing of the international Secretariat both on the part of Member Governments and on the part of those who bear the principal responsibility for the management of the international civil service. The central Secretariat in particular must be restructured and strengthened so as to be able to provide intellectual direction on issues of system-wide concern.

7. Functions Not Yet Adequately Performed in the Institutional Structure

There are certain vital functions which are not now being performed adequately by any global economic agencies. While our Group has not had time to explore the whole range of international economic questions in detail, our work has already identified a number of obvious gaps in the institutional system. For example, there is the absence of an agreed system of balance-of-payments adjustment and international reserve creation. There is need for a more integrated system for the exchange of information so that investment decisions, particularly in industrial sectors, may be taken with greater knowledge of developments in other countries. There is need for improved institutions to provide greater price stability, access to markets and fair returns to the producers of primary commodities while assuring security of supply to the consumer of these commodities. There is also need for institutions to cope with various dimensions of the energy problem and issues of science and technology, particularly to assist countries to devise strategies and develop indigenous resources to achieve their economic and social objectives.

8. Problems of Universality of Membership

For historical reasons which are well known, there is less than universal participation in some of the global international economic institutions that are part of, or are associated with, the United Nations system. A number of countries do not participate in such specialized agencies as the World Bank, the International Monetary Fund and the Food and Agriculture Organization of the United Nations (FAO). In addition, the General Agreement on Tariffs and Trade (GATT), an agency with no formal links with the United Nations system, has far from universal participation. We do not underestimate the problems involved in moving towards the universal participation that was envisaged at the founding of the United Nations. Nevertheless, we believe that ways should be sought to promote truly universal participation in trade and monetary and development co-operation, and that further attention will be required on this important question.

9. Regional Structures

On the question of decentralizing United Nations economic and social activities and strengthening the regional commissions, the following problems can be identified: inadequate implementation of United Nations resolutions on decentralization of economic and social activities; lack of adequate co-ordination at the regional level between policy formulation, planning and programming, on the one hand, and operational activities, on the other; insufficient co-ordination between the regional commissions and the regional offices of the specialized agencies and other organizations of the system; membership patterns in some regional commissions.

Concluding Remarks

Our Group has had neither the time nor the resources to develop fully detailed answers to the nine basic structural problems identified above. What we have sought to do in this report is to provide, in broad outline, a picture of what a restructured United Nations system might look like, and a number of practical first steps to implement that institutional design. We have confined ourselves to recommending reforms that can be initiated by the General Assembly itself and which do not require amendment of the Charter. We recognize that many of the proposals made in this report will require some time for their full discussion and implementation, yet we believe that some of them can and should be set in motion by the General Assembly this year to provide a clear signal to the world that the urgently needed process of institutional revitalization has in fact begun. Without that, talk of structural reform will lack real credibility.

Structural Changes Proposed

Our Group is proposing major changes in the central structures of the United Nations. Our proposals call for new approaches to the handling of economic items in the General Assembly, a major reform in the Economic and Social Council and its subsidiary bodies, and new consultative procedures to encourage agreed solutions leading to speedy implementation by Governments. They also call for the creation of the new post of Director-General for Development and International Economic Co-operation to provide leadership to the central Secretariat and the entire United Nations system, and for the consolidation of funds for technical co-operation and preinvestment activities in a United Nations Development Authority (UNDA), headed by an Administrator who would serve as a deputy to the Director-General.

In moving towards the institutional design put forward in this report, it will be essential to ensure that at every stage in the reform process the enlightened self-interest of Member States in development and international co-operation will be promoted rather than sacrificed. Decisions taken to strengthen the central institutions are inevitably linked to decisions in some key sectoral areas.

For example, some members of our Group feel that the appointment of a Director-General for Development and International Economic Co-operation, as envisaged in this report, and the agreement that he should be a national from a developing country when the Secretary-General is from a developed country, should be conditioned upon the gradual incorporation into the central Secretariat of those portions of the UNCTAD [United Nations Conference on Trade and Development] secretariat that are not dealing with sectoral trade questions. For other members of our Group, however, the creation of UNCTAD reflected the widespread feeling that the then existing structure of the Economic and Social Council was not serving the international community and especially the developing countries sufficiently well. These members feel that the incorporation into the central structure of those portions of the UNCTAD secretariat not dealing with trade questions, and especially those concerned with development financing and international monetary issues, should only take place when developing countries are satisfied that the new central structure is able to deal adequately with such questions. In their view, progress in the field of monetary reform, especially revisions in the distribution of voting rights under the weighted voting system of the World Bank and the International Monetary Fund, is an essential prerequisite. The same principle applies to the incorporation of the intergovernmental organs of UNCTAD into the revitalized central structure. These members feel, moreover, that pending the development of an adequate institutional framework for dealing comprehensively with trade questions—an International Trade Organization (ITO) or other device—it would not be realistic to expect any such incorporation of either the Secretariat or the intergovernmental components of UNCTAD into the central system.

To take account of the above concerns, the Group recommends that, in its first biennial period, the Economic and Social Council should not establish negotiating groups of the kind outlined in chapter II, section D below to deal with subjects under consideration in UNCTAD. At the end of this initial two-year period there should be a review to decide whether the central structures are working sufficiently well to warrant further progress in the direction of strengthening the central institutions. The Group further agrees that during this transitional period, the decision-making process of UNCTAD should be improved by the application of the consultative procedures proposed in this report.

Similarly, with respect to the subject of operational activities, in chapter II, section F below, some members of our Group feel that the eventual consolidation of various existing funds into the new UNDA and the designation of the Administrator of UNDA as deputy to the Director-General for Development and International Economic Co-operation must be dependent upon the negotiation of satisfactory arrangements regarding the composition of the new Operations Board and the division of responsibility between that Board and the Council and the UNDA Administrator, as well as a satisfactory definition of the status of the Administrator. The Group, therefore, recommends that these views be accepted as part of the general understanding governing the implementation of the proposals regarding the new UNDA, while noting its expectation that such concerns can be taken care of in negotiations within a two-year period.

The Group envisages a process of institutional restructuring which could be initiated immediately by the seventh special session of the General Assembly and unfold over a five-year transitional period, during which the many difficult questions involved could be resolved to the satisfaction of all the Members. At every stage during the five-year period the General Assembly could examine the measures needed to implement the restructuring with a view to ensuring a fair balance of advantages to different groups of Member States, and all the measures would be reviewed at the end of the five-year period to ensure that the restructuring in the centre and the sectoral areas was mutually compatible and regarded as satisfactory by the membership as a whole.

Chapter II

Central Structures for Global Policy Making, Programming, Planning and Operational Activities
A. General Assembly

...The group...recommends that the General Assembly decide that:

(a) Whenever issues of global significance need urgent and separate consideration, special sessions of the General Assembly, on the pattern of the sixth and seventh special sessions, or special sessions of the proposed "Development Committee" *(see...below)*, should, after careful preparation, be convened rather than *ad hoc* world conferences;...

(b) There should not be a fixed periodicity for any global conferences; a decision as to the best timing and approach and the most suitable arrangements for the consideration of a given issue should be taken by the Assembly, on a case-by-case basis, in the light of developments. For this purpose, the possibility of convening special sessions of the General Assembly or special sessions of the proposed Development Committee should be explored....

The Group, therefore, recommends that:

(a) The Second Committee of the General Assembly should be renamed the Committee on Development and International Economic Co-operation (to be known as the "Development Committee"). Consideration should be given to transferring from the Third Committee to the Second Committee, on a case-by-case basis, those items on social development that might more appropriately be dealt with in the Second Committee, bearing in mind the need to avoid overloading the Second Committee's agenda;

(b) The agenda of this Committee should be organized around meaningful clusters of issues (rather than be based on a mechanical con-solidation of some of the items that traditionally appear on the agenda of the Second and Third Committees), reflecting an integrated approach to the economic and social aspects of development;

(c) Some days during the meeting of this Committee should be organized for discussions and decision making at senior or ministerial level on key issues that are ready for decision;

(d) The Economic and Social Council should be consulted in the elabora-tion of the Committee's agenda and should be asked to prepare its dis-cussions and submit draft recommendations for action by the Committee;

(e) The Third Committee should be renamed the Committee on Social Problems, Human Rights and Humanitarian Activities.

The Group believes that the above arrangements will also help to clarify the respective roles of the Assembly and the Economic and Social Council. Without prejudice to the functions of the General Assembly under the Charter, the Group views these arrangements as ones whereby the Assembly establishes the over-all policy strategies and pronounces itself upon the negotiations to be carried on within the framework of the Council, where ways of implementing in practice the strategies formulated by the Assembly would be worked out. At the same time, the Council should identify major issues and policies requiring action at the General Assembly level, and act as the main preparatory body for the proposed Development Committee of the Assembly by laying the groundwork and conceptual framework for its discussions....

B. Economic and Social Council
1. Revitalization of the Council

...The council's decisions, at present, lack the necessary degree of authority. In spite of repeated reaffirmations of its role under the Charter, the Council has never been given adequate means to follow up and ensure the effective implementation of its recommendations. At the same time, the continued growth in the functions assigned to the Council, and the number of reports reviewed by it, prevent it from addressing itself in a selective manner to major developments in the economic sphere. The recent increase in its membership, however, has created the necessary preconditions for entrusting to the Council a strengthened role.

The Group recommends that the General Assembly at its forthcoming special session should reaffirm the Council's central role with respect to global policy formulation and implementation and the setting of priorities for the system as a whole....

2. The Council's Calendar and Programme of Work

As a first step towards achieving these objectives, the Group recommends that the Council organize its programme on a biennial basis, with its calendar subdivided into frequent subject-oriented sets of short sessions spread throughout the calendar year (except during the General Assembly period). These sessions would take place in New York, Geneva or in other cities, such as Nairobi, depending on the subject-matter and the location of the relevant secretariat units....

3. Negotiating Groups

Another important innovation which the Group recommends in the functioning of the Council is the establishment by the Council of small negotiating groups to deal with key economic issues identified by it as requiring further negotiations with a view to bringing about agreed solutions.... While it would be necessary for the Council to be kept informed of the progress being made by these groups and to discuss the subjects being considered by them, the groups would be given the necessary time and means to carry out their tasks effectively, and would be permitted one to two years to seek agreed solutions. During the one- to two-year period, the General Assembly and the Council would be free to vote resolutions on these subjects but, in addressing themselves to these questions, the Assembly and the Council would presumably take into account the progress of the negotiations within the respective groups. It should be understood, of course, that the Assembly and the Council could not be expected to post-pone taking decisions if there were an excessively large number of negotiating groups which were all active at the same time. The proposed procedures for the functioning of these groups further provide that, during the one- to two-year period, proposals emanating from the groups which do not appear acceptable to the Council's membership would be referred back to the groups with new guidelines.

4. Type and Level of Representation

A major aim and, it is hoped, one of the main results of this new pattern of meetings is the attendance at the Council's sessions of higher-level and more specialized government representatives. Indeed, such representation is a necessary prerequisite to ensure that the arrangements referred to above result in a substantial enhancement of the Council's effectiveness....

In view of the special importance it attaches to the question of the level and type of representation in the Council, the Group suggests that the adoption of the above measures be accompanied by a recommendation by the General Assembly to Member States to take all the steps necessary to ensure the systematic attendance of higher-level and more specialized government representatives at the Council's meetings, it being understood that the composition of such delegations would be governed by the specific subject-matter to be considered at any given session....

5. The Council's Subsidiary Machinery

...The Group recommends that the Council assume direct responsibility for the work now performed by its existing subsidiary bodies. As a result, the permanent commissions and committees of the Council would be dis-continued, except for the following bodies: the regional commissions; the Statistical Commission; the Commission on Narcotic Drugs; the Com-mittee for Development Planning; the Commission on Transnational Cor-porations; and the Commission on Human Rights....

The Group recognizes that the discontinuance of a number of subsidiary bodies dealing with sectoral areas could create considerably greater pressure for representation in the Council. One means of dealing with this problem, on which the Group agreed, would be that, as already provided for in the Council's rules of procedure, any country not a member of the Coun-cil which was especially interested in a particular sectoral issue would be permitted to participate in the relevant discussion, with all the rights of membership except the right to vote. The Group recognizes, however, that this device may not be fully adequate to resolve the problem satisfactorily. The Group believes that the revitalized Council will be able to perform its function only if it is adequately representative of all regions and interests....

In summary, the Group recommends that the following changes be made with respect to the Council's subsidiary machinery and the other bodies related to the Council:

The Council should assume direct responsibility for the work now performed by the Committee on Natural Resources, the Committee on Science and Technology for Development, the Committee on Review and Appraisal, the Committee on Crime Prevention and Control, the Population Commission, the Commission for Social Development, the Commission on the Status of Women, and the Committee on Housing, Building and Planning, all of which would cease to exist.

Science

The Committee on the Application of Science and Technology to Development should cease to exist. Instead, to provide the United Nations in general and the Economic and Social Council in particular with ready access to the resources of the world scientific community, the Group recommends that small *ad hoc* groups of scientists be convened on a case-by-case basis to study specific problems and formulate recommendations which would then be taken into account by the Council in the formulation of relevant policies. [Footnote: The United Nations Scientific Committee on the Effects of Atomic Radiation, being a subsidiary body of the General Assembly, would not be affected. On the other hand, the United Nations Scientific Advisory Committee would be discontinued.] The establishment of such groups, which would be based on rosters of scientists representing a wide range of scientific disciplines, would provide the Council with the necessary flexibility to deal, as appropriate, with diverse and constantly changing issues. The Group further recommends the appointment of a science adviser to the Secretary-General who should be an individual of international eminence and recognized competence, to serve as a link between the Secretary-General and the world scientific community. His main function would be to provide timely advice to the Secretary-General to help him anticipate the impact of advances in science and technology and identify the options that their application presents, especially for the benefit of the developing countries.

Environment

The Group recommends that the Council should assume direct responsibility, through the device of subject-oriented sessions as described above, for the policy functions in respect of environmental issues at present being carried out by the Governing Council of the United Nations Environment Programme (UNEP). Inasmuch as responsibility for managing the UNEP Fund would be assumed by the proposed Operations Board responsible for all pre-investment funds, as recommended in section F below, the Governing Council of UNEP would be discontinued. The environment secretariat would remain in Nairobi, subject to the authority of the Director-General for Development and International Economic Co-operation.

Human Rights

With respect to the structural arrangements of the United Nations in the field of human rights, some members of the Group are of the view that a

Council on Human Rights should be created to replace the Trusteeship Council and serve as a principal organ of the Organization, discharging all the functions in the field of human rights that are now the responsibility of the Economic and Social Council and the Commission on Human Rights and, perhaps, also the functions of the Commission on the Status of Women. In addition, this new Council could perform the tasks that the entry into force of the Covenants on Human Rights will entail. It was recognized that the implementation of this idea would require an amendment to the Charter. Other members of the Group feel that the Commission on Human Rights should be maintained but that the Council should simply transmit the Commission's reports to the General Assembly without debate.

C. Secretariat Support Facilities

1. Objectives

The Group strongly believes that the increasing recognition of the interdependence of economic issues, and the resulting changes in the responsibilities of the central organs, require that the Secretariat's capacity for intersectoral analysis and synthesis of policy options be greatly strengthened.

2. Reorientation of the Functions of the Department of Economic and Social Affairs

In the view of the Group, a first necessary step towards strengthening the analytical capabilities of the Secretariat and enabling it to concentrate its efforts on the task of providing support, on an interdisciplinary basis, for the policy-making function of the Council, is to divest the Department of Economic and Social Affairs of its sectoral technical functions in the economic and social field and, particularly, of its sectoral operational responsibilities....

3. Director-General for Development and International Economic Co-operation

...[T]he Group recommends the establishment, within the Secretariat, of a new post of Director-General for the Development and International Economic Co-operation. This official would be directly responsible to the Secretary General, would serve as *primus inter pares* among the heads of United Nations organizations and agencies dealing with economic and social affairs and would be in charge of directing all activities at present being carried out by the Department of Economic and Social Affairs and the various United Nations offices and programmes with respect to research, policy-making support, interagency co-ordination and operational activities. The autonomous position of the specialized agencies would, of course, not be affected, but the new Director-General would seek to promote improved system-wide co-operation. He would chair the proposed Advisory Committee on Economic Co-operation and Development, mentioned in the following subsection. He would need to be assisted in this task by two Deputy Directors-General, one for Research and Policy, and the other to serve as Administrator of the new United Nations Development Authority. Under these arrangements, the existing post of Under-Secretary-General for Economic and Social Affairs would cease to exist....

The Group recommends that the post of Director-General should be assigned to a national of a developing country, at least during those years when the post of Secretary-General is occupied by a national of a developed country. If the post of Secretary-General were occupied by a national of a developing country, this arrangement would have to be reviewed. (It should be understood that the reference to developed and developing countries is to be interpreted as embracing countries with different social systems.) The post of Administrator of the new United Nations Development Authority and that of Deputy Director-General for Research and Policy could then be allocated, respectively, to a national of a developed country and a national of a developing country. The Group further recommends that the Director-General be elected for his five-year term at the same time as the Secretary-General is elected for his five-year term. It also recommends, however, that if the proposals in this report are accepted, the Director-General could be appointed on an interim basis in time for his appointment to be confirmed by the General Assembly at its thirtieth session.

As noted above, a major function of the new Director-General and his staff should be to assist the central organs of the United Nations in the development of global policies, the formulation of system-wide decisions and priorities and the overview of the implementation of such decisions by the various components of the system. As it builds its capacity for global intersectoral analysis, this secretariat should progressively be able to function as an early-warning system geared to providing timely and effective advice to the intergovernmental organs on major emerging developments in the economic sphere requiring their urgent action. In order to play this role effectively, the secretariat should have at its disposal a flexible mechanism for drawing upon the expertise and knowledge of existing international organizations, national Governments and the private sector generally.

4. Advisory Committee on Economic Co-operation and Development

During the past three decades, the programmes, organizations and agencies of the United Nations system dealing with economic, social and financial questions have acquired substantial experience and carried out extensive research in the field of development. At present, however, although there is wide realization of the need for an integrated and multidisciplinary approach to development, there are no joint mechanisms for effectively pooling the results of this work.

The Group believes that one effective measure to this end would be the establishment of a new interagency mechanism, to be known as the Advisory Committee on Economic Co-operation and Development, under the chairmanship of the new Director-General for Development and International Economic Co-operation. The Managing Director of IMF, the President of the World Bank, the Secretary-General of UNCTAD, the Executive Director of UNIDO [United Nations Industrial Development Organization], the Directors-General of the ILO, FAO, UNESCO and WHO, the Executive Secretaries of the regional commissions, the Deputy Director-General for Research and Policy and the Administrator of the new United Nations Development Authority would be ex officio members of this Committee. The Director-General of GATT would also be invited to join the Committee, and the executive heads of other United Nations agencies and programmes would be invited, as necessary, to attend.

The main task of the Committee would be to review the world economic and social situation and bring to the attention of high-level meetings of the Economic and Social Council, together with its own assessment and recommendations, all issues which, in its view, require international decisions and actions. Whenever possible, alternative policy options should be developed for submission to the Council, either by the Committee as a whole or by any of its members.

5. Joint Research, Planning and Programming Staff

Another condition for the effective functioning of the new secretariat structure, as regards both its ability for in-depth intersectoral analysis of development issues and its capacity to ensure coherent implementation of decisions, is the development of built-in mechanisms whereby the expertise and experience of the specialized agencies would be available to the central Secretariat on a continuing basis.

To this end, the Group recommends the establishment of a small "joint unit" within the new Director-General's Office to be composed of high-level staff seconded by the various organizations of the system—for a longer or shorter duration depending on central requirements—and such other highly qualified officials as may be required by the Director-General....

As regards the functioning of this joint staff, the Group believes that the seconded officials should bring to the central office the expertise and perspective of their organizations, but should be responsible to the new Director-General and would not, therefore, formally represent the agencies to which they belong.

The functions of this joint staff would be:

(a) To serve as a centre for global policy analysis and assessment, in support of the work of the Advisory Committee and the Economic and Social Council; and

(b) To serve as a system-wide planning bureau for the elaboration, on the basis of general policies and priorities laid down by the Council, of short and medium-term plans to serve as guidelines for the programmes of individual organizations. It would also develop budgetary proposals for joint programmes in close collaboration and consultation with the Department of Administration and Management of the United Nations Secretariat and the relevant organs and offices of the specialized agencies.

6. Functions of the Director-General's Staff

...The Group believes that, in order to ensure harmony between planning and operations, it would be useful to establish a post of Administrator of the United Nations Development Authority, who would be responsible for the functions now being carried out by the Administrator of UNDP and the executive heads of other United Nations voluntary programmes and funds for technical assistance and preinvestment activities (excluding, for the time being, the Executive Director of the United Nations Children's Fund (UNICEF)...). In addition, this official would also serve as a Deputy to the Director-General for Development and International Economic Co-operation. At the same time, the Group recognizes that the eventual consolidation of United Nations funds in the new UNDA and the designation of the Administrator of UNDA as Deputy to the Director-General for Development and International Economic Co-operation must be dependent on the negotiation of satisfactory arrangements regarding the composition of the new Operations Board and the division of responsibility between the Board and the Economic and Social Council and the Administrator of UNDA, as well as a satisfactory definition of the status of the Administrator. It is the Group's expectation that these negotiations could be concluded within a two-year period.

7. Co-ordination Arrangements

...In addition to the Administrative Committee for Co-ordination [ACC], there are at present two other interagency co-ordinating bodies attended by the executive heads of the United Nations agencies and programmes: the Inter-Agency Consultative Board (IACB) of UNDP, chaired by the Administrator, which has no formal relationship to ACC although its meetings are usually held in conjunction with those of ACC; and the Environment Co-ordination Board (ECB), which is chaired by the Executive Director of UNEP and has been established "within the framework of ACC". The Group believes that a merger of these two bodies with ACC would not only bring about a needed measure of streamlining in the structure of the co-ordination machinery, but would also serve to promote the establishment of a closer link between research and operational functions—an objective to which several of the foregoing recommendations have been addressed.

At the same time, the Group believes that there would be merit in maintaining the two subsidiary bodies which now back up IACB and ECB at the working level, namely, the Programme Working Group and the Meeting of Environmental "Focal Points", which would function as two subsidiary bodies of ACC....

8. Personnel Practices and Policies

...Steps should be taken to increase the proportion of women in the professional category, especially at the senior level;

A United Nations Fellows Programme should be established to bring to the United Nations system young people of superior ability from all regions of the world.

The Group of Experts believes that measures should be taken to upgrade the skills of United Nations staff members, bring them up to date on new developments in their fields, improve their morale and enhance prospects for career development. Accordingly, the Group recommends that:

...Consideration should be given to reviving the Staff College project as part of the development of new and improved training facilities....

D. Consultative Procedures

...The consultative procedures here proposed are designed to promote agreement on major policy issues where agreement might otherwise be unobtainable. With this end in view, the procedures would normally be initiated at an early stage in the discussion of a given subject and before the stage of the passing of resolutions, but the procedures could also be initiated at the end of a process of debate or even after a decision where this seemed to be appropriate. It would be for the Economic and Social Council, if the recommendations in this section were accepted, to work out these consultative arrangements in appropriate rules of procedure which would specify, among other things, the kinds of subjects on which consultative procedures could take place....

Consultative groups would be so composed as to be representative of the United Nations membership, including countries with a particular interest in the subject-matter. The groups would be given from one to two years, as the case might be, to bring in agreed recommendations. Each group would be served by a full-time chairman with the responsibility of defining issues for consideration, structuring the discussion and generally working with the parties in the search for an agreed solution....

During the initial two-year period, negotiating groups would only be constituted by majority vote of the General Assembly or the Council;...the General Assembly and the Council would be free to consider subjects under discussion in the groups and to vote resolutions thereon, but in deciding upon whether to vote a particular resolution, the General Assembly and the Council would take into account the progress of the negotiations....

Each negotiating group would operate on the basis of unanimity. When a negotiating group reached agreement, it would report to the Council, which would adopt the agreement, refer the matter back to the negotiating group for further consideration, or take such other action as it deemed appropriate. Upon approval by the Council, the agreement would be passed to the General Assembly, which could approve the agreement, refer the matter back to the group, or take some other action....

E. Planning, Programming and Budgeting

...The United Nations regular budget is put together in a piecemeal way as a result of independent decisions taken by various units within the

Secretariat and the several dozen boards, commissions and committees to which they are responsible, such as the organs functional organizations like UNCTAD and UNIDO, subordinate organs of the Economic and Social Council like the Committee on Natural Resources and the regional commissions. It is a budget, in short, that is put together from the bottom up, rather than from the top down, an aggregation of demands from specialized constituencies without any systematic evaluation of their relative importance and without any over-all conception of the purposes for which the regular budget should be spent....

As a long-term goal, the United Nations should work towards a single body to advise the Economic and Social Council as well as the General Assembly with respect to the review, approval and evaluation of both programmes and budgets. This could be a small body representative of the different groups of Member States composed of highly qualified individuals nominated by Governments but serving in their personal capacity. The ACABQ, whose small membership of 13 adequately balances the groups of developed countries, developing countries and socialist countries, might eventually be transformed into such a body. Alternatively, the membership of CPC might be adjusted to make it the small, balanced group necessary for this task....

F. Operational Activities

1. Introduction and Background

...Over the years, initiatives to establish new voluntary funds have contributed decisively to expanding the scope and intensity of international co-operation. The establishment of new funds, by their appeal to special constituencies, has resulted in a mobilization of additional resources for international co-operation. The question arises, however, whether the costs of this process in terms of administrative duplication and inefficiency and resulting difficulties for the administrations of recipient countries, are not beginning to outweigh the benefits heretofore derived from the multiplication of separate funds. The Group believes that this evolution is beginning to undermine efforts to programme the activities of the United Nations system in a more rational and comprehensive manner and more in accordance with the real needs of developing countries....

2. Recommendations

(a) Consolidation of Operational Activities and Funds

All United Nations funds for technical assistance and pre-investment activities should be consolidated for the purpose of more effective policy making, administration and management into a new United Nations Development Authority. Certain small funds for capital investment should also be consolidated, as hereinafter specified, in UNDA. The Group believes that the consolidation here proposed will lead to substantial administrative economies and a useful flexibility in the blending of funds for certain kinds of projects, for example, the use of development and environment funds for projects related to soil and forestry resources. The Group also believes that this consolidation will better meet the needs of all recipient countries. The Group does not recommend the inclusion, for the time being, of UNICEF in this consolidation. This move could, however, be considered at some future stage, taking into account the unique character of UNICEF's role within the system. With respect to trust funds established by individual donors, their future disposition would be subject to further study and negotiation among interested parties.

(b) Maintenance of Separate Identity of Funds

In the consolidation of funds under a single administrative and management structure, the separate identity of the funds would be maintained so that donors would continue to have the right to earmark contributions for particular purposes, a right which the Group believes will encourage a higher level of total contributions....

(c) Integration of Intergovernmental Policy-Making Organs

Under the present intergovernmental arrangements, the governing bodies of the various funds for the most part perform a dual function, being responsible for both policy making and management of the operational programmes and funds under their authority. In lieu of this arrangement the Group of Experts proposes that there should be a single governing body responsible for reviewing the operational activities of the United Nations system as a whole and providing over-all policy guidance within the context of global development strategies. In the opinion of the Group, the Economic and Social Council is the appropriate body to perform this policy-making function since it is fitting that global policy making on operational activities be part of the responsibilities of the body charged with the task of formulating global development policies. This arrangement would not only promote the integration of global policy and operations but would also avoid the duplication of discussions that debates in the various governing bodies and the subsequent Council review of reports of the voluntary programmes and funds entail. For this purpose,...the Economic and Social Council should include in its programme of work an annual session devoted to a global review of operational activities.

(d) Integration of Management Bodies

...The Group recommends that there should be a consolidation, as early as possible and under appropriate administrative arrangements, of intergovernmental structures such as the UNDP Governing Council, the UNEP Governing Council, the United Nations/FAO Intergovernmental Committee of the World Food Programme and the Board of Governors of the Special Fund, and that these bodies should be replaced by a single Operations Board which would be responsible for the conduct of the general operations of UNDA and would exercise all the power delegated to it by the Economic and Social Council.

The mandate of the Operations Board would extend to all operational funds currently administered by the United Nations, UNDP (including the Capital Development Fund, the United Nations Volunteers programme and the United Nations Revolving Fund for Natural Resources), the United Nations Fund for Population Activities (UNFPA), UNEP (including the United Nations Habitat Human Settlements Foundation), the World Food Programme (WFP) and the Special Fund. Its membership should be relatively small (18-27) and equitably balanced between net donors and net recipient countries. There should also be appropriate representation of countries with different social systems. It would be in a position to function on a year-round basis, as necessary, and would not be confined to members of the Economic and Social Council. It could establish subgroups to deal with subjects not directly related to economic and social development, such as a subgroup for disaster relief and emergency assistance, and a subgroup for drug abuse control or other activities. The Board and its subgroups would be in close contact with the Administrator to assist in management functions.

(e) Integration at the Secretariat Level

...In the consolidation of funds under the proposed United Nations Development Authority, the separate identities of certain administrative units should be maintained, notably in the case of population, environment and other areas where this would facilitate fund raising or operations;

Under the arrangement set forth above, the present Department of Economic and Social Affairs, which would become part of the secretariat under the authority of the Deputy Director-General for Research and Policy, should be relieved of the responsibilities at present performed by the Office of Technical Co-operation, which would be transferred to UNDA, when established. The sectoral/technical functions of ESA should be progressively transferred to other parts of the system as soon as satisfactory arrangements can be worked out, with the understanding that certain technical functions would remain at the centre....

(k) Relations With IBRD and Other Agencies

The value of the United Nations development work in the past has been reduced because of a somewhat inadequate working relationship between the United Nations and the International Bank for Reconstruction and Development. There has been a danger in the United Nations undertaking, on a smaller scale, with more limited resources, some of the same functions as the Bank....

The Group believes that it is of the greatest importance that the new UNDA establish the closest possible working relations with the World Bank. Moreover, the recommended merger of the other voluntary funds with the new UNDA will make it possible for the country programmes to cover a broader range of operations, including those in the fields of population, environment and so on. The Group, therefore, recommends that the country programmes of UNDA and the World Bank should, in the future, be co-ordinated and harmonized....

Chapter III

Structures for Sectoral Activities
Introduction

In view of the limited time available to discharge the task entrusted to it, the Group of Experts, in reviewing sectoral activities, concentrated its attention on developments in the fields of trade, international monetary reform, development financing, agriculture and food, and industrialization, in compliance with its mandate under the relevant paragraphs of General Assembly resolution 3343 (XXIX)....

A. Trade

The Group recommends that:

...GATT and the United Nations enter into a mutually satisfactory agreement providing for a formal relationship, including exchange of information and closer administrative collaboration;

As a longer-term objective, there should be an evolution towards the creation of an international trade organization to deal with trade issues in a comprehensive manner....

B. International Monetary Reform

1. Issues in International Monetary Reform....

Recycling of petrodollars through IMF, to help both developed and developing countries deal with balance-of-payment problems related to the higher costs of energy, food, fertilizer and other imports.

Ways of rectifying the imbalance between countries that has characterized the process of international liquidity creation over the past four years, both between developed and developing countries, on the one hand, and within these two groups of countries, on the other....

Better international management of global liquidity, with special drawing rights (SDR) becoming the principal reserve asset and the role of gold and reserve currencies being reduced.

The need for interim steps in the direction of longer-term reform, including the possibility of establishing a gold substitution account in the International Monetary Fund which would permit the substitution of monetary gold stocks for SDR and the redistribution of some parts of the resulting book-keeping profits to the developing countries.

Measures to enable developing countries, particularly those most seriously affected, to adjust to a higher level of international prices in a manner consistent with their development needs, possibly through the establishment of facilities within the International Monetary Fund; in this context, the trust fund category of proposals would require consideration as one possibility....

2. Recommendations

The Group of Experts recommends that:

...The distribution of voting rights under the weighted voting system in the International Monetary Fund be revised to reflect the new balance of economic power and the legitimate interest of developing countries in a greater voice in the operation of that institution.

C. Development Financing

...The Group of Experts recommends that....

The distribution of voting rights under the weighted voting system in the World Bank be revised to reflect the new balance of economic power and the legitimate interest of developing countries in a greater voice in the operations of that institution....

D. Agriculture and Food

...Owing to the pressure of time, the Group was not able to deal with the complex matter of food and agriculture in the detailed manner that it felt was warranted. Furthermore, the Group believed that at this early stage in the implementation of the World Food Conference initiatives, it would be premature and inappropriate to pass judgment on this important area by way of recommendations for structural change.

The Group, therefore, makes no recommendation for food and agriculture.

Industrialization

...The Group recommends that UNIDO should assume the task of examining global trends concerning supply and demand in the various industrial and related sectors with a view to the better exchange of information on sectoral economic policies....

...The Group of Experts envisages the strengthening of the central institutions of the United Nations system, specifically the General Assembly and the Economic and Social Council, so that industry will be treated like other sectoral activities carried out within the United Nations system....

Chapter IV
Means of Implementation

Our Group has carefully considered the next steps which might be taken to implement the recommendations in this report. Some of our recommendations call for action by the General Assembly. Other recommendations require implementation by the Economic and Social Council, other intergovernmental bodies, and the Secretary-General. Moreover, the administrative and financial implications of some of our recommendations will require further examination. As we suggested earlier, the process of restructuring that we are recommending here will need to be implemented in stages over a period of five years in order to ensure that the interests of all the Members are adequately protected.

The Group therefore suggests that the Secretary-General appoint a committee on the structure of the United Nations system, to study and report regularly to the General Assembly on the progress of the restructuring effort....

FORD ADDRESS AT NATO SUMMIT
May 29, 1975

President Gerald R. Ford told European leaders May 29 that the recent collapse of U.S.-supported governments in Indochina did not mean that American commitments for European defense had altered. American pledges to the North Atlantic Treaty Organization (NATO) were "juridically binding" and they "command broad support in the United States," Ford assured NATO's Council at a meeting in Brussels.

His strong affirmations apparently were intended to clear up substantial doubts among U.S. allies. One NATO official had indicated that the main purpose of the conference was to dispel "uncertainties" created by the fall of Cambodia and Vietnam a month earlier (see p. 279). The following day, however, Ford said at a news conference that, in private meetings with European leaders following his speech, "many allies stressed that they did not feel the need of any special American reassurance."

Nevertheless, American steadfastness was a prominent theme of Ford's remarks in Brussels, the first stop on his first trip to Europe as President. Shortly after his arrival May 28, Ford asserted that NATO was "the cornerstone of U.S. foreign policy" and, at the news conference prior to his departure from Brussels two days later, he again stressed America's "firm and vigorous" purpose with regard to European defense.

NATO Problems

Ford's speech came at a time when the Atlantic alliance was troubled by other factors as well. Two member states, Portugal and Italy, then appeared to be moving toward Communist-dominated governments, while Turkey

353

and Greece, bitter enemies in the wake of their 1974 conflict over Cyprus, had threatened to withdraw from the alliance. Greece did withdraw from the military structure of NATO, as France had done some years earlier. Other problems included nationalistic rivalries over military commands and defense contracts, plus a recession-caused resistance to military spending in numerous member states.

The President addressed a number of these problems and proposed several new initiatives, including NATO membership for Spain and attention to "the issues of population, food, and raw materials." Ford's appeal on behalf of Spain was interpreted as a gesture to soften difficulties encountered in current U.S.-Spanish negotiations over American bases in that country. However, the appeal was rebuffed by the conference. British Prime Minister Harold Wilson asserted that a democratic government in Spain was an "essential precondition" to its acceptance in NATO, and the communique issued at the end of the conference May 30 made no mention of Spain.

Ford's reference to the global scope of economic and social problems, a concern voiced earlier by West German Chancellor Helmut Schmidt, was acknowledged in the final communique which declared the "allies...resolved to cooperate with the other members of the international community on global problems such as those of population, food, energy, raw materials and the environment." [In September the United Nations called a special session on raw materials and related questions; see p. 587.]

On the subject of the Warsaw Pact, the East European equivalent of NATO, Ford urged a reduction of tensions. The May 30 communique went further, noting that the "armed forces of the Warsaw Pact continue to grow in strength beyond any apparent defensive needs," forcing a NATO level of defense incompatible with "the worldwide economic situation."

No "Partial Membership"

In his speech Ford warned that the alliance could not tolerate "partial membership or special arrangements," a reference to Greece, not France, according to a later Presidential statement.

In private meetings with Greek Prime Minister Constantine Caramanlis and Turkey's Suleyman Demirel, Ford discussed Cyprus but reportedly was told by both leaders that they would resolve their differences without American intervention. Ford also apparently raised the question of Communist influence in a talk with Vasco Goncalves, then Portuguese premier, who responded that his nation was not "NATO's Trojan horse" but was "a loyal European state and intends to remain a NATO member." American concern had focused on the Azores, site of an American base likely to be of vital importance as a refueling stop in the event of a Middle East crisis.

Text of address delivered May 29, 1975, by President
Gerald R. Ford at a meeting in Brussels of heads of state or

government of member nations of the North Atlantic Treaty Organization:

Mr. Secretary General, members of the Council:

President Truman, in 1949, transmitted the text of the North Atlantic Treaty to the Congress of the United States with his assessment of its importance. "Events of this century," he wrote, "have taught us that we cannot achieve peace independently. The world has grown too small. The security and welfare of each member of this community depends on the security and welfare of all. None of us alone can achieve economic prosperity or military security. None of us alone can assure the continuance of freedom." So spoke President Truman. These words, describing the interdependence of the North Atlantic Nations, are as accurate today as they were a quarter century ago.

On the twenty-fifth anniversary of the signing of the North Atlantic Treaty, leaders of the NATO nations met here in Brussels to reaffirm the Declaration on Atlantic Relations, the fundamental purposes of an Alliance that had fulfilled its promises by providing for the security, promoting the welfare, and maintaining the freedom of its members.

We meet here today to renew our commitment to the Alliance. We meet to remind our citizens in the 15 member nations, by our presence, of the strength and stability of the transatlantic ties that unite us and to restate our pledge to collective self-defense. We are assembled to address the serious problems we face and to review the steps we must take to deal with them.

Renewal of our commitment to the Alliance is the most important of these purposes. The United States of America unconditionally and unequivocally remains true to the commitments undertaken when we signed the North Atlantic Treaty, including the obligation in Article 5 to come to the assistance of any NATO nation subject to armed attack. As treaties are the supreme law of my land, these commitments are juridically binding in the United States. These commitments are strategically sound, politically essential, and morally justifiable and, therefore, command broad support in the United States. They remain the firm foundation, as they have for 26 years, on which our relationship rests. This foundation has well served the purposes for which it was created. It will go on serving these purposes, even in the face of new difficulties, as long as we continue our common resolve.

In the treaty we signed 26 years ago, and from which we drew confidence and courage, we pledged:

—To live in peace with all peoples and all governments;

—To safeguard the freedom, common heritage, and civilization of our peoples founded on the principles of democracy, individual liberty, and the rule of law;

—To promote stability and well-being in the North Atlantic area;

—To settle by peaceful means any international dispute in which any one of us may be involved;

—To eliminate conflict in international economic policies and encourage economic collaboration;

—To maintain and develop our individual and collective capacity to resist armed attack by means of continuous and effective self-help and mutual aid;

—To consult together when any one of us is threatened;

—To consider an armed attack against one as an armed attack against all.

Matters of Concern

There is no need today to improve on that statement of principles and purposes. It remains as clear, as resolute, and as valid today as when first adopted. But it is worth reminding ourselves of these pledges as we turn our attention and energies to the problems we now face both outside and within the Alliance—problems very different from those we confronted 26 years ago. As NATO heads of governments and friends, we have a duty to be frank and realistic with one another. Therefore, I must cite the following matters of concern to the United States and of importance to the Alliance:

—In Indochina, the events of recent months have resulted in enormous human suffering for the people of Cambodia and Vietnam, an ordeal that touches all human hearts. Because of the United States' long involvement in Indochina, these events have led some to question our strength and reliability. I believe that our strength speaks for itself: Our military power remains and will continue to remain second to none—of this let there be no doubt; our economy remains fundamentally sound and productive; and our political system has emerged from the shocks of the past year stronger for the way in which it met a severe internal test. Our actions will continue to confirm the durability of our commitments.

—There have been strains and difficulties within the Alliance during the past year. Serious disagreements have marred relations among some members. The unity of the Alliance and our common resolve have come into question.

—There are some problems that relate directly to our defense capabilities. I refer to increasing pressures to reduce the level of military commitments to NATO, despite the fact that the forces of our potential enemies have grown stronger. We also face basic problems of military effectiveness. A generation after its creation, the Alliance wastes vast sums each year, sacrificing military effectiveness. We have simply not done enough to standardize our weapons. We must correct this. We must also agree among ourselves on a sensible division of weapons development programs and production responsibilities. And we must do more to enhance our mutual capacity to support each other both in battle and logistically. The pressures on defense budgets throughout the Alliance should by now have convinced each of us that we simply must rationalize our collective defense.

—In the field of energy, we are still not immune from the political pressures that result from a heavy dependence on external sources of energy. Indeed, we are becoming more vulnerable each month. We have made joint progress in offsetting the effect of the action taken last year by the major oil producing countries, but we have far more to do.

—In the Middle East, there remains a possibility of a new war that not only could involve the countries in the area but also sow discord beyond the Middle East itself, perhaps within our Alliance.

This is a formidable array of problems. However, we have faced formidable problems before. Let us master these new challenges with all the courage, conviction, and cohesion of this great Alliance. Let us proceed. It is time for concerted action.

Primary Tasks for NATO

At this important stage in the history of the Alliance we must pledge ourselves to six primary tasks:

Defense

—First, we must maintain a strong and credible defense. This must remain the foremost objective of the Alliance. If we fail in this task, the others will be irrelevant. A society that does not have the vigor and dedication to defend itself cannot survive—neither can an alliance. For our part, our commitment not to engage in any unilateral reduction of U.S. forces committed to NATO remains valid. But that is not enough. We must make more effective use of our defense resources. We need to achieve our longstanding goals of common procedures and equipment. Our research and development efforts must be more than the sum of individual parts. Let us become truly one in our allocation of defense tasks, support, and production.

Unqualified Participation

—Second, we must preserve the quality and integrity of this Alliance on the basis of unqualified participation, not on the basis of partial membership or special arrangements. The commitment to collective defense must be complete if it is to be credible. It must be unqualified if it is to be reliable.

Consultation

—Third, let us improve the process of political consultation. We have made considerable progress in recent months, but there is—as each of us knows—room for improvement by all parties if we are to maintain our solidarity. This is of particular importance if we are to move forward together in our efforts to reduce the tensions that have existed with the Warsaw Pact nations for more than a quarter of a century. We should further cultivate the habit of discussing our approaches to those matters which touch the interests of all, so that we can develop common policies to deal with common problems.

Détente

—Fourth, let us cooperate in developing a productive and realistic agenda for détente, an agenda that serves our interests and not the interests of

357

others who do not share our values. I envision an agenda that anticipates and precludes the exploitation of our perceived weaknesses. One item on that agenda must be to assure that the promises made in the Conference on Security and Cooperation in Europe are translated into action to advance freedom and human dignity for all Europeans. [The final conference declaration was signed in Helsinki Aug. 1, 1975; see p. 559.] Only by such realistic steps can we keep CSCE in perspective, whatever euphoric or inflated emphasis the Soviet Union or other participants may try to give it. Another agenda item should be the negotiations on mutual and balanced force reductions in Europe. We in NATO should be prepared to take appropriate initiatives in these negotiations if they will help us to meet our objectives. But the Soviet Union and its allies should also be prepared to respond in good faith on the common objectives both sides should be working toward—undiminished security for all, but at a lower level of forces.

Spain

—Fifth, let us look to the future of the West itself. We must strengthen our own democratic institutions and encourage the growth of truly democratic processes everywhere. Let us also look beyond our Alliance as it stands today. As an important topic on this agenda, we should begin now to consider how to relate Spain with Western defense. Spain has already made and continues to make an important contribution to Western military security as a result of its bilateral relationship with the United States.

Population, Food, Raw Materials

—Sixth, we should rededicate ourselves to the Alliance as a great joint enterprise, as a commitment to follow common approaches to shared aspirations. We must build on the contribution our Alliance already makes through the Committee on the Challenges of Modern Society in coping with the environmental problems of industrialized societies. We must address the issues of population, food, and raw materials. We must find ways to strengthen the world trading and monetary system and to meet the imperatives of energy development and conservation. With the wealth and technological skills which are the products of our free systems, we can make progress toward a better standard of life in all of our countries if we work together.

These six primary tasks of the Alliance illustrate the breadth and depth of our responsibilities and opportunities. They reflect how very complex the world has become and how much more difficult it is to manage the Alliance today than a generation ago. Then, our problems were relatively simple to define; it was easier to agree on common solutions. Today, the problem of definition seems more complicated. In many of our countries there has been a fragmentation of public and parliamentary opinion, which has made it more difficult for governments to mobilize support for courses of action of importance to the Alliance.

But there are constants as well, and they are—in the final analysis—more important than the complexities. Together we continue to be the greatest reservoir of economic, military, and moral strength in the world. We must use that strength to safeguard our freedom and to address the grave problems that confront us.

I am proud of America's role in NATO, and I am confident of the future of our Alliance.

As President of the United States—but also as one who has been a participant and close observer of the American political scene for close to 30 years—I assure you that my country will continue to be a strong partner. On occasion, in the public debate of our free society, America may seem to stray somewhat off course. But the fact is that we have the willpower, the technical capability, the spiritual drive, and the steadiness of purpose that will be needed. Today, we in the United States face our NATO commitments with new vision, new vigor, new courage, and renewed dedication.

America's emphasis is on cooperation, cooperation within NATO and throughout the world. From diversity we can forge a new unity. Together, let us build to face the challenges of the future.

REVIEW OF THE NUCLEAR NONPROLIFERATION TREATY

May 31, 1975

Five years after the Nuclear Nonproliferation Treaty (NPT) came into effect, most of its signatories were in agreement that it had failed to check the arms race between the superpowers or curtail the nuclear-weapons ambitions of some other nations. A majority of the representatives of 65 nations meeting at Geneva to review the pact expressed strong dissatisfaction in a communique approved May 31. Although the declaration named no offenders, delegates were known to be highly critical of the United States and the Soviet Union for failing to reach agreement on reduction of their nuclear arsenals. Signatories of the Nonproliferation Treaty had pledged to conclude such agreements "at an early date."

A bloc of developing nations attending the conference pushed for a strong condemnation of the superpowers and for guarantees of preferential treatment for NPT nations in the transfer of nuclear technology for peaceful purposes. The final document represented a compromise on these issues between the demands of the self-described non-aligned nations on the one hand and the United States and Soviet Union on the other. All parties to the conference agreed to stricter safeguards. These grew out of shared concern over the uneven application of regulations for the transfer of nuclear materials and technology to non-nuclear nations. In May 1974 India had exploded its first nuclear device, built with materials supplied for a nuclear power reactor by Canada.

Although India declared at the time of the 1974 test explosion that its "peaceful intentions" provided a sufficient guarantee against misuse of its nuclear capability, it was just this spread of uncontrolled atomic facilities that the treaty was designed to prevent. The major provisions of the treaty, which was concluded in 1968 and came into effect in 1970, bound signatories with nuclear weapons not to transfer them to non-nuclear nations. The latter agreed not to accept or construct such weapons, in return for free access to nuclear technology and the materials for peaceful use of that technology, subject to inspection by the United Nations International Atomic Energy Agency (IAEA).

Summary of Treaty

Article I of the Nonproliferation Treaty prohibited the transfer of nuclear weapons to signatory non-nuclear-weapon states. It also forbade the nuclear states to assist non-nuclear states in the manufacture of nuclear weapons.

Article II prohibited participating non-nuclear-weapon states from receiving or manufacturing nuclear weapons.

Article III, Section 1, bound participating non-nuclear-weapon states to accept safeguards making it possible to ascertain that nuclear materials made available to them for peaceful uses were not used to produce weapons. Section 2 bound participating nuclear-weapon states to transfer nuclear materials only if they would be subject to specified safeguards.

Article IV, Section 1, affirmed the "inalienable right" of all parties to pursue research and development of nuclear energy for peaceful purposes. Section 2 promoted the exchange of equipment, materials and technical information for peaceful uses and directed attention to the special needs of "developing areas of the world."

Article V guaranteed the access of non-nuclear-weapon states to the "benefits" from "any peaceful applications of nuclear explosions." These benefits were to be made available on a non-discriminatory basis at low cost.

Article VI bound signatories to "undertake to pursue negotiations in good faith on effective measures relating to cessation of the nuclear arms race at an early date and to nuclear disarmament, and on a treaty on general and complete disarmament under strict and effective international control."

Article VII affirmed the right of signatories to enter into regional treaties "to assure the total absence of nuclear weapons from their respective territories."

Article VIII specified procedures for amending the treaty and provided for reviews of its efficacy at five-year intervals.

Article IX contained provisions for the signing and ratification of the treaty.

Subsequent Developments

The Nonproliferation Treaty was approved by the United Nations General Assembly June 12, 1968, with France, a nuclear nation, abstaining. The People's Republic of China, also a nuclear nation, had refused an invitation to participate in the NPT negotiations at Geneva and had repeatedly denounced the treaty as a United States-Soviet "plot." In March 1970 the treaty came into effect when 43 nations had ratified it.

By 1975 only three of the world's six nuclear powers, the United States, Great Britain and the Soviet Union, were parties to NPT. American and Soviet testing, production and deployment of nuclear arms continued and only preliminary steps toward nuclear disarmament had been taken (see Historic Documents 1972, p. 431 and Historic Documents of 1974, p. 535, 955). The other three nations that had detonated nuclear devices, France, India and China, gave no indication that they would participate in the agreement. And the treaty had failed to win approval of a number of other prospective nuclear powers including Argentina, Brazil, Israel, Japan, Pakistan and South Africa.

The United States was widely criticized during 1974 for offering to sell Israel and Egypt each a 600 megawatt nuclear power reactor. The offer came during Middle East peace negotiations, and arms-control proponents questioned whether the belligerent nations might not divert the nuclear materials to military uses. Neither Israel nor Egypt was an NPT signatory.

For most nations the drive for nuclear capability, fired by national pride and defense needs, gained new impetus after the 1973 oil crisis. South African spokesman Dr. Louw Alberts, for example, announced in July 1974 that his country had the capability to produce a nuclear bomb and to process uranium. (South African uranium comprises one quarter of the known world supply of that mineral.) Alberts added that: "We have now a bargaining position equal to that of any Arab country with a lot of oil."

Reaction to Review

The Geneva review session elicited little official comment. On July 7 West Germany concluded an agreement to sell Brazil a "full cycle" nuclear complex which would enable that country to establish a self-sufficient atomic power industry. Brazil was not an NPT signatory but it pledged the facilities to peaceful purposes and agreed to open them to IAEA inspection. In September, The New York Times reported that Washington was attempting to work out with the major supplying nations an agreement on safeguards and controls to govern the export to other countries of certain nuclear materials and technology. The major nuclear suppliers were designated as Britain, Canada, France, Japan, the Soviet Union and West Germany, in addition to the United States.

Text of the Final Declaration *of the Review Conference of the Parties to the Treaty on the Non-Proliferation of Nuclear Weapons, adopted at Geneva May 30, 1975:*

Preamble

The States Party to the Treaty on the Non-Proliferation of Nuclear Weapons which met in Geneva in May 1975, in accordance with the Treaty, to review the operation of the Treaty with a view to assuring that the purposes of the Preamble and the provisions of the Treaty are being realized,

Recognizing the continuing importance of the objectives of the Treaty,

Affirming the belief that universal adherence to the Treaty would greatly strengthen international peace and enhance the security of all States,

Firmly convinced that, in order to achieve this aim, it is essential to maintain, in the implementation of the Treaty, an acceptable balance of mutual responsibilities and obligations of all States Party to the Treaty, nuclear-weapon and non-nuclear-weapon States,

Recognizing that the danger of nuclear warfare remains a grave threat to the survival of mankind,

Convinced that the prevention of any further proliferation of nuclear weapons or other nuclear explosive devices remains a vital element in efforts to avert nuclear warfare and that the promotion of this objective will be furthered by more rapid progress towards the cessation of the nuclear arms race and the limitation and reduction of existing nuclear weapons, with a view to the eventual elimination from national arsenals of nuclear weapons, pursuant to a Treaty on general and complete disarmament under strict and effective international control,

Recalling the determination expressed by the Parties to seek to achieve the discontinuance of all test explosions of nuclear weapons for all time,

Considering that the trend towards détente in relations between States provides a favourable climate within which more significant progress should be possible towards the cessation of the nuclear arms race,

Noting the important role which nuclear energy can, particularly in changing economic circumstances, play in power production and in contributing to the progressive elimination of the economic and technological gap between developing and developed States,

Recognizing that the accelerated spread and development of peaceful applications of nuclear energy will, in the absence of effective safeguards, contribute to further proliferation of nuclear explosive capability,

Recognizing the continuing necessity of full co-operation in the application and improvement of International Atomic Energy Agency (IAEA) safeguards on peaceful nuclear activities,

Recalling that all Parties to the Treaty are entitled to participate in the fullest possible exchange of scientific information for, and to contribute alone or in co-operation with other States to, the further development of the applications of atomic energy for peaceful purposes,

Reaffirming the principle that the benefits of peaceful applications of nuclear technology, including any technological by-products which may be derived by nuclear-weapon States from the development of nuclear explosive devices, should be available for peaceful purposes to all Parties to the Treaty, and

Recognizing that all States Parties have a duty to strive for the adoption of tangible and effective measures to attain the objectives of the Treaty,

Declare as follows:

Purposes

The States Party to the Treaty reaffirm their strong common interest in averting the further proliferation of nuclear weapons. They reaffirm their strong support for the Treaty, their continued dedication to its principles and objectives, and their commitment to implement fully and more effectively its provisions.

They reaffirm the vital role of the Treaty in international efforts

—to avert further proliferation of nuclear weapons

—to achieve the cessation of the nuclear arms race and to undertake effective measures in the direction of nuclear disarmament, and

—to promote co-operation in the peaceful uses of nuclear energy under adequate safeguards.

Review of Articles I and II

The review undertaken by the Conference confirms that the obligations undertaken under Articles I and II of the Treaty have been faithfully observed by all Parties. The Conference is convinced that the continued strict observance of these Articles remains central to the shared objective of averting the further proliferation of nuclear weapons.

Review of Article III

The Conference notes that the verification activities of the IAEA under Article III of the Treaty respect the sovereign rights of States and do not hamper the economic, scientific or technological development of the Parties to the Treaty or international co-operation in peaceful nuclear activities. It urges that this situation be maintained. The Conference attaches considerable importance to the continued application of safeguards under Article III, 1, on a non-discriminatory basis, for the equal benefit of all States Party to the Treaty.

The Conference notes the importance of systems of accounting for and control of nuclear material, from the standpoints both of the responsibilities of States Party to the Treaty and of co-operation with the IAEA in order to facilitate the implementation of the safeguards provided for in Article III, 1. The Conference expresses the hope that all States having peaceful nuclear activities will establish and maintain effective accounting and control systems and welcomes the readiness of the IAEA to assist States in so doing.

The Conference expresses its strong support for effective IAEA safeguards. In this context it recommends that intensified efforts be made towards the standardization and the universality of application of IAEA safeguards, while ensuring that safeguard agreements with non-nuclear-weapon States not Party to the Treaty are of adequate duration, preclude diversion to any nuclear explosive devices and contain appropriate provisions for the continuance of the application of safeguards upon re-export.

The Conference recommends that more attention and fuller support be given to the improvement of safeguards techniques, instrumentation, data-handling and implementation in order, among other things, to ensure optimum cost-effectiveness. It notes with satisfaction the establishment by the Director General of the IAEA of a standing advisory group on safeguards implementation.

The Conference emphasizes the necessity for the States Party to the Treaty that have not yet done so to conclude as soon as possible safeguards agreements with the IAEA.

With regard to the implementation of Article III, 2 of the Treaty, the Conference notes that a number of States suppliers of nuclear material or equipment have adopted certain minimum, standard requirements for IAEA safeguards in connexion with their exports of certain such items to non-nuclear-weapon States not Party to the Treaty (IAEA document INFCIRC/209 and Addenda). The Conference attaches particular importance to the condition, established by those States, of an undertaking of non-diversion to nuclear weapons or other nuclear explosive devices, as included in the said requirements.

The Conference urges that:

(a) in all achievable ways, common export requirements relating to safeguards be strengthened, in particular by extending the application of safeguards to all peaceful nuclear activities in importing States not Party to the Treaty;

(b) such common requirements be accorded the widest possible measure of acceptance among all suppliers and recipients;

(c) all Parties to the Treaty should actively pursue their efforts to these ends.

The Conference takes note of:

(a) the considered view of many Parties to the Treaty that the safeguards required under Article III, 2 should extend to all peaceful nuclear activities in importing States;

(b) (i) the suggestion that it is desirable to arrange for common safeguards requirements in respect of nuclear material processed, used or produced by the use of scientific and technological information transferred in tangible form to non-nuclear-weapon States not Party to the Treaty;

(ii) the hope that this aspect of safeguards could be further examined.

The Conference recommends that, during the review of the arrangements relating to the financing of safeguards in the IAEA which is to be undertaken by its Board of Governors at an appropriate time after 1975, the less favourable financial situation of the developing countries be fully taken into account. It recommends further that, on that occasion, the Parties to the Treaty concerned seek measures that would restrict within appropriate limits the respective shares of developing countries in safeguards costs.

The Conference attaches considerable importance, so far as safeguards inspectors are concerned, to adherence by the IAEA to Article VII.D of its Statute, prescribing, among other things, that "due regard shall be paid...to the importance of recruiting the staff on as wide a geographical basis as possible"; it also recommends that safeguards training be made available to personnel from all geographic regions.

The Conference, convinced that nuclear materials should be effectively protected at all times, urges that action be pursued to elaborate further, within the IAEA, concrete recommendations for the physical protection of nuclear material in use, storage and transit, including principles relating to the responsibility of States, with a view to ensuring a uniform, minimum level of effective protection for such material.

It calls upon all States engaging in peaceful nuclear activities (i) to enter into such international agreements and arrangements as may be necessary to ensure such protection; and (ii) in the framework of their respective physical protection systems, to give the earliest possible effective application to the IAEA's recommendations.

Review of Article IV

The Conference reaffirms, in the framework of Article IV, 1, that nothing in the Treaty shall be interpreted as affecting, and notes with satisfaction that nothing in the Treaty has been identified as affecting, the inalienable right of all the Parties to the Treaty to develop research, production and use of nuclear energy for peaceful purposes without discrimination and in conformity with Articles I and II of the Treaty.

The Conference reaffirms, in the framework of Article IV, 2, the undertaking by all Parties to the Treaty to facilitate the fullest possible exchange of equipment, materials and scientific and technological information for the peaceful uses of nuclear energy and the right of all Parties to the Treaty to participate in such exchange and welcomes the efforts made towards that end. Noting that the Treaty constitutes a favourable framework for broadening international co-operation in the peaceful uses of nuclear energy, the Conference is convinced that on this basis, and in conformity with the Treaty, further efforts should be made to ensure that the benefits of peaceful applications of nuclear technology should be available to all Parties to the Treaty.

The Conference recognizes that there continues to be a need for the fullest possible exchange of nuclear materials, equipment and technology, including up-to-date developments, consistent with the objectives and safeguards requirements of the Treaty. The Conference reaffirms the under-taking of the Parties to the Treaty in a position to do so to co-operate in con-tributing, alone or together with other States or international organizations, to the further development of the applications of nuclear energy for peaceful purposes, especially in the territories of non-nuclear-weapon States Party to the Treaty, with due consideration for the needs of the developing areas of the world. Recognizing, in the context of Article IV, 2, those growing needs of developing States the Conference considers it necessary to continue and increase assistance to them in this field bilaterally and through such mul-tilateral channels as the IAEA and the United Nations Development Programme.

The Conference is of the view that, in order to implement as fully as possible Article IV of the Treaty, developed States Party to the Treaty should consider taking measures, making contributions and establishing programmes, as soon as possible, for the provision of special assistance in the peaceful uses of nuclear energy for developing States Party to the Treaty.

The Conference recommends that, in reaching decisions on the provision of equipment, materials, services and scientific and technological informa-tion for the peaceful uses of nuclear energy, on concessional and other appropriate financial arrangements and on the furnishing of technical assistance in the nuclear field, including co-operation related to the con-tinuous operation of peaceful nuclear facilities, States Party to the Treaty should give weight to adherence to the Treaty by recipient States. The Conference recommends, in this connexion, that any special measures of co-operation to meet the growing needs of developing States Party to the Trea-ty might include increased and supplemental voluntary aid provided bilaterally or through multilateral channels such as the IAEA's facilities for administering funds-in-trust and gifts-in-kind.

The Conference further recommends that States Party to the Treaty in a position to do so, meet, to the fullest extent possible, "technically sound" requests for technical assistance, submitted to the IAEA by developing States Party to the Treaty, which the IAEA is unable to finance from its own resources, as well as such "technically sound" requests as may be made by developing States Party to the Treaty which are not Members of the IAEA.

The Conference recognizes that regional or multinational nuclear fuel cycle centres may be an advantageous way to satisfy, safely and economically, the needs of many States in the course of initiating or ex-panding nuclear power programmes, while at the same time facilitating physical protection and the application of IAEA safeguards and con-tributing to the goals of the Treaty.

The Conference welcomes the IAEA's studies in this area, and recommends that they be continued as expeditiously as possible. It con-siders that such studies should include, among other aspects, identification of the complex practical and organizational difficulties which will need to be dealt with in connexion with such projects.

The Conference urges all Parties to the Treaty in a position to do so to co-operate in these studies, particularly by providing to the IAEA where possible economic data concerning construction and operation of facilities such as chemical reprocessing plants, plutonium fuel fabrication plants, waste management installations, and longer-term spent fuel storage, and by assistance to the IAEA to enable it to undertake feasibility studies concerning the establishment of regional nuclear fuel cycle centres in specific geographic regions.

The Conference hopes that, if these studies lead to positive findings, and if the establishment of regional or multinational nuclear fuel cycle centres is undertaken, Parties to the Treaty in a position to do so, will co-operate in, and provide assistance for, the elaboration and realization of such projects.

Review of Article V

The Conference reaffirms the obligation of Parties to the Treaty to take appropriate measures to ensure that potential benefits from any peaceful applications of nuclear explosions are made available to non-nuclear-weapon states Party to the Treaty in full accordance with the provisions of Article V and other applicable international obligations. In this connexion, the Conference also reaffirms that such services should be provided to non-nuclear-weapon States Party to the Treaty on a non-discriminatory basis and that the charge to such Parties for the explosive devices used should be as low as possible and exclude any charge for research and development.

The Conference notes that any potential benefits could be made available to non-nuclear-weapon States not Party to the Treaty by way of nuclear explosion services provided by nuclear-weapon States, as defined by the Treaty, and conducted under the appropriate international observation and international procedures called for in Article V and in accordance with other applicable international obligations. The Conference considers it imperative that access to potential benefits of nuclear explosions for peaceful purposes not lead to any proliferation of nuclear explosive capability.

The conference considers the IAEA to be the appropriate international body, referred to in Article V of the Treaty, through which potential benefits from peaceful applications of nuclear explosions could be made available to any non-nuclear-weapon State. Accordingly, the Conference urges the IAEA to expedite work on identifying and examining the important legal issues involved in, and to commence consideration of, the structure and content of the special international agreement or agreements contemplated in Article V of the Treaty, taking into account the views of the Conference of the Committee on Disarmament (CCD) and the United Nations General Assembly and enabling States Party to the Treaty but not Members of the IAEA which would wish to do so to participate in such work.

The Conference notes that the technology of nuclear explosions for peaceful purposes is still at the stage of development and study and that there are a number of interrelated international legal and other aspects of such explosions which still need to be investigated.

The Conference commends the work in this field that has been carried out within the IAEA and looks forward to the continuance of such work pursuant to United Nations General Assembly resolution 3261 D (XXIX). It emphasizes that the IAEA should play the central role in matters relating to the provision of services for the application of nuclear explosions for peaceful purposes. It believes that the IAEA should broaden its consideration of this subject to encompass, within its area of competence, all aspects and implications of the practical applications of nuclear explosions for peaceful purposes. To this end it urges the IAEA to set up appropriate machinery within which intergovernmental discussion can take place and through which advice can be given on the Agency's work in this field.

The Conference attaches considerable importance to the consideration by the CCD, pursuant to United Nations General Assembly resolution 3261 D (XXIX) and taking due account of the views of the IAEA, of the arms control implications of nuclear explosions for peaceful purposes.

The Conference notes that the thirtieth session of the United Nations General Assembly will receive reports pursuant to United Nations General Assembly resolution 3261 D (XXIX) and will provide an opportunity for States to discuss questions related to the application of nuclear explosions for peaceful purposes. The Conference further notes that the results of discussion in the United Nations General Assembly at its thirtieth session will be available to be taken into account by the IAEA and the CCD for their further consideration.

Review of Article VI

The Conference recalls the provisions of Article VI of the Treaty under which all Parties undertook to pursue negotiations in good faith on effective measures relating

—to the cessation of the nuclear arms race at an early date and

—to nuclear disarmament and

—to a treaty on general and complete disarmament under strict and effective international control.

While welcoming the various agreements on arms limitation and disarmament elaborated and concluded over the last few years as steps contributing to the implementation of Article VI of the Treaty, the Conference expresses its serious concern that the arms race, in particular the nuclear arms race, is continuing unabated.

The Conference therefore urges constant and resolute efforts by each of the Parties to the Treaty, in particular by the nuclear-weapon States, to achieve an early and effective implementation of Article VI of the Treaty.

The Conference affirms the determination expressed in the preamble to the 1963 Partial Test Ban Treaty and reiterated in the preamble to the Non-Proliferation Treaty to achieve the discontinuance of all test explosions of nuclear weapons for all time. The Conference expresses the view that the conclusion of a treaty banning all nuclear weapons tests is one of the most important measures to halt the nuclear arms race. It expresses the hope that the nuclear-weapon States Party to the Treaty will take the lead in reaching an early solution of the technical and political difficulties on this issue. It appeals to these States to make every effort to reach agreement on the conclusion of an effective comprehensive test ban. To this end, the desire was expressed by a considerable number of delegations at the Conference that the nuclear-weapon States Party to the Treaty should as soon as possible enter into an agreement, open to all States and containing appropriate provisions to ensure its effectiveness, to halt all nuclear weapons tests of adhering States for a specified time, whereupon the terms of such an agreement would be reviewed in the light of the opportunity, at that time, to achieve a universal and permanent cessation of all nuclear weapons tests. The Conference calls upon the nuclear-weapon States signatories of the Treaty on the Limitation of Underground Nuclear Weapons tests, meanwhile, to limit the number of their underground nuclear weapons tests to a minimum. The Conference believes that such steps would constitute an incentive of particular value to negotiations for the conclusion of a treaty banning all nuclear weapons test explosions for all time.

The Conference appeals to the nuclear-weapon States Parties to the negotiations on the limitation of strategic arms to endeavour to conclude at the earliest possible date the new agreement that was outlined by their leaders in November 1974. The Conference looks forward to the commencement of follow-on negotiations on further limitations of, and significant reductions in, their nuclear weapons systems as soon as possible following the conclusion of such an agreement.

The Conference notes that, notwithstanding earlier progress, the CCD has recently been unable to reach agreement on new substantive measures to advance the objectives of Article VI of the Treaty. It urges, therefore, all members of the CCD Party to the Treaty, in particular the nuclear-weapon States Party, to increase their efforts to achieve effective disarmament agreements on all subjects on the agenda of the CCD.

The Conference expresses the hope that all States Party to the Treaty, through the United Nations and the CCD and other negotiations in which they participate, will work with determination towards the conclusion of arms limitation and disarmament agreements which will contribute to the goal of general and complete disarmament under strict and effective international control.

The Conference expresses the view that, disarmament being a matter of general concern, the provision of information to all governments and peoples on the situation in the field of the arms race and disarmament is of great importance for the attainment of the aims of Article VI. The Conference therefore invites the United Nations to consider ways and means of improving its existing facilities for collection, compilation and dissemination of information on disarmament issues, in order to keep all governments as well as world public opinion properly informed on progress achieved in the realization of the provisions of Article VI of the Treaty.

Review of Article VII and the Security of Non-Nuclear Weapon States

Recognizing that all States have need to ensure their independence, territorial integrity and sovereignty, the Conference emphasizes the particular importance of assuring and strengthening the security of non-nuclear-weapon States Parties which have renounced the acquisition of nuclear weapons. It acknowledges that States Parties find themselves in different security situations and therefore that various appropriate means are necessary to meet the security concerns of States Parties.

The Conference underlines the importance of adherence to the Treaty by non-nuclear-weapon States as the best means of reassuring one another of their renunciation of nuclear weapons and as one of the effective means of strengthening their mutual security.

The Conference takes note of the continued determination of the Depositary States to honour their statements, which were welcomed by the United Nations Security Council in resolution 255 (1968), that, to ensure the security of the non-nuclear-weapon States Party to the Treaty, they will provide or support immediate assistance, in accordance with the Charter, to any non-nuclear-weapon State Party to the Treaty which is a victim of an act or an object of a threat of aggression in which nuclear weapons are used.

The Conference, bearing in mind Article VII of the Treaty, considers that the establishment of internationally recognized nuclear-weapon-free zones on the initiative and with the agreement of the directly concerned States of the zone, represents an effective means of curbing the spread of nuclear weapons, and could contribute significantly to the security of those States. It welcomes the steps which have been taken toward the establishment of such zones.

The Conference recognizes that for the maximum effectiveness of any Treaty arrangements for establishing a nuclear-weapon-free zone the co-operation of the nuclear-weapon States is necessary. At the Conference it was urged by a considerable number of delegations that nuclear-weapon States should provide, in an appropriate manner, binding security assurances to those States which become fully bound by the provisions of such regional arrangements.

At the Conference it was also urged that determined efforts must be made especially by the nuclear weapon States Party to the Treaty, to ensure the security of all non-nuclear-weapon States Parties. To this end the Conference urges all States, both nuclear-weapon States and non-nuclear-weapon States to refrain, in accordance with the Charter of the United Nations, from the threat or the use of force in relations between States, involving either nuclear or non-nuclear-weapons. Additionally, it stresses the responsibility of all Parties to the Treaty and especially the nuclear-weapon States, to take effective steps to strengthen the security of non-nuclear-weapon States and to promote in all appropriate fora the consideration of all practical means to this end, taking into account the views expressed at this Conference.

Review of Article VIII

The Conference invites States Party to the Treaty which are Members of the United Nations to request the Secretary-General of the United Nations to include the following item in the provisional agenda of the thirty-first session of the General Assembly: "Implementation of the conclusions of the first Review Conference of the Parties to the Treaty on the Non-Proliferation of Nuclear Weapons".

The States Party to the Treaty participating in the Conference propose to the Depositary Governments that a second Conference to review the operation of the Treaty be convened in 1980.

The Conference accordingly invites States Party to the Treaty which are Members of the United Nations to request the Secretary-General of the United Nations to include the following item in the provisional agenda of the thirty-third session of the General Assembly: "Implementation of the conclusions of the first Review Conference of the Parties to the Treaty on the Non-Proliferation of Nuclear Weapons and establishment of a preparatory committee for the second Conference."

Review of Article IX

The five years that have passed since the entry into force of the Treaty have demonstrated its wide international acceptance. The Conference welcomes the recent progress towards achieving wider adherence. At the same time, the Conference notes with concern that the Treaty has not as yet achieved universal adherence. Therefore, the Conference expresses the hope that States that have not already joined the Treaty should do so at the earliest possible date.

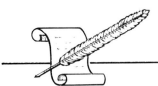
June

CALIFORNIA FARM-LABOR LAW

June 5, 1975

Landmark state labor legislation, the first to protect collective bargaining rights of farm workers, cleared the California legislature May 29 and was signed into law June 5 by Governor Edmund G. Brown Jr. Under the act, field workers in California's multi-million-dollar agriculture industry gained the right to vote by secret ballot in organizing elections and to strike to gain contract terms. Agricultural workers, perhaps the lowest paid and least protected segment of the nation's labor force, were not covered by the federal statutes enforced by the National Labor Relations Board. The California measure was widely hailed as prototype legislation in that field. It was passed only after a marathon bargaining session, called by Brown, had ensured the support of major growers, the International Brotherhood of Teamsters and the AFL-CIO United Farm Workers Union (UFW) led by Cesar Chavez. The two unions had been locked in an acrimonious, often violent, jurisdictional dispute for five years prior to passage of the bill.

The first UFW contracts, signed by table-grape growers in 1970, promised an end to many decades of futile efforts to organize farm workers. Particularly in California, the profits of major growers had always depended on the availability of cheap labor, mostly foreign-born. Japanese, Filipinos, "Okies" and Mexicans in succession had tended California's lush fields and harvested the crops under conditions which Winthrop Griffith, writing in The New York Times, *characterized as a "lingering form of slavery." The fieldhands lived in extreme poverty and worked without protection from pesticides and other occupational hazards, dependent on an employment system controlled by independent labor contractors.*

In 1962 former fieldhand Chavez began organizing farm workers in central California. By the late sixties, the movement, La Causa, had caught the attention of the liberal press and gained the support of many church leaders and prominent politicians. As a young seminarian, Governor Brown had marched with Chavez. A nationwide boycott of table grapes and iceberg lettuce and well-publicized field strikes finally forced a grudging recognition of UFW by growers in 1970. Three years after the first UFW contracts, the union had negotiated agreements with 300 growers affecting more than 60,000 workers.

During the years when UFW control was expanding most rapidly, the Teamsters union, which already controlled produce truckers, loaders and processors, moved to take over control of field workers. Initially the Teamsters bargained directly with the growers, excluding workers from the negotiations. Under the first Teamster contracts, workers earned less than under the UFW contracts, and in December 1972 the California Supreme Court ruled against certain of the Teamster contracts. Finding that Salinas Valley growers had shown "the ultimate form of favoritism" in switching to the Teamsters, the court judged that "at least a substantial number and probably the majority" of affected workers preferred UFW representation.

Teamster competition continued, moving into a violent phase in 1973 when confrontations in the fields between Chavistas and Teamster organizers resulted in numerous arrests and hundreds of serious injuries on both sides, and at least one death. Chavez renewed the national consumer boycott but with less effect than in the late sixties when the issue of unionization had been more clearly defined.

By 1974 the Teamsters began to stress consultations with workers, attractive contracts and efficient organization, markedly superior to what UFW could offer. Chavistas continued to claim spiritual loyalty to La Causa, but they signed petitions for Teamster representation. UFW shrank to fewer than 10,000 members.

Provisions of the California law, which closely follows the National Labor Relations Act, allowed contracts signed before the law went into effect Aug. 28, 1975, to be nullified by secret-ballot elections if they were called for by workers. Chavez predicted that these provisions of the act would pave the way for his union's resurgence. Balloting during September and October seemed to bear out Chavez' optimism. Figures released Oct. 30 by the California Agricultural Labor Relations Board, established by the new bill, indicated that UFW had won 142 elections with 16,219 workers voting in its favor, and the Teamsters had won 91 contests with 9,059 votes. The majority of these contests had not been certified by the Board, however. The elections uncovered several troublesome facets of the new law that were likely to require correction. One was the question of access to, or the right to approach, workers in the field. The second, which displeased the Teamsters *and other unions, was the fact that the act limited each employer to one union and thereby raised the possibility that skilled workers might be forced to join UFW.*

> *Text of the California Agricultural Labor Relations Act, signed into law June 5, 1975, by Governor Edmund G. Brown Jr.:*

The people of the State of California do enact as follows:

SECTION 1. In enacting this legislation the people of the State of California seek to ensure peace in the agricultural fields by guaranteeing justice for all agricultural workers and stability in labor relations.

This enactment is intended to bring certainty and a sense of fair play to a presently unstable and potentially volatile condition in the state. The Legislature recognizes that no law in itself resolves social injustice and economic dislocations.

However, in the belief the people affected desire a resolution to this dispute and will make a sincere effort to work through the procedures established in this legislation, it is the hope of the Legislature that farm laborers, farmers, and all the people of California will be served by the provisions of this act.

SEC. 1.5. It is the intent of the Legislature that collective-bargaining agreements between agricultural employers and labor organizations representing the employees of such employers entered into prior to the effective date of this legislation and continuing beyond such date are not to be automatically canceled, terminated or voided on that effective date; rather, such a collective-bargaining agreement otherwise lawfully entered into and enforceable under the laws of this state shall be void upon the Agricultural Labor Relations Board certification of that election after the filing of an election petition by such employees pursuant to Section 1156.3 of the Labor Code.

SEC. 2. Part 3.5 (commencing with Section 1140) is added to Division 2 of the Labor Code, to read:

Part 3.5. Agricultural Labor Relations

Chapter 1. General Provisions and Definitions

1140. This part shall be known and may be referred to as the Alatorre-Zenovich-Dunlap-Berman Agricultural Labor Relations Act of 1975.

1140.2. It is hereby stated to be the policy of the State of California to encourage and protect the right of agricultural employees to full freedom of association, self-organization, and designation of representatives of their own choosing, to negotiate the terms and conditions of their employment, and to be free from the interference, restraint, or coercion of employers of labor, or their agents, in the designation of such representatives or in self-organization or in other concerted activities for the purpose of collective bargaining or other mutual aid or protection. For this purpose this part is adopted to provide for collective-bargaining rights for agricultural employees.

1140.4. As used in this part:

(a) The term "agriculture" includes farming in all its branches, and, among other things, includes the cultivation and tillage of the soil, dairying, the production, cultivation, growing, and harvesting of any agricultural or horticultural commodities (including commodities defined as agricultural commodities in Section 1141j(g) of Title 12 of the United States Code), the raising of livestock, bees, furbearing animals, or poultry, and any practices (including any forestry or lumbering operations) performed by a farmer or on a farm as an incident to or in conjunction with such farming operations, including preparation for market and delivery to storage or to market or to carriers for transportation to market.

(b) The term "agricultural employee" or "employee" shall mean one engaged in agriculture, as such term is defined in subdivision (a). However, nothing in this subdivision shall be construed to include any person other than those employees excluded from the coverage of the National Labor Relations Act, as amended, as agricultural employees, pursuant to Section 2(3) of the Labor Management Relations Act (Section 152(3), Title 29, United States Code), and Section 3(f) of the Fair Labor Standards Act (Section 203(f), Title 29, United States Code).

Further, nothing in this part shall apply, or be construed to apply, to any employee who performs work to be done at the site of the construction, alteration, painting, or repair of a building, structure, or other work (as these terms have been construed under Section 8(e) of the Labor Management Relations Act, 29 USC Section 158(e)) or logging or timber-clearing operations in initial preparation of land for farming, or who does land leveling or only land surveying for any of the above.

As used in this subdivision, "land leveling" shall include only major land moving operations changing the contour of the land, but shall not include annual or seasonal tillage or preparation of land for cultivation.

(c) The term "agricultural employer" shall be liberally construed to include any person acting directly or indirectly in the interest of an employer in relation to an agricultural employee, any individual grower, corporate grower, cooperative grower, harvesting association, hiring association, land management group, any association of persons or cooperatives engaged in agriculture, and shall include any person who owns or leases or manages land used for agricultural purposes, but shall exclude any person supplying agricultural workers to an employer, any farm labor contractor as defined by Section 1682, and any person functioning in the capacity of a labor contractor. The employer engaging such labor contractor or person shall be deemed the employer for all purposes under this part.

(d) The term "person" shall mean one or more individuals, corporations, partnerships, associations, legal representatives, trustees in bankruptcy, receivers, or any other legal entity, employer, or labor organization having an interest in the outcome of a proceeding under this part.

(e) The term "representatives" includes any individual or labor organization.

(f) The term "labor organization" means any organization of any kind, or any agency or employee representation committee or plan, in which employees participate and which exists, in whole or in part, for the purpose of dealing with employers concerning grievances, labor disputes, wages, rates of pay, hours of employment, or conditions of work for agricultural employees.

(g) The term "unfair labor practice" means any unfair labor practice specified in Chapter 4 (commencing with Section 1153) of this part.

(h) The term "labor dispute" includes any controversy concerning terms, tenure, or conditions of employment, or concerning the association or representation of persons in negotiating, fixing, maintaining, changing, or seeking to arrange terms or conditions of employment, regardless of whether the disputants stand in the proximate relation of employer and employee.

(i) The term "board" means Agricultural Labor Relations Board.

(j) The term "supervisor" means any individual having the authority, in the interest of the employer, to hire, transfer, suspend, lay off, recall, promote, discharge, assign, reward, or discipline other employees, or the responsibility to direct them, or to adjust their grievances, or effectively to recommend such action, if, in connection with the foregoing, the exercise of such authority is not of a merely routine or clerical nature, but requires the use of independent judgment.

Chapter 2. Agricultural Labor Relations Board

Article 1. Agricultural Labor Relations Board: Organization

1141. (a) There is hereby created in state government the Agricultural Labor Relations Board, which shall consist of five members.

(b) The members of the board shall be appointed by the Governor with the advice and consent of the Senate. The term of office of the members shall be five years, and the terms shall be staggered at one-year intervals. Upon the initial appointment, one member shall be appointed for a term ending January 1, 1977, one member shall be appointed for a term ending January 1, 1978, one member shall be appointed for a term ending January 1, 1979, one member shall be appointed for a term ending January 1, 1980, and one member shall be appointed for a term ending January 1, 1981. Any individual appointed to fill a vacancy of any member shall be appointed only for the unexpired term of the member to whose term he is succeeding. The Governor shall designate one member to serve as chairperson of the board. Any member of the board may be removed by the Governor, upon notice and hearing, for neglect of duty or malfeasance in office, but for no other cause.

1142. (a) The principal office of the board shall be in Sacramento, but it may meet and exercise any or all of its power at any other place in California.

(b) Besides the principal office in Sacramento, as provided in subdivision (a), the board may establish offices in such other cities as it shall deem necessary. The board may delegate to the personnel of these offices such powers as it deems appropriate to determine the unit appropriate for the purpose of collective bargaining, to investigate and provide for hearings, to determine whether a question of representation exists, to direct an election by a secret ballot pursuant to the provisions of Chapter 5 (commencing with Section 1156), and to certify the results of such election, and to investigate, conduct hearings and make determinations relating to unfair labor practices. The board may review any action taken pursuant to the authority delegated under this section upon a request for a review of such action filed with the board by an interested party. Any such review made by the board shall not, unless specifically ordered by the board, operate as a stay of any action taken. The entire record considered by the board in considering or acting upon any such request or review shall be made available to all parties prior to such consideration or action, and the board's findings and action thereon shall be published as a decision of the board.

1143. The board shall, at the close of each fiscal year, make a report in writing to the Legislature and to the Governor stating in detail the cases it has heard, the decisions it has rendered, the names, salaries, and duties of all employees and officers in the employ or under the supervision of the board, and an account of all moneys it has disbursed.

1144. The board may from time to time make, amend, and rescind, in the manner prescribed in Chapter 4.5 (commencing with Section 11371) of Part 1 of Division 3 of Title 2 of the Government Code, such rules and regulations as may be necessary to carry out the provisions of this part.

1145. The board may appoint an executive secretary and such attorneys, hearing officers, administrative law officers, and other employees as it may from time to time find necessary for the proper performance of its duties. Attorneys appointed pursuant to this section may, at the discretion of the board, appear for and represent the board in any case in court.

1146. The board is authorized to delegate to any group of three or more board members any or all the powers which it may itself exercise. A vacancy in the board shall not impair the right of the remaining members to exercise all the powers of the board, and three members shall at all times constitute a quorum. A vacancy shall be filled in the same manner as an original appointment.

1147. The annual salary of a member of the board shall be forty-two thousand five hundred dollars ($42,500).

1148. The board shall follow applicable precedents of the National Labor Relations Act, as amended.

1149. There shall be a general counsel of the board who shall be appointed by the Governor, subject to confirmation by a majority of the

Senate, for a term of four years. The general counsel shall have the power to appoint such attorneys, administrative assistants, and other employees as necessary for the proper exercise of his duties. The general counsel of the board shall exercise general supervision over all attorneys employed by the board (other than administrative law officers and legal assistants to board members), and over the officers and employees in the regional offices. He shall have final authority, on behalf of the board, with respect to the investigation of charges and issuance of complaints under Chapter 6 (commencing with Section 1160) of this part, and with respect to the prosecution of such complaints before the board. He shall have such other duties as the board may prescribe or as may be provided by law. In case of a vacancy in the office of the general counsel, the Governor is authorized to designate the officer or employee who shall act as general counsel during such vacancy, but no person or persons so designated shall so act either (1) for more than 40 days when the Legislature is in session unless a nomination to fill such vacancy shall have been submitted to the Senate, or (2) after the adjournment sine die of the session of the Senate in which such nomination was submitted.

1150. Each member of the board and the general counsel of the board shall be eligible for reappointment, and shall not engage in any other business, vocation, or employment.

Article 2. Investigatory Powers

1151. For the purpose of all hearings and investigations, which, in the opinion of the board, are necessary and proper for the exercise of the powers vested in it by Chapters 5 (commencing with Section 1156) and 6 (commencing with Section 1160) of this part:

(a) The board, or its duly authorized agents or agencies, shall at all reasonable times have access to, for the purpose of examination, and the right to copy, any evidence of any person being investigated or proceeded against that relates to any matter under investigation or in question. The members of the board or their designees or their duly authorized agents shall have the right of free access to all places of labor. The board, or any member thereof, shall upon application of any such party to such proceedings, forthwith issue to such party subpoenas requiring the attendance and testimony of witnesses or the production of any evidence in such proceeding or investigation requested in such application. Within five days after the service of a subpoena on any person requiring the production of any evidence in his possession or under his control, such person may petition the board to revoke, and the board shall revoke, such subpoena if in its opinion the evidence whose production is required does not relate to any matter under investigation, or any matter in question in such proceedings, or if in its opinion such subpoena does not describe with sufficient particularity the evidence whose production is required. Any member of the board, or any agent or agency designated by the board for such purposes, may administer oaths and affirmations, examine witnesses, and receive evidence. Such attendance of witnesses and the production of such evidence may be required from any place in the state at any designated place of hearing.

(b) In case of contumacy or refusal to obey a subpoena issued to any person, any superior court in any county within the jurisdiction of which the inquiry is carried on, or within the jurisdiction of which such person allegedly guilty of contumacy or refusal to obey is found or resides or transacts business, shall, upon application by the board, have jurisdiction to issue to such person an order requiring such person to appear before the board, its member, agent, or agency, there to produce evidence if so ordered, or there to give testimony touching the matter under investigation or in question. Any failure to obey such order of the court may be punished by such court as a contempt thereof.

1151.2. No person shall be excused from attending and testifying, or from producing books, records, correspondence, documents, or other evidence in obedience to the subpoena of the board, on the ground that the testimony or evidence required of him may tend to incriminate him or subject him to a penalty or forfeiture. However, no individual shall be prosecuted or subjected to any penalty or forfeiture for or on account of any transaction, matter, or thing concerning which he is compelled, after having claimed his privilege against self-incrimination, to testify or produce evidence, except that such individual so testifying shall not be exempt from prosecution and punishment for perjury committed in so testifying.

1151.3. Any party shall have the right to appear at any hearing in person, by counsel, or by other representative.

1151.4. (a) Complaints, orders, and other process and papers of the board, its members, agents, or agency, may be served either personally or by registered mail or by telegraph, or by leaving a copy thereof at the principal office or place of business of the person required to be served. The verified return by the individual so serving the same setting forth the manner of such service shall be proof of the same, and the return post office receipt or telegraph receipt therefor when registered and mailed or telegraphed as provided in this subdivision shall be proof of service of the same. Witnesses summoned before the board, its members, agents, or agency, shall be paid the same fees and mileage that are paid witnesses in the courts of the state, and witnesses whose depositions are taken and the persons taking the same shall severally be entitled to the same fees as are paid for like services in the courts of the state.

(b) All process of any court to which application may be made under this part may be served in the county where the defendant or other person required to be served resides or may be found.

1151.5. The several departments and agencies of the state upon request by the board, shall furnish the board all records, papers, and information in their possession, not otherwise privileged, relating to any matter before the board.

1151.6. Any person who shall willfully resist, prevent, impede, or interfere with any member of the board or any of its agents or agencies in the performance of duties pursuant to this part shall be guilty of a misdemeanor, and shall be punished by a fine of not more than five thousand ($5,000) dollars.

Chapter 3. Rights of Agricultural Employees

1152. Employees shall have the right to self-organization, to form, join, or assist labor organizations, to bargain collectively through representatives of their own choosing, and to engage in other concerted activities for the purpose of collective bargaining or other mutual aid or protection, and shall also have the right to refrain from any or all of such activities except to the extent that such right may be affected by an agreement requiring membership in a labor organization as a condition of continued employment as authorized in subdivision (c) of Section 1153.

Chapter 4. Unfair Labor Practices and Regulation of Secondary Boycotts

1153. It shall be an unfair labor practice for an agricultural employer to do any of the following:

(a) To interfere with, restrain, or coerce agricultural employees in the exercise of the rights guaranteed in Section 1152.

(b) To dominate or interfere with the formation or administration of any labor organization or contribute financial or other support to it. However, subject to such rules and regulations as may be made and published by the board pursuant to Section 1144, an agricultural employer shall not be prohibited from permitting agricultural employees to confer with him during working hours without loss of time or pay.

(c) By discrimination in regard to the hiring or tenure of employment, or any term or condition of employment, to encourage or discourage membership in any labor organization.

Nothing in this part, or in any other statute of this state, shall preclude an agricultural employer from making an agreement with a labor organization (not established, maintained, or assisted by any action defined in this section as an unfair labor practice) to require as a condition of employment, membership therein on or after the fifth day following the beginning of such employment, or the effective date of such agreement whichever is later, if such labor organization is the representative of the agricultural employees as provided in Section 1156 in the appropriate collective-bargaining unit covered by such agreement. No employee who has been required to pay dues to a labor organization by virtue of his employment as an agricultural worker during any calendar month, shall be required to pay dues to another labor organization by virtue of similar employment during such month. For purposes of this chapter, membership shall mean the satisfaction of all reasonable terms and conditions uniformly applicable to other members in good standing; provided, that such membership shall not be denied or terminated except in compliance with a constitution or bylaws which afford full and fair rights to speech, assembly, and equal voting and membership privileges for all members, and which contain adequate procedures to assure due process to members and applicants for membership.

(d) To discharge or otherwise discriminate against an agricultural employee because he has filed charges or given testimony under this part.

(e) To refuse to bargain collectively in good faith with labor organizations certified pursuant to the provisions of Chapter 5 (commencing with Section 1156) of this part.

(f) To recognize, bargain with, or sign a collective-bargaining agreement with any labor organization not certified pursuant to the provisions of this part.

1154. It shall be an unfair labor practice for a labor organization or its agents to do any of the following:

(a) To restrain or coerce:

(1) Agricultural employees in the exercise of the rights guaranteed in Section 1152. This paragraph shall not impair the right of a labor organization to prescribe its own rules with respect to the acquisition or retention of membership therein.

(2) An agricultural employer in the selection of his representatives for the purposes of collective bargaining or the adjustment of grievances.

(b) To cause or attempt to cause an agricultural employer to discriminate against an employee in violation of subdivision (c) of Section 1153, or to discriminate against an employee with respect to whom membership in such organization has been denied or terminated for reasons other than failure to satisfy the membership requirements specified in subdivision (c) of Section 1153.

(c) To refuse to bargain collectively in good faith with an agricultural employer, provided it is the representative of his employees subject to the provisions of Chapter 5 (commencing with Section 1156) of this part.

(d) To do either of the following: (i) To engage in, or to induce or encourage any individual employed by any person to engage in, a strike or a refusal in the course of his employment to use, manufacture, process, transport, or otherwise handle or work on any goods, articles, materials, or commodities, or to perform any services; or (ii) to threaten, coerce, or restrain any person; where in either case (i) or (ii) an object thereof is any of the following:

(1) Forcing or requiring any employer or self-employed person to join any labor or employer organization or to enter into any agreement which is prohibited by Section 1154.5.

(2) Forcing or requiring any person to cease using, selling, transporting, or otherwise dealing in the products of any other producer, processor, or manufacturer, or to cease doing business with any other person, or forcing or requiring any other employer to recognize or bargain with a labor organization as the representative of his employees unless such labor organization has been certified as the representative of such employees. Nothing contained in this paragraph shall be construed to make unlawful, where not otherwise unlawful, any primary strike or primary picketing.

(3) Forcing or requiring any employer to recognize or bargain with a particular labor organization as the representative of his agricultural employees if another labor organization has been certified as the representative of such employees under the provisions of Chapter 5 (commencing with Section 1156) of this part.

(4) Forcing or requiring any employer to assign particular work to employees in a particular labor organization or in a particular trade, craft, or class, unless such employer is failing to conform to an order or certification of the board determining the bargaining representative for employees performing such work.

Consumer Boycotts Permitted

Nothing contained in this subdivision (d) shall be construed to prohibit publicity, including picketing for the purpose of truthfully advising the public, including consumers, that a product or products or ingredients thereof are produced by an agricultural employer with whom the labor organization has a primary dispute and are distributed by another employer, as long as such publicity does not have an effect of inducing any individual employed by any person other than the primary employer in the course of his employment to refuse to pick up, deliver, or transport any goods, or not to perform any services at the establishment of the employer engaged in such distribution, and as long as such publicity does not have the effect of requesting the public to cease patronizing such other employer.

However, publicity which includes picketing and has the effect of requesting the public to cease patronizing such other employer, shall be permitted only if the labor organization is currently certified as the representative of the primary employer's employees.

Further, publicity other than picketing, but including peaceful distribution of literature which has the effect of requesting the public to cease patronizing such other employer, shall be permitted only if the labor organization has not lost an election for the primary employer's employees within the preceding 12-month period, and no other labor organization is currently certified as the representative of the primary employer's employees.

Nothing contained in this subdivision (d) shall be construed to prohibit publicity, including picketing, which may not be prohibited under the United States Constitution or the California Constitution.

Nor shall anything in this subdivision (d) be construed to apply or be applicable to any labor organization in its representation of workers who are not agricultural employees. Any such labor organization shall continue to be governed in its intrastate activities for nonagricultural workers by Section 923 and applicable judicial precedents.

(e) To require of employees covered by an agreement authorized under subdivision (c) of Section 1153 the payment, as a condition precedent to becoming a member of such organization, of a fee in an amount which the board finds excessive or discriminatory under all circumstances. In making such a finding, the board shall consider, among other relevant factors, the practices and customs of labor organizations in the agriculture industry and the wages currently paid to the employees affected.

(f) To cause or attempt to cause an agricultural employer to pay or deliver, or agree to pay or deliver, any money or other thing of value, in the nature of an exaction, for services which are not performed or not to be performed.

(g) To picket or cause to be picketed, or threaten to picket or cause to be picketed, any employer where an object thereof is either forcing or requiring an employer to recognize or bargain with a labor organization as the representative of his employees, or forcing or requiring the employees of an employer to accept or select such labor organization as their collective-bargaining representative, unless such labor organization is currently certified as the representative of such employees, in any of the following cases:

(1) Where the employer has lawfully recognized in accordance with this part any other labor organization and a question concerning representation may not appropriately be raised under Section 1156.3.

(2) Where within the preceding 12 months a valid election under Chapter 5 (commencing with Section 1156) of this part has been conducted.

Nothing in this subdivision shall be construed to prohibit any picketing or other publicity for the purpose of truthfully advising the public (including consumers) that an employer does not employ members of, or have a contract with, a labor organization, unless an effect of such picketing is to induce an individual employed by any other person in the course of his employment, not to pick up, deliver, or transport any goods or not to perform any services.

Nothing in this subdivision (g) shall be construed to permit any act which would otherwise be an unfair labor practice under this section.

(h) To picket or cause to be picketed, or threaten to picket or cause to be picketed, any employer where an object thereof is either forcing or requiring an employer to recognize or bargain with the labor organization as a representative of his employees unless such labor organization is currently certified as the collective-bargaining representative of such employees.

(i) Nothing contained in this section shall be construed to make unlawful a refusal by any person to enter upon the premises of any agricultural employer, other than his own employer, if the employees of such employer are engaged in a strike ratified or approved by a representative of such employees whom such employer is required to recognize under this part.

Prohibited Secondary Boycotts

1154.5. It shall be an unfair labor practice for any labor organization which represents the employees of the employer and such employer to enter into any contract or agreement, express or implied, whereby such employer ceases or refrains, or agrees to cease or refrain, from handling, using, selling, transporting, or otherwise dealing in any of the products of any other employer, or to cease doing business with any other person, and any contract or agreement entered into heretofore or hereafter containing such an agreement shall be, to such extent, unenforceable and void. Nothing in this section shall apply to an agreement between a labor organization and an employer relating to a supplier of an ingredient or ingredients which are integrated into a product produced or distributed by such employer where the labor organization is certified as the representative of the employees of such supplier, but no collective-bargaining agreement between such supplier and such labor organization is in effect. Further, nothing in this section shall apply to an agreement between a labor organization and an agricultural employer relating to the contracting or subcontracting of work to be done at the site of the farm and related operations. Nothing in this part shall prohibit the enforcement of any agreement which is within the foregoing exceptions.

Nor shall anything in this section be construed to apply or be applicable to any labor organization in its representation of workers who are not agricultural employees. Any such labor organization shall continue to be governed in its intrastate activities for nonagricultural workers by Section 923 and applicable judicial precedents.

1154.6. It shall be an unfair labor practice for an employer or labor organization, or their agents, willfully to arrange for persons to become employees for the primary purpose of voting in elections.

1155. The expressing of any views, arguments, or opinions, or the dissemination thereof, whether in written, printed, graphic, or visual form, shall not constitute evidence of an unfair labor practice under the provisions of this part, if such expression contains no threat of reprisal or force, or promise of benefit.

1155.2. (a) For purposes of this part, to bargain collectively in good faith is the performance of the mutual obligation of the agricultural employer and the representative of the agricultural employees to meet at reasonable times and confer in good faith with respect to wages, hours, and other terms and conditions of employment, or the negotiation of an agreement, or any questions arising thereunder, and the execution of a written contract incorporating any agreement reached if requested by either party, but such obligation does not compel either party to agree to a proposal or require the making of a concession.

(b) Upon the filing by any person of a petition not earlier than the 90th day nor later than the 60th day preceding the expiration of the 12-month period following initial certification, the board shall determine whether an employer has bargained in good faith with the currently certified labor organization. If the board finds that the employer has not bargained in good faith, it may extend the certification for up to one additional year, effective immediately upon the expiration of the previous 12-month period following initial certification.

1155.3. (a) Where there is in effect a collective-bargaining contract covering agricultural employees, the duty to bargain collectively shall also mean that no party to such contract shall terminate or modify such contract, unless the party desiring such termination or modification does all of the following:

(1) Serves a written notice upon the other party to the contract of the proposed termination or modification not less than 60 days prior to the expiration date thereof, or, in the event such contract contains no expiration date, 60 days prior to the time it is proposed to make such termination or modification.

(2) Offers to meet and confer with the other party for the purpose of negotiating a new contract or a contract containing the proposed modifications.

(3) Notifies the Conciliation Service of the State of California within 30 days after such notice of the existence of a dispute, provided no agreement has been reached by that time.

(4) Continues in full force and effect, without resorting to strike or lockout, all the terms and conditions of the existing contract, for a period of 60 days after such notice is given, or until the expiration date of such contract, whichever occurs later.

(b) The duties imposed upon agricultural employers and labor organizations by paragraphs (2), (3), and (4) of subdivision (a) shall become inapplicable upon an intervening certification of the board that the labor organization or individual which is a party to the contract has been superseded as, or has ceased to be the representative of the employees, subject to the provisions of Chapter 5 (commencing with Section 1156) of this part, and the duties so imposed shall not be construed to require either party to discuss or agree to any modification of the terms and conditions contained in a contract for a fixed period, if such modification is to become effective before such terms and conditions can be reopened under the provisions of the contract. Any agricultural employee who engages in a strike within the 60-day period specified in this section shall lose his status as an agricultural employee of the agricultural employer engaged in the particular labor dispute, for the purposes of Section 1153 to 1154 inclusive, and Chapters 5 (commencing with Section 1156) and 6 (commencing with Section 1160) of this part, but such loss of status for such employee shall terminate if and when he is reemployed by such employer.

1155.4. It shall be unlawful for any agricultural employer or association of agricultural employers, or any person who acts as a labor relations expert, adviser, or consultant to an agricultural employer, or who acts in the interest of an agricultural employer, to pay, lend, or deliver, any money or other thing of value to any of the following:

(a) Any representative of any of his agricultural employees.

(b) Any agricultural labor organization, or any officer or employee thereof, which represents, seeks to represent, or would admit to membership, any of the agricultural employees of such employer.

(c) Any employee or group or committee of employees of such employer in excess of their normal compensation for the purpose of causing such employee or group or committee directly or indirectly to influence any other employees in the exercise of the right to organize and bargain collectively through representatives of their own choosing.

(d) Any officer or employee of an agricultural labor organization with intent to influence him in respect to any of his actions, decisions, or duties as a representative of agricultural employees or as such officer or employee of such labor organization.

1155.5. It shall be unlawful for any person to request, demand, receive, or accept, or agree to receive or accept, any payment, loan, or delivery of any money or other thing of value prohibited by Section 1155.4.

1155.6. Nothing in Section 1155.4 or 1155.5 shall apply to any matter set forth in subsection (c) of Section 186 of Title 29 of the United States Code.

1155.7. Nothing in this chapter shall be construed to apply or be applicable to any labor organization in its representation of workers who are not agricultural employees. Any such labor organization shall continue to be governed in its intrastate activities for nonagricultural workers by Section 923 and applicable judicial precedents.

Chapter 5. Labor Representatives and Elections

1156. Representatives designated or selected by a secret ballot for the purposes of collective bargaining by the majority of the agricultural employees in the bargaining unit shall be the exclusive representatives of all the agricultural employees in such unit for the purpose of collective bargaining with respect to rates of pay, wages, hours of employment, or other conditions of employment. Any individual agricultural employee or a group of agricultural employees shall have the right at any time to present grievances to their agricultural employer and to have such grievances adjusted, without the intervention of the bargaining representative, as long as the adjustment is not inconsistent with the terms of a collective-bargaining contract or agreement then in effect, if the bargaining representative has been given opportunity to be present at such adjustment.

1156.2. The bargaining unit shall be all the agricultural employees of an employer. If the agricultural employees of the employer are employed in two or more contiguous geographical areas, the board shall determine the appropriate unit or units of agricultural employees in which a secret ballot election shall be conducted.

1156.3. (a) A petition which is either signed by, or accompanied by authorization cards signed by, a majority of the currently employed employees in the bargaining unit may be filed in accordance with such rules and regulations as may be prescribed by the board, by an agricultural employee or group of agricultural employees, or any individual or labor organization acting in their behalf alleging all the following:

(1) That the number of agricultural employees currently employed by the employer named in the petition, as determined from his payroll immediately preceding the filing of the petition, is not less than 50 percent of his peak agricultural employment for the current calendar year.

(2) That no valid election pursuant to this section has been conducted among the agricultural employees of the employer named in the petition within the 12 months immediately preceding the filing thereof.

(3) That no labor organization is currently certified as the exclusive collective-bargaining representative of the agricultural employees of the employer named in the petition.

(4) That the petition is not barred by an existing collective-bargaining agreement.

Upon receipt of such a signed petition, the board shall immediately investigate such petition, and, if it has reasonable cause to believe that a bona fide question of representation exists, it shall direct a representation election by secret ballot to be held, upon due notice to all interested parties and within a maximum of seven days of the filing of the petition. If at the time the election petition is filed a majority of the employees in a bargaining unit are engaged in a strike, the board shall, with all due diligence, attempt to hold a secret ballot election within 48 hours of the filing of such petition. The holding of elections under strike circumstances shall take precedence over the holding of other secret ballot elections.

The board shall make available at any election under this chapter ballots printed in English and Spanish. The board may also make available at such election ballots printed in any other language as may be requested by an agricultural labor organization, or agricultural employee eligible to vote under this part. Every election ballot, except ballots in runoff elections where the choice is between labor organizations, shall provide the employee with the opportunity to vote against representation by a labor organization by providing an appropriate space designated "No Labor Organizations".

(b) Any other labor organization shall be qualified to appear on the ballot if it presents authorization cards signed by at least 20 percent of the employees in the bargaining unit at least 24 hours prior to the election.

(c) Within five days after an election, any person may file with the board a signed petition asserting that allegations made in the petition filed pursuant to subdivision (a) were incorrect, that the board improperly determined the geographical scope of the bargaining unit, or objecting to the conduct of the election or conduct affecting the results of the election.

Upon receipt of a petition under this subdivision, the board, upon due notice, shall conduct a hearing to determine whether the election shall be certified. Such hearing may be conducted by an officer or employee of a regional office of the board. He shall make no recommendations with respect thereto. If the board finds, on the record of such hearing, that any of the assertions made in the petition filed pursuant to this subdivision are correct, or that the election was not conducted properly, or misconduct affecting the results of the election occurred, the board may refuse to certify the election. Unless the board determines that there are sufficient grounds to refuse to do so, it shall certify the election.

(d) If no petition is filed pursuant to subdivision (c) within five days of the election the board shall certify the election.

(e) The board shall decertify a labor organization if the United States Equal Employment Opportunity Commission has found, pursuant to Section 2000(e) (5) of Title 42 of the United States Code, that the labor organization engaged in discrimination on the basis of race, color, national origin, religion, sex or any other arbitrary or invidious classification in violation of Subchapter VI of Chapter 21 of Title 42 of the United States Code during the period of such labor organization's present certification.

Harvest-time Strikes

1156.4. Recognizing that agriculture is a seasonal occupation for a majority of agricultural employees, and wishing to provide the fullest scope for employees' enjoyment of the rights included in this part, the board shall not consider a representation petition or a petition to decertify as timely filed unless the employer's payroll reflects 50 percent of the peak agricultural employment for such employer for the current calendar year for the payroll period immediately preceding the filing of the petition.

In this connection, the peak agricultural employment for the prior season shall alone not be a basis for such determination, but rather the board shall estimate peak employment on the basis of acreage and crop statistics which shall be applied uniformly throughout the State of California and upon all other relevant data.

1156.5. The board shall not direct an election in any bargaining unit where a valid election has been held in the immediately preceding 12-month period.

1156.6. The board shall not direct an election in any bargaining unit which is represented by a labor organization that has been certified within the immediately preceding 12-month period or whose certification has been extended pursuant to subdivision (b) of Section 1155.2.

1156.7. (a) No collective-bargaining agreement executed prior to the effective date of this chapter shall bar a petition for an election.

(b) A collective-bargaining agreement executed by an employer and a labor organization certified as the exclusive bargaining representative of his employees pursuant to this chapter shall be a bar to a petition for an election among such employees for the term of the agreement, but in any event such bar shall not exceed three years, provided that both the following conditions are met:

(1) The agreement is in writing and executed by all parties thereto.

(2) It incorporates the substantive terms and conditions of employment of such employees.

(c) Upon the filing with the board by an employee or group of employees of a petition signed by 30 percent or more of the agricultural employees in a bargaining unit represented by a certified labor organization which is a party to a valid collective-bargaining agreement, requesting that such labor organization be decertified, the board shall conduct an election by secret ballot pursuant to the applicable provisions of this chapter, and shall certify the results to such labor organizations and employer.

However, such a petition shall not be deemed timely unless it is filed during the year preceding the expiration of a collective-bargaining agreement which would otherwise bar the holding of an election, and when the number of agricultural employees is not less than 50 percent of the employer's peak agricultural employment for the current calendar year.

(d) Upon the filing with the board of a signed petition by an agricultural employee or group of agricultural employees, or any individual or labor organization acting in their behalf, accompanied by authorization cards signed by a majority of the employees in an appropriate bargaining unit, and alleging all the conditions of paragraphs (1), (2), and (3), the board shall immediately investigate such petition and, if it has reasonable cause to believe that a bona fide question of representation exists, it shall direct an election by secret ballot pursuant to the applicable provisions of this chapter:

(1) That the number of agricultural employees currently employed by the employer named in the petition, as determined from his payroll immediately preceding the filing of the petition, is not less than 50 percent of his peak agricultural employment for the current calendar year.

(2) That no valid election pursuant to this section has been conducted among the agricultural employees of the employer named in the petition within the 12 months immediately preceding the filing thereof.

(3) That a labor organization, certified for an appropriate unit, has a collective-bargaining agreement with the employer which would otherwise bar the holding of an election and that this agreement will expire within the next 12 months.

1157. All agricultural employees of the employer whose names appear on the payroll applicable to the payroll period immediately preceding the filing of the petition of such an election shall be eligible to vote. An economic striker shall be eligible to vote under such regulations as the board shall find are consistent with the purposes and provisions of this part in any election, provided that the striker who has been permanently replaced shall not be eligible to vote in any election conducted more than 12 months after the commencement of the strike.

In the case of elections conducted within 18 months of the effective date of this part which involve labor disputes which commenced prior to such effective date, the board shall have the jurisdiction to adopt fair, equitable, and appropriate eligibility rules, which shall effectuate the policies of this part, with respect to the eligibility of economic strikers who were paid for work performed or for paid vacation during the payroll period immediately preceding the expiration of a collective-bargaining agreement or the commencement of a strike; provided, however, that in no event shall the board afford eligibility to any such striker who has not performed any services for the employer during the 36-month period immediately preceding the effective date of this part.

1157.2. In any election where none of the choices on the ballot receives a majority, a runoff shall be conducted, the ballot providing for a selection between the two choices receiving the largest and second largest number of valid votes cast in the election.

1157.3. Employers shall maintain accurate and current payroll lists containing the names and addresses of all their employees, and shall make such lists available to the board upon request.

1158. Whenever an order of the board made pursuant to Section 1160.3 is based in whole or in part upon the facts certified following an investigation pursuant to Sections 1156.3 to 1157.2 inclusive, and there is a petition for review of such order, such certification and the record of such investigation shall be included in the transcript of the entire record required to be filed under Section 1160.8 and thereupon the decree of the court enforcing, modifying, or setting aside in whole or in part the order of the board shall be made and entered upon the pleadings, testimony, and proceedings set forth in such transcript.

1159. In order to assure the full freedom of association, self-organization, and designation of representatives of the employees own choosing, only labor organizations certified pursuant to this part shall be parties to a legally valid collective-bargaining agreement.

Chapter 6. Prevention of Unfair Labor Practices and Judicial Review and Enforcement

1160. The board is empowered, as provided in this chapter, to prevent any person from engaging in any unfair labor practice, as set forth in Chapter 4 (commencing with Section 1153) of this part.

1160.2. Whenever it is charged that any person has engaged in or is engaging in any such unfair labor practice, the board, or any agent or agency designated by the board for such purposes, shall have power to issue and cause to be served upon such person a complaint stating the charges in that respect, and containing a notice of hearing before the board or a member thereof, or before a designated agency or agencies, at a place therein fixed, not less than five days after the serving of such complaint. No complaint shall issue based upon any unfair labor practice occurring more than six months prior to the filing of the charge with the board and the service of a copy thereof upon the person against whom such charge is made, unless the person aggrieved thereby was prevented from filing such charge by reason of service in the armed forces, in which event the six-month period shall be computed from the day of his discharge. Any such complaint may be amended by the member, agent, or agency conducting the hearing, or the board in its discretion, at any time prior to the issuance of an order based thereon. The person so complained against shall have the right to file an answer to the original or amended complaint and to appear in person or otherwise and give testimony at the place and time fixed in the complaint. In the discretion of the member, agent, or agency conducting the hearing or the board, any other person may be allowed to intervene in the proceeding and to present testimony. Any such proceeding shall, so far as practicable, be conducted in accordance with the Evidence Code. All proceedings shall be appropriately reported.

1160.3. The testimony taken by such member, agent, or agency, or the board in such hearing shall be reduced to writing and filed with the board. Thereafter, in its discretion, the board, upon notice, may take further testimony or hear argument. If, upon the preponderance of the testimony taken, the board shall be of the opinion that any person named in the complaint has engaged in or is engaging in any such unfair labor practice, the board shall state its findings of fact and shall issue and cause to be served on such person an order requiring such person to cease and desist from such unfair labor practice, to take affirmative action, including reinstatement of employees with or without backpay, and making employees whole, when the board deems such relief appropriate, for the loss of pay resulting from the employer's refusal to bargain, and to provide such other relief as will effectuate the policies of this part. Where an order directs reinstatement of an employee, backpay may be required of the employer or labor organization, as the case may be, responsible for the discrimination suffered by him. Such order may further require such person to make reports from time to time showing the extent to which it has complied with the order. If, upon the preponderance of the testimony taken, the board shall be of the opinion that the person named in the complaint has not engaged in or is not engaging in any unfair labor practice, the board shall state its findings of fact and shall issue an order dismissing the complaint. No order of the board shall require the reinstatement of any individual as an employee who has been suspended or discharged, or the payment to him of any backpay, if such individual was suspended or discharged for cause. In case the evidence is presented before a member of the board, or before an administrative law officer thereof, such member, or such administrative law officer, as the case may be, shall issue and cause to be served on the parties to the proceedings a proposed report, together with a recommended order, which shall be filed with the board, and, if no exceptions are filed within 20 days after service thereof upon such parties, or within such further period as the board may authorize, such recommended order shall become the order of the board and become effective as therein prescribed.

Until the record in a case shall have been filed in a court, as provided in this chapter, the board may, at any time upon reasonable notice and in such manner as it shall deem proper, modify or set aside, in whole or in part, any finding or order made or issued by it.

1160.4. The board shall have power, upon issuance of a complaint as provided in Section 1160.2 charging that any person has engaged in or is engaging in an unfair labor practice, to petition the superior court in any county wherein the unfair labor practice in question is alleged to have occurred, or wherein such person resides or transacts business, for appropriate temporary relief or restraining order. Upon the filing of any such petition, the board shall cause notice thereof to be served upon such person, and thereupon the court shall have jurisdiction to grant to the board such temporary relief or restraining order as the court deems just and proper.

1160.5. Whenever it is charged that any person has engaged in an unfair labor practice within the meaning of paragraph (4) of subdivision (d) of Section 1154, the board is empowered and directed to hear and determine the dispute out of which such unfair labor practice shall have arisen, unless within 10 days after notice that such charge has been filed, the parties to such dispute submit to the board satisfactory evidence that they have adjusted, or agreed upon methods for the voluntary adjustment of the dispute. Upon compliance by the parties to the dispute with the decision of the board or upon such voluntary adjustment of the dispute, such charge shall be dismissed.

1160.6. Whenever it is charged that any person has engaged in an unfair labor practice within the meaning of paragraph (1), (2), or (3) of subdivision (d), or of subdivision (g), of Section 1154, or of Section 1155, the preliminary investigation of such charge shall be made forthwith and given priority over all other cases except cases of like character in the office where it is filed or to which it is referred. If, after such investigation, the officer or regional attorney to whom the matter may be referred has reasonable cause to believe such charge is true and that a complaint should issue, he shall, on behalf of the board, petition the superior court in the county in which the unfair labor practice in question has occurred, is alleged to have occurred, or where the person alleged to have committed the unfair labor practice resides or transacts business, for appropriate injunctive relief pending the final adjudication of the board with respect to the matter. The officer or regional attorney shall make all reasonable efforts to advise the party against whom the restraining order is sought of his intention to seek such order at least 24 hours prior to doing so. In the event the officer or regional attorney has been unable to advise such party of his intent at least 24 hours in advance, he shall submit a declaration to the court under penalty of perjury setting forth in detail the efforts he has made. Upon the filing of any such petition, the superior court shall have jurisdiction to grant such injunctive relief or temporary restraining order as it deems just and proper. Upon the filing of any such petition, the board shall cause notice thereof to be served upon any person involved in the charge and such person, including the charging party, shall be given an opportunity to appear by counsel and present any relevant testimony. For the purposes of this section, the superior court shall be deemed to have jurisdiction of a labor organization either in the county in which such organization maintains its principal office, or in any county in which its duly authorized officers or agents are engaged in promoting or protecting the interests of employee members. The service of legal process upon such officer or agent shall constitute service upon the labor organization and make such organization a party to the suit. In situations where such relief is appropriate, the procedures specified herein shall apply to charges with respect to paragraph (4) of subdivision (d) of Section 1154.

1160.7. Whenever it is charged that any person has engaged in an unfair labor practice within the meaning of subdivision (c) of Section 1153 or subdivision (b) of Section 1154, such charge shall be given priority over all other cases except cases of like character in the office where it is filed or to which it is referred and cases given priority under Section 1160.6.

1160.8. Any person aggrieved by the final order of the board granting or denying in whole or in part the relief sought may obtain a review of such order in the court of appeal having jurisdiction over the county wherein the unfair labor practice in question was alleged to have been engaged in, or wherein such person resides or transacts business, by filing in such court a written petition requesting that the order of the board be modified or set aside. Such petition shall be filed with the court within 30 days from the date of the issuance of the board's order. Upon the filing of such petition, the court shall cause notice to be served upon the board and thereupon shall have jurisdiction of the proceeding. The board shall file in the court the record of the proceeding, certified by the board within 10 days after the clerk's notice unless such time is extended by the court for good cause shown. The court shall have jurisdiction to grant to the board such temporary relief or restraining order it deems just and proper and in like manner to make and enter a decree enforcing, modifying and enforcing as so modified, or setting aside in whole or in part, the order of the board. The findings of the board with respect to questions of fact if supported by substantial evidence on the record considered as a whole shall in like manner be conclusive.

An order directing an election shall not be stayed pending review, but such order may be reviewed as provided in Section 1158.

If the time for review of the board order has lapsed, and the person has not voluntarily complied with the board's order, the board may apply to the superior court in any county in which the unfair labor practice occurred or wherein such person resides or transacts business for enforcement of its order. If after the hearing, the court determines that the order was issued pursuant to procedures established by the board and that the person refuses to comply with the order, the court shall enforce such order by writ of injunction or other proper process. The court shall not review the merits of the order.

1160.9. The procedures set forth in this chapter shall be the exclusive method of redressing unfair labor practices.

Chapter 7. Suits Involving Employers and Labor Organizations

1165. (a) Suits for violation of contracts between an agricultural employer and an agricultural labor organization representing agricultural employees, as defined in this part, or between any such labor organizations, may be brought in any superior court having jurisdiction of the parties, without respect to the amount in controversy.

(b) Any agricultural labor organization which represents agricultural employees and any agricultural employer shall be bound by the acts of its agents. Any such labor organization may sue or be sued as an entity and in behalf of the employees whom it represents in the courts of this state. Any money judgment against a labor organization in a superior court shall be enforceable only against the organization as an entity and against its assets, and shall not be enforceable against any individual member or his assets.

1165.2. For the purpose of this part, the superior court shall have jurisdiction over a labor organization in this state if such organization maintains its principal office in this state, or if its duly authorized officers or agents are engaged in representing or acting for employee members.

1165.3. The service of summons, subpoena, or other legal process of any superior court upon an officer or agent of a labor organization, in his capacity as such, shall constitute service upon the labor organization.

1165.4. For the purpose of this part, in determining whether any person is acting as an agent of another person so as to make such other person responsible for his acts, the question of whether the specific acts performed were actually authorized or subsequently ratified shall not be controlling.

Chapter 8. Limitations

1166. Nothing in this part, except as specifically provided for herein, shall be construed so as either to interfere with or impede or diminish in any way the right to strike, or to affect the limitations or qualifications on such right.

1166.2. Nothing in this part shall prohibit any individual employed as a supervisor from becoming or remaining a member of a labor organization, but no employer subject to this part shall be compelled to deem individuals defined herein as supervisors as employees for the purpose of any law, either national or local, relating to collective bargaining.

1166.3. (a) If any provision of this part, or the application of such provision to any person or circumstances, shall be held invalid, the remainder of this part, or the application of such provision to persons or circumstances other than those as to which it is held invalid, shall not be affected thereby.

(b) If any other act of the Legislature shall conflict with the provisions of this part, this part shall prevail.

SEC. 3. No appropriation is made by this act, nor is any obligation created thereby under Section 2231 of the Revenue and Taxation Code, for the reimbursement of any local agency for any costs that may be incurred by it in carrying on any program or performing any service required to be carried on or performed by it by this act.

ROCKEFELLER COMMISSION REPORT ON CENTRAL INTELLIGENCE AGENCY

June 10, 1975

On Dec. 22, 1974, The New York Times *published assertions that the Central Intelligence Agency (CIA) had launched "a massive, illegal domestic intelligence operation during the Nixon administration against the antiwar movement and other dissident groups." Times reporter Seymour Hersh said the agency had amassed files on American citizens and engaged in unlawful "break-ins, wiretapping and surreptitious interception of mail" far beyond the limits of its statutory authority. These and subsequent published charges of CIA complicity in the assassination of foreign heads of state set in train a series of investigations, unprecedented in scope, of the entire U.S. intelligence community.*

The first official report to the nation on charges against the CIA came June 10 when President Ford released the findings of a prestigious commission chaired by Vice President Nelson A. Rockefeller. Special congressional investigatory committees with broader mandates covering, in addition to the CIA, the Federal Bureau of Investigation (FBI), the National Security Agency (NSA), and other federal intelligence and law enforcement units began releasing their findings in November (see p. 709). Ford had established the Rockefeller panel in January to examine the charges publicized by the Times, and he subsequently suggested that the panel also look into published accounts of CIA involvement in plots in the early 1960s to assassinate such foreign leaders as Cuban Premier Fidel Castro, Dominican Republic President Rafael Trujillo and South Vietnamese President Ngo Dinh Diem.

Panel Findings

The Rockefeller panel found that certain activities undertaken by the CIA were "plainly unlawful and...improper invasions upon the rights of Americans." But it concluded that the "great majority" of the agency's domestic activities were in keeping with provisions of the 1947 act creating the CIA. Although the commission confirmed to a large extent the newspaper accounts of domestic improprieties, it considered such improprieties as lapses of judgment rather than parts of a coordinated, "massive" domestic program.

The panel also disclosed previously unreported questionable or illegal actions, including:

● President Nixon's acquisition of classified CIA data—on the Bay of Pigs invasion, the Cuban missile crisis, and events in Vietnam—"to serve the President's personal political ends";
● A 20-year agreement under which the Justice Department authorized the CIA to investigate crimes allegedly committed by its agents and decide whether or not prosecution was warranted. The commission found no evidence of abuses but concluded that the arrangement was "an abdication by the Justice Department of its statutory responsibilities";
● A "clearly illegal" CIA program testing the influence of drugs on human behavior. In 1953 the tests led to the death of one person following administration of the hallucinogen LSD, the report said.

The commission did not publish results of its unfinished inquiry into charges of CIA involvement in foreign assassinations. Information already gathered was turned over to the President, who promised to pass it on to the congressional committees and to the Justice Department for possible prosecution. Numerous recommendations to tighten congressional and executive control over the CIA were included in the Rockefeller report, but the outlook for their acceptance was clouded by the failure of earlier attempts to make the CIA more accountable to Congress.

Previous Allegations

Charges of serious abuses of power by the CIA had been accruing since 1972, when columnist Jack Anderson accused the agency of improper interference in the internal affairs of Chile at the behest of the International Telephone & Telegraph corporation. Prior to that time, the only scandal of any consequence to touch the CIA had come to light in 1967 when the National Student Association admitted that the agency, over a period of ten years or longer, had funneled more than $3-million to that association through various foundations. This covert support to the nation's largest college student organization had financed international activities, including educational exchange programs and sending American students to conferences abroad.

Testimony before a Senate subcommittee in 1973 corroborated Anderson's charges that an ITT official and a former CIA director had approached then-CIA Director Richard Helms in 1970 with an offer to provide corporate funds to help the agency block the election of Marxist Salvador Allende Gossens as president of Chile. It later became known that the CIA itself had been authorized to spend more than $8-million, following Allende's election, to "destabilize" the new Chilean government. The acknowledgement was made in House testimony in April 1974 by CIA Director William E. Colby (see Historic Documents of 1974, p. 805). (Allende's government was overthrown and Allende met his death in a military coup in September 1973.)

The CIA had already been seriously compromised by the disclosure in 1973 of its participation in illegal projects originating in the Nixon White House. In 1971 the agency had furnished equipment to aid in the burglary of the office of Daniel Ellsberg's psychiatrist. The break-in was part of a White House effort to discredit Ellsberg, who had made the top secret Pentagon Papers on U.S. policy during the Vietnam War available for publication. CIA psychiatrists had also prepared two "personality profiles" on Ellsberg at the request of the White House. When these and other unlawful government actions were disclosed, espionage charges against Ellsberg were dismissed (see Historic Documents 1973, p. 537).

Reaction to Rockefeller Report

Members of Congress and editorial writers generally praised the report of the eight-man Rockefeller commission but looked to ongoing House and Senate investigations to provide answers about the assassination charges and alleged transgressions by the FBI, NSA and military intelligence operations.

In the wake of the panel's report, the Justice Department gave up the special arrangement regarding prosecution of CIA employees. President Ford had prepared his own proposals for reorganizing the intelligence community, according to a Washington Post *report in October. The proposals were said to follow commission recommendations for a White House-based inspector general to oversee the agency and a joint congressional oversight committee modeled after the Joint Committee on Atomic Energy.*

Summary of the Investigation, *Part I of the* Report to the President by the Commission on CIA Activities within the United States *(the Rockefeller Commission), published June 10, 1975:*

Chapter 1

The Fundamental Issues

In announcing the formation of this Commission, the President noted that an effective intelligence and counterintelligence capability is essential to provide "the safeguards that protect our national interest and help avert armed conflicts."

While it is vital that security requirements be met, the President continued, it is equally important that intelligence activities be conducted without "impairing our democratic institutions and fundamental freedoms."

The Commission's assessment of the CIA's activities within the United States reflects the members' deep concern for both individual rights and national security.

A. Individual Rights

The Bill of Rights in the Constitution protects individual liberties against encroachment by government. Many statutes and the common law also reflect this protection.

The First Amendment protects the freedoms of speech and of the press, the right of the people to assemble peaceably, and the right to petition the government for redress of grievances. It has been construed to protect freedom of peaceable political association. In addition, the Fourth Amendment declares:

> The right of the people to be secure in their persons, houses, papers, and effects, against unreasonable searches and seizures, shall not be violated....

In accordance with the objectives enunciated in these and other Constitutional amendments, the Supreme Court has outlined the following basic Constitutional doctrines:

> 1. Any intrusive investigation of an American citizen by the government must have a sufficient basis to warrant the invasion caused by the particular investigative practices which are utilized;
> 2. Government monitoring of a citizen's political activities requires even greater justification;
> 3. The scope of any resulting intrusion on personal privacy must not exceed the degree reasonably believed necessary;
> 4. With certain exceptions, the scope of which are not sharply defined, these conditions must be met, at least for significant investigative intrusions, to the satisfaction of an uninvolved governmental body such as a court.

These Constitutional standards give content to an accepted principle of our society—the right of each person to a high degree of individual privacy.

In recognition of this right, President Truman and the Congress—in enacting the law creating the CIA in 1947—included a clause providing that the CIA should have no police, subpoena, law-enforcement powers or internal security functions.

Since then, Congress has further outlined citizen rights in statutes limiting electronic surveillance and granting individuals access to certain information in government files, underscoring the general concern of Congress and the Executive Branch in this area.

B. Government Must Obey the Law

The individual liberties of American citizens depend on government observance of the law.

Under our form of Constitutional government, authority can be exercised only if it has been properly delegated to a particular department or agency by the Constitution or Congress.

Most delegations come from Congress; some are implied from the allocation of responsibility to the President. Wherever the basic authority resides, however, it is fundamental in our scheme of Constitutional government that agencies—including the CIA—shall exercise only those powers properly assigned to them by Congress or the President.

Whenever the activities of a government agency exceed its authority, individual liberty may be impaired.

C. National Security

Individual liberties likewise depend on maintaining public order at home and in protecting the country against infiltration from abroad and armed attack. Ensuring domestic tranquility and providing for a common defense are not only Constitutional goals but necessary preconditions for a free, democratic system. The process of orderly and lawful change is the essence of democracy. Violent change, or forcing a change of government by the stealthy action of "enemies, foreign or domestic," is contrary to our Constitutional system.

The government has both the right and the obligation within Constitutional limits to use its available power to protect the people and their established form of government. Nevertheless, the mere invocation of the "national security" does not grant unlimited power to the government. The degree of the danger and the type of action contemplated to meet that danger require careful evaluation, to ensure that the danger is sufficient to justify the action and that fundamental rights are respected.

D. Resolving the Issues

Individual freedoms and privacy are fundamental in our society. Constitutional government must be maintained. An effective and efficient intelligence system is necessary; and to be effective, many of its activities must be conducted in secrecy.

Satisfying these objectives presents considerable opportunity for conflict. The vigorous pursuit of intelligence by certain methods can lead to invasions of individual rights. The preservation of the United States requires an effective intelligence capability, but the preservation of individual liberties within the United States requires limitations or restrictions on gathering of intelligence. The drawing of reasonable lines—where legitimate intelligence needs end and erosion of Constitutional government begins—is difficult.

In seeking to draw such lines, we have been guided in the first instance by the commands of the Constitution as they have been interpreted by the Supreme Court, the laws as written by Congress, the values we believe are reflected in the democratic process, and the faith we have in a free society. We have also sought to be fully cognizant of the needs of national security, the requirements of a strong national defense against external aggression and internal subversion, and the duty of the government to protect its citizens.

In the final analysis, public safety and individual liberty sustain each other.

Chapter 2

The Need for Intelligence

During the period of the Commission's inquiry, there have been public allegations that a democracy does not need an intelligence apparatus. The Commission does not share this view. Intelligence is information gathered for policymakers in government which illuminates the range of choices available to them and enables them to exercise judgment. Good intelligence will not necessarily lead to wise policy choices. But without sound intelligence, national policy decisions and actions cannot effectively respond to actual conditions and reflect the best national interest or adequately protect our national security.

Intelligence gathering involves collecting information about other countries' military capabilities, subversive activities, economic conditions, political developments, scientific and technological progress, and social activities and conditions. The raw information must be evaluated to determine its reliability and relevance, and must then be analyzed. The final products—called "finished intelligence"—are distributed to the President and the political, military and other governmental leaders according to their needs.

Intelligence gathering has changed rapidly and radically since the advent of the CIA in 1947. The increased complexity of international political, economic, and military arrangements, the increased destructiveness of the weapons of modern warfare, and the advent of electronic methods of surveillance have altered and enlarged the needs for sophisticated intelligence.

Intelligence agencies have had to rely more and more on scientific and technological developments to help meet these needs.

Despite the increasing complexity and significance of intelligence in national policymaking, it is also important to understand its limits. Not all information is reliable, even when the most highly refined intelligence methods are used to collect it. Nor can any intelligence system ensure that its current estimates of another country's intentions or future capacities are accurate or will not be outrun by unforeseen events. There are limits to accurate forecasting, and the use of deception by our adversaries or the penetration of our intelligence services increases the possibility that intelligence predictions may prove to be wrong. Nevertheless, informed decision-making is impossible without an intelligence system adequately protected from penetration.

Therefore, a vital part of any intelligence service is an effective counterintelligence program, directed toward protecting our own intelligence system and ascertaining the activities of foreign intelligence services, such as espionage, sabotage, and subversion, and toward minimizing or counteracting the effectiveness of these activities.

Foreign Invasions of United States Privacy

This Commission is devoted to analyzing the domestic activities of the CIA in the interest of protecting the privacy and security rights of American citizens. But we cannot ignore the invasion of the privacy and security rights of Americans by foreign countries or their agents. This is the other side of the coin—and it merits attention here in the interest of perspective.

Witnesses with responsibilities for counterintelligence have told the Commission that the United States remains the principal intelligence target of the communist bloc.

The communists invest large sums of money, personnel and sophisticated technology in collecting information—within the United States—on our military capabilities, our weapons systems, our defense structure and our social divisions. The communists seek to penetrate our intelligence services, to compromise our law enforcement agencies and to recruit as their agents United States citizens holding sensitive government and industry jobs. In addition, it is a common practice in communist bloc countries to inspect and open mail coming from or going to the United States.

In an open society such as ours, the intelligence opportunities for our adversaries are immeasurably greater than they are for us in their closed societies. Our society must remain an open one, with our traditional freedoms unimpaired. But when the intelligence activities of other countries are flourishing in the free environment we afford them, it is all the more essential that the foreign intelligence activities of the CIA and our other intelligence agencies, as well as the domestic counterintelligence activities of the FBI, be given the support necessary to protect our national security and to shield the privacy and rights of American citizens from foreign intrusion.

The Commission has received estimates that communist bloc intelligence forces currently number well over 500,000 worldwide.

The number of communist government officials in the United States has tripled since 1960, and is still increasing. Nearly 2,000 of them are now in this country—and a significant percentage of them have been identified as members of intelligence or security agencies. Conservative estimates for the number of unidentified intelligence officers among the remaining officials raise the level to over 40 percent.

In addition to sending increasing numbers of their citizens to this country openly, many of whom have been trained in espionage, communist bloc countries also place considerable emphasis on the training, provision of false identification and dispatching of "illegal" agents—that is, operatives for whom an alias identity has been systematically developed which enables them to live in the United States as American citizens or resident aliens without our knowledge of their true origins.

While making large-scale use of human intelligence sources, the communist countries also appear to have developed electronic collection of intelligence to an extraordinary degree of technology and sophistication for use in the United States and elsewhere throughout the world, and we believe that these countries can monitor and record thousands of private telephone conversations. Americans have a right to be uneasy if not seriously disturbed at the real possibility that their personal and business activities which they discuss freely over the telephone could be recorded and analyzed by agents of foreign powers.

This raises the real specter that selected American users of telephones are potentially subject to blackmail that can seriously affect their actions, or even lead in some cases to recruitment as espionage agents.

Chapter 3

Summary of Findings, Conclusions, and Recommendations

As directed by the President, the Commission has investigated the role and authority of the CIA, the adequacy of the internal controls and external supervision of the Agency, and its significant domestic activities that raise questions of compliance with the limits on its statutory authority. This chapter summarizes the findings and conclusions of the Commission and sets forth its recommendations.

A. Summary of Charges and Findings

The initial public charges were that the CIA's domestic activities had involved:

1. Large-scale spying on American citizens in the United States by the CIA, whose responsibility is foreign intelligence.

2. Keeping dossiers on large numbers of American citizens.

3. Aiming these activities at Americans who have expressed their disagreement with various government policies.

These initial charges were subsequently supplemented by others including allegations that the CIA:

—Had intercepted and opened personal mail in the United States for 20 years;

—Had infiltrated domestic dissident groups and otherwise intervened in domestic politics;

—Had engaged in illegal wiretaps and break-ins; and,

—Had improperly assisted other government agencies.

In addition, assertions have been made ostensibly linking the CIA to the assassination of President John F. Kennedy.

It became clear from the public reaction to these charges that the secrecy in which the Agency necessarily operates, combined with the allegations of wrongdoing, had contributed to widespread public misunderstanding of the Agency's actual practices.

A detailed analysis of the facts has convinced the Commission that the great majority of the CIA's domestic activities comply with its statutory authority.

Nevertheless, over the 28 years of its history, the CIA has engaged in some activities that should be criticized and not permitted to happen again—both in light of the limits imposed on the Agency by law and as a matter of public policy.

Some of these activities were initiated or ordered by Presidents, either directly or indirectly.

Some of them fall within the doubtful area between responsibilities delegated to the CIA by Congress and the National Security Council on the one hand and activities specifically prohibited to the Agency on the other.

Some of them were plainly unlawful and constituted improper invasions upon the rights of Americans.

The Agency's own recent actions, undertaken for the most part in 1973 and 1974, have gone far to terminate the activities upon which this investigation has focused. The recommendations of the Commission are designed to clarify areas of doubt concerning the Agency's authority, to strengthen the Agency's structure, and to guard against recurrences of these improprieties.

B. The CIA's Role and Authority

The Central Intelligence Agency was established by the National Security Act of 1947 as the nation's first comprehensive peacetime foreign intelligence service. The objective was to provide the President with coordinated intelligence, which the country lacked prior to the attack on Pearl Harbor.

The Director of Central Intelligence reports directly to the President. The CIA receives its policy direction and guidance from the National Security Council, composed of the President, the Vice President, and the Secretaries of State and Defense.

The statute directs the CIA to correlate, evaluate, and disseminate intelligence obtained from United States intelligence agencies, and to perform such other functions related to intelligence as the National Security Council directs. Recognizing that the CIA would be dealing with sensitive, secret materials, Congress made the Director of Central Intelligence responsible for protecting intelligence sources and methods from unauthorized disclosure.

At the same time, Congress sought to assure the American public that it was not establishing a secret police which would threaten the civil liberties of Americans. It specifically forbade the CIA from exercising "police, subpoena, or law-enforcement powers or internal security functions." The CIA was not to replace the Federal Bureau of Investigation in conducting domestic activities to investigate crime or internal subversion.

Although Congress contemplated that the focus of the CIA would be on foreign intelligence, it understood that some of its activities would be conducted within the United States. The CIA necessarily maintains its headquarters here, procures logistical support, recruits and trains employees, tests equipment, and conducts other domestic activities in support of its foreign intelligence mission. It makes necessary investigations in the United States to maintain the security of its facilities and personnel.

Additionally, it has been understood from the beginning that the CIA is permitted to collect foreign intelligence—that is, information concerning foreign capabilities, intentions, and activities—from American citizens within this country by overt means.

Determining the legal propriety of domestic activities of the CIA requires the application of the law to the particular facts involved. This task involves consideration of more than the National Security Act and the directives of the National Security Council; Constitutional and other statutory provisions also circumscribe the domestic activities of the CIA. Among the applicable Constitutional provisions are the First Amendment, protecting freedom of speech, of the press, and of peaceable assembly; and the Fourth Amendment, prohibiting unreasonable searches and seizures. Among the statutory provisions are those which limit such activities as electronic eavesdropping and interception of the mails.

The precise scope of many of these statutory and Constitutional provisions is not easily stated. The National Security Act in particular was drafted in broad terms in order to provide flexibility for the CIA to adapt to changing intelligence needs. Such critical phrases as "internal security functions" are left undefined. The meaning of the Director's responsibility to protect intelligence sources and methods from unauthorized disclosure has also been a subject of uncertainty.

The word "foreign" appears nowhere in the statutory grant of authority, though it has always been understood that the CIA's mission is limited to matters related to foreign intelligence. This apparent statutory ambiguity, although not posing problems in practice, has troubled members of the public who read the statute without having the benefit of the legislative history and the instructions to the CIA from the National Security Council.

The evidence within the scope of this inquiry does not indicate that fundamental rewriting of the National Security Act is either necessary or appropriate.

The evidence does demonstrate the need for some statutory and administrative clarification of the role and function of the Agency.

Ambiguities have been partially responsible for some, though not all, of the Agency's deviations within the United States from its assigned mission. In some cases, reasonable persons will differ as to the lawfulness of the activity; in others, the absence of clear guidelines as to its authority deprived the Agency of a means of resisting pressures to engage in activities which now appear to us improper.

Greater public awareness of the limits of the CIA's domestic authority would do much to reassure the American people.

The requisite clarification can best be accomplished (a) through a specific amendment clarifying the National Security Act provision which delineates the permissible scope of CIA activities, as set forth in Recommendation 1, and (b) through issuance of an Executive Order further limiting domestic activities of the CIA, as set forth in Recommendation 2.

Recommendation (1)

Section 403 of the National Security Act of 1947 should be amended in the form set forth in Appendix VI to this Report. These amendments, in summary, would:

a. Make explicit that the CIA's activities must be related to *foreign* intelligence.

b. Clarify the responsibility of the CIA to protect intelligence sources and methods from unauthorized disclosure. (The agency would be responsible for protecting against unauthorized disclosures within the CIA, and it would be responsible for providing guidance and technical assistance to other agency and department heads in protecting against unauthorized disclosures within their own agencies and departments.)

c. Confirm publicly the CIA's existing authority to collect foreign intelligence from willing sources within the United States, and, except as specified by the President in a published Executive Order, [Footnote: The Executive Order authorized by this statute should recognize that when the collection of foreign intelligence from persons who are not United States citizens results in the incidental acquisition of information from unknowing citizens, the Agency should be permitted to make appropriate use or disposition of such information. Such collection activities must be directed at foreign intelligence sources, and the involvement of American citizens must be incidental.] prohibit the CIA from collection efforts within the United States directed at securing foreign intelligence from unknowing American citizens.

411

Recommendation (2)

The President should by Executive Order prohibit the CIA from the collection of information about the domestic activities of United States citizens (whether by overt or covert means), the evaluation, correlation, and dissemination of analyses or reports about such activities, and the storage of such information, with exceptions for the following categories of persons or activities:

a. Persons presently or formerly affiliated, or being considered for affiliation, with the CIA, directly or indirectly, or others who require clearance by the CIA to receive classified information;

b. Persons or activities that pose a clear threat to CIA facilities or personnel, provided that proper coordination with the FBI is accomplished;

c. Persons suspected of espionage or other illegal activities relating to foreign intelligence, provided that proper coordination with the FBI is accomplished.

d. Information which is received incidental to appropriate CIA activities may be transmitted to an agency with appropriate jurisdiction, including law enforcement agencies.

Collection of information from normal library sources such as newspapers, books, magazines and other such documents is not to be affected by this order.

Information currently being maintained which is inconsistent with the order should be destroyed at the conclusion of the current congressional investigations or as soon thereafter as permitted by law.

The CIA should periodically screen its files and eliminate all material inconsistent with the order.

The order should be issued after consultation with the National Security Council, the Attorney General, and the Director of Central Intelligence. Any modification of the order would be permitted only through published amendments.

C. Supervision and Control of the CIA

1. External Controls (Chapter 7)

The CIA is subject to supervision and control by various executive agencies and by the Congress.

Congress has established special procedures for review of the CIA and its secret budget within four small subcommittees. [Footnote: Subcommittees of the Appropriations Committees and the Armed Services Committees of the two houses.] Historically, these subcommittees have been composed of members of Congress with many other demands on their time. The CIA has not as a general rule received detailed scrutiny by the Congress.

The principal bodies within the Executive Branch performing a supervisory or control function are the National Security Council, which gives the CIA its policy direction and control; the Office of Management and Budget, which reviews the CIA's budget in much the same fashion as it reviews budgets of other government agencies; and the President's Foreign Intelligence Advisory Board, which is composed of distinguished citizens, serving part time in a general advisory function for the President on the quality of the gathering and interpretation of intelligence.

None of these agencies has the specific responsibility of overseeing the CIA to determine whether its activities are proper.

The Department of Justice also exercises an oversight role, through its power to initiate prosecutions for criminal misconduct. For a period of over 20 years, however, an agreement existed between the Department of Justice and the CIA providing that the Agency was to investigate allegations of crimes by CIA employees or agents which involved Government money or property or might involve operational security. If, following the investigation, the Agency determined that there was no reasonable basis to believe a crime had been committed, or that operational security aspects precluded prosecution, the case was not referred to the Department of Justice.

The Commission has found nothing to indicate that the CIA abused the function given it by the agreement. The agreement, however, involved the Agency directly in forbidden law enforcement activities, and represented an abdication by the Department of Justice of its statutory responsibilities.

Some improvement in the congressional oversight system would be helpful. The problem of providing adequate oversight and control while maintaining essential security is not easily resolved. Several knowledgeable witnesses pointed to the Joint Committee on Atomic Energy as an appropriate model for congressional oversight of the Agency. That Committee has had an excellent record of providing effective oversight while avoiding breaches of security in a highly sensitive area.

One of the underlying causes of the problems confronting the CIA arises out of the pervading atmosphere of secrecy in which its activities have been conducted in the past. One aspect of this has been the secrecy of the budget.

A new body is needed to provide oversight of the Agency within the Executive Branch. Because of the need to preserve security, the CIA is not subject to the usual constraints of audit, judicial review, publicity or open congressional budget review and oversight. Consequently, its operations require additional external control. The authority assigned the job of supervising the CIA must be given sufficient power and significance to assure the public of effective supervision.

The situation whereby the Agency determined whether its own employees would be prosecuted must not be permitted to recur.

Recommendation (3)

The President should recommend to Congress the establishment of a Joint Committee on Intelligence to assume the oversight role currently played by the Armed Services Committees.

Recommendation (4)

Congress should give careful consideration to the question whether the budget of the CIA should not, at least to some extent, be made public, particularly in view of the provisions of Article I, Section 9, Clause 7 of the Constitution.

Recommendation (5)

a. The functions of the President's Foreign Intelligence Advisory Board should be expanded to include oversight of the CIA. This expanded oversight board should be composed of distinguished citizens with varying backgrounds and experience. It should be headed by a full-time chairman and should have a full-time staff appropriate to its role. Its functions related to the CIA should include:

    1. Assessing compliance by the CIA with its statutory authority.

    2. Assessing the quality of foreign intelligence collection.

    3. Assessing the quality of foreign intelligence estimates.

    4. Assessing the quality of the organization of the CIA.

    5. Assessing the quality of the management of the CIA.

    6. Making recommendations with respect to the above subjects to the President and Director of Central Intelligence, and, where appropriate, the Attorney General.

b. The Board should have access to all information in the CIA. It should be authorized to audit and investigate CIA expenditures and activities on its own initiative.

c. The Inspector General of the CIA should be authorized to report directly to the Board, after having notified the Director of Central Intelligence, in cases he deems appropriate.

Recommendation (6)

The Department of Justice and the CIA should establish written guidelines for the handling of reports of criminal violations by employees of the Agency or relating to its affairs. These guidelines should require that the criminal investigation and the decision whether to prosecute be made by the Department of Justice, after consideration of Agency views regarding the impact of prosecution on the national security. The Agency should be permitted to conduct such investigations as it requires to determine whether its operations have been jeopardized. The Agency should scrupulously avoid exercise of the prosecutorial function.

2. Internal Controls (Chapter 8)

The Director's duties in administering the intelligence community, handling relations with other components of the government, and passing on broad questions of policy leave him little time for day-to-day supervision of the Agency. Past studies have noted the need for the Director to delegate greater responsibility for the administration of the Agency to the Deputy Director of Central Intelligence.

In recent years, the position of Deputy Director has been occupied by a high-ranking military officer, with responsibilities for maintaining liaison with the Department of Defense, fostering the Agency's relationship with the military services, and providing top CIA management with necessary experience and skill in understanding particular intelligence requirements of the military. Generally speaking, the Deputy Directors of Central Intelligence have not been heavily engaged in administration of the Agency.

Each of the four directorates within the CIA—Operations, Intelligence, Administration, and Science and Technology—is headed by a deputy director who reports to the Director and Deputy Director of Central Intelligence. These four deputies, together with certain other top Agency officials such as the Comptroller, form the Agency Management Committee, which makes many of the administrative and management decisions affecting more than one directorate.

Outside the chain of command, the primary internal mechanism for keeping the Agency within bounds is the Inspector General. The size of this office was recently sharply reduced, and its previous practice of making regular reviews of various Agency departments was terminated. At the present time, the activities of the office are almost entirely concerned with coordinating Agency responses to the various investigating bodies, and with various types of employee grievances.

The Office of General Counsel has on occasion played an important role in preventing or terminating Agency activities in violation of law, but many of the questionable or unlawful activities discussed in this report were not brought to the attention of this office. A certain parochialism may have resulted from the fact that attorneys in the office have little or no legal experience outside the Agency. It is important that the Agency receive the best possible legal advice on the often difficult and unusual situations which confront it.

In the final analysis, the proper functioning of the Agency must depend in large part on the character of the Director of Central Intelligence. The best assurance against misuse of the Agency lies in the appointment to that position of persons with the judgment, courage and independence to resist improper pressure and importuning, whether from the White House, within the Agency or elsewhere.

Compartmentation within the Agency, although certainly appropriate for security reasons, has sometimes been carried to extremes which prevent proper supervision and control.

The Agency must rely on the discipline and integrity of the men and women it employs. Many of the activities we have found to be improper or unlawful were in fact questioned by lower-level employees. Bringing such situations to the attention of upper levels of management is one of the purposes of a system of internal controls.

Recommendation (7)

a. Persons appointed to the position of Director of Central Intelligence should be individuals of stature, independence, and integrity. In making

415

this appointment, consideration should be given to individuals from outside the career service of the CIA, although promotion from within should not be barred. Experience in intelligence service is not necessarily a prerequisite for the position; management and administrative skills are at least as important as the technical expertise which can always be found in an able deputy.

b. Although the Director serves at the pleasure of the President, no Director should serve in that position for more than 10 years.

Recommendation (8)

a. The Office of Deputy Director of Central Intelligence should be reconstituted to provide for two such deputies, in addition to the four heads of the Agency's directorates. One deputy would act as the administrative officer, freeing the Director from day-to-day management duties. The other deputy should be a military officer, serving the functions of fostering relations with the military and providing the Agency with technical expertise on military intelligence requirements.

b. The advice and consent of the Senate should be required for the appointment of each Deputy Director of Central Intelligence.

Recommendation (9)

a. The Inspector General should be upgraded to a status equivalent to that of the deputy directors in charge of the four directorates within the CIA.

b. The Office of Inspector General should be staffed by outstanding, experienced officers from both inside and outside the CIA, with ability to understand the various branches of the Agency.

c. The Inspector General's duties with respect to domestic CIA activities should include periodic reviews of all offices within the United States. He should examine each office for compliance with CIA authority and regulations as well as for the effectiveness of their programs in implementing policy objectives.

d. The Inspector General should investigate all reports from employees concerning possible violations of the CIA statute.

e. The Inspector General should be given complete access to all information in the CIA relevant to his reviews.

f. An effective Inspector General's office will require a larger staff, more frequent reviews, and highly qualified personnel.

g. Inspector General reports should be provided to the National Security Council and the recommended executive oversight body. The Inspector General should have the authority, when he deems it appropriate, after notifying the Director of Central Intelligence, to consult with the executive oversight body on any CIA activity (see Recommendation 5).

Recommendation (10)

a. The Director should review the composition and operation of the Office of General Counsel and the degree to which this office is consulted to determine whether the Agency is receiving adequate legal assistance and representation in view of current requirements.

b. Consideration should be given to measures which would strengthen the office's professional capabilities and resources including, among other things, (1) occasionally departing from the existing practice of hiring lawyers from within the Agency to bring in seasoned lawyers from private practice as well as to hire law school graduates without prior CIA experience; (2) occasionally assigning Agency lawyers to serve a tour of duty elsewhere in the government to expand their experience; (3) encouraging lawyers to participate in outside professional activities.

Recommendation (11)

To a degree consistent with the need for security, the CIA should be encouraged to provide for increased lateral movement of personnel among the directorates and to bring persons with outside experience into the Agency at all levels.

Recommendation (12)

a. The Agency should issue detailed guidelines for its employees further specifying those activities within the United States which are permitted and those which are prohibited by statute, Executive Orders, and NSC and DCI directives.

b. These guidelines should also set forth the standards which govern CIA activities and the general types of activities which are permitted and prohibited. They should, among other things, specify that:

— Clandestine collection of intelligence directed against United States citizens is prohibited except as specifically permitted by law or published Executive Order.

— Unlawful methods or activities are prohibited.

— Prior approval of the DCI shall be required for any activities which may raise questions of compliance with the law or with Agency regulations.

c. The guidelines should also provide that employees with information on possibly improper activities are to bring it promptly to the attention of the Director of Central Intelligence or the Inspector General.

D. Significant Areas of Investigation

Domestic activities of the CIA raising substantial questions of compliance with the law have been closely examined by the Commission to determine the context in which they were performed, the pressures of the times, the relationship of the activity to the Agency's foreign intelligence assignment and to other CIA activities, the procedures used to authorize and conduct the activity, and the extent and effect of the activity.

In describing and assessing each such activity, it has been necessary to consider both that activity's relationship to the legitimate national security needs of the nation and the threat such activities might pose to individual rights of Americans and to a society founded on the need for government, as well as private citizens, to obey the law.

1. The CIA's Mail Intercepts (Chapter 9)

At the time the CIA came into being, one of the highest national intelligence priorities was to gain an understanding of the Soviet Union and its worldwide activities affecting our national security.

In this context, the CIA began in 1952 a program of surveying mail between the United States and the Soviet Union as it passed through a New York postal facility. In 1953 it began opening some of this mail. The program was expanded over the following two decades and ultimately involved the opening of many letters and the analysis of envelopes, or "covers," of a great many more letters.

The New York mail intercept was designed to attempt to identify persons within the United States who were cooperating with the Soviet Union and its intelligence forces to harm the United States. It was also intended to determine technical communications procedures and mail censorship techniques used by the Soviets.

The Director of the Central Intelligence Agency approved commencement of the New York mail intercept in 1952. During the ensuing years, so far as the record shows, Postmasters General Summerfield, Day, and Blount were informed of the program in varying degrees, as was Attorney General Mitchell. Since 1958, the FBI was aware of this program and received 57,000 items from it.

A 1962 CIA memorandum indicates the Agency was aware that the mail openings would be viewed as violating federal criminal laws prohibiting obstruction or delay of the mails.

In the last year before the termination of this program, out of 4,350,000 items of mail sent to and from the Soviet Union, the New York intercept examined the outside of 2,300,000 of these items, photographed 33,000 envelopes, and opened 8,700.

The mail intercept was terminated in 1973 when the Chief Postal Inspector refused to allow its continuation without an up-to-date high-level approval.

The CIA also ran much smaller mail intercepts for brief periods in San Francisco between 1969 and 1971 and in the territory of Hawaii during 1954 and 1955. For a short period in 1957, mail in transit between foreign countries was intercepted in New Orleans.

While in operation, the CIA's domestic mail opening programs were unlawful. United States statutes specifically forbid opening the mail.

The mail openings also raise Constitutional questions under the Fourth Amendment guarantees against unreasonable search, and the scope of the New York project poses possible difficulties with the First Amendment rights of speech and press.

Mail cover operations (examining and copying of envelopes only) are legal when carried out in compliance with postal regulations on a limited and selective basis involving matters of national security. The New York mail intercept did not meet these criteria.

The nature and degree of assistance given by the CIA to the FBI in the New York mail project indicate that the CIA's primary purpose eventually became participation with the FBI in internal security functions. Accordingly, the CIA's participation was prohibited under the National Security Act.

Recommendation (13)

a. The President should instruct the Director of Central Intelligence that the CIA is not to engage again in domestic *mail openings* except with express statutory authority in time of war. (See also Recommendation 23.)

b. The President should instruct the Director of Central Intelligence that *mail cover* examinations are to be in compliance with postal regulations; they are to be undertaken only in furtherance of the CIA's legitimate activities and then only on a limited and selected basis clearly involving matters of national security.

2. Intelligence Community Coordination (Chapter 10)

As a result of growing domestic disorder, the Department of Justice, starting in 1967 at the direction of Attorney General Ramsey Clark, coordinated a series of secret units and interagency groups in an effort to collate and evaluate intelligence relating to these events. These efforts continued until 1973.

The interagency committees were designed for analytic and not operational purposes. They were created as a result of White House pressure which began in 1967, because the FBI performed only limited evaluation and analysis of the information it collected on these events. The stated purpose of the CIA's participation was to supply relevant foreign intelligence and to furnish advice on evaluation techniques.

The CIA was reluctant to become unduly involved in these committees, which had problems of domestic unrest as their principal focus. It repeatedly refused to assign full-time personnel to any of them.

The most active of the committees was the Intelligence Evaluation Staff, which met from January 1971 to May 1973. A CIA liaison officer [Footnote: The liaison officer was Chief of the CIA's Special Operations Group which ran Operation CHAOS, discussed in Chapter 11 of this Report.] attended over 100 weekly meetings of the Staff, some of which concerned drafts of reports which had no foreign aspects. With the exception of one instance, there is no evidence that he acted in any capacity other than as an adviser on foreign intelligence, and, to some degree, as an editor.

On one occasion the CIA liaison officer appears to have caused a CIA agent to gather domestic information which was reported to the Intelligence Evaluation Staff.

419

The Commission found no evidence of other activities by the CIA that were conducted on behalf of the Department of Justice groups except for the supplying of appropriate foreign intelligence and advice on evaluation techniques.

The statutory prohibition on internal security functions does not preclude the CIA from providing foreign intelligence or advice on evaluation techniques to interdepartmental intelligence evaluation organizations having some domestic aspects. The statute was intended to promote coordination, not compartmentation of intelligence between governmental departments.

The attendance of the CIA liaison officer at over 100 meetings of the Intelligence Evaluation Staff, some of them concerned wholly with domestic matters, nevertheless created at least the appearance of impropriety. The Director of Central Intelligence was well advised to approach such participation reluctantly.

The liaison officer acted improperly in the one instance in which he directed an agent to gather domestic information within the United States which was reported to the Intelligence Evaluation Staff.

Much of the problem stemmed from the absence in government of any organization capable of adequately analyzing intelligence collected by the FBI on matters outside the purview of CIA.

Recommendation (14)

a. A capability should be developed within the FBI, or elsewhere in the Department of Justice, to evaluate, analyze, and coordinate intelligence and counterintelligence collected by the FBI concerning espionage, terrorism, and other related matters of internal security.

b. The CIA should restrict its participation in any joint intelligence committees to foreign intelligence matters.

c. The FBI should be encouraged to continue to look to the CIA for such foreign intelligence and counter-intelligence as is relevant to FBI needs.

3. Special Operations Group— "Operation CHAOS" (Chapter 11)

The late 1960's and early 1970's were marked by widespread violence and civil disorders. Demonstrations, marches and protest assemblies were frequent in a number of cities. Many universities and college campuses became places of disruption and unrest. Government facilities were picketed and sometimes invaded. Threats of bombing and bombing incidents occurred frequently. In Washington and other major cities, special security measures had to be instituted to control the access to public buildings.

Responding to Presidential requests made in the face of growing domestic disorder, the Director of Central Intelligence in August 1967 established a Special Operations Group within the CIA to collect, coordinate, evaluate and report on the extent of foreign influence on domestic dissidence.

The Group's activities, which later came to be known as Operation CHAOS, led the CIA to collect information on dissident Americans from CIA field stations overseas and from the FBI.

Although the stated purpose of the Operation was to determine whether there were any foreign contacts with American dissident groups, it resulted in the accumulation of considerable material on domestic dissidents and their activities.

During six years, the Operation compiled some 13,000 different files, including files on 7,200 American citizens. The documents in these files and related materials included the names of more than 300,000 persons and organizations, which were entered into a computerized index.

This information was kept closely guarded within the CIA. Using this information, personnel of the Group prepared 3,500 memoranda for internal use; 3,000 memoranda for dissemination to the FBI; and 37 memoranda for distribution to White House and other top level officials in the government.

The staff assigned to the Operation was steadily enlarged in response to repeated Presidential requests for additional information, ultimately reaching a maximum of 52 in 1971. Because of excessive isolation, the Operation was substantially insulated from meaningful review within the Agency, including review by the Counterintelligence Staff—of which the Operation was technically a part.

Commencing in late 1969, Operation CHAOS used a number of agents to collect intelligence abroad on any foreign connections with American dissident groups. In order to have sufficient "cover" for these agents, the Operation recruited persons from domestic dissident groups or recruited others and instructed them to associate with such groups in this country.

Most of the Operation's recruits were not directed to collect information domestically on American dissidents. On a number of occasions, however, such information was reported by the recruits while they were developing dissident credentials in the United States, and the information was retained in the files of the Operation. On three occasions, an agent of the Operation was specifically directed to collect domestic intelligence.

No evidence was found that any Operation CHAOS agent used or was directed by the Agency to use electronic surveillance, wiretaps or break-ins in the United States against any dissident individual or group.

Activity of the Operation decreased substantially by mid-1972. The Operation was formally terminated in March 1974.

Some domestic activities of Operation CHAOS unlawfully exceeded the CIA's statutory authority, even though the declared mission of gathering intelligence abroad as to foreign influence on domestic dissident activities was proper.

Most significantly, the Operation became a repository for large quantities of information on the domestic activities of American citizens. This information was derived principally from FBI reports or from overt sources and not from clandestine collection by the CIA, and much of it was not directly related to the question of the existence of foreign connections.

It was probably necessary for the CIA to accumulate an information base on domestic dissident activities in order to assess fairly whether the activities had foreign connections. The FBI would collect information but would not evaluate it. But the accumulation of domestic data in the Operation exceeded what was reasonably required to make such an assessment and was thus improper.

The use of agents of the Operation on three occasions to gather information within the United States on strictly domestic matters was beyond the CIA's authority. In addition the intelligence disseminations and those portions of a major study prepared by the Agency which dealt with purely domestic matters were improper.

The isolation of Operation CHAOS within the CIA and its independence from supervision by the regular chain of command within the clandestine service made it possible for the activities of the Operation to stray over the bounds of the Agency's authority without the knowledge of senior officials. The absence of any regular review of these activities prevented timely correction of such missteps as did occur.

Recommendation (15)

a. Presidents should refrain from directing the CIA to perform what are essentially internal security tasks.

b. The CIA should resist any efforts, whatever their origin, to involve it again in such improper activities.

c. The Agency should guard against allowing any component (like the Special Operations Group) to become so self-contained and isolated from top leadership that regular supervision and review are lost.

d. The files of the CHAOS project which have no foreign intelligence value should be destroyed by the Agency at the conclusion of the current congressional investigations, or as soon thereafter as permitted by law.

4. Protection of the Agency Against Threats of Violence—Office of Security (Chapter 12)

The CIA was not immune from the threats of violence and disruption during the period of domestic unrest between 1967 and 1972. The Office of Security was charged throughout this period with the responsibility of ensuring the continued functioning of the CIA.

The Office, therefore, from 1967 to 1970, had its field officers collect information from published materials, law enforcement authorities, other agencies and college officials before recruiters were sent to some campuses. Monitoring and communications support was provided to recruiters when trouble was expected.

The Office was also responsible, with the approval of the Director of Central Intelligence, for a program from February 1967 to December 1968, which at first monitored, but later infiltrated, dissident organizations in the Washington, D.C., area to determine if the groups planned any activities against CIA or other government installations.

At no time were more than 12 persons performing these tasks, and they performed them on a part-time basis. The project was terminated when the Washington Metropolitan Police Department developed its own intelligence capability.

In December, 1967, the Office began a continuing study of dissident activity in the United States, using information from published and other voluntary knowledgeable sources. The Office produced weekly Situation Information Reports analyzing dissident activities and providing calendars of future events. Calendars were given to the Secret Service, but the CIA made no other disseminations outside the Agency. About 500 to 800 files were maintained on dissenting organizations and individuals. Thousands of names in the files were indexed. Report publication was ended in late 1972, and the entire project was ended in 1973.

The program under which the Office of Security rendered assistance to Agency recruiters on college campuses was justified as an exercise of the Agency's responsibility to protect its own personnel and operations. Such support activities were not undertaken for the purpose of protecting the facilities or operations of other governmental agencies, or to maintain public order or enforce laws.

The Agency should not infiltrate a dissident group for security purposes unless there is a clear danger to Agency installations, operations or personnel, and investigative coverage of the threat by the FBI and local law enforcement authorities is inadequate. The Agency's infiltration of dissident groups in the Washington area went far beyond steps necessary to protect the Agency's own facilities, personnel and operations, and therefore exceeded the CIA's statutory authority.

In addition, the Agency undertook to protect other government departments and agencies—a police function prohibited to it by statute.

Intelligence activity directed toward learning from what sources a domestic dissident group receives its financial support within the United States, and how much income it has, is no part of the authorized security operations of the Agency. Neither is it the function of the Agency to compile records on who attends peaceful meetings of such dissident groups, or what each speaker has to say (unless it relates to disruptive or violent activity which may be directed against the Agency).

The Agency's actions in contributing funds, photographing people, activities and cars, and following people home were unreasonable under the circumstances and therefore exceeded the CIA's authority.

With certain exceptions, the program under which the Office of Security (without infiltration) gathered, organized and analyzed information about dissident groups for purposes of security was within the CIA's authority.

The accumulation of reference files on dissident organizations and their leaders was appropriate both to evaluate the risks posed to the Agency and to develop an understanding of dissident groups and their differences for security clearance purposes. But the accumulation of information on domestic activities went beyond what was required by the Agency's legitimate security needs and therefore exceeded the CIA's authority.

423

Recommendation (16)

The CIA should not infiltrate dissident groups or other organizations of Americans in the absence of a written determination by the Director of Central Intelligence that such action is necessary to meet a clear danger to Agency facilities, operations, or personnel and that adequate coverage by law enforcement agencies is unavailable.

Recommendation (17)

All files on individuals accumulated by the Office of Security in the program relating to dissidents should be identified, and, except where necessary for a legitimate foreign intelligence activity, be destroyed at the conclusion of the current congressional investigations, or as soon thereafter as permitted by law.

5. Other Investigations by the Office of Security (Chapter 13)

A. Security Clearance Investigations of Prospective Employees and Operatives

The Office of Security routinely conducts standard security investigations of persons seeking affiliation with the Agency. In doing so, the Office is performing the necessary function of screening persons to whom it will make available classified information. Such investigations are necessary, and no improprieties were found in connection with them.

B. Investigations of Possible Breaches of Security

1. Persons Investigated

The Office of Security has been called upon on a number of occasions to investigate specific allegations that intelligence sources and methods were threatened by unauthorized disclosures. The Commission's inquiry concentrated on those investigations which used investigative means intruding on the privacy of the subjects, including physical and electronic surveillance, unauthorized entry, mail covers and intercepts, and reviews of individual federal tax returns.

The large majority of these investigations were directed at persons affiliated with the Agency—such as employees, former employees, and defectors and other foreign nationals used by the Agency as intelligence sources.

A few investigations involving intrusions on personal privacy were directed at subjects with no relationship to the Agency. The Commission has found no evidence that any such investigations were directed against any congressman, judge, or other public official. Five were directed against newsmen, in an effort to determine their sources of leaked classified information, and nine were directed against other United States citizens.

The CIA's investigations of newsmen to determine their sources of classified information stemmed from pressures from the White House and were partly a result of the FBI's unwillingness to undertake such investigations. The FBI refused to proceed without an advance opinion that the Justice Department would prosecute if a case were developed.

Investigations of allegations against Agency employees and operatives are a reasonable exercise of the Director's statutory duty to protect intelligence sources and methods from unauthorized disclosure if the investigations are lawfully conducted. Such investigations also assist the Director in the exercise of his unreviewable authority to terminate the employment of any Agency employee. They are proper unless their principal purpose becomes law-enforcement or the maintenance of internal security.

The Director's responsibility to protect intelligence sources and methods is not so broad as to permit investigations of persons having no relationship whatever with the Agency. The CIA has no authority to investigate newsmen simply because they have published leaked classified information. Investigations by the CIA should be limited to persons presently or formerly affiliated with the Agency, directly or indirectly.

Recommendation (18)

a. The Director of Central Intelligence should issue clear guidelines setting forth the situations in which the CIA is justified in conducting its own investigation of individuals presently or formerly affiliated with it.

b. The guidelines should permit the CIA to conduct investigations of such persons only when the Director of Central Intelligence first determines that the investigation is necessary to protect intelligence sources and methods the disclosure of which might endanger the national security.

c. Such investigations must be coordinated with the FBI whenever substantial evidence suggesting espionage or violation of a federal criminal statute is discovered.

Recommendation (19)

a. In cases involving serious or continuing security violations, as determined by the Security Committee of the United States Intelligence Board, the Committee should be authorized to recommend in writing to the Director of Central Intelligence (with a copy to the National Security Council) that the case be referred to the FBI for further investigation, under procedures to be developed by the Attorney General.

b. These procedures should include a requirement that the FBI accept such referrals without regard to whether a favorable prosecutive opinion is issued by the Justice Department. The CIA should not engage in such further investigations.

Recommendation (20)

The CIA and other components and agencies of the intelligence community should conduct periodic reviews of all classified material originating within those departments or agencies, with a view to declassifying as much of that material as possible. The purpose of such review would be to assure the public that it has access to all information that should properly be disclosed.

Recommendation (21)

The Commission endorses legislation, drafted with appropriate safeguards of the constitutional rights of all affected individuals, which would make it a criminal offense for employees or former employees of the CIA wilfully to divulge to any unauthorized person classified information pertaining to foreign intelligence or the collection thereof obtained during the course of their employment.

2. Investigative Techniques

Even an investigation within the CIA's authority must be conducted by lawful means. Some of the past investigations by the Office of Security within the United States were conducted by means which were invalid at the time. Others might have been lawful when conducted, but would be impermissible today.

Some investigations involved physical surveillance of the individuals concerned, possibly in conjunction with other methods of investigation. The last instance of physical surveillance by the Agency within the United States occurred in 1973.

The investigation disclosed the domestic use of 32 wiretaps, the last in 1965; 32 instances of bugging, the last in 1968; and 12 break-ins, the last in 1971. None of these activities was conducted under a judicial warrant, and only one with the written approval of the Attorney General.

Information from the income tax records of 16 persons was obtained from the Internal Revenue Service by the CIA in order to help determine whether the taxpayer was a security risk with possible connections to foreign groups. The CIA did not employ the existing statutory and regulatory procedures for obtaining such records from the IRS.

In 91 instances, mail covers (the photographing of the front and back of an envelope) were employed, and in 12 instances letters were intercepted and opened.

The state of the CIA records on these activities is such that it is often difficult to determine why the investigation occurred in the first place, who authorized the special coverage, and what the results were. Although there was testimony that these activities were frequently known to the Director of Central Intelligence and sometimes to the Attorney General, the files often are insufficient to confirm such information.

The use of physical surveillance is not unlawful unless it reaches the point of harassment. The unauthorized entries described were illegal when conducted and would be illegal if conducted today. Likewise, the review of individuals' federal tax returns and the interception and opening of mail violated specific statutes and regulations prohibiting such conduct.

Since the constitutional and statutory constraints applicable to the use of electronic eavesdropping (bugs and wiretaps) have been evolving over the years, the Commission deems it impractical to apply those changing standards on a case-by-case basis. The Commission does believe that while some of the instances of electronic eavesdropping were proper when conducted, many were not. To be lawful today, such activities would require at least the written approval of the Attorney General on the basis of a finding that the national security is involved and that the case has significant foreign connections.

Recommendation (22)

The CIA should not undertake physical surveillance (defined as systematic observation) of Agency employees, contractors or related personnel within the United States without first obtaining written approval of the Director of Central Intelligence.

Recommendation (23)

In the United States and its possessions, the CIA should not intercept wire or oral communications [Footnote: As defined in the Omnibus Crime Control and Safe Streets Act.] or otherwise engage in activities that would require a warrant if conducted by a law enforcement agency. Responsibility for such activities belongs with the FBI.

Recommendation (24)

The CIA should strictly adhere to established legal procedures governing access to federal income tax information.

Recommendation (25)

CIA investigation records should show that each investigation was duly authorized, and by whom, and should clearly set forth the factual basis for undertaking the investigation and the results of the investigation.

C. Handling of Defectors

The Office of Security is charged with providing security for persons who have defected to the United States. Generally a defector can be processed and placed into society in a few months, but one defector was involuntarily confined at a CIA installation for three years. He was held in solitary confinement under spartan living conditions. The CIA maintained the long confinement because of doubts about the bona fides of the defector. This confinement was approved by the Director of Central Intelligence; and the FBI, Attorney General, United States Intelligence Board and selected members of Congress were aware to some extent of the confinement. In one other case a defector was physically abused; the Director of Central Intelligence discharged the employee involved.

Such treatment of individuals by an agency of the United States is unlawful. The Director of Central Intelligence and the Inspector General must be alert to prevent repetitions.

6. Involvement of the CIA in Improper Activities for the White House (Chapter 14)

During 1971, at the request of various members of the White House staff, the CIA provided alias documents and disguise material, a tape recorder, camera, film and film processing to E. Howard Hunt. It also prepared a psychological profile of Dr. Daniel Ellsberg.

Some of this equipment was later used without the knowledge of the CIA in connection with various improper activities, including the entry into the office of Dr. Lewis Fielding, Ellsberg's psychiatrist.

Some members of the CIA's medical staff who participated in the preparation of the Ellsberg profile knew that one of its purposes was to support a public attack on Ellsberg. Except for this fact, the investigation has disclosed no evidence that the CIA knew or had reason to know that the assistance it gave would be used for improper purposes.

President Nixon and his staff also insisted in this period that the CIA turn over to the President highly classified files relating to the Lebanon landings, the Bay of Pigs, the Cuban missile crisis, and the Vietnam War. The request was made on the ground that these files were needed by the President in the performance of his duties, but the record shows the purpose, undisclosed to the CIA, was to serve the President's personal political ends.

The Commission has also investigated the response of the CIA to the investigations following the Watergate arrests. Beginning in June 1972, the CIA received various requests for information and assistance in connection with these investigations. In a number of instances, its responses were either incomplete or delayed and some materials that may or may not have contained relevant information were destroyed. The Commission feels that this conduct reflects poor judgment on the part of the CIA, but it has found no evidence that the CIA participated in the Watergate break-in or in the post-Watergate cover-up by the White House.

Providing the assistance requested by the White House, including the alias and disguise materials, the camera and the psychological profile on Ellsberg, was not related to the performance by the Agency of its authorized intelligence functions and was therefore improper.

No evidence has been disclosed, however, except as noted in connection with the Ellsberg profile, that the CIA knew or had reason to know that its assistance would be used in connection with improper activities. Nor has any evidence been disclosed indicating that the CIA participated in the planning or carrying out of either the Fielding or Watergate break-ins. The CIA apparently was unaware of the break-ins until they were reported in the media.

The record does show, however, that individuals in the Agency failed to comply with the normal control procedures in providing assistance to E. Howard Hunt. It also shows that the Agency's failure to cooperate fully with ongoing investigations following Watergate was inconsistent with its obligations.

Finally, the Commission concludes that the requests for assistance by the White House reflect a pattern for actual and attempted misuse of the CIA by the Nixon administration.

Recommendation (26)

a. A single and exclusive high-level channel should be established for transmission of all White House staff requests to the CIA. This channel should run between an officer of the National Security Council staff designated by the President and the office of the Director or his Deputy.

b. All Agency officers and employees should be instructed that any direction or request reaching them directly and out of regularly established channels should be immediately reported to the Director of Central Intelligence.

7. Domestic Activities of the Directorate of Operations (Chapter 15)

In support of its responsibility for the collection of foreign intelligence and conduct of covert operations overseas, the CIA's Directorate of Operations engages in a variety of activities within the United States.

A. Overt Collection of Foreign Intelligence Within the United States

One division of the Directorate of Operations collects foreign intelligence within the United States from residents, business firms, and other organizations willing to assist the Agency. This activity is conducted openly by officers who identify themselves as CIA employees. Such sources of information are not compensated.

In connection with these collection activities, the CIA maintains approximately 50,000 active files which include details of the CIA's relationships with these voluntary sources and the results of a federal agency name check.

The division's collection efforts have been almost exclusively confined to foreign economic, political, military, and operational topics.

Commencing in 1969, however, some activities of the division resulted in the collection of limited information with respect to American dissidents and dissident groups. Although the focus was on foreign contacts of these groups, background information on domestic dissidents was also collected. Between 1969 and 1974, when this activity was formally terminated, 400 reports were made to Operation CHAOS.

In 1972 and 1973, the division obtained and transmitted, to other parts of the CIA, information about telephone calls between the Western Hemisphere (including the United States) and two other countries. The information was limited to names, telephone numbers, and locations of callers and recipients. It did not include the content of the conversations.

This division also occasionally receives reports concerning criminal activity within the United States. Pursuant to written regulations, the source or a report of the information received is referred to the appropriate law enforcement agency.

The CIA's efforts to collect foreign intelligence from residents of the United States willing to assist the CIA are a valid and necessary element of its responsibility. Not only do these persons provide a large reservoir of foreign intelligence; they are by far the most accessible source of such information.

The division's files on American citizens and firms representing actual or potential sources of information constitute a necessary part of its legitimate intelligence activities. They do not appear to be vehicles for the collection or communication of derogatory, embarrassing, or sensitive information about American citizens.

The division's efforts, with few exceptions, have been confined to legitimate topics.

The collection of information with respect to American dissident groups exceeded legitimate foreign intelligence collection and was beyond the proper scope of CIA activity. This impropriety was recognized in some of the division's own memoranda.

The Commission was unable to discover any specific purpose for the collection of telephone toll call information or any use of that information by the Agency. In the absence of a valid purpose, such collection is improper.

B. Provision and Control of Cover for CIA Personnel

CIA personnel engaged in clandestine foreign intelligence activities cannot travel, live or perform their duties openly as Agency employees. Accordingly, virtually all CIA personnel serving abroad and many in the United States assume a "cover" as employees of another government agency or of a commercial enterprise. CIA involvement in certain activities, such as research and development projects, are also sometimes conducted under cover.

CIA's cover arrangements are essential to the CIA's performance of its foreign intelligence mission. The investigation has disclosed no instances in which domestic aspects of the CIA's cover arrangements involved any violations of law.

By definition, however, cover necessitates an element of deception which must be practiced within the United States as well as within foreign countries. This creates a risk of conflict with various regulatory statutes and other legal requirements. The Agency recognizes this risk. It has installed controls under which cover arrangements are closely supervised to attempt to ensure compliance with applicable laws.

C. Operating Proprietary Companies

The CIA uses proprietary companies to provide cover and perform administrative tasks without attribution to the Agency. Most of the large operating proprietaries—primarily airlines—have been liquidated, and the remainder engage in activities offering little or no competition to private enterprise.

The only remaining large proprietary activity is a complex of financial companies, with assets of approximately $20 million, that enable the Agency to administer certain sensitive trusts, annuities, escrows, insurance arrangements, and other benefits and payments provided to officers or contract employees without attribution to CIA. The remaining small operating proprietaries, generally having fewer than ten employees each, make non-attributable purchases of equipment and supplies.

Except as discussed in connection with the Office of Security (see Chapters 12 and 13), the Commission has found no evidence that any proprietaries have been used for operations against American citizens or investigation of their activities. All of them appear to be subject to close supervision and multiple financial controls within the Agency.

D. Development of Contacts With Foreign Nationals

In connection with the CIA's foreign intelligence responsibilities, it seeks to develop contacts with foreign nationals within the United States. American citizens voluntarily assist in developing these contacts. As far as the Commission can find, these activities have not involved coercive methods.

These activities appear to be directed entirely to the production of foreign intelligence and to be within the authority of the CIA. We found no evidence that any of these activities have been directed against American citizens.

E. Assistance in Narcotics Control

The Directorate of Operations provides foreign intelligence support to the government's efforts to control the flow of narcotics and other dangerous drugs into this country. The CIA coordinates clandestine intelligence collection overseas and provides other government agencies with foreign intelligence on drug traffic.

From the beginning of such efforts in 1969, the CIA Director and other officials have instructed employees to make no attempt to gather information on Americans allegedly trafficking in drugs. If such information is obtained incidentally, it is transmitted to law enforcement agencies.

Concerns that the CIA's narcotics-related intelligence activities may involve the Agency in law enforcement or other actions directed against American citizens thus appear unwarranted.

Beginning in the fall of 1973, the Directorate monitored conversations between the United States and Latin America in an effort to identify narcotics traffickers. Three months after the program began, the General Counsel of the CIA was consulted. He issued an opinion that the program was illegal, and it was immediately terminated.

This monitoring, although a source of valuable information for enforcement officials, was a violation of a statute of the United States. Continuation of the operation for over three months without the knowledge of the Office of the General Counsel demonstrates the need for improved internal consultation. (See Recommendation 10.)

8. Domestic Activities of the Directorate of Science and Technology (Chapter 16)

The CIA's Directorate of Science and Technology performs a variety of research and development and operational support functions for the Agency's foreign intelligence mission.

Many of these activities are performed in the United States and involve cooperation with private companies. A few of these activities were improper or questionable.

As part of a program to test the influence of drugs on humans, research included the administration of LSD to persons who were unaware that they were being tested. This was clearly illegal. One person died in 1953, apparently as a result. In 1963, following the Inspector General's discovery of these events, new stringent criteria were issued prohibiting drug testing by the CIA on unknowing persons. All drug testing programs were ended in 1967.

In the process of testing monitoring equipment for use overseas, the CIA has overheard conversations between Americans. The names of the speakers were not identified; the contents of the conversations were not disseminated. All recordings were destroyed when testing was concluded. Such testing should not be directed against unsuspecting persons in the United States. Most of the testing undertaken by the Agency could easily have been performed using only Agency personnel and with the full knowledge of those whose conversations were being recorded. This is the present Agency practice.

Other activities of this Directorate include the manufacture of alias credentials for use by CIA employees and agents. Alias credentials are necessary to facilitate CIA clandestine operations, but the strictest controls and accountability must be maintained over the use of such documents. Recent guidelines established by the Deputy Director for Operations to control the use of alias documentation appear adequate to prevent abuse in the future.

As part of another program, photographs taken by CIA aerial photography equipment are provided to civilian agencies of the government. Such photographs are used to assess natural disasters, conduct route surveys and forest inventories, and detect crop blight. Permitting civilian use of aerial photography systems is proper. The economy of operating but one aerial photography program dictates the use of these photographs for appropriate civilian purposes.

Recommendation (27)

In accordance with its present guidelines, the CIA should not again engage in the testing of drugs on unsuspecting persons.

Recommendation (28)

Testing of equipment for monitoring conversations should not involve unsuspecting persons living within the United States.

Recommendation (29)

A civilian agency committee should be reestablished to oversee the civilian uses of aerial intelligence photography in order to avoid any concerns over the improper domestic use of a CIA-developed system.

9. CIA Relationships With Other Federal, State, and Local Agencies (Chapter 17)

CIA operations touch the interest of many other agencies. The CIA, like other agencies of the government, frequently has occasion to give or receive assistance from other agencies. This investigation has concentrated on those relationships which raise substantial questions under the CIA's legislative mandate.

A. Federal Bureau of Investigation

The FBI counterintelligence operations often have positive intelligence ramifications. Likewise, legitimate domestic CIA activities occasionally cross the path of FBI investigations. Daily liaison is therefore necessary between the two agencies.

Much routine information is passed back and forth. Occasionally joint operations are conducted. The relationship between the agencies has, however, not been uniformly satisfactory over the years. Formal liaison was cut off from February 1970 to November 1972, but relationships have improved in recent years.

The relationship between the CIA and the FBI needs to be clarified and outlined in detail in order to ensure that the needs of national security are met without creating conflicts or gaps of jurisdiction.

Recommendation (30)

The Director of Central Intelligence and the Director of the FBI should prepare and submit for approval by the National Security Council a detailed agreement setting forth the jurisdiction of each agency and providing for effective liaison with respect to all matters of mutual concern. This agreement should be consistent with the provisions of law and with other applicable recommendations of this Report.

B. Narcotics Law Enforcement Agencies

Beginning in late 1970, the CIA assisted the Bureau of Narcotics and Dangerous Drugs (BNDD) to uncover possible corruption within that organization. The CIA used one of its proprietary companies to recruit agents for BNDD and gave them short instructional courses. Over two and one-half years, the CIA recruited 19 agents for the BNDD. The project was terminated in 1973.

The Director was correct in his written directive terminating the project. The CIA's participation in law enforcement activities in the course of these activities was forbidden by its statute. The Director and the Inspector General should be alert to prevent involvement of the Agency in similar enterprises in the future.

C. The Department of State

For more than 20 years, the CIA through a proprietary conducted a training school for foreign police and security officers in the United States under the auspices of the Agency for International Development of the Department of State. The proprietary also sold small amounts of licensed firearms and police equipment to the foreign officers and their departments.

The CIA's activities in providing educational programs for foreign police were not improper under the Agency's statute. Although the school was conducted within the United States through a CIA proprietary, it had no other significant domestic impact.

Engaging in the firearms business was a questionable activity for a government intelligence agency. It should not be repeated.

D. Funding Requests From Other Federal Agencies

In the spring of 1970, at the request of the White House, the CIA contributed $33,655.68 for payment of stationery and other costs for replies to persons who wrote the President after the invasion of Cambodia.

This use of CIA funds for a purpose unrelated to intelligence is improper. Steps should be taken to ensure against any repetition of such an incident.

E. State and Local Police

The CIA handles a variety of routine security matters through liaison with local police departments. In addition, it offered training courses from 1966 to 1973 to United States police officers on a variety of law enforcement techniques, and has frequently supplied equipment to state and local police.

In general, the coordination and cooperation between state and local law enforcement agencies and the CIA has been exemplary, based upon a desire to facilitate their respective legitimate aims and goals.

Most of the assistance rendered to state and local law enforcement agencies by the CIA has been no more than an effort to share with law enforcement authorities the benefits of new methods, techniques, and equipment developed or used by the Agency.

On a few occasions, however, the Agency has improperly become involved in actual police operations. Thus, despite a general rule against providing manpower to local police forces, the CIA has lent men, along with radio-equipped vehicles, to the Washington Metropolitan Police Department to help monitor antiwar demonstrations. It helped the same Department surveil a police informer. It also provided an interpreter to the Fairfax County (Virginia) Police Department to aid in a criminal investigation.

In compliance with the spirit of a recent Act of Congress, the CIA terminated all but routine assistance to state and local law enforcement agencies in 1973. Such assistance is now being provided state and local agencies by the FBI. There is no impropriety in the CIA's furnishing the FBI with information on new technical developments which may be useful to local law enforcement.

For several years the CIA has given gratuities to local police officers who had been helpful to the Agency. Any such practice should be terminated.

The CIA has also received assistance from local police forces. Aside from routine matters, officers from such forces have occasionally assisted the Office of Security in the conduct of investigations. The CIA has occasionally obtained police badges and other identification for use as cover for its agents.

Except for one occasion when some local police assisted the CIA in an unauthorized entry, the assistance received by the CIA from state and local law enforcement authorities was proper. The use of police identification as a means of providing cover, while not strictly speaking a violation of the Agency's statutory authority as long as no police function is performed, is a practice subject to misunderstanding and should be avoided.

10. Indices and Files on American Citizens (Chapter 18)

Biographical information is a major resource of an intelligence agency. The CIA maintains a number of files and indices that include biographical information on Americans.

As a part of its normal process of indexing names and information of foreign intelligence interest, the Directorate of Operations has indexed some 7,000,000 names of all nationalities. An estimated 115,000 of these are believed to be American citizens.

Where a person is believed to be of possibly continuing intelligence interest, files to collect information as received are opened. An estimated 57,-000 out of a total of 750,000 such files concern American citizens. For the most part, the names of Americans appear in indices and files as actual or potential sources of information or assistance to the CIA. In addition to these files, files on some 7,200 American citizens, relating primarily to their domestic activities, were, as already stated, compiled within the Directorate of Operations as part of Operation CHAOS.

The Directorate of Administration maintains a number of files on persons who have been associated with the CIA. These files are maintained for security, personnel, training, medical and payroll purposes. Very few are maintained on persons unaware that they have a relationship with the CIA. However, the Office of Security maintained files on American citizens associated with dissident groups who were never affiliated with the Agency because they were considered a threat to the physical security of Agency facilities and employees. These files were also maintained, in part, for use in future security clearance determinations. Dissemination of security files is restricted to persons with an operational need for them.

The Office of Legislative Counsel maintains files concerning its relationships with congressmen.

Although maintenance of most of the indices, files, and records of the Agency has been necessary and proper, the standards applied by the Agency at some points during its history have permitted the accumulation and indexing of materials not needed for legitimate intelligence or security purposes. Included in this category are many of the files related to Operation CHAOS and the activities of the Office of Security concerning dissident groups.

Constant vigilance by the Agency is essential to prevent the collection of information on United States citizens which is not needed for proper intelligence activities. The Executive Order recommended by the Commission (Recommendation 2) will ensure purging of nonessential or improper materials from Agency files.

11. Allegations Concerning the Assassination of President Kennedy (Chapter 19)

Numerous allegations have been made that the CIA participated in the assassination of President John F. Kennedy. The Commission staff investigated these allegations. On the basis of the staff's investigation, the Commission concludes that there is no credible evidence of CIA involvement.

AEROSOL SPRAYS AND
THE ATMOSPHERE
June 12, 1975

A federal task force recommended June 12 that certain aerosol spray-can propellants be banned by January 1978, because there was a strong probability that they diluted the earth's ozone layer and thereby threatened an increase in the incidence of skin cancer. The suspected chemicals, fluorocarbons 11 and 12 (usually known commercially as Freon), had been used in the packaging of a wide variety of household products and as coolants in refrigerators and air conditioning systems. The proposal to ban the chemicals was made in a report by a twelve-agency group, the Federal Task Force on Inadvertent Modification of the Stratosphere (IMOS), which had spent five months evaluating the potential hazards of fluorocarbons.

Concern about harm to the ozone layer had, in 1971, been a major factor in defeating an administration plan to build a prototype supersonic transport (SST) plane. The latest threat to the fragile ozone shield had been suggested a year before the IMOS report appeared. In June 1974 Frank S. Rowland and Mario J. Molina, University of California (Irvine campus) research chemists, attracted wide attention with an article in Nature *magazine about the possible harmful effects of fluorocarbons. The major controversy centered on whether the industrial and commercial use of Freon would, indeed, threaten terrestrial life by destroying ozone, a thin, chemically active form of oxygen concentrated 16 to 19 miles above the earth.*

Rowland and Molina postulated that fluorocarbons, when released, were not broken down by chemical reactions in the lower atmosphere but moved slowly, unchanged, into the stratosphere. There they were converted into

437

chlorine atoms, which attacked and destroyed ozone, exposing the earth to potentially lethal doses of ultraviolet rays from the sun. The possible consequences of this bombardment, Rowland, Molina and other atmospheric researchers warned, include destruction of plant and marine life and drastic changes in world weather patterns, in addition to increases in abnormal and malignant skin growths.

Theory Disputed

Rowland's and Molina's findings did not go unchallenged. Julius London and Jean Kelly, two University of Colorado scientists, had reported in May 1974 that the distribution of ozone at high altitudes actually increased during the 1960s, a period when aerosol production was expanding. Spokesmen for the $8-billion-a-year fluorocarbon industry and other scientists maintained that very little is known about the ozone layer and that the chemical reactions obtained thus far in various research laboratories had not been verified by reliable data.

"A Cause for Concern"

Acknowledging the speculative nature of its findings, the IMOS group still judged the "fluorocarbon releases to the environment...a legitimate cause for concern." Should a National Academy of Sciences (NAS) study on "man-made impacts on the stratosphere" concur, government regulation ought to be instituted, the report said. In July the NAS issued an interim report stressing the urgent need for more data and noting that if nothing were done until fluorocarbons "produced a directly measured reduction in the ozone layer, it would then be too late to avoid further, more drastic long-term effects." The NAS was to make its final report in the spring of 1976.

The proposed ban would apply primarily to fluorocarbons used as propellants. These constraints could be lifted if later scientific research reversed current theories, the report noted. In addition to the NAS study, independent research was being carried out by private companies and the National Aeronautics and Space Administration, which expects final results by the end of 1977.

The IMOS task force, headed by the President's Council on Environmental Quality and the Federal Council for Science and Technology, also recommended immediate regulations requiring that aerosol products using fluorocarbons be so labeled and quick passage of legislation providing wide government authority to regulate fluorocarbon manufacture and distribution.

On June 1, just prior to publication of the IMOS report, Oregon became the first state to enact a law banning the sale of aerosol cans containing fluorocarbons (after March 1977).

Federal action seemed far away, however. At Senate hearings in September 1975 the majority of witnesses—representatives of industry, the administration and the scientific community—agreed that the issue needed further study and that there was currently insufficient data to warrant an immediate ban on production of fluorocarbons. A few witnesses worried that by the time studies were completed irreparable harm might have been done.

Excerpts from Fluorocarbons and the Environment, *a report of the Federal Task Force on Inadvertent Modification of the Stratosphere (IMOS), released June 12, 1975, in Washington, D.C.:*

I.

Executive Summary

One year ago the first scientific paper was published that postulated serious damage to the earth's ozone shield in the stratosphere as a result of the use on earth, and release to the atmosphere, of certain man-made fluorocarbon compounds, used widely as refrigerants, as propellants for aerosol products, and for other uses. Calculations reported in that paper led the authors to believe that fluorocarbons-11 and -12 (F-11 and F-12), developed and valued largely because of their useful chemical properties, apparently are not destroyed in chemical reactions in the lower atmosphere but slowly diffuse upward into the upper atmosphere. Upon reaching the stratosphere, they are decomposed by ultraviolet (UV) radiation from the sun, with the resulting release of free chlorine atoms. The free chlorine atoms then act to decrease gradually the average concentration of ozone by means of catalytic chain reactions. These chlorine chain reactions are postulated to be three times more effective in reducing ozone than the similar processes of ozone destruction by nitrogen oxides (on a molecule for molecule basis), which have been of recent concern in conjunction with the effects of emissions from aircraft operating in or near the stratosphere.

Ozone is a form of oxygen that exists in minor quantities in the atmosphere; it is concentrated primarily in the stratosphere, where it is maintained in a dynamic equilibrium by natural processes through which it is continually being formed and destroyed. The principal reason why fluorocarbon releases to the atmosphere are considered to be of such potential importance is that a reduction in the average long-term concentration of ozone would result in an increase in the amount of harmful UV radiation reaching the earth's surface. In addition to postulated human health effects (such as increased incidence of skin cancer), it is feared that the growth and development of certain plant and animal species might be altered and that the balance of delicate ecosystems might be disturbed. Concern has also been expressed that significant changes in the stratosphere could affect the earth's climate.

439

The Interagency Task Force on Inadvertent Modification of the Stratosphere has conducted a 5-month intensive study of these matters. The general conclusions of the report are highlighted below....

Stratospheric Effects

Although the theory of possible ozone reduction by F-11 and F-12 cannot presently be supported by direct atmospheric measurements, the matter has been carefully studied independently by many scientists. Thus far, the validity of the theory and the predicted amounts of ozone reduction have not been seriously challenged. More research is required and will be undertaken, but there seems to be legitimate cause for serious concern.

Fluorocarbons are produced in large quantities. World production of F-11 and F-12 (excluding the U.S.S.R. and Eastern European countries) was 1.7 billion pounds in 1973, which represented an 11% growth over the 1972 production. Approximately 50% of that world production and use occurs in the U.S. Almost all are ultimately released to the atmosphere—sooner in the case of aerosols than in the case of refrigerants, which are released principally through leakage and at the time of recharging or eventual disposal of refrigeration and air-conditioning systems.

These fluorocarbons are found in the atmosphere in concentrations that seem consistent with the total world release to date. It is expected that a significant fraction of the total fluorocarbon release eventually reaches the stratosphere through atmospheric circulation and upward diffusion, and recent measurements have detected the presence of F-11 in the stratosphere. There are no known significant natural "sinks" (mechanisms for removal) for their destruction other than stratospheric processes.

Slow Recovery

Several scientists have independently calculated possible reductions in ozone concentration to date and expectations of future reductions based on alternate patterns of future release to the atmosphere. Despite varying assumptions, the findings of these scientists agree within about a factor of two. The best estimates are that past fluorocarbon releases to the atmosphere may have resulted in a reduction to date of between about 0.5 and 1% and possibly as large as 2% in the natural equilibrium ozone level. It is believed that even if no more F-11 or F-12 were released, the average ozone concentration in the stratosphere would continue to decrease and eventually undergo as much as a 1.3% to 3% reduction because of the delayed effects of past releases of fluorocarbons. An important aspect of the theoretical reduction of ozone by fluorocarbons is its projected decrease for about a decade after cessation of releases to the atmosphere, with very slow subsequent recovery to normal values taking place over as much as a century or more.

Other current calculations predict an eventual reduction of about 7% in the equilibrium ozone concentration, presuming a continuation of fluorocarbon release at the 1972 rate.

The validity of these calculations could be questioned if: (1) major unexpected natural sinks for chlorine atoms were discovered, or (2) large amounts of chlorine from natural sources were measured in the stratosphere, of such magnitude that would overwhelm the amounts attributed to man-made compounds and that were outside the range of present understanding of the dynamics of the stratosphere.

Limits of Predictions

There are uncertainties in predicted values of reduction in ozone levels because of the uncertainties in estimated rates of mixing and transport in the stratosphere and in estimates of the chemical reaction rates for several reactions. The degree of uncertainty introduced from these estimates, however, does not seem to be sufficient, even under the best of circumstances, to eliminate the concern about past and future releases of fluorocarbons.

Ideally, the proof or rejection of the model calculations could be found in measurements of the change in the equilibrium ozone concentration in the stratosphere over time. However, there are natural variations in ozone concentration from day to day, between seasons, from year to year, and at different latitudes that are larger than those that could be attributed to fluorocarbon releases to date. A 5 to 10% average decrease, persisting and measured for several years, would be required before a change could be attributed to human activity with any reasonable statistical reliability. Ozone levels in the northern hemisphere seem to have increased by about 5 to 10% during the period 1955-1970. The ozone concentration, however, has been on the decline since 1970 (approximately 1 to 2%). These fluctuations probably represent primarily natural variations, possibly related to solar activity.

Although human-induced reductions in stratospheric ozone levels may be quite small when compared to natural fluctuations, these reductions may be of considerable significance because the average ozone concentration is affected; therefore, the cumulative exposure to UV-B radiation over time would be increased.

Carbon tetrachloride (CCl_4) also has been measured in the troposphere in significant quantities and is a potential source of free chlorine in the stratosphere. It is suspected to have caused a 0.5 to 2% decrease to date in the equilibrium level of ozone. The extent to which its presence has arisen from natural or man-made sources (or both) has yet to be determined, however, and restrictions upon its use are believed to have resulted in recent substantial decreases in the amounts released to the atmosphere. Nonetheless, it may be of stratospheric concern, and will require additional study. Other man-made chemicals may be of concern with respect to possible reduction of stratospheric ozone. However, most appear at this time not to be as important, either because they are expected to be removed more răpidly in the lower atmosphere or because they are produced and released in substantially lesser amounts. These chemicals will be the subjects of further study.

Climatic Effects of Ozone Reduction

Some scientists postulate that changes in stratospheric ozone levels would cause changes in temperature, wind patterns, precipitation, and other weather elements. The nature and extent of these changes and their effects on the earth's climate, however, cannot be predicted on the basis of present knowledge.

Biological and Health Effects
of Ozone Reduction

There is persuasive, although not absolutely conclusive, clinical and epidemiological evidence of a direct link between solar radiation and the historically observed incidence of several generally non-fatal (non-melanomal) types of skin cancer in humans,... (The death rate in the U.S. from these types of cancer is estimated to be about 1% of the non-melanoma cases.) There is, for example, an observed doubling of non-melanoma skin cancers with each 8° to 11° decrease in latitude, which is presumed to relate to the correlated increase in UV radiation reaching the earth with decrease in latitude. Estimates based upon observed changes in incidence of skin cancer with variations in latitude for each percent reduction in average ozone concentration range from 2,100 to 15,000 (6,000 median) new cases of non-melanoma skin cancer per year among light-skinned individuals in the U.S. at steady state. (The National Cancer Institute estimates the current incidence of non-melanoma skin cancers in the U.S. to be about 300,000 cases per year.)

This clinical and epidemiological evidence is strongly supported by the unequivocal induction of skin cancers in animals exposed to increased UV radiation.

There is some evidence, although much less conclusive, to support a correlation between UV-B radiation and melanoma, a considerably more frequently fatal form of skin cancer (median survival time of 7 years). Other expected health effects include greater incidence of sunburning in populations at risk and earlier onset of skin aging. Additional possible effects that have been less studied are eye damage and excessive synthesis of vitamin D in the skin.

Because of the sensitivity of other living organisms to UV-B radiation, any increase in the cumulative dosage of this radiation might be of considerable biological and agricultural significance.

Possible biological and agricultural effects, for which more investigation is required before any definite conclusions can be made, include changes in physiological, biochemical, anatomical, and growth characteristics of certain plant and animal species; health effects on livestock; disturbances in the balance of aquatic and terrestrial ecosystems; and changes in the stability and effectiveness of agricultural chemicals. Any significant climatic changes resulting from reduction in stratospheric ozone levels might be expected to have some agricultural effects, such as reduction of the yield of some crops, especially in areas where production of a crop is marginal.

The Fluorocarbon Industry

Fluorocarbons are produced by six companies in the U.S. and by at least 48 companies in more than 23 other nations. U.S. production has been doubling about every 6 years, with an annual increase of between 10 and 20%. However, there are indications that the rapid growth may be slowing in the U.S. There are no known plans for new construction to expand production in the next 3 years. In 1974 total aerosol sales (not restricted to those using fluorocarbon propellants) were reported by industry to have decreased about 5 to 10% from 1973 sales of 3 billion units, compared with a growth rate of 10.5% in 1972. It is expected that future expansion of fluorocarbon production to meet market demands would be greater in other parts of the world than in the U.S. (again, presuming the absence of any regulation) because other countries are farther from market saturation.

Fluorocarbon Uses

Approximately one-half of U.S. fluorocarbon production is used in aerosol propellants. Fluorocarbons constitute the propellant in 50 to 60% of the aerosol units sold. By far the largest amounts of fluorocarbons used in aerosols (more than 90%) are for personal products, especially hair care products, deodorants, and antiperspirants, as opposed to household products, most of which contain propellants other than fluorocarbons.

About 28% of U.S. fluorocarbon production is used as refrigerants in residential and commercial air conditioning and refrigeration, food storage and display, and automobile air conditioning. Estimates are that F-11, F-12, and F-22 ($CHClF_2$) constitute about 92% of U.S. refrigerants.

Fluorocarbons are also used as agents in the production of foams, and as solvents and fire extinguishers.

Substitutes

The problem of finding adequate substitutes for fluorocarbons is easier in the case of propellants than refrigerants. Acceptable alternate propellants are available for many aerosol applications; for others, no alternate propellants are known to be suitable, especially in personal products where a fine, well controlled spray is desirable. Non-propellant packaging can be used for many products now utilizing the aerosol, however, and may be less

443

expensive for the consumer. Numerous deodorants and antiperspirants in non-aerosol packaging have been marketed successfully for many years; hair care products are also available with manual atomizers. Improvements in mechanical pumping devices, currently believed to be under investigation by industry, could make such products more widely accepted.

It has been reported by industry representatives that no suitable alternatives are presently known for the majority of refrigeration uses employing F-11 and F-12. It has been suggested that F-22 and other fluorocarbons that might not pose as significant a stratospheric hazard as F-11 and F-12 (because of their anticipated greater chemical reactivity in the lower atmosphere) could be used as alternative refrigerants. Although F-22 does not have properties that would allow it to be used as a propellant in aerosol products, it now constitutes about 30% of the refrigeration market. F-22 probably cannot be substituted in new equipment presently designed for use of F-11 and F-12 without substantial and costly design changes. This possibility should be further investigated, however. It is expected that greater problems would be encountered in switching to presently known non-fluorocarbon refrigerants (e.g., ammonia) because of toxic and other hazardous properties. Substitution of other refrigerants for F-11 and F-12 could not generally be made in existing equipment because the equipment is designed and constructed for the properties of specific compounds.

Development of chemical substitutes for each fluorocarbon use would in nearly all cases be a long and costly process. It is hoped, however, that this will not be necessary—that if restrictions on fluorocarbons are required, substitute delivery systems could be used for most aerosol products presently using fluorocarbon propellants, and that the refrigeration problem might be partially solved through reduction of leakage and recovery of the fluorocarbons for recycling at the time of eventual disposal. Some preliminary study indicates that there may be a potential for controlling a significant portion of the emissions from refrigeration systems during their operation with only relatively minor modifications of existing technology. These matters demand intensive additional study as to technological possibilities and economic feasibility.

Impact on Industry

Present data do not permit precise judgment on the number of workers and dollar value of business that might be affected by restrictions on fluorocarbon production or use, especially because any future development of alternatives cannot be predicted. Any restrictions would result in some adverse impacts, which would vary in severity for different occupations and different companies. Industry estimates that more than 1 million jobs may be associated with the use of fluorocarbons (of which 4,000 are associated with fluorocarbon production). The fraction of these 1 million workers who would be affected by restrictions upon fluorocarbon uses would depend upon the nature of the restrictions. It is not probable, for example, that persons associated with refrigeration and air-conditioning sales would be significantly affected by any restrictions likely to be considered. Industry representatives also estimate that the refrigeration and air-conditioning industry as a whole accounts for about $5.5 billion of the gross national product and that aerosol products containing fluorocarbon propellants account for about an additional $2 billion.

Detailed studies of substitution possibilities and of various socio-economic impacts of regulation are currently underway and are expected to be taken into account by the regulatory agencies in determining the exact nature of any regulations and timetables that might be considered.

Federal Authorities and
Recommended Federal Actions

Products that release fluorocarbons ultimately reaching the stratosphere can be divided into four categories according to how they may be regulated.

Fluorocarbons that are used as propellants in foods, drugs, and cosmetic products can be regulated by the Food and Drug Administration. These same compounds used to propel pesticide products can be regulated by the Environmental Protection Agency. Any other product (except automobiles) produced for distribution to, or use by, consumers can be regulated by the Consumer Product Safety Commission.

There is, however, no Federal authority governing any of the other fluorocarbon uses such as automobile air conditioning, industrial and commercial applications for air conditioning and refrigeration, and uses as a foaming agent or fire retardant. The proposed Toxic Substances Control Act now pending before Congress would provide for effective control of all uses of fluorocarbons if required and, in addition, would provide a regulatory base for control of a wide variety of potentially harmful substances with broad environmental consequences. This is the preferred approach in lieu of narrower specific legislation for fluorocarbons. The task force urges rapid passage of this legislation to fill these important gaps in the applicable Federal Authorities.

Cause for Concern

The task force has concluded that fluorocarbon releases to the environment are a legitimate cause for concern. Moreover, unless new scientific evidence is found to remove the cause for concern, it would seem necessary to restrict uses of fluorocarbons-11 and -12 to replacement of fluids in existing refrigeration and air-conditioning equipment and to closed recycled systems or other uses not involving release to the atmosphere.

The National Academy of Sciences is currently conducting an in-depth scientific study of man-made impacts on the stratosphere and will report in less than a year. If the National Academy of Sciences confirms the current task force assessment, it is recommended that the Federal regulatory agencies initiate rulemaking procedures for implementing regulations to restrict fluorocarbon uses. Such restrictions could reasonably be effective by January 1978—a date that, given the concern expressed now, should allow time for consideration of further research results and for the affected industries and consumers to initiate adjustments.

In order to reduce the chance of unduly penalizing producers and marketers of aerosol products that do not use F-11 and F-12, the task force recommends that the regulatory agencies proceed immediately with consideration of a requirement that all aerosol products using fluorocarbons be labeled to indicate their fluorocarbon content.

International Cooperation

International cooperation is strongly urged, inasmuch as the U.S. produces and uses only about one-half of the world-wide fluorocarbons, and effects on stratospheric ozone from ground release transcend national boundaries. The State Department will initiate and coordinate a program of international exchange of information, cooperative research, and proposals for international action to help implement uniform policy actions on a world-wide basis. U.S. concern will be expressed and coordination will be initiated in the Organization for Economic Cooperation and Development (OECD), other international organizations, and through bilateral channels.

Research Programs

Much relevant research on the fluorocarbon question has already been conducted or is currently in progress through basic research programs in the atmospheric sciences and through applied research such as the recent Climatic Impact Assessment Program. [A Department of Transportation study of the impact of aircraft emissions on the stratosphere.]

In addition to Federally sponsored research, the chemical industries affected are also conducting research programs. The research supported by 19 fluorocarbon producers around the world will amount to about a $3.75 to $5 million program over 3 years, which might be increased upon consideration of further research proposals. The program will emphasize measuring and monitoring chlorine levels in the stratosphere, modeling atmospheric dynamics, and determining critical rates of reaction. It will also include other studies relevant to determining the validity of the theories of ozone reduction. The program is coordinated through a Fluorocarbons Technical Panel under the auspices of the Manufacturing Chemists Association.

The National Aeronautics and Space Administration (NASA) has accepted lead agency responsibility for the development and testing of instruments and measuring systems for the sampling of trace atmospheric constituents and is chairing an interagency subcommittee of the Interdepartmental Committee for Atmospheric Sciences (ICAS) to develop an expanded program in these areas. Ozone monitoring is conducted by the National Oceanic and Atmospheric Administration (NOAA) and NASA. Other atmospheric research will be conducted by NOAA; NASA; the Departments of Defense and Transportation; Energy Research and Development Administration; Environmental Protection Agency; and the National Science Foundation and will be coordinated through ICAS. This research includes refining critical rates of reaction, searching for additional sinks for chlorine, studying the total chlorine burden of the stratosphere and its sources, monitoring fluorocarbons and other trace gases in the troposphere and stratosphere, and modeling the atmosphere. The entire program amounts to about $14 million in FY 1975, and funds are being sought to continue and expand this effort in future years.

Research on the agricultural, biological, and human health effects of ozone reduction will be conducted by the U.S. Department of Agriculture, the National Institute of Environmental Health Sciences, and the National Cancer Institute. This includes research on effects of increased UV radiation on agricultural crops, timber, natural vegetation, livestock, insects, and aquatic and terrestrial ecosystems; studies of biological mechanisms for resisting UV radiation and alleviating stress; models of effects of potential climatic changes; development of instrumentation for simulating natural UV-B radiation; analyses of the causes and incidence of skin cancer, and toxicological studies of the relationship between UV radiation and various types of skin cancer.

The regulatory agencies will conduct further studies of the socioeconomic impacts of any restrictions on fluorocarbons....

II.
Conclusions and Federal Actions

In June 1974 the first scientific paper was published raising the issue of possible harmful effects from discharges of fluorocarbon gases, principally $CFCl_3$ (Fluorocarbon-11) and CF_2Cl_2 (fluorocarbon-12), into the atmosphere. Since that time numerous other scientific groups have reported on the issue.

The Interagency Task Force on Inadvertent Modification of the Stratosphere (IMOS) has investigated this subject and found that:

(1) Fluorocarbons are produced in large quantities; ultimately almost all are released into the atmosphere.

(a) Approximately 13.8 billion pounds of fluorocarbons-11 and -12 (F-11 and F-12) have been produced to date in the world (exclusive of the U.S.S.R. and Eastern European countries).

(b) 1.7 billion pounds of this total were produced in 1973.

(c) Total U.S. production has been doubling about every 5 to 7 years since the early 1950's; world-wide production (exclusive of the U.S.S.R. and Eastern European countries) in 1973 was 11% over 1972 production.

(d) Approximately 50% of the world production and use of these fluorocarbons (exclusive of the U.S.S.R. and Eastern European countries) occurs in the U.S.

(2) F-11 and F-12 are not appreciably chemically decomposed in the lower atmosphere.

(a) They are virtually inert chemically in the troposphere.

(b) They have very low solubility in water and therefore are not washed out of the atmosphere by precipitation.

(c) They are found in the atmosphere in concentrations that seem to be consistent with the total world release to date.

(3) No significant natural "sinks" other than stratospheric processes are known to exist for fluorocarbons in the environment.

(a) The amount of fluorocarbons contained in the oceans, in soil, in subsurface ground water, and frozen in the polar ice caps is probably insignificant when compared with the atmospheric content.

(4) A significant fraction of the fluorocarbons is expected eventually to move by atmospheric circulation and diffusion up into the stratosphere.

(a) Recent measurements have detected the presence of F-11 in the stratosphere.

(b) It is estimated that it would take several years for a significant fraction of the total volume of fluorocarbons discharged in a given year to reach the stratosphere.

(5) In the stratosphere above 25 km (about 80,000 ft.), fluorocarbons are expected to:

(a) Be reactive due to dissociation by UV radiation from the sun which penetrates only as far as the stratosphere.

(b) Yield chlorine atoms (Cl) and a fluorocarbon radical.

(c) Dissociate within days to months depending upon the altitude.

(6) Although it has yet to be confirmed by direct stratospheric measurements, it is assumed that the fluorocarbon radical will probably dissociate until all of the chlorine atoms are released. Cl may react catalytically with either an oxygen atom (O) or ozone (O_3) before forming less reactive hydrogen chloride (HCl) and diffusing downward to the troposphere.

(a) Under these conditions the chlorine atoms (Cl) or as the free radical ClO for at least several days, and in this interval would be expected to react with thousands of oxygen atoms or ozone molecules.

Ozone

(7) Ozone is a minor, but extremely important, constituent gas in the stratosphere.

(a) It is generated by the splitting of a normal oxygen molecule (O_2) by ultraviolet (UV) solar radiation and subsequent combination of the liberated oxygen atoms with another oxygen molecule to form ozone.

(b) The rate of formation of ozone is believed to depend almost exclusively upon the amount of incoming UV solar radiation and is therefore virtually independent of human influence.

(8) Ozone is maintained in the stratosphere in a dynamic equilibrium; i.e., there is an approximate balancing of the rate of ozone formation with that of ozone destruction.

(a) The naturally occurring ozone-destroying reactions include the interaction of ozone with oxygen atoms (O), with nitrogen oxides (NO_x), with hydrogen species (H, OH, HO_2) and possibly other natural stratospheric components. The rate of loss to the troposphere by transport into the stratosphere is much smaller than the rate of loss by chemical reaction.

(b) Most of the ozone in the atmosphere resides in the stratosphere.

(c) The concentration of ozone between the earth and the sun at mid-latitudes fluctuates daily on the average of 10% in the winter and 5% in the summer and 25% between seasons.

(d) The total ozone equilibrium concentration of the stratosphere also varies considerably with latitude; ozone occurs in greater amounts over the polar regions than at lower latitudes.

(9) Because of the large natural variations in ozone content, a 5 to 10% average decrease, persisting and measured for several years, would be required before a change could be attributed to human activity with any reasonable statistical reliability.

(a) Total ozone levels in the northern hemisphere seem to have increased by about 5 to 10% during the period 1955-1970. The ozone concentration has been on the decline since 1970 (approximately 1 to 2%). These fluctuations probably represent primarily natural variations, possibly related to solar activity.

(10) It is expected that any relase to the atmosphere of man-made chemicals that reach the stratosphere and react to destroy ozone would create additional decreases in the stratospheric ozone content over and above those caused naturally....

(13) Although there are some uncertainties in the calculations, the best estimates are that fluorocarbon production and release to the environment to date may:

(a) Have resulted in a current reduction in average ozone concentration estimated to be most likely between 0.5 and 1% and possibly as large as 2%.

(b) Eventually result in as much as a 1.3 to 3% reduction in the equilibrium ozone concentration.

Duration of Change

(14) Because of slow diffusion of fluorocarbons into the stratosphere, any changes in ozone from fluorocarbon release would be delayed.

(a) Even if no additional fluorocarbons were released after a certain date, further reduction of average ozone concentration would continue, reaching a maximum in about a decade or more later.

(b) It is expected that reduced levels of ozone would last to some extent for as much as a century or more after cessation of fluorocarbon releases.

(15) Current model calculations predict that if release of fluorocarbons were to continue at the 1972 rate, a maximum reduction of about 7% in the equilibrium ozone concentration would be expected after several decades.

Effects of Ozone Reduction

(1) Stratospheric ozone screens UV-B radiation in sunlight from the earth's surface....

Any significant decrease in the stratospheric ozone layer resulting in increased UV-B radiation reaching the earth would cause environmental effects that are predominantly harmful.

(1) There is persuasive, although not absolutely conclusive, clinical and epidemiological evidence of a direct correlation between solar radiation and the historically observed incidence of several generally non-fatal (non-melanoma) skin cancers in humans. (The death rate in the U.S. is estimated to be about 1% of the non-melanoma cases.) This is strongly supported by the unequivocal induction of skin cancers in animals exposed to increased UV radiation....

(b) An increase of approximately 2% (range 0.7 to 5%) in the incidence of non-melanoma skin cancers in the U.S. is predicted for a 1% reduction in average ozone concentration (with a disproportionately greater increase in cancer for higher percentages of reduction in ozone levels)....

(2) There is some evidence, although much less conclusive, to support a similar correlation between UV-B radiation and melanoma—a much less common, but considerably more frequently fatal, form of skin cancer (median survival time of 7 years).

(3) Other expected health effects include greater incidence of sunburning in population at risk and earlier onset of skin aging.

(4) Other possible effects that have been less studied are eye damage and excessive synthesis of vitamin D in the skin.

(5) Possible biological and agricultural effects, for which more investigation is required before any definite conclusions can be made, include:

(a) Changes in physiological, biochemical, anatomical, and growth characteristics of certain plant species sensitive to UV-B radiation, including some food crops.

(b) Disturbances in aquatic and terrestrial ecosystems.

(c) Effects on the behavior of insects, including those beneficial to agriculture.

(d) Effects on the stability and effectiveness of agricultural chemicals.

(e) Effects on livestock, e.g., increases in certain types of cancer.

(f) Reduction in the yield of some crops, especially in areas of marginal agricultural production, as the result of any significant climatic changes resulting from reduction of stratospheric ozone levels.

(6) Some scientists postulate that changes in stratospheric ozone levels would cause changes in temperature, wind patterns, precipitation, and other weather elements. The nature and extent of these changes and their effects on the earth's climate, however, cannot be predicted on the basis of present knowledge.

Assessment of Validity of Stratospheric Models

...The fact that current models are consistent with the behavior of currently measurable chemical species and reactions suggests that characterizations by the models of other as yet unmeasured reactions are likely to be reasonably predictive.

Therefore, unless future measurements are found to be totally inconsistent with predicted values, there would be no reason to challenge the basic validity of the stratospheric models. For example, a contraindication would be the discovery of natural sources of chlorine in the stratosphere grossly in excess of the amount that could otherwise be accounted for by current understanding.

Calculations of possible reduction in stratospheric ozone by F-11 and F-12 have been made independently by several scientists. Despite varying assumptions and parameters, the findings of these experts agree within a factor of two—an agreement that is somewhat better than the uncertainty in each of the calculations....

It is not expected, however, that further refinements in the calculations will affect the conclusions of the task force because, even at the most optimistic end of the currently reported range of uncertainty, there is still a basis for concern about possible stratospheric alterations from past and future releases of fluorocarbons to the atmosphere....

Assessment of Validity of Expected Effects of Ozone Reduction

...Because of the short time frame in which biological studies were conducted on increased UV-B radiation under CIAP [Climatic Impact Assessment Program, Department of Transportation] and because of the difficulties of UV-B simulation and measurement, most presently available results are only preliminary. Considerably more research is needed to determine baseline data on present UV-B levels reaching the earth's surface and the biological impact of increased UV-B radiation before definitive statements can be made of the nature and magnitude of any changes that may occur....

Despite uncertainties concerning the actual amount of decrease in average ozone levels that might occur or the exact nature and magnitude of the resulting effects, the task force concludes that the prospects of a reduction in the equilibrium ozone concentration in the stratosphere from present and future releases of F-11 and F-12 and other atmospheric pollutants may represent a potentially serious problem of long-range consequences that would warrant increased attention on a national and international basis.

Considerations in Reaching a Decision

Most well recognized hazards until recent years have been characterized by direct and immediate or almost immediate effects (e.g., food poisoning, unshielded machinery in the workplace, faulty automobile equipment). The inherent risks for these types of hazards are usually measurable directly at the first indication of a problem, and actions can be taken quickly to alleviate the risk. The decision whether to regulate or modify the risk largely depends on whether or not an unacceptable effect has occurred.

Lately, however, many hazards, particularly those related to the environment, have been identified for which the effects are not immediately apparent. Cancer induced by chemicals in the environment is one example; the fluorocarbon-ozone question described in this report is another.

For this latter form of hazard, the harmful effects occur far removed in time and space from their cause. In the case of cancer induced by chemical agents in the environment, or the fluorocarbon-ozone question, the time delay is typically on the order of tens of years. The existence of a long time lag between causes and effects requires that decisions about the possible control of such hazards be made on a somewhat different basis from those acute hazards whose effects can be directly and immediately observed or simulated....

In an attempt to judge what is an acceptable level of risk, as soon as there is reasonable assurance that the predicted effects will indeed occur, the decisionmaker must take into account the equity factors and treat the potential future effects as if they were occurring today. If the hazard poses potentially serious effects, the decisionmaker may not be able to wait for the measurement of the effects. Great caution has to be exercised in reacting to relatively unsupported hypotheses. On the other hand, when presented with well founded scientific theory, confirmed by statistically reasonable experimental evidence, it may be necessary to act....

Timetable For Action

The task force has concluded that fluorocarbon releases to the environment are a legitimate cause for concern. Moreover, unless new scientific evidence is found to remove the cause for concern, it would seem necessary to restrict uses of F-11 and F-12 to replacement of fluids in existing refrigeration and air-conditioning equipment and to closed recycled systems or other uses not involving release to the atmosphere.

The National Academy of Sciences is currently conducting an in-depth scientific study of man-made impacts on the stratosphere and will report its findings in less than a year. If the National Academy of Sciences study confirms the current task force assessment, it is recommended that the Federal regulatory agencies initiate rulemaking procedures for implementing regulations to restrict fluorocarbon uses. Such restrictions could reasonably be effective by January 1978—a date that, given the concern expressed now, should allow time for consideration of further results and for the affected industries and consumers to initiate adjustments....

Currently, the Environmental Protection Agency has jurisdiction over pesticides under the Federal Insecticide, Fungicide, and Rodenticide Act as amended. The Food and Drug Administration has authority over aerosol-propelled foods, drugs, and cosmetics under the Federal Food, Drug, and Cosmetic Act. The Consumer Product Safety Commission has authority over all other consumer aerosol products, home air conditioners, home refrigerators, and any other consumer products except automobiles under the Consumer Product Safety Act. There is, however, no Federal authority governing any of the remaining uses of fluorocarbons such as automobile air conditioning, industrial and commercial applications for air conditioning and refrigeration, and uses as a foaming agent or fire retardant. The proposed Toxic Substances Control Act now pending before Congress would provide for effective control of all uses of fluorocarbons, if required, and also would provide a regulatory base for control of a wide variety of potentially harmful substances with broad environmental consequences, including other compounds that may be of stratospheric concern. This is the preferred approach in lieu of narrower specific legislation for fluorocárbons.

The Congress is, therefore, urged to act promptly to enact toxic substances control legislation so that, if necessary, the Federal Government will have sufficient authority to address any potentially serious problems involving such substances. [As of Dec. 31, 1975, the legislation, first introduced in 1971, was still pending.]

In order to reduce the chance of unduly penalizing manufacturers of aerosol products that do not employ F-11 and F-12 (approximately 40 to 50% of the market), the task force recommends that the regulatory agencies proceed immediately with consideration of a requirement that all aerosol products using fluorocarbons be labeled to indicate their fluorocarbon content....

PROPOSED NEW APPEALS COURT
June 20, 1975

When a panel of prominent lawyers in 1972 urged the creation of a "national court of appeals," opponents of the plan objected that the proposed tribunal would foreclose the possibility of final appeal to the Supreme Court in certain types of cases (see Historic Documents 1972, p. 953). Three years later, the massive and still growing caseload of the high court prompted a second panel of legal experts to again recommend an appellate court with national jurisdiction. After a 15-month study of the federal courts, a congressional commission chaired by Sen. Roman L. Hruska (R Neb.) proposed the creation of a seven-judge court to hear cases referred to it by the Supreme Court or by the existing circuit appellate courts.

The commission's recommendations, released June 20 in its final report, stressed improvement of the nation's judicial system as a whole, whereas the 1972 plan had focused more narrowly on screening the Supreme Court's caseload. The commission stated that the new court would provide prompt, nationally binding decisions on important cases which the Supreme Court would probably not review, because of the Court's crowded docket or because of limitations in the scope of the cases. However, since the rulings of the proposed new court would still be subject to Supreme Court review upon petition, critics of the plan complained that it would simply add a fourth layer to the nation's judicial system without substantially lightening the high court's work load.

One of the plan's most prominent critics, Associate Justice William O. Douglas, contended that, as proposed, the new court would sustain the "quite conservative" bias of lower state and federal court judges. "[T]he mounting pleas of individuals are not heard and the [Supreme] Court will no longer take on highly controversial issues," Douglas wrote to Senator Hruska.

Douglas was one of four justices known to oppose the creation of a new appellate court; the other five, in varying degrees, supported the proposal. Chief Justice Warren E. Burger formally endorsed the proposal in a June 3 letter to Hruska. Since his 1969 appointment to the bench, Burger had repeatedly warned that the Supreme Court's burgeoning caseload threatened the quality of its judgments. He had handpicked the panel which recommended a new court in 1972.

Pressures for Change

Fundamental changes in the American judicial system have been rare. The last was in 1925 when Congress gave the Supreme Court almost complete discretion in selecting the cases on which it would rule. In recent years the number of cases appealed to the Court had skyrocketed; according to the commission's report, the number rose from about 1,200 in 1951 to around 4,000 in 1974. New areas of dispute "relatively unknown to the law a few short years ago," such as environmental law, occupational safety and consumer rights, had added substantially to the Court's burden. And the increased burden tended to restrict court decisions more and more to constitutional questions and such federal statutes as labor and antitrust laws. A second tier of cases of wide impact, often involving conflicting circuit court opinions, rarely reach the high court docket. Although these cases, concerned with tax law, patents and similar matters, are considered of "less intrinsic merit," they still require "definitive declaration[s] of national law," the commission asserted. The proposed new court could be expected to hand down 150 rulings a year, approximately the same number as the Supreme Court. Although the Supreme Court might have to review some of the decisions of the new court, the capacity of the federal system of justice to deliver final and nationally binding decisions more promptly would be markedly enhanced.

Other Changes Recommended

While the focus of the commission's report was the proposed new appellate court, it also recommended a number of other changes including:

● Appointment of additional federal judges to handle the mounting caseload in the lower courts;

● Increasing the salaries of federal judges;

● Reducing or omitting oral arguments under certain circumstances in federal court cases;

● Requiring some written explanation of every appellate decision, but in certain circumstances substituting memorandums or other short unsigned forms for signed opinions;

● Easing retirement age requirements for appellate court judges.

Creation of the proposed new appellate court would require the approval of the Congress and the President. Although Hruska planned to introduce enabling legislation in the 94th Congress, observers did not expect immediate action on the measure. When the commission's report was submitted to President Ford in June, he refrained from commenting on its recommendations but urged Congress to give the plan "serious study."

Excerpts from Structure and Internal Procedures: Recommendations for Change, *the report of the Commission on Revision of the Federal Court Appellate System, published June 20, 1975:*

Summary of Recommendations

1. The Commission recommends that Congress establish a National Court of Appeals, consisting of seven Article III judges appointed by the President with the advice and consent of the Senate.

2. The court would sit only en banc and its decisions would constitute precedents binding upon all other federal courts and, as to federal questions, upon state courts as well, unless modified, or overruled by the Supreme Court.

3. The National Court of Appeals would have jurisdiction to hear cases (a) referred to it by the Supreme Court (reference jurisdiction), or (b) transferred to it from the regional courts of appeals, the Court of Claims and the Court of Customs and Patent Appeals (transfer jurisdiction).

(a) *Reference jurisdiction.* With respect to any case before it on petition for certiorari, the Supreme Court would be authorized:

(1) to retain the case and render a decision on the merits;

(2) to deny certiorari without more, thus terminating the litigation;

(3) to deny certiorari and refer the case to the National Court of Appeals for that court to decide on the merits;

(4) to deny certiorari and refer the case to the National Court, giving that court discretion either to decide the case on the merits or to deny review and thus terminate the litigation.

The Supreme Court would also be authorized to refer cases within its obligatory jurisdiction, excepting only those which the Constitution requires it to accept. Referral in such cases would always be for decision on the merits.

(b) *Transfer jurisdiction.* If a case filed in a court of appeals, the Court of Claims or the Court of Customs and Patent Appeals is one in which an immediate decision by the National Court of Appeals is in the public interest, it may be transferred to the National Court provided it falls within one of the following categories:

(1) the case turns on a rule of federal law and federal courts have reached inconsistent conclusions with respect to it; or

(2) the case turns on a rule of federal law applicable to a recurring factual situation, and a showing is made that the advantages of a prompt and definitive determination of that rule by the National Court of Appeals outweigh any potential disadvantages of transfer; or

(3) the case turns on a rule of federal law which has theretofore been announced by the National Court of Appeals, and there is a substantial question about the proper interpretation or application of that rule in the pending case.

The National Court would be empowered to decline to accept the transfer of any case. Decisions granting or denying transfer, and decisions by the National Court accepting or rejecting cases, would not be reviewable under any circumstances, by extraordinary writ or otherwise.

4. Any case decided by the National Court of Appeals, whether upon reference or after transfer, would be subject to review by the Supreme Court upon petition for certiorari....

A National Court of Appeals

The Commission recommends the creation of a new national court of appeals, designed to increase the capacity of the federal judicial system for definitive adjudication of issues of national law, subject always to Supreme Court review. Such a tribunal will help assure that differences in legal rules applied by the circuits do not result in unequal treatment of citizens with respect, for example, to their rights under the social security laws, their liability to criminal sanctions, or their immunity from discrimination in employment. It will assure consistency and uniformity by resolving conflicts between circuits after they have developed, and it will, by anticipating and avoiding possible future conflicts, eliminate years of repetitive litigation and uncertainty as to the state of the federal law. It will, in short, contribute to that stability in the law which makes it possible for the courts and the bar to serve society more effectively.

Consistent with its Congressional mandate, the Commission has focused its studies on those areas in which deficiencies have been demonstrated and for which a more effective and efficient structure can be designed. A close and careful study of the considerations discussed below has led to the conclusion that a National Court of Appeals is needed today, and, if the demands of society continue to grow, will be indispensable in the years ahead.

The Need for a New Court

Current Capacity: Numbers

The United States Supreme Court is today the only court with the power to hand down judgments which constitute binding precedents in all state and federal courts. It is charged with maintaining a harmonious body of national law through its power of review of the judgments in cases brought before it by way of certiorari and appeal. As the number of cases brought to the Supreme Court for review has burgeoned, the number disposed of on the merits after argument has remained relatively constant. Obviously, the major variable has been in the number of cases not accorded plenary review.

The figures are dramatic. In 1951 about 1,200 cases were filed in the Court. Twenty years later the number had tripled to about 3,600. The volume continues to rise: in the most recent complete term over 4,000 cases were filed. By contrast, as Erwin N. Griswold observes, the Court was "hearing about 150 cases on the merits in 1925; it was hearing about 150 cases on the merits twenty five years ago. It hears about 150 cases on the merits today." Elaborating on the same point, he continues:

> The number of cases argued orally in 1951 was 128. The number of cases argued orally at the 1973 Term was 170. But there were a considerable number of occasions when two or more cases were heard at a single argument. Thus, there were approximately 150 oral arguments, and this number has been more or less constant for a number of years. It is, in fact, the maximum number that the Court can be expected to hear on the merits.

The significance of these figures is summarized by Griswold as follows:

> ... Putting it another way, about eighteen percent of paid cases (appeals and certiorari) were heard on the merits twenty years ago, while about six percent of paid cases were heard on the merits during the 1973 Term. What became of the other twelve percent of paid cases? ...they were lost in the 1973 Term simply because of inadequate appellate capacity to hear cases on a national basis.

The figures discussed above do not include summary dispositions of cases within the Court's appeal docket. While these dispositions are binding on lower courts, a dismissal or a summary affirmance with bare recitation of result and without citation cannot be considered the equivalent of plenary disposition for purposes of providing an adequate body of precedents on recurring issues of national law. The Court itself has recognized as much. Mr. Justice Rehnquist, speaking for the Court, observed last year that "obviously, they [summary affirmances] are not of the same precedential value as would be an opinion of this Court treating the question on the merits." More recently the Chief Justice in a concurring opinion wrote: "When we summarily affirm, without opinion, the judgment of a three-judge District Court we affirm the judgment but not necessarily the reasoning by which it was reached." He emphasized that "upon fuller consideration of an issue under plenary review, the Court has not hesitated to discard a rule which a line of summary affirmances may appear to have established."

Supreme Court filings may already be an inadequate measure of the real needs of the country for definitive adjudication of national issues. As the needs increase and the proportion of cases accorded review decreases, the number of filings becomes even less likely to reflect the real need accurately. Fewer litigants will seek review, not necessarily because their cause is unimportant by traditional criteria, but rather because there is so little chance of persuading the Court to hear the case. Professors Casper and

Posner make the point effectively in their recently-published *Study of the Supreme Court's Caseload:* "[T]he value of filing an application for review with the Supreme Court," they write, "is a function of the probability that review will be granted, and as that probability declines over time due to increases in the number of cases filed coupled with the Court's inability to increase significantly the number of cases it accepts for review, the value of seeking review will fall, and, other things being equal, the number of cases should decline."

Impact of Caseload

The implication of this analysis is clear. In the words of the authors: "[S]hould the Court's caseload level off or even decline in the coming years, this would *not* refute the existence of a serious workload problem—the caseload might simply have become so large in relation to the Court's ability to decide cases that litigants were discouraged from seeking review by the low probability of obtaining it."

There is evidence that this phenomenon has already had its impact and that the data we have discussed may in fact understate the problem today. We know that in cases which the Solicitor General considered "certworthy," he has refused to request review because of a sensitivity to the Court's workload and a concern that review would be jeopardized in cases of even greater importance. Similarly, private practitioners refer to what has been termed the "hidden docket," those cases in which counsel chose not to seek review only because the probability of a decision on the merits is too low to warrant the expense.

The pressure of this increased competition for the attention of the Supreme Court is not distributed equally in all categories of cases. Understandably, an increasing proportion of the Court's decisions have involved constitutional issues. Since the total number of decisions has remained constant, the result is that the number dealing with non-constitutional issues has been decreasing. Prior to 1960, the Harvard Law Review reported in 1971, non-constitutional holdings "almost uniformly made up two-thirds to three-quarters of the Court's decisions. In more recent years, the proportions have almost been reversed: constitutional cases have comprised between one-half and two-thirds of the Court's plenary decisions. Congressional enactments have imposed federal standards in such areas as occupational health and safety, protection of the environment, product safety, and economic stabilization, to name but a few. Thus, while the scope of federal regulatory legislation—typically including provisions for judicial review—has been steadily broadening, the number of definitive decisions interpreting that legislation has been diminishing. What this means, in absolute figures, is that in each term the Supreme Court can be expected to hand down no more than 80, and perhaps as few as 55, plenary decisions in all areas of federal nonconstitutional law. The question is whether this number of decisions is adequate to meet the country's needs for authoritative exposition of recurring issues of national law.

No single conclusion follows inexorably from the raw statistics discussed above. We do not know the minimum number of cases which must be decided each year by a court of nationwide authority in order to maintain a stable and harmonious law. The data suggest either that there were many cases decided by the Supreme Court a quarter of a century ago which need not have been decided by that Court then; or that there are many cases deserving decision by a national tribunal today which are not being decided in such a forum; or that conditions have changed in a way which reduces, rather than increases, the proportion of cases which must be decided by a national tribunal in order to assure a stable, harmonious and authoritative national law.

Questions About the Future

At the least, the data raise serious questions about the future. They provide no basis for confidence that the Supreme Court can be expected adequately to satisfy the need for stability and harmony in the national law as the demands continue to increase in the decades ahead.

There are those who suggest that the solution lies in persuading the Supreme Court to accept a greater number of cases each year for decision on the merits. Specifically, it has been urged that the Supreme Court increase its capacity for decision, particularly with respect to the resolution of inter-circuit conflicts, by resorting to truncated procedures. Rather than accord the litigants a full scale hearing, the Court should simply choose, as one witness put it, "the most appealing opinion among [those] of the courts of appeals." We reject any approach which would call upon the Court to increase the number of cases decided on the merits without full briefing or oral argument. In our view, a solution to the lack of capacity should not be sought by resort to measures which would adversely affect the Court's processes or the public's confidence in them. To do so would be a disservice to the judicial system and litigants alike; it would incur the risk of permanent damage for what may well prove the ephemeral benefit of temporary relief.

More basically, we cannot recommend any solution which would increase the Court's burden. There is ample evidence that the workload of the Justices is such that they are already subject, in the words of Mr. Justice Blackmun, to "greater and more constant pressure" than busy practitioners or hard-working appellate judges, pressure which "relents little even during the summer months." The issue is not whether the Justices find it possible to keep abreast of present work. The evidence is that more than one does so by giving up the "normal extracurricular enjoyments of life"; six or seven days of work a week are not unknown as a regular pattern. Whether or not such burdens should be viewed as an appropriate norm, it hardly seems a desirable solution to increase the number of cases which the Court should be expected to decide. On the contrary, given the complexity and significance of the issues which only the Supreme Court can decide, it may be appropriate to reduce the number of cases which the Court must decide. Both Mr. Justice White and Mr. Justice Rehnquist have invited consideration of this alternative.

It should be emphasized that the primary focus of our inquiry has not been the burden on the Supreme Court. It has rather been to determine whether the need for definitive declaration of the national law in all its facets is being met, and, if it is not being met, how best to assure that it will be met. As Mr. Justice Rehnquist puts it:

> [T]he desirability of a national court of appeals turns not on the workload of the Supreme Court but rather on the sufficiency of judicial capacity within the federal system to review issues of federal constitutional and statutory law. While the adoption of the Commission's proposal might enable the Supreme Court to make some changes in the way it exercises its discretionary jurisdiction, the principal objective of the proposal is not "relief" for the Supreme Court but "relief" for litigants who are left at sea by conflicting decisions on questions of federal law.

At the least it must be clear that we cannot seek solutions by requiring the Court to assume the added burden of an increased caseload. We cannot do so today; assuredly, we cannot expect to do so as the need increases in the years ahead.

The Experience of Participants in the System

The perceptions of participants in the federal judicial system are valuable in assessing the extent to which the present structure of the federal courts is adequate to meet the needs of the country. Particularly significant are the views of the Justices of the Supreme Court of the United States.

Mr. Justice White is convinced that there are cases "which should be decided after plenary consideration but which the Supreme Court now either declines to review or resolves summarily," and that they exist in substantial numbers, sufficient "to warrant the creation of another appellate court." After expressing agreement with Mr. Justice White, Mr. Justice Powell adds:

> [T]he burgeoning caseload of the federal courts is not likely to diminish, and this Court can hardly serve the national appellate needs of our country as adequately today as it could when petitions filed here were about 1,000 per year as contrasted with the present 4,000 plus.

Mr. Justice Blackmun has put the matter in another way. He refers to the cases "that almost assuredly would have been taken twenty years ago," but which are now denied review, and to the "worry" occasioned the Justices themselves by the need to deny. The concerns expressed by Justice White, Justice Powell, and Justice Blackmun are elaborated by Mr. Justice Rehnquist:

> Conflicting views on questions of federal law remain unresolved because of the Supreme Court's unwillingness, which is reflected in the exercise of its discretionary jurisdiction each year, to undertake to decide more than about 150 cases on the merits during each Term. This reluctance reflects the institutional view that thorough and deliberative decision-making,

and not quantity of output, is the Court's primary consideration. A generation ago, when I was a law clerk to Justice Jackson, this order of priorities imposed no hardship to litigants. The Supreme Court's capacity to decide important issues of federal constitutional and statutory law was adequate for the needs of the country.

I think the Commission's report documents the case that the capacity of this Court is no longer adequate for that purpose. While the number of unresolved conflicts between courts of appeals which were not resolved by this Court is not numerically large, it is significant and, I think everyone would agree that it is bound to increase. Congressional action that would constrict this Court's appellate jurisdiction and thereby increase our ability to resolve direct conflicts through exercise of our discretionary jurisdiction would affect only the immediacy of the need for a national court of appeals, and not the ultimate need for expanded capacity.

A somewhat different problem is underscored by the Chief Justice:

[O]ne element of the Court's historic function is to give binding resolution to important questions of national law. Under present conditions, filings have almost tripled in the past 20 years; even assuming that levels off, the quality of the Court's work will be eroded over a period of time.

The risk of an erosion of quality must be of particular concern at a time when the importance of the issues presented to the Supreme Court is undiminished and the volume increased.

As the Chief Justice states:

The changes brought on in the 20th century and the new social, political, and economic developments have surely not diminished the importance of the questions presented to the Supreme Court and have vastly increased the volume of important questions which can have an impact of great significance on the country.

The Chief Justice "conclude[s] by saying that if no significant changes are made in federal jurisdiction, including that of the Supreme Court, the creation of an intermediate appellate court in some form will be imperative."

The perspective of other participants in the system is also instructive. Erwin Griswold served as Solicitor General of the United States for six terms of the United States Supreme Court, from 1967 until June 1973. One of his responsibilities was to pass on nearly every case in which any officer or agency of the Federal Government had lost in a lower court and wanted to take the case to the Supreme Court, either by appeal or by certiorari. Reviewing the experience of those six terms, Griswold elaborated on the need for the Solicitor General to refuse to recommend Supreme Court review in a substantial number of cases because of the workload of the Court. There are, he concluded, "at least twenty government cases every year which are fully worthy of review by an appellate court with national jurisdiction and...the Government and the legal system suffer...from the lack of authoritative decisions which would come from such review and would serve as a guide to government agencies and the lower courts." This statement, made by one in a unique position to observe the flow of cases and the trends of the law in the federal courts, is important evidence that a problem exists.

"...Fewer Than One Per Cent"

Judge Shirley Hufstedler of the Ninth Circuit has spoken in even stronger terms. The Supreme Court, she observes, "now hears fewer than 1 per cent of the cases decided by the federal courts of appeals." Courts of appeals, she continues, "can be neither right nor harmonious 99 per cent of the time. One per cent supervision is patently inadequate." Views may differ on the importance to be attributed to the precise percentage of cases receiving Supreme Court review. The basis of Judge Hufstedler's conclusion is what is most significant. As she herself notes, it is the experience of adjudicating federal cases appealed to a busy court, and the "informed tuition" which derives from that experience.

Not all judges may be expected to share Judge Hufstedler's views, and indeed there is evidence of dissent. It may be, too, that the Court of Appeals for the Ninth Circuit has been beleaguered more than most. But it is indisputable that if the present growth pattern should continue, the percentages of cases accorded review by the Supreme Court will continue to diminish. It seems clear that at some point the percentage of cases accorded review will have dipped below the minimum necessary for effective monitoring of the nation's courts on issues of federal statutory and constitutional law.

The Consequences of Inadequate Capacity

The studies of the Commission show four major consequences of the failure of the federal judicial system to provide adequate capacity for the declaration of national law. In a very real sense, however, each of the four is but a different facet of the same phenomenon: unnecessary and undesirable uncertainty. For the judge, uncertainty is the lack of a body of precedents adequate for confident decision; for the practitioner, it is a lack of stability sufficient to provide predictability adequate for effective service to clients and society.

Some uncertainty is, of course, inevitable. No lawyer steeped in the tradition of case-by-case development of the law, or sensitive to the inevitable problems of applying even a settled rule to a given fact situation, would pursue the chimera of certainty as an absolute. Moreover, we would not, if we could, accept certainty at the price of stifling new wisdom and needed change. Yet, to recognize the inevitability of some uncertainty does not require that subordination of clarity and stability which results in wasteful proliferation of litigation and threatens public as well as private interests. A prudent balance must be struck.

Inter-Circuit Conflict

Clarity and stability are, of course, conclusory terms. It is helpful to identify specifically and to describe briefly the four major consequences referred to above, with fuller treatment in the sections which follow and in the Appendix to this report. First is the unresolved inter-circuit conflict: two contradictory statements of the same rule of national law, each of equal force within specified territorial limits. Imposing, as it does, different obligations for the payment of taxes, or for environmental control, or occupational safety standards, by reason of the accident of geography, the direct conflict is perhaps the most visible of the consequences of inadequate appellate capacity; certainly it is the most frequently discussed in the literature.

Delay

A second consequence of inadequate appellate capacity for definitive decision on a national basis is delay, which is significant and substantial in terms of its impact. The fact that a conflict is ultimately resolved does not eliminate the cost exacted by the delay; a fortiori, it cannot mean that the system is working in optimal fashion. Resolution may come only after years of uncertainty, confusion and, inevitably, forum shopping by litigants eager to take advantage of the situation. Even where the Supreme Court acts expeditiously to resolve conflicts which have been brought to its attention, a decade or more may have passed from the time the conflict first began to develop.

"Trivial" Cases

A third consequence of the lack of adequate capacity for declaration of national law is the burden upon the Supreme Court to hear cases otherwise not worthy of its resources. The Supreme Court alone can provide definitive answers on issues which have divided the circuits. Although no longer convinced that, as the leading authorities put it in 1951, "it is required to grant certiorari where a conflict exists," the existence of a conflict remains an important reason for granting plenary review. The result is that, each year, the Justices hear and consider a number of cases which, in terms of their intrinsic importance, might well be thought unworthy of the time and effort which they demand of the Court. Inevitably, opinions will differ as to the importance of particular issues and the desirability of their resolution by the United States Supreme Court. Issues which some may consider trivial will appear to others to be quite significant in terms of the human values which the Court must be alert to protect. Moreover, as long as the Court remains the only tribunal empowered to resolve conflicts among the circuits or among state courts on federal questions, no one would fault it for granting review solely for that purpose. The elimination of conflict is, in itself, an important value in our federalism, even if the issue is conceded to be relatively unimportant in terms of development of national law. The question, however, is whether, in light of the other demands placed upon the Court, and considering the interests of the system as a whole, some issues might better be decided by another tribunal empowered to hand down precedents of national effect. An alternate forum for resolving conflicts would allow the Supreme Court greater freedom to hear, or to refuse to hear, such cases, relieved of the pressure to adjudicate solely because two courts have disagreed.

Uncertainty

Finally, the lack of capacity for definitive declaration of the national law frequently results in uncertainty even though a conflict never develops. The possibility of conflict, not knowing whether a potential conflict will mature into an actual conflict, is yet another consequence of our present system. In many cases there are years of uncertainty during which hundreds, sometimes thousands, of individuals are left in doubt as to what rule will be applied to their transactions. Moreover, such uncertainty breeds repetitive litigation as (for instance) successive taxpayers, or employers, or producers litigate the identical issue in circuit after circuit, encouraged by the hope of developing a conflict. Whether or not their hope is ever realized, the relitigation is costly both to their adversaries and to the system as a whole. By the same token, the United States frequently persists in enforcing a policy despite adverse rulings in several circuits, not only in tax cases, but also in other areas of federal regulation.

A caveat is in order. There are some issues as to which "successive considerations by several courts, each re-evaluating and building upon the preceding decisions" will improve the quality of adjudication. As to these, there may be reason to avoid premature adjudication by a tribunal whose decisions are nationally binding. In discussing the consequences of inadequate capacity, we do not speak of such cases. We speak here of those cases as to which, to borrow Erwin Griswold's words, "the gain from maturation of thought from letting the matter simmer for awhile is not nearly as great as the harm which comes from years of uncertainty." In short, we have endeavored throughout to put to one side cases in which delayed adjudication is appropriate; we would not sacrifice the quality of either process or product for speed or for the appearance of efficiency. However, we find no value in a system which fosters prolonged uncertainty and delay because the design of the system cannot accommodate more rapid resolution.

The focus of the preceding discussion has been on conflicts, both real and potential, with respect to a rule of law. Even where there is neither disagreement nor uncertainty about the governing rule of law, in some situations litigation will continue to arise, focusing instead on whether the facts put a case on one side of the line or the other. In such situations, the greater the number of nationally authoritative decisions pricking out the contours of a rule, specifying whether it does or does not apply to the facets of a particular record, the easier it is to achieve predictability and consistency throughout the country in still other factual settings.

Forum Shopping

The problem has been particularly acute in the field of patent law. The Commission's consultants, Professor James B. Gambrell of New York

University and Donald R. Dunner, Esq., confirmed what has long been asserted: the perceived disparity in results in different circuits leads to widespread forum shopping. "[M]ad and undignified races," Judge Henry Friendly describes them, "between a patentee who wishes to sue for infringement in one circuit believed to be benign toward patents, and a user who wants to obtain a declaration of invalidity or non-infringement in one believed to be hostile to them."

Such forum shopping, write Professor Gambrell and Mr. Dunner, "demeans the entire judicial process and the patent system as well." At the root of the problem, in their view, is the "lack of guidance and monitoring by a single court whose judgments are nationally binding." The Supreme Court has set, and can be expected to continue to set, national policy in the area of patent law as in other areas of federal law. However, the Court should not be expected to perform a monitoring function on a continuing basis in this complex field. The additional appellate capacity for nationally binding decisions which a national court of appeals would provide can be expected to fulfill this function.

A final point.... A litigant's failure to seek Supreme Court review...does not indicate that a national resolution may not have been desired or desirable. The stakes for any one litigant may not have justified pursuing a case beyond the first level of appeal. Counsel may have concluded that the chance of obtaining Supreme Court review was too small to be worth the expense of filing a petition for certiorari. The prospect of further delay in the resolution of the particular controversy may have loomed large. The persevering uncertainty with respect to the venue provisions governing a corporate plaintiff is one example. Today, there is no alternative to Supreme Court review but under the transfer provision of the Commission's national court proposal, it would be possible, in an appropriate case, to obtain a definitive resolution without requiring the parties to litigate in three levels of courts. This provision would thus permit the federal system to provide final answers to issues that are recurring and that affect numerous cases, yet are not of sufficient significance in any one case to induce the losing litigant to seek a second level of review.

These, in broad outline, are the major consequences of inadequate capacity for definitive declaration of the national law in the present system....

COURT ON CONFINEMENT
OF THE MENTALLY ILL
June 26, 1975

In its first consideration of the rights of mentally ill citizens, the Supreme Court ruled unanimously June 26 that a state cannot confine such persons against their will in psychiatric hospitals which fail to provide treatment. Although the case, O'Connor v. Donaldson, had been widely expected to elicit a ruling on a constitutional "right to treatment," the Court explicitly avoided that and other "difficult issues of constitutional law" raised by involuntary commitment of the mentally ill. It simply decided that the plaintiff, Kenneth Donaldson, had been improperly denied his constitutional right to liberty during the 15 years he had been compelled to remain, untreated, in a Florida state mental hospital.

With Justice Potter Stewart writing for the Court, the justices stated: "A finding of 'mental illness' alone cannot justify a state's locking a person up against his will and keeping him indefinitely in simple custodial confinement....[T]here is still no constitutional basis for confining such persons involuntarily if they are dangerous to no one and can live safely in freedom."

As developed in lower-court rulings, the right-to-treatment doctrine denied a state the power to confine the mentally ill without providing adequate psychiatric treatment.

History of the Plaintiff

Fearing that his 48-year-old son was suffering from "delusions," Kenneth Donaldson's elderly father had had him committed to the state hospital

469

in January 1957. There he remained until 1971 despite his repeated efforts to be released. He was never found dangerous to himself or others. He received little, if any, treatment. It appeared likely that he could survive and support himself outside the hospital, and friends sought to aid his efforts by requesting that he be released in their care.

Finally, in 1971, Donaldson went to court. He filed a federal suit against the hospital superintendent, Dr. J. B. O'Connor, and other staff members, claiming that they had intentionally and maliciously deprived him of his constitutional right to liberty. Shortly thereafter, Donaldson was released and declared mentally competent.

The trial jury ruled in Donaldson's favor, awarding him $38,500 in damages against O'Connor and another hospital staff member. The court of appeals, fifth circuit, agreed, and went on to hold that persons who are involuntarily civilly committed to state mental hospitals have a constitutional right to treatment—a right denied to Donaldson.

No Right to Treatment

The Supreme Court found "no reason" in the case as it stood "to decide whether mentally ill persons dangerous to themselves or to others have a right to treatment upon compulsory confinement by the State"; nor, in the opinion of the Court, did the case raise the related question of whether enforced hospitalization for the purpose of treatment could be imposed on persons who are mentally ill but not demonstrably dangerous to themselves or society.

In a concurring opinion Chief Justice Warren Burger wrote at length against the presumptive right to treatment. "Despite many recent advances in medical knowledge," Burger said, "it remains a stubborn fact that there are many forms of mental illness which are not understood, some of which are untreatable...." In light of this fact, "few things would be more fraught with peril than to irrevocably condition a State's power to protect the mentally ill upon the providing of 'such treatment as will give (them) a realistic opportunity to be cured.' "

The Supreme Court's ruling was hailed by the New York Civil Liberties Union as "a landmark legal victory,...." and Donaldson's ACLU attorney predicted that the Court's action would force mental hospitals "to reevaluate the status of each patient." But the narrowness of the decision and the imprecision of the Court's criteria for release disappointed many psychiatric law experts. No mass releases of mental patients materialized as a result of the ruling. Thomas Szasz, professor of psychiatry at the State University of New York and an outspoken opponent of state intervention in psychiatric treatment, faulted the Court for failing to decide "on what grounds, if any, may an individual be deprived of liberty by being incarcerated in a mental hospital."

The Court's decision came at a time when trends in the practice of psychiatry were reducing the necessity for civil commitment of the mentally ill. The use of new tranquilizing drugs and the growth of community mental health centers had more than halved the population of mental institutions since Donaldson's original commitment.

Excerpts from the Supreme Court decision of June 26, 1975, on the confinement of the mentally ill:

Full Text of Opinions

No. 74-8

J. B. O'Connor, Petitioner, *v.* Kenneth Donaldson.	On Writ of Certiorari to the United States Court of Appeals for the Fifth Circuit.

[June 26, 1975]

MR. JUSTICE STEWART delivered the opinion of the Court.

The respondent, Kenneth Donaldson, was civilly committed to confinement as a mental patient in the Florida State Hospital at Chattahoochee in January of 1957. He was kept in custody there against his will for nearly 15 years. The petitioner, Dr. J. B. O'Connor, was the hospital's superintendent during most of this period. Throughout his confinement Donaldson repeatedly, but unsuccessfully, demanded his release, claiming that he was dangerous to no one, that he was not mentally ill, and that, at any rate, the hospital was not providing treatment for his supposed illness. Finally, in February of 1971, Donaldson brought this lawsuit...in the United States District Court for the Northern District of Florida, alleging that O'Connor, and other members of the hospital staff, named as defendants, had intentionally and maliciously deprived him of his constitutional right to liberty. After a four-day trial, the jury returned a verdict assessing both compensatory and punitive damages against O'Connor and a codefendant. The Court of Appeals for the Fifth Circuit affirmed the judgment.... We granted O'Connor's petition for certiorari...because of the important constitutional questions seemingly presented.

I

Donaldson's commitment was initiated by his father, who thought that his son was suffering from "delusions." After hearings before a county judge of Pinellas County, Florida, Donaldson was found to be suffering from "paranoid schizophrenia" and was committed for "care, maintenance, and treatment" pursuant to Florida statutory provisions that have since been repealed. The state law was less than clear in specifying the grounds necessary for commitment, and the record is scanty as to Donaldson's condition at the time of the judicial hearing. These matters are, however, irrelevant, for this case involves no challenge to the initial commitment, but is focused, instead, upon the nearly 15 years of confinement that followed.

The evidence at the trial showed that the hospital staff had the power to release a patient, not dangerous to himself or others, even if he remained mentally ill and had been lawfully committed. Despite many requests, O'Connor refused to allow that power to be exercised in Donaldson's case. At the trial, O'Connor indicated that he had believed that Donaldson would have been unable to make a "successful adjustment outside the institution," but could not recall the basis for that conclusion. O'Connor retired as superintendent shortly before this suit was filed. A few months thereafter, and before the trial, Donaldson secured his release and a judicial restoration of competency, with the support of the hospital staff.

The testimony at the trial demonstrated, without contradiction, that Donaldson has posed no danger to others during his long confinement, or indeed at any point in his life. O'Connor himself conceded that he had no personal or secondhand knowledge that Donaldson had ever committed a dangerous act. There was no evidence that Donaldson had ever been suicidal or been thought likely to inflict injury upon himself. One of O'Connor's codefendants acknowledged that Donaldson could have earned his own living outside the hospital. He had done so for some 14 years before his commitment, and immediately upon his release he secured a responsible job in hotel administration.

Furthermore, Donaldson's frequent requests for release had been supported by responsible persons willing to provide him any care he might need on release. In 1963, for example, a representative of Helping Hands, Inc., a halfway house for mental patients, wrote O'Connor asking him to release Donaldson to its care. The request was accompanied by a supporting letter from the Minneapolis Clinic of Psychiatry and Neurology, which a codefendant conceded was a "good clinic." O'Connor rejected the offer, replying that Donaldson could be released only to his parents. That rule was apparently of O'Connor's own making. At the time, Donaldson was 55 years old, and, as O'Connor knew, Donaldson's parents were too elderly and infirm to take responsibility for him. Moreover, in his continuing correspondence with Donaldson's parents, O'Connor never informed them of the Helping Hands offer. In addition, on four separate occasions between 1964 and 1968, John Lembcke, a college classmate of Donaldson's and a longtime family friend, asked O'Connor to release Donaldson to his care. On each occasion O'Connor refused. The record shows that Lembcke was a serious and responsible person, who was willing and able to assume responsibility for Donaldson's welfare.

The evidence showed that Donaldson's confinement was a simple regime of enforced custodial care, not a program designed to alleviate or cure his supposed illness. Numerous witnesses, including one of O'Connor's codefendants, testified that Donaldson had received nothing but custodial care while at the hospital. O'Connor described Donaldson's treatment as "milieu therapy." But witnesses from the hospital staff conceded that, in the context of this case, "milieu therapy" was a euphemism for confinement in the "milieu" of a mental hospital. For substantial periods, Donaldson was simply kept in a large room that housed 60 patients, many of whom were under criminal commitment. Donaldson's requests for ground privileges, occupational training, and an opportunity to discuss his case with O'Connor or other staff members were repeatedly denied.

At the trial, O'Connor's principal defense was that he had acted in good faith and was therefore immune from any liability for monetary damages. His position, in short, was that state law, which he had believed valid, had authorized indefinite custodial confinement of the "sick," even if they were not given treatment and their release could harm no one.

The trial judge instructed the members of the jury that they should find that O'Connor had violated Donaldson's constitutional right to liberty if they found that he had

> "confined [Donaldson] against his will, knowing that he was not mentally ill or dangerous or knowing that if mentally ill he was not receiving treatment for his mental illness....

> "Now the purpose of involuntary hospitalization is treatment and not mere custodial care or punishment if a patient is not a danger to himself or others. Without such treatment there is no justification from a constitutional standpoint for continued confinement unless you should also find that [Donaldson] was dangerous either to himself or others." [Footnote: The District Court defined treatment as follows: "You are instructed that a person who is involuntarily civilly committed to a mental hospital does have a constitutional right to receive such treatment *as will give him a realistic opportunity to be cured or to improve his mental condition.*" (Emphasis added.) O'Connor argues that this statement suggests that a mental patient has a right to treatment even if confined by reason of dangerousness to himself or others. But this is to take the above paragraph out of context, for it is bracketed by paragraphs making clear the trial judge's theory that treatment is constitutionally required only if mental illness alone, rather than danger to self or others, is the reason for confinement. If O'Connor had thought the instructions ambiguous on this point, he could have objected to them and requested a clarification. He did not do so. We accordingly have no occasion here to decide whether persons committed on grounds of dangerousness enjoy a "right to treatment."...]

The trial judge further instructed the jury that O'Connor was immune from damages if he

> "reasonably believed in good faith that detention of [Donaldson] was proper for the length of time he was so confined....
> "However, mere good intentions which do not give rise to a reasonable belief that detention is lawfully required cannot justify [Donaldson's] confinement in the Florida State Hospital."

The jury returned a verdict for Donaldson against O'Connor and a codefendant, and awarded damages of $38,500, including $10,000 in punitive damages.

The Court of Appeals affirmed the judgment of the District Court in a broad opinion dealing with "the far-reaching question whether the

Fourteenth Amendment guarantees a right to treatment to persons involuntarily civilly committed to state mental hospitals." ...The appellate court held that when, as in Donaldson's case, the rationale for confinement is that the patient is in need of treatment, the Constitution requires that minimally adequate treatment in fact be provided.... The court further expressed the view that, regardless of the grounds for involuntary civil commitment, a person confined against his will at a state mental institution has "a constitutional right to receive such individual treatment as will give him a reasonable opportunity to be cured or to improve his mental condition." ...Conversely, the court's opinion implied that it is constitutionally permissible for a State to confine a mentally ill person against his will in order to treat his illness, regardless of whether his illness renders him dangerous to himself or others....

II

We have concluded that the difficult issues of constitutional law dealt with by the Court of Appeals are not presented by this case in its present posture. Specifically, there is no reason now to decide whether mentally ill persons dangerous to themselves or to others have a right to treatment upon compulsory confinement by the State, or whether the State may compulsorily confine a nondangerous, mentally ill individual for the purpose of treatment. As we view it, this case raises a single, relatively simple, but nonetheless important question concerning every man's constitutional right to liberty.

The jury found that Donaldson was neither dangerous to himself nor dangerous to others, and also found that, if mentally ill, Donaldson had not received treatment. That verdict, based on abundant evidence, makes the issue before the Court a narrow one. We need not decide whether, when, or by what procedures, a mentally ill person may be confined by the State on any of the grounds which, under contemporary statutes, are generally advanced to justify involuntary confinement of such a person—to prevent injury to the public, to ensure his own survival or safety, or to alleviate or cure his illness.... For the jury found that none of the above grounds for continued confinement was present in Donaldson's case.

Given the jury's findings, what was left as justification for keeping Donaldson in continued confinement? The fact that state law may have authorized confinement of the harmless mentally ill does not itself establish a constitutionally adequate purpose for the confinement. ...Nor is it enough that Donaldson's original confinement was founded upon a constitutionally adequate basis, if in fact it was, because even if his involuntary confinement was initially permissible, it could not constitutionally continue after that basis no longer existed....

A finding of "mental illness" alone cannot justify a State's locking a person up against his will and keeping him indefinitely in simple custodial confinement. Assuming that that term can be given a reasonably precise content and that the "mentally ill" can be identified with reasonable accuracy, there is still no constitutional basis for confining such persons involuntarily if they are dangerous to no one and can live safely in freedom.

May the State confine the mentally ill merely to ensure them a living standard superior to that they enjoy in the private community? That the State has a proper interest in providing care and assistance to the unfortunate goes without saying. But the mere presence of mental illness does not disqualify a person from preferring his home to the comforts of an institution. Moreover, while the State may arguably confine a person to save him from harm, incarceration is rarely if ever a necessary condition for raising the living standards of those capable of surviving safely in freedom on their own or with the help of family or friends....

May the State fence in the harmless mentally ill solely to save its citizens from exposure to those whose ways are different? One might as well ask if the State, to avoid public unease, could incarcerate all who are physically unattractive or socially eccentric. Mere public intolerance or animosity cannot constitutionally justify the deprivation of a person's physical liberty....

In short, a State cannot constitutionally confine without more a non-dangerous individual who is capable of surviving safely in freedom by himself or with the help of willing and responsible family members or friends. Since the jury found, upon ample evidence, that O'Connor, as an agent of the State, knowingly did so confine Donaldson, it properly concluded that O'Connor violated Donaldson's constitutional right to freedom.

III

O'Connor contends that in any event he should not be held personally liable for monetary damages because his decisions were made in "good faith." Specifically, O'Connor argues that he was acting pursuant to state law which, he believed, authorized confinement of the mentally ill even when their release would not compromise their safety or constitute a danger to others, and that he could not reasonably have been expected to know that the state law as he understood it was constitutionally invalid. A proposed instruction to this effect was rejected by the District Court.

The District Court did instruct the jury, without objection, that monetary damages could not be assessed against O'Connor if he had believed reasonably and in good faith that Donaldson's continued confinement was "proper," and that punitive damages could be awarded only if O'Connor had acted "maliciously or wantonly or oppressively." The Court of Appeals approved those instructions. But that court did not consider whether it was error for the trial judge to refuse the additional instruction concerning O'Connor's claimed reliance on state law as authorization for Donaldson's continued confinement. Further, neither the District Court nor the Court of Appeals acted with the benefit of this Court's most recent decision on the scope of the qualified immunity possessed by state officials....

Under that decision, the relevant question for the jury is whether O'Connor "knew or reasonably should have known that the action he took within his sphere of official responsibility would violate the constitutional rights of

[Donaldson], or if he took the action with the malicious intention to cause a deprivation of constitutional rights or other injury to [Donaldson]." ...For purposes of this question, an official has, of course, no duty to anticipate unforeseeable constitutional developments....

Accordingly, we vacate the judgment of the Court of Appeals and remand the case to enable that court to consider, in light of *Wood* v. *Strickland*, whether the District Judge's failure to instruct with regard to the effect of O'Connor's claimed reliance on state law rendered inadequate the instructions as to O'Connor's liability for compensatory and punitive damages.

It is so ordered.

MR. CHIEF JUSTICE BURGER, concurring.

Although I join the Court's opinion and judgment in this case, it seems to me that several factors merit more emphasis than it gives them. I therefore add the following remarks.

I

With respect to the remand to the Court of Appeals on the issue of official immunity, it seems to me not entirely irrelevant that there was substantial evidence that Donaldson consistently refused treatment that was offered to him, claiming that he was not mentally ill and needed no treatment. The Court appropriately takes notice of the uncertainties of psychiatric diagnosis and therapy, and the reported cases are replete with evidence of the divergence of medical opinion in this vexing area. ...Nonetheless, one of the few areas of agreement among behaviorial specialists is that an uncooperative patient cannot benefit from therapy and that the first step in effective treatment is acknowledgement by the patient that he is suffering from an abnormal condition. ...Donaldson's adamant refusal to do so should be taken into account in considering petitioner's good-faith defense.

Perhaps more important to the issue of immunity is a factor referred to only obliquely in the Court's opinion. On numerous occasions during the period of his confinement Donaldson unsuccessfully sought release in the Florida courts; indeed, the last of these proceedings was terminated only a few months prior to the bringing of this action. ...Whatever the reasons for the state courts' repeated denials of relief, and regardless of whether they correctly resolved the issue tendered to them, petitioner and the other members of the medical staff at Florida State Hospital would surely have been justified in considering each such judicial decision as an approval of continued confinement and an independent intervening reason for continuing Donaldson's confinement. Thus, this fact is inescapably related to the issue of immunity and must be considered by the Court of Appeals on remand and, if a new trial is ordered, by the District Court.

II

As the Court points out...the District Court instructed the jury in part that "a person who is involuntarily civilly committed to a mental hospital does have a *constitutional* right to receive such treatment as will give him a realistic opportunity to be cured," (emphasis added) and the Court of Appeals unequivocally approved this phrase, standing alone, as a correct statement of the law. ...The Court's opinion plainly gives no approval to that holding and makes clear that it binds neither the parties to this case nor the courts of the Fifth Circuit. ...Moreover, in light of its importance for future litigation in this area, it should be emphasized that the Court of Appeals' analysis has no basis in the decisions of this Court.

A

There can be no doubt that involuntary commitment to a mental hospital, like involuntary confinement of an individual for any reason, is a deprivation of liberty which the State cannot accomplish without due process of law. ...Commitment must be justified on the basis of a legitimate state interest, and the reasons for committing a particular individual must be established in an appropriate proceeding. Equally important, confinement must cease when those reasons no longer exist....

The Court of Appeals purported to be applying these principles in developing the first of its theories supporting a constitutional right to treatment. It first identified what it perceived to be the traditional bases for civil commitment—physical dangerousness to oneself or others, or a need for treatment—and stated:

> "[W]here, as in Donaldson's case, the rationale for confinement is the *'parens patriae'* rationale that the patient is in need of treatment, the due process clause requires that minimally adequate treatment be in fact provided.... 'To deprive any citizen of his or her liberty upon the altruistic theory that the confinement is for humane therapeutic reasons and then fail to provide adequate treatment violates the very fundamentals of due process.' "...

The Court of Appeals did not explain its conclusion that the rationale for respondent's commitment was that he needed treatment. The Florida statutes in effect during the period of his confinement did not require that a person who had been adjudicated incompetent and ordered committed either be provided with psychiatric treatment or released, and there was no such condition in respondent's order of commitment. ...More important, the instructions which the Court of Appeals read as establishing an absolute constitutional right to treatment did not require the jury to make any findings regarding the specific reasons for respondent's confinement or to focus upon any rights he may have had under state law. Thus, the premise of the Court of Appeals' first theory must have been that, at least with respect to persons who are not physically dangerous, a State has no power to confine the mentally ill except for the purpose of providing them with treatment.

That proposition is surely not descriptive of the power traditionally exercised by the States in this area. Historically, and for a considerable period of time, subsidized custodial care in private foster homes or boarding houses was the most benign form of care provided incompetent or mentally ill persons for whom the States assumed responsibility. Until well into the 19th century the vast majority of such persons were simply restrained in poorhouses, almshouses, or jails. ...The few States that established institutions for the mentally ill during this early period were concerned primarily with providing a more humane place of confinement and only secondarily with "curing" the persons sent there....

As the trend toward state care of the mentally ill expanded, eventually leading to the present statutory schemes for protecting such persons, the dual functions of institutionalization continued to be recognized. While one of the goals of this movement was to provide medical treatment to those who could benefit from it, it was acknowledged that this could not be done in all cases and that there was a large range of mental illness for which no known "cure" existed. In time, providing places for the custodial confinement of the so-called "dependent insane" again emerged as the major goal of the State's programs in this area and continued to be so well into this century....

In short, the idea that States may not confine the mentally ill except for the purpose of providing them with treatment is of very recent origin, and there is no historical basis for imposing such a limitation on state power. Analysis of the sources of the civil commitment power likewise lends no support to that notion. There can be little doubt that in the exercise of its police power a State may confine individuals solely to protect society from the dangers of significant antisocial acts or communicable disease. ...Additionally, the States are vested with the historic *parens patriae* power, including the duty to protect "persons under legal disabilities to act for themselves." ...The classic example of this role is when a State undertakes to act as " 'the general guardian of all infants, idiots, and lunatics.' "...

Of course, an inevitable consequence of exercising the *parens patriae* power is that the ward's personal freedom will be substantially restrained, whether a guardian is appointed to control his property, he is placed in the custody of a private third party, or committed to an institution. Thus, however the power is implemented, due process requires that it not be invoked indiscriminately. At a minimum, a particular scheme for protection of the mentally ill must rest upon a legislative determination that it is compatible with the best interests of the affected class and that its members are unable to act for themselves. ...Moreover, the use of alternative forms of protection may be motivated by different considerations, and the justifications for one may not be invoked to rationalize another....

However, the existence of some due process limitations on the *parens patriae* power does not justify the further conclusion that it may be exercised to confine a mentally ill person only if the purpose of the confinement is treatment. Despite many recent advances in medical knowledge, it remains a stubborn fact that there are many forms of mental illness which are not understood, some which are untreatable in the sense that no effective therapy has yet been discovered for them, and that rates of "cure" are generally low. ...There can be little responsible debate regarding "the uncertainty of diagnosis in this field and the tentativeness of professional judgment." ...Similarly, as previously observed, it is universally recognized as fundamental to effective therapy that the patient acknowledge his illness and cooperate with those attempting to give treatment; yet the failure of a large proportion of mentally ill persons to do so is a common phenomenon. ...It may be that some persons in either of these categories, and there may be others, are unable to function in society and will suffer real harm to themselves unless provided with care in a sheltered environment. ...At the very least, I am not able to say that a state legislature is powerless to make that kind of judgment....

B

Alternatively, it has been argued that a Fourteenth Amendment right to treatment for involuntarily confined mental patients derives from the fact that many of the safeguards of the criminal process are not present in civil commitment. The Court of Appeals described this theory as follows:

> "[A] due process right to treatment is based on the principle that when the three central limitations on the government's power to detain—that detention be in retribution for a specific offense; that it be limited to a fixed term; and that it be permitted after a proceeding where the fundamental procedural safeguards are observed—are absent, there must be a *quid pro quo* extended by the government to justify confinement. And the *quid pro quo* most commonly recognized is the provision of rehabilitative treatment."...

To the extent that this theory may be read to permit a State to confine an individual simply because it is willing to provide treatment, regardless of the subject's ability to function in society, it raises the gravest of constitutional problems, and I have no doubt the Court of Appeals would agree on this score. As a justification for a constitutional right to such treatment, the *quid pro quo* theory suffers from equally serious defects.

It is too well established to require extended discussion that due process is not an inflexible concept. Rather, its requirements are determined in particular instances by identifying and accommodating the interests of the individual and society. ...Where claims that the State is acting in the best interests of an individual are said to justify reduced procedural and substantive safeguards, this Court's decisions require that they be "candidly appraised." ...However, in so doing judges are not free to read their private notions of public policy or public health into the Constitution....

The *quid pro quo* theory is a sharp departure from, and cannot coexist with, these due process principles. As an initial matter, the theory presupposes that essentially the same interests are involved in every situation where a State seeks to confine an individual; that assumption, however, is incorrect. It is elementary that the justification for the criminal process and the unique deprivation of liberty which it can impose requires that it be invoked only for commission of a specific offense prohibited by legislative enactment. ...But it would be incongruous to apply the same limitation when quarantine is imposed by the State to protect the public from a highly communicable disease....

A more troublesome feature of the *quid pro quo* theory is that it elevates a concern for essentially procedural safeguards into a new substantive constitutional right. Rather than inquiring whether strict standards of proof or periodic redetermination of a patient's condition are required in civil confinement, the theory accepts the absence of such safeguards but insists that the State provide benefits which, in the view of a court, are adequate "compensation" for confinement. In light of the wide divergence of medical opinion regarding the diagnosis of and proper therapy for mental abnormalities, that prospect is especially troubling in this area and cannot be squared with the principle that "courts may not substitute for the judgments of legislators their own understanding of the public welfare, but must instead concern themselves with the validity of the methods which the legislature has selected." ...Of course, questions regarding the adequacy of procedure and the power of a State to continue particular confinements are ultimately for the courts, aided by expert opinion to the extent that is found helpful. But I am not persuaded that we should abandon the traditional limitations on the scope of judicial review.

C

In sum, I cannot accept the reasoning of the Court of Appeals and can discern no other basis for equating an involuntarily committed mental patient's unquestioned constitutional right not to be confined without due process of law with a constitutional right to *treatment*. Given the present state of medical knowledge regarding abnormal human behavior and its treatment, few things would be more fraught with peril than to irrevocably condition a State's power to protect the mentally ill upon the providing of "such treatment as will give [them] a realistic opportunity to be cured." Nor can I accept the theory that a State may lawfully confine an individual thought to need treatment and justify that deprivation of liberty solely by providing some treatment. Our concepts of due process would not tolerate such a "trade-off." Because the Court of Appeals' analysis could be read as authorizing those results, it should not be followed.

SOLZHENITSYN ON DETENTE

June 30, 1975

Nobel laureate Alexander Solzhenitsyn, whose harsh and persisting criticism of the Soviet system led finally to his expulsion from the U.S.S.R. in 1974, delivered in Washington on June 30 a strongly worded attack on current U.S. efforts to reduce East-West tensions. In his first major public address in the West, the exiled author urged the United States to "interfere as much as you can" in the internal affairs of the Soviet Union by withholding trade and disarmament agreements, the substance of détente, as long as the Communist regime in his native land suppresses basic human rights.

The fervor and direction of Solzhenitsyn's lengthy address disconcerted many observers. The Washington Post *called him "a shocking figure," reporting that the audience of labor leaders and government officials "went away fatigued and puzzled by his powerful presence." Solzhenitsyn's anguished warnings also appeared to embarrass the administration, just two months away from the signing of a major East-West pact (see p. 559). The chief architect of détente, Secretary of State Henry A. Kissinger, advised President Ford not to receive the outspoken Russian during his Washington visit. This snub and Ford's apparent lack of candor—initially the White House had simply said the President was "too busy" to meet with Solzhenitsyn—stirred angry reaction. By mid-July the White House had received approximately 500 letters on the subject, all critical of Ford's action, according to a presidential spokesman. Sen. Jesse A. Helms of North Carolina declared on the Senate floor that it was "a sad day for our country if [it] must tremble...for fear of offending Communists...." Helms had sponsored a bill to confer honorary American citizenship on Solzhenitsyn.*

Although Ford finally offered an "open invitation" to the controversial visitor, Solzhenitsyn let it be known that he would respond only to a formal invitation from the White House, which was not forthcoming.

Solzhenitsyn's Views

Since his forced departure from the Soviet Union in February 1974 (see Historic Documents of 1974, p. 129), Solzhenitsyn's bold views had startled some of his admirers. In a letter to Soviet authorities released shortly after his arrival in the West, the deeply religious author called upon the Soviet government to repudiate Marxism, relinquish control of all non-Russian ethnic nationalities, resist urbanization and industrialization, and turn away from the West toward spiritual and "slavic" values. These views contrasted sharply with those of other well-known Soviet dissidents such as historian Roy A. Medvedev and physicist Andrei D. Sakharov, who have urged internal reforms of the existing state and closer East-West relations. Their differences had previously been obscured by the dissidents' unanimous condemnation of Soviet policies on human rights. The proximate cause of Solzhenitsyn's expulsion from the Soviet Union had been the publication in 1973 of his massive report on the Soviet penal system, The Gulag Archipelago. Solzhenitsyn himself was imprisoned 11 years in forced-labor camps for making anti-Stalinist remarks in letters written while serving in the Soviet army during World War II.

Solzhenitsyn's host at the Washington dinner was AFL-CIO president George Meany, a durable and vehement foe of communism. Meany's dislike of détente was well-known; he told the Senate Foreign Relations Committee in 1974 that current U.S. policy toward Russia amounted to one-sided appeasement. On another occasion he said that he prayed that "Kissinger won't give the Russians the Washington Monument—he's given them every goddam thing else." However, Meany testified during the 1974 hearings that he supported "genuine détente," a notion which also appeared in Solzhenitsyn's Washington speech.

Solzhenitsyn made a second major address in New York on July 9, again under the auspices of the AFL-CIO. He took that occasion to amplify some of his earlier remarks, denying that he had voiced "an appeal to the United States to liberate us from communism." He had, he said, always urged his own countrymen not to "wait for assistance" from the West but to stand on their own feet. What he did ask was that the West cut off all aid to the Soviet economy. "When they bury us in the ground alive...please do not send them shovels," he pleaded. As for détente, "relations between [the two nations] should be such that there would be no deceit in the question of armaments, that there would be no concentration camps...."

> *Excerpts from an English translation of the address by the Russian novelist Alexander Solzhenitsyn at a banquet given in his honor by the AFL-CIO in Washington, D.C., June 30, 1975:*

....There is...[a] Russian proverb: "The yes-man is your enemy, but your friend will argue with you." It is precisely because I am the friend of the United States, precisely because my speech is prompted by friendship, that I have come to tell you: My friends, I'm not going to tell you sweet words. The situation in the world is not just dangerous, it isn't just threatening, it is catastrophic.

Something that is incomprehensible to the ordinary human mind has taken place. We over there, the powerless, average Soviet people, couldn't understand, year after year and decade after decade, what was happening. How were we to explain this? England, France, the United States, were victorious in World War II. Victorious states always dictate peace; they receive firm conditions; they create the sort of situation which accords with their philosophy, their concept of liberty, their concept of national interest.

Instead of this, beginning in Yalta, your statesmen of the West, for some inexplicable reason, have signed one capitulation after another. Never did the West or your President Roosevelt impose any conditions on the Soviet Union for obtaining aid. He gave unlimited aid, and then unlimited concessions. Already in Yalta, without any necessity, the occupation of Mongolia, Moldavia, Estonia, Latvia, Lithuania was silently recognized. Immediately after that, almost nothing was done to protect eastern Europe, and seven or eight more countries were surrendered....

And after that, for another 30 years, the constant retreat, the surrender of one country after another, to such a point that there are Soviet satellites even in Africa; almost all of Asia is taken over by them; Portugal is rolling down the precipice.

During those 30 years, more was surrendered to totalitarianism than any defeated country has ever surrendered after any war in history. There was no war, but there might as well have been.

For a long time we in the East couldn't understand this. We couldn't understand the flabbiness of the truce concluded in Vietnam. Any average Soviet citizen understood that this was a sly device which made it possible for North Vietnam to take over South Vietnam when it so chose. And suddenly, this was rewarded by the Nobel Prize for Peace—a tragic and ironic prize.

A very dangerous state of mind can arise as a result of this 30 years of retreat: give in as quick as possible,...peace and quiet at any cost....

This is very dangerous for one's view of the world when this feeling comes on: "Go ahead, give it up." We already hear voices in your country and in the West—"Give up Korea and we will live quietly. Give up Portugal, of course; give up Japan, give up Israel, give up Taiwan, the Philippines, Malaysia, Thailand, give up 10 more African countries. Just let us live in peace and quiet. Just let us drive our big cars on our splendid highways; just let us play tennis and golf, in peace and quiet; just let us mix our cocktails in peace and quiet as we are accustomed to doing; just let us see the beautiful toothy smile with a glass in hand on every advertisement page of our magazines."

America..."Least Guilty"

But look how things have turned out: Now in the West this has all turned into an accusation against the United States. Now, in the West, we hear very many voices saying, "It's your fault, America." And, here, I must decisively defend the United States against these accusations.

I have to say that the United States, of all the countries of the West, is the least guilty in all this and has done the most in order to prevent it. The United States has helped Europe to win the First and the Second World Wars. It twice raised Europe from post-war destruction—twice—for 10, 20, 30 years it has stood as a shield protecting Europe while European countries were counting their nickels, to avoid paying for their armies (better yet to have none at all) to avoid paying for armaments, thinking about how to leave NATO, knowing that in any case America will protect them anyway. These countries started it all, despite their thousands of years of civilization and culture, even though they are closer and should have known better.

I came to your continent—for two months I have been traveling in its wide open spaces and I agree: here you do not feel the nearness of it all, the immediacy of it all. And here it is possible to miscalculate. Here you must make a spiritual effort to understand the acuteness of the world situation. The United States of America has long shown itself to be the most magnanimous, the most generous country in the world. Wherever there is a flood, an earthquake, a fire, a natural disaster, disease, who is the first to help? The United States. Who helps the most and unselfishly? The United States.

And what do we hear in reply? Reproaches, curses, "Yankee Go Home." American cultural centers are burned, and the representatives of the Third World jump on tables to vote against the United States.

But this does not take the load off America's shoulders. The course of history—whether you like it or not—has made you the leaders of the world. Your country can no longer think provincially. Your political leaders can no longer think only of their own states, of their parties, of petty arrangements which may or may not lead to promotion. You must think about the whole world, and when the new political crisis in the world will arise (I think we have just come to the end of a very acute crisis and the next one will come any moment) the main decisions will fall anyway on the shoulders of the United States of America.

And while already here, I have heard some explanations of the situation. Let me quote some of them: "It is impossible to protect those who do not have the will to defend themselves." I agree with that, but this was said about South Vietnam. In one-half of today's Europe and in three-quarters of today's world the will to defend oneself is even less than it was in South Vietnam.

We are told: "We cannot defend those who are unable to defend themselves with their own human resources." But against the overwhelming powers of totalitarianism, when all of this power is thrown against a country—no country can defend itself with its own resources. For instance, Japan doesn't have a standing army.

We are told, "We should not protect those who do not have full democracy." This is the most remarkable argument of the lot. This is the Leitmotif I hear in your newspapers and in the speeches of some of your political leaders. Who in the world, ever, on the front line of defense against totalitarianism has been able to sustain full democracy? You, the united democracies of the world, were not able to sustain it. America, England, France, Canada, Australia together did not sustain it. At the first threat of Hitlerism, you stretched out your hands to Stalin. You call that sustaining democracy?

And there is more of the same (there were many of these speeches in a row): "If the Soviet Union is going to use détente for its own ends, then we...." But what will happen then? The Soviet Union has used détente in its own interests, is using it now and will continue to use it in its own interests! For example, China and the Soviet Union, both actively participating in détente, have quietly grabbed three countries of Indochina. True, perhaps as a consolation, China will send you a Ping-Pong team....

Detente From the Other Side

To understand properly what détente has meant all these 40 years—friendships, stabilization of the situation, trade, etc. I would have to tell you something, which you have never seen or heard, of how it looked from the other side. Let me tell you how it looked. Mere acquaintance with an American, and God forbid that you should sit with him in a cafe or restaurant, meant a 10-year term for suspicion of espionage....

In 1945-46 through our prison cells passed a lot of persons—and these were not ones who were cooperating with Hitler, although there were some of those, too. These were not guilty of anything, but rather persons who had just been in the West and had been liberated from German prison camps by the Americans. This was considered a criminal act: liberated by the Americans. That means he has seen the good life. If he comes back he will talk about it. The most terrible thing is not what he did but what he would talk about. And all such persons got 10-year terms.

During Nixon's last visit to Moscow your American correspondents were reporting in the western way from the streets of Moscow. I am going down a Russian street with a microphone and asking the ordinary Soviet citizen: "Tell me please, what do you think about the meeting between Nixon and Brezhnev?" And, amazingly, every last person answered: "Wonderful. I'm delighted. I'm absolutely overjoyed!"

What does this mean? If I'm going down a street in Moscow and some American comes up to me with a microphone and asks me something, then I know that on the other side of him is a member of the state security, also with a microphone who is recording everything I say. You think that I'm going to say something that is going to put me in prison immediately? Of course I say: "It's wonderful; I'm overjoyed."....

"Impossible To Understand"

The Soviet system is so closed that it is almost impossible for you to understand from here. Your theoreticians and scholars write works trying to understand and explain how things occur there. Here are some naive explanations which are simply funny to Soviet citizens. Some say that the Soviet leaders have now given up their inhumane ideology. Not at all. They haven't given it up one bit.

Some say that in the Kremlin there are some on the left, some on the right. And they are fighting with each other, and we've got to behave in such a way as not to interfere with those on the left side. This is all fantasy: left...right. There is some sort of a struggle for power, but they all agree on the essentials.

There also exists the following theory, that now, thanks to the growth of technology, there is a technocracy in the Soviet Union, a growing number of engineers and the engineers are now running the economy and will soon determine the fate of the country, rather than the party. I will tell you, though, that the engineers determine the fate of the economy just as much as our generals determine the fate of the Army. That means zero. Everything is done the way the party demands. That's our system. Judge it for yourself.

It's a system where for 40 years there haven't been genuine elections but simply a comedy, a farce. Thus a system which has no legislative organs. It's a system without an independent press; a system without an independent judiciary; where the people have no influence either on external or internal policy; where any thought which is different from what the state thinks is crushed.

And let me tell you that electronic bugging in our country is such a simple thing that it's a matter of everyday life. You had an instance in the United States where a bugging caused an uproar which lasted for a year and a half. For us it's an everyday matter. Almost every apartment, every institution has got its bug and it doesn't surprise us in the least—we are used to it.

It's a system where unmasked butchers of millions like Molotov and others smaller than him have never been tried in the courts but retire on tremendous pensions in the greatest comfort. It's a system where the show still goes on today and to which every foreigner is introduced surrounded by a couple of planted agents working according to a set scenario. It's a system where the very constitution has never been carried out for one single day; where all the decisions mature in secrecy, high up in a small irresponsible group and then are released on us and on you like a bolt of lightning.

And what are the signatures of such persons worth? How could one rely on their signatures to documents of détente? You yourselves might ask your specialists now and they'll tell you that precisely in recent years the Soviet Union has succeeded in creating wonderful chemical weapons, missiles, which are even better than those used by the United States.

True Detente

So what are we to conclude from that? Is détente needed or not? Not only is it needed, it's as necessary as air. It's the only way of saving the earth—instead of a world war to have détente, but a true détente, and if it has already been ruined by the bad word which we use for it—"détente"—then we should find another word for it.

I would say that there are very few, only three, main characteristics of such a true détente.

In the first place, there would be disarmament—not only disarmament from the use of war but also from the use of violence. We must stop using not only the sort of arms which are used to destroy one's neighbors, but the sort of arms which are used to oppress one's fellow countrymen. It is not détente if we here with you today can spend our time agreeably while over there people are groaning and dying in psychiatric hospitals. Doctors are making their evening rounds, for the third time injecting people with drugs which destroy their brain cells.

The second sign of détente, I would say, is the following: that it be not one based on smiles, not on verbal concessions, but it has to be based on a firm foundation. You know the words from the Bible: "Build not on sand, but on rock." There has to be a guarantee that this will not be broken overnight and for this the other side—the other party to the agreement—must have its acts subject to public opinion, to the press, and to a freely elected parliament. And until such control exists there is absolutely no guarantee.

The third simple condition—what sort of détente is it when they employ the sort of inhumane propaganda which is proudly called in the Soviet Union "ideological warfare." Let us not have that. If we're going to be friends, let's be friends, if we're going to have détente, then let's have détente, and an end to ideological warfare.

Funeral of Eastern Europe

The Soviet Union and the Communist countries can conduct negotiations. They know how to do this. For a long time they don't make any concessions and then they give in a little bit. Then everyone says triumphantly, "Look, they've made a concession; it's time to sign." The European negotiators of the 35 countries for two years now have painfully been negotiating and their nerves were stretched to the breaking point and they finally gave in. [Reference to Conference on Security and Cooperation in Europe (CSCE), the final act of which was signed Aug. 1 at Helsinki, Finland, *see p. 559]* A few women from the Communist countries can now marry foreigners. And a few newspapermen are now going to be permitted to travel a little more than before. They give 1/1,000th of what natural law should provide. Matters which people should be able to do even before such negotiations are undertaken. And already there is joy. And here in the West we hear many voices, saying: "Look, they're making concessions; it's time to sign."

During these two years of negotiations, in all the countries of eastern Europe, the pressure has increased, the oppression intensified, even in Yugoslavia and Romania, leaving aside the other countries. And it is precisely now that the Austrian chancellor says, "We've got to sign this agreement as rapidly as possible."

What sort of an agreement would this be? The proposed agreement is the funeral of eastern Europe. It means that western Europe would finally, once and for all, sign away eastern Europe, stating that it is perfectly willing to see eastern Europe be crushed and overwhelmed once and for all, but please don't bother us. And the Austrian chancellor thinks that if all these countries are pushed into a mass grave, Austria at the very edge of this grave will survive and not fall into it also.

And we, from our lives there, have concluded that violence can only be withstood by firmness.

You have to understand the nature of communism. The very ideology of communism, all of Lenin's teachings, are that anyone is considered to be a fool who doesn't take what's lying in front of him. If you can take it, take it. If you can attack, attack. But if there's a wall, then go back. And the Communist leaders respect only firmness and have contempt and laugh at persons who continually give in to them. Your people are now saying—and this is the last quotation I am going to give you from the statements of your leaders—"Power, without any attempt at conciliation, will lead to a world conflict." But I would say that power with continual subservience is no power at all.

"Firmness of Spirit"

But from our experience I can tell you that only firmness will make it possible to withstand the assaults of Communist totalitarianism. We see many historic examples, and let me give you some of them. Look at little Finland in 1939, which by its own forces withstood the attack. You, in 1948, defended Berlin only by your firmness of spirit, and there was no world conflict. In Korea in 1950 you stood up against the Communists, only by your firmness, and there was no world conflict. In 1962 you compelled the rockets to be removed from Cuba. Again it was only firmness, and there was no world conflict....

We, we the dissidents of the USSR, don't have any tanks, we don't have any weapons, we have no organization. We don't have anything. Our hands are empty. We have only a heart and what we have lived through in the half century of this system. And when we have found the firmness within ourselves to stand up for our rights, we have done so. It's only by firmness of spirit that we have withstood. And if I am standing here before you, it's not because of the kindness or the good will of communism, not thanks to détente, but thanks to my own firmness and your firm support. They knew that I would not yield one inch, not one hair. And when they couldn't do more they themselves fell back.

This is not easy. In our conditions this was taught to me by the difficulties of my own life. And if you yourselves—any one of you—were in the same difficult situation, you would have learned the same thing. Take Vladimir Bukovsky, whose name is now almost forgotten. Now, I don't want to mention a lot of names because however many I might mention there are more still. And when we resolve the question with two or three names it is as if we forget and betray the others. We should rather remember figures. There are tens of thousands of political prisoners in our country and—by the calculation of English specialists—7,000 persons are now under compulsory psychiatric treatment. Let's take Vladimir Bukovsky as an example. It was proposed to him, "All right, we'll free you. Go to the West and shut up." And this young man, a youth today on the verge of death, said: "No, I won't go this way. I have written about the persons whom you have put in insane asylums. You release them and then I'll go West." This is what I mean by that firmness of spirit to stand up against granite and tanks.

Finally, to evaluate everything that I have said to you, I would say we need not have had our conversation on the level of business calculations. Why did such and such a country act in such and such a way? What were they counting on? We should rather rise above this to the moral level and, say: "In 1933 and in 1941 your leaders and the whole western world, in an unprincipled way, made a deal with totalitarianism." We will have to pay for this, some day this deal will come back to haunt us. For 30 years we have been paying for it and we're still paying for it. And we're going to pay for it in a worse way.

"What Is Honorable..."

One cannot think only in the low level of political calculations. It's necessary to think also of what is noble, and what is honorable—not only what is profitable. Resourceful western legal scholars have now introduced the term "legal realism." By legal realism, they want to push aside any moral evaluation of affairs. They say, "Recognize realities; if such and such laws have been established in such and such countries by violence, these laws still must be recognized and respected."

At the present time it is widely accepted among lawyers that law is higher than morality—law is something which is worked out and developed, whereas morality is something inchoate and amorphous. That isn't the case. The opposite is rather true! Morality is higher than law! While law is our human attempt to embody in rules a part of that moral sphere which is above us. We try to understand this morality, bring it down to earth and present it in a form of laws. Sometimes we are more successful, sometimes less. Sometimes you actually have a caricature of morality, but morality is always higher than law. This view must never be abandoned. We must accept it with heart and soul.

It is almost a joke now in the western world, in the 20th century, to use words like "good" and "evil." They have become almost old-fashioned concepts, but they are very real and genuine concepts. These are concepts from a sphere which is higher than us. And instead of getting involved in base, petty, shortsighted political calculations and games we have to recognize that the concentration of World Evil and the tremendous force of hatred is there and it's flowing from there throughout the world. And we have to stand up against it and not hasten to give to it, give to it, give to it, everything that it wants to swallow.

Today there are two major processes occurring in the world. One is the one which I have just described to you which has been in progress more than 30 years. It is a process of shortsighted concessions; a process of giving up, and giving up and giving up and hoping that perhaps at some point the wolf will have eaten enough.

"Liberation of the Spirit"

The second process is one which I consider the key to everything and which, I will say now, will bring all of us our future; under the cast-iron shell of communism—for 20 years in the Soviet Union and a shorter time in other Communist countries—there is occurring a liberation of the human spirit. New generations are growing up which are steadfast in their struggle with evil; which are not willing to accept unprincipled compromises; which prefer to lose everything—salary, conditions of existence and life itself—but are not willing to sacrifice conscience; not willing to make deals with evil.

This process has now gone so far that in the Soviet Union today, Marxism has fallen so low that it has become an anecdote, it's simply an object of contempt. No serious person in our country today, not even university and high school students, can talk about Marxism without smiling, without laughing. But this whole process of our liberation, which obviously will entail social transformations, is slower than the first one—the process of concessions. Over there, when we see these concessions, we are frightened. Why so quickly? Who so precipitously? Why yield several countries a year?

I started by saying that you are the allies of our liberation movement in the Communist countries. And I call upon you: let us think together and try to see how we can adjust the relationship between these two processes. Whenever you help the persons persecuted in the Soviet Union, you not only display magnanimity and nobility, you're defending not only them but yourselves as well. You're defending your own future.

So let us try and see how far we can go to stop this senseless and immoral process of endless concessions to the aggressor—these clever legal arguments for why we should give up one country after another. Why must we hand over to Communist totalitarianism more and more technology—complex, delicate, developed technology which it needs for armaments and for crushing its own citizens? If we can at least slow down that process of concessions, if not stop it all together—and make it possible for the process of liberation to continue in the Communist countries—ultimately these two processes will yield us our future.

"Interfere More and More"

On our crowded planet there are no longer any internal affairs. The Communist leaders say, "Don't interefere in our internal affairs. Let us strangle our citizens in peace and quiet." But I tell you: Interfere more and more. Interfere as much as you can. We beg you to come and interfere....

I would like to call upon America to be more careful with its trust and prevent those wise persons who are attempting to establish even finer degrees of justice and even finer legal shades of equality—some because of their distorted outlook, others because of shortsightedness and still others out of self-interest—from falsely using the struggle for peace and for social justice to lead you down a false road. Because they are trying to weaken you; they are trying to disarm your strong and magnificent country in the face of this fearful threat—one which has never been seen before in the history of the world. Not only in the history of your country, but in the history of the world.

And I call upon you: ordinary working men of America—as represented here by your trade union movement—do not let yourselves become weak. Do not let yourselves be taken in the wrong direction. Let us try to slow down the process of concessions and help the process of liberation!

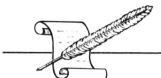

July

SCHLESINGER ON NUCLEAR POLICY
July 1, 1975

Secretary of Defense James R. Schlesinger told newsmen July 1 that the United States had never relinquished the option of first use of nuclear weapons if faced with defeat in a conventional war. Schlesinger's remarks were intended to clarify changes, initiated in 1974, in the nation's policy on nuclear weapons. The shift was away from a 20-year doctrine of "mutual assured destruction," under which both the United States and the Soviet Union targeted strategic (long-range) nuclear missiles on each other's cities. Under that doctrine each side could absorb a first strike and still destroy the other's population centers, thus each supposedly would be deterred from launching a first strike.

In January 1974 Schlesinger had announced that the United States would develop a so-called "counterforce" capability, which meant reliance on missiles powerful and accurate enough to be targeted on particular Soviet missile sites. If the Soviet Union launched a nuclear attack on a U.S. military target, the counterforce program would give the United States the option of responding "in kind" rather than unleashing massive strikes against population centers.

Schlesinger's remarks in July in effect joined the counterforce concept with that of first use, a conjunction which was viewed with considerable alarm by arms-control advocates. "This rattling of the nuclear sword is suicidal," warned Rep. Richard L. Ottinger (D N.Y.) the day after Schlesinger spoke.

The defense secretary termed a U.S. first strike "a very, very low probability" but rejected suggestions that U.S. policy on first use had changed.

495

Schlesinger's attempt to clarify U.S. nuclear policy was prompted by statements made the previous week by President Ford at a June 25 news conference. In answer to questions, the President had refused to affirm or rule out first use of tactical nuclear weapons if North Korea attacked South Korea. The questions arose in the context of widespread doubts about U.S. foreign commitments in the wake of Communist victories in Cambodia and South Vietnam (see p. 279). America's "strong deterrent force" in Korea would be "used in a flexible way in our own national interest," Ford said.

Long-Standing Nuclear Policy

The "first-use" doctrine was rooted in President Truman's decision to drop atomic bombs on Hiroshima and Nagasaki near the end of World War II 30 years ago. During the 1960s, however, the Kennedy and Johnson administrations had deemphasized nuclear weapons. The Nixon administration continued this trend; in 1970, Secretary of Defense Melvin R. Laird wrote Sen. Edward W. Brooke (R Mass.) to assure him that "we have not developed, and are not seeking to develop, a weapon system having, or which could reasonably be construed as having, a first-strike potential." If Laird's letter to Brooke were interpreted as "excluding American response to a major Soviet movement towards counterforce capabilities," Schlesinger said, then U.S. nuclear policy had indeed changed. As he indicated repeatedly in his talk, however, the United States never had renounced first use of nuclear weapons if faced with defeat in a conventional war. The Defense Department issued a separate news release June 30 quoting past Presidents and secretaries of defense in support of Schlesinger's assertion.

In Schlesinger's opinion, the very existence of nuclear weapons implied their possible use "If one accepts the no-first-use doctrine, one is accepting a self-denying ordinance that weakens deterrence," he said. But in any event the basic thrust of U.S. defense policy was to "raise the nuclear threshold" by developing more effective conventional weapons, the secretary noted.

At the time Schlesinger spoke, the 1968 Treaty on the Non-Proliferation of Nuclear Weapons was widely conceded to have failed, largely because the two superpowers had not curtailed their own nuclear arms spending (see p. 361). Early in 1975 the United States had nearly 30,000 nuclear weapons based throughout the world, according to figures published by the Center for Defense Information, an independent research organization often critical of Pentagon policies. Eight thousand of these weapons were considered strategic weapons, to be delivered from land-based missile sites, submarines or bombers. Because bilateral U.S.-Soviet arms control negotiations (see Historic Documents 1972, p. 431) had dealt only with strategic weapons, the buildup of tactical nuclear weapons proceeded apace, unaffected by international agreements. In NATO countries alone, the U.S. had 7,000 tactical weapons, the Center estimated.

Public statements and Pentagon budget requests indicated that the United States was still several years away from actual deployment of the counterforce systems urged by Schlesinger.

> *Excerpts from remarks by Secretary of Defense James R. Schlesinger before the Godfrey Sperling Group (an informal group of journalists which holds breakfast meetings with public officials) July 1, 1975:*

Q: Mr. Secretary, I would like to return to trivial business, and that is the question that was raised at the press conference at the White House the other day [June 25] about nuclear weapons. It stated that it was consistent American policy not to keep open the option of first use. Is that an accurate statement, and if not, what has been consistent?

A: I'm glad you raised that question.... The question included a faulty premise so we reached a faulty conclusion. The United States has consistently refrained from disavowing the first use of nuclear weapons. It has been under pressure from various quarters basically for more than twenty-five years to disavow first use. I will mention a bit of the history here and I have some quotations, if any of you are interested, but they show a consistent pattern of either direct endorsement of first use or a refusal to rule out first use. The American policy on this has been unchanged for many years. The changes that have occurred, in fact, have been the result of a gradual evolution towards increasing stress on the conventional components, a diminution on the threat of immediate recourse to nuclear weapons. This has, I think, been an evolution that has been followed for the past twenty years, but under no circumstances could we disavow the first use of nuclear weapons.

If one goes back to the early or mid-1950s, one finds a statement of national strategy enshrined in the policy of massive retaliation by Secretary Dulles, that we would use nuclear weapons at times and in places of our own choosing. At the same time, on the military side, Secretary Wilson as well as President Eisenhower indicated that nuclear weapons were being introduced and were becoming virtually conventional weapons in the force structure; that the distinction between conventional and nuclear weapons should be abridged. I think from that period of time there has been a gradual movement away from the tendency to erode the distinction between nuclear and conventional weapons, but we have always retained in all of our strategies the necessity of not declaring against first use. NATO strategy since the 1950s has been based either on the so-called trip-wire strategy, which prevails into the 1960s and formally prevailed to 1967 when it was shifted to flexible response. The trip-wire strategy, sometimes called the plate glass window, was designed to have a small force sometimes referred to as a corporal's guard up front so that the nuclear bell could ring. The intention was to respond to conventional attack with a nuclear response. Throughout the period since the 1950s we have put emphasis upon the availability of tactical nuclear weapons but I think that the emphasis has gradually shifted towards conventional weapons without in any way reducing the role that nuclear weapons play in deterrence.

Q: Do you want to keep a substantial firebreak between the tac nukes [tactical nuclear] and conventional weapons?

A: I think that we should keep in mind the distinction and that we should be careful and all aware of the firebreak. The purpose of this Administration's military strategy has been to raise the nuclear threshold in the only way that it can be effectively raised, which is to have a solid, conventional posture. Without a solid conventional posture you are driven willy-nilly to the threat of early recourse to nuclear weapons which this Administration, and the President specifically, has rejected. What we want to do is to raise the nuclear threshold and you can only do that by improving the conventional posture.

Now let me add just a few more words on this subject. If one looks back, one sees that in the early 1950s the Soviets pressed us very hard for a declaration against first use; that was in a period in which they had, or were perceived to have, overwhelming conventional strength in Europe and they were in a relatively insignificant posture in terms of nuclear weapons. In that period of time they pressed us hard. In the 1960s their interest in such a declaration waned as their nuclear posture improved and perhaps as they became aware of the intractable difficulties associated with their southeast frontier. So that pressure has disappeared. On the other hand, the Chinese now for obvious reasons have begun to talk about no first use. If one accepts the no-first-use doctrine, one is accepting a self-denying ordinance that weakens deterrence. The underlying purpose and premise of U.S. military policy is to deter attack on the U.S. itself and our Allies and part of the deterrent, a major part of the deterrent, is the existence of our tactical nuclear force. Consistently in Europe we have stated, as we recently restated in the ministerial guidance, the close relationship between conventional capabilities and tactical nuclear capabilities as well as strategic capabilities in the NATO triad and the mutual reinforcement amongst these we felt was what deferred any possibility of Warsaw Pact probing.

Q: How is this Chinese pressure manifested?...

A: I would say it is reflected in Chinese statements repeatedly and has been repeatedly stated ever since the detonation of their first nuclear device in 1964.

First Strike or First Use?

Q: Mr. Secretary, do you make a distinction between first use and first strike? Confusion seems to come in, especially at the present time, about first strike and first use, one being the strategic response, and the other more tactical. Do you make that distinction, or does first use in your mind include the possibility of first strike?

A: First strike in this case is a term that has been applied in the strategic area. I think that distinctions between the strategic and theater areas have probably been somewhat overdrawn, but one needs, for example, a high degree of invulnerability in the theater nuclear forces as we do in the strategic forces. But I do draw a distinction between first strike and first use in the case of the strategic forces because it is a relevant distinction as it applies to the strategic forces. Let me say that there is a problem in this area that the terminology has become somewhat confused and hard-target kill, first strike, disarming first strike are all used interchangeably.

What the United States Government has said of late is that neither side can acquire a disarming first-strike capability. That the nuclear forces of both superpowers are so extensive that irrespective of the deployments of additional forces for the foreseeable future, neither side could hope to eliminate the retaliatory capability of the other side against its own cities. So there is no possibility, as we would see it, of a disarming first strike. Now, we also have added that it is desirable that both sides avoid seeking a disarming first-strike capability. I think that this is the underlying point that the questions are designed to elicit.

While the United States does reject the notion that acquisition of the disarming first-strike capability by either side is desirable, what we have said is as long as the Soviets continue to press ahead with the acquisition of their new weaponry, that the United States will not permit itself to be unilaterally put in a secondary position with regard to counterforce capabilities. But those counterforce capabilities will not reach the level of a disarming first strike.

Q: Mr. Secretary the question is really of whether we have ruled in first use, we have not ruled it out, let me put it that way. We have not really ruled it out, all we're talking about is that disarming first-strike capabilities, is not desirable?

A: No, what I said is that it is not feasible. We cannot obtain it, the Soviets cannot obtain it, for the foreseeable future and as long as both sides are intelligent about their deployment, neither side can obtain a disarming first strike, so it's not feasible and in addition we have indicated that we do not desire ourselves or the Soviets to achieve a disarming first strike. Now that does not mean that we will declare against the first use of strategic weapons. We are pledged as we have been for many years to deterrence of attack upon and defense of Western Europe and we are prepared, should the need arise, to use those weapons in that way.

Let me remind you that U.S. forces are designed for deterrence across the entire spectrum of risk and that one should not select out some particular component of those forces and ask what will happen when they are used or will they be used; rather one should look at the total composite and inquire whether this composite contributes to deterrence. Our doctrine and our force structure, we believe, can make deterrence effective with regard to NATO and the United States.

Enforcement of Agreements

Q: About the disarming first strikes; President Ford at the press conference said that he was satisfied that the Soviets have not cheated on

SALT I [Strategic Arms Limitation Talks]. There are reports that you testified very strongly before the [Sen. Henry] Jackson Armed Forces Subcommittee of certain evidence of the Soviet violations in SALT I. There have been a number of articles; Tad Szulc had a very detailed article in the *New Republic*. *Aviation Week* has had a number of highly technical articles on alleged jamming of American telemetry measurements and other forms of cheating. Are you satisfied in your own mind, there has been no Soviet cheating on SALT I? Are you satisfied that verification procedures for SALT II will be adequate?

A: I think what the President indicated was that we have no firm evidence or proof that the Soviets have indeed violated the SALT I Agreement. When questions arise they go to the standing Consultative Commission. A number of ambiguities have arisen and have gone to the Commission for review. Some of the answers that we have received have been satisfactory up to a point. Other answers are yet to be delivered, but, as yet, we have no demonstrated case of violation by the Soviet Union. There have been ambiguities in a number of areas. I think that with regard to the second half of your question, one must recognize that verification in the forthcoming SALT Agreement cannot be absolutely foolproof. What we must have is a verification procedure that gives us very high confidence that any significant amount of testing of violation overtime would be detected by our intelligence apparatus and therefore by insuring that verification would preclude significant violation, we diminish substantially the incentive for those very small violations that might have no effect on the strategic balance.

Q: But what about the replacement of the SS-11 with the 19 [nuclear-tipped missiles]? The President said that the Russians have not exploited the loopholes, you said the 19, in your testimony, was three to four times the throw-weight of the 11, which would certainly represent a significant increase, as defined by our unilateral ban on—

A: It is plain, I think, that the deployment by the Soviets of the SS-19 is inconsistent with the American unilateral statement that was made in Moscow in 1972. It is wholly inconsistent with the statement. The Soviets did not then accept that statement; witness the fact that it was a unilateral statement by the United States. Consequently, the Soviets are not bound by their treaty or agreement obligations to refrain from this deployment of this larger missile which we very much regret. I think that it does raise a question as to the inherent worth of unilateral statements....

Q: Mr. Secretary, I'd like to follow up that question on the 19's; wasn't that anticipated in the Vladivostok Accords [of 1974]?

A: Anticipated may be the wrong verb, but—

Q: We assumed they were going to do this, didn't we?

A: By that time, it was evident that they were moving ahead in light of their R&D testing of the SS-19 and the 17, which had a throw-weight very substantially in excess of the U.S. definition of what constituted a light missile in 1972, and that they were going ahead with that.

Q: Wasn't it the volume that was the test?

A: In the Agreement, the volume is the test. I think you may have missed what I said just a moment ago. The American Unilateral Statement in 1972 declared that any missile that was larger than the largest light missile then deployed would be construed by the United States as a heavy missile. That was the American Unilateral Statement. As you indicate, the agreement itself referred only to increasing the silo dimensions....

Violations or Ambiguities

[T]here are ambiguities that must be resolved by reference through the standing Consultative Commissions.... Those who are too impatient to allow the deliberative processes or consultative processes established by the Moscow Agreement and Treaty in the form of the standing Consultative Commission are not patient enough to wait for those processes to work themselves out and therefore they are prepared to leap to conclusions, but let me reassert that all of the issues are ambiguous and for that reason they must be discussed in the negotiating framework if we are to make any kind of an agreement on arms control work....

Q: Could you resolve some ambiguities about that first use? You have held out that we will not disavow first use. Does this apply [imply that] the first use in a tactical sense could involve a Trident missile from Charleston, South Carolina, on the one hand and on the other hand, would you tell us where the target would be; would the Soviet Union itself be included or excluded in the target area in tactical use?

A: I think that this is fairly clear in terms of our nuclear doctrine in the posture statement and elsewhere. First use could conceivably, let me underscore conceivably, involve what we define as strategic forces and possibly, possibly, underscore possibly, involve selective strike at the Soviet Union. We do not necessarily exclude that, but it is indeed a very, very low probability....

Q: Could you just tell us how this Consultative Commission would adjudicate differences on these questions, how it works?

A: Each side raises questions about possible violations or ambiguities as it sees them, that the other side has undertaken. The parties then return to their respective governments and bring back whatever response or clarification of the practice is made available by the governments, and the other party sees whether this indeed resolves the issue, removes the ambiguity sufficiently so that the issue can be withdrawn....

Q: I was wondering, sir, if you could characterize your view of the spirit in which the Soviets have carried out the present SALT agreements. We've been focusing on the details here and we get into a debate over violations vs. ambiguities. Are they pressing to the very limits repeatedly, are you dissatisfied in this sense with their performance under the agreement, or how would you characterize that?

A: I think that the Soviets have been inclined to probe a little bit more into gray areas than we would prefer. But, generally, overall, they have been respectful of the broad outlines of the agreement not only in letter but I believe generally in spirit. In certain areas they have not been overly meticulous and those are areas in which ambiguities have arisen which are a disappointment to us and we are seeking clarification....

Limited Nuclear War

Q: What makes you think that a selective strike is a feasible option as distinguished from your predecessors who rejected the concept that you could keep the firebreak between nuclear and conventional weapons from getting out of hand? In other words, their conclusion was there is no such thing as a small nuclear war; President Ford told a couple of reporters yesterday that he regarded your nuclear strategy as "no serious change," which would indicate there's been some change....

A: The notion that a nuclear firebreak if ever breached must inevitably lead to escalation to the top has been supported neither in American military planning nor doctrine nor policy statements. You can check back through the years and you will find that the various Secretaries of Defense might have been more or less optimistic with regard to interfering with the process of escalation, but none of them thought that the probability was so small that it was not desirable to take advantage of it.

Now, the notion that if one uses nuclear weapons that inevitably it must go all the way is one that I understand psychologically, but I do not understand the underlying logic or presumed logic of that statement. Presumably escalation is a conscientious choice; there will be very powerful incentives as have been pointed out by Secretary [Robert S.] McNamara; Secretary [Clark] Clifford; Secretary [Melvin R.] Laird, very powerful incentives.

Under such circumstances, to avoid further escalation and for the parties to compose their differences without further damage, I would point out that in the case of Vietnam, that even though nuclear weapons were not involved and were never, so far as I know, seriously considered, that there was very, very great restraint on the pace of escalation outside of the nuclear sphere. But I think that it demonstrates that conscious policy choice indeed has on occasion controlled escalation, perhaps wisely, perhaps unwisely, but it has controlled that escalation and it certainly indicates that it can do so in the future; the possibility cannot be dismissed.

Q: Since you're reading the record back, just one last point. Secretary Laird has said, even in recent weeks, that he very definitely tried to avoid the appearance of preparing for a first strike, that he did not want to let the Russians read our preparations into that. Are you saying there's no change in your policy because you're changing the targeting of your missiles to...?

A: You've got two things here, a moment ago you were talking about nuclear threshold.

Policy Change?

Q: I'm asking about first-strike appearances?
A: I think that if you read the letters to Senator [Edward W.] Brooke

that the underlying thrust of those letters was that the United States would not seek a disarming first strike. As I've indicated, we would prefer that neither side move in the direction of major counterforce capabilities or disarming first strike if that were attainable, but that the United States is not prepared to see the Soviet Union unilaterally attain that option and that capability and that we will not be second in this regard. To that extent if you define the letters to Senator Brooke as excluding American response to a major Soviet movement towards counterforce capabilities, then the policy has changed. But as you phrase the policy—Secretary Laird indicated that he would prefer not to move in this direction in order to avoid giving this appearance to the Soviet Union; presumably so that they would not feel obliged to respond to an American initiative. In this case, as the questions earlier indicated, the questions about the increase of the throw-weight of the SS-19 or SS-17 by a factor of three or four, the questions about purported violation of the SALT agreement, the Soviets are plowing ahead toward the acquisition of major counterforce capabilities, and if you study Soviet doctrine there is no inhibition expressed whatsoever on going after U.S. strategic capability. That inhibition is something that one sees in the writings of arms controllers; but in Soviet military doctrine they indicate that they are going first and immediately after U.S. strategic forces and the rest of U.S. forces....

I should reiterate that last year when the issue came up, we offered a kind of swap with the Soviets. We offered in the posture statement and outside of it, to restrain the growth of our own strategic forces if they would exhibit some restraint, restraint within the guidelines permitted within the agreement. As has been indicated, they have stated that they are going to go ahead with anything that is not precluded by the SALT agreement or treaty and in the case of throw-weights they have increased their throw-weights by three or fourfold in conflict at least with the American unilateral statement made at Moscow at the time of the SALT I agreement....

Let me reiterate that any use of nuclear weapons would be a most agonizing decision for any political leader. That the purpose and thrust of U.S. military strategy in recent years has been to raise the nuclear threshold so that we have serious conventional options that will not drive us to early recourse to nuclear weapons. That is the main thrust. We cannot exclude the possibility of using nuclear weapons, but our thrust has been towards reliance upon conventional capabilities to the extent that we can. Therefore, I would not expect, given any reasonable stalwartness of our conventional capabilities, early resourse to nuclear weapons should we be faced with serious aggression likely to result in defeat in an area of very great importance to the United States in terms of foreign policy. This has clearly been the case in Western Europe for many years and has been stated again and again by all Secretaries and all Presidents going back to the 1950s with regard to NATO....

Q: But the target is Eastern Europe, not the homeland?

A: Quite right. But the point that I was making is that one cannot sharply distinguish between theater weapons and weapons in what have been described as essential strategic capabilities of the United States in terms of employments as opposed to terms of deployment. Now with regard to the selective strikes on the Soviet Union, I attempted to indicate first that that was a very low, low probability event. Secondly, that we desire to raise the nuclear threshold to have a stalwart conventional capability that would permit us to have options other than recourse to nuclear weapons and, of course, the possibility you mentioned would be the most serious possible use of nuclear weapons.

Soviet Buildup

Q: If the policy hasn't changed, then apparently our appreciation of Soviet efforts and capabilities has. If Secretary Laird feared exciting the Russians to new research and development efforts in his letters to Senator Brooke, we seem to have come around a full circle now, for you're casting the United States' role as one responding to the Soviet. Could you chart that 180 degree turn from Laird's concern about exciting the Soviet Union to our current posture now of what following their initiative in responding? When did that appreciation start to change?

A: I would say that our perception of the Soviet Program began to emerge after the SALT Agreements in May 1972. There was an explosion, an explosion of R&D activity at that time, in the strategic area. Whether it was planned that way or not, it happened. A considerable expansion, a dramatic expansion of R&D activity took place after May of 1972....

Korea

Q: Can you amplify what the President did not say and what you have said about the nuclear situation with regard to Korea, which is very much in the minds of people at that Presidential news conference of last week? We laymen assume we're talking about tactical weapons when we talk about Korea obviously, maybe we're not but can you clarify that at all?

A: Yes, I thought I might reiterate what I did say at that press conference. I indicated that the ground-forces balance in the Korean Peninsula was not unsatisfactory. I reiterated the significant fact that since 1945 no nuclear weapons had been fired in anger; I stated then, as I have stated today that the purpose and thrust of our military policy has been to raise the nuclear threshold and I also indicated that we cannot foreclose the nuclear option. I think that what one is saying here is that the President of the United States should not disclose what he intends to do and he should not disclose his plans [about what] he will refrain from doing. It is, I believe, known that we have deployed nuclear weapons in Europe and Korea along with our forces and that those nuclear weapons are available as options to the President, but I reiterate that the main thrust of U.S. policy has been to raise the nuclear threshold. We will not foreclose the use of nuclear weapons....

NATO

Q: Mr. Secretary, to what extent have NATO leaders been consulted and acquiesced in the first-use doctrine that you've just outlined this morning?

A: As I've indicated, first use has been NATO strategy back to the 1950s. If there were any hint from the United States Government that we were to accept the blandishments of a few people in the arms-control community or a few people on the Hill that we would refrain from first use, that would have a devastating effect on NATO because NATO depends, in large degree, psychologically as well as in terms of force structure, on nuclear reinforcement of conventional capabilities should that be necessary. It is agreed NATO strategy. It was reiterated in the Ministerial guidance that reflects the shift to flexible response in 1967. With regard to the strategic aspect of things, the change in doctrine announced a year and a half ago towards greater selectivity and flexibility has been universally welcomed in Europe for obvious reasons and it serves to recouple to the extent that it had decoupled our strategic and tactical nuclear forces....

U.N. WORLD CONFERENCE
ON STATUS OF WOMEN

July 2, 1975

The first major inter-governmental meeting ever held to discuss the status of women was concluded July 2 in Mexico City with the unanimous adoption of a World Plan of Action *to improve the position of women in all countries. The conference delegates also approved a controversial document, the* Declaration of Mexico, *which condemned Zionism, imperialism and racism and demanded international economic reforms. Only the United States and Israel voted against the* Declaration, *but the delegates from a number of countries abstained.*

Sponsored by the United Nations, which had designated 1975 as International Women's Year, the conference was attended by approximately 1,-300 delegates representing the governments of 133 countries. An uncounted number of women established a parallel, unofficial "Tribune." Its sessions focused on radical feminist issues and were attended primarily by American and Mexican women. The two weeks of public debates in Mexico were often interrupted by noisy confrontations reflecting a deep ideological division between women from industrialized countries and those from developing nations. While women from the so-called Third World insisted that creation of a "new international economic order" must necessarily precede the emancipation of women, Western delegates, particularly those from the United States, regarded elimination of discrimination against women as the first priority.

Both the World Plan of Action *and the* Declaration of Mexico *dealt largely with issues not always relevant to women of industrialized societies. For example, the* Declaration *condemned "forced marriage and marriage as a commercial transaction," and both documents urged agricultural im-*

provements as well as advances in women's literacy, health, nutrition and housing. The goals of women from developed nations appeared in proposals for equal legal status for women and men, equal access to professional advancement, and elimination of stereotyped sex roles. Neither document mentioned abortion, a major issue within women's movements.

The 49-page action plan set a five-year deadline for 14 "minimum" goals, but since the document was purely advisory, the implementation of these proposals depended on whether the delegates themselves could persuade their governments to take action.

The plan was the latest in a series of U.N. agreements relating to women's rights dating back to 1965, when the International Labor Organization (ILO) adopted the Convention on Equal Remuneration for Men and Women Workers for Work of Equal Value. *Subsequent conventions urged political rights for women (1952), equality of opportunity and treatment in employment (1958) and non-discriminatory education (1960).*

Current Status of Women

United Nations studies available at the time of the Mexico City conference indicated that despite dramatic advances, women were still subject to various forms of discrimination, overt or subtle, in nearly every country. Although women made up about one-half of the world's population, they were vastly underrepresented in public life almost everywhere. Nine nations still did not give women full political rights. The marriage laws in several countries deprived women of personal rights as well as property rights. The results of over-population and insufficient resources fell most heavily on women, who "usually lose out if they must compete with men for limited educational facilities and limited job opportunities," according to Margaret K. Bruce, deputy director of the U.N. Centre for Social Development and Humanitarian Affairs.

According to U.N. statistics, as much as 50 per cent of the food in developing countries was produced by women and often under extremely harsh working conditions because of the lack of modern improvements in agricultural technology and mechanization. Also, in many tribal societies women and female children were discriminated against in food distribution during famine periods.

In industrialized nations, many women were subject to discriminatory pay practices. An International Labor Organization (ILO) report in June 1975 found that women's wages amounted to only about 50 to 80 per cent of those received by men. These figures were based on comparisons between the wage earnings of men and women in manufacturing—often the only sector for which statistics were available. But women's wages had been increasing at a faster rate than those of men, the ILO stated. It reported substantial improvement in the status of working women and mentioned Western European nations, the United States, Japan and Arab states as countries that have worked toward ending discrimination against female workers.

At the time of the Mexico City conference some women's organizations in the United States were calling for the establishment of a Cabinet-level department to deal with women's issues. The Equal Rights Amendment (ERA) to prohibit discrimination on the basis of sex had been approved by 34 of the 38 states required for ratification.

Introduction *and* Plan for National Action, *excerpted from the* World Plan of Action for the Implementation of the Objectives of the International Women's Year, *adopted by the U.N.-sponsored World Conference of the International Women's Year at Mexico City July 2, 1975:*

Introduction

1. In subscribing to the Charter, the peoples of the United Nations undertook specific commitments: "to save succeeding generations from the scourge of war...to reaffirm faith in fundamental human rights, in the dignity and worth of the human person, in the equal rights of men and women and of nations large and small, and...to promote social progress and better standards of life in larger freedom".

2. The greatest and most significant achievement during recent decades has been the liberation of a large number of peoples and nations from alien colonial domination, which has permitted them to become members of the community of free peoples. Technological progress has also been achieved in all spheres of economic activity during the past three decades, thus offering substantial possibilities for improving the well-being of all peoples. However, the last vestiges of alien and colonial domination, foreign occupation, racial discrimination, *apartheid* and neo-colonialism in all its forms are still among the greatest obstacles to the full emancipation and progress of developing countries and of all the peoples concerned. The benefits of technological progress are not shared equitably by all members of the international community. The developing countries, which account for 70 per cent of the population of the world, receive only 30 per cent of world income. It has proved impossible to achieve uniform and balanced development of the international community under the present economic order, and, for this reason, it is urgent to implement a new international economic order in accordance with General Assembly resolution 3201 (S-VI).

3. Conventions, declarations, formal recommendations and other instruments have been adopted since the Charter came into force with a view to reinforcing, elaborating and implementing these fundamental principles and objectives. Some of them seek to safeguard and promote the human rights and fundamental freedoms of all persons without discrimination of any kind. Others deal with promotion of economic and social progress and development and the need to eliminate all forms of alien domination, dependence, neo-colonialism, and include international strategies, programmes and plans of action. Some have the more specific purpose of eliminating discrimination on the ground of sex and promoting the equal

rights of men and women. These documents reflect the ever-increasing awareness in the international community of the uneven development of peoples, and of the tragedy of all forms of discrimination be it on the ground of race, sex or any other ground, and the evident will to promote progress and development in conditions of peace, equity and justice.

4. In these various instruments the international community has proclaimed that the full and complete development of a country, the welfare of the world and the cause of peace require the maximum participation of women as well as men in all fields. It has declared that all human beings without distinction have the right to enjoy the fruits of social and economic progress and should, on their part, contribute to it. It has condemned sex discrimination as fundamentally unjust, an offence against human dignity and an infringement of human rights. It has included the full integration of women in the total development effort as a stated objective of the International Development Strategy for the decade of the 1970s.

5. Despite these solemn pronouncements and notwithstanding the work accomplished in particular by the United Nations Commission on the Status of Women and the specialized agencies concerned, progress in translating these principles into practical reality is proving slow and uneven. The difficulties encountered in the preparation and implementation of these many instruments are attributable to the complexities created by the considerable differences between countries, regions, etc.

6. History has attested the active role which women played, together with men, in accelerating the material and spiritual progress of peoples and in the process of the progressive renewal of society; in our times, women's role will increasingly emerge as a powerful revolutionary social force.

National Differences in Status of Women

7. There are significant differences in the status of women in different countries and regions of the world which are rooted in the political, economic and social structure, the cultural framework and the level of each country, and in the social category of women within a given country. However, basic similarities unite women to fight differences wherever they exist in the legal, economic, social, political and cultural status of women and men.

8. As a result of the uneven development which prevails in the international economic relations, three quarters of humanity is faced with urgent and pressing social and economic problems. The women among them are even more affected by such problems and the new measures taken to improve their situation as well as their role in the process of development must be an integral part of the global project for the establishment of a new economic order.

Need for Technical Assistance

9. In many countries women form a large part of the agricultural work force. Because of this and because of their important role in agricultural

production and in the preparation, processing and marketing of food, they constitute a substantial economic resource. Nevertheless, if the rural worker's lack of technical equipment, education and training is taken into account, it will be seen that in many countries the status of women in this sector is doubly disadvantaged.

10. While industrialization provides jobs for women and constitutes one of the main means for the integration of women in the process of development, women workers are disadvantaged in many respects because of the fact that the technological structure of production in general has been oriented towards man and his requirements. Therefore special attention must be made to the situation of the woman worker in industry and in services. Women workers feel painfully the effects of the present economic crisis, the growth of unemployment, inflation, mass poverty, lack of resources for education and medical care, unexpected and unwanted side-effects of urbanization and other migration, etc.

11. Scientific and technological developments have had both positive and negative repercussions on the situation of women in many countries. Political, economic and social factors are important in overcoming any adverse effects of such developments.

12. During the last decades women's movements and millions of women together with other progressive forces acting in many countries have focused public opinion at the national and international levels on all these problems.

13. However, that public opinion often overlooks the many women of regions under alien domination, particularly those subjected to *apartheid* who experience daily the terror of repression and who struggle tirelessly for the recovery of the most elementary rights of the human person.

14. The reality of the problems which women still meet in their daily life in many countries of the world in their efforts to participate in the economic and social activities in the decision-making process and the political administration of their countries, and the loss represented by the under-utilization of the potentialities of approximately 50 per cent of the world's adult population, have prompted the United Nations to proclaim 1975 as International Women's Year, and to call for intensified action to ensure the full integration of women in the total development effort, and to involve women widely in international co-operation and strengthening of world peace on the basis of equal rights, opportunities, and responsibilities of women and men. The objective of International Women's Year is to define a society in which women participate in a real and full sense in economic, social and political life and to devise strategies whereby such societies could develop.

15. This Plan of Action is intended to strengthen the implementation of the instruments and programmes which have been adopted concerning the status of women, and to broaden and place them in a more timely context. Its purpose is mainly to stimulate national and international action to solve the problems of underdevelopment and of the socio-economic structure which places women in an inferior position, and in order to achieve the goals of International Women's Year.

Reassessment of Sex Roles

16. The achievement of equality between men and women implies that they should have equal rights, opportunities and responsibilities to enable them to develop their talents and capabilities for their own personal fulfilment and the benefit of society. To that end, a reassessment of the functions and roles traditionally allotted to each sex within the family and the community at large is essential. The necessity of a change in the traditional role of men as well as of women must be recognized. In order to allow for women's equal (fuller) participation in all societal activities, socially organized services should be established and maintained to lighten household chores, and especially services for children should be provided. All efforts should be made to change social attitudes—based mainly on education—in order to bring about the acceptance of shared responsibilities for home and children by both men and women.

17. In order to promote equality between women and men Governments should ensure for both women and men equality before the law, the provision of facilities for equality of educational opportunities and training, equality in conditions of employment, including remuneration and adequate social security. Governments should recognize and undertake measures to implement men's and women's rights to employment on equal conditions, regardless of marital status and their access to the whole range of economic activities. The State has also the responsibility to create conditions that promote the implementation of legal norms providing for equality of men and women and in particular the opportunity for all individuals to receive free general and primary education, and eventually compulsory general secondary education, equality in conditions of employment, and maternity protection.

18. Governments should strive to ameliorate the hard working conditions and unreasonably heavy work load, especially that fall upon large groups of women in many countries and particularly among underprivileged social groups. Governments should ensure improved access to health services, better nutrition and other social services that are essential to the improvement of the condition of women and their full participation in development on an equal basis with men.

Family Planning

19. Individuals and couples have the right freely and responsibility to determine the number and spacing of their children and to have the information and the means to do so. The exercise of this right is basic to the attainment of any real equality between the sexes and without its achievement women are disadvantaged in their attempt to benefit from other reforms.

20. Child-care centres and other child-minding facilities are means to supplement the training and care that the children get at home. At the same time they are of vital importance in promoting equality between men and women. Governments have therefore a responsibility to see to it that

such centres and facilities are available in the first place for those children, whose parents or parent are employed, in self-employment and particularly in agriculture for rural women, in training or in education or wish to take up employment, training or education.

21. The primary objective of development being to bring about sustained improvement in the well-being of the individual and of society and to bestow benefits on all, development should be seen not only as a desirable goal in itself but also as the most important means for furthering equality of the sexes and the maintenance of peace.

22. The integration of women in development will necessitate widening their activities to embrace all aspects of social, economic, political and cultural life. They must be provided with the necessary technical training to make their contribution more effective in terms of production, and to ensure their greater participation in decision-making, planning and implementation of all programmes and projects. Full integration also implies that women receive their fair share of the benefits of development, thereby helping to ensure a more equitable distribution of income among all sectors of the population.

"New Economic Order"

23. The promotion and protection of human rights for all is one of the fundamental principles of the United Nations Charter whose achievement is the goal of all people. An essential element for securing the protection of human rights and full equality between men and women throughout the world is sustained international co-operation based on peace, justice and equity for all and the elimination of all sources of conflict. True international co-operation must be based, in accordance with the Charter of the United Nations, on fully equal rights, the observance of national independence and sovereignty including sovereignty over natural resources and the right of their exploitation, non-interference in internal affairs, the right of peoples to defend their territorial integrity, and the inadmissibility of acquisition or attempts to acquire territory by force, mutual advantage, the avoidance of the use or the threat of force, and the promotion and maintenance of a new just world economic order, which is the basic purpose of the Charter of Economic Rights and Duties of States. International co-operation and peace requires national liberation and political and economic independence, the elimination of colonialism and neo-colonialism, fascism and other similar ideologies, foreign occupation and *apartheid,* racism and discrimination in all its forms as well as recognition of the dignity of the individual and appreciation of the human person and his or her self-determination. To this end, the Plan calls for the full participation of women in all efforts to promote and maintain peace. True peace cannot be achieved unless women share with men the responsibility for establishing a new international economic order.

24. It is the aim of the Plan to ensure that the original and multidimensional contribution—both actual and potential—of women is not overlooked in existing concepts for development action programmes and an

improved world economic equilibrium. Recommendations for national and international action are proposed with the aim of accelerating the necessary changes in all areas, and particularly in those where women have been especially disadvantaged.

25. Since the integral development of the personality of the woman as a human being is directly connected with her participation in the development process as mother, worker and citizen, policies should be developed to promote the co-ordination of these different roles of the woman so as to give the most favourable conditions for the harmonious development of her personality—an aim which is equally relevant to the development of man.

I. National Action

26. This Plan provides guidelines for national action over the 10-year period from 1975 to 1985 as part of a sustained, long-term effort to achieve the objectives of the International Women's Year. The recommendations are not exhaustive, and should be considered in addition to the other existing international instruments and resolutions of the United Nations bodies which deal with the condition of women and the quality of life. They constitute rather the main areas for priority action within the decade.

27. The recommendations for national action in this Plan are addressed primarily to Governments, and to all public and private institutions, women's and youth organizations, employers, trade unions, mass communications media, non-governmental organizations, political parties and other groups.

28. Since there are wide divergencies in the situation of women in various societies, cultures and regions, reflected in differing needs and problems, each country should decide upon its own national strategy, and identify its own targets and priorities within the present World Plan. Given the changing conditions of society today, [an] operative mechanism for assessment should be established and targets should be linked to those set out, in particular, in the International Development Strategy for the Second United Nations Development Decade, and in the World Population Plan of Action.

29. Changes in social and economic structures should be promoted which would make possible the full equality of women and their free access to all types of development, without discrimination of any kind, and to all types of education and employment.

30. There should be a clear commitment at all levels of government to take appropriate action to implement these targets and priorities. Commitment on the part of Governments to the ideals of equality and integration of women in society cannot be fully effective outside the larger context of commitment to transform fundamental relationships within a society in order to ensure a system that excludes the possibility of exploitation.

31. In elaborating national strategies and development plans in which women should participate, measures should be adopted to ensure that the set targets and priorities should take fully into account women's interests and needs, and make adequate provision to improve their situation and in-

crease their contribution to the development process. There should be equitable representation of women at all levels of policy—and decision-making. Appropriate national machinery and procedures should be established if they do not already exist.

32. National plans and strategies for the implementation of this Plan should be sensitive to the needs and problems of different categories of women and of women of different age groups. However, Governments should pay special attention to improving the situation of women in areas where they have been most disadvantaged and especially of women in rural and urban areas.

33. While integrated programmes for the benefit of all members of society should be the basis for action in implementing this plan, special measures on behalf of women whose status is the result of particularly discriminatory attitudes will be necessary.

Need for Special Government Agencies

34. The establishment of interdisciplinary and multisectoral machinery within government, such as national commissions, women's bureaux and other bodies, with adequate staff and budget, can be an effective transitional measure for accelerating the achievement of equal opportunity for women and their full integration in national life. The membership of such bodies should include both women and men, representative of all groups of society responsible for making and implementing policy decisions in the public sector. Government ministries and departments (especially those responsible for education, health, labour, justice, communications and information, culture, industry, trade, agriculture, rural development, social welfare, finance and planning), as well as appropriate private and public agencies should be represented on them.

35. Such bodies should investigate the situation of women in all fields and at all levels and make recommendations for needed legislation, policies and programmes establishing priorities. Follow-up programmes should be maintained to monitor and evaluate the progress achieved within the country to assess the implementation of the present Plan in national plans.

36. These national bodies should also co-operate in the co-ordination of similar regional and international activities, as well as those undertaken by non-governmental organizations, and self-help programmes devised by women themselves.

Role of Legislation

37. Constitutional and legislative guarantees of the principle of non-discrimination on the ground of sex and of equal rights and responsibilities of women and men are essential. Therefore, general acceptance of the principles embodied in such legislation and a change of attitude with regard to them should be encouraged. It is also essential to ensure that the adoption and enforcement of such legislation can in itself be a significant means of influencing and changing public and private attitudes and values.

38. Governments should review their legislation affecting the status of women in the light of human rights principles and internationally accepted standards. Wherever necessary, legislation should be enacted or updated to bring national laws into conformity with the relevant international instruments. Adequate provision should also be made for the enforcement of such legislation, especially in each of the areas dealt with in chapter II of the Plan. Where they have not already done so, Governments should take steps to ratify the relevant international conventions and fully implement their provisions. It should be noted that there are States whose national legislation guarantees women certain rights which go beyond those embodied in the relevant international instruments.

39. Appropriate bodies should be specifically entrusted with the responsibility of modernizing, changing or repealing outdated national laws and regulations, keeping them under constant review, and ensuring that their provisions are applied without discrimination. These bodies could include, for example, law commissions, human rights commissions, civil liberties unions, appeals boards, legal advisory boards and the office of *ombudsman*. Such bodies should have full governmental support to enable them to carry out their functions effectively. Non-governmental organizations could also play an important role in ensuring that relevant legislation is adequate, up to date and applied without discrimination.

40. Appropriate measures should be taken to inform and advise women of their rights and to provide them with every other type of assistance. Accordingly, the awareness of the mass communication media should be heightened so that they may offer their broad co-operation through public education programmes. Non-governmental organizations can and/or should be encouraged to play similar roles with regard to women. In this context, special attention should be paid to the women of rural areas, whose problem is most acute.

41. Efforts to widen opportunities for women to participate in development and to eliminate discrimination against them will require a variety of measures and action by society at large through its governmental machinery and other institutions.

42. While some of the measures suggested could be carried out at minimum cost, implementation of this Plan will require a redefinition of certain priorities and a change in the pattern of government expenditure. In order to ensure adequate allocation of funds, Governments should explore all available sources of support, which are acceptable to Governments and in accordance with Governments' goals.

43. Special measures should also be envisaged to assist Governments whose resources are limited in carrying out specific projects or programmes. The Fund for International Women's Year established under Economic and Social Council resolution 1851 (LVI), in addition to multilateral and bilateral assistance which is vital for the purpose, should be extended provisionally pending further consideration as to its ultimate disposition in order to assist Governments whose resources are limited in carrying out specific programmes or projects. Women in countries holding special finan-

cial responsibilities entrusted by the United Nations and its specialized agencies with a view to assisting developing countries are called upon to make their contribution to the implementation of the goals set in connexion with the governmental assistance earmarked for improving the status of women especially of those in the under-developed States.

44. It is recognized that some of the objectives of this Plan have already been achieved in some countries, while in others they may only be accomplished progressively. Moreover, some measures by their very nature will take longer to implement than others. Governments are therefore urged to establish short-, medium- and long-term targets and objectives to implement the Plan.

45. On the basis of this World Plan of Action the United Nations Secretariat should elaborate a two-year plan of its own, containing several most important objectives, aiming at the implementation of the World Plan of Action under the current control of the Commission on the Status of Women and the over-all control of the General Assembly.

Recommended Five-Year Goals

46. By the end of the first five-year period (1975-1980) the achievement of the following should be envisaged as a minimum:

(a) Marked increase in literacy and civic education of women, especially in rural areas;

(b) The extension of co-educational technical and vocational training in basic skills to women and men in the industrial and agricultural sectors;

(c) Equal access at every level of education, compulsory primary school education and the measures necessary to prevent school drop-outs;

(d) Increased employment opportunities for women, reduction of unemployment and increased efforts to eliminate discrimination in the terms and conditions of employment;

(e) The establishment and increase of the infrastructural services required in both rural and urban areas;

(f) The enactment of legislation on voting and eligibility for election on equal terms with men and equal opportunity and conditions of employment including remuneration and on equality in legal capacity and the exercise thereof;

(g) To encourage a greater participation of women in policy-making positions at the local, national and international levels;

(h) Increased provision for comprehensive measures for health education and services, sanitation, nutrition, family education, family planning and other welfare services;

(i) Provision for parity in the exercise of civil, social and political rights such as those pertaining to marriage, citizenship and commerce;

(j) Recognition of the economic value of women's work in the home in domestic food production and marketing and voluntary activities not traditionally remunerated;

(k) To direct formal, non-formal and life-long education towards the reevaluation of the man and woman, in order to ensure their full realization as an individual in the family and in society;

(l) The promotion of women's organizations as an interim measure within workers' organizations and educational, economic and professional institutions;

(m) The development of modern rural technology, cottage industry, pre-school day centres, time and energy saving devices so as to help reduce the heavy work load of women, particularly those living in rural sectors and for the urban poor and thus facilitate the full participation of women in community, national and international affairs;

(n) The establishment of an inter-disciplinary and multi-sectoral machinery within the government for accelerating the achievement of equal opportunities for women and their full integration into national life.

47. These minimum objectives should be developed in more specific terms in regional plans of action.

48. The active involvement of non-governmental women's organizations in the achievement of the goals of the 10-year World Plan of Action at every level and especially by the effective utilization of volunteer experts and in setting up and in running of institutions and projects for the welfare of women and the dissemination of information for their advancement.

> *Excerpts from the* Declaration of Mexico on the Equality of Women and Their Contribution to Development and Peace, 1975, *adopted by the World Conference of the International Women's Year at Mexico City July 2, 1975; the conference was sponsored by the United Nations:*

The World Conference of the International Women's Year,....

Decides to promulgate the following principles:

1. Equality between women and men means equality in their dignity and worth as human beings as well as equality in their rights, opportunities and responsibilities.

2. All obstacles that stand in the way of enjoyment by women of equal status with men must be eliminated in order to ensure their full integration into national development and their participation in securing and in maintaining international peace.

3. It is the responsibility of the State to create the necessary facilities so that women may be integrated into society while their children receive adequate care.

4. National non-governmental organizations should contribute to the advancement of women by assisting women to take advantage of their opportunities, by promoting education and information about women's rights, and by co-operating with their respective Governments.

Equal Rights and Responsibilities

5. Women and men have equal rights and responsibilities in the family and in society. Equality between women and men should be guaranteed in

the family, which is the basic unit of society and where human relations are nurtured. Men should participate more actively, creatively and responsibly in family life for its sound development in order to enable women to be more intensively involved in the activities of their communities and with a view to combining effectively home and work possibilities of both partners.

6. Women, like men, require opportunities for developing their intellectual potential to the maximum. National policies and programmes should therefore provide them with full and equal access to education and training at all levels, while ensuring that such programmes and policies consciously shall orient them towards new occupations and new roles consistent with their need for self-fulfilment and the needs of national development.

7. The right of women to work, to receive equal pay for work of equal value, to be provided with equal conditions and opportunities for advancement in work, and all other women's rights to full and satisfying economic activity are strongly reaffirmed. Review of these principles for their effective implementation is now urgently needed, considering the necessity of restructuring world economic relationships. This restructuring offers greater possibilities for women to be integrated into the stream of national economic, social, political and cultural life.

8. All means of communication and information as well as all cultural media should regard as a high priority their responsibility for helping to remove the attitudinal and cultural factors that still inhibit the development of women and for projecting in positive terms the value to society of the assumption by women of changing and expanding roles.

9. Necessary resources should be made available in order that women may be able to participate in the political life of their countries and of the international community since their active participation in national and world affairs at decision-making and other levels in the political field is a prerequisite of women's full exercise of equal rights as well as of their further development, and of the national well-being.

10. Equality of rights carries with it corresponding responsibilities; it is therefore a duty of women to make full use of opportunities available to them and to perform their duties to the family, the country and humanity.

11. It should be one of the principal aims of social education to teach respect for physical integrity and its rightful place in human life. The human body, whether that of a woman or man, is inviolable and respect for it is a fundamental element of human dignity and freedom.

12. Every couple and every individual has the right to decide freely and responsibly whether or not to have children as well as to determine their number and spacing, and to have information, education and means to do so.

13. Respect for human dignity encompasses the right of every woman to decide freely for herself whether or not to contract matrimony.

14. The issue of inequality, as it affects the vast majority of the women of the world, is closely linked with the problem of under-development, which exists as a result not only of unsuitable internal structures, but also of a profoundly unjust world economic system.

15. The full and complete development of any country requires the maximum participation of women as well as of men in all fields: the underutilization of the potential of approximately half of the world's population is a serious obstacle to social and economic development.

16. The ultimate end of development is to achieve a better quality of life for all, which means not only the development of economic and other material resources but also the physical, moral, intellectual and cultural growth of the human person.

17. In order to integrate women into development, States should undertake the necessary changes in their economic and social policies because women have the right to participate and contribute to the total development effort.

Economic Reforms Necessary

18. The present state of international economic relations poses serious obstacles to a more efficient utilization of all human and material potential for accelerated development and for the improvement of living standards in developing countries aimed at the elimination of hunger, child mortality, unemployment, illiteracy, ignorance and backwardness, which concern all of humanity and women in particular. It is therefore essential to establish and implement with urgency the New International Economic Order of which the Charter of Economic Rights and Duties of States constitutes a basic element, founded on equity, sovereign equality, interdependence, common interest, co-operation among all States irrespective of their social and economic systems, on the principles of peaceful co-existence and on the promotion by the entire international community of economic and social progress of all countries, especially developing countries, and on the progress of States comprising the international community.

19. The principle of full and permanent sovereignty of every State over its natural resources, wealth and all economic activities as well as its inalienable right of nationalization as an expression of this sovereignty, constitute fundamental prerequisites in the process of economic and social development.

20. The attainment of economic and social goals, so basic to the realization of the rights of women, does not, however, of itself bring about the full integration of women in development on a basis of equality with men unless specific measures are undertaken for the elimination of all forms of discrimination against them. It is therefore, important to formulate and implement models of development that will promote the participation and advancement of women in all fields of work, provide them with equal educational opportunities, and such services as would facilitate housework.

21. Modernization of the agricultural sector of vast areas of the world is an indispensable element for progress, particularly as it creates opportunities for millions of rural women to participate in development. Governments, the United Nations, its specialized agencies and other competent regional and international organizations should support projects

designed to utilize the maximum potential and to develop the self-reliance of rural women.

22. It must be emphasized that, given the required economic, social and legal conditions as well as the appropriate attitudes conducive to the full and equal participation of women in society, efforts and measures aimed at a more intensified integration of women in development can be successfully implemented only if made an integral part of over-all social and economic growth. Full participation of women in the various economic, social, political and cultural sectors is an important indication of the dynamic progress of peoples and their development. Individual human rights can only be realized within the framework of total development.

Right of Nations to Self-Determination

23. The objectives considered in this Declaration can be achieved only in a world in which the relations between States are governed, *inter alia,* by the following principles: the sovereign equality of States, the free self-determination of peoples, the unacceptability of acquisition or attempted acquisition of territories by force and the prohibition of recognition of such acquisition, territorial integrity, and the right to defend it, and non-interference in the domestic affairs of States, in the same manner as relations between human beings should be governed by the supreme principle of the equality of rights of women and men.

24. International co-operation and peace require the achievement of national liberation and independence, the elimination of colonialism and neo-colonialism, foreign occupation, zionism, *apartheid,* and racial discrimination in all its forms as well as the recognition of the dignity of peoples and their right to self-determination.

25. Women have a vital role to play in the promotion of peace in all spheres of life: in the family, the community, the nation and the world. As such, women must participate equally with men in the decision-making processes which help to promote peace at all levels.

26. Women as well as men together should eliminate colonialism, neo-colonialism, imperialism, foreign domination and occupation, zionism, *apartheid,* racial discrimination, the acquisition of land by force and the recognition of such acquisition, since such practices inflict incalculable suffering on women, men and children.

27. The solidarity of women in all countries of the world should be supported in their protest against violations of human rights condemned by the United Nations. All forms of repression and inhuman treatment of women, men and children, including imprisonment, torture, massacres, collective punishment, destruction of homes, forced eviction and arbitrary restriction of movement shall be considered crimes against humanity and in violation of the Universal Declaration of Human Rights and other international instruments.

28. Women all over the world should unite to eliminate violations of human rights committed against women and girls such as: rape,

prostitution, physical assault, mental cruelty, child marriage, forced marriage and marriage as a commercial transaction.

29. Peace requires that women as well as men should reject any type of intervention in the domestic affairs of States, whether it be openly or covertly carried on by other States or by transnational corporations. Peace also requires that women as well as men should also promote respect for the sovereign right of a State to establish its own economic, social and political system without undergoing political and economic pressures or coercion of any type.

30. Women as well as men should promote real, general and complete disarmament under effective international control, starting with nuclear disarmament. Until genuine disarmament is achieved, women and men throughout the world must maintain their vigilance and do their utmost to achieve and maintain international peace.

Wherefore,
The World Conference of the International Women's Year,

1. *Affirms* its faith in the objectives of the International Women's Year, which are equality, development and peace;

2. *Proclaims* its commitment to the achievement of such objectives;

3. *Strongly urges* Governments, the entire United Nations system, regional and international intergovernmental organizations and the international community as a whole to dedicate themselves to the creation of a just society where women, men and children can live in dignity, freedom, justice and prosperity.

COLBY REPORT ON THE CIA
July 8, 1975

Almost a month after the Rockefeller Commission submitted its report on improper domestic activities of the Central Intelligence Agency (CIA), the CIA itself unexpectedly made public unclassified portions of an earlier inquiry of its own into possible wrongdoing. The report, consisting of a six-page letter by CIA Director William E. Colby and supporting documents, had been sent to President Ford on Dec. 24, 1974, two days after The New York Times *published allegations that the CIA had carried on "massive" illegal surveillance of U.S. citizens during the Nixon administration. While the agency's internal review had turned up certain "improper actions" in the past, Colby wrote, the CIA was "not conducting activities comparable to those alleged" in* The Times. *What missteps the agency had taken were "few" and "quite exceptional," Colby added.*

The basis of the Colby report was a 1973 review ordered by then CIA Director James R. Schlesinger. The publication of a truncated version of this review—the Colby report—was apparently spurred by preliminary steps in a lawsuit seeking its release. The legal action had been taken under provisions of the Freedom of Information Act by Morton Halperin, a consultant to a Washington public-interest project on national security. Halperin, a staff member of the National Security Council in 1969, told the Washington Post *that the report as released and Colby's cover letter summarizing its findings were "just an absolute cover-up."*

The document did not add substantially to the public record on CIA activities. However, Colby confirmed that two years earlier the chairmen of the congressional Armed Services Committees had been briefed on the contents of the Schlesinger report. In June Rep. Lucien N. Nedzi (D Mich.) had been ousted as chairman of the special House committee investigating the CIA after five committee members charged that he had failed to disclose similar briefings.

Colby's report differed from the Rockefeller Commission findings on a CIA mail interception project which, Colby said, had from its inception in 1953 been "fully coordinated" with the Federal Bureau of Investigation. The Rockefeller Commission had placed FBI coordination in 1958.

> *Text of a letter to President Gerald R. Ford from CIA Director William E. Colby, summarizing findings of an agency inquiry into possible wrongdoing; the letter, dated Dec. 24, 1974, was made public July 8, 1975. Supporting documents ("annexes") omitted:*

Dear Mr. President:

This report is in response to your request for my comments on *The New York Times* article of December 22nd alleging CIA involvement in a "massive" domestic intelligence effort. While CIA has made certain errors, it is not accurate to characterize it as having engaged in "massive domestic intelligence activity."

The National Security Act of 1947 states that CIA shall have no "police, subpoena, law-enforcement powers, or internal security functions." The Agency's functions thus relate solely to *foreign* intelligence. Included in this responsibility is foreign counterintelligence, as stated in National Security Council Intelligence Directive No. 5. This provides that CIA shall, *inter alia,* conduct clandestine counterintelligence outside the United States and its possessions. Under this charge, CIA for many years has maintained liaison with the intelligence and security services of other nations and has conducted independent counterintelligence activities abroad. Whenever such matters relate to the internal security of the United States, information derived from such operations is passed to the Federal Bureau of Investigation and other Departments or Agencies of the Government when appropriate. In addition, CIA has responded to requests from the Federal Bureau of Investigation, and on occasion other Departments, for counterintelligence work abroad.

In 1967, when concern grew in the United States Government over domestic dissidence, questions were raised as to whether there might be stimulation or support of such activity from outside the United States. As a result, the Director of Central Intelligence on 15 August established within the CIA counterintelligence office a program to identify possible foreign links with American dissident elements (Annex A). Later that same year, this became a part of an interagency program (Annex B). In November 1967, the Agency produced a study, *International Connections of US Peace Groups,* in response to a request by the President. In late 1967 or early 1968 the Assistant to the President for National Security Affairs [Walt W. Rostow] requested an assessment of possible foreign links with American dissident student groups (SDS) [Students for a Democratic Society]. In mid-1968 the Agency produced an assessment of youth movements throughout the world, including a section analyzing the American scene to complete the picture. This study concluded that: "There is no convincing evidence of control, manipulation, sponsorship, or significant financial support of student dissidents by any international Communist authority."

In September 1969 the Director [Richard Helms] reviewed the counterintelligence program and stated that he believed it to be proper, "while strictly observing the statutory and *de facto* prescriptions on Agency domestic involvements" (Annex C).

In 1970, in the so-called Huston Plan, the Directors of the FBI [Federal Bureau of Investigation], DIA [Defense Intelligence Agency], NSA [National Security Agency], and CIA signed a report to the President recommending an integrated approach to the coverage of domestic unrest. While not explicit in the Plan, CIA's role would have been to contribute foreign intelligence and counterintelligence. The Huston Plan itself was not implemented but was followed by the establishment on 3 December 1970 of the Interagency Evaluation Committee which was coordinated by the Counsel to the President, Mr. John Dean. This committee was chaired by a Department of Justice officer, Mr. Robert Mardian, and included representatives from CIA, FBI, DOD [Department of Defense], State, Treasury, and NSA. Pursuant to the Government-wide effort, CIA continued its counterintelligence interest in possible foreign links with American dissidents. A full description of the CIA project, prepared on 1 June 1972, is attached (Annex D).

Because of CIA's effort during these years, some CIA employees, not directly involved in the program, misinterpreted it as being more focused on American dissidents than on their possible connections with foreign governments. In addition, however, there were individual cases in which actions were taken which overstepped proper bounds. For example, the Agency recruited or inserted individuals into American dissident circles to establish their credentials for operations abroad against those foreign elements which might be supporting, encouraging, or directing dissidence in the United States. In the course of their preparatory work or on completion of a phase of their mission abroad, these individuals reported on the activities of the American dissidents with whom they came in contact. Significant information thereby derived was reported to the FBI, but in the process CIA files were established on the individuals named.

In 1972, with the approval of the Director, the Executive Director [William E. Colby] issued an internal memorandum to senior CIA officials describing the program in order to clarify its scope and to invite reports of any departures from its policy:

> "To carry out its responsibilities for counterintelligence, CIA is interested in the activities of foreign nations or intelligence services aimed at the U.S. To the extent that these activities lie outside the U.S., including activities aimed at the U.S. utilizing U.S. citizens or others, they fall within CIA's responsibilities.

Responsibility for coverage of the activities within the U.S. lies with the FBI, as an internal security function. CIA's responsibility and authority are limited to the foreign intelligence aspect of the problem, and any action of a law enforcement or internal security nature lies with the FBI or local police forces."
(Annex E)

On 9 May 1973, the Director [James R. Schlesinger] issued a bulletin to all employees requesting them to report any indication of any activity they believed might be outside CIA's charter (Annex F.). Responses from some employees referred to the counterintelligence program. As a result, on 29 August 1973 the Director issued specific direction to the managers of the program reemphasizing that the focus of the program was to be clearly on the foreign organizations and individuals involved in links with American dissidents and only incidentally on the American contacts involved (Annex G).

In March 1974 the Director terminated the program and issued specific guidance that any collection of counterintelligence information on Americans would only take place abroad and would be initiated only in response to requests from the FBI or in coordination with it; furthermore, any such information obtained as a by-product of foreign intelligence activities would be reported to the FBI (Annex H).

Files on U.S. Citizens

In the course of this program, files were developed on American citizens. The total index of these Americans amounts to 9,944 counterintelligence files. Approximately two-thirds of these consisted of the by-product coverage of the activities outlined above or stemmed from specific requests from the FBI for information on the activities of Americans abroad. One-third consisted of FBI reports on American Communists. We have for the past several months been in the process of eliminating material not justified by CIA's counterintelligence responsibilities, and about 1,000 such files have been removed from the active index but not destroyed.

Aside from our Congressional liaison working records, we hold files on fourteen past and present Members of Congress. These were opened prior to their election to office and were caused either by the process of clearing them for work with the Agency or because we were interested in them for foreign intelligence purposes. There is no, and to my knowledge never has been any, surveillance—technical or otherwise—of any Members of Congress.

Improper Actions

The New York Times article makes a number of specific allegations of improper activity domestically by CIA and relates these to the above program. In the 1973 compilation by the Agency of all activities which might be questionable, a number of items were raised which were not related to that program. The Agency's action in most of these cases was founded upon the section of the National Security Act of 1947 which provides that the Director of Central Intelligence is responsible for protecting intelligence sources and methods from unauthorized disclosure. Over the many years in which CIA has been operating, some actions have been taken which were improper extensions of the charge contained in this language. Apparently *The New York Times* reporter learned of some of these items and erroneously associated them with the above program. Examples include:

a. Unauthorized entry of the premises of three individuals, a defector and two former employees, to determine whether they had classified documents, and in one case to recover them (in 1966, 1970 and 1971). Two of these incidents involved breaking and entering.

b. Electronic surveillance (telephone tap) of two newspaper reporters (1963) and physical surveillance of five reporters (in 1971 and 1972) to determine the sources of classified information published by them. Similar physical surveillance of three ex-employees of the CIA who were suspected of unauthorized possession of classified documents (1969, 1971, and 1972).

c. Development of paid informants among construction workers at the time of construction of the Agency building (1960-1961) to protect against the placement of electronic taps therein.

d. During the period 1967-1971, agents were also developed to monitor dissident groups in the Washington area considered to be potential threats to Agency personnel and installations, and Agency security field officers in the US also collected information on similar dissident groups, to advise the Agency of potential threats to its personnel and installations.

e. A list of individuals suspected of particular offenses considered to pose a security vulnerability was collected over a number of years prior to 1973. This practice was terminated and the file destroyed in 1973.

f. From May-September 1971 a long-time CIA source was under surveillance in the US in connection with a reported plot to assassinate or kidnap Vice President Agnew and the DCI [Director of Central Intelligence]. The individual covered was a Latin American revolutionary, but the surveillance expanded to cover several American citizen contacts in New York and Detroit.

A final category of questionable activity identified during the 1973 survey was related to the Agency's mission to collect foreign intelligence. In some cases the Agency exceeded proper bounds or its activities were subject to misconstruction as being aimed at purposes outside its charter. The following examples, for instance, may be related to the charges made in *The New York Times* article, although they have no connection with the program first discussed above:

a. Records were made of the identities and addresses of individuals exchanging correspondence between the United States and certain communist countries, as an aid to determining possible leads to potential operations. This program included the surreptitious opening of certain first-class mail to extract positive intelligence or data valuable for the development of foreign intelligence operations against the communist country. This program was initiated in 1953, and from its inception was fully coordinated with the FBI, which received much of its product. The operation was approved by three Postmasters General and one Attorney General. The program was terminated in 1973.

b. We obtained names and addresses of persons telephoning a communist country so that we could follow up for possible operational leads.

c. Individuals were recruited or inserted into dissident groups in the US to establish their credentials to collect foreign intelligence overseas. By-product information reflecting planned violence or similar activity was passed to the FBI.

The items listed above are those questionable activities relating to matters covered in *The New York Times* article, Obviously, I am prepared to brief you fully on such matters, as I did the Chairmen of the Congressional Armed Services Committee.

Following our identification of all these matters in 1973, I issued detailed and specific instructions dealing with each activity. Some were terminated; others were continued but only as fully authorized by our statute and in accordance with law (Annex I).

The New York Times article also states that I am considering the possibility of asking the Attorney General to institute legal action against some of those who had been involved in these activities. I have conferred with the Acting Attorney General, Mr. Silberman, as to my responsibilities with respect to evidence relating to possible illegal activities by Agency personnel. On December 21st I agreed with him that I would review the questionable activities noted in this letter and others to determine whether these should be brought to his attention for legal review. I will certainly keep you advised of any such action.

As I stated to you on the telephone, Mr. President, you have my full assurance that the Agency is not conducting activities comparable to those alleged in *The New York Times* article. Even in the past, I believe the Agency essentially conformed to its mission of foreign intelligence. There were occasions over the years in which improper actions were taken as noted above, but I believe these were few, were quite exceptional to the thrust of the Agency's activities, and have been fully terminated. Agency personnel are instructed each year to advise me of any activity they consider questionable, and I am resolved to follow your directive that no improper activity be conducted by this Agency.

Respectfully,
W.E. Colby, Director

RAILROAD REORGANIZATION
July 28, 1975

In 1973 Congress authorized a sweeping reorganization of seven bankrupt freight and passenger railroads serving the Northeast and Midwest. The Final System Plan (FSP) for that reorganization was made public July 28, 1975, by the United States Railway Association (USRA), a quasi-governmental agency created to assist in and oversee the reorganization. According to the USRA, the final plan embodied the largest corporate restructuring in U.S. history. Basically, it provided for a federally financed Consolidated Rail Corporation (ConRail) and a government-created private competitor. ConRail and its competitor, between them, would take over operation of more than 15,000 miles of rail lines currently run by the Penn Central and six other bankrupt carriers in 17 states. An additional 5,700 miles of underused (light density) track would be abandoned.

The start-up costs of $2.5-billion would be financed by the federal government through loans and stock purchases, but the planners expected that ConRail would become independent and operate at a profit by 1979. To foster competition and allay investors' fears of railroad nationalization, the plan proposed that federal funds be used to induce solvent carriers, principally the Chessie System, to pick up sections of the bankrupt lines.

The federal plan had its origins in the 1970 collapse of the Penn Central Transportation Company, the largest freight and passenger carrier in the United States. When Penn Central filed bankruptcy proceedings in June of that year, the action signaled a new phase in the prolonged, industry-wide railroad crisis. Competition from airlines and trucks, inflexible government regulation, inefficient management and labor costs were all blamed for the chronic financial woes and deteriorating service of the nation's rail carriers.

*Within three years, six more eastern and midwestern railroads had gone in-
to bankruptcy. Together, the failed carriers transported almost half of the
freight in the eastern United States. After several unsuccessful attempts to
bail out the Penn Central, Congress in 1973 finally authorized the planning
of the new hybrid railroad corporation. Opinion was divided as to whether
the legislation represented a last attempt to save the railroads as private
carriers or a first step toward railroad nationalization.*

Criticism of FSP

*The 1973 act (PL 93-236) provided that the final plan devised by USRA
was to become effective Nov. 10, 1975, 60 days after its publication, unless
Congress rejected it. By November, the bankrupt railroads were losing more
than $1-million a day, according to USRA figures.*

*Although the 60-day period for congressional disapproval passed without
formal action, congressional opposition to key features of the plan raised the
possibility that it might be changed in several respects during the
appropriations process. The abandonment of light-density lines evoked the
most public concern. Many members of Congress, particularly in the
House, were angry over the exclusion of unprofitable lines in their districts
from the new system. Residents of the affected rural areas and small towns
feared severe economic and social dislocations.*

*Another major problem raised about the FSP was its treatment of the
claims of creditors holding securities of Penn Central and other insolvent
lines. Soon after the 1973 act became law, it was challenged by Penn
Central creditors who feared that stock they would receive in the new entity
might prove as worthless as their current holdings. In December 1974 the
Supreme Court upheld the constitutionality of the act, ruling that the
railroads involved would not be giving up their property in the reorganization without adequate compensation. The Supreme Court's decision was
satisfactory to most of the parties concerned, for while the reorganization
could continue, creditors could file suit against the federal government in
the U.S. Court of Claims to retrieve any losses—which could amount to
billions of dollars.*

*Another supposed flaw in the plan involved ConRail's financial struc-
ture, which provided, in effect, for temporary public ownership and a
gradual return to private control. The Interstate Commerce Commission
(ICC), which had been directed by the 1973 act to review for Congress the
final USRA plan, concluded that ConRail would probably never be
profitable enough to attract private investors. Though the ICC was "in substantial agreement" with FSP, it said that ConRail's capital structure was
"tantamount to nationalization," in an agency report issued Aug. 25, 1975.
"This is not because we believe [ConRail] cannot be profitable, but because
we doubt that it will be as profitable as the pro formas [financial forecasts]
indicate, and because we think the capital structure burdens it with too*

much debt...," the ICC said. The agency recommended that ConRail either forgo payment of dividends entirely or postpone such payments. It also disapproved of FSP provisions for restricting membership on ConRail's board of directors mostly to government officials during the initial reorganization period. Instead, the ICC urged that "holders of the securities awarded the debtor estates [should] be awarded a majority of seats on the Board...so they will have an opportunity to demonstrate whether private enterprise management...can or cannot succeed." Yet another potential obstacle to implementation of FSP was President Ford's insistence on substantial deregulation of railroads by the ICC.

The only recent precedent for the creation by Congress of a hybrid corporation to provide an essential public service appeared to be the 1970 Postal Reorganization Act (PL 91-375). That measure converted the inefficient, deficit-ridden federal service into a semi-private corporation with an annual federal subsidy. The expectation was that postal efficiency would rise and the service would become self-supporting when it was run in a "businesslike" manner. Similar claims were made for ConRail. In the case of the postal corporation, mail rates shot up but consumers complained that service had worsened. By 1975 solvency appeared a distant or impossible goal. A three-year loss totaling $2.9-billion prompted the House of Representatives in September 1975 to revoke the Postal Service's financial independence.

Excerpts from Introduction and Summary *of the* Final System Plan *of the United States Railway Association, published July 28, 1975:*

Causes of the Decline of Railroading

The financial problems of the railroad industry are due to a number of interrelated factors.

● Railroad facilities are old by the standards of other industries—often poorly located, physically run-down or simply obsolete. A large portion of railroad costs is related to fixed facilities, which makes adaptation to changing circumstances difficult and often contributes to inadequate allocation of fixed facilities costs to specific commodities or movements. Costing difficulties contribute to problems of managing and marketing rail services. Railroad cost structures differ sharply from those of competing modes, a circumstance which poses difficulties in achieving balanced public policy toward all transport modes.

● The rapid rate of technological development in rival forms of transportation since 1920 radically changed the competitive position of the rail industry. Large-scale public support has promoted development of the newer auto, truck, barge, pipeline and airline technologies. Innovations in trucking and the development of modern highway systems have enabled motor

531

carriers to capture 23 percent of total intercity freight ton-miles. The water carrier industry has matured with the development of extensive waterway improvements and modern efficient barge technology. Pipelines now move fluid petroleum and natural gas, and development of coal slurry (particles of coal suspended in water) pipelines may permit this mode to penetrate another key railroad market. The emergence of the automobile and bus and the development of the high-speed, pressurized airplane for medium and long distance travel effectively eliminated the train as a competitor for long distance passenger services.

• Basic changes have taken place in underlying market conditions, such as shifts in the location of industrial activity and changes in types of freight normally suited to rail transportation. Railroads in the older eastern production centers have heavy investments in fixed facilities oriented toward these centers. As manufacturers relocate plants to newer growth centers, rail traffic at the old locations declines and excess rail capacity results. Industries which consume bulk raw materials from the agriculture, mining and forestry sectors of the economy, historically the basic generators of railroad freight, have been declining as a share of GNP as service-oriented, high technology industries advance.

• Railroads were the first large business to be regulated by the federal government and few other industries are regulated so pervasively. Regulation of railroads is related to the industry's technology, industrial organization and financial structure. Railroads are big businesses, ordinarily, because railroad operations are most efficient when conducted on a large volume, mass production basis; the high fixed investment associated with rail technology likewise implies large enterprise. The railroads' large scale of operations and a cost structure that enabled them to price some services monopolistically while engaging in "predatory" competition for other business led to regulation of the industry. Regulation, in turn, has contributed to the inflexibility of rail operations and investment, principally with respect to setting rates, abandoning costly routes and services and changing the corporate structure of the industry. In addition, public policy has restricted the rail industry from taking advantage of different methods of moving goods, except in the case of "grandfather" trucking rights owned by certain railroads.

• For a variety of reasons, there have been insufficient internal funds to maintain and upgrade facilities which, coupled with the lack of private capital or public funds, has resulted in deferred maintenance, further weakening the competitive position of the lines involved, thus completing the vicious cycle.

All these problems must be attacked if satisfactory rail freight service is to exist in the future. Progress can come from within the industry through improvement of operations and general management. Burdens imposed by public policy can be lessened and intermodal transport policies made more fair. If these changes are accomplished, the railroad industry will be able to overcome its current infirmities and become a more dynamic part of the American industrial economy.

Goals and Issues Underlying the FSP

In enacting the Regional Rail Reorganization Act of 1973 (Act), Congress provided a means for revitalizing rail service in the Northeast and Midwest Region. The declared purposes of the Act are:

- Identification of an adequate rail service system for the Region,
- Reorganization of the Region's railroads into an economically viable system capable of providing adequate and efficient service,
- The establishment of the United States Railway Association and the Consolidated Rail Corporation.
- Assistance to the states and local and regional authorities for continuation of local rail services threatened with cessation and
- Necessary federal financial assistance at the lowest possible cost to the general taxpayer.

The statutory goals guiding preparation of the Final System Plan (FSP) are outlined in section 206 of the Act. These goals complement the purposes of the Act and offer further direction to the United States Railway Association (Association or USRA) and those who review the Association's work. The Act stipulates that the restructured regional rail system should:

- Be financially self-sustaining,
- Meet regional rail transportation needs adequately,
- Promote improved high-speed rail passenger service in the Northeast Corridor and reflect USRA's identification of other corridors in which major up-grading of track for high-speed passenger operation would yield substantial public benefits.
- Preserve, as much as possible, existing patterns of service,
- Preserve facilities and service for coal transport and conserve scarce energy resources,
- Retain and promote competition,
- Attain and maintain desirable environmental standards,
- Achieve efficiency in train operations and
- Minimize unemployment and adverse effects on communities....

The Regional Rail System (Chapter 1)

The Association recommends a rail structure for the Region made up of these key components:

- ConRail, which combines most of the services of the Penn Central Transportation Co. (PC), the Central Railroad of New Jersey (CNJ), the Lehigh Valley (LV), the Lehigh & Hudson River (LHR), the Pennsylvania-Reading Seashore Lines (PRSL) [Footnote: PRSL is not in bankruptcy but has been included in USRA's planning process.], a limited section of the Ann Arbor Railroad (AA) and small portions of the Erie Lackawanna (EL) and Reading (RDG);

• The Chessie System, which is offered most EL freight services east of Sterling (Akron), Ohio, most Reading services, access to some CNJ traffic in the Greater Newark, N.J. area and the PC markets in the Charleston, W.Va. area;

• The Norfolk & Western Railroad (N&W), which essentially will continue in its present configuration but which is offered a few route extensions to improve connections with its own or affiliated lines;

• The Delaware & Hudson (D&H), with route extensions necessary to provide it with direct connections to the South and West;

• The other smaller railroads in the Region essentially maintaining their existing route structures;

• Southern Railway (SOU), which is offered the PC main lines on the Delmarva Peninsula and the car float from Cape Charles to Norfolk; and

• Amtrak, which is designated to acquire the Northeast Corridor from Boston to Washington for the development of high-speed passenger service. Most through freight service is expected to be provided over a bypass route, as described in Chapter 2....

This basic structure will offer competition between at least two railroads in major markets of the Region, supplemented by the services of the smaller railroads. It will enable such major railroads as Chessie and N&W to continue as solvent carriers, without undermining the chances for ConRail to attain solvency in the private sector. It also should serve to stabilize and in several instances enhance performance of the smaller solvent railroads....

Structure in Detail

Under the FSP, ConRail will account for about 37 percent of the Region's total net ton-miles yearly, the expanded Chessie System 32 percent, N&W 21 percent and the smaller solvent lines 10 percent. Besides the major transfer of EL and RDG properties, USRA proposes a number of trackage-rights exchanges and projects aimed at coordinating facilities and services among railroads. The aim is to reduce needless duplication and improve traffic routing patterns without reducing competition in major markets.

USRA recommends that the Region's rail system consist of service by three major railroads and several smaller solvent carriers, as follows:

ConRail.—The Consolidated Rail Corp. will be a dominant east-west carrier between New England-New York/Newark-Philadelphia-Baltimore and Chicago-St. Louis. Its major north-south routes will connect Cincinnati to Detroit and Chicago and Washington, D.C. to Newark, upstate New York and New England.

Chessie.—Chessie's acquisition of most of the Reading and the Erie Lackawanna and access to some CNJ traffic would give Chessie a strong base in the Newark, Philadelphia and Allentown markets and would allow it to provide single-line service between Newark-Philadelphia-Baltimore and the Chicago-St. Louis markets. In conjunction with D&H and the

Boston & Maine, it would become a major carrier between New England and the West and South. It will remain a significant carrier of West Virginia coal to the Virginia Tidewater and the Great Lakes and a major merchandise carrier in the North Central states.

Norfolk & Western.—N&W will continue to be a main conveyor of Pocahontas coal from the West Virginia fields to Norfolk in the east and Lake Erie in the north. Its Lake and Western Regions (former Nickel Plate and Wabash railroads) provide it with a comprehensive merchandise route structure in the Midwest....

Conclusion

A task so complex as the restructuring of the rail system in the Region must be evolutionary. The American economy owes its essential dynamism to the ability of individual firms to shift, to adjust, to adapt, to give incentives and to test new ideas and new markets. Other parties and interests must take this view of the restructuring plan. What is important is that economic forces be allowed to work themselves out within an established framework of fairness and guaranteed continuation of essential services. The very nature of the competitive market place requires flexibility so that corporations may adapt to changing conditions.

The major solvent carriers in the nation earn rates of return on investment that are low compared to most other industries. ConRail will be neither better nor worse than the major solvents and like them obviously will be vulnerable to economic fluctuations; thus, a 5-year plan for rehabilitation during an economic downturn may become a 7 or 10 year plan.

The Association has made no attempt to define precisely how Chessie might integrate operations of the Erie Lackawanna and Reading, or how N&W might adjust to changes in traditional connecting patterns. USRA's outline of ConRail's operating plan, similarly, is just that—an outline. It represents a best estimate of how the Association believes the system initially should be set up, although 10 years from now it easily could look very different. Indeed, the Association *could not* make such final determinations, for shippers and other carriers in the Region, acting on their own business instincts and exercising their transportation options, continually will make decisions that will alter any "definitive" plans USRA might adopt at this time....

Passenger Services (Chapter 2)

....The Association supports the establishment of a discrete high-speed passenger route in the Northeast Corridor consonant with the recommendations of the Secretary of Transportation's report of September 1971. The Corridor improvements should be completed by the earliest practicable date. USRA recommends that ConRail shift its through freight operation to parallel Reading/Lehigh Valley routes north of Philadelphia and acquire and improve the Chessie property between Washington and Philadelphia if satisfactory terms for such a transfer can be negotiated. USRA has worked closely with Amtrak, the Federal Railroad Administration and Chessie System in developing detailed plans for this alternative route. ConRail should not bear any acquisition and upgrading costs of this line in excess of those which would be incurred by ConRail in acquiring and rehabilitating the PC route; costs above that level should be borne by an entity other than ConRail. USRA contemplates continued through freight operations on the Corridor passenger route until such services can be transferred to the parallel route. Local freight services will be maintained on the Corridor.

In the PSP, USRA identified a number of short to medium distance routes outside the Corridor where upgrading for passenger service might return substantial benefits. With only minor revisions, the FSP reaffirms those identifications.

Outside the Northeast Corridor, ConRail should own all lines over which Amtrak operates, except for those already owned or leased by state or local transportation authorities and three lines that USRA proposes Amtrak or state agencies purchase or lease because of dominant or exclusive passenger use: Philadelphia to Harrisburg, Pa., New Haven, Conn. to Springfield, Mass. and Porter, Ind. to Kalamazoo, Mich. Amtrak and the states also should have the option to purchase or lease passenger related facilities outside the Northeast Corridor. Transfers to Amtrak of properties outside the Northeast Corridor would require amendments to the Act and USRA recommends that such amendments be made.

Further discussions with Amtrak have been aimed at assuring un-interrupted intercity passenger service and to coordinate ConRail's activities with improved passenger service. USRA also has been in close contact with state and local transportation authorities to ensure orderly and continued operation of vital commuter services in the Region.

Financial Analysis (Chapter 3)

...Approach to the Financial Forecasts. The Association developed a financial plan for ConRail in the form of a complete 10-year financial forecast incorporating the operating, marketing and capital improvement plans made by the Association for ConRail. Revenue and tonnage forecasts were prepared by consultants under contract to USRA. These forecasts are based on 10-year projections for the American economy which show a minor recession in 1978 followed by steady growth through 1985. The Association adjusted the revenue and tonnage forecasts for the 10-year planning period to include traffic diversions and selective rate increases. Traffic flows were simulated to determine the best operating network for ConRail. Estimates of annual expenses were prepared to reflect new operating efficiencies and improvements of roadbed and other new facilities....

Although the total amount of expenditures on road property would be the same under any accounting method, USRA turned to depreciation accounting as the most satisfactory way to present ConRail's earnings. Of the two other alternatives examined, USRA concluded that betterment accounting masked financial reality and modified betterment accounting would be difficult for ConRail to implement and therefore might not receive unqualified acceptance from the accounting profession.

Since a realistic analysis requires consideration of anticipated increases in general price levels, the Association developed inflation indices for each major expense factor in the ICC accounting system. These inflated financial forecasts are the most relevant set of estimates for projecting ConRail's cash requirements.

A computerized financial model was designed to generate *pro forma* financial forecasts for the various industry structure options studied by the Association. The model uses forecasts of uninflated revenues, expenses, capital programs, inflation indices and interest rates to calculate financial forecasts in accord with conditions specified by USRA. These conditions include: specification of the debt and equity configuration, rate increases estimated to be permitted by the regulatory agency (ICC) in recognition of increased costs, the value of assets to be conveyed, payment of dividends and alternative accounting methods.

The model then forecasts results directly in *pro forma* statement format. The generated statements fall into four general categories:
- Statements of net income (loss),
- Statements of financial condition (balance sheets),
- Statements of sources and uses of funds and required financing,
- Supplemental financial and statistical information.

Summary of Results. Figures 1, 2, and 3 summarize the financial forecasts and portray the financial condition of ConRail for the years 1976 through 1985.

Figure 1 illustrates projections that:

- ConRail will realize positive income from operations beginning in 1979 and
- ConRail will generate positive cash flow from operations beginning in 1979 and each year thereafter.

Figure 2 illustrates projections that:

- Government funding will total $1.85 billion and no new cash funding will be required after 1980.

To achieve improvements in operating efficiency and in earnings, ConRail must make very large expenditures to rehabilitate the existing road facilities and to purchase additional freight equipment.

Figure 3 shows that:

- Road property expenditures capitalized will total $4.2 billion during the period 1976 through 1985,

FIGURE 1—*Annual Income and Fund Flow From Operations*

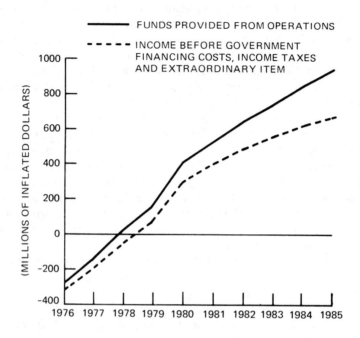

FIGURE 2—*Cumulative Funding Requirement—Government*[1]

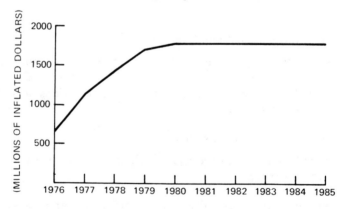

---

[1] Exclusive of Series A Preferred Stock issued in lieu of interest and dividends.

FIGURE 3—*Annual additions to operating assets and equipment financing*

NOTE: 1976 property and equipment additions shown...include the assets conveyed from the railroads in reorganization and are reflected in the initial balance sheet as follows: 1) Road properties of $334 million which includes $44 million for land and 2) Equipment of $340 million.

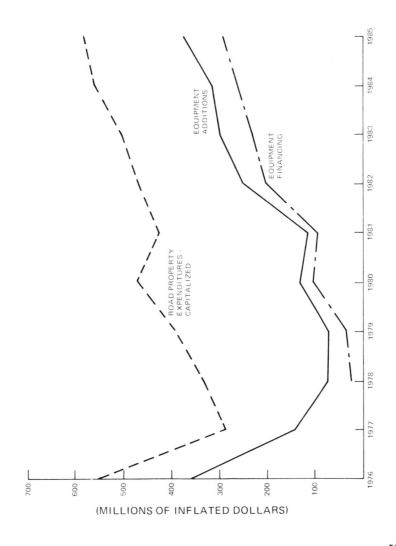

- Equipment additions will total $1.8 billion from 1976 through 1985 and
- New equipment financing will total $1.3 billion from 1976 through 1985.

Capital Structure and Financial Programs (Chapter 4)

....The capital structure is based on the projections of ConRail's operating performance. According to the *pro forma* financial statements, ConRail's needs for funds during the first 5 years of its operation will exceed its internally generated funds and funds from identifiable external sources, other than the government, including private sector equipment financing. The total needs are projected to be $1.85 billion. These funds will be required for rehabilitation and other capital improvements, equipment purchases, working capital needs and to make up operating losses.

Private sector financing is not available to provide these funds and therefore this funding requirement must be met by the federal government. It is proposed that the government finance ConRail through the purchase of the company's Debentures and Series A Preferred Stock. The $1.85 billion funding requirement will be met through the issuance of $1.0 billion of Debentures and $0.85 billion of Series A Preferred Stock to USRA.

The Debentures will pay interest at 7.5% and the Series A Preferred Stock will pay dividends at the same rate. ConRail will be authorized to pay interest on the Debentures and dividends on the Series A Preferred in the form of additional shares of Series A Preferred Stock during the years when cash is not available for these purposes.

USRA also proposes that an additional $250 million of budget authority be provided to USRA for possible purchase of additional ConRail securities. This amount will provide a reasonable margin of safety for ConRail to meet potential contingencies, possibly exceeding the projected requirement of $1.85 billion. The additional funding would be made available to ConRail at the discretion of the Government Investment Committee of the USRA Board, comprised of the Chairman of USRA and the Secretaries of Transportation and the Treasury. The Committee would operate in consultation with the USRA Board. The Association also supports the authorization of $400 million to be used in the discretion of the Secretary of Transportation for ConRail or otherwise to further the purposes of the Act, as amended.

USRA proposes that the estates of the railroads in reorganization receive Series B Preferred Stock, Common Stock and Certificates of Value. The Certificates of Value would be redeemable by the Association within 12 years under certain circumstances should the Series B Preferred and Common Stock fail to represent fair and equitable consideration for the rail properties acquired by ConRail....

Manpower (Chapter 6)

The economic impact of the FSP on individual employees is minimized by the employee protection provisions contained in Title V of the Act. The Act authorizes $250 million to fund the program....

Five factors were critical in determining ConRail's manpower requirements: industry structure, transactions with solvent carriers, volume projections, efficiency improvements and rehabilitation. ConRail's manpower requirements were determined by assessing the impact of these factors on several categories of employment: maintenance of way and structures, maintenance of equipment and stores, transportation and executive, professional and clerical staff.

Under the Act, ConRail will offer employment to approximately 90,000 employees of the railroads in reorganization at the time of conveyance. In addition, USRA estimates that approximately 8,100 employees will be offered jobs with solvent railroads acquiring properties from the railroads in reorganization, although this figure could vary.

USRA projects that during 1976 ConRail will require approximately 3,400 additional employees. The bulk of new manpower requirements is in maintenance of way and communications and signals due to the planned ConRail rehabilitation program. USRA projects a surplus of 3,300 employees in other crafts. These employees are protected by the displacement allowance, separation allowance, termination allowance and moving expense benefit provisions of the Act. Surplus employees will be offered an opportunity to fill the estimated 5,400 vacancies per year to be created by attrition. USRA expects, however, that many employees will choose not to accept a vacancy that requires a change in residence and instead will take the separation allowance.

It is not possible to determine precisely how many employees will be offered and accept jobs with the acquiring carriers and how many will elect to separate from ConRail rather than accept employment in a new location. There is uncertainty inherent in predicting job decisions to be made by individual employees and as a result USRA has come up with a wide range of estimated employee protection costs. Depending on initial assumptions, cumulative employee protection costs could range from $162 million to $200 million....

Light Density Lines and Community Impact (Part III/Chapter 9)

....Light density lines are an important part of the total economic problem of railroads in the Region. Overcapacity and overlapping service, poor physical condition of the lines, operating deficits and high upgrading costs make continuation of service on many light density lines a costly proposition.

USRA has reaffirmed its basic line analysis method and the policy that only financially self-sufficient lines should be included in the system. Such lines have at least one of the following characteristics:

● They have the capability of generating sufficient revenue to cover the cost incurred on the light density line and the cost of serving branch-line generated traffic beyond the branch itself.

- Although not currently self-sustaining, they can be made viable by reasonable rate adjustments.
- Although not currently self-sustaining, they can be made so because of identifiable traffic growth in the near future.

All other lines automatically become available for participation in the Act's subsidy program. If a line is not designated for inclusion in ConRail, and if the state and local interests fail to provide the subsidy, the Act permits the discontinuance of service and abandonment of the line.

USRA believes subsidies can ease many of the negative effects of the abandonment of light density lines. Rail service continuation subsidies can be used to cover the "cost of operating adequate and efficient rail service, including necessary improvement and maintenance of track and related facilities" (section 402(j)). The federal share of the subsidy for any light density line is 70 percent, with state and/or local government contributing the remaining 30 percent of the cost.

The restructured rail system for the Region will serve 97.8 percent of the freight currently carried by the railroads in reorganization. Excluded from the FSP are about 6,900 miles of roadway, of which about 5,750 miles are currently in service and 1,150 miles are out of service. In 1973 these lines carried only about 2.2 percent of all freight carried by the railroads in reorganization. Service on these lines may be maintained under the Act's service continuation subsidy program.

The total operating loss resulting from continuing service for the first year on all active light density lines not included in ConRail will be about $38 million. This means the federal share of the required subsidy would be about $27 million, with about $11 million being borne by state or local authorities. The cost of upgrading these lines to meet Class I safety standards (10 m.p.h.) is estimated to be at least $51 million....

Community Impact. Abandonment of rail service on individual light-density lines not included in ConRail will have isolated or relatively small impacts on communities, according to studies prepared under contract to USRA. Only seven counties of the total 279 having lines not recommended for inclusion in the PSP faced a change in employment exceeding 2 percent of total county employment. In 15 counties, the 1-percent level was exceeded. In only seven counties was the percentage change in income generated greater than 2 percent of total county personal income. The estimated change in income generated was greater than 1 percent in 22 counties. Only a single county was estimated to sustain a loss in real income close to 2 percent.

Net increases in employment and incomes from increased maintenance expenditures and rehabilitation should offset any negative impacts which might occur as a consequence of line abandonments.

USRA investigated the extent of increased employment and income that would result between 1976 and 1985 from the large new investment program envisioned in the FSP. A full report of these studies will be published subsequently.

▼▼▼

HEW REGULATIONS
ON FETAL RESEARCH
July 29, 1975

Caspar W. Weinberger, Secretary of Health, Education and Welfare (HEW), approved July 29 new regulations governing research on human fetuses. His action ended a lengthy federal moratorium which had denied public funding of the controversial research except in cases where an experimental procedure might directly save the life of the unborn infant (therapeutic research).

The new rules permitted research both on fetuses inside the mother's womb and, in certain cases, on aborted fetuses which might live briefly outside the womb but were insufficiently developed to survive. Procedures which would cause the death of an aborted fetus or which would artificially prolong its life for experimental purposes were prohibited. Proposals for nontherapeutic research—that which did not directly benefit a pregnant woman or a fetus scheduled for abortion—would be reviewed by a new national board if the research involved "more than a minimal risk or would not be acceptable" to an infant carried to term.

The regulations were developed after four months of public hearings and study by the newly established National Commission on the Protection of Human Subjects of Biomedical and Behavioral Research. Weinberger adopted the panel's findings with only minor modifications and the rules went into effect Aug. 8.

The commission, made up of prominent medical researchers, lawyers and ethicists, had been created by the National Research Act of 1974 (PL 93-348). It had been charged with identifying the basic ethical principles which should guide federal funding for research involving human subjects. Special

attention was to be directed toward research and therapeutic procedures in-
volving children, prisoners, and the institutionalized mentally infirm. The
panel's first priority, by congressional mandate, was to determine the "cir-
cumstances (if any) under which such research [involving the human fetus]
may be conducted or supported" by HEW. The act also barred federal sup-
port of fetal research until the commission could make its recommen-
dations, confirming federal policy already in effect for more than a year. In
April 1973 the National Institutes of Health (NIH) had announced it would
not fund fetal research.

Concern Over Human Experimentation

Congressional hearings in 1973 and the disclosure of abuses of human
subjects in federally funded research and medical care programs had
directed new attention that year to problems posed by experimentation on
human beings. One of the most widely criticized experiments was a 40-year-
old Public Health Service study of syphilis in which more than 400 black,
impoverished victims of the disease had gone untreated so that doctors
could study the long-term effects of the illness. The study, which took place
in Tuskegee, Ala., was first made public in August 1972.

Public concern about the ethics of fetal research in particular arose after
the Supreme Court ruled in 1973 on the legality of abortion (see Historic
Documents 1973, p. 101). *Many anti-abortionists feared a massive escala-*
tion of fetal research, which they considered morally repugnant. The
Court's decision cited the mother's right to privacy and passed over the con-
cept of fetal rights advanced by abortion opponents. While the decision
barred state intervention in abortion until the fetus became viable, it did
not precisely define viability.

In April 1974 Dr. Kenneth Edelin, chief obstetrics resident at a Boston
hospital, was indicted for manslaughter in connection with the death of a
fetus resulting from a late-term, legal abortion he had performed. The same
day, four other Boston doctors who had used tissues from legally aborted
dead fetuses for medical research were also indicted under a 19th-century
law against grave-robbing. The research in question, performed in 1971-72
with federal support, evaluated the effectiveness of two antibiotics against
certain fetal infections, such as congenital syphilis. Edelin was found guilty
Feb. 15, 1975. (The cases of the four other physicians had not yet been
tried.) One member of the Edelin jury acknowledged that his vote against
Edelin was based on his feeling that the "baby [fetus] should have had the
chance to prove his own viability."

The Case for Research

Medical researchers opposed to the HEW and congressional bans con-
tended that properly conducted research on nonviable fetuses did not

violate human rights. Moreover, major medical discoveries which could not have been achieved by any other means were said to have saved thousands of lives. Further advances were necessary to improve the survival rate and health of future unborn human beings, the scientists asserted.

Both points of view were represented in the membership of the new commission and in extensive studies contracted for by the panel. In one such study Battelle Columbus Laboratories, a private research institute in Ohio, identified four major medical developments which would have been foreclosed or substantially delayed by a total ban on fetal research. One of these, development of treatment for Rh Hemolytic disease, had prevented the stillbirth of approximately 450,000 fetuses between 1930 and 1975, the Battelle report estimated. Other papers reviewed by the panel dealt with ethical and legal aspects of the problem.

Without directly addressing "the issues of personhood and the civil status of the fetus," the commission nevertheless concluded that "moral concern should extend to all who share human genetic heritage, and that the fetus...should be treated respectfully." The commission said that its summary section covering "deliberations and conclusions" on ethical and medical issues was to be read as a part of the final regulations.

One panel member, Dr. David W. Louisell, filed a dissenting opinion with the commission's final report. Dr. Louisell, professor of law at the University of California at Berkeley, objected particularly to the regulations which allowed certain types of research on a fetus scheduled for abortion or during the abortion procedure. These threatened harm to an unborn individual who could not consent, Louisell held. "The good in much of the report cannot blind me to its departure from our society's most basic moral commitment: the essential equality of all human beings...," Louisell wrote.

Deliberations and Conclusions *and* Recommendations, *excerpted from Department of Health, Education and Welfare regulations,* Protection of Human Subjects, Fetuses, Pregnant Women, in Vitro Fertilization, *approved July 29, 1975, by HEW Secretary Caspar W. Weinberger and published Aug. 8, 1975, in the* Federal Register:

VIII. Deliberations and Conclusions

The charge to the Commission is to investigate and study research involving the living fetus and to make recommendations to the Secretary, DHEW [Department of Health, Education and Welfare], on "policies defining the circumstances (if any) under which such research may be conducted or supported."...

...This section of the Commission's report summarizes the reasoning and conclusions that emerged during the deliberations. Section IX of the report sets forth the Commission's Recommendations to the Secretary, DHEW.

These Recommendations arise from and are consistent with the Deliberations and Conclusions of the Commission. The Recommendations should be considered only within the context of the Deliberations that precede them.

A. Preface to Deliberations and Conclusions. Throughout the deliberations of the Commission, the belief has been affirmed that the fetus as a human subject is deserving of care and respect. Although the Commission has not addressed directly the issues of the personhood and the civil status of the fetus, the members of the Commission are convinced that moral concern should extend to all who share human genetic heritage, and that the fetus, regardless of life prospects, should be treated respectfully and with dignity.

The members of the Commission are also convinced that medical research has resulted in significant improvements in the care of the unborn threatened by death or disease, and they recognize that further progress is anticipated. Within the broad category of medical research, however, public concern has been expressed with regard to the nature and necessity of research on the human fetus. The evidence presented to the Commission was based upon a comprehensive search of the world's literature and a review of more than 3000 communications in scientific periodicals. The preponderance of all research involved experimental procedures designed to benefit directly a fetus threatened by premature delivery, disease or death, or to elucidate normal processes or development. Some research constituted an element in the health care of pregnant women. Other research involved only observation or the use of noninvasive procedures bearing little or no risk. A final class of investigation (falling outside the present mandate of the Commission) has made use of tissues of the dead fetus, in accordance with accepted standards for treatment of the human cadaver. The Commission finds that, to the best of its knowledge, these types of research have not contravened accepted ethical standards.

Nonetheless, the Commission notes that there have been instances of abuse in the area of fetal research. Moreover, differences of opinion exist as to whether desired results could have been attained without the use of the human fetus in nontherapeutic research.

Concern has also been expressed that the poor and minority groups may bear an inequitable burden as research subjects. The Commission believes that those groups which are most vulnerable to inequitable treatment should receive special protection.

The Commission concludes that some information which is in the public interest and which provides significant advances in health care can be attained only through the use of the human fetus as a research subject. The Recommendations which follow express the Commission's belief that, while the exigencies of research and the moral imperatives of fair and respectful treatment may appear to be mutually limiting, they are not incompatible.

B. Ethical Principles and Requirements Governing Research on Human Subjects with Special Reference to the Fetus and the Pregnant Woman.

The Commission has a mandate to develop the ethical principles underlying the conduct of all research involving human subjects. Until it can adequately fulfill this charge, its statement of principles is necessarily limited. In the interim, it proposes the following as basic ethical principles for use of human subjects in general, and research involving the fetus and the pregnant woman in particular.

Scientific inquiry is a distinctly human endeavor. So, too, is the protection of individual integrity. Freedom of inquiry and the social benefits derived therefrom, as well as protection of the individual are valued highly and are to be encouraged. For the most part, they are compatible pursuits. When occasionally they appear to be in conflict, efforts must be made through public deliberation to effect a resolution.

In effecting this resolution, the integrity of the individual is preeminent. It is therefore the duty of the Commission to specify the boundaries that respect for the fetus must impose upon freedom of scientific inquiry. The Commission has considered the principles proposed by ethicists in relation to the exigencies of scientific inquiry, the requirements and present limitations of medical practice, and legal commentary. Among the general principles for research on human subjects judged to be valid and binding are: (1) To avoid harm whenever possible, or at least to minimize harm; (2) to provide for fair treatment by avoiding discrimination between classes or among members of the same class; and (3) to respect the integrity of human subjects by requiring informed consent. An additional principle pertinent to the issue at hand is to respect the human character of the fetus.

To this end, the Commission concludes that in order to be considered ethically acceptable, research involving the fetus should be determined by adequate review to meet certain general requirements:

(1) Appropriate prior investigations using animal models and nonpregnant humans must have been completed.

(2) The knowledge to be gained must be important and obtainable by no reasonable alternative means.

(3) Risks and benefits to both the mother and the fetus must have been fully evaluated and described.

(4) Informed consent must be sought and granted under proper conditions.

(5) Subjects must be selected so that risks and benefits will not fall inequitably among economic, racial, ethnic and social classes.

These requirements apply to all research on the human fetus. In the application of these principles, however, the Commission found it helpful to consider the following distinctions: (1) therapeutic and nontherapeutic research; (2) research directed toward the pregnant woman and that directed toward the fetus; (3) research involving the fetus-going-to-term and the fetus-to-be-aborted; (4) research occurring before, during or after an abortion procedure; and (5) research which involves the nonviable fetus *ex utero* and that which involves the possibly viable infant. The first two distinctions encompass the entire period of the pregnancy through delivery; the latter three refer to different portions of the developmental continuum.

The Commission observes that the fetus is sometimes an unintended subject of research when a woman participating in an investigation is incorrectly presumed not to be pregnant. Care should be taken to minimize this possibility.

C. Application to Research Involving the Fetus. The application of the general principles enumerated above to the use of the human fetus as a research subject presents problems because the fetus cannot be a willing participant in experimentation. As with children, the comatose and other subjects unable to consent, difficult questions arise regarding the balance of risk and benefit and the validity of proxy consent.

In particular, some would question whether subjects unable to consent should ever be subjected to risk in scientific research. However, there is general agreement that where the benefits as well as the risks of research accrue to the subject, proxy consent may be presumed adequate to protect the subject's interests. The more difficult case is that where the subject must bear risks without direct benefit.

The Commission has not yet studied the issues surrounding informed consent and the validity of proxy consent for nontherapeutic research (including the difficult issue of consent by a pregnant minor). These problems will be explored under the broader mandate of the Commission. In the interim, the Commission has taken various perspectives into consideration in its deliberations about the use of the fetus as a subject in different research settings. The Deliberations and Conclusions of the Commission regarding the application of general principles to the use of the fetus as a human subject in scientific research are as follows:

1. In therapeutic research directed toward the fetus, the fetal subject is selected on the basis of its health condition, benefits and risks accrue to that fetus, and proxy consent is directed toward that subject's own welfare. Hence, with adequate review to assess scientific merit, prior research, the balance of risks and benefits, and the sufficiency of the consent process, such research conforms with all relevant principles and is both ethically acceptable and laudable. In view of the necessary involvement of the woman in such research, her consent is considered mandatory; in view of the father's possible ongoing responsibility, his objection is considered sufficient to veto.

2. Therapeutic research directed toward the pregnant woman may expose the fetus to risk for the benefit of another subject and thus is at first glance more problematic. Recognizing the woman's priority regarding her own health care, however, the Commission concludes that such research is ethically acceptable provided that the woman has been fully informed of the possible impact on the fetus and that other general requirements have been met. Protection for the fetus is further provided by requiring that research put the fetus at minimum risk consistent with the provision of health care for the woman. Moreover, therapeutic research directed toward the pregnant woman frequently benefits the fetus, though it need not necessarily do so. In view of the woman's right to privacy regarding her own health care, the Commission concludes that the informed consent of the woman is both necessary and sufficient.

In general, the Commission concludes that therapeutic research directed toward the health condition of either the fetus or the pregnant woman is, in principle, ethical. Such research benefits not only the individual woman or fetus but also women and fetuses as a class, and should therefore be encouraged actively.

The Commission, in making recommendations on therapeutic and non-therapeutic research directed toward the pregnant woman (Recommendations (2) and (3)), in no way intends to preclude research on improving abortion techniques otherwise permitted by law and government regulation.

3. Nontherapeutic research directed toward the fetus in utero or toward the pregnant woman poses difficult problems because the fetus may be exposed to risk for the benefit of others.

Here, the Commission concludes that where no additional risks are imposed on the fetus (e.g., where fluid withdrawn during the course of treatment is used additionally for nontherapeutic research), or where risks are so minimal as to be negligible, proxy consent by the parent(s) is sufficient to provide protection. (Hence, the consent of the woman is sufficient provided the father does not object.) The Commission recognizes that the term "minimal" involves a value judgment and acknowledges that medical opinion will differ regarding what constitutes "minimal risk." Determination of acceptable minimal risk is a function of the review process.

When the risks cannot be fully assessed, or are more than minimal, the situation is more problematic. The Commission affirms as a general principle that manifest risks imposed upon nonconsenting subjects cannot be tolerated. Therefore, the Commission concludes that only minimal risk can be accepted as permissible for nonconsenting subjects in nontherapeutic research.

The Commission affirms that the woman's decision for abortion does not, in itself, change the status of the fetus for purposes of protection. Thus, the same principles apply whether or not abortion is contemplated; in both cases, only minimal risk is acceptable.

Differences of opinion have arisen in the Commission, however, regarding the interpretation of risk to the fetus-to-be-aborted and thus whether some experiments that would not be permissible on a fetus-going-to-term might be permissible on a fetus-to-be-aborted. Some members hold that no procedures should be applied to a fetus-to-be-aborted that would not be applied to a fetus-going-to-term. Indeed, it was also suggested that any research involving fetuses-to-be-aborted must also involve fetuses-going-to-term. Others argue that, while a woman's decision for abortion does not change the status of the fetus *per se,* it does make a significant difference in one respect—namely, in the risk of harm to the fetus. For example, the injection of a drug which crosses the placenta may not injure the fetus which is aborted within two weeks of injection, where it might injure the fetus two months after injection. There is always, of course, the possibility that a woman might change her mind about the abortion. Even taking this into account, however, some members argue that risks to the fetus-to-be-aborted may be considered "minimal" in research which would entail more than minimal risk for a fetus-going-to-term.

There is basic agreement among Commission members as to the validity of the equality principle. There is disagreement as to its application to individual fetuses and classes of fetuses. Anticipating that differences of interpretation will arise over the application of the basic principles of equality and the determination of "minimal risk," the Commission recommends review at the national level. The Comission believes that such review would provide the appropriate forum for determination of the scientific and public merit of such research. In addition, such review would facilitate public discussion of the sensitive issues surrounding the use of vulnerable nonconsenting subjects in research.

The question of consent is a complicated one in this area of research. The Commission holds that procedures that are part of the research design should be fully disclosed and clearly distinguished from those which are dictated by the health care needs of the pregnant woman or her fetus. Questions have been raised regarding the validity of parental proxy consent where the parent(s) have made a decision for abortion. The Commission recognizes that unresolved problems both of law and of fact surround this question. It is the considered opinion, however, that women who have decided to abort should not be presumed to abandon thereby all interest in and concern for the fetus. In view of the close relationship between the woman and the fetus, therefore, and the necessary involvement of the woman in the research process, the woman's consent is considered necessary. The Commission is divided on the question of whether her consent alone is sufficient. Assignment of an advocate for the fetus was proposed as an additional safeguard; this issue will be thoroughly explored in connection with the Commission's review of the consent process. Most of the Commissioners agree that in view of the father's possible responsibility for the child, should it be brought to term, the objection of the father should be sufficient to veto. Several Commissioners, however, hold that for non-therapeutic research directed toward the pregnant woman, the woman's consent alone should be sufficient and the father should have no veto.

4. Research on the fetus during the abortion procedure or on the non-viable fetus ex utero raises sensitive problems because such a fetus must be considered a dying subject. By definition, therefore, the research is non-therapeutic in that the benefits will not accrue to the subject. Moreover, the question of consent is complicated because of the special vulnerability of the dying subject.

The Commission considers that the status of the fetus as dying alters the situation in two ways. First, the question of risk becomes less relevant, since the dying fetus cannot be "harmed" in the sense of "injured for life." Once the abortion procedure has begun, or after it is completed, there is no chance of a change of mind on the woman's part which will result in a living, injured subject. Second, however, while questions of risk become less relevant, considerations of respect for the dignity of the fetus continue to be of paramount importance, and require that the fetus be treated with the respect due to dying subjects. While dying subjects may not be "harmed" in the sense of "injured for life," issues of violation of integrity are nonetheless central. The Commission concludes, therefore, that out of respect for the dying subjects, no nontherapeutic interventions are permissible which would alter the duration of life of the nonviable fetus *ex utero*.

Additional protection is provided by requiring that no significant changes are made in the abortion procedure strictly for purposes of research. The Commission was divided on the question of whether a woman has a right to accept modifications in the timing or method of the abortion procedure in the interest of research, and whether the investigator could ethically request her to do so. Some Commission members desired that neither the research nor the investigator in any way influence the abortion procedure; others felt that modifications in timing or method of abortion were acceptable provided no new elements of risk were introduced. Still others held that even if modifications increased the risk, they would be acceptable provided the woman had been fully informed of all risks, and provided such modifications did not postpone the abortion beyond the 20th week of gestational age (5 lunar months; four and one-half calendar months). Despite this division of opinion, the Recommendation of the Commission on this matter is that the design and conduct of a nontherapeutic research protocol should not determine the recommendations by a physician regarding the advisability, timing or method of abortion. No members of the Commission desired less stringent measures.

Furthermore, it is possible that, due to mistaken estimation of gestational age, an abortion may issue in a possibly viable infant. If there is any danger that this might happen, research which would entail more than minimal risk could be absolutely prohibited. In order to avoid that possibility the Commission recommends that, should research during abortion be approved by national review, it be always on condition that estimated gestational age be below 20 weeks. There is, of course, a moral and legal obligation to attempt to save the life of a possibly viable infant.

Finally, the Commission has been made aware that certain research, particularly that involving the living nonviable fetus, has disturbed the moral sensitivity of many persons. While it believes that its Recommendations would preclude objectionable research by adherence to strict review processes, problems of interpretation or application of the Commission's Recommendations may still arise. In that event, the Commission proposes ethical review at a national level in which informed public disclosure and assessment of the problems, the type of proposed research and the scientific and public importance of the expected results can take place.

D. Review Procedures. The Commission will conduct comprehensive studies of existing review mechanisms in connection with its broad mandate to develop guidelines and make recommendations concerning ethical issues involved in research on human subjects. Until the Commission has completed these studies, it can offer only tentative conclusions and recommendations regarding review mechanisms.

In the interim, the Commission finds that existing review procedures required by statute (Pub. L. 93-348) and DHEW regulations (45 CFR 46) suffice for all therapeutic research involving the pregnant woman and the fetus, and for all nontherapeutic research which imposes minimal or no risk and which would be acceptable for conduct on a fetus *in utero* to be carried to term or on an infant. Guidelines to be employed under the existing review procedures include: (1) importance of the knowledge to be gained; (2) completion of appropriate studies on animal models and nonpregnant humans and existence of no reasonable alternative; (3) full evaluation and disclosure of the risks and benefits that are involved; and (4) supervision of the conditions under which consent is sought and granted, and of the information that is disclosed during that process.

The case is different, however, for nontherapeutic research directed toward a pregnant woman or a fetus if it involves more than minimal risk or would not be acceptable for application to an infant. Questions may arise concerning the definition of risk or the assessment of scientific and public importance of the research. In such cases, the Commission considers current review procedures insufficient. It recommends these categories be reviewed by a national review body to determine whether the proposed research could be conducted within the spirit of the Commission's recommendations. It would interpret these recommendations and apply them to the proposed research, and in addition, assess the scientific and public value of the anticipated results of the investigation.

The national review panel should be composed of individuals having diverse backgrounds, experience and interests, and be so constituted as to be able to deal with the legal, ethical, and medical issues involved in research on the human fetus. In addition to the professions of law, medicine, and the research sciences, there should be adequate representation of women, members of minority groups, and individuals conversant with the various ethical persuasions of the general community.

Inasmuch as even such a panel cannot always judge public attitudes, panel meetings should be open to the public, and, in addition, public participation through written and oral submissions should be sought.

E. Compensation. The Commission expressed a strong conviction that considerable attention be given to the issue of provision of compensation to those who may be injured as a consequence of their participation as research subjects.

Concerns regarding the use of inducements for participation in research are only partially met by the Commission's Recommendation (14) on the prohibition of the procurement of an abortion for research purposes. Compensation not only for injury from research but for participation in research as a normal volunteer or in a therapeutic situation will be part of later Commission deliberations.

F. Research Conducted Outside the United States. The Commission has considered the advisability of modifying its standards for research which is supported by the Secretary, DHEW, and is conducted outside the United States. It has concluded that its recommendations should apply as a single minimal standard, but that research should also comply with any more stringent limitations imposed by statutes or standards of the country in which the research will be conducted.

G. The Moratorium on Fetal Research. The Commission notes that the restrictions on fetal research (imposed by section 213 of Pub. L. 93-348) have been construed broadly throughout the research community, with the result that ethically acceptable research, which might yield important biomedical information, has been halted. For this reason, it is considered in the public interest that the moratorium be lifted immediately, that the Secretary take special care thereafter that the Commission's concerns for the protection of the fetus as a research subject are met, and appropriate regulations based upon the Commission's recommendations be implemented within a year from the date of submission of this report to the Secretary, DHEW. Until final regulations are published, the existing review panels at the agency and institutional levels should utilize the Deliberations and Recommendations of the Commission in evaluating the acceptability of all grant and contract proposals submitted for funding.

H. Synthesis. The Commission concludes that certain prior conditions apply broadly to all research involving the fetus, if ethical considerations are to be met. These requirements include evidence of pertinent investigations in animal models and nonpregnant humans, lack of alternative means to obtain the information, careful assessment of the risks and benefits of the research, and procedures to ensure that informed consent has been sought and granted under proper conditions. Determinations as to whether these essential requirements have been met may be made under existing review procedures, pending study by the Commission of the entire review process.

In the judgment of the Commission, therapeutic research directed toward the health care of the pregnant woman or the fetus raises little concern, provided it meets the essential requirements for research involving the fetus, and is conducted under appropriate medical and legal safeguards.

For the most part, nontherapeutic research involving the fetus to be carried to term or the fetus before, during or after abortion is acceptable so long as it imposes minimal or no risk to the fetus and, when abortion is involved, imposes no change in the timing or procedure for terminating pregnancy which would add any significant risk. When a research protocol or procedure presents special problems of interpretation or application of these guidelines, it should be subject to national ethical review; and it should be approved only if the knowledge to be gained is of medical importance, can be obtained in no other way, and the research proposal does not offend community sensibilities.

IX. Recommendations

1. Therapeutic research directed toward the fetus may be conducted or supported, and should be encouraged, by the Secretary, DHEW, provided such research (a) conforms to appropriate medical standards, (b) has received the informed consent of the mother, the father not dissenting, and (c) has been approved by existing review procedures with adequate provision for the monitoring of the consent process. (Adopted unanimously.)

2. Therapeutic research directed toward the pregnant woman may be conducted or supported, and should be encouraged, by the Secretary, DHEW, provided such research (a) has been evaluated for possible impact on the fetus, (b) will place the fetus at risk to the minimum extent consistent with meeting the health needs of the pregnant woman, (c) has been approved by existing review procedures with adequate provision for the monitoring of the consent process, and (d) the pregnant woman has given her informed consent. (Adopted unanimously.)

3. Nontherapeutic research directed toward the pregnant woman may be conducted or supported by the Secretary, DHEW, provided such research (a) has been evaluated for possible impact on the fetus, (b) will impose minimal or no risk to the well-being of the fetus, (c) has been approved by existing review procedures with adequate provision for the monitoring of the consent process, (d) special care has been taken to assure that the woman has been fully informed regarding possible impact on the fetus, and (e) the woman has given informed consent. (Adopted unanimously.)

It is further provided that nontherapeutic research directed at the pregnant woman may be conducted or supported (f) only if the father has not objected, both where abortion is not at issue (adopted by a vote of 8 to 1) and where an abortion is anticipated (adopted by a vote of 5 to 4).

4. Nontherapeutic research directed toward the fetus in utero (other than research in anticipation of, or during, abortion) may be conducted or supported by the Secretary, DHEW, provided (a) the purpose of such research is the development of important biomedical knowledge that cannot be obtained by alternative means, (b) investigation on pertinent animal models and nonpregnant humans has preceded such research, (c) minimal or no risk to the well-being of the fetus will be imposed by the research, (d) the research has been approved by existing review procedures with adequate provision for the monitoring of the consent process, (e) the informed consent of the mother has been obtained, and (f) the father has not objected to the research. (Adopted unanimously.)

5. Nontherapeutic research directed toward the fetus in anticipation of abortion may be conducted or supported by the Secretary, DHEW, provided such research is carried out within the guidelines for all other nontherapeutic research directed toward the fetus *in utero*. Such research presenting special problems related to the interpretation or application of these guidelines may be conducted or supported by the Secretary, DHEW, provided such research has been approved by a national ethical review body. (Adopted by a vote of 8 to 1.)

6. Nontherapeutic research directed toward the fetus during the abortion procedure and nontherapeutic research directed toward the nonviable fetus ex utero may be conducted or supported by the Secretary, DHEW, provided (a) the purpose of such research is the development of important biomedical knowledge that cannot be obtained by alternative means, (b) investigation on pertinent animal models and nonpregnant humans (when appropriate) has preceded such research, (c) the research has been approved by existing review procedures with adequate provision for the monitoring of the consent process, (d) the informed consent of the mother has been obtained, and (e) the father has not objected to the research; and provided further that (f) the fetus is less than 20 weeks gestational age, (g) no significant procedural changes are introduced into the abortion procedure in the interest of research alone, and (h) no intrusion into the fetus is made which alters the duration of life. Such research presenting special problems related to the interpretation or application of these guidelines may be conducted or supported by the Secretary, DHEW, provided such research has been approved by a national ethical review body. (Adopted by a vote of 8 to 1).

7. Nontherapeutic research directed toward the possibly viable infant may be conducted or supported by the Secretary, DHEW, provided (a) the purpose of such research is the development of important biomedical knowledge that cannot be obtained by alternative means, (b) investigation on pertinent animal models and nonpregnant humans (when appropriate) has preceded such research, (c) no additional risk to the well-being of the infant will be imposed by the research, (d) the research has been approved by existing review procedures with adequate provision for the monitoring of the consent process, and (e) informed consent of either parent has been given and neither parent has objected. (Adopted unanimously.)

8. Review Procedures. Until the Commission makes its recommendations regarding review and consent procedures, the review procedures mentioned above are to be those presently required by the Department of Health, Education, and Welfare. In addition, provision for monitoring the consent process shall be required in order to ensure adequacy of the consent process and to prevent unfair discrimination in the selection of research subjects, for all categories of research mentioned above. A national ethical review, as required in Recommendations (5) and (6), shall be carried out by an appropriate body designated by the Secretary, DHEW, until the establishment of the National Advisory Council for the Protection of Subjects of Biomedical and Behavioral Research. In order to facilitate public attitudes toward special problems reviewed by the national review body, appropriate provision should be made for public attendance and public participation in the national review process. (Adopted unanimously, one abstention.)

9. Research on the Dead Fetus and Fetal Tissue. The Commission recommends that use of the dead fetus, fetal tissue and fetal material for research purposes be permitted, consistent with local law, the Uniform Anatomical Gift Act and commonly held convictions about respect for the dead. (Adopted unanimously, one abstention.)

10. The design and conduct of a nontherapeutic research protocol should not determine recommendations by a physician regarding the advisability, timing or method of abortion. (Adopted by a vote of 6 to 2.)

11. Decisions made by a personal physician concerning the health care of a pregnant woman or fetus should not be compromised for research purposes, and when a physician of record is involved in a prospective research protocol, independent medical judgment on these issues is required. In such cases, review panels should assure that procedures for such independent medical judgment are adequate, and all conflict of interest or appearance thereof between appropriate health care and research objectives should be avoided. (Adopted unanimously.)

12. The Commission recommends that research on abortion techniques continue as permitted by law and government regulation. (Adopted by a vote of 6 to 2.)

13. The Commission recommends that attention be drawn to Section 214(d) of the National Research Act (Pub. L. 93-348) which provides that:

> "No individual shall be required to perform or assist in the performance of any part of a health service program or research activity funded in whole or in part by the Secretary of Health, Education, and Welfare, if his performance or assistance in the performance of such part of such program or activity would be contrary to his religious beliefs or moral convictions." (Adopted unanimously.)

14. No inducements, monetary or otherwise, should be offered to procure an abortion for research purposes. (Adopted unanimously.)

15. Research which is supported by the Secretary, DHEW, to be conducted outside the United States should at the minimum comply in full with the standards and procedures recommended herein. (Adopted unanimously.)

16. The moratorium which is currently in effect should be lifted immediately, allowing research to proceed under current regulations but with the application of the Commission's Recommendations to the review process. All the foregoing Recommendations of the Commission should be implemented as soon as the Secretary, DHEW, is able to promulgate regulations based upon these Recommendations and the public response to them. (Adopted by a vote of 9 to 1.)

August

FINAL ACT OF EUROPEAN SECURITY CONFERENCE

August 1, 1975

After 22 months of negotiations the 35-nation Conference on Security and Cooperation in Europe (CSCE) reached final agreement Aug. 1 on general principles "guiding their mutual relations." These principles were spelled out in a lengthy document, known as the conference's Final Act, which was adopted at the conclusion of a summit meeting in Helsinki, Finland.

In effect, the document legitimized all national boundaries established in the aftermath of World War II. The pact pledged signatories to endeavor to resolve future disputes "by peaceful means in such a manner as not to endanger international peace and security..." It was signed by heads of government of the United States, Canada, and every Eastern and Western European nation except Albania.

Major provisions confirmed the "inviolability" of national frontiers and prohibited intervention by one state in the affairs of any other. The inclusion of both these provisions had been a longstanding goal of the Soviet Union. A third feature of the act which had been sought by the Western nations was a set of broadly worded measures committing participating states to "take positive action" in the sphere of personal liberties. These were aimed at relaxing restrictions on travel and communications for journalists and other individuals, at facilitating the reunion of families and the issuance of entry or exit permits to persons wishing to marry a citizen of another nation. Soviet-bloc governments had enforced stringent limitations in such areas, as indicated by protests of prominent Eastern European and Soviet dissidents published in the West (see p. 915).

American Reaction

How effective the CSCE Act would be was open to question. It was non-binding and had no legal status. United States participation in the conference had stirred considerable criticism among conservatives and opponents of détente, who feared that American prestige had been traded for what they viewed as empty Soviet pledges. Emigrants from Soviet-bloc nations deplored the treaty's apparent confirmation of the current status of the Baltic states, East Germany and other areas that had come under Moscow's domination during or after World War II. Sen. Henry M. Jackson (D Wash.) called American acceptance of the agreement a retreat from "a crucial point of principle"—the right of self-determination for states currently under Soviet hegemony. Exiled novelist Alexander Solzhenitsyn warned that the good intentions expressed in the act were unlikely to ease Soviet policies on human rights (see p. 481). Many critics questioned whether the Soviet Union, which had invaded Hungary in 1956 and Czechoslovakia in 1968, would respect the non-intervention clauses.

Supporters of the treaty said that it was an important first step toward easing international tensions. The "ratification" of postwar national boundaries was defended as a practical recognition of longstanding realities.

The night before he left for Helsinki to sign the agreement, President Ford cited the non-binding nature of the act as proof that the United States had not abandoned its position on Latvia, Lithuania and Estonia, the three Baltic states whose absorption by the Soviet Union had never been formally recognized by the United States. The strength of CSCE lay in its "political and moral commitments aimed at lessening tensions and opening further the lines of communication between the peoples of East and West," Ford said. The President reiterated a widely publicized opinion that merely to obtain a "public commitment by the leaders of the more closed and controlled countries to a greater measure of freedom...for individuals..." would be beneficial.

Origins of CSCE

Efforts to bring about such a pact date from 1954 when the Soviet Union called, at a conference of foreign ministers in Berlin, for liquidation of the North Atlantic Treaty Organization and its replacement by a security pact open to all European nations "irrespective of their social systems." Exclusion of the United States blocked this scheme, but East European governments continued to advance various European security plans. All such efforts foundered on the issue of German reunification. Not until 1969, when Willy Brandt became chancellor, did West Germany begin to move toward acceptance of the status quo. By 1972 East-West agreements ratifying existing boundaries between the two Germany's and Poland were in place. The Nixon administration, pushing for overall East-West détente, then indicated interest in European security talks. Preliminary talks began that year and negotiations started in 1973.

Incidents occurring after the Helsinki conference seemed to support skeptical views of the effectiveness of the CSCE humanitarian clauses. By mid-August, two Soviet citizens had been permitted to join relatives in the United States, according to State Department records, but the records also indicated that as many as 641 individuals known to the American Embassy in Moscow wished to emigrate. Prospects for freer circulation of Western publications behind the Iron Curtain were dimmed by a vigorous Soviet press campaign against their alleged "decadence" and their inflammatory character. And Soviet authorities in November turned down a visa application of Physicist Andrei Sakharov to visit Norway to receive the Nobel Peace Prize that had been awarded him. Sakharov was a prominent critic of what he considered to be repressive policies of the Soviet government. (See p. 915.)

The CSCE agreement called for a final session in 1976 to review the measure's effectiveness.

> *Excerpts from* Final Act of the Conference on Security and Cooperation in Europe (CSCE), *adopted in Helsinki, Finland, Aug. 1, 1975:*

1.

Declaration on Principles Guiding Relations Between Participating States

The participating States,

Reaffirming their commitment to peace, security and justice and the continuing development of friendly relations and co-operation;

Recognizing that this commitment, which reflects the interest and aspirations of peoples, constitutes for each participating State a present and future responsibility, heightened by experience of the past;

Reaffirming, in conformity with their membership in the United Nations and in accordance with the purposes and principles of the United Nations, their full and active support for the United Nations and for the enhancement of its role and effectiveness in strengthening international peace, security and justice, and in promoting the solution of international problems, as well as the development of friendly relations and co-operation among States;

Expressing their common adherence to the principles which are set forth below and are in conformity with the Charter of the United Nations, as well as their common will to act, in the application of these principles, in conformity with the purposes and principles of the Charter of the United Nations;

Declare their determination to respect and put into practice, each of them in its relations with all other participating States, irrespective of their political, economic or social systems as well as of their size, geographical location or level of economic development, the following principles, which all are of primary significance, guiding their mutual relations:

I. Sovereign Equality, Respect for the Rights Inherent in Sovereignty

The participating States will respect each other's sovereign equality and individuality as well as all the rights inherent in and encompassed by its sovereignty, including in particular the right of every State to juridical equality, to territorial integrity and to freedom and political independence. They will also respect each other's right freely to choose and develop its political, social, economic and cultural systems as well as its right to determine its laws and regulations.

Within the framework of international law, all the participating States have equal rights and duties. They will respect each other's right to define and conduct as it wishes its relations with other States in accordance with international law and in the spirit of the present Declaration. They consider that their frontiers can be changed, in accordance with international law, by peaceful means and by agreement. They also have the right to belong or not to belong to international organizations, to be or not to be a party to bilateral or multilateral treaties including the right to be or not to be a party to treaties of alliance; they also have the right to neutrality.

II. Refraining From the Threat or Use of Force

The participating States will refrain in their mutual relations, as well as in their international relations in general, from the threat or use of force against the territorial integrity or political independence of any State, or in any other manner inconsistent with the purposes of the United Nations and with the present Declaration. No consideration may be invoked to serve to warrant resort to the threat or use of force in contravention of this principle.

Accordingly, the participating States will refrain from any acts constituting a threat of force or direct or indirect use of force against another participating State. Likewise they will refrain from any manifestation of force for the purpose of inducing another participating State to renounce the full exercise of its sovereign rights. Likewise they will also refrain in their mutual relations from any act of reprisal by force.

No such threat or use of force will be employed as a means of settling disputes, or questions likely to give rise to disputes, between them.

III. Inviolability of Frontiers

The participating States regard as inviolable all one another's frontiers as well as the frontiers of all States in Europe and therefore they will refrain now and in the future from assaulting these frontiers.

Accordingly, they will also refrain from any demand for, or act of, seizure and usurpation of part or all of the territory of any participating State.

IV. Territorial Integrity of States

The participating States will respect the territorial integrity of each of the participating States.

Accordingly, they will refrain from any action inconsistent with the purposes and principles of the Charter of the United Nations against the territorial integrity, political independence or the unity of any participating State, and in particular from any such action constituting a threat or use of force.

The participating States will likewise refrain from making each other's territory the object of military occupation or other direct or indirect measures of force in contravention of international law, or the object of acquisition by means of such measures or the threat of them. No such occupation or acquisition will be recognized as legal.

V. Peaceful Settlement of Disputes

The participating States will settle disputes among them by peaceful means in such a manner as not to endanger international peace and security, and justice.

They will endeavour in good faith and a spirit of co-operation to reach a rapid and equitable solution on the basis of international law.

For this purpose they will use such means as negotiation, enquiry, mediation, conciliation, arbitration, judicial settlement or other peaceful means of their own choice including any settlement procedure agreed to in advance of disputes to which they are parties.

In the event of failure to reach a solution by any of the above peaceful means, the parties to a dispute will continue to seek a mutually agreed way to settle the dispute peacefully.

Participating States, parties to a dispute among them, as well as other participating States, will refrain from any action which might aggravate the situation to such a degree as to endanger the maintenance of international peace and security and thereby make a peaceful settlement of the dispute more difficult.

VI. Non-intervention in Internal Affairs

The participating States will refrain from any intervention, direct or indirect, individual or collective, in the internal or external affairs falling within the domestic jurisdiction of another participating State, regardless of their mutual relations.

They will accordingly refrain from any form of armed intervention or threat of such intervention against another participating State.

They will likewise in all circumstances refrain from any other act of military, or of political, economic or other coercion designed to subordinate to their own interest the exercise by another participating State of the rights inherent in its sovereignty and thus to secure advantages of any kind.

Accordingly, they will, inter alia, refrain from direct or indirect assistance to terrorist activities, or to subversive or other activities directed towards the violent overthrow of the regime of another participating State.

VII. Respect for Human Rights and Fundamental Freedoms, Including the Freedom of Thought, Conscience, Religion or Belief

The participating States will respect human rights and fundamental freedoms, including the freedom of thought, conscience, religion or belief, for all without distinction as to race, sex, language or religion.

They will promote and encourage the effective exercise of civil, political, economic, social, cultural and other rights and freedoms all of which derive from the inherent dignity of the human person and are essential for his free and full development.

Within this framework the participating States will recognize and respect the freedom of the individual to profess and practise, alone or in community with others, religion or belief acting in accordance with the dictates of his own conscience.

The participating States on whose territory national minorities exist will respect the right of persons belonging to such minorities to equality before the law, will afford them the full opportunity for the actual enjoyment of human rights and fundamental freedoms and will, in this manner, protect their legitimate interests in this sphere.

The participating States recognize the universal significance of human rights and fundamental freedoms, respect for which is an essential factor for the peace, justice and well-being necessary to ensure the development of friendly relations and co-operation among themselves as among all States.

They will constantly respect their rights and freedoms in their mutual relations and will endeavour jointly and separately, including in co-operation with the United Nations, to promote universal and effective respect for them.

They confirm the right of the individual to know and act upon his rights and duties in this field.

In the field of human rights and fundamental freedoms, the participating States will act in conformity with the purposes and principles of the Charter of the United Nations and with the Universal Declaration of Human Rights. They will also fulfil their obligations as set forth in the international declarations and agreements in this field, including inter alia the International Covenants on Human Rights, by which they may be bound.

VIII. Equal Rights and Self-determination of Peoples

The participating States will respect the equal rights of peoples and their right to self-determination, acting at all times in conformity with the purposes and principles of the Charter of the United Nations and with the relevant norms of international law, including those relating to territorial integrity of States.

By virtue of the principle of equal rights and self-determination of peoples, all peoples always have the right, in full freedom, to determine, when and as they wish, their internal and external political status, without external interference, and to pursue as they wish their political, economic, social and cultural development.

The participating States reaffirm the universal significance of respect for and effective exercise of equal rights and self-determination of peoples for the development of friendly relations among themselves as among all States; they also recall the importance of the elimination of any form of violation of this principle.

IX. Co-operation Among States

The participating States will develop their co-operation with one another and with all States in all fields in accordance with the purposes and principles of the Charter of the United Nations.

In developing their cooperation the participating states will place special emphasis on the fields as set forth within the framework of the Conference on Security and Co-operation in Europe, with each of them making its contribution in conditions of full equality.

They will endeavour, in developing their co-operation as equals, to promote mutual understanding and confidence, friendly and good-neighbourly relations among themselves, international peace, security and justice. They will equally endeavour, in developing their co-operation, to improve the well-being of peoples and contribute to the fulfilment of their aspirations through, inter alia, the benefits resulting from increased mutual knowledge and from progress and achievement in the economic, scientific, technological, social, cultural and humanitarian fields. They will take steps to promote conditions favourable to making these benefits available to all; they will take into account the interest of all in the narrowing of differences in the levels of economic development, and in particular the interest of developing countries throughout the world.

They confirm that governments, institutions, organizations and persons have a relevant and positive role to play in contributing toward the achievement of these aims of their co-operation.

They will strive, in increasing their co-operation as set forth above, to develop closer relations among themselves on an improved and more enduring basis for the benefit of peoples.

X. Fulfilment in Good Faith of Obligations Under International Law

The participating States will fulfil in good faith their obligations under international law, both those obligations arising from the generally recognized principles and rules of international law and those obligations arising from treaties or other agreements, in conformity with international law, to which they are parties.

In exercising their sovereign rights, including the right to determine their laws and regulations, they will conform with their legal obligations under international law; they will furthermore pay due regard to and implement the provisions in the Final Act of the Conference on Security and Co-operation in Europe.

The participating States confirm that in the event of a conflict between the obligations of the members of the United Nations under the Charter of the United Nations and their obligations under any treaty or other international agreement, their obligations under the Charter will prevail, in accordance with Article 103 of the Charter of the United Nations.

All the principles set forth above are of primary significance and, accordingly, they will be equally and unreservedly applied, each of them being interpreted taking into account the others.

The participating States express their determination fully to respect and apply these principles, as set forth in the present Declaration, in all aspects, to their mutual relations and co-operation in order to ensure to each participating State the benefits resulting from the respect and application of these principles by all.

The participating States, paying due regard to the principles above and, in particular, to the first sentence of the tenth principle, "Fulfilment in good faith of obligations under international law", note that the present Declaration does not affect their rights and obligations, nor the corresponding treaties and other agreements and arrangements.

The participating States express the conviction that respect for these principles will encourage the development of normal and friendly relations and the progress of co-operation among them in all fields. They also express the conviction that respect for these principles will encourage the development of political contacts among them which in turn would contribute to better mutual understanding of their positions and views.

The participating States declare their intention to conduct their relations with all other States in the Spirit of the principles contained in the present Declaration.

2.

Document on Confidence-building Measures and Certain Aspects of Security and Disarmament

The participating States,....

Have adopted the following:

Prior notification of major military manoeuvres

They will notify their major military manoeuvres to all other participating States through usual diplomatic channels in accordance with the following provisions:

Notification will be given of major military manoeuvres exceeding a total of 25,000 troops, independently or combined with any possible air or naval components (in this context the word "troops" includes amphibious and airborne troops). In the case of independent manoeuvres of amphibious or airborne troops, or of combined manoeuvres involving them, these troops will be included in this total. Furthermore, in the case of combined manoeuvres which do not reach the above total but which involve land forces together with significant numbers of either amphibious or airborne troops, or both, notification can also be given.

Notification will be given of major military manoeuvres which take place on the territory, in Europe, of any participating State as well as, if applicable, in the adjoining sea area and air space....

Notification will be given 21 days or more in advance of the start of the manoeuvre or in the case of a manoeuvre arranged at shorter notice at the earliest possible opportunity prior to its starting date.

Notification will contain information of the designation, if any, the general purpose of and the States involved in the manoeuvre, the type or types and numerical strength of the forces engaged, the area and estimated time-frame of its conduct. The participating States will also, if possible, provide additional relevant information, particularly that related to the components of the forces engaged and the period of involvement of these forces....

Exchange of observers

The participating States will invite other participating States, voluntarily and on a bilateral basis, in a spirit of reciprocity and goodwill towards all participating States, to send observers to attend military manoeuvres....

Questions relating to disarmament

The participating States recognize the interest of all of them in efforts aimed at lessening military confrontation and promoting disarmament which are designed to complement political détente in Europe and to strengthen their security. They are convinced of the necessity to take effective measures in these fields which by their scope and by their nature constitute steps towards the ultimate achievement of general and complete disarmament under strict and effective international control, and which should result in strengthening peace and security throughout the world....

Co-operation in the Field of Economics, of Science and Technology and of the Environment

The participating States,

Will encourage the expansion of trade on as broad a multilateral basis as possible, thereby endeavouring to utilize the various economic and commercial possibilities;....

Will endeavour to reduce or progressively eliminate all kinds of obstacles to the development of trade;....

Recognize that possibilities exist for further improving scientific and technological co-operation, and to this end, express their intention to remove obstacles to such co-operation, in particular through:

—the improvement of opportunities for the exchange and dissemination of scientific and technological information among the parties interested in scientific and technological research and co-operation including information related to the organization and implementation of such co-operation;

—the expeditious implementation and improvement in organization, including programmes, of international visits of scientists and specialists in connexion with exchanges, conferences and co-operation;

—the wider use of commercial channels and activities for applied scientific and technological research and for the transfer of achievements obtained in this field while providing information on and protection of intellectual and industrial property rights;

Cooperation in Humanitarian and Other Fields

1. Human Contacts

The participating States,...

Make it their aim to facilitate freer movement and contacts, individually and collectively, whether privately or officially, among persons, institutions and organizations of the participating States, and to contribute to the solution of the humanitarian problems that arise in that connexion,

Declare their readiness to these ends to take measures which they consider appropriate and to conclude agreements or arrangements among themselves, as may be needed, and

Express their intention now to proceed to the implementation of the following:

(a) Contacts and Regular Meetings on the Basis of Family Ties

In order to promote further development of contacts on the basis of family ties the participating States will favourably consider applications for travel with the purpose of allowing persons to enter or leave their territory temporarily, and on a regular basis if desired, in order to visit members of their families.

Applications for temporary visits to meet members of their families will be dealt with without distinction as to the country of origin or destination: existing requirements for travel documents and visas will be applied in this spirit. The preparation and issue of such documents and visas will be effected within reasonable time limits....

(b) Reunification of Families

The participating States will deal in a positive and humanitarian spirit with the applications of persons who wish to be reunited with members of their family, with special attention being given to requests of an urgent character—such as requests submitted by persons who are ill or old.

They will deal with applications in this field as expeditiously as possible.

They will lower where necessary the fees charged in connexion with these applications to ensure that they are at a moderate level.

Applications for the purpose of family reunification which are not granted may be renewed at the appropriate level and will be reconsidered at reasonably short intervals by the authorities of the country of residence or destination, whichever is concerned; under such circumstances fees will be charged only when applications are granted.

Persons whose applications for family reunification are granted may bring with them or ship their household and personal effects; to this end the participating States will use all possibilities provided by existing regulations....

(c) Marriage Between Citizens of Different States

The participating States will examine favourably and on the basis of humanitarian considerations requests for exit or entry permits from persons who have decided to marry a citizen from another participating State.

The processing and issuing of the documents required for the above purposes and for the marriage will be in accordance with the provisions accepted for family reunification.

In dealing with requests from couples from different participating States, once married, to enable them and the minor children of their marriage to transfer their permanent residence to a State in which either one is normally a resident, the participating States will also apply the provisions accepted for family reunification.

(d) Travel for Personal or Professional Reasons

The participating States intend to facilitate wider travel by their citizens for personal or professional reasons and to this end they intend in particular:

—gradually to simplify and to administer flexibly the procedures for exit and entry;

—to ease regulations concerning movement of citizens from the other participating States in their territory, with due regard to security requirements....

They confirm that religious faiths, institutions and organizations, practising within the constitutional framework of the participating States, and their representatives can, in the field of their activities, have contacts and meetings among themselves and exchange information....

—grant to permanently accredited journalists of the participating States, on the basis of arrangements, multiple entry and exit visas for specified periods;

—facilitate the issue to accredited journalists of the participating States of permits for stay in their country of temporary residence and, if and when these are necessary, of other official papers which it is appropriate for them to have;

—ease, on a basis of reciprocity, procedures for arranging travel by journalists of the participating States in the country where they are exercising their profession, and to provide progressively greater opportunities for such travel, subject to the observance of regulations relating to the existence of areas closed for security reasons;

—ensure that requests by such journalists for such travel receive, in so far as possible, an expeditious response, taking into account the time scale of the request;

—increase the opportunities for journalists of the participating States to communicate personally with their sources, including organizations and official institutions;

—grant to journalists of the participating States the right to import, subject only to its being taken out again, the technical equipment (photographic, cinematographic, tape recorder, radio and television) necessary for the exercise of their profession;....

September

EGYPTIAN-ISRAELI SINAI ACCORD
September 1, 16 and 17, 1975

At separate ceremonies in Alexandria and Jerusalem Sept. 1, representatives of Egypt and Israel initialed an interim agreement declaring that the Middle East conflict should not be "resolved by military force." The agreement provided for further Israeli troop withdrawals in the Sinai Peninsula and the placement of up to 200 American civilians to monitor the truce at key Sinai passes. The U.S.-mediated accord, which was formally adopted in Geneva Sept. 4, was intended to provide another stepping stone toward a final peace agreement among the Arab nations and Israel. Under the terms of the accord the United States for the first time would be directly involved in Middle East peacekeeping.

The agreement reached in Alexandria and Jerusalem contained four documents: 1) an Agreement Between Egypt and Israel *outlining the basic provisions of the accord; 2) an* Annex *providing details for negotiators in Geneva to follow in working out the particulars of a final pact; 3) a* Proposal *relating to the role of the American technicians in the Sinai buffer zone and 4) a* Memorandum of Agreement *between Israel and the United States.*

Under the terms of the Agreement, *Egyptian forces would be allowed to advance to the eastern edge of the U.N. zone established by an accord between the two nations reached in January 1974. In addition, the Israeli-controlled Abu Rudeis oil fields along the Gulf of Suez were to be returned to Egypt.*

In return for the Israeli concessions, Egypt pledged that it would not resort to the threat or use of force or continue a military blockade against Israel in the Strait of Bab el Mandeb linking the Red Sea with the Indian Ocean.

The Egyptians also agreed to a provision stating that "nonmilitary cargoes destined to or coming from Israel shall be permitted through the Suez Canal." Although agreed to privately in 1974, this concession had never been carried out. The new agreement would open the waterway to Israel for the first time since 1956.

Foreign Aid Pledges

The text of the private Memorandum *detailing U.S. pledges of military and economic assistance to Israel was obtained by the* Washington Post *and published Sept. 16. Two additional "secret" documents were published unofficially Sept. 17. One dealt with United States "assurances" to Egypt relating to future Middle East negotiations and American technical aid. In the second, the United States promised Israel it would continue to refuse to recognize or negotiate with the Palestine Liberation Organization unless the PLO changed its stance toward Israel. All the documents were considered to be part of the truce agreement. The White House and the State Department resisted pressures from Congress to release these "understandings," contending that to do so would breach diplomatic confidentiality. Texts of the three agreements were nevertheless made available Oct. 6 at a hearing conducted by the Senate Foreign Relations Committee.*

Congressional Action on Pact

The plan to use American cease-fire monitors instead of an international team and the promises of foreign aid (estimated at $2.3-billion for Israel and $800-million for Egypt) raised fears in Congress that the accord might be a first step toward committing the United States to a major role as a peace guarantor in the Middle East. Senate Majority Leader Mike Mansfield (D Mont.), who flatly opposed the involvement of Americans in the early-warning system in the Sinai, said "one Vietnam is enough." Congressional approval of the monitoring and foreign-aid provisions of the accord was required. Israel indicated Sept. 4, when the agreements were signed, that it would not consider the pact to be in effect until Congress had endorsed the establishment of an American presence in the Sinai. Both Middle East countries had insisted on the use of American monitors as a condition for agreeing to the accord. After considering the proposal for more than a month, Congress finally gave its final approval on Oct. 9. Supporters of the resolution said it was absolutely essential to the implementation of the Mideast accord and thus to the hopes for lasting peace in the troubled area.

Soviet and Arab Displeasure

The Sinai accord was the first Middle East pact since the preliminary truces that marked the end of hostilities in the 1973 war (see Historic

Documents 1973, p. 931 and Historic Documents of 1974, p. 29 and 435). *Like the earlier agreements, it was negotiated by Secretary of State Henry A. Kissinger in a round of "shuttle diplomacy." The Soviet Union, apparently annoyed at being excluded from the negotiations, did not send a representative to the formal signing at Geneva. The United States also stayed away from the signing ceremony, presumably in deference to the Russians. (The United States and the U.S.S.R. were co-chairmen of the Middle East peace conference which met, for two days, in Geneva in December 1973.)*

As soon as terms of the accord became known, Egypt's President Anwar Sadat faced accusations by other Arab leaders that he was seeking a separate peace with Israel. Syria's ruling Baath Party denounced the Sinai accord Sept. 4 and Syrian President Hafez Assad refused to receive the Egyptian vice president who had been sent to Damascus to discuss the agreement with him. In an hour-long speech on Egyptian television Sept. 4, Sadat sought to dismiss Arab charges of disloyalty by revealing that Egypt had turned down an Israeli offer to return the entire Sinai Peninsula if Egypt would agree to end the state of war between the two nations. "Egypt refused these offers...because it is faithful to its Arab vocation and respects its commitment towards its allies," Sadat said. "If our aim was solely the recovery of Sinai, we would have achieved far more than we did," he added. (The Sinai accord left in Israeli hands about 87 per cent of the peninsula occupied by Israel since the 1967 war.)

In Israel, the Tel Aviv newspaper Davar, *a semi-official government organ, stated that "to a considerable degree the agreement was the result of pressure from Washington, which seeks to strengthen its position with Egypt and the other Arab countries."*

> *Texts of the Sinai accords initialed in Alexandria and Jerusalem Sept. 1, 1975, and signed in Geneva Sept. 4, 1975 (Israeli representatives at Geneva initialed the documents to indicate that their government would not implement the accord until the U.S. Congress approved the provision for American truce monitors).*
>
> *The* Agreement *and the* Annex *were initialed in Jerusalem by Avraham Kidron, director general of the Foreign Ministry, and Gen. Mordechai Gur, chief of staff. In Alexandria, the Egyptian chief of staff, Gen. Mohammed Ali Fahmy, and Ahmed Osman, Egyptian representative at the United Nations offices in Geneva, initialed the same agreement.*
>
> *The* Proposal *for an American monitoring team in the Sinai was signed in Israel by Secretary of State Henry A. Kissinger and Prime Minister Yitzhak Rabin and in Egypt by Kissinger and Prime Minister Mamdouh Salem.*

Agreement Between Egypt and Israel

The Government of the Arab Republic of Egypt and the Government of Israel have agreed that:

Article I

The conflict between them and in the Middle East shall not be resolved by military force but by peaceful means.

The Agreement concluded by the Parties January 18, 1974, within the framework of the Geneva Peace Conference, constituted a first step towards a just and durable peace according to the Provisions of Security Council Resolution 338 of October 22, 1973.

They are determined to reach a final and just peace settlement by means of negotiations called for by Security Council Resolution 338, this Agreement being a significant step towards that end.

Article II

The Parties hereby undertake not to resort to the threat or use of force or military blockage against each other.

Article III

The Parties shall continue scrupulously to observe the ceasefire on land, sea and air and to refrain from all military or para-military actions against each other.

The Parties also confirm that the obligations contained in the Annex and, when concluded, the Protocol shall be an integral part of this Agreement.

Article IV

A. The military forces of the Parties shall be deployed in accordance with the following Principles:

(1) All Israeli Forces shall be deployed east of the lines designated as lines JA and M on the attached map.

(2) All Egyptian Forces shall be deployed west of the line designated as Line E on the attached map.

(3) The area between the lines designated on the attached map as lines E and F and the area between the lines designated on the attached map as lines J and KA shall be limited in armament and forces.

(4) The limitations on armament and forces in the areas described by Paragraph (3) above shall be agreed as described in the attached Annex.

(5) The zone between the lines designated on the attached map as lines E and J, will be a Buffer Zone. In this zone the United Nations Emergency Force will continue to perform its functions as under the Egyptian-Israeli Agreement of January 18, 1974.

(6) In the area south from Line E and west from Line M, as defined on the attached map, there will be no military forces, as specified in the attached Annex.

B. The details concerning the new lines, the redeployment of the forces and its timing, the limitation on armaments and forces, aerial reconnaissance, the operation of the early warning and surveillance installations and the use of the roads, the United Nations functions and other arrangements will all be in accordance with the provisions of the Annex and map which are an integral part of this Agreement and of the Protocol which is a result from negotiations pursuant to the Annex and which, when concluded, shall become an integral part of this Agreement.

Article V

The United Nations Emergency Force is essential and shall continue its functions and its mandate shall be extended annually.

Article VI

The Parties hereby establish a Joint Commission for the duration of this Agreement. It will function under the Aegis of the Chief Coordinator of the United Nations Peacekeeping Missions in the Middle East in order to consider any problem arising from this Agreement and to assist the United Nations Emergency Force in the execution of its mandate. The Joint Commission shall function in accordance with procedures established in the Protocol.

Article VII

Non-military cargoes destined for or coming from Israel shall be permitted through the Suez Canal.

Article VIII

This Agreement is regarded by the Parties as a significant step toward a just and lasting peace.

It is not a final peace agreement.

The Parties shall continue their efforts to negotiate a final peace agreement within the framework of the Geneva Peace Conference in accordance with Security Council Resolution 338.

Article IX

This Agreement shall enter into force upon signature of the Protocol and remain in force until superseded by a new Agreement.

Annex to Egypt-Israel Agreement

Within five days after the signature of the Egypt-Israeli Agreement, representatives of the two Parties shall meet in the military working group of the Middle East peace conference at Geneva to begin preparation of a detailed protocol for the implementation of the Agreement. The working group will complete the protocol within two weeks. In order to facilitate preparation of the protocol and implementation of the Agreement, and to assist in maintaining the scrupulous observance of the ceasefire and the elements of the Agreement, the two Parties have agreed on the following principles, which are an integral part of the Agreement, as guidelines for the working group.

1. Definitions of the Lines and Areas

The deployment lines, areas of limited forces and armaments, buffer zones, the area south from line E and west from line M, other designated areas, road sections for common use and other features referred to in Article IV of the Agreement shall be as indicated on the attached map.

2. Buffer Zones

(A) Access to the buffer zones will be controlled by the United Nations emergency force, according to procedures to be worked out by the working group and the United Nations emergency force.

(B) Aircraft of either party will be permitted to fly freely up to the forward line of that party. Reconnaissance aircraft of either party may fly up to the middle line of the buffer zone between E and J on an agreed schedule.

(C) In the buffer zone, between lines E and J there will be established under Article IV of the Agreement an early warning system entrusted to United States civilian personnel as detailed in a separate proposal, which is a part of this Agreement.

(D) Authorized personnel shall have access to the buffer zone for transit to and from the early warning system; the manner in which this is carried out shall be worked out by the working group and the United Nations emergency force.

3. Area South of Line E and West of Line M

(A) In this area, the United Nations emergency force will assure that there are no military or para-military forces of any kind, military for-tifications and military installations; it will establish checkpoints and have the freedom of movement necessary to perform this function.

(B) Egyptian civilians and third country civilian oil field personnel shall have the right to enter, exit from, work, and live in the above indicated area, except for buffer zones 2A, and 2B and the United Nations posts. Egyptian civilian police shall be allowed in the area to perform normal civil police functions among the civilian population in such numbers and with such weapons and equipment as shall be provided for in the protocol.

(C) Entry to and exit from the area, by land, by air or by sea, shall be only through United Nations emergency force checkpoints. The United Nations emergency force shall also establish checkpoints along the road, the dividing line and at other points, with the precise locations and number to be included in the protocol.

(D) Access to the airspace and the coastal area shall be limited to unarmed Egyptian civilian vessels and unarmed civilian helicopters and transport planes involved in the civilian activities of the area as agreed by the working group.

(E) Israel undertakes to leave intact all currently existing civilian installations and infrastructures.

(F) Procedures for use of the common sections of the coastal road along the Gulf of Suez shall be determined by the working group and detailed in the protocol.

4. Aerial Surveillance

There shall be a continuation of aerial reconnaissance missions by the United States over the areas covered by the agreement (the area between lines F and K), following the same procedures already in practice. The missions will ordinarily be carried out at a frequency of one mission every 7 to 10 days, with either party or the United Nations emergency force empowered to request an earlier mission. The United States Government will make the mission results available expeditiously to Israel, Egypt and the chief coordinator of the United Nations peacekeeping mission in the Middle East.

5. Limitation of Forces and Armaments

(A) Within the areas of limited forces and armaments (the areas between lines J and K and lines E and F) the major limitations shall be as follows:

(1) Eight (8) standard infantry battalions

(2) Seventy-five (75) tanks

(3) Seventy-two (72) artillery pieces, including heavy mortars (E.E. with caliber larger than 120 MM), whose range shall not exceed twelve (12) KM.

(4) The total number of personnel shall not exceed eight thousand (8,000).

(5) Both Parties agree not to station or locate in the area weapons which can reach the line of the other side.

(6) Both Parties agree that in the areas between lines J and K, and between line A (Of the Disengagement Agreement of January 18, 1974) and line E, they will construct no new fortifications or installations for forces of a size greater than that agreed herein.

(B) The major limitations beyond the areas of limited forces and armament will be:

(1) Neither side will station nor locate any weapon in areas from which they can reach the other line.

(2) The Parties will not place anti-aircraft missiles within an area of ten (10) kilometres each of line K and west of line F, respectively.

(C) The United Nations Emergency Force will conduct inspections in order to ensure the maintenance of the agreed limitations within these areas.

6. Process of Implementation

The detailed implementation and timing of the redeployment of forces, turnover of oil fields, and other arrangements called for by the Agreement, Annex and Protocol shall be determined by the Working Group, which will agree on the stages of this process, including the phased movement of Egyptian troops to line E and Israeli troops to line J. The first phase will be the transfer of the oil fields and installations to Egypt. This process will begin two weeks from the signature of the Protocol with the introduction of the necessary technicians, and it will be completed no later than eight weeks after it begins. The details of the phasing will be worked out in the Military Working Group.

Implementation of the redeployment shall be completed within 5 months after signature of the Protocol.

Proposal

In connection with the early warning system referred to in Article IV of the Agreement between Egypt and Israel concluded on this date and as an integral part of that Agreement, (hereafter referred to as the Basic Agreement), the United States proposes the following:

1. The early warning system to be established in accordance with Article IV in the area shown on the map attached to the Basic Agreement will be entrusted to the United States. It shall have the following elements:

A. There shall be two surveillance stations to provide strategic early warning, one operated by Egyptian and one operated by Israeli personnel. (Their locations are shown on the map attached to the Basic Agreement.) Each station shall be manned by not more than 250 technical and administrative personnel. They shall perform the functions of visual and electronic surveillance only within their stations.

B. In support of these stations, to provide tactical early warning and to verify access to them, three watch stations shall be established by the United States in the Mitla and Giddi Passes as will be shown on the map attached to the agreement. These stations shall be operated by United States civilian personnel. In support of these stations, there shall be established three unmanned electronic sensor fields at both ends of each Pass and in the general vicinity of each station and the roads leading to and from those stations.

2. The United States civilian personnel shall perform the following duties in connection with the operation and maintenance of these stations.

A. At the two surveillance stations described in paragraph 1A, above, United States personnel will verify the nature of the operations of the stations and all movement into and out of each station and will immediately report any detected divergency from its authorized role of visual and electronic surveillance to the Parties to the Basic Agreement and to the United Nations emergency force.

B. At each watch station described in paragraph 1B, above, the United States personnel will immediately report to the Parties to the Basic Agreement and to the United Nations emergency force any movement of armed forces, other than the United Nations emergency force, into either Pass and any observed preparations for such movement.

C. The total number of United States civilian personnel assigned to functions under this proposal shall not exceed 200. Only civilian personnel shall be assigned to functions under this proposal.

3. No arms shall be maintained at the stations and other facilities covered by this proposal, except for small arms required for their protection.

4. The United States personnel serving the early warning system shall be allowed to move freely within the area of the system.

5. The United States and its personnel shall be entitled to have such support facilities as are reasonably necessary to perform their functions.

6. The United States personnel shall be immune from local criminal, civil, tax and customs jurisdiction and may be accorded any other specific privileges and immunities provided for in the United Nations emergency force agreement of February 13, 1957.

7. The United States affirms that it will continue to perform the functions described above for the duration of the Basic Agreement.

8. Notwithstanding any other provision of this proposal, the United States may withdraw its personnel only if it concludes that their safety is jeopardized or that continuation of their role is no longer necessary. In the latter case the Parties to the Basic Agreement will be informed in advance in order to give them the opportunity to make alternative arrangements. If both Parties to the Basic Agreement request the United States to conclude its role under this proposal, the United States will consider such requests conclusive.

9. Technical problems including the location of the watch stations will be worked out through consultation with the United States.

Texts of the Memorandum *relating to the Sinai agreement among the United States, Egypt and Israel published in unauthorized version Sept. 16, 1975:*

Memorandum of Agreement Between
U.S. and Israel

The United States recognizes that the Egypt-Israel Agreement initialed on Sept. 1, 1975 (hereinafter referred to as the agreement), entailing the withdrawal from vital areas in Sinai, constitutes an act of great significance on Israel's part in the pursuit of final peace. That agreement has full United States support.

1

The United States Government will make every effort to be fully responsive, within the limits of its resources and Congressional authorization and appropriation, on an on-going and long-term basis, to Israel's military equipment and other defense requirements, to its energy requirements and to its economic needs. The needs specified in paragraphs 2, 3 and 4 below shall be deemed eligible for inclusion within the annual total to be requested in FY '76 and later fiscal years.

2

Israel's long-term military supply needs from the United States shall be the subject of periodic consultations between representatives of the U.S. and Israeli defense establishments, with agreement reached on specific items to be included in a separate U.S.-Israeli memorandum. To this end, a joint study by military experts will be undertaken within three weeks. In conducting this study, which will include Israel's 1976 needs, the United States will view Israel's requests sympathetically, including its request for advanced and sophisticated weapons.

3

Israel will make its own independent arrangements for oil supply to meet its requirements through normal procedures. In the event Israel is unable to secure its needs in this way, the United States Government, upon notification of this fact by the Government of Israel, will act as follows for five years, at the end of which period either side can terminate this arrangement on one year's notice.

(a) If the oil Israel needs to meet all its normal requirements for domestic consumption is unavailable for purchase in circumstances where no quantitative restrictions exist on the ability of the United States to procure oil to meet its normal requirements, the United States Government will promptly make oil available for purchase by Israel to meet all of the aforementioned normal requirements of Israel. If Israel is unable to secure the necessary means to transport such oil to Israel, the United States Government will make every effort to help Israel secure the necessary means of transport.

(b) If the oil Israel needs to meet all of its normal requirements for domestic consumption is unavailable for purchase in circumstances where quantitative restrictions through embargo or otherwise also prevent the

United States from procuring oil to meet its normal requirements, the United States Government will promptly make oil available for purchase by Israel in accordance with the International Energy Agency conservation and allocation formula as applied by the United States Government, in order to meet Israel's essential requirements. If Israel is unable to secure the necessary means to transport such oil to Israel, the United States Government will make every effort to help Israel secure the necessary means of transport.

Israeli and U.S. experts will meet annually or more frequently at the request of either party, to review Israel's continuing oil requirement.

4

In order to help Israel meet its energy needs, and as part of the over-all annual figure in paragraph 1 above, the United States agrees:

(a) In determining the overall annual figure which will be requested from Congress, the United States Government will give special attention to Israel's oil import requirements and, for a period as determined by Article 3 above, will take into account in calculating that figure Israel's additional expenditures for the import of oil to replace that which would have ordinarily come from Abu Rudeis and Ras Sudar (4.5 million tons in 1975).

(b) To ask Congress to make available funds, the amount to be determined by mutual agreement, to the Government of Israel necessary for a project for the construction and stocking of the oil reserves to be stored in Israel, bringing storage reserve capacity and reserve stocks, now standing at approximately six months, up to one year's need at the time of the completion of the project. The project will be implemented within four years. The construction, operation and financing and other relevant questions of the project will be the subject of early and detailed talks between the two Governments.

5

The United States Government will not expect Israel to begin to implement the agreement before Egypt fulfills its undertaking under the January, 1974, disengagement agreement to permit passage of all Israeli cargoes to and from Israeli ports through the Suez Canal.

6

The United States Government agrees with Israel that the next agreement with Egypt should be a final peace agreement.

7

In case of an Egyptian violation of any of the provisions of the agreement, the United States Government is prepared to consult with Israel as to the significance of the violation and possible remedial action by the United States Government.

8

The United States Government will vote against any Security Council resolution which in its judgment affects or alters adversely the agreement.

9

The United States Government will not join in and will seek to prevent efforts by others to bring about consideration of proposals which it and Israel agree are detrimental to the interests of Israel.

10

In view of the long-standing U.S. commitment to the survival and security of Israel, the United States Government will view with particular gravity threats to Israel's security or sovereignty by a world power. In support of this objective, the United States Government will in the event of such threat consult promptly with the Government of Israel with respect to what support diplomatic or otherwise, or assistance it can lend to Israel in accordance with its constitutional practices.

11

The United States Government and the Government of Israel will, at the earliest possible time, and if possible within two months after the signature of this document, conclude the contingency plan for a military supply operation to Israel in an emergency situation.

12

It is the United States Government's position that Egyptian commitments under the Egypt-Israel agreement, its implementation, validity and duration are not conditional upon any act or developments between the other Arab states and Israel. The United States Government regards the agreement as standing on its own.

13

The United States Government shares the Israeli position that under existing political circumstances negotiations with Jordan will be directed toward an over-all peace settlement.

14

In accordance with the principle of freedom of navigation on the high seas and free and unimpeded passage through and over straits connecting international waters, the United States Government regards the Strait of Bab el Mandeb and the Strait of Gibraltar as international waterways. It will support Israel's right to free and unimpeded passage through such straits. Similarly, the United States Government recognizes Israel's right to freedom of flights over the Red Sea and such straits and will support diplomatically the exercise of that right.

15

In the event that the United Nations Emergency Force or any other United Nations organ is withdrawn without the prior agreement of both parties to the Egypt-Israel agreement and the United States before this agreement is superseded by another agreement, it is the United States view that the agreement shall remain binding in all its parts.

16

The United States and Israel agree that signature of the protocol of the Egypt-Israel agreement and its full entry into effect shall not take place before approval by the United States Congress of the U.S. role in connection with the surveillance and observation functions described in the agreement and its annex. The United States has informed the Government of Israel that it has obtained the Government of Egypt agreement to the above.

Addendum on Arms to Israel

On the question of military and economic assistance to Israel, the following conveyed by the U.S. to Israel augments what the memorandum of agreement states.

The United States is resolved to continue to maintain Israel's defensive strength through the supply of advanced types of equipment, such as the F-16 aircraft. The United States Government agrees to an early meeting to undertake a joint study of high technology and sophisticated items, including the Pershing ground-to-ground missiles with conventional warheads, with the view to giving a positive response. The U.S. Administration will submit annually for approval by the U.S. Congress a request for military and economic assistance in order to help meet Israel's economic and military needs.

Texts of U.S.-Egypt agreement and U.S.-Israel agreement relating to the Geneva peace conference, published in unauthorized versions Sept. 17, 1975:

Assurances to Egypt

1. The United States intends to make a serious effort to help bring about further negotiations between Syria and Israel, in the first instance through diplomatic channels.

2. In the event of an Israeli violation of the agreement, the United States is prepared to consult with Egypt as to the significance of the violation and possible remedial action by the United States.

3. The United States will provide technical assistance to Egypt for the Egyptian early-warning station.

U.S.-Israel Agreement on Geneva

1. The Geneva peace conference will be reconvened at a time coordinated between the United States and Israel.

2. The United States will continue to adhere to its present policy with respect to the Palestine Liberation Organization, whereby it will not recognize or negotiate with the Palestine Liberation Organization so long as the Palestine Liberation Organization does not recognize Israel's right to exist and does not accept Security Council Resolutions 242 and 338. The United States Government will consult fully and seek to concert its position and strategy at the Geneva peace conference on this issue with the Government of Israel. Similarly, the United States will consult fully and seek to concert its position and strategy with Israel with regard to the participation of any other additional states. It is understood that the participation at a subsequent phase of the conference of any possible additional state, group or organization will require the agreement of all the initial participants.

3. The United States will make every effort to insure at the conference that all the substantive negotiations will be on a bilateral basis.

4. The United States will oppose and, if necessary, vote against any initiative in the Security Council to alter adversely the terms of reference of the Geneva peace conference or to change Resolutions 242 and 338 in ways which are incompatible with their original purpose.

5. The United States will seek to insure that the role of the co-sponsors will be consistent with what was agreed in the memorandum of understanding between the United States Government and the Government of Israel of Dec. 20, 1972.

6. The United States and Israel will concert action to assure that the conference will be conducted in a manner consonant with the objectives of this document and with the declared purpose of the conference, namely the advancement of a negotiated peace between Israel and its neighbors.

ECONOMIC COOPERATION AND THE UNITED NATIONS

September 1 and 16, 1975

A special session of the United Nations General Assembly approved on Sept. 16 a framework for international economic negotiations aimed at "redressing the economic imbalances" between industrialized nations and developing countries. The seven-point program represented a compromise between demands of Third World leaders for "a new world economic order" involving global redistribution of wealth, and flat rejection of this concept by the industrialized nations led by the United States.

Adoption of the compromise program followed a major policy review by U.S. State Department and Treasury officials which resulted in a substantial change in the American position. The United States' new, more conciliatory position was announced Sept. 1 at the opening of the seventh U.N. special session on economic cooperation and development. A lengthy address by Secretary of State Henry A. Kissinger, read by Daniel P. Moynihan, U.S. Representative to the United Nations, responded directly to many Third World demands and contained more than 40 specific proposals.

Neither Kissinger's speech nor the final U.N. plan endorsed a new economic order as such, but both included numerous proposals for increased assistance to and preferential treatment of Third World countries. The U.N. resolution also included several proposals opposed by the United States. However, the American delegation, after expressing reservations on those aspects of the plan, voted for the program as a whole. The vote concluded the 16-day special General Assembly session on economic development, the second such session in less than two years (see Historic Documents of 1974, p. 255).

Plight of Developing Nations

Since the Arab oil embargo of 1973, the marginal economic position of the underdeveloped nations had worsened dramatically. Long impoverished by the gap between their earnings from commodity exports and what they had to pay for imports from industrial countries, the poorest Asian, African and Latin nations were thrust into still graver trouble by the fourfold increase in prices of oil and related products such as fertilizer. Unremitting inflation steadily eroded their meager purchasing power. Whereas 25 tons of natural rubber bought six tractors in 1960, it could buy only two in 1975, according to a Wall Street Journal *estimate. Moreover, extreme fluctuations in world markets effectively prevented long-range development to diversify the economic bases of these countries. And, in recent years, the recession had forced industrial nations to reduce their purchases of raw materials.*

In 1974, as the financial situation of the poor nations deteriorated, they launched a drive to shift the flow of wealth away from the industrial powers and toward their countries. They threatened cartel action, similar to that of the Organization of Petroleum Exporting Countries (OPEC), to force concessions; the OPEC nations, particularly Algeria, encouraged such action. At regional conferences and at the United Nations, militant Third World representatives read strongly worded denunciations of the Western world and pushed through resolutions designed to redress what they considered economic injustice on a global scale. Frequent confrontations disrupted U.N. sessions. In 1975 this trend set in motion the first attempt to change the structure of the United Nations itself (see p. 325)

U.S. Policy Shift

Western European nations, almost wholly dependent on the Middle East for oil, tended to be somewhat sympathetic to Third World demands. But the various initiatives for a new economic order were given little chance of success because of the unyielding opposition of the United States to such a concept and because the Third World nations, apart from the oil producers, lacked the economic power to force radical changes in the economic order.

A softening of the American position was signaled May 27, 1975, when Kissinger announced at a ministerial-level meeting of the International Energy Agency (IEA) that the United States was willing to discuss raw-materials prices on a case-by-case basis. (Non-aligned nations had demanded an overall international price-support system.) A month earlier U.S. refusal to permit any discussion of commodity prices at oil meetings had broken up preliminary producer-consumer talks in Paris. But Kissinger told the IEA ministers that it had "become clear as a result of the April preparatory meeting that the dialogue between the producers and consumers will not progress unless it is broadened to include the general issue of the relationship between developing and developed countries."

U.S. and U.N. Proposals

Substantive American proposals to better that relationship followed in Kissinger's September speech at the U.N. General Assembly. Among other things, Kissinger advocated: establishment of a $10-billion fund to enable poor nations to cope with broad swings in the prices of their commodity exports; preferential trade agreements between advanced and developing nations; provisions for sharing technological and scientific advances; easier access to capital markets; and increased funds for development loans administered by international lending facilities such as the World Bank and the International Monetary Fund.

The U.N. resolution synthesized these proposals with additional Third World demands to which the U.S. objected. One such demand was to "index" or adjust the prices of raw materials to those of finished goods exported by the advanced nations. The United States objected also to setting 0.7 per cent of gross national product as an end-of-the-decade target for each developed nation's assistance to the developing nations.

Many of the trade and foreign-aid proposals would require congressional or executive action before the United States could act upon them. Observers looked to a meeting of producing and consuming nations beginning in December in Paris as the first test of how, and to what extent, the U.N. proposals would be implemented. But representatives of both advanced and developing countries viewed the September resolution as a promising start. Ambassador Moynihan, often critical of Third World tactics (see p. 645), declared that in this case "genuine accord had been reached." A spokesman for Mexico, one of the leading proponents of the Third World position, stated that "a friendly dialogue had begun...."

> *Excerpts from* Global Consensus and Economic Development, *an address by Secretary of State Henry A. Kissinger read at the seventh special session of the U.N. General Assembly, Sept. 1, 1975, by Daniel P. Moynihan, U.S. Representative to the United Nations:*

We assemble here this week with an opportunity to improve the condition of mankind. We can let this opportunity slip away, or we can respond to it with vision and common sense.

The United States has made its choice. There are no panaceas available—only challenges. The proposals that I shall announce today on behalf of President Ford are a program of practical steps responding to the expressed concerns of developing countries....

The developing nations have stated their claim for a greater role, for more control over their economic destiny, and for a just share in global prosperity. The economically advanced nations have stated their claim for reliable supplies of energy, raw materials, and other products at a fair price; they seek stable economic relationships and expanding world trade, for these are important to the well-being of their own societies....

We profoundly believe that neither the poor nor the rich nations can achieve their purposes in isolation. Neither can extort them from the other—the developing countries least of all, for they would pay the greater cost of division of the planet, which would cut them off needlessly from sources of capital and markets essential to their own progress.

Global Approach Required

The reality is that ample incentives exist for cooperation on the basis of mutual respect. It is not necessarily the case that if some grow worse off, others will be worse off. But there is an opposite proposition, which we believe is true: that an economic system thrives if all who take part in it thrive. This is no theory; it is our own experience. And it is an experience that we, a people uniquely drawn from all the other peoples of the world, truly desire and hope to share with others.

Therefore it is time to go beyond the doctrines left over from a previous century that are made obsolete by modern reality.

History has left us the legacy of strident nationalism—discredited in this century by its brutal excesses a generation ago and by its patent inadequacy for the economic needs of our time. The economy is global. Recessions, inflation, trade relations, monetary stability, gluts and scarcities of products and materials, the growth of transnational enterprises—these are international phenomena and call for international responses....

The reality is that the world economy is a single global system of trade and monetary relations on which hinges the development of all our economies. The advanced nations have an interest in the growth of markets and production in the developing world; with equal conviction we state that the developing countries have a stake in the markets, technological innovation, and capital investment of the industrial countries....

Need for Consensus

So let us get down to business. Let us put aside the sterile debate over whether a new economic order is required or whether the old economic order is adequate. Let us look forward and shape the world before us. Change is inherent in what we do and what we seek. But one fact does not change: that without a consensus on the realities and principles of the development effort, we will achieve nothing.

—There must be consensus, first and foremost, on the principle that our common development goals can be achieved only by cooperation, not by the politics of confrontation.

—There must be consensus that acknowledges our respective concerns and our mutual responsibilities. All of us have rights, and all of us have duties.

—The consensus must embrace the broadest possible participation in international decisions. The developing countries must have a role and voice in the international system, especially in decisions that affect them. But those nations who are asked to provide resources and effort to carry out the decisions must be accorded a commensurate voice....

The determination of the developing nations to mobilize their own effort is indispensable. Without it, no outside effort will have effect. Government policies to call forth savings, to institute land reform, to use external aid and capital productively, to manage and allocate national resources wisely, to promote family planning—for these there are no substitutes.

But there must be international as well as national commitment. The United States is prepared to do its part. The senior economic officials of our government have joined with me in developing our approach. Treasury Secretary Simon, with whom I have worked closely on our program, will discuss it tomorrow in relation to the world economy. The large congressional delegation that will attend the session, and the seriousness with which they and the executive branch have collaborated in preparing these proposals, are evidence of my country's commitment.

We ask in return for a serious international dialogue on the responsibilities which confront us all.

Insuring Economic Security

...Developing economies are by far the most vulnerable to natural and man-made disasters—the vagaries of weather and of the business cycle. Sharp increases in the prices of oil and food have a devastating effect on their livelihood. Recessions in the industrial countries depress their export earnings.

Thus economic security is the minimum requirement of an effective strategy for development. Without this foundation, sound development programs cannot proceed and the great efforts that development requires from poor and rich alike cannot be sustained.

And because economic security is a global problem, it is a global challenge:

—The industrial nations must work together more effectively to restore and maintain their noninflationary expansion;

—Nations which supply vital products must avoid actions which disrupt that expansion; and

—The international community must undertake a new approach to reduce drastic fluctuations in the export earnings of the developing countries....

Security of Supply

Global economic security depends, secondly, on the actions of suppliers of vital products.

Thus the United States has believed that the future of the world economy requires discussions on energy and other key issues among oil consuming and producing nations. The Government of France is inviting in-

591

dustrialized, oil-producing, and developing nations to relaunch a dialogue this fall [rescheduled for December] on the problems of energy, development, raw materials, and related financial issues. The United States has supported this proposal and worked hard to establish the basis for successful meetings....

Stabilization of Earnings

The third basic factor in economic security is the stability of export earnings. The development programs—indeed, the basic survival—of many countries rest heavily on earnings from exports of primary products which are highly vulnerable to fluctuations in worldwide demand....

The question of stabilization of income from primary products has become central in the dialogue on international economic concerns. Price stabilization is not generally a promising approach. For many commodities it would be difficult to achieve without severe restrictions on production or exports, extremely expensive buffer stocks, or price levels which could stimulate substitutes and thereby work to the long-range disadvantage of producers. Even the most ambitious agenda for addressing individual commodities would not result in stabilization arrangements for all of them in the near term. And focusing exclusively on stabilizing commodity prices would not provide sufficient protection to the many developing countries whose earnings also depend on the exports of manufactured goods.

Measures for Price Stabilization

The U.S. Government has recently completed a review of these issues. We have concluded that, because of the wide diversity among countries, commodities, and markets, a new, much more comprehensive approach is required—one which will be helpful to exporters of all commodities and manufactured goods as well.

Let me set forth our proposal. The United States proposes creation in the International Monetary Fund (IMF) of a new development security facility to stabilize overall export earnings.

—The facility would give loans to sustain development programs in the face of export fluctuations; up to $2.5 billion, and possibly more, in a single year and a potential total of $10 billion in outstanding loans.

—Assistance would be available to all developing countries which need to finance shortfalls in export earnings, unless the shortfalls are caused by their own acts of policy.

—The poorest countries would be permitted to convert their loans into grants under prescribed conditions. These grants would be financed by the proceeds of sales of IMF gold channeled through the proposed $2 billion Trust Fund now under negotiation.

—Eligible countries could draw most, or under certain conditions all, of their IMF quotas in addition to their normal drawing rights. Much of that could be drawn in a single year, if necessary; part automatically, part subject to balance-of-payments conditions, and part reserved for cases of particularly violent swings in commodity earnings.

—Shortfalls would be calculated according to a formula geared to future growth as well as current and past exports. In this way the facility helps countries protect their development plans.

—This facility would replace the IMF's compensatory finance facility; it would not be available for industrial countries....

This new source of funds also reinforces our more traditional types of assistance; without the stabilization of earnings, the benefits of concessional aid for developing countries are vitiated. [Concessional aid refers to loans made at less than the current rate of interest, also known as "soft" loans.] For industrialized countries, it means a more steady export market. For developing countries, it helps assure that development can be pursued without disruption and makes them more desirable prospects in international capital markets....

Accelerating Economic Growth

It is not enough to insure the minimal economic security of the developing countries. Development is a process of growth, acceleration, greater productivity, higher living standards, and social change. This is a process requiring the infusion of capital, technology, and managerial skills on a massive scale....

To put it frankly, the political climate for bilateral aid has deteriorated. In the industrial countries, support for aid has been eroded by domestic economic slowdown, compounded by energy problems; in the developing countries, there is resentment at forms of assistance which imply dependence.

The oil exporters have only begun to meet their responsibility for assistance to the poorer countries. Last year their concessionary aid disbursements were roughly $2 billion; they could, and must, rise substantially this year.

But the industrial nations and the oil exporters cannot, even together, supply all the new resources needed to accelerate development. It follows inescapably that the remaining needs for capital and technology can only be met, directly or indirectly, from the vast pool of private sources. This investment will take place only if the conditions exist to attract or permit it. The United States therefore believes it is time for the world community to address the basic requirements for accelerating growth in developing countries:...

Access to Capital Markets

....First, the United States will support a major expansion of the resources of the World Bank's International Finance Corporation, the investment banker with the broadest experience in supporting private enterprise in developing countries. We propose a large increase in the IFC's capital, from the present $100 million to at least $400 million.

Second, the United States proposes creation of an International Investment Trust to mobilize portfolio capital for investment in local enterprises. The trust would attract new capital by offering investors a unique opportunity: participation in a managed broad selection of investments in developing country firms, public, private, and mixed. The International Finance Corporation would manage it and perhaps provide seed capital, but most of its funds would come from government and private investors. Investors would have their exposure to major losses limited by a $200 million loss reserve provided by governments of industrialized, oil-producing, and developing nations. This institution could be a powerful link between the capital markets and the developing world and could provide billions of dollars of essential resources.

Third, the United States will contribute actively to the work of the IMF-World Bank Development Committee to find ways to assist developing countries in their direct borrowing in the capital markets....

Finally, we believe that all industrial countries should systematically review the conditions for developing-country access to their national markets to assure that they offer fair and open opportunity. The United States is prepared to provide technical assistance and expertise to developing countries ready to enter long-term capital markets, and we ask others to join us.

Transfer of Technology

....For technology to spur development, it must spur growth in priority areas: energy, food, other resources strategic to the developing economies, and industrialization itself.

First, energy is critical for both agricultural and industrial development....

The United States invites other nations to join us in an increase of bilateral support for training and technical assistance to help developing countries find and exploit new sources of fossil fuel and other forms of energy.

Methods of discovering and using less accessible or low-grade resources must be fully utilized. So must technology to produce solar and geothermal power. And these techniques must be suited to the conditions of the developing countries.

The United States believes the topic of energy cooperation should be high on the agenda for the forthcoming dialogue between consumers and producers. We will propose, in this dialogue, creation of an International Energy Institute bringing together developed and developing, consumer and producer, on the particular problem of energy development. The International Energy Agency and the International Atomic Energy Agency should both find ways to give technical assistance and support to this institute.

A second critical area for technological innovation is *food production and improvement of nutrition.*

During the past decade, a number of international agricultural research centers have been established to adapt techniques to local needs and conditions. In 1971 the Consultative Group for International Agricultural Research was formed to coordinate these efforts. The United States is prepared to expand the capacity of these institutions. In collaboration with national research organizations with more skilled manpower and funds, they could grow into a worldwide research network for development of agricultural technology.

We are also supporting legislation in the Congress to enable our universities to expand their technical assistance and research in the agricultural field.

Nonfood agricultural and forestry products are a third strategic area for technological assistance. The export earnings of many of the poorest countries—and the livelihood of many millions of their people—depend on such products as timber, jute, cotton, and natural rubber, some of which have encountered serious problems in the face of synthetics. They urgently need assistance to improve the productivity and competitiveness of these products and to diversify their economies.

The United States therefore proposes creation of an organization to coordinate and finance such assistance. Its task will be to attract manpower and capital for research. The financing of this effort should be a priority task for the new International Fund for Agricultural Development....

Institute Proposed

[T]he United States supports creation of an International Industrialization Institute to sponsor and conduct research on industrial technology together with the governments, industries, and research facilities of developing countries.

We support creation of an international center for the exchange of technological information, as a clearinghouse for the sharing of ongoing research and new findings relevant to development.

We will expand our bilateral support of industrial technology appropriate to developing country needs.

We will work with others in this organization in preparing guidelines for the transfer of technology and in the planning of a conference on science and technology for development.

Transnational Enterprises

....Transnational enterprises have been power instruments of modernization both in the industrial nations—where they conduct most of their operations—and in the developing countries, where there is often no substitute for their ability to marshal capital, management skills, technology, and initiative. Thus the controversy over their role and conduct is itself an obstacle to economic development....

The United States therefore believes that the time has come for the international community to articulate standards of conduct for both enterprises and governments. The United Nations Commission on Transnational Corporations and other international bodies have begun such an effort. We must reach agreement on balanced principles. These should apply to transnational enterprises in their relations with governments, and to governments in their relations with enterprises and with other governments. They must be fair principles, for failure to reflect the interests of all parties concerned would exacerbate rather than moderate the frictions which have damaged the environment for international investment. Specifically, the United States believes that:

—Transnational enterprises are obliged to obey local law and refrain from unlawful intervention in the domestic affairs of host countries. Their activities should take account of public policy and national development priorities. They should respect local customs. They should employ qualified local personnel, or qualify local people through training.

—Host governments in turn must treat transnational enterprises equitably, without discrimination among them, and in accordance with international law. Host governments should make explicit their development priorities and the standards which transnational enterprises are expected to meet, and maintain them with reasonable consistency.

—Governments and enterprises must both respect the contractual obligations that they freely undertake. Contracts should be negotiated openly, fairly, and with full knowledge of their implications....

—Principles established for transnational enterprises should apply equally to domestic enterprises, where relevant. Standards should be addressed not only to privately owned corporations, but also to state-owned and mixed transnational enterprises, which are increasingly important in the the world economy.

A statement of principles is not the only or necessarily a sufficient way of resolving many of the problems affecting transnational enterprises. We must develop others:

—Governments must harmonize their tax treatment of these enterprises. Without coordination, host-country and home-country policies may inhibit productive investment.

—Factfinding and arbitral procedures must be promoted as means for settling investment disputes. The World Bank's International Center for the Settlement of Investment Disputes and other third-party facilities should be employed to settle the important disputes which inevitably arise.

—Laws against restrictive business practices must be developed, better coordinated among countries, and enforced.... We condemn restrictive practices in setting prices or restraining supplies, whether by private or state-owned transnational enterprises or by the collusion of national governments.

—Insurance for foreign private investors should to the extent possible be multilateralized and should include financial participation by developing countries to reflect our mutual stake in encouraging foreign investment in the service of development.

—And there must be more effective bilateral consultation among governments to identify and resolve investment disputes before they become irritants in political relations....

Trade and Development

...[T]oday the global trading system is threatened by the most serious recession since the Second World War. We face the danger of proliferating artificial barriers and unfair competition reminiscent of the 1930's, which contributed to economic and political disaster. Every day that economic recovery is delayed, the temptation grows to restrict imports, subsidize exports, and control scarce commodities. Concerted action is necessary now to safeguard and improve the open trading system on which the future well-being of all our countries depends....

The United States therefore believes that a major goal of the multilateral trade negotiations [then under way in Geneva] should be to make the trading system better serve development goals. Let me briefly outline our policy.

—First, there must be fundamental structural improvement in the relationship of the developing countries to the world trading system. In the earlier stages of their development, they should receive special treatment through a variety of means—such as preferences, favorable concessions, and exceptions which reflect their economic status. But as they progress to a higher level of development, they must gradually accept the same obligations of reciprocity and stable arrangements that other countries undertake. At some point they must be prepared to compete on more equal terms, even as they derive growing benefits.

—Second, we must improve opportunities for the manufacturing sectors of developing countries. These provide the most promising new areas for exports at the critical stage in development, but the tariffs of industrial countries are a substantial obstacle. To ease this problem the United States has agreed to join other industrial countries in instituting generalized tariff preferences to permit developing countries enhanced access to the markets of industrialized nations.

I am pleased to announce today that the U.S. program will be put into effect on January 1, 1976. And before that date, we will begin consultations and practical assistance to enable exporting countries to benefit from the new trade opportunities in the American market, the largest single market for the manufactured goods of developing countries.

—Third, in keeping with the Tokyo Declaration [1973], we should adapt rules of nontariff barriers to the particular situation of developing countries. In setting international standards for government procurement practices, for example, the United States will negotiate special consideration for the developing countries. We will also negotiate on the basis that under

prescribed conditions, certain subsidies may be permitted without triggering countervailing duties for a period geared to achieving particular
development objectives.

—Fourth, we will work for early agreement on tariffs for tropical
products, which are a major source of earnings for the developing world.
Moreover, the United States will implement its tariff cuts on these products
as soon as possible.

—Finally, we are ready to join with other participants in Geneva to
negotiate changes in the system of protection in the industrialized countries
that favors the import of raw materials over other goods....

The developing countries have obligations in return. The world needs a
system in which no nation, developed or developing, arbitrarily withholds
or interferes with normal exports of materials. This practice—by depriving
other countries of needed goods—can trigger unemployment, cut production, and fuel inflation. It is therefore as disruptive as any of the other trade
barriers I have discussed. We urge negotiations on rules to limit and govern
the use of export restraints, a logical extension of existing rules on imports.
The United States will join others in negotiating supply-access commitments as part of the reciprocal exchange of concessions....

Commodity Trade and Production

....[B]oth industrial and developing countries would benefit from more
stable conditions of trade and an expansion of productive capacity in commodities.

Many solutions have been put forward to benefit producers of particular
products: cartelization, price indexing, commodity agreements, and other
methods. But reality demonstrates the interdependence of all our
economies and therefore the necessity for approaches that serve global
rather than narrow interests.

Food Security

....The U.S. [food] policy is now one of maximum production. At home,
we want a thriving farm economy and moderate prices for consumers. Internationally, we wish cooperative relations with nations that purchase from
us, an open and growing market, and abundant supplies to meet the needs
of the hungry through both good times and bad....

The United States believes that a global approach to food security, which
contains elements that can apply to other commodities, should follow these
basic principles:

—The problem must be approached globally, comprehensively, and
cooperatively, by consultation and negotiation among all significant
producers and consumers;

—Producers should recognize the global interest in stability of supply,
and consumers should recognize the interest of producers in stability of
markets and earnings;

—Special consideration should be given to the needs of developing countries; and

—Where volatile demand is combined with limited ability to make short-term increases in production, buffer stocks may be the best approach to achieving greater security for both consumers and producers.

At the World Food Conference last November, which was convened at our initiative, the United States proposed a comprehensive international cooperative approach to providing food security *[See Historic Documents of 1974, p. 939.]* We proposed an international system of nationally held grain reserves, to meet emergencies and improve the market. The United States has since then offered specific proposals and begun negotiations. But the international effort lagged when improved harvests seemed to diminish the immediate danger of worldwide shortage.

My government today declares that it is time to create this reserve system. If we do not, future crises are inevitable. Specifically, we propose:

—To meet virtually all potential shortfalls in food grains production, total world reserves must reach at least 30 million tons of wheat and rice. We should consider whether a similar reserve is needed in coarse grains.

—Responsibility for holding reserves should be allocated fairly, taking into account wealth, production, and trade. The United States is prepared to hold a major share.

—Acquisition and release of reserves should be governed by quantitative standards such as anticipated surpluses and shortfalls in production.

—Full participants in the system should receive assured access to supplies. Among major producers, full participation should require complete exchange of information and forecasts.

—Special assistance should be extended to developing countries that participate, to enable them to meet their obligation to hold a portion of global reserves....

Other Primary Commodities

And let us apply the same approach of cooperation to other primary commodities that are similarly beset by swings of price and supply—and that are similarly essential to the global economy.

There is no simple formula that will apply equally to all commodities. The United States therefore proposes to discuss new arrangements in individual commodities on a case-by-case basis.

Buffer stocks can be an effective technique to moderate instability in supplies and earnings. On the other hand, price-fixing arrangements distort the market, restrict production, and waste resources for everyone. It is developing countries that can least afford this waste. Restricted production idles the costly equipment and economic infrastructure that takes years to build. Artificially high prices lead consumers to make costly investment in domestic substitutes, ultimately eroding the market power of the traditional producers.

Accordingly, the United States proposes the following approach to commodity arrangements:

—We recommend that a consumer-producer forum be established for every key commodity to discuss how to promote the efficiency, growth, and stability of its market. This is particularly important in the case of grains, as I have outlined. It is also important in copper, where priority should be given to creating a forum for consumer-producer consultation.

—The first new formal international agreement being concluded is on tin. We have participated actively in its negotiation. President Ford has authorized me to announce that the United States intends to sign the tin agreement, subject to congressional consultations and ratification. We welcome its emphasis on buffer stocks, its avoidance of direct price fixing, and its balanced voting system. We will retain our right to sell from our strategic stockpiles, and we recognize the right of others to maintain a similar program.

—We are participating actively in negotiations on coffee. We hope they will result in a satisfactory new agreement that reduces the large fluctuations in prices and supplies entering the market.

—We will also join in the forthcoming cocoa and sugar negotiations. Their objective will be to reduce the risks of investment and moderate the swings in prices and supplies.

—We will support liberalization of the International Monetary Fund's financing of buffer stocks, to assure that this facility is available without reducing other drawing rights.

I have already announced my government's broad proposal of a development security facility, a more fundamental approach to stabilizing the overall earnings of countries dependent on commodities trade. My government also believes that an effective approach to the commodities problem requires a comprehensive program of investment to expand worldwide capacity in minerals and other critical raw materials....

The United States therefore proposes a major new international effort to expand raw material resources in developing countries.

The World Bank and its affiliates, in concert with private sources, should play a fundamental role. They can supply limited amounts of capital directly; more importantly, they can use their technical, managerial, and financial expertise to bring together funds from private and public sources. They can act as intermediary between private investors and host governments and link private and public effort by providing cross-guarantees on performance. World Bank loans could fund government projects, particularly for needed infrastructure, while the International Finance Corporation [soft loan facility of the World Bank] could join private enterprise in providing loans and equity capital. The World Bank Group should aim to mobilize $2 billion in private and public capital annually.

In addition, the United States will contribute to and actively support the new United Nations revolving fund for natural resources. This fund will encourage the worldwide exploration and exploitation of minerals and thus promote one of the most promising endeavors of economic development.

The Poorest Nations

....No international order can be considered just unless one of its fundamental principles is cooperation to raise the poorest of the world to a decent standard of life.

This challenge has two dimensions. We must look to elemental economic security and the immediate relief of suffering. And we must give preference to these countries' needs for future economic growth.

Elemental Economic Security

First, security means balance-of-payments support for the poorest countries during periods of adversity....

To provide greater balance-of-payments support at more acceptable rates of interest for the poor nations, the United States last November proposed a Trust Fund in the International Monetary Fund of up to $2 billion for emergency relief. Although this proposal met with wide support, it has been stalled by a dispute over an unrelated issue: the role of gold in the international monetary system. We cannot let this delay continue....

Second, security requires stable export earnings. The new approach that we are proposing today for earnings stabilization can provide major new economic insurance in the form of loans and grants for the poorest countries.

Third, security means having enough to eat. There must be determined international cooperation on food....

Another priority in the poorest countries must be to reduce the tragic waste of losses after harvest from inadequate storage, transport, and pest control. There are often simple and inexpensive techniques to resolve these problems. Investment in such areas as better storage and pesticides could have a rapid and substantial impact on the world's food supply; indeed, the saving could match the total of all the food aid being given around the world. Therefore we urge that the Food and Agriculture Organization, in conjunction with the U.N. Development Program and the World Bank, set a goal of cutting in half these postharvest losses by 1985, and develop a comprehensive program to this end.

Finally, security means good health and easing the strains of population growth.... One of the most promising approaches to these problems is the integrated delivery of basic health services at the community level, combining medical treatment, family planning, and nutritional information and using locally trained paramedical personnel. The United States will support a major expansion of the efforts already underway, including those in cooperation with the World Health Organization, to develop and apply these methods. We strongly urge the help of all concerned nations.

Future Economic Growth

Programs to achieve minimum economic security, however essential, solve only part of the problem. We must help the poorest nations break out of their present stagnation and move toward economic growth....

601

The special financial needs of the poorest countries can be met particularly well by expanded low-interest loans of the international financial
institutions. The International Development Association of the World Bank
Group is a principal instrument whose great potential has not been fully
realized. After congressional consultations, the United States will join
others in a substantial fifth replenishment of the resources of the International Development Association, provided that the oil-exporting
countries also make a significant contribution.

An effective strategy for sustained growth in the poorest countries must
expand their agricultural production....

Traditional bilateral aid programs to boost agricultural production remain indispensable. President Ford is asking Congress for authorization to
double our bilateral agricultural assistance this year to $582 million. We
urge the other affluent nations to increase their contributions as well.

Clearly a massive program of international cooperation is also required.
More research is needed to improve agricultural yields, make more efficient
use of fertilizer, and find better farm management techniques. Technical
assistance and information exchange are needed for training and for
technological advance. Better systems of water control, transportation, and
land management are needed to tap the developing countries' vast reserves
of land, water, and manpower.

To mobilize massive new concessional resources for these purposes, the
United States proposes the early establishment of the new International
Fund for Agricultural Development. President Ford has asked me to announce that he will seek authorization of a direct contribution of $200
million to the fund, provided that others will add their support for a combined goal of at least $1 billion....

The Political Dimension

...The United States believes that participation in international decisions
must be widely shared, in the name of both justice and effectiveness. We
believe the following principles should apply:

The process of decision should be fair. No country or group of countries
should have exclusive power in the areas basic to the welfare of others. This
principle is valid for oil. It also applies to trade and finance.

The methods of participation must be realistic. We must encourage the
emergence of real communities of interest between nations, whether they
are developed or developing, producer or consumer, rich or poor....

The process of decision should be responsive to change. On many issues
developing countries have not had a voice that reflects their role. This is
now changing. It is already the guiding principle of two of the most
successful international bodies, the IMF and the World Bank, where the
quotas of oil-producing states will soon be at least doubled—on the basis of
objective criteria. Basic economic realities, such as the size of economies,
participation in world trade, and financial contributions, must carry great
weight.

Finally, participation should be tailored to the issues at hand. We can usefully employ many different institutions and procedures. Sometimes we should seek broad consensus in universal bodies, as we are doing this week in this Assembly; sometimes negotiations can more usefully be focused in more limited forums, such as the forthcoming consumer-producer dialogue; sometimes decisions are best handled in large specialized bodies such as the IMF and World Bank, where voting power is related to responsibility; and sometimes most effective action can be taken in regional bodies.... In our view, an improved U.N. organization must include:

—Rationalization of the U.N.'s fragmented assistance programs;

—Strengthened leadership within the central Secretariat and the entire U.N. system for development and economic cooperation;

—Streamlining of the Economic and Social Council;

—Better consultative procedures to insure effective agreement among members with a particular interest in a subject under consideration; and

—A mechanism for independent evaluation of the implementation of programs.

The United States proposes that 1976 be dedicated as a year of review and reform of the entire U.N. development system....

U.S. Commitment

My government does not offer these proposals as an act of charity, nor should they be received as if due. We know that the world economy nourishes us all; we know that we live on a shrinking planet. Materially as well as morally, our destinies are intertwined.

There remain enormous things for us to do. We can say once more to the new nations: We have heard your voices. We embrace your hopes. We will join your efforts. We commit ourselves to our common success.

Excerpts from the United Nations resolution entitled Development and International Economic Cooperation (3362 [S-VII]) *adopted by the General Assembly Sept. 16, 1975:*

The General Assembly,

...Believing that the over-all objective of the new international economic order is to increase the capacity of developing countries, individually and collectively, to pursue their development,

Decides, to this end and in the context of the foregoing, to set in motion the following measures as the basis and framework for the work of the competent bodies and organizations of the United Nations system:

I. International Trade

1. Concerted efforts should be made in favour of the developing countries towards expanding and diversifying their trade, improving and diversifying their productive capacity, improving their productivity and increasing their

export earnings, with a view to counteracting the adverse effects of inflation—thereby sustaining real incomes—and with a view to improving the terms of trade of the developing countries and in order to eliminate the economic imbalance between developed and developing countries....

3. An important aim of the fourth session of the United Nations Conference of Trade and Development, in addition to work in progress elsewhere, should be to reach decisions on the improvement of market structures in the field of raw materials and commodities of export interest to the developing countries, including decisions with respect to an integrated programme and the applicability of elements thereof. In this connexion, taking into account the distinctive features of individual raw materials and commodities, the decisions should bear on the following:

(a) Appropriate international stocking and other forms of market arrangements for securing stable, remunerative and equitable prices for commodities of export interest to developing countries and promoting equilibrium between supply and demand, including, where possible, long-term multilateral commitments;

(b) Adequate international financing facilities for such stocking and market arrangements;

(c) Where possible, promotion of long-term and medium-term contracts;

(d) Substantially improve facilities for compensatory financing of export revenue fluctuations through the widening and enlarging of the existing facilities....

(e) Promotion of processing of raw materials in producing developing countries and expansion and diversification of their exports, particularly to developed countries;

(f) Effective opportunities to improve the share of developing countries in transport, marketing and distribution of their primary commodities and to encourage measures of world significance for the evolution of the infrastructure and secondary capacity of developing countries from the production of primary commodities to processing, transport and marketing, and to the production of finished manufactured goods, their transport, distribution and exchange, including advanced financial and exchange institutions for the remunerative management of trade transactions....

5. A number of options are open to the international community to preserve the purchasing power of developing countries. These need to be further studied on a priority basis. The Secretary-General of the United Nations Conference on Trade and Development should continue to study direct and indirect indexation schemes and other options with a view to making concrete proposals before the Conference at its fourth session.

6. The Secretary-General of the United Nations Conference on Trade and Development should prepare a preliminary study on the proportion between prices of raw materials and commodities exported by developing countries and the final consumer price, particularly in developed countries....

7. Developed countries should fully implement agreed provisions on the principle of standstill as regards imports from developing countries, and any departure should be subjected to such measures as consultations and multilateral surveillance and compensation, in accordance with internationally agreed criteria and procedures. [The principle of standstill as stated in GATT (General Agreement on Tariffs and Trade) holds that developed nations should not subject underdeveloped nations to import controls except under "compelling" circumstances.]

Reduction of Trade Barriers

8. Developed countries should take effective steps within the framework of multilateral trade negotiations for the reduction or removal, where feasible and appropriate, of non-tariff barriers affecting the products of export interest to developing countries on a differential and more favourable basis for developing countries. The Generalized Scheme of Preferences should not terminate at the end of the period of ten years originally envisaged and should be continuously improved through wider coverage, deeper cuts and other measures, bearing in mind the interests of those developing countries which enjoy special advantages and the need for finding ways and means for protecting their interests.

9. Countervailing duties should be applied only in conformity with internationally agreed obligations. [Countervailing duties are taxes levied on imports whose production is subsidized by the producer nation with harmful effects on the market in which they are sold.] Developed countries should exercise maximum restraint within the framework of international obligations in the imposition of countervailing duties on the imports of products from developing countries. The multilateral trade negotiations under way should take fully into account the particular interests of developing countries with a view to providing them differential and more favourable treatment in appropriate cases.

10. Restrictive business practices adversely affecting international trade, particularly that of developing countries, should be eliminated and efforts should be made at the national and international levels with the objective of negotiating a set of equitable principles and rules.

11. Special measures should be undertaken by developed countries and developing countries in a position to do so to assist in the structural transformation of the economy of the least developed, land-locked and island developing countries....

II. Transfer of Real Resources for Financing the Development of Developing Countries and International Monetary Reforms

1. Concessional financial resources to developing countries need to be increased substantially, their terms and conditions ameliorated and their flow made predictable, continuous and increasingly assured so as to facilitate

the implementation by developing countries of long-term programmes for economic and social development. [Concessional financial resources are loans made at less than the current rate of interest, also known as "soft" loans.] Financial assistance should, as a general rule, be untied [that is, the nation receiving the loan is not obligated to spend it in the nation making the loan].

2. Developed countries confirm their continued commitment in respect of the targets relating to the transfer of resources, in particular the official development assistance target of 0.7 per cent of gross national product, as agreed to in the International Development Strategy for the Second United Nations Development Decade, and adopt as their common aim an effective increase in official development assistance with a view to achieving these targets by the end of the decade. Developed countries which have not yet made a commitment in respect of these targets undertake to make their best efforts to reach these targets in the remaining part of this decade.

3. The establishment of a link between the special drawing rights and development assistance should form part of the consideration by the International Monetary Fund of the creation of new special drawing rights as and when they are created according to the needs of international liquidity. [Special drawing rights are a monetary unit developed by the International Monetary Fund to replace gold and the dollar in calculating currency exchanges between nations; *see Historic Documents of 1974, p. 497.]* Agreement should be reached at an early date on the establishment of a trust fund, to be financed partly through the International Monetary Fund gold sales and partly through voluntary contributions and to be governed by an appropriate body, for the benefit of developing countries. Consideration of other means of transfer of real resources which are predictable, assured and continuous should be expedited in appropriate bodies.

4. Developed countries and international organizations should enhance the real value and volume of assistance to developing countries and ensure that the developing countries obtain the largest possible share in the procurement of equipment, consultants and consultancy services. Such assistance should be on softer terms and, as a general rule, untied.

Augmented Lending Resources

5. In order to enlarge the pool of resources available for financing development, there is an urgent need to increase substantially the capital of the World Bank Group, and in particular the resources of the International Development Association, to enable it to make additional capital available to the poorest countries on highly concessional terms.

6. The resources of the development institutions of the United Nations system, in particular the United Nations Development Programme, should also be increased. The funds at the disposal of the regional development banks should be augmented. These increases should be without prejudice to bilateral development assistance flows....

8. The burden of debt on developing countries is increasing to a point where the import capacity as well as reserves have come under serious

strain. At its fourth session the United Nations Conference on Trade and Development shall consider the need for, and the possibility of, convening as soon as possible a conference of major donor, creditor and debtor countries to devise ways and means to mitigate this burden....

9. Developing countries should be granted increased access on favourable terms to the capital markets of developed countries.... Consideration should be given to the examination of an international investment trust and to the expansion of the International Finance Corporation capital without prejudice to the increase in resources of other intergovernmental financial and development institutions and bilateral assistance flows.

10. Developed and developing countries should further co-operate through investment of financial resources and supply of technology and equipment to developing countries....

12. Developed countries should improve terms and conditions of their assistance so as to include a preponderant grant element for the least developed, land-locked and island developing countries....

Increased Liquidity

15. The role of national reserve currencies should be reduced and the special drawing rights should become the central reserve asset of the international monetary system in order to provide for greater international control over the creation and equitable distribution of liquidity and in order to limit potential losses as a consequence of exchange rate fluctuations. Arrangements for gold should be consistent with the agreed objective of reducing the role of gold in the system and with equitable distribution of new international liquidity and should in particular take into consideration the needs of developing countries for increased liquidity.

16. The process of decision-making should be fair and responsive to change and should be most specially responsive to the emergence of new economic influence on the part of developing countries....

17. The compensatory financing facility now available through the International Monetary Fund should be expanded and liberalized. In this connexion, early consideration should be given by the Fund and other appropriate United Nations bodies to various proposals made at the current session—including the examination of a new development security facility—which would mitigate export earnings shortfalls of developing countries, with special regard to the poorest countries, and thus provide greater assistance to their continued economic development....

18. Drawing under the buffer stock financing facility of the International Monetary Fund should be accorded treatment with respect to floating alongside the gold tranche, similar to that under the compensatory financing facility, [That is, if a nation draws from the buffer stock financing facility to stabilize its earnings, its capacity to draw from the International Monetary Fund for other purposes will not be lessened; "tranche" is a technical term referring to the process whereby the IMF determines how much and what type of assistance a country can receive from the fund,

based on its contributions to the fund.] and the Fund should expedite its study of the possibility of an amendment of the Articles of Agreement, to be presented to the Interim Committee, if possible in its next meeting, that would permit the Fund to provide assistance directly to international buffer stocks of primary products.

III. Science and Technology

1. Developed and developing countries should co-operate in the establishment, strengthening and development of the scientific and technological infrastructure of developing countries. Developed countries should also take appropriate measures, such as contribution to the establishment of an industrial technological information bank and consideration of the possibility of regional and sectoral banks, in order to make available a greater flow to developing countries of information permitting the selection of technologies, in particular advanced technologies. Consideration should also be given to the establishment of an international centre for the exchange of technological information for the sharing of research findings relevant to developing countries....

3. All States should co-operate in evolving an international code of conduct for the transfer of technology, corresponding, in particular, to the special needs of the developing countries. Work on such a code should therefore be continued within the United Nations Conference on Trade and Development and concluded in time for decisions to be reached at the fourth session of the Conference, including a decision on the legal character of such a code with the objective of the adoption of a code of conduct prior to the end of 1977. International conventions on patents and trade marks should be reviewed and revised to meet, in particular, the special needs of the developing countries, in order that these conventions may become more satisfactory instruments for aiding developing countries in the transfer and development of technology. National patents systems should, without delay, be brought into line with the international patent system in its revised form.

4. ....Inasmuch as in market economies advanced technologies with respect to industrial production are most frequently developed by private institutions, developed countries should facilitate and encourage these institutions in providing effective technologies in support of the priorities of developing countries.

5. Developed countries should give developing countries the freest and fullest possible access to technologies whose transfer is not subject to private decision.

6. Developed countries should improve the transparency of the industrial property market in order to facilitate the technological choices of developing countries. In this respect, relevant organizations of the United Nations system, with the collaboration of developed countries, should undertake projects in the fields of information, consultancy and training for the benefit of developing countries.

7. A United Nations Conference on Science and Technology for Development should be held in 1978 or 1979 with the main objectives of strengthening the technological capacity of developing countries to enable them to apply science and technology to their own development....

10. Since the outflow of qualified personnel from developing to developed countries seriously hampers the development of the former, there is an urgent need to formulate national and international policies to avoid the "brain drain" and to obviate its adverse effects.

IV. Industrialization

2. ....Developed countries should facilitate the development of new policies and strengthen existing policies, including labour market policies, which would encourage the redeployment of their industries which are less competitive internationally to developing countries, thus leading to structural adjustments in the former and a higher degree of utilization of natural and human resources in the latter. Such policies may take into account the economic structure and the economic, social and security objectives of the developed countries concerned and the need for such industries to move into more viable lines of production or into other sectors of the economy....

4. The Executive Director of the United Nations Industrial Development Organization should take immediate action to ensure the readiness of that organization to serve as a forum for consultations and negotiation of agreements in the field of industry....

6. Developed countries should, whenever possible, encourage their enterprises to participate in investment projects within the framework of the development plans and programmes of the developing countries which so desire; such participation should be carried out in accordance with the laws and regulations of the developing countries concerned....

V. Food and Agriculture

1. The solution to world food problems lies primarily in increasing rapidly food production in the developing countries. To this end, urgent and necessary changes in the pattern of world food production should be introduced and trade policy measures should be implemented, in order to obtain a notable increase in agricultural production and the export earnings of developing countries.

2. To achieve these objectives, it is essential that developed countries and developing countries in a position to do so should substantially increase the volume of assistance to developing countries for agriculture and food production, and that developed countries should effectively facilitate access to their markets for food and agricultural products of export interest to developing countries, both in raw and processed form, and adopt adjustment measures, where necessary.

3. Developing countries should accord high priority to agricultural and fisheries development, increase investment accordingly and adopt policies which give adequate incentives to agricultural producers. It is a responsibility of each State concerned, in accordance with its sovereign judgement

and development plans and policies, to promote interaction between expansion of food production and socio-economic reforms, with a view to achieving an integrated rural development. The further reduction of post-harvest food losses in developing countries should be undertaken as a matter of priority, with a view to reaching at least a 50 per cent reduction by 1985. All countries and competent international organizations should co-operate financially and technically in the effort to achieve this objective. Particular attention should be given to improvement in the systems of distribution of food-stuffs....

5. ...Developed countries should adopt policies aimed at ensuring a stable supply and sufficient quantity of fertilizers and other production inputs to developing countries at reasonable prices. They should also provide assistance to, and promote investments in, developing countries to improve the efficiency of their fertilizer and other agricultural input industries....

6. In order to make additional resources available on concessional terms for agricultural development in developing countries, developed countries and developing countries in a position to do so should pledge, on a voluntary basis, substantial contributions to the proposed International Fund for Agricultural Development so as to enable it to come into being by the end of 1975, with initial resources of SDR 1,000 million. Thereafter, additional resources should be provided to the Fund on a continuing basis....

8. ....In view of the importance of food aid as a transitional measure, all countries should accept both the principle of a minimum food aid target and the concept of forward planning of food aid. The target for the 1975-1976 season should be 10 million tons of food grains. They should also accept the principle that food aid should be channelled on the basis of objective assessment of requirements in the recipient countries....

10. Developed countries and developing countries in a position to do so should provide food grains and financial assistance on most favourable terms to the most seriously affected countries, to enable them to meet their food and agricultural development requirements within the constraints of their balance-of-payments position. Donor countries should also provide aid on soft terms, in cash and in kind, through bilateral and multilateral channels, to enable the most seriously affected countries to obtain their estimated requirements of about 1 million tons of plant nutrients during 1975-1976.

11. Developed countries should carry out both their bilateral and multilateral food aid channelling in accordance with the procedures of the Principles of Surplus Disposal of the Food and Agriculture Organization of the United Nations so as to avoid causing undue fluctuations in market prices or the disruption of commercial markets for exports of interest to exporting developing countries.

12. All countries...should build up and maintain world food-grain reserves, to be held nationally or regionally and strategically located in developed and developing, importing and exporting countries, large enough to cover foreseeable major production shortfalls....

VI. Co-operation Among Developing Countries

1. Developed countries and the United Nations system are urged to provide, as and when requested, support and assistance to developing countries in strengthening and enlarging their mutual co-operation at sub-regional, regional and interregional levels....

2. The Secretary-General, together with the relevant organizations of the United Nations system, is requested to continue to provide support to ongoing projects and activities, and to commission further studies through institutions in developing countries, which would take into account the material already available within the United Nations system, including in particular the regional commissions and the United Nations Conference on Trade and Development, and in accordance with existing subregional and regional arrangements. These further studies, which should be submitted to the General Assembly at its thirty-first session, should, as a first step, cover:

(a) Utilization of know-how, skills, natural resources, technology and funds available within developing countries for promotion of investments in industry, agriculture, transport and communications;

(b) Trade liberalization measures including payments and clearing arrangements, covering primary commodities, manufactured goods and services, such as banking, shipping, insurance and reinsurance;

(c) Transfer of technology.

3. These studies on co-operation among developing countries, together with other initiatives, would contribute to the evolution towards a system for the economic development of developing countries.

VII. Restructuring of the Economic and Social Sectors of the United Nations System

1. With a view to initiating the process of restructuring the United Nations system so as to make it more fully capable of dealing with problems of international economic co-operation and development in a comprehensive and effective manner...an *Ad Hoc* Committee on the Restructuring of the Economic and Social Sectors of the United Nations System, which shall be a committee of the whole of the General Assembly open to the participation of all states, is hereby established to prepare detailed action proposals. The *Ad Hoc* Committee should start its work immediately and inform the General Assembly at its thirtieth session on the progress made, and submit its report to the Assembly at its thirty-first session, through the Economic and Social Council at its resumed session. The *Ad Hoc* Committee should take into account its work, *inter alia,* the relevant proposals and documentation submitted in preparation for the seventh special session of the General Assembly...and other relevant decisions, including the report of the Group of Experts on the Structure of the United Nations System, entitled *A New United Nations Structure for Global Economic Co-operation....*

COLEMAN ON DESEGREGATION

September 4, 1975

James S. Coleman, sociologist and principal author of a landmark 1966 study on school segregation, asserted in a report published Sept. 4 that compulsory busing had failed to integrate 22 of the nation's largest central city school systems. The report, prepared for the Urban Institute by Coleman and two associates, found that white flight from desegregating school systems appeared to reverse the desired effects of court-ordered measures, primarily busing, "intensifying that problem [segregation] rather than reducing it." According to the report, busing creates "a temporary, but fast eroding increase in interracial contact among children in the central city." Coleman predicted that if white reactions against busing continued, full-scale efforts to produce desegregation could, in certain cities "[transform] schools to nearly all black in a single year." Coleman also noted that this trend was most pronounced in major metropolitan areas; similar "resegregation" in smaller school districts was far less acute.

Coleman's findings, first disclosed April 2 in a speech to a professional education group in Washington, formed a somber epilogue to his 1966 report which had frequently been cited by courts to justify school desegregation. The earlier study had concluded that predominantly black schools provided educational opportunities inferior to those offered by predominantly white schools. Black schools had fewer facilities, larger class sizes and—though this conclusion was somewhat impressionistic—"less able" teachers. Students at these schools scored lower than whites on achievement tests and the school dropout rate for blacks was almost double that for whites. Further, although more than ten years had passed since the Supreme Court had declared segregated education unconstitutional (Brown *v.* Board of Education, 1954), *large majorities of white and black children still attended classes where 90 to 100 per cent of their classmates were of the same race. The 1966 study had been ordered by Congress in the 1964 Civil Rights Act.*

Desegregation Strategies

Since Coleman's original report, district-wide busing had become the courts' remedy of choice where deliberately discriminatory policies on the part of school systems could be proved. One strategy developed to counteract segregating effects of housing patterns, by forming metropolitan school districts from predominantly black central city districts and mostly white suburbs, had failed in the courts (see Historic Documents 1974, p. 639), *with the exception of Louisville. Because that city had once operated a dual school system, a U.S. circuit court in 1973 ordered a county-wide desegregation plan to go into effect in 1975.*

By the early seventies, busing to achieve school integration, previously limited to the South, had moved to northern cities as well, often with explosive results. The 1974-75 school year in Boston, that city's first experience with large-scale busing, was marred by riots and demonstrations, largely by whites. In September 1975, the month in which the Urban Institute officially issued Coleman's latest report, Boston was again the scene of anti-busing protests, as was Louisville. National Guard troops were alerted in both cities; in Louisville, armed guards rode school buses to prevent further disruptions.

Reactions to Report

Proponents of school integration interpreted Coleman's report—especially early versions which included more material on policy implications—as a major setback. Roy Wilkins, executive director of the National Association for the Advancement of Colored People (NAACP) told a June 13 news conference that civil rights leaders and educators were "stunned" by Coleman's findings. At its national convention in July, the NAACP drafted a resolution which asserted that Coleman's study neglected "the many variables, e.g., increase in crime, pollution, urban blight, the movement of industry from the cities, which may be correlated with 'white flight' from urban areas." The resolution, adopted unanimously Sept. 8 by the NAACP's national committee, also suggested that Coleman had attempted "to use a research base to espouse racist positions."

Academic experts in race relations attacked Coleman's methods. Sociologists Robert L. Green of Michigan State University and Thomas F. Pettigrew of Harvard told the June press conference, where Wilkins spoke, that Coleman's findings were "premature" and that he had failed to explore other causes for the white exodus to the suburbs. At a Brookings Institution symposium on desegregation and white flight in August, University of Michigan demographer Reynolds Farley disputed Coleman's conclusions. Farley reported that his analysis of data from 125 of the nation's largest cities between 1967 and 1972 showed no "significant relationship between school integration and the white flight."

Coleman Defends Views

Speaking to the question of whether desegregation alone had caused the white exodus from central cities, Coleman told The New York Times *that "in those large cities that didn't desegregate, there was much less increase in the loss of whites over this period than in cities that did desegregate." In a lengthy interview published Aug. 24 Coleman also claimed that his original report in 1966 had not actually stated that equal educational opportunity required racial integration. "We found that children from disadvantaged backgrounds did somewhat better in schools that were predominantly middle-class than in schools that were homogeneously lower class," Coleman said. And, "since a high proportion of blacks come from disadvantaged backgrounds," this particular educational benefit could be achieved "primarily through racial integration." Coleman's view a decade after his original report was that although there were measurable benefits from integrating lower class children with those from the middle class, the advantage was "not very large, not nearly as great as the effects of the child's own home background."*

Coleman told The Times *that although he was still a "great proponent" of integration, he was concerned about the polarization in racial attitudes which busing had produced. The courts, he said, should not attempt to achieve complete desegregation but should limit their efforts to redrawing of school district lines and similar measures to redress segregationist "state actions." As for other solutions, Coleman looked to improved income among blacks, racial intermarriage and changing residential patterns. "It's time," Coleman observed, "we recognized that some problems don't have immediate solutions."*

> *Excerpts from* Trends in School Segregation, 1968-73, *a report prepared for the Urban Institute by James S. Coleman, Sara D. Kelly and John A. Moore and officially released Sept. 4, 1975 (includes revisions published Oct. 22, 1975):*

Introduction

School desegregation has been a major issue in the United States in the 1960's and 1970's. In 1954, the Supreme Court decision in the *Brown* case initiated a set of activities which has culminated in the current desegregation efforts in large cities of the North.

"Desegregation" has meant many things during the period since 1954. The term initially referred to elimination of dual school systems, in which one set of attendance zones was used to assign white children to one set of schools, and a second set of attendance zones was used to assign black children to a different set of schools. The classic and plaintive query of the black mother in the South was why should her child be bused to a school far away, past a nearby school, merely because of the color of his skin. The extent of the change is that the same plaintive query is now heard, primarily from white mothers, primarily in large cities, where busing has begun to be used, not to segregate children by race, but to integrate them.

This change is reflected in a change in meaning of the term desegregation. From the initial meaning of eliminating a system of dual assignment, the term desegregation has come to mean reduction of any segregation within a system, and in the strongest meaning of the term, elimination of any racial imbalance among schools in the system. Thus desegregation, which initially meant abolition of a legally-imposed segregation, has come to mean, in many cases, affirmative integration.

However, except for one court case (in Detroit) which was later reversed in the Supreme Court *[see Historic Documents 1974, p. 639]*, desegregation has not come to mean elimination of racial imbalance between school districts. Nor, except in a few instances, have two or more school systems combined or cooperated to reduce segregation due to residence in different districts. Thus social policy in school desegregation, although changing over time and different in different districts, has almost wholly been confined to desegregation of schools within a school district.

"The Opposite Effect"

Given the policies that have been applied, by local school systems, by the Department of Health, Education, and Welfare, and by the courts, we can ask a series of questions concerning the actual state of racial integration in schools, and recent trends in that state. For actions taken by one branch of government and at one level of government interact with actions taken by individuals and by other branches and levels of government. The actual state of school integration is a result of this interaction. It is different than it would be in the absence of the policies designed to bring about integration; but it is more than a simple consequence of the policies. Indeed, there are numerous examples of government policy in which the result of the interaction between policy and response is precisely the opposite of the result intended by those who initiated the policy. It is especially important in the case of school desegregation to examine this interaction, because many of the actions taken by individuals, and some of those taken by their local government bodies, have precisely the opposite effect on school desegregation to that intended by federal government policy. The most obvious such individual action, of course, is a move of residence to flee school integration.

To examine the status and trends in school segregation, the primary (and virtually singular) data source are the statistical reports collected by the Department of Health, Education, and Welfare [HEW]. Beginning in 1968 and continuing to the present, the Office for Civil Rights (OCR) of HEW has obtained from school systems throughout the United States statistics showing the racial composition of each school in the district, the racial composition of teaching staffs, and related information. The data for 1968, 69, 70, 71, 72, and 73 have been processed and are available for analysis. These data allow a detailed statistical analysis of the status and trends in school segregation by race throughout the United States. They are unique in this; and the opportunity they offer is the opportunity to examine what has actually occurred throughout the period 1968-73 during which there have been policies at local, state, and federal levels, in courts, legislatures, executive and administrative branches of government related to school desegregation. Most of these policies have been aimed at bringing about desegregation, though in a few cases, such as anti-busing actions in Congress, they have been aimed at preventing certain kinds of desegregation.

Not all the questions surrounding school desegregation can be answered by these data, as will be evident in subsequent pages, but some can be, in a more complete way than before.

Limits of Research

Of the various policy aims that have been the objects of school desegregation policies, these statistical data can give evidence only on a subset of the aims. And from this subset, we will examine a still smaller subset: the aim of eliminating racial segregation among schools within a system, whatever its source, and the aim of eliminating racial segregation between districts....

The data do not allow, on the other hand, for a study of segregation among classes within a school (often known as "tracking"), because there is no good information on pupil assignment to classes within a school. The Office for Civil Rights attempted, in its 1971 questionnaire, to obtain these data from school systems, but abandoned the effort in 1972. A more detailed and intensive mode of data collection is probably necessary if data of sufficient quality on assignment within schools are to be obtained.

Policy Implications

No implication is attended by the examination to be carried out below that the policy aim of eliminating segregation among schools with a system, whatever its source, is the "correct" one, and other policies which would either go less far (such as eliminating only that school segregation not due to residence) or further (such as eliminating all segregation among classes within a school) are not correct. The question of what is correct policy depends not only on the implicitly aimed-for social consequences, but upon the realm of legitimate authority of the governmental units applying the policy. This in turn depends on just which individual rights citizens have vested in their government for collective use, through the Constitution and legislative acts. For example, to accomplish the policy aim of eliminating all segregation among schools, whatever its source, the most effective implementation would be federally-specified pupil assignment to schools to create precise racial balance, disregarding school district and state lines. However, such a policy would be using collectively certain rights that individuals have retained to themselves or vested in a more local level of government. As another example, citizens have vested certain authority in the court, such as constitutional protection, but a wider range of authority in elected legislatures. Thus certain policy aims such as elimination of segregation among schools whatever its source may be appropriate for legislative action if it achieves certain desired consequences, but not appropriate for court action, which must be directed not toward achieving desirable social goals, but insuring constitutional protection for all citizens. It is useful also to point out that data such as these which show the indirect and unintended consequences of school desegregation actions may be relevant for certain desegregation decisions, but not for others. They are relevant for an executive or legislative body which is attempting in its action to achieve a desirable social consequence. They are not relevant for a court decision which is acting to insure equal protection under the 14th Amendment.

Despite the fact that only two aims, student desegregation among schools in a district regardless of the source of segregation, and desegregation between school districts, can be studied, there are a number of important questions that can be answered with these data. In particular, these data show the result of government desegregation actions and individual segregating actions taken together, and allow some assessment of the effects of each. In this way, they suggest the limits of government policy, or at least the limits of policies carried out in the conflict mode that has characterized school desegregation policy.

We will begin by examining the state of racial integration among schools within a district in 1968, and then move to an examination of the changes that occurred over the period 1968-1973. What will be of special interest is the differential changes that occurred over that period of time in different kinds of school settings: in different regions of the country, in school districts of different sizes, and in particular large cities. For different things were happening in different places during this time, giving rise to very different trends in different places.

For much of the analysis in examining trends, two separate series must be used. The even years, 1968, 1970, 1972, constitute a census of U.S. school districts, covering 90% of the children in school, and excluding only a few very small districts. The odd years include only a sample of school systems, representing those districts in which most minority pupils are found. When examining trends over time in individual districts the odd-numbered years can be safely included, because each district is either included as a whole, or excluded. But for average across the country, across regions, across states, and even metropolitan areas, the odd years cannot be included, and the series must end with 1972.

The Measures of School Integration

A principal consequence of school desegregation that is of major societal interest is the amount of contact between children of different racial groups. Furthermore, most of the attention has been focussed on the amount of contact of "minority" children (principally blacks and Spanish-American children) with "majority whites." Much attention both of courts and legislatures has been directed toward elimination of patterns that result in schools which are overwhelmingly or predominantly minority.

For these reasons, a directly relevant statistical measure on a school system is the proportion of white children in the same school with the average black child. This gives a measure of the experience of the "average black child" in that school district with whites. A similar measure may be calculated for the proportion of children of each racial group in the school of the average child from each racial group.

This measure is affected not only by the degree of segregation between two groups in different schools in the system, but also by the overall proportion of children in each group. If there are few white children in the system, for example, then whether or not there is the same proportion of whites in each school, the average black child will have a small proportion of white children in his school. Because of this, it is valuable also to have a measure of just how far from an even distribution across the schools the actual distribution is, that is, a measure that is standardized for the number of whites in the system. Such a measure can be constructed, having a value of 0 if there is no segregation between the two groups in question, and a value of 1.0 if segregation is complete.

It is important to note, however, that although the standardized measure is a measure of segregation of children in one group from those of another, it is the unstandardized measure which measures directly the presence of children of a group in schools attended by children of another group. Thus the proportion of white schoolmates for the average black child may be low, as in Washington, D.C., where only 3% of the children are white, without the measure of segregation being especially high.

Integration in 1968

In 1968 in the United States, 15% of the children in public schools (grades 1-12) were black, 6% were of another minority, and 79% were majority whites. But the average black child in U.S. schools went to a school which had 74% black children in it, and only 22% white children (and 4% other minorities). Meanwhile, the average majority white child was in a school which was 93% white and only 4% black.

These numbers show that the interracial contact in American schools in 1968 was quite low. Black children had more contact with whites than whites had with blacks, due to the disparity in overall numbers; but the separation was quite marked. Using the standardized measure described earlier...the segregation between blacks and whites is .72.

Racial Contact and Segregation in the 22 Largest Central-City Districts

...[S]egregation is most pronounced in the largest school districts, which tend to be located in the largest cities. Table 6...shows for the twenty-two largest central-city districts (1972 enrollment) the proportion of schoolmates of the other race in columns 3 and 4, and the measure of segregation in column 5. [Footnote: These 22 largest central city schools districts are classified according to 1972 enrollment and an Office of Education metropolitan status classification. They represent 22 of the 23 largest central city districts; Albuquerque is excluded (the 22nd largest) because it is not among the largest 50 cities in total population.] The first seventeen of these are in the 100,000+ size category;... the last five are in the 25-100,000 class. In only three cities (Columbus, Boston, and San Diego) did the average black child have more than a quarter of his schoolmates white, and in only six cities (Philadelphia, Detroit, Baltimore, New Orleans, New York, and San Francisco, excluding Washington, D.C., which is an aberrant case, almost racially homogeneous) did the average white child have more than 15% of his schoolmates black. This low degree of contact is reflected by the segregation measures, eight of which are .80 or above, and only three of which are below .60. These figures [indicate]...that segregation in large cities in 1968 was not concentrated in any region of the country, but appeared to a similar degree in all regions.

Table 6: Black-White Contact and School Segregation in 1968 For 22 Largest Central City School Districts

(Districts ranked by 1972 Enrollment)

	Proportion		Schoolmates		Segre-
			Whites for average	Blacks for average	gation within
	White	Black	black	white	district
1. New York	.44	.31	.31	.17	.47
2. Los Angeles	.54	.23	.07	.03	.86
3. Chicago	.38	.53	.05	.08	.86
4. Philadelphia	.39	.59	.14	.21	.64
5. Detroit	.39	.59	.13	.20	.66
6. Houston	.53	.33	.06	.04	.89
7. Baltimore	.35	.65	.10	.19	.71
8. Dallas	.61	.31	.06	.03	.91
9. Cleveland	.42	.56	.06	.09	.85
10. Wash., D.C.	.06	.93	.03	.44	.53
11. Memphis	.46	.54	.04	.04	.92
12. Milwaukee	.73	.24	.18	.06	.75
13. San Diego	.76	.12	.26	.04	.66
14. Columbus	.74	.26	.30	.10	.60
15. Tampa	.74	.19	.16	.04	.78
16. St. Louis	.36	.64	.07	.12	.82
17. New Orleans	.31	.67	.09	.19	.72
18. Indianapolis	.66	.34	.22	.11	.67
19. Boston	.68	.27	.27	.11	.60
20. Atlanta	.38	.62	.06	.09	.85
21. Denver	.66	.14	.20	.04	.69
22. San Francisco	.41	.28	.25	.17	.38

Altogether, the picture of racial segregation in U.S. schools in 1968 is one with several components:

1. High segregation in the largest cities of the country, where the proportions of blacks are greatest;

2. Sharply lower segregation in smaller districts everywhere but the South (and slightly lower there), but much smaller proportions of blacks in these smaller districts—except in the South;

3. A large contribution to total segregation in some northern regions due to blacks and whites living in different districts, so that the difference in

total segregation between North and South is considerably less than their difference in segregation within districts;

4. Greater segregation at elementary than at secondary levels, due at least in part to the smaller, more homogeneous areas served by elementary schools;

5. A seeming paradox: the region with the highest degree of segregation, the Southeast, is also the region in which the average white child had the highest proportion of black schoolmates.... The reason, of course, lies in the higher proportion of blacks in the Southeast.

It is clear from these data that by 1968, desegregation of schools was a far from accomplished task in cities and towns of all sizes in the South; but that in the largest cities it was equally high in many places where dual school systems had never existed. But this was the picture in 1968, before the major thrust of desegregation in schools had occurred. The next four years show strong trends toward desegregation. It is these trends to which we now turn.

Trends in Within-System Segregation

Between 1968 and 1972, there was a sharp reduction in black-white segregation in the United States. In 1972, 16% of public school children were black, and 77% white. The average black child in 1972 went to a school that was 61% black (compared to 74% in 1968) and 34% white. And the average majority white child was in a school which was 89% white and 7% black. The comparison below shows the change from 1968 to 1972:

	Proportion		Schoolmates		Black-white segregation	
			whites for average	blacks for average	within	
	white	black	black	white	district	Total
1968	.79	.15	.22	.04	.63	.72
1972	.77	.16	.34	.07	.37	.56

The change from 1968 to 1972 is substantial. Indeed, the average within-district segregation in 1972 between blacks and whites may not be greater than that between some pairs of white ethnic groups. But the change from 1968 to 1972 consists of very different changes in different locales. ...There is a radical drop in the Southeast, from highest at .75 in 1968 to lowest at .19 in 1972. Among the other regions, there are rather large declines in West South Central, Mountain, and Pacific regions. In New England, Middle Atlantic, and East North Central regions, there has been virtually no change in segregation. These trends show that school desegregation during this period (the period during which most desegregation took place) was almost wholly a southern affair, with the far West being the only exception. This concentration in the South was of course largely the consequence of federal requirements, supported by legal decisions in the courts, aimed at removing segregation where dual school systems had not been eliminated.

The graph suggests, however, that the segregation removed was not only that due to dual systems; it was also that due to individual residential location within districts that has led in the North to within-district segregation of .40-.60.... Districts greater than 100,000 in size changed very little; and the amount of change increased steadily as the district size decreased. Among districts 10,000 or below in size, segregation is small indeed, less than .15. [The data show] the very great effectiveness of desegregation policies in the smaller districts (though we have not yet examined the effects on total segregation), and the much lesser effectiveness in the largest districts.

Differential Changes

But these differential changes in different sized districts can be somewhat misleading because of the fact that desegregation policy was located primarily in the South, and most of the blacks in smaller districts were located in the South...great amounts of desegregation did take place in small districts in those regions where small-district segregation existed: the Southeast and West South Central regions: The [data] show in addition several points: even outside the South, some desegregation within districts occurred in the smaller districts, though essentially none in the largest districts. The decline in segregation in Mountain, Pacific, and Border states occurred in the medium and medium-large districts, not the largest. And finally, there was a reduction of segregation in the largest districts in one region only, the Southeast.... In a four-year period (and primarily in the two-year period 1968-70), school districts of all sizes in the Southeast changed from being the most segregated in the nation to among the least segregated.

Changes in Segregation at Elementary and Secondary Levels

...In the two regions where federal and court actions toward integration were strongest, the Southeast and West South Central and in the Border states, the drop in segregation was greater in high schools than in elementary ones. But in each of the other regions the decrease in segregation was greater in elementary schools. In fact, in three of the northern regions (New England, Middle Atlantic, East North Central), segregation *increased* among secondary schools from 1968-70, while no region showed an increase in segregation among elementary schools."

Causes of Increased Segregation

This increase in segregation among secondary schools appears likely to be due to segregating movement among white families with high-school age children. One form of movement that would bring about such an increase is movement from an attendance zone serving a school with many blacks to an attendance zone serving a school with fewer blacks, but within the same school system. Another, and more likely, is differential movement of families with high school age children out of central city districts with many blacks: greater movement out of the district on the part of white families whose children were in largely white schools.

Table 10: Black-White Segregation and Contact of Blacks With Whites in 22 Largest Central City School Districts, 1968-1973

(Districts ranked by 1972 Enrollment)

	Segregation Measures			Proportion white schoolmates for average black		
	1968	1973	change (1973-1968)	1968	1973	change (1973-1968)
1. New York	.47	.50	+.03	.23	.17	−.06
2. Los Angeles	.86	.79	−.07	.08	.09	+.01
3. Chicago	.86	.88	+.02	.05	.04	−.01
4. Philadelphia	.64	.72	+.08	.14	.10	−.04
5. Detroit	.66	.62	−.04	.13	.11	−.02
6. Houston	.89	.73	−.17	.06	.11	+.05
7. Baltimore	.71	.69	−.02	.10	.09	−.01
8. Dallas	.91	.69	−.22	.06	.15	+.09
9. Cleveland	.85	.87	+.02	.07	.05	−.02
10. Washington, D.C.	.53	.49	−.04	.03	.02	−.01
11. Memphis	.92	.31	−.61	.04	.22	+.18
12. Milwaukee	.76	.73	−.03	.18	.18	−.01
13. San Diego	.66	.53	−.13	.26	.34	+.08
14. Columbus	.60	.57	−.03	.30	.30	0
15. Tampa	.78	.04	−.74	.16	.72	+.56
16. St. Louis	.82	.85	+.03	.07	.05	−.02
17. New Orleans	.72	.57	−.15	.09	.09	0
18. Indianapolis	.67	.39	−.28	.22	.35	+.13
19. Boston	.60	.63	+.03	.27	.21	−.06
20. Atlanta	.85	.48	−.37	.06	.09	+.03
21. Denver	.69	.31	−.38	.20	.39	+.19
22. San Francisco	.38	.07	−.31	.26	.28	+.02

...A final picture of change in within-district segregation is the change in the 22 largest central-city districts. The left side of Table 10 shows the segregation of each in 1968 and 1973, together with the change, in column 3. The table shows the dramatic reduction in some southern cities, joined by Indianapolis among the northern cities, Denver and San Francisco in the West. It shows, however, an increase in five northern cities and one Border city, showing that even during this period of major desegregation, and even within the city boundaries themselves, there were residential movements increasing the segregation in these cities. There are no more northern cities within which segregation was reduced than there are within which segregation increased.

But this does not tell the whole story, even before examining the question of segregation between districts. There have been substantial population shifts in some of these cities, and we can ask the question: given these population shifts, to what extent does the decrease in segregation, where it occurred, result in an increase in the proportion of white schoolmates for the average black? The right hand side of Table 10 answers that question by comparing the proportion of white schoolmates for the average black in each of these districts in 1968 with the proportion in 1973. The figures show that although segregation decreased in 16 of the 22 cities, the proportion of white schoolmates for the average black increased only in ten of those sixteen. In four it decreased, and it remained unchanged in two. Thus although segregation was reduced in most of the 22 cities, the contact of the average black with white schoolmates has increased in less than half of them. Only in those cities where desegregation was great did the contact increase substantially—and even in Atlanta, where there was great desegregation, from .85 to .48, the proportion of white schoolmates for the average black child increased only .03, from .06 to .09—because of the great loss in numbers of white school children in Atlanta. (In Atlanta, the white school population in 1973 was only 38% of its size in 1968.)

This last result leads directly to a set of further questions about the larger effects of school desegregation over the 1968-72 or 1968-73 period. The desegregation policies have been confined wholly to within-district desegregation. But as has been evident in earlier examination, there was, especially in the North, substantial segregation due to residence of blacks and whites in different districts—in particular, larger proportions of blacks in large districts and larger proportion of whites in small districts. We can ask, then, what has been the trend, over this period of time, not merely in within-district segregation, as examined so far, but in overall segregation. And we can ask just what has been the change in segregation between districts during this period. Has it increased, as appears likely, and if so, to what extent? Finally, we can ask just what has been the effect of desegregation within districts on the behavior that increases segregation between districts: the movement of whites from districts with high proportions of blacks and low segregation to districts with smaller proportions of blacks.

Factors in Integration

The importance of these questions for educational policy lies in the fact that the distribution of children by race in schools is a result not merely of policies by the Federal government, nor of court orders, nor of policies by state and local governments. It is also the result of individuals' decisions about where they will live, and about whether they will send their children to public or nonpublic schools. Increasingly, as incomes increase, more families have these options open to them, though residential options are more restricted for black families due to residential discrimination. Thus the resulting distribution of children among schools is the result of the interaction of the collective decisions by governmental units and the individual family decisions. In areas of economic policy, governments have recognized that final outcomes are not merely the direct result of a policy, and are as concerned with the indirect effects of a policy as with the direct ones. In areas of social policy that are not economic, they usually have not, and have proceeded blindly, as if the policies directly controlled the final outcomes.

School segregation can show well these indirect effects, because the indirect effects have their principal impact on the distribution of whites and blacks among districts, and thus upon segregation between districts, while the direct effects of government policy have been on the distribution of whites and blacks among schools within a district....

Changes in Total Segregation and Segregation Between Districts

...[W]hile there were reductions in segregation within districts, due to desegregation policies, there were at the same time increases in segregation between districts, due primarily to the movement of white students to districts with few blacks....

The comparisons of elementary and secondary levels in 1968 show that in every region the between-district segregation was greater at the elementary level than at the secondary level. This indicates that elementary children were more residentially segregated by race throughout the country than secondary children were—a strong indication that the greater within-district segregation found earlier at the elementary level is not due merely to the smaller size and greater neighborhood focus of the elementary school, but is due to a greater tendency to segregate at the elementary level. For between-district segregation is not affected by the size of school or the size of its attendance zone, since the district contains both elementary and high schools for those who live within its boundaries.

When we look at changes from 1968 to 1972, there is an increase in every region but Border states at both levels. But the increases vary by region and by level. In all regions, the increase was either the same at both levels or greater at the secondary level.

What appears to occur is this: As suggested by the earlier data, the general movement of whites to areas with few blacks during this period was greater at the secondary level, very likely due to the greater age and affluence of families with children of high school age. The result of that greater movement was to increase the between-district segregation more among secondary school students than among elementary students. Whether the loss of white children when desegregation occurred was greater at secondary than at elementary levels cannot, however, be inferred from these results. That question will be discussed again in a subsequent section.

Within- and Between-District Segregation in Metropolitan Areas

Another way of seeing what is happening in school segregation in the largest metropolitan areas is to examine trends in the segregation between different school districts in the metropolitan area. Most large cities have a separate school district from that of the surrounding suburbs (although many districts in the South are countywide). And just as there is racial segregation due to blacks and whites attending different schools in the same district, there is racial segregation due to blacks and whites living in different districts. Although the former (within-district segregation) has been reduced in a number of cities, especially in the South, the latter (between-district segregation) has been increasing in each of the metropolitan areas containing the 22 largest central city districts except for Washington, D.C....

The data show that already in 1972, the between district segregation is substantial in many of these metropolitian areas.... In Washington, D.C. and San Francisco, it exceeds the segregation within the central city district itself. Furthermore, the projections of these trends to 1976 show that it may be expected to grow substantially in many metropolitan areas. And in two metropolitan areas in addition to Washington and San Francisco—Detroit and Atlanta—it will exceed the within-district segregation of these cities (assuming that the latter does not change). [Footnote: Of course, desegregation within Boston in 1974 and in Detroit in 1975 reduces sharply the within-district segregation in those cities.] These projections indicate that the segregation of the future in metropolitan areas is as much a matter of segregation between districts as it is a matter of segregation within districts.

Washington, D.C.

The Washington metropolitan area, as the one metropolitan area in which between-district segregation is decreasing, is especially interesting, because it illustrates the kind of process that may be expected to occur in many metropolitan areas as an outgrowth of present patterns of within-district school desegregation, and continuing residential segregation. Washington schools became almost completely racially homogeneous (6% white in 1968, and 3% in 1973), with the between-district segregation of whites and blacks increasing (highest among all these cities in 1968 and 1972), until finally the between-district segregation had nowhere to go but down. This pattern, of course, involves the central city first turning nearly all black before there is reduction of the city-suburb segregation.

All the changes described so far suggest a strong individual response to school desegregation on the part of families, especially where desegregation has been great....

The Size of Individual Segregating Responses to Desegregation

It is clear from the preceding sections that there is a segregating process occurring through individual movement, primarily of white families, from schools and districts in which there is greater integration or a greater proportion of blacks, to schools and districts in which there is less integration or a smaller proportion of blacks. The consequences of this, of course, are to partially nullify the effects of school desegregation as carried out by various governmental or legal agencies.

What is not yet clear is whether desegregation itself induces an increased movement of whites from the desegregated district. This is a difficult but important question to answer, because desegregation in particular school districts is a direct outcome of social policy or legal rulings, and it is important to ask whether there are indirect consequences of desegregation itself which partly nullify it, and if so, what the size of this response is under various circumstances....

The question is difficult because casual observation shows that desegregation has evoked differing reactions in different cities, and because desegregation has taken place in very different settings. For example, in many areas of the South, school systems are countywide, encompassing both a city and the surrounding suburbs. Leaving a desegregated system in that setting entails leaving the public school system itself, or a rather distant move (unless adjacent counties have also desegregated, which was a common occurrence in the early 1970's in the South). This, of course, is more difficult than a move to a separate predominantly white suburban school system, which is the common pattern in the North. Another variation is in city size, which creates nearly a qualitative difference in the character of desegregation. For full-scale desegregation in a large city entails mixing student populations that are much more socially distinct and more residentially separated than in small cities.

Limits on Analysis

Additional complications include these:

a. Most desegregation in this period took place in the South, so that except as there was a similar response in those few places in the North that did segregate, the generalization of results to northern cities must remain a question.

b. There was a general loss during this time of whites from central cities, a loss which preliminary analysis indicates is greater as the size of the city is greater, and as the proportion black in the city is greater.

c. The available data show simply the student populations of each race for each of the six years, 1968-73, so that only changes in student populations are directly measured. This is not exactly the same as movement, although something about net movement of a racial group out of the district's schools can be inferred from these measures of gain or loss. [Footnote: Fertility changes among whites also affect the change in numbers of white children in the schools. Fertility of whites in the years preceding this period was declining, which leads to a general decline in white student populations. This affects the constant term in the regression equations, but not the indicated effects of desegregation, unless the decline in white fertility was by some chance greater in those cities that desegregated. The covariance analyses even controls for that possibility....]

d. If there is a loss of whites when desegregation occurs, it is not clear what the time progression of this loss is. When does it begin? Does it continue, and accelerate as the proportion white in the schools declines, or is it a one-time response which does not continue once the degree of desegregation is constant? Or does it in fact reverse itself, with whites returning to the district's schools a year or so after they have desegregated? Initial observation of particular cities which have fully desegregated suggests that a loss due to desegregation begins in the *same* year that desegregation takes place, but its subsequent course is less clear.... The cities to be examined are divided into two groups because of the indications that response to desegregation differs considerably in very large cities from the response in smaller ones: 1)twenty-one of the twenty-three largest districts in the country classified as central-city districts; 2) forty-six of the next forty-seven largest central-city districts....

Results

[The data] suggest that the impact of desegregation is quite large for the largest 21 districts, of the same order of magnitude as other effects; but that for the next 46 cities, the impact is much less, considerably smaller than that due to other factors. (The average loss of whites per year in the largest 21 cities was 5.6% of those present at the beginning of the year, and in the next 46, 3.7%.) It should be remembered also that this is an effect for the year of desegregation only; we do not yet know about subsequent effects....

Differences Among Cities

A next step which can be taken (or two steps at once) is to attempt to consider two more factors which differ among cities which have experienced desegregation, factors which may affect the rate of loss of whites. One is location in the South or North. This factor we do not expect to affect the *general* loss of whites, but only their loss when desegregation occurs. Thus we can ask what is the effect of desegregation of .2 for southern cities, and what is the effect for northern cities? Second, cities differ in the degree to which a suburban alternative is available. Some cities, either because the school district encompasses all or most of the metropolitan area, or because the rest of the metropolitan area is about the same racial composition as the central city, have no such available havens. Thus we can ask how the loss of whites is affected by the racial disparity between city and suburbs, or what we have called in an earlier section, the between-district segregation....

A regression equation which includes these two variables gives results...which allow the following estimates:

Estimated increase in loss of whites in one year as a function of reduction of .2 in index of segregation:

	South	North
Largest 21	6.8%	4.0%
Next 46	1.9%	*

*No reliable estimate for the North can be made since the correlation between Δr and Δrx South is .983 (i.e., nearly all changes in segregation occurred in the South in these 46 cities).

These results show that indeed there has been a greater loss of whites when desegregation has taken place in large southern cities than when it has taken place in large northern cities, with the estimate nearly twice for the southern cities what it is for northern ones. For the smaller cities, there is a smaller loss for the Southern cities though no effect can be estimated for the North in these smaller cities.

For this analysis with the two additional variables, we can also ask what differences in loss of whites are associated with a difference between 0 and 50% black in the city schools and a difference between 0 between-district segregation and .4 between-district segregation.

Estimated increase in loss of whites in one year as a function of 50% black in city school district and between-district segregation of .4:

	50% black	Between-district segregation of .4
Largest 21	2.2%	6.6%
Next 46	1.7%	4.4%

The estimates show that the loss which was earlier seen as resulting from the proportion black in the city can in fact in considerable part be accounted for by the between-district segregation, which is a function of the *difference* between proportion black in the city and that in the suburbs. Thus, the frequent observation that the loss of whites from central-city school systems depends on the existence of suburban systems with high proportions of whites is certainly confirmed by these data. Note, however, that this is a *generally* greater loss of whites under such conditions, not related to the period of desegregation. The question of whether there is additional loss at the time of desegregation can be answered by a further analysis, to which we now turn.

Additional Analysis

In this analysis, we include not only the possibilities that have already been examined, but three others as well:

a) The possibility that there is a generally different loss rate of whites from central cities in the South than in the North, in the absence of desegregation

b) the possibility that desegregation produces different rates of loss when the proportion black in the city differs (interaction between proportion black and change in segregation)

c) the possibility that desegregation produces different rates of loss when the inter-district segregation differs....

The most striking from these illustrative estimates are two effects. One is the large increase in the effect of desegregation on rate of white loss as the proportion black in the district increases. This effect exists in both size cities, though it is more pronounced in the largest 21. There is a similarly large increase in the effect of desegregation on white loss if there are suburban alternatives, as measured by a high value for between-district segregation. In this case, the estimated augmentation effect is high both for the smaller cities and for the large ones.... [T]here is no evidence for a return to city schools in the second or third year after desegregation nor any strong evidence for a delayed loss in the second and third years after desegregation. (There is, however, an indirect effect in subsequent years through the increase in proportion black that occurs during the first year.)

Other Factors In Loss of Whites

There is another more stringent test of segregating effects of school desegregation than those we have examined so far. Each city, with its own particular housing patterns, suburban configurations, crime levels, distribution of racial prejudices, industrial growth or decline, and other factors, has rates of white loss that are specific to it. A rough test of this sort can be carried out for the largest cities by using the white student loss that occurred in each city in 1968-69, before much desegregation occurred in any of these cities (except for Denver), and observing what occurred from 1969 to 1973....

...[W]e [can] compare districts that have desegregated with their own expected rates of loss in the absence of desegregation, to discover any additional loss of whites due to desegregation. This is obviously a much more stringent test because it controls for the general characteristics of each city. The equations used in the analysis include proportion black, logarithm of number of students, and between-district segregation, with the addition of a dummy variable for each city. The results of the analysis give coefficients for Δr of .258 (.058) for the largest wl city districts, and .143 (.034) for the smaller cities. These coefficients correspond closely to those found in earlier equations, indicating that the estimate of the average additional loss rate during desegregation is a stable one, and not due to uncontrolled characteristics of the cities.

Finally, it is possible to carry out a full analysis of covariance [a statistical technique], in which we can not only control for the characteristics of the individual cities, but also estimate the loss rate under desegregation for each city which underwent substantial desegregation. These estimates are probably as close as we can obtain to the actual effects of desegregation on white loss in the year of desegregation. They show that the estimated white loss does vary considerably from city to city, and that the average loss rate specified earlier obscures very different loss rates in different cities....

"Only Estimates"

These rates must still be regarded as only estimates because there are other things varying concurrently with desegregation. For three of these, proportion black, between-district segregation, and size of district, the equation has controlled the general effects; but the specific effects of each of these variables (as well as others) may differ from city to city. Nevertheless, these figures do indicate where the losses due to segregation are especially great, and where they are small....

"A One-Time Effect"

...[I]nsofar as we can determine, the effect of desegregation is a one-time effect. The present data give no good evidence that there is a continuing increased loss of whites from city schools after desegregation has taken place. On the other hand, there are secondary impacts of the initial loss: it increases the proportion of blacks in the schools, which itself increases the rate of loss. And it increases the racial disparity between suburbs and city, also increasing the rate of loss. Yet these are second-order effects and their overall impact is not clear....

The [data] give considerably different projections, but perhaps the most important point is that the impact of desegregation, as a one-time impact, matters less in the overall population composition of the central city than does the continuing loss of whites with or without desegregation....

Less Interracial Contact

These projections show that under all conditions, there is an extensive decline in interracial contact over the ten years. The interracial contact under desegregation is projected to remain higher after 10 years than it was in year 0 under no desegregation; but the projected erosion is great, and especially so under desegregation. Most of the intended benefits of desegregation will have been lost at the end of 10 years—in part to the loss of white students upon desegregation, but due even more to the general loss of white students from city schools, with or without desegregation. Nothing here can be said, of course, about the quality of interracial contact in the two situations.

It is important again to emphasize that these are projections for a hypothetical city with the given characteristics; as is evident in the earlier analysis, the estimated impact of changes in segregation differs from city to city, and in some cities is estimated to be absent.

Altogether, these projections emphasize what data from earlier projections have shown: that the emerging patterns of segregation are those between large cities which are becoming increasingly black, and everywhere else, which is becoming increasingly white. Desegregation in central cities hastens this process of residential segregation but not by a great deal under the conditions specified in the example. It provides a temporary, but fast eroding, increase in interracial contact among children within the central city. In districts with certain characteristics, however, (such as about 75% black and about .4 between-district segregation, as in Detroit, Baltimore, Philadelphia, or Chicago), the impact of full-scale desegregation would be, according to [our] estimates very large, moving the city's schools to nearly all black in a single year. What would happen in a particular city is unknown; the point here is that the white loss depends very much on the extent of desegregation, the proportion black in the central city and the black-white differential between central city and suburb....

Results

Altogether then, what does this analysis of effects of desegregation in cities indicate? Several results can be specified with some assurance:

1. In the large cities (among the largest 22 central city school districts) there is a sizeable loss of whites when desegregation takes place.

2. There is a loss, but less than half as large, from small cities. These differences due to city size continue to hold when the reduced opportunity of white flight into surrounding school districts in the smaller cities is taken into account.

3. The estimated loss is less in northern cities which have undergone desegregation than in southern ones.

4. In addition to effects of desegregation on white loss, both the absolute proportion of blacks in the central city and their proportion relative to those in the surrounding metropolitan areas have strong effects on loss of whites from the central-city district.

5. Apart from their general effect on white loss, a high absolute proportion of blacks in the central city and a high difference in racial composition between the central-city district and the remaining metropolitan area both intensify the effects of desegregation on rates of white loss.

6. When general rates of white loss for individual cities are taken into account, the desegregation effects still hold to about the same degree as estimated from comparisons among cities.

7. No conclusive results have been obtained concerning the direct effect of desegregation in subsequent years after the first. The indirect effect, however, through increasing the proportion black in the city and the segregation between the city district and suburban ones, is to accelerate the loss of whites.

8. The effect of desegregation on white loss has been widely different among different cities where desegregation has taken place.

9. Because, insofar as we can estimate, the loss of whites upon desegregation is a one-time loss, the long-term impact of desegregation is considerably less than that of other continuing factors. The continuing white losses produce an extensive erosion of the interracial contact that desegregation of city schools brings about.

Conclusions

All this leads to general conclusions consistent with those from earlier sections of this examination: that the emerging problem with regard to school desegregation is the problem of segregation between central city and suburbs; and in addition, that current means by which schools are being desegregated are intensifying that problem, rather than reducing it. The emerging problem of school segregation in large cities is a problem of metropolitan area residential segregation, black central cities and white suburbs, brought about by a loss of whites from the central cities. This loss is intensified by extensive school desegregation in those central cities, but in cities with high proportions of blacks and predominantly white suburbs, it proceeds at a relatively rapid rate with or without desegregation.

BURNS ON INFLATION
AND UNEMPLOYMENT
September 19, 1975

Attributing inflation and unemployment to "the changing character of economic institutions" rather than federal policy, Federal Reserve Board Chairman Arthur F. Burns Sept. 19 urged sweeping economic reforms, including government-created low-wage jobs for unemployed persons. Burns told a University of Georgia audience that the nation's two-year recession—the worst since the thirties—and intractable inflation had made conventional economic wisdom "inadequate and out of date." New tactics were needed, Burns said, and he offered a program of his own. In addition to last-resort government employment, he recommended "modest" voluntary wage and price restraints. Sharp cuts in unemployment benefits and other federal welfare programs would finance his proposed jobs program.

The wage and job proposals were considered a major departure for the conservative economist, who had consistently opposed such measures. But the Burns proposals were in line with the deep concern he had previously expressed about the troubled American economy (see Historic Documents 1972, p. 961, Historic Documents of 1974, p. 419)

Between 1973 and August 1975 the U.S. jobless rate had soared from 4.9 per cent to 8.4 per cent, with a high of 9.2 per cent in May 1975. During the summer months the job picture brightened somewhat but only for skilled workers and heads of households. The overall rate was unchanged and for certain groups it was far higher. Department of Labor statistics cited in October by Nat Goldfinger, AFL-CIO director of research, placed unemployment at 20 per cent among construction workers, 21 per cent among teenagers and "close to" 40 per cent for black teenagers. For 20- to

24-year-old men, the figure was 15 per cent, a condition which indicated to Goldfinger that a substantial portion of the population was closed out of the economic "mainstream," probably for three to five years given Ford administration policies. "I think that kind of condition could tear the country apart," Goldfinger said in a Forbes *magazine interview.*

Worry Over Inflation

Despite high unemployment, prices continued to rise. It was this kind of relationship between inflation and unemployment that had alarmed Burns. Traditional economic theories held that wages and prices declined during periods of recession, but during the recent downturn this had not been the case. "Whatever may have been true in the past, there is no longer a meaningful trade-off between unemployment and inflation," Burns said.

Administration proposals to cure unemployment had been outlined the previous February in the fiscal 1976 budget (see p. 83). In his congressional budget message at that time, President Ford had called for rebates of personal and corporation income taxes to stimulate the economy, but he acknowledged that budget measures aimed at controlling deficit spending and conserving energy were likely to prolong 8 per cent unemployment and double-digit inflation into 1976. On Sept. 20 Ford told the editorial board of the Los Angeles Times *that he thought the "emphasis" of efforts to provide more jobs should be "in the private sector." He said he "respectfully disagreed" with Burns' proposal for government-guaranteed jobs.*

Congressional action in 1975 focused on providing temporary relief to the jobless by extending regular benefit periods and by providing benefits for certain workers not previously covered. Congressional efforts to beef up the number of public service jobs made no headway. In November unemployment figures showed that 8.3 per cent of the work force or approximately 8 million Americans were out of work. The totals did not include persons who had given up looking for a job.

Excerpts from address delivered by Arthur F. Burns at the University of Georgia in Athens, Georgia, Sept. 19, 1975:

...Our country is now engaged in a fateful debate. There are many who declare that unemployment is a far more serious problem than inflation, and that monetary and fiscal policies must become more stimulative during the coming year even if inflation quickens in the process. I embrace the goal of full employment, and I shall suggest ways to achieve it. But I totally reject the argument of those who keep urging faster creation of money and still larger governmental deficits. Such policies would only bring us additional trouble; they cannot take us to the desired goal....

The basic cause of the recession was our nation's failure to deal effectively with the inflation that got underway in the mid-sixties and soon became a dominant feature of our economic life. As wage and price increases quickened, seeds of trouble were sown across the economy. With abundant credit readily available, the construction of new homes, condominiums, and office buildings proceeded on a scale that exceeded the underlying demand. Rapidly rising prices eroded the purchasing power of workers' incomes and savings. Managerial practices of business enterprises became lax and productivity languished, while corporate profits—properly reckoned—kept falling. Inventories of raw materials and other supplies piled up as businessmen reacted to fears of shortages and still higher prices. Credit demands, both public and private, soared and interest rates rose to unprecedented heights. The banking system became overextended, the quality of loans tended to deteriorate, and the capital position of many banks was weakened.

During the past year many of these basic maladjustments have been worked out of the economic system by a painful process that could have been avoided if inflation had not gotten out of control. As the demand for goods and services slackened last winter, business managers began to focus more attention on efficiency and cost controls. Prices of industrial materials fell substantially, price increases at later stages of processing became less extensive, and in many instances business firms offered price concessions to clear their shelves. With the rate of inflation moderating, confidence of the general public was bolstered, and consumer spending strengthened....

These self-corrective forces internal to the business cycle were aided by fiscal and monetary policies that sought to cushion the effects of economic adversity and to provide some stimulus to economic recovery.... With the base for economic recovery thus established, business activity has recently begun to improve....

Renewed Inflation

Along with these favorable developments, however, some ominous signs have emerged. Despite an occasional pause, inflation once again may be accelerating. By the second quarter of this year, the annual rate of increase in the general price level was down to 5½ per cent—about half the rate of inflation registered in the same period a year earlier. But over the summer, prices began to rise more briskly.

This behavior of prices is particularly worrisome in view of the large degree of slack that now exists in most of our nation's industries. Price increases in various depressed industries—aluminum, steel, autos, industrial chemicals, among others—are a clear warning that our long-range problem of inflation is unsolved and therefore remains a threat to sustained economic recovery.

History suggests that at this early stage of a business upturn, confidence in the economic future should be strengthening steadily. A significant revival of confidence is indeed underway, but it is being hampered by widespread concern that a fresh outburst of double-digit inflation may before long bring on another recession. By now, thoughtful Americans are well aware of the profoundly disruptive consequences of inflation for our economy. They also recognize that these consequences are not solely of an economic character. Inflation has capricious effects on the income and wealth of a nation's families, and this inevitably causes disillusionment and discontent. Social and political frictions tend to multiply, and the very foundations of a society may be endangered. This has become evident in other nations around the world, where governments have toppled as a result of the social havoc wrought by inflation....

Causes Of Inflation

Our long-run problem of inflation has its roots in the structure of our economic institutions and in the financial policies of our government. All too frequently, this basic fact is clouded by external events that influence the rate of inflation—such as a crop shortfall that results in higher farm prices, or the action of a foreign cartel that raises oil prices. The truth is that, for many years now, the economies of the United States and many other countries have developed a serious underlying bias toward inflation. This tendency has simply been magnified by the special influences that occasionally arise.

A major cause of this inflationary bias is the relative success that modern industrial nations have had in moderating the swings of the business cycle. Before World War II, cyclical declines of business activity in our country were typically longer and more severe than they have been during the past thirty years. In the environment then prevailing, the price level typically declined in the course of a business recession, and many months or years elapsed before prices returned to their previous peak.

Prices and Wages Constant

In recent decades, a new pattern of wage and price behavior has emerged. Prices of many individual commodities still demonstrate a tendency to decline when demand weakens. The average level of prices, however, hardly ever declines. Wage rates have become even more inflexible. Wage reductions are nowadays rare even in severely depressed industries and the average level of wage rates continues to rise inexorably in the face of widespread unemployment.

These developments have profoundly altered the economic environment. When prices are pulled up by expanding demand in a time of prosperity, and are also pushed up by rising costs during a slack period, the decisions of the economic community are sure to be influenced, and may in fact be dominated, by expectations of continuing inflation.

Thus, many businessmen have come to believe that the trend of production costs will be inevitably upward, and their resistance to higher prices—whether of labor, or materials, or equipment—has therefore diminished. Labor leaders and workers now tend to reason that in order to achieve a gain in real income, they must bargain for wage increases that allow for advances in the price level as well as for such improvements as may occur in productivity. Lenders in their turn expect to be paid back in cheaper dollars, and therefore tend to hold out for higher interest rates....

These patterns of thought are closely linked to the emphasis that governments everywhere have placed on rapid economic growth throughout the postwar period. Western democracies, including our own, have tended to move promptly to check economic recession, but they have moved hesitantly in checking inflation. Western governments have also become more diligent in seeking ways to relieve the burdens of adversity facing their peoples. In the process they have all moved a considerable distance towards the welfare state.

In the United States, for example, the unemployment insurance system has been greatly liberalized.... Social security benefits too have been expanded materially, thus facilitating retirement or easing the burden of job loss for older workers. Welfare programs have been established for a large part of the population.... Protection from economic hardship has been extended by our government to business firms as well....

Impact of Government, Business, Labor

Many, perhaps most, of these governmental programs have highly commendable objectives, but they have been pursued without adequate regard for their cost or method of financing.... In the past ten years, Federal expenditures have increased by 175 per cent. Over that interval, the fiscal deficit of the Federal Government, including government-sponsored enterprises, has totalled over $200 billion. In the current fiscal year alone, we are likely to add another $80 billion or more to that total. In financing these large and continuing deficits, pressure has been placed on our credit mechanisms, and the supply of money has frequently grown at a rate inconsistent with general price stability.

Changes in market behavior have contributed to the inflationary bias of our economy. In many businesses, price competition has given way to other forms of rivalry—advertising, changes in product design, and "hard-sell" salesmanship. In labor markets, when an excessive wage increase occurs, it is apt to spread faster and more widely than before, partly because workmen have become more sensitive to wage developments elsewhere, partly also because many employers have found that a stable work force can be best maintained by emulating wage settlements in unionized industries. For their part, trade unions at times seem to attach higher priority to wage increases than to the jobs of their members. Moreover, the spread of trade unions to the rapidly expanding public sector has fostered during recent years numerous strikes, some of them clearly illegal....

The growth of our foreign trade and of capital movements to and from the United States has also increased the susceptibility of the American economy to inflationary trends. National economies around the world are now more closely interrelated, so that inflationary developments in one country are quickly communicated to others and become mutually reinforcing. Moreover, the adoption of a flexible exchange rate system—though beneficial in dealing with large-scale adjustments of international payments, such as those arising from the sharp rise in oil prices—may have made the Western world more prone to inflation by weakening the discipline of the balance of payments. Furthermore, since prices nowadays are more flexible upwards than downwards, any sizable decline in the foreign exchange value of the dollar is apt to have larger and more lasting effects on our price level than any offsetting appreciation of the dollar.

The long-run upward trend of prices in this country thus stems fundamentally from the financial policies of our government and the changing character of our economic institutions. This trend has been accentuated by new cultural values and standards, as is evidenced by pressures for wage increases every year, more holidays, longer vacations, and more liberal coffee breaks. The upward trend of prices has also been accentuated by the failure of business firms to invest sufficiently in the modernization and improvement of industrial plant. In recent years, the United States has been devoting a smaller part of its economic resources to business capital expenditures than any other major industrial nation in the world. All things considered, we should not be surprised that the rate of improvement in output per manhour has weakened over the past fifteen years, or that rapidly rising money wages have overwhelmed productivity gains and boosted unit labor costs of production.

Economic Theories Inadequate

Whatever may have been true in the past, there is no longer a meaningful trade-off between unemployment and inflation. In the current environment, a rapidly rising level of consumer prices will not lead to the creation of new jobs. On the contrary, it will lead to hesitation and sluggish buying, as the increase of the personal savings rate in practically every industrial nation during these recent years of rapid inflation indicates. In general, stimulative financial policies have considerable merit when unemployment is extensive and inflation weak or absent; but such policies do not work well once inflation has come to dominate the thinking of a nation's consumers and businessmen. To be sure, highly expansionary monetary and fiscal policies might, for a short time, provide some additional thrust to economic activity. But inflation would inevitably accelerate—a development that would create even more difficult economic problems than we have encountered over the past year.

Conventional thinking about stabilization policies is inadequate and out of date. We must now seek ways of bringing unemployment down without becoming engulfed by a new wave of inflation. The areas that need to be explored are many and difficult, and we may not find quickly the answers we seek. But if we are to have any chance of ridding our economy of its inflationary bias, we must at least be willing to reopen our economic minds....

Proposed Remedies

First, governmental efforts are long overdue to encourage improvements in productivity through larger investment in modern plant and equipment. This objective would be promoted by overhauling the structure of Federal taxation, so as to increase incentives for business capital spending and for equity investments in American enterprises.

Second, we must face up to the fact that environmental and safety regulations have in recent years played a troublesome role in escalating costs and prices and in holding up industrial construction across our land. I am concerned, as are all thoughtful citizens, with the need to protect the environment and to improve in other ways the quality of life. I am also concerned, however, about the dampening effect of excessive governmental regulations on business activity. Progress towards full employment and price stability would be measurably improved, I believe, by stretching out the timetables for achieving our environmental and safety goals.

Third, a vigorous search should be made for ways to enhance price competition among our nation's business enterprises. We need to gather the courage to reassess laws directed against restraint of trade by business firms and to improve the enforcement of these laws. We also need to reassess the highly complex governmental regulations affecting transportation, the effects on consumer prices of remaining fair trade laws, the monopoly of first-class mail by the Postal Service, and the many other laws and practices that impede the competitive process.

Fourth, in any serious search for noninflationary measures to reduce unemployment, governmental policies that affect labor markets have to be reviewed. For example, the Federal minimum wage law is still pricing many teenagers out of the job market. The Davis-Bacon Act continues to escalate construction costs and damage the depressed construction industry. Programs for unemployment compensation now provide benefits on such a generous scale that they may be blunting incentives to work. Even in today's environment, with about 8 per cent of the labor force unemployed, there are numerous job vacancies—perhaps because job seekers are unaware of the opportunities, or because the skills of the unemployed are not suitable, or for other reasons. Surely, better results could be achieved with more effective job banks, more realistic training programs, and other labor market policies.

Full Employment the Ultimate Objective

I believe that the ultimate objective of labor market policies should be to eliminate all involuntary unemployment. This is not a radical or impractical goal. It rests on the simple but often neglected fact that work is far better than the dole, both for the jobless individual and for the nation. A wise government will always strive to create an environment that is conducive to high employment in the private sector. Nevertheless, there may be no way to reach the goal of full employment short of making the government an employer of last resort. This could be done by offering public employment—for example, in hospitals, schools, public parks, or the like—to anyone who is willing to work at a rate of pay somewhat below the Federal minimum wage.

With proper administration, these public service workers would be engaged in productive labor, not leaf-raking or other make-work. To be sure, such a program would not reach those who are voluntarily unemployed, but there is also no compelling reason why it should do so. What it would do is to make jobs available for those who need to earn some money.

It is highly important, of course, that such a program should not become a vehicle for expanding public jobs at the expense of private industry. Those employed at the special public jobs will need to be encouraged to seek more remunerative and more attractive work. This could be accomplished by building into the program certain safeguards—perhaps through a Constitutional amendment—that would limit upward adjustment in the rate of pay for these special public jobs. With such safeguards, the budgetary cost of eliminating unemployment need not be burdensome. I say this, first, because the number of individuals accepting the public service jobs would be much smaller than the number now counted as unemployed; second, because the availability of public jobs would permit sharp reduction in the scope of unemployment insurance and other governmental programs to alleviate income loss. To permit active searching for a regular job, however, unemployment insurance for a brief period—perhaps 13 weeks or so—would still serve a useful function.

Wage and Price Controls

Finally, we also need to rethink the appropriate role of an incomes policy in the present environment. Lasting benefits cannot be expected from a mandatory wage and price control program, as recent experience indicates. It might actually be helpful if the Congress renounced any intention to return to mandatory controls, so that businesses and trade unions could look forward with confidence to the continuance of free markets. I still believe, however, that a modest form of incomes policy, in some cases relying on quiet governmental intervention, in others on public hearings and the mobilization of public opinion, may yet be of significant benefit in reducing abuses of private economic power and moving our nation towards the goal of full employment and a stable price level.

Structural reforms of our economy, along some such lines as I have sketched, deserve more attention this critical year from members of the Congress and from academic students of public policy than they are receiving. Economists in particular have tended to concentrate excessively on over-all fiscal and monetary policies of economic stimulation. These traditional tools remain useful and even essential; but once inflationary expectations have become widespread, they must be used with great care and moderation.

This, then, is the basic message that I want to leave with you: our nation cannot now achieve the goal of full employment by pursuing fiscal and monetary policies that rekindle inflationary expectations. Inflation has weakened our economy; it is also endangering our economic and political system based on freedom. America has become enmeshed in an inflationary web, and we need to gather our moral strength and intellectual courage to extricate ourselves from it....

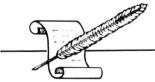
October

MOYNIHAN ON DEMOCRACY
October 3, 1975

American diplomacy at the United Nations turned toward tactics of confrontation at the 30th session of the General Assembly, which began Sept. 16. In a series of unusually blunt speeches Ambassador Daniel Patrick Moynihan, U.S. Representative to the United Nations, challenged anti-Western biases of the Third World bloc, continuing a trend begun by his predecessor John Scali. Near the end of the stormy 29th session, during which a number of actions had been approved over U.S. objections (see p. 325), Scali had characterized the U.N. coalition of Latin, Asian and African states as "a tyranny of the majority." But while Scali's address was followed immediately by supporting speeches from representatives of other Western nations, Moynihan's aggressive defense of democracy often discomfited U.S. allies and, in some instances, apparently embarrassed the State Department. The major complaint against Moynihan involved the ambassador's provocative style which, it was feared, precluded the possibility of compromise on many issues.

Perhaps Moynihan's most controversial statement was his endorsement of a New York Times editorial calling Uganda's president Idi Amin a "racist murderer." The epithet referred to charges that since seizing power in 1971 Amin had systematically used murder to silence political opponents and rid that African country of Indian residents. The International Commission of Jurists had charged that the Amin regime was responsible for the deaths of at least 25,000 and possibly as many as 250,000 persons.

Three days before Moynihan's speech, Amin, while visiting the U.N., had urged the "extinction of Israel as a state." In a message read to the General

Assembly by the Ugandan representative, Amin, who was present at the session, had also advised Americans to "rid their society of the Zionists" who, he claimed, controlled banking, media and other key U.S. institutions.

Moynihan's reply to Amin came in an address on Oct. 3 in San Francisco at the annual AFL-CIO convention. In the context of a broad discussion of what he considered the decline of the democratic ideal, Moynihan said he considered it "no accident" that the Ugandan leader had become head of the Organization of African Unity (OAU), whose member states were largely non-democratic. Moynihan was later criticized for his charge against the OAU because Amin had actually assumed leadership of the African organization in July when the post went by normal rotation to Uganda.

African, Arab Response

Moynihan's remarks stirred angry reactions among African and Arab representatives at the U.N. Although many African leaders were known to be privately critical of Amin, they were offended by Moynihan's attack on the OAU, particularly since the organization had resisted pressures to adopt an anti-Israel resolution at its meeting the previous July. Tiamiou Adjibade of Dahomey, a spokesman for the 46-member African bloc at the U.N., told the General Assembly that if the U.S. representative confused his work in the United Nations with the defense of Zionism, he should "go to Israel as soon as possible." Speaking on behalf of the 20 members of the Arab League, Libyan delegate Mansur R. Kikhja deplored Moynihan's "uncivil attacks" and repeated Amin's assertion that the United States was in "the total grip of international Zionism."

Administration Support

After the San Francisco speech, the White House let it be known that the President felt that Moynihan had "said what had to be said," but journalists reported that Secretary of State Henry A. Kissinger was angered by the tone of the speech, which had not been cleared in advance with Washington. A month later, after Moynihan called a U.N. anti-Zionism resolution "obscene" (see p. 825), the British representative at the U.N., Ambassador Ivor Richard, complained publicly that Moynihan's behavior had the effect of "encouraging enemies, irritating friends and isolating [his] country." Because diplomatic observers assumed that Richard's remarks were cleared with the British Foreign Office which, in turn, would have informed the State Department, the incident was widely interpreted as an indirect admonition of Moynihan by State. Moynihan threatened to quit and decided to stay on only after a White House meeting Nov. 24 produced a statement that "The President and Secretary Kissinger encouraged Ambassador Moynihan to continue to speak out candidly and forcefully on major issues coming before the U.N."

Moynihan's Background

Moynihan, a former Harvard professor and adviser to four Presidents, was no stranger to controversy. In 1965, when he was Lyndon Johnson's assistant secretary of labor, Moynihan had been attacked by liberals and civil rights leaders for writing a report that attributed social instability among blacks to the prevalence of broken homes in the black population. Five years later, in 1970, Moynihan drew fire for a memorandum to President Richard M. Nixon in which he advised a policy of "benign neglect" concerning "the issue of race" in view of the improving status of blacks, on the one hand, and the concurrent rise of black extremism on the other.

From 1971 to 1973 Moynihan had maintained a low profile as U.S. ambassador to India. But during the last months of his two-year tour in that country, he wrote a lengthy account of what he saw as the "massive failure of American diplomacy" to deal effectively with Third World insults and demands for assistance. He was appointed to the U.N. post after this analysis appeared in the March issue of Commentary. *"It is past time," he wrote, "we ceased to apologize for an imperfect democracy.... It is time we asserted that inequalities in the world may be not so much a matter of condition as of performance."*

> *Excerpts from speech of Daniel Patrick Moynihan, U.S. Representative to the United Nations, delivered Oct. 3, 1975, in San Francisco:*

...In his statement yesterday [AFL-CIO president] George Meany said that the "nation has never suffered more foreign policy defeats than it has in the past year." If what he means is "never recently,"—we can agree, can we not, that when the British burned Washington it was a sort of setback, and there have been others—if he means "never recently" then I think most of us would agree. But here again there is a crisis of confidence, for many Americans would not at all agree with the list of events which President Meany regards as defeats. Some would see them as victories, some as standoffs, some as opening rather than concluding events.

Saying that, I agree with George Meany far more than I disagree with him. Let me say here that I would not agree that the conclusion of the Helsinki Conference on Security and Cooperation in Europe was a defeat. In the terms that President Ford spelled out at the Conference, in the terms in which Secretary Kissinger carried out those negotiations, the Conference was something that had to come, and came as much on our terms as the realities of power allowed. *(See p. 559)*

It is these realities that assail us, and to suppose otherwise is to court self-deception and even worse setbacks.

The realities of power are in the first instance economic. The industrial world—the United States included—is in the midst of the worst recession since the 1930's. This time, however, we suffer not only from internal disorders, but from external attack. The oil producing nations of the world have brought about—without retaliation or redress—an increase in the price of energy that has proved jolting to the most advanced economies of the world and devastating to the least advanced.

If, as I think, it is a sign of strength that such measures can occur without retaliation—when America and its allies speak about respecting the territorial integrity and independence of other countries, we mean it—it is no less a sign of weakness that such measures can have such effects. The rest of the world cannot but note.

Democracy Assailed

Nor fail, I fear, to gloat. For this is the second reality of power that assails us, the reality, as George Meany said yesterday, that "Democracy has come under increasing attack."

It is hard, I suppose, for us to understand this. Too easy perhaps to ascribe it to the wrong doings of democracy itself, to mistakes that we have made that have brought on inevitable, justified, even admirable retaliation. Again, this crisis of confidence: the trouble we have in trusting ourselves. But let me say that we distrust ourselves to our utmost period. For democracy is indeed under increasing attack, the West is under increasing attack, and increasingly the attack succeeds. Increasingly the attack is *seen* to succeed.

I see it every day at the United Nations. Every day, on every side, we are assailed. There are those in this country whose pleasure, or profit, it is to believe that our assailants are motivated by what is wrong about us. *They* are wrong. We are assailed because of what is right about us. We are assailed because we are a democracy.

A quarter century ago the future looked good enough for democracy, at least in most parts of the world. The old democracies of Europe were reviving. Old autocracies such as Japan seemed to be following the evolution that had given way to democracy in Western Europe and would have done in Eastern Europe had not the Bolsheviks seized power. One by one the colonies of Africa and Asia were becoming independent. And one by one they were establishing democratic regimes.

All this has changed. One by one the new democracies have disappeared, and even some of the old ones. President Meany included India in his list of recent disasters in American foreign relations, and again he was right to do so. Not that events there were the result of anything America did, but simply because of what those events do to America. When half the people in the world with democratic rights lose those rights—lose them in a sequence of government repression that began, typically, with the breaking of a strike and the imprisonment of trade union leaders—then the American democracy suffers, too. It is too soon to write off India, but hardly too soon to take note of what is happening there. [Indian Prime Minister Indira Gandhi June 26 declared a national state of emergency in India. The action suspended civil rights and authorized military operations to maintain public order.]

And elsewhere. In the United Nations today there are in the range of two dozen democracies left. Totalitarian Communist regimes and assorted ancient and modern despotisms make up all the rest. And nothing so unites these nations as the conviction that their success ultimately depends on our failure.

Amin Criticized

It is no accident that on Wednesday, "His Excellency Field Marshal Al Hadji Idi Amin Dada, President of the Republic of Uganda"—to give him his U.N. title—called for "the extinction of Israel as a state." And it is no accident, I fear, this "racist murderer"—as one of our leading newspapers called him this morning—is head of the Organization of African Unity. For Israel is a democracy and it is simply the fact that despotisms will seek whatever opportunities come to hand to destroy that one which threatens them most, which is democracy. At this very moment in New York, for example, Mr. Leonard Garment, Counsel to the U.S. Delegation, is fighting back the latest such move, a resolution now before the Third Committee which equates "Zionism" with "racism", calling for the eradication of both. I put it to you that this outrage is likely as not to be voted for by a majority of the membership of the United Nations.

I hope and trust that members of the Organization of African Unity will disavow Amin and all he stands for. Certainly it was African countries at the last OAU meeting in Kampala, which broke the gathering force of the movement to suspend Israel from the General Assembly. Just Wednesday that issue was quietly put to rest. But then hours later Amin commenced yet a new campaign.

There will be more campaigns. They will not abate, for it is sensed in the world that democracy is in trouble. There is blood in the water and the sharks grow frenzied. They commence, of course, to consume one another and the chaos mounts. Let me offer you a statistic. There are 142 members of the U.N. We calculated last evening for the benefit of this occasion just what was the length of time in which the typical U.N. member had enjoyed a relatively stable government without violent overthrow or usurpation, including revolution. We put ourselves down for 199 years, Belgium for 144, France for 127, Australia for 74. And what did the median come out to be? 11 years. 11 years since the last overthrow of government in the median member of the U.N. In a world where technologists in the field of nuclear energy measure the length of storage of reactor wastes in what they have come to term "geological time": five thousand years, 30,000 years. Such are the issues we are handling with governments which can not survive even eleven years.

Communist Influence

A year ago I was far more optimistic about all this than I am today. It seemed to me then that many of the new countries of the world had inherited, mostly from Western Europe, a decent and honorable tradition of democratic socialism which if it had a certain anti-American bias was nonetheless a tradition we could work with and respect. A year later I am not at all sure about that. Such has been the success of Communist arms, Communist intrigue, Communist treachery in Asia and Africa that the reputation of democracy in those regions has all but collapsed.

Certainly it has done so where I work. There is much that the United Nations has done in its 30 years that is honorable and good. But it has done damn all for democracy. All that talk of freedom gets frighteningly close to the Orwellian inversion: War is Peace; Slavery is Liberty; Injustice is Justice. What the U.N. has done is simply to extend the nation state to the farthest reaches of the inhabited world. Now that was going to happen, I assume, and the U.N. is hardly to blame if it happened under its auspices. But let there be no illusions: Most of the new states and most of the old ones have ended up enemies of freedom as we would know it, as we have inherited it, and as we have tried to preserve it.

What is to be done? as someone once said. This it seems to me obvious enough. It is to set for ourselves the agenda the labor movement has set at home and abroad—and not least to see the connection between the two.

Let me speak to the issues in which is now my field, that of foreign affairs, and especially that aspect of foreign affairs which tends to legitimate or delegitimate democratic practices and private institutions.

If we have fallen back, we have also shortened our lines; and if we have taken more than a little punishment, it may be it has served to wake us up to what is going on.

What is going on is a systematic effort to create an international society in which government is the one only legitimate institution. The old dream of a new international economic order in which one single nation dominated is being replaced by a not different vision of the domination of a single idea, the idea of the all-encompassing state, a state which has no provision for the liberties of individuals, much less for the liberties of collections of individuals, such as trade unions.

American Response

I think we are in a position to respond to this. Everyone has been talking about the new international order, and as the United States has already indicated in Secretary Kissinger's address on September 1, we stand ready to participate in the creation of a world from which starvation would be eliminated and in which everyone would be assured a basic minimum of economic sustenance. [See p. 587.] It must be clear, however, that the United States doesn't wish to do this because we accept responsibility for the economic condition of the Third and Fourth Worlds. We repudiate the charge that we have exploited or plundered other countries, or that our own prosperity has ever rested on any such relation. We are prosperous because we are—or were—an energetic and productive people who have lived under a system which has encouraged the development of our productive capacities and energies. We also consider that we have been reasonably helpful and generous in our economic dealings with other countries. We do not, then, wish to contribute toward the creation of a new international order out of guilt or as a matter of reparations. The idea of reparations implies a debt incurred as a result of past wrongs. The United States acknowledges no such debt.

What we acknowledge is a common humanity and a common concern arising out of our own sense of what we can and ought to do.

Not guilt, then, and not fear. We are moved as a matter of free choice and out of a growing willingness in our culture to broaden the boundaries of fellow feeling beyond those which define the territories of the nation-state. We elect to act because the plight of people in other countries increasingly presses itself upon us and we wish to take whatever effective measures we can to alleviate suffering that can be alleviated and to eliminate such causes of suffering as can be eliminated.

Conditions of U.S. Assistance

But it is important to stress—as important, it seems to me, as any thing can be—that this willingness of ours has as its object the fate of *individuals.* Ours is a culture based on the primacy of the individual—the rights of the individual, the welfare of the individual, the claims of the individual against those of the state. We have no wish, therefore, to participate in any new economic arrangements whose beneficiaries will be the state rather than the individual, leaders rather than the individual, politicians and bureaucrats rather than the individual. If there is to be an increased flow of wealth to the countries of the South, the United States will insist that it be channeled into the pockets of individuals and not into Swiss bank accounts, and we will insist that necessary precautions be taken to that effect.

The United States will also insist on another point. We will insist on broadening the definition of welfare to include not only the economic condition of the individual but his political condition as well. If there is to be a new international order, the United States will insist that the right to a minimum standard of political and civil liberty is no less fundamental than the right to a minimum standard of material welfare. President Ford affirmed our commitment to universal human rights at Helsinki, and we reaffirm it here.

The new nations when we say things like that respond, and understandingly in some cases, that we talk about individual rights but they care about economic rights. There is, or so it seems to me, one indisputably valid response to this point. It is for the United States Government to put the utmost emphasis, in multilateral relations and in bilateral relations, on the single most important area where individual rights and economic rights can be seen to merge, to complement one another, to reinforce one another, and that is the area of trade union rights, and trade union responsibilities. Things we know and believe-in things. Rights that are here for any honest eye to see. Rights to be seen in at least half the world, and maybe more. For one of the lessons of the 20th century is that democratic trade unions can be a lot tougher than democratic governments....

FINAL WATERGATE REPORT
October 16, 1975

The Watergate Special Prosecution Force published Oct. 16 a summary report on its 28-month investigation of the major political scandal of the century, the illegal activities connected with the 1972 presidential campaign of Richard M. Nixon (see Watergate-related entries in Historic Documents 1973 and 1974). *The 277-page report recommended a number of changes in federal statutes and government practices. But it added no new facts to the public record and left unanswered several critical questions about the scandal.*

Adverse press commentary focused on the failure of the prosecutor's office to ascertain who was responsible for erasing 18½ minutes of a taped conversation between Nixon and H. R. Haldeman, his chief of staff (see Historic Documents of 1974, p. 23). *The conversation had taken place June 20, 1972, three days after the break-in at the Democratic National Committee headquarters.*

Favorable comment stressed the accomplishments of the Watergate prosecutor: in two and one-half years the office had helped force Nixon's resignation (see Historic Documents of 1974, p. 683) *and had won the convictions of 50 men, including two former Attorneys General (John N. Mitchell and Richard Kleindienst), and 19 corporations.*

In its most far-reaching recommendation, the report said Congress should consider passage of a constitutional amendment to clarify whether or not an incumbent President could be indicted and, if so, for what kinds of crimes. Calling its proposals "modest," the prosecution force also recommended closer scrutiny of domestic intelligence-gathering agencies, disclosure of the standards which currently govern the President and Attorney General in ordering warrantless foreign intelligence searches and seizures, including electronic surveillance, and a prohibition against naming persons who took leading roles in presidential campaigns as heads of federal law enforcement agencies. (Mitchell, convicted for obstructing justice and committing other crimes, was Nixon's campaign manager in 1968 and 1972.)

Omissions From Report

The report omitted all evidence which could not support an indictment. These omissions represented a departure from the stated intention of the first Watergate prosecutor, Archibald Cox, to make the final report a vehicle for full disclosure of the results of his inquiry. In March 1973 then prosecutor-designate Cox told the Senate Judiciary Committee he thought it was "important not only that prosecutions be brought...but that the reasons for not bringing other prosecutions or...for not indicting other figures, the exculpatory facts, if there were any...all those things [should] be included certainly in the final report." However, the third special prosecutor, Henry S. Ruth Jr., who was responsible for issuing the report, held that publication of damaging evidence would be improper because no legal action was contemplated and the individuals implicated would never have an opportunity to answer the charges in court. Ruth's decision was in accord with accepted legal practice.

Besides the question of responsibility for the 18½-minute gap, the report referred to several other questions which had not been resolved and which were apparently to be left unanswered. These included inquiries into:

● The Nixon administration's 1971 antitrust settlement with the International Telephone and Telegraph Corp. ITT had made a sizable contribution to help finance the Republican convention of 1972. (See Historic Documents of 1974, p. 407.)

●Unreported cash contributions totaling $100,000 made in 1970 by billionaire Howard Hughes to Nixon associate C. G. (Bebe) Rebozo. Rebozo insisted he had returned the cash to Hughes in 1973.

● Wiretaps, ordered by the White House, on government officials and newsmen between 1969 and 1971.

The October report was originally intended to be the final summary of the special prosecutor's work but was designated an "interim" report after Attorney General Edward H. Levi, early in October, ordered that the office continue in existence, as an independent arm of the Justice Department, to deal with appeals and a few remaining investigations.

Excerpts from the Watergate Special Prosecution Force Report, *published Oct. 16, 1975:*

Brief History of the
Watergate Special Prosecution Force

Agents of the Committee to Re-Elect the President (CRP) broke into the Democratic National Committee headquarters in the Watergate office complex on June 17, 1972. The resulting conspiracy, burglary, and wiretapping charges produced convictions of seven men the following January in a trial before Chief Judge John J. Sirica of the U.S. District Court for the District of Columbia. By that time various public allegations had created suspicions that high-level officials of CRP and the Nixon Administration had engaged in a variety of illegal activities connected with the 1972 campaign, of which the Watergate break-in was only one. As a result, the Senate established its Select Committee on Presidential Campaign Activities, chaired by Senator Sam J. Ervin, Jr.

On March 19, 1973, before the Select Committee hearings started, James W. McCord, one of the convicted Watergate burglars, wrote an explosive letter to Judge Sirica who was to sentence him 4 days later. McCord's letter, revealed in open court, claimed that Government witnesses had committed perjury during his trial and that the trial had failed to identify others involved in the Watergate operation. Throughout April, news accounts based on the reopening of the criminal investigation, the initial Select Committee inquiries and press investigations—as well as public statements by the Administration—increased public doubt about the conduct of high White House and campaign officials. These doubts heightened at the end of April with the dismissal of the counsel to the President [John W. Dean III], and the resignation of the Attorney General [John N. Mitchell], the acting director of the Federal Bureau of Investigation [L. Patrick Gray III], and two of the President's closest aides [John D. Ehrlichman and H. R. Haldeman]. Further public concern arose about the desirability of the U.S. Attorney's office continuing its investigation, especially in light of publicly assumed interference from Justice Department and White House officials. During his confirmation hearings before the Senate Judiciary Committee, the newly designated Attorney General, Elliot Richardson, pledged to appoint an independent special prosecutor to take over the inquiry.

Charge to Prosecutor

With the approval of the Judiciary Committee, Richardson and Archibald Cox, his ultimate choice for the post of Special Prosecutor, agreed upon the terms of Cox's charter. The resulting statement, entitled "Duties and Responsibilities of the Special Prosecutor," became part of Department of Justice regulations and defined the Special Prosecutor's jurisdiction in these terms:

> The Special Prosecutor shall have full authority for investigating and prosecuting offenses arising out of the unauthorized entry into Democratic National Committee headquarters at the Watergate, all offenses arising out of the 1972 presidential election for which the Spe-

cial Prosecutor deems it necessary and appropriate to assume responsibility, allegations involving the President, members of the White House
staff, or presidential appointees, and any other matters which he consents to have assigned to him by the Attorney General.

Richardson also pledged to Cox adequate funding, complete independence in hiring and supervising his staff, and sole responsibility for
contesting any "executive privilege" or "national security" claims which
might be raised to prevent the acquisition of evidence. Cox could decide
whether to seek grants of immunity (subject to the Attorney General's
approval as required by statute), and whether and to what extent he would
inform or consult with the Attorney General about his work. Richardson
further agreed that he would not "countermand or interfere with the
Special Prosecutor's decisions or actions," and that he could remove Cox
from office only for "extraordinary improprieties." On May 25, 1973, Cox
was sworn in as Special Prosecutor and the Watergate Special Prosecution
Force (WSPF) was officially established within the Department of Justice.

May 25—October 20, 1973

Richardson had told the Senate Judiciary Committee that Cox's jurisdiction would include the Watergate case, the activities of alleged political
saboteur Donald Segretti, the office burglary of Dr. Lewis Fielding, Daniel
Ellsberg's psychiatrist, and illegal activity involving 1972 campaign contributions that Cox chose to investigate. Richardson later referred to Cox
certain allegations, including possible perjury in Senate hearings relating to
Administration handling of an antitrust suit against the International
Telephone and Telegraph Corporation (ITT). When the Justice
Department's Criminal and Tax Divisions were conducting any investigations regarding matters related to his jurisdiction, they would inform
the Special Prosecutor and ascertain if he wanted to take responsibility. In
addition, after initial discussions and inquiries, the Special Prosecutor
arranged to use the FBI for investigative work and to send investigative requests directly to the Bureau without transmittal through the Attorney
General.

One of Cox's first problems was the possible impact on his work of the
Senate Select Committee's televised hearings, which had begun about a
week before he took office. Although the Committee and the Special
Prosecutor's office were investigating many of the same allegations about
Watergate and other Nixon Administration activities, each meant to use
the information it would gather for a different purpose, in accord with its
particular responsibilities. The Committee sought to bring facts before the
public in order to propose legislative remedies for any abuses it might uncover; the Special Prosecutor had the responsibility of investigating and
prosecuting specific criminal charges. The danger existed that legislative
hearings might frustrate the criminal proceedings. For example, in order to
obtain the testimony of several important witnesses, the Committee
planned to immunize them, thus barring any prosecution that could be
shown to be based on any direct or indirect use of their Senate testimony. In

addition, the televised hearings might create adverse publicity about potential defendants in criminal trials, especially a Watergate trial that then seemed likely to begin in a few months. For these reasons, Cox requested that the Committee postpone its hearings; the Committee quickly rejected this request.

Before two Committee witnesses were immunized, Cox acted to reduce the chance that a future criminal case against either of them would be "tainted" by evidence obtained as a result of their testimony. He arranged to have the evidence already gathered against each of them deposited under seal with the District Court before they testified at the Committee hearings. And, to minimize possible pretrial publicity and ensure maximum fairness to potential defendants, he [Cox] sought a court order that the Committee's grants of immunity be conditioned on its holding hearings in executive session, or at least without radio and television coverage. However, Judge Sirica concluded that he had no power to issue such an order to a Congressional committee, and Cox decided not to appeal the decision, since a prolonged conflict with the Committee would have kept both groups from their investigative work and the likelihood of a successful appeal was doubtful. In the end, the continuation of public hearings through the summer of 1973, among other benefits, brought to public attention testimony relating to alleged White House involvement in the Watergate cover-up and other crimes and thereby helped create for the Special Prosecutor's investigation a base of public and Congressional support that did much to force the reestablishment of WSPF after the President's attempt to abolish it later that year.

This early conflict over the possible harm that the Committee's televised hearings would inflict on the cover-up investigation soon subsided. In other WSPF matters, the Committee's staff had commenced its investigation some months before the prosecutors were appointed and had gathered much information of value to WSPF. Most of this information was placed on computer tapes, which the Committee agreed to provide to the prosecutors. WSPF decided to undertake a similar computer operation, and arranged to use the same Library of Congress computer system so that information gathered from other sources could be cross-referenced with that obtained by the Committee.

Meanwhile, Cox was selecting a staff that eventually numbered, in permanent positions, 37 attorneys, 16 other professionals, and 32 supporting personnel by August 1974. The bulk of the investigative work was divided among five task forces, each responsible for a broad area of investigation—the Watergate break-in and cover-up; the allegations about ITT and possible perjury during 1972 Senate hearings; the activities of the White House "Plumbers" group, including the break-in at Ellsberg's psychiatrist's office; Segretti's activities and other alleged campaign "dirty tricks"; and illegal conduct in the financing of the various Presidential campaigns of 1972.

Assisting and providing support for the task forces were several other groups. A counsel's office was established to provide legal advice to the

Special Prosecutor and the task force. An information section went to work summarizing and cross-indexing the masses of Congressional and grand jury testimony that had already been gathered, and creating a filing and reference system that would give any WSPF investigator access to whatever information was already available in the area of his inquiry. An office of public affairs handled relations with the press—an especially sensitive task in view of the dual demands of the First Amendment's free-press guarantees and the right of a potential defendant to a trial unprejudiced by publicity about his conduct. An administrative office dealt with the many problems of space allocation, payroll, supplies, equipment, clerical help, and messenger service. The FBI and IRS supplied personnel who worked closely with WSPF in some of its investigations, while the Federal Protective Service provided security services for WSPF's offices in a private building in downtown Washington.

The Assistant U.S. Attorneys who had handled the initial Watergate investigation—Earl Silbert, Seymour Glanzer, and Donald Campbell —worked with WSPF until the end of June, when they returned to the U.S. Attorney's office for the District of Columbia. The grand jury that had brought the original Watergate indictment in the fall of 1972, and had received new evidence in the spring of 1973, continued to hear evidence gathered by WSPF in the Watergate cover-up case. In August a second grand jury was empaneled to hear evidence in other cases, and a third grand jury was added in January 1974. Because the original grand jury was so familiar with the Watergate case, special legislation in December 1973 extended its term beyond the normal 18 months.

Taped Evidence

As the various task forces were absorbing information already gathered by other investigators and beginning to interview witnesses and bring them before the grand jury, the Senate Select Committee continued its hearings. In June, former White House counsel John Dean gave testimony implicating President Nixon and his closest advisors in the Watergate cover-up. On July 16, a former White House official [Alexander P. Butterfield] told the Committee that President Nixon in 1971 had installed in the White House a taping system designed to record his meetings and telephone conversations. This revelation opened up the possibility of obtaining evidence that could resolve the conflicting testimony about alleged involvement of Administration officials in various crimes.

On July 23, the Special Prosecutor, after unsuccessful attempts to obtain such material from the President on a voluntary basis, issued a subpoena on behalf of the grand jury for the tapes, notes, and memoranda of nine conversations which the available evidence indicated were relevant and necessary to the investigation. The President opposed the subpoena, and appealed Judge Sirica's order enforcing it to the U.S. Court of Appeals for the District of Columbia Circuit. After first suggesting that Cox and the White House seek a compromise—which they were unable to do—the appellate court on

October 12 affirmed Judge Sirica's order with modifications sought by the Special Prosecutor. The Court directed Judge Sirica to listen to the tapes to determine whether they contained discussions subject to a valid claim of executive privilege, and then turn over any unprivileged sections of the tapes to the grand jury.

The First Guilty Pleas

While the litigation over the subpoenaed tapes had delayed the Watergate and other WSPF investigations, the prosecutors had made considerable progress in the first six months of their work. The Watergate investigation had produced guilty pleas from Fred LaRue, Jeb Magruder, and John Dean on charges of conspiracy to obstruct justice. Donald Segretti had pleaded guilty to charges of conspiracy and distributing campaign literature without properly identifying its source, in connection with his "dirty tricks" operation. Egil Krogh, Jr. had been indicted for lying to the grand jury in prior testimony regarding the "Plumbers' " activities. Three large corporations—American Airlines, Goodyear Tire and Rubber, and Minnesota Mining and Manufacturing—had entered guilty pleas to making illegal corporate contributions in the 1972 Presidential election, as had the responsible officers of two of them. Dwayne Andreas and his First Interoceanic Corporation had been charged with the same offenses. Other investigations had progressed, and were expected to produce additional indictments and guilty pleas. In the negotiations leading to their guilty pleas, Segretti, LaRue, Magruder, and Dean had agreed to disclose to WSPF what they knew about the Watergate case and other matters under investigation.

Tape Compromise Rejected

Dean's guilty plea and agreement to cooperate with the prosecutors came October 19, the last day for the President to seek Supreme Court review of the decision ordering him to produce the tapes. Instead of asking the Supreme Court to hear the case, he announced a proposed compromise: Senator John Stennis would listen to the tapes and review a statement of their contents; if verified by Stennis the statement would then be given to the Special Prosecutor and the grand jury. Under an integral part of the proposal, Cox would agree not to litigate further with respect to the nine tapes or to seek additional tapes in the future.

In a news conference the following day, Cox stated his reasons for not accepting the proposal. Edited summaries, he noted, probably would not be admissible as evidence in court. His agreement not to seek additional tapes would prevent WSPF from conducting its investigations thoroughly. And the order to accept the compromise terms, he said, was inconsistent with the pledge of independence he had received from Attorney General Richardson at the time of his appointment.

Cox Fired

That evening, October 20, the White House announced the events that came to be known as the "Saturday Night Massacre": President Nixon ordered Attorney General Richardson to dismiss Cox for his refusal to accept the White House proposal; Richardson resigned rather than carry out the order, and Deputy Attorney General William Ruckelshaus was fired for his refusal to obey; finally, Solicitor General Robert Bork, next in seniority at the Justice Department, dismissed Cox as Special Prosecutor. Also on White House orders, agents of the FBI occupied the offices of WSPF, the Attorney General, and the Deputy Attorney General in order to prevent the removal of any documents. WSPF staff members, gathered in their offices, were informed that they would work henceforth as part of the Justice Department's Criminal Division.

The events leading to Cox's dismissal had been foreshadowed by a number of his contacts with Attorney General Richardson over the previous months. On several occasions Richardson had asked whether particular matters Cox appeared to be investigating were under his jurisdiction and had expressed concern that Cox's inquiries were going into areas not contemplated when WSPF was established. Some of these questions were inherent in the apparent breadth of Cox's charter. Other questions rose from Richardson's own misgivings, and those of White House officials.

The actions which Richardson raised in conversation with Cox included WSPF's possible inquiry into the financing of President Nixon's two homes, its broad letters to several Federal agencies asking their policies and practices in electronic surveillance, the interviewing of a former White House aide [Tom Charles Huston] who had prepared a controversial plan for intelligence gathering by the executive branch, investigation of wiretaps claimed to be justified by national security, and an inquiry into the handling of campaign contributions by a close friend of the President. In July, because both he and Cox were uneasy about the prospect of a series of politically motivated referrals to WSPF of charges against the President or his Administration, with attendant publicity, Richardson had suggested that the Criminal Division screen all allegations to determine whether they were substantial and fell within WSPF's jurisdiction before sending them on to Cox. Cox quickly rejected this proposal and Richardson did not pursue it. In August, citing the concerns of White House officials that Cox was reaching beyond his charter, Richardson proposed revising the Special Prosecuter's charter to define his jurisdiction with more precise limitations, and appointing a special consultant on national security matters to serve as an expediting intermediary between the Special Prosecutor and agencies from which he was seeking information regarding such matters. Cox felt that it was his own responsibility to determine what matters fell within the terms of his existing charter, and rejected any charter revisions as unnecessary. Cox also disagreed with the idea of a national security consultant because he saw such an official as a possible hindrance rather than an aid to obtaining necessary information.

Richardson also informed Cox of White House positions on various issues, including the production of evidence in response to the Special Prosecutor's requests. Despite their willingness to take independent positions on such legal issues as executive privilege and national security, Richardson and Cox had also made efforts to reach agreement on such issues. During the period just before his resignation and Cox's dismissal, Richardson had made efforts to achieve a compromise on the question of the Special Prosecutor's access to the subpoenaed tapes.

October 20, 1973—August 9, 1974

The "Saturday Night Massacre" did not halt the work of WSPF, and the prosecutors resumed their grand jury sessions as scheduled the following Tuesday. Bork placed Assistant Attorney General Henry Petersen, head of the Criminal Division, in charge of the investigations WSPF had been conducting. Both men assured the staff that its work would continue with the cooperation of the Justice Department and without interference from the White House. Upon WSPF's request, Judge Sirica issued a protective order to limit access to, and prevent removal of, WSPF files. Despite their anger over Cox's dismissal and their doubts about the future of their office, the staff members, in a series of meetings, decided to continue their work for the time being.

Nevertheless, the dismissal of Cox and the President's refusal to produce the subpoenaed tapes provoked what one White House official called a "firestorm" of public criticism and serious talk of impeachment on Capitol Hill. In an abrupt reversal, the President announced on October 23 that he would comply with the grand jury subpoena and on October 26 that Bork would appoint a new Special Prosecutor who would have "total cooperation from the executive branch." While the President said he would be unwilling to produce additional White House tapes or other evidence that he considered privileged, he placed no restrictions on the new Special Prosecutor's authority to seek such evidence through the courts.

On November 1, the President announced that he would nominate Senator William B. Saxbe as the new Attorney General. Later that day, Acting Attorney General Bork announced his appointment of Leon Jaworski as Special Prosecutor. Jaworski, who was sworn into office November 5, was assured the same jurisdiction and guarantees of independence as Cox, with the additional provision the he could be dismissed, or his jurisdiction limited, only with consent of a bipartisan group of eight Congressional leaders. Three days after taking office, Jaworksi told a House subcommittee that the continuity of WSPF operations had been restored and that the office's staff would remain intact.

Efforts to Protect Office

Meanwhile, a number of bills had been introduced in Congress to provide for judicial appointment or other safeguards of the independence of the

Special Prosecutor. In the wake of the "Saturday Night Massacre," many people thought it impossible to assure an independent investigation by anyone appointed solely by the executive branch of Government or subject to dismissal without Congressional approval. Others including Chief Judge Sirica and some of his fellow judges opposed the idea of a court-appointed prosecutor, and Saxbe testified that he had accepted his nomination only on the condition that Jaworski's investigation would remain independent. Jaworski testified that he would welcome any legislation protecting his independence further, but was satisfied with his charter and the assurances he had been given. In mid-November, ruling on a civil suit that challenged the dismissal of Cox, District Judge Gerhard Gesell held that Cox's firing had been illegal. However, noting that Cox had not sought reinstatement, the judge said there was no reason to interfere with Jaworski's tenure. As a result of all these events, Congress abandoned the idea of establishing a special prosecutor's office by legislation.

Missing and Incomplete Tapes

Less than a week after the President's attorney had told Judge Sirica that the nine subpoenaed tapes would be produced for his examination, another White House lawyer announced that two of the conversations for which tapes had been sought had in fact never been recorded. Shortly thereafter, during a court inquiry into the question of the President's compliance with the subpoena, White House lawyers disclosed that the tape of a third conversation contained a substantial "gap"—a humming sound which obliterated some 18½ minutes of one of the President's conversations—and that dictabelts of the President's recollections of two of the conversations contained shorter gaps. A panel of experts chosen by White House and WSPF lawyers reported in January 1974 that the 18½-minute gap had been caused by a series of deliberate erasures, and that it was impossible to retrieve the original conversation. Judge Sirica thereupon referred the matter to a grand jury. A lengthy investigation, conducted by WSPF and the FBI, concluded that only a small number of people had had the opportunity to make the erasures but was unable to fix criminal responsibility on any particular individual or individuals.

Additional Indictments and Guilty Pleas

Meanwhile, the task force investigations continued. By the end of 1973, five more corporations—Braniff Airways, Ashland Petroleum Gabon Inc., Gulf Oil Corporation, Phillips Petroleum Company, and Carnation Company—and their responsible officers had pleaded guilty to making corporate contributions to 1972 Presidential campaigns. Former Presidential aide Dwight Chapin had been indicted for making false statements to the grand jury in connection with Segretti's activities. Egil Krogh, Jr., former head of the White House "Plumbers," had entered a guilty plea to conspiring to violate the rights of Dr. Fielding, whose office had been broken into in a vain attempt to obtain Daniel Ellsberg's psychiatric records.

The new year brought additional indictments and guilty pleas. Herbert Porter, a former aide in the President's re-election campaign, pleaded guilty to making false statements in connection with the original investigation of the Watergate case. Jake Jacobsen, an attorney who had helped milk producer cooperatives make campaign contributions and obtain an increase in milk price supports, was indicted on charges of making false statements to the grand jury. Herbert Kalmbach, the President's personal lawyer and an active campaign fundraiser, pleaded guilty to a felony violation of the Federal Corrupt Practices Act in his fund-raising for candidates in the 1970 Congressional elections and to a charge of promising an ambassadorship to a campaign contributor.

More Evidence Sought

Efforts to obtain additional recordings and other documents from the White House, for use as evidence in various grand jury investigations, continued during the winter of 1973-74. For a short period after Jaworski took office, the White House offered limited cooperation by supplying some of the numerous tapes and documents requested by WSPF over the past four months. In January, however, the President retained as counsel James St. Clair, whose major concern appeared to be protecting him against possible impeachment. The President stopped his initial cooperation with Jaworski, and WSPF requests were soon met by unusual delays and claims that some materials could not be located. Other materials, the President said, were unnecessary to the grand jury investigations. To furnish them would be inconsistent with his constitutional responsibilities.

During the winter, and again in the late spring of 1974, Jaworski met periodically with General Alexander Haig, the President's chief of staff. For the most part, these meetings involved attempts by Jaworski to persuade Haig that the President should provide WSPF with materials it was seeking. Haig complained about particular actions by WSPF staff members, including their intensive questioning of White House witnesses in the grand jury and their efforts to have FBI agents interview White House staff members in connection with the investigation of the 18½ minute tape gap.

On March 1, the grand jury returned an indictment in the Watergate cover-up case of seven men formerly associated with the White House or CRP—Charles Colson, John Ehrlichman, H. R. Haldeman, Robert Mardian, John Mitchell, Kenneth Parkinson, and Gordon Strachan—on charges of conspiracy, obstruction of justice, and, as to some, perjury and false declarations. A week later six men—Bernard Barker, Colson, Felipe DeDiego, Ehrlichman, Gordon Liddy, and Eugenio Martinez—were indicted for conspiring to violate Dr. Fielding's civil rights in connection with the illegal entry of his office, and Ehrlichman was charged in addition with making false statements to the FBI and the grand jury about the case.

Nixon a Participant in Cover-up

The grand jury hearing evidence in the Watergate case concluded that President Nixon had been a participant in the cover-up. However, after extensive legal research in the office, Jaworski concluded that it would be improper to indict an incumbent President for such a crime when the House of Representatives' Judiciary Committee had already begun a formal impeachment inquiry. He believed, in addition, that such an indictment would be challenged and ultimately overturned by the Supreme Court, and that the fruitless litigation would delay the trial of the seven cover-up defendants and possibly also temporarily halt the impeachment inquiry. The grand jury then authorized the Special Prosecutor to name President Nixon as an unindicted co-conspirator in the cover-up case. Since this finding was relevant to the impeachment investigation, WSPF asked the grand jury to report to the court all of its evidence relating to the President's alleged involvement in the cover-up, with a recommendation that Judge Sirica forward the report to the House Judiciary Committee. The grand jury did so and by order of Judge Sirica, upheld by the Court of Appeals, the report was delivered to the Committee on March 26.

Discussions had been held between Committee attorneys and WSPF several months before. The prosecutors felt obligated to assist the Committee to the extent that such assistance was legally proper and would not jeopardize WSPF's investigations. In February, with the consent of White House counsel, WSPF had provided the Committee with a list of tapes and documents it had received from the White House, and in March the office supplied a list of those items requested from White House files but not received. As soon as the existence of the grand jury report became public knowledge, the President's counsel agreed to supply the Committee with all materials that had been supplied to the Special Prosecutor, and he subsequently did so. Later in the spring, when the Committee sought access to various records under seal of the court, the Special Prosecutor on most occasions indicated his approval. WSPF's task force heads also met on several occasions with Committee attorneys to provide relevant information. Necessary ground rules protected the secrecy of grand jury proceedings and the confidentiality of WSPF sources of information. The prosecutors suggested what witnesses the Committee should interview on what subjects, and what lines of inquiry were likely to prove fruitless for their purposes.

After months of frustrating efforts to obtain grand jury and trial evidence from the White House, including recordings of Presidential conversations, Jaworski decided that he would have to resort, as his predecessor had, to judicial process. A grand jury subpoena of March 15 had resulted in the production of campaign contribution documents from White House files but had not called for Presidential tapes. At Jaworski's request, Judge Sirica issued a trial subpoena on April 18 in the cover-up case for recordings and documents related to 64 specified Presidential conversations. Unlike the previous subpoenas, which had been issued by the grand juries in connection with their investigations, this one was issued by the court so that

WSPF could prepare adequately for the trial in the Watergate case, then scheduled to begin early in September.

Edited Transcripts Released

On April 30, two days before the date for compliance with the trial subpoena, the President released to the public edited transcripts of some of the recorded conversations which had been subpoenaed by both the House Committee and WSPF, claiming that "the materials...will tell it all." The next day, he formally refused to provide the tapes to Judge Sirica contending that some of the materials covered by the subpoena were protected by executive privilege, that disclosure would be "contrary to the public interest," and that the subpoena was invalid because the tapes would be inadmissible as evidence. His attorneys filed a motion to quash the subpoena.

Jaworski informed Haig [General Alexander Haig, Nixon's chief of staff] and St. Clair a few days later that imminent argument in court by WSPF in an effort to enforce the subpoena would require the statement that the President had been named as an unindicted co-conspirator. Jaworski offered to withdraw the subpoena, thus postponing disclosure of the President's status until later trial proceedings, if the White House supplied voluntarily 16 specified tape recordings that WSPF considered crucial. A few days later, after listening to the tapes in question, the President sent word to Jaworski that his proposed compromise was unacceptable.

During ensuing litigation over the White House motion to quash the subpoena, the President's counsel asserted that the Special Prosecutor, as an employee of the executive branch, lacked authority to seek evidence from the White House by judicial process. This renewed the argument used seven months earlier to justify the dismissal of Cox. In accordance with a promise he had made when appointed, Jaworski immediately informed the chairmen of the Senate Judiciary Committee and House Judiciary Committee of the new challenge to his independence. By resolution the following day, the Senate Committee affirmed its support of Jaworski's right to take the President to court, and urged Attorney General Saxbe to "use all reasonable and appropriate means to guarantee the independence" of the Special Prosecutor. Two days later, Saxbe promised the Committee that he would support WSPF's independence.

On May 20, Judge Sirica denied the President's motion to quash and ordered him to comply with the subpoena. After the President's lawyers announced their decision to appeal this order, Jaworski asked the Supreme Court to consider the matter as soon as possible, bypassing the Court of Appeals in order to avoid unnecessary delays. The Supreme Court agreed to do so, over White House opposition.

Court Orders Compliance

After legal briefs and oral arguments had been scheduled in an unusual summer session, the Court ruled unanimously on July 24 that the President must comply with the subpoena. While recognizing for the first time the Constitutional doctrine of executive privilege, the Court held that "the generalized assertion of privilege must yield to the demonstrated specific need for evidence in a pending criminal trial." The President announced that he would comply with the Court's ruling and with the subpoena.

In the days that followed, the House Judiciary Committee concluded its inquiry by adopting three articles of impeachment to be reported to the full House of Representatives for its consideration.

Nixon Resigns

On August 5, the President released to the public transcripts of portions of recorded conversations held six days after the Watergate break-in. His accompanying statement acknowledged that in the conversations he had ordered steps taken to conceal from the FBI the involvement of White House and campaign officials, and he admitted that he had kept this evidence from his own lawyers and Congressional supporters. On August 9, in the face of overwhelming support for impeachment in the House and almost certain conviction in the Senate, he resigned the Presidency.

The Special Prosecutor's efforts to obtain Watergate trial evidence from President Nixon did not inhibit other WSPF investigations and prosecutions. A trial jury convicted Dwight Chapin of lying about his knowledge of campaign "dirty tricks." Gordon Liddy, one of the men convicted in the original Watergate break-in case, was indicted, tried, and convicted of contempt of Congress, for his refusal to testify before a House committee. The ITT investigations resulted in two convictions: former Attorney General Richard Kleindienst pleaded guilty to giving inaccurate testimony to a Senate Committee, and Lieutenant Governor Ed Reinecke of California, who chose to stand trial, was convicted of perjury.

Investigations of campaign contribution activity also continued during the spring and summer of 1974. Diamond International Corporation, Northrop Corporation, Lehigh Valley Cooperative Farmers, and National By-Products, Inc., all entered guilty pleas to making illegal campaign contributions. The principal officer of Diamond, two officers of Lehigh Valley, and two officers of Northrop pleaded guilty to similar charges. American Ship Building Company and its chairman George Steinbrenner were indicted for making illegal contributions, and Steinbrenner was also charged with conspiracy and obstruction of the grand jury's inquiry. Another official of American Ship Building acknowledged guilt as an accessory to an illegal contribution. A jury in New York found John Mitchell and Maurice Stans, two former members of President Nixon's cabinet, not guilty of charges connected with contributions by financier Robert Vesco, and a federal judge in Minnesota acquitted the First Interoceanic Corporation and Dwayne Andreas of illegal contribution charges.

The investigation into the campaign activities of Associated Milk Producers, Inc. (AMPI) resulted in several prosecutions. Former AMPI officials Harold Nelson and David Parr pleaded guilty to conspiracy charges, with Nelson also acknowledging his part in a conspiracy to make an illegal payment to a public official. AMPI entered a guilty plea to charges of conspiracy and making five corporate contributions. The perjury charge against attorney Jake Jacobsen had been dismissed on technical grounds, but he pleaded guilty to a later charge of making illegal payments to a public official. The same indictment charged former Treasury Secretary John Connally with accepting such payments and with conspiracy and perjury. Later in the summer of 1974, Norman Sherman and John Valentine pleaded guilty to aiding and abetting unlawful AMPI contributions.

While WSPF's subpoena of White House tapes for the Watergate trial was pending before Judge Sirica, Judge Gerhard Gesell was hearing pretrial motions in the Fielding break-in case. Because of doubts about the legal effect of a previous grant of immunity to defendant Felipe DeDiego, the judge dismissed the charges against him. Judge Gesell also ruled against a defense argument that the entry into Dr. Fielding's office had been justified by considerations of national security. Shortly after this ruling, one of the defendants, former White House aide Charles Colson, pleaded guilty to obstructing justice in the federal criminal case brought against Daniel Ellsberg after his public release of the Pentagon Papers. Colson admitted that White House efforts to discredit Ellsberg by public release of derogatory information were intended to interfere with his fair trial. As a result of this plea and his agreement to disclose what he knew about matters under the Special Prosecutor's jurisdiction, the charges against Colson in the Watergate case and the original charges against him in the Fielding break-in case were dropped. The break-in trial began June 26 and ended July 12 with the convictions of the four remaining defendants—Bernard Barker, John Ehrlichman, Gordon Liddy, and Eugenio Martinez.

August 9, 1974—October 1, 1975

The Nixon resignation presented WSPF with an immediate question: should the former President be prosecuted as a private citizen for whatever crimes he might have committed while in office? Jaworski, after announcing that he had reached no agreement or understanding with anyone about the former President's possible prosecution, said he intended to defer a decision on whether to seek any indictments. The WSPF staff needed time to analyze all the relevant factors. But, on September 8, before the Special Prosecutor had decided whether to seek an indictment, President Ford pardoned his predecessor for any and all Federal crimes he might have committed while President.

President Nixon's resignation also raised questions of access to the White House papers and recordings which WSPF needed in its investigations of possible criminal conduct during his Administration. President Ford's counsel assured WSPF on August 15 that the former President's files would be kept in White House custody until their ownership had been resolved. However, when he announced the pardon September 8, President Ford also revealed an agreement—made without any prior notice to the Special Prosecutor—giving the former President control over access to the files, which would be kept in a Government installation near the Nixon residence in California. President Ford based his position on a Justice Department opinion that the former President was the legal owner of the materials, and on his belief that their physical security could be assured by maintaining them in Government custody. The Special Prosecutor disagreed with the President's view of the situation and suggested that he might challenge the September 8 agreement in court. Resulting discussions among WSPF, Justice Department, and White House officials produced an agreement whereby the Nixon files would remain in White House custody pending review of the question of WSPF's access to them.

Control of Presidential Materials Disputed

On October 17, the former President filed a lawsuit to compel enforcement of the September 8 agreement giving him control over access to his White House files. The court issued a temporary restraining order prohibiting access to the materials without the consent of attorneys for both the former President and President Ford. On November 9, based on President Ford's determination that the needs of justice required direct access to the Nixon files by the Special Prosecutor's office, the President's counsel, along with the directors of the General Services Administration and the Secret Service, agreed in writing with the Special Prosecutor on procedures for direct access by WSPF. The Special Prosecutor's office then began discussions with former President Nixon's counsel to obtain his consent to this agreement.

Because of the needs of all parties to prepare adequately for trial, the Watergate cover-up trial was postponed from September 9 to October 1 pursuant to a suggestion from the Court of Appeals to Judge Sirica. Doubts about the effect on the prosecution's case of grants of immunity to defendant Gordon Strachan led to his severance from the trial. On October 12, shortly after the jury had been sequestered, Special Prosecutor Jaworski announced that he would resign as of October 26, stating that the bulk of the office's work had been completed. He also announced that he had decided not to challenge President Ford's pardon of former President Nixon in the courts because he did not believe such a challenge would have any chance of prevailing. Thus WSPF ended its consideration of the former President as a possible defendant. Jaworski was succeeded October 26 by Henry S. Ruth, Jr., who had served as deputy to both of the previous Special Prosecutors.

During the months following President Nixon's resignation, WSPF obtained additional indictments and convictions. George Steinbrenner and the American Ship Building Company pleaded guilty to charges of conspiracy and making an illegal campaign contribution, and "DKI for '74," a committee supporting the re-election of Senator Daniel Inouye, pleaded guilty to failing to report a contribution received from Steinbrenner. Guilty pleas for illegal contributions were entered by LBC&W, Inc. and its principal officer, Greyhound Corporation, Ashland Oil, Inc., Ratrie, Robbins, and Schweitzer, Inc. and its principal officers, and the principal officer of HMS Electric Corporation. Tim Babcock, an executive of Occidental Petroleum, Inc. and formerly Governor of Montana, pleaded guilty to making a campaign contribution in another person's name. Oklahoma lawyer Stuart Russell and Minnesota lawyer Jack Chestnut were both indicted in connection with milk-producer contribution activities. Jack Gleason and Harry Dent, former White House aides, pleaded guilty to violating the Federal Corrupt Practices Act in their fund-raising for the 1970 Congressional elections. Edward Morgan, a former Deputy Counsel in the White House, pleaded guilty to conspiracy to defraud the Government in connection with an income tax deduction taken by former President Nixon.

Cover-up Trial

Most of these actions occurred as the Watergate cover-up trial was taking place during the autumn of 1974 in Judge Sirica's courtroom. Efforts to obtain former President Nixon's testimony at the trial were frustrated when three court-appointed physicians reported that his serious illness prevented his testimony for several months. After a three-month trial, defendants Ehrlichman, Haldeman, Mardian and Mitchell were found guilty by the jury, and defendant Parkinson was acquitted.

Work Nears Completion

Early in 1975, WSPF's staff began a steady reduction as investigations and prosecutions were completed, but office business continued through the spring and summer. Los Angeles lawyer Frank DeMarco and Chicago book dealer and appraiser Ralph Newman were indicted on conspiracy and other charges related to their roles in the preparation of former President Nixon's income tax returns. Former Secretary of Commerce Maurice Stans, who had headed the Finance Committee to Re-Elect the President, pleaded guilty to three violations of the Federal Election Campaign Act's reporting requirements and to two violations of accepting corporate contributions. Former Treasury Secretary Connally was found not guilty by a jury on charges of accepting illegal payments, and the remaining charges against him were dismissed. A New York City jury convicted Jack Chestnut of a felony for aiding and abetting an illegal milk-producer contribution and a San Antonio, Texas, jury convicted Stuart Russell of three felonies for conspiracy and aiding and abetting other dairy industry contributions. Former Congressman Wendell Wyatt pleaded guilty to a reporting violation under the Federal Election Campaign Act.

Discussions with the former President's counsel about WSPF access to Nixon Administration tapes and documents resulted in an understanding that permitted the prosecutors to obtain relevant evidence. Beginning in February 1975, with an index prepared by Government archivists, the prosecutors designated the particular files they wanted searched for documents and recordings related to specified investigations. The file searches were conducted by archivists under the supervision of President Ford's counsel; former President Nixon's attorney reviewed all requested recordings of Presidential conversations and provided copies of those which might be pertinent to WSPF's investigations. Between February and June, WSPF obtained numerous documents and tapes generated in the White House during the Nixon Administration. On June 23 and 24, after negotiations with the former President's counsel, several WSPF attorneys and two members of the grand jury took Nixon's testimony under oath near his California residence.

A considerable portion of the prosecutors' work in 1975 involved the numerous appeals that followed convictions at trial and other court actions. Matters on appeal included the convictions in the 1973 Watergate trial, the later Watergate cover-up trial, the Fielding break-in trial, the trials of Dwight Chapin, Ed Reinecke, and Stuart Russell, and the sentence imposed on Tim Babcock. The prosecutors unsuccessfully sought reversal of a court order moving the trials of Frank DeMarco and Ralph Newman to two separate cities and intervened in litigation to oppose Mr. Nixon's contention that the Presidential Recordings and Materials Preservation Act of 1974 deprived him unconstitutionally of his Presidential papers. The appellate process in some cases is expected to extend at least through 1976.

The grand juries which had heard evidence obtained by WSPF were dismissed when their terms expired. The first, originally empaneled on June 5, 1972, and extended by legislation was dismissed on December 4, 1974. After having sat for the standard 18-month term, the second was dismissed February 12, 1975, and the third, July 3, 1975....

Concluding Observations and Recommendations

Normally when prosecutors are asked to recommend reforms, the questions are limited to the criminal justice system. But most of what WSPF personnel experienced in criminal justice was dramatically atypical of criminal justice generally. The prosecutors had adequate resources; defendants were not jailed for long periods of time prior to trial; the courts had time and resources to meet all the demands of Watergate litigation in a detached, unhurried atmosphere; private defense counsel brought all their skills to thorough pretrial investigation, legal attack, trial strategy and fully-briefed appeals; the sections of Federal prisons in which convicted Watergate defendants served their terms all lacked the small, inhuman spaces in which most American criminals reside, locked into their idleness for 17 hours each day; and constant press and public scrutiny provided a careful watchdog to make sure that Government investigations proceeded without abuse of power or undue leniency. Watergate did not educate American citizens about the normal, day-to-day criminal justice process.

In considering what recommendations to include in this report, WSPF concentrated on what it did observe: criminal abuse of power by Government officials in high places; historical growth of secrecy in the Federal executive branch unchecked by Americans and their elected Congress; un-challenged, subjective judgments by the executive branch in identifying persons and organizations that constitute an impermissible threat to the national interest and to executive policy; an undemocratic condition wherein money is power, and skillful, cynical public relations cements that power; and finally, a silent, sometimes grudging, sometimes willful conclusion by some Government representatives that ethical standards are irrelevant because quick implementation of policy goals is mandatory, but achievable only by social and personal injustices to others.

These conclusions all arose from observing how Government officials and agencies actually grapple with the legitimate demands upon them. The demands of national security require extraordinary judgment. The separation of powers concept requires judicious use of the privilege doctrine. Politicians cannot be elected without extensive campaign funds and loyal friends who want rewards. Individual requirements for personal success seem always to demand that one must "ride with the system." And a leader hoping to implement his policies is loathe to choose anyone whose independence or unpredictable mind may eventually undermine or delay those goals.

These demands have always had, and will continue to have, inherent potential for abuse of power. National security can easily be used to justify unconstitutional actions, and executive privilege can then be invoked to justify the failure to disclose these actions. Subjective distrust can be identified mistakenly with a national need that justifies massive intelligence systems with permanent storage and illicit use of personal information. Political survival, rationalized by one's perceived ability to accomplish the national will, can too easily justify the acceptance of "big money" and the granting of instant access to any friend of one's cause or one's administration. The leader who sets out to accomplish his goals may appoint as executives only those who helped him along the political path and who will give him support that disregards independent analysis or the demands of personal will and courage.

This brief and, by no means, original or exclusive catalog should sound familiar to all readers of this report. Many of the Watergate phenomena had their historical precedents. Many had grown with no deterrence from other branches of Government. Others had grown without questions from the people and from the press. Watergate should not be analyzed merely in the context of each individual abuse of power that prosecutors were told to investigate. As with any coalescing of activities that lead to a national crisis, so too did Watergate grow from historical roots that presaged abuses of institutional power.

Need for Vigilance

If Watergate was an insidious climax to recent and hitherto subtle historical trends, the formulation of recommendations must begin with the simple, but basic, observation that democracies do not survive unless elected officials do what they are supposed to do and citizens maintain vigilance to see that they do. The public unfolding of Watergate abuses resulted from citizen, press and official actions. Nothing can replace that kind of vigilance; and recommendations for new laws or new institutions are insignificant when compared to the stubborn, plodding, daily work of Americans and their elected representatives in watching over and channeling the power of their national Government, the power of concentrated wealth, the power of officially spoken and written words, and the power of secret bureaucracies.

As prosecutors searching only for facts that disclose or disclaim criminal activity, WSPF lacks the expertise to propose a broad base of political and social change. The recommendations that follow are not so intended. The proposals are modest but their implementation would probably help. Most appear easy and obvious. But that is a good way to start testing a Nation's willingness to learn from its past.

Recommendations

Protecting the Integrity and Effectiveness of the Prosecution Function

The integrity of Government officials, from the President down, depends in part on the credibility of criminal statutes as a deterrent to misconduct. This credibility in turn depends on the capacity of the system of justice to investigate and prosecute wrongdoing wherever it occurs. At a minimum, this means that the Department of Justice must be capable of exercising its prosecution functions free of undue influence or conflicts of interest. At the same time, many of the functions of the Department are legitimate subjects of Presidential concern on a policy level, and the President needs as Attorney General a legal adviser in whom he has full confidence. If the Department is properly insulated from partisan politics and from service to an Administration's purely political interests, it would not seem necessary to take the major institutional steps of making the Attorney General's office elective or creating a permanent special prosecutor's office.

Independence of Department of Justice Officials. The President should not nominate and the Senate should not confirm as Attorney General, or as any other appointee in high Department of Justice posts, a person who has served as the President's campaign manager or in a similar high-level campaign role. A campaign manager seeks support for his candidate and necessarily incurs obligations to political leaders and other individuals throughout wide geographical areas. If he then takes a high position in the Justice Department, he may take—or appear to take—official actions on the basis of those commitments rather than on appropriate legal and policy grounds. The Attorney General and other Justice Department appointees should be lawyers with their own reputations in the legal profession, with capacity and willingness to make independent judgments, and with the authority to choose similarly qualified persons for subordinate positions. In advising and consenting on Presidential nominees, Senators should apply to Justice Department appointees standards of character and independence similar to those they apply to nominees for the Supreme Court. Similar standards should attach to the appointment and confirmation of United States Attorneys.

The Hatch Act, which prohibits most Federal employees from taking an active part in political management or campaigns, should be amended to apply to all employees of the Department of Justice, including the Attorney General. However, the amendment should make clear that high Department officials are not violating the prohibition of political activity when they discuss and defend Department policies and actions on their merits in public forums.

Contacts About Pending Cases. In August 1973, Attorney General Richardson issued Order No. 532-73, requiring all Justice Department employees to record in memorandum form each oral communication "concerning a case or other matter pending before the Department with a non-involved party indicating an interest in the case or matter." This order was meant to deter improper contacts by creating a written record of any attempt to influence Department handling of cases.

Subsequent debate within the Department of Justice has questioned the breadth of the order and the lack of an enforcement mechanism....

The Attorney General should resolve these problems of coverage and reissue the Order. Attempted political persuasion and other efforts by non-involved parties to secure direct, out-of-channel access to Department personnel should all be part of official records.

Increased Federal Efforts Against Corruption Without Creation of a Permanent Special Prosecutor. The Senate Select Committee reacted to their Watergate hearings by recommending the creation of a permanent special prosecutor's office. The proposed new officer would be appointed by the judiciary and confirmed by the Senate. He would be independent of the Attorney General in making all his decisions and have jurisdiction over most corrupt acts committed by Federal employees and also over political campaign crimes.

The principal reason cited for such an institution is the perceived incapacity of the Justice Department to investigate fully allegations of criminal conduct by high officials. Since the Attorney General is a Presidential appointee, it is argued, his subordinates cannot be expected to seek or uncover misconduct by high officials whose prosecution might embarrass the President. The problem is most acute, of course, when the alleged wrongdoer is the President himself; but it is substantial when the subject of investigations is a Presidential appointee at any level. Justice Department investigators may be equally frustrated in efforts to prosecute the President's judicial appointees or political allies in Congress; even members of Congress who belong to the opposing party may be immune from prosecution because of a "live and let live" political tradition that survives changes of Administration and protects politicians even after they leave office. An independent special prosecutor, not subject to such considerations, would pursue wrongdoing in Government solely on an objective basis.

No one who has watched "Watergate" unfold can doubt that the Justice Department has difficulty investigating and prosecuting high officials, or that an independent prosecutor is freer to act according to politically neutral principles of fairness and justice. But the question is whether such independence should be institutionalized on a permanent basis. Do the advantages of such a step outweigh its disadvantages?

WSPF is opposed to the idea of extending the special prosecutor concept on a permanent basis. Central to the question is the fact that such a public officer would be largely immune from the accountability that prosecutors and other public officials constantly face. Lack of accountability of an official on a permanent basis carries a potential for abuse of power that far exceeds any enforcement gains that might ensue. An independent prosecutor reports directly on ongoing investigations to no one, takes directions from no one and could easily abuse his power with little chance of detection. Although matters that reach court obviously invoke court control over a prosecutor's public conduct, the discretionary process of initiating and conducting investigations bears great potential for hidden actions that are unfair, arbitrary, dishonest, or subjectively biased.

Ordinarily, prosecutors are accountable either directly to the electorate or indirectly through the elected officials who appoint them. Under proposed legislation, a permanent special prosecutor would not be subject to such accountability. In extraordinary situations such as "Watergate," an independent prosecutor can be held accountable directly to the public because his actions are subject to intense and continuous press scrutiny. But such high visibility cannot be expected for a permanent office dealing day to day with less explosive matters.

Much of the Watergate and preceding abuses resulted from the public's delegation of public responsibilities to powerful men whose judgments were trusted and whose claimed need for secrecy was always accepted. Men with unchecked power and unchallenged trust too often come to believe that their own perceptions of priorities and the common good coincide with the national will. There is no reason to believe that, in the long run, an independent special prosecutor's office would avoid this status.

Other problems exist. Anyone who has observed bureaucracies realizes that a "special" organization rarely retains its "special" qualities beyond a 3-year period. New organizations, large or small, start with a burst of speed, energy, imagination, enthusiasm, flexibility, long daily hours, and almost uniform high quality of personnel. That level is hardly ever maintained over a long period by a permanent organization in either the public or private sector. This is a problem for Government generally and should be addressed as such, not just as to law enforcement. But there is no reason to believe that a permanent special prosecutor's office would be immune from the rigidity that comes over most organizations after the initial period. Indeed, this would probably happen to the Watergate Special Prosecution Force if it were to continue beyond the period in which it has been needed. Such rigidity is especially likely, and especially harmful, in an agency that is as unaccountable as a permanent special prosecutor would be.

A third reason for opposing the proposed new office relates to problems with which WSPF constantly wrestled. Should our interpretation of the campaign laws, the coverage of statutes of limitation, and the perjury, false statement, and obstruction statutes coincide with those of the Justice Department? Should our policies regarding the use of various intrusive investigative techniques coincide with the Attorney General's? One is moved to answer in the affirmative, since those policies are promulgated under normal democratic conditions of accountability and since different policies easily lead to unequal justice. These policy determinations provide great potential for a special prosecutor's abuse of power. He can easily stretch from proper investigative techniques or attempt unfairly to widen the conduct or the persons included within a criminal sanction. Thus, that relatively small group of persons falling within a permanent special prosecutor's jurisdiction could be subject to a much heavier hammer of Federal criminal law than the rest of the Nation which is subject to Department of Justice standards.

In looking for alternatives to a permanent, independent prosecutor, one must first turn to the problem of resource allocation. When the Department of Justice commenced a specialized, intensive effort against organized crime in 1958—with a dramatic expansion in 1961—prosecutors found a nationwide string of racketeering enterprises that only a few enforcement personnel had thought existed. So too, in recent years, with adequate resources and personnel the United States Attorneys for the Southern District of New York, the Northern District of Illinois, Maryland, Florida, New Jersey and elsewhere were able to uncover extensive Federal corruption. Thus, these Justice Department representatives have prosecuted Federal executives, members of Congress and a Vice President.

This visible, concentrated effort should be institutionalized within the Department of Justice. An effort similar to that devoted to organized crime should be placed in an expanded section within the Criminal Division or similar to the proposal of Senators Baker and Percy, in a new Division of Government Crimes with an Assistant Attorney General appointed by the President. This new office should also have constant coordination and monitoring responsibilities with the various Inspectors General who now inquire into possible corruption in the Federal executive departments.

In addition, the Attorney General should freely exercise his existing power to appoint special assistants as prosecutors, with independence for particular investigations and cases, whenever a real or apparent conflict of interest threatens public confidence in the enforcement system. On several occasions, WSPF borrowed lawyers from the Department and special assistants can be afforded the same advantage for their staffs.

Finally, the absence of a permanent, independent prosecutor need not dispel the idea that an independent prosecution office can be appointed in the future when activities by the executive, legislative or judicial branches of Government show the necessity of a temporary office similar to WSPF.

Congress has the power to enact a statute requiring the President or Attorney General to appoint such a prosecutor, with appropriate safeguards of his jurisdiction and independence, and two-thirds majorities of both Houses have the power to override a Presidential veto of such legislation if necessary. In addition, the nature of the relationship between Congress and the executive branch provides other means of compelling such an appointment. WSPF was created because the Senate insisted on such action as a condition of confirming the nomination of an Attorney General. Congress can similarly use its power to appropriate funds and the Senate can use its confirmation power to force such action if necessary. The remedy of impeachment remains available as a last resort.

Attorney Representation of Multiple Interests in Grand Jury Proceedings. In almost every investigation which centers on the criminal activity of one or more members of a hierarchical structure—whether a corporation, labor union, a Government agency, or a less formally organized group—the prosecutor is confronted with a witness who has been called to testify about his employers. Many times, the witness is represented by an attorney who also represents the employer and perhaps is compensated by him. Although the legal profession's *Code of Professional Responsibility* forbids a lawyer from representing conflicting or even potentially conflicting interests, lawyers and judges historically have been reluctant to enforce the Code's mandate strictly. They have taken the position that, so long as the witness understands that his attorney also represents the person or entity about which he will be asked to testify and that he has the right to a lawyer of his own choosing, he cannot be forced to retain new counsel.

No lay witness, however, can realistically be expected to appreciate all the legal and practical ramifications of his attorney's dual loyalties, and in many cases he will be precluded from giving adequate consideration to the possibility of cooperating with the Government by the fear that the fact of his cooperation will be revealed to his employer. A mere inquiry by the judge in open court concerning the witness' preference is not likely to elicit a truthful response. It is necessary, therefore, for the court to intervene more directly by making a factual determination as to the existence of the conflict of interest and then requiring the witness to retain, or appointing for him, counsel who has no such conflict. Although there will obviously be great reluctance to interfere with the individual's freedom to select his own attorney, the suggested course is the only one that can preserve the equally valid right of the Government to his full and truthful testimony.

Both the courts and the various bar groups should be alerted to the serious issues of professional responsibility arising out of the representation of multiple interests during grand jury investigations, and Government counsel should press on every justifiable occasion for a judicial ruling on the question of conflict of interest and, where a conflict is found, for the replacement of the attorney involved.

Clarification of the Status under the Freedom of Information Act of Information Obtained in Confidence by Criminal Investigators. Under the

Freedom of Information Act as amended in 1974, a prosecutor's investigative files are exempt from disclosure, but only to the extent that production would:

    (A) interfere with enforcement proceedings,

    (B) deprive a person of a right to a fair trial or an impartial adjudication,

    (C) constitute an unwarranted invasion of personal privacy,

    (D) disclose the identity of a confidential source and, in the case of a record compiled by a criminal law enforcement authority in the course of a criminal investigation, or by an agency conducting a lawful national security intelligence investigation, confidential information furnished only by the confidential source,

    (E) disclose investigative techniques and procedures, or

    (F) endanger the life or physical safety of law enforcement personnel.

Much of the information received by WSPF was received either upon an express assurance of confidentiality or upon a reasonable understanding that the information would not be disclosed except as necessary in court proceedings. In some cases, disclosure of such information would not interfere with ongoing investigations or prosecutions, or constitute an unwarranted invasion of anyone's privacy. The question then arises whether the disclosures of such information, even if the source has been identified publicly, would "interfere with enforcement proceedings" and hence be protected from disclosure.

The statute can and should be interpreted to protect the confidentiality of such information. Successful investigation and prosecution, particularly in the areas of official corruption and "white-collar" crime, often depend heavily on the voluntary cooperation of the subjects of the investigation or their close associates. This cooperation would diminish substantially if information from such sources was subject to ready disclosure under the Freedom of Information Act after the inquiry was closed.

In this sense, public disclosure would interfere with law enforcement proceedings and the information would be protected under the current language of the statute. However, the language is sufficiently ambiguous that its interpretation could involve litigation that would extend for several years. The very existence of such litigation, putting in doubt the validity of prosecutors' assurances to sources of information, might deter many persons from cooperating with Federal law enforcement authorities. The statute's language suggests that Congress weighed the value of such cooperation against the value of disclosure and concluded that the former should receive greater weight. The statute should be amended to make clear that information furnished on a confidential basis to a Federal law enforcement agency is protected from disclosure.

Protecting the Integrity of Executive Branch Functions in Law Enforcement

Some of the actual abuses of "Watergate", and many attempted abuses, can be traced to pressures upon agencies with law-enforcement functions by requests or directives from White House staff members whose purpose was to serve the President's political interest. Executive branch agencies with these kinds of responsibilities, such as the Secret Service, the Federal Bureau of Investigation and the Internal Revenue Service, should respond to Presidential direction in broad policy areas and should be generally accountable to the President for the performance of their functions. But their responsiveness should not be such as to make them part of the President's political apparatus, particularly since their powers and duties involve basic rights of citizens.

Independence of Agency Heads and Staff. The persons appointed by the President and confirmed by the Senate to head such agencies as the FBI, IRS and the Secret Service should, like the Attorney General, be highly qualified individuals, with independent reputations, who had not taken leading roles in the President's political campaigns. They should be capable of making independent judgments and authorized to appoint similarly qualified subordinates. In exercising their power to advise and consent to Presidential nominations of such officials, Senators should stress the sensitivity of the respective agencies' functions and the danger of their over-responsiveness to political concerns.

Congressional Oversight. The oversight powers and responsibilities of Congress can provide an effective restraint on possible misuse of such sensitive agencies. Congress should exercise effective policy oversight in areas subject to abuse, such as law enforcement and intelligence functions. Recent disclosures about some of the activities of the CIA, FBI, and IRS suggest that such oversight has been seriously deficient in the past. Oversight should include regular review of agency policies, the nature of priority programs, allocations of resources, intelligence programs, internal inspection procedures, compliance with audit requirements, and similar indications of the manner in which such agencies are performing their sensitive functions. The oversight function can and should include, without the need for new laws, a regular monitoring of the nature and frequency of White House action directives about individuals subject to possible scrutiny by the enforcement agencies. Policy oversight, however, should not be allowed to become Congressional intervention in particular matters, such as criminal and tax investigations, in which the agencies are engaged; over-responsiveness to the personal or political interests of Members of Congress is no less evil than over-responsiveness to the White House.

Liability of an Incumbent President to Criminal Prosecution. One of the most difficult legal and policy questions WSPF faced was whether to seek an indictment of President Nixon along with the indictment of several of his former aides in connection with the Watergate cover-up conspiracy. After careful deliberation, Special Prosecutor Jaworski concluded that an indictment of President Nixon for such crimes would not be upheld by the Supreme Court, and that the litigation leading to such an adverse decision would be prolonged and might complicate the impeachment inquiry then underway in the House of Representatives. Because of these conclusions and because the evidence regarding President Nixon was clearly relevant to the House inquiry, the Special Prosecutor chose to ask the grand jury to transmit an evidentiary report to the Committee considering the President's impeachment.

The Special Prosecutor's conclusion about the President's indictability was not easily reached, and the legal standard needs clarification. Should such a question arise in the future, it would be helpful to know with more certainty whether the Constitution permits the indictment of an incumbent President, and if so, for what kinds of crimes, and what relationship such a prosecution has to the exercise of Congress' impeachment power. The worst time to answer such questions is when they arise; perhaps the best time is the present, while the memory of relevant events is fresh. Congress should consider these issues and clarify them by constitutional amendment.

Control of the Intelligence and National Security Functions

The executive branch of government exercises its greatest enforcement powers when its agents identify persons or groups as a threat to internal order or to the Nation's security. Acting without court approval, law enforcement agencies can gather, store and use large amounts of information about these persons and groups. These activities have been scrutinized, and are under scrutiny, by many organizations—the Rockefeller Commission on CIA Activities [see p. 401], the Senate and House Select Committees on Intelligence [see p. 873] and subcommittees of the House and Senate Judiciary Committees. Since many of these activities spanned two decades and others did not involve Presidential appointees or White House staff members, WSPF investigations covered only part of these prior federal enforcement efforts. The recommendations of the inquiry groups mentioned above should be given immediate consideration by the executive and legislative branches. The following two suggestions arose from WSPF's work.

Policies Regarding the Intelligence Function. Much of what goes awry in intelligence functions can be laid to secret, subjective judgments about the establishment of priorities for intelligence-gathering, the selection of the kinds of information to be gathered, a failure to analyze gathered information adequately and the stubborn failure to reappraise decisions over time. The intelligence function should be subject to the same policy procedures as any other important government enterprise.

Therefore, each agency with significant intelligence-gathering responsibilities, including the CIA, FBI, and IRS, should formulate written policies that include the purposes for which intelligence is to be gathered, the methods to be used in obtaining information, the kinds of information to be sought, and provisions for periodic review of priorities and purging of records that no longer serve an important or legitimate purpose.

These policy statements should be submitted to a Presidentially-appointed domestic intelligence policy review board that includes agency heads and representatives of the public. The board would hear the justifications for each policy and have the authority to make public recommendations.

The general policy statements of each agency should be made public. This can be accomplished without any threat to the effectiveness of the intelligence function and can serve as guides for press and citizen scrutiny of agency operations.

"National Security" Exception to the Warrant Requirement for Searches and Seizures. In *United States* v. *Ehrlichman,* which charged that the entry into the office of Daniel Ellsberg's psychiatrist by the White House "Plumbers" constituted a violation of the Fourth Amendment, the Special Prosecutor maintained both in the District Court and in the Court of Appeals that interests of "national security" cannot justify the lack of a judicially-authorized search warrant to enter a citizen's home or office, in order to seize or copy documents. Although the Special Prosecutor acknowledged that Attorneys General in the past in foreign intelligence cases had authorized warrantless physical trespasses to place electronic eavesdropping devices, he argued that no Attorney General and no President had claimed the constitutional power to authorize or, in fact had authorized warrantless entries to seize documents from citizens. To WSPF's knowledge, that remains a fact.

In the Court of Appeals, however, the Department of Justice filed a brief stating the Department's view on "the legality of forms of surveillance in the United States without a warrant in cases involving foreign espionage or intelligence." The brief continued:

> It is the position of the Department of Justice that such activities must be very carefully controlled. There must be solid reason to believe that foreign espionage or intelligence is involved. In addition, the intrusion into any zone of expected privacy must be kept to the minimum and there must be personal authorization by the President or the Attorney General. The United States believes that activities so controlled are lawful under the Fourth Amendment.
>
> In regard to warrantless searches related to foreign espionage or intelligence, the Department does not believe there is a constitutional difference between searches conducted by wiretapping and those involving physical entries into private premises. One form of search is no less serious than another. It is and has long been the Department's view that warrantless searches involving physical entries into private premises are justified under the proper circumstances when related to foreign espionage or intelligence....

The Department's long-held "view" is based solely on policies and authorized practices with regard to electronic surveillance and is not based on any historical record involving authorized physical break-ins to seize tangible items. Moreover, in dealing with the Department on this matter,

WSPF found that the historical record even with respect to electronic surveillance is not entirely clear. Attorneys General over the years have not always taken positions consistent with those of their predecessors, and there is no centralized, complete record of prior practices and policies.

This is obviously a matter of great public importance, affecting not only basic constitutional rights but also the national security. Although ultimately the courts must answer the constitutional question—what power if any the President and his chief legal officer (the Attorney General) have to authorize warrantless searches and seizures in the name of national security—the current policy of the executive should be subject to thorough Congressional and public scrutiny. Accordingly, it is recommended:

(a) Past memoranda setting forth the policy positions of the Presidents and Attorneys General should be disclosed publicly, and

(b) The Administration should promulgate publicly its current policy, stating the precise power claimed by the President and setting forth in as great detail as possible the factors and standards that now govern the President's and Attorney General's exercise of discretion in authorizing warrantless foreign intelligence searches and seizures.

Political Financing and Campaign Tactics

Campaign Financing and Reporting. WSPF's experience in attempting to enforce the campaign financing and reporting laws, some newly enacted and others on the books for many years, suggests that continuing enforcement efforts can be improved and that such efforts would be aided by certain changes in the statutory requirements and prohibitions.

1. *Proactive Enforcement Policy.* In many of WSPF's election law investigations and prosecutions, defense counsel contended that there had been a long history of non-enforcement of the applicable criminal statutes, and that the Special Prosecutor's office should take that history into account by deciding either that no charges should be brought or that some mitigation of proposed charges would be appropriate. This argument had its greatest force with respect to the registration and reporting provisions of the universally criticized Federal Corrupt Practices Act, which has been repealed. Only one reported prosecution had ever been brought, in 1934, and the Justice Department had long followed a policy, enunciated by Attorney General Herbert Brownell in 1954, of not initiating investigations except upon referral by the Clerk of the House of Representatives or the Secretary of the Senate, the officials to whom reports were required to be made. Such referrals rarely occurred. With respect to the prohibition against contributions by Government contractors (18 U.S.C. §611), no reported prosecutions had ever been brought. In the case of the prohibition against corporate or labor union contributions (18 U.S.C. §610) the record was somewhat better: a number of unions and union officials had been prosecuted, and some corporations had also been charged, but generally the individual corporate officers responsible for the making of illegal contributions had not been charged.

It is important to the integrity of both law enforcement and the electoral process that this history not be repeated. The Department of Justice should use the resources and make the effort necessary to monitor actively areas of possible abuse and begin investigations without waiting for formal referrals or complaints. The Department should announce its intent to pursue an aggressive policy of enforcement of the election laws. To give further notice of such an enforcement policy, individual notices should be mailed to candidates for federal office, political committees and their officers, and corporations, labor unions, and their officers.

As a result of the 1974 amendments to the Federal Election Campaign Act, the Federal Elections Commission has a clear responsibility to monitor and investigate campaign violations and make civil dispositions or refer criminal matters to the Department of Justice for possible prosecution. The Commission presumably will discharge its duties responsibly and effectively, but the existence of the Commission should not inhibit the development and promulgation of new Justice Department enforcement policies, particularly in view of the ongoing legal challenges to the Commission's own enforcement powers. Vigorous enforcement efforts by the Justice Department would have a marked deterrent effect on would-be violators of the election laws.

2. *Federal Election Campaign Act* (FECA)

a. *Reporting responsibility of the chairman of a political committee under 2 U.S.C. §434(a).* This statute places sole responsibility for filing reports of campaign receipts and expenditures on the treasurer of a political committee. This approach tends to focus the law's requirements on a campaign official who often is not an important figure in the committee hierarchy but merely acts as the chairman's agent. A committee chairman can therefore attempt to avoid responsibility for his committee's reporting violations by claiming that the statute imposes no reporting duty on him. While the "aiding and abetting" provisions of federal criminal law can be used under some circumstances to hold a chairman liable for such violations, the treasurer-centered language of §434(a) permits the raising of a false issue which can mislead a court or jury. The statute should be amended to place equal reporting responsibility on the chairman and treasurer of a political committee.

b. *Penalty provisions of 2 U.S.C. §441.* This section, establishing penalties for FECA violations, appears to pose an ambiguity. It reads as follows:

§441. Penalties for violations

(a) Any person who violates any of the provisions of this chapter shall be fined not more than $1,000 or imprisoned not more than one year, or both.

(b) In case of any conviction under this chapter, where the punishment inflicted does not include imprisonment, such conviction shall be deemed a misdemeanor conviction only.

This language raised problems in two cases brought by WSPF in which defendants entered guilty pleas to misdemeanor FECA violations and then argued that Section (b) of the statute would not permit the judge to sentence them to imprisonment. WSPF argued that the statute permits a prison sentence for a misdemeanor and does not create any felony designation. In neither case did the sentencing judge accept the defense contention. However, the statute should be amended to clarify Congress' intent, and it is recommended that §441(b) be eliminated as superfluous.

c. *Statute of limitations: 2 U.S.C. §455(a).* The FECA was amended in 1974 to require that any prosecution for violations of its provisions, and certain other criminal statutes dealing with campaign financing, be commenced within 3 years of the violation. Before the amendment, under both the FECA and its predecessor the Federal Corrupt Practices Act, the period of limitation had been 5 years, as it is for almost all Federal crimes. It is often difficult, in dealing with "white-collar" crime generally, to uncover violations and bring violators to indictment even within the normal 5-year period. The difficulty increases when campaign-law violators, including both givers and receivers of contributions, make efforts to conceal the illegal nature of their activities, as many did in the 1972 campaigns. Under such circumstances, with a 3-year statute of limitations, the chances are excellent that many violations will be barred from prosecution by the time they are discovered. Another advantage of a 5-year limitation period is that it permits a new Administration to prosecute violations that might have occurred at any time during the previous President's last term of office, making it impossible for the previous Administration to cover up its election violations and bar pursuit of those crimes by a new Administration circumscribed by the short, 3-year limitations. No convincing reasons have been advanced for granting this special privilege to Federal candidates, and the statute should be amended to readopt the 5-year period now applicable to all other persons in the criminal code.

d. *Intent-centered definitions in 2 U.S.C. §431(e) and (f).* The Act requires the reporting of "contributions" and "expenditures" by political committees; these subsections define those terms for reporting purposes as contributions or expenditures made "for the purpose of...influencing" nominations, primaries, or general elections. This definition seems unnecessarily narrow, permitting campaign officials to contend that contributions received or expenditures made after an election has taken place need not be reported because they could not have been made with the requisite intent to influence the election. Similarly, it has been argued that the campaign-fund expenditures that resulted in "hush-money" payments to the Watergate defendants in 1972 were not reportable because they were not made for the purpose of influencing the election. If the policy behind the Act is to promote disclosure of the financial dealings of political campaign committees, the "definitions" section should be amended to require that committees report all financial transactions in which they engage (subject to the existing minimum dollar amounts), regardless of the purpose of the transaction or whether it occurred before or after an election.

3. *Solicitation and Receipt of Contributions in Federal Buildings (18 U.S.C. §603).* During the course of its investigations, the Campaign Contributions Task Force learned of instances where members of Congress or other Federal employees accepted voluntary campaign contributions from private citizens in Federal Office buildings. This practice appears on its face to be prohibited by this felony statute, which, in essence, prohibits any person from soliciting or receiving a contribution in any Federal building. The statute's legislative history, however, indicates that it was intended to protect Federal civil service employees from coercion and thus prohibit the solicitation or receipt of contributions only from such employees. Any other interpretation of the statute would give felony status to any person who merely received campaign funds from any other person in a Federal building, even though the funds were unsolicited and neither person was a Government employee, when the identical conduct if performed a short distance away, i.e., on the sidewalk outside the building, would involve no criminal act at all.

On the basis of that legislative history, the Watergate Special Prosecution Force declined to prosecute in those cases. Some might argue that the solicitation or receipt of political contributions in Federal buildings from non-Federal employees by elected Federal officials should be permitted, but there are strong policy considerations which would support a prohibition against such action by appointed Federal officials, such as cabinet officers or other executive branch officials.

Because of this conflict between the plain meaning of the present statute and the legislative history of this Act, the statute should be amended to state whether it does or does not apply only to contributions to and from Federal employees, and to clarify the question of its applicability to elected as well as appointed officials.

4. *Contributions of Corporate or Union Funds Under 18 U.S.C. §610.*
a. *Designation of corporate violations as felony or misdemeanor.* The amended statute imposes a fine of $25,000 for each violation by a corporation or labor union, but does not specify whether such a violation is a felony or misdemeanor. This omission sometimes leads to confusion when a corporation or union pleads guilty to an information alleging a violation of §610, and an individual is charged under 18 U.S.C. §2 with causing, aiding, or abetting the violation. The absence of a penalty of imprisonment for such conduct suggests that it is a misdemeanor, but the size of the maximum fine is reserved for the felony classification defined elsewhere in the Federal criminal statutes. Section 610 should be amended to designate a violation by a corporation or union as either a felony or a misdemeanor.
b. *Definition of the term "officer."* The section prohibits an officer of a corporation or union from consenting to a contribution of corporate or union funds, but does not define the term "officer." WSPF has taken the position, and a trial court has agreed in one case, that the term applies to anyone who performs the managerial functions that an officer ordinarily would perform, regardless of title. But the lack of a definition permits defendants in certain

cases to argue that the term applies only to individuals holding a position specifically entitled "officer" in the corporate charter or by-laws, or the laws of the State of incorporation. A definition of "officer" should be added to Section 610 to include all corporate or union employees who perform the functions of an officer.

c. *Definition of "willful" consent.* The section prohibits corporate or union officers, and campaign officials who receive contributions, from consenting to contributions of corporate or union funds, and distinguishes between the misdemeanor of "consent" and the felony of "willful consent." WSPF has taken the position that "willful consent" by a donor requires only the knowledge of the operative facts and action taken with that knowledge which results in the making of an illegal contribution, rather than the affirmative knowledge that the contribution is illegal. But that position has not been fully tested in litigation and leaves open the question of what is a "nonwillful" violation—i.e., what defenses of good faith or reliance on advice of counsel will reduce the violation from a felony to a misdemeanor. A related question is whether the language penalizing "nonwillful" violations imposes a standard of strict liability, making a corporate or union officer liable for consenting to a contribution even if he had no knowledge of its corporate or union source. Similarly, in prosecuting recipients WSPF has taken the position that a "willful" violation requires actual knowledge of a contribution's corporate or union source, while a "non-willful" violation is established by reckless disregard of the possibility that a contribution comes from such a source. But it is possible to interpret the statute as one imposing strict liability on recipients as well as donors.

A collateral question is whether there can be a conspiracy to commit a "non-willful" §610 violation. While one court in a case unrelated to WSPF's work has held that such a conspiracy can be charged, the basis for this finding is unclear in §610.

Section 610 should be amended to clarify the definitions of "willful" and "non-willful" conduct, preferably as WSPF has interpreted the terms, and to make clear whether a "non-willful" violation can be the object of a conspiracy.

5. *Contributions by Government Contractors Under 18 U.S.C. §611*

a. *Nature of requisite contractual relationship.* The statute prohibits the giving of a campaign contribution by anyone who has entered into a contract with the United States "either for the rendition of personal services or furnishing any material, supplies, or equipment to the United States...or for selling any land or building to the United States...," if the contract payment includes funds appropriated by Congress. This language leaves open the question whether a person or firm leasing property to the government is a contractor within the statute's meaning. Based on the section's legislative history, the Department of Justice has taken the position, to which WSPF has adhered, that such a person or firm is not a contractor under the section. However, that position seems inconsistent with the statute's general purpose of preventing improper influence on decisions about spending government funds. The section should be amended to cover lessors of property along with other contractors.

b. *Liability of individual partners in partnerships.* Section 611 applies to corporations, partnerships, and individuals—anyone holding a contract with the government. Because a corporation is a separate entity from the individuals who own its stock, the Department of Justice and WSPF have taken the position that shareholders of corporations holding government contracts may make contributions of funds they receive from corporate dividends without being in violation of §611. Under the provisions of §610, officers and employees of such a corporation also may contribute personal funds, including those derived from corporate dividends, to a political fund established to make campaign contributions with corporate identity. However, because a partnership is not an entity separate from its individual partners, the Justice Department has taken the position that partners may not make personal contributions if their partnership holds a government contract. This leads to the anomalous situation in which corporate shareholders and employees may contribute personal funds either individually or jointly with corporate identity without being in violation of §611, but members of a partnership which holds a government contract are prohibited from giving similar support to the candidates of their choice. The statute should be amended to place partners and corporate officers and shareholders of firms holding government contracts on the same footing.

c. *General scope of §611.* The evident purpose of this section is to prohibit the possible use of campaign contributions as a means of influencing Government actions that affect potential contributors. But its coverage is limited to potential donors having a contractual relationship with the Government. Other donors that do not necessarily hold any Government contracts might have an equally if not more compelling interest in influencing Government action—for example, airlines which depend on Government decisions about routes or oil companies depending on Government decisions about import quotas. At the same time, §611 is broad enough to include any person or firm having any contractual relationship with the Government, no matter how small or insignificant that contract may be in the person's or firm's overall business. In enforcing §611, WSPF exercised its discretion to limit prosecutions under the statute to firms whose contracts with the Government provided at least 20 percent of their gross receipts for the year in question, and it would seem reasonable to amend the statute to narrow its coverage along those lines. At the same time, the statute should be redrafted to cover contributions by persons or firms whose possible interest in improperly influencing Government action is based on either contracts with the Government or other relationships, such as the regulated character of the person's or firm's business.

Such an amendment might also involve reduction of the disparity of penalties under both §610 and §611. As the law now stands, an officer of a corporation with a substantial interest in Government regulatory action, but with no contractual relationship, can be sentenced to two years' imprisonment if he willfully consents to a contribution of corporate funds, while an individual holding a small contract with the Government can be sentenced to five years' imprisonment for making a personal contribution to any federal candidate. It might be appropriate to reduce the maximum penalty under §611, while broadening the statute's subject-matter coverage. A contribution made for the purpose of influencing a Government action is already subject to a bribery charge.

Questionable Campaign Practices. In addition to its inquiries into possible violations of campaign financing and reporting laws, WSPF investigated allegations of other campaign activities generally known as "dirty tricks." Many of these activities seemed clearly at odds with prevailing standards of acceptable campaign conduct, but did not appear to be covered by existing federal criminal statutes. [Footnote: The Federal criminal code...prohibits publication or distribution of campaign literature without a designation of its true source, as well as misrepresentation by a candidate or his agent that he is acting on behalf of another candidate or campaign.] As a result, the Senate Select Committee recommended legislation to prohibit the following activities during political campaigns:

> (1) obtaining or causing another to obtain employment in a campaign by false pretenses in order to spy on or obstruct the campaign;
> (2) requesting or knowingly disbursing campaign funds for the purpose of promoting or financing violations of election laws;
> (3) stealing, taking by false pretenses, or copying without authorization campaign documents which are not available for public dissemination;
> (4) fraudulently misrepresenting oneself as representing a candidate (applying to any person, not just candidates and their agents as in §617.)

In addition, legislation has been introduced to prohibit any payment to another person for actions that violate any election law (covering payments of campaign funds and funds from other sources), and to make any violation of State or Federal law a separate Federal offense if committed for the purpose of interfering with or affecting the outcome of a Federal election.

These proposals, designed to eliminate practices which are clearly disruptive of the political process, raise serious questions about the proper role of the criminal justice system in policing day-to-day campaign activities. There are stronger reasons for legislating against corrupt campaign financing practices than for using criminal sanctions to enforce standards of behavior during the heat of a political campaign. In the former instance, corruption is likely to influence not only the outcome of the campaign but also decisions of elected officials on matters of interest to their contributors; by contrast, "dirty tricks" perpetrated during a campaign have, at most, only a temporary effect, if any.

Several other considerations complicate the question of whether to outlaw "dirty tricks" not encompassed by existing legislation. First, the criminal justice system is not a desirable watch-dog over the daily operations of political campaigns. Proper enforcement efforts would produce a tremendous drain on law enforcement resources and could inhibit the legitimate activities of candidates and their supporters, as well as create dangers of prosecutorial misconduct. In addition, many "dirty tricks" are exposed during the course of a political campaign, to the detriment of the candidate on whose behalf they are conducted. The experience of WSPF also suggests that most campaign "pranksters" are persons who, because of their youthful inexperience, fail to appreciate the nature of their conduct. Finally, there is the problem of defining prohibited conduct in this area so as to give adequate notice to potential offenders, while at the same time avoiding infringement on the First Amendment rights of candidates and their supporters.

All these considerations suggest the wisdom of keeping criminal prohibitions to a minimum. Both the Constitution and the nation's experience as a democracy suggest that broad criminal restraints on political activity and expression are unnecessary and unwise. Even so, some reforms are desirable. In terms of the criminal law, it might be advisable to prohibit the copying, stealing or taking by false pretenses of campaign documents not available to the public.

The suggestion that campaign "dirty tricks" be dealt with chiefly by the political process is based also on the theory that the recently created Federal Election Commission, if given expanded powers, would be able to detect and expose improper campaign practices. The Commission is presently empowered to receive complaints and conduct investigations of alleged violations of §617, as well as transgressions of campaign financing laws. The Commission's authority should be broadened to include investigation of violations of §612 and of any other legal prohibitions enacted in the future as to campaign tactics. The Commission should also be empowered to adopt standards of campaign conduct to define what behavior is not acceptable in political campaigns, and to enforce such standards through its investigative powers, its authority to assess civil penalties, and its authority to issue public reports describing instances or patterns of misconduct in particular campaigns.

Lesson of Watergate

One final note, albeit a personal one. One hundred years ago, an America still recovering from its devastating Civil War wrestled with the pay-off scandals of the Grant Administration and approached its centennial celebration. Historians report that few candidates reached the United States Senate without financial support from the "special interests"— railroads, oil companies, textile concerns, the iron and steel industry and mining companies. The Nation had grown so weary that even the usually optimistic Longfellow wrote:

> Ah, woe is me
> I hoped to see my country rise to heights
> Of happiness and freedom yet unreached

By other nations, but the climbing wave
Pauses, lets go its hold, and slides again
Back to the common level, with a hoarse
Death rattle in its throat. I am too old
To hope for better days.

Now again, at the Bicentennial, the Nation has grown weary. Much contributed to this, but few can deny that uncovering years of actual and alleged Government abuses has played its part. Institutions once again had to earn the faith of the people in whose names they acted.

That lesson became clear. When Archibald Cox was fired, Americans rose in anger. The telegrams came to us from Middle America—small cities, towns, and hamlets that only the residents had ever heard of. The national Government had offended its people's sense of justice. The citizens wanted to control what would happen, and they eventually did. When vigilance erupted, institutions responded. One must believe that unresponsive power, both public and private, can never overcome that will.

SURVEY OF COMPETENCY
OF ADULT AMERICANS

October 29, 1975

One-fifth of adult Americans—more than 23 million—are too poorly educated to function successfully in a complex society, according to a report published Oct. 29 by the U.S. Office of Education, which funded the project. An additional 40 million adults were found to have difficulties with the reading, writing and computing required by such tasks as applying for a job, following a doctor's instructions or making out a personal check. The four-year project, entitled the Adult Performance Level Study (APL), represented the first nationwide effort to assess the "functional competence" of Americans—that is, their ability to use basic skills in day-to-day life. The study's conclusion that more than one-half of the nation's adults were not proficient in these skills prompted U.S. Education Commissioner Terrell H. Bell to urge "major rethinking of education on several levels."

The findings of the APL survey were not the only indication of serious trouble in the nation's schools. A Senate staff report had pointed out in April (see p. 207) that widespread violence and vandalism in the schools were diverting needed funds from educational programs and demoralizing teachers and students. Student performance on many standardized tests, moreover, was worsening year by year. The College Entrance Examination Board reported in September that average verbal and mathematical scores on its Scholastic Aptitude Test (SAT) in 1975 had fallen 10 and 8 points respectively from the previous year, continuing a 12-year decline.

High school students as a whole, in apparent contrast to the college-bound aspirants taking the SAT test, showed a two per cent improvement

in "functional literacy"—mastery of simple reading matter—between 1971
and 1974, according to a September report of the National Assessment of
Educational Progress (NAEP). But the federally subsidized project had
reported earlier, in March 1975, that high school students in the same
period of time had fallen behind in their knowledge of science. And in
November the NAEP reported there had been a steady drop in writing skills
of young Americans, with "increases in awkwardness, run-on sentences and
incoherent paragraphs."

Not surprisingly, confidence in schools was also down, according to a
national survey conducted by the Gallup organization. Results published in
the December issue of the professional educators' journal, Phi Delta Kap-
pan, showed that significantly fewer adults than in 1974 considered local
schools "excellent." Also, a majority polled expressed a preference for
schools emphasizing discipline and "the Three R's."

Criticism and New Programs

Several developments accompanied the decline in student performance. Standardized tests and other traditional measures of achievement
often came under fire from minority group spokesmen who charged that
such methods of evaluating students were culture-bound to the white
middle class and failed to measure the abilities of other groups in American
society. At the same time, a growing "accountability of schools" movement
focusing on basic skills reflected dissatisfaction among middle-class
parents.

Schools and school systems began experimenting with granting credits for
demonstrated skills in such areas as consumer economics and communications or, as in Oregon, requiring this type of proficiency for high
school graduation. In the most far-reaching of these new programs, California offered 16- and 17-year-olds an optional proficiency test of basic
skills—reading, writing and math—and practical expertise. Those who
passed the four-hour exam would receive a certificate of proficiency and
could choose to leave school before the mandatory attendance age of 18. In
announcing the new policy, which was to take effect in January 1976,
California superintendent of schools Wilson Riles predicted that the
proficiency certificate would compare favorably to a high school diploma
because, unlike a diploma, the certificate would at least guarantee that a
student could read.

APL Test Methods

In constructing its national test for "functional competence" in adults
the APL team, based at the University of Texas, consulted educators,
professionals in business and management as well as "undereducated and
unemployed" persons to find out what types of skills an adult needed to

function successfully in American society of the seventies. "Success" was defined in terms of income, education and job status. Testing was conducted by a professional opinion-sampling organization which interviewed a total of 7,500 adults in five separate national surveys. The fifth survey, using a composite of test items derived from a review of the previous four series of interviews, included 1,500 persons. The APL estimates of functional competence were based on the results of the last survey. The report, completed in March 1975, was circulated among educators before it was released by the Office of Education in October.

Excerpts from Adult Functional Competency: A Summary, *published by the U.S. Office of Education, Oct. 29, 1975:*

I. OBJECTIVES

The ability to use skills and knowledge with the functional competence needed for meeting the requirements of adult living is often called "functional literacy," "survival literacy," or occasionally "coping skills." The central objectives of the Adult Performance Level (APL) project are to specify the competencies which are functional to economic and educational success in today's society and to develop devices for assessing those competencies of the adult population of the United States....

II. A THEORY AND METHODOLOGY OF ADULT FUNCTIONAL COMPETENCY

The APL theory of functional competency was arrived at in the following manner. The staff focused on the first objective of the project which was to identify basic requirements for adult living. Rather than rely upon expert opinion, four simultaneous lines of research were pursued.

1. *Review of related literature and research....*

2. An extensive *survey of state and federal agencies and foundations* was conducted in order to identify characteristics which distinguished the successful from the unsuccessful adult. The assumption was that a major source of knowledge of minimum performance criteria existed in the experiences, accumulated data, and reports of professionals who deal with the minimally performing adult....

3. A series of *conferences on adult needs* was conducted in different regions of the country. Adult educators, members of the private sector (e.g., supervisors and personnel managers), and members of different state and federal agencies were brought together to review APL progress....

4. A continuing series of semi-structured *interviews with undereducated and underemployed persons* was begun in order to gather some first-hand data on their felt needs.

"Literacy" Redefined

The result of these activities, which occupied much of the first year of the study, was a taxonomy of adult needs which finally came to be called "general knowledge areas." These general areas, which may be considered as the content of adult literacy, are now known as (1) consumer economics, (2) occupational (or occupationally-related) knowledge, (3) community resources, (4) health, and (5) government and law.

Having identified the general knowledge areas which seemed to be the most critical to adult performance related to the acquisition of literacy, data which had been obtained were then reanalyzed. This time, however, the concern was not with the content of literacy, but with the skills involved. Four primary skills seemed to account for the vast majority of requirements placed on adults. These skills were named (1) communication skills (reading, writing, speaking, and listening), (2) computation skills, (3) problem solving skills, and (4) interpersonal relations skills.

By this time it should be clear that the concern of the APL project is much more than the stereotypical notion of literacy. Because the term "literacy" popularly connotes a low level of functioning (e.g., the ability to read and write one's name) which may have nothing to do with functional competence, we have chosen to excise the word "literacy" from the rest of this exposition. Instead, we will consistently use the phrase "functional competency." This practice seems to be preferable to reeducating the whole world concerning the true meaning of literacy....

Methodology

1. *Specification of competencies....*

2. *Development of performance indicators.* Performance indicators are written for each competency. These are not "test items" in the traditional sense. Because they reflect requirements taken from adult life, they are small simulations of what is demanded of the adult by his or her society, and they require the adult to employ communication, computation, problem-solving, and interpersonal relations skills in a variety of adult-related situations.

3. *Field test and subsequent revision.* Initial versions of the performance indicators were field tested with undereducated and underemployed adults. An initial round of field testing involving some 3,500 adults was conducted with the cooperation of Adult Basic Education programs in 30 states. Since that time, several thousand more adults have been tested in a number of states with subsequent versions of the performance indicators. Field testing and subsequent revision of performance indicators is a continuous, rather than one-time process,...

Information gathered during the field test stage is used to respecify objectives and to improve the quality of performance indicators....

4. *National assessment of competency.* The next step in the APL research process is to determine national levels of performance with regard to the objectives. Performance indicators are formatted into a series of interview schedules. With the assistance of a subcontractor (Opinion Research Corporation, Princeton, New Jersey) a representative sample of adults is drawn from the continental United States, excluding Alaska and Hawaii, and data are obtained from this sample. To date, five independent samples of the population have been drawn, each with a size of not less than 1,500, for a total of 7,500 adults. The overall precision of each sample is about 4% at the 95% confidence level for an item which breaks at the 50-50 level.

5. *Determination of competency levels.* The final stage of the process is to determine meaningful and well-defined competency levels from data gathered in the various national surveys. This determination is accomplished by (1) examining the performance of the population on an objective-by-objective basis, and (2) describing overall competency in terms of three levels based on an aggregate index (This aggregate index of functional competency is defined below). In essence, the nationally representative survey data are used to develop "competency profiles" which are associated with different levels of adult success as measured by income, job status, and education. Three such levels have been chosen and are called simply APL 1, APL 2, and APL 3.

APL 1 (Adults Who Function With Difficulty)

APL 1's are those adults whose mastery of competency objectives is associated with:

1. Inadequate income of poverty level or less
2. Inadequate education of eight years of school or fewer
3. Unemployment or occupations of low job status

APL 2 (Functional Adults)

APL 2's are those adults whose mastery of competency objectives is associated with:

1. Income of more than poverty level but no discretionary income
2. Education of nine to eleven years of school
3. Occupations falling in medial job status range

APL 3 (Proficient Adults)

APL 3's are those adults whose mastery of competency objectives is associated with:

1. High levels of income or varying amounts of discretionary income
2. High levels of education, high school completion or more
3. High levels of job status

...Those persons classified as APL 1 are, by and large, "functionally incompetent" or adults who function with difficulty. APL 2's are competent, or adults functioning on a minimal level; and APL 3's are proficient in that their mastery of competency objectives is associated with the highest levels of income, job status and education.

Since the sample data are nationally representative, it is possible to estimate the proportion of the U.S. adult population which comprises each APL level....

III. HOW FUNCTIONALLY COMPETENT ARE U.S. ADULTS?

In general, the answer to the question posed by this section is "not as competent as we thought." Overall, approximately one-fifth of U.S. adults are functioning with difficulty. This estimate is based on a representative sample of adults performing on indicators which cover the five general knowledge areas and four skills.

The results of the APL national survey on functional competency will be presented as follows: (1) For each general knowledge area and skill area, the proportion of the population estimated to be in levels 1, 2, or 3 are reported; and (2) For each major demographic grouping, the proportion of the population estimated to be in levels 1, 2, or 3 are presented.

Competency levels by knowledge area and skills. The percentages of the adult population which are in APL levels 1, 2 or 3 as determined by performance on those indicators in the survey which measure knowledge and skills are presented in the following table.

Areas	APL Competency Levels		
	1	2	3
Occupational Knowledge	19.1	31.9	49.0
Consumer Economics	29.4	33.0	37.6
Government and Law	25.8	26.2	48.0
Health	21.3	30.3	48.3
Community Resources	22.6	26.0	51.4
Reading	21.7	32.2	46.1
Problem Solving	28.0	23.4	48.5
Computation	32.9	26.3	40.8
Writing	16.4	25.5	58.1
Overall Competency Levels	19.7	33.9	46.3

In terms of the general knowledge areas, the greatest area of difficulty appears to be Consumer Economics. Almost 30% of the population falls into the lowest level (APL 1), while one-third of the population is categorized as APL 2. Translated into population figures, some 34.7 million adult Americans function with difficulty and an additional 39 million are functional, (but not proficient) in coping with basic requirements that are related to Consumer Economics.

The highest proportion of proficient persons (most able to cope) is found in relation to Community Resources. Over half of the U.S. population falls into APL level 3. This is followed by Occupational Knowledge; again, almost half of the population is estimated to be proficient in dealing with occupationally related tasks. Although the least proportion of persons in comparison to all areas are in level 1 of Occupational Knowledge, this still indicates that about one of every five adults in the U.S. function with difficulty or are unable to perform correctly on occupationally related performance indicators.

A greater proportion of people is unable to perform basic computations than the other skills. Approximately one-third of the population, or 39 million adults, functions with difficulty, and a little over one-fourth, or 29.5 million adults, is functional but not proficient in task performance on items requiring mathematical manipulation. The area of greatest competency in comparison with other skills is in writing. However, even though almost three-fifths of the population performed adequately on tasks requiring writing skills, 16% of the adults in the U.S., or, some 18.9 million persons, are unable to cope successfully.

Competency levels by demographic groupings.... In general, the three success indices (level of education, family income and job status) demonstrate a positive relationship with performance. The percent of the population estimated to be in APL levels 1, 2, and 3 for each reporting group of relevant demographic variables as indicated by task performance is presented in the following table.

Demographic Variables	APL Competency Levels		
	1	**2**	**3**
Education			
0-3 years	85%	10%	6%
4-5	84	16	0
6-7	49	37	14
8-11	18	55	27
High school completed	11	37	52
Some college	9	27	64
College graduate plus	2	17	80
Family Income			
under $5,000	40%	39%	21%
$5,000-$6,999	20	44	36
$7,000-$9,999	24	39	37
$10,000-$14,999	14	34	52
$15,000 plus	8	26	66
Job Status			
Unskilled	30%	38%	32%
Semi-skilled	29	42	29
Skilled	24	33	43
Clerical-Sales	8	38	54
Professional-Managerial	11	28	61
Age			
18-29	16%	35%	49%
30-39	11	29	60
40-49	19	32	49
50-59	28	37	35
60-65	35	40	24

	1	2	3
Sex			
Male	17%	31%	52%
Female	23	35	42
Ethnicity			
White	16%	34%	50%
Black	44	39	17
Spanish-surname	56	26	18
Other	26	41	33
Occupational Status			
Employed	15%	28%	57%
Unemployed	36	30	34
Housewives	27	38	35
Number in Household			
1 person	21%	23%	56%
2-3	20	35	45
4-5	19	31	50
6-7	21	33	46
8 plus	43	22	35
Region			
Northeast	16%	36%	48%
North Central	15	42	43
South	25	37	38
West	15	35	50
Metropolitan Areas			
1 million plus	21%	39%	40%
under 1 million	15	38	47
Suburb	21	32	47
Urban	14	29	57

Success Variables

In relation to the "success" variables, for level of education the percentage of APL 1's rises steadily from about 2% for college graduates to about 85% for adults with less than 4 years of formal schooling. For family income, the percentage of functionally incompetent persons rises from about 8% for incomes of $15,000 or greater to 40% for those under $5,000 a year income. For occupation of chief wage earner, the percentage of APL 1's rises from about 11% for the professional and managerial category to approximately 30% for the unskilled.

There is a generally negative relationship between age and performance. Although the youngest group (18-29) does not have the lowest level of functionally incompetent adults, still the general trend is that the older the individual, the more likely that he/she is incompetent. It appears that males and females perform about the same; although there are minor differences with males estimated to have a greater percentage of APL 3's than females. As for ethnic groups, it appears that there are great differences between Whites and all other minority groups. While 16% of the Whites are estimated to be functionally incompetent, about 44% of the Black and 56% of the Spanish-surname groups are estimated to be so. Here, as with other variables that have been discussed, the differences are probably due to the relatively lower levels of income, education, job status, and job opportunity found among minority groups in this country.

The demographic comparison of regions of the U.S. indicates that while the Northeast, Northcentral and Western parts of the U.S. have about the same percentage of APL 1's, 2's and 3's, the South has more APL 1's and less APL 3's. While all other regions of the country are estimated to have about 16% functionally incompetent adults, approximately 25% in the South are predicted to be APL 1's. Thus, a greater percentage of adults in the South appear to be in need of educational assistance than other parts of the country.

Rural areas have the greatest estimated percentage of APL 1's (27%) with cities over one million and suburbs slightly less (about 21%), and cities under one million and other urban areas having the least percentage of APL 1's.

IV. THE VALIDITY AND RELIABILITY OF APL

Validity. A strong case can be made for the validity of the APL objectives and the performance data which relate to them. Consider the following argument:

1. The objectives derive from inputs from the appropriate segments of society....

2. Great care was taken to construct performance indicators which were, within budgetary and time constraints, the best possible measures of the objectives. In addition to a technical review by consultants, performance indicators were also reviewed by the groups mentioned in 1 above, and were processed through several cycles of field testing and redesigning before being used on a national sample....

3. Great care was also taken to design a national sample of adults and to exercise the proper control over field procedures in order to produce meaningful and precise results. As mentioned earlier, the sample design is straightforward, has a known precision, and is reproducible in the scientific sense....

Reliability. Although the term "reliability" is quite often used to refer to different constructs, "reliability" means temporal stability in the context of the APL project. That is, APL performance indicators are reliable to the extent that, assuming no major changes have taken place in either societal requirements or in the level of achievements of the general population, repeated measures produce identical results....

The traditional method of estimating reliability is repeated testing of a given sample. Coefficients of reliability calculated from total scores are used as decision variables for the estimation of reliability. No such coefficients are available at this time for APL measures, for two good reasons;

(1) Reliability coefficients are based on total scores. Total scores are never calculated in the development of competency levels from APL data. (2) A test-retest design for a national sample would have cost at least $100,000. This was money which was better spent on development and validation of objectives. There are, however, two valuable sources of information which are relevant to a discussion of the reliability of APL measures:

1. The fifth APL national survey consisted of a composite battery of items which had been used in previous surveys. Although changes were made in many of the items, some useful comparisons can be made on an item-by-item basis between results from earlier surveys and results of the final survey. Theoretically, if an item had not been changed at all, the estimates from two independent samples should differ only by the precision which each sample affords. For two independent samples of size 1,500, most items require a difference of 4% or more to indicate statistically significant differences (.05 level).

For the 39 items which were not changed between surveys, the mean absolute difference was 5.5% with most items having slightly higher p-values on the second sample than on the first. Although 5.5% is somewhat higher than the anticipated 4%, the reason for these results is quite clear. In order to minimize interview length (and maximize budgets), respondents in earlier surveys who failed to get a specified number of items correct during the initial portion of the interview were discontinued, under the assumption that most, if not all, of the remaining responses would be incorrect (items were arranged in order of difficulty). For the final survey, this criterion was omitted, so that every respondent completed all parts of the interview. The net effect was a desirable one—all respondents attempted practically every item. A side effect, however, was that p-values for easier items placed later in the interview tended to rise when compared with earlier results. Consequently, the overall difference between the samples is exaggerated. Most of that difference is due to a change in the criterion for completion, rather than factors relative to sample size, item format, or field procedure.

2. Another independent sample, drawn specifically for the State of Texas,...was simultaneous with the final national survey. Although detailed results are too numerous to mention here, data from the Texas effort, which replicated the national one, are remarkably consistent with national trends....

A final note of caution regarding the interpretation of APL results, particularly those dealing with the three levels of competency, must be sounded here. Those who are familiar with the APL objectives know very well that each one comprises a broad sector of human behavior. Clearly, it is fruitless to try to list and to measure all the behaviors which are embedded within a particular APL objective. Ultimately, one must operationalize the objective by selecting a set of behaviors as measures of that particular objective. All APL estimates of competency are based on such operational definitions, and their limitations must be kept in mind.

V. HOW DO WE MEET THE NEED?

The United States has been in a preeminent position of world power and influence for decades. Citizens of this country are justifiably proud of their country's accomplishments in industry, science, technology, the arts, and, perhaps most of all, in their system of universal free public education. Millions of mothers and fathers have intuitively subscribed to that tenet of the American dream which holds that education is the major avenue to success for their daughters and sons. Accordingly, Americans are, by many standards, the best educated and the most affluent people on earth.

OBJECTIVES FOR FUNCTIONAL COMPETENCY

Occupational Knowledge

GOAL: To develop a level of occupational knowledge which will enable adults to secure employment in accordance with their individual needs and interests.

1. Objective: To build an oral and written vocabulary related to occupational knowledge.

2. Objective: To identify sources of information (e.g., radio broadcasts, newspapers, etc.) which may lead to employment.

3. Objective: To define occupational categories in terms of the education and job experience required, and to know minimum requirements of given occupations.

4. Objective: To be aware of vocational testing and counseling methods which help prospective employees recognize job interests and qualifications.

5. Objective: To understand the differences among commercial employment agencies, government employment agencies and private employers.

6. Objective: To prepare for job applications and interviews.

7. Objective: To know standards of behavior for various types of employment.

8. Objective: To know attributes and skills which may lead to promotion.

9. Objective: To know the financial and legal aspects of employment.

10. Objective: To understand aspects of employment other than financial which would affect the individual's satisfaction with a job.

Consumer Economics

GOAL: To manage a family economy and to demonstrate an awareness of sound purchasing principles.

1. Objective: To build an oral and written consumer economics vocabulary. This should be an ongoing process through each objective.
2. Objective: To be able to count and convert coins and currency, and to convert weights and measures using measurement tables and mathematical operations.
3. Objective: To understand the concepts of sales tax and income tax.
4. Objective: To be aware of the basic principles of money management, including knowing the basics of consumer decision-making.
5. Objective: To use catalogs, consumer guides and other reference documents to select goods and services.
6. Objective: To be aware of factors that affect costs of goods and services and to determine the most economical places to shop.
7. Objective: To be aware of the principles of comparison shopping, and to be aware of the relationship of price to quality among brand names, and between "firsts" and "seconds" and to be able to substitute economy for quality according to individual needs.
8. Objective: To know the various methods by which goods are packaged and to know which methods are most cost-effective in terms of quality and storage.
9. Objective: To be able to take advantage of sales by knowing where to find them, by planning for their eventuality, and by being able to determine which are of worthwhile value to the individual.
10. Objective: To be aware of advertising techniques and to recognize appropriate and inappropriate forms of selling and advertising.
11. Objective: To know how to order food and to tip in a restaurant.
12. Objective: To be aware of different stores where home furnishings can be purchased and to determine the best buys for essential and luxury items based on individual needs and resources.
13. Objective: To determine housing needs and to know how to obtain housing and utilities based on those needs.
14. Objective: To know how to buy and maintain a car economically.
15. Objective: To know basic procedures for the care and upkeep of personal possessions (home, furniture, car, clothing, etc.) and to be able to use resources relating to such care.
16. Objective: To know the various media of exchange and to be familiar with banking services in the community.
17. Objective: To develop understanding of credit systems.
18. Objective: To collect information concerning the types of insurance available and to be able to select the best insurance for the individual and his family.
19. Objective: To know the recourses available to the consumer in the face of misleading and/or fraudulent product/service claims or tactics.

20. Objective: To understand the implication of consumption vis-a-vis finite world resources and to recognize that each individual's pattern of consumption influences the general welfare.

Health

GOAL: To insure good mental and physical health for the individual and his family.

1. Objective: To develop a working vocabulary related to health, especially as it related to basic medical and physiological terminology, for accurate reporting of symptoms and following a doctor's directions in applying treatments.

2. Objective: To understand how basic safety measures can prevent accidents and injuries and to recognize potential hazards, especially as such hazards relate to home and occupational safety.

3. Objective: To know medical and health services in the community.

4. Objective: To understand the physical and psychological influences on pregnancy as well as the need for proper prenatal care.

5. Objective: To understand the importance of family planning, its physical, psychological, financial and religious implications; and to have knowledge of both effective and ineffective methods of birth control.

6. Objective: To understand general child rearing practices and procedures for guarding the health and safety of a child and to apply proper action in accordance with needs and resources.

7. Objective: To understand the special health needs and concerns of the adolescent (and his parents) and to become acquainted with some ways to ease the transition from childhood to adulthood.

8. Objective: To understand what contributes to good mental health and physical health and to apply this understanding toward preventive care and health maintenance.

9. Objective: To understand the interaction of self as a member of small groups (family, work, club, class) and to use this understanding to promote effective interpersonal coping skills.

10. Objective: To be able to apply first aid in emergencies and to inform proper authorities of sudden illnesses, various accidents or natural disasters.

11. Objective: To plan for health or medical insurance and to be aware of available financial assistance for medical or health problems.

12. Objective: To understand what constitutes a proper diet and to plan meals according to individual needs and resources.

13. Objective: To understand federal control of various drugs and items for health protection and to understand how public reaction influences this control.

Government and Law

GOAL: To promote an understanding of society through government and law and to be aware of governmental functions, agencies and regulations which define individual rights and obligations.

1. Objective: To develop a working vocabulary related to government and law in order to understand their functions in society and in the personal life of the individual. This should be an ongoing process as each objective is covered.

2. Objective: To develop an understanding of the structure and functioning of the federal government.

3. Objective: To investigate the relationship between the individual citizen and the government.

4. Objective: To understand the relationship between the individual and the legal system.

5. Objective: To obtain a working knowledge of the various legal documents which the individual will need as a member of society.

6. Objective: To explore the relationship between government services and the American tax system.

Community Resources

GOAL: To understand that community resources, including transportation systems, are utilized by individuals in society in order to obtain a satisfactory mode of living.

1. Objective: To build an oral and written vocabulary pertaining to community resources and to define community resources in terms of (a) services to community members and (b) services to persons outside the community or non self-supporting members of society (unemployed, criminals, insane, etc.)

2-3. Objective: To know the types of community services provided for members of society including the purposes of and how to gain access to these services.

4. Objective: To understand how and when to apply for community services, such as Social Security, and Medicare.

5. Objective: To know various recreational services available in the community.

6. Objective: To be able to utilize information services of the community.

7. Objective: To be aware of the people and agencies in the community whose job it is to register and act upon citizen complaints.

SUBSET: Transportation

8. Objective: To build an oral and written vocabulary of transportation terms, including car insurance terms.

9. Objective: To be able to recognize and utilize signs related to transportation needs.

10. Objective: To develop a familiarity with transportation schedules, and to calculate fares.

11. Objective: To be able to find and utilize information facilities.

12. Objective: To learn the use of maps relating to travel needs.

13. Objective: To recognize time zone boundaries and understand the concept of daylight savings time.

14. Objective: To request information on and make verbal and written travel and overnight accommodations/reservations.

15. Objective: To understand the relationship between transportation and public problems.

16. Objective: To understand driving regulations, including safety, courtesy, and rules such as having a driver's license, car license plates, etc.

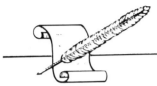

November

CIA ASSASSINATION PLOTS AND NSA CABLE INTERCEPTS

November 6 and 20, 1975

Beginning in November, the Senate Select Intelligence Committee published a series of reports on its eleven-month investigation of U.S. intelligence activities. The most disturbing of the reports disclosed that the Central Intelligence Agency (CIA) had directly plotted the assassination of two foreign leaders and had been involved in covert action against three other foreign officials who were subsequently assassinated. These findings were contained in a 347-page document made public Nov. 20 over last-minute objections of the Ford administration.

Earlier in the month, on Nov. 6, committee chairman Sen. Frank Church (D Idaho) had released a lengthy statement describing a secret cable-monitoring program called "Operation Shamrock," which the National Security Agency (NSA) initiated during the Truman administration. Subsequent committee reports in early December dealt with political abuses of the FBI and covert CIA action in Chile (see p. 873). All were designated "interim" accounts, released in advance of a final, comprehensive report scheduled for February 1976.

The Senate investigation was one of three comprehensive inquiries into U.S. intelligence and law enforcement activities launched early in 1975 after New York Times *reporter Seymour Hersh, in December 1974, had attributed to the CIA "massive" illegal domestic spying during the Nixon administration. The Senate action was also prompted by allegations of CIA involvement in assassinations of foreign leaders, and by a* Washington Post *report that the FBI had kept files of derogatory information on members of Congress. Creation of the Senate committee marked the first time Congress had approved a thorough probe of the activities of the post-World War II intelligence community.*

The other two investigative panels were a House committee with a broad mandate similar to that of the Senate committee and a presidential commission on the CIA chaired by Vice President Nelson A. Rockefeller. The Rockefeller Commission's final report, published in June, omitted the panel's findings on the assassination charges because the available evidence was considered incomplete as well as extremely sensitive. President Ford subsequently turned over the commission's assassination data to the congressional committees, and to the Justice Department for possible prosecution. (See p. 401.)

Assassination Report

Release of the Church committee's assassination report came after a rare secret session of the Senate Nov. 20 to consider the impact of its publication. CIA Director William E. Colby had called a press conference the previous day to ask that at least certain names in the report be withheld from the public. And the administration mounted an intense last-minute lobbying campaign against the release, including a personal letter from President Ford to the Senate leadership citing national security concerns, that continued "right up until the doors were closed," according to Church. The committee had already voted 12-0, with John G. Tower (R Texas) abstaining, to release the report, contending that it was the committee's prerogative and not the Senate's to make that decision.

Church justified publication of the damaging material on the basis of the public's right to know "what instrumentalities of their government have done." Church also told the closed Senate session that because portions of the report's findings were already public knowledge the committee felt that such "piecemeal disclosures [were] unfair to the individuals involved" and did not constitute a sound basis for public policy decisions. Church acknowledged that the committee had agreed to use pseudonyms or simply titles in the report for more than half of the individuals for whom the administration requested protection.

The report revealed CIA involvement in assassination plots against Premiers Fidel Castro of Cuba and Patrice Lumumba of the Congo (now Zaire). Two other leaders, General Rafael Trujillo of the Dominican Republic and President Ngo Dinh Diem of South Vietnam, were targets of CIA covert activity and were eventually assassinated, but the committee could find no direct link between their deaths and the agency. Similarly, the committee found no CIA complicity in the murder of Chilean General Rene Schneider in 1970, although the agency was known to have supported groups who tried to kidnap him for his opposition to a military coup against Marxist President Salvador Allende.

While evidence available to the panel strongly implied that President Eisenhower had "authorized" the assassination of Lumumba, the committee said it could not establish that any President had directly ordered the killing of a foreign leader. The report recommended legislation making it a criminal offense to assassinate or conspire to kill a foreign official.

NSA Cable Monitoring

Church's Nov. 6 statement on the NSA cable monitoring program was also made over strenuous administration protests. Late in October the committee had initiated an unprecedented public investigation of the activities of the National Security Agency, a component of the Defense Department responsible for foreign intelligence gathering by electronic means as well as for developing and breaking secret communications codes.

Drawing the committee's attention was the agency's 1967-73 monitoring of international cable and telephone traffic to spot Americans suspected of narcotics dealings, terrorism and anti-Vietnam War activities. Testimony during the hearings revealed that the NSA had scanned cable communications of persons and organizations designated by such agencies as the CIA, the FBI and the Secret Service. Despite administration objections, the committee decided to release its report on the project, which Church said "appeared to be unlawful." Much of the Senate committee's effort paralleled an investigation conducted by the House Government Operations Government Information and Individual Rights Subcommittee chaired by Bella S. Abzug (D N.Y.). During a hearing by the subcommittee Oct. 23, Abzug had revealed that government agents for years had monitored and photographed private international cables sent to and from Washington.

> *Excerpts from* Alleged Assassination Plots Involving Foreign Leaders, *an interim report published Nov. 20, 1975, by the Senate Select Committee on Intelligence:*

I. INTRODUCTION AND SUMMARY

This interim report covers allegations of United States involvement in assassination plots against foreign political leaders. The report also examines certain other instances in which foreign political leaders in fact were killed and the United States was in some manner involved in activity leading up to the killing, but in which it would be incorrect to say that the purpose of United States involvement had been to encourage assassination.

The evidence establishes that the United States was implicated in several assassination plots. The Committee believes that, short of war, assassination is incompatible with American principles, international order, and morality. It should be rejected as a tool of foreign policy.

Our inquiry also reveals serious problems with respect to United States involvement in coups directed against foreign governments. Some of these problems are addressed here on the basis of our investigation to date; others we raise as questions to be answered after our investigation into covert action has been completed.

We stress the interim nature of this report. In the course of the Committee's continuing work, other alleged assassination plots may surface, and new evidence concerning the cases covered herein may come to light. However, it is the Committee's view that these cases have been developed in sufficient detail to clarify the issues which are at the heart of the Committee's mandate to recommend legislative and other reforms....

A. Committee's Mandate

Senate Resolution 21 instructs the Committee to investigate the full range of governmental intelligence activities and the extent, if any, to which such activities were "illegal, improper or unethical." In addition to that broad general mandate, the Committee is required to investigate, study and make recommendations concerning various specific matters, several of which relate to the assassination issue. [Footnote: For example, S Res 21 requires the Committee to study and investigate the following: The extent and necessity of***covert intelligence activities***abroad; [The] nature and extent of executive branch oversight of all United States intelligence activities; The need for improved, strengthened, or consolidated oversight of United States intelligence activities by the Congress...and the need for new legislation.]

Although the Rockefeller Commission initiated an inquiry into reported assassination plots, the Commission declared it was unable, for a variety of reasons, to complete its inquiry. At the direction of the President, the Executive Branch turned over to the Select Committee the work the Commission has done, along with certain other documents relating to assassination.

B. Committee Decision to Make Report Public

This report raises important questions of national policy. We believe that the public is entitled to know what instrumentalities of their Government have done. Further, our recommendations can only be judged in light of the factual record. Therefore, this interim report should be made public.

The Committee believes the truth about the assassination allegations should be told because democracy depends upon a well-informed electorate. We reject any contention that the facts disclosed in this report should be kept secret because they are embarrassing to the United States. Despite the temporary injury to our national reputation, the Committee believes that foreign peoples will, upon sober reflection, respect the United States more for keeping faith with its democratic ideal than they will condemn us for the misconduct revealed. We doubt that any other country would have the courage to make such disclosures.

The fact that portions of the story have already been made public only accentuates the need for full disclosure. Innuendo and misleading partial disclosures are not fair to the individuals involved. Nor are they a responsible way to lay the groundwork for informed public policy judgments.

C. Scope of Committee's Investigation

Investigating the assassination issue has been an unpleasant duty, but one that the Committee had to meet. The Committee has compiled a massive record in the months that the inquiry has been underway. The record comprises over 8,000 pages of sworn testimony taken from over 75 witnesses during 60 hearing days and numerous staff interviews. The documents which the Committee has obtained include raw files from agencies and departments, the White House, and the Presidential libraries of the Administrations of former Presidents Dwight Eisenhower, John Kennedy and Lyndon Johnson.

We have obtained two types of evidence: *first,* evidence relating to the general setting in which the events occurred, the national policy of the time, and the normal operating procedures, including channels of command and control; and *second,* evidence relating to the specific events.

A Senate Committee is not a court. It looks to the past, not to determine guilt or innocence, but in order to make recommendations for the future. When we found the evidence to be ambiguous—as we did on some issues—we have set out both sides, in order that the evidence may speak for itself.

Limitations in Evidence

Despite the number of witnesses and documents examined by the Committee, the available evidence has certain shortcomings.

Many of the events considered occurred as long as fifteen years ago. With one exception, they occurred during the administrations of Presidents now dead. Other high officials whose testimony might have shed additional light on the thorny issues of authorization and control are also dead. Moreover, with the passage of time, the memories of those still alive have dimmed.

The Committee has often faced the difficult task of distinguishing refreshed recollection from speculation. In many instances, witnesses were unable to testify from independent recollection and had to rely on documents contemporaneous with the events to refresh their recollections. While informed speculation is of some assistance, it can only be assigned limited weight in judging specific events.

Although assassination is not a subject on which one would expect many records or documents to be made or retained, there were, in fact, more relevant contemporaneous documents than expected. In addition, in 1967 the Central Intelligence Agency had made an internal study of the Castro, Trujillo and Diem assassination allegations. That study was quite useful, particularly in suggesting leads for uncovering the story of the actual assassination activity. Unfortunately, the working papers relating to that investigation were destroyed upon the completion of the Report, pursuant to instructions from CIA Director

Richard Helms. (Memorandum for the Record, 5/23/67) These notes were destroyed because of their sensitivity and because the information they contained had already been incorporated into the Report. In fairness to Director Helms, it should be added, however, that he was responsible for requesting the preparation of the Inspector General's Report and for preserving the Report.

Some ambiguities in the evidence result from the practice of concealing CIA covert operations from the world and performing them in such a way that if discovered, the role of the United States could be plausibly denied. An extension of the doctrine of "plausible deniability" had the result that communications between the Agency and high Administration officials were often convoluted and imprecise.

The evidence contains sharp conflicts, some of which relate to basic facts. But the most important conflicts relate not so much to basic facts as to differing perceptions and opinions based upon relatively undisputed facts. With respect to both kinds of conflicts, the Committee has attempted to set forth the evidence extensively so that it may speak for itself, and in our section on findings and conclusions, we suggest resolutions for some of the conflicts. However, because the Committee's main task is to find lessons for the future, resolving conflicts in the evidence may be less important than making certain that the system which produced the ambiguities is corrected....

D. Summary of Findings and Conclusions

...The Committee investigated alleged United States involvement in assassination plots in five foreign countries: [Footnote: In addition to the plots discussed in the body of this report, the Committee received some evidence of CIA involvement in plans to assassinate President Sukarno of Indonesia and "Papa Doc" Duvalier of Haiti. Former Deputy Director for Plans Richard Bissell testified that the assassination of Sukarno had been "contemplated" by the CIA, but that planning had proceeded no farther than identifying an "asset" whom it was believed might be recruited to kill Sukarno. Arms were supplied to dissident groups in Indonesia, but, according to Bissell, those arms were not intended for assassination. (Bissell, 6/11/75, p. 89)

Walter Elder, Executive Assistant to CIA Director John McCone, testified that the Director authorized the CIA to furnish arms to dissidents planning the overthrow of Haiti's dictator, Duvalier. Elder told the Committee that while the assassination of Duvalier was not contemplated by the CIA, the arms were furnished "to help [the dissidents] take what measures were deemed necessary to replace the government", and it was realized that Duvalier might be killed in the course of the overthrow. (Elder, 8/13/75, p. 79)]....

The evidence concerning each alleged assassination can be summarized as follows:

Patrice Lumumba (Congo/Zaire).—In the Fall of 1960, two CIA officials were asked by superiors to assassinate Lumumba. Poisons were sent to the Congo and some exploratory steps were taken toward gaining access to Lumumba. Subsequently, in early 1961, Lumumba was killed by Congolese rivals. It does not appear from the evidence that the United States was in any way involved in the killing.

Fidel Castro (Cuba).—United States Government personnel plotted to kill Castro from 1960 to 1965. American underworld figures and Cubans hostile to Castro were used in these plots, and were provided encouragement and material support by the United States.

Rafael Trujillo (Dominican Republic).—Trujillo was shot by Dominican dissidents on May 31, 1961. From early in 1960 and continuing to the time of the assassination, the United States Government generally supported these dissidents. Some Government personnel were aware that the dissidents intended to kill Trujillo. Three pistols and three carbines were furnished by American officials, although a request for machine guns was later refused. There is conflicting evidence concerning whether the weapons were knowingly supplied for use in the assassination and whether any of them were present at the scene.

Ngo Dinh Diem (South Vietnam).—Diem and his brother, Nhu, were killed on November 2, 1963, in the course of a South Vietnamese Generals' coup. Although the United States Government supported the coup, there is no evidence that American officials favored the assassination. Indeed, it appears that the assassination of Diem was not part of the Generals' pre-coup planning but was instead a spontaneous act which occurred during the coup and was carried out without United States involvement or support.

General Rene Schneider (Chile).—On October 25, 1970, General Schneider died of gunshot wounds inflicted three days earlier while resisting a kidnap attempt. Schneider, as Commander-in-Chief of the Army and a constitutionalist opposed to military coups, was considered an obstacle in efforts to prevent Salvador Allende from assuming the office of President of Chile. The United States Government supported, and sought to instigate a military coup to block Allende. U.S. officials supplied financial aid, machine guns and other equipment to various military figures who opposed Allende. Although the CIA continued to support coup plotters up to Schneider's shooting, the record indicates that the CIA had withdrawn active support of the group which carried out the actual kidnap attempt on October 22, which resulted in Schneider's death. Further, it does not appear that any of the equipment supplied by the CIA to coup plotters in Chile was used in the kidnapping. There is no evidence of a plan to kill Schneider or that United States officials specifically anticipated that Schneider would be shot during the abduction.

Assassination capability (Executive action).—In addition to these five cases, the Committee has received evidence that ranking Government officials discussed, and may have authorized, the establishment within the CIA of a generalized assassination capability. During these discussions, the concept of assassination was not affirmatively disavowed....

3. Summary of Findings and Conclusions on the Issues of Authority and Control

To put the inquiry into assassination allegations in context, two points must be made clear. First, there is no doubt that the United States Government opposed the various leaders in question. Officials at the highest levels objected to the Castro and Trujillo regimes, believed the accession of Allende to power in Chile would be harmful to American interests, and thought of Lumumba as a dangerous force in the heart of Africa. Second, the evidence on assassinations has to be viewed in the context of other, more massive activities against the regimes in question. For example, the plots against Fidel Castro personally cannot be understood without considering the fully authorized, comprehensive assaults upon his regime, such as the Bay of Pigs invasion in 1961 and Operation MONGOOSE in 1962.

Once methods of coercion and violence are chosen, the probability of loss of life is always present. There is, however, a significant difference between a coldblooded, targeted, intentional killing of an individual foreign leader and other forms of intervening in the affairs of foreign nations. Therefore, the Committee has endeavored to explore as fully as possible the questions of how and why the plots happened, whether they were authorized, and if so, at what level.

The picture that emerges from the evidence is not a clear one. This may be due to the system of deniability and the consequent state of the evidence which, even after our long investigation, remains conflicting and inconclusive. Or it may be that there were in fact serious shortcomings in the system of authorization so that an activity such as assassination could have been undertaken by an agency of the United States Government without express authority.

Ambiguities in Control System

The Committee finds that the system of executive command and control was so ambiguous that it is difficult to be certain at what levels assassination activity was known and authorized. This situation creates the disturbing prospect that Government officials might have undertaken the assassination plots without it having been uncontrovertibly clear that there was explicit authorization from the Presidents. It is also possible that there might have been a successful "plausible denial" in which Presidential authorization was issued but is now obscured. Whether or not the respective Presidents knew of or authorized the plots, as chief executive officer of the United States, each must bear the ultimate responsibility for the activities of his subordinates.

The Committee makes four other major findings. The first relates to the Committee's inability to make a finding that the assassination plots were authorized by the Presidents or other persons above the governmental agency or agencies involved. The second explains why certain officials may have perceived that, according to their judgment and experience, assassination was an acceptable course of action. The third criticizes agency officials for failing on several occasions to disclose their plans and activities to superior authorities, or for failing to do so with sufficient detail and clarity. The fourth criticizes Administration officials for not ruling out assassination, particularly after certain Administration officials had become aware of prior assassination plans and the establishment of a general assassination capability.

There is admittedly a tension among the findings. This tension reflects a basic conflict in the evidence. While there are some conflicts over facts, it may be more important that there appeared to have been two differing perceptions of the same facts. This distinction may be the result of the differing backgrounds of those persons experienced in covert operations as distinguished from those who were not. Words of urgency which may have meant killing to the former, may have meant nothing of the sort to the latter.

While we are critical of certain individual actions, the Committee is also mindful of the inherent problems in a system which relies on secrecy, compartmentation, circumlocution, and the avoidance of clear responsibility. This system creates the risk of confusion and rashness in the very areas where clarity and sober judgment are most necessary. Hence, before reviewing the evidence relating to the cases, we briefly deal with the general subject of covert action.

II. COVERT ACTION AS A VEHICLE FOR FOREIGN POLICY IMPLEMENTATION

Covert action is activity which is meant to further the sponsoring nation's foreign policy objectives, and to be concealed in order to permit that nation to plausibly deny responsibility.

The National Security Act of 1947 which established the Central Intelligence Agency did not include specific authority for covert operations. However, it created the National Security Council, and gave that body authority to direct the CIA to "perform such other functions and duties related to intelligence affecting the national security as the National Security Council may from time to time direct." At its first meeting in December 1947, the NSC issued a top secret directive granting the CIA authority to conduct covert operations. From 1955 to 1970, the basic authority for covert operations was a directive of the National Security Council, NSC5412/2.

This directive instructed the CIA to counter, reduce and discredit "International Communism" throughout the world in a manner consistent with United States foreign and military policies. It also directed the CIA to undertake covert operations to achieve this end and defined covert operations as any covert activities related to propaganda, economic warfare, political action (including sabotage, demolition and assistance to resistance movements) and all activities compatible with the directive. [Footnote: By contrast NSDM (National Security Decision Memorandum) 40 of 1970 described covert actions as those secret activities designed to further official United States programs and policies abroad. It made no reference to communism.] In 1962, the CIA's General Counsel rendered the opinion that the Agency's activities were "not inhibited by any limitations other than those broadly set forth in NSC 5412/2." (CIA General Counsel Memorandum 4/6/62)

A. Policy Development and Approval Mechanism

In his 1962 memorandum, CIA's General Counsel made it clear that the CIA considered itself responsible for developing proposals and plans to implement the objectives of NSC 5412/2. The memorandum also stated that even in developing ideas or plans it was incumbent on the Agency not only to coordinate with other executive departments and agencies, but also to "obtain necessary policy approval." The Committee has been faced with determining whether CIA officials thought it was "necessary" to obtain express approval for assassination plans and, if so, whether such approval was in fact either sought or granted.

Authorization for Operations

Beginning in 1955, the responsibility for authorizing CIA covert action operations lay with the Special Group, a subcommittee of the National Security Council composed of the President's Assistant for National Security Affairs, the Director of Central Intelligence, the Deputy Secretary of Defense and the Under Secretary of State for Political Affairs. Today this group is known as the 40 Committee, and its membership has been expanded to include the Chairman of the Joint Chiefs of Staff. During 1962 another NSC subcommittee was established to oversee covert operations in Cuba. This subcommittee was the Special Group (Augmented); its membership included the Special Group, the Attorney General, and certain other high officials.

In exercising control over covert operations, the Special Group was charged with considering the objectives of proposed activities, determining whether the activities would accomplish the objectives, assessing the likelihood of success, and deciding whether the activities would be "proper" and in the national interest. The Chairman of the Special Group was usually responsible for determining which projects required Presidential consideration and for keeping him abreast of developments.

Authorization procedures, however, have not always been clear and tidy, nor have they always been followed. Prior to 1955, there were few formal procedures. Procedures from 1955 through 1963 were characterized in an internal CIA memorandum as "somewhat cloudy and * * * based on value judgments by the DCI." (Memorandum for the Record, C/CA/PEG, "Policy Coordination of CIA's Covert Action Operations", 2/21/67)

Alternative Procedures

The existence of formal procedures for planning and implementing covert actions does not necessarily rule out the possibility that other, more informal procedures might be used. The granting of authority to an executive agency to plan covert action does not preempt Presidential authority to develop and mandate foreign policy. Formal procedures may be disregarded by either high Administration officials or officers in the CIA. In the Schneider incident, for example, President Nixon instructed CIA officials not to consult with the 40 Committee or other policy-making bodies. [Footnote: The Special Group was renamed the 303 Committee in 1964. In 1970 its name was changed again—this time to the 40 Committee.] In the plot to assassinate Castro using underworld figures, CIA officials decided not to inform the Special Group of their activities. One CIA operation, an aspect of which was to develop an assassination capability, was assigned to a senior case officer as a special task. His responsibility to develop this capability did not fall within the Special Group's review of covert operations, even though this same officer was responsible to the Special Group (Augmented) on other matters.

CIA Organization

The Central Intelligence Agency also has a formal chain of command. At the top of the structure of the CIA is the Director of Central Intelligence (DCI) and his immediate subordinate, the Deputy Director of Central Intelligence (DDCI). Together they are responsible for the administration and supervision of the Agency. Beneath the DCI and directly responsible to him, are the four operational components of the Agency. During the period covered by this report, the component responsible for clandestine operations was the Directorate of Plans, headed by the Deputy Director for Plans (DDP). The Directorate of Plans was organized around regional geographic divisions. These divisions worked with their respective overseas stations (headed by a Chief of Station (COS)) in planning and implementing the Directorate's operations. The divisions which played a part in the events considered in this report were the Western Hemisphere Division (WH) which was responsible for Latin America, the African Division (AF), and the Far Eastern Division (FE).

In addition to the regional divisions, the Directorate of Plans also included three staff-level units which provided some oversight and coordination of division projects. The staff units had no approval authority over the divisions. However, they could criticize and suggest modifications of projects sponsored by divisions. The three staffs were: Foreign Intelligence, Counterintelligence, and Covert Action.

When functioning in accordance with stated organizational procedures, the Directorate of Plans operated under a graduated approval process. Individual project proposals generally originated either from the field stations or from the divisions and were approved at varying levels within the Directorate, depending on the estimated cost and risk of the operation. Low-cost, low-risk projects could be approved at the Deputy Director for Plans level;

extremely high-cost, high-risk projects required the approval of the DCI. Covert action proposals also required approval of the Special Group.

Also within the Directorate of Plans was a Technical Services Division (TSD) which developed and provided technical and support material required in the execution of operations. A separate Directorate, the Directorate of Support, handled financial and administrative matters. The Office of Security, a component of the Directorate of Support, was largely responsible for providing protection for clandestine installations and, as discussed at length in the Castro study, was occasionally called on for operational assistance.

B. The Concept of "Plausible Denial"

Non-attribution to the United States for covert operations was the original and principal purpose of the so-called doctrine of "plausible denial."

Evidence before the Committee clearly demonstrates that this concept, designed to protect the United States and its operatives from the consequences of disclosures, has been expanded to mask decisions of the President and his senior staff members. A further consequence of the expansion of this doctrine is that subordinates, in an effort to permit their superiors to "plausibly deny" operations, fail to fully inform them about those operations.

"Plausible denial" has shaped the processes for approving and evaluating covert actions. For example, the 40 Committee and its predecessor, the Special Group, have served as "circuit breakers" for Presidents, thus avoiding consideration of covert action by the Oval office.

"Plausible denial" can also lead to the use of euphemism and circumlocution, which are designed to allow the President and other senior officials to deny knowledge of an operation should it be disclosed. The converse may also occur; a President could communicate his desire for a sensitive operation in an indirect, circumlocutious manner. An additional possibility is that the President may, in fact, not be fully and accurately informed about a sensitive operation because he failed to receive the "circumlocutious" message. The evidence discussed below reveals that serious problems of assessing intent and ensuring both control and accountability may result from the use of "plausible denial."

III. ASSASSINATION PLANNING AND THE PLOTS

A. Congo

INTRODUCTION

The Committee has received solid evidence of a plot to assassinate Patrice Lumumba. Strong hostility to Lumumba, voiced at the very highest levels of government may have been intended to initiate an assassination operation; at the least it engendered such an operation. The evidence indicates that it is likely that President Eisenhower's expression of strong concern about Lumumba at a meeting of the National Security Council on August 18, 1960, was taken by Allen Dulles as authority to assassinate Lumumba. There is, however, testimony by Eisenhower Administration officials, and ambiguity and lack of clarity in the records of high-level policy meetings, which tends to contradict the evidence that the President intended an assassination effort against Lumumba.

The week after the August 18 NSC meeting, a presidential advisor reminded the Special Group of the "necessity for very straight-forward action" against Lumumba and prompted a decision not to rule out consideration of "any particular kind of activity which might contribute to getting rid of Lumumba." The following day, Dulles cabled a CIA Station Officer in Leopoldville, Republic of the Congo [now Zaire], that "in high quarters" the "removal" of Lumumba was "an urgent and prime objective." Shortly thereafter the CIA's clandestine service formulated a plot to assassinate Lumumba. The plot proceeded to the point that lethal substances and instruments specifically intended for use in an assassination were delivered by the CIA to the Congo Station. There is no evidence that these instruments of assassination were actually used against Lumumba...

Background

In the summer of 1960, there was great concern at the highest levels in the United States government about the role of Patrice Lumumba in the Congo. Lumumba, who served briefly as Premier of the newly independent nation, was viewed with alarm by United States policymakers because of what they perceived as his magnetic public appeal and his leanings toward the Soviet Union.

Under the leadership of Lumumba and the new President, Joseph Kasavubu, the Congo declared its independence from Belgium on June 30, 1960. In the turbulent month that followed, Lumumba threatened to invite Soviet troops to hasten the withdrawal of Belgian armed forces. The United Nations Security Council requested Belgium's withdrawal and dispatched a neutral force to the Congo to preserve order. In late July, Lumumba visited Washington and received pledges of economic aid from Secretary of State Christian Herter. By the beginning of September, Soviet airplanes, trucks, and technicians were arriving in the province where Lumumba's support was strongest.

In mid-September, after losing a struggle for the leadership of the government to Kasavubu and Joseph Mobutu, Chief of Staff of the Congolese armed forces, Lumumba sought protection from the United Nations forces in Leopoldville. Early in December, Mobutu's troops captured Lumumba while he was traveling toward his stronghold at Stanleyville and imprisoned him. On January 17, 1961, the central government of the Congo transferred Lumumba to the custody of authorities in Katanga province, which was then asserting its own independence from the Congo. Several weeks later, Katanga authorities announced Lumumba's death.

Accounts of the circumstances and timing of Lumumba's death vary. The United Nations investigation concluded that Lumumba was killed on January 17, 1961....

4. The Plot to Assassinate Lumumba

In the Summer of 1960, DDP Richard Bissell asked the Chief of the Africa Division, Bronson Tweedy, to explore the feasibility of assassinating Patrice Lumumba. Bissell also asked a CIA scientist, Joseph Scheider, to make preparations to assassinate or incapacitate an unspecified "African leader." According to Scheider, Bissell said that the assignment had the "highest authority." Scheider procured toxic biological materials in response to Bissell's request, and was then ordered by Tweedy to take these materials to the Station Officer in Leopoldville. According to Scheider, there was no explicit requirement that the Station check back with Headquarters for final approval before proceeding to assassinate Lumumba. Tweedy maintained, however, that whether or not he had explicitly levied such a requirement, the Station Officer was not authorized to move from exploring means of assassination to actually attempting to kill Lumumba without referring the matter to Headquarters for a policy decision.

In late September, Scheider delivered the lethal substances to the Station Officer in Leopoldville and instructed him to assassinate Patrice Lumumba. The Station Officer testified that after requesting and receiving confirmation from CIA Headquarters that he was to carry out Scheider's instructions, he proceeded to take "exploratory steps" in furtherance of the assassination plot. The Station Officer also testified that he was told by Scheider that President Eisenhower had ordered the assassination of Lumumba. Scheider's testimony generally substantiated this account, although he acknowledged that his meetings with Bissell and Tweedy were the only bases for his impression about Presidential authorization. Scheider's mission to the Congo was preceded and followed by cables from Headquarters urging the "elimination" of Lumumba transmitted through an extraordinarily restricted "Eyes Only" channel—including two messages bearing the personal signature of Allen Dulles [CIA Director].

The toxic substances were never used. But there is no evidence that the assassination operation was terminated before Lumumba's death. There is, however, no suggestion of a connection between the assassination plot and the events which actually led to Lumumba's death....

5. The Question of a Connection Between the Assassination Plot and Other Actions of CIA Officers and Their Agents in the Congo

Michael Mulroney, a senior CIA officer in the Directorate for Plans, testified that in October 1960 he had been asked by Richard Bissell to go to the Congo to carry out the assassination of Lumumba. Mulroney said that he refused to participate in an assassination operation, but proceeded to the Congo to attempt to draw Lumumba away from the protective custody of the U.N. guard and place him in the hands of Congolese authorities. (Mulroney, 6/9/75, pp. 11-14)

Shortly after Mulroney's arrival in the Congo, he was joined by QJ/WIN, a CIA agent with a criminal background. Late in 1960, WI/ROGUE, one of

[CIA Congo Station Officer Victor] Hedgman's operatives approached QJ/WIN with a proposition to join an "execution squad." (CIA Cable, Leopoldville to Director, 12/7/70)

It is unlikely that Mulroney was actually involved in implementing the assassination assignment. Whether there was any connection between the assassination plot and either of the two operatives—QJ/WIN and WI/ROGUE—is less clear....

Mulroney testified that in October of 1960, Bissell asked him to undertake the mission of assassinating Patrice Lumumba:...

> I told him that I would absolutely not have any part of killing Lumumba. He said, I want you to go over and talk to Joseph Scheider. (Mulroney, 6/9/75, p. 12)

Mulroney said that it was "inconceivable that Bissell would direct such a mission without the personal permission of Allen Dulles":

> I assumed that he had authority from Mr. Dulles in such an important issue, but it was not discussed [with me], nor did he purport to have higher authority to do it. (Mulroney 9/9/75, pp. 15, 44)...

[Footnote: When asked at the conclusion of his testimony to add anything to the record that he felt was necessary to present a full picture of the operation against Lumumba, Mulroney volunteered a statement about the moral climate in which it took place:

"All the people that I knew acted in good faith. I think they acted in the light of * * * maybe not their consciences, but in the light of their concept of patriotism. [T]hey felt that this was in the best interests of the U.S. I think that we have too much of the 'good German' in us, in that we do something because the boss says it is okay. And they are not essentially evil people. But you can do an awful lot of wrong in this"....

Earlier in his testimony, Mulroney succinctly summarized his philosophical opposition to assassinating Lumumba: "murder corrupts." (Mulroney, 9/11/75, p. 9)]

Mulroney said that in one of his two conversations with Bissell about Lumumba, he raised the prospect "that conspiracy to commit murder being done in the District of Columbia might be in violation of federal law." He said that Bissell "airily dismissed" this prospect. (Mulroney, 6/9/75, p. 14)

Although he refused to participate in assassination, Mulroney agreed to go to the Congo on a general mission to "neutralize" Lumumba "as a political factor" (Mulroney, 9/11/75, pp. 43-44)....

According to Mulroney there was a "very, very high probability" that Lumumba would receive capital punishment at the hands of the Congolese authorities. But he "had no compunction about bringing him out and then having him tried by a jury of his peers." (Mulroney, 6/9/75, pp. 24, 14)....

6. The Question of Whether the CIA Was Involved in Bringing About Lumumba's Death in Katanga Province

...The contemporaneous cable traffic shows that the CIA was kept informed of Lumumba's condition and movements in January of 1961 by the

Congolese and that the CIA continued to consider Lumumba a serious political threat. Despite the fact that the Station Officer knew of a plan to deliver Lumumba into the hands of his enemies at a time when the CIA was convinced that "drastic steps" were necessary to prevent Lumumba's return to power, there is no evidence of CIA involvement in this plan or in bringing about the death of Lumumba in Katanga....

On January 17, authorities in Leopoldville placed Lumumba and two of his leading supporters, Maurice Mpolo and Joseph Okito, aboard an airplane bound for Bakwanga. Apparently the aircraft was redirected in midflight to Elisabethville in Katanga Province "when it was learned that United Nations troops were at Bakwanga airport." On February 13, the government of Katanga reported that Lumumba and his two companions escaped the previous day and died at the hands of hostile villagers. (U.N. Report, 11/12/61, pp. 98-100, 109)

The United Nations Commission on Investigation was "not convinced by the version of the facts given by the provincial government of Katanga." The Commission concluded instead, that Lumumba was killed on January 17, almost immediately after his arrival in Katanga, probably with the knowledge of the central government and at the behest of the Katanga authorities. (U.N. Report, 11/11/61, pp. 100, 117)....

Cables from the Station Officer demonstrated no CIA involvement in the plan to transport Lumumba to Bakwanga. But the Station Officer clearly had prior knowledge of the plan to transfer Lumumba to a state where it was probable that he would be killed. Other supporters of Lumumba who had been sent to Bakwanga earlier by Leopoldville authorities

> Were killed there in horrible circumstances, and the place was known as the 'slaughterhouse.' It was therefore improbable that Mr. Lumumba and his companions would have met a different fate at Bakwanga if they had been taken there. (U.N. Report, 11/11/61, p. 109)....

Two days after Lumumba was flown to Katanga, the CIA Base Chief in Elizabethville sent an unusual message to headquarters:

THANKS FOR PATRICE. IF WE HAD KNOWN HE WAS COMING WE WOULD HAVE BAKED A SNAKE.

The cable also reported that the Base's sources had provided "no advance word whatsoever" of Lumumba's flight to Katanga and that the Congolese central government "does not plan to liquidate Lumumba." (CIA Cable, Elisabethville to Director, 1/19/61)

This cable indicates that the CIA did not have knowledge of the central government's decision to transfer Lumumba from Thysville military camp to a place where he would be in the hands of his avowed enemies. This cable indicates that the CIA was not kept informed of Lumumba's treatment after he arrived in Katanga because, according to the report of the United Nations Commission, Lumumba had already been killed when the cable was sent....

B. Cuba

1. The Assassination Plots

...We have found concrete evidence of at least eight plots involving the CIA to assassinate Fidel Castro from 1960 to 1965. Although some of the assassination plots did not advance beyond the stage of planning and preparation, one plot, involving the use of underworld figures, reportedly twice progressed to the point of sending poison pills to Cuba and dispatching teams to commit the deed. Another plot involved furnishing weapons and other assassination devices to a Cuban dissident. The proposed assassination devices ran the gamut from high-powered rifles to poison pills, poison pens, deadly bacterial powders, and other devices which strain the imagination.

The most ironic of these plots took place on November 22, 1963—the very day that President Kennedy was shot in Dallas—when a CIA official offered a poison pen to a Cuban for use against Castro while at the same time an emissary from President Kennedy was meeting with Castro to explore the possibility of improved relations....

(a) Plots: Early 1960

(i) Plots to Destroy Castro's Public Image

Efforts against Castro did not begin with assassination attempts.

From March through August 1960, during the last year of the Eisenhower Administration, the CIA considered plans to undermine Castro's charismatic appeal by sabotaging his speeches. According to the 1967 Report of the CIA's Inspector General, an official in the Technical Services Division (TSD) recalled discussing a scheme to spray Castro's broadcasting studio with a chemical which produced effects similar to LSD, but the scheme was rejected because the chemical was unreliable. During this period, TSD impregnated a box of cigars with a chemical which produced temporary disorientation, hoping to induce Castro to smoke one of the cigars before delivering a speech. The Inspector General also reported a plan to destroy Castro's image as "The Beard" by dusting his shoes with thallium salts, a strong depilatory that would cause his beard to fall out. The depilatory was to be administered during a trip outside Cuba, when it was anticipated Castro would leave his shoes outside the door of his hotel room to be shined. TSD procured the chemical and tested it on animals, but apparently abandoned the scheme because Castro cancelled his trip. (I.G. Report, pp. 10-13)....

(iii) Poison Cigars

A notation in the records of the Operations Division, CIA's Office of Medical Services, indicates that on August 16, 1960, an official was given a box of Castro's favorite cigars with instructions to treat them with lethal poison. (I.G. Report, p. 21) The cigars were contaminated with a botulinum toxin so potent that a person would die after putting one in his mouth. (I.G. Report, p. 22) The official reported that the cigars were ready on October 7, 1960; TSD notes indicate that they were delivered to an unidentified person on February 13, 1961. (I.G. Report [CIA Inspector General's Report of 1967], p. 22) The record does not disclose whether an attempt was made to pass the cigars to Castro.

(b) Use of Underworld Figures—Phase I (Pre-Bay of Pigs)

(i) The Initial Plan

In August 1960, the CIA took steps to enlist members of the criminal underworld with gambling syndicate contacts to aid in assassinating Castro. The origin of the plot is uncertain. According to the 1967 Inspector General's Report,

> Bissell recalls that the idea originated with J. C. King, then Chief of W[estern] H[emisphere] Division, although King now recalls having only had limited knowledge of such a plan and at a much later date—about mid-1962. (I. G. Report, p. 14)

The earliest concrete evidence of the operation is a conversation between DDP Bissell and Colonel Sheffield Edwards, Director of the Office of Security. Edwards recalled that Bissell asked him to locate someone who could assassinate Castro. (Edwards, 5/30/75, pp. 2-3) Bissell confirmed that he requested Edwards to find someone to assassinate Castro and believed that Edwards raised the idea of contacting members of a gambling syndicate operating in Cuba. (Bissell, 6/9/75, pp. 71-73)....

Edwards and the Support Chief decided to rely on Robert A. Maheu to recruit someone "tough enough" to handle the job. (O.C. [an individual whose identity the committee chose to protect], 5/30/75, p. 8) Maheu was an ex-FBI agent who had entered into a career as a private investigator in 1954. A former FBI associate of Maheu's was employed in the CIA's Office of Security and had arranged for the CIA to use Maheu in several sensitive covert operations in which "he didn't want to have an Agency person or a government person get caught." (O.C., 5/30/75, p. 158) Maheu was initially paid a monthly retainer by the CIA of $500, but it was terminated after his detective agency became more lucrative. (O.C., 5/30/75, pp. 13-14; I. G. Report, p. 15)

Rosselli Recruited

...Sometime in late August or early September 1960, the Support Chief approached Maheu about the proposed operation. (O.C. 5/30/75, p. 9; Maheu, 7/29/75, p. 6) as Maheu recalls the conversation, the Support Chief asked him to contact John Rosselli, an underworld figure with possible gambling contacts in Las Vegas, to determine if he would participate in a plan to "dispose" of Castro (Maheu, 7/29/75, p. 8) The Support Chief testified, on the other hand, that it was Maheu who raised the idea of using Rosselli. (O.C., 5/30/75, pp. 15-16)

Maheu had known Rosselli since the late 1950's. (Maheu, 7/29/75, pp. 58-60) Although Maheu claims not to have been aware of the extent of Rosselli's underworld connections and activities, he recalled that "it was certainly evident to me that he was able to accomplish things in Las Vegas when nobody else seemed to get the same kind of attention." (Maheu, 7/29/75, p. 60)

The Support Chief had previously met Rosselli at Maheu's home. (Maheu, 7/29/75, p. 8). The Support Chief and Maheu each claimed that the other had raised the idea of using Rosselli, and Maheu said the Chief was aware that Rosselli had contacts with the gambling syndicate. (Maheu, 7/29/75, p. 8; O.C., 5/30/75, pp. 15-16)

At first Maheu was reluctant to become involved in the operation because it might interfere with his relationship with his new client, Howard Hughes [the millionaire recluse]. He finally agreed to participate because he felt that he owed the Agency a commitment. (O.C., 5/30/75, pp. 12-13, 103)....

(ii) Contact With the Syndicate

According to Rosselli, he and Maheu met at the Brown Derby Restaurant in Beverly Hills in early September 1960. Rosselli testified that Maheu told him that "high government officials" needed his cooperation in getting rid of Castro, and that he asked him to help recruit Cubans to do the job. (Rosselli, 6/24/75, p. 8) Maheu's recollection of that meeting was that "I informed him that I had been asked by my Government to solicit his cooperation in this particular venture." (Maheu, 7/29/75, p. 9)

Maheu stated that Rosselli "was very hesitant about participating in the project, and he finally said that he felt that he had an obligation to his government, and he finally agreed to participate." (Maheu, 7/29/75, p. 10) Maheu and Rosselli both testified that Rosselli insisted on meeting with a representative of the Government. (Maheu, 7/29/75, p. 9; Rosselli, 6/24/75, p. 9)

A meeting was arranged for Maheu and Rosselli with the Support Chief at the Plaza Hotel in New York. The Inspector General's Report placed the meeting on September 14, 1960. (I.G. Report, p. 16) Rosselli testified that he could not recall the precise date of the meeting, but that it had occurred during Castro's visit to the United Nations, which the New York Times Index places from September 18 through September 28, 1960. (Rosselli, 6/24/75, p. 10)

The Support Chief testified that he was introduced to Rosselli as a business associate of Maheu. He said that Maheu told Rosselli that Maheu represented international business interests which were pooling money to pay for the assassination of Castro. (O.C. 5/30/75, p. 26) Rosselli claimed that Maheu told him at that time that the Support Chief was with the CIA. (Rosselli, 6/24/75, pp. 11, 85) [Footnote: The weight of the testimony indicates that Rosseli realized the CIA was behind the assassination attempt at an early stage. Maheu substantially confirmed his account (Maheu, 7/29/75, p. 111). The support chief recalled that about three weeks after the New York meeting, Rosseli told him, "I am not kidding, I know who you work for." (O.C., 5/30/75, p. 26)]

Rosselli Recruits for Assassination

It was arranged that Rosselli would go to Florida and recruit Cubans for the operation. (Rosselli, 6/24/75, pp. 11-12) Edwards informed Bissell that contact had been made with the gambling syndicate. (Bissell, 6/9/75, pp. 20-21; I. G. Report, p. 17)

During the week of September 24, 1960 the Support Chief, Maheu, and Rosselli met in Miami to work out the details of the operation. (O.C. 5/30/75, pp. 25-26; Rosselli, 6/24/75, p. 12; I.G. Report, p. 18) Rosselli used the cover name "John Rawlston" and represented himself to the Cuban contacts as an agent of "* * * some business interests of Wall Street that had * * * nickel interests and properties around in Cuba, and I was getting financial assistance from them." (Rosselli, 6/24/75, pp. 9, 17)

Maheu handled the details of setting up the operation and keeping the Support Chief informed of developments. After Rosselli and Maheu had been in Miami for a short time, and certainly prior to October 18. Rosselli introduced Maheu to two individuals on whom Rosselli intended to rely: "Sam Gold," who would serve as a "back-up man" (Rosselli, 6/24/75, p. 15), or "key" man (Maheu, 7/29/75, p. 17), and "Joe," whom "Gold" said would serve as a courier to Cuba and make arrangements there. (I.G., Report p. 19) The Support Chief, who was using the name "Jim Olds," said he had met "Sam" and "Joe" once, and then only briefly. (O.C., 5/30/75, pp. 26-29)

The Support Chief testified that he learned the true identities of his associates one morning when Maheu called and asked him to examine the "Parade" supplement to the *Miami Times.* An article on the Attorney General's ten-most-wanted criminals list revealed that "Sam Gold" was Momo Salvatore Giancana, a Chicago-based gangster, [Footnote: Sam Giancana was murdered in his home on June 20, 1975.] and "Joe" was Santos Trafficante, the Cosa Nostra chieftain in Cuba. (I.G., Report, p. 19) The Support Chief reported his discovery to Edwards, (O.C. 5/30/75, pp. 31, 33) but did not know whether Edwards reported this fact to his superiors. (O.C., 5/30/75, pp. 32, 41) The Support Chief testified that this incident occurred after "we were up to our ears in it," a month or so after Giancana had been brought into the operation, but prior to giving the poison pills to Rosselli. (O.C. 5/30/75, pp. 30, 44)

Maheu recalled that it was Giancana's job to locate someone in Castro's entourage who could accomplish the assassination. (Maheu, 7/29/75, p. 19) and that he met almost daily with Giancana over a substantial period of time. (Maheu, 7/29/75, p. 18) Although Maheu described Giancana as playing a "key role," (Maheu, 7/29/75, p. 34) Rosselli claimed that none of the Cubans eventually used in the operation were acquired through Giancana's contacts. (Rosselli, 6/24/75, p. 15)

(iii) Las Vegas Wiretap

In late October 1960, Maheu arranged for a Florida investigator, Edward DuBois, to place an electronic "bug" in a room in Las Vegas. (Maheu, 7/29/75, p. 36)....

The Committee received conflicting evidence on whether the Agency was consulted prior to the installation of the tap....

The Committee...received conflicting evidence concerning whether the tap had been placed to keep Giancana in Miami or to check on security leaks. The Support Chief testified that during the early stages of negotiations with the gambling syndicate, Maheu informed him that a girl friend of Giancana was having an affair with the target of the tap. Giancana wanted Maheu to bug that person's room....

There is some evidence, however, suggesting that the CIA itself may have instituted the tap to determine whether Giancana was leaking information about his involvement in an assassination attempt against Castro....

Edwards told Maheu that if he was "approached by the FBI, he could refer them to me to be briefed that he was engaged in an intelligence operation directed at Cuba". (Memo, Edwards to Attorney General, 5/14/62) FBI records indicate that on April 18, 1961, Maheu informed the FBI that the tap involved the CIA, and suggested that Edwards be contacted. (Memo 4/20/61) Edwards subsequently informed the Bureau that the CIA would object to Maheu's prosecution because it might reveal sensitive information relating to the abortive Bay of Pigs invasion.

In a memo dated April 24, 1962, Herbert J. Miller, Assistant Attorney General, Criminal Division, advised the Attorney General that the "national interest" would preclude any prosecutions based upon the tap. Following a briefing of the Attorney General by the CIA, a decision was made not to prosecute.

(iv) Poison Is Prepared And Delivered to Cuba

The Inspector General's Report described conversations among Bissell, Edwards, and the Chief of the Technical Services Division (TSD), concerning the most effective method of poisoning Castro. (I.G. Report, pp. 23-33) There is some evidence that Giancana or Rosselli originated the idea of depositing a poison pill in Castro's drink to give the "asset" a chance to escape. (I.G. Report, p. 25) The Support Chief recalled Rosselli's request for something "nice and clean, without getting into any kind of out and out ambushing", preferably a poison that would disappear without a trace. (O.C. 5/30/75, p. 116) The Inspector General's Report cited the Support Chief as stating that the Agency had first considered a "gangland-style killing" in which Castro would be gunned down. Giancana reportedly opposed the idea because it would be difficult to recruit someone for such a dangerous operation, and suggested instead the use of poison. (I.G. Report, p. 25)

Edwards rejected the first batch of pills prepared by TSD because they would not dissolve in water. A second batch, containing botulinum toxin, "did the job expected of them" when tested on monkeys. (I.G. Report pp. 25-26; O.C. 5/30/75, p. 43) The Support Chief received the pills from TSD, probably in February 1961, with assurances that they were lethal, and then gave them to Rosselli. (O.C., 5/30/75, p. 43)

The record clearly establishes that the pills were given to a Cuban for delivery to the island some time prior to the Bay of Pigs invasion in mid-April 1961....

[A leading] Cuban [exile] claimed to have a contact inside a restaurant frequented by Castro. (Rosselli, 6/24/75, p. 21) As a prerequisite to the deal, he demanded cash and $1,000 worth of communications equipment.

The record does clearly reflect,...that communications equipment was delivered to the Cuban and that he was paid advance money to cover his expenses, probably in the amount of $10,000. (I.G. Report, p. 32) The money and pills were delivered at a meeting between Maheu, Rosselli, Trafficante, and the Cuban at the Fountainebleau Hotel in Miami....

The attempt met with failure. According to the Inspector General's Report, Edwards believed the scheme failed because Castro stopped visiting the restaurant where the "asset" was employed. Maheu suggested an alternative reason. He recalled being informed that after the pills had been delivered to Cuba, "the go signal still had to be received before in fact they were administered." (Maheu, 9/23/75, p. 42)....

(c) Use of Underworld Figures: Phase II (Post Bay of Pigs)

(i) Change in Leadership

The Inspector General's Report divides the gambling syndicate operation into Phase I, terminating with the Bay of Pigs, and Phase II, continuing with the transfer of the operation to William Harvey in late 1961. [Footnote: Harvey had a long background in clandestine activities. At the time the gambling syndicate operation was moved under Harvey's supervision, he was responsible for a number of important activities and soon thereafter was selected to head of Task Force W, the CIA component of the Kennedy Administration's cover effort to oust Castro.] The distinction between a clearly demarcated Phase I and Phase II may be an artificial one, as there is considerable evidence that the operation was continuous, perhaps lying dormant for the period immediately following the Bay of Pigs....

(ii) The Operation Is Reactivated

In early April 1962, Harvey, who testified that he was acting on "explicit orders" from [Richard] Helms [DDP], (Harvey, 7/11/75, p. 18), requested Edwards to put him in touch with Rosselli: (Edwards memo, 5/14/62)

[Poison] pills were passed to Harvey, who arrived in Miami on April 21, and found Rosselli already in touch with the same Cuban who had been involved in the pre-Bay of Pigs pill passage. (I.G. Report, p. 47) He gave the pills to Rosselli,...

Rosselli kept Harvey informed of the operation's progress. Sometime in May 1962, he reported that the pills and guns had arrived in Cuba, (Harvey, p. 64; Rosselli, 6/24/75, pp. 34, 42-43) On June 21, he told Harvey that the Cuban had dispatched a three-man team to Cuba. The Inspector General's report described the team's mission as "vague" and conjectured that the team would kill Castro or recruit others to do the job, using the poison pills if the opportunity arose. (I.G. Report, 6/2/75, p. 51)

Harvey met Rosselli in Miami on September 7 and 11, 1962. The Cuban was reported to be preparing to send in another three-man team to penetrate Castro's bodyguard....

The second team never left for Cuba, claiming that "conditions" in Cuba were not right. (I.G. Report, pp. 51-52) During early January 1963, Harvey paid Rosselli $2,700 to defray the Cuban's expenses. (I.G. Report, p. 52).

Harvey terminated the operation in mid-February 1963. At a meeting with Rosselli in Los Angeles, it was agreed that Rosselli would taper off his communications with the Cubans.

Patriotic Motives

The agency personnel who dealt with Rosselli attributed his motivation to patriotism [Footnote: Rosselli claims that he was motivated by "honor and dedication." (Roselli, 6/24/75, p. 59) In 1943, Rosselli had been convicted of extorting money from motion picture producers to insure studios against labor strikes, and during the period of his contacts with the CIA, Rosselli was deeply involved in hotel and gambling operations in Las Vegas. (File R-505, Summary of FBI Documents) It is possible that he believed cooperating with the government in the assassination operation might serve him well in the future.] and testified that he was not paid for his services. According to the Support Chief, Rosselli "paid his way, he paid his own hotel fees, he paid for his own travel. ***And he never took a nickel, he said, no, as long as it is for the Government of the United States, this is the least I can do, because I owe it a lot." (O.C., 5/30/75, p. 27)

Edwards agreed that Rosselli was "never paid a cent," (Edwards, 5/30/75, p. 16) and Maheu testified that "Giancana was paid nothing at all, not even for expenses, and that Mr. Rosselli was given a pittance that did not even begin to cover his expenses." (Maheu, 7/29/75, p. 68) It is clear, however, that the CIA did pay Rosselli's hotel bill during his stay in Miami in October 1960. The CIA's involvement with Rosselli caused the Agency some difficulty during Rosselli's subsequent prosecutions for fraudulent gambling activities and living in the country under an assumed name.

(d) Plans in Early 1963

Two plans to assassinate Castro were explored by Task Force W, the CIA section then concerned with covert Cuban operations, in early 1963. Desmond Fitzgerald (now deceased), Chief of the Task Force, asked his assistant to determine whether an exotic seashell, rigged to explode, could be deposited in an area where Castro commonly went skin diving. (Assistant, 9/18/75, p. 28) The idea was explored by the Technical Services Division and discarded as impractical. (Helms, 6/13/75, p. 135; I.G. Report, p. 77)

A second plan involved having James Donovan (who was negotiating with Castro for the release of prisoners taken during the Bay of Pigs operation) present Castro with a contaminated diving suit. (Colby, 5/21/75, pp. 38-39)

The Inspector General's Report dates this operation in January 1963, when Fitzgerald replaced Harvey as Chief of Task Force W, although it is unclear whether Harvey or Fitzgerald conceived the plan. (I.G. Report, p. 75) It is likely that the activity took place earlier, since Donovan had completed his negotiations by the middle of January 1963. Helms characterized the plan as "cockeyed." (Helms, 6/13/75, p. 135)

The Technical Services Division bought a diving suit, dusted the inside with a fungus that would produce a chronic skin disease (Madura foot), and contaminated the breathing apparatus with a tubercule bacillus. The Inspector General's Report states that the plan was abandoned because Donovan gave Castro a different diving suit on his own initiative. (I.G., Report, p. 75) Helms testified that the diving suit never left the laboratory. (Helms, 6/13/75, p. 135)

(e) AM/LASH

(i) Origin of the Project

In early 1961, a CIA official met with a highly-placed Cuban official to determine if the Cuban would cooperate in efforts against the Castro regime. (I.G. Report, p. 78) The Cuban was referred to by the cryptonym AM/LASH. The meeting was inconclusive, but led to subsequent meetings at which AM/LASH agreed to cooperate with the CIA.

The CIA regarded AM/LASH as an important "asset" inside Cuba. As a high-ranking leader who enjoyed the confidence of Fidel Castro, AM/LASH could keep the CIA informed of the internal workings of the regime. (Case Officer 2, 8/1/75, pp. 23, 40) It was also believed that he might play a part in fomenting a coup within Cuba. (Case Officer 2, 8/1/75, p. 43)

From the first contact with AM/LASH until the latter part of 1963, it was uncertain whether he would defect or remain in Cuba. His initial requests to the CIA and FBI for aid in defecting were rebuffed. (I.G. Report, pp. 80, 82-83) When Case Officer 1 joined the operation in June 1962, his assignment was to ensure that AM/LASH would "stay in place and report to us." (Case Officer 1, 8/11/75, p. 38) At a meeting in the fall of 1963, AM/LASH 1 stated that he would remain in Cuba if he "could do something really significant for the creation of a new Cuba" and expressed a desire to plan the "execution" of Fidel Castro. (Case Officer 1 Contact Report) The subject of assassinating Castro was again discussed by AM/LASH and the case officer at another meeting a few days later. The case officer's contact report states that assassination was raised in discussing AM/LASH's role in Cuba, and that M/LASH was visibly upset. "It was not the act that he objected to, but merely the choice of the word used to describe it. 'Eliminate' was acceptable." (Case Officer 1, Contact Report)

Each case officer testified that he did not ask AM/LASH to assassinate Castro....

Helms recalled that he told Fitzgerald to "go ahead and say [to AM/LASH] that from the standpoint of political support, the United States government will be behind you if you are successful. This had nothing to do with killings. This had only to do with the political action part of it." (Helms, 6/13/75, p. 131)

Fitzgerald met AM/LASH in late fall 1963 and promised him that the United States would support a coup against Castro. When later interviewed for the Inspector General's Report, Fitzgerald recalled that AM/LASH repeatedly requested an assassination weapon, particularly a "high-powered rifle with telescopic sights that could be used to kill Castro from a distance." Fitzgerald stated that he told AM/LASH that the United States would have "no part of an attempt on Castro's life." (I.G. Report, p. 90)

Case Officer 2 recalled that AM/LASH raised the prospect of assassinating Castro, but did not propose an explicit plan. (Case Officer 2, 8/1/75, pp. 62, 85) AM/LASH was, however, "convinced that Castro had to be removed from power before a coup could be undertaken in Cuba." (Case Officer 2, 8/1/75, p. 61)

AM/LASH also requested high-powered rifles and grenades. (Case Officer 2, 8/1/75, p. 77) A memorandum by Case Officer 2 states:

> C/SAS [Fitzgerald] approved telling AM/LASH he would be given a cache inside Cuba. Cache could, if he requested it, include *** high-powered rifles with scopes ***.

AM/LASH was told on November 22, 1963 that the cache would be dropped in Cuba. (Case Officer 2, 8/1/75, p. 92)

(ii) The Poison Pen Device

Another device offered to AM/LASH was a ball-point pen rigged with a hypodermic needle. (Case Officer 2, 8/1/75, p. 110) The needle was designed to be so fine that the victim would not notice its insertion. (Case Officer 2, 8/1/75, p. 103)

According to the Inspector General's Report, when Case Officer 2 was interviewed in 1967, he stated that AM/LASH had requested the Agency to "devise some technical means of doing the job that would not automatically cause him to lose his own life in the try." (I.G. Report, p. 92)

The Report concluded that: "although none of the participants so stated, it may be inferred that they were seeking a means of assassination of a sort that AM/LASH might reasonably have been expected to have devised himself." (I.G. Report, p. 92)

Fitzgerald's assistant told the Committee that the pen was intended to show "bona fides" and "The orders were to do something to get rid of Castro *** and we thought this other method might work whereas a rifle wouldn't." (Assistant, 9/18/75, p. 26)

Helms confirmed that the pen was manufactured "to take care of a request from him that he have some device for getting rid of Castro, for killing him, murdering him, whatever the case may be." (Helms, 6/13/75, p. 113)

"* * * [t]his was a temporizing gesture." (Helms, 6/11/75, p. 133)

On November 22, 1963, Fitzgerald and the case officer met with AM/LASH and offered him the poison pen, recommending that he use Blackleaf-40, a deadly poison which is commercially available. (Case Officer 2, 8/1/75, p. 112) The Inspector General's Report noted that "it is likely that at the very moment President Kennedy was shot, a CIA officer was meeting with a Cuban agent * * * and giving him an assassination device for use against Castro." (I.G. Report, p. 94)

The case officer later recalled that AM/LASH did not "think much of the device," and complained that CIA could surely "come up with something more sophisticated than that." (I.G. Report, p. 93a)....

(iii) Providing AM/LASH with Arms

CIA cables indicate that one cache of arms for AM/LASH was delivered in Cuba in March 1964 and another in June....

2. At What Level Were the Castro Plots Known About or Authorized Within the Central Intelligence Agency?

(a) The Question Presented

As explained in the preceding section, Richard Bissell clearly authorized the two attempts to assassinate Cuban leaders that occurred during his tenure as Deputy Director of Plans—the incident involving a Cuban in contact with Raul Castro and the attempt involving underworld figures that took place prior to the Bay of Pigs. It is also clear that Bissell's successor, Richard Helms, authorized and was aware of the attempt on Castro's life involving underworld figures that took place the year following the Bay of Pigs, although the degree of Helms' participation in the details of the plot is not certain. [Footnote: William Harvey testified that he kept Helms informed of the operation involving the underworld at all stages. (Harvey, 6/25/75, pp. 65-66)]

...Helms' recollection was less certain. Helms did recall that he was briefed by Harvey when Harvey first contacted Rosselli in April 1962. He remembered that he "reluctantly" had approved the operation, but that he had no confidence that it would succeed. (Helms, 7/17/75, p. 23)

When asked if he authorized sending the poison pills to Florida, Helms testified:

"I believe they were poison pills, and I don't recall necessarily approving them, but since Harvey alleges to have them and says that he took them to Miami, I must have authorized them in some fashion." (Helms, 6/13/75, p. 44)]

Helms also authorized and was aware of the AM/LASH operation, although it is not certain that he knew that AM/LASH intended to assassinate Castro. The evidence indicates that the exploding seashell and diving suit schemes were abandoned at the laboratory stage and that no authorization was sought for their development or eventual use.

This section deals with whether the Director of Central Intelligence, Allen Dulles, and his successor, John McCone, authorized or were aware of the assassination plots. Dulles served as DCI from 1953 to November 1961. McCone was DCI from November 1961 to April 1965. General Charles Cabell served as Deputy Director of Central Intelligence under Dulles and continued into the early months of McCone's term. He was replaced as DDCI in April 1962 by General Marshall Carter.

In summary, the evidence relating to Dulles and McCone (and their respective Deputy DCI's) is as follows:

(i) *Dulles.*—Bissell and Edwards testified that they were certain that both Dulles and his Deputy General [Charles] Cabell were aware of and authorized the initial phase of the assassination plot involving underworld figures. They acknowledged, however, that Dulles and Cabell were not told about the plot until after the underworld figures had been contacted. The words said to have been used to brief the Director and his Deputy—"an intelligence operation"—do not convey on their face that the plot involved assassination, although Bissell and Edwards insist that the real meaning must have been understood. Certain other evidence before the Committee suggests that Dulles and Cabell did know about the assassination plots; other evidence suggests that they did not. (See subsection (b) below.)

(ii) McCone.—McCone testified that he did not know about or authorize the plots. Helms, Bissell and Harvey all testified that they did not know whether McCone knew of the assassination plots. Each said, however, that he did not tell McCone of the assassination efforts either when McCone assumed the position of DCI in November 1961 or at any time thereafter until August 1963, when Helms gave McCone a memorandum from which McCone concluded that the operation with underworld figures prior to the Bay of Pigs had involved assassination. The Inspector General's Report states that Harvey received Helms' approval not to brief McCone when the assassination efforts were resumed in 1962. Harvey testified this accorded with his recollection. On other occasions when it would have been appropriate to do so, Helms and Harvey did not tell McCone about assassination activity. Helms did not recall any agreement not to brief McCone, but he did not question the position taken by Harvey or the Inspector General's Report. Helms did say that McCone never told him not to assassinate Castro....

Evidence concerning what Dulles Was Told.—Bissell recalled that "in the latter part of September" there was "a meeting in which Col. Edwards and I briefed Mr. Dulles and General Cabell" about the plan to assassinate Castro. (Bissell, 6/9/75, p. 20) Bissell testified that "Colonel Edwards outlined in somewhat circumlocutious terms the plan that he had discussed with syndicate representatives." (Bissell, 6/9/75, p. 22)....

> The discussion was circumspect. Edwards deliberately avoided the use of any "bad words." The descriptive term used was "an intelligence operation." Edwards is quite sure that the DCI and the DDCI clearly understood the nature of the operation he was discussing. He recalls describing the channel as being "from A to B to C." As he then envisioned it, A was Maheu, B was Rosselli, and C was the principal in Cuba. Edwards recalls that Mr. Dulles merely nodded, presumably in understanding and approval. Certainly there was no opposition. Edwards states that, while there was no formal approval as such, he felt that he clearly had tacit approval to use his own judgment. (I.G. Report, pp. 17-18)

Bissell testified that the description sounded "highly plausible." (Bissell, 6/9/75, p. 24) Edwards said it was "accurate." (Edwards, 5/30/75, p. 11)....

When asked by the Chairman why, in this context, persons within the Agency talked "in riddles to one another," Bissell replied that:

> * * * I think there was a reluctance to spread even on an oral record some aspects of this operation.
>
> Chairman. Did the reluctance spring from the fact that it simply grated against your conscience to have to speak more explicitly?

Bissell. I don't think it grated against my conscience. I think it may have been a feeling that the Director preferred the use of the sort of language that is described in the Inspector General's Report. (Bissell, 6/9/75, p. 25)

McCone's testimony.—McCone testified that he was not aware of the plots to assassinate Castro which took place during the years in which he was DCI, and that he did not authorize those plots. (McCone, 6/6/75, pp. 33, 44-45) He testified that he was not briefed about the assassination plots by Dulles, Bissell, Helms, or anyone else when he succeeded Dulles as Director in November 1961 (McCone, 6/6/75, pp. 6-7, 17), and that if he had ever been asked about the plots, he would have disapproved....

(ii) Testimony of Helms, Bissell, and other Subordinate Agency Employees.—Bissell was DDP under McCone for three months, from November 1961 until February 1962. Helms assumed the duties of DDP from Bissell and served throughout the balance of McCone's terms as director....

Q. Your testimony is that you never discussed assassination with Mr. McCone?

A. That is correct.

Q. ***[D]id you tell McCone anything about that conversation with Mr. Harvey in which you at least told him to take over the relationship with the criminal syndicate?

A. I don't remember so doing. (Bissell, 6/11/75, p. 19)

Helms testified that he did not recall ever having discussed the assassination plots with McCone while the plots were continuing. When asked whether McCone was aware of the assassination plots against Castro, Helms testified:

No, it isn't my impression that I told him, at least I don't have any impression, unfortunately * * *. Mr. McCone is an honorable man. He has done his own testifying and all I can say is that I do not know specifically whether he was aware or not. (Helms, 6/13/75, pp. 90, 101-102)....

Senator Mondale. If you were a member of this Committee wouldn't you assume that Mr. McCone was unaware of the assassination attempts while they were underway?

Helms. I don't know how to answer that, Senator Mondale. He was involved in this up to his scuppers just the way everybody else was that was in it, and I just don't know. I have no reason to impugn his integrity. On the other hand, I don't understand how it was he didn't hear about some of these things that he claims that he didn't. (Helms, 7/17/75, pp. 32-33)....

3. At What Level Were the Castro Plots Authorized or Known About Outside of the Central Intelligence Agency?

...(a) The Question of Knowledge and Authorization Outside The Central Intelligence Agency in The Eisenhower Administration

The evidence as to whether Allen Dulles, CIA Director during the Eisenhower Administration, was informed of the Castro assassination operation is not clear.

Even assuming that Dulles was informed, authorization outside the CIA for a Castro assassination could, according to the testimony, only have come from President Eisenhower, from someone speaking for him, or from the Special Group. At issue, then is whether President Eisenhower, his close aides, or the Special Group authorized or had knowledge of the Castro assassination plots.

The Committee took testimony on this issue from Richard Bissell and from President Eisenhower's principal staff assistants. In summary, the evidence was:

(a) Bissell testified that he did not inform the Special Group or President Eisenhower of the Castro assassination operation, and that he had no personal knowledge that Allen Dulles had informed either President Eisenhower or the Special Group. However, Bissell expressed the belief that Allen Dulles would have advised President Eisenhower (but not the Special Group) in a "circumlocutious" or "oblique" way. Bissell based this "pure personal opinion" on his understanding of Dulles' practice regarding other particularly sensitive covert operations. But Bissell testified that Dulles never told him that he had so advised President Eisenhower about the Castro assassination operation, even though Dulles had told Bissell when he had employed this "circumlocutious" approach to the President on certain other occasions.

(b) Gordon Gray, Eisenhower's Special Assistant for National Security Affairs and the President's representative on the Special Group, testified that the Special Group never approved a Castro assassination, and that President Eisenhower had charged the Special Group with the responsibility of authorizing all important covert operations. A review of the records of Special Group meetings shows that a query concerning a plan to take "direct positive action" against Castro caused Allen Dulles' Deputy, General Cabell, to advise that such action was beyond the CIA's capability. Gray, Andrew Goodpaster (the President's staff secretary responsible for national security operational matters) and John Eisenhower (Assistant Staff Secretary) each stated that he believed that President Eisenhower would not have considered such a matter in a private meeting with Dulles, would not have approved Castro's assassination, and would not have discussed such a matter without telling him. Each concluded as a matter of opinion that President Eisenhower was never told, and each denied having heard anything about any assassination.

(iii) In addition to the Inspector General's Report (which concluded that it could not say that any assassination activity carried on during this period was responsive to Administration pressure), the documentary evidence shows that Castro's removal was discussed at two meetings of the National Security Council and the Special Group in March 1960. The minutes of these meetings indicate that the discussions involved a general consideration of a proposal to train a Cuban exile force to invade Cuba and an assessment that Castro's overthrow might result in a Communist takeover. Gray and Admiral Arleigh Burke, Chief of Naval Operations from 1955 through 1961, testified that these discussions of Castro's removal did not refer to assassination, but rather to the problem of creating an anti-Castro exile force strong enough to ensure a non-Communist successor to the Castro regime. Apparently there was no assassination activity stemming directly from those meetings. Another Special Group document stated that planning for "direct positive action" against Cuban leaders was raised at a meeting in the Fall of 1960, shortly after Phase I of the CIA/underworld assassination operation was initiated. The DDCI told the Special Group, however, that such action was beyond the CIA's capability....

(iii) Testimony of White House Officials

(1) Gordon Gray

Gordon Gray served as President Eisenhower's Special Assistant for National Security Affairs from July 1958 to January 20, 1961. (Gray, 7/9/75, p. 4) Gray was also the President's representative on the Special Group. (Gray, 7/9/75, p. 4) President Eisenhower instructed Gray that all covert actions impinging on the sovereignty of other countries must be deliberated by the Special Group. (Gray, 7/9/75, p. 6) Gray testified that from July 1958 to January 20, 1961, the Special Group never approved an action to assassinate Castro (Gray, 7/9/75, p. 6) and that no such suggestion was made by Bissell. (Gray, 7/9/75, p. 37)

Gray testified that:

> I find it very difficult to believe, and I do not believe, that Mr. Dulles would have gone independently to him [President Eisenhower] with such a proposal without, for that matter, my knowing about it from Mr. Dulles (Gray, 7/9/75, p. 35)

Gray further testified that his relationship with President Eisenhower was such that President Eisenhower "would discuss with me anything that came to his attention independently of me." (Gray, 7/9/75, p. 7) And Gray testified that President Eisenhower never discussed with him the subject of a Castro assassination or of the use of the underworld figures and Cubans in such an effort. (Gray, 7/9/75, p. 7)....

(4) John Eisenhower

John Eisenhower was [Andrew] Goodpaster's Assistant Staff Secretary from mid-1958 to the end of his father's Administration. (Eisenhower, 7/18/75, pp. 5, 9) Eisenhower testified that his father had confided in him about secret matters "to a very large extent." (Eisenhower, 7/18/75, p. 3) For example, he said that after the Potsdam Conference in July 1945, his father had told him that the United States had developed the atomic bomb (Eisenhower, 7/18/75, p. 3) and that as early as 1956, President Eisenhower had told him of the secret U-2 flights. (Eisenhower, 7/18/75, p. 4)

John Eisenhower said that President Eisenhower never told him of any CIA activity involving an assassination plan or attempt concerning Castro....

(b) The Question of Knowledge and Authorization Outside The Central Intelligence Agency During the Kennedy Administration

...(i) Pre-Bay Of Pigs Assassination Plot

The testimony was essentially the same as for the Eisenhower Administration. Bissell again said he assumed and believed that Dulles had met with President Kennedy and informed him, in a circumlocutious fashion, that the operation had been planned and was being attempted. Bissell also testified that he (Bissell) informed neither the President nor any other officials outside the CIA about the assassination efforts. Each Kennedy Administration official who testified said that he had not known about or authorized the plots, and did not believe the President would have authorized an assassination.

(1) Bissell's Testimony Concerning His Assumption That Dulles Told The President.—Richard Bissell continued as DDP, the principal agency official responsible for efforts against the Castro regime, including both the Bay of Pigs operation and the assassination plots, when Kennedy became President in January, 1961. Bissell is the only surviving CIA policy maker with first hand knowledge of high-level decisions in the pre-Bay of Pigs phase of the Castro assassination plot involving underworld figures. Although Bissell testified that Allen Dulles never told him that Dulles had informed President Kennedy about the underworld plot, Bissell told the Committee that he believed Dulles had so informed President Kennedy and that the plot had accordingly been approved by the highest authority....

Bissell repeatedly coupled Eisenhower and Kennedy when he speculated that the Presidents would have been advised in a manner calculated to maintain "plausible deniability." (Bissell, 6/9/75, pp. 38, 57; 6/11/75, pp. 5-6):

> In the case of an operation of high sensitivity of the sort that we are discussing, there was a further objective that would have been pursued at various levels, and that was specifically with respect to the President, to protect the President. And, therefore, the way in which I believe that Allen Dulles would have attempted to do that was to have indicated to the two successive Presidents the general objective of the operation that was contemplated, to make that sufficiently clear so that the President—either President Eisenhower or President Kennedy—could have ordered the termination of the operation, but to give the President just as little information about it as possible beyond an understanding of its general purpose. Such an approach to the President would have had as its purpose to leave him in the position to deny knowledge of the operation if it should surface....

(3) Kennedy Administration Officials Testimony.—The Committee has taken testimony from all living officials high in the Kennedy Administration who dealt with Cuban affairs. The theme of their testimony was that they had no knowledge of any assassination plan or attempt by the United

States government before or after the Bay of Pigs invasion, and that they did not believe President Kennedy's character or style of operating would be consistent with approving assassination.

Secretary of Senate [State] Dean Rusk testified: "I never had any reason to believe that anyone that I ever talked to knew about had any active planning of assassination underway." (Rusk, 7/10/75, p. 65)

Secretary of Defense Robert McNamara stated that he had "no knowledge or information about * * * plans or preparations for a possible assassination attempt against Premier Castro." (McNamara 7/11/75, p. 7)

Roswell Gilpatric, Deputy Secretary of Defense under McNamara, said that killing Castro was not within the mandate of the Special Group, which he construed as having been only to weaken and undermine "the Cuban economy." (Gilpatric, 7/8/75, p. 28)

General Maxwell Taylor, who later chaired Special Group meetings on Operation Mongoose, stated that he had "never heard" of an assassination effort against Castro, and that he never raised the question of assassination with anyone. (Taylor, 7/9/75, pp. 7-8, 72, 19)

McGeorge Bundy stated that it was his "conviction" that "no one in the Kennedy Administration, in the White House, or in the cabinet, ever gave any authorization, approval, or instruction of any kind for any effort to assassinate anyone by the CIA." (Bundy, 7/11/75, p. 54) Bundy said that he was never told that assassination efforts were being conducted against Castro. (Bundy, 7/11/75, p. 63)

Walt W. Rostow, who shared national security duties with Bundy before moving to the Department of State, testified that during his entire tenure in government, he "never heard a reference" to an intention to undertake an assassination effort. (Rostow, 7/9/75, pp. 10, 12-13, 38)

Asked if he had ever been told anything about CIA efforts to assassinate Castro, Richard Goodwin, Assistant Special Counsel to the President replied, "No, I never heard of such a thing." (Goodwin, 7/18/75, p. 13)

Sorensen concluded his testimony with the following exchange:

> Q. Would you think it would be possible that * * * the Agency, the CIA could somehow have been under the impression that they had a tacit authorization for assassination due to a circumspect discussion that might have taken place in any of these meetings?
>
> Sorensen. It is possible, indeed, I think the President on more than one occasion felt that Mr. Dulles, by making rather vague and sweeping references to particular countries was seeking tacit approval without ever asking for it, and the President was rather concerned that he was not being asked for explicit directives and was not being given explicit information, so it is possible. But on something of this kind, assassination, I would doubt it very much. Either you are for it or you are not for it, and he was not for it. (Sorensen 7/21/75, pp. 32-33)....

(4) The Question of Whether Assassination Efforts Were Disclosed in Various Briefings of Administration Officials.

a. Briefing of the President-Elect

In the latter part of November 1960, after the Presidential election, Dulles and Bissell jointly briefed President-elect Kennedy on "the most important details with respect to the operation which became the Bay of Pigs." (Bissell, 6/9/75, p. 34) Bissell testified that he did not believe the ongoing assassination efforts were mentioned to the President-elect at that meeting. (Bissell, 6/9/75, pp. 27, 35-36) Bissell surmised that the reasons he and Dulles did not tell Kennedy at that initial meeting were that they had "apparently" thought it was not an important matter, and that they "would have thought that that was a matter of which he should be advised upon assuming office rather than in advance." (Bissell, 6/9/75, p. 35) Bissell's latter comment led to the following exchange:

> The Chairman. Isn't it a strange distinction that you draw that on the one hand (as) a Presidential designate, as President-elect, he should have all of the details concerning a planned invasion of Cuba, but that he should not be told about an ongoing attempt to assassinate Fidel Castro?....
>
> Mr. Bissell. Well, Mr. Chairman, it is quite possible that Mr. Dulles did say something about an attempt to or the possibility of making use of syndicate characters for this purpose. I do remember his doing so at that briefing. My belief is that had he done so, he probably would have done so in rather general terms and that neither of us was in a position to go into detail on the matter. (Bissell, 6/9/75, p. 35)....

FBI Director [J. Edgar] Hoover sent the Attorney General a memorandum about the Las Vegas wire tap on May 22, 1961. [Footnote: A handwritten note from the Attorney General to his assistant on the face of the memorandum indicates that the Attorney General had seen the document.] An attachment to that memorandum quoted Sheffield Edwards as saying that Bissell, in his "recent briefings" of [General Maxwell] Taylor and [Attorney General Robert] Kennedy "told the Attorney General that some of the associated planning included the use of Giancana and the underworld against Castro."....

Language Used To Describe Plot

The examination of Bissell on whether he had discussed a pre-Bay of Pigs plot with the Attorney General or General Taylor and, if so, why he used such obscure and indirect language, elicited the following testimony:

> Q. Did you, sometime in May of 1961 communicate the state of your awareness to the Attorney General in your briefing to him?
>
> Bissell. Well, there is a report which I was shown, I think it was last week, I believe it also came from the FBI, but I could be wrong about that, or indicating that I did, at that time in May, brief the Attorney General, and I think General Taylor to the

effect that the Agency had been using—I don't know whether Giancana was mentioned by name, but in effect, the Underworld against the Castro regime.

Q. Did you tell them—them being the Attorney General and General Taylor—that this use included actual attempts to assassinate Mr. Castro?

Bissell. I have no idea whether I did [.] I have no idea of the wording. I think it might quite possibly have been left in the more general terms of using the underworld against the Castro regime, or the leadership of the Castro regime.

Q. Mr. Bissell, given the state of your knowledge at that time, wouldn't that have been deliberately misleading information?

Bissell. I don't think it would have been. We were indeed doing precisely that. We were trying to use elements of the underworld against Castro and the Cuban leadership.

Q. But you had information, didn't you, that you were, in fact, trying to kill him?

Bissell. I think that is a way of using these people against him.

Q. That's incredible. You're saying that in briefing the Attorney General you are telling him you are using the underworld against Castro, and you intended that to mean, Mr. Attorney General, we are trying to kill him?

Bissell. I thought it signaled just exactly that to the Attorney General, I'm sure....

(5) Conversation Between President Kennedy and Senator George Smathers

George Smathers, former Senator from Florida, testified that the subject of a possible assassination of Castro arose in a conversation Smathers had with President Kennedy on the White House lawn in 1961....

It was Smathers' "impression" that President Kennedy raised the subject of assassination with Smathers because someone else "had apparently discussed this and other possibilities with respect to Cuba" with the President. (Smathers, 7/23/75, pp. 16, 25)....

Senator Smathers concluded his testimony by indicating that on Cuban affairs in general, he felt he was "taking a tougher stance than was the President." (Smathers, 7/23/75, p. 24) Smathers said he was "positive" that Kennedy opposed assassination. (Smathers, 7/23/75, p. 16)....

(7) The Question of Whether or not the Assassination Operation Involving Underworld Figures was Known about by Attorney General Kennedy or President Kennedy as Revealed by Investigations of Giancana and Rosselli....

....[A]ll living CIA officials who were involved in the underworld assassination attempt or who were in a position to have known of the attempt have testified that they never discussed the assassination plot with the President. By May 1961, however, the Attorney General and Hoover were aware that the CIA had earlier used Giancana in an operation against Cuba and FBI files contained two memoranda which, if simultaneously reviewed, would have led one to conclude that the CIA operation had involved assassination. There is no evidence that any one within the FBI concluded that the CIA had used Giancana in an assassination attempt. The Committee has uncovered a chain of events, however, which would have given Hoover an opportunity to have assembled the entire picture and to have reported the information to the President.

Evidence before the Committee indicates that a close friend of President Kennedy had frequent contact with the President from the end of 1960 through mid-1962. FBI reports and testimony indicate that the President's friend was also a close friend of John Rosselli and Sam Giancana and saw them often during this same period. [Footnote: White House telephone logs show 70 instances of phone contact between the White House and the President's friend whose testimony confirms frequent phone contact with the President himself.

Both the President's friend and Rosselli testified that the friend did not know about either the assassination operation or the wiretap case. Giancana was killed before he was available for questioning. (In a December 1975 press conference in San Diego Judith Campbell Exner identified herself as "the President's friend.")]

On February 27, 1962, Hoover sent identical copies of a memorandum to the Attorney General and Kenneth O'Donnell, Special Assistant to the President. The memorandum stated that information developed in connection with a concentrated FBI investigation of John Rosselli revealed that Rosselli had been in contact with the President's friend. The memorandum also reported that the individual was maintaining an association with Sam Giancana, described as "a prominent Chicago underworld figure." Hoover's memorandum also stated that a review of the telephone toll calls from the President's friend's residence revealed calls to the White House. The President's secretary ultimately received a copy of the memorandum and said she believed she would have shown it to the President.

The association of the President's friend with the "hoodlums" and that person's connection with the President was again brought to Hoover's attention in a memorandum preparing him for a meeting with the President planned for March 22, 1962. Courtney Evans [FBI liaison with the Attorney General] testified that Hoover generally required a detailed summary of information in the FBI files for drafting important memoranda or preparing for significant meetings. (Evans, 8/28/75, pp. 70, 72) The FBI files on Giancana then contained information disclosing Giancana's connection with the CIA as well as his involvement in assassination plotting. (Memoranda of 10/18/60 and 5/22/61)

On March 22, Hoover had a private luncheon with President Kennedy. There is no record of what transpired at that luncheon. According to the White House logs, the last telephone contact between the White House and the President's friend occurred a few hours after the luncheon.

The fact that the President and Hoover had a luncheon at which one topic was presumably that the President's friend was also a friend of Giancana and Rosselli raised several possibilities. The first is, assuming that Hoover did in fact receive a summary of FBI information relating to Giancana prior to his luncheon with the President, whether that summary reminded the Director that Giancana had been involved in a CIA operation against Cuba that included "dirty business" and further indicated that Giancana had talked about an assassination attempt against Castro. A second is whether Hoover would then have taken the luncheon as an opportunity to fulfill his duty to bring this information to the President's attention. What actually transpired at that luncheon may never be known, as both participants are dead and the FBI files contain no records relating to it....

Post-Bay Of Pigs Underworld Plot—MONGOOSE Period

This section discusses evidence bearing on whether the post-Bay of Pigs operation to assassinate Castro involving underworld figures—which began in April 1962, and continued at least through the Cuban missile crisis in October of that year—was authorized or known about by Administration officials outside of the CIA.

This issue must be considered in light of the differing perceptions of Helms and his subordinates, on the one hand, and of other members of the Kennedy Administration, including the Director of the CIA, on the other. While Helms testified that he never received a direct order to assassinate Castro, he fully believed that the CIA was at all times acting within the scope of its authority and that Castro's assassination came within the bounds of the Kennedy Administration's effort to overthrow Castro and his regime. Helms said that he inherited the Rosselli program from Bissell, and due to its sensitive and unsavory character, it was not the type of program one would discuss in front of high officials. He stated that he never informed McCone or any other officials of the Kennedy Administration of the assassination plot. However, McCone and the surviving members of the Kennedy Administration testified that they believed a Castro assassination was impermissible without a direct order, that assassination was outside the parameters of the Administration's anti-Castro program, and each testified that to his knowledge no such order was given to Helms.

An understanding of the Kennedy Administration's 1962 covert action program for Cuba is essential to an evaluation of the testimony on the issue of authorization. That program, which was designed to overthrow the Castro regime, and the events in 1961 leading up to it are discussed below....

(1) Events Preceding the Establishment of MONGOOSE

On April 22, 1961, following the Bay of Pigs failure, the President requested General Maxwell Taylor to conduct a reevaluation of "our practices and programs in the areas of military and paramilitary, guerilla and anti-guerilla activity which fall short of outright war." Taylor was to give special attention to Cuba (Letter to Maxwell Taylor, 4/22/61) and Robert Kennedy was to be his principal colleague in the effort....

By July 1961, the Special Group had agreed that "the basic objective toward Cuba was to provide support to a U.S. program to develop opposition to Castro...."

In early November 1961 Tad Szulc [Footnote: A reporter in the Washington Bureau of the *New York Times*. Szulc had visited Cuba in May-June 1961, following the Bay of Pigs invasion. During the course of that trip, Szulc had a "series of very long conversations" with Castro. (Szulc, 6/10/75, p. 24)] was asked by Richard Goodwin, a Special Assistant to President Kennedy, to meet with Attorney General Robert Kennedy on November 8 to discuss the situation in Cuba. The meeting was "off-the-record." Szulc attended as a friend of Goodwin's, and not as a reporter. (Szulc, 6/10/75, p. 24) During the meeting with Robert Kennedy, the discussion centered on "the situation in Cuba following the [Bay of Pigs] invasion [and] the pros and cons of some different possible actions by the United States Government in that context." (Szulc, 6/10/75, p. 25) According to Szulc the subject of assassination was not mentioned during this meeting. (Szulc, 6/10/75, p. 31)

At the close of the meeting, Robert Kennedy asked Szulc to meet with the President. (Szulc, 6/10/75, p. 25) The next day Szulc, accompanied by Goodwin, met with President Kennedy for over an hour in the Oval Office....

Szulc testified that after [a] general discussion, the President asked "what would you think if I ordered Castro to be assassinated." (Szulc, 6/10/75, pp. 26, 27; Szulc Notes of conversation with President Kennedy, 11/9/61) Szulc testified that he replied that an assassination would not necessarily cause a change in the Cuban system, and that it was Szulc's personal view that the United States should not be party to murders and political assassinations. (Szulc, 6/10/75, p. 26) Szulc said that the President responded, "I agree with you completely." Szulc stated:

> He [President Kennedy] then went on for a few minutes to make the point how strongly he and his brother felt that the United States for moral reasons should never be in a situation of having recourse to assassination. (Szulc, 6/10/75, p. 27)....

Szulc stated that it is "possible" and he "believed" that President Kennedy used such words as "someone in the intelligence business," to describe the source of the pressure for a Castro assassination. (Szulc, 6/10/75, p. 29) The President did not specifically identify the source of the pressure. (Szulc, 6/10/75, p. 27)

There is no evidence other than Szulc's testimony that the President was being pressured. This lack of evidence was particularly troublesome since everyone else questioned by the Committee denied ever having discussed assassination with the President, let alone having pressed him to consider it....

(2) Operation MONGOOSE

In November 1962 the proposal for a major new covert action program to overthrow Castro was developed. The President's Assistant, Richard Goodwin, and General Edward Lansdale, who was experienced in counter-insurgency operations, played major staff roles in creating this program, which was named Operation MONGOOSE. Goodwin and Lansdale worked closely with Robert Kennedy, who took an active interest in this preparatory stage, and Goodwin advised the President that Robert Kennedy "would be the most effective commander" of the proposed operation. (Memo, Goodwin to the President, 11/1/61, p. 1) In a memorandum to Robert Kennedy outlining the MONGOOSE proposal, Lansdale stated that a "picture of the situation has emerged clearly enough to indicate what needs to be done and to support your sense of urgency concerning Cuba." (Memo, 11/15/61)

At the end of the month, President Kennedy issued a memorandum recording his decision to begin the MONGOOSE project to "use our available assets * * * to help Cuba overthrow the Communist regime." (Memo from the President to the Secretary of State, et al., 11/30/61)

The establishment of Operation MONGOOSE resulted in important organizational changes.

(1) The Special Group (Augmented) (SGA)

A new control group, the Special Group (Augmented) (SGA) was created to oversee Operation MONGOOSE. The SGA comprised the regular Special Group members (*i.e.*, McGeorge Bundy, Alexis Johnson of the Department of State, Roswell Gilpatric of the Department of Defense, John McCone, and General Lyman Lemnitzer of the Joint Chiefs) augmented by Attorney General Robert Kennedy and General Maxwell Taylor. Although Secretary of State Rusk and Secretary of Defense McNamara were not formal members of the Special Group or the Special Group (Augmented), they sometimes attended meetings.

(2) General Lansdale named Chief-of-Operations of MONGOOSE....
(3) CIA Organization for MONGOOSE

In late 1961 or early 1962, William Harvey was put in charge of the CIA's Task Force W, the CIA unit for MONGOOSE Operations. Task Force W operated under guidance from the Special Group (Augmented) and employed a total of approximately 400 people at CIA headquarters and its Miami Station....

B. Lansdale's Theory and Objective for MONGOOSE

In the fall of 1961, Lansdale was asked by President Kennedy to examine the Administration's Cuba policy and to make recommendations. Lansdale testified that he reported to President Kennedy that "Castro * * * had aroused considerable affection for himself personally with the Cuban population * * *" (Lansdale, 7/8/75, p. 4), and that the United States "should take a very different course" from the "harassment" operations that had been directed against Castro up to that time. (Lansdale, 7/8/75, p. 3) Lansdale informed the President that these prior United States operations were conceived and led by Americans. (Lansdale, 7/8/75, p. 5) In contrast, Lansdale proposed in Operation MONGOOSE that the United States work with exiles, particularly professionals, who had opposed Batista and then became disillusioned with Castro. (Lansdale, 7/8/75, pp. 4, 10-11) Lansdale's ultimate objective was to have "the people themselves overthrow the Castro regime rather than U.S. engineered efforts from outside Cuba." (Lansdale, 7/8/75, p. 41)....

According to the Assistant to the head of Task Force W, sometime early in the fall of 1961, Bissell was "chewed out in the Cabinet Room of the White House by both the President and the Attorney General for, as he put it, sitting on his ass and not doing anything about getting rid of Castro and the Castro regime." (Assistant, 6/18/75, p. 8)....

On January 19, 1962, a meeting of principal MONGOOSE participants was held in Attorney General Kennedy's office. (McManus, 7/22/75, p. 6) Notes taken at the meeting by George McManus, Helms' Executive Assistant, contain the following passages:

> Conclusion Overthrow of Castro is Possible.
>
> "* * * a solution to the Cuban problem today carried top priority in U.S. Gov[ernmen]t. No time, money, effort—or manpower is to be spared."...

McManus attributed the words "the top priority in the U.S. Gov-[ernmen]t—no time, money, effort or manpower is to be spared" to the Attorney General. (McManus, 7/22/75, pp. 8-9)

Helms stated that those words reflected the "kind of atmosphere" in which he had perceived the assassination was implicitly authorized. (Helms, 7/17/75, pp. 60-61) McManus agreed that Robert Kennedy "was very vehement in his speech" and "really wanted action," but McManus disagreed with Helms' perception, stating that "it never occurred to me" that Kennedy's exhortation included permission to assassinate Castro. Nor did the spirit of the meeting as a whole leave McManus with the impression that assassination was either contemplated or authorized. (McManus, 7/22/75, pp. 9-10)

E. General Lansdale's MONGOOSE Planning Tasks

....In a memorandum to the Attorney General on January 27, 1962, Lansdale referred to the possibility that "we might uncork the touchdown play independently of the institutional program we are spurring." (Memo, Lansdale to Attorney General, 1/27/62) Lansdale testified that the phrase "touchdown play" was a "breezy way of referring to a Cuban revolt to overthrow the regime" rather than to Castro's assassination. (Lansdale, 7/8/75, p. 45) The examples of such plays cited in the memorandum (e.g., "stir up workers in Latin America and Cuba," work through "ethnic language groups," "youth elements," or "families through the Church") do not contain any indication of assassination. (Memo, Lansdale to Attorney General, 1/27/62, p. 1)

On January 19, 1962, Lansdale added an additional task to those assigned on January 18. "Task 33" involved a plan to "incapacitate" Cuban sugar workers during the harvest by the use of chemical warfare means. Lansdale testified that the plan involved using nonlethal chemicals to sicken Cubans temporarily and keep them away from the fields for a 24-48 hour period "without ill effects." The task was initially approved for planning purposes with the notation that it would require "policy determination" before final approval. After a study showed the plan to be unfeasible, it was cancelled without ever being submitted to the SGA for debate. (Lansdale, 7/8/75, p. 29; SGA Minutes, 1/30/62, p. 1)....

Lansdale testified that early in the MONGOOSE operation he had suggested that working level representatives of the MONGOOSE agencies get in touch with "criminal elements" to obtain intelligence and for "possible actions against the police structure" in Cuba. (Lansdale, 7/8/75, p. 104) Lansdale conceded that his proposal to recruit gangster elements for attacks on "key leaders" contemplated the targeted killing of individuals, in addition to the casualties that might occur in the course of the revolt itself. (Lansdale, 7/8/75, p. 107)

Lansdale's 33 plans were never approved for implementation by the SGA.... [T]he SGA tabled Lansdale's six phase plan altogether in February 1962, and directed him to plan for and conduct an intelligence collection plan only. (SGA Minutes, 3/5/62)....

H. The Pattern of MONGOOSE Action

The Kennedy Administration pressed the MONGOOSE operation with vigorous language. Although the collection of intelligence information was the central objective of MONGOOSE until August 1962, sabotage and paramilitary actions were also conducted, including a major sabotage operation aimed at a large Cuban copper mine. Lansdale described the sabotage acts as involving "blowing up bridges to stop communications and blowing up certain production plants." (Lansdale, 7/8/75, p. 36) During the Missile Crisis in the fall of 1962, sabotage was increasingly urged.

Despite the Administration's urgings, the SGA shied away from sabotage and other violent action throughout 1962, including the period of the Missile Crisis. Helms noted in a memorandum of a meeting on October 16, 1962, that Robert Kennedy, in expressing the "general dissatisfaction of the President" with MONGOOSE, "pointed out that [MONGOOSE] had been underway for a year * * * that there had been no acts of sabotage and that even the one which had been attempted had failed twice." (Memo by Helms, 10/16/62)....

On August 20, Taylor told the President that the SGA saw no likelihood that Castro's Government would be overturned by internal means without direct United States military intervention, and that the SGA favored a more aggressive MONGOOSE program. (Memo, Taylor to the President, 8/20/62) On August 23, McGeorge Bundy issued NSC Memorandum No. 181, which stated that, at the President's directive, "the line of activity projected for Operation MONGOOSE Plan B plus should be developed with all possible speed." On August 30, the SGA instructed the CIA to submit a list of possible sabotage targets and noted that: "The Group, by reacting to this list, could define the limits within which the Agency could operate on its own initiative." (Minutes of 8/30/62)

The onset of the Cuban Missile Crisis initially caused a reversion to the stepped-up Course B plan...the SGA decided that "considerably more sabotage" should be undertaken, and that "all efforts should be made to develop new and imaginative approaches with the possibility of getting rid of the Castro regime." (Minutes of SGA Meeting, 10/14/62, p. 3) However, on October 30, 1962, the Special Group (Augmented) ordered a halt to all sabotage operations. (Lansdale Memo for the record, 10/30/62)

Theodore Sorensen, a member of the Executive Committee established to deal with the Missile Crisis, testified that Cuba was the "No. 1 priority" during the Crisis. He said that although "all alternatives, plans, possibilities were exhaustively surveyed" during that time, the subject of assassination was never raised in the National Security Council or the Executive Committee. (Sorensen, 7/21/75, p. 11)

(3) Evidence Bearing on Knowledge of and Authorization for the Assassination Plot, Phase II

As discussed below, both Helms and the high Kennedy Administration officials who testified agreed that no direct order was ever given for Castro's assassination and that no senior Administration officials, including McCone, were informed about the assassination activity. Helms testified, however, that he believed the assassination activity was permissible and that it was within the scope of authority given to the Agency. McCone and other Kennedy Administration officials disagreed, testifying that assassination was impermissible without a direct order and that Castro's assassination was not within the bounds of the MONGOOSE operation.

As DDP, Helms was in charge of covert operations when the poison pills were given to Rosselli in Miami in April 1962. Helms had succeeded to this post following Bissell's retirement in February 1962. He testified that after the Bay of Pigs:

> Those of us who were still [in the Agency] were enormously anxious to try and be successful at what we were being asked to do by what was then a relatively new Administration. We wanted to earn our spurs with the President and with other officers of the Kennedy Administration. (Helms 7/17/75, p. 4)

A. Helms' Testimony Concerning Authority

Helms testified that he doubted that he was informed when Harvey gave poison pills to Rosselli and that he did not recall having authorized Castro's assassination by that means. He said, however, that he had authorized that assassination plot because "we felt that we were operating as we were supposed to operate, that these things if not specifically authorized, at least were authorized in general terms." (Helms, 6/13/75, p. 61)

(1) Helms' Perception of Authority

Helms testified that the "intense" pressure exerted by the Kennedy Administration to overthrow Castro had led him to perceive that the CIA was acting within the scope of its authority in attempting Castro's assassination, even though assassination was never directly ordered....

Helms recalled that during the MONGOOSE period, "it was made abundantly clear * * * to everybody involved in the operation that the desire was to get rid of the Castro regime and to get rid of Castro * * * the point was that no limitations were put on this injunction." (Helms, 7/17/75, pp. 16-17)....

Helms said that he was never told by his superior to kill Castro, (Helms, 7/17/75, p. 15) but that:

> No member of the Kennedy Administration * * * ever told me that [assassination] was proscribed, [or] ever referred to it in that fashion * * *. Nobody ever said that [assassination] was ruled out * * * (Helms, 7/17/75, pp. 18, 43)

Helms said that the delivery of poison pills for assassinating Castro:

> "with all the other things that were going on at that time * * * seemed to be within the permissible part of this effort * * *. In the perceptions of the time and the things we were trying to do this was one human life against many other human lives that were being lost." (Helms, 6/13/75, pp. 64, 99)

(2) Helms' Testimony Concerning the Absence of a Direct Order and Why He Did Not Inform Administration Officials

...When asked if President Kennedy had been informed of any assassination plots, Helms pointed out that "nobody wants to embarrass a President of the United States by discussing the assassination of foreign leaders in his presence." (Helms, 6/13/75, p. 29) He added that the Special Group was "the mechanism that was set up *** to use as a circuit breaker so that these things did not explode in the President's face and that he was not held responsible for them." (Helms, 6/13/75, p. 29) He said that he had "no knowledge that a Castro assassination was ever authorized" by the SGA. (Helms, 6/13/75, pp. 28-29)....

(4) Helms' Testimony as to Why he Did Not Obtain a Direct Order

Helms testified that assassination "was not part of the CIA's policy" and was not part of its "armory." (Helms, 6/13/75, pp. 87-88) Helms said that he "never liked assassination," and banned its use five years after he became Director of Central Intelligence. (Helms, 6/13/75, p. 166) Helms also testified to his "very grave doubts about the wisdom" of dealing with underworld figures when Harvey proposed contacting Rosselli to see if gangster links to Cuba could be developed. (Helms, 6/13/75, p. 33; 7/18/75, p. 31)

Despite these reservations, Helms did not seek approval for the assassination activity. He said this was because assassination was not a subject which should be aired with higher authority....

Helms gave additional testimony in response to questions concerning his failure to seek explicit authorization for assassination activity.

Senator Huddleston. * * * it did not occur to you to inquire of the Attorney General or of the Special Group or of anyone that when they kept pushing and asking for action * * * to clarify that question of whether you should actually be trying to assassinate?

Mr. Helms. I don't know whether it was in training, experience, tradition or exactly what one points to, but I think to go up to a Cabinet officer and say, am I right in assuming that you want me to assassinate Castro or to try to assassinate Castro, is a question it wouldn't have occurred to me to ask....

Senator Morgan. In light of your previous statement that this is a Christian country and that this Committee has to face up to the prime moral issue of whether or not killing is * * * acceptable * * * don't you think it would have taken affirmative permission or authority to kill, rather than just saying it was not eliminated from the authority or you were not restricted * * *?

Mr. Helms. *** killing was not part of the CIA's policy. It was not part of the CIA's armory * * * but in this Castro operation * * * I have testified as best I could about the atmosphere of the time, what I understood was desired [and] that this was getting rid of Castro, if he had been gotten rid of by this means that this would have been acceptable to certain individuals * * * I was just doing my best to do what I thought I was supposed to do. (Helms, 6/13/75, pp. 87-88).... I do not recall ever having been convinced that any attempt was really made on Castro's life. And since I didn't believe any attempt had been made on Castro's life, I saw no reason to pursue the matter further. (Helms, 7/18/75, pp. 31-32)

C. Testimony of Kennedy Administration Officials

The Committee took testimony from the Kennedy Administration officials principally involved in the MONGOOSE operation, all of whom testified that the assassination plots were not authorized....

McCone said that although the Cuban problem was discussed in terms of "dispose of Castro," or "knock off Castro," those terms were meant to refer to "the overthrow of the Communist Government in Cuba," and not to assassination. (McCone, 6/6/75, p. 44; Memo to Helms, April 14, 1967)

Taylor served as Chairman of the SGA during the MONGOOSE Operation (Taylor, 7/9/75, p. 12), and as President Kennedy's Military Representative and Intelligence Advisor after the Bay of Pigs until his appointment as Chairman of the Joint Chiefs of Staff in November 1962. (Taylor, 7/9/75, p. 11; Bundy, 7/11/75, p. 25) He testified that a plan to assassinate Castro was "never" submitted to the SGA, either orally or in writing. (Taylor, 7/9/75, p. 41) He said the SGA was never told of the poison pills given to Rosselli in April 1962, and that the passage of those pills without the knowledge of the SGA was "entirely, completely out of [the] context and character of the way the [SGA] operated or the way it would accept" that an operation was properly authorized. (Taylor, 7/9/75, p. 43)....

[McGeorge] Bundy served as President Kennedy's Special Assistant for National Security Affairs throughout the Kennedy Administration (Bundy, 7/11/75, p. 2) and participated in the planning that led to the creation of Operation MONGOOSE. He was also a member of the SGA. (Bundy, 7/11/75, pp. 34, 87) Bundy worked on an intimate basis with the President and the Attorney General during the entire Kennedy Administration.

Bundy testified that it was his conviction that "no one in the Kennedy Administration, in the White House * * * ever gave any authorization, approval, or instruction of any kind for any effort to assassinate anyone by the CIA." (Bundy, 7/11/75, p. 54) He said that Castro's assassination was "mentioned from time to time," but "never that I can recall by the President." (Bundy, 7/11/75, p. 73) Bundy emphasized that the question came up "as something to talk about rather than to consider." (Bundy, 7/11/75, p. 73)

> ...[Mr. Bundy]. Let me say one other thing about these two men, and that is that there was something that they really wanted done, they did not leave people in doubt, so that on the one hand, I would say about their character, their purposes, and their nature and the way they confronted international affairs that I find it incredible that they would have ordered or authorized explicitly or implicitly an assassination of Castro. I also feel that if, contrary to everything that I know about their character, they had had such a decision and such a purpose, people would not have been in any doubt about it. (Bundy, 7/11/75, pp. 98-99)....

McNamara's Testimony

McNamara served as Secretary of Defense throughout the Kennedy Administration. He represented the Department on the Special Group and the SGA during the MONGOOSE operations.

McNamara stated that he had never heard either the President or the Attorney General propose Castro's assassination. (McNamara, 7/11/75, p. 4) He noted that: "We were hysterical about Castro at the time of the Bay of Pigs and thereafter, and that there was pressure from [President Kennedy and the Attorney General] to do something about Castro. But I don't believe we contemplated assassination. We did, however, contemplate overthrow." (McNamara, 7/11/75, p. 93)

An exchange that occurred during McNamara's testimony captures the dilemma posed by the evidence:

> The Chairman. We also have received evidence from your senior associates that they never participated in the authorization of an assassination attempt against Castro nor ever directed the CIA to undertake such attempts.
>
> We have much testimony establishing the chain of command where covert action was concerned, and all of it has been to the effect that the Special Group or the Special Group (Augmented)

had full charge of covert operations, and that in that chain of command any proposal of this character or any other proposal having to do with covert operations being directed against the Castro regime, or against Castro personally, were to be laid before the Special Group (Augmented) and were not to be undertaken except with the authority of that group and at the direction of that group.

Now, at the same time we know from the evidence that the CIA was in fact engaged during the period in a series of attempts to assassinate Castro.

Now, you see what we are faced with is this dilemma. Either the CIA was a rogue elephant rampaging out of control, over which no effective direction was being given in this matter of assassination, or there was some secret channel circumventing the whole structure of command by which the CIA and certain officials in the CIA were authorized to proceed with assassination plots and assassination attempts against Castro. Or the third and final point that I can think of is that somehow these officials of the CIA who were so engaged misunderstood or misinterpreted their scope of authority....

Mr. McNamara: I can only tell you what will further your uneasiness. Because I have stated before and I believe today that the CIA was a highly disciplined organization, fully under the control of senior officials of the government, so much so that I feel as a senior official of the government I must assume responsibility for the actions of the two, putting assassination aside just for the moment. But I know of no major action taken by CIA during the time I was in the government that was not properly authorized by senior officials. And when I say that I want to emphasize also that I believe with hindsight we authorized actions that were contrary to the interest of the Republic but I don't want it on the record that the CIA was uncontrolled, was operating with its own authority and we can be absolved of responsibility for what CIA did, again with exception of assassination, again which I say I never heard of.

The second point you say that you have, you know that CIA was engaged in a series of attempts of assassination. I think to use your words. I don't know that. I accept the fact that you do and that you have information I was not aware of. I find that impossible to reconcile. I just can't understand how it could have happened and I don't accept the third point, that they operated on the basis of misunderstanding....

I find it almost inconceivable that the assassination attempts were carried on during the Kennedy Administration days without the senior members knowing it, and I understand the contradiction that this carries with respect to the facts. (McNamara, 7/11/75, p. 90)

(4) The August 10, 1962 Special Group (Augmented) Meeting

The question of liquidating Cuban leaders was raised at a meeting of the SGA on August 10, 1962. On August 13, 1962, Lansdale directed Harvey to include in a proposed plan for Phase II of MONGOOSE, an option for the "liquidation of leaders."

At the outset, it should be noted that the documents and testimony about the meeting indicate that the discussion of assassination on August 10 was unrelated to the assassination activity undertaken by Harvey and Rosselli, or to any other plans or efforts to assassinate Castro....

The minutes of the August 10 meeting contain no reference to assassination. (Memo for Record, Special Group Augmented Meeting, August 10, 1962, hereafter "August 10 Minutes") Thomas Parrott, who authored the August 10 Minutes, testified that he did not recall a discussion of assassination at that meeting, but that the fact that the minutes reflect no such discussion does not necessarily indicate that the matter had not come up....

Parrott testified that he did not record proposals that were quickly rejected. (Parrott, 7/10/75, p. 35) He said that, although he had no recollection of a discussion of Castro's assassination at the meeting, he would infer from the related documents [the Lansdale and Harvey Memoranda of August 13 and 14, respectively] that the subject was raised but "it never got off the ground * * *. Therefore, I did not record it." (Parrott, 7/10/75, p. 35) ...Lansdale recalled that the subject of Castro's assassination had surfaced at the August 10 meeting. He testified that the "consensus was * * * hell no on this and there was a very violent reaction." (Lansdale, 7/8/75, p. 20) Lansdale was questioned as to why he subsequently asked Harvey for a Castro assassination plan:

> Senator Baker. Why did you, three days later if they all said, hell no, [go] ahead with it?
>
> General Lansdale. * * * the meeting at which they said that was still on a development of my original task, which was a revolt and an overthrow of regime. At the same time, we were getting intelligence accumulating very quickly of something very different taking place in Cuba than we had expected, which was the Soviet technicians starting to come in and the possibilities of Soviet missiles being placed there *** At that time, I thought it would be a possibility someplace down the road in which there would be some possible need to take action such as that [assassination] (Lansdale, 7/8/75, p. 21)....

The Question of Whether the AM/LASH Plot (1963-1965) Was Known About or Authorized by Administration Officials Outside the CIA

This section examines evidence relating to whether officials in the Kennedy or Johnson Administrations were aware of or authorized the CIA's use of AM/LASH as a potential assassin. The question is examined in light of the policies of those Administrations toward Cuba as well as the evidence bearing more directly on the authorization issues.

The evidence falls into a pattern similar to that described in the discussion of post-Bay of Pigs activity in the Kennedy Administration. Administration officials testified that they had never been informed about the plot and that they never intended to authorize assassination. Richard Helms, on the other hand, testified that he had believed that assassination was permissible in view of the continuing pressure to overthrow the Castro regime exerted by the respective Administrations and the failure of either Administration to place limits on the means that could be used to achieve that end.

The Question of Authorization in the Johnson Administration

a. Summary of the Assassination Activity

The CIA delivered arms to AM/LASH in Cuba in March and June of 1964. Early in 1965, after AM/LASH had become more insistent that Castro's assassination was necessary and had asked for a silenced weapon, the Agency put AM/LASH in contact with the leader of an anti-Castro group, "B-1," with the intention that AM/LASH obtain his desired weapon from that group. The Agency subsequently learned that AM/LASH had received a silencer and other special equipment from B-1 and was preparing to assassinate Castro.

b. The Issue of Authorization

The issue of authority in the Johnson Administration is similar to that in the Kennedy Administration. The principal officials of the Kennedy Administration (and DDP Helms) continued in their positions during the relevant period of the Johnson Administration (Robert Kennedy left the Administration in September 1964). Helms testified that he believed Castro's assassination was within the scope of the CIA's authority in view of Administration policy toward Cuba reflected in the AM/LASH operation in both 1963 and 1964-65. (Helms, 6/13/75, pp. 137-138) Again, there was no direct evidence that McCone or anyone outside the Agency authorized or knew about the AM/LASH plot....

c. The Covert Action Program Against Cuba in 1964-1965

According to the minutes of a Special Group meeting on April 7, 1964, President Johnson decided to discontinue the use of CIA-controlled sabotage raids against Cuba. (Memorandum of Special Group Meeting, 4/7/64) A McCone memorandum indicated that in reaching that decision, President Johnson had abandoned the objective of Castro's overthrow. [Footnote: In a memorandum the day after President Johnson's decision to stop CIA-controlled sabotage operations, McCone stated: "the real issue to be considered at the meeting and by the President was a question of whether we wished to implement the policy (outlined in certain memoranda) or abandon the basic objective of bringing about the liquidation of the Castro Communist entourage and the elimination of Communist presence in Cuba and thus rely on future events of an undisclosed nature which might accomplish this objective". (Memorandum by McCone, 4/8/64)

In the context of the Special Group's discussion, McCone's use of the words "liquidation" and "elimination" appears to be another example of inartful language. A literal interpretation of these words leaves one with the impression that assassination was contemplated. But the context of the discussion does not bear out such an interpretation....]

e. Helms' Report to Rusk

In 1966 Helms sent a memorandum to Rusk reporting the CIA's relations with AM/LASH. The memorandum stated that the CIA's contact with AM/LASH was for "the express purpose" of intelligence collection.... Noting allegations that had come to his attention that AM/LASH had been involved with the CIA in a Castro assassination plot, Helms stated:

> The Agency was not involved with [AM/LASH] in a plot to assassinate Fidel Castro. * * * nor did it ever encourage him to attempt such an act.

Helms' memorandum made no mention of the fact that CIA officers, with Helms' knowledge, had offered a poison pen to AM/LASH on November 22, 1963, that the CIA had supplied arms to AM/LASH in 1964, or that the CIA had put AM/LASH in touch with B-1 to obtain a silenced weapon to assassinate Castro.

Helms told the Committee that this memorandum to Rusk was "inaccurate" and not factual. (Helms, 6/13/75, p. 115)....

C. Institutionalizing Assassination: The "Executive Action" Capability

In addition to investigating actual assassination plots, the Committee has examined a project known as Executive Action which included, as one element, the development of a general, standby assassination capability. As with the plots, this examination focused on two broad questions: What happened? What was the extent and nature of authorization for the project?

I. Introduction

Sometime in early 1961, Bissell instructed Harvey, who was then Chief of a CIA Foreign Intelligence staff, to establish an "executive action capability," which would include research into a capability to assassinate foreign leaders. (Bissell, 6/9/75, p. 51; Harvey, 6/25/75, pp. 36-37) At some point in early 1961 Bissell discussed the Executive Action capability with Bundy. The timing of that conversation and whether "the White House" urged that a capability be created were matters on which the evidence varied widely,...

Bissell, Harvey and Helms all agreed that the "generalized" capability was never used. (Bissell 6/9/75, p. 87; Harvey 6/25/75; p. 45; Helms 6/13/75, p. 52)

"Executive Action" was a CIA euphemism, defined as a project for research into developing means for overthrowing foreign political leaders, including a "capability to perform assassinations." (Harvey, 6/25/75, p. 34) Bissell indicated that Executive Action covered a "wide spectrum of actions" to "eliminate the effectiveness" of foreign leaders, with assassination as the "most extreme" action in the spectrum. (Bissell, 7/22/75, p. 32) The

Inspector General's Report described executive action as a "general standby capability" to carry out assassination when required. (I.G. Report, p. 37) The project was given the code name ZR/RIFLE by the CIA.

A single agent ("asset") was given the cryptonym QJ/WIN, and placed under Harvey's supervision for the ZR/RIFLE project. He was never used in connection with any actual assassination efforts. Helms described QJ/WIN's "capability":

> If you needed somebody to carry out murder, I guess you had a man who might be prepared to carry it out. (Helms, 6/13/75, p. 50)

Harvey used QJ/WIN, to spot "individuals with criminal and underworld connections in Europe for possible multi-purpose use." (Harvey, 6/25/75, p. 50) For example, QJ/WIN reported that a potential asset in the Middle East was "the leader of a gambling syndicate" with "an available pool of assassins." (CIA file, ZR/RIFLE/Personality Sketches) However, Harvey testified that:

> During the entire existence of the entire ZR/RIFLE project * * * no agent was recruited for the purpose of assassination, and no even tentative targeting or target list was ever drawn. (Harvey, 6/25/75, p. 45)

In general, project ZR/RIFLE involved assessing the problems and requirements of assassination and developing a stand-by assassination capability; more specifically, it involved "spotting" potential agents and "researching" assassination techniques that might be used. (Bissell, 7/17/75, p. 11 and 6/9/75, p. 73; Harvey, 6/25/75, pp. 37-A., 45) Bissell characterized ZR/RIFLE as "internal and purely preparatory." (Bissell, 7/22/75, p. 32) The 1967 Inspector General's Report found "no indication in the file that the Executive Action capability of ZR/RIFLE-QJ/WIN was ever used," but said that "after Harvey took over the Castro operation, he ran it as one aspect of ZR/RIFLE." (I.G. Report, pp. 40-41)

2. The Question of White House Initiation, Authorization, or Knowledge of the Executive Action Project

Harvey testified that Bissell had told him that "the White House" had twice urged the creation of such a capability and the Inspector General's Report quoted notes of Harvey's (no longer in existence) to that effect. Bissell did not recall any specific conversation with the "White House," but in his initial testimony before the Committee he assumed the correctness of Harvey's notes and stated that, while he could have created the capability on his own, any urgings would have come from Bundy or Walt Rostow. In a later appearance, however, Bissell said he merely informed Bundy of the capability and that the context was a briefing by him and not urging by Bundy. Bundy said he received a briefing and gave no urging, though he raised no objections. Rostow said he never heard of the project.

William Harvey testified that he was "almost certain" that on January 25 and 26, 1961, he met with two CIA officials: Joseph Scheider, who by then had become Chief of the Technical Services Division, and a CIA recruiting officer, to discuss the feasibility of creating a capability within the Agency for "Executive Action." (Harvey, 6/25/75, p. 52)....

The testimony regarding the relationship between "the White House" and the Executive Action capability is summarized as follows:

Harvey.—Harvey testified that his missing notes which had been destroyed had indicated that Bissell mentioned White House urgings to develop an Executive Action capability. (Harvey, 6/25/75, p. 37) Harvey said that he "particularly remember[ed]" that Bissell said that he received "more than one" urging from the White House. (Harvey, 6/25/75, pp. 36-37; 7/11/75, p. 59)....

But Harvey had no direct evidence that Bissell actually had any such discussion with "the White House." No specific individual in the White House was named to Harvey by Bissell. (Harvey, 6/25/75, p. 31) Harvey said that it would have been "improper" for him to have asked Bissell whom he had talked to and "grossly improper" for Bissell to have volunteered that name. (Harvey, 6/25/75, p. 37)

Bissell.—Bissell specifically recalled assigning Harvey to investigate the capability. (Bissell, 6/9/75, p. 51) However, Bissell did not recall "a specific conversation with anybody in the White House as the origin" of his instruction to Harvey. (Bissell, 6/9/75, p. 51)

During the course of several appearances before the Committee, Bissell's testimony varied as to whether or not he had been urged by the White House to develop an Executive Action capability....

Bissell said that he and [McGeorge] Bundy had discussed an untargeted "capability" rather than the plan or approval for an assassination operation. (Bissell, 7/17/75, p. 11) Bissell said that although he does not have a specific recollection, he "might have" mentioned Castro, Lumumba, and Trujillo in the course of a discussion of Executive Action "because these were the sorts of individuals at that moment in history against whom such a capability might possibly have been employed." (Bissell, 6/11/75, p. 51)

Bissell said his impression was that in addition to expressing no unfavorable reaction to the project, Bundy actually might have given a more affirmative response. (Bissell, 7/22/75, pp. 25, 28) Bissell testified that he might have interpreted Bundy's reaction as approval (or at least no objection) for the Executive Action concept. (Bissell, 7/22/75, p. 30)....

Bundy.—McGeorge Bundy also testified to a conversation with Bissell, during which the Executive Action capability was discussed. Bundy's testimony comports with Bissell's on the fact that they discussed an untargeted capability, rather than an assassination operation. But Bundy said that the capability included "killing the individual." (Bundy, 7/11/75, p. 5) Bundy's impression was that the CIA was "testing my reaction," not "seeking authority." (Bundy, 7/11/75, p. 15) Bundy said:

> I am sure I gave no instruction. But it is only fair to add that I do not recall that I offered any impediment either. (Bundy, 7/11/75, p. 10)

Bundy said that he did not take steps to halt the development of the Executive Action capability or "pursue the matter at all" (Bundy, 7/11/75, p. 19) because he was satisfied.

> That this was not an operational activity, and would not become such without two conditions: first, that there be a desire or a request or a guidance that there should be planning against some specific individual; and second, that there should be a decision to move against the individual. (Bundy, 7/11/75, p. 7).

Bundy believed that neither of these conditions had been fulfilled. (Bundy, 7/11/75, p. 7)....

The Committee has sought to determine whether the CIA development of an Executive Action capability was related in any way to the actual assassination efforts. One question raised by this inquiry is whether the participants in the assassination operations might have perceived the Executive Action capability as in some way lending legitimacy to the actual assassination efforts....

Bissell and Bundy both testified, however, that their discussion on the development of the capability for assassination did not involve any mention of actual assassination plans or attempts.... There is no testimony to the contrary. The account of this conversation raises a question as to whether Bissell acted properly in withholding from Bundy the fact that assassination efforts against Castro had already been mounted and were moving forward. Bundy was responsible to a new President for national security affairs and Bissell was his principal source of information about covert operations at the CIA....

D. Trujillo

1. Summary

Rafael Trujillo came to power in the Dominican Republic in 1930. For most of his tenure, the United States Government supported him and he was regarded throughout much of the Caribbean and Latin America as a protege of the United States. Trujillo's rule, always harsh and dictatorial, became more arbitrary during the 1950's. As a result, the United States' image was increasingly tarnished in the eyes of many Latin Americans.

Increasing American awareness of Trujillo's brutality and fear that it would lead to a Castro-type revolution caused United States' officials to consider various plans to hasten his abdication or downfall.

As early as February 1960, the Eisenhower Administration gave high level consideration to a program of covert aid to Dominican dissidents. (Special Group Minutes, 2/10/20) In April 1960 President Eisenhower approved a contingency plan for the Dominican Republic....

3. Initial Contact With Dissidents and Request for Arms

During the spring of 1960, the U.S. Ambassador to the Dominican Republic, Joseph Farland, made initial contact with dissidents who sought to free their country from Trujillo's grasp. They asked for sniper rifles. Although documentary evidence indicates that a recommendation to provide these rifles was approved both within the State Department and the CIA, the rifles were never provided....

Events occurring during the Summer of 1960 further intensified hemispheric opposition to the Trujillo regime. In June, agents of Trujillo tried to assassinate Venezuelan President Betancourt. As a result, the OAS [Organization of American States] censured the Trujillo government. At the same time, in August 1960, the United States interrupted diplomatic relations with the Dominican Republic and imposed economic sanctions.

With the interruption of diplomatic relations, the United States closed its Embassy. Most American personnel, including the CIA Chief of Station, left the Dominican Republic. With the departure of the CIA Chief of Station, [Henry] Dearborn [formerly Deputy-Chief-of-Mission] became *de facto* CIA Chief of Station and was recognized as such by both CIA and the State Department. Although in January 1961, a new CIA Chief of Station came to the Dominican Republic, Dearborn continued to serve as a link to the dissidents.

*(b) Dearborn reports assassination may be only way
to overthrow Trujillo regime*

Dearborn came to believe that no effort to overthrow the Trujillo government could be successful unless it involved Trujillo's assassination. He communicated this opinion to both the State Department and the CIA. In July 1960, he advised Assistant Secretary Rubottom that the dissidents were

> * * * in no way ready to carry on any type of revolutionary activity in the foreseeable future except the assassination of their principal enemy. (Letter, Dearborn to Rubottom, 7/14/60)

It is uncertain what portion of the information provided by Dearborn to State was passed above the Assistant Secretary level. Through August of 1960, only Assistant Secretary Rubottom, his Deputy, Lester Mallory, and his Staff Assistant, were, within the Latin American Division of the Department, aware of Dearborn's "current projects." (Letter, Staff Assistant to Dearborn, 8/15/60)

[Assistant Secretary for Inter-American Affairs Thomas] Mann solicited Dearborn's comments concerning plans under discussion for forcing Trujillo from power. Dearborn replied in a detailed letter which concluded:

> One further point which I should probably not even make. From a purely practical standpoint, it will be best for us, for the OAS, and for the Dominican Republic if the Dominicans put an end to Trujillo before he leaves this island. If he has his millions and is a free agent, he will devote his life from exile to preventing stable government in the D.R.... If you recall Dracula, you will remember it was necessary to drive a stake through his heart to prevent a continuation of his crimes.... (Letter, Dearborn to Mann, 10/27/60)...

6. January 20, 1961—April 17, 1971 (The Kennedy Administration Through the Bay of Pigs)

On January 20, 1961, the Kennedy Administration took office. Three of the four members of the Special Group (all except Allen Dulles) retired.

Prior to the failure of the Bay of Pigs invasion on April 17, 1961, a number of significant events occurred. These events included meetings with Dominican dissidents in which specific assassination plans were discussed, requests by dissidents for explosive devices, the passage by United States officials of pistols and carbines to dissidents inside the Dominican Republic and the pouching to the Dominican Republic of machine guns which had been requested by the dissidents for use in connection with an assassination attempt.... [Materials sent by diplomatic pouch are not subject to customs inspection.]

In a March 15, 1961 cable, a Station officer reported that Dearborn had asked for three .38 caliber pistols for issue to several dissidents....

Dearborn testified that he had asked for a single pistol for purposes completely unrelated to any assassination activity. (Dearborn, 7/29/75, pp. 29-31) He said he had been approached by a Dominican contact who lived in a remote area and who was concerned for the safety of his family in the event of political reprisals. Dearborn testified that he had believed the man's fears were well-founded and had promised to seek a pistol.

Although there is no direct evidence linking any of these pistols to the assassination of Trujillo, a June 7, 1961, CIA memorandum, unsigned and with no attribution as to source, states that two of the three pistols were passed by a Station officer to a United States citizen who was in direct contact with the action element of the dissident group. It should also be noted that the assassination was apparently conducted with almost complete reliance upon hand weapons. Whether one or more of these .38 caliber Smith & Wesson pistols eventually came into the hands of the assassins and, if so, whether they were used in connection with the assassination, remain open questions.

Both Dearborn and the Station officer testified that they regarded the pistols as weapons for self-defense purposes and that they never considered them to be connected, in any way, with the then-current assassination plans. (Dearborn 7/29/75, p. 70; Didier, 7/8/75, pp. 38, 73) However, none of the Headquarters cables inquired as to the purpose for which the handguns were sought and the Station's cable stated only that Dearborn wanted them for passage to dissidents. (Cable, Station to HQ, 3/15/61) Indeed, the March 24, 1961, cable advising that the pistols were being pouched was sent in response to a request by the dissidents for machine guns to be used in an assassination effort. As with the carbines discussed below, it appears that little, if any, concern was expressed within the Agency over passing these weapons to would-be assassins.

(1) Request by the Station and by Dearborn and approval by CIA

In a March 26, 1961, cable to CIA Headquarters, the Station asked for permission to pass to the dissidents three 30 caliber M1 carbines. The guns had been left behind in the Consulate by Navy personnel after the United States interrupted formal diplomatic relations in August 1960. Dearborn testified that he knew of and concurred in the proposal to supply the carbines to the dissidents. (Dearborn, 7/29/75, pp. 42, 43) On March 31, 1961, CIA Headquarters cabled approval of the request to pass the carbines. (Cable, HQ to Station, 3/31/61)

(2) Were the carbines related to assassination?

The carbines were passed to the action group contact on April 7, 1961. (Cable, HQ to Station. 4/8/61) Eventually, they found their way into the hands of one of the assassins, Antonio de la Maza. (Cable, Station to HQ, 4/26/61; I.G. Reports, pp. 46, 49) Both Dearborn and a Station officer testified that the carbines were at all times viewed as strictly a token show of support, indicating United States support of the dissidents' efforts to overthrow Trujillo. (Dearborn, 7/29/75, pp. 46-48; Didier, 7/8/75, p. 39)....

(iv) Requests for and Pouching of the Machine Guns

(1) Requests for Machine Guns

...On March 20, 1961, the Station cabled a dissident request for five M3 or comparable machine guns specifying their wish that the arms be sent via the diplomatic pouch or similar means. The dissidents were said to feel that delivery by air drop or transfer at sea would overly-tax their resources. (Cable, Station to HQ, 3/20/61)

The machine guns sought by the dissidents were clearly identified, in the Station cable, as being sought for use in connection with an attempt to assassinate Trujillo. This plan was to kill Trujillo in the apartment of his mistress....

On April 7, 1961 a Pouch Restriction Waiver Request and Certification was submitted seeking permission to pouch "four M3 machine guns and 240 rounds of ammunition on a priority basis for issuance to a small action group to be used for self protection." (Pouch Restriction Waiver Request, 4/7/61)....

The machine guns were pouched to the Dominican Republic and were received by the Station on April 19, 1961. (I.G. Report, p. 42; Cable, Station to HQ, 4/19/61)....

7. April 17, 1961—May 31, 1961 (Bay of Pigs Through Trujillo Assassination)

...(a) Decision not to pass the machine guns and unsuccessful United States attempt to stop assassination effort

By April 17, 1961, the Bay of Pigs invasion had failed. As a result, there developed a general realization that precipitous action should be avoided in the Dominican Republic until Washington was able to give further consideration to the consequences of a Trujillo overthrow and the power vacuum which would be created. (Bissell, 6/11/75, p. 113) A cable from Headquarters to the Station, on April 17, 1961, advised that it was most important that the machine guns not be passed without additional Headquarters approval.

The machine guns arrived in the Dominican Republic on April 19, 1961, and Headquarters was so advised....

Headquarters restated that there was no approval to pass any additional arms to the dissidents and requested the Station to advise the dissidents that the United States was simply not prepared at that time to cope with the aftermath of the assassination. (See C/S comments. Cable, Station to HQ, 4/27/61)....

Dearborn recalls receiving instructions that an effort be made to turn off the assassination attempt and testified that efforts to carry out the instructions were unsuccessful. In effect, the dissidents informed him that this was their affair and it could not be turned off to suit the convenience of the United States government. (Dearborn, 7/29/75, p. 52)....

E. Diem
1. Summary

South Vietnamese President Ngo Dinh Diem and his brother, Ngo Dinh Nhu, were assassinated during a coup by Vietnamese generals on November 2, 1963. Evidence before the Committee indicates that the United States government offered encouragement for the coup, but neither desired nor was involved in the assassinations. Rather, Diem's assassination appears to have been a spontaneous act by Vietnamese generals, engendered by anger at Diem for refusing to resign or put himself in the custody of the leaders of the coup.

On one occasion, General Duong Van Minh ("Big Minh") outlined to a CIA officer the possible assassination of Nhu and another brother, Ngo Dinh Can, as one of three methods being considered for changing the government in the near future. Ambassador Henry Cabot Lodge and Deputy Chief of Mission William Trueheart were informed of this possibility by the Saigon Chief of Station, who recommended that "we do not set ourselves irrevocably against the assassination plot, since the other two alternatives mean either a bloodbath in Saigon or a protracted struggle which would rip the Army and the country asunder." (CIA cable, Saigon Station to DCI, 10/5/63) Upon being informed, Director McCone sent two cables. The first stated "[w]e cannot be in the position of stimulating, approving, or supporting assassination," and the second directed that the recommendation be withdrawn because "we cannot be in position actively condoning such course of action and thereby engaging our responsibility therefor." (CIA cable, DCI to Saigon, 10/5/63; CIA cable, DCI to Saigon, 10/6/63)....

F. Schneider
1. Summary

On September 4, 1970, Dr. Salvador Allende Gossens won a plurality in Chile's Presidential election. [Footnote: Dr. Allende, a long-time Senator and founder of the Socialist Party in Chile, was a candidate of the Popular

Unity Coalition. The Coalition was made up of Communists, Socialists, Social Democrats, Radicals, and dissident Christian Democrats. Allende was a self-proclaimed Marxist....] Since no candidate had received a majority of the popular vote, the Chilean constitution required that a joint session of its Congress decide between the first and second place finishers. This constitutional requirement had, in the past, been pro forma. The Congress had always selected the candidate who received the highest popular vote. The date set for the Congressional joint session was October 24, 1970.

On September 15, 1970, President Richard Nixon informed CIA Director Richard Helms that an Allende regime in Chile would not be acceptable to the United States. The CIA was instructed by President Nixon to play a direct role in organizing a military coup d'etat in Chile to prevent Allende's accession to the presidency. The Agency was to take this action without coordination with the Departments of State or Defense and without informing the U.S. Ambassador in Chile. [This activity was known as Track II; concurrent CIA covert activities in Chile approved by the 40 Committee were referred to as Track I.] While coup possibilities in general and other means of seeking to prevent Allende's accession to power were explored by the 40 Committee throughout this period, the 40 Committee was never informed of this direct CIA role. In practice, the Agency was to report, both for informational and approval purposes, to the President's Assistant for National Security Affairs, Henry Kissinger, or his deputy.

Between October 5 and October 20, 1970, the CIA made 21 contacts with key military and Carabinero (police) officials in Chile. Those Chileans who were inclined to stage a coup were given assurances of strong support at the highest levels of the U.S. Government, both before and after a coup.

One of the major obstacles faced by all the military conspirators in Chile was the strong opposition to a coup by the Commander-in-Chief of the Army, General Rene Schneider, who insisted the constitutional process be followed. As a result of his strong constitutional stand, the removal of General Schneider became a necessary ingredient in the coup plans of all the Chilean conspirators. Unable to have General Schneider retired or reassigned, the conspirators decided to kidnap him. An unsuccessful abduction attempt was made on October 19, 1970, by a group of Chilean military officers whom the CIA was actively supporting. A second kidnap attempt was made the following day, again unsuccessfully. In the early morning hours of October 22, 1970, machine guns and ammunition were passed by the CIA to the group that had failed on October 19. That same day General Schneider was mortally wounded in an attempted kidnap on his way to work. The attempted kidnap and the shooting were apparently conducted by conspirators other than those to whom the CIA had provided weapons earlier in the day.

A Chilean military court found that high-ranking military officers, both active and retired, conspired to bring about a military coup and to kidnap General Schneider. Several of the officers whom the CIA had contacted and encouraged in their coup conspiracy were convicted of conspiring to kidnap General Schneider. Those convicted of carrying out the actual kidnap attempt and the killing of General Schneider were associates of retired General Roberto Viaux, who had initially been thought by the CIA to be the best hope. However, later the CIA discouraged General Viaux because the Agency felt other officers, such as General Camilo Valenzuela, were not sufficiently involved. General Viaux was convicted by the military court and received a twenty-year prison sentence for being the "intellectual author" of the Schneider kidnap attempt. General Valenzuela was sentenced by the military court to three years in exile for taking part in the conspiracy to prevent Allende's assumption of office. The military court found that the two Generals had been in contact throughout the coup plotting.

Principal Facts Leading Up to the Death of General Schneider

...1. By the end of September 1970, it appeared that the only feasible way for the CIA to implement the Presidential order to prevent Allende from coming to power was to foment a coup d'etat.

2. All of the known coup plots developed within the Chilean military entailed the removal of General Schneider by one means or another.

3. United States officials continued to encourage and support Chilean plans for a coup after it became known that the first step would be to kidnap General Schneider.

4. Two unsuccessful kidnap attempts were made, one on October 19, the other on October 20. Following these attempts, and with knowledge of their failure, the CIA passed three submachine guns and ammunition to Chilean officers who still planned to kidnap General Schneider.

5. In a third kidnap attempt on October 22, apparently conducted by Chileans other than those to whom weapons had been supplied, General Schneider was shot and subsequently died. The guns used in the abortive kidnapping of General Schneider were, in all probability, not those supplied by the CIA to the conspirators. The Chilean military court which investigated the Schneider killing determined that Schneider had been murdered by handguns, although one machine gun was at the scene of the killing. [Footnote: The Committee has not been able to determine whether or not the machine gun at the scene of the Schneider killing was one of the three supplied by the CIA.]

6. While there is no question that the CIA received a direct instruction from the President on September 15th to attempt to foment a coup, the Committee received sharply conflicting testimony about whether the White House was kept informed of, and authorized, the coup efforts in Chile after October 15. On one side of the conflict is the testimony of Henry Kissinger and General Alexander Haig; on the other, that of CIA officials. Kissinger testified that the White House stood down CIA efforts to promote a military coup d'etat in Chile on October 15, 1970. After that date, Kissinger testified—and Haig agreed—that the White House neither knew of, nor specifically approved, CIA coup activities in Chile. CIA officials, on the other hand, have testified that their activities in Chile after October 15 were known to and thus authorized by the White House.

This conflict in testimony, which the Committee has been unable to resolve through its hearings or the documentary record, leaves unanswered the most serious question of whether the CIA was acting pursuant to higher authority (the CIA's view) or was pursuing coup activities in Chile without sufficient communication (the Kissinger/Haig view).

2. The President's Initial Instruction and Background

(a) September 15 White House meeting

On September 15, 1970, President Nixon met with his Assistant for National Security Affairs, Henry Kissinger, CIA Director Richard Helms, and Attorney General John Mitchell at the White House. The topic was Chile. Handwritten notes taken by Director Helms at that meeting reflect both its tenor and the President's instructions:

One in 10 chance perhaps, but save Chile!

worth spending

not concerned risks involved

no involvement of Embassy

$10,000,000 available, more if necessary

full-time job—best men we have

game plan

make the economy scream

48 hours for plan of action.

In his testimony before the Select Committee, Director Helms recalled coming away from the meeting on September 15 with:

* * * [the] impression * * * that the President came down very hard that he wanted something done, and he didn't much care how and that he was prepared to make money available. * * * This was a pretty all-inclusive order. * * * If I ever carried a marshall's baton in my knapsack out of the Oval Office, it was that day. (Helms, 7/15/75, pp. 6, 10, 11)

However, none of the CIA officers believed that assassination was within the guidelines Helms had been given....

United States Government concern over an Allende regime in Chile did not begin with President Nixon's September instruction to the CIA. *[For the Senate Select Intelligence Committee's report on CIA involvement in Chile, see p. 873.]...*

4. CIA Efforts to Promote a Coup

Anti-Allende coup plotting in Chile centered around several key individuals. One of these was retired General Roberto Viaux, the General who had led the "Tacnazo" insurrection a year before. Following the "Tacnazo" revolt, and his dismissal from the Army, Viaux retained the support of many non-commissioned and junior officers as well as being the recognized leader of several right-wing civilian groups. (CIA Briefing Paper, "Special

Mandate from the President on Chile," 7/15/75) Another individual around which plotting centered was General Camilo Valenzuela, Commander of the Santiago Garrison, who was in league with several other Chilean officers....

The CIA's initial task in Chile was to assess the potential within the Chilean military to stage a coup. It recognized quickly that anti-Allende currents did exist in the military and the Carabineros (police), but were immobilized by "the tradition of military respect for the Constitution" and "the public and private stance of General Schneider, Commander-in-Chief of the Army, who advocated strict adherence to the Constitution." (CIA Report on Chilean Task Force Activities, 11/18/70), p. 17) The Agency's task, then, was to overcome "the apolitical, constitutional-oriented inertia of the Chilean military." (Ibid, p. 2)

Since the very top of the Chilean military, embodied by General Schneider and his second-in-command, General Prats, were hostile to the idea of a coup against Allende, discreet approaches were made to the second level of general officers. They were to be informed that the U.S. Government would support a coup both before and after it took place. (Cable 611, Hq. to Sta., 10/7/70) This effort began in earnest on October 5 when the attache informed both an Army General ("Station's priority contact") and an Air Force General of the pro-coup U.S. policy. (Santiago 469, October 5; Santiago 473, October 6.) Three days later the Chief of Station told a high ranking Carabinero official that "the U.S. Government favors a military solution and is willing to support it in any manner short of outright military intervention." (Task Force Log, 10/9/70) The official informed the COS that there was no chance of a coup by the Chilean Army high command. (Task Force Log, 10/10/70)

On October 7, the attache approached members of the War Academy in Santiago who in turn asked him to provide light weapons. This was the attache's first contact with the Army officer to whom he would ultimately pass three submachine guns on October 22....

During the first week of intensive efforts chances of success looked bleak. The Chile Task Force Log commented:

> * * * the highest levels of the armed forces unable to pull themselves together to block Allende. The Chilean military's tradition of non-intervention, Frei's reluctance to tarnish his historical image, General Schneider's firm constitutional stand, and most importantly, the lack of leadership within the government and military are working against a military takeover. (Task Force Log, 10/8/70)....

If Viaux was the CIA's only hope of staging a coup, things were bleak indeed. His own colleagues, including General Valenzuela, described him as "a General without an army." (Cable 495, Sta. to Hq., 10/9/70) Yet in the first two weeks of October he came to be regarded as the best hope for carrying out the CIA's Track II mandate....

To summarize, by October 15 General Viaux had advertised to his contact a desire to proceed with a coup, had indicated he would deal with the

Schneider obstacle by kidnapping him, had met at least once with General Valenzuela and had once postponed his coup plans.

On October 15 Thomas Karamessines met with Henry Kissinger and Alexander Haig at the White House to discuss the situation in Chile.... A decision was made at the meeting "to de-fuse the Viaux coup plot, at least temporarily".... [Karamessines was CIA Deputy Director for Plans.]

The decision to "de-fuse" General Viaux was passed to a Viaux associate on October 17. The associate responded that it did not matter because they had decided to proceed with the coup in any case. (Cable 533, Sta. to Hq., 10/17/70)....

U.S. Provides Arms

On the evening of October 17, the U.S. military attache met with the Chilean Army officer and the Navy officer. They requested 8 to 10 tear gas grenades, three 45-caliber machine guns and 500 rounds of ammunition. The Navy officer said he had three machine guns himself "but can be identified by serial numbers as having been issued to him. Therefore unable to use them." (Cable 562, Sta. to H., 10/18/70) The attache and the Chief of Station have testified that the officers wanted the machine guns for self-protection. The question, of course, is whether the arms were intended for use, or were used, in the kidnapping of General Schneider. The fact that the weapons were provided the Army officer and the Navy officer and that Viaux associates were convicted of the Schneider killing suggests that the guns were not involved.

The machine guns and ammunition were sent from Washington by diplomatic pouch on the morning of October 19, although Headquarters was puzzled about their purpose: "Will continue make effort provide them but find our credulity stretched by Navy officer leading his troops with sterile guns. What is special purpose for these guns? We will try send them whether you can provide explanation or not." (Cable 854, Hq. to Sta., 10/18/70)....

(e) The Shooting of General Schneider

In the early morning hours of October 22 (2 a.m.), the attache delivered the three submachine guns with ammunition to the Army officer in an isolated section of Santiago.

At about 7 a.m. that day the group that intended to kidnap General Schneider met to discuss last-minute instructions. According to the findings of the Chilean Military Court which investigated the Schneider killing, neither the Army officer nor the Navy officer were there. Shortly after 8 a.m., General Schneider's car was intercepted on his way to work by the abductors and he was mortally wounded when he drew his handgun in self-defense. The Military Court determined that hand guns had been used to kill General Schneider, although it also found that one unloaded machine gun was at the scene of the killing....

5. CIA/White House Communication
During Track II

The testimony given to the Committee by Henry Kissinger and General Haig conflicts with that given by CIA officials.

Kissinger and Haig testified that on October 15, 1970, the White House stood down CIA efforts to promote a military coup d'etat in Chile. Both testified that after that date they were neither informed of, nor authorized, CIA Track II activities, including the kidnap plans of General Schneider and the passage of weapons to the military plotters.

By contrast, CIA officials testified that they operated before and after October 15 with the knowledge and approval of the White House....

IV. FINDINGS AND CONCLUSIONS

In evaluating the evidence and arriving at findings and conclusions, the Committee has been guided by the following standards. We believe these standards to be appropriate to the constitutional duty of a Congressional committee.

1. The Committee is not a court. Its primary role is not to determine individual guilt or innocence, but rather to draw upon the experiences of the past to better propose guidance for the future.

2. It is necessary to be cautious in reaching conclusions because of the amount of time that has passed since the events reviewed in this report, the inability of three Presidents and many other key figures to speak for themselves, the conflicting and ambiguous nature of much of the evidence, and the problems in assessing the weight to be given to particular documents and testimony.

3. The Committee has tried to be fair to the persons involved in the events under examination, while at the same time responding to a need to understand the facts in sufficient detail to lay a basis for informed recommendations.

With these standards in mind, the Committee has arrived at the following findings and conclusions.

A. Findings Concerning the Plots Themselves

1. Officials of the United States Government Initiated Plots to Assassinate Fidel Castro and Patrice Lumumba

The Committee finds that officials of the United States Government initiated and participated in plots to assassinate Patrice Lumumba and Fidel Castro.

The plot to kill Lumumba was conceived in the latter half of 1960 by officials of the United States Government, and quickly advanced to the point of sending poisons to the Congo to be used for the assassination.

The effort to assassinate Castro began in 1960 and continued until 1965. The plans to assassinate Castro using poison cigars, exploding seashells, and a contaminated diving suit did not advance beyond the laboratory phase. The plot involving underworld figures reached the stage of producing poison pills, establishing the contacts necessary to send them into Cuba, procuring potential assassins within Cuba, and apparently delivering the pills to the island itself. One 1960 episode involved a Cuban who initially had no intention of engaging in assassination, but who finally agreed, at the suggestion of the CIA, to attempt to assassinate Raul Castro if the opportunity arose. In the AM/LASH operation, which extended from 1963 through 1965, the CIA gave active support and encouragement to a Cuban whose intent to assassinate Castro was known, and provided him with the means of carrying out an assassination.

2. No Foreign Leaders Were Killed as a Result of Assassination Plots Initiated by Officials of the United States

The poisons intended for use against Patrice Lumumba were never administered to him, and there is no evidence that the United States was in any way involved in Lumumba's death at the hands of his Congolese enemies. The efforts to assassinate Castro failed.

3. American Officials Encouraged or Were Privy to Coup Plots Which Resulted in the Deaths of Trujillo, Diem, and Schneider

American officials clearly desired the overthrow of Trujillo, offered both encouragement and guns to local dissidents who sought his overthrow and whose plans included assassination. American officials also supplied those dissidents with pistols and rifles.

American officials offered encouragement to the Vietnamese generals who plotted Diem's overthrow, and a CIA official in Vietnam gave the generals money after the coup had begun. However, Diem's assassination was neither desired nor suggested by officials of the United States.

The record reveals that United States officials offered encouragement to the Chilean dissidents who plotted the kidnapping of General Rene Schneider, but American officials did not desire or encourage Schneider's death. Certain high officials did know, however, that the dissidents planned to kidnap General Schneider.

As Director Colby testified before the Committee, the death of a foreign leader is a risk foreseeable in any coup attempt. In the cases we have considered, the risk of death was in fact known in varying degrees. It was widely known that the dissidents in the Dominican Republic intended to assassinate Trujillo. The contemplation of coup leaders at one time to assassinate Nhu, President Diem's brother, was communicated to the upper levels of the United States Government. While the CIA and perhaps the White House knew that the coup leaders in Chile planned to kidnap General Schneider, it was not anticipated that he would be killed, although the possibility of his death should have been recognized as a forseeable risk of his kidnapping.

4. The Plots Occurred in a Cold War Atmosphere Perceived To Be of Crisis Proportions

The Committee fully appreciates the importance of evaluating the assassination plots in the historical context within which they occurred. In the preface to this report, we described the perception, generally shared within the United States during the depths of the Cold War, that our country faced a monolithic enemy in Communism. That attitude helps explain the assassination plots which we have reviewed, although it does not justify them. Those involved nevertheless appeared to believe they were advancing the best interests of their country.

5. American Officials Had Exaggerated Notions About Their Ability to Control the Actions of Coup Leaders

Running throughout the cases considered in this report was the expectation of American officials that they could control the actions of dissident groups which they were supporting in foreign countries. Events demonstrated that the United States had no such power. This point is graphically demonstrated by cables exchanged shortly before the coup in Vietnam. Ambassador Lodge cabled Washington on October 30, 1963, that he was unable to halt a coup; a cable from William Bundy in response stated that "we cannot accept conclusion that we have no power to delay or discourage a coup." The coup took place three days later.

Shortly after the experience of the Bay of Pigs, CIA Headquarters requested operatives in the Dominican Republic to tell the dissidents to "turn off" the assassination attempt, because the United States was not prepared to "cope with the aftermath." The dissidents replied that the assassination was their affair and that it could not be turned off to suit the convenience of the United States Government.

6. CIA Officials Made Use of Known Underworld Figures in Assassination Efforts

Officials of the CIA made use of persons associated with the criminal underworld in attempting to achieve the assassination of Fidel Castro. These underworld figures were relied upon because it was believed that they had expertise and contacts that were not available to law-abiding citizens.

Foreign citizens with criminal backgrounds were also used by the CIA in two other cases that we have reviewed. In the development of the Executive Action capability, one foreign national with a criminal background was used to "spot" other members of the European underworld who might be used by the CIA for a variety of purposes, including assassination, if the need should arise. In the Lumumba case, two men with criminal backgrounds were used as field operatives by CIA officers in a volatile political situation in the Congo.

B. Conclusions Concerning the Plots Themselves

1. The United States Should Not Engage in Assassination

We condemn the use of assassination as a tool of foreign policy. Aside from pragmatic arguments against the use of assassination supplied to the Committee by witnesses with extensive experience in covert operations, we find that assassination violates moral precepts fundamental to our way of life.

In addition to moral considerations, there were several practical reasons advanced for not assassinating foreign leaders. These reasons are discussed in the section of this report recommending a statute making assassination a crime.

(a) Distinction between targeted assassinations instigated by the United States and support for dissidents seeking to overthrow local governments

Two of the five principal cases investigated by the Committee involved plots to kill foreign leaders (Lumumba and Castro) that were instigated by American officials. Three of the cases (Trujillo, Diem, and Schneider) involved killings in the course of coup attempts by local dissidents. These latter cases differed in the degree to which assassination was contemplated by the leaders of the coups and in the degree the coups were motivated by United States officials.

The Committee concludes that targeted assassinations instigated by the United States must be prohibited.

Coups involve varying degrees of risk of assassination. The possibility of assassination in coup attempts is one of the issues to be considered in determining the propriety of United States involvement in coups, particularly in those where the assassination of a foreign leader is a likely prospect.

This country was created by violent revolt against a regime believed to be tyrannous, and our founding fathers (the local dissidents of that era) received aid from foreign countries. Given that history, we should not today rule out support for dissident groups seeking to overthrow tyrants. But passing beyond that principle, there remain serious questions: for example, whether the national interest of the United States is genuinely involved; whether any such support should be overt rather than covert; what tactics should be used; and how such actions should be authorized and controlled by the coordinate branches of government. The Committee believes that its recommendations on the question of covert actions in support of coups must await the Committee's final report which will be issued after a full review of covert action in general.

(b) The setting in which the assassination plots occurred explains, but does not justify them

The Cold War setting in which the assassination plots took place does not change our view that assassination is unacceptable in our society. In addition to the moral and practical problems discussed elsewhere, we find three principal defects in any contention that the tenor of the period justified the assassination plots:

First, the assassination plots were not necessitated by imminent danger to the United States. Among the cases studied, Castro alone posed a physical threat to the United States, but then only during the period of the Cuban missile crisis. Attempts to assassinate Castro had begun long before that crisis, and assassination was not advanced by policymakers as a possible course of action during the crisis.

Second, we reject absolutely any notion that the United States should justify its actions by the standards of totalitarians. Our standards must be higher, and this difference is what the struggle is all about. Of course, we must defend our democracy. But in defending it, we must resist undermining the very virtues we are defending.

Third, such activities almost inevitably become known. The damage to American foreign policy, to the good name and reputation of the United States abroad, to the American people's faith and support of our government and its foreign policy is incalculable. This last point—the undermining of the American public's confidence in its government—is the most damaging consequence of all.

Two documents which have been supplied to the Committee graphically demonstrate attitudes which can lead to tactics that erode and could ultimately destroy the very ideals we must defend.

The first document was written in 1954 by a special committee formed to advise the President on covert activities. The United States may, it said, have to adopt tactics "more ruthless than [those] employed by the enemy" in order to meet the threat from hostile nations. The report concluded that "long standing American concepts of American fair play must be reconsidered." [Footnote: The full text of the passage is as follows: "* * * another important requirement is an aggressive covert psychological, political, and paramilitary organization far more effective, more unique, and, if necessary, more ruthless than that employed by the enemy. No one should be permitted to stand in the way of the prompt, efficient, and secure accomplishment of this mission.

"The second consideration, it is now clear that we are facing an implacable enemy whose avowed objective is world domination by whatever means at whatever cost. There are no rules in such a game. Hitherto acceptable norms of human conduct do not apply. If the U.S. is to survive, long standing American concepts of American fair play must be reconsidered."]

Although those proposals did not involve assassinations, the attitudes underlying them were, as Director Colby testified, indicative of the setting within which the assassination plots were conceived. (Colby, 6/4/75, p. 117).

We do not think that traditional American notions of fair play need be abandoned when dealing with our adversaries. It may well be ourselves that we injure most if we adopt tactics "more ruthless than the enemy."

A second document which represents an attitude which we find improper was sent to the Congo in the fall of 1960 when the assassination of Patrice Lumumba was being considered. The chief of CIA's Africa Division recommended a particular agent—WI/ROGUE—because:

He is indeed aware of the precepts of right and wrong, but if he is given an assignment which may be morally wrong in the eyes of the world, but necessary because his case officer ordered him to carry it out, then it is right, and he will dutifully undertake appropriate action for its execution without pangs of conscience. In a word, he can rationalize all actions.

The Committee finds this rationalization is not in keeping with the ideals of our nation.

2. The United States Should Not Make Use of Underworld Figures for Their Criminal Talents

We conclude that agencies of the United States must not use underworld figures for their criminal talents in carrying out Agency operations. In addition to the corrosive effect upon our government, [Footnote: The corrosive effect of dealing with underworld figures is graphically demonstrated by the fact that Attorney General Robert Kennedy, who had devoted much of his professional life to fighting organized crime, did not issue an order against cooperating with such persons when he learned in May 1961 that the CIA had made use of Sam Giancana in a sensitive operation in Cuba.

In May, 1962, the Attorney General learned that the operation—which was described to him as terminated—had involved assassination. According to a CIA witness, the Attorney General was angered by the report and told those briefing him that he must be consulted before underworld figures were used again. He did not, however, direct that underworld figures must never again be used.] the use of underworld figures involves the following dangers:

a. The use of underworld figures for "dirty business" gives them the power to blackmail the government and to avoid prosecution, for past or future crimes. For example, the figures involved in the Castro assassination operation used their involvement with the CIA to avoid prosecution. The CIA also contemplated attempting to quash criminal charges brought in a foreign tribunal against QJ/WIN.

b. The use of persons experienced in criminal techniques and prone to criminal behavior increases the likelihood that criminal acts will occur. Sometimes agents in the field are necessarily given broad discretion. But the risk of improper activities is increased when persons of criminal background are used, particularly when they are selected precisely to take advantage of their criminal skills or contacts.

c. There is the danger that the United States Government will become an unwitting accomplice to criminal acts and that criminal figures will take advantage of their association with the government to advance their own projects and interests.

d. There is a fundamental impropriety in selecting persons because they are skilled at performing deeds which the laws of our society forbid.

The use of underworld figures by the United States Government for their criminal skills raises moral problems comparable to those recognized by Justice Brandeis in a different context five decades ago:

Our government is the potent, the omnipresent teacher. For good or for ill, it teaches the whole people by its example. Crime is contagious. If the Government becomes a law-breaker, it breeds contempt for law; it invites every man to become a law unto himself. To declare that in the administration of the criminal law the end justifies the means—to declare that the Government may commit crimes in order to secure the conviction of the private criminal—would bring terrible retribution. Against that pernicious doctrine this Court should resolutely set its face. [*Olmstead* v. *U.S.*....(1927)]

e. The spectacle of the Government consorting with criminal elements destroys respect for government and law and undermines the viability of democratic institutions.

C. Findings and Conclusions Relating to Authorization and Control

In the introduction to this report, we set forth in summary form our major conclusions concerning whether the assassination plots were authorized. The ensuing discussion elaborates and explains those conclusions.

The Committee analyzed the question of authorization for the assassination activities from two perspectives. First, the Committee examined whether officials in policymaking positions authorized or were aware of the assassination activities. Second, the Committee inquired whether the officials responsible for the operational details of the plots perceived that assassination had the approval of their superiors, or at least was the type of activity that their superiors would not disapprove.

No doubt, the CIA's general efforts against the regimes discussed in this report were authorized at the highest levels of the government. However, the record is unclear and serious doubt remains concerning whether assassination was authorized by the respective Presidents. Even if the plots were not expressly authorized, it does not follow that the Agency personnel believed they were acting improperly.

1. The Apparent Lack of Accountability in the Command and Control System Was Such that the Assassination Plots Could Have Been Undertaken Without Express Authorization

As emphasized throughout this report, we are unable to draw firm conclusions concerning who authorized the assassination plots. Even after our long investigation it is unclear whether the conflicting and inconclusive state of the evidence is due to the system of plausible denial or whether there were, in fact, serious shortcomings in the system of authorization which made it possible for assassination efforts to have been undertaken by agencies of the United States Government without express authority from officials above those agencies.

Based on the record of our investigation, the Committee finds that the system of Executive command and control was so inherently ambiguous that it is difficult to be certain at what level assassination activity was known and authorized. This creates the disturbing prospect that assassination activity might have been undertaken by officials of the United States Government without its having been incontrovertibly clear that there was explicit authorization from the President of the United States. At the same time, this ambiguity and imprecision leaves open the possibility that there was a successful "plausible denial" and that a Presidential authorization was issued but is now obscured.

Whether or not assassination was authorized by a President of the United States, the President as the chief executive officer of the United States Government must take ultimate responsibility for major activities during his Administration. Just as these Presidents must be held accountable, however, their subordinates throughout the Government had a concomitant duty to fully disclose their plans and activities.

As part of their responsibility, these Presidents had a duty to determine the nature of major activities and to prevent undesired activities from taking place. This duty was particularly compelling when the Presidents had reason to believe that major undesired activities had previously occurred or were being advocated and might occur again. Whether or not the Presidents in fact knew about the assassination plots, and even if their subordinates failed in their duty of full disclosure, it still follows that the Presidents should have known about the plots. This sets a demanding standard, but one the Committee supports. The future of democracy rests upon such accountability.

2. Findings Relating to the Level at Which the Plots were Authorized

(a) Diem

We find that neither the President nor any other official in the United States Government authorized the assassination of Diem and his brother Nhu. Both the DCI and top State Department officials did know, however, that the death of Nhu, at least at one point, had been contemplated by the coup leaders. But when the possibility that the coup leaders were considering assassination was brought to the attention of the DCI, he directed that the United States would have no part in such activity, and there is some evidence that this information was relayed to the coup leaders.

(b) Schneider

We find that neither the President nor any other official in the United States Government authorized the assassination of General Rene Schneider. The CIA, and perhaps the White House, did know that coup leaders contemplated a kidnapping, which, as it turned out resulted in Schneider's death.

(c) Trujillo

The Presidents and other senior officials in the Eisenhower and Kennedy Administrations sought the overthrow of Trujillo and approved or condoned actions to obtain that end.

The DCI and the Assistant Secretary of State for Inter-American Affairs knew that the Dominican dissidents viewed the removal of Trujillo as critical to any plans to overthrow his regime and that they intended to assassinate Trujillo if given the opportunity. It is uncertain precisely when officials at higher levels of government with responsibility for formulating policy learned that the dissidents equated assassination with overthrow. Clearly by early May 1961 senior American officials, including President Kennedy, knew that the dissidents intended to assassinate Trujillo. The White House and State Department, as well as the CIA, knew that the United States had provided the dissidents with rifles and pistols and that the dissidents had requested machine guns which they intended to use in connection with an assassination effort.

Thereafter, on May 16, 1961 President Kennedy approved National Security Council recommendations that the United States not initiate the overthrow of Trujillo until it was known what government would succeed the dictator. That recommendation was consistent with earlier attempts initiated by the CIA to discourage the planned assassination and thereby avoid potential problems from a power vacuum which might arise. After deciding to discourage the planned assassination, the DCI directed that the machine guns not be passed to the Dominican dissidents. That policy was reconfirmed by the State Department, the Special Group, and, in a cable of May 29, 1961, by President Kennedy himself.

The day before the assassination, President Kennedy cabled the State Department representative in the Dominican Republic that the United States "as [a] matter of general policy cannot condone assassination." However, the cable also stated that if the dissidents planning the imminent assassination of Trujillo succeeded, and thereby established a provisional government, the United States would recognize and support them.

The President's cable has been construed in several ways. One reading stresses the President's opposition to assassination "as a matter of general policy." Another stresses those portions of the cable which discuss pragmatic matters, including the risk that the United States' involvement might be exposed, and suggests that the last minute telegram was designed to avoid a charge that the United States shared responsibility for the assassination. A third construction would be that both of the prior readings are correct and that they are not mutually exclusive. However the cable is construed, its ambiguity illustrates the difficulty of seeking objectives which can only be accomplished by force—indeed, perhaps only by the assassination of a leader—and yet not wishing to take specific actions which seem abhorrent.

(d) Lumumba

The chain of events revealed by the documents and testimony is strong enough to permit a reasonable inference that the plot to assassinate Lumumba was authorized by President Eisenhower. Nevertheless, there is enough countervailing testimony by Eisenhower Administration officials and enough ambiguity and lack of clarity in the records of high-level policy meetings to preclude the Committee from making a finding that the President intended an assassination effort against Lumumba.

It is clear that the Director of Central Intelligence, Allen Dulles, authorized an assassination plot. There is, however, no evidence of United States involvement in bringing about the death of Lumumba at the hands of Congolese authorities.

Strong expressions of hostility toward Lumumba from the President and his National Security Assistant, followed immediately by CIA steps in furtherance of an assassination operation against Lumumba, are part of a sequence of events that, at the least, make it appear that Dulles believed assassination was a permissible means of complying with pressure from the President to remove Lumumba from the political scene.

Robert Johnson's testimony that he understood the President to have ordered Lumumba's assassination at an NSC meeting does, as he said, offer a "clue" about Presidential authorization. His testimony, however, should be read in light of the fact that NSC records during this period do not make clear whether or not the President ordered Lumumba's assassination and the fact that others attending those meetings testified that they did not recall hearing such a Presidential order.

Richard Bissell assumed that Presidential authorization for assassinating Lumumba had been communicated to him by Dulles, but Bissell had no specific recollection concerning when that communication occurred. The impression shared by the Congo Station Officer and the DDP's Special Assistant Joseph Scheider that the President authorized an assassination effort against Lumumba was derived solely from conversations Scheider had with Bissell and Bronson Tweedy. However, the impression thus held by Scheider and the Station Officer does not, in itself, establish Presidential authorization because neither Scheider nor the Station Officer had first-hand knowledge of Allen Dulles' statements about Presidential authorization, and because Scheider may have misconstrued Bissell's reference to "highest authority."

(c) Castro

There was insufficient evidence from which the Committee could conclude that Presidents Eisenhower, Kennedy, or Johnson, their close advisors, or the Special Group authorized the assassination of Castro.

The assassination plots against Castro were clearly authorized at least through the level of DDP. We also find that DCI Allen Dulles approved "thorough consideration" of the "elimination" of Castro. Further, it is also likely that Dulles knew about and authorized the actual plots that occurred during his tenure. Bissell and Edwards testified that they had briefed Dulles (and Cabell) on the plot involving underworld figures "circumlocutiously," but that they were certain that he had understood that the plot involved assassination. Their testimony is buttressed by the fact that Dulles knew about the plot to assassinate Lumumba which was being planned at the same time, and which also involved Bissell. We can find no evidence that McCone was aware of the plots which occurred during his tenure. His DDP, Richard Helms, testified that he never discussed the subject with McCone and was never expressly authorized by anyone to assassinate Castro.

The only suggestion of express Presidential authorization for the plots against Castro was Richard Bissell's opinion that Dulles would have informed Presidents Eisenhower and Kennedy by circumlocution only after the assassination had been planned and was underway. The assumptions underlying this opinion are too attenuated for the Committee to adopt it as a finding. First, this assumes that Dulles himself knew of the plot, a matter which is not entirely certain. Second, it assumes that Dulles went privately to the two Presidents—a course of action which Helms, who had far more covert action experience than Bissell, testified was precisely what the doctrine of plausible denial forbade CIA officials from doing. Third, it necessarily assumes that the Presidents would understand from a "circumlocutious" description that assassination was being discussed.

In view of the strained chain of assumptions and the contrary testimony of all the Presidential advisors, the men closest to both Eisenhower and Kennedy, the Committee makes no finding implicating Presidents who are not able to speak for themselves.

Helms and McCone testified that the Presidents under which they served never asked them to consider assassination.

There was no evidence whatsoever that President Johnson knew about or authorized any assassination activity during his Presidency.

3. CIA Officials Involved in the Assassination Operations Perceived Assassination to Have Been a Permissible Course of Action

The CIA officials involved in the targeted assassination attempts testified that they had believed that their activities had been fully authorized.

In the case of the Lumumba assassination operation, Richard Bissell testified that he had no direct recollection of authorization, but after having reviewed the cables and Special Group minutes, testified that authority must have flowed from Dulles through him to the subordinate levels in the Agency.

In the case of the assassination effort against Castro, Bissell and Sheffield Edwards testified they believed the operation involving underworld figures had been authorized by Dulles when they briefed him shortly after the plot had been initiated. William Harvey testified he believed that the plots "were completely authorized at every appropriate level within and beyond the Agency," although he had "no personal knowledge whatever of the individuals' identities, times, exact words, or channels through which such authority may have passed." Harvey stated that he had been told by Richard Bissell that the effort against Castro had been authorized "from the highest level," and that Harvey had discussed the plots with Richard Helms, his immediate superior. Helms testified that although he had never discussed assassination with his superiors, he believed:

> *** that in these actions we were taking against Cuba and against Fidel Castro's government in Cuba, that they were what we had been asked to do. *** In other words we had been asked to get rid of Castro and *** there were no limitations put on the means, and we felt we were acting well within the guidelines that we understoood to be in play at this particular time.

The evidence points to a disturbing situation. Agency officials testified that they believed the effort to assassinate Castro to have been within the parameters of permissible action. But Administration officials responsible for formulating policy, including McCone, testified that they were not aware of the effort and did not authorize it. The explanation may lie in the fact that orders concerning overthrowing the Castro regime were stated in broad terms that were subject to differing interpretations by those responsible for carrying out those orders.

The various Presidents and their senior advisors strongly opposed the regimes of Castro and Trujillo, the accession to power of Allende, and the potential influence of Patrice Lumumba. Orders concerning action against those foreign leaders were given in vigorous language. For example, President Nixon's orders to prevent Allende from assuming power left Helms feeling that "if I ever carried a marshall's baton in my knapsack out of the Oval Office, it was that day." Similarly, General Lansdale described the Mongoose effort against Cuba as "a combat situation," and Attorney General Kennedy emphasized that "a solution to the Cuba problem today carries top priority." Helms testified that the pressure to "get rid of Castro and the Castro regime" was intense, and Bissell testified that he had been ordered to "get off your ass about Cuba."

It is possible that there was a failure of communication between policymakers and the agency personnel who were experienced in secret, and often violent, action. Although policymakers testified that assassination was not intended by such words as "get rid of Castro." Some of their subordinates in the Agency testified that they perceived that assassination was desired and that they should proceed without troubling their superiors.

The 1967 Inspector General's Report on assassinations appropriately observed:

The point is that of frequent resort to synecdoche—the mention of a part when the whole is to be understood, or vice versa. Thus, we encounter repeated references to phrases such as "disposing of Castro," which may be read in the narrow, literal sense of assassinating him, when it is intended that it be read in the broader figurative sense of dislodging the Castro regime. Reversing the coin, we find people speaking vaguely of "doing something about Castro" when it is clear that what they have specifically in mind is killing him....

Differing perceptions between superiors and their subordinates were graphically illustrated in the Castro context. [Footnote: Senator Mathias. Let me draw an example from history. When Thomas Becket was proving to be an annoyance, as Castro, the King said, "who will rid me of this troublesome priest?" He didn't say, "go out and murder him." He said, "who will rid me of this man," and let it go at that.

Mr. Helms. That is a warming reference to the problem....

Senator Mathias. And that is typical of the kind of thing which might be said, which might be taken by the Director or by anybody else as presidential authorization to go forward?...] McCone [interpreted phrases such as "dispose of Castro" or "knock off Castro" to mean] "the overthrow of the Communist government in Cuba...."

Helms, who had considerable experience as a covert operator, gave precisely the opposite meaning to the same words, interpreting them as conveying authority for assassination.

Helms repeatedly testified that he felt that explicit authorization was unnecessary for the assassination of Castro in the early 1960's, but he said he did not construe the intense pressure from President Nixon in 1970 as providing authority to assassinate anyone. As Helms testified, the difference was not that the pressure to prevent Allende from assuming office was any less than the pressure to remove the Castro regime, but rather that "I had already made up my mind that we weren't going to have any of that business when I was Director."

Certain CIA contemporaries of Helms who were subjected to similar pressures in the Castro case rejected the thesis that implicit authority to assassinate Castro derived from the strong language of the policymakers. Bissell testified that he had believed that "formal and explicit approval" would be required for assassination, and Helms' assistant, George McManus, testified that "it never occurred to me" that the vigorous words of the Attorney General could be taken as authorizing assassination. The differing perceptions may have resulted from their different backgrounds and training. Neither Bissell (an acdemician whose Agency career for the six years before he became DDP had been in the field of technology) nor McManus (who had concentrated on intelligence and staff work) were experienced in covert operations.

The perception of certain Agency officials that assassination was within the range of permissible activity was reinforced by the continuing approval of violent covert actions against Cuba that were sanctioned at the Presidential level, and by the failure of the successive admissions to make clear that assassination was not permissible. This point is one of the subjects considered in the next section.

4. The Failure in Communication Between Agency Officials in Charge of the Assassination Operations and Their Superiors in the Agency and in the Administration Was Due to: (A) the Failure of Subordinates to Disclose Their Plans and Operations to Their Superiors; and (B) the Failure of Superiors in the Climate of Violence and Aggressive Covert Actions Sanctioned by the Administrations to Rule Out Assassinations as a Tool of Foreign Policy; to Make Clear to Their Subordinates That Assassination Was Impermissible; or to Inquire Further After Receiving Indications That it Was Being Considered

While we cannot find that officials responsible for making policy decisions knew about or authorized the assassination attempts (with the possible exception of the Lumumba case), Agency operatives at least through the level of DDP nevertheless perceived assassination to have been permissible. This failure in communication was inexcusable in light of the gravity of assassination. The Committee finds that the failure of Agency officials to inform their superiors was reprehensible, and that the reasons that they offered for having neglected to inform their superiors are unacceptable. The Committee further finds that Administration officials failed to be sufficiently precise in their directions to the Agency, and that their attitude toward the possibility of assassination was ambiguous in the context of the violence of other activities that they did authorize.

(a) Agency officials failed on several occasions to reveal the plots to their superiors, or to do so with sufficient detail and clarity

Several of the cases considered in this report raise questions concerning whether officials of the CIA sufficiently informed their superiors in the Agency or officials outside the Agency about their activities.

(i) Castro

The failure of Agency officials to inform their superiors of the assassination efforts against Castro is particularly troubling.

On the basis of the testimony and documentary evidence before the Committee, it is not entirely certain that Dulles was ever made aware of the true nature of the underworld operation. The plot continued into McCone's term, apparently without McCone's or the Administration's knowledge or approval.

On some occasions when Richard Bissell had the opportunity to inform his superiors about the assassination effort against Castro, he either failed to inform them, failed to do so clearly, or misled them.

Bissell testified that he and Edwards told Dulles and Cabell about the assassination operation using underworld figures, but that they did so "circumlocutiously", and then only after contact had been made with the underworld and a price had been offered for Castro's death.

Perhaps Bissell should have checked back with Dulles at an earlier stage after having received approval to give "thorough consideration" to Castro's "elimination" from Dulles in December 1959.

Bissell further testified that he never raised the issue of assassination with non-CIA officials of either the Eisenhower or Kennedy Administration. His reason was that since he was under Dulles in the chain of command, he would normally have had no duty to discuss the matter with these Presidents or other Administration officials, and that he assumed that Dulles would have "circumlocutiously" spoken with Presidents Eisenhower and Kennedy about the operation. These reasons are insufficient. It was inexcusable to withhold such information from those responsible for formulating policy on the unverified assumption that they might have been "circumlocutiously" informed by Dulles.

Opportunities for Disclosure

The failure either to inform those officials or to make certain that they had been informed by Dulles was particularly reprehensible in light of the fact that there were many occasions on which Bissell should have informed them, and his failure to do so was misleading. In the first weeks of the Kennedy Administration, Bissell met with Bundy and discussed the development of an assassination capability within CIA—Executive Action. But Bissell did not mention that an actual assassination attempt was underway. Bissell appeared before the Taylor-Kennedy Board of Inquiry which was formed to report to the President on the Bay of Pigs and the Cuban situation, but he testified that he did not inform the Board of the assassination operation. As chief of the CIA directorate concerned with clandestine operations and the Bay of Pigs, Bissell frequently met with officials in the Eisenhower and Kennedy Administrations to discuss Cuban operations, and his advice was frequently sought. He did not tell them that the CIA had undertaken an effort to assassinate Castro, and did not ask if they favored proceeding with the effort. He was present at the meeting with Dulles and President Kennedy at which the new President was briefed on covert action in Cuba, but neither Dulles nor Bissell mentioned the assassination operation that was underway. Dulles himself may not have always been candid. On December 11, 1959, he approved the CIA's giving "thorough consideration to the elimination of Fidel Castro," but told the Special Group in a meeting the following month that "we do not have in mind the quick elimination of Castro, but rather actions designed to enable responsible opposition leaders to get a foothold."

The failures to make forthright disclosures to policy-makers continued during the time that Richard Helms was DDP. Helms' failure to inform McCone about the underworld operation (when it was reactivated under Harvey and poison pills were sent to Cuba) was a grave error in judgment, and Helms' excuses are unpersuasive. In May 1962 the Attorney General was told that the CIA's involvement in an assassination plot had terminated with the Bay of Pigs. Not only did Edwards, who had briefed the Attorney General, know that the operation had not been terminated, but Helms did not inform the Attorney General that the operation was still active when he learned that the Attorney General had been misled. Helms did not inform McCone of the plot until August 1963, and did so then in a manner which indicated that the plot had been terminated before McCone became Director. Helms' denial that AM/LASH had been involved in an assassination effort in response to Secretary of State Rusk's inquiries was, as Helms conceded, not factual.

When Helms briefed President Johnson on the Castro plots, he apparently described the activities that had occurred during prior administrations but did not describe the AM/LASH operation which had continued until 1965. Helms also failed to inform the Warren Commission of the plots because the precise question was not asked. [Footnote: John McCone was Director of the CIA and at least knew about the pre-Bay of Pigs plot during the Warren Commission's inquiry. McCone failed to disclose the plot to the Commission. Allen Dulles was on the Warren Commission. He did not inform the other members about the plots that had occurred during his term as DCI.]

Helms told the Committee that he had never raised the assassination operation with McCone or other Kennedy Administration officials because of the sensitivity of the matter, because he had assumed that the project had been previously authorized, and because the aggressive character of the Kennedy Administration's program against the Castro regime led him to believe that assassination was permissible, even though he did not receive an express instruction to that effect. He added that he had never been convinced that the operation would succeed, and that he would have told McCone about it if he had ever believed that it would "go anyplace."

Non-Disclosure Held Unacceptable

Helms' reasons for not having told his superiors about the assassination effort are unacceptable; indeed, many of them were reasons why he should have specifically raised the matter with higher authority. As Helms himself testified, assassination was of a high order of sensitivity. Administration policymakers, supported by intelligence estimates furnished by the Agency, had emphasized on several occasions that successors to Castro might be worse than Castro himself. In addition, the Special Group (Augmented) required that plans for covert actions against Cuba be submitted in detail for its approval. Although the Administration was exerting intense pressure on the CIA to do something about Castro and the Castro regime, it was a serious error to have undertaken so drastic an operation without making certain that there was full and unequivocal permission to proceed.

William Harvey, the officer in charge of the CIA's attempt using underworld figures to assassinate Castro, testified that he never discussed the plot with McCone or officials of the Kennedy Administration because he believed that it had been fully authorized by the previous Director, because he was uncertain whether it had a chance of succeeding, and because he believed that it was not his duty to inform higher authorities.

Nonetheless, the Committee believes there were occasions on which it was incumbent on Harvey to have disclosed the assassination operation. As head of Task Force W, the branch of the CIA responsible for covert operations in Cuba, Harvey reported directly to General Lansdale and the Special Group (Augmented). The Special Group (Augmented) had made it known that covert operations in Cuba should be first approved by it, both by explicit instruction and by its practice that particular operations be submitted in "nauseating detail". Yet Harvey did not inform either General Lansdale or the Special Group (Augmented) of the assassination operation, either when he was explicitly requested to report to McCone, General Taylor, and the Special Group on his activities in Miami in April 1962, or when the subject of assassination was raised in the August 1962 meeting and McCone voiced his disapproval. Harvey testified that a matter as sensitive as assassination would never be raised in a gathering as large as the Special Group (Augmented).

The Committee finds the reasons advanced for not having informed those responsible for formulating policy about the assassination operation inadequate, misleading, and inconsistent. Some officials viewed assassination as too important and sensitive to discuss with superiors, while others considered it not sufficiently important. Harvey testified that it was premature to tell McCone about the underworld operation in April 1962, because it was not sufficiently advanced; but too late to tell him about it in August 1962, since by that time Harvey had decided to terminate it. On other occasions, officials thought disclosure was someone else's responsibility; Bissell said he thought it was up to Dulles, and Harvey believed it was up to Helms.

The Committee concludes that the failure to clearly inform policymakers of the assassination effort against Castro was grossly improper. The Committee believes that it should be incumbent on the DDP to report such a sensitive operation to his superior, the DCI, no matter how grave his doubts might be about the possible outcome of the operation. It follows that the DCI has the same duty to accurately inform his superiors.

(ii) Trujillo

In the Trujillo case there were several instances in which it appears that policymakers were not given sufficient information, or were not informed in a timely fashion.

At a meeting on December 29, 1960, Bissell presented a plan to the Special Group for supporting Dominican exile groups and local dissidents, and stated that the plan would not bring down the regime without "some decisive stroke against Trujillo himself." At a meeting on January 12, 1961, the Special Group authorized the passage of "limited supplies of small arms and other materials" to Dominican dissidents under certain conditions.

At this time, the fact that the dissidents had been contemplating the assassination of Trujillo had been known in the State Department at least through the level of the Assistant Secretary of State for Inter-American Affairs, and by senior officials of the CIA, including the DCI. Yet the internal State Department memorandum which was furnished to Undersecretary Livingston Merchant, and which was said to have been the basis for the Special Group's agreeing to the limited supply of small arms and other material (i.e., explosive devices), did not mention assassination. Instead, it spoke of "sabotage potential" and stated that there "would be no thought of toppling the [government] by any such minor measure [as the supplying of small arms and explosives]."

At a meeting of the Special Group on February 14, 1961, representatives of the CIA briefed the new members of the Group on outstanding CIA projects. The Dominican Republic was one of the briefing topics. The minutes of that meeting indicate that Mr. Bundy requested a memorandum for "higher authority" on the subject of what plans could be made for a successor government to Trujillo. Bissell had no clear recollection as to the details of the February 14 briefing and was unable to recall whether or not the method of overthrow to be attempted by the dissidents was discussed. It is not known, therefore, whether the new members of the Special Group learned, at that time, of Bissell's assessment that overthrow of the regime required a decisive stroke against Trujillo himself. Robert McNamara recalled no mention at that meeting of any dissident plans to assassinate Trujillo.

On February 15 and 17, 1961, memoranda were prepared for the President by Secretary of State Rusk and by Richard Bissell respectively. Although both the Department of State and the CIA then had information concerning the dissidents' intent to assassinate Trujillo if possible, neither memorandum referred to such a contingency. Rusk disclaimed any knowledge of the dissidents intent to assassinate Trujillo until shortly before the event occurred, but Bissell admitted personal awareness of the assassination plans.

Bissell's February 17 memorandum indicated that dissident leaders had informed the CIA of "their plan of action which they felt could be implemented if they were provided with arms for 300 men, explosives, and remote control detonation devices." Various witnesses testified that supplying arms for 300 men would, standing alone, indicate a "non-targeted" use for the arms. One possible method of assassinating Trujillo which had long been discussed by the dissidents and which was the favored approach at the time of Bissell's memorandum envisioned assassination by means of a bomb detonated by remote control. But the memorandum made no reference to the use to which the explosive devices might be put. (There is no record of any query from recipients of the briefing paper as to the nature of the dissidents' "plan of action" or the uses for which the arms and explosives were intended.)

Arms Supply Hidden

The passage of the carbines was approved by CIA Headquarters on March 31, 1961. Although the State Department's representative in the Dominican Republic concurred in the decision to pass the carbines, he was requested by the CIA not to communicate this information to State Department officials in Washington, and he complied with that request. Accordingly, neither the State Department nor the White House was aware of the passage for several weeks. Similarly, there was no contemporaneous disclosure outside the CIA, other than to the State Department representative in the Dominican Republic, that machine guns had been sent to the Dominican Republic via the diplomatic pouch.

A memorandum prepared by Adolph Berle, the State Department official from whom the CIA sought permission to pass the machine guns, states that "on cross-examination it developed that the real plan was to assassinate Trujillo and they wanted guns for that purpose." (Berle, Memorandum of Conversation, 5/3/61) Berle's memorandum states that he informed the CIA officials that "we did not wish to have anything to do with any assassination plots anywhere, any time." The CIA official reportedly said he felt the same way, even though on the previous day he had been one of the signers of a draft CIA cable which would have permitted passage of the machine guns to the dissidents for "* * * their additional protection on their proposed endeavor." (Draft HQs to Station Cable, 5/2/61)

Although the report of a new anti-Trujillo plot was discussed at a meeting of the Special Group on May 4, 1961, there is no indication that Berle, who was the Chairman of the Inter-Agency Task Force having responsibility for contingency planning for Cuba, the Dominican Republic, and Haiti, disclosed to higher authority the assassination information which he discovered by "cross-examination." The National Security Council met the next day and noted the President's view that the United States should not initiate the overthrow of Trujillo before it was known what government would succeed him. That National Security Council Record of Action was approved by the President on May 16, 1961. There is no record indicating whether Berle communicated to the President, or to members of the National Security Council, his knowledge as to the lethal intent of the dissidents who would be carrying out the overthrow of Trujillo.

(iii) Schneider

The issue here is not whether the objectives of the CIA were contrary to those of the Administration. It is clear that President Nixon desired to prevent Allende from assuming office, even if that required fomenting and supporting a coup in Chile. Nor did White House officials suggest that tactics employed (including as a first step kidnapping General Schneider) would have been unacceptable as a matter of principle. Rather, the issue posed is whether White House officials were consulted, and thus given an opportunity to weigh such matters as risk and likelihood of success, and to apply policy-making judgments to particular tactics. The record indicates that up to October 15 they were; after October 15 there is some doubt.

The documentary record with respect to the disputed post-October 15 period gives rise to conflicting inferences. On the one hand, Karamessines' calendar shows at least one White House contact in the critical period prior to the kidnapping of General Schneider on October 22. However, the absence of any substantive memoranda in CIA files—when contrasted with several such memoranda describing contacts with the White House between September 15 and October 15—may suggest a lack of significant communication on the part of the CIA as well as a lack of careful supervision on the part of the White House.

The standards applied within the CIA itself suggest a view that action which the Committee believes called for top-level policy discussion and decision was thought of as permissible, without any further consultation, on the basis of the initial instruction to prevent Allende from assuming power. Machine guns were sent to Chile and delivered to military figures there on the authority of middle level CIA officers without consultation even with the CIA officer in charge of the program. We find no suggestion of bad faith in the action of the middle level officers, but their failure to consult necessarily establishes that there was no advance permission from outside the CIA for the passage of machine guns. And it also suggests an unduly lax attitude within the CIA toward consultation with superiors. Further, this case demonstrates the problems inherent in giving an agency a "blank check" to engage in covert operations without specifying which actions are permissible and which are not, and without adequately supervising and monitoring these activities.

(b) Administration officials failed to rule out assassination as a tool of foreign policy, to make clear to their subordinates that assassination was impermissible or to inquire further after receiving indications that assassination was being considered

While we do not find that high Administration officials expressly approved of the assassination attempts, we have noted that certain agency officials nevertheless perceived assassination to have been authorized. Although those officials were remiss in not seeking express authorization for their activities, their superiors were also at fault for giving vague instructions and for not explicitly ruling out assassination. No written order prohibiting assassination was issued until 1972, and that order was an internal CIA directive issued by Director Helms.

(i) Trujillo

Immediately following the assassination of Trujillo, there were a number of high-level meetings about the Dominican Republic attended by the policymakers of the Kennedy Administration. All relevant facts concerning CIA and State Department support of the Dominican dissidents were fully known. No directive was issued by the President or the Special Group criticizing any aspect of United States involvement in the Dominican affair.

Similarly, there is no record of any action having been taken prohibiting future support or encouragement of groups or individuals known to be planning the assassination of a foreign leader. The meetings and discussions following the Trujillo assassination represent another missed opportunity to establish an administration policy against assassination and may partially account for the CIA's assessment of the Dominican operation as a success a few years later. They may also have encouraged Agency personnel, involved in both the Trujillo and the Castro plots, in their belief that the Administration would not be unhappy if the Agency were able to make Castro disappear. No such claim, however, was made in testimony by any agency official.

(ii) Schneider

As explained above, there is no evidence that assassination was ever proposed as a method of carrying out the Presidential order to prevent Allende from assuming office. The Committee believes, however, that the granting of *carte blanche* authority to the CIA by the Executive in this case may have contributed to the tragic and unintended death of General Schneider. This was also partially due to assigning an impractical task to be accomplished within an unreasonably short time. Apart from the question of whether any intervention in Chile was justified under the circumstances of this case, the Committee believes that the Executive in any event should have defined the limits of permissible action.

(iii) Lumumba

We are unable to make a finding that President Eisenhower intentionally authorized an assassination effort against Lumumba due to the lack of absolute certainty in the evidence. However, it appears that the strong language used in discussions at the Special Group and NSC, as reflected in minutes of relevant meetings, led Dulles to believe that assassination was desired. The minutes contain language concerning the need to "dispose of" Lumumba, an "extremely strong feeling about the necessity for straightforward action," and a refusal to rule out any activity that might contribute to "getting rid of" Lumumba.

(iv) Castro

The efforts to assassinate Fidel Castro took place in an atmosphere of extreme pressure by Eisenhower and Kennedy Administration officials to discredit and overthrow the Castro regime. Shortly after Castro's ascendancy to power, Allen Dulles directed that "thorough consideration" be given to the "elimination" of Castro. Richard Helms recalled that:

> I remember vividly [that the pressure] was very intense. And therefore, when you go into the record, you find a lot of nutty schemes...borne of the intensity of the pressure....

Another CIA official stated that sometime in the Fall of 1961 Bissell was:

> *** chewed out in the Cabinet Room in the White House by both the President and the Attorney General for, as he put it, sitting on his ass and not doing anything about getting rid of Castro and the Castro Regime.

General Lansdale informed the agencies cooperating in Operation MONGOOSE that "you're in a combat situation where we have been given full command." Secretary of Defense McNamara confirmed that "we were hysterical about Castro at the time of the Bay of Pigs and thereafter."

Many of the plans that were discussed and often approved contemplated violent action against Cuba. The operation which resulted in the Bay of Pigs as a major paramilitary onslaught that had the approval of the highest government officials, including the two Presidents. Thereafter, Attorney General Kennedy vehemently exhorted the Special Group (Augmented) that "a solution to the Cuban problem today carried top priority *** no time, money, effort—or manpower is to be spared." [Footnote: The Attorney General himself took a personal interest in the recruitment and development of assets within Cuba, on occasion recommending Cubans to the CIA as possible recruits and meeting in Washington and Florida with Cuban exiles active in the covert war against the Castro Government.] Subsequently, Operation MONGOOSE involved propaganda and sabotage operations aimed toward spurring a revolt of the Cuban people against Castro. Measures which were considered by the top policymakers included incapacitating sugar workers during harvest season by the use of chemicals; blowing up bridges and production plants; sabotaging merchandise in third countries—even those allied with the United States—prior to its delivery to Cuba; and arming insurgents on the island. Programs undertaken at the urging of the Administration included intensive efforts to recruit and arm dissidents within Cuba, and raids on plants, mines, and harbors. Consideration and approval of these measures may understandably have led the CIA to conclude that violent actions were an acceptable means of accomplishing important objectives.

Discussions at the Special Group and NSC meetings might well have contributed to the perception of some CIA officials that assassination was a permissible tool in the effort to overthrow the Castro Regime. At a Special Group meeting in November 1960, Undersecretary Merchant inquired whether any planning had been undertaken for "direct, positive action" against Che Guevara, Raul Castro, and Fidel Castro. Cabell replied that such a capability did not exist, but he might well have left the meeting with the impression that assassination was not out of bounds. Lansdale's plan, which was submitted to the Special Group in January 1962, aimed at inducing "open revolt and overthrow of the Communist regime." Included in its final phase an "attack on the cadre of the regime, including key leaders."

The proposal stated that "this should be a 'Special Target' operation * * *. Gangster elements might provide the best recruitment potential against police * * *." Although Lansdale's proposal was shelved, the type of aggressive action contemplated was not formally ruled out. Minutes from several Special Group meetings contain language such as "possible removal of Castro from the Cuban scene."

Ambiguous Administration Reactions

On several occasions, the subject of assassination was discussed in the presence of senior Administration officials. Those officials never consented to actual assassination efforts, but they failed to indicate that assassination was impermissible as a matter of principle.

In early 1961, McGeorge Bundy was informed of a CIA project described as the development of a capability to assassinate. Bundy raised no objection and, according to Bissell, may have been more affirmative [Footnote: The Inspector General's Report states that Harvey's notes (which no longer exist) quoted Bissell as saying to Harvey: "The White House has twice urged me to create such a capability."] Bissell stated that he did not construe Bundy's remarks as authorization for the underworld plot against Castro that was then underway. But the fact that he believed that the development of an assassination capability had, as he subsequently told Harvey, been approved by the White House, may well have contributed to the general perception that assassination was not prohibited. [Footnote: Bundy, as the National Security Advisor to the President, had an obligation to tell the President of such a grave matter, even though it was only a discussion of a capability to assassinate. His failure to do so was a serious error.]

Documents received by the Committee indicate that in May 1961, Attorney General Kennedy and the Director of the FBI received information that the CIA was engaged in clandestine efforts against Castro which included the use of Sam Giancana and other underworld figures. The various documents referred to "dirty business," "clandestine efforts," and "plans" which were still "working" and might eventually "pay off." The Committee is unable to determine whether Hoover and the Attorney General ever inquired into the nature of the CIA operation, although there is no evidence that they did so inquire. The Committee believes that they should have inquired, and that their failure to do so was a dereliction of their duties.

Documents indicate that in May 1962, Attorney General Kennedy was told that the CIA had sought to assassinate Castro prior to the Bay of Pigs. According to the CIA officials who were present at the briefing, the Attorney General indicated his displeasure about the lack of consultation rather than about the impropriety of the attempt itself. There is no evidence that the Attorney General told the CIA that it must not engage in assassination plots in the future.

At a meeting of the Special Group (Augmented) in August 1962, well after the assassination efforts were underway, Robert McNamara is said to have raised the question of whether the assassination of Cuban leaders should be explored, and General Lansdale issued an action memorandum assigning the CIA the task of preparing contingency plans for the assassination of Cuban leaders. While McCone testified that he had immediately made it clear that assassination was not to be discussed or condoned, Harvey's testimony and documents which he wrote after the event indicate that Harvey may have been confused over whether McCone had objected to the use of assassination, or whether he was only concerned that the subject not be put in writing. In any event, McCone went no further. He issued no general order banning consideration of assassination within the Agency.

One of the programs forwarded to General Lansdale by the Defense Department in the MONGOOSE program was entitled "Operation Bounty" and envisioned dropping leaflets in Cuba offering rewards for the assassination of Government leaders. Although the plan was vetoed by Lansdale, it indicates that persons in agencies other than the CIA perceived that assassination might be permissible.

While the ambivalence of Administration officials does not excuse the misleading conduct by Agency officials or justify their failure to seek explicit permission, this attitude displayed an insufficient concern about assassination which may have contributed to the perception that assassination was an acceptable tactic in accomplishing the Government's general objectives.

Moreover, with the exception of the tight guidelines issued by the Special Group (Augmented) concerning Operation MONGOOSE, precise limitations were never imposed on the CIA requiring prior permission for the details of other proposed covert operations against Cuba.

Assassination Banned in 1972

No general policy banning assassination was promulgated until Helms' intra-agency order in 1972. Considering the number of times the subject of assassination had arisen, Administration officials were remiss in not explicitly forbidding such activity.

The committee notes that many of the occasions on which CIA officials should have informed their superiors of the assassination efforts but failed to do so, or did so in a misleading manner, were also occasions on which Administration officials paradoxically may have reinforced the perception that assassination was permissible.

For example, when Bissell spoke with Bundy about an Executive Action capability, Bissell failed to indicate that an actual assassination operation was underway, but Bundy failed to rule out assassination as a tactic.

In May 1962, the Attorney General was misleadingly told about the effort to assassinate Castro prior to the Bay of Bigs, but not about the operation that was then going on. The Attorney General, however, did not state that assassination was improper.

When a senior administration official raised the question of whether assassination should be explored at a Special Group meeting, the assassination operation should have been revealed. A firm written order against engaging in assassination should also have been issued by McCone if, as he testified, he had exhibited strong aversion to assassination.

5. Practices Current at the Time in Which the Assassination Plots Occurred Were Revealed by the Record to Create the Risk of Confusion, Rashness and Irresponsibility in the Very Areas Where Clarity and Sober Judgment Were Most Necessary

Various witnesses described elements of the system within which the assassination plots were conceived. The Committee is disturbed by the custom that permitted the most sensitive matters to be presented to the highest levels of Government with the least clarity. We view the following points as particularly dangerous:

(1) The expansion of the doctrine of "plausible denial" beyond its intended purpose of hiding the involvement of the United States from other countries into an effort to shield higher officials from knowledge, and hence responsibility, for certain operations.

(2) The use of circumlocution or euphemism to describe serious matters—such as assassination—when precise meanings ought to be made clear.

(3) The theory that general approval of broad covert action programs is sufficient to justify specific actions such as assassination or the passage of weapons.

(4) The theory that authority granted, or assumed to be granted, by one DCI or one Administration could be presumed to continue without the necessity for reaffirming the authority with successor officials.

(5) The creation of covert capabilities without careful review and authorization by policymakers, and the further risk that such capabilities, once created, might be used without specific authorization.

(a) The danger inherent in overextending the doctrine of "plausible denial"

The original concept of "plausible denial" envisioned implementing covert actions in a manner calculated to conceal American involvement if the actions were exposed. The doctrine was at times a delusion and at times a snare. It was naive for policymakers to assume that sponsorship of actions as big as the Bay of Pigs invasion could be concealed. The Committee's investigation of assassination and the public disclosures which preceded the inquiry demonstrate that when the United States resorted to cloak-and-dagger tactics, its hand was ultimately exposed. We were particularly disturbed to find little evidence that the risks and consequences of disclosure were considered.

We find that the likelihood of reckless action is substantially increased when policymakers believe that their decisions will never be revealed. Whatever can be said in defense of the original purpose of plausible denial—a purpose which intends to conceal United States involvement from the outside world—the extension of the doctrine to the internal decision-making process of the Government is absurd. Any theory which, as a matter of doctrine, places elected officials on the periphery of the decision-making process is an invitation to error, an abdication of responsibility, and a perversion of democratic government. The doctrine is the antithesis of accountability.

(b) The danger of using "Circumlocution" and "Euphemism"

According to Richard Bissell, the extension of "plausible denial" to internal decision-making required the use of circumlocution and euphemism in speaking with Presidents and other senior officials.

Explaining this concept only heightens its absurdity. On one hand, it assumes that senior officials should be shielded from the truth to enable them to deny knowledge if the truth comes out. On the other hand, the concept assumes that senior officials must be told enough, by way of double talk, to grasp the subject. As a consequence, the theory fails to accomplish its objective and only increases the risk of misunderstanding. Subordinate officials should describe their proposals in clear, precise, and brutally frank language; superiors are entitled to, and should demand, no less.

Euphemism may actually have been preferred—not because of "plausible denial"—but because the persons involved could not bring themselves to state in plain language what they intended to do. In some instances, moreover, subordinates may have assumed, rightly or wrongly, that the listening superiors did not want the issue squarely placed before them. "Assassinate," "murder" and "kill" are words many people do not want to speak or hear. They describe acts which should not even be proposed, let alone plotted. Failing to call dirty business by its rightful name may have increased the risk of dirty business being done.

(c) The danger of generalized instructions

Permitting specific acts to be taken on the basis of general approvals of broad strategies (e.g., keep Allende from assuming office, get rid of the Castro regime) blurs responsibility and accountability. Worse still, it increases the danger that subordinates may take steps which would have been disapproved if the policymakers had been informed. A further danger is that policymakers might intentionally use loose general instructions to evade responsibility for embarrassing activities.

In either event, we find that the gap between the general policy objectives and the specific actions undertaken to achieve them was far too wide.

It is important that policymakers review the manner in which their directives are implemented, particularly when the activities are sensitive, secret, and immune from public scrutiny.

(d) The danger of "Floating Authorization"

One justification advanced by Richard Helms and William Harvey for not informing John McCone about the use of underworld figures to attempt to assassinate Fidel Castro was their assertion that the project had already been approved by McCone's predecessor, Allan Dulles, and that further authorization was unnecessary, at least until the operation had reached a more advanced stage.

We find that the idea that authority might continue or "float" from one administration or director to the next and that there is no duty to reaffirm authority inhibits responsible decision-making. Circumstances may change or judgments differ. New officials should be given the opportunity to review significant programs.

(e) The problems connected with creating new covert capabilities

The development of a new capability raises numerous problems. Having a capability to engage in certain covert activity increases the probability that the activity will occur, since the capability represents a tool available for use. There is the further danger that authorization for the mere creation of a capability may be misunderstood as permitting its use without requiring further authorization.

Finally, an assassination capability should never have been created.

V. RECOMMENDATIONS

The Committee's long investigation of assassination has brought a number of important issues into sharp focus. Above all stands the question of whether assassination is an acceptable tool of American foreign policy. Recommendations on other issues must await the completion of our continuing investigation and the final report, but the Committee needs no more information to be convinced that a flat ban against assassination should be written into law.

We condemn assassination and reject it as an instrument of American policy. Surprisingly, however, there is presently no statute making it a crime to assassinate a foreign official outside the United States. Hence, for the reasons set forth below, the Committee recommends the prompt enactment of a statute making it a Federal crime to commit or attempt an assassination, or to conspire to do so.

A. General Agreement That the United States Must Not Engage in Assassination

Our view that assassination has no place in America's arsenal is shared by the Administration.

President Ford, in the same statement in which he asked this Committee to deal with the assassination issue, stated:

> I am opposed to political assassination. This administration has not and will not use such means as instruments of national policy. (Presidential Press Conference, 6/9/75....)

The witnesses who testified before the Committee uniformly condemned assassination. They denounced it as immoral, described it as impractical, and reminded us that an open society, more than any other, is particularly vulnerable to the risk that its own leaders may be assassinated. As President Kennedy reportedly said: "We can't get into that kind of thing, or we would all be targets." (Goodwin, 7/18/75, p. 4)

The current Director of Central Intelligence and his two predecessors testified emphatically that assassination should be banned. William Colby said:

> With respect to assassination, my position is clear. I just think it is wrong. And I have said so and made it very clear to my subordinates. (Colby, *** 5/21/75, p. 89)

Richard Helms, who had been involved in an assassination plot before he became DCI, said he had concluded assassination should be ruled out for both moral and practical reasons:

> As a result of my experiences through the years, when I became Director I had made up my mind that this option *** of killing foreign leaders, was something that I did not want to happen on my watch. My reasons for this were these:
> There are not only moral reasons but there are also some other rather practical reasons.
> It is almost impossible in a democracy to keep anything like that secret ***. Somebody would go to a Congressman, his Senator, he might go to a newspaper man, whatever the case may be, but it just is not a practical alternative, it seems to me, in our society.
> Then there is another consideration *** if you are going to try by this kind of means to remove a foreign leader, then who is going to take his place running that country, and are you essentially better off as a matter of practice when it is over than you were before? And I can give you I think a very solid example of this which happened in Vietnam when President Diem was eliminated from the scene. We then had a revolving door of prime ministers after that for quite some period of time, during which the Vietnamese Government at a time in its history when it should have been strong was nothing but a caretaker government * * *. In other words, that whole exercise turned out to the disadvantage of the United States.
> * * * there is no sense in my sitting here with all the experience I have had and not sharing with the Committee my feelings this day. It isn't because I have lost my cool, or because I have lost my guts, it simply is because I don't think it is a viable option in the United States of America these days.
> ...Chairman Church. Since we do like a free society and since these secrets are going to come out in due course, the revelation

will then do serious injury to the good name and reputation of the United States. Would you agree with that?

Mr. Helms. Yes. I would.

Chairman Church. And finally, if we were to reserve to ourselves the prerogative to assassinate foreign leaders, we may invite reciprocal action from foreign governments who assume that if it's our prerogative to do so, it is their prerogative as well, and that is another danger that we at least invite with this kind of action, wouldn't you agree?

Mr. Helms: Yes, sir. (Helms, 6/13/75, pp. 76-78)

John McCone said he was opposed to assassinations because:

I didn't think it was proper from the standpoint of the U.S. Government and the Central Intelligence Agency. (McCone, 6/6/75, p. 15)

B. CIA Directives Banning Assassination

Helms in 1972 and Colby in 1973 issued internal CIA orders banning assassination.

C. The Need for a Statute

Commendable and welcome as they are, these CIA directives are not sufficient. Administrations change, CIA directors change, and someday in the future what was tried in the past may once again become a temptation. Assassination plots did happen. It would be irresponsible not to do all that can be done to prevent their happening again. A law is needed. Laws express our nation's values; they deter those who might be tempted to ignore those values and stiffen the will of those who want to resist the temptation.

The Committee recommends a statute which would make it a criminal offense for persons subject to the jurisdiction of the United States (1) to conspire, within or outside the United States, to assassinate a foreign official; (2) to attempt to assassinate a foreign official, or (3) to assassinate a foreign official.

Present law makes it a crime to kill, or to conspire to kill, a foreign official or foreign official guest while such a person is in the United States.... However, there is no law which makes it a crime to assassinate, to conspire to assassinate, or to attempt to assassinate a foreign official while such official is outside the United States. The Committee's proposed statute is designed to close this gap in the law.

Subsection (a) of the proposed statute would punish conspiracies within the United States; subsection (b) would punish conspiracies outside the United States. Subsection (b) is necessary to eliminate the loophole which would otherwise permit persons to simply leave the United States and conspire abroad. Subsections (c) and (d), respectively, would make it an offense to attempt to kill or to kill a foreign official outside the United States.

Subsections (a), (b), (c), and (d) would apply expressly to any "officer or employee of the United States" to make clear that the statute punishes conduct by United States Government personnel, as well as conduct by private citizens. In addition, subsection (a), which covers conspiracies within the United States, would apply to "any other person," regardless of citizenship. Non-citizens who conspired within the United States to assassinate a foreign official would clearly come within the jurisdiction of the law. Subsections (b), (c), and (d), which deal with conduct abroad, would apply to United States citizens, and to officers or employees of the United States, regardless of their citizenship. Criminal liability for acts committed abroad by persons who are not American citizens or who are not officers or employees of the United States is beyond the jurisdiction of the United States.

"Foreign official" is defined in subsection (e) (2) to make clear that an offense may be committed even though the "official" belongs to an insurgent force, an unrecognized government, or a political party. The Committee's investigation—as well as the reality of international politics—has shown that officials in such organizations are potential targets for assassination. Killing, attempting to kill, or conspiring to kill would be punishable under the statute only if it were politically motivated. Political motivation would encompass acts against foreign officials because of their political views, actions, or statements.

The definition of "foreign official" in section (e) (2) also provides that such person must be an official of a foreign government or movement "with which the United States is not at war pursuant to a declaration of war or against which the United States Armed Forces have not been introduced into hostilities or situations pursuant to the provisions of the War Powers Resolution". This definition makes it clear that, absent a declaration of war or the introduction of United States Armed Forces pursuant to the War Powers Resolution, the killing of foreign officials on account of their political views would be a criminal offense.

During the Committee's hearings, some witnesses, while strongly condemning assassination, asked whether assassination should absolutely be ruled out in a time of truly unusual national emergency. Adolf Hitler was cited as an example. Of course, the cases which the Committee investigated were not of that character. Indeed, in the Cuban missile crisis—the only situation of true national danger considered in this report—assassination was not even considered and, if used, might well have aggravated the crisis.

In a grave emergency, the President has a limited power to act, not in violation of the law, but in accord with his own responsibilities under the Constitution to defend the Nation. As the Supreme Court has stated, the Constitution "is not a suicide pact." (Kennedy v. Mendoza-Martinez ...(1963).)

During an unprecedented emergency, Abraham Lincoln claimed unprecedented power based on the need to preserve the nation:

> *** my oath to preserve the Constitution to the best of my ability, imposed upon me the duty of preserving, by every indispensable means, that government—that nation—of which that Constitution was the organic law. Was it possible to lose the nation, and yet preserve the Constitution? By general law, life and limb must be protected; yet often a limb must be amputated to save a life; but a life is never wisely given to save a limb. I felt that measures, otherwise unconstitutional, might become lawful, by becoming indispensable to the preservation of the Constitution, through the preservation of the nation ***.

Whatever the extent of the President's own constitutional powers, it is a fundamental principle of our constitutional system that those powers are checked and limited by Congress, including the impeachment power. As a necessary corollary, any action taken by a President pursuant to his limited inherent powers and in apparent conflict with the law must be disclosed to Congress. Only then can Congress judge whether the action truly represented, in Lincoln's phrase, an "indispensable necessity" to the life of the Nation....

EPILOGUE

The Committee does not believe that the acts which it has examined represent the real American character. They do not reflect the ideals which have given the people of this country and of the world hope for a better, fuller, fairer life. We regard the assassination plots as aberrations....

The United States must not adopt the tactics of the enemy. Means are as important as ends. Crisis makes it tempting to ignore the wise restraints that make men free. But each time we do so, each time the means we use are wrong, our inner strength, the strength which makes us free, is lessened.

Despite our distaste for what we have seen, we have great faith in this country. The story is sad, but this country has the strength to hear the story and to learn from it. We must remain a people who confront our mistakes and resolve not to repeat them. If we do not, we will decline; but, if we do, our future will be worthy of the best of our past.

> *Sen. Frank Church's statement of Nov. 6, 1975, on "Operation Shamrock," the National Security Agency cable-monitoring program:*

I. Introductory

"SHAMROCK" was the cover name given to a message-collection program in which the Government persuaded three international telegraph companies—RCA Global, ITT World Communications, and Western Union International—to make available in various ways certain of their international telegraph traffic to the United States Government. For almost thirty years, copies of most international telegrams originating in or forwarded through the United States were turned over to the National Security Agency and its predecessor agencies.

As we discuss more fully below, the evidence appears to be that in the midst of the program, the Government's use of the material turned over by the companies changed. At the outset, the purpose apparently was only to extract international telegrams relating to certain foreign targets. Later, the Government began to extract the telegrams of certain United States citizens. In defense of the companies, the fact is that the Government did not tell them that it was selecting out and analyzing the messages of certain U.S. citizens. On the other hand, the companies knew they were turning over to the Government most international telegrams, including those of United States citizens and organizations. There is no evidence to suggest that they ever asked what the Government was doing with that material or took steps to make sure the Government did not read the private communications of Americans.

II. The Committee's Investigation

The Select Committee made its first inquiries into this operation last May. It was not until early September, however, that the Select Committee received a response to its questions. At that time, we obtained preliminary briefings from NSA operational personnel.

Subsequently, we examined three NSA officials, including former Deputy Director Louis Tordella. These persons were the only ones at NSA with substantial knowledge of the SHAMROCK operation. The Committee also reviewed all existing documentation relating to the operation.

The Select Committee again examined NSA officials in executive sessions. Subsequently, the companies which had participated were contacted. Sworn testimony was taken from officials in each company, and company counsel have worked with the Committee to reconstruct, as nearly as possible, what has taken place over the last thirty years.

III. History

During World War II, all international telegraph traffic was screened by military censors, located at the companies, as part of the wartime censorship program. During this period, messages of foreign intelligence targets were turned over to military intelligence.

According to documents in possession of the Department of Defense, the Department sought in 1947 to renew the part of this arrangement whereby the telegraph traffic of foreign intelligence targets had been turned over to it. At that time, most of these foreign targets did use the paid message facilities of the international carriers to transmit messages.

At meetings with Secretary of Defense James Forrestal in 1947, representatives of the three companies were assured that if they cooperated with the Government in this program, they would suffer no criminal liability and no public exposure, at least as long as the current administration was in office. They were told that such participation was in the highest interests of national security.

Secretary Forrestal also explained that the arrangements had the approval of President Truman and his Attorney General, Tom C. Clark. Forrestal explained to the companies, however, that he could not bind his successors by these assurances. He told the companies, moreover, that Congress would consider legislation in its forthcoming session which would make clear that such activity was permissible. In fact, no such legislation was ever introduced.

In 1949, the companies sought renewed assurances from Forrestal's successor, Louis D. Johnson, and were told again that President Truman and Attorney General Clark had been consulted and had given their approval of these arrangements. As I will explain later in this statement, neither the Department of Defense nor any of the participating private companies has any evidence that such assurances were ever sought again.

The Army Security Agency was the first Government agency which had operational responsibility for SHAMROCK. When the Armed Forces Security Agency was created in 1949, however, it inherited the program; and, similarly, when NSA was created in 1952, it assumed operational control.

IV. Early Operation of SHAMROCK

There are no documents at NSA or the Department of Defense which reflect the operational arrangements between the Government and the telegraph companies. (The companies decided at the outset that they did not want to keep any documents and the Government has none today other than those relating to the 1947 and 1949 discussions which I previously covered.)

According to the testimony given to us, it appears, however, that the companies were given to understand at the outset that only traffic of foreign intelligence targets would be gleaned by NSA.

In practice, the arrangements with each company varied somewhat. RCA Global and ITT World Communications provided NSA with the great bulk of their international message traffic, which NSA then selected for traffic of foreign intelligence reports. Western Union International sorted the traffic itself and provided NSA only with copies of the traffic of certain foreign targets and all the traffic to one country.

In the beginning, the Government received paper tapes of messages that had been transmitted by overseas cables, as well as microfilm copies of messages that had been sent by radio. These were, at the outset, sorted by hand apparently for certain foreign intelligence targets only; such traffic could be readily identified by special codes in the heading of each telegram.

As a practical matter, the inherent limitations of manual sorting precluded the traffic from being sorted on its content.

V. Later Operation of SHAMROCK

In the early 1960s, there was a change in technology which had a significant impact upon the way in which SHAMROCK was run. RCA Global and ITT World Communications began to store their international paid message traffic on magnetic tapes, and these were turned over to NSA. Thereafter, the telegrams were selected in precisely the same way in which NSA selects its information from other sources. This meant, for example, that telegrams to or from, or even mentioning, United States citizens whose names appeared on the Watch List in the late 1960s and early 1970s would have been sent to NSA analysts, and many would subsequently be disseminated to other agencies.

The NSA officials examined by us had no recollection of NSA's ever informing the companies how NSA was handling the information they were providing. They furthermore had no recollection of any of the companies making such an inquiry, even after NSA began receiving magnetic tapes from two of the companies. Several company officials corroborated this testimony, stating that they had no knowledge of any inquiry by their respective companies or that NSA ever volunteered any information in this regard.

Only the Director, Deputy Director, and a lower-level manager at NSA had operational responsibility for SHAMROCK at any one time. Moreover, their contacts with company officials were extremely rare; in fact, the Director never met with company representatives and the Deputy Director only met once with a company official. Any communications with the companies were usually relayed by NSA couriers which made routine pick-ups and deliveries at the companies.

No one examined from NSA or the companies knew of any effort by the companies since 1949 to seek renewed assurances from the Government for their continued participation in SHAMROCK. Indeed, each of the companies has given sworn statements to the Committee that they did not think the arrangements with NSA were ever considered by the executive levels of their respective companies. Moreover, Dr. Tordella, the former Deputy Director, told us that he would have known if additional assurances had ever been sought and testified that to his knowledge they were not.

NSA and company officials likewise knew of no compensation given the companies by the Government for their participation in SHAMROCK, and testified that they knew of no incident where favoritism was shown any of the participating companies by an agency of the Federal Government. Again, Dr. Tordella has stated under oath that he would have been told about such an incident if it had taken place.

NSA never received any domestic telegrams from these companies. Indeed, none of these companies, at least since 1963, has had domestic operations.

Approximately 90 percent of the messages collected in SHAMROCK came from New York. Company offices in Washington, San Francisco, and, for a short while, Miami, also participated in a similar fashion. In Washington, the companies turned over copies of particular traffic of foreign intelligence targets to agents of the FBI. These were later delivered to NSA.

Of all the messages made available to NSA each year, it is estimated that NSA in recent years selected about 150,000 messages a month for NSA analysts to review. Thousands of these messages in one form or another were distributed to other agencies in response to "foreign intelligence requirements."

VI. Knowledge and Authorization of SHAMROCK

Until the current controversy arose, only a handful of officials in the Executive Branch over the last thirty years were apparently aware of the SHAMROCK operation. Dr. Tordella testified that to the best of his knowledge no President since Truman had been informed of it.

VII. Termination of SHAMROCK

SHAMROCK terminated by order of the Secretary of Defense on May 15, 1975.

QUINLAN DECISION: A QUESTION OF DEATH

November 10, 1975

For more than two months during the fall of 1975, a New Jersey lawsuit concerning the fate of a comatose young woman with irreversible brain damage occupied national attention. The Roman Catholic parents of 21-year-old Karen Ann Quinlan, with the support of their parish priest, had sought removal of a mechanical respirator which had sustained their daughter's biological functions since April, when she had been brought unconscious to a hospital. The cause for her illness was not known.

After medical experts advised that she would not recover from a "persistent vegetative state," and that she could not continue to breathe without mechanical intervention, the Quinlans had decided that she should be removed from the respirator and allowed to die "with grace and dignity." When the attending physician in the case, Dr. Robert J. Morse, refused to turn off the respirator, the Quinlans sought a court order appointing her father, Joseph Quinlan, as her legal guardian for the purpose of ordering the cessation of what the parents considered to be extraordinary life-sustaining measures.

The resulting legal action, which attracted extensive news coverage and editorial comment across the country, was widely expected to elicit a legal definition of death, substituting the recently developed concept of "brain death" (cessation of organized brain waves) for the traditional criterion of loss of vital signs including heartbeat and respiration. In a Nov. 10 decision, Judge Robert Muir Jr. of the New Jersey Superior Court ruled that Quinlan "is by any legal and medical definition alive." He refused to authorize removal of the respirator, holding that that decision lay in the realm of medicine rather than law.

The Quinlan case prompted introduction of a "determination-of-death" bill in the New Jersey state legislature. It also evoked a public debate on the issue by high Vatican officials.

Controversy Over Definition of Death

The legal definition of death became an ethical question with the arrival of the age of the heart transplant. Doctors soon discovered that the ideal donor prospect was an individual with a healthy heart suffering from a fatal brain injury. The usual procedure in such a case was to keep the circulatory system of the donor functioning by mechanical means after he had suffered "brain death" and until doctors were ready to remove his heart and implant it in the recipient. This raised the question of whether doctors showed undue haste in declaring a heart donor dead.

In a 1970 paper Dr. Henry K. Beecher of Harvard Medical School described dying as "a continuous process," adding that, "While death may occur at a discrete time, we are not able to pinpoint it (except in certain traumatic situations). We can only describe its presence when it occurs."

By late 1975 nine states had given statutory recognition to the concept of brain death, and the American Bar Association had adopted a resolution stating that "for all legal purposes, a human body with irreversible cessation of total brain function, according to usual and customary standards of medical practice, shall be considered dead." However, the American Medical Association had refused to formulate a statement on death, holding that this determination should only be made on a case-by-case basis by individual physicians.

Medical officials acknowledged to reporters that the Quinlans' request did not differ from requests often honored at American hospitals, generally for patients with terminal illnesses. But these officials pointed out that such decisions were becoming increasingly difficult in the context of current well-publicized controversies over medical malpractice insurance and medical ethics.

No Precedent

Dr. Morse maintained simply that he could find no medical precedent for terminating Karen Quinlan's life. The New York Times reported in September that there was "no record of an American court ever authorizing cessation of supportive medical devices to sustain life," whether or not brain death was involved.

The Quinlans contended that in the absence of any possibility for a meaningful human life, their daughter should be allowed to die. They also stated that on more than one occasion prior to her illness Miss Quinlan had said that she would not want her life to be prolonged by extraordinary artificial means.

Judge Muir appointed a legal guardian, whose concurrence with future medical decisions regarding Miss Quinlan would be required. An appeal from the decision was scheduled in the New Jersey Supreme Court in January 1976

Opinion of New Jersey Superior Court Judge Robert J. Muir In the Matter of Karen Quinlan, *handed down Nov. 10, 1975, at Morristown, New Jersey:*

IN THE MATTER OF KAREN QUINLAN, : AN ALLEGED INCOMPETENT. :	SUPERIOR COURT OF NEW JERSEY CHANCERY DIVISION MORRIS COUNTY Docket No. C-201-75 OPINION

Decided: November 10, 1975

In his initial pleading, Joseph Quinlan, father of 21-year old Karen Ann Quinlan, seeks, on grounds of mental incompetency, to be appointed the guardian of the person and property of his daughter. He alleges her "vital processes are artificially sustained via the extraordinary means of a mechanical MA-1 Respirator." He imprecates the Court grant "the express power of authorizing the discontinuance of all extraordinary means of sustaining the vital processes of his daughter."

Plaintiff initially asserted that Karen Quinlan is legally and medically dead but altered this position prior to trial by admitting she is not dead" according to any legal standard recognized by the State of New Jersey."...

It is stipulated by all parties that Karen Ann Quinlan is unfit and unable to manage her own affairs.

Medical History

The Court's findings of fact are as hereinafter set forth:

Karen Ann Quinlan, one of three children of Joseph and Julia Quinlan, was born April 24, 1954. She was baptized and raised a Roman Catholic. She attended Roman Catholic Church affiliated elementary and secondary schools. She is a member of her parents' local Roman Catholic Church in Mount Arlington, New Jersey. The parish priest is Father Thomas A. Trapasso.

Sometime in late 1974 or early 1975, Karen Quinlan moved from her parents' home. Thereafter, she had at least two subsequent residences, with the last being a lake cottage in Sussex County, New Jersey.

On the night of April 15, 1975, friends of Karen summoned the local police and emergency rescue squad, and she was taken to Newton Memorial Hospital. The precise events leading up to her admission to Newton Memorial Hospital are unclear. She apparently ceased breathing for at least two fifteen minute periods. Mouth to mouth resuscitation was applied by her friends the first time and by a police respirator the second time. The exact amount of time she was without spontaneous respiration is unknown.

Upon her admission to Newton Memorial, urine and blood tests were administered, which indicated the presence of quinine, aspirin, barbiturates in normal range and traces of valium and librium. The drugs found present were indicated by Dr. Robert Morse, the neurologist in charge of her care at St. Clare's, to be in the therapeutic range and the quinine consistent with mixing in drinks like soda water.

The cause of the unconsciousness and periodic cessations of respiration is undetermined. The interruption in respiration apparently caused anoxia—insufficient supply of oxygen in the blood—resulting in her present condition.

Hospital records at the time of admission reflected Karen's vital signs to be normal, a temperature of 100, pupils unreactive, unresponsivity to deep pain, legs rigid and curled up with decorticate brain activity. Her blood oxygen level was low at the time. She was placed upon a respirator at Newton Hospital.

At 10 p.m. on April 16, 1975, Dr. Morse examined Karen at the request of her then attending physician. He found her in a state of coma with evidence of decortication indicating altered level of consciousness. She required the respirator for assistance. She did not trigger the respirator, which means she did not breathe spontaneously nor independently of it at any time during the examination. Due to her decorticate posturing, no reflexes could be elicited.

In the decorticate posturing, the upper arms are drawn into the side of the body. The forearms are drawn in against the chest with the hands generally at right angles to the forearms, pointing towards the waist. The legs are drawn up against the body, knees are up, feet are in near the buttocks and extended in a ballet type pose.

He found her oculocephalic and oculovestibular reflexes normal. The oculocephalic reflex test consists of turning the head from side to side with the eyes open. In a positive response, when the head is rotated to the right, the eyes deviate to the left. As part of this test the head is also moved front and back, the neck is flexed in the back movement, causing the eyelids to open. This phenomenon is called "doll's-eyelid response". (Dr. Morse found that reflex intact on April 26th according to hospital records.) The oculovestibular reflex ascertained by a caloric stimulation test consists of the slow introduction of ice water into the ear canal. The eyes drift or move toward the irrigated ear. It is a lateral eye movement test.

He also found pupillary reaction to light in both eyes.

Her weight at the time was 115 pounds.

Dr. Morse could not obtain any initial history (i.e., the circumstances and events occurring prior to Karen's becoming unconscious). There was no information available from her friends. He speculated at the outset on the possibility of an overdose of drugs, past history of lead poisoning, foul play, or head injury due to a fall. He indicated that the lack of an initial history seriously inhibits a diagnosis.

Karen was transferred to the Intensive Care Unit (I.C.U.) of St. Clare's Hospital, under the care of Dr. Morse. At the time of her transfer, she was still unconscious, still on a respirator, a catheter was inserted into her bladder and a tracheostomy had been performed.

Upon entry to the St. Clare's I.C.U. she was placed on a MA-1 Respirator,... The machine takes over completely the breathing function when the patient does not breathe spontaneously.

Subsequently, the serial blood gas or arterial blood gas examinations were made.... Dr. Javed, the attending pulmonary internist, indicated some 300 tests were conducted.

Dr. Javed testified the blood tests were all normal while Karen was on the respirator.

In an effort to ascertain the cause of the coma, Dr. Morse conducted a brain scan, an angiogram, an electroencephalogram (EEG), a lumbar tap and several other tests. The first three are related to the brain and are conducted, according to the testimony, with the object of finding an injury or insult to the brain, such as a subdural hematoma or the like, or for ascertaining any abnormality in the brain activity patterns. The latter is particularly true of the EEG where electrodes are placed on the skull. The measurement is made of cortical neurons. The neuron is basically a conducting cell of nervous energy. The recordings are made on awake and sleep cycles. The awake recorded data, referred to in the testimony as alpha rhythm or activity, indicates a frequency of pattern which can be compared against normal frequencies or patterns to determine whether any abnormality exists. The EEG establishes the existence or non-existence of normal patterns. It does not precisely locate the insult or lesion causing, in this case, the unconsciousness. Dr. Morse indicated the EEG performed at the outset established nothing abnormal for a comatose person and did not establish the offending agent to her central nervous system which caused her unconsciousness. Subsequent EEGs provided no further information. All indicated brain rhythm or activity.

Subsequent tests and examinations did not further the establishment of the precise location and cause of Karen's comatose condition.

Treatment Limited

Dr. Morse testified concerning the treatment of Karen at St. Clare's. He averred she receives oral feedings since intravenous feeding is insufficient to sustain her. She is fed a high caloric nutrient called "Vivenex" which she receives through a small nasal gastro tube inserted in her gastro-intestinal system. He asserts this is necessary to keep her "viable". She has apparently lost considerable weight, being described as emaciated by most of the examining experts, who also indicate her weight condition to be good under the circumstances.

There is constant threat of infection, according to Dr. Morse. Antibiotics are administered to thwart potential infection with tests constantly being made to keep a check on this threat. The hospital records indicate specialists consulted with respect to the cleaning, utilization and operation of the urethral catheter and with respect to the treatment and care of decubiti (lesions commonly known as bed sores) generated by her continuous repose.

Condition of Patient Described

The day-by-day charts entitled "Vital Signs", kept by nurses who give her 24-hour care indicate, in part, the following:

1. Her color was generally pale, her skin warm, she was almost constantly suffering from diaphoresis (sweating), many times profusely but occasionally moderately or not at all;

2. there was always a reaction to painful stimuli, she responded decerebrately to pain, she sometimes would grimace as if in pain, which would be followed by increased rigidity of her arms and legs;

3. there would be periodic contractions and spasms, periodic yawning, periodic movements of spastic nature;

4. pupils were sometimes dilated, sometimes normal but almost always sluggish to light;

5. body waste disposal through the urethral catheter and the bowel was indicated to occur;

6. feedings of Vivinex were given alternately with water on various nurses shifts;

7. the nurses were constantly moving, positioning, and bathing her;

8. body rashes occurred at times; decubiti [bed sores] were treated with heat lamps on occasions;

9. sometimes she would trigger and assist the respirator; other times she would go for periods without triggering it at all;

10. her extremities remained rigid with contraction of them being described as severe at times;

11. on May 7th, nurses indicated she blinked her eyes two times when asked to and appeared responsive by moving her eyes when talked to but there is no further evidence of this type reaction thereafter.

Dr. Javed indicated efforts were made to wean or remove Karen from the respirator. The hospital records support this. Dr. Javed testified for weaning to be successful, the patient must have a stable respiratory pattern. Karen was taken off the respirator for short periods of time. Each time, her respiratory rate, rate of breathing, went up and the volume of air intake would decrease. He indicated her breathing rate would more than double in intensity while her "tidal volume" or air intake would drop 50 percent. The longest period of time she was off the respirator was one-half hour. He further indicated during removal from the respirator her pO_2 dropped. He stated the respiratory problem is secondary to the neurological problem, and without improvement in the latter she cannot be removed from the respirator since she would be unable to maintain her vital processes without its assistance.

Dr. Morse's hospital notes indicate there is no neurological improvement from the time of her admission to St. Clare's to date. He testified Karen changed from a sleeping comatose condition to a sleep-awake type comatose condition but described this as normal in comatose patients and not any indication of improvement. During the awake cycle, she is still unconscious.

Damage to Brain

In Dr. Morse's opinion, the cause of Karen's condition is a lesion on the cerebral hemispheres and a lesion in the brain stem....

In absence of a clear history, Dr. Morse relied basically upon the decorticate posturing of Karen Quinlan and the respiratory difficulty for reaching his conclusion as to the brain lesion locations. He contrasted the decorticate posture to decerebrate posture of a patient for drawing his conclusions.

Brain Death Criteria

He asserted with medical certainty that Karen Quinlan is not brain dead. He identified the Ad Hoc Committee of Harvard Medical School Criteria as the ordinary medical standard for determining brain death and said that Karen satisfied none of the criteria. These criteria are set forth in a 1968 report entitled "Report of the Ad Hoc Committee of Harvard Medical School to Examine the Definition of Brain Death": A Definition of "Irreversible Coma,"....

The report reflects that it is concerned "only with those comatose individuals who have discernible central nervous system activity" and the problem of determining the characteristics of a permanently non-functioning brain. The criteria as established are:

"1. Unreceptivity and Unresponsitivity—There is a total unawareness to externally applied stimuli and inner need and complete unresponsiveness.... Even the most intensely painful stimuli evoke no vocal or other response, not even a groan, withdrawal of a limb, or quickening of respiration.

"2. No Movements or Breathing—Observations covering a period of at least one hour by physicians is adequate to satisfy the criteria of no spontaneous muscular movement or spontaneous respiration or response to stimuli such as a pain, touch, sound or light. After the patient is on a mechanical respirator, the total absence of spontaneous breathing may be established by turning off the respirator for three minutes and observing whether there is any effort on the part of the subject to breathe spontaneously....

"3. No Reflexes—Irreversible coma with abolition of central nervous system activity is evidenced in part by the absence of elicitable reflexes. The pupil will be fixed and dilated and will not respond to a direct source of bright light. Since the establish-

811

ment of a fixed, dilated pupil is clear-cut in clinical practice, there would be no uncertainty as to its presence. Ocular movement (to head turning and to irrigation of ears with ice water) and blinking are absent. There is no evidence of postural activity (deliberate or other). Swallowing, yawning, vocalization are in abeyance. Corneal and pharyngeal reflexes are absent.

As a rule the stretch of tendon reflexes cannot be elicited; i.e., tapping the tendons of the biceps, triceps, and pronator muscles, quadriceps and gastrocnemius muscles with reflex hammer elicits no contraction of the respective muscles. Plantar or noxious stimulation gives no response.

"4. Flat—Electroencephalogram—of great confirmatory value is the flat or isoelectric EEG....

All tests must be repeated at least 24 hours later with no change.

The validity of such data as indications of irreversible cerebral damage depends on the exclusion of two conditions: hypothermia (temperature below 90F.) or central nervous system depressants, such as barbiturates."

Recovery Unlikely

Dr. Morse reflected carefully in his testimony on Karen's prognosis. He described her condition as a chronic or "persistent vegetative state." Dr. Fred Plum, a creator of the phrase, describes its significance by indicating the brain as working in two ways. "We have an internal vegetative regulation which controls body temperature, which controls breathing, which controls to a considerable degree blood pressure, which controls to some degree heart rate, which controls chewing, swallowing and which controls sleeping and waking. We have a more highly developed brain, which is uniquely human, which controls our relation to the outside world, our capacity to talk, to see, to feel, to sing, to think.... Brain death necessarily must mean the death of both of these functions of the brain, vegetative and the sapient. Therefore, the presence of any function which is regulated or governed or controlled by the deeper parts of the brain which in layman's terms might be considered purely vegetative would mean that the brain is not biologically dead."

Dr. Morse, in reflecting on the prognosis, notes Karen's absence of awareness of anything or anyone around her. In response to a direct question he noted she is not suffering from locked-in syndrome in which a patient is conscious but so totally paralyzed that communications can be made only through a complex system of eye or eyelid movements.

Dr. Morse states Karen Quinlan will not return to a level of cognitive function (i.e., that she will be able to say "Mr. Coburn [her court-appointed guardian] I'm glad you are my guardian.") What level or plateau she will reach is unknown. He does not know of any course of treatment that can be given and cannot see how her condition can be reversed but is unwilling to say she is in an irreversible state or condition. He indicated there is a possibility of recovery but that level is unknown particularly due to the absence of pre-hospital history.

Concurring Medical Opinions

Karen Ann Quinlan was examined by several experts for the various parties. All were neurologists with extensive experience and backgrounds. Some had done research in the area of brain injury, conscious and comatose behavior. The qualifications of all were admitted....

Their testimonies did not vary significantly....

All agree she is in a persistent vegetative state. She is described as having irreversible brain damage; no cognitive or cerebral functioning; chances for useful sapient life or return of discriminative functioning are remote. The absence of knowledge on the events precipitating the condition, and the fact that other patients have been comatose for longer periods of time and recovered to function as a human made Dr. Stuart Cook qualify his statement as to the return to discriminative functioning. All agree she is not brain dead by present known medical criteria and that her continued existence away from the respirator is a determination for a pulmonary internist.

Dr. Sidney Diamond examined Karen and testified on behalf of the State.... He states Karen is not brain dead within the Harvard Criteria.

He considered "empirical data" which included Dr. Javed's weaning attempts and said he was convinced there is no evidence she can continue to exist physically without the respirator. His opinion is that no physician would interrrupt the use of the respirator and that the continued use of the respirator does not deviate from standard medical practice.

Dr. Julius Korein testified as an expert on behalf of the plaintiff....

He described her condition as a persistent vegetative state.

In response to questions concerning her dependency on the respirator, he acknowledged that the information of Dr. Javed showing respiratory difficulty and low oxygen in the blood while off the respirator establishes her need to continue on it if her life is to continue....

He is the only expert who testified on the concepts of "ordinary" and "extraordinary" medical treatment. Essentially, he considers use of a respirator at the admission of a patient an "ordinary" medical practice. He equates the usage of it with an "extraordinary" practice when it is used for a prolonged period of time in concert with other hospital resources including extensive nursing care. He acknowledges the term "extraordinary" lacks precision in definition.

Testimony of other doctors reflects an inclination that the use of the respirator is an ordinary medical practice.

Quinlans' Decision

The decision to request removal of their daughter from the respirator, understandably, came tortuously, arduously to the Quinlans. At the outset, they authorized Dr. Morse to do everything he could to keep her alive, believing she would recover. They participated in a constant vigil over her with other family members. They were in constant contact with the doctors, particularly Dr. Morse, receiving day by day reports concerning her prognosis which, as time passed, became more and more pessimistic and more and more discouraging to them.

Mrs. Quinlan and the children were the first to conclude Karen should be removed from the respirator. Mrs. Quinlan, working at the local parish church, had ongoing talks with Father Trapasso, who supported her conclusion and indicated that it was a permissible practice within the tenets of Roman Catholic teachings.

Mr. Quinlan was slower in making his decision. His hope for recovery continued despite the disheartening medical reports. Neither his wife nor Father Trapasso made any attempt to influence him. A conflict existed between letting her natural body functioning control her life and the hope for recovery. Precisely when he came to a decision is not clear. By his testimony he indicated early September but he signed a release to the hospital dated July 31, 1975, hereafter referred to, which makes it reasonably inferrable the decision was made in July. Once having made the decision, he sought Father Trapasso's encouragement, which he received.

Position of Church

Father Trapasso based his support of the position taken by the Quinlans on the traditional, moral precepts of the Roman Catholic faith and upon a declaration, designated an *allocutio,* by Pope Pius XII made on November 24, 1957. Speaking to a group of anesthesiologists the Pope was requested to respond to the question: "When the blood circulation and the life of a patient who is deeply unconscious because of a central paralysis are maintained only through artificial respiration, and no improvement is noted after a few days, at what time does the Catholic Church consider the patient 'dead', or when must he be declared dead according to natural law?" The Papal response was "Where the verification of the fact in particular cases is concerned, the answer cannot be deduced from any religious and moral principle and, under this aspect, does not fall within the competence of the Church. Until an answer can be given, the question must remain open. But considerations of a general nature allow us to believe that human life continues for as long as its vital functions—distinguished from the simple life of organs—manifest themselves spontaneously or even with the help of artificial processes. A great number of these cases are the object of insoluble doubt, and must be dealt with according to the presumptions of law and of fact of which we have spoken."

Father Trapasso acknowledges it is not a sinful act under the church teachings or the Papal *allocutio* to either continue extraordinary treatment or discontinue it. It is acknowledged to be a matter left optional to a Roman Catholic believer. Mr. Quinlan indicates had Roman Catholic traditions and morals considered it a sin, he would not be seeking termination of the respiratorial support. Mr. Quinlan avers Karen's natural bodily functions should be allowed to operate free of the respirator. He states then if it is

God's will to take her she can go on to life after death and that is a belief of Roman Catholics. He asserts he does not believe or support the concept of euthanasia.

Once having made the determination, the Quinlans approached hospital officials to effectuate their decision....

The Quinlans on July 31, 1975, signed the following:

> "We authorize and direct Doctor Morse to discontinue all ex-traordinary measures, including the use of a respirator for our daughter Karen Quinlan.
>
> "We acknowledge that the above named physician has thor-oughly discussed the above with us and that the consequences have been fully explained to us. Therefore, we hereby RELEASE from any and all liability the above named physician, associates and assistants of his choice, Saint Clare's Hospital and its agents and employees."

Extraordinary Means Questioned

The Quinlans, upon signing the release, considered the matter decided. Dr. Morse, however, felt he could not and would not agree to the cessation of the respirator assistance. He testified, characterizing the issue of extraor-dinary treatment and the termination of it as something brought up suddenly in July—he advised the Quinlans prior to the time of the release, that he wanted to check into the matter further before giving his approval. After checking on other medical case histories, he concluded to terminate the respirator would be a substantial deviation from medical tradition, that it involved ascertaining "quality of life", and that he would not do so.

Karen Quinlan is quoted as saying she never wanted to be kept alive by extraordinary means. The statements attributed to her by her mother, sister and a friend are indicated to have been made essentially in relation to instances where close friends or relatives were terminally ill.... Mrs. Quinlan testified her daughter was very full of life, that she loved life and did not want to be kept alive in any way she would not enjoy life to the fullest.

No testimony was elicited concerning the nature and extent of the assets of Karen Quinlan. By affidavit in support of the application, Joseph Quinlan indicates she receives $157.70 per month from a Federal Supplemental Security Income program and has a personal estate valued at approximately $300 consisting primarily of personal possessions....

Plaintiff...contends under the equitable doctrine of substituted judgment this Court can act in Karen Quinlan's best interest by authorizing the cessation of the respirator. He asserts Karen Quinlan and her family have by virtue of the constitutional right of privacy a right of self-determination which extends to the decision to terminate "futile use of extraordinary medical measures." Also asserted are the constitutional right of free exer-cise of religious belief and freedom from cruel and unusual punishment as grounds for granting the sought relief.

All defendants...challenge the constitutional claims asserting no constitutional right to die exists and arguing a compelling State interest in
favor of preserving human life.

They all, essentially, contend, since Karen Quinlan is medically and
legally alive, the Court should not authorize termination of the respirator,
that to do so would be homicide and an act of euthanasia....

The case presented is:

Given the facts that Karen Quinlan is now an incompetent in a persistent
vegetive state, that at the outset of her unconsciousness her parents placed
her under the care and treatment of Dr. Morse, and through him Dr. Javed
and St. Clare's Hospital, urging everything be done to keep her alive, that
the doctors and hospital introduced life sustaining techniques, does this
Court have the power and right, under the mantle of either its equity
jurisdiction, the constitutional rights of free exercise of religion, right of
privacy or privilege against cruel and unusual punishment, to authorize the
withdrawing of the life sustaining techniques?

I.

I pause to note the scope of my role. I am concerned only with the facts of
this case and the issues presented by them. It is not my function to render
an advisory opinion. In this age of advanced medical science the prolonga-
tion of life and organ transplants, it is not my intent nor can it be, to resolve
the extensive civil and criminal legal dilemmas engendered.

The absence of specific legal precedence does not delimit the scope of my
determination. The principles of prior decisions are to be considered,
although as Cardozo points out, little faith should be placed on dic-
ta.... [Footnote: It is suggested to make "the life or death" decision here involves apotheosis and should therefore be avoided entirely. It is the nature
of the judicial process, once set in motion, to deal with an issue no matter
how grave its consequences. To carry out the judicial process, I most humbly
suggest is NOT an effort to exercise Divine Powers. The onus of the judicial
process for me, in this instance, is unparalleled.]

II.

The matter is presented to the Court, aside from constitutional considerations, in the principle framework of inherent equitable concepts and,
corollary thereto, declaratory relief.

Plaintiff invokes the inherent power of an Equity Court as the protector
and general guardian of all persons under a disability. He urges under the
doctrine of *parens patriae,* the Court as representative of the sovereign, may
intervene "in the best interests" of Karen Quinlan and allow her to die a
natural death. The doctrine has been utilized in this State in the management and administration of an incompetent's estate....but not in his personal affairs. The doctrine has been extended to the personal affairs of in-
competents and others suffering under disability in other jurisdictions....

The nature and extent to which that authority is to be exercised requires
analysis.

It has been stated that the power of equity is "the power possessed by judges—and even the duty resting upon them—to decide every case according to the high standard of morality and abstract right; that is the power and duty of a judge to do justice..."...

It involves the obedience to dictates of morality and conscience.... It may not disregard statutory law and it looks to the intent rather than the form.

These dictates set the framework for the authority this Court may exercise on Karen's behalf.

Judicial Conscience

Equity speaks of conscience. That conscience is not the personal conscience of the judge. For, if it were, the compassion, empathy, sympathy I feel for Mr. and Mrs. Quinlan and their other two children would play a *very* significant part in the decision. It is a judicial conscience, "a metaphorical term, designating the common standard of civil right and expediency combined, based upon general principles, and limited by established doctrines to which the court appeals, and by which it tests the conduct and right of the suitors".... The rationale behind not allowing the personal conscience and therefore the noted emotional aspects are that while it may result in a decision based on a notion of what is right for these individuals, the precedential effect on future litigation, particularly in light of the raging issue of euthanasia, would be legally detrimental.

Equity also speaks of morality. The morality involved is that of society. The standards evolved through social advancement in a stabilized community life.

Karen Quinlan is by legal and medical definition alive. She is not dead by the Ad Hoc Committee of Harvard Medical School standards nor by the traditional definition, the stoppage of blood circulation and related vital functions. [Footnote: The advent of life supportive techniques and advanced medical knowledge have raised a controversy over an adequate legal definition of death. *Black's Law Dictionary*...defines death as:

> The cessation of life; the ceasing to exist; defined by physicians as a total stoppage of the circulation of the blood, and a cessation of the animal and vital functions consequent thereon, such as respiration, pulsation, etc.

The difficulty with a definition which involves blood circulation develops in clinical situations, as present here, where the patient's cardio-respiratory system is mechanically supported, causing the blood to circulate and the related vital functions to continue. There obviously can be no death under *Black's* traditional definition as long as the heart and lungs remain intact. Yet, all other signs of life as reflected in the Ad Hoc Committee of Harvard Medical School can cease.

In clinical situations, such as the case at bar, the need for adoption of brain death as a legal definition is urged by many authorities. The establishment of an appropriate modern day legal definition of death and the criteria to be followed are the subject of a plethora of written material....]

The quality of her living is described as a persistent vegetative state, a description that engenders total sorrow and despair in an emotional sense. She does not exhibit cognitive behavior (i.e., the process of knowing or perceiving). Those qualities unique to man, the higher mental functions, are absent. Her condition is categorized as irreversible and the chance of returning to discriminate functioning remote. Nevertheless, while her condition is neurologically activated, due to the absence of a pre-hospital history, and in light of medical histories showing other comatose patients surviving longer coma periods, there is some medical qualification on the issue of her returning to discriminative functioning and on whether she should be removed from the respirator. There is a serious question whether she can live off the respirator and survive (at least two physicians indicated she could not). It is also apparent that extensive efforts to wean her from the respirator created a danger of more extensive brain injury. There is no treatment suggested.

Ethical Strictures on Physicians

The judicial conscience and morality involved in considering whether the Court should authorize Karen Quinlan's removal from the respirator are inextricably involved with the nature of medical science and the role of the physician in our society and his duty to his patient.

When a doctor takes a case, there is imposed upon him the duty "to exercise in the treatment of his patient the degree of care, knowledge and skill ordinarily possessed and exercised in similar situations by the average member of the profession practicing in his field".... If he is a specialist he "must employ not merely the skill of a general practitioner, but also that special degree of skill normally possessed by the average physician who devotes special study and attention to the particular organ or disease or injury involved, having regard to the present state of scientific knowledge".... This is the duty that establishes his legal obligations to his patients.

There is a higher standard, a higher duty, that encompasses the uniqueness of human life, the integrity of the medical profession and the attitude of society toward the physician and therefore the morals of society. A patient is placed, or places himself, in the care of a physician with the expectation that he (the physician) will do everything in his power, everything that is known to modern medicine, to protect the patient's life. He will do all within his human power to favor life against death.

The attitudes of society have over the years developed a significant respect for the medical profession. Society has come to request and expect this higher duty.

But the doctor is dealing in a science which lacks exactitude...a science that has seen significant changes in recent years, a science that will undoubtedly have prodigious advancements in the future but a science which still does not know the cause of some afflictions and which does not know all the inter-relationships of the body functions. In recent years, open heart surgery and organ transplantation have made continuation of life possible where the patient is suffering from a fatal disability. The cause of cancer remains to a major extent unknown, but advances have been made in cures and remissions. The brain, the only organ incapable of transplant to date, as Dr. Morse points out, is still, even among neuroanatomists, unknown insofar as the interrelationships of some of its parts and how these parts are controlled.

Medical Decision Required

Doctors, therefore, to treat a patient, must deal with medical tradition and past case histories. They must be guided by what they do know. The extent of their training, their experience, consultations with other physicians, must guide their decision making processes in providing care to their patient. The nature, extent and duration of care by societal standards is the responsibility of a physician. The morality and conscience of our society places this responsibility in the hands of the physician. What justification is there to remove it from the control of the medical profession and place it in the hands of the courts? Aside from the constitutional arguments, plaintiff suggests because medical science holds no hope for her recovery, because if Karen was conscious she would elect to turn off the respirator and finally because there is no duty to keep her alive.

None of the doctors testified there was *no* hope. The hope for recovery is remote but no doctor talks in the absolute. Certainly he cannot and be credible in light of the advancements medical science has known and the inexactitudes of medical science.

There *is* a duty to continue the life assisting apparatus, if within the treating physician's opinion, it should be done. Here Dr. Morse has refused to concur in the removal of Karen from the respirator. It is his considered position that medical tradition does not justify that act. There is no mention in the doctor's refusal of concern over criminal liability and the Court concludes that such is not the basis for his determination. It is significant that Dr. Morse, a man who demonstrated strong empathy and compassion, a man who has directed care that impressed all the experts, is unwilling to direct Karen's removal from the respirator.

The assertion that Karen would elect, if competent, to terminate the respirator requires careful examination.

She made these statements at the age of twenty. In the words of her mother, she was full of life. She made them under circumstances where another person was suffering, suffering in at least one instance from severe pain. While perhaps it is not too significant, there is no evidence she is now in pain. Dr. Morse describes her reacting to noxious stimuli—pain—as reflex but not indicative that she is sensing the pain as a functioning human being does. The reaction is described as stereotyped and her reflexes show no adjustment that would indicate she mentally experiences pain.

The conversations with her mother and friends were theoretical ones. She was not personally involved. It was not under the solemn and sobering fact that death is a distinct choice.... Karen Quinlan while she was in complete control of her mental faculties to reason out the staggering magnitude of the decision not to be "kept alive" did not make a decision....

While the repetition of the conversations indicates an awareness of the problems of terminal illness, the elements involved—the vigor of youth that espouses the theoretical good and righteousness, the absence of being presented the question as it applied to her—are not persuasive to establish a probative weight sufficient to persuade this Court that Karen Quinlan would elect her own removal from the respirator.

Authorization Denied

The breadth of the power to act and protect Karen's interests is, I conclude, controlled by a judicial conscience and morality that dictate the determination whether or not Karen Ann Quinlan be removed from the respirator is to be left to the treating physician. It is a medical decision, not a judicial one. I am satisfied that it may be concurred in by the parents but not governed by them. This is so because there is always the dilemma of whether it is the conscious beings relief or the unconscious beings welfare that governs the parental motivation.

It is also noted the concept of the Court's power over a person suffering under a disability is to *protect* and aid the best interests.... Here the authorization sought, if granted, would result in Karen's death. The natural processes of her body are now shown to be sufficiently strong to sustain her by themselves. The authorization, therefore, would be to permit Karen Quinlan to die. This is not protection. It is not something in her best interests, in a temporal sense, and it is in a temporal sense that I must operate whether I believe in life after death or not. The single most important temporal quality Karen Ann Quinlan has is life. This Court will not authorize that life to be taken from her.

As previously indicated, equity follows the law. When positive statutory law exists, an Equity Court cannot supersede or abrogate it. The Common Law concept of homicide, the unlawful killing of one person by another, is reflected in our codified law.... The intentional taking of another's life, regardless of motive, is sufficient grounds for conviction.... Humanitarian motives cannot justify the taking of a human life.... The fact that the victim is on the threshold of death or in terminal condition is no defense to a homicide charge....

New Jersey has adopted the principles of the Common Law against homicide.... It is a reasonable construction that the law of this State would preclude the removal of Karen Quinlan from the respirator. As such, a Court of Equity must follow the positive statutory law; it cannot supersede it. [Footnote: Certainly the question must be asked, did the Common Law contemplate the continued existence of a human being, where that human being, although medically and legally alive, has been given all the diagnostic and therapeutic treatment available and should not the natural functions of that human being be permitted to progress in a normal way without the law against homicide being a deterrent?]

A significant amount of the legal presentation to the court has involved whether the act of removing Karen from the respirator constitutes an affirmative act, or could be considered an act of omission. An intricate discussion on semantics and form is not required since the substance of the sought for authorization would result in the taking of the life of Karen Quinlan when the law of the State indicates that such an authorization would be homicide.

III.

The proceeding brings considerable attention and focus on the physical condition of Karen Quinlan. The results thereof are that in the future the decisions and determinations of the treating doctors and the hospital will be the subject of abnormal scrutiny.

The hospital, through amendment to the pretrial order, seeks a determination "whether the use of the criteria developed and enunciated by the Ad Hoc Committee of Harvard Medical School on or about August 5, 1968, as well as similar criteria, by a physician to assist him in determination of the death of a patient whose cardiopulmonary functions are being artificially sustained, is in accordance with ordinary and standard medical practice."

The scope of that request is extremely broad. It deals not with the question of Karen Quinlan but a theoretical patient. To the extent that it goes beyond this case, it is a request to make a determination in the abstract and not a proper subject for judicial determination....

Counsel for the hospital, to avoid the objection that the request deals in an abstraction and therefore constitutes a proscribed advisory opinion, by letter subsequent to trial, suggests a refinement of the stated issue to refer specifically to Karen Quinlan....

The controversy, however, must have matured and not be something sought in advance of its occurrence....

The application is prospective and in advance of the controversy. The doctors do not seek the determination—in fact, they oppose it.

Additionally, just as the matter of the nature and extent of care and treatment of a patient and therefore the patient's removal from a respirator is a medical decision based upon ordinary practice, so, too, is the decision whether a patient is dead and by what medical criteria. Whether Karen Quinlan one day becomes brain dead and therefore should be removed from the respirator is a decision that will have to be based upon the extant ordinary medical criteria at the time.

IV.

A. Right of Privacy—Right of Self Determination

The "Right of Privacy", identified as such, was first recognized in *Griswold* v. *Connecticut*,...(1965). The source of this right has various explanations.

Justice Blackmun, writing for the [U.S. Supreme] Court in [*Roe v.*] *Wade*, [1972] indicated:

> The Constitution does not explicitly mention any right of
> privacy.... [T]he Court has recognized that a right of personal

privacy, or a guarantee of certain areas or zones of privacy does exist under the Constitution. In varying contexts the Court or individual Justices have, indeed, found at least the roots of that right in the First Amendment...; in the Fourth and Fifth Amendments,...; in the penumbras of the Bill of Rights,...in the Ninth Amendment, ...; or in the concept of liberty guaranteed by the first section of the Fourteenth Amendment,....   These decisions make it clear that only personal rights that can be deemed "fundamental" or "implicit in the concept of ordered liberty," ..., are included in this guarantee of personal privacy....

Plaintiff suggests,... that the right of self determination and right of privacy are synonomous. He also suggests the right is exercisable by a parent for his child.

It is not significant to this opinion whether or not the right of self-determination is within the scope of the right of privacy. What is significant is the extent to which it is subject to a compelling State interest,... and whether the right can be exercised by the parent for his child.

The majority of cases dealing with the refusal of an individual to accept treatment which created an exposure to death involved mature, competent adults.... None, however, dealt with an incompetent adult, as here, totally unaware of the problem.

The disability places the Court in a *parens patriae* circumstance, significantly different from the instance of a competent adult's effort to control his body....

The judicial power to act in the incompetent's best interest in this instance selects continued life and to do so is not violative of a constitutional right.

The majority of the right of privacy cases,... involved a claim which asserted a *life* practice for the individual involved. The compelling state interest found lacking in [these cases] is appropriate here in the state's interest in preservation of life and the extension of the Court's protection to an incompetent....

The power of the parents to exercise the constitutional right is found lacking on several grounds: First, the only cases where a parent has standing to pursue a constitutional right on behalf of an infant are those involving continuing life styles.... Second, the parents urged Dr. Morse to do everything at the outset to save Karen's life. The parents now ask him to abandon his conscience and allow her life to end. In *Roe* v. *Wade,* the court refused to hold that the right of privacy included the unlimited right to body control. In a like manner, the right to privacy, being urged through a parent, must be fettered, when in conflict with a doctor's duty to provide life giving care.

There is no constitutional right to die that can be asserted by a parent for his incompetent adult child.

B. Free Exercise

Religious beliefs are absolute under the Free Exercise Clause but practice in pursuit thereof is not free from governmental regulation....

The religious belief here asserted is twofold:

(1) that the discontinuance of extraordinary care to Karen Quinlan is not a mortal sin; and (2) to interfere with her natural body functions prevents her from reaching a better life in the hereafter.

The absence of mortal sin contention is based, according to Father Trapasso, on the Papal *allocutio* of November 24, 1957 and Roman Catholic traditions and morals. The impetus of the thought is that it is neither a mortal sin to continue nor discontinue "extraordinary" means of support for the body functions. The Court does not consider the "extraordinary" versus "ordinary" discussions viable legal distinctions. The essence of the contention is that it is optional with the Roman Catholic involved and to do either does not conflict with the teachings of the Church. It is not a dogma of the Church. It is not a claim "rooted in religious belief". There is no governmental or other interference with religious belief here that is caused by the Court's refusal to authorize the termination of the respirator.

The temporal world is what the Free Exercise clause deals with—not the hereafter. All instances where a religious belief has been freed of attempted governmental interference dealt with *life* styles and *life* circumstances.

...[T]his Court recognizes the State's interest in preserving life, particularly in this instance where the Court sits in the capacity of *parens patriae.* There is a presumption that one chooses to go on living. The presumption is not overcome by the prior statements of Karen Quinlan. As previously noted, she did not make the statements as a personal confrontation. Additionally, it is not Karen who asserts her religious belief but her parents. In those instances where the parental standing to assert the religious belief has been upheld, it dealt with future life conduct of their children, not the ending of life....

The right to life and the preservation of it are "interests of the highest order" and this Court deems it constitutionally correct to deny Plaintiff's request.

C. Cruel and Unusual Punishment

It is argued to deny the suspension of the "futile use of extraordinary measures after the dignity, beauty, promise and meaning of earthly life have vanished", is cruel and unusual punishment proscribed by the Eighth Amendment of the United States Constitution....

The nature and scope of the Cruel and Unusual Punishment concept is set forth in *Furman* v. *Georgia*... (1972). All of the concurring and dissenting opinions in *Furman* make it clear the proscription is directed to state imposed criminal sanctions, not the situation presented here. Justice Douglas in his concurring opinion, in discussing the fact that the Eighth Amendment may have found its source in the English Bill of Rights of 1689 indicates the concern was "primarily with selection or irregular application of harsh penalties and that its aim was to forbid arbitrary and discriminatory penalties of a severe nature".... The impetus for the concept was to preclude judicial or legislative imposition of punishment in the guise or nature of criminality....

Continuation of medical treatment, in whatever form, where its goal is the sustenance of life is not something degrading, arbitrarily inflicted, unacceptable to contemporary society or unnecessary.

The Eighth Amendment has no applicability to this civil action.

V.

Joseph Quinlan applies to be appointed guardian ad litem for the case of his daughter's person and property.... As next of kin, Mr. Quinlan qualifies to be her guardian,... unless it is shown his appointment would be contrary to Karen's best interest.... The guardian ad litem opposes his appointment.

The responsibility of the guardian over property is to manage the business affairs of the incompetent. There is no reason that Mr. Quinlan should not serve in this capacity.

The responsibility of the guardian over the person of the incompetent is to make the decisions, in this instance that relate to her welfare insofar as those decisions are within the person's control. I have ruled it is a medical decision whether or not Karen should be removed from the respirator. Just as that decision is a medical one, the continued care and treatment of Karen is a medical one. There will be, however, from time to time medical decisions relating to further treatment that will require a guardian's counsel, advice and concurrence. This is reflected by the testimony of Dr. Morse.

Mr. Quinlan impressed me as a very sincere, moral, ethical and religious person. He very obviously anguished over his decision to terminate what he considers the extraordinary care of his daughter. That anguish would be continued and magnified by the inner conflicts he would have if he were required to concur in the day by day decisions on the future care and treatment of his daughter. These conflicts would have to offset his decision making processes. I, therefore find it more appropriate and in Karen's interests if another is appointed.

For the same reasons, I do not feel Mrs. Quinlan should be appointed.

Daniel Coburn, Esq., who has acted on Karen's behalf throughout this proceeding, is appointed the guardian of her person....

U.N. ANTI-ZIONISM RESOLUTION
November 10, 1975

In a move immediately condemned by President Ford and by Congress, the United Nations General Assembly adopted Nov. 10 a resolution equating Zionism with racism. The vote was the strongest anti-Israeli action taken at the U.N. up to that time. The General Assembly had opened its 30th session in September amid rumors that Third World and Communist members would attempt to expel Israel from the United Nations. Israel's U.N. ambassador Chaim Herzog, expressing his nation's outrage over the resolution, declared on the day the vote was taken that the organization was "on its way to becoming the world center of anti-Semitism." Herzog pointed out that the anti-Zionism resolution was adopted on the anniversary of the 1938 anti-Semitic Kristallnacht demonstrations in Nazi Germany, during which Jewish businesses and synagogues were defaced, looted, and burned and individuals were attacked.

Those who defended the resolution maintained that the imposition of an exclusively Jewish state on Palestinian territory had been comparable to the earlier establishment of "racist" colonial regimes in various parts of the world by Western European nations. Current Israeli policies which based citizenship and civil rights on an individual's ethnic origin were, in fact, "racial discrimination...[according to] the approved, formal, authoritative definition of the United Nations," Dr. Abdallah al-Sayegh of Kuwait contended during the General Assembly debate.

The anti-Zionist resolution was adopted by a vote of 72-35 with 32 abstentions. It was solidly supported by Arab countries and the Communist bloc and by a large number of less-developed nations. Among them were some

*that have relatively close links with the United States or receive substantial
U.S. assistance. Included among these were Egypt, Turkey, Jordan, Cyprus
and Mexico.*

American Disapproval

*President Ford condemned the General Assembly's action in a statement
which said:*

*"...the United States deplores the characterization of Zionism as a form
of racism and believes that the adoption of this resolution undermines the
principles on which the United Nations is based. But...will not consider
withdrawal."*

*Only a week before the vote, Ford had submitted to Congress an annual
presidential report on U.S. participation in the United Nations in which he
warned of "divisive actions" taken by the organization in 1974 (see p. 325).*

*The House and Senate adopted separate resolutions Nov. 11 condemning
the General Assembly's vote. In further response, members 1) called for
hearings by the foreign relations committees on future United States
relations with the world body, 2) issued critical statements on the U.N. vote,
and 3) proposed various retaliatory actions including U.S. withdrawal from
the organization and reductions in or a cutoff of U.S. contributions.*

*The General Assembly's vote was the most recent of a series of U.N. ac-
tions that had irritated members of Congress. In 1974, Congress barred
further funding of the U.N. Educational, Scientific and Cultural Organization (UNESCO) because of its anti-Israel actions. On Nov. 6 the United
States notified the International Labor Organization, another U.N. agency,
that it would withdraw in two years unless the agency reversed its trend
toward involvement in increasingly political activities. Further funding had
been terminated by Congress in the State Department appropriations
bill.*

*Text of resolution on Zionism adopted by the General
Assembly of the United Nations Nov. 10, 1975:*

The General Assembly,
Recalling its Resolution 1904 (XVIII) of 20 November, 1963, proclaiming
the United Nations declaration on the elimination of all forms of racial discrimination, and in particular its affirmation that "any doctrine of racial
differentiation or superiority is scientifically false, morally condemnable
and social unjust and dangerous" and its expression of alarm at "the mani-
festations of racial discrimination still in evidence in some areas in the
world, some of which are imposed by certain governments by means of
legislative, administrative or other measures,"
Recalling also that, in its Resolution 3151 G (XXVIII) of 14 December
1973, the General Assembly condemned, inter alia, the unholy alliance
between South African racism and Zionism,

Taking note of the declaration of Mexico on the equality of women and their contribution to development and peace, proclaimed by the World Conference of the International Women's Year, held at Mexico City from 19 June to 2 July 1975, which promulgated the principle that "international co-operation and peace require the achievement of national liberation and independence, the elimination of colonialism and neocolonialism, foreign occupation, Zionism, apartheid, and racial discrimination in all its forms as well as the recognition of the dignity of peoples and their right to self-determination" *[see p. 507]*.

Taking note also of Resolution 77 (XII) adopted by the assembly of heads of state and government of the Organization of African Unity at its 12th ordinary session, held in Kampala from 28 July to 1 Aug., 1975, which considered "that the racist regime in occupied Palestine and racist regimes in Zimbabwe and South Africa have a common imperialist origin, forming a whole and having the same racist structure and being organically linked in their policy aimed at repression of the dignity and integrity of the human being,"

Taking note also of the political declaration and strategy to strengthen international peace and security and to intensify solidarity and mutual assistance among nonaligned countries, adopted at the Conference of Ministers for Foreign Affairs of nonaligned countries held at Lima from 25 to 30 Aug. 1975, which most severely condemned Zionism as a threat to world peace and security and called upon all countries to oppose this racist and imperialist ideology,

Determines that Zionism is a form of racism and racial discrimination.

CRITICISM OF IRS OPERATIONS
November 16, 1975

The Internal Revenue Service often subjected taxpayers to procedures which were "whimsical, inconsistent, unpredictable and highly personal," according to a government study made public Nov. 16. In the first outside review of IRS operations in three decades, a group of consultants to the Administrative Conference of the United States found numerous instances of "dissimilar treatment of similarly situated taxpayers." While IRS agents possessed extraordinary powers, they were subject to few procedural regulations, the study showed. This factor, combined with pressures from an IRS quota system, had produced broad and unjust variations in audit and settlement processes, collection of delinquent taxes and application of civil penalties, the study group concluded.

In addition, contrary to a general public impression that tax returns are confidential, the group reported that numerous federal agencies and the White House had regular access to information on returns or to the actual forms filed by taxpayers. Furthermore, the Justice Department's practice of scanning tax returns of individuals under criminal investigation appeared to violate constitutional guarantees against self-incrimination.

The panel did find that the IRS had made efforts to curb some of these practices. But the report's negative findings, coming on top of previous revelations of political abuses of the IRS during the Nixon administration, prompted The New York Times and other newspapers to urge immediate action to protect the credibility of the service.

The report was the latest of several damaging disclosures about the IRS during 1975. Initially, criticism had focused on improper intelligence-

gathering activities, particularly those of the Special Service Staff (SSS) of the IRS. Established by the Nixon administration in 1969 as an information-gathering office, the SSS had concentrated on political activist groups until its termination in 1973. In December 1974 Sen. Sam J. Ervin Jr. (D N.C.) had characterized SSS operations as "a dangerous abuse of the enormous powers Americans have given the tax-collection arm of the government." A class-action suit brought in March 1975 by the New York branch of the American Civil Liberties Union alleged that the SSS had investigated more than 11,000 individuals and organizations because of "their political beliefs and activities."

A House Government Operations subcommittee conducting oversight hearings into charges of Internal Revenue Service misconduct sought to determine May 14, 1975, whether the IRS was emphasizing its law enforcement functions more than its tax-collection duties. Two months earlier the Miami Daily News had published an article describing the service's "Operation Leprechaun," an effort in 1972 to collect data on the sex and drinking habits of dozens of individuals in the Miami area. IRS officials, after disclaiming any such activity, finally admitted its occurrence when a former IRS informant told the Florida newspaper that she had spied on a number of prominent officials, including the Dade County state's attorney who was then investigating Watergate. An IRS report on the operation published in June said the program had involved only one agent, who had obtained information on 70 persons.

Later in the year, IRS Commissioner Donald C. Alexander came under fire for suspending a broad IRS inquiry into illegal tax shelters for wealthy Americans in the Bahamas and Caribbean Islands. Alexander had acted in August after learning of evidence acquired by what he considered improper methods. The investigation was re-instituted in October with the "tainted" data excluded.

Within days after the Administrative Conference issued its November report, Alexander said he was reviewing its contents and looked forward to "constructive comment." The Administrative Conference is an independent agency established by Congress in 1964 to evaluate the operations of federal agencies. The year-long study of IRS was headed by Charles Davenport, then professor of law at the University of California at Davis.

Excerpts from report on IRS operations published Nov. 16, 1975, by the Administrative Conference of the United States:

Chapter 1 - The Audit and Settlement Processes

Selection of Returns for Examination

Congress has directed the Internal Revenue Service "to the extent...practicable...to proceed, from time to time, through each internal revenue dis-

trict and inquire after...all persons...who may be liable to pay any...tax...."
The Service is further empowered to review books and records relating to
tax returns. For the individual income tax, the Service has heeded the
Congressional direction by each year examining some taxpayers' returns for
accuracy and demanding substantiation of the entries on the return. Such
examinations are called audits.

The Service does not have enough people to audit each of the 80 million
individual income tax returns filed each year. Instead only a small percentage is examined. Such audits increase revenue, and also have a major purpose to induce "voluntary compliance" with the tax laws. The program of
examinations to achieve this end appears to be based on the assumption
that the public will be encouraged to comply if there is a credible possibility
that any particular return may be audited....

A projection of returns to be audited from each of [seven] classes is determined at the beginning of each fiscal year and is communicated to Service
personnel as the Annual Audit Plan. "The Plan" is a management projection developed by the national office with substantial assistance from
management personnel at the district and regional offices. It un-
questionably is management's most important tool for planning and
monitoring the Service's audit activities, and its impact on the auditing
process itself is substantial. Accomplishments toward fulfilling the projected goals are collected monthly, quarterly, and annually, and are
tabulated by district. District management personnel use such statistics in
monitoring the district's success in meeting its assigned objectives, and a
desire to "make the plan" is naturally transmitted to and felt by those who
do the auditing. What results is a sometimes subtle pressure on the examining officer to increase his productivity as measured by number of audits
completed.

The selection of returns for examination begins at the ten IRS Service
Centers, where returns are received from the taxpayer and reviewed
manually and by machine, for math errors and obvious other errors apparent on the return. If errors (either in favor of or against the taxpayer) are
detected, the taxpayer is notified by the Service Center, and the issues so
raised are resolved with its personnel if possible. If not, the return may be
audited.

The computer at the Service Center also gives every return a score for the
tax change that might result from an audit of the return. A high score
means there is a correspondingly high probability that an audit would
result in either a significant increase or decrease of the tax liability shown
on the return ("tax change"). The formula upon which such scoring is based
is developed from the results of an intensive survey of sample tax returns
known as the Taxpayer Compliance Measurement Program (TCMP).

Intensive Audits

This program, conducted in periodic cycles, consists of auditing a random
sample of all returns filed in a particular year. From this sample,

characteristics of returns which have significant tax changes are identified. These characteristics are then built into a formula called the Discriminant Function (DIF) which gives each characteristic and combinations of characteristics on a return a weight related to the amount of tax change found on the sample returns with similar characteristics. The total weight constitutes the DIF score, which purports to indicate the probability of a tax change if the return were audited.

In numerical terms, TCMP examinations are relatively insignificant. About 30,000 returns were examined under this program in the last cycle covering tax year 1971, a small number when compared to the more than 1.6 million taxpayers who were audited under other programs. [But]...standards of examination are more stringent than are standards for other audits.... As a result this audit, done primarily for research purposes, imposes considerable costs in time, money, and frustration on the taxpayer. Furthermore, since the sample is purely a random one, not geared to the potentiality of error, the cost of improving the audit system as a whole is largely borne by those unfortunate and presumably faultless taxpayers who are selected for intensive audit under the TCMP....

[I]t is recommended that the Service establish units of especially skilled examiners to perform TCMP examinations. *(Recommendation 1-V).*

....[T]he fashion in which most returns are chosen for audit [is that] they are routinely forwarded in batches by the Service Center to the district office and ultimately assigned to an examiner. Because several persons along the way consider the suitability of each return for audit, there is only a slight possibility that such Service personnel might abuse their screening power and exercise it maliciously or capriciously.

Non-Routine Selection

Other returns are individually selected for examination at the initiative of examiners in the district or branch offices. The examiner's discretion to requisition returns from the Service Center is relatively unchecked, and therefore presents a greater potential for abuse. For example, an examiner may, as a result of findings during an audit, decide that the return of another taxpayer should be examined. The Department of Justice may request that a particular return be examined. Or information suggesting that a taxpayer be audited may be sent to the Service from outside sources. In such cases, individual Service personnel exercise a high degree of discretion in deciding whether the individual returns should be examined. Indeed, the examiner may initiate the requisition entirely for reasons of his own. The examiner need only obtain his immediate supervisor's approval to request a return for audit.... The examiner's discretion is further enhanced by the fact that supervisors generally seem to consider approval a mere ministerial duty. There exists, then, the danger that a return may be requisitioned for examination by reason of the whim or malice of an examiner. A similar potential for abuse lies in the examining agent's power to earmark the return of a taxpayer he is currently auditing for audit in a future year.

Again, approval is perfunctory, and no directives require the supervisor to scrutinize the request for necessity and propriety....

[I]t is recommended that each examining officer's requisition of a return be supported by written reasons, for review by his manager. *(Recommendation 1-I).*

Second, if the Service carried out a systematic, ongoing evaluation of the reasons assigned for the selection of returns for audit, improper return selection could be restricted. *It is therefore recommended* that the IRS develop procedures to permit such verification, in a fashion that will simplify review by the Service's Internal Audit Division and facilitate Congressional oversight of the audit selection process. *(Recommendation 1-IV).* One such procedure was begun during the course of this study.

Third...*it is recommended* that each taxpayer be notified of the reason that his return was selected for audit, that programs and criteria for selection be established in advance to the maximum extent feasible, and that the Service publish annual statistics pertinent to each of its selection programs and criteria. *(Recommendation 1-II)....*

The Examination

....Despite sincere efforts on the part of the Service to lessen...apprehensions, the confrontation between the tax auditor and the taxpayer remains essentially an adversary proceeding. Its adversary nature is heightened by the differing attitudes of examiner and taxpayer. The examiner tends to believe that tax returns in general contain many intentional or careless inaccuracies. As to the particular return before him, he knows that it was probably scientifically selected by a computer.... In the back of the examiner's mind is the knowledge that his failure to find a tax change in a large number of returns may result in a review of his returns or a discussion of his skills, or both. It seems significant that examinations have long been referred to as "enforcement activity." (The 1974 Annual Report, issued as this study was nearing completion, used the word "compliance" in place of "enforcement.")...

Likewise, the taxpayer enters the fray with his own well-established notions and indignation at being called for audit. He also may be resentful about well-publicized tax law preferences, such as real estate tax shelters, or some real or presumed special treatment given to more prominent personalities. His irritation is compounded by the knowledge that the audit experience will cost him time and perhaps money in additional tax assessments or the need to hire professional help.

Further, the average taxpayer is bewildered by the complexity of the tax law and of the auditing procedures, and often learns only then of the degree of verification of items listed on his return that will be required. To reduce this lack of knowledge about the requirement for verification during audit, *it is recommended* that the Service annually include, along with the blank tax forms sent to taxpayers, information telling taxpayers: (1) that all supporting records should be retained for at least three years; (2) that an audit, if there is to be one, is not likely to commence for some time after the return has been filed, and (3) that receipt of a refund does not preclude audit. *(Recommendation 1-VI).*

Study of Motivations for Compliance

The Service regards the audit process as its primary implement to induce voluntary compliance with the laws requiring the filing of accurate returns and payment of taxes.... There may be techniques other than audit that would encourage greater compliance with the law. The Internal Revenue Service does not really claim to understand the complexities of the taxpayer motivations involved in compliance or noncompliance.... The Service has limited resources, and Congress has not to this time provided funds for a study that would evaluate various methods to measure and promote compliance with the tax laws. *It is recommended* that Congress provide funds for such a study. *(Recommendation 1-VII)....*

Settlement Results and Their Variations

Disputatious taxpayers seem to fare better as they progress up the administrative settlement ladder. In 1971, for example, District Conferees settled for approximately 42 percent of the amount originally assessed by the examiners, whereas Appellate Conferees settled their cases at about 30 percent of the initial claim. Cases settled at the Tax Court level resulted in a 32 percent collection rate, while in cases actually tried by the court the Service collected 41 percent. These disparities are understandable because of the differing settlement standards and strategies employed at each level of the process.

Less understandable, though, are the significant geographical variations in settlement results, both at the District Conference level and the regional Appellate Conference level. In 1971, for instance, the Cincinnati District sustained only 19 percent of the initial assessments while the Newark District sustained 84 percent. Similar variations occurred at the Appellate Conferee stage. Of course some part of these disparities might be explainable by differences in examiner expertise, or by the degree to which different District Directors emphasize the preliminary informal conference procedure, but the extent of such discrepancies raises doubt about whether similarly situated taxpayers have been receiving substantially equivalent treatment in the audit and settlement process. The Service, to its credit, has adopted a number of procedures aimed at encouraging increased consultation and uniformity within and among districts. However, in order better to inform itself as well as the public about settlement variations, *it is recommended* that the Service should annually publish an analysis of a representative sample of District and Appellate Conference settlements.... *(Recommendation 1-VIII).*

The recommended study ought to shed light on the reasons for the tendency of the Service to settle cases involving large sums of money for a lower percentage of the proposed assessment than cases involving relatively small sums of money. This phenomenon no doubt can be explained in part by the simple observation that the larger assessments will be resisted more tenaciously by the taxpayer, whose threat of appeal and suit is more credible. This tendency undoubtedly is also related to the tendency that the quality of the taxpayer's representation increases as the amount at issue increases.

Taxpayer Representation Recommended

...Although the Service has made efforts to promote objectivity on the part of its examiners and conferees, and has instructed them not to take advantage of the unrepresented, the unrepresented taxpayer is nevertheless at a great disadvantage in the essentially adversary audit and settlement processes....

This imbalance could be at least partially redressed by establishment of an organization to offer advice and representational assistance to some taxpayers. Accordingly, *it is recommended* that Congress establish a Taxpayer Assistance Center, independent of the Department of the Treasury, to offer advice, assistance and representation to certain classes of individual income taxpayers. The Center would advise and represent taxpayers in the preparation for and conduct of audits and appeals therefrom. The Center should be authorized to charge a reasonable and standard fee to taxpayers who have an ability to pay such a fee. For reasons to be mentioned presently, it is suggested that the assistance of the Center be made available to individual income taxpayers who have been notified that they will undergo examination of their returns by means of office or correspondence audits, in contrast to field audits. *(Recommendation 1-IX)*.

Concededly, it would be a difficult task for Congress to draw an appropriate line between those who should have access to such assistance and those who should not. One approach would distinguish the predominant purposes of the Service in its application of the audit function to various categories of taxpayers—whether the purpose is primarily to raise additional revenue or is primarily to maintain credibility in enforcement of the tax laws. Where the revenue motive is predominant, and returns in a given category are regularly expected to yield substantial additional revenue, it is also likely to be worthwhile from the standpoint of taxpayers in that category to endure ultimate audit rather than to file returns resolving all doubts in the government's favor....

At the other extreme are non-business tax returns showing under $10,000 of income. Although audits of these returns are on the whole cost-efficient to the Service because they raise more revenue than the cost of performing the audits, they are not nearly as remunerative as other audits in higher income brackets. The audit of low income returns is justified by the Service's desire to maintain an enforcement "presence" at each income level.... [T]he audit and appeal system is not cost-effective for this person. For the amounts involved, the cost of commercial or professional assistance in most cases will far exceed the potential saving in taxes....

The line between giving assistance and not giving assistance would lie somewhere between these extremes. Until that line is authoritatively drawn in some other fashion, a practical division can be made by viewing returns subjected to field audits as generally being examined primarily to raise revenue, and viewing office and correspondence audits as being conducted primarily for enforcement purposes. Under the approach outlined, the latter category would be considered for assistance.

Chapter 2 - Collection of Delinquent Taxes

Congress has conferred drastic powers upon the Internal Revenue Service forcibly to collect taxes from delinquent taxpayers. By law, the IRS is authorized without an adjudicatory hearing, summarily to place a lien on, to levy upon, or to seize and sell any or all property and rights to property belonging to a taxpayer with a tax delinquency.

At the same time Congress has provided little guidance on how the IRS should use its collection powers. Nor has there been much judicial direction supplied by the courts. The result is a large body of discretionary authority given to the IRS to collect taxes forcibly. Inevitably, such discretionary power is not uniformly exercised and is open to administrative abuse....

In 1973, 77.7 million individual tax returns were filed. Slightly less than 3 million of them showed an unpaid balance due. Another 1.6 million revealed a tax deficiency after the Service Center's mathematical check. In all, 4.6 million individual returns indicated that taxpayer contact was necessary to collect the missing revenues.

Once detected, the errors or omissions trigger a series of Service Center computer-printed notices to taxpayers whose accounts show a balance due. As many as four such notices may be mailed to a taxpayer.

Notice and Demand

....It is [the fourth] Final Notice Before Seizure which, by formal notice of delinquency and demand for payment thereof, lays the legal groundwork for subsequent imposition of the Service's potent summary powers of collection. The present practices of the Service in regard to this notice create the possibility of unfairness and unnecessary irritation for the taxpayer....

If the computer-printed notices do not produce payment, a Service Center automatically will issue a Taxpayer Delinquent Account (TDA) for any deficiency above a specified minimum dollar amount set by the Service. The TDA is forwarded to the District Office, where it is screened by the Office Branch, which attempts to collect the tax from the taxpayer through office interviews, correspondence or limited field contact. Three out of four delinquent taxpayer accounts are settled in the District Office without application of any of the Service's formidable forcible collection powers.

In principle, no Final Notice Before Seizure should be sent to a taxpayer unless it is clear that the circumstances will warrant the application of levy or seizure power. Since these notices are computer-generated by Service Centers without benefit of the sort of investigation of a taxpayer's circumstances that can be undertaken by the District Office, many Final Notices in response to which the taxpayer does not promptly pay his account will in fact not be followed by a decision to seize the taxpayer's property. Since decisions to seize property are not automated, but made by Service personnel (now by Revenue Officers—in the future by Group Managers, if *Recommendation 2-IV.A.* is adopted) on a case-by-case basis, the timing of the decisions is far from uniform, nor is it as prompt as the Final Notice Before Seizure implies it will be, i.e., 10 days after. The longer the interval between the mailing of the Final Notice and the initiation of forcible action to collect the tax, the greater the possibility of surprise to the taxpayer and resentment by him when forcible action is actually taken....

Liens

In legal theory under the tax code, a lien in favor of the government arises against all taxpayer property and rights to property, whether real or personal, the moment the Internal Revenue Service assesses any tax liability against a taxpayer. The tax code also seems to provide, still as a matter of theory, that the lien attaches the moment, following a demand for payment of the Service-assessed tax liability, when the taxpayer "neglects or refuses to pay the same." For any practical purpose, it appears that a lien, in the amount of the assessed tax liability, only takes priority over the rights of third parties when the Service files for official public record a notice of the lien. When notice of a lien is filed, generally speaking in places prescribed by state law, the lien becomes an encumbrance on the taxpayer's property which very substantially reduces his ability to make legally effective dispositions thereof.... *[I]t is recommended* that the Internal Revenue Service provide specific guidance to make the determination as to whether and when to file notices of liens. *(Recommendation 2-II(1).)*

As a matter of legal theory under the tax code, a tax lien continues until the tax liability has been satisfied or has become legally unenforceable.... The practical effects of a lien of which notice has been filed in a public record are likely to persist until a certificate of release of the lien has been filed wherever the notice of lien was filed. However, there is no assurance that this will take place. Since the Service has no legal obligation, procedure, or practice to notify a taxpayer when a notice of lien is filed, he may not know it and may, therefore, not seek a formal release certificate—or, if he does, may not know where to file it. Furthermore, nothing mandates the Service to initiate release of a lien, to notify the taxpayer if and when it does so, or to file a certificate of discharge wherever notice of a lien was filed. Nor has the Service adopted a regular and reliable practice of doing any of these things. There can be no possible justification for a taxpayer to have to suffer disadvantage, embarrassment, or other inconvenience due to the persistence of a shadow on his clear interest in property created by a recorded lien that has not been discharged on the record. Accordingly, *it is recommended* that the Internal Revenue Service adopt procedures that will notify a taxpayer whenever notice of a lien is filed against his property in any public record and that will provide, without application by the taxpayer, for the recording of a certificate of discharge of any such lien, upon its release, wherever notice of the lien was filed. *(Recommendations 2-II(2) & (3).)*

Levies

A more powerful instrument available to the Collection Division of the IRS to collect delinquent taxes is its levy authority. Although it is imposed in the cases of only a small number of the taxpayers who have failed to meet their tax obligations, those with regard to whom it is imposed frequently suffer severely. In the fiscal year ending June 30, 1974, 582,701 notices of levy were made.

The levy procedure is applied to third parties, such as employers, stock brokers, insurance agents, and bankers holding any asset—usually liquid—owned by the taxpayer. Levies attach to earned salaries and wages, bank accounts, investment accounts, and all accounts receivable. The third-party served with notice of a tax levy is obligated to surrender the property on demand. If he refuses, he is held personally liable for the tax due, interest charges, costs, and penalties, unless he has a reasonable cause for his refusal.

A court judgment or court order is not required before the imposition of a levy, nor is notification of the taxpayer required, beyond the computer-printed Final Notice Before Seizure, except in cases where his salary is to be garnished.

As in most summary actions, the Revenue Officer has enormous discretion in deciding to impose a levy. The Service instructs only that his action be "judicious" in the application of levy. But judiciousnes is interpreted differently by different members of the IRS and in some cases in such a manner as to preclude the delinquent taxpayer from paying voluntarily. The Service suggests but does not require that the officer contact the taxpayer to advise him of the possible consequences. One of the few restrictions the officer faces in deciding when to exercise levy is a requirement that he consider the impact his action may have in what the Service refers to as "significant" cases, i.e., those which might cause embarrassment to the Service by adversely affecting large numbers of innocent third parties whose circumstances would be disrupted by levy action. Examples would be levies in case of a hospital, a newspaper, or a large, "viable" business. Avoiding levy in such cases, while perhaps saving the IRS potential embarrassment, does not constitute even-handed treatment of all taxpayers in similar tax-delinquent situations. Accordingly, *it is recommended* that the Internal Revenue Service establish guidelines that will assure judicious and even-handed application of the levy power and that will specify the circumstances constituting a reasonable opportunity for the taxpayer to pay his tax liability to avoid levy on his property. *(Recommendation 2-III.A.)...*

It is recommended that the Internal Revenue Service establish more specific criteria and procedures to make application of the undue hardship principle more uniform. There should be criteria for common necessaries of life.... In addition, the Service should allow a minimum subsistence exemption from the initial levy on the salary or wages of a taxpayer being subject to levy for the first time. *(Recommendations 2-V, 2-III.B.)*

Seizure and Sale

The power of the Internal Revenue Service to seize a taxpayer's property for sale is virtually absolute. Seizure may be made to collect taxes, interest, and additions to the tax in the form of penalties.

There are very few seizures of property in comparison with the number of lien notice filings or levies on wages and salaries and other liquid assets. Seizures are imposed in case of well under 1 percent of taxpayer delinquent accounts; they are ordinarily applied to tangible property in the taxpayer's possession. The exercise of seizure power has been delegated to journeymen Revenue Officers. There is no requirement for the Revenue Officer to give specific prior notice of seizure to the taxpayer beyond the general warning contained in the Service Center's computer-printed Final Notice Before Seizure. There is no requirement that the Revenue Officer seek approval of his superior before he seizes property, although he often does so in practice. There is no requirement that seizure of an individual taxpayer's property be made on a last-resort-basis as there is in case of delinquent business taxpayers. Consequently, Revenue Officers have broad and essentially unguided discretion in deciding to exercise this confiscatory power.

From the time property is seized, the Service becomes responsible for the seized property until it is sold and may incur expenses, such as insurance or guards, to protect it. The proceeds of sale of seized property are applied first, to pay the expenses of seizure, protection, and sale of the property, next, to pay any specific unpaid Federal tax liability on the property itself, and finally, to pay the delinquent tax of the taxpayer on account of which the property was seized and sold....

As might be expected, the present Service guidelines, confusing as they are, lean strongly toward protecting the government. In spite of this, there have been many cases when the proceeds of sales of seized property have not even been sufficient to pay the Service's expenses of seizure, protection, and sale of the property. In any such case, the taxpayer's situation is worsened, with little or no benefit to the government, as a result of the Service's action....

The risk of imprudent and unfair seizures and sales is especially great when property to be seized is subject to an encumbrance with priority over the Federal tax lien for the delinquency involved. This makes it more difficult to fix a fair minimum sale price and to estimate what the character of bidding at the sale will be. In spite of these difficulties, it seems clear that the Service should never seize or sell a taxpayer's residual (after allowance for any prior encumbrance) interest in property, or "equity [in property] under the lien" as the Service calls it, unless the proceeds of sale will substantially exceed the Service's costs and expenditures....

Absence of Data

A serious obstacle to formulating Service guidelines for the making of decisions about when to exercise the power of seizure and sale to collect delinquent tax accounts is the absence of adequate, systematic data about the Service's practices and their consequences. The Service has records of the number of seizures of property which it makes. However, it has no overall records of how many sales ensue, of the gross proceeds of sales, of its expenses of seizure, protection, and sale of property, of the amount of funds obtained from sales applied to reduction of tax liabilities, of the personnel and other overhead costs incurred in seizure and sale proceedings, of the number of or reasons for releases back to taxpayers of seized property. Ad hoc selective studies by the Service's Internal Audit Division have identified serious deficiencies in achieving the Service's own existing policy objectives in relation to seizures and sales. Thus, *it is recommended* that in order better to evaluate and execute its policies and procedures, the Internal Revenue Service should, at least from time to time, collect, tabulate, and analyze data relative to all the matters identified above. *(Recommendation 2-IV-B).*

Jeopardy and Termination Assessments

....Under certain exceptional circumstances, when collection of a tax deficiency appears to be in jeopardy, the IRS is empowered by the tax code to collect forcibly unpaid taxes through jeopardy or termination assessment procedures, followed by seizure and sale, without any prior notice to the taxpayer. Although these procedures are applied to few tax delinquents, even their infrequent use has had crushing impact upon some taxpayers and has led to numerous charges of misuse of IRS power.

Despite the havoc which can be wrought by jeopardy assessments, the sole criterion specified in the tax code (Section 6861) to determine whether such assessment will be made is a *belief* by the IRS that collection of a tax deficiency "will be jeopardized by delay."

How is a taxpayer actually selected by the Service for jeopardy assessments? Until recently revenue agents, who are likely to be the prime movers in initiating such assessments, have been advised by the Service that "certain conditions and circumstances can properly be considered establishing prima facie cases" in which a jeopardy assessment should be made. These prima facie cases include: present and former major operators in the criminal field; bookies and gamblers; border hoppers; "individuals engaged in other activities generally regarded as illegal"; and taxpayers consistently suffering business or personal losses. Generally speaking, these classifications provide no factual basis for a belief that collection of any particular taxpayer's tax will be jeopardized by delay, and they thereby create a reservoir of discretion to initiate a jeopardy assessment without regard to whether collection of a tax deficiency actually is in jeopardy....

Impact of Jeopardy Assessments

The total number of taxpayers subjected to jeopardy assessment has been small. In fiscal year 1972, for example, there were 375. In the first nine months of fiscal year 1974 there were 479. Nevertheless, the consequences can be disastrous for those individual taxpayers selected and whose assets are seized immediately. In one case a jeopardy assessment of $533,000 was made when the maximum tax liability was probably $58,000. In another case an assessment of $3 million was made after revenue agents had testified in a criminal case that the tax liability did not exceed $300,000. The impact of immediate seizure and inordinately high assessment tends to leave the taxpayer with very little with which to post a bond and in many cases reduces him to penury overnight....

Although a jeopardy assessment and consequent seizure can be made without prior notice to the taxpayer, the Service is obliged within 60 days thereafter to send the taxpayer a Statutory Notice of Deficiency. By the time the taxpayer receives this notice it is likely, due to levy and seizure action, that he will not have the wherewithal to pay the asserted deficiency, which he must do as a precondition to contesting the assessment by a suit for refund in the U.S. Court of Claims or a U.S. District Court. However, when he receives the Statutory Notice, he may, without first paying the tax, contest the deficiency in the Tax Court whose jurisdiction is based only on notice of deficiency being given. The Tax Court can abate the assessment if it is excessive, withdraw it altogether if no collection jeopardy is found, and, of course, release any or all assets levied or seized. The impact of the jeopardy assessment may be so crushing as to make it difficult for the taxpayer to take advantage of his right to Tax Court review of the Service's action—but the right exists. The same is not true in the case of termination assessments as will be explained below.

Termination Assessments

As practiced by the Service, termination assessment is a summary collection tool more dangerously powerful than jeopardy assessment and subject to still greater potential abuse....

[T]here are instances when the Service may need to act promptly before any tax is due, in order to safeguard from evasive taxpayer conduct its opportunity to collect taxes that will become due in the future. To meet this need, the tax code (Section 6851) empowers the Service without any prior notice, to terminate a taxpayer's taxable year at any time that it finds that the taxpayer "designs quickly to depart from the United States or to remove his property therefrom, or to conceal himself or his property..., or to do any other act tending..." to frustrate future collection of the current or

841

preceding year's income tax. Termination of the taxable year has the effect
of making immediately due and payable income tax for the current (or
preceding) year and thereby creating the basis for the Service to assess a tax
deficiency and move summarily (by levy or seizure) to collect it....

An assessment after termination of tax year is potentially more damaging
to a taxpayer than a jeopardy assessment because it may leave him with absolutely no judicial review recourse to contest the tax deficiency, the legality of the assessment (and consequent levy or seizure), or the amount of the
assessment. The reason for this is that the Service does not issue a
Statutory Notice of Deficiency in connection with a termination
assessment. As a consequence, the tax-year-terminated taxpayer, whose opportunity to sue for a refund is as blighted as that of a jeopardy assessee,
cannot even have access to the Tax Court....

Punitive Uses of Assessments

In many cases the size of the assessment has been equal to the value of
goods seized in police raids. The obvious conclusion is that its size is the
result of pure guesswork. The service, hence, has used termination
assessments as a means of summary, extra-judicial punishment for
criminality which neither the tax code nor the agency was established to
impose. In any event, the size of the assessment is frequently in excess of the
taxpayer's net worth thereby leaving him [in] a position unable to pay the
tax and without access to the courts.

Although the tax code provision for tax-year-termination calls for IRS
findings of taxpayer behavior which, if made, constitute presumptive
evidence of jeopardy, the Service has given "prima facie" cases, referred to
above, the same triggering significance for tax-year-termination as for
jeopardy assessment. The availability of this basis for decision-making
about both jeopardy and termination may have contributed to the prostitution of these powers to serve goals of criminal law enforcement unrelated, or
very marginally related, to the collection of taxes as occurred, for example,
in the so-called Narcotics Traffickers Program of the early 1970's. It appears
that Commissioner of Internal Revenue Donald C. Alexander put an end to
the program in 1974. However, there is no published evidence in IRS
guidelines to indicate how the Service's procedures have been altered to
help guard against renewed misapplication of IRS summary tax collection
powers to some future anti-crime initiative....

Alternatives to Forcible Collection

....[E]xperience has shown that most of the delinquencies will be collected
eventually—either as offsets to future tax refunds, as voluntary payments,
or because the addition of subsequent liabilities, accumulated penalties
and interest charges raise the amount above the tolerance level, leading to
collection action....

The tax code, while enumerating a number of methods for forcible collection of delinquent taxes, is silent on the payment of delinquent taxes by installments. This silence is interpreted by the IRS as the denial of a right to pay by such a method. Consequently, Service personnel are directed to request immediate satisfaction of the tax debt. If the taxpayer cannot comply, he is requested to fill out a financial statement. If there are no assets to seize, the Service has no choice but to accept installment payments.... [T]he IRS should be encouraged to liberalize installment payment procedures, at least to the extent that they involve smaller liabilities.

In 1973, collection efforts were suspended on 313,884 delinquent accounts—representing $397,459,356—which were reported uncollectible. During the same year, the Service's field offices received nearly 3 million new delinquent accounts representing over $5 billion. Hence, the Service appears to write off accounts on a grand scale, but the influx of new accounts requires that some limit be placed on efforts to collect old ones.

At some point the cost of collection exceeds the amount to be collected, particularly on small-delinquency accounts. Cost considerations do seem to outweigh any undesirable impact on voluntary compliance which might result from writing off accounts. Despite this, some accounts listed as uncollectible were reported as such merely because the tax debt could not be satisfied immediately. IRS Collection personnel commonly indicate that if a balance due can be paid only in installments and the schedule of payments is too long or their size too small, the account will be written off....

Employer Tax Delinquents

....Federal Tax Deposits (FTDs) consisting of the funds withheld from employees are required to be paid over to designated depository banks within three banking days after they have been withheld. Employer reports of tax withholdings are required on a quarterly basis....

....In times of high interest rates and a stagnant economy, money owed the government can constitute a source of ready and cheap capital to unscrupulous or financially troubled employers. Until July, 1975, the interest on withholding tax deficiencies was only 6 percent per year. There is a one-time penalty for underpayment of withheld taxes in the amount of 5 percent of the deficiency, and a monthly penalty of 0.5 percent of the unpaid balance limited to a maximum of 25 percent. Starting July 1, 1975, the interest rate on deficiencies was raised to 9 percent, which may curtail, at least for the time being, the tendency of businesses hard-pressed for cash to borrow withheld taxes from the government.

The cheaper cost of "borrowing" from the government resulted in 1973 in 2.3 million "balance due" returns filed by employers. Another 180,000 returns contained errors in arithmetic or preparation which, when corrected, resulted in a balance due to the government. In all, 15 percent of 1973 quarterly returns were not fully paid. While many of these balances were quickly satisfied in response to demands for payment, the Service assigned more than 1.5 million TDA's [Taxpayer Deficiency Accounts] to local offices for collection of $2.5 billion in overdue withheld taxes. Although there are no accurate statistics available, the consensus is that at least 50 percent of the employers on whom TDA's are issued have been delinquent in the past....

Uneven Enforcement

The Service has not had as high a success rate in dealing with delinquent employers as it has with individuals in protecting Federal revenues. Part of this failure stems from the reluctance of Revenue Officers to seize assets of a going-business to enforce the government claim. It further appears that the larger the business and the longer it has been established, the less likely it is that the Service will move forcibly. The Service's relatively lighthanded treatment of business delinquents may reflect undue concern about the repercussions that firmer treatment might arouse among their employees and in their communities.

Business taxpayers should be treated even-handedly and firmly where collection of delinquent taxes is involved, except perhaps when it is clear that hasty, forcible collection would result in very serious, long-term damage to the local economy. The Internal Revenue Service does not have authority to decide to go easy on businesses that do not pay taxes in a timely fashion.

Compounding the difficulty of tax collection efforts from delinquent business taxpayers is the reluctance of the judiciary and U.S. Attorneys to deal with business tax enforcement cases generated by the Service. Judicial reluctance is manifested in the light penalties imposed on business officers. This galls the Service because whether they are paid over or not, withheld taxes must be credited to employee accounts. U.S. Attorneys prefer not to handle the cases at all....

Chapter 3 - Civil Penalties

The Internal Revenue Code contains a complex and in some ways overlapping assortment of civil penalties that the Internal Revenue Service can impose on the taxpayer. Such penalties call for money payments in addition to the tax, as a consequence of culpable conduct, and are regarded as necessary for assuring compliance with the tax laws. The existence of such penalties, routinely utilized and substantial in relation to the amount of tax, is thought to deter intentional violations and to discourage negligence.

There is, though, a lack of information to support the generally held rationale that the civil penalties are an effective method for achieving compliance with the tax laws. The Internal Revenue Service does not possess figures on how many penalties are assessed, the size of the penalties in relation to taxes due, how often the penalties are litigated, or how often penalties are disposed of in the settlement process. Such information obviously is of importance in determining the deterrent value of the penalty system and how effectively and fairly it is working. *It is recommended* that the Internal Revenue Service publish an annual study on the assessment and collection of civil penalties. *(Recommendation 3-I.)...*

Penalties for Underpayment of Taxes

There is a serious question, however, whether the present system of penalties for underpayment of tax is so structured and administered that it properly fulfills its punitive and deterrent roles. A basic shortcoming in the present system is a lack of gradations in the penalties, with the result that the punishment does not always fit the offense. Too often, for example, conduct amounting to or approaching fraud is penalized as mere negligence. *It is recommended,* therefore, that a more flexible range of penalties be established, to cover intentional violations that may fall short of fraud. *(Recommendation 3-II.)*

The most serious penalty is for fraud. It is also the most ill-defined and most unevenly applied penalty.... [C]ivil fraud has come to mean something different from mere intentional inaccuracy in a tax return. Rather, it has come to be nearly equated with criminal tax evasion, which involves an aggravated willful attempt to evade taxes and carries with it a penalty of imprisonment or fine. But there are administrative distinctions between criminal and civil fraud cases.... Within the Service, however, there appears to be a reluctance to press civil fraud. An internal review by the Service last year showed considerable variation in the use of the civil fraud penalty from district to district. The review focussed on cases that were referred back by the Intelligence Division. In the Wilmington District, examining agents assessed civil fraud penalties in 77 percent of the cases, and in the Cincinnati district it was 55 percent. But the figure was only 36 percent in New Orleans, 20 percent in Philadelphia and six percent in Dallas.

Several reasons appear for this uneven use of the civil fraud penalty. Examining agents are under pressure to complete a large volume of agreed cases, and assertion of fraud tends to delay completion of a case. The belief has grown among agents that cases not involving larger dollar amounts will not be pressed by management, and management in turn has come to the conclusion that the courts will limit penalties to situations involving highly flagrant behavior. Consequently, in many districts, the civil fraud penalty is reserved for cases in which criminal fraud is likely to be present....

...[J]udicial and administration constructions that have broadened the definition of negligence and narrowed the definition of fraud reflect a defect in the tax statutes as they presently are enforced. There is no penalty between the mild five percent penalty for negligence and the 50 percent penalty reserved for highly culpable conduct. However, an immense middle ground exists. There is an endless array of cases which involve reckless or intentional overstatement of deductions or understatements of income where the inaccuracy fails to reach the level of quasi-criminality now required to establish fraud. In effect, there is a vast "excluded middle" in the penalty system....

[One] approach...*that is recommended* is creation of a new intermediate penalty of, say, 25 percent. *(Recommendation 3-II(3).)* This penalty would apply to conduct more culpable than negligence but less culpable than quasi-criminal fraud or willful evasion. This approach would have the advantage of preserving the small but useful five percent penalty for negligence and the heavy 50 percent for aggravated tax evasion. The new intermediate penalty would be sufficiently severe that a taxpayer would have to weigh it in making any plans to cheat....

The new in-between penalty would clearly cover conduct not serious enough to constitute willful tax evasion under the present civil fraud penalties but more egregious than ordinary carelessness. It would cover both intentionally inaccurate returns and those where the taxpayer proceeded despite his lack of knowledge that the figures on his return were correct.

In asserting the new penalty, it would be important to impose the burden of proof on the taxpayer to demonstrate that his conduct was not reckless or intentional.... In civil fraud, the burden of proof is placed on the government, reflecting the quasi-criminal nature of the charge. Under court rulings, the government has the additional burden of demonstrating bad faith or intentional wrong-doing, which means establishing the taxpayer's state of mind in preparing a return. Indeed, many rather obvious cases of intentional cheating fail to be treated as fraud under present law because of the onerous burden placed on the IRS of establishing the taxpayer's state of mind. Under the lesser intermediate penalty, the same burden of proof should not be imposed on the government. In effect, the government is waiving charges of civil fraud, which intentional inaccuracies might have amounted to in many cases. In return, the taxpayer should assume the burden of demonstrating that his conduct was not reckless or intentional. There would be a difference, however, in the standards of proof. In civil fraud, the government must prove its case in a clear and convincing fashion. With the proposed intermediate penalty, the taxpayer should only have to prove his case by a preponderance of the evidence....

Assessment of Penalties for Different Degrees of Culpability

Under present law, the IRS, in assessing fraud penalties, does not distinguish between deficiencies caused by fraud or intentional errors and those caused by negligence or honest mistakes. The practice is to impose the 50 percent penalty for fraud on the entire deficiency even though only part of the deficiency is attributable to fraud.

The result quite frequently is a disproportionate and unfair penalty. For example, a taxpayer may have fraudulently evaded $5,000 in taxes. At the same time he may have another deficiency of $80,000 for claiming excessive depreciation, which occurred because of a good-faith but erroneous use of the wrong method of depreciation, and thus, at most, should be subject to the five percent penalty for negligence. Under present practice, the tax-payer would be required to pay a civil fraud penalty of $42,500—or 50 percent of the total deficiency of $85,000—even though only $5,000 of the deficiency was clearly attributable to fraud....

It is therefore recommended that, in imposing any of the penalties for underpayment of tax, each penalty rate should be applied only to that portion of the underpayment as is attributable to conduct that is liable for such rate....

Publicity of Civil Fraud Penalties

By law and by practice, a distinction is drawn between the publicity given criminal tax convictions and penalties imposed for civil fraud. The IRS publicizes criminal tax convictions, both those arising from guilty pleas as well as those from guilty verdicts. Such publicity obviously is viewed by the IRS as essential if criminal tax law enforcement is to have a deterrent impact upon the taxpaying public.

But the IRS does not publicize the imposition of the 50 percent civil penalty for fraud. If the taxpayer litigates the penalty, his name will appear in a court-reported case, but generally the press and the public would take no notice. If the taxpayer settles his case administratively, there is no publicity at all.... Most civil fraud cases are quasi-criminal in nature, characterized by highly blameworthy conduct, much worse than garden-variety tax chiseling. It can be argued that taxpayers who engage in such fraud have forfeited their right to privacy of tax data; that publicity for the penalty would increase its deterrent effect; and moreover, that publicity in itself would be a severe sanction, to many persons worse than any money penalty....

Penalties for Delinquencies in Filing Returns and Paying Taxes

The Internal Revenue Code (Section 6651) provides a penalty for failure to file a tax return on time. The penalty is five percent of the amount of the tax in the first month and an additional five percent for each succeeding month, up to a total penalty not exceeding 25 percent of the tax. However, the penalty is not imposed if the taxpayer establishes that his late filing "is due to reasonable cause and not due to willful neglect."

....There is a question, however, whether the penalty for non-filing does not escalate too quickly and terminate too soon. The five percent penalty for the first month obviously provides an incentive for the taxpayer to get his return in on time. But after the first month, the penalty escalates at an effective annual rate, 60 percent on the entire tax, that generally would be viewed as very steep, particularly so when the penalty for failure to pay a tax shown on a return is at the rate of only 1/2 of one percent per month or six percent annually. Moreover, the rapid escalation of the penalty seems to create an undesired side effect of encouraging procrastination on the part of the taxpayer after five months. When the maximum penalty has been reached after five months, the penalty creates no additional pressure to file.

It is recommended, therefore, that the penalty be stretched out over a longer period of time, and that after the first month the rate at which the penalty accrues be reduced....

Administrative and Judicial Review of Late-Filing and Failure-to-Pay Penalties

The taxpayer who is assessed a penalty for late filing (or for failure to pay the full tax with his return) finds himself with little administrative or judicial recourse to overturn what may be an arbitrary decision on the part of the IRS. Such penalties are generated by computers at regional IRS Service Centers.

In principle, the penalty can be abated if the taxpayer can demonstrate that his delinquency is "due to reasonable cause and not due to willful neglect."...

No doubt many of the explanations submitted by taxpayers are accepted by IRS officials. But if an explanation is rejected, the options open to the taxpayer are markedly different and more limited than those available to a taxpayer who has undergone audit. The audit procedures are available to inaccuracy penalties, but not failure-to-file or late payment penalties. If a deficiency is claimed after an audit, an elaborate negotiating procedure is open to the taxpayer before he has to pay the tax (and/or penalty.)...

....The taxpayer may send a letter to a tax examiner at the Service Center or speak over the telephone toll-free with an IRS employee. After his account has been declared a Tax Delinquency Account, he can try to convince the collection officers to whom the case has been assigned. But in order to negotiate further with the IRS, he must pay the penalty and file a claim for refund. If his claim is denied, he can litigate only in a Federal district court or the Court of Claims. The Tax Court, with its more informal and less expensive procedures, is not open to him.

In view of the muddiness of many reasonable cause determinations, the administrative and judicial review available to delinquent taxpayers seems most inadequate. It is doubted that a taxpayer (especially an uneducated one) should be expected to present his case in the form of a detailed written statement that will satisfy a harassed tax examiner in the Service Center. If he writes only that he was sick or that his accountant made a mistake, that will probably not be enough....

Recourse to the Federal district courts or the Court of Claims, after paying the penalties, is not adequate for many taxpayers, particularly those with lower incomes....

Accordingly, *it is recommended* that the appellate audit and settlement processes of the IRS, and the procedures of the Tax Court, be opened up to taxpayers disputing penalties for late filing or failure to pay with a tax return. *(Recommendation 3-V.)*....

Chapter 6 - Confidentiality of Tax Returns

The individual taxpayer expects that his income tax return will be treated as confidential by his government. It is a reasonable expectation since the taxpayer, under pain of financial penalties or even imprisonment, is required to provide information on his tax return that provides a skeletal yet revealing profile of his personal and financial life.

To a large though decreasing degree, the expectation is fulfilled. Information contained in tax returns is not made available to the general public. In fact, there have long been penalties under the tax code against unauthorized disclosure of information in tax returns by Federal or state employees. Since information on tax returns generally has not been available to the public, there is a widespread impression that tax returns are confidential documents. Indeed, public figures have contributed to this impression by consistently referring to tax returns as if they were documents locked away in the Internal Revenue Service's vaults. Increasingly over the past half century, however, this public impression has been more myth than reality.

Beginning about 1920, without a change in the tax code, there has been a gradual administrative erosion of the confidentiality of tax returns. The government continues to maintain their confidentiality so far as the general public is concerned. Within the government, however, the returns more and more have come to be viewed as a general resource available for purposes going far beyond the administration of the tax laws. Tax returns have become readily available sources of information, used by the government to study the population in general and to investigate individuals in particular.

Dissemination of Returns

As a result, within the government there has been a dissemination of tax returns going far beyond the Internal Revenue Service. Federal agencies, such as the Census Bureau, receive "raw" tax data from tax returns in the form of IRS computer tapes for use in a host of business and economic studies and analyses. States receive tax return information to help in the administration of their tax laws. Committees of Congress, including those not involved in the writing of tax laws, can and do obtain tax return information. The Department of Justice systematically obtains returns for use in civil cases as well as for use in developing criminal charges that do not involve violation of the tax laws. The White House and other Executive agencies routinely obtain "tax check" reports on persons under consideration for government jobs. In the wake of the Watergate affair, there also are questions as to whether the White House has not obtained access to tax returns for political purposes.

One of the striking features of the broadening dissemination of tax returns within the government is that it has occurred largely through regulations prepared only by the Executive branch rather than as a result of laws passed by Congress. Certainly, a practice that is based on largely unpublicized administrative decisions and which departs significantly from concepts of confidentiality commonly held by the public and Congress is open to question and needs basic reexamination.

Disclosure of Tax Returns to Other Executive Agencies

The extent to which tax returns should be available for legitimate functions of the Federal government apart from collection of taxes is a question fraught with deep and difficult philosophical and legal issues. At least in principle, a strong case can be made that tax returns should be an instrument for administering the tax laws and nothing more. Certainly, the opportunity for invasion of citizen privacy increases when a tax return escapes the grasp of the Internal Revenue Service. On the other side, an argument can be made that non-revenue use of tax returns can frequently serve a meritorious social purpose. Some uses would seem more meritorious and less intrusive than others. For example, some would see little harm in the use by the Census Bureau of computerized tax return information to distill purely statistical data about the population in general, but would shudder at the thought of the Department of Justice "fishing" through individual tax returns to develop leads in non-tax criminal cases. Others, however, might consider it the duty as well as the right of the government to use all information available to it, including tax returns, in the drive against organized crime....

The dichotomy between tax returns being viewed as confidential documents and as governmental assets is embodied in the tax code itself. Section 6103, which is the basic policy provision in the code dealing with confidentiality, states that tax returns "shall constitute public records" and "shall be open to inspection only upon orders of the President and under rules and regulations prescribed by the Secretary [of the Treasury] or his delegate and approved by the President." The result is an outwardly contradictory and confusing concept that tax returns are to be "public" records but are to be made available only at the order of the President. By interpretation and practice, "public" has come to mean records belonging to the government rather than the general public....

By 1920...government agencies other than the Treasury Department were permitted, at the discretion of the Secretary of the Treasury, to inspect both corporate and individual income tax returns. At the same time, the Executive branch repealed a regulation, dating back to the 1909 law, permitting public access to certain corporate returns. Thereafter, the public would be denied unrestricted access to any returns, but governmental access to returns would be broadened. State tax officials were added in 1921 to the governmental group permitted access to returns. In 1930, President Hoover set a significant precedent by approving a regulation authorizing the Department of Commerce to inspect returns for statistical purposes. In 1933, President Roosevelt approved a regulation permitting a special Senate Committee investigating air mail contracts to examine returns, and in 1935 the examination rights were extended to another non-tax-writing

Congressional committee. These precedents were but the first drops of a gentle rain which nearly became a downpour, with later presidents issuing at least 110 Executive orders permitting various Congressional committees to inspect tax returns.

A broad overhaul of the regulations in 1938 greatly facilitated access to returns by United States Attorneys and attorneys of the Justice Department for use in cases not involving tax violations. Later the same year, the regulations were amended to permit any government agency to obtain tax return information for evidentiary use in proceedings conducted by or before it and to which the United States was a party. The 1940's, 1950's, and 1960's were marked by almost unrestrained growth in the access to tax returns by government agencies, largely for statistical purposes.

Efforts to Restrict Dissemination

The early 1970's saw the first steps to stem, if not yet reverse, this tide toward ever greater governmental access to tax returns. The processing of requests by U.S. Attorneys, or by attorneys of the Department of Justice, for returns to be used in non-tax litigation, or for use in grand jury proceedings, was shifted from District Directors of the Internal Revenue Service to the National Office of IRS. Regulations were amended to deny to Justice Department attorneys access to tax returns for examining prospective jurors. After Congressional protests, a proposed regulation authorizing the Agriculture Department access to tax returns of farmers for a proposed economic study of the farming industry was withdrawn. More detailed rules for White House access to tax returns were developed. And finally, the definition of "return" was broadened to include any information related to the return "or other written statements filed on behalf of the taxpayer." It was provided that these internal documents relating to a taxpayer's return could be available "only in the discretion of the Secretary [of the Treasury] or the Commissioner [of Internal Revenue] or the delegate of either."...

Public Belief in Confidentiality

Despite the growth in governmental access, the thought persists in Congress, and among the public as well, that tax returns are generally confidential. There seems to be little public awareness that the principle of confidentiality has been progressively eroded by administrative process. For all its ambiguity, the current statutory language is more consistent with the concept of confidentiality than with present governmental practices. Given this fact, and the public assumption that tax returns are confidential, there seems little to justify the exploitation of tax returns for investigative purposes, particularly on a dragnet basis, as is now done by the Justice Department. There is no use of tax returns more in conflict with the principle of confidentiality than their use for investigative purposes. Information on tax returns which most people assume is confidential, and which is obtained under compulsion, is being used by the government to investigate crimes unrelated to the tax laws.

Methods for Obtaining Returns

There are basically two methods by which government agencies obtain tax returns from the IRS. One is under a so-called "catchall" regulation which permits an agency to have its executive head request inspection by an agency employee in connection with a matter officially before the agency. The request must be in writing, signed by the agency head, and must set forth the name and address of the taxpayer, the type of tax, the period covered by the return, and the reason for the inspection. Nominally, the Secretary of the Treasury or the Commissioner of Internal Revenue retain discretion to deny inspection. In practice, however, such discretion is rarely exercised....

The second method to obtain tax returns is through the existence of so-called "blanket" authority, approved by the President, for an agency to inspect returns. The regulations providing for "blanket" authority generally state the circumstances under which inspection will be permitted and do not impose the procedural requirements of naming a taxpayer, giving an address, stating the type of tax and return period. While the language of such regulations states that the Treasury Department "may" furnish the requested information, this has not generally been interpreted as giving the Department discretionary authority to refuse the information....

"Investigative Regulations"

The inspection of tax returns by Justice Department attorneys and U.S. Attorneys is governed by a separate set of special "investigative" regulations. These provide that a "return...shall be open to inspection by a United States Attorney or by an attorney of the Department of Justice where necessary in the performance of his duties." Under these regulations, the request must be signed by either the Attorney General, Deputy Attorney General or an Assistant Attorney General if the information is needed by a Justice Department attorney, or by a United States Attorney if the return is needed by him. The regulations specify that the request must state "the reason why inspection is desired," but most of the requests do not make precisely clear why access to a tax return is needed. Another "investigative" provision provides that a United States Attorney, or an attorney of the Department of Justice, may obtain tax returns "for official use in proceedings before a United States grand jury, or in litigation in any court, if the United States is interested in the result, or for use in preparation for such proceedings."...

The tax information supplied by the IRS varies considerably, depending upon whether it is requested under the "catchall" or "blanket" regulations. In the "catchall," investigative request, the IRS tends to turn over the actual return of a taxpayer. Under the "blanket" authority, most agencies do not get the return itself but only data taken from the return....

What information is made available by the IRS under an investigative request is complicated by the Service's bifurcated definition of what constitutes a "return." A return is first defined as including "information returns, schedules, lists and other written statements filed by or on behalf of the taxpayer" as well as audit reports, claims for refund, and notices of over-assessment or adjustments. Under the "catchall" regulations, a Federal agency is entitled to obtain all information falling within these categories. There is, however, a second grouping of information, embracing, for the most part, material prepared within the Service, such as work papers of examiners, cover letters, reports of special agents, and inter-office communications. This latter material (which embraces information obtained from third parties, including voluntary informants, IRS investigative reports, and data obtained by third-party summonses) is not available as a matter of right to the requesting agency but "only in the discretion" of the Secretary of Treasury or the Commissioner of Internal Revenue. In response to investigative requests, however, the Service usually will produce both the documents filed by the taxpayer as well as most material prepared inside the IRS, including conferences' and revenue agents' reports. Some information, such as work papers of examiners, cover letters, reports of special agents, and inter-office communications, may be obtained only with the express authorization of the Assistant Commissioner for Compliance....

Agency Use of Tax Information

The principal, most consistent users of tax return information have been the Department of Justice, the various United States Attorneys, the Bureaus of the Census and of Economic Analysis of the Department of Commerce, the Social Security Administration, and the Federal Trade Commission. In addition, over the years, such tax information has been used by more than two dozen other departments and agencies, largely for investigative purposes. The purposes have ranged from investigation of profits on charter flights by the Civil Aeronautics Board to alleged kickbacks by a borrower from the Rural Electrification Administration....

Most statistical uses of income tax information are for compiling what are regarded as essential economic data for government planning. In many cases, the tax return information serves the purpose of identifying further sources of information. In other instances, the return information itself is converted into statistical information. Most of the tax return information is transmitted by the IRS in a form that makes identification of the individual taxpayer either difficult or impossible. Not only is the anonymity of taxpayers preserved, but also the material is handled by department and agency offices and bureaus having no power to take actions affecting directly the taxpayers whose returns are furnished. Hence, this type of disclosure of tax information would seem the least offensive of all as an infringement upon the complete confidentiality of tax returns. Whatever small infringement may exist, it appears to be far outweighed by the benefits of obtaining objective information on which to base national government economic and social policies.

IRS Restrictions

To the concern of the Census Bureau, the Service recently has adopted new procedures which may reduce the availability of tax data for statistical purposes. The Service apparently has concluded that income tax data should be available for statistical purposes only if (1) the data are absolutely essential and (2) no satisfactory substitute can be found. The revised procedures apparently reflect a new policy emphasis by the IRS upon protecting the confidentiality of tax returns.

Another potential restriction on the dissemination of tax return information is presented by the Privacy Act enacted in 1974. One of the principal purposes of the Act is to restrict the use by Federal agencies of information about individuals to the purposes for which it was obtained.... In a key provision, the Act provides that no agency shall disclose any individual's record to another agency except with the written consent of the individual to whom the record pertains. The provision, however, contains exceptions, pertinent to the use of tax returns, stating that consent is not required for either "routine use" of the record or for "civil or criminal law enforcement activity."...

Use by Justice Department

Aside from statistical purposes, the largest use of tax return information by government agencies is for investigating possible violations of laws other than the tax code by the Justice Department, United States Attorneys and the Securities and Exchange Commission.

The majority of the returns requested by the Justice Department are for criminal investigations, particularly by "strike forces," the interagency task force created some 15 years ago to provide a coordinated attack on organized crime. The strike force concept has become inextricably linked to the use of tax returns for investigative purposes. Service representatives from the Audit and Intelligence Divisions have been assigned to the strike forces to help single out individuals for investigation. In addition, the Service has placed itself in the position of volunteering tax information to the Justice Department, particularly when it desires to have a taxpayer selected as a strike force target. The IRS engages in this act of voluntary disclosure by sending the name of a suspected law violator to the Justice Department with the notation that the Service may have information on the taxpayer which Justice may find useful. Under the appropriate regulation, the Justice Department then requests and obtains the information from the IRS. To do this, the IRS has had to make a dubious interpretation of a provision in the tax code (Section 7213) which prohibits disclosure of tax returns by IRS personnel. The IRS rationale is that the prohibitions apply to information in the tax return and not to the name of the taxpayer. From June 1, 1973 through October 31, 1974, 240 taxpayers were so "voluntarily" identified to the Justice Department by the IRS.

Among U.S. Attorneys there has been a growing demand for tax returns for investigative purposes as they have adopted the task force approach toward crime. Disclosure of tax return information to U.S. Attorneys poses a particular problem in protecting the confidentiality of such information. U.S. Attorneys are political appointees who very often harbor political ambitions. Placing confidential material in their hands raises a potential for political abuse.

The use of tax returns for investigative purposes generally raises a multitude of legal and administrative problems. By far the most serious problem is whether the disclosure of information, provided by the individual taxpayer on his tax return, for use in prosecution for non-tax crimes, violates the Fifth Amendment protection against self-incrimination. The preparation and filing of truthful and accurate tax returns is compelled for reasons unrelated to criminal law....

Administratively, the IRS's close involvement in criminal law enforcement raises the serious problem that the Service may be diverting resources and energies away from its primary job of collecting taxes and enforcing the tax laws and in the process acquiring a punitive public image as a law enforcement agency. It was a possibility recognized by Commissioner of Internal Revenue Donald C. Alexander, who in a 1974 speech warned that the emphasis on non-tax criminal law enforcement could "be jeopardizing our traditional tax administration processes....[Alexander also announced] that the Service would withdraw the Audit Division representative from Strike Force teams....

Express Authorization for Disclosure Urged

The most general and perhaps most fundamental recommendation growing out of this report is that disclosures of income tax returns and tax return information (as covered by the Service's present definition of "return") of individuals and decedents, by the Internal Revenue Service to any persons or officials outside the Service should be made only as permitted by express statutory authorization designating the persons to whom and the purposes for which disclosure may be made, the procedures governing such disclosure, and limitations on use or redisclosure that shall govern such disclosure. *(Recommendation 6-I.)...*

The purpose of this recommendation is to lodge exclusively in the Congress the responsibility for determining what uses and disclosures of tax returns, pertaining to individuals and decedents, may be made for purposes other than those necessary for the administration of the Federal revenue laws by the Internal Revenue Service....

Another principal recommendation growing out of this report is to constrain the authority of the Internal Revenue Service to transfer tax return data pertaining to individuals and decedents to other Executive agencies. The Service should be prohibited from disclosing individual and decedent tax return and associated information to another government agency for use in criminal or civil investigations unrelated to administration of the tax laws....

White House Access to Tax Returns

In recent decades there has been a lingering suspicion that given the awesome power of the presidency over the bureaucracy, the White House had undue access to tax returns and was perhaps using them for political purposes. The suspicions seemed to be confirmed by events in recent presidencies. Early in the Kennedy Administration, Carmine S. Bellino, a special consultant to the President, entered into arrangements with the IRS to inspect tax returns and associated documents. Similarly, in the Nixon Administration, Clark R. Mollenhoff, Deputy Counsel to the President, reached an understanding with the Commissioner of Internal Revenue concerning the inspection of tax returns. So far as is known, neither individual had an actual presidential order to inspect tax returns. They merely exercised the influence of the White House to obtain access to tax information. In the course of the Watergate investigations, further evidence was developed that tax return information was improperly transmitted to the White House.

The Watergate experience made it clear that the unfettered ability of White House employees to obtain tax return information presents distinct potential for abuse. This was acknowledged by President Ford, who, a few weeks after assuming the presidency, issued an Executive order designed to control White House access to tax information....

If reform is needed in this area—and it seems agreed that it is—the question is whether it should take the form of administrative change, such as that ordered by President Ford, or statutory change by Congress in the basic law. Statutory change has the advantage of relative permanency. An Executive order, on the other hand, is subject to modification at the discretion, or even the whim, of a President....

A statutory change which falls short of a complete restriction would still constitute a considerable improvement over present law and practice. Accordingly, *it is recommended* that legislation be enacted restricting the availability of tax returns to the Executive Office of the President. *(Recommendation 6-III)* If such legislation is to be effective, it must incorporate certain safeguards. First, the request for tax data should be signed by the President personally. Second, the request should designate, by name, the White House employee or employees to whom the tax data may properly be furnished by the IRS. Third, the presidential request should state in a full and complete manner why the tax return information is desired. Fourth, some procedures should be required to control dissemination of the information once it is obtained by the White House and to provide for its eventual return to the Internal Revenue Service. Fifth, an outside group, such as the Congressional committees having jurisdiction over tax matters, should periodically be informed by the Service of the instances in which the White House has requested tax information....

Tax Checks

Another questionable tax practice initiated by the White House and now widely followed within the Executive branch is the somewhat secretive check on the tax status of individuals under consideration of appointment to federal jobs. Since 1961, the so-called "tax checks" have become part of the "character investigations" of prospective appointees conducted by the Federal Bureau of Investigation. Upon a request by the FBI, the Service furnishes information on whether the individual has paid income taxes, liens, criminal tax investigations or civil penalties for fraud or negligence. Tax checks are an example of how a practice, which started out as a device to check on a few high-level presidential appointees, can be copied and spread throughout the Executive branch. The White House requests tax checks concerning all its own appointees—from gardeners to cabinet ministers. Other departments of the Executive branch usually reserve the tax checks for high level positions.

During the recent years, the White House and other Executive agencies have requested total numbers of tax checks as shown in the following table:

	1966	1967	1968	1969	1970	1971	1972	1973	1974
White House	547	583	880	1263	868	1134	915	1081	1045
Department of Justice	547	495	517	1424	1162	1274	772	999	335
Department of Treasury	91	240	89	258	412	233	393	397	775
Department of State	242	16	9	5	4	76	105	113	148
Department of Commerce	75	67	74	113	133	94	114	121	106
Department of Agriculture	0	0	0	69	183	72	—	—	—
Export-Import Bank	0	0	0	0	16	17	9	13	15

Apparently there are two rationalizations for the tax check. The first is that the tax status information has some relevance to the competence or fitness of the individual for a public job. The second is to spare the President the embarassment of appointing someone with serious recent or current tax trouble....

Some procedural steps have been taken by the Service to lessen the likelihood of abuse....

Access to Tax Information by Congressional Committees

Three Congressional committees—the House Committee on Ways and Means, the Senate Committee on Finance and the Joint Committee on Internal Revenue Taxation—are specifically authorized under the tax code to receive and inspect tax returns. Such inspection presumably is needed either as part of their tax oversight function or as an aid in the drafting of tax legislation.

Other Congressional committees, to obtain access to tax returns, must request a Presidential Executive order, with the request stating the general purpose of the inspection. Since the 1930's, it has been the general practice of the White House to comply with such requests from Congressional committees. Surveys show, however, that the number of tax returns requested by the committees are relatively few in number. It is estimated that no more than a half-dozen requests for income tax returns have been made by the three tax law writing committees in the last ten years. Other Congressional committees authorized by executive orders to obtain tax returns also have used the authority sparingly.

While Congressional examination of individual tax returns may serve a legislative purpose, quite obviously there is a thin dividing line between obtaining tax information for purposes of legislating and obtaining such information for purely investigative purposes. It would appear that some committees use tax data for the purpose of developing investigative leads. To the extent that such information is used for public hearings or is forwarded to prosecutorial agencies, the Congressional practice of using income tax returns for investigative purposes would seem to raise the same problems of infringement upon confidentiality presented by the Justice Department's access to tax returns. Furthermore, with tax returns in the hands of Congressional investigators, there is an obvious potential for political abuse....

Inspection of Tax Returns by State and Local Governments

Since 1935, the tax code has permitted inspection of Federal tax returns by state tax administrators (Section 6103 (b)). Returns may be inspected only for state tax purposes or to obtain information to be furnished local tax authorities. Eleven states have chosen to make this inspection by examining and copying returns in an office of the Service. Another 38 states carry out inspection by obtaining computer tapes drawn from the IRS Individual Master File, which contains enough information to compute taxable income but not enough to reproduce the return of a taxpayer.

The release of Federal tax information to state officials raises an obvious concern over maintaining the confidentiality of the tax returns once they are in state hands. To a large extent, this concern is now met through so-called Agreements on Coordination of Tax Administration entered into between the Federal government and the individual states. All states except Texas and Nevada have entered into such agreements. The agreements spell out the mutual obligations in handling the tax returns and usually require the states to make available certain tax information to the Federal government. Recently the agreement has been tightened by imposing additional requirements for safeguarding tax information....

Unauthorized Access to Returns by IRS Employees

With the multitude of records that exists in numerous forms in Service files, there obviously is a potential problem that a taxpayer's right to confidentiality may be violated by unauthorized examination or improper use of tax return information by employees of the Service. Abuse of tax returns by Service employees may be motivated by any number of reasons. During the Watergate investigation, instances were uncovered of employee access to tax returns solely for political purposes.

Every year, IRS employees make about 18 million requests for tax return information on file in Federal Record Centers. The objective of course is to make sure that all of these requests are legitimate. Information stored on computer tapes seems to be fairly well guarded against unauthorized access, but the Service's procedures for guarding hard copies of returns appear somewhat casual. In the millions of requests processed by the Federal Records Centers, a permanent record of who requested the return is maintained in only about two-thirds of the cases. If no action is taken on a requested return, the return is refiled and the requisitioning document identifying the Service employee is destroyed. In such "no action" cases, abuses obviously could arise with a photocopy quickly made of a return, which would then be returned to the file with no record showing that it had ever been removed.

Partly as a result of the disclosures in the Watergate investigations, the Service is now moving to improve and strengthen its internal procedures for protecting returns against unauthorized access....

Notice to the Public About Tax Return Disclosure

To maximize citizens' awareness of the ways in which their tax return information may be used, *it is recommended* that the Internal Revenue Service place on tax return forms a concise statement describing the disclosure, for uses unrelated to the administration of Federal tax laws, that may be made of information supplied in such returns....

AID TO NEW YORK CITY
November 26, 1975

In a Thanksgiving-eve turnaround, President Ford announced that he would approve unprecedented federal assistance, amounting to $2.3-billion annually in short-term loans, to rescue New York City from imminent bankruptcy. Ford's action ended an eight-month period during which the city tottered on the brink of default while its officials lobbied vigorously in Washington and across the nation for federal intervention.

Until his announcement at an evening press conference Nov. 26, Ford had repeatedly vowed that he would block congressional efforts to aid New York. His position had been that the city would have to slash spending and, if necessary, declare bankruptcy to pave the way toward regaining fiscal responsibility.

The President retracted his opposition to federal aid for the nation's largest city one day after the New York state legislature approved a package of stiff new taxes and other rigorous measures, including a moratorium on repayment of some of the city's debts. The measure, which provided that private holders of short-term city securities exchange them for long-term bonds, appeared to many observers to be a default in everything but name. However, for the moment a formal declaration of bankruptcy had been averted. In light of the state's legislative action, Ford asserted Nov. 26 in reply to a reporter's question, his latest decision did not constitute a reversal of his earlier position. New York had "bailed itself out," he said, indicating that his insistence on self-help had been vindicated. "We have always felt that they could do enough, but only because we were firm have they moved ahead to accomplish what they have done now."

Genesis of the Crisis

New York's predicament symbolized the deep-rooted problems of many large, older cities. They too faced erosion of their tax base due to suburban flight, rising costs of providing services and paying municipal wages, and growing inner-city concentrations of poorer citizens needing special services. But New York's woes were exacerbated by the expenses of costly social services, liberal municipal salaries and municipal employee pension plans financed entirely by the city.

The fiscal crisis first surfaced in May when Mayor Abraham Beame and New York Governor Hugh Carey met privately with Ford, who recommended budget cuts and restructuring of the city's debt to ease its repayment. During the summer months the New York legislature created a new entity, the Municipal Assistance Corporation (MAC) to renegotiate the city's debt. By August, however, it was clear that MAC had been unable to find buyers for new New York bond issues. Layoffs of city employees also began in the summer, but these had little immediate impact on the financial crisis and were overshadowed by the effective exclusion of the city from the credit market.

Congressional Action

In Congress, the New York aid issue provoked one of the most heated battles of the legislative year. Supporters argued that the federal government could not let the nation's largest city and financial capital collapse. Opponents objected vehemently to the precedent of "bailing out" a city that had mismanaged its financial affairs for years.

Until late in the year, the federal government clung to a spectator role in the fast-paced drama surrounding New York City's repeated brushes with financial disaster. But growing awareness of the potential national impact of the city's problems appeared to have strengthened support for some kind of federal action.

At first, Ford administration officials and most members of Congress tended to dismiss New York's plight as the price it finally had to pay for years of living beyond its means. But key members of Congress began to push for federal help in September and October as events started to wear down the traditional congressional hostility toward New York.

The city tottered dramatically on the edge of default Oct. 17 until, two hours before the deadline, the city's teachers' union finally agreed to make the investments providing the cash the city needed to pay off debts falling due that day and to meet payrolls. The Senate and House banking committees accelerated their work on aid legislation after the near-default and eventually both committees developed legislation that would have allowed the federal government to guarantee bonds issued to help the city meet its expenses. In the meantime, however, Ford had vowed Oct. 29 to veto any bill designed to "bail out" New York before a default. Without federal action, a city default in early December was considered certain, and state officials maintained that New York state could default soon after.

In ending his opposition to pre-default aid to New York City, President Ford asked Congress to approve federal loans to the city on a seasonal basis through June 30, 1978. Faced with a Dec. 11 deadline—the date set for New York's default—the House and Senate laid aside bond-guarantee measures and moved swiftly to approve the President's proposals for short-term loans. Ford signed the bill (PL 94-143) Dec. 9. Even its supporters conceded that the measure might not be enough to save New York from default. The "problem will come back to haunt us," predicted Rep. Henry S. Reuss (D Wis.). Just in case federal aid did not prevent a New York default, the House and Senate passed legislation (PL 94-143) during the week of Dec. 8 that would make it easier for cities like New York to use municipal bankruptcy proceedings to adjust repayment of their debts.

> *Statement by President Gerald R. Ford, and answers to reporters' questions on New York City's financial situation, at White House news conference Nov. 26, 1975, followed by White House summaries of actions taken to relieve situation:*

Since early this year, and particularly in the last few weeks, the leaders of New York State and of New York City have been working to overcome the financial difficulties of the city which as a result of many years of unsound fiscal practices, unbalanced budgets, and increased borrowing, threaten to bring about municipal bankruptcy of an unprecedented magnitude.

As you know, I have been steadfastly opposed to any Federal help for New York City which would permit them to avoid responsibility for managing their own affairs. I will not allow the taxpayers of other States and cities to pay the price of New York's past political errors. It is important to all of us that the fiscal integrity of New York City be restored and that the personal security of 8 million Americans in New York City be fully assured.

It has always been my hope that the leaders of New York, when the chips were down, face up to their responsibilities and take the tough decisions that the facts of the situation require. That is still my hope, and I must say that it is much, much closer to reality today than it was last spring.

I have, quite frankly, been surprised that they have come as far as they have. I doubted that they would act unless ordered to do so by a Federal court. Only in the last month after I made it clear that New York would have to solve its fundamental financial problems without the help of the Federal taxpayer has there been a concerted effort to put the finances of the city and the State on a sound basis. They have today informed me of the specifics of New York's self-help program.

This includes: meaningful spending cuts have been approved to reduce the cost of running the city; two, more than $200 million in new taxes have been voted; three, payments to the city's noteholders will be postponed and interest payments will be reduced through the passage of legislation by New York State; four, banks and other large institutions will have agreed to wait to collect on their loans and to accept lower interest rates; five, for the first time in years members of municipal unions will be required to bear part of the cost of pension contributions and other reforms will be made in union pension plans; six, the city pension system is to provide additional loans up to $2.5 billion to the city. All of these steps, adding up to $4 billion, are part of an effort to provide financing and to bring the city's budget into balance by the fiscal year beginning July 1, 1977.

Only a few months ago we were told that all of these reforms were impossible and could not be accomplished by New York alone. Today they are being done.

This is a realistic program. I want to commend all of those involved in New York City and New York State for their constructive efforts to date. I have been closely watching their progress in meeting their problem.

Loans Necessary

However, in the next few months New York will lack enough funds to cover its day-to-day operating expenses. This problem is caused by the city having to pay its bills on a daily basis throughout the year while the bulk of its revenues are received during the spring. Most cities are able to borrow short-term funds to cover these needs, traditionally repaying them within their fiscal year.

Because the private credit markets may remain closed to them, representatives of New York have informed me and my Administration that they have acted in good faith, but they still need to borrow money on a short-term basis for a period of time each of the next 2 years in order to provide essential services to the 8 million Americans who live in the Nation's largest city.

Therefore, I have decided to ask the Congress when it returns from recess for authority to provide a temporary line of credit to the State of New York to enable it to supply seasonal financing of essential services for the people of New York City.

There will be stringent conditions. Funds would be loaned to the State on a seasonal basis, normally from July through March, to be repaid with interest in April, May, and June, when the bulk of the city's revenues comes in. All Federal loans will be repaid in full at the end of each year.

There will be no cost to the rest of the taxpayers of the United States.

This is only the beginning of New York's recovery process, and not the end. New York officials must continue to accept primary responsibility. There must be no misunderstanding of my position. If local parties fail to carry out their plan, I am prepared to stop even the seasonal Federal assistance.

I again ask the Congress promptly to amend the Federal bankruptcy laws so that if the New York plan fails, there will be an orderly procedure available. A fundamental issue is involved here—sound fiscal management is an imperative of self-government. I trust we have all learned the hard lesson that no individual, no family, no business, no city, no State, and no nation can go on indefinitely spending more money than it takes in.

As we count our Thanksgiving blessings, we recall that Americans have always believed in helping those who help themselves. New York has finally taken the tough decisions it had to take to help itself. In making the required sacrifices, the people of New York have earned the encouragement of the rest of the country.

Questions and Answers

Q. Mr. President, I notice that you don't put any dollar figure on the amount of the loans that you would be offering. I wonder if you could supply us with a figure and also why were loans necessary rather than loan guarantees?

A. The amount in the proposed legislation, which is a maximum ceiling—not necessarily would they have to go up to the ceiling—but the figure is $2.3 billion per year, all of it to be repaid at the end of each fiscal year.

The reason we made it a loan rather than a loan guarantee is very simple. It's a much cleaner transaction between the Federal Government and the state and/or the city. If you have a loan guarantee, you involve other parties and we think it's much better—we have better control over it—if we make it a direct loan from the Federal Government....

Changed Stance

Q. Mr. President, in a nationally televised speech before the National Press Club on October 29 you said, and I quote, "I can tell you now that I am prepared to take to veto any bill that has as its purpose a Federal bailout of New York City to prevent a default," end of quote. What has happened in the interim, sir, to make you change your mind and, secondly, do you regard your proposal as a Federal bailout of New York City?

A. The answer is very simple. New York has bailed itself out, because on October 29 when I made the speech before the press club it was anticipated that on June 30 of 1976 there would be a cash deficit of $3,950,000,000 in the New York City situation. Under the plan that I have embraced, on June 30, 1976, New York City will have a zero cash balance, so New York City by what they had done in conjunction with New York State, with the noteholders, with the labor organization, the pension fund people, they have bailed out themselves.

Terms of Loan

Q. Mr. President, the private sector will not invest in New York City apparently because they think it's too great of a gamble to invest any longer in New York City. Can you tell us why you are willing to risk Federal money in investing in New York City when the private sector thinks the risks are too great?

A. Unfortunately, because a period of 10 or 12 years where the finances of New York City have been badly handled, there has been a loss of confidence in the private money markets.

In order to get New York City to restore their credibility in the money markets, they have taken these steps which have eliminated a $3.95 billion cash deficit and by the fiscal year that begins July 1, 1977, they will be on a balanced budget basis.

Therefore, in the interim while they're restoring their credit credibility, I decided that it was needed and necessary to give short-term financing on a seasonal basis. This, I think, is what we can do without any loss of taxpayers' money and let me show you what the precautions are that we've taken.

We have said that the money will be loaned to New York City at a rate no less than the Federal Government borrows itself and with the option of the Secretary of the Treasury to impose an additional up to 1 percent on the city when they do borrow from us.

And secondly, we include in the legislation a lien for the Federal Government so that the Federal Government has the priority claim against any other creditor for the repayment of any seasonal loan made by the Federal Government.

The net result is the Federal Government will be held harmless and the taxpayers won't have to lose a penny and the City of New York will straighten out its fiscal situation.

Q. Mr. President, that's a pretty good deal, 1 percent loan. What will you do tomorrow when other mayors around the country call up and say, "Mr. President, how do we get in on that?"

A. Mr. Schieffer, I think you misunderstood. They will have to pay the same interest rate that the Federal Government pays when it borrows money plus up to 1 percent extra. So they're in effect, reimbursing us over and above what the Federal Government has to pay to borrow its money....

Now, other cities, we hope, won't have to be in that situation....

Tactics Questioned

Q. Mr. President, Mayor Beame in New York was asking as long ago as September for short-term Federal assistance. How is the plan that you propose tonight different from what he was seeking then?

A. Significantly different. As I pointed out a minute ago, when the Governor and the Mayor were asking for any kind of help—short-term or long-term—there was the anticipated deficit for the current fiscal year in New

York City of $4 billion. In the meantime the Mayor and the other public officials in New York City, along with the help of private citizens, have reduced that fiscal deficit for this current year to zero. So there's quite a different circumstance.

Q. Well, you seem to be suggesting, Mr. President, that your opposition earlier to assistance for New York was based primarily on a tactical maneuver to get them to make the hard decisions that you say they have now made. Why couldn't you have said then that the aid would be forthcoming if they did all those things?

A. Well, we have always felt that they could do enough, but only because we were firm have they moved ahead to accomplish what they have done now, which is a bailout of New York City by New York officials.

If we had shown any give, I think they wouldn't have made the hard decisions that they have made in the last week or so....

Summary of the New York City Seasonal Financing Act of 1975

The act provides for Federal short-term loans to the city or any agency authorized by the state to act for the city, in an aggregate outstanding amount not to exceed $2.3 billion. Such loans will have a maturity date not later than the last day of the fiscal year of the city in which the loan was issued.

According to New York City, the anticipated amount of such Federal seasonal assistance required is $1.3 billion in fiscal 1976 and $2.1 billion in each of the following two fiscal years.

Loans by the Federal Government will bear interest at a rate 1 percentage point higher than the Treasury borrowing rate. No loan will be provided unless all matured loans have been repaid in accordance with their terms and there is compliance with the terms of any such outstanding loans.

A loan may be made only if the Secretary determines that there is a reasonable prospect of repayment. Loans will bear such terms and conditions as may be established by the Secretary of the Treasury to insure repayment of such obligations in accordance with their terms. The Secretary may require such security as he deems appropriate.

To offset any claim that the United States may have against New York Cith under the Act, the Secretary will be authorized to withhold any payments from the United States to the city, either directly or through the state, which may be due under any law.

The authority of the Secretary to make new loans will terminate on June 30, 1978.

Actions by New York City and New York State

Governor Carey and Mayor Beame have informed Administration officials that the actions listed below are being implemented. New York State and city officials are delivering documentation verifying such actions for the Administration to review.

The following actions are designed to insure a balanced city budget by June 30, 1978:

A. The three-year Emergency Financial Control Board [E.F.C.B.] plan will produce a modest surplus in the city's expense budget by fiscal year 1977-78.

B. The State Legislature has voted over $200 million of additional city taxes, which will be imposed by the E.F.C.B.

C. A portion of annual city contributions to the pension system has been shifted to the employees by legislation. On an annual basis the savings to the city would be $85 million and the impact on the employees would be $107 million per annum.

D. The city has laid off about 22,000 employees since Jan. 1 and increased taxes over $300 million this past summer. Additional personnel reductions of over 40,000 employees are contemplated in fiscal year 1977-1978.

E. A partial wage deferral was imposed this fall.

F. The city has reduced its subsidy to the City University by $32 million.

G. The New York City transit fare has been increased from 35c to 50c.

The following actions are designed to enable New York City to meet its financing requirements:

A. Moratorium legislation has been enacted with respect to $2.6 billion of city short-term notes.

B. An exchange offer has been approved by the M.A.C. [Municipal Assistance Corporation] Board for an exchange of 10-year 8 percent bonds for the $1.6 billion of city notes held by the public.

C. The New York banks and pension systems have agreed to take 10-year 6 percent securities as part of the moratorium in exhange for $1 billion of city notes.

D. The New York banks and pension systems have agreed to take 10-year 6 percent bonds in exchange for $1.7 billion of M.A.C. bonds bearing higher interest rates and/or shorter maturities.

E. New York City pension systems have agreed to purchase $2.5 billion of new M.A.C. and/or city securities over the next three years. This commitment is subject to appropriate trustee indemnification.

F. M.A.C. has provided about $3.5 billion of financing to the city, of which $1.5 billion is refinancing of short-term debt.

The city and state have implemented the following management changes:

A. Creation of M.A.C. and E.F.C.B. control mechanisms.

B. Extensive management changes are being made in the city, including a new Deputy Mayor for Finance and a new Chief of Planning.

The following proposals have been made to reform the New York City pension program:

A. The E.F.C.B. has passed a resolution directing the city to terminate the practice of using, for budgetary purposes, all income of the pension systems in excess of 4 percent per annum. In the year beginning July 1, 1976, this will result in approximately $136 million per annum of additional income to the pension system and a commensurate increase in the city's expenses.

The E.F.C.B. has also directed the city management to take action and report back within 30 days with respect to termination of the practices resulting in the abuse of overtime in the last year of employment, thereby creating excessive pension burdens on the city.

B. Governor Carey has directed Richard Shinn, president of the Metropolitan Life Insurance Company, to report to the E.F.C.B. by Dec. 31 on the actuarial soundness of the city pension funds.

The E.F.C.B. has directed the city to prepare and submit to the Control Board such legislative requests and other amendments as may be necessary as a result of the Shinn study to put the funds on a sound actuarial basis and to have those recommendations to the Control Board no later than Jan. 31, 1976.

December

SENATE REPORTS ON FBI ABUSES AND CIA ROLE IN CHILE

December 3 and 4, 1975

In conjunction with hearings on FBI and CIA improprieties, the Senate Select Intelligence Committee made public on Dec. 3 and 4 two staff reports which confirmed widespread allegations that the FBI had spied on political figures and that the CIA had conducted a well-financed, decade-long campaign against the late Salvador Allende of Chile. These documents were part of a series of interim reports on activities of federal intelligence and law enforcement agencies which the committee, chaired by Sen. Frank Church (D Idaho), had begun releasing in November (see p. 709).

The staff report on the FBI, together with information developed in the hearings, showed a pattern of improper and unlawful bureau actions ranging over three decades. The report focused on political abuses, beginning with President Franklin D. Roosevelt's orders for wiretaps on the telephones of his closest personal aides and reports on private citizens expressing opposition to his defense policies. In its study the committee concluded that Presidents Roosevelt, Truman, Eisenhower, Kennedy, Johnson and Nixon had received reports from the FBI on journalists, political opponents and critics of administration policies.

"The FBI intelligence system developed to a point where no one inside or outside the bureau was willing or able to tell the difference between legitimate national security or law enforcement information and purely political intelligence," the staff report stated. When L. Patrick Gray, as acting FBI director, in 1973 gave FBI reports to various presidential aides whom the FBI should have been investigating after the Watergate break-in, "he just carried to the extreme an established practice of service to the White House," according to the report.

Earlier Disclosures

At the time the Senate committee published its December report, the public image of the FBI had already been tarnished by disclosures of other improprieties. On Nov. 18 and 19 the Church committee made public a detailed 20-year history of FBI activities to disrupt U.S. protest groups and movements. The committee's investigation of the bureau revealed an undercover FBI effort to discredit civil rights leader Dr. Martin Luther King Jr. that involved blackmail, bugging and intimidation. The campaign to discredit King, committee investigators said, was directed from the top, in the office of then Director J. Edgar Hoover.

The campaign began in earnest in 1963, when the bureau first employed telephone taps and hidden microphones. The bugs apparently revealed sensitive personal information about King which the bureau tried to turn against him in 1964. Shortly before the civil rights leader was to receive the 1964 Nobel Peace Prize, the FBI sent him an anonymous letter, accompanied by transcripts from the hotel room bugs, which the committee investigators said implied that King should commit suicide.

According to a draft found in FBI files, the note read: "King, there is only one thing left for you to do. You know what it is. You have just 34 days (apparently, the period before the Nobel ceremony) in which to do it.... You are done. There is but one way out for you."

The campaign against King was just one of a range of FBI efforts to disrupt political movements under its counter-intelligence program, according to the testimony. Many of the bureau's activities were directed against such groups as the Ku Klux Klan, black nationalist organizations, the Socialist Workers Party and the New Left.

CIA in Chile

American intervention in Chile had been publicly acknowledged in September 1974 by President Ford. He told a press conference that U.S. activities there had been limited to assisting in "the preservation of opposition newspapers and electronic media and to preserve political parties." He concluded that the program was in the "best interest" of both the United States and the Chilean people (see Historic Documents of 1974, p. 805).

In its Dec. 4 CIA report the Senate committee cleared the agency of alleged direct responsibility for the 1973 coup in which the elected government of Marxist President Salvador Allende was overthrown and Allende lost his life. But it gave a detailed picture of massive CIA intervention in Chilean media and politics which had lasted ten years and cost more than $13-million. The report contained few surprises, for much of the material it covered had previously been reported in the press. Also, the committee's Nov. 20 report on assassinations of foreign political leaders had included a section on the death in 1970 of Chilean General Rene Schneider during an abortive coup linked to CIA activities.

New information contained in the latest report included details of massive financial support of Allende's conservative opponent in the 1970 presidential elections—undertaken by U.S. corporations with the benefit of advice from the CIA. Other disclosures dealt with agency briefings which the committee said had influenced a Time *magazine cover story on Chile in 1970, and with substantial subsidizing of the anti-Allende Chilean daily,* El Mercurio. *The report was based on secret government documents and on closed-session testimony by CIA and other government officials, including Secretary of State Henry A. Kissinger.*

The cumulative effect of ongoing intelligence investigations began to be felt as early as November when President Ford announced his intention to replace the current director of the Central Intelligence Agency, William E. Colby, with George Bush, then U.S. representative in the People's Republic of China. In early December the Gallup Poll registered a significant drop in public esteem for the FBI and the CIA. Whereas 84 per cent of Americans had indicated a "highly favorable" view of the FBI in 1965, only 37 per cent still held that view, and only 14 per cent were reported as having a "highly favorable" opinion of the CIA.

> *Text of the Senate Select Intelligence Committee's staff report on political abuses of the Federal Bureau of Investigation, published Dec. 3, 1975:*

The political abuse of the FBI did not begin in the 1960s. Although this Committee has concentrated its investigations on the events of the '60s and '70s, the story cannot be fully understood by looking at just the last 15 years.

Therefore, the first objective of this report is to lay out some of the historical context for more-recent political abuses of the Bureau.

The second objective is to describe some of the results of our investigation which show the various types of political abuse to which the FBI is susceptible.

Some have been in response to the desires of the Bureau's superiors.

Others have been generated by the Bureau itself.

And there is the added possibility, suggested by some of the documents we have seen and some of the witnesses we have interviewed, that certain political abuses resulted from the inexorable dynamics of the FBI's intelligence-gathering process itself: in other words, that the FBI intelligence system developed to a point where no one inside or outside the Bureau was willing or able to tell the difference between legitimate national-security or law-enforcement information and purely political intelligence.

Whether any particular abuse resulted from outside demands, from the FBI's own desires, or from the nature of the intelligence process is a question for the Committee to answer when all the evidence is in.

Background of Abuse of FBI

The historical background of political abuse of the FBI involves at least three dimensions.

The first is the Bureau's subservience to the Presidency, its willingness to carry out White House requests without question. When L. Patrick Gray, as acting FBI Director, destroyed documents and gave FBI reports to presidential aides whom the FBI should have been investigating after the Watergate break-in, he just carried to the extreme an established practice of service to the White House.

The other side of this practice was the Bureau's volunteering political intelligence to its superiors, not in response to any specific request.

And the third historical dimension was the FBI's concerted effort to promote its public image and discredit its critics.

Early examples of the Bureau's willingness to do the President's bidding occur under Franklin D. Roosevelt. In 1940 it complied with a request to run name checks, open files, and make reports on hundreds of persons who sent telegrams to the President that were—to quote the letter from the President's secretary to J. Edgar Hoover—"all more or less in opposition to national defense," or that expressed approval of Col. Charles Lindbergh's criticism of the President.

Another example came to light in recent years when Maj. Gen. Harry Vaughan, who was President Truman's military aide, disclosed that President Roosevelt had ordered wiretaps on the home telephones of his closest aides. Shortly after Mr. Truman had taken office, someone had presented General Vaughan with transcripts of the wiretaps. He took them to President Truman, who said, according to General Vaughan: "I don't have time for that foolishness." This story is generally confirmed by the Committee staff's inquiry into J. Edgar Hoover's "Official and Confidential Files," where an index to the logs of these wiretaps was located.

Political Intelligence Offered

Historical illustrations of the FBI's practice of volunteering political intelligence to its superiors appear in virtually every Administration.

President Roosevelt's Attorney General, Francis Biddle, recalled in his autobiography how J. Edgar Hoover shared with him some of the "intimate details" of what his fellow Cabinet members did and said—"their likes and dislikes, their weaknesses and their associations." Attorney General Biddle confessed that he enjoyed hearing these derogatory and sometimes "embarrassing" stories and that Director Hoover "knew how to flatter his superior."

President Truman and his aides received regular letters from Hoover labeled "Personal and Confidential" and containing tidbits of political intelligence. Sometimes they reported on possible Communist influence behind various lobbying efforts, such as activities in support of civil-rights legislation. On other occasions they reported allegations that a Communist sympathizer had helped write a Senator's speech, and inside information about the negotiating position of a non-Communist labor union.

Some of the letters were undoubtedly of political value to the President. One related the activities of a former Roosevelt aide who was trying to influence the Truman Administration's appointments. Another advised that the FBI had learned from a confidential source that a "scandal" was brewing and that it would be "very embarrassing to the Democratic Administration." A third contained the report of a "very confidential source" about a meeting of newspaper representatives in Chicago to plan publication of a series of stories exposing organized crime and corrupt politicians. The stories were going to be critical of the Attorney General and the President.

The Truman White House also received a copy of an FBI memorandum reporting the contents of an in-house communication from *Newsweek* magazine reporters to their editors about a story they had obtained from the State Department.

An example from the Eisenhower Administration shows how White House requests and FBI initiative were sometimes mixed together. President Eisenhower asked Director Hoover to brief the Cabinet on racial tensions in early 1956. What the Cabinet received was a report not only on incidents of violence, but also on the activities of Southern Governors and Congressmen in groups opposing integration, as well as the role of Communists in civil-rights lobbying efforts and the NAACP's plans to push for legislation.

No one appears to have questioned the propriety of the FBI reporting such political intelligence, or Director Hoover's competence to do so.

Reaction to Criticism

The third source of abuse throughout the Bureau's history was its concern for its image and hostility to any critics. One example each from the Truman and Eisenhower years shows how the Bureau checked and reported on its critics.

In 1949 the National Lawyers Guild planned to issue a report denouncing FBI surveillance activities revealed in a court case. The FBI provided the Attorney General advance information from its source about the Lawyers Guild plans, as well as a full report on everything about the group in Bureau files. Attorney General Howard McGrath passed the report on to the President, and J. Edgar Hoover advised the White House directly about last-minute changes in the Guild's plans. The FBI's inside information gave the Attorney General the opportunity to prepare a rebuttal well in advance of the expected criticism.

The second instance took place in 1960, when the Tennessee Advisory Committee to the U.S. Civil Rights Commission announced it would investigate charges by the Knoxville Area Human Relations Council that federal agencies, including the FBI, were practicing racial discrimination. The FBI conducted name checks on the 11 members of the council's board of directors. The results were sent to Attorney General William Rogers,

Deputy Attorney General Lawrence Walsh, and Special Assistant to the Attorney General Harold R. Tyler, Jr.

Derogatory information on four of these individuals included allegations of subversive connections from as far back as the late '30s and early '40s, an allegation that one board member had "corrupt political associates" in 1946, and the characterization of another as having "unorthodox attitudes" and sending flowers and "mash" notes to a woman in his church. The FBI's report also made the flat statement: "As you know, this Bureau does not practice racial segregation or discrimination." (The Committee will recall that it has previously received information as to the number of black FBI agents in the early 1960s.)

Thus, the Bureau's more distant history shows the development of its political services for higher authorities and its concern for its own political position.

Name Checks

The staff's investigation of alleged abuses in the 1960s and '70s discloses a wide variety of questionable name checks, sometimes for Presidents and sometimes in the Bureau's own interest.

An examination of these name-check reports shows the peculiarly damaging nature of the Bureau's practice. No new investigation was done to verify the allegations stored away for years in FBI files. Anything anyone ever told the FBI about the individual was pulled together, including charges that the Bureau may never have substantiated. FBI files inevitably include misinformation because people bear grudges or make mistakes. Sometimes the Bureau verifies the charge, but frequently there is no reason to do so, and it is just recorded in the files. Such charges can be retrieved by a name check and reported without further substantiation.

The request by the Nixon White House for a name check on CBS correspondent Daniel Schorr, which the FBI turned into a full field investigation, has been examined extensively elsewhere. The staff has determined that President Johnson asked for name-check reports on at least seven other journalists, including NBC commentator David Brinkley, Associated Press reporter Peter Arnett and columnist Joseph Kraft.

Another political abuse of FBI name checks occurred in the closing days of the 1964 presidential-election campaign, when Johnson aide Bill Moyers asked the Bureau to report on all persons employed in Senator Goldwater's office. Moyers has publicly recounted his role in the incident, and his account is confirmed by FBI documents.

Some of President Johnson's requests parallel those of President Roosevelt 25 years earlier. The FBI complied with White House requests for name checks on dozens of persons who signed telegrams critical of U.S. Vietnam policy in 1965. The names of other presidential critics were also sent to the Bureau to be checked and reported on, as were the names of critics of the Warren Commission. The FBI also volunteered reports on presidential critics.

The White House requests for name checks are episodic in comparison to the name checks conducted as a matter of systematic Bureau policy for the use of FBI Director Hoover. The Crime Records Division prepared namecheck memoranda for Director Hoover regularly on Congressmen, other public officials, and prominent persons of interest to the Director. Many of these special memoranda were filed by the Crime Records Division. Others found their way into Director Hoover's "Official and Confidential Files."

The Committee staff has located in these "O and C Files" such special memoranda on the author of a critical book about the FBI, and on all the members of the Senate subcommittee chaired by Senator Long which threatened to investigate the FBI in the mid-1960s. Some of these name-check reports and special memoranda contained derogatory information and, in the case of the author, information from his income-tax returns and personal information about his wife. The reports on members of the Long committee were compiled in a briefing book, with tabs on each Senator.

Therefore, these incidents demonstrate the potential for abuse inherent in the Bureau's unregulated name-check procedure. White House requests bypassed the Attorney General, and the FBI Director's own requests took place totally within the Bureau. The real meaning of the long-standing fear that the FBI had so-called dossiers on Congressmen and other prominent persons was that FBI officials could have name-check reports prepared for his use on anyone he desired to know more about.

Abuse of Investigative Powers

The next category is abuse of the FBI's investigative powers.

There is a vivid example under the Kennedy Administration involving the FBI's late-night and early-morning interviews of a steel-company executive and several reporters who had written stories about the steel executive. Former Assistant FBI Director Courtney Evans, who was informal liaison with Attorney General Kennedy, has told the Committee that he was given no reason for the request.

Another example arises out of the Bobby Baker case. In 1965 the FBI declined a request of the Justice Department Criminal Division to "wire" a witness in the investigation of former Johnson Senate aide Bobby Baker. Although the FBI refused on grounds that there was not adequate security, the Criminal Division had the Bureau of Narcotics in the Treasury Department "wire" the witness as a legitimate alternative. When the Baker trial began in 1967, this became known. Presidential aide Marvin Watson told the FBI that President Johnson was quite "exercised," and the FBI was ordered to conduct a discreet "rundown" on the head of the Criminal Division in 1965 and four persons in Treasury and the Narcotics Bureau, including specifically any associations with former Attorney General Robert Kennedy.

Another incident occurred in 1966 when Mr. Watson requested that the FBI monitor the televised hearings of the Senate Foreign Relations Committee on Vietnam and prepare a memorandum comparing statements of

Senators Fulbright and Morse with "the Communist Party line."

At the request of President Johnson, made directly to FBI executive Cartha DeLoach, the FBI passed purely political intelligence about United States Senators to the White House which was obtained as a by-product of otherwise legitimate national-security electronic surveillance of foreign-intelligence targets. This practice also continued under the Nixon Administration at the request of Mr. H. R. Haldeman.

Electronic Surveillance

It is more difficult to place the label "abuse" automatically on presidential requests for electronic surveillance to investigate leaks of classified information. Attorney General Kennedy authorized wiretaps in 1962 on *New York Times* reporter Hanson Baldwin and his secretary, and they lasted for about one month.

In addition to the wiretap on *New York Times* reporter Hanson Baldwin in 1962, the Committee has received materials from the FBI reflecting authorization by Attorney General Robert Kennedy of a wiretap for *Newsweek* magazine in 1961 during the investigation of another leak of classified information. Further materials reflect authorization by Attorney General Nicholas Katzenbach of a wiretap on the editor of an anti-Communist newsletter in 1965, also during the investigation of a leak of classified information.

The Committee has received materials from the FBI reflecting authorization by Attorney General Robert F. Kennedy of wiretaps on at least six American citizens, including three executive-branch officials, a congressional staff member and two registered lobbying agents for foreign interests. The materials also reflect that these wiretaps related to an investigation of efforts by foreign interests to influence United States economic policies.

The wiretaps under the Nixon Administration of journalists and current or former White House and other executive officials have been widely publicized.

The staff's inquiry into this matter has determined that, according to available records, at least one of these wiretaps had nothing to do with leaks and was conducted solely for personal information about the target. Nevertheless, the wiretapping to investigate leaks under Attorneys General Kennedy and Katzenbach and of President Roosevelt's aides were undoubtedly precedents J. Edgar Hoover had in mind when he told President Nixon and Dr. Kissinger in 1969 that wiretaps had been used for these purposes in the past.

Surveillance of King, Agnew

Another abuse of FBI investigative powers under the Johnson Administration was the surveillance conducted at the 1964 Democratic National Convention in Atlantic City. The most-sensitive details of the plans and tactics of persons supporting the Mississippi Freedom Democratic Party delegate challenge went to the White House from the FBI's wiretap on Dr. [Martin Luther] King and other types of FBI surveillance. The responsible White House official at the time, Mr. Walter Jenkins, has told the Committee that he can recall no political use made of these reports. Nevertheless, an unsigned document has been located at the Johnson Library recording at least one political use of Mr. DeLoach's phone reports.

As Theodore H. White's account of the 1964 campaign ["The Making of the President 1964"] makes clear, the most important single issue that might have disturbed President Johnson at the Atlantic City Convention was the Mississippi challenge. And the FBI's own inquiry into the Atlantic City events reports several FBI agents' recollection that one purpose of the Bureau operation was to help avoid "embarrassment to the President."

The Committee must weigh all the evidence in deciding whether this abuse of the FBI resulted from a White House request, from FBI officials volunteering information to serve and please the President, or from a legitimate civil-disorders intelligence operation which got out of hand because no one was willing to shut off the political-intelligence by-product.

It should also be noted that an aide to Vice President Hubert Humphrey contacted the FBI to request assistance at the 1968 Chicago [Democratic] Convention. Nothing appears to have come of this request, largely because Attorney General Ramsey Clark turned down FBI requests for authorization to wiretap protest-demonstration leaders at the Chicago Convention.

According to materials provided to the Committee by the FBI, President Johnson asked the FBI to conduct physical surveillance on Mrs. Anna Chennault, prominent Republican woman leader, on Oct. 30, 1968, in the final days of the election campaign. The FBI instituted this surveillance to cover her activities in Washington, D.C., and New York City. The results of this physical surveillance were disseminated to J. Bromley Smith, executive secretary of the National Security Council, who had conveyed Johnson's request to Cartha DeLoach of the FBI. On Nov. 7, 1968, Smith called DeLoach and stated that President Johnson wanted the FBI to abandon its physical surveillance of Mrs. Chennault.

On Nov. 13, 1968, at the instruction of President Johnson, the FBI checked the toll-call telephone records in Albuquerque, N.M., to determine if vice-presidential candidate Spiro Agnew had called Mrs. Chennault or the South Vietnamese Embassy on Nov. 2, 1968, when he was in Albuquerque. No such records were located. President Johnson was furnished with this information on Nov. 13, 1968. Also, the arrival and departure times of Agnew in and out of Albuquerque on Nov. 2, 1968, were verified at the request of the White House.

The FBI has reviewed its files on this matter and has advised that the apparent reason the White House was interested in the activities of Mrs. Chennault and Spiro Agnew was to determine whether the South Vietnamese had secretly been in touch with supporters of presidential candidate Nixon, possibly through Mrs. Chennault, as President Johnson was apparently suspicious that the South Vietnamese were trying to sabotage his peace negotiations in the hope that Nixon would win the election and then take a harder line towards North Vietnam.

The FBI also states that physical surveillance of Mrs. Chennault was consistent with FBI responsibilities to determine if her activities were in violation of certain provisions of the Foreign Agents Registration Act (Section 601, et seq., Title 22, USC) and of the Neutrality Act (Section 953, Title 18, USC).

(Further details of these events involving electronic surveillance remain classified "Top Secret.")

Actions on Ellsberg, Abernathy

Finally, there are two additional examples of political abuse of the FBI or by the FBI in the 1970s.

In July 1971, three months after the supposed end of FBI COINTEL-PRO [counterintelligence program] operations, the FBI leaked to a newsman derogatory public-record information about Daniel Ellsberg's lawyer. Copies of the article were sent to the Attorney General, the Deputy Attorney General and presidential aide H. R. Haldeman, with the specific approval of Director Hoover, with no indication it was generated by the FBI.

In May 1970, the FBI provided Vice President Agnew at his request with derogatory public-record information and other allegations about Rev. Ralph David Abernathy, the president of the Southern Christian Leadership Conference. This occurred following a telephone conversation between Director Hoover and Mr. Agnew during which, according to FBI records, the Vice President "said he thought he was going to have to start destroying Abernathy's credibility."

Thus, in summary, political abuse of the FBI and by the FBI has extended over the years through Administrations of both parties.

> *Excerpts from* Covert Action in Chile: 1963-1973, *a staff report of the Senate Select Intelligence Committee published Dec. 4, 1975:*

I. Overview and Background

A. Overview: Covert Action in Chile

Covert United States involvement in Chile in the decade between 1963 and 1973 was extensive and continuous. The Central Intelligence Agency spent three million dollars in an effort to influence the outcome of the 1964 Chilean presidential elections. Eight million dollars was spent, covertly, in the three years between 1970 and the military coup in September 1973, with over three million dollars expended in fiscal year 1972 alone. [Footnote: Moreover, the bare figures are more likely to understate than to exaggerate the extent of U.S. covert action. In the years before the 1973 coup, especially, CIA dollars could be channeled through the Chilean black market where the unofficial exchange rate into Chilean *escudos* often reached five times the official rate.]

It is not easy to draw a neat box around what was "covert action." The range of clandestine activities undertaken by the CIA includes covert action, clandestine intelligence collection, liaison with local police and intelligence services, and counterintelligence. The distinctions among the types of activities are mirrored in organizational arrangements, both at Headquarters and in the field. Yet it is not always so easy to distinguish the effects of various activities. If the CIA provides financial support to a political party, this is called "covert action"; if the Agency develops a paid "asset" in that party for the purpose of information gathering, the project is "clandestine intelligence collection."...

The pattern of United States covert action in Chile is striking but not unique. It arose in the context not only of American foreign policy, but also of covert U.S. involvement in other countries within and outside Latin America. The scale of CIA involvement in Chile was unusual but by no means unprecedented....

C. Historical Background to Recent United States-Chilean Relations

1. Chilean Politics and Society: An Overview

....Chile's history has been one of remarkable continuity in civilian, democratic rule. From independence in 1818 until the military *coup d'etat* of September 1973, Chile underwent only three brief interruptions of its democratic tradition. From 1932 until the overthrow of Allende in 1973, constitutional rule in Chile was unbroken.

Chile defies simplistic North American stereotypes of Latin America. With more than two-thirds of its population living in cities, and a 1970 per capita GNP of $760, Chile is one of the most urbanized and industrialized countries in Latin America. Nearly all of the Chilean population is literate. Chile has an advanced social welfare program, although its activities did not reach the majority of the poor until popular participation began to be exerted in the early 1960's. Chileans are a largely integrated mixture of indigenous American with European immigrant stock. Until September 1973, Chileans brokered their demands in a bicameral parliament through a multi-party system and through a broad array of economic, trade union, and, more recently, managerial and professional associations.

2. U.S. Policy Toward Chile

The history of United States policy toward Chile followed the patterns of United States diplomatic and economic interests in the hemisphere. In the same year that the United States recognized Chilean independence, 1823, it also proclaimed the Monroe Doctrine. This unilateral policy pronouncement of the United States was directed as a warning toward rival

European powers not to interfere in the internal political affairs of this hemisphere.

The U.S. reaction to Fidel Castro's rise to power suggested that while the Monroe Doctrine had been abandoned, the principles which prompted it were still alive. Castro's presence spurred a new United States hemispheric policy with special significance for Chile—the Alliance for Progress. There was little disagreement among policymakers either at the end of the Eisenhower Administration or at the beginning of the Kennedy Administration that something had to be done about the alarming threat that Castro was seen to represent to the stability of the hemisphere.

The U.S. reaction to the new hemispheric danger—communist revolution—evolved into a dual policy response. Widespread malnutrition, illiteracy, hopeless housing conditions and hunger for the vast majority of Latin Americans who were poor; these were seen as communism's allies. Consequently, the U.S. undertook loans to national development programs and supported civilian reformist regimes, all with an eye to preventing the appearance of another Fidel Castro in our hemisphere.

But there was another component in U.S. policy toward Latin America. Counterinsurgency techniques were developed to combat urban or rural guerrilla insurgencies often encouraged or supported by Castro's regime. Development could not cure overnight the social ills which were seen as the breeding ground of communism. New loans for Latin American countries' internal national development programs would take time to bear fruit. In the meantime, the communist threat would continue. The vicious circle plaguing the logic of the Alliance for Progress soon became apparent. In order to eliminate the short-term danger of communist subversion, it was often seen as necessary to support Latin American armed forces, yet frequently it was those same armed forces who were helping to freeze the status quo which the Alliance sought to alter.

Of all the countries in the hemisphere, Chile was chosen to become the showcase for the new Alliance for Progress. Chile had the extensive bureaucratic infrastructure to plan and administer a national development program; moreover, its history of popular support for Socialist, Communist and other leftist parties was perceived in Washington as flirtation with communism. In the years between 1962 and 1969, Chile received well over a billion dollars in direct, overt United States aid, loans and grants both included. Chile received more aid per capita than any country in the hemisphere. Between 1964 and 1970, $200 to $300 million in short-term lines of credit was continuously available to Chile from private American banks.

3. Chilean Political Parties: 1958-1970

The 1970 elections marked the fourth time Salvador Allende had been the presidential candidate of the Chilean left. His personality and his program were familiar to Chilean voters. His platform was similar in all three elections: efforts to redistribute income and reshape the Chilean economy, beginning with the nationalization of major industries, especially the copper companies; greatly expanded agrarian reform; and expanded relations with socialist and communist countries.

Allende was one of four candidates in the 1958 elections. His principal opponents were Jorge Alessandri, a conservative, and Eduardo Frei, the candidate of the newly formed Christian Democratic Party, which contended against the traditionally centrist Radical Party. Allende's coalition was an uneasy alliance, composed principally of the Socialist and Communist Parties, labeled the Popular Action Front (FRAP). Allende himself, a self-avowed Marxist, was considered a moderate within his Socialist Party, which ranged from the extreme left to moderate social democrats. The Socialists, however, were more militant than the pro-Soviet, bureaucratic—though highly organized and disciplined—Communist Party.

Allende finished second to Alessandri in the 1958 election by less than three percent of the vote....

The 1964 election shaped up as a three-way race. Frei was once again the Christian Democratic candidate, and the parties of the left once again selected Allende as their standard-bearer. The governing coalition, the Democratic Front, chose Radical Julio Duran as their candidate. Due in part to an adverse election result in a March 1964 by-election in a previously conservative province, the Democratic Front collapsed. The Conservatives and Liberals, reacting to the prospect of an Allende victory, threw their support to Frei, leaving Duran as the standard-bearer of only the Radical Party.

After Frei's decisive majority victory, in which he received 57 percent of the vote, he began to implement what he called a "revolution in liberty." That included agrarian, tax, and housing reform. To deal with the American copper companies, Frei proposed "Chileanization," by which the state would purchase majority ownership in order to exercise control and stimulate output.

Frei's reforms, while impressive, fell far short of what he had promised....

Frei's relations with the United States were cordial, although he pursued an independent foreign policy. His government established diplomatic relations with the Soviet Union immediately after taking power and in 1969 reestablished trade relations with Cuba....

III. Major Covert Action Programs and Their Effects

This section outlines the major programs of covert action undertaken by the United States in Chile, period by period. In every instance, covert action was an instrument of United States foreign policy, decided upon at the highest levels of the government.

A. The 1964 Presidential Election

1. United States Policy

The United States was involved on a massive scale in the 1964 presidential election in Chile. The Special Group authorized over three million dollars during the 1962-64 period to prevent the election of a Socialist or Communist candidate. [The Special Group was the predecessor of the 40 Committee, a sub-Cabinet level body of the Executive Branch whose mandate is to review proposed major covert actions. The Committee has existed in similar form since the 1950's under a variety of names: 5412 Panel, Special Group (until 1964), 303 Committee (to 1969), and 40 Committee (since 1969). Currently chaired by the President's Assistant for National Security Affairs, the Committee includes the Undersecretary of State for Political Affairs, the Deputy Secretary of Defense, the Chairman of the Joint Chiefs of Staff, and the Director of Central Intelligence.] A total of nearly four million dollars was spent on some fifteen covert action projects ranging from organizing slum dwellers to passing funds to political parties.

The goal, broadly, was to prevent or minimize the influence of Chilean Communists or Marxists in the government that would emerge from the 1964 election. Consequently, the U.S. sought the most effective way of opposing FRAP (Popular Action Front), an alliance of Chilean Socialists, Communists, and several miniscule non-Marxist parties of the left which backed the candidacy of Salvador Allende. Specifically, the policy called for support of the Christian Democratic Party, the Democratic Front (a coalition of rightist parties), and a variety of anti-communist propaganda and organizing activities.

The groundwork for the election was laid early in 1961 by establishing operational relationships with key political parties and by creating propaganda and organizational mechanisms capable of influencing key sectors of the population. Projects that had been conducted since the 1950's among peasants, slum dwellers, organized labor, students, and the media provided a basis for much of the pre-election covert action.

The main problem facing the United States two years before the election was the selection of a party and/or candidate to support against the leftist alliance. The CIA presented two papers to the Special Group on April 2, 1962. One of these papers proposed support for the Christian Democratic Party, while the other recommended support of the Radical Party, a group to the right of the Christian Democrats. The Special Group approved both proposals. Although this strategy appears to have begun as an effort to hedge bets and support two candidates for President, it evolved into a strategy designed to support the Christian Democratic candidate.

On August 27, 1962, the Special Group approved the use of a third-country funding channel and authorized $180,000 in fiscal year 1963 for the Chilean Christian Democrats. The Kennedy Administration had preferred a center-right government in Chile, consisting of the Radicals on the right and the Christian Democrats in the center. However, political events in Chile in 1962-1963—principally the creation of a right-wing alliance that included the Radical Party—precluded such a coalition. Consequently, throughout 1963, the United States funded both the Christian Democrats and the right-wing coalition, the Democratic Front.

After a by-election defeat in May 1964 destroyed the Democratic Front, the U.S. threw its support fully behind the Christian Democratic candidate. However, CIA funds continued to subsidize the Radical Party candidate in order to enhance the Christian Democrats' image as a moderate progressive party being attacked from the right as well as the left.

2. Covert Action Techniques

Covert action during the 1964 campaign was composed of two major elements. One was direct financial support of the Christian Democratic campaign. The CIA underwrote slightly more than half of the total cost of that campaign. After debate, the Special Group decided not to inform the Christian Democratic candidate, Eduardo Frei, of American covert support of his campaign. A number of intermediaries were therefore mobilized to pass the money to the Christian Democrats. In addition to the subsidies for the Christian Democratic Party, the Special Group allocated funds to the Radical Party and to private citizens' groups.

In addition to support for political parties, the CIA mounted a massive anti-communist propaganda campaign. Extensive use was made of the press, radio, films, pamphlets, posters, leaflets, direct mailings, paper streamers, and wall painting. It was a "scare campaign," which relied heavily on images of Soviet tanks and Cuban firing squads and was directed especially to women. Hundreds of thousands of copies of the anti-communist pastoral letter of Pope Pius XI were distributed by Christian Democratic organizations. They carried the designation, "printed privately by citizens without political affiliation, in order to more broadly disseminate its content." "Disinformation" and "black propaganda"— material which purported to originate from another source, such as the Chilean Communist Party—were used as well.

The propaganda campaign was enormous. During the first week of intensive propaganda activity (the third week of June 1964), a CIA-funded propaganda group produced twenty radio spots per day in Santiago and on 44 provincial stations; twelve-minute news broadcasts five times daily on three Santiago stations and 24 provincial outlets; thousands of cartoons, and much paid press advertising. By the end of June, the group produced 24 daily newscasts in Santiago and the provinces, 26 weekly "commentary" programs, and distributed 3,000 posters daily. The CIA regards the anti-communist scare campaign as the most effective activity undertaken by the U.S. on behalf of the Christian Democratic candidate.

The propaganda campaign was conducted internationally as well, and articles from abroad were "replayed" in Chile. Chilean newspapers reported: an endorsement of Frei by the sister of a Latin American leader, a public letter from a former president in exile in the U.S., a "message from the women of Venezuela," and dire warnings about an Allende victory from various figures in military governments in Latin America.

The CIA ran political action operations independent of the Christian Democrats' campaign in a number of important voter blocks, including slum dwellers, peasants, organized labor, and dissident Socialists. Support was given to "anti-communist" members of the Radical Party in their efforts to achieve positions of influence in the party hierarchy, and to prevent the party from throwing its support behind Allende.

3. U.S. Government Organization for the 1964 Chilean Election

To manage the election effort, an electoral committee was established in Washington, consisting of the Assistant Secretary of State for Inter-American Affairs, Thomas Mann; the Western Hemisphere Division Chief of the CIA, Desmond Fitzgerald; Ralph Dungan and McGeorge Bundy from the White House; and the Chief of the Western Hemisphere Division Branch Four, the branch that has jurisdiction over Chile. This group was in close touch with the State Department Office of Bolivian and Chilean Affairs. In Santiago there was a parallel Election Committee that coordinated U.S. efforts. It included the Deputy Chief of Mission, the CIA Chief of Station, and the heads of the Political and Economic Sections, as well as the Ambassador. The Election Committee in Washington coordinated lines to higher authority and to the field and other agencies. No special task force was established, and the CIA Station in Santiago was temporarily increased by only three officers.

4. Role of Multinational Corporations

A group of American businessmen in Chile offered to provide one and a half million dollars to be administered and disbursed covertly by the U.S. Government to prevent Allende from winning the 1964 presidential election. This offer went to the 303 Committee (the name of the Special Group after June 1964) which decided not to accept the offer. It decided that offers from American business could not be accepted, that they were neither a secure way nor an honorable way of doing business. This decision was a declaration of policy which set the precedent for refusing to accept such collaboration between CIA and private business. However, CIA money, represented as private money, was passed to the Christian Democrats through a private businessman.

5. Role of the Chilean Military

On July 19, 1964, the Chilean Defense Council, which is the equivalent of the U.S. Joint Chiefs of Staff, went to President Alessandri to propose a *coup d'etat* if Allende won. This offer was transmitted to the CIA Chief of Station, who told the Chilean Defense Council through an intermediary that the United States was absolutely opposed to a coup. On July 20, the Deputy Chief of Mission at the U.S. Embassy was approached by a Chilean Air Force general who threatened a coup if Allende won. The DCM reproached him for proposing a *coup d'etat* and there was no further mention of it. Earlier, the CIA learned that the Radical candidate for election, several other Chileans, and an ex-politician from another Latin American country had met on June 2 to organize a rightist group called the Legion of Liberty. They said this group would stage a *coup d'etat* if Allende won, or if Frei won and sought a coalition government with the Communist Party. Two of the Chileans at the meeting reported that some military officers wanted to stage a *coup d'etat* before the election if the United States Government would promise to support it. Those approaches were rebuffed by the CIA.

6. Effects of Covert Action

A CIA study concludes that U.S. intervention enabled Eduardo Frei to win a clear majority in the 1964 election, instead of merely a plurality. What U.S. Government documents do not make clear is why it was necessary to assure a majority, instead of accepting the victory a plurality would have assured. CIA assistance enabled the Christian Democratic Party to establish an extensive organization at the neighborhood and village level. That may have lent grassroots support for reformist efforts that the Frei government undertook over the next several years.

Some of the propaganda and polling mechanisms developed for use in 1964 were used repeatedly thereafter, in local and congressional campaigns, during the 1970 presidential campaign, and throughout the 1970-1973 Allende presidency. Allegations of CIA involvement in the campaign, and press allegations of CIA funding of the International Development Foundation contributed to the U.S. reluctance in 1970 to undertake another massive pre-election effort.

B. Covert Action: 1964-1969

During the years between the election of Christian Democratic President Eduardo Frei in 1964 and the presidential election campaign of 1970, the CIA conducted a variety of covert activities in Chile. Operating within different sectors of society, these activities were all intended to strengthen groups which supported President Frei and opposed Marxist influences.

The CIA spent a total of almost $2 million on covert action in Chile during this period, of which one-fourth was covered by 40 Committee authorizations for specific major political action efforts. The CIA conducted twenty covert action projects in Chile during these years.

1. Covert Action Methods

In February 1965 the 303 Committee approved $175,000 for a short-term political action project to provide covert support to selected candidates in the March 1965 congressional elections in Chile. According to the CIA, twenty-two candidates were selected by the Station and the Ambassador; nine were elected. The operation helped defeat up to 13 FRAP candidates who would otherwise have won congressional seats.

Another election effort was authorized in July 1968, in preparation for the March 1969 congressional election. The 40 Committee authorized $350,-

000 for this effort, with the objective of strengthening moderate political forces before the 1970 presidential election. The program consisted of providing financial support to candidates, supporting a splinter Socialist Party in order to attract votes away from Allende's socialist party, propaganda activities, and assisting independent groups. The CIA regarded the election effort as successful in meeting its limited objective; ten of the twelve candidates selected for support won their races, including one very unexpected victory. The support provided to the dissident socialist group deprived the Socialist Party of a minimum of seven congressional seats.

The 303 Committee also approved $30,000 in 1967 to strengthen the right wing of the Radical Party.

A number of other political actions not requiring 303 Committee approval were conducted. The project to increase the effectiveness and appeal of the Christian Democratic Party and to subsidize the party during the 1964 elections continued into late 1965 or 1966, as did a project to influence key members of the Socialist Party toward orthodox European socialism and away from communism. During this period, the CIA dealt with a Chilean official at the cabinet level, though with scant result.

Covert action efforts were conducted during this period to influence the political development of various sectors of Chilean society. One project, conducted prior to the 1964 elections to strengthen Christian Democratic support among peasants and slum dwellers, continued to help train and organize "anti-communists" in these and other sectors until public exposure of CIA funding in 1967 forced its termination. A project to compete organizationally with the Marxists among the urban poor of Santiago was initiated shortly after the 1964 election, and was terminated in mid-1969 because the principal agent was unwilling to prejudice the independent posture of the organization by using it on a large scale to deliver votes in the 1969 and 1970 presidential elections. In the mid-1960's, the CIA supported an anti-communist women's group active in Chilean political and intellectual life.

Two projects worked within organized labor in Chile. One, which began during the 1964 election period, was a labor action project to combat the communist-dominated *Central Unica de Trabajadores Chilenos* (CUTCh) and to support democratic labor groups. Another project was conducted in the Catholic labor field.

Various CIA projects during this period supported media efforts. One, begun in the early 1950's, operated wire services. Another, which was an important part of the 1964 election effort, supported anti-communist propaganda activities through wall posters attributed to fictitious groups, leaflet campaigns, and public heckling.

A third project supported a right-wing weekly newspaper, which was an instrument of the anti-Allende campaign during and for a time after the 1970 election campaign. Another project funded an asset who produced regular radio political commentary shows attacking the political parties on the left and supporting CIA-selected candidates. After the Soviet invasion of Czechoslovakia, this asset organized a march on the Soviet Embassy which led to major police action and mass media coverage. Other assets funded under this project placed CIA-inspired editorials almost daily in *El Mercurio,* Chile's major newspaper and, after 1968, exerted substantial control over the content of that paper's international news section.

The CIA also maintained covert liaison relations with Chile's internal security and intelligence services, civilian and military. The primary purpose of these arrangements was to enable the Chilean services to assist CIA in information collection about foreign targets. A subsidiary purpose of these relationships was to collect information and meet the threat posed by communists and other groups of the far left within Chile.

2. Effects of Covert Action

The CIA's evaluations of the 1965 and 1969 election projects suggest that those efforts were relatively successful in achieving their immediate goals. On the other hand, the labor and "community development" projects were deemed rather unsuccessful in countering the growth of strong leftist sentiment and organization among workers, peasants and slum dwellers. For instance, neither of the labor projects was able to find a nucleus of legitimate Chilean labor leaders to compete effectively with the communist-dominated CUTCh.

The propaganda projects probably had a substantial cumulative effect over these years, both in helping to polarize public opinion concerning the nature of the threat posed by communists and other leftists, and in maintaining an extensive propaganda capability. Propaganda mechanisms developed during the 1960's were ready to be used in the 1970 election campaign. At the same time, however, in a country where nationalism, "economic independence" and "anti-imperialism" claimed almost universal support, the persistent allegations that the Christian Democrats and other parties of the center and right were linked to the CIA may have played a part in undercutting popular support for them.

C. The 1970 Election: A "Spoiling" Campaign

1. United States Policy and Covert Action

Early in 1969, President Nixon announced a new policy toward Latin America, labelled by him "Action for Progress." It was to replace the Alliance for Progress which the President characterized as paternalistic and unrealistic. Instead, the United States was to seek "mature partnership" with Latin American countries, emphasizing trade and not aid. The reformist trappings of the Alliance were to be dropped; the United States announced itself prepared to deal with foreign governments pragmatically.

The United States program of covert action in the 1970 Chilean elections reflected this less activist stance. Nevertheless, that covert involvement was substantial. In March 1970, the 40 Committee decided that the United States should not support any single candidate in the election but should instead wage "spoiling" operations against the Popular Unity coalition which supported the Marxist candidate, Salvador Allende. In all, the CIA spent from $800,000 to $1,000,000 on covert action to affect the outcome of the 1970 Presidential election. Of this amount, about half was for major efforts approved by the 40 Committee. By CIA estimates, the Cubans provided about $350,000 to Allende's campaign, with the Soviets adding an additional, undetermined amount. The large-scale propaganda campaign which was undertaken by the U.S. was similar to that of 1964: an Allende victory was equated with violence and repression.

2. Policy Decisions

Discussions within the United States Government about the 1970 elections began in the wake of the March 1969 Chilean congressional elections. The CIA's involvement in those elections was regarded by Washington as relatively successful, even though the Christian Democrats' portion of the vote fell from 43 per cent in 1965 to 31 per cent in 1969. In June 1968 the 40 Committee had authorized $350,000 for that effort, of which $200,000 actually was spent. Ten of the twelve CIA-supported candidates were elected.

The 1970 election was discussed at a 40 Committee meeting on April 17, 1969. It was suggested that something be done, and the CIA representative noted that an election operation would not be effective unless it were started early. But no action was taken at that time.

The 1970 Presidential race quickly turned into a three-way contest. The conservative National Party, buoyed by the 1969 congressional election results, supported 74-year-old, ex-President Jorge Alessandri. Radomiro Tomic became the Christian Democratic nominee. Tomic, to the left of President Frei, was unhappy about campaigning on the Frei government's record and at one point made overtures to the Marxist left. Salvador Allende was once again the candidate of the left, this time formed into a Popular Unity coalition which included both Marxist and non-Marxist parties. Allende's platform included nationalization of the copper mines, accelerated agrarian reform, socialization of major sectors of the economy, wage increases, and improved relations with socialist and communist countries.

In December 1969, the Embassy and Station in Santiago forwarded a proposal for an anti-Allende campaign. That proposal, however, was withdrawn because of the State Department's qualms about whether or not the United States should become involved at all. The CIA felt it was not in a position to support Tomic actively because ambassadorial "ground rules" of the previous few years had prevented the CIA from dealing with the Christian Democrats. The Agency believed that Alessandri, the apparent front runner, needed more than money; he needed help in managing his campaign.

On March 25, 1970, the 40 Committee approved a joint Embassy/CIA proposal recommending that "spoiling" operations—propaganda and other activities—be undertaken by the CIA in an effort to prevent an election victory by Allende. Direct support was not furnished to either of his opponents. This first authorization was for $135,000, with the possibility of more later.

On June 18, 1970, the Ambassador, Edward Korry, submitted a two-phase proposal to the Department of State and the CIA for review. The first phase involved an increase in support for the anti-Allende campaign. The second was a $500,000 contingency plan to influence the congressional vote in the event of a vote between the candidates finishing first and second. In response to State Department reluctance, the Ambassador responded by querying: if Allende were to gain power, how would the U.S. respond to those who asked what actions it had taken to prevent it?

On June 27, the 40 Committee approved the increase in funding for the anti-Allende "spoiling" operation by $300,000. State Department officials at the meeting voted "yes" only reluctantly. They spoke against the contingency plan, and a decision on it was deferred pending the results of the September 4 election.

CIA officials met several times with officials from ITT [International Telephone and Telegraph Corp.] during July. The CIA turned down ITT's proposal to make funds available for CIA transmission to Alessandri but did provide the company advice on how to pass money to Alessandri. Some $350,000 of ITT money was passed to Alessandri during the campaign—$250,000 to his campaign and $100,000 to the National Party. About another $350,000 came from other U.S. businesses. According to CIA documents, the Station Chief informed the Ambassador that the CIA was advising ITT in funding the Alessandri campaign, but not that the Station was aiding ITT in passing money to the National Party.

The 40 Committee met again on August 7 but did not give further consideration to supporting either Alessandri or Tomic. As the anti-Allende campaign in Chile intensified, senior policy makers turned to the issue of U.S. policy in the event of an Allende victory. A study done in response to National Security Study Memorandum 97 was approved by the Interdepartmental Group (IG) on August 18. The approved paper set forth four options, one in the form of a covert annex. The consensus of the Interdepartmental Group favored maintaining minimal relations with Allende, but the Senior Review Group deferred decision until after the elections. Similarly, a paper with alternatives was circulated to 40 Committee members on August 13, but no action resulted.

3. "Spoiling" Operations

The "spoiling" operations had two objectives: (1) undermining communist efforts to bring about a coalition of leftist forces which could gain control of the presidency in 1970; and (2) strengthening non-Marxist political leaders and forces in Chile in order to develop an effective alternative to the Popular Unity coalition in preparation for the 1970 presidential election.

In working toward these objectives, the CIA made use of half-a-dozen covert action projects. Those projects were focused into an intensive propaganda campaign which made use of virtually all media within Chile and which placed and replayed items in the international press as well. Propaganda placements were achieved through subsidizing right-wing women's and "civic action" groups. A "scare campaign," using many of the same themes as the 1964 presidential election program, equated an Allende victory with violence and Stalinist repression. Unlike 1964, however, the 1970 operation did not involve extensive public opinion polling, grass-roots organizing, or "community development" efforts, nor, as mentioned, direct funding of any candidate.

In addition to the massive propaganda campaign, the CIA's effort prior to the election included political action aimed at splintering the non-Marxist Radical Party and reducing the number of votes which it could deliver to the Popular Unity coalition's candidate. Also, "black propaganda"—material purporting to be the product of another group—was used in 1970 to sow dissent between Communists and Socialists, and between the national labor confederation and the Chilean Communist Party.

The CIA's propaganda operation for the 1970 elections made use of mechanisms that had been developed earlier. One mechanism had been used extensively by the CIA during the March 1969 congressional elections.

During the 1970 campaign it produced hundreds of thousands of high-quality printed pieces, ranging from posters and leaflets to picture books, and carried out an extensive propaganda program through many radio and press outlets. Other propaganda mechanisms that were in place prior to the 1970 campaign included an editorial support group that provided political features, editorials, and news articles for radio and press placement; a service for placing anti-communist press and radio items; and three different news services.

There was a wide variety of propaganda products: a newsletter mailed to approximately two thousand journalists, academicians, politicians, and other opinion makers; a booklet showing what life would be like if Allende won the presidential election; translation and distribution of chronicles of opposition to the Soviet regime; poster distribution and sign-painting teams. The sign-painting teams had instructions to paint the slogan *"su paredón"* (your wall) on 2,000 walls, evoking an image of communist firing squads. The "scare campaign" *(campaña de terror)* exploited the violence of the invasion of Czechoslovakia with large photographs of Prague and of tanks in downtown Santiago. Other posters, resembling those used in 1964, portrayed Cuban political prisoners before the firing squad, and warned that an Allende victory would mean the end of religion and family life in Chile.

Still another project funded individual press assets. One, who produced regular radio commentary shows on a nationwide hookup, had been CIA-funded since 1965 and continued to wage propaganda for CIA during the Allende presidency. Other assets, all employees of *El Mercurio,* enabled the

Station to generate more than one editorial per day based on CIA guidance. Access to *El Mercurio* had a multiplier effect, since its editorials were read throughout the country on various national radio networks. Moreover, *El Mercurio* was one of the most influential Latin American newspapers, particularly in business circles abroad. A project which placed anti-communist press and radio items was reported in 1970 to reach an audience of well over five million listeners.

The CIA funded only one political group during the 1970 campaign, in an effort to reduce the number of Radical Party votes for Allende.

4. Effects

The covert action "spoiling" efforts by the United States during the 1970 campaign did not succeed: Allende won a plurality in the September 4 election. Nevertheless, the "spoiling" campaign had several important effects. First, the "scare campaign" contributed to the political polarization and financial panic of the period. Themes developed during the campaign were exploited even more intensely during the weeks following September 4, in an effort to cause enough financial panic and political instability to goad President Frei or the Chilean military into action.

Second, many of the assets involved in the anti-Allende campaign became so visible that their usefulness was limited thereafter. Several of them left Chile. When Allende took office, little was left of the CIA-funded propaganda apparatus. Nevertheless, there remained a nucleus sufficient to permit a vocal anti-Allende opposition to function effectively even before the new President was inaugurated.

D. Covert Action Between September 4 and October 24, 1970

On September 4, 1970, Allende won a plurality in Chile's presidential election. Since no candidate had received a majority of the popular vote, the Chilean Constitution required that a joint session of its Congress decide between the first- and second-place finishers. The date set for the congressional session was October 24, 1970.

The reaction in Washington to Allende's plurality victory was immediate. The 40 Committee met on September 8 and 14 to discuss what action should be taken prior to the October 24 congressional vote. On September 15, President Nixon informed CIA Director Richard Helms that an Allende regime in Chile would not be acceptable to the United States and instructed the CIA to play a direct role in organizing a military *coup d'etat* in Chile to prevent Allende's accession to the Presidency.

Following the September 14 meeting of the 40 Committee and President Nixon's September 15 instruction to the CIA, U.S. Government efforts to prevent Allende from assuming office proceeded on two tracks. [Footnote: The terms Track I and Track II were known only to CIA and White House officials who were knowledgeable about the President's September 15 order to the CIA.] Track I comprised all covert activities approved by the 40 Committee, including political, economic and propaganda activities. These activities were designed to induce Allende's opponents in Chile to prevent his assumption of power, either through political or military means. Track II activities in Chile were undertaken in response to President Nixon's September 15 order and were directed toward actively promoting and encouraging the Chilean military to move against Allende.

1. Track I

A. Political Action: Initially, both the 40 Committee and the CIA fastened on the so-called Frei re-election gambit as a means of preventing Allende's assumption of office. This gambit, which was considered a constitutional solution to the Allende problem, consisted of inducing enough congressional votes to elect Alessandri over Allende with the understanding that Alessandri would immediately resign, thus paving the way for a special election in which Frei would legally become a candidate. At the September 14 meeting of the 40 Committee, the Frei gambit was discussed, and the Committee authorized a contingency fund of $250,000 for covert support of projects which Frei or his associates deemed important. The funds were to be handled by Ambassador Korry and used if it appeared that they would be needed by the moderate faction of the Christian Democratic Party to swing congressional votes to Alessandri. The only proposal for the funds which was discussed was an attempt to bribe Chilean Congressmen to vote for Alessandri. That quickly was seen to be unworkable, and the $250,-000 was never spent.

CIA's Track I aimed at bringing about conditions in which the Frei gambit could take place. To do this, the CIA, at the direction of the 40 Committee, mobilized an interlocking political action, economic, and propaganda campaign. As part of its political action program, the CIA attempted indirectly to induce President Frei at least to consent to the gambit or, better yet, assist in its implementation. The Agency felt that pressures from those whose opinion and views he valued—in combination with certain propaganda activities—represented the only hope of converting Frei. In Europe and Latin America, influential members of the Christian Democratic movement and the Catholic Church were prompted either to visit or contact Frei. In spite of these efforts, Frei refused to interfere with the constitutional process, and the re-election gambit died.

B. Propaganda Campaign: On September 14, the 40 Committee agreed that a propaganda campaign should be undertaken by the CIA to focus on the damage that would befall Chile under an Allende government. The campaign was to include support for the Frei re-election gambit. According to a CIA memorandum, the campaign sought to create concerns about Chile's future if Allende were elected by the Congress; the propaganda was designed to influence Frei, the Chilean elite, and the Chilean military.

The propaganda campaign included several components. Predictions of economic collapse under Allende were replayed in CIA-generated articles in European and Latin American newspapers. In response to criticisms of *El*

Mercurio by candidate Allende, the CIA, through its covert action resources, orchestrated cables of support and protest from foreign newspapers, a protest statement from an international press association, and world press coverage of the association's protest. In addition, journalists—agents and otherwise—traveled to Chile for on-the-scene reporting. By September 28, the CIA had agents who were journalists from ten different countries in or en route to Chile. This group was supplemented by eight more journalists from five countries under the direction of high-level agents who were, for the most part, in managerial capacities in the media field.

Second, the CIA relied upon its own resources to generate anti-Allende propaganda in Chile. These efforts included: support for an underground press; placement of individual news items through agents; financing a small newspaper; indirect subsidy of *Patria y Libertad,* a group fervently opposed to Allende, and its radio programs, political advertisements, and political rallies; and the direct mailing of foreign news articles to Frei, his wife, selected leaders, and the Chilean domestic press.

Third, special intelligence and "inside" briefings were given to U.S. journalists, at their request. One *Time* cover story was considered particularly noteworthy. According to CIA documents, the *Time* correspondent in Chile apparently had accepted Allende's protestations of moderation and constitutionality at face value. Briefings requested by *Time* and provided by the CIA in Washington resulted in a change in the basic thrust of the *Time* story on Allende's September 4 victory and in the timing of that story.

A few statistics convey the magnitude of the CIA's propaganda campaign mounted during the six-week interim period in the Latin American and European media. According to the CIA, partial returns showed that 726 articles, broadcasts, editorials, and similar items directly resulted from Agency activity. The Agency had no way to measure the scope of the multiplier effect—i.e., how much its "induced" news focused media interest on the Chilean issues and stimulated additional coverage—but concluded that its contribution was both substantial and significant.

C. Economic Pressures: On September 29, 1970, the 40 Committee met. It was agreed that the Frei gambit had been overtaken by events and was dead. The "second-best option"—the cabinet resigning and being replaced with a military cabinet—was also deemed dead. The point was then made that there would probably be no military action unless economic pressures could be brought to bear on Chile. It was agreed that an attempt would be made to have American business take steps in line with the U.S. government's desire for immediate economic action.

The economic offensive against Chile, undertaken as a part of Track I, was intended to demonstrate the foreign economic reaction to Allende's accession to power, as well as to preview the future consequences of his regime. Generally, the 40 Committee approved cutting off all credits, pressuring firms to curtail investment in Chile and approaching other nations to cooperate in this venture.

These actions of the 40 Committee, and the establishment of an inter-agency working group to coordinate overt economic activities towards Chile (composed of the CIA's Western Hemisphere Division Chief and representatives from State, the NSC, and Treasury), adversely affected the Chilean economy; a major financial panic ensued. However, U.S. efforts to generate an economic crisis did not have the desired impact on the October 24 vote, nor did they stimulate a military intervention to prevent Allende's accession.

2. Track II

As previously noted, U.S. efforts to prevent Allende's assumption of office operated on two tracks between September 4 and October 24. Track II was initiated by President Nixon on September 15 when he instructed the CIA to play a direct role in organizing a military *coup d'etat* in Chile. The Agency was to take this action without coordination with the Departments of State or Defense and without informing the U.S. Ambassador. While coup possibilities in general and other means of seeking to prevent Allende's accession to power were explored by the 40 Committee throughout this period, the 40 Committee never discussed this direct CIA role. In practice, the Agency was to report, both for informational and approval purposes, to the White House.

Between October 5 and October 20, 1970, the CIA made 21 contacts with key military and *Carabinero* (police) officials in Chile. Those Chileans who were inclined to stage a coup were given assurances of strong support at the highest levels of the U.S. Government both before and after a coup.

Tracks I and II did, in fact, move together in the month after September 15. Ambassador Korry, who was formally excluded from Track II, was authorized to encourage a military coup, provided Frei concurred in that solution. At the 40 Committee meeting on September 14, he and other "appropriate members of the Embassy mission" were authorized to intensify their contacts with Chilean military officers to assess their willingness to support the "Frei gambit." The Ambassador was also authorized to make his contacts in the Chilean military aware that if Allende were seated, the military could expect no further military assistance (MAP) from the United States. Later, Korry was authorized to inform the Chilean military that all MAP and military sales were being held in abeyance pending the outcome of the congressional election on October 24.

The essential difference between Tracks I and II, as evidenced by instructions to Ambassador Korry during this period, was not that Track II was coup-oriented and Track I was not. Both had this objective in mind. There were two differences between the two tracks: Track I was contingent on at least the acquiescence of Frei; and the CIA's Track II direct contacts with the Chilean military, and its active promotion and support for a coup, were to be known only to a small group of individuals in the White House and the CIA.

Despite these efforts, Track II proved to be no more successful than Track I in preventing Allende's assumption of office. Although certain elements within the Chilean army were actively involved in coup plotting, the plans of the dissident Chileans never got off the ground. A rather disorganized coup attempt did begin on October 22, but aborted following the shooting of General Schneider.

On October 24, 1970, Salvador Allende was confirmed as President by Chilean Congress. On November 3, he was inaugurated. U.S. efforts, both overt and covert, to prevent his assumption of office had failed.

E. Covert Action During the Allende Years, 1970-1973

1. United States Policy and Covert Action

In his 1971 State of the World Message, released Feb. 25, 1971, President Nixon announced: "We are prepared to have the kind of relationship with the Chilean government that it is prepared to have with us." This public articulation of American policy followed internal discussions during the NSSM 97 exercise. Charles Meyer, Assistant Secretary of State for Inter-American Affairs, elaborated that "correct but minimal" line in his 1973 testimony before the Senate Foreign Relations Subcommittee on Multinational Corporations:

> Mr. Meyer. The policy of the Government, Mr. Chairman, was that there would be no intervention in the political affairs of Chile. We were consistent in that we financed no candidates, no political parties before or after September 8, or September 4.... The policy of the United States was that Chile's problem was a Chilean problem, to be settled by Chile. As the President stated in October of 1969, "We will deal with governments as they are."...

Yet, public pronouncements notwithstanding, after Allende's inauguration the 40 Committee approved a total of over seven million dollars in covert support to opposition groups in Chile. That money also funded an extensive anti-Allende propaganda campaign. Of the total authorized by the 40 Committee, over six million dollars was spent during the Allende presidency and $84,000 was expended shortly thereafter for commitments made before the coup. The total amount spent on covert action in Chile during 1970-73 was approximately $7 million, including project funds requiring 40 Committee approval.

Broadly speaking, U.S. policy sought to maximize pressures on the Allende government to prevent its consolidation and limit its ability to implement policies contrary to U.S. and hemispheric interests. That objective was stated clearly in National Security Decision Memorandum (NSDM) 93, issued in early November 1970. Other governments were encouraged to adopt similar policies, and the U.S. increased efforts to maintain close relations with friendly military leaders in the hemisphere. The "cool but correct" overt posture denied the Allende government a handy foreign enemy to use as a domestic and international rallying point. At the same time, covert action was one reflection of the concerns felt in Washington:

the desire to frustrate Allende's experiment in the Western Hemisphere and thus limit its attractiveness as a model; the fear that a Chile under Allende might harbor subversives from other Latin American countries; and the determination to sustain the principle of compensation for U.S. firms nationalized by the Allende government.

Henry Kissinger outlined several of these concerns in a background briefing to the press on September 16, 1970, in the wake of Allende's election plurality:

> Now it is fairly easy for one to predict that if Allende wins, there is a good chance that he will establish over a period of years some sort of Communist government. In that case you would have one not on an island off the coast which has not a traditional relationship and impact on Latin America, but in a major Latin American country you would have a Communist government, joining, for example, Argentina, which is already deeply divided, along a long frontier; joining Peru, which has already been heading in directions that have been difficult to deal with, and joining Bolivia, which has also gone in a more leftist, anti-U.S. direction, even without any of these developments.
>
> So I don't think we should delude ourselves that an Allende takeover in Chile would not present massive problems for us, and for democratic forces and for pro-U.S. forces in Latin America, and indeed to the whole Western Hemisphere. What would happen to the Western Hemisphere Defense Board, or to the Organization of American States, and so forth, is extremely problematical.... It is one of those situations which is not too happy for American interests....

As the discussion of National Intelligence Estimates in Section IV of this paper makes clear the more extreme fears about the effects of Allende's election were ill-founded: there never was a significant threat of a Soviet military presence; the "export" of Allende's revolution was limited, and its value as a model more restricted still; and Allende was little more hospitable to activist exiles from other Latin American countries than his predecessor had been. Nevertheless, those fears, often exaggerated, appear to have activated officials in Washington.

The "cool but correct" public posture and extensive clandestine activites formed two-thirds of a triad of official actions. The third was economic pressure, both overt and covert, intended to exacerbate the difficulties felt by Chile's economy. The United States cut off economic aid, denied credits, and made efforts—partially successful—to enlist the cooperation of international financial institutions and private firms in tightening the economic "squeeze" on Chile. That international "squeeze" intensified the effect of the economic measures taken by opposition groups within Chile, particularly the crippling strikes in the mining and transportation sectors. For instance, the combined effect of the foreign credit squeeze and domestic copper strikes on Chile's foreign exchange position was devastating.

Throughout the Allende years, the U.S. maintained close contact with the Chilean armed forces, both through the CIA and through U.S. military attaches. The basic purpose of these contacts was the gathering of intelligence, to detect any inclination within the Chilean armed forces to intervene. But U.S. officials also were instructed to seek influence within the

Chilean military and to be generally supportive of its activities without appearing to promise U.S. support for military efforts which might be premature. For instance, in November 1971, the Station was instructed to put the U.S. government in a position to take future advantage of either a political or a military solution to the Chilean dilemma, depending on developments within the country and the latter's impact on the military themselves.

There is no hard evidence of direct U.S. assistance to the coup, despite frequent allegations of such aid. Rather the United States—by its previous actions during Track II, its existing general posture of opposition to Allende, and the nature of its contacts with the Chilean military—probably gave the impression that it would not look with disfavor on a military coup. And U.S. officials in the years before 1973 may not always have succeeded in walking the thin line between monitoring indigenous coup plotting and actually stimulating it.

2. Techniques of Covert Action

A. Support for Opposition Political Parties: More than half of the 40 Committee-approved funds supported the opposition political parties: the Christian Democratic Party (PDC), the National Party (PN), and several splinter groups. Nearly half-a-million dollars was channeled to splinter groups during the Allende years. Early in 1971 CIA funds enabled the PDC and PN to purchase their own radio stations and newspapers. All opposition parties were passed money prior to the April 1971 municipal elections and a congressional by-election in July. In November 1971 funds were approved to strengthen the PDC, PN, and splinter groups. An effort was also made to induce a breakup of the UP coalition. CIA funds supported the opposition parties in three by-elections in 1972, and in the March 1973 congressional election. Money provided to political parties not only supported opposition candidates in the various elections, but enabled the parties to maintain an anti-government campaign throughout the Allende years, urging citizens to demonstrate their opposition in a variety of ways.

Throughout the Allende years, the CIA worked to forge a united opposition. The significance of this effort can be gauged by noting that the two main elements opposing the Popular Unity government were the National Party, which was conservative, and the reformist Christian Democratic Party, many of whose members had supported the major policies of the new government.

B. Propaganda and Support for Opposition Media: Besides funding political parties the 40 Committee approved large amounts to sustain opposition media and thus to maintain a hard-hitting propaganda campaign. The CIA spent $1.5 million in support of El Mercurio, the country's largest newspaper and the most important channel for anti-Allende propaganda. According to CIA documents, these efforts played a significant role in setting the stage for the military coup of September 11, 1973.

The 40 Committee approvals in 1971 and early 1972 for subsidizing El Mercurio were based on reports that the Chilean government was trying to close the *El Mercurio* chain. In fact, the press remained free throughout the Allende period, despite attempts to harass and financially damage opposition media. The alarming field reports on which the 40 Committee decisions to support *El Mercurio* were based are at some variance with intelligence community analyses. For example, an August 1971 National Intelligence Estimate—nine months after Allende took power—maintained that the government was attempting to dominate the press but commented that *El Mercurio* had managed to retain its independence. Yet one month later the 40 Committee voted $700,000 to keep *El Mercurio* afloat. And CIA documents in 1973 acknowledge that *El Mercurio* and, to a lesser extent, the papers belonging to opposition political parties, were the only publications under pressure from the government.

The freedom of the press issue was the single most important theme in the international propaganda campaign against Allende. Among the books and pamphlets produced by the major opposition research organization was one which appeared in October 1972 at the time of the Inter-American Press Association (IAPA) meeting in Santiago. As in the 1970 period, the IAPA listed Chile as a country in which freedom of the press was threatened.

The CIA's major propaganda project funded a wide range of propaganda activities. It produced several magazines with national circulation and a large number of books and special studies. It developed material for placement in the *El Mercurio* chain (amounting to a total daily circulation of over 300,000); opposition party newspapers; two weekly newspapers; all radio stations controlled by opposition parties; and on several regular television shows on three channels. *El Mercurio* was a major propaganda channel during 1970-73, as it had been during the 1970 elections and pre-inauguration period.

The CIA also funded progressively a greater portion—over 75 percent in 1975—of an opposition research organization. A steady flow of economic and technical material went to opposition parties and private sector groups. Many of the bills prepared by opposition parliamentarians were actually drafted by personnel of the research organization.

C. Support for Private Sector Organizations: The Committee has taken testimony that 40 Committee-approved funds were used to help maintain and strengthen the democratic opposition in Chile. It has been stressed that CIA had nothing to do with the truck owners' strike and the disorders that led to the coup. The question of CIA support to Chilean private sector groups is a matter of considerable concern because of the violent tactics used by several of these groups in their efforts to bring about military intervention.

The issue of whether to support private groups was debated within the Embassy and the 40 Committee throughout late 1972 and 1973. In September 1972, the 40 Committee authorized $24,000 for "emergency support" of a powerful businessmen's organization, but decided against financial support to other private sector organizations because of their possible involvement in anti-government strikes. In October 1972, the Committee approved $100,000 for three private sector organizations—the businessman's organization, associations of large and small businessmen and an umbrella organization of opposition groups—as part of a $1.5 million approval for support to opposition groups. According to CIA testimony, this limited financial support to the private sector was confined to specific activities in support of the opposition electoral campaign, such as voter registration drives and a get-out-the-vote campaign.

After the March 1973 elections, in which opposition forces failed to achieve the two-thirds majority in the Senate that might have permitted them to impeach Allende and hold new elections, the U.S. Government reassessed its objectives. There seemed little likelihood of a successful military coup, but there did appear to be a possibility that increasing unrest in the entire country might induce the military to re-enter the Allende government in order to restore order. Various proposals for supporting private sector groups were examined in the context, but the Ambassador and the Department of State remained opposed to any such support because of the increasingly high level of tension in Chile, and because the groups were known to hope for military intervention.

Nevertheless, on August 20, the 40 Committee approved a proposal granting $1 million to opposition parties and private sector groups, with passage of the funds contingent on the concurrence of the Ambassador, Nathaniel Davis, and the Department of State. None of these funds were passed to private sector groups before the military coup three weeks later.

While these deliberations were taking place, the CIA Station asked Headquarters to take soundings to determine whether maximum support could be provided to the opposition, including groups like the truck owners. The Ambassador agreed that these soundings should be taken but opposed a specific proposal for $25,000 of support to the strikers. There was a CIA recommendation for support to the truck owners, but it is unclear whether or not that proposal came before the 40 Committee. On August 25—16 days before the coup—Headquarters advised the Station that soundings were being taken, but the CIA Station's proposal was never approved.

The pattern of U.S. deliberations suggests a careful distinction between supporting the opposition parties and funding private sector groups trying to bring about a military coup. However, given turbulent conditions in Chile, the interconnections among the CIA-supported political parties, the various militant trade associations *(gremios)* and paramilitary groups prone to terrorism and violent disruption were many. The CIA was aware that links between these groups and the political parties made clear distinctions difficult.

The most prominent of the right-wing paramilitary groups was *Patria y Libertad* (Fatherland and Liberty), which formed following Allende's September 4 election, during so-called Track II. The CIA provided *Patria y Libertad* with $38,500 through a third party during the Track II period, in an effort to create tension and a possible pretext for intervention by the Chilean military. After Allende took office, the CIA occasionally provided the group small sums through third parties for demonstrations or specific propaganda activity. Those disbursements, about seven thousand dollars in total, ended in 1971. It is possible that CIA funds given to political parties reached *Patria y Libertad* and a similar group, the Rolando Matus Brigade, given the close ties between the parties and these organizations.

Throughout the Allende presidency, *Patria y Libertad* was the most strident voice opposing all compromise efforts by Christian Democrats, calling for resistance to government measures, and urging insurrection in the armed forces. Its tactics came to parallel those of the Movement of the Revolutionary Left (MIR) at the opposite end of the political spectrum. *Patria y Libertad* forces marched at opposition rallies dressed in full riot gear. During the October 1972 national truckers' strike, *Patria y Libertad* was reported to strew "miguelitos" (three-pronged steel tacks) on highways in order to help bring the country's transportation system to a halt. On July 13, 1973, *Patria y Libertad* placed a statement in a Santiago newspaper claiming responsibility for an abortive coup on June 29, and on July 17, *Patria y Libertad* leader Roberto Thieme announced that his groups would unleash a total armed offensive to overthrow the government.

With regard to the truckers' strike, two facts are undisputed. First, the 40 Committee did not approve any funds to be given directly to the strikers. Second, all observers agree that the two lengthy strikes (the second lasted from July 13, 1973, until the September 11 coup) could not have been maintained on the basis of union funds. It remains unclear whether or to what extent CIA funds passed to opposition parties may have been siphoned off to support strikes. It is clear that anti-government strikers were actively supported by several of the private sector groups which received CIA funds. There were extensive links between these private sector organizations and the groups which coordinated and implemented the strikes. In November 1972 the CIA learned that one private sector group had passed $2,800 directly to strikers, contrary to the Agency's ground rules. The CIA rebuked the group but nevertheless passed it additional money the next month.

3. United States Economic Policies Toward Chile: 1970-1973

A. Covert Action and Economic Pressure: The policy response of the U.S. Government to the Allende regime consisted of an interweaving of diplomatic, covert, military, and economic strands. Economic pressure exerted by the United States formed an important part of the mix. It is impossible to understand the effect of covert action without knowing the economic pressure which accompanied it.

B. Chilean Economic Dependence: The demise of the brief Allende experiment in 1970-73 came as the cumulative result of many factors—external and internal. The academic debate as to whether the external or the internal factors weighed more heavily is endless. This is not the place to repeat it. A brief description of the Chilean economy will suffice to suggest the probable effect on Chile of U.S. economic actions and the possible interactions between economic and political factors in causing Allende's downfall.

Chile's export-oriented economy remained, in 1970, dependent for foreign exchange earnings on a single product—copper—much as it had depended on nitrate in the 19th century. However, the Allende Administration consciously adopted a policy of beginning to diversify Chile's trade by expanding ties with Great Britain, the rest of the Western European countries, and Japan, and by initiating minor trade agreements with the Eastern Bloc countries.

Nevertheless, Chilean economic dependence on the United States remained a significant factor during the period of the Allende government. In 1970, U.S. direct private investment in Chile stood at $1.1 billion, out of an estimated total foreign investment of $1.672 billion. U.S. and foreign corporations played a large part in almost all of the critical areas of the Chilean economy. Furthermore, United States corporations controlled the production of 80 percent of Chile's copper, which in 1970 accounted for four-fifths of Chile's foreign exchange earnings. Hence, the Allende government faced a situation in which decisions of foreign corporations had significant ramifications throughout the Chilean economy.

Chile had accumulated a large foreign debt during the Frei government, much of it contracted with international and private banks. Chile was able, through the Paris Club, to re-negotiate $800 million in debts to foreign governments and medium-term debt to major U.S. banks in early 1972. It also obtained in 1972 some $600 million in credits and loans from socialist bloc countries and Western sources; however, a study done by the Inter-American Committee on the Alliance for Progress concluded that these credits were "tied to specific development projects and [could] be used only gradually."

Even with a conscious policy of diversifying its foreign trading patterns, in 1970 Chile continued to depend on the import of essential replacement parts from United States firms. The availability of short-term United States commercial credits dropped from around $300 million during the Frei years to around $30 million in 1972. The drop, a result of combined economic and political factors, seriously affected the Allende government's ability to purchase replacement parts and machinery for the most critical sectors of the economy: copper, steel, electricity, petroleum, and transport.

By late 1972, the Chilean Ministry of the Economy estimated that almost one-third of the diesel trucks at Chuquicamata Copper Mine, 30 percent of the privately owned city buses, 21 percent of all taxis, and 33 percent of state-owned buses in Chile could not operate because of the lack of spare parts or tires. In overall terms, the value of United States machinery and transport equipment exported to Chile by U.S. firms declined from $152.6 million in 1970 to $110 million in 1971.

C. The Instruments of United States Foreign Economic Policy Toward Allende: United States foreign economic policy toward Allende's government was articulated at the highest levels of the U.S. government, and coordinated by interagency task forces. The policy was clearly framed during the Track II period. Richard Helms' notes from his September 15, 1970, meeting with President Nixon, the meeting which initiated Track II, contain the indication: "Make the economy scream." A week later Ambassador Korry reported telling Frei, through his Defense Minister, that "not a nut or bolt would be allowed to reach Chile under Allende."

While the Chilean economy was vulnerable to U.S. pressures over a period of a few years, it was not in the short run. That judgment was clearly made by intelligence analysts in the government, but its implications seem not to have affected policy-making in September and October of 1970. A February 1971 Intelligence Memorandum noted that Chile was not immediately vulnerable to investment, trade or monetary sanctions imposed by the United States. In fact, the imposition of sanctions, while it would hurt Chile eventually, was seen to carry one possible short-run benefit—it would have given Chile a justification for renouncing nearly a billion dollars of debt to the United States.

The policy of economic pressure—articulated in NSDM 93 of November 1970—was to be implemented through several means. All new bilateral foreign assistance was to be stopped, although disbursements would continue under loans made previously. The U.S. would use its predominant position in international financial institutions to dry up the flow of new multilateral credit or other financial assistance. To the extent possible, financial assistance or guarantees to U.S. private investment in Chile would be ended, and U.S. businesses would be made aware of the government's concern and its restrictive policies.

The bare figures tell the story. U.S. bilateral aid, $35 million in 1969, was $1.5 million in 1971.... U.S. Export-Import Bank credits, which had totalled $234 million in 1967 and $29 million in 1969, dropped to zero in 1971. Loans from the multilateral Inter-American Development Bank (IDB), in which the U.S. held what amounted to a veto, had totalled $46 million in 1970; they fell to $2 million in 1972 (United States A.I.D. figures). The only new IDB loans made to Chile during the Allende period were two small loans to Chilean universities made in January 1971. [Footnote: As with bilateral aid, disbursements were continued under previous commitments. $54 million was disbursed between December 1970 and December 1972. (IDB figures).] Similarly, the World Bank made no new loans to Chile between 1970 and 1973. However, the International Monetary Fund extended Chile approximately $90 million during 1971 and 1972 to assist with foreign exchange difficulties.

Reaction to events in Chile accounted for much of the momentum in the United States Government for the development of a policy on expropriation. In what came to be known as the Allende Doctrine, Chile proposed to deduct a calculation of "excess profits" (over and above reinvestments and a 10-12 percent profit margin) from any compensation paid to nationalized firms in the copper sector. By this calculation, U.S. copper companies were in fact told they owed money. The reaction of the U.S. Government was strong. In January 1972, President Nixon announced that, when confronted with such situations, the U.S. would cut off bilateral aid and "withhold its support from loans under consideration in multilateral development banks."

While the State Department, the CIA, and the Department of Commerce all participated in the United States economic policy toward Chile, a central point in the execution of this policy was the Department of the Treasury. The Department instructs U.S. representatives on multilateral lending institutions. In the IDB, for instance, the U.S. controlled 40 percent of the votes, sufficient to veto any "soft" IDB loans. Loan proposals submitted to the IDB were held under study, never coming up for a vote by the IDB Board. Whether U.S. actions, and those of the multilaterial institutions, were motivated by political interests or economic judgments of Chile's "credit worthiness" is a debate not yet definitively settled. However, it seems clear from the pattern of U.S. economic actions and from the nature of debates within the Executive Branch that American economic policy was driven more by political opposition to an Allende regime than by purely technical judgments about Chile's finances.

The posture of the Export-Import Bank, a United States public institution, reflected the tone of U.S. economic policy toward Chile during the Allende period. In the fall of 1970, the Bank dropped Chile's credit rating from "B," the second category, to "D," the last category. Insofar as the rating contributed to similar evaluations by private U.S. banks, corporations, and international private investors, it aggravated Chile's problem of attracting and retaining needed capital inflow through private foreign investment. In mid-August 1971 the Bank decided that a $21 million credit for Boeing passenger jets would be deferred pending a resolution of the controversy over compensation for nationalized U.S. copper companies. That Bank decision came one month after the nationalization and two months before the final decision on compensation. In fact, the Boeing decision had been first announced in May, *before* the nationalization occurred.

The United States linked the question of indemnization for U.S. copper companies with Chile's multilateral foreign debt. That foreign debt, an inheritance from the obligations incurred by the Alessandri and Frei governments, was the second highest foreign debt per capita of any country in the world. Yet, in the 1972 and 1973 Paris Club foreign debt negotiations with Chile's principal foreign creditor nations, the United States alone refused to consider rescheduling Chile's foreign debt payments until there was movement toward indemnization for the U.S. copper companies. The United States also exerted pressure on each of the other foreign creditor nations not to renegotiate Chile's foreign debt as a group.

4. U.S. Relations with the Chilean Military

United States relations with the Chilean military during 1970-1973 must be viewed against the backdrop not only of the tradition of close cooperation between the American and Chilean military services and of continuing intelligence collection efforts, but also in the context of Track II—an attempt to foment a military coup. Track II marked a break in the nature of relations between U.S. officials and the Chilean military.

Close personal and professional cooperation between Chilean and U.S. officers was a tradition of long standing. The American military presence in Chile was substantial, consisting both of military attaches, the Embassy, and members of the Military Group who provided training and assistance to the Chilean armed services. In the late 1960's the Military Group numbered over fifty; by the Allende period, it was reduced to a dozen or so, for reasons which had primarily to do with U.S. budget-cutting.

A. Pre-Track II: In July 1969 the CIA Station in Santiago requested and received Headquarters approval for a covert program to establish intelligence assets in the Chilean armed Services for the purpose of monitoring coup plotting. The program lasted for four years: it involved assets drawn from all three branches of the Chilean military and included command-level officers, field- and company-grade officers, retired general staff officers and enlisted men. From 1969 to August 1970, the project adhered closely to its stated objective of monitoring and reporting coup-oriented activity within the Chilean military.

During August, September and October of 1969, it became increasingly clear from the agents' reports that the growing dissatisfaction and unrest within the armed forces was leading to an unstable military situation. These events culminated in the abortive military revolt of October 1969—the *Tacnazo,* named after the Tacna regiment in Santiago. How close the amateurish *Tacnazo* came to success was a lesson to remember, particularly in light of the upcoming Presidential election of 1970 and the strong possibility that Salvador Allende would emerge victorious.

B. Track II: The Track II covert action effort to organize a military coup to deny Allende the Presidency caught the Santiago Station unprepared. Its two assets in the Chilean military were not in a position to spark a coup. To accomplish the mission directed by Washington, the Station had to use a U.S. military attache and other hastily developed contacts with the two main coup plotting groups in the Chilean military. These contacts not only reported the plans of the groups but also relayed the Station's advice about mechanics and timing, and passed on indications of U.S. Government support following a successful coup. With the death of Schneider, the plotters' effort collapsed in disarray, leaving the Station with only its initial assets in the military. It took the Station another ten months to rebuild a network of agents among the cautious Chilean military.

As part of its attempt to induce the Chilean military to intervene before the October 24 congressional vote, the United States had threatened to cut off military aid if the military refused to act. That was accompanied by a promise of support in the aftermath of a coup. However, military assistance was *not* cut off at the time of Allende's confirmation.... Military sales jumped sharply from 1972 to 1973 and even more sharply from 1973 to 1974 after the coup.... Training of Chilean military personnel in Panama also rose during the Allende years....

C. 1970-73: After the failure of Track II, the CIA rebuilt its network of contacts and remained close to Chilean military officers in order to monitor developments within the armed forces. For their part, Chilean officers who were aware that the United States once had sought a coup to prevent Allende from becoming president must have been sensitive to indications of continuing U.S. support for a coup.

By September 1971 a new network of agents was in place and the Station was receiving almost daily reports of new coup plotting. The Station and Headquarters began to explore ways to use this network. At the same time, and in parallel, the Station and Headquarters discussed a "deception operation" designed to alert Chilean officers to real or purported Cuban involvement in the Chilean army. Throughout the fall of 1971, the Station and Headquarters carried on a dialogue about both the general question of what to do with the intelligence network and the objectives of the specific operation....

The Station proposed, in September, to provide information—some of it fabricated by the CIA—which would convince senior Chilean Army officers that the Carabineros' *Investigaciones* unit, with the approval of Allende was acting in concert with Cuban intelligence (DGI) to gather intelligence prejudicial to the Army high command. It was hoped that the effort would arouse the military against Allende's involvement with the Cubans, inducing the armed services to press the government to alter its orientation and to move against it if necessary. A month later CIA Headquarters suggested that the deception operation be shelved, in favor of passing "verifiable" information to the leader of the coup group which Headquarters and the Station perceived as having the highest probability of success.

After a further Station request, Headquarters agreed to the operation, with the objective of educating senior Chilean officers and keeping them on alert. In December 1971 a packet of material, including a fabricated letter, was passed to a Chilean officer outside Chile. The CIA did not receive any subsequent reports on the effect, if any, this "information" had on the Chilean military. While the initial conception of the operation had included a series of such passages, no further packets were passed.

The Station/Headquarters dialogue over the use of the intelligence network paralleled the discussion of the deception operation. In November the Station suggested that the ultimate objective of the military penetration program was a military coup. Headquarters responded by rejecting that formulation of the objective, cautioning that the CIA did not have 40 Committee approval to become involved in a coup. However, Headquarters acknowledged the difficulty of drawing a firm line between monitoring coup plotting and becoming involved in it. It also realized that the U.S. government's desire to be in clandestine contact with military plotters, for whatever purpose, might well imply to them U.S. support for their future plans.

During 1970-73, the Station collected operational intelligence necessary in the event of a coup—arrest lists, key civilian installations and personnel that needed protection, key government installations which needed to be taken over, and government contingency plans which would be used in case of a military uprising. According to the CIA, the data was collected only against the contingency of future Headquarters requests and was never passed to the Chilean military.

The intelligence network continued to report throughout 1972 and 1973 on coup plotting activities. During 1972 the Station continued to monitor the group which might mount a successful coup, and it spent a significantly greater amount of time and effort penetrating this group than it had on previous groups. This group had originally come to the Station's attention in October 1971. By January 1972 the Station had successfully penetrated it and was in contact through an intermediary with its leader.

During late 1971 and early 1972, the CIA adopted a more active stance *vis a vis* its military penetration program, including a short-lived effort to subsidize a small anti-government news pamphlet directed at the armed services, its compilation of arrest lists and other operational data, and its deception operation.

Intelligence reporting on coup plotting reached two peak periods, one in the last week of June 1973 and the other during the end of August and the first two weeks in September. It is clear the CIA received intelligence reports on the coup planning of the group which carried out the successful September 11 coup throughout the months of July, August and September...

The CIA's information-gathering efforts with regard to the Chilean military included activity which went beyond the mere collection of information.... They put the United States Government in contact with those Chileans who sought a military alternative to the Allende presidency.

F. Post-1973

1. Chile Since the Coup

Following the September 11, 1973, coup, the military Junta, led by General Augusto Pinochet, moved quickly to consolidate its newly acquired power. Political parties were banned, Congress was put in indefinite recess, press censorship was instituted, supporters of Allende and others deemed opponents of the new regime were jailed, and elections were put off indefinitely.

The prospects for the revival of democracy in Chile have improved little over the last two years. A 1975 National Intelligence Estimate stated that the Chilean armed forces were determined to oversee a prolonged political moratorium and to revamp the Chilean political system. The NIE stated that the Junta had established tight, authoritarian controls over political life in Chile which generally continued in effect. It had outlawed Marxist parties in Chile as well as other parties which had comprised Allende's coalition. In addition, the Christian Democratic and National parties had been placed in involuntary recess. These two parties were forbidden from engaging in political activity and restricted to...housekeeping functions.

In addition, charges concerning the violation of human rights in Chile continue to be directed at the Junta. Most recently, a United Nations report on Chile charged that "torture centers" are being operated in Santiago and other parts of the country. The lengthy document, issued October 14, 1975, listed 11 centers where it says prisoners are being questioned "by methods amounting to torture." The Pinochet government had originally offered full cooperation to the U.N. group, including complete freedom of movement in Chile. However, six days before the group's arrival in Santiago, the government reversed itself and notified the group that the visit was cancelled.

2. CIA Post-Coup Activities in Chile

The covert action budget for Chile was cut back sharply after the coup and all the anti-Allende projects except for one, a major propaganda project, were terminated. Covert activities in Chile following the coup were either continuations or adaptations of earlier projects, rather than major new initiatives.

The goal of covert action immediately following the coup was to assist the Junta in gaining a more positive image, both at home and abroad, and to maintain access to the command levels of the Chilean government. Another goal, achieved in part through work done at the opposition research organization before the coup, was to help the new government organize and implement new policies. Project files record that CIA collaborators were involved in preparing an initial overall economic plan which has served as the basis for the Junta's most important economic decisions.

With regard to the continuing propaganda project, a number of activities, including the production of books, a mailing effort, a military collection program, and the media coordination effort were terminated. However, access to certain Chilean media outlets was retained in order to enable the CIA Station in Santiago to help build Chilean public support for the new government as well as to influence the direction of the government, through pressures exerted by the mass media. These media outlets attempted to present the Junta in the most positive light for the Chilean public and to assist foreign journalists in Chile to obtain facts about the local situation. Further, two CIA collaborators assisted the Junta in preparing a *White Book of the Change of Government in Chile.* The *White Book,* published by the Junta shortly after the coup, was written to justify the overthrow of Allende. It was distributed widely both in Washington and in other foreign capitals.

After the coup, the CIA renewed liaison relations with the Chilean government's security and intelligence forces, relations which had been disrupted during the Allende period. Concern was expressed within the CIA that liaison with such organizations would lay the Agency open to charges of aiding political repression; officials acknowledged that, while most of CIA's support to the various Chilean forces would be designed to assist them in controlling subversion from abroad, the support could be adaptable to the control of internal subversion as well. However, the CIA made it clear to the Chileans at the outset that no CIA support would be provided for use in internal political repression. Furthermore, the CIA attempted to influence the Junta to maintain the norms the Junta had set in its "Instructions for Handling of Detainees" which closely followed the standards on human rights set by the 1949 Geneva Convention.

IV. Chile: Authorization, Assessment, and Oversight
A. 40 Committee Authorization and Control:
Chile, 1969-1973

1. 40 Committee Functions and Procedures

Throughout its history, the 40 Committee and its direct predecessors— the 303 Committee and the Special Group—have had one overriding purpose; to exercise political control over covert operations abroad. The 40 Committee is charged with considering the objectives of any proposed activity, whether or not it would accomplish these aims, and in general whether or not it would be "proper" and in the American interest. Minutes and summaries of 40 Committee meetings on Chile indicate that, by and large, these considerations were discussed and occasionally debated by 40 Committee members....

Before covert action proposals are presented to the Director for submission to the 40 Committee, an internal CIA instruction states that they *should* be coordinated with the Department of State and that, *ordinarily,* concurrence by the ambassador to the country concerned is required. "Should," and "ordinarily" were underscored for an important reason—major covert action proposals are not always coordinated among the various agencies....

B. Intelligence Estimates and Covert Action

The intelligence community produces several kinds of assessments for policy makers. Of these, the most important are National Intelligence Estimates (NIEs)—joint, agreed assessment of foreign politics and capabilities—produced by the U.S. intelligence community....

There have been persistent criticisms of NIEs....the documents are least-common-denominator compromises and thus are of little value to policy makers; they are oriented toward short-range predictions rather than long-run assessments. Another criticism deals not with the NIEs themselves but with their use or abuse. It is charged that policy makers ignore NIEs or consult them only when estimates confirm their pre-existing policy preferences.

A number of comments can be made concerning [Chile intelligence estimates] and their relation to decisions about covert action:

(a) Despite the view expressed by the Interdepartmental Group, and reported in a CIA Intelligence Memorandum, that the U.S. had no vital national interest in Chile, the decision was made by the Executive Branch to intervene in that nation's internal political and economic affairs, before the [1970] election, between it and the congressional vote and during Allende's tenure in office.

It appears that the Chile NIEs were either, at best, selectively used or, at worst, disregarded by policy makers when the time came to make decisions regarding U.S. covert involvement in Chile. 40 Committee decisions regarding Chile reflected greater concern about the internal and international consequences of an Allende government than was reflected in the intelligence estimates. At the same time as the Chile NIEs were becoming less shrill, the 40 Committee authorized greater amounts of money for covert operations in Chile. The amounts authorized by the 40 Committee rose from $1.5 million in 1970 to $3.6 million in 1971, $2.5 million in 1972, and, during the first eight months of 1973, $1.2 million. Covert action decisions were not, in short, entirely consistent with intelligence estimates.

(b)...NIEs are designed to provide economic and political assessments and an analysis of trends. As such, they are vulnerable to being interpreted by policymakers to support whatever conclusions the policymakers wish to draw from them. The estimates do, however, serve to narrow the range of uncertainty about future events in Chile, and thus narrow the range of justifiable U.S. policies. But a range remained.

For example, a 1971 estimate stated that, on the one hand, Allende was moving skillfully and confidently toward his declared goal of building a revolutionary nationalistic, socialist society on Marxist principles, but, on the other hand, the consolidation of the Marxist political leadership in Chile was not inevitable, and Allende had a long, hard way to go to achieve this. As a further example, a 1973 NIE which addressed the possibility of enhanced Soviet influence in Chile stated that the Soviets were interested both in increasing their influence in South America and in Allende's successful coalition of leftist parties as a model for a Marxist revolution through election. Yet, the estimate went on to say that the Soviets did not want another Cuba on their hands and they were reluctant to antagonize the U.S.

(c) The Committee has determined that the analysts responsible for drawing up the Chile NIEs were not privy to information concerning covert operations approved by the 40 Committee and being implemented in Chile by the CIA operators. The explanation for this is CIA compartmentation. Analysts and operators often exist in separate worlds. Information available to the Operations Directorate is not always available to the Intelligence Directorate. As a result, those who were responsible for preparing NIEs on Chile appear not to have had access to certain information which could have added to, or substantially revised, their assessments and predictions. That flaw was telling. It meant, for example, that the 1972 assessment of the durability of opposition sectors was written without knowledge of covert American funding of precisely those sectors. Thus, there was no estimate of whether those sectors would survive *absent* U.S. money.

C. Congressional Oversight

With regard to covert action in Chile between April 1964 and December 1974, CIA's consultation with its Congressional oversight committees—and thus Congress' exercise of its oversight function—was inadequate. The CIA did not volunteer detailed information; Congress most often did not seek it

...Based on CIA records, there were a total of fifty-three CIA Congressional briefings on Chile between 1964 and 1974. At thirty-one of these meetings, there was some discussion of covert action; special releases of funds for covert action were discussed at twenty-three of them. After January 1973 these briefings were concerned with past CIA covert activity. From information currently in the possession of the Committee and public sources, several tentative conclusions emerge: on several important occasions the CIA did not report on covert action until quite long after the fact; and in one case—Track II—it omitted discussion of an important, closely held operation, but one whose outcome reverberated on the foreign policy of the United States and carried implications for domestic affairs as well.

Of the thirty-three covert action projects undertaken in Chile with 40 Committee approval during the period 1963-1974, Congress was briefed in some fashion on eight. [Footnote: Under section 622 of the Foreign Assistance Act of 1974, the Director of Central Intelligence is required to notify six Congressional oversight committees of *every* 40 Committee approval once the President has issued a finding that the project is necessary for the national security of the United States.] Presumably the twenty-five others were undertaken without Congressional consultation. These twenty-five projects included: the $1.2 million authorization in 1971, half of which was spent to purchase radio stations and newspapers while the other half went to support municipal candidates and anti-Allende political parties; and the additional expenditure of $815,000 in late 1971 to provide support to opposition parties.

Of the total of over thirteen million dollars actually spent by the CIA on covert action operations in Chile between 1963 and 1974, Congress received some kind of briefing (sometimes before, sometimes after the fact) on projects totaling about 7.1 million dollars. Further, Congressional oversight committees were not consulted about projects which were not viewed by the full 40 Committee. One of these was the Track II attempt to foment a military coup in 1970. The other—a later CIA project involving contacts with Chilean military officers—was an intelligence collection project and thus did not come before the 40 Committee, even though in this instance the political importance of the project was clear.

SAKHAROV'S ACCEPTANCE
OF NOBEL PEACE PRIZE
December 10 and 11, 1975

Andrei D. Sakharov, the first Soviet citizen to win the Nobel peace prize, renewed his appeals for global cooperation and amnesty for political prisoners in speeches read by his wife, Yelena Bonner Sakharov, at ceremonies in Oslo, Norway, on Dec. 10 and 11. Sakharov also urged "genuine disarmament" and restoration of personal liberties in his homeland. In a brief speech accepting the Nobel prize Dec. 10, he spoke of his pleasure that the award "stressed the link between defense of peace and defense of human rights." In an hour-long lecture read the following evening, the Soviet dissident emphasized the need for international cooperation to control runaway technologies. He also asserted that without an open society the nations of the world could never reach the confidence and mutual understanding which were required to prevent nuclear or ecological disasters.

Most of the human rights for which Sakharov pleaded, including freedom of information and freedom to travel, publish and emigrate, had been af- firmed the previous August by the final act of the Conference on European Security and Cooperation (see p. 559). Although the Soviet Union sub- scribed to that pact, Moscow had refused to let Sakharov attend the Nobel ceremonies. His visa request was denied in November on the ground that he was a security risk. A brilliant nuclear physicist, Sakharov had played a leading role in the development of the Soviet hydrogen bomb.

As his wife delivered his Nobel addresses, Sakharov maintained a vigil in Vilnius, Lithuania, where he attempted—without success—to attend the trial of a fellow dissident. Mrs. Sakharov had been permitted to leave the

Soviet Union to seek medical treatment in the West before the peace award to her husband had been made known.

Sakharov had come to international attention as a critic of the Soviet system in 1968 upon publication of an essay entitled Progress, Co-existence and Intellectual Freedom. *After Alexander Solzhenitsyn was deported in 1974 (see Historic Documents of 1974, p. 129), Sakharov had in effect become the leader of the dissident movement. Solzhenitsyn, who won the Nobel prize for literature in 1970, had also been prevented by Soviet authorities from receiving the award in person.*

Although Sakharov shared his compatriot's horror of the Soviet penal system and repression of political dissent, his views differed markedly from Solzhenitsyn's distaste for détente, technological advances and the democratic process. (For Solzhenitsyn's views on détente, see p. 481). *His Dec. 11 lecture, in an apparent reference to Solzhenitsyn, warned that "any attempt to reduce the tempo of scientific and technological progress...to call for isolationism, patriarchal ways of life...would be unrealistic."*

By 1975 Sakharov had abandoned his scientific career for a life of protest and political action. Although he was subject to some harassment for his views, he had escaped more severe penalties, apparently because of his international scientific reputation. A virulent campaign against him in the Soviet press in 1973 had prompted the National Academy of Sciences of the United States to warn Soviet officials that further actions against Sakharov could endanger scientific cooperation between the two nations. Nevertheless, the October announcement of Sakharov's award launched a renewed series of published attacks. Seventy-two members of the Soviet Academy of Sciences condemned the award and a Soviet labor newspaper characterized Sakharov as "Judas" and the prize as "political pornography."

In its nomination the Nobel committee cited Sakharov's stand against the armaments race and his insistence on "the inviolable rights of man...as the only sure foundation for...international cooperation." Further, the committee found that Sakharov had "succeeded very effectively, and under trying conditions, in reinforcing respect for such values as all true friends of peace are anxious to support." He was "the spokesman for the conscience of mankind...."

The peace prize was awarded by a selection committee appointed by the Norwegian parliament under procedures designated in the will of the Swedish millionaire, Alfred Nobel. When the Nobel Foundation was established in 1900, Sweden and Norway were united in a political union. The other Nobel prizes are awarded by Swedish institutions and presented in Stockholm.

> *Texts of English translations of Andrei D. Sakharov's speech accepting the Nobel peace prize on Dec. 10, 1975, and of a lecture delivered Dec. 11 before the Nobel Com-*

mittee of the Norwegian Parliament at the University Festival Hall in Oslo, Norway. Both speeches were read in Russian by Sakharov's wife, Yelena Bonner Sakharov.

I am very grateful and very proud. I am proud to see my name placed together with the names of many outstanding people, among whom is Albert Schweitzer.

Thirty years ago nothing but ruins were left of half of my country and half of Europe. Millions of people mourned and still continue to mourn their dear ones. For all those who went through the experience of the most terrible war in history, World War II, conception of war as the worst catastrophe and evil for all mankind has become not only an abstract idea but a deep personal feeling, the basis for one's entire outlook on the world. To keep one's self-respect one must therefore act in accordance with the general human longing for peace, for true détente, for genuine disarmanent. This is the reason why I am so deeply moved by your appreciation of my activity as a contribution to peace.

Human Rights Essential for Peace

But what made me particularly happy was to see that the committee's decision stressed the link between defense of peace and defense of human rights, emphasizing that the defense of human rights guarantees a solid ground for genuine long-term international cooperation. Not only did you thus explain the meaning of my activity, but you also granted it a powerful support.

Granting the award to a person who defends political and civil rights against illegal and arbitrary actions means an affirmation of principles which play such an important role in determining the future of mankind. For hundreds of people, known or unknown to me, many of whom pay a high price for the defense of these same principles—the price being loss of freedom, unemployment, poverty, persecution, exile from one's country—your decision was a great personal joy and a gift.

I am aware of all this, but I am also aware of another fact: In the present situation, it is an act of intellectual courage and great equity to grant the award to a man whose ideas do not coincide with official concepts of the leadership of a big and powerful state. This, in fact, is how I value the decision of the Nobel Committee. I also see in it a manifestation of tolerance and of the true spirit of détente. I want to hope that even those who at present view your decision skeptically or with irritation some day will come to share this point of view.

The authorities of my country denied me the right to travel to Oslo on the alleged grounds that I am acquainted with state and military secrets. I think that actually it would not have been difficult to solve this security problem in a way acceptable to our authorities, but unfortunately this was not done.

I was unable to participate personally in today's ceremony. I think my friends who live abroad and who honored me by being my guests here. I had also invited friends from my country—Valentin Turchin, Yuri Orlov and two of the most noble defenders of the cause of justice, legality, honor and honesty, Sergei Kovalev and Andrei Tverdokhlebov, both of whom are at present in jail awaiting trial. Not only the latter two but none of them could come: In the U.S.S.R. when it comes to obtaining a permit to travel abroad, there is not much difference between their respective situations. Still, I beg you to kindly consider all of them my official guests.

I would like to end my speech expressing the hope in a final victory of the principles of peace and human rights. The best sign that such hopes can come true would be a general political amnesty in all the world, liberation of all prisoners of conscience everywhere. The struggle for a general political amnesty is the struggle for the future of mankind.

I am deeply grateful to the Nobel Committee for awarding me the Nobel Peace Prize for 1975, and I beg you to remember that the honor which was thus granted to me is shared by all prisoners of conscience in the Soviet Union and in other Eastern European countries as well as by all those who fight for their liberation.

Peace, Progress, Human Rights

Peace, progress, human rights—these three goals are insolubly linked to one another: it is impossible to achieve one of these goals if the other two are ignored. This is the dominant idea that provides the main theme of my lecture. I am deeply grateful that this great and significant prize, the Nobel Peace Prize, has been awarded to me, and that I have been given the opportunity of speaking to you here today. It was particularly gratifying for me to note the Committee's citation, which emphasises the defence of human rights as the only sure basis for genuine and lasting international cooperation. I consider that this idea is very important; I am convinced that international confidence, mutual understanding, disarmament, and international security are inconceivable without an open society with freedom of information, freedom of conscience, the right to publish, and the right to travel and choose the country in which one wishes to live. I am likewise convinced that freedom of conscience, together with the other civic rights, provides the basis for scientific progress and constitutes a guarantee that scientific advances will not be used to despoil mankind, providing the basis for economic and social progress, which in turn is a political guarantee for the possibility of an effective defence of social rights. At the same time I should like to defend the thesis of the original and decisive significance of civil and political rights in moulding the destiny of mankind. This view differs essentially from the widely accepted Marxist view, as well as the technocratic opinions, according to which it is precisely material factors and social and economic conditions that are of decisive importance. (But in saying this, of course, I have no intention of denying the importance of people's material circumstances.)

I should like to express all these theses in my lecture, and I should like in particular to dwell on a number of concrete problems affecting the violation of human rights. It seems to me that a solution of these problems is imperative, and that the time at our disposal is short.

This is the reason why I have called my lecture "Peace, Progress, Human Rights". There is, naturally, a conscious parallel with the title of my article of 1968, "Thoughts on Progress, Peaceful Coexistence, and Intellectual Freedom", with which my lecture, both in its contents and its implications, has very close affinities.

There is a great deal to suggest that mankind, at the threshold of the second half of the twentieth century, entered a particularly decisive and critical period of its history.

Disquieting Trends

Nuclear missiles, which in principle are capable of annihilating the whole of mankind, exist; this is the greatest danger threatening our age. Thanks to economic, industrial, and scientific advances, the so-called "conventional" arms have likewise grown incomparably more dangerous, not to mention chemical and bacteriological instruments of war.

There is no doubt that industrial and technological progress is the most important factor in overcoming poverty, famine, and disease. But this progress leads at the same time to ominous changes in the environment in which we live and the exhaustion of our natural resources. In this way mankind faces grave ecological dangers.

Rapid changes in traditional forms of life have resulted in an unchecked demographic explosion which is particularly noticeable in the developing countries of the third world. The growth in population has already created exceptionally complicated economic, social, and psychological problems, and will in the future inevitably pose still more serious problems. In a great many countries, particularly in Asia, Africa, and Latin America, the lack of food will be an overriding factor in the lives of many hundreds of millions of people, who from the moment of birth are condemned to a wretched existence on the starvation level. In view of this, future prospects are menacing, and in the opinion of many specialists tragic, despite the undoubted success of the "green revolution".

And yet in the developed countries, too, people are face to face with serious problems. One of these is the pressure resulting from excessive urbanisation, all the changes that disrupt the community's social and psychological stability, the incessant pursuit of fashion and trends, and overproduction, the senseless and crazy tempo of life, the increase in the number of nervous and mental disorders, the growing number of people deprived of contact with nature and of normal human lives in the traditional sense of the word, the dissolution of the family and the loss of simple human joys and delights, the decline in the community's moral and ethic principles, and the sense that more and more people no longer feel that they have any reasonable goal in life. Against this background we witness a whole host of disquieting phenomena: an increase in crime, in alcoholism, in drug addiction, in acts of terror, and so forth. The imminent exhaustion of the world's resources, the threat of overpopulation, the constant and deep-rooted international, political, and social problems are making a more and more forceful impact on the developed countries too, and will deprive—or at any rate threaten to deprive—a great many people who have long been used to abundance, affluence, and creature comforts.

However, in the pattern of problems facing the world today a more decisive and important role is played by the global political polarisation of mankind, which is divided into the so-called first world (which is conventionally called the western world), the second (socialist), and the third (the developing countries). Two powerful socialist states, in fact, have become hostile totalitarian empires, in which a single party and the State exercise immoderate power in all spheres of life. They possess an enormous potential for expansion, striving to increase their influence to cover large areas of the globe. One of these states—the Chinese People's Republic—has as yet reached only a relatively modest stage of economic development, whereas the other—the Soviet Union—by exploiting its unique natural resources, by taxing to the utmost the powers of its inhabitants and their ability to suffer continued privation, has today built up a tremendous war potential and a relatively high—though one-sided—economic development. But in the Soviet Union, too, the people's standard of living is low, and civic rights more restricted than in less socialist countries. Highly complicated global problems are also involved in the third world, where a relatively stagnant economy may be seen hand in hand with growing international political activity.

Moreover, this polarisation further reinforces the very serious dangers threatening the world—the danger of nuclear annihilation, famine, pollution of the environment, exhaustion of resources, over-population, and dehumanisation.

Retreat Not Possible

If we consider the whole of this complex of urgent problems and contradictions, I am convinced that the first point that must be made is that any attempt to reduce the tempo of scientific and technological progress, to reverse the process of urbanisation, to call for isolationism, patriarchal ways of life, and a renaissance based on a return to sound national traditions from times long past, would be unrealistic. Progress is indispensable, and to bring it to a halt would involve the decline and fall of our civilisation.

It is not so very long since men were unfamiliar with artificial fertilisers, mechanised farming, toxic chemicals, and intensive agricultural methods. There are voices calling for a return to more traditional and possibly less dangerous forms of agriculture. But can this be put into practice in a world in which hundreds of millions of people are suffering the pangs of hunger?

On the contrary, there is no doubt that we need increasingly intensive methods of farming, and we need to spread modern methods all over the world, including the developing countries. We cannot reject the idea of a more and more widespread use of the results of medical research or the extension of research in all its branches, including bacteriology and virology, neurophysiology, human genetics, and gene surgery, no matter what potential dangers lurk in their abuse and the undesirable social consequences of this research. This also applies to research which aims at creating systems for imitating intellectual processes and research involving the control of mass human behaviourism, the setting up of a unified global system of communication, systems for selecting and storing of information, and so forth. It is quite clear that in the hands of irresponsible, bureaucratic authorities operating under cover of secretiveness, all this research may prove exceptionally dangerous, but at the same time it may prove extremely important and necessary to mankind, if it is carried out under state control, testing, and socio-scientific analysis. We cannot reject the wider and wider application of artificial materials, synthetic food, or the modernisation of every aspect of life; we cannot object to the growing automatisation and increase in industrial production, irrespective of the social problems these may involve.

We cannot object to the construction of bigger and bigger nuclear power stations or research into nuclear physics, since energetics is one of the bases of our civilisation. In this connection I should like to remind you of the fact that twenty-five years ago I and my teacher, the winner of the Nobel Prize for Physics, Igor Jeugenivich Tamm, laid the basis for nuclear physical research in our country. This research has achieved a tremendous scope, extending into the most varied directions, from the classical setup for magnetic heat insulation to methods for the use of lasers.

We cannot object to the exertions which aim at control not only of those parts of the universe that surround our earth, as well as other sections of the cosmos, including the attempts to intercept signals from civilisations outside our own earth. The chance of experiments of this kind proving successful are probably small, but precisely for this reason the results may well be tremendous.

Control of Progress Essential

I have only mentioned a few examples, but there are undoubtedly many others. In actual fact all important aspects of progress are closely interwoven; not one of them can be dispensed with without a risk of destroying the entire setup of our civilisation. Progress is indivisible. But intellectual factors play a special role in the mechanism of progress. The attempt to underestimate these factors is particularly widespread in the socialist countries, no doubt owing to the populist-ideological dogmas of official philosophy, and may well result in a distorted picture of progress or even its cessation and stagnation. Progress is possible and innocuous only when it is subject to the control of reason. The highly important problem involving the preservation of the environment is one of the examples in which the role of public opinion, the open society, and freedom of conscience is particularly obvious. The partial liberalisation that took place in our country after the death of Stalin made it possible for us to engage in public debate on this problem during the early sixties. But an effective solution of the problem demands increased tightening of social and international control. The military application of scientific results and controlled disarmament are an equally critical area, in which international confidence depends on public opinion and the open society. The example I mentioned involving the control of mass human behaviourism is already a highly topical one, even though this may appear far-fetched.

Freedom of conscience, the existence of an informed public opinion, a system of education of a pluralist nature, freedom of the press, and access to other sources of information, all these are in very short supply in the socialist countries. This is a result of the economic, political, and ideological monism which is characteristic of these nations. At the same time these conditions are a vital necessity, not only if all abuse of progress, witting or unwitting, is to be avoided, but also if we wish to strengthen it. It is particularly important that an effective system of education and a creative sense of heredity from one generation to another is only possible in an atmosphere of intellectual freedom. And conversely: intellectual bondage, the power and conformism of a pitiful bureaucracy which from the very start acts as a blight on humanist fields of knowledge, literature, and art, results eventually in a general intellectual decline, bureaucratisation and formalisation of the entire system of education, a decline of scientific research, and the thwarting of all incentive to creative work, to stagnation, and to dissolution.

Conditions for Detente

In the polarised world the totalitarian states, thanks to détente, enjoy the opportunity today of indulging in a special form of intellectual sponging. And it seems that, if the inner changes, which we all consider necessary, do not take place, they will soon be forced to adopt an approach of this kind. This is precisely one of the many results of détente. If it does take place, the danger of an explosion in the world situation will merely increase. Cooperation on a wide front between the western countries, the socialist countries, and the developing countries is a vital necessity for peace, and it involves an exchange of scientific results, technology, trade, and mutual economic aid, particularly where food is concerned. But this cooperation must be based on mutual trust between open societies, or—to put it another way—with an open mind, on the basis of genuine equality, and not on the basis of the democratic countries' fear of their totalitarian neighbours. If that were the case, cooperation would merely involve an attempt at ingratiating oneself with a formidable neighbour. But a policy of this kind would merely mean postponing the evil day, which would soon return, through another door, in tenfold strength. This is simply another version of the Munich policy. The success of détente can only be assured if from the very outset it goes hand in hand with continual observation of openness on the part of all countries, an aroused sense of public opinion, free exchange of information, absolute respect in all countries for civic and political rights. In short: in addition to détente in the material sphere, with disarmament and trade, détente should take place in the intellectual and ideological sphere. The President of France, Giscard d'Estaing, expressed this in an admirable fashion during his visit to Moscow. It was worth listening to criticism from shortsighted pragmatists among one's own countrymen when the maintenance of an important principle was at stake!

Uses of International Organizations

Before dealing with the problem of disarmament I should like to take this opportunity once again of reminding you of some of my proposals of a general nature. This applies first and foremost to the idea of setting up an international consultative committee for questions related to disarmament, human rights, and the protection of the environment, under the aegis of the United Nations. In my opinion a committee of this kind should have the right to receive binding replies from all governments to their enquiries and recommendations. A committee of this kind could become an important working body in securing international discussion and information on the most important problems affecting the future of mankind. I am waiting for this idea to receive support and to be discussed.

I should also like to emphasise that I consider it particularly important for United Nations armed forces to be used more generally for the purpose of restricting armed conflicts between states and ethnic groups. I have a very high regard for the United Nations' potential and necessary role, and I consider the institution to be one of mankind's most important hopes for a better future. Recent years have proved difficult and critical for this organisation. I have written on this subject in my book *My Country and the World,* but after it came out a deplorable event took place: the General Assembly adopted—practically without any real debate—a resolution declaring Zionism a form of racism and racial discrimination. *[See p. 825.]* All impartial persons know that Zionism is the ideology of a national rebirth of the Jewish people after two thousand years of separation, and that this ideology is not directed against any other people. The adoption of a resolution of this kind has, in my opinion, dealt the prestige of the United Nations a hard blow. But despite motions of this kind, which are frequently tabled as the result of insufficient sense of responsibility among the leaders of some of the younger member-nations of UN, I believe nevertheless that the Organisation may sooner or later be in a position to play a worthy role in the life of mankind, in accordance with the clause in which the Organisation's aims are set forth.

Steps Toward Disarmament

Let me now tackle one of the central questions of the present age, the problem of disarmament. I have described in detail just what my position is in the book *My Country and the World.* It is imperative to promote confidence between nations, and carry out measures of control with the aid of international inspection groups. This is only possible if detente is extended to the ideological sphere, and it presupposes greater social openness. In my book I have stressed the need for international agreements on the limitation of arms supplies to other states, a halt in the production of new weapon systems based on a mutual agreement, treaties banning secret rearmament, the elimination of strategically uncertain factors, and in particular a ban on multi-warhead nuclear missiles.

What do I consider would be the ideal international agreement on disarmament on the technical plane?

I believe that prior to an agreement of this kind we must have an official declaration—though not necessarily official in the initial stages—on the extent of military potential (ranging from the number of nuclear warheads to forecast figures on the number of personnel liable for military service), with, for example, an indication of areas of "potential confrontation". The first step in this agreement would be to ensure that for every single strategic area and for all sorts of military potential an adjustment would be made in every case to iron out the superiority of one party to the agreement in relation to the other. (Naturally this is the kind of pattern that would be liable to some adjustment.) This would in the first place obviate the possibility of an agreement in one strategic area (Europe, for instance) being utilised to strengthen military positions in another area (e.g. the Soviet-Chinese border). In the second place potential injustices based on quantitive comparison with regard to the significance of different types of potential would be excluded. (It would, for example, be difficult to say how many batteries of the ABM type would correspond to a cruiser, and so on.) The next step in disarmament would have to be proportional and simultaneous de-escalation for all countries and in all strategic areas. A formula of this kind for "balanced" two-stage disarmament would ensure continuous security for all countries, an interrelated equilibrium between armed forces in all areas where there is a potential danger of confrontation, while at the same time providing a radical solution to the economic and social problems that have arisen as a result of militarisation. In the course of time a great many experts and politicians have launched similar views, but hitherto these have not made much significant advance. However, now that humanity is faced with a real threat of annihilation in the holocaust of nuclear explosion, I hope that human reason will not hesitate to take this step. Radical and balanced disarmament is in effect both necessary and possible, constituting an integral part of a manifold and complicated process for the solution of the menacing and urgent problems facing the world. The new phase in international relations which has been called détente, and which appears to have culminated with the Helsinki Conference, does in principle open up certain possibilities for a move in this direction.

Soviet Violations of Human Rights

The final agreement reached at the Helsinki Conference has a special claim on our attention, because here for the first time official expression is given to a nuanced approach which appears to be the only possible one for a solution of international security problems. This document contains far-reaching declarations on the relationship between international security and the preservation of human rights, freedom of information, and freedom of movement. These rights are guaranteed by solemn obligations entered into by the participating nations. Obviously we cannot speak here of a guaranteed result, but we can speak of fresh possibilities that can only be realised as a result of long-term planned activities, in which the participating nations, and in particular the democracies, maintain a unified and consistent attitude.

This is in particular bound up with the problem of human rights, to which I have devoted the final portion of my lecture. I should like to speak mainly of my own country. During the months that have ensued since the Helsinki Conference there has been absolutely no real improvement in this direction. In fact in some cases attempts on the part of hard-liners can be noted to "give the screw another turn".

This also applies to important problems involving an international exchange of information, the freedom to choose the country in which one wishes to live, travel abroad for studies, work, or health reasons, as well as ordinary tourist travel. In order to provide concrete examples for my assertion, I should like to give you a few instances—chosen at random and without any attempt to provide a complete picture.

You all know, even better than I do, that children, e.g. from Denmark, can get on their bicycles and cycle off to the Adriatic. No-one would ever think of suggesting that they were "teen-age spies". But Soviet children are not allowed to do this! I am sure that you can all find analogous examples of this and similar situations.

As you know, the General Assembly, as a result of pressure on the part of the socialist countries, resolved to restrict the liberty to make TV transmissions via satellite. I believe, now that the Helsinki Conference has taken place, that there is every reason to deal afresh with this problem. For millions of Soviet citizens this is both important and interesting.

In the Soviet Union there is a great shortage of artificial limbs and similar aids for invalids. But no Soviet invalid, even though he may be in receipt of a formal invitation from a foreign firm, is allowed to travel abroad in response to an invitation of this kind.

Soviet newsstands do not sell foreign anti-Communist papers, and it is not even possible to buy every issue of the Communist periodicals. Even informative periodicals such as *America* are in very short supply. They are on sale only in a very small number of kiosks, and are immediately snapped up by eager buyers, generally with a "makeweight" of non-saleable printed matter.

Any person wishing to emigrate from the Soviet Union must have a formal invitation from a close relative. For many people this is an insoluble problem, e.g. for 300,000 Germans who wish to travel to the German Federal Republic (the emigration quota for Germans is 5,000 a year, which means that one's plans would have to cover a sixty-year period!). This is an enormous tragedy. The position of persons who wish to be reunited with relatives in non-Socialist countries is particularly tragic. They have no-one to plead their case, and on such occasions the arbitrary behaviour of the authorities knows no bounds.

Freedom to travel, freedom to choose where one wishes to work and live, these are still violated in the case of millions of kolkhoz workers, and in the case of hundreds of thousands of Crimean Tartars, who thirty years ago were cruelly and brutally deported from the Crimea and who to this day have been denied the right to return to the land of their fathers.

The Helsinki Treaty confirms yet again the principle of freedom of conscience. However, a stern and relentless struggle will have to be carried on if the contents of this treaty are to be given reality. In the Soviet Union today many thousands of people are persecuted because of their convictions, both by judicial and by non-judicial organs, for the sake of their religious beliefs and for their desire to bring their children up in the spirit of religion, for reading and disseminating—often only to a few acquaintances—literature which is unwelcome to the State, but which in accordance with ordinary democratic practice is absolutely legitimate, e.g. religious literature, and for attempts to leave the country. On the moral plane the persecution of persons who have defended other victims of unjust treatment, who have worked to publish and in particular to distribute information regarding the persecution and trials of persons with deviant opinions, and of conditions in places of internment, is particularly important.

Plea for Prisoners

It is unbearable to consider that at this very moment that we are gathered together in this hall on this festive occasion hundreds and thousands of prisoners of conscience are suffering from undernourishment, as the result of year-long hunger, and of an almost total lack of proteins and vitamins in their daily food, of a shortage of medicines (there is a ban on the sending of vitamins and medicines to internees), and of overexertion. They shiver with cold, damp, and exhaustion in ill-lit dungeons, where they are forced to wage a ceaseless struggle for their human dignity and their conviction against the "indoctrination machine", in fact against the very destruction of their souls. The very special feature of the concentration-camp system is carefully concealed. All the sufferings a handful of people have undergone because they have drawn aside the veil to reveal this, provide the best proof of the truth of their allegations and accusations. Our concepts of human dignity demand an immediate change in this system for all interned persons, no matter how guilty they may be. But what about the sufferings of the innocent? Worst of all is the hell that exists in the special psychiatric clinics in Dnieperopetrovsk, Sytshevk, Blagoveshensk, Kazan, Chernakovsk, Oriol, Leningrad, Tashkent,...

There is no time for me today to describe in detail particular trials, or the fates of particular persons. There is a wealth of literature on this subject: may I draw your attention to works published by the Chronica Press in New

York, which specialises in offprints of the Soviet Samizdat periodical "Survey of Current Events", and which publishes similar bulletins of current information. Here in this hall I should just like to mention the names of some of the internees I am acquainted with. As you were told yesterday, I would ask you to remember that all prisoners of conscience and all political prisoners in my country share with me the honour of the Nobel Prize. Here are some of the names that are known to me: Plyush, Bukovsky, Glusman, Moros, Maria Semionova, Nadeshda Svetlishnaya, Stefania Shabatura, Irina Klynets-Stasiv, Irina Senik, Niyola Sadunaite, Anait Karapetian, Osipov, Kornid Ljubarsky, Shumuk, Vins, Rumachek, Khaustov, Superfin, Paulaitis, Simutis, Karavanskiy, Valery, Martshenko, Shuchevich, Pavlenkov, Chernoglas, Abanckin, Suslenskiy, Meshener, Svetlichny, Sofronov, Rode, Shakirov, Heifetz, Afanashev, Mo-Chun, Butman, Lukianenko, Ogurtsov, Sergeyenko, Antoniuk, Lupynos, Ruban, Plachotniuk, Kovgar, Belov, Igrunov, Soldatov, Miattik, Kierend, Jushkevich, Zdorovyy, Tovmajan, Shachverdjan, Zagrobian, Arikian, Markoshan, Arshakian, Mirauskas, Stus, Sverstiuk, Chandyba, Uboshko, Romaniuk, Vorobiov, Gel, Pronjuk, Gladko, Malchevsky, Grazis, Prishliak, Sapeliak, Kolynets, Suprei, Valdman, Demidov, Bernitshuk, Shovkovy, Gorbatiov, Berchov, Turik, Ziukauskas, Bolonkin, Lisovoi, Petrov, Chjekalin, Gorodetsky, Chjernovol, Balakonov, Bondar, Kalintchenko, Kolomin, Plumpa, Jaugelis, Fedoseyev, Osadchij, Budulak-Sharigin, Makarenko, Malkin, Shtern, Lazar Liubarsky, Feldman, Roitburt, Shkolnik, Murzienko, Fedorov, Dymshits, Kuznetsov, Mendelevich, Altman, Penson, Knoch, Vulf, Zalmanson, Izrail Zalmanson, and many, many others. Among those in exile are Anatoly Martshenko, Nashpits, and Zitlenok.

Mustafa Dziemilev, Kovalev, and Tverdochlebov are awaiting their verdicts. There is no time to mention all the prisoners of whose fate I am aware, and there are still larger numbers whom I do not know, or of whom I have insufficient knowledge. But their names are all implicit in what I have to say, and I should like all those whose names I have not mentioned to forgive me. Every single name, mentioned as well as unmentioned, represents a hard and heroic human destiny, years of suffering, years of struggling for human dignity.

Action on Prisoners Urged

The main solution to the problem of persecuting persons with deviant views must be liberation on the basis of international agreements—a liberation of all political prisoners, of all prisoners of conscience in prisons, internment camps, and psychiatric clinics, if necessary on the basis of a resolution passed by the General Assembly of the United Nations. This proposal involves no intervention in the internal affairs of any country. After all, it would apply to every country on the same basis—to the Soviet Union, to Indonesia, to Chile, to the Republic of South Africa, to Spain, Brazil, and to every other country. Since the protection of human rights has been proclaimed in the United Nations Declaration of Human Rights, this cannot for this reason be said to be a matter of purely internal or domestic concern. In order to achieve this great goal, no exertions are too great, however long the road may seem. And that the road is long was clearly shown during the recent sitting of the United Nations, in the course of which the United States tabled a proposal for political amnesty, only to withdraw it after attempts had been made by a number of countries—in the opinion of the USA—to extend unduly the framework that would cover the concept of amnesty. I much regret what took place. A problem cannot be taken out of circulation. I am profoundly convinced that it would be better to liberate a certain number of people—even though they might be guilty of some offence or other—than to keep thousands of innocent people locked up and exposed to torture.

Without losing sight of an overall solution of this kind, we must today fight for every individual person separately against injustice and the violation of human rights. Much of our future depends on this.

In struggling to protect human rights we must, I am convinced, first and foremost act as protectors of the innocent victims of regimes installed in various countries, without demanding the destruction or total condemnation of these regimes. We need reform, not revolution. We need a pliant, pluralist, tolerant community, which selectively and tentatively can bring about a free, undogmatic use of the experiences of all social systems. What is détente? What is rapprochement? We are concerned not with words, but with a willingness to create a better and more friendly society, a better world order.

Thousands of years ago tribes of human beings suffered great privations in the struggle to survive. In this struggle it was important not only to be able to handle a club, but also to possess the ability to think reasonably, to take care of the knowledge and experience garnered by the tribe, and to develop the links that would provide cooperation with other tribes. Today the entire human race is faced with a similar test. In infinite space many civilisations are bound to exist, among them civilisations that are also wiser and more "successful" than ours. I support the cosmological hypothesis which states that the development of the universe is repeated in its basic features an infinite number of times. In accordance with this, other civilisations, including more "successful" ones, should exist an infinite number of time on the "preceding" and the "following" pages of the Book of the Universe. Yet this should not minimise our sacred endeavours in this world of ours, where, like faint glimmers of light in the dark, we have emerged for a moment from the nothingness of dark unconsciousness into material existence. We must make good the demands of reason and create a life worthy of ourselves and of the goals we only dimly perceive.

CUMULATIVE INDEX, 1972-75

CUMULATIVE INDEX, 1972-1975

A

C

F

J

N

963

Q

R

RABIN, YITZHAK
  Nixon Mideast Trip, 451, 464-467 *(1974)*
RABORN, ADM. WILLIAM F.
  Pentagon Papers: Final Installment, 492-493 *(1972)*
RACE AND RACISM. *See also* Blacks. Indians, American.
  Arafat U.N. Speech, 921-937 *(1974)*
  International Women's Year Conference, 507-522 *(1975)*
  Moynihan on Democracy, 645 *(1975)*
  Navy Race Relations, 901-906 *(1972)*
  South Africa, 326, 826, 827 *(1975)*
  Voter Turnout, Nov. '72, 38 *(1973)*
RADIATION
  Aerosol Sprays and the Atmosphere, 437-453 *(1975)*
  Solar Radiation and SST, 235-244 *(1973)*
RAIFFA, HOWARD
  Science and World Problems, 833-835 *(1972)*
RAILROADS
  Annual Economic Report, 87-89 *(1974)*
  Reorganization of Bankrupt Lines, 529-542 *(1975)*
  Steel Industry Pact, 438 *(1973)*
RAILSBACK, TOM (R Ill.)
  Impeachment Report, 733, 760, 762 *(1974)*
RAND CORPORATION
  Pentagon Papers Trial, 537-548 *(1973)*
RANGEL, CHARLES B. (D N.Y.)
  Impeachment Report, 714, 734, 744, 747, 750 *(1974)*
RATHER, DAN
  Conversation with President Nixon, 3-13 *(1972)*
RAW MATERIALS. *See* Natural Resources.
REBOZO, CHARLES G. "BEBE"
  Cronkite Interview, 975-981 *(1973)*
  Nixon Campaign Contributions, 898, 906, 907 *(1973)*; 599, 605 *(1974)*
RECESSION
  Burns on Inflation and Unemployment, 635-642 *(1975)*
  Democrats' Emergency Plan, 34-36 *(1975)*
  Economic Report, 69, 75 *(1974)*; 99, 106 *(1975)*
  Ford on Economy, 975-980 *(1974)*; 28 *(1975)*
  Foreign Economic Policy Report, 190 *(1975)*
  Nixon Budget, 95, 97 *(1974)*
  Nixon News Conference, 150 *(1974)*
  State of the Union, 42, 46, 53, 56-57 *(1974)*; 19, 27 *(1975)*

REDISTRICTING
  Apportionment in State Legislatures, 277-289 *(1973)*
REFUGEES
  Anderson Papers, 31-32, 36 *(1972)*
  Kennedy Speech at Dacca University, 165 *(1972)*
  Kissinger Press Conference, 267-277 *(1975)*
  Last Flight from Da Nang, 201-204 *(1975)*
REGIONAL GOVERNMENT
  American Party Platform, 621 *(1972)*
  Democratic Party Platform, 550 *(1972)*
REHABILITATION OF OFFENDERS
  Democratic Party Platform, 567-568 *(1972)*
  Republican Party Platform, 681 *(1972)*
REHNQUIST, WILLIAM H. *See also* Supreme Court.
  Abortion Guidelines, 102, 110, 114 *(1973)*
  Apportionment in State Legislatures, 277, 278, 280-284 *(1973)*
  Cruel and Unusual Punishment, 505 *(1972)*
  Jury Service for Women, 55, 63-66 *(1975)*
  Miranda Ruling Limits, 474, 475-482 *(1974)*
  Nixon Tapes Ruling, 621, 637 *(1974)*
  Obscenity Scope Narrowed, 516-519, 520 *(1974)*
  Social Security for Widowers, 178, 185 *(1975)*
RELIGION. *See also* Prayer in Schools.
  European Security and Cooperation Conference (CSCE), 564 *(1975)*
  Evolution or Creation, 843-844 *(1972)*
  Public Aid to Nonpublic Schools, 641-658 *(1973)*
RENT ADVISORY BOARD, 47, 53 *(1973)*
REORGANIZATION OF EXECUTIVE BRANCH. *See* Executive Branch.
REPUBLICAN NATIONAL COMMITTEE
  Watergate Investigation, 413-425 *(1973)*
REPUBLICAN PARTY
  Convention 1972
    Agnew, Nixon speeches, 711-725 *(1972)*
    ITT Role, 3-5, 16, 20-21 *(1974)*
    Party Platform, 651-709 *(1972)*
  McGovern at Oxford, 90 *(1973)*
  Nixon Tax Payments, 236 *(1974)*
  Nixon's Press Relations, 634 *(1973)*
  Nixon's Second-Term Plans, 886 *(1972)*
  State of the Union, 74 *(1972)*
  Victory and Concession, 893-895 *(1972)*
  Watergate, Emergence of Scandal, 413-425 *(1973)*
  Watergate: White House Shake-up, 499-512 *(1973)*
  Youth Vote Turnout '72, 36 *(1973)*

T

U

X, Y, Z